OXFORD WORLD'S CLA

HOBSON-JOBS(

Henry Yule (1820–89) spent over twenty years in India as a Bengal Engineer, working as a soldier, engineer, surveyor, and diplomat. He worked on two of the major British engineering projects in India: the extension of the canal and railway systems. As Secretary to a mission to Ava, he published the official account of the 1855 expedition to Burma. In retirement, Yule reinvented himself as historical geographer. He edited books of medieval European travels to the East and published the definitive edition of Marco Polo's travels. An acknowledged expert on Asian affairs, Yule occupied various posts of scholarly and governmental responsibility: he was a member of the Council of India, vice-president of the Royal Geographical Society, and president of both the Royal Asiatic Society and the Hakluyt Society (which produced editions of early travel texts). Yule's multifaceted career and varied interests fed directly into *Hobson-Jobson*, the encyclopaedic glossary of Anglo-Indian terms, which he compiled in collaboration with A.C. Burnell.

Arthur Coke Burnell (1840-82) was a phenomenally gifted linguist who worked as a magistrate and judge in South India. Primarily a Sanskrit scholar, Burnell was also proficient in southern Indian languages, Javanese, Coptic, and Tibetan (not to mention Portuguese, Dutch, and Italian). He published translations of Hindu law, editions of Sanskrit texts, and studies of South Indian scripts. He supplied Yule with the necessary linguistic expertise for *Hobson-Jobson*. Their collaboration lasted around a decade, but Burnell's health was never strong. Forced to retire in 1880, Burnell died prematurely, at the age of 42. He did not live to see the glossary's publication.

Kate Teltscher is Reader in English Literature at Roehampton University. She is the author of *India Inscribed: European and British writing on India 1600-1800* (1995) and *The High Road to China: George Bogle, the Panchen Lama and the First British Expedition to Tibet* (2006).

OXFORD WORLD'S CLASSICS

For over 100 years Oxford World's Classics have brought readers closer to the world's great literature. Now with over 700 titles—from the 4,000-year-old myths of Mesopotamia to the twentieth century's greatest novels—the series makes available lesser-known as well as celebrated writing.

The pocket-sized hardbacks of the early years contained introductions by Virginia Woolf, T. S. Eliot, Graham Greene, and other literary figures which enriched the experience of reading. Today the series is recognized for its fine scholarship and reliability in texts that span world literature, drama and poetry, religion, philosophy, and politics. Each edition includes perceptive commentary and essential background information to meet the changing needs of readers.

OXFORD WORLD'S CLASSICS

HENRY YULE AND A. C. BURNELL

Hobson-Jobson

The Definitive Glossary of British India

Selected with an Introduction and Notes by

KATE TELTSCHER

UNIVERSITY PRESS

OXFORD
UNIVERSITY PRESS

Great Clarendon Street, Oxford, OX2 6DP
United Kingdom

Oxford University Press is a department of the University of Oxford.
It furthers the University's objective of excellence in research, scholarship,
and education by publishing worldwide. Oxford is a registered trade mark of
Oxford University Press in the UK and in certain other countries

First published 2013
First published as an Oxford World's Classics paperback 2015

Impression: 9

Published in the United States of America by Oxford University Press
198 Madison Avenue, New York, NY 10016, United States of America

British Library Cataloguing in Publication Data
Data available

Library of Congress Control Number: 2015933310

ISBN 978–0–19–871800–0

Printed and bound in Great Britain by Clays Ltd, Elcograf S.p.A.

To the memory of my father

WILLIAM TELTSCHER

(1923–2010)

who spoke six languages

and loved playing with words

ACKNOWLEDGEMENTS

WHENEVER I mention that I am working on *Hobson-Jobson*, I am rewarded with smiles of recognition. Many people feel a particular affection towards *Hobson-Jobson*, the kind of attachment that only truly idiosyncratic books can generate. This response has buoyed me up in my research, as much as the support of specific individuals and institutions.

I would like to thank Elleke Boehmer and Nicki Humble for their initial encouragement in this project. Judith Luna has provided insightful editorial guidance throughout. I am grateful to Roehampton University for granting me study leave to prepare this edition. Jonathan Katz first introduced me to *Hobson-Jobson* many years ago, and has provided invaluable linguistic assistance. Kathryn Tempest kindly helped me with translation. Rachel Beattie at the John Murray Archive has always been extremely prompt in answering my queries.

Invitations to deliver papers at conferences have prompted me to pursue new directions in my research. I am grateful to Indra Sengupta and Daud Ali for inviting me to the 'Knowledge Production and Pedagogy in Colonial India' conference at the German Historical Institute; to Kingsley Bolton, Sam Kaislaniemi, and Anna Winterbottom for asking me to speak at 'The East India Company and Language' symposium at Hong Kong University; and to Janet Montefiore and Kaori Nagai for inviting me to the 'International Kipling' conference at the University of London.

I have benefited greatly from the opportunity to give papers while holding visiting fellowships in the English departments at the universities of Delhi and Jadavpur. I was made to feel extremely welcome by Udaya Kumar and Sumanyu Satpathy at Delhi, by Swapan Chakravorty and Amlan Das Gupta at Jadavpur. I would also like to thank Elleke Boehmer for inviting me to speak at the Postcolonial Writing and Theory Seminar at Oxford University, Ruvani Ranasinha at the Postcolonial Seminar at Kings College London, Andrea Major at the South Asian Studies Seminar at Leeds University, and Nile Green at UCLA.

I am grateful to Amitav Ghosh, Javed Majeed, and Charlotte

Brewer for their comments. It has been a great pleasure to work as consultant on a feature on *Hobson-Jobson* for BBC Radio 4 with Mukti Jain Campion and Daljit Nagra. I would like to thank my colleagues at the Department of English and Creative Writing at Roehampton University for all their support, in particular Jenny Hartley, Ian Haywood, Zach Leader, Susan Matthews, Laura Peters, Martin Priestman, Sarah Turvey, and Cathy Wells-Cole.

Julian Loose is my endlessly patient and kind first reader. Jacob and Isaac now know more about English words with Asian origins than most boys their age.

CONTENTS

HOBSON-JOBSON

INTRODUCTION

A. C. Burnell and Henry Yule's *Hobson-Jobson* (1886) is a glossary unlike any other. Multilingual and encyclopaedic in range, *Hobson-Jobson* traces the relations between Asia and Europe through the histories of words. For Salman Rushdie, it is 'the legendary dictionary of British India'.[1] Some fourteen years in the making, the glossary embraces aspects of the peoples, customs, government, geography, commerce, cuisine, and botany of Asia. It is a unique work of unparalleled scholarship: a lexicon of words and phrases that enter English from Spanish, Portuguese, Arabic, Persian, Indian, and Chinese sources—and vice versa. But *Hobson-Jobson* wears its learning lightly. Definitions frequently slip into anecdote, reminiscence, and digression. The book defies easy classification: 'neither glossary, vocabulary, dictionary or anything else that may be described in one word, but simply—*Hobson-Jobson*', to quote the young Rudyard Kipling.[2]

But what is 'Hobson-Jobson'? The peculiarity of the title is entirely characteristic. Contemporaries like Kipling deemed the title uncouth, but it was both catchy and intriguing. The phrase 'Hobson-Jobson' refers to a communal religious celebration or, to quote the book itself, a 'native festal excitement' (p. 261). 'Hobson-Jobson' is the distorted, anglicized version of the mourning cries of 'Ya Hassan! Ya Hosain!' at the Shia festival of Muharram. Used as a title, the phrase *Hobson-Jobson* signals the lexicon's interest in the cross-cultural transformation of words. With its nursery-rhyme echoes, it would have sounded reassuringly familiar, far removed from the obscurities of oriental scholarship.

If the title is memorably concise, the subtitle is anything but: 'A GLOSSARY OF COLLOQUIAL ANGLO-INDIAN WORDS AND PHRASES, AND OF KINDRED TERMS; ETYMOLOGICAL, HISTORICAL, GEOGRAPHICAL AND DISCURSIVE'. The term 'Anglo-Indian' here refers to the British community in India, rather than people of

[1] Salman Rushdie, 'Hobson-Jobson', in *Imaginary Homelands: Essays and Criticism 1981–1991* (London: Granta & Penguin, 1992), 81.

[2] Rudyard Kipling, 'Hobson-Jobson', *Civil and Military Gazette* (15 Apr. 1886); repr. in Thomas Pinney (ed.), *Kipling's India: Uncollected Sketches 1884–1888* (London: Macmillan, 1986), 158.

mixed British and Indian descent. With its emphasis on the vernacular, *Hobson-Jobson* catches the precise nuances of slang terms and the official jargon of the Raj. But the glossary is not confined to the language and culture of Anglo-India. In its expansiveness, the subtitle enacts something of the sprawling waywardness of the glossary itself. *Hobson-Jobson* demonstrates that imperial confidence which assumes mastery over multiple disciplines and languages, that speaks with equal authority on matters as diverse as satin, Siam, sugar, and the Supreme Court.

Hobson-Jobson was a product of the Victorian enthusiasm for lexicography. This was the era of the grandest of all lexicographical projects, the *New English Dictionary* (*NED*), later renamed the *Oxford English Dictionary*, an immense undertaking which would finally be published in ten volumes between 1884 and 1928. Yule and Burnell organized their glossary on similar historical principles to the *NED*, demonstrating usage and dating the entry of words into English through textual quotation. The compilers of the two lexicons were in correspondence; Yule sent the proofs of *Hobson-Jobson* to James Murray, the first editor of the *NED*. Many of *Hobson-Jobson*'s definitions and quotations went straight into the *NED*, both with and without acknowledgement. This initial borrowing was further augmented in subsequent editions resulting in some 500 citations of *Hobson-Jobson* in the *OED*. The entry of words of Asian origin into the national lexicon is a striking example of the manner in which India remade British culture.

In its breadth of reference, *Hobson-Jobson* spans literary and colloquial usage, high and popular culture, the local and the global. Its remarkable range reflects the omnivorous intellectual appetites of its two compilers. The main author, Colonel (later Sir) Henry Yule, was a retired Bengal Engineer turned historical geographer. His co-author, Arthur Coke Burnell, who died before the book was completed, was a judge in the Madras Civil Service and scholar of Sanskrit. Both men were extraordinarily well read in the European literature of Asia and steeped in the culture of Anglo-India. To compile *Hobson-Jobson*, they drew as much on their own experience and personal recollection as on their voluminous reading and prodigious learning.

Victorian Polymaths: Henry Yule and Arthur Coke Burnell

The Yule family had extensive connections with India. Henry Yule's father, Major William Yule, like many eighteenth-century Scots, sought advancement through service with the East India Company. He held appointments as assistant resident at the courts of Lucknow and Delhi, the latter post under Sir David Ochterlony (famous for his flamboyantly acculturated lifestyle and harem of thirteen Indian wives). William Yule developed a taste for Persian and Arabic literature, amassing a collection of manuscripts which he later donated to the British Museum.

Raised in such a household, it is not surprising that Henry Yule should abandon his legal studies at University College London in favour of a career in India. He was following the example set by his two elder brothers: George, who had joined the Indian Civil Service, and Robert who had entered the military. Henry trained at the East India Company's Military College at Addiscombe and at the Chatham headquarters of the Royal Engineers, before embarking for India in 1840.

Aptitude, tenacity, self-confidence, and good connections could take a man far in India. Yule managed to establish close relations with the Governor General of India, Lord Dalhousie (a fellow Scot), and his successor and first viceroy of India, Lord Canning. He was involved in two of the major engineering projects undertaken by the British in India: the expansion of the canal system and the development of the railway network. In 1855, Yule's career took a diplomatic turn when he was appointed secretary to Colonel Arthur Phayre's mission to Ava, the capital of Burma. Yule compiled the official report on the expedition which was published as *A Narrative of the Mission sent by the Governor-General of India to the Court of Ava in 1855* (1858), illustrated by Yule's own sketches. The lavishly produced book offered the Victorian public the first detailed account of Burma. A number of Yule's Burmese observations would later find their way into *Hobson-Jobson*.

The *Narrative* went to press during the tumultuous months of the Indian Rebellion (1857–8). Yule's brother, Robert, died in the uprising at Delhi. The Rebellion (or Mutiny, as the British called it) lived on long in the British imagination. A number of Mutiny sites were held sacred by the British, none more so than the well at Kanpur, which contained the remains of 125 British civilians, mostly women and children. The viceroy and his wife commissioned Yule to design a memorial at the well. Working from a sketch by Lady Canning, Yule designed a massive, neo-Gothic, octagonal screen to enclose the well, and composed inscriptions and selected biblical texts to sanctify the space. Yule seems to have caught the prevailing British mood absolutely; a reverential visit to the memorial provided the culmination of the popular Mutiny tour undertaken by large numbers of Britons in the last decades of the nineteenth century.

But by the time that the monument was erected, Yule had left the army and India for good. He resigned his post in 1862, to accompany the departing viceroy back to Britain in the hope that Canning's influence would procure him a new position. But Canning's unexpected death deprived him of a patron. Failing to find a suitable post, Yule opted instead for European travels with his wife and daughter. In 1864, the family settled in Palermo, a climate supposed to be beneficial to his invalid wife's health.

In Sicily, Yule settled into a highly productive life of scholarship, remaking himself as historical geographer. He embarked on a long association with the Hakluyt Society, the scholarly society devoted to the publication of early voyages and travels. In the 1860s he edited two volumes of medieval European travels to the East for the Hakluyt Society: *Mirabilia Descripta* (1863) and *Cathay and the Way Thither* (1866). Yule's research on early travel texts would later prove invaluable for *Hobson-Jobson*. In the early 1870s, he also acquired the reputation of a Central Asian expert with the timely publication of his 'Essay on the Geography of the Valley of the Oxus' (1872), just as diplomatic negotiation between Britain and Russia focused on the Upper Oxus as the proposed northern border of Afghanistan.

Yule's magnum opus was his monumental edition of Marco Polo's travels, *The Book of Ser Marco Polo*, published in two illustrated volumes in 1871 by John Murray, the leading publisher for literary, scientific, and travel works. Yule considered the travels a great puzzle which he strove to solve. He did not doubt that Marco Polo had visited the various regions mentioned in his account, and devoted all his energies to verifying Polo's claims. Reviewers hailed the work as a masterpiece of scholarship; the Geographical Society of Italy awarded him a gold medal, and the Royal Geographical Society, a founder's medal. So closely did Yule identify with Marco Polo that he adopted the pseudonym Marcus Paulus Venetus (or M.P.V.) when writing to the press. For the second edition of *Marco Polo*, he even inserted an account of an imagined visit by Marco Polo to contemporary Britain, composed in mock medieval French. Such whimsical gestures set the tone for *Hobson-Jobson*, where Yule would cite his own 'found' manuscript of the Indian travels of Sir John Mandeville.

In 1875, the year that the second edition of *Marco Polo* appeared, Yule's wife died, and he returned to London. Two years later, Yule remarried. Mary Skipwith was twenty years his junior, the daughter of one of Yule's friends; their marriage lasted four years, until Mary's premature death in 1881. In his newly established London home, Yule took up all the scholarly and political opportunities open to an erudite and well-connected old India hand. He embarked on a series of articles for the ninth edition of the *Encyclopaedia Britannica* on Asian regions and travellers. He was appointed to the Council of India, the fifteen-strong advisory body that met weekly to discuss matters of policy with the Secretary of State for India. 'We have all rather the look of old hulks laid up in dock', one of Yule's fellow councillors wrote, 'and are men who have said good-bye to active service.'[3]

The Council of India was supposed to act as a check on the Secretary of State. The members had the opportunity to intervene in the political controversies of the day. Yule did not often voice his dissent, but soon after his appointment, he opposed the removal of duty on the Indian importation of Manchester-manufactured cotton textiles, for fear that it would damage Indian cloth production. He also registered his dissent to the Vernacular Press Act of 1878. The Act required printers and publishers of Indian language newspapers to pledge not to print articles that might spread opposition to the British government, and gave the authorities the power to close down offending presses. 'This is not a modification of the law. It is a suspension of the law', thundered Yule.[4] In the event, the Act proved unworkable and was repealed three years later.

But Yule was not consistently liberal in his attitudes; indeed he grew increasingly disillusioned with liberalism in later years. 'He

[3] Alfred Comyn Lyall writing to his brother James in 1888, from Sir Mortimer Durand, *The Life of the Right Hon. Sir Alfred Comyn Lyall* (Edinburgh & London: William Blackwood & Sons, 1913), 322.

[4] *Opinions, and Reasons for the same, entered in the Minutes of the Proceedings of the Council of India, relating to the Vernacular Press Act, 1878.* Lytton Collection MSS Eur E218/146, Asia, Pacific and Africa Collections, British Library.

was never in any sense a party man', his daughter wrote, 'but often called himself "one of Mr. Gladstone's converts," i.e. one whom Gladstonian methods had compelled to break with liberal tradition and prepossessions.'[5] Yule objected to Gladstone's support for Home Rule for Ireland, and thought that he had behaved dishonourably in delaying the dispatch of a relief force to General Gordon, besieged at Khartoum. In the late 1880s, Yule found himself increasingly drawn to the fierce patriotism of Lord Wolseley, who blamed party politics, and Gladstone in particular, for sapping the country of manly honesty and depleting the strength of the armed forces. Some of these political views would resurface in the pages of *Hobson-Jobson*.

In addition to his involvement with the council, Yule took on various posts of scholarly responsibility. From 1877 to 1889, he was president of the Hakluyt Society, overseeing the production of editions of early travels. Recognition of his status as Asian expert came in 1885, with Yule's election to a two-year term as president of the Royal Asiatic Society. Towards the end of his life, Yule's achievements were acknowledged with the vice-presidency of the Royal Geographical Society (1887–9) and a knighthood (1889).

With these various institutional affiliations, Yule was at the heart of imperial networks of scholarship and authority. His multifaceted career and wide interests suggest that he was a man who could turn his hand, mind, and pen to virtually anything. Of unbounded intellectual confidence and energy, Yule turned out streams of articles, sat on countless scholarly and governmental committees, and corresponded with scholars across the world. Yule falls into that type of 'gentleman-officer-scholar' whom Douglas M. Peers has identified as crucial to the production of colonial knowledge in India.[6]

Yule's habits, enthusiasms, connections, and varied pursuits uniquely qualified him for his role as author of *Hobson-Jobson*. 'Colonel Yule represents the ideal glossologist', asserted the curator and critic George Birdwood. 'There is no writer among Anglo-Indians, living or dead, who has attained to his degree of eminence in extent or variety of knowledge, in exactitude of workmanship, in shrewd discrimination of the relative value of the fanciful and the

[5] Amy Frances Yule, 'Memoir of Sir Henry Yule', in Henry Yule, *The Book of Ser Marco Polo*, 3rd edn. (London: John Murray, 1903), p. lxviii.

[6] Doulas M. Peers, 'Colonial Knowledge and the Military in India, 1780–1860', *Journal of Imperial and Commonwealth History*, 33/2 (May 2005), 157–80.

practical, and in the capacity of lucid exposition.'[7] But even Yule could not compile *Hobson-Jobson* alone.

The linguistic expertise for the glossary was provided by Arthur Coke Burnell. 'He is one of the best Sanskrit (and other) scholars in the Civil Service', Yule wrote of Burnell to the publisher John Murray in May 1877. 'He supplies learning & I supply—what you may please to call it.'[8] Twenty years Yule's junior, Burnell was also born into a family with East India Company connections: his father had served in the Marine Service. It seems that Burnell senior was a Dutch Jew who had anglicized his name. Burnell made a point of telling his friends about his Jewish origins because he did not like his family's habit of concealing them.[9]

Burnell attended King's College London, and gained a place in the Indian Civil Service, offering Arabic as his oriental language. Then he turned his attention to Sanskrit and south Indian languages, gaining a proficiency which would later earn him the title of 'Burnell Shastri' ('one learned in the shastras'). Over the course of his life, in addition to Portuguese, Dutch, and Italian, Burnell would master Javanese, Coptic, and Tibetan (studied during a homeward voyage).

Burnell's professional duties in the Madras Civil Service, first as assistant magistrate and revenue official, then as district judge, took him to various south Indian districts. In his spare time he amassed an extensive collection of Sanskrit manuscripts, regularly contributed articles to scholarly journals, and published translations of Hindu law and editions of Sanskrit texts. His work on south Indian scripts, *Elements of South Indian Palaeography* (1874), gained him an honorary doctorate from the University of Strasbourg. Fêted by institutions overseas, he felt that he lacked official recognition from the government of India. The governor of Madras requested that Burnell catalogue the collection of Sanskrit manuscripts held at the palace at Tanjore (over 12,000 in number), but did not offer relief from his official duties. The decade-long task broke new scholarly ground, but also Burnell's health.

[7] *Quarterly Review*, 164/327 (Jan. 1887), 144.

[8] Henry Yule to John Murray, 7 May 1877, MS 41319, John Murray Archive (JMA), National Library of Scotland (NLS).

[9] Friedrich Max Müller, Obituary of Dr A. C. Burnell, *The Academy*, 546 (21 Oct. 1882), 295; Edward Nicholson, 'In Memoriam: The Late Dr. A. Burnell', *The Academy*, 548 (4 Nov. 1882), 329; Henry Yule to James Sutherland Cotton, 25 Nov. 1882, Arthur Coke Burnell letters, the John Rylands University Library, Eng MS 740/16.

The Making of Hobson-Jobson

Yule and Burnell first met at the India Office Library in London around 1872. When they discovered that they shared a common interest in the language of Anglo-India, Yule proposed a joint glossary. The idea of such a glossary was not entirely novel. Indian glossaries and word lists were an established genre, sometimes appearing as appendices, sometimes as discrete volumes. But most were purely utilitarian or technical in nature, focusing on terms that were required for work, trade, or domestic life, drawn from Persian and the various Indian languages. The definitions tended to be brief and explanatory, as befitted a handbook. What made *Hobson-Jobson* unique was its ambition to marry serious philological work with discursive commentary, to entertain as much as inform, and to organize the glossary on historical principles, supplying extensive illustrative quotations.

The collaboration proceeded through correspondence, since Yule was based in Sicily, and Burnell in India. Yule assumed responsibility for producing the text, compiling the definitions and composing the glosses, gathering and transcribing quotations. Yule was a compulsive annotator, both as reader and editor. According to George Birdwood, he always took heed of the eccentric Captain Cuttle's catchphrase from Dickens's *Dombey and Son*: 'when found, make a note of'.[10] In the works that Yule edited, the apparatus far outweighed the text. *Hobson-Jobson* is perhaps the fullest expression of the art of annotation. Each term is elucidated and illustrated at whatever length Yule sees fit (perhaps influenced by the form of the encyclopaedic essay, some extend to several pages). In the lexicon's ordered prolixity, Yule found his perfect form.

The entries were set out conventionally, with a headword in bold, followed by an abbreviation identifying the part of speech, then a definition. But there was no pattern to what followed. It could be a surprising etymology, a learned account of the evolution of a term, a commentary on the thing itself, a political aside or nostalgic reminiscence. To read the glossary is to encounter the unexpected. The entry on 'Mosquito', for instance, moves from epigrammatic definition to anecdotal digression:

[10] *Quarterly Review*, 164/327 (Jan. 1887), 166. The phrase was borrowed as the motto of that most miscellaneous of scholarly publications, *Notes & Queries.*

MOSQUITO s. A gnat is so called in the tropics. The word is Spanish and Port. (dim. of *mosca*, 'a fly'), and probably came into familiar English use from the East Indies, though the earlier quotations show that it was *first* brought from S. America. A friend annotates here: "Arctic mosquitoes are worst of all; and the Norfolk ones (in the Broads) beat Calcutta!"

It is related of a young Scotch lady of a former generation who on her voyage to India had heard formidable, but vague accounts of this terror of the night, that on seeing an elephant for the first time, she asked: "Will yon be what's called a **musqueetae**?" (p. 362)

Each term is illustrated by a selection of literary quotations, mainly in English, but also in French, Italian, Latin, and Greek. The sources for *Hobson-Jobson* testify to the remarkable breadth of Yule and Burnell's reading. It was perhaps Yule's involvement with the Hakluyt Society that contributed most to the lexicon. Travel texts formed the bulk of the sources for illustrative quotation. 'No work has been more serviceable in the compilation of the Glossary', Yule comments of John Fryer's *New Account of East India and Persia* (1698) which is cited more than 300 times (p. 35). Other fertile sources include *Purchas His Pilgrimes* (1625), the *Voyages* of the Dutch traveller Jan Huygen van Linschoten (1596) which Burnell edited for the Hakluyt Society, and the *Travels* of the Arabic traveller Ibn Batuta (1355). Yule also relied heavily on travel texts that he himself edited; there are some 400 references in all to *Cathay and the Way Thither*, *The Book of Ser Marco Polo,* and his edition of the *Diary* of William Hedges, the first East India Company agent in Bengal (1886).

The dependence on travel accounts is evident too in the length of entries. Some of the longest reflect the stereotypes of Indian travel writing. The entry for 'tiger' runs to two and a half pages, 'elephant' to four, 'suttee' (the rite of widow burning) to four and a half, and five separate entries detail the synonyms for 'dancing girl'. The quotations, far in excess of their illustrative function, grow into short narratives. But the lexicon sometimes defies expectation. For instance the two-page article on 'Juggurnaut' (the image of Krishna, carried in an enormous ceremonial car) reproduces the common story of devotees committing suicide under the car's wheels, but suggests that such reports are grossly exaggerated.

While the lexicon documents some of the customs associated with Indian religions (particularly the more sensational), it tends to neglect theological or philosophical concepts. As Ivor Lewis has pointed out, there are no entries for terms such as 'karma' or 'kismet' (fate) that were current in nineteenth-century English texts.[11] Such omissions may relate to Burnell's personal beliefs. He was a Positivist, a follower of the secular doctrine founded by Auguste Comte which influenced a number of Victorian intellectuals.[12] Positivism proposed a moral system without God or the supernatural. Human thought, according to Comte, always progressed through three stages: the theological or fictitious; the metaphysical or abstract; and ultimately, the positive or scientific. Burnell's Positivist belief seems to have led him to dismiss Indian intellectual traditions entirely. 'Considering the long intercourse with India,' he wrote in a draft introduction to *Hobson-Jobson*, 'it is noteworthy that the additions which have thus accrued to the English language are, from the intellectual standpoint, of no intrinsic value. Nearly all the borrowed words refer to material facts, or to peculiar customs and stages of society . . . they do not represent new ideas' (p. 21).

Such cultural arrogance is of course a common feature of imperial discourse. *Hobson-Jobson* is capable of both endorsing and undermining colonial stereotypes and policy. There are precise delineations of imperial attitudes, as in the much-quoted definition of 'Baboo': 'often used with a slight savour of disparagement, as characterizing a superficially cultivated, but too often effeminate, Bengali' (p. 72). But we also find more subversive comments, such as the commentary on the word 'Dustoor' ('custom'): 'That commission or percentage on the money passing in any cash transaction which, with or without acknowledgment or permission, sticks to the fingers of the agent of payment. Such "customary" appropriations are, we believe, very nearly as common in England as in India' (p. 217). There are occasional hints of colonial anxiety. The convoluted gloss on 'sahib', the title so resonant of British authority, suggests both a blurring of social distinctions and the possibility of native disrespect: 'The title by which, all over India, European gentlemen, and it may be said Europeans generally, are addressed, and spoken of, when no disrespect is intended, by natives' (p. 450). At times, British policy is criticized; the entry for 'Piece-goods' (cotton cloth) attacks the duties

[11] Ivor Lewis, *Sahibs, Nabobs and Boxwallahs: A Dictionary of the Words of Anglo-India* (Bombay: Oxford University Press, 1991), 4.

[12] For Burnell's Positivist beliefs see Nicholson, 'In Memoriam: The Late Dr. A. Burnell', 329–30.

which stifled Indian cloth manufacture (reiterating Yule's opposition on the Council of India). On the other hand, the British devastation of the Japanese city of Kagoshima in 1863 is justified in terms of political necessity (p. 455).

There are also some significant omissions. The commentary on 'Opium', for instance, overlooks the East India Company monopoly on the cultivation of the drug, its illegal export to China, and the two destructive Opium Wars. Equally, there is scant reference in *Hobson-Jobson* to the political opposition to British rule that led to the foundation of the Indian National Congress in 1885. Little mention is made of the extensive Anglo-Indian vocabulary of abuse. On the rare occasion that an obscenity is noted, the glossary shies away from a clear definition, taking refuge instead in euphemism or allusion.

At times, *Hobson-Jobson* evinces a clear sense of cultural superiority. In the customary nineteenth-century manner, the glossary condemns the pidgin English of the Chinese ports and the various forms of Indian English as corrupt jargons. But for all their disdain, Yule and Burnell identify some of the main grammatical elements of Indian English. According to the linguist Braj B. Kachru, *Hobson-Jobson* remained in 1980 the 'only existing dictionary which closely approximates serious lexical work' in Indian English.[13]

One of the central concerns of *Hobson-Jobson* is the intersection of languages and cultures under colonial rule: the linguistic borrowing and mutual mishearing, the hybrid words and puns. As its title suggests, *Hobson-Jobson* is preoccupied with the transformations of words across languages, the 'striving after meaning' of sound association, a process sometimes termed folk etymology. By the end of the nineteenth century, the phrase 'the law of Hobson-Jobson' had entered the vocabulary of linguists to describe the adaptation of a word from a foreign language to suit the sound system of another.

Delight in language animates the whole glossary. For Yule and Burnell, *Hobson-Jobson* was an absorbing hobby. It provided Yule with a nostalgic return to the language of his youth. As his contemporary Alexander Allardyce observed in *Blackwood's Edinburgh Magazine*, 'Anglo-Indianisms entwine themselves into men's habits and modes

[13] Braj B. Kachru, 'The New Englishes and Old Dictionaries: Directions in Lexicographical Research on Non-Native Varieties of English', in Ladislav Zguta (ed.), *Theory and Method in Lexicography: Western and Non-Western Perspectives* (Columbia, SC: Hornbeam Press, 1980), 80.

of thinking . . . they take a hold upon the sentimental feelings, and draw people together as if by a sort of freemasonry.'[14] For Yule, the book was something of a family affair with contributions by his friends and relatives. Among the illustrative quotations, we find extracts from letters sent by family and acquaintances, texts edited by Yule himself, even Yule's own speeches and anonymous verse. In a wonderfully self-referential moment, Yule provides textual evidence of the word 'Pundit' (as applied to Indian surveyors who secretly mapped regions of Central Asia) by reference to a speech he himself made at the Royal Geographical Society when he accepted the Victoria medal on behalf of the pundit surveyor Nain Singh (p. 431).

The eclectic range of sources, idiosyncratic approach, and long-distance collaboration meant that the glossary grew haphazardly. Yule and Burnell found it hard to resist a word with an engaging past, an unlikely etymology, or a personal resonance. One of the most frequently used terms in the commentaries is 'curious', and in a sense, *Hobson-Jobson* is a cabinet of linguistic curiosities. It followed the contours of its authors' particular interests. 'The subject, indeed, had taken so comprehensive a shape,' wrote Yule, 'that it was becoming difficult to say where its limits lay, or why it should ever end' (p. 5).

Despite the lexicon's unruly growth, it is possible to determine some broad categories into which most of the entries fall. *Hobson-Jobson*'s core lexis derives from the earliest Asian–European trading contacts. The association of language with commerce is evident from the first line of *Hobson-Jobson*'s introduction which invokes the wares of seventeenth-century England: '*calico*, *chintz*, and *gingham* had already effected a lodgment in English warehouses and shops, and were lying in wait for entrance into English literature' (p. 11). Language follows the routes of trade in *Hobson-Jobson* with the names of manufactured goods and raw commodities, fabrics and foods, weights and measures, currencies and ships.

Trade relies on geographical knowledge, and the glossary is concerned to document the regions of Asia. As Yule once observed, 'names are half geography'.[15] Drawing on his expertise as historical geographer, Yule provides entries on major towns, principalities, and

[14] Alexander Allardyce, 'The Anglo-Indian Tongue', *Blackwood's Edinburgh Magazine* (1877), 541–51; repr. in Kingsley Bolton and Braj. B. Kachru (eds.), *Asian Englishes*, i. *South Asian English 1837–1938* (London: Routledge, 2006), 83–93.

[15] Yule to H. W. Bates, 2 Nov. 1871, CB6, Royal Geographical Society Archives.

geographical features of India and beyond. The glossary also records the flora and fauna of Asia, detailing the properties of plants, animals, and crops throughout the region.

There is an ethnographic strand to *Hobson-Jobson* which describes the religious practices, social customs, and foods of various groups. We might here include the British community, for *Hobson-Jobson* provides what Javed Majeed has termed an 'auto-ethnographic' account of Anglo-Indian life.[16] The glossary is interested in preserving the obsolete language and practices of previous generations of Anglo-Indians. But there is also an emphasis on contemporary terms and the official language of the administration. In part, *Hobson-Jobson* operates as a working handbook for the British in India.

Publication and Reception

Burnell and Yule's collaboration was to last ten years; but Burnell's health was failing. He suffered an attack of cholera and frequent bouts of pneumonia; in 1880, he was afflicted with partial paralysis and was forced to retire. He returned to Britain, but spent the winters in the kinder climate of San Remo in Italy. He only lasted two more years. He met his premature death at the age of 42.

The first edition of *Hobson-Jobson* bore a memorial portrait of Burnell, and the preface paid handsome tribute to Burnell's linguistic expertise and untiring search for quotations; but Yule clearly claimed the work as his own: 'Indeed, in bulk, nearly seven-eighths of it is so' (p. 6). He himself wrote, and rewrote, the glossary at least four times. In a letter to John Murray of April 1888, Yule argued that he deserved the lion's share of royalties for *Hobson-Jobson*. 'The task of the book fell so largely upon me that I should consider an equal division of profits—whatever they may be—between Burnell's heirs & me by no means fair!'[17] Later the same year, Yule paid off Burnell's brother and executor with 'a lump sum of £25 in acquittance of all claims'.[18]

At the time of his death, Burnell had nearly completed his contribution to the glossary. But *Hobson-Jobson* would not be published for

[16] Javed Majeed, '"The Bad Habit": *Hobson-Jobson*, British Indian Glossaries, and Intimations of Mortality', *Henry Sweet Society Bulletin*, 46–7 (Nov. 2006), 7–22.

[17] Yule to John Murray, 27 Apr. 1888, Acc12604/199, MS 42733, JMA, NLS.

[18] Yule to John Murray 2 Aug. 1888, Acc12604/199, MS 42733, JMA, NLS.

another four years. Yule himself was not in good health; however, he was not wrestling with the glossary entirely alone. It is possible that there was another, unacknowledged collaborator in the person of his daughter, Amy, who was an author in her own right. She had revised and corrected one of John Murray's famous series of Handbooks for Travellers, the *Handbook for Travellers in Greece* (1884). In a memoir of her father, Amy Yule wrote of *Hobson-Jobson* as 'an abiding interest' to both her father and herself. 'Contributions of illustrative quotations came from most diverse and unexpected sources, and the arrival of each new word or happy quotation was quite an event, and gave such pleasure to the recipients as can only be fully understood by those who have shared in such pursuits.'[19] It is unclear how far Amy Yule shared in the book's production, but her account of the excitement generated by the arrival of the mail certainly suggests the extent of Yule's network of correspondents.[20]

The glossary was in proof form by the summer of 1883. Yule requested that it be printed in slips, so that additions and corrections could be made. By October 1884, the glossary was advertised in *The Times* as forthcoming, but the main alphabet was printed only in May 1885. In July of that year, Yule was shocked to discover that a rival publication had just appeared: George Whitworth's *An Anglo-Indian Dictionary* (1885). 'The book is poor in the extreme', Yule wrote to John Murray in July 1885, 'but of course its appearance with the title it bears, may injure the market for mine.' He was particularly exercised by a review in the *St James Gazette* which suggested 'that a vocabulary of this kind has never hitherto been published . . . although it is well known that Col Yule contemplated issuing one'. Yule immediately wrote to the *Gazette*'s editor, 'pointing out the injurious implication that I had abandoned the intention'. His concluding remarks to Murray justified the long delay in delivering the manuscript: 'By the bye the Gazette's statement that "a vocabulary of this kind" had never hitherto been published is erroneous.

[19] Amy Yule, 'Memoir', p. lxvii.

[20] Among those whose assistance Yule acknowledged were the curator Sir George Birdwood; Sir Joseph Hooker, director of Kew Gardens (who checked the botanical entries); William Robertson-Smith, professor of Arabic at Cambridge and editor-in-chief of the *Encyclopaedia Britannica* (to which Yule contributed a raft of articles); Dr James Murray, editor of the *New English Dictionary* (who read the dictionary in proof form). These exalted scholars were joined by the professor of Indo-Chinese philology at University College London, the India Office librarian, the bishop of mid-China, the consul-general in Korea, and two retired generals.

There are several of the kind of Mr Whitworth's—none of the kind of mine.'[21] In September the same year, Yule assured Murray that he had been 'working every moment I could get to the completion of the Glossary', and again dismissed the *Anglo-Indian Dictionary* as 'a very cutcha concern (vide the real Glossary!)'.[22] *Hobson-Jobson* finally appeared six months later, in March 1886.

The publication of *Hobson-Jobson* was in a sense the culmination of Yule's life and work. Into its pages, Yule poured the scholarly obsessions and personal recollections of his long and varied career. He was in his mid-sixties when it was published, and would die three years later. But the collaborative method of composition, the number of contributors, and wide range of illustrative quotation also made it a collective enterprise. *Hobson-Jobson* was at once an intensely individual text and a record of the language of the Anglo-Indian tribe. In its way, it was as much a monument to British India as Yule's earlier Kanpur memorial to the Mutiny dead; a lexicon that both preserved and fashioned Anglo-Indian identity.

The year of *Hobson-Jobson*'s publication saw imperial sentiment running high. Over the summer of 1886, over five-and-a-half million people thronged to South Kensington in London to view the Colonial and Indian Exhibition. A lavish celebration of commerce and power, this imperial spectacle granted India pride of place. Britain's global economic and political dominance depended on India—hence its pre-eminent position in the exhibition. A significant supplier of raw goods for British industry, India was also a captive market for British manufactured goods. The subcontinent was the great recruiting ground of empire, supplying manpower—at Indian expense—to fight Britain's battles overseas.

With its empire-wide focus, the Colonial and Indian Exhibition inevitably exceeded *Hobson-Jobson*'s geographic range, but both were hugely ambitious projects that aimed at encyclopaedic coverage. They were manifestations of a similar curatorial impulse to organize a haphazard collection in a manner intended to educate and entertain. Both featured India in its commercial, ethnographic, and administrative aspects. Indeed, Yule was a member of the Royal Commission for the exhibition, and the *Official Catalogue* referred twice to his newly

[21] Henry Yule to John Murray, 30 July 1885, MS 41319, JMA, NLS.
[22] Henry Yule to John Murray, 17 Sept. 1885, MS 41319, JMA, NLS.

published glossary in its discussion of the products on display.[23] Together, the exhibition and lexicon celebrated the extent of India's enrichment of British culture—through objects and words.

It was clearly an opportune moment to publish *Hobson-Jobson*. Reviewers were unanimous in their praise. The *Scottish Geographical Magazine* considered *Hobson-Jobson* 'a work not only of vast and enduring utility, but marked by a humour, a quaintness, a purity of treatment and style, and a ripeness of scholarship' that was distinctive of Yule (who, it should be noted, was one of the vice-presidents of the Scottish Geographical Society which published the journal).[24] In India, the young Rudyard Kipling predicted that *Hobson-Jobson* would 'take its place among the standard works on the East, gathering bulk as it goes, from decade to decade'.[25] Publications as unlikely as *The Girls' Own Paper* deemed it 'very amusing and instructive'.[26] Sir George Birdwood, who himself contributed to the glossary, reviewed *Hobson-Jobson* anonymously for both *The Athenaeum* and the *Quarterly Review* (published by John Murray). He declared *Hobson-Jobson* 'a library of entertaining knowledge'. Like Samuel Johnson's *Dictionary*, it could be read for both profit and pleasure, and was 'already an Anglo-Indian classic'.[27]

Hobson-Jobson *in the Twentieth Century*

By 1900 *Hobson-Jobson* was out of print. It was, in any case, somewhat unwieldy to use, with its 120-page supplement and without the index which Yule had originally planned. For years, the ethnographer, folklorist, and retired Indian magistrate William Crooke had been gathering materials on Anglo-Indian words, amassing notes and quotations on over a thousand terms, with a view to revising *Hobson-Jobson*. In February 1900 Crooke approached John Murray, setting out his qualifications for the role of editor: 'I served for 25 years in the Bengal Civil Service during which time I devoted much of my leisure to philology and anthropology.'[28] He listed his major publications on

[23] *Official Catalogue Colonial and Indian Exhibition 1886* (London: W. Clowes, 1886), 74, 80.

[24] *Scottish Geographical Magazine*, 2 (1886), 249.

[25] Pinney, *Kipling's India*, 159.

[26] *The Girls Own Paper*, 308 (4 June 1887).

[27] *The Athenaeum*, 3062 (3 July 1886), 8; *Quarterly Review* 164/327 (Jan. 1887), 148, 166.

[28] William Crooke to John Murray, 19 Feb. 1900, MS 40295, JMA, NLS.

the peoples, religion, folklore, and language of north-western India, and his editorship of the scholarly journal, *North Indian Notes and Queries*. With Amy Yule's approval, Murray commissioned Crooke to prepare a second edition of *Hobson-Jobson*.

Much of Crooke's preparatory work did not in fact find its way into the new edition. He decided on a light editorial touch. 'It is clear that no attempt should be made to interfere with the discussions of the book, which is its greatest charm', Crooke told Murray. The book should 'be edited tenderly, preserving as far as possible the original form'. He proposed to incorporate the appendix and list of errata into the main body of the text and to correct other errors. The book should be supplemented with examples drawn from contemporary writers: 'Kipling and other modern writers of his school must be read for new words and illustrations.'[29]

But, in the event, Amy Yule must have expressed some reservations over the inclusion of Kipling, who was then at the height of his fame. The exact nature of her objections remains uncertain, but it is evident that she was responsible for a change of editorial direction. Throughout her correspondence with Murray, Amy Yule was keen to respect her dead father's wishes and preserve his approach. It may have been that Yule himself objected to Kipling's work or political views. In an early short story, 'The Taking of Lungtungpen', Kipling had made fun of Lord Wolseley, Yule's great hero. Or Amy Yule herself may have disliked the increasingly strident tone of Kipling's later political opinions. 'In deference to Miss Yule's wishes', Crooke wrote to Murray when he submitted the final manuscript in 1902, 'I have quoted Kipling I think only twice.'[30] In fact, Crooke smuggled in eleven references to Kipling's work.

In general, Crooke attempted to follow Yule's lead as closely as possible, quoting from precisely the kinds of texts that Yule himself used. He drew supplementary quotations from recent Hakluyt Society publications and editions of early East India Company letter books. Recognizing Yule's habit of self-reference, Crooke quoted from Yule's own edition of the *Diary of William Hedges*. Like Yule, Crooke corresponded with a circle of experts on specialist matters. All additions were marked by square brackets, so that Crooke's voice did not obtrude into the original. He managed to supply one of the

[29] William Crooke to John Murray, 13 Apr. 1900, MS 40295 JMA, NLS.
[30] William Crooke to John Murray, 23 Jan. 1902, MS 40295 JMA, NLS.

most glaring omissions of the first edition, a literary quotation from the *Oriental Sporting Magazine* (1829) for the eponymous 'Hobson-Jobson' itself: 'the folks makes sich a noise, firing and troompeting and shouting **Hobson Jobson, Hobson Jobson**' (p. 262).

It was the 1903 edition that was repeatedly reissued both in India and Britain, over the course of the twentieth and twenty-first centuries. The book's longevity suggests something of its enduring appeal to writers, historians, and the general reader alike. To historians of colonial India, *Hobson-Jobson* provides an unrivalled resource; its eccentric, gentlemanly scholarship may well constitute the acceptable face of the Raj, for there is surely an element of Raj nostalgia in the lexicon's popularity, both in Britain and India.

In the early 1990s there were two attempts to update *Hobson-Jobson*: Ivor Lewis's *Sahibs, Nabobs and Boxwallahs* (1991) and Nigel Hankin's *Hanklyn-Janklyn* (1992). Two decades later, with the rise of Indian English as a global language and the advent of the Internet, an entirely new form of glossary was born. Launched in 2011, *Samosapedia* is a wiki that celebrates the inventiveness of South Asian English. Contributors supply words, definitions, and examples to catalogue the worldwide growth of South Asian English. It is irreverent, self-referential, colloquial, and very up to date: an evolving, collaborative resource that translates *Hobson-Jobson* for the Internet age and the diasporic South Asian community.

The playful exploration of words constitutes much of *Hobson-Jobson*'s appeal. Those who enjoy the history and texture of language, particularly writers, have long prized *Hobson-Jobson*. As Priya Joshi has noted, *Hobson-Jobson* legitimated 'a bastard, hybrid, colloquial English'; in effect, the glossary made the vernacular available for literary use.[31] It is therefore appropriate that Kipling, *the* poet of the Anglo-Indian vernacular, should have been one of the glossary's first reviewers. Kipling wrote that '[e]very one in the East . . . should possess himself of *Hobson-Jobson* and once possessed of it should apply himself diligently thereto'.[32] How far did Kipling follow his own advice? He certainly rivalled Yule as a connoisseur of slang and linguistic idiosyncrasy. The glossary gleefully notes rhyming reduplications such as *naukar-chākar* ('the servants') as 'one of those jingling

[31] Priya Joshi, *In Another Country: Colonialism, Culture, and the English Novel in India* (Delhi: Oxford University Press, 2002), 255.

[32] Pinney *Kipling's India*, 160.

double-barrelled phrases in which Orientals delight even more than Englishmen . . . As regards Englishmen, compare hugger-mugger, hurdy-gurdy, tip-top, highty-tighty, higgledy-piggledy, hocus-pocus, tit for tat, topsy-turvy, harum-scarum, roly-poly, fiddle-faddle, rump and stump, slip-slop' (p. 377). The list—to which we could of course add 'Hobson-Jobson'—enacts the irrepressible inventiveness of such formations. Kipling certainly shared in that pleasure. Compare, for example, these lines describing army pack camels or 'Oonts' ('Unts' to rhyme with 'fronts', as pronounced by the British soldier) from the poem of the same name in *Barrack Room Ballads* (1892): 'the hairy scary oont', 'the floppin', droppin' oont', 'the floatin', bloatin' oont' (ll. 13, 29, 37).

For some British writers, *Hobson-Jobson* offered a nostalgic return to the Raj. Anthony Burgess, a former colonial teacher in Malaya, read *Hobson-Jobson* for its evocation of British India 'in the days when it seemed it must last for ever . . . the smell, taste, rustle of the place'.[33] Nostalgia also infused Tom Stoppard's representation of *Hobson-Jobson* in his 1995 play, *Indian Ink*, set in a fictitious princely state in the closing decades of imperial rule, during the nationalist protests of the 1930s. Stoppard, who spent four years of his childhood in India, explores Indo-British relations and cultural influence through the characters of Flora Crewe, an English poet on a lecture tour, and Nirad Das, an Indian portrait painter. The Anglophile Das is painting Crewe's portrait, and their highly charged sittings veer between formality and flirtation. At one point, they play the Hobson-Jobson game; taking turns to make up sentences using as many Anglo-Indian words as possible:

FLORA: While having tiffin on the verandah of my bungalow I spilled kedgeree on my dungarees and had to go to the gymkhana in my pyjamas looking like a coolie.

DAS: I was buying chutney in the bazaar when a thug escaped from the choky and killed a box-wallah for his loot, creating a hullabaloo and landing himself in the mulligatawny.[34]

Hobson-Jobson has always appealed to Anglophile Indians, none more so than the Bengali writer Nirad C. Chaudhuri. For Chaudhuri, *Hobson-Jobson* offered a complex and paradoxical vision of British

[33] Anthony Burgess, 'Foreword' to H. Yule and A. C. Burnell, *Hobson-Jobson* (London: Routledge, 1985), p. viii.

[34] Tom Stoppard, *Indian Ink* (London: Faber, 1995), 18.

India, 'at the same time noble and mean, serious and trivial, pathetic and cruel, comical and tragic'.[35] Chaudhuri saw *Hobson-Jobson* as a work not only of historical significance, but of relevance to contemporary upper-class Indians. The mentality and behaviour of the Indian elite was shaped by the British, Chaudhuri argued, so present-day Indians should regard *Hobson-Jobson* not just as a reference work, but read it 'as if they were performing the *Srādh* [death anniversary] ceremony of their ancestors'.[36] In a typically contentious flourish, Chaudhuri reimagined the colonial lexicon as Hindu ritual text.

In fashioning a literary Indian English, writers such as Salman Rushdie and Amitav Ghosh are drawn to the hybrid language of *Hobson-Jobson*, even as they reject the glossary's colonial assumptions. Vijay Mishra has suggested that Rushdie's distinctive style, particularly his fondness for rhyming reduplication and anglicized Hindi/Urdu, is heavily indebted to *Hobson-Jobson*.[37] Rushdie himself celebrates 'the unparalleled intermingling that took place between English and the languages of India'. But where, he asks, are the terms of abuse: 'No *kaffir*, no *gully*, not even a *wog*'?[38] These striking absences point to Rushdie's ambivalence towards the text: 'To spend a few days with *Hobson-Jobson* is, almost, to regret the passing of the intimate connection that made this linguistic *kedgeree* possible. But then one remembers what sort of connection it was . . .'.[39]

Hobson-Jobson evokes a similarly contradictory response from Amitav Ghosh. The first volume of his *Ibis* trilogy, *Sea of Poppies* (2008), comes equipped in its US edition with a light-hearted glossary, 'The *Ibis* Chrestomathy', which is in constant dialogue with *Hobson-Jobson* ('The Glossary'). Its compiler, Neel Rattan Halder (one of the characters in the novel), both defers to and takes issue with his 'guru, Sir Henry'. Neel comments tellingly on the violence that lies latent in Anglo-Indian grammar: 'Is it not a commentary on the relationship of England and India', Neel asks, 'that most of the Hind. candidates for the Peerage of the English Verb pertain to grappling, grasping, binding, tying and whipping?'[40] On his deathbed,

[35] Nirad C. Chaudhuri, 'A Historical Perspective', introduction to H. Yule and A. C. Burnell, *Hobson-Jobson* (Sittingbourne, Kent: Linguasia, 1994), p. xv.

[36] Ibid.

[37] Vijay Mishra, 'Rushdie-Wushdie: Salman Rushdie's Hobson-Jobson', *New Literary History*, 40/2 (Spring 2009), 407.

[38] Rushdie, *Imaginary Homelands*, 82.

[39] Ibid. 83.

[40] http://www.amitavghosh.com/Chrestomathy.pdf, 6, 32.

Neel enjoins his descendants to continue work on the Chrestomathy. In a curious echo of Chaudhuri's injunction, Neel's last words turn the Chrestomathy into a ceremonial death ritual, linking the family to its founder. The linguistic cross-fertilization that occurred under British rule, Chaudhuri and Neel suggest, has become integral to a sense of Indian identity.

For a number of contemporary writers, *Hobson-Jobson* offers a way into the cultural (and other) liaisons of the colonial period. To quote Pico Iyer, 'three centuries of backstairs meetings seem to hide out in this monumental dictionary'.[41] In 'This Be the Pukka Verse' (2011), the British poet Daljit Nagra adopts a swaggering Anglo-Indian idiom of comic excess, but as the poem proceeds, it darkens to narrate a tale of lust and greed:

> the nautch that leads to ayahs
> and passer-by *goodies* snookered
>
> for sahibs sport that ends
> in the hushed-up betzi births
> of half-breed bastards growing up
> cursed as mad dogs and vagabonds
> in a jolly good lingam-land overflowing
> with Hobson-Jobsons of Holi,
> and opium and silk and spice
> and all the gems of the shafted earth![42]

The verse is full of unlikely alliterative phrases and compound words, the 'Hobson-Jobsons of Holi' that promiscuously mix English, Muslim, and Hindu terms. By the end, the Anglo-Indian diction and the Anglo-Indian offspring seem almost interchangeable, both blighted by their colonial origins.

Over the century and a quarter since its first publication, *Hobson-Jobson* has grown into something more than itself. From the start, its entries swelled the pages of what would become the *OED*. Over the course of the twentieth century, the glossary has been updated and imitated, but never surpassed. *Hobson-Jobson* not only breathes life into the language of the Raj, but has also influenced the prose style of

[41] Pico Iyer, 'English in India: Still All the Raj', *New York Times* (10 Aug. 1997).

[42] Daljit Nagra, *Tippoo Sultan's Incredible White-Man-Eating Tiger Toy Machine* (London: Faber & Faber, 2011), 17.

some of the leading Indian English writers of recent generations. Its literary afterlife suggests that the glossary is one of the most enduring—and perhaps one of the few endearing—imperial bequests. Yule imagined *Hobson-Jobson* in architectural terms as a 'portly double-columned edifice' (p. 5). It has indeed become a monument to Anglo-Indian language, a metonym for imperial cultural exchange, and ultimately, a symbol of British India itself.

NOTE ON THE TEXT

The task of compiling *Hobson-Jobson* lasted fourteen years. Seven years into Yule and Burnell's collaboration, twenty-two sample entries were published as 'Specimens of a Discursive Glossary of Anglo-Indian Terms' in *The Indian Antiquary* (1879). The taster gave an idea of the distinctive approach of the glossary and announced the publisher, but it would be a further seven years before the book actually appeared. John Murray published the first edition of *Hobson-Jobson* in octavo in March 1886, at the price of 36*s.*, with a print run of 1,000. Twenty-five copies were purchased by the London office of the Calcutta-based booksellers, Thacker, Spink & Co. for sale in India. The main body of the text ran to 751 double-columned pages, with a supplement of 118 pages.

John Murray issued the second edition of the glossary, edited by William Crooke, in 1903. Crooke did not greatly expand the entries of the glossary, but rather corrected and augmented them with additional textual examples. The book was now more than 1,000 pages long. All new material was marked in square brackets. Crooke integrated the 1886 supplement into the text and added an index, compiled by Charles Partridge.

The present edition is an abridged version of the 1903 edition, chosen because it integrates the 1886 supplement, and clearly indicates all additional material with square brackets. This abridgement is approximately half the length of the 1903 edition. Individual entries have not been shortened (except on rare occasions where the notes explain what has been cut). The entries have been selected on the basis of their historical, literary, and linguistic significance. Every effort has been made to preserve the range and idiosyncrasy of the original, albeit on a smaller scale.

It might be considered redundant to attempt to annotate *Hobson-Jobson*, since the glossary is a bravura performance of the art of annotation itself, but the Notes on the Entries aim to enhance the reader's understanding of the lexicon's cultural significance and its colonial context. The notes provide translations of foreign language passages in the glosses, but not of foreign language extracts in the illustrative quotations. These are left to stand, to give a sense of the extraordinary range of Yule and Burnell's literary references. The editorial notes are signalled by an asterisk in the text, which, in the case of the main entries, precedes the headword.

As Yule points out in the Introductory Remarks, the glossary employs the 'popular, or . . . vulgar quasi-English spellings' in the headwords (pp. 22–3). The headwords are followed by a more precise transliteration in Roman script. No words are supplied in their original scripts. The illustrative quotations provide variant spellings for the headword. The system of transliteration is set out in the 'Nota Bene'. However, Yule acknowledges that he has not been consistent, either in his spelling or transliteration. Indeed, he makes a virtue of this inconsistency, suggesting that greater scholarly rigour would be pedantic (or Germanic) in a popular work.

The present edition has retained Yule's spelling which, it should be noted, frequently varies from forms of romanization current today. When looking up a word in the glossary, readers should bear in mind the following principles:

Vowels

A short ă is usually represented in the glossary by **u**. So **baksheesh** becomes **bucksheesh**.

A short ă is occasionally represented by **o**. So Hindi **chappar** becomes the Anglo-Indian **chopper**.

A long ā is often represented either by **au** or **aw**. So Hindi **ghāṭ** becomes **ghaut**, and **pānī** becomes **pawnee**.

A long ā may sometimes be represented by **o**. So **chāp** becomes **chop**.

ai may be represented by **y**. So **maidān** becomes **mydan**.

au may be represented by **o**. So Hindi **caukīdār** becomes **chokidar**.

au may also be represented by **ow**. So Hindi **cauk** becomes **chowk**.

A long ī is frequently represented by **ee**. So Hindi **bībī** becomes **beebee**.

A short ŭ is sometimes represented by **o**. So Hindi/Urdu **mufassal** becomes **mofussil**.

A short ŭ may occasionally be represented by **oo**. So Sanskrit **tulasī** becomes **toolsy**.

A long ū is often represented by **oo**. So **Bābū** becomes **Baboo**.

Consonants

An initial **k** may be represented by **c**. So Hindi **kamarband** becomes **cummerbund**.

A **sh** may occasionally be represented by **s**. So Sanskrit **śālagrāma** becomes **saligram**.

A **v** or **w** may be represented by **b**. So **navāb** becomes **nabob**.

Aspirated consonants (e.g. **th, kh**), especially at the beginning of a word, may lose the aspiration (**h**) in the Anglo-Indian derived word. So Hindi **thānadār** becomes **tanadar**.

SELECT BIBLIOGRAPHY

Primary Texts

Allardyce, Alexander, 'The Anglo-Indian Tongue', *Blackwood's Edinburgh Magazine*, 121 (1877); repr. in Kingsley Bolton and Braj B. Kachru (eds.), *Asian Englishes*, i. *South Asian English 1837–1938* (London: Routledge, 2006), 83–93.

Burnell, Arthur Coke, *Elements of South-Indian Palaeography*, 2nd edn. (London: Trübner & Co., 1874).

—— *The Ordinances of Manu*, ed. Edward W. Hopkins (London: Trübner & Co., 1884).

Hotten, John Camden, *A Dictionary of Modern Slang, Cant and Vulgar Words* (London: John Camden Hotten, 1859).

Leland, Charles G., *Pidgin-English Sing-Song or Songs and Stories in the China-English Dialect with a Vocabulary* (London: Trübner & Co., 1876).

MacMillan, Michael, 'Anglo-Indian Words and Phrases', in *The Globe Trotter in India Two Hundred Years Ago and Other Indian Studies* (London: Sonnenschein, 1895); repr. in Kingsley Bolton and Braj B. Kachru (eds.), *Asian Englishes*, i. *South Asian English 1837–1938* (London: Routledge, 2006), 247–84.

Müller, Friedrich Max, *Lectures on the Science of Language* (London: Longman, 1864).

Murray, James A. H., 'Preface to Volume I', *A New English Dictionary on Historical Principles . . .*, i. *A and B* (Oxford: Clarendon Press, 1888).

Palmer, Abram Smythe, *Folk Etymology: A Dictionary of Verbal Corruptions or Words Perverted in Form or Meaning, by False Derivation or Mistaken Analogy* (London: George Bell, 1882).

Schuchardt, Hugo, *Pidgin & Creole Languages*, trans. Glen. G. Gilbert (orig. German 1891; Cambridge: Cambridge University Press, 1988).

Skeat, Walter W., *A Concise Etymological Dictionary of the English Language* (Oxford: Clarendon Press, 1882).

Small, George, *A Laskari Dictionary or Anglo-Indian Vocabulary of Nautical Terms and Phrases in English and Hindustani Chiefly in the Corrupt Jargon in use among Laskars or Indian Sailors* (London: W. H. Allen, 1882).

Stocqueler, J. H., *The Oriental Interpreter and Treasury of East India Knowledge* (London: James Madden, 1848).

Whitworth, George Clifford, *An Anglo-Indian Dictionary: A Glossary of Indian Terms used in English, and of such English or other non-Indian Terms as have obtained special Meanings in India* (London: Kegan Paul, Trench & Co., 1885).

Wood, John, *A Journey to the Source of the River Oxus, with an Essay on the Geography of the Valley of the Oxus by Colonel Henry Yule* (London: John Murray, 1872).

Yule, Henry, *The Book of Ser Marco Polo*, 2 vols. (London: John Murray, 1871).

——articles for the *Encyclopaedia Britannica*, 9th edn. (London, 1875–89): Achin, Afghanistan, Andaman Islands, Cambodia, Gaur, Ghazni, Gilgit, Hindu-Kush, Hwen T'sang, Ibn Batuta, Kafiristan, Lhasa, Marco Polo, Maldive Islands, Mandeville, Odoric, Ormus, Prester John, Rennell, Rubruquius.

——*A Narrative of the Mission to the Court of Ava in 1855* (1858; Kuala Lumpur: Oxford University Press, 1968).

Biographical

Yule, Amy Frances, 'Memoir of Sir Henry Yule', in Henry Yule, *The Book of Ser Marco Polo*, 3rd edn. (London: John Murray, 1903).

Language & Lexicography

Benson, Phil, *Ethnocentrism and the English Dictionary* (London: Routledge, 2001).

Bolton, Kingsley, 'Language and Hybridization: Pidgin Tales from the China Coast', *Interventions*, 2/1 (2000), 35–52.

Burke, Peter, and Porter, Roy, *Languages and Jargon: Contributions Towards a Social History of Language* (Cambridge: Polity Press, 1995).

Chaudhuri, Nirad C., 'A Historical Perspective', introduction to Yule and Burnell, *Hobson-Jobson* (Sittingbourne, Kent: Linguasia, 1994), pp. vi–xv.

Dowling, Linda, 'Victorian Oxford and the Science of Language', *PMLA* 97/2 (1982), 160–78.

Errington, Joseph, *Linguistics in a Colonial World: A Story of Language, Meaning & Power* (Oxford: Blackwell, 2008).

Ghosh, Amritav, 'Of Fanás and Forecastles: The Indian Ocean and Some Lost Languages of the Age of Sail', *Economic and Political Weekly* (21 June 2008), 56–62.

——'The Ibis Chrestomathy', appended to *Sea of Poppies* (New York: Farrar, Straus, Giroux, 2008) also available at http://www.amitavghosh.com/Chrestomathy.pdf

Harpham, Geoffrey Galt, 'Roots, Races and the Return to Philology', *Representations*, 106 (Spring 2009), 34–62.

Iyer, Pico, 'A Far-off Affair', *Sun After Dark: Flights into the Foreign* (New York: Vintage Books, 2004), 204–13.

Lehrer, Seth, *Inventing English: A Portable History of the Language* (New York: Columbia University Press, 2007).

Majeed, Javed, 'The Bad Habit: *Hobson-Jobson*, British Indian Glossaries and Intimations of Mortality', *Henry Sweet Society Bulletin*, 46–7 (Nov. 2006), 7–22.

Mishra, Vijay, 'Rushdie-Wushdie: Salman Rushdie's Hobson-Jobson', *New Literary History*, 40/2 (Spring 2009), 385–410.

Nagle, Traci, '"There is much, very much, in the name of a book": or, the Famous Title of *Hobson-Jobson* and How It Got That Way', in Michael Adams (ed.), *'Cunning Passages, Contrived Corridors': Unexpected Essays in the History of Lexicography* (Monza: Polimetrica, 2010), 111–27.

Pechey, Graham, 'Exotic to Demotic: Folk Etymology in the Context of Empire', *Critical Quarterly*, 47/4 (2005), 67–86.

Rushdie, Salman, '*Hobson-Jobson*', in *Imaginary Homelands: Essays and Criticism 1981–1991* (London: Granta & Penguin, 1992), 81–3.

Teltscher, Kate, 'The Floating Lexicon: *Hobson-Jobson* and the *OED*', in Indra Sengupta and Daud Ali (eds.), *Knowledge Production, Pedagogy, and Institutions in Colonial India* (New York: Palgrave Macmillan, 2011).

Willinsky, John, *Empire of Words: The Reign of the OED* (Princeton: Princeton University Press, 1994).

Historical Context

Ballantyne, Tony, *Orientalism and Race* (Basingstoke: Palgrave, 2002).

Bayly, C. A., *Empire and Information: Intelligence Gathering and Social Communication in India, 1780–1870* (Cambridge: Cambridge University Press, 1996).

—— *Indian Society and the Making of the British Empire* (Cambridge: Cambridge University Press, 1988).

Chang, Elizabeth H., *Britain's Chinese Eye: Literature, Empire and Aesthetics in the Nineteenth Century* (Stanford: Stanford University Press, 2010).

Cohn, Bernard S., *Colonialism and Its Forms of Knowledge: The British in India* (Princeton: Princeton University Press, 1996).

Collingham, E. M., *Imperial Bodies: The Physical Experience of the Raj c. 1800–1947* (Cambridge: Polity, 2001).

Edney, Matthew H., *Mapping an Empire: The Geographical Construction of British India, 1765–1843* (Chicago: Chicago University Press, 1997).

Hevia, James L., *English Lessons: The Pedagogy of Imperialism in Nineteenth-Century China* (Durham, NC: Duke University Press, 2003).

Hillemann, Ulrike, *Asian Empire and British Knowledge: China and the Networks of British Imperial Expansion* (Basingstoke: Palgrave Macmillan, 2009).

Hopkirk, Peter, *The Great Game: On Secret Service in High Asia* (London: John Murray, 2006).

Liu, Lydia H., *The Clash of Empires: The Invention of China in Modern World Making* (Cambridge, Mass.: Harvard, 2004).

Mathur, Saloni, *India by Design: Colonial History and Cultural Display* (Berkeley: University of California Press, 2007).

Metcalf, Thomas R., *Ideologies of the Raj* (Cambridge: Cambridge University Press, 1994).

Peers, Douglas M., 'Colonial Knowledge and the Military in India, 1780–1860', *Journal of Imperial and Commonwealth History*, 33/2 (May 2005), 157–80.

Sinha, Mrinalini, *Colonial Masculinities: The Manly Englishman and the Effeminate Bengali in the Late Nineteenth Century* (Manchester: Manchester University Press, 1995).

Teltscher, Kate, '"The Rubicon between the Empires": The River Oxus in the Nineteenth-Century British Geographical Imaginary', in Nile Green (ed.), *Writing Travel in Central Asian History* (Bloomington: Indiana University Press, 2013).

Trautmann, Thomas R., *Aryans and British India* (Berkeley: University of California Press, 1997).

Further Reading in Oxford World's Classics

Baden-Powell, Robert, *Scouting for Boys*, ed. Elleke Boehmer.

Empire Writing, ed. Elleke Boehmer.

Fowler, H. W., *A Dictionary of Modern English Usage*, ed. David Crystal.

Kipling, Rudyard, *Kim*, ed. Alan Sandison.

Steele, Flora Annie, and Gardiner, Grace, *The Complete Indian Housekeeper and Cook*, ed. Ralph Crane and Anna Johnston.

A CHRONOLOGY OF HENRY YULE AND ARTHUR COKE BURNELL

1820 Henry Yule born 1 May at Inveresk, near Edinburgh, to Major William Yule and Elizabeth (née Paterson), youngest of three sons.

1824 First Anglo-Burmese War begins (to 1826).

1827 H.Y.'s mother dies.

1829 Abolition of sati.

1830 H.Y. attends the Royal High School, Edinburgh. Sent for private tuition to the mathematician Revd Henry Parr Hamilton, then the astronomer Revd James Challis (to 1836).

1832 The Reform Act extends the franchise in Britain.

1836 H.Y. briefly studies law at University College London.

Lord Auckland appointed Governor General of India.

W. E. Sleeman, *Ramseeana or a Vocabulary of the Peculiar Language used by Thugs*

1837 H.Y. attends East India Company's Military College, Addiscombe.

Accession of Queen Victoria.

1839 H.Y. trains with the Royal Engineers at Chatham.

Beginning of First Opium War and First Afghan War (both to 1842).

Philip Meadows Taylor, *Confessions of a Thug*

1840 H.Y. joins the Bengal Engineers. Arrives Calcutta. Arthur Coke Burnell born 11 July at St Briavels, Gloucestershire, to Arthur Burnell and Mary (née Coke).

Queen Victoria marries Prince Albert.

1841 H.Y. sent to survey Khasi Hills, Shillong.

China cedes Hong Kong to Britain.

1842 H.Y. works on canals in North-Western Provinces.

Lord Ellenborough appointed Governor General of India.

1843 During period of leave in Britain, H.Y. marries his cousin, Anna Maria. Returns to India to work on canals.

Annexation of Sind. Abolition of slavery in British India.

James Cowles Prichard, *Natural History of Man*

1845 H.Y. engaged in campaign against Sikhs (bridges Sutlej River).

First Anglo-Sikh War begins (to 1846). Lord Hardinge appointed Governor General of India.

1846 H.Y. works on the Ganges Canal.

1848 H.Y. at Battle of Chilianwallah (British defeat by Sikhs).

Second Anglo-Sikh War begins (to 1849). Lord Dalhousie appointed Governor General of India.

William Makepeace Thackeray, *Vanity Fair*

1849 Annexation of the Punjab.

1850 H.Y. on leave in Britain. Railway construction begins in India.

1851 A.B. attends Bedford Grammar School.

First Indian telegraph line laid. Great Exhibition staged in London.

1852 H.Y.'s daughter, Amy, born. H.Y. returns to India.

Second Anglo-Burmese War begins (to 1853). Annexation of Lower Burma.

1853 H.Y. sent to survey Aracan–Burma border, report on defences of the Straits Settlement. On return to Calcutta, H.Y. appointed deputy consulting engineer for railways.

First Indian railway opens. Introduction of competitive exam to enter East India Company service.

1854 Opening of Ganges Canal. Crimean War begins (to 1856).

1855 H.Y. appointed under-secretary for public works. H.Y. serves as secretary to Colonel Arthur Phayre's mission to Burma.

Horace Hayman Wilson, *A Glossary of Judicial and Revenue Terms*

1856 H.Y. on leave in Britain.

Lord Canning appointed Governor General of India. Annexation of Oudh. Second Opium War begins (to 1860).

1857 H.Y. responsible for defence of Allahabad, and troop accommodation. A.B. attends King's College London.

Indian Rebellion begins (to 1858). Foundation of Calcutta, Bombay, and Madras Universities. Philological Society of London proposes new English dictionary.

1858 H.Y. appointed secretary for public works.

Government of India Act abolishes East India Company and brings India under Crown rule. Lord Canning becomes the first viceroy of India.

Yule, *A Narrative of the Mission . . . to the Court of Ava in 1855*

1859 A.B. passes Indian Civil Service examination.

1859 Charles Darwin, *On the Origin of Species*

1860 A.B. arrives in Madras, serves as magistrate and revenue official in the Malabar, Tanjore, Chingleput, and Nellore districts (to 1868).

Indian Penal Code.

1861 H.Y. designs Memorial Well at Kanpur.

Indian Councils Act. Lord Elgin appointed viceroy.

Friedrich Max Müller, *Lectures on the Science of Language* (first series)

1862 H.Y. designs tomb for Lady Canning. H.Y. and Lord Canning retire from India. Lord Canning dies in London.

1863 H.Y. awarded CB (Companion of the Order of the Bath).

Sir John Lawrence appointed viceroy.

Yule, *Mirabilia Descripta: The Wonders of the East*

1864 H.Y. and family settle in Palermo, Sicily.

Friedrich Max Müller, *Lectures on the Science of Language* (2nd series)

George Otto Trevelyan, *The Competition Wallah*

1865 First telegraph connection between India and Europe.

1866 Yule, *Cathay and the Way Thither*

1867 Second Reform Bill extends franchise in Britain.

1868 A.B. on sick leave in Britain.

J. Forbes Watson, *The People of India*

Wilkie Collins, *The Moonstone*

1869 Opening of the Suez Canal.

1870 A.B. returns to India as district judge in various districts in Madras Presidency (to 1880).

Brewer's *Dictionary of Phrase and Fable*

1871 A.B. appointed to catalogue over 12,000 Sanskrit manuscripts in the palace at Tanjore (to 1880).

Indian Criminal Tribes Act.

Charles Darwin, *The Descent of Man*

Henry Sumner Maine, *Village Communities*

Yule, *Book of Ser Marco Polo* (awarded founder's medal of Royal Geographical Society, 1872)

1872 H.Y. and A.B. decide to collaborate on Anglo-Indian glossary.

Lord Northbrook appointed viceroy.

Yule, 'Essay on the Geography of the Valley of the Oxus'

Charles Leland, *Pidgin-English Sing-Song*

1873 Bengal famine.

1874 A.B. awarded honorary doctorate from the University of Strasbourg.

Burnell, *Elements of South Indian Palaeography*

1875 Death of Anna, H.Y.'s wife. H.Y. returns to Britain. Appointed to the Council of India (to 1889). Contributes articles to the *Encyclopaedia Britannica* (to 1886).

Foundation of Arya Samaj, Hindu reform movement. Foundation of the Theosophical Society in New York. British government purchases majority holding of shares in the Suez Canal.

Burnell, *The Aindra School of Sanskrit Grammarians*

1876 Queen Victoria proclaimed empress of India. Lord Lytton appointed viceroy. Famine in south India (to 1878).

1877 H.Y. marries Mary Skipwith. H.Y. president of the Hakluyt Society (to 1889).

Imperial Durbar held in Delhi.

1878 India's Vernacular Press Act. Second Afghan War begins (to 1880).

1879 James Murray begins work on *New English Dictionary*.

Edwin Arnold, *The Light of Asia*

1880 A.B. retires to Britain through ill health, over-winters in Italy.

Lord Ripon appointed viceroy. First Boer War begins (to 1881). Closure of India Museum, London; contents dispersed to South Kensington Museum, British Museum, Natural History Museum, and Kew Gardens.

George Birdwood, *The Industrial Arts of India*

Alfred, Lord Tennyson, 'The Defence of Lucknow'

Burnell, *Classified Index to the Sanskrit MSS in the Palace at Tanjore*

1881 Death of Mary, H.Y.'s second wife.

1882 A.B. dies (12 October).

Britain occupies Egypt and assumes control of Egyptian finances.

Bankimcandra Chatterji, *Anandamath* (contains 'Vande Mataram', which would become India's national song)

Toru Dutt, *Ancient Ballads and Legends of Hindustan*

1883 Opposition to the Ilbert Bill (enables Indian magistrates to judge Europeans).

1883 John Seeley, *The Expansion of England*

1884 H.Y. awarded honorary LLD from Edinburgh University.
Lord Dufferin appointed viceroy.
Publication of first fascicle of *New English Dictionary* (continues to 1928).

1885 H.Y. president of the Royal Asiatic Society (to 1887).
Penjdeh Incident on Afghan–Russian border raises tensions between Britain and Russia. Death of General Gordon. Third Anglo-Burmese War. Foundation of Indian National Congress.
Burnell, *Translation of the Ordinances of Manu* (completed by E. W. Hopkins)
Linschoten's *East Indies*, ed. Burnell (completed by P. A. Tiele)

1886 Annexation of Upper Burma. Colonial and Indian Exhibition.
Yule & Burnell, *Hobson-Jobson*

1887 H.Y. vice-president of the Royal Geographical Society (to 1889).
Yule, *Diary of Sir William Hedges*

1888 Lord Lansdowne appointed viceroy. Sikkim War.
Rudyard Kipling, *Plain Tales from the Hills*
William Crooke, *Glossary of North Indian Peasant Life*

1889 H.Y. created KCSI (Knight Commander of the Order of the Star of India). H.Y. dies (30 Dec.).
Flora Annie Steele, *The Complete Indian Housekeeper and Cook*

1890 Arthur Conan Doyle, *The Sign of Four*

1891 Age of Consent Act (India) raises age of marriage from 10 to 12.
Herbert Hope Risley, *The Tribes and Castes of Bengal*
Arthur Conan Doyle, *The Adventures of Sherlock Holmes*

1892 Indian Councils Act introduces Indian members to viceroy's Legislative Council.
Rudyard Kipling, *Barrack Room Ballads*

1893 Durand Line fixes border between British India and Afghanistan.

1894 Lord Elgin appointed viceroy. Linguistic Survey of India begins (to 1927).

1896 William Crooke, *Tribes and Castes of the North-Western Provinces*
William Crooke, *The Popular Religion and Folklore of Northern India*

1897 Queen Victoria's Diamond Jubilee. Foundation of Ramakrishna Mission, devoted to relief work and education.

1898 Lord Curzon appointed viceroy. Second Boer War begins (to 1902).

1901 Death of Queen Victoria, accession of Edward VII. Creation of North-Western Frontier Province.

Rudyard Kipling, *Kim*

1903 British invasion of Tibet (to 1904).

Second edition of Yule and Burnell's *Hobson-Jobson*, edited by William Crooke

HOBSON-JOBSON

["Wee have forbidden the severall Factoryes from wrighting words in this languadge and refrayned itt our selves, though in bookes of coppies we feare there are many which by wante of tyme for perusall we cannot rectefie or expresse."—Surat Factors to Court, Feb. 26, 1617: I. O. Records: O. C. No. 450. (Evidently the Court had complained of a growing use of "Hobson-Jobsons.")]*

"Οὐδὲ γὰρ πάντως τὴν αὐτήν διασώζει διάνοιαν μεθερμηνευόμενα τὰ ὀνόματα ἀλλ' ἔστι τινὰ, καὶ καθ' ἕκαστον ἔθνος ἰδιώματα, ἀδύνατα εἰς ἄλλο ἔθνος διὰ φωνῆς σημαίνεσθαι."—IAMBLICHUS, *De Mysteriis*, vii. cap. v.

i.e. "For it is by no means always the case that translated terms preserve the original conception; indeed every nation has some idiomatic expressions which it is impossible to render perfectly in the language of another."

"As well may we fetch words from the *Ethiopians*, or East or West *Indians*, and thrust them into our Language, and baptize all by the name of *English*, as those which we daily take from the *Latine* or Languages thereon depending; and hence it cometh, (as by often experience is found) that some *English-men* discoursing together, others being present of our own Nation ... are not able to understand what the others say, notwithstanding they call it *English* that they speak."—R. V(ERSTEGAN), *Restitution of Decayed Intelligence*, ed. 1673, p. 223.*

"Utque novis facilis signatur cera figuris,
Nec manet ut fuerat, nec formas servat easdem,
Sed tamen ipsa eadem est; VOCEM sic semper eandem
Esse, sed in varias doceo migrare figuras."

Ovid. Metamorph. xv. 169–172 (adapt.).*

"... *Take this as a good fare-well draught of* English-Indian *liquor.*"—PURCHAS, *To the Reader* (*before* Terry's Relation of East India), ii. 1463 (misprinted 1464).

"Nec dubitamus multa esse quae et nos praeterierint. Homines enim sumus, et occupati officiis; subsicivisque temporibus ista curamus." —C. PLINII SECUNDI, *Hist. Nat. Praefatio, ad Vespasianum.**

"Haec, si displicui, fuerint solatia nobis:
Haec fuerint nobis praemia, si placui."

MARTIALIS, *Epigr.* II. xci.*

HOBSON-JOBSON

A GLOSSARY OF COLLOQUIAL ANGLO-INDIAN WORDS AND PHRASES, AND OF KINDRED TERMS, ETYMOLOGICAL, HISTORICAL, GEOGRAPHICAL AND DISCURSIVE

BY COL. HENRY YULE, R.E., C.B.
AND A. C. BURNELL, PH.D., C.I.E.

NEW EDITION EDITED BY
WILLIAM CROOKE, B.A.

LONDON
JOHN MURRAY, ALBEMARLE STREET
1903

[*Dedication to Sir George Udny Yule, C.B., K.C.S.I.*]*

G. U. Y.

FRATRI OPTIMO DILECTISSIMO

AMICO JUCUNDISSIMO

HOC TRIUM FERME LUSTRORUM

OBLECTAMENTUM ET SOLATIUM

NEC PARVI LABORIS OPUS

ABSOLUTUM TANDEM

SENEX SENI

DEDICAT

H. Y.

PREFACE

THE objects and scope of this work are explained in the Introductory Remarks which follow the Preface. Here it is desired to say a few words as to its history.

The book originated in a correspondence between the present writer, who was living at Palermo, and the late lamented ARTHUR BURNELL, of the Madras Civil Service, one of the most eminent of modern Indian scholars, who during the course of our communications was filling judicial offices in Southern and Western India, chiefly at Tanjore. We had then met only once—at the India Library; but he took a kindly interest in work that engaged me, and this led to an exchange of letters, which went on after his return to India. About 1872—I cannot find his earliest reference to the subject—he mentioned that he was contemplating a vocabulary of Anglo-Indian words, and had made some collections with that view. In reply it was stated that I likewise had long been taking note of such words, and that a notion similar to his own had also been at various times floating in my mind. And I proposed that we should combine our labours.

I had not, in fact, the linguistic acquirements needful for carrying through such an undertaking alone; but I had gone through an amount of reading that would largely help in instances and illustrations, and had also a strong natural taste for the kind of work.

This was the beginning of the portly double-columned edifice which now presents itself, the completion of which my friend has not lived to see. It was built up from our joint contributions till his untimely death in 1882, and since then almost daily additions have continued to be made to the material and to the structure. The subject, indeed, had taken so comprehensive a shape, that it was becoming difficult to say where its limits lay, or why it should ever end, except for the old reason which had received such poignant illustration: *Ars longa, vita brevis.** And so it has been wound up at last.

The work has been so long the companion of my *horae subsicivae*, a thread running through the joys and sorrows of so many years, in the search for material first, and then in their handling and adjustment to the edifice—for their careful building up has been part of my duty from the beginning, and the whole of the matter has, I suppose, been written and re-written with my own hand at least four times—and the work has been one of so much interest to dear friends, of whom not a few are no longer here to welcome its appearance in print,[1] that I can hardly speak of the work except as mine.

Indeed, in bulk, nearly seven-eighths of it is so. But BURNELL contributed so much of value, so much of the essential; buying, in the search for illustration, numerous rare and costly books which were not otherwise accessible to him in India; setting me, by his example, on lines of research with which I should have else possibly remained unacquainted; writing letters with such fulness, frequency, and interest on the details of the work up to the summer of his death; that the measure of bulk in contribution is no gauge of his share in the result.

In the *Life of Frank Buckland* occur some words in relation to the church-bells of Ross, in Herefordshire, which may with some aptness illustrate our mutual relation to the book:

> "It is said that the Man of Ross" (John Kyrle) "was present at the casting of the tenor, or great bell, and that he took with him an old silver tankard, which, after drinking claret and sherry, he threw in, and had cast with the bell."

John Kyrle's was the most precious part of the metal run into the mould, but the shaping of the mould and the larger part of the material came from the labour of another hand.

At an early period of our joint work BURNELL sent me a fragment of an essay on the words which formed our subject, intended as the basis of an introduction. As it stands, this is too incomplete to print, but I have made use of it to some extent, and given some extracts from it in the Introduction now put forward.[2]

The alternative title (*Hobson-Jobson*) which has been given to this book (not without the expressed assent of my collaborator), doubtless requires explanation.

A valued friend of the present writer many years ago published a book, of great acumen and considerable originality, which he

1 The dedication was sent for press on 6th January; on the 13th, G. U. Y. departed to his rest.

2 Three of the mottoes that face the title were also sent by him.

called *Three Essays*, with no Author's name; and the resulting amount of circulation was such as might have been expected. It was remarked at the time by another friend that if the volume had been entitled *A Book, by a Chap*, it would have found a much larger body of readers. It seemed to me that *A Glossary* or *A Vocabulary* would be equally unattractive, and that it ought to have an alternative title at least a little more characteristic. If the reader will turn to *Hobson-Jobson* in the Glossary itself, he will find that phrase, though now rare and moribund, to be a typical and delightful example of that class of Anglo-Indian *argot* which consists of Oriental words highly assimilated, perhaps by vulgar lips, to the English vernacular; whilst it is the more fitted to our book, conveying, as it may, a veiled intimation of dual authorship. At any rate, there it is; and at this period my feeling has come to be that such *is* the book's name, nor could it well have been anything else.

In carrying through the work I have sought to supplement my own deficiencies from the most competent sources to which friendship afforded access. Sir JOSEPH HOOKER has most kindly examined almost every one of the proof-sheets for articles dealing with plants, correcting their errors, and enriching them with notes of his own. Another friend, Professor ROBERTSON SMITH, has done the like for words of Semitic origin, and to him I owe a variety of interesting references to the words treated of, in regard to their occurrence, under some cognate form, in the Scriptures. In the early part of the book the Rev. GEORGE MOULE (now Bishop of Ningpo), then in England, was good enough to revise those articles which bore on expressions used in China (not the first time that his generous aid had been given to work of mine). Among other friends who have been ever ready with assistance I may mention Dr. REINHOLD ROST, of the India Library; General ROBERT MACLAGAN, R.E.; Sir GEORGE BIRDWOOD, C.S.I.; Major-General R. H. KEATINGE, V.C., C.S.I.; Professor TERRIEN DE LA COUPERIE; and Mr. E. COLBORNE BABER, at present Consul-General in Corea. Dr. J. A. H. MURRAY, editor of the great English Dictionary, has also been most kind and courteous in the interchange of communications, a circumstance which will account for a few cases in which the passages cited in both works are the same.

My first endeavour in preparing this work has been to make it accurate; my next to make it—even though a Glossary—interesting.

In a work intersecting so many fields, only a fool could imagine that he had not fallen into many mistakes; but these when pointed out, may be amended. If I have missed the other object of endeavour, I fear there is little to be hoped for from a second edition.

H. YULE.

5th January 1886.

PREFACE TO THE SECOND EDITION

THE twofold hope expressed in the closing sentence of Sir Henry Yule's Preface to the original Edition of this book has been amply justified. More recent research and discoveries have, of course, brought to light a good deal of information which was not accessible to him, but the general accuracy of what he wrote has never been seriously impugned—while those who have studied the pages of *Hobson-Jobson* have agreed in classing it as unique among similar works of reference, a volume which combines interest and amusement with instruction, in a manner which few other Dictionaries, if any, have done.

In this edition of the *Anglo-Indian Glossary* the original text has been reprinted, any additions made by the Editor being marked by square brackets. No attempt has been made to extend the vocabulary, the new articles being either such as were accidentally omitted in the first edition, or a few relating to words which seemed to correspond with the general scope of the work. Some new quotations have been added, and some of those included in the original edition have been verified and new references given. An index to words occurring in the quotations has been prepared.

I have to acknowledge valuable assistance from many friends. Mr. W. W. SKEAT has read the articles on Malay words, and has supplied many notes. Col. Sir R. TEMPLE has permitted me to use several of his papers on Anglo-Indian words, and has kindly sent me advance sheets of that portion of the Analytical Index to the first edition by Mr. C. PARTRIDGE, which is being published in the *Indian Antiquary*. Mr. R. S. WHITEWAY has given me numerous extracts from Portuguese writers; Mr. W. FOSTER, quotations from unpublished records in the India Office; Mr. W. IRVINE, notes on the later Moghul period. For valuable suggestions and information on disputed points I am indebted to Mr. H. BEVERIDGE, Sir G. BIRDWOOD, Mr. J. BRANDT, Prof. E. G. BROWNE, Mr. M. LONGWORTH DAMES, Mr. G. R. DAMPIER, Mr. DONALD FERGUSON, Mr. C. T. GARDNER, the late Mr. E. J. W. GIBB, Prof. H. A. GILES, Dr. G. A. GRIERSON, Mr. T. M. HORSFALL, Mr. L. W.

King, Mr. J. L. Myres, Mr. J. Platt, jun., Prof. G. U. Pope, Mr. V. A. Smith, Mr. C. H. Tawney, and Mr. J. Weir.

W. Crooke.

14*th November* 1902.

INTRODUCTORY REMARKS

WORDS of Indian origin have been insinuating themselves into English ever since the end of the reign of Elizabeth and the beginning of that of King James, when such terms as *calico*, *chintz*, and *gingham* had already effected a lodgment in English warehouses and shops, and were lying in wait for entrance into English literature. Such outlandish guests grew more frequent 120 years ago, when, soon after the middle of last century, the numbers of Englishmen in the Indian services, civil and military, expanded with the great acquisition of dominion then made by the Company; and we meet them in vastly greater abundance now.

Vocabularies of Indian and other foreign words, in use among Europeans in the East, have not unfrequently been printed. Several of the old travellers have attached the like to their narratives; whilst the prolonged excitement created in England, a hundred years since, by the impeachment of Hastings* and kindred matters, led to the publication of several glossaries as independent works; and a good many others have been published in later days. At the end of this Introduction will be found a list of those which have come under my notice, and this might no doubt be largely added to.[1]

Of modern Glossaries, such as have been the result of serious labour, all, or nearly all, have been of a kind purely technical, intended to facilitate the comprehension of official documents by the explanation of terms used in the Revenue department, or in other branches of Indian administration. The most notable examples are (of brief and occasional character), the Glossary appended to the famous *Fifth Report* of the Select Committee of 1812, which was compiled by Sir Charles Wilkins; and (of a far more vast and comprehensive sort), the late Professor Horace Hayman Wilson's *Glossary of Judicial and Revenue Terms* (4to, 1855) which leaves far behind every other attempt in that kind.[2]

1 See Note A. at end of Introduction.

2 Professor Wilson's work may perhaps bear re-editing, but can hardly, for its purpose, be superseded. The late eminent Telugu scholar, Mr. C. P. Brown, interleaved, with criticisms and addenda, a copy of Wilson, which is now in the India Library. I have gone through it, and borrowed a few notes, with acknowledgment by the initials C. P. B. The amount of improvement does not strike me as important.

That kind is, however, not ours, as a momentary comparison of a page or two in each Glossary would suffice to show. Our work indeed, in the long course of its compilation, has gone through some modification and enlargement of scope; but hardly such as in any degree to affect its distinctive character, in which something has been aimed at differing in form from any work known to us. In its original conception it was intended to deal with all that class of words which, not in general pertaining to the technicalities of administration, recur constantly in the daily intercourse of the English in India, either as expressing ideas really not provided for by our mother-tongue, or supposed by the speakers (often quite erroneously) to express something not capable of just denotation by any English term. A certain percentage of such words have been carried to England by the constant reflux to their native shore of Anglo-Indians, who in some degree imbue with their notions and phraseology the circles from which they had gone forth. This effect has been still more promoted by the currency of a vast mass of literature, of all qualities and for all ages, dealing with Indian subjects; as well as by the regular appearance, for many years past, of Indian correspondence in English newspapers, insomuch that a considerable number of the expressions in question have not only become familiar in sound to English ears, but have become naturalised in the English language, and are meeting with ample recognition in the great Dictionary* edited by Dr. Murray at Oxford.

Of words that seem to have been admitted to full franchise, we may give examples in *curry*, *toddy*, *veranda*, *cheroot*, *loot*, *nabob*, *teapoy*, *sepoy*, *cowry*; and of others familiar enough to the English ear, though hardly yet received into citizenship, *compound*, *batta*, *pucka*, *chowry*, *baboo*, *mahout*, *aya*, *nautch*,[1] first-*chop*, competition-*wallah*, *griffin*, &c. But beyond these two classes of words, received within the last century or so, and gradually, into half or whole recognition, there are a good many others, long since fully assimilated, which really originated in the adoption of an Indian word, or the modification of an Indian proper name. Such words are the three quoted at the beginning of these remarks, *chintz*, *calico*,

1 *Nautch*, it may be urged, *is* admitted to full franchise, being used by so eminent a writer as Mr. Browning. But the fact that his use is entirely *misuse*, seems to justify the classification in the text (see GLOSS., s.v.). A like remark applies to *compound*. See for the tremendous fiasco made in its intended use by a most intelligent lady novelist, the last quotation s.v. in GLOSS.

gingham, also *shawl, bamboo, pagoda, typhoon, monsoon, mandarin, palanquin*,[1] &c., and I may mention among further examples which may perhaps surprise my readers, the names of three of the boats of a man-of-war, viz. the *cutter*, the *jolly-boat*, and the *dingy*, as all (probably) of Indian origin.[2] Even phrases of a different character—slang indeed, but slang generally supposed to be vernacular as well as vulgar—*e.g.* 'that is the *cheese*';[2] or supposed to be vernacular and profane—*e.g.* 'I don't care a *dam*'[2]—are in reality, however vulgar they may be, neither vernacular nor profane, but phrases turning upon innocent Hindustani vocables.

We proposed also, in our Glossary, to deal with a *selection* of those administrative terms, which are in such familiar and quotidian use as to form part of the common Anglo-Indian stock, and to trace all (so far as possible) to their true origin—a matter on which, in regard to many of the words, those who hourly use them are profoundly ignorant—and to follow them down by quotation from their earliest occurrence in literature.

A particular class of words are those indigenous terms which have been adopted in scientific nomenclature, botanical and zoological. On these Mr. Burnell remarks:—

"The first Indian botanical names were chiefly introduced by Garcia de Orta (*Colloquios*, printed at Goa in 1563), C. d'Acosta (*Tractado*, Burgos, 1578), and Rhede van Drakenstein (*Hortus Malabaricus*, Amsterdam, 1682). The Malay names were chiefly introduced by Rumphius (*Herbarium Amboinense*, completed before 1700, but not published till 1741). The Indian zoological terms were chiefly due to Dr. F. Buchanan, at the beginning of this century. Most of the N. Indian botanical words were introduced by Roxburgh."

It has been already intimated that, as the work proceeded, its scope expanded somewhat, and its authors found it expedient to introduce and trace many words of Asiatic origin which have disappeared from colloquial use, or perhaps never entered it, but which occur in old writers on the East. We also judged that it would add to the interest of the work, were we to investigate and make out the

1 Gloss., s.v. (note p. 397, col. *b*), contains quotations from the Vulgate of the passage in Canticles iii. 9, regarding King Solomon's *ferculum* of Lebanon cedar. I have to thank an old friend for pointing out that the word *palanquin* has, in this passage, received solemn sanction by its introduction into the Revised Version.

2 See these words in Gloss.

pedigree of a variety of geographical names which are or have been in familiar use in books on the Indies; take as examples *Bombay, Madras, Guardafui, Malabar, Moluccas, Zanzibar, Pegu, Sumatra, Quilon, Seychelles, Ceylon, Java, Ara, Japan, Doab, Punjab*, &c., illustrating these, like every other class of word, by quotations given in chronological series.

Other divagations still from the original project will probably present themselves to those who turn over the pages of the work, in which we have been tempted to introduce sundry subjects which may seem hardly to come within the scope of such a glossary.

The words with which we have to do, taking the most extensive view of the field, are in fact organic remains deposited under the various currents of external influence that have washed the shores of India during twenty centuries and more. Rejecting that derivation of *elephant*[1] which would connect it with the Ophir trade of Solomon, we find no existing Western term traceable to that episode of communication; but the Greek and Roman commerce of the later centuries has left its fossils on both sides, testifying to the intercourse that once subsisted. *Agallochum, carbasus, camphor, sandal, musk, nard, pepper* (πέπερι, from Skt. *pippali*, 'long pepper'), *ginger* (ζιγγίβερις, see under *Ginger*), *lac, costus, opal, malabathrum* or *folium indicum, beryl, sugar* (σάκχαρ, from Skt. *sarkara*, Prak. *sakkara*), *rice* (ὄρυζα, but see s.v.), were products or names, introduced from India to the Greek and Roman world, to which may be added a few terms of a different character, such as Βραχμᾶνες, Σαρμάνες (*śramaṇas*, or Buddhist ascetics), ξύλα σαγαλίνα καὶ σασαμίνα (logs of teak and shīsham), the σάγγαρα (rafts) of the Periplus; whilst *dīnāra, dramma*, perhaps *kastīra* ('tin,' κασσίτερος), *kastūrī* ('musk,' καστόριον, properly a different, though analogous animal product), and a very few more, have remained in Indian literature as testimony to the same intercourse.[2]

The trade and conquests of the Arabs both brought foreign words to India and picked up and carried westward, in form more or less corrupted, words of Indian origin, some of which have in one way or other become part of the heritage of all succeeding foreigners in the East. Among terms which are familiar items in the Anglo-Indian

1 See this word in GLOSS.

2 See A. Weber, in *Indian Antiquary*, ii. 143 *seqq*. Most of the other Greek words, which he traces in Sanskrit, are astronomical terms derived from books.

colloquial, but which had, in some shape or other, found their way at an early date into use on the shores of the Mediterranean, we may instance *bazaar*, *cazee*, *hummaul*, *brinjaul*, *gingely*, *safflower*, *grab*, *maramut*, *dewaun* (dogana, douane, &c.). Of others which are found in medieval literature, either West-Asiatic or European, and which still have a place in Anglo-Indian or English vocabulary, we may mention *amber*-gris, *chank*, *junk*, *jogy*, *kincob*, *kedgeree*, *fanam*, *calay*, *bankshall*, *mudiliar*, *tindal*, *cranny*.

The conquests and long occupation of the Portuguese, who by the year 1540 had established themselves in all the chief ports of India and the East, have, as might have been expected, bequeathed a large number of expressions to the European nations who have followed, and in great part superseded them. We find instances of missionaries and others at an early date who had acquired a knowledge of Indian languages, but these were exceptional.[1] The natives in contact with the Portuguese learned a bastard variety of the language of the latter, which became the *lingua franca* of intercourse, not only between European and native, but occasionally between Europeans of different nationalities. This Indo-Portuguese dialect continued to serve such purposes down to a late period in the last century, and has in some localities survived down nearly to our own day.[2] The number of people in India claiming to be of Portuguese descent was, in the 17th century, very large. Bernier, about 1660, says:—

"For he (Sultan Shujā', Aurangzeb's brother) much courted all those *Portugal* Fathers, Missionaries, that are in that Province. ... And they were indeed capable to serve him, it being certain that in the kingdom of *Bengale* there are to be found not less than eight or nine thousand families of *Franguis*, *Portugals*, and these either Natives or Mesticks." (*Bernier*, E.T. of 1684, p. 27.)

A. Hamilton, whose experience belonged chiefly to the end of the same century, though his book was not published till 1727, states:—

"Along the Sea-coasts the *Portuguese* have left a Vestige of their Language, tho' much corrupted, yet it is the Language that most

1 Varthema, at the very beginning of the 16th century, shows some acquaintance with Malayālam, and introduces pieces of conversation in that language. Before the end of the 16th century, printing had been introduced at other places besides Goa, and by the beginning of the 17th, several books in Indian languages had been printed at Goa, Cochin, and Ambalakkādu.—(A. B.)

2 "At Point de Galle, in 1860, I found it in common use, and also, somewhat later, at Calecut."—(A. B.)

Europeans learn first to qualify them for a general Converse with one another, as well as with the different inhabitants of *India*." (*Preface*, p. xii.)

Lockyer, who published 16 years before Hamilton, also says:—

"This they (the *Portugueze*) may justly boast, they have established a kind of *Lingua Franca* in all the Sea Ports in *India*, of great use to other *Europeans*, who would find it difficult in many places to be well understood without it." (*An Account of the Trade in India*, 1711, p. 286.)

The early Lutheran Missionaries in the South, who went out for the S.P.C.K., all seem to have begun by learning Portuguese, and in their diaries speak of preaching occasionally in Portuguese.[1] The foundation of this *lingua franca* was the Portuguese of the beginning of the 16th century; but it must have soon degenerated, for by the beginning of the last century it had lost nearly all trace of inflexion.[2]

It may from these remarks be easily understood how a large number of our Anglo-Indian colloquialisms, even if eventually traceable to native sources (and especially to Mahratti, or Dravidian originals) have come to us through a Portuguese medium, and often bear traces of having passed through that alembic. Not a few of these are familiar all over India, but the number current in the South is larger still. Some other Portuguese words also, though they can hardly be said to be recognized elements in the Anglo-Indian colloquial, have been introduced either into Hindustani generally, or into that shade of it which is in use among natives in habitual contact with Europeans. Of words which are essentially Portuguese, among Anglo-Indian colloquialisms, persistent or obsolete, we may quote *goglet*, *gram*, *plantain*, *muster*, *caste*, *peon*, *padre*, *mistry* or *maistry*, *almyra*,

1 See "Notices of Madras and Cuddalore, &c., by the earlier Missionaries." Longman, 1858, *passim*. See also *Manual*, &c. in BOOK-LIST, *infra* p. xxxix. Dr Carey, writing from Serampore as late as 1800, says that the children of Europeans by native women, whether children of English, French, Dutch, or Danes, were all called Portuguese. *Smith's Life of Carey*, 152.

2 See Note B. at end of Introductory Remarks. "Mr. Beames remarked some time ago that most of the names of places in South India are greatly disfigured in the forms used by Europeans. This is because we have adopted the Portuguese orthography. Only in this way it can be explained how Kolladam has become *Coleroon*, Solamandalam, *Coromandel*, and Tuttukkudi, *Tuticorin*." (A. B.) Mr. Burnell was so impressed with the excessive corruption of S. Indian names, that he would hardly ever willingly venture any explanation of them, considering the matter all too uncertain.

aya, cobra, mosquito, pomfret, cameez, palmyra, still in general use; *picotta, rolong, pial, fogass, margosa,* preserved in the South; *batel, brab, foras, oart, vellard* in Bombay; *joss, compradore, linguist* in the ports of China; and among more or less obsolete terms, *Moor,* for a Mahommedan, still surviving under the modified form *Moorman,* in Madras and Ceylon; *Gentoo,* still partially kept up, I believe, at Madras in application to the Telugu language, *mustees, castees, bandeja* ('a tray'), *Kittysol* ('an umbrella,' and this survived ten years ago in the Calcutta customs tariff), *cuspadore* ('a spittoon'), and *covid* ('a cubit or ell'). Words of native origin which bear the mark of having come to us through the Portuguese may be illustrated by such as *palanquin, mandarin, mangelin* (a small weight for pearls, &c.), *monsoon, typhoon, mango, mangosteen, jack-fruit, batta, curry, chop, congee, coir, cutch, catamaran, cassanar, nabob, avadavat, betel, areca, benzoin, corge, copra.*[1] A few examples of Hindustani words borrowed from the Portuguese are *chābī* ('a key'), *bāola* ('a portmanteau'), *bāltī* ('a bucket'), *martol* ('a hammer'), *tauliya* ('a towel,' Port. *toalha*), *sābūn* ('soap'), *bāsan* ('plate' from Port. *bacia*), *līlām* and *nīlām* ('an auction'), besides a number of terms used by Lascars on board ship.

The Dutch language has not contributed much to our store. The Dutch and the English arrived in the Indies contemporaneously, and though both inherited from the Portuguese, we have not been the heirs of the Dutch to any great extent, except in Ceylon, and even there Portuguese vocables had already occupied the colloquial ground. *Petersilly,* the word in general use in English families for 'parsley,' appears to be Dutch. An example from Ceylon that occurs to memory is *burgher.* The Dutch admitted people of mixt descent to a kind of citizenship, and these were distinguished from the pure natives by this term, which survives. *Burgher* in Bengal means 'a rafter,' properly *bargā.* A word spelt and pronounced in the same way had again a curiously different application in Madras, where it was a corruption of *Vaḍagar,* the name given to a tribe in the Nilgherry hills;—to say nothing of Scotland, where Burghers and

1 The nasal termination given to many Indian words, when adopted into European use, as in *palanquin, mandarin,* &c., must be attributed mainly to the Portuguese; but it cannot be entirely due to them. For we find the nasal termination of *Achīn,* in Mahommedan writers, and that of *Cochin* before the Portuguese time, whilst the conversion of *Pasei,* in Sumatra, into *Pacem,* as the Portuguese call it, is already indicated in the *Basma* of Marco Polo.

Antiburghers* were Northern tribes (*veluti* Gog *et* Magog!*) which have long been condensed into elements of the United Presbyterian Church——!

Southern India has contributed to the Anglo-Indian stock words that are in hourly use also from Calcutta to Peshawur (some of them already noted under another cleavage), *e.g. betel, mango, jack, cheroot, mungoose, pariah, bandicoot, teak, patcharee, chatty, catechu, tope* ('a grove'), *curry, mulligatawny, congee. Mamooty* (a digging tool) is familiar in certain branches of the service, owing to its having long had a place in the nomenclature of the Ordnance department. It is Tamil, *manvĕtti*, 'earth-cutter.' Of some very familiar words the origin remains either dubious, or matter only for conjecture. Examples are *hackery* (which arose apparently in Bombay), *florican, topaz.*

As to Hindustani words adopted into the Anglo-Indian colloquial the subject is almost too wide and loose for much remark. The habit of introducing these in English conversation and writing seems to prevail more largely in the Bengal Presidency than in any other, and especially more than in Madras, where the variety of different vernaculars in use has tended to make their acquisition by the English less universal than is in the north that of Hindustani, which is so much easier to learn, and also to make the use in former days of Portuguese, and now of English, by natives in contact with foreigners, and of French about the French settlements, very much more common than it is elsewhere. It is this bad habit of interlarding English with Hindustani phrases which has so often excited the just wrath of high English officials, not accustomed to it from their youth, and which (*e.g.*) drew forth in orders the humorous indignation of Sir Charles Napier.*

One peculiarity in this use we may notice, which doubtless exemplifies some obscure linguistic law. Hindustani *verbs* which are thus used are habitually adopted into the quasi-English by converting the imperative into an infinitive. Thus to *bunow*, to *lugow*, to *foozilow*, to *puckarow*, to *dumbcow*, to *sumjow*, and so on, almost *ad libitum*, are formed as we have indicated.[1]*

It is curious to note that several of our most common adoptions

1 The first five examples will be found in GLOSS. *Banāo*, is imperative of *banā-nā*, 'to fabricate'; *lagāo of lagā-nā*, 'to lay alongside,' &c.; *sumjhāo*, of *samjhā-nā*, 'to cause to understand,' &c.

are due to what may be most especially called the Oordoo (*Urdū*) or 'Camp' language, being terms which the hosts of Chinghiz* brought from the steppes of North Eastern Asia—*e.g.* "The old *Bukshee* is an awful *bahadur*, but he keeps a first-rate *bobachee*." That is a sentence which might easily have passed without remark at an Anglo-Indian mess-table thirty years ago—perhaps might be heard still. Each of the outlandish terms embraced in it came from the depths of Mongolia in the thirteenth century. *Chick* (in the sense of a cane-blind), *ḍaroga*, *oordoo* itself, are other examples.

With the gradual assumption of administration after the middle of last century, we adopted into partial colloquial use an immense number of terms, very many of them Persian or Arabic, belonging to technicalities of revenue and other departments, and largely borrowed from our Mahommedan predecessors. Malay has contributed some of our most familiar expressions, owing partly to the ceaseless rovings among the Eastern coasts of the Portuguese, through whom a part of these reached us, and partly doubtless to the fact that our early dealings and the sites of our early factories lay much more on the shores of the Eastern Archipelago than on those of Continental India. *Paddy*, *godown*, *compound*, *bankshall*, *rattan*, *durian*, *a-muck*, *prow*, and *cadjan*, *junk*, *crease*, are some of these. It is true that several of them may be traced eventually to Indian originals, but it seems not the less certain that we got them through the Malay, just as we got words already indicated through the Portuguese.

We used to have a very few words in French form, such as *boutique* and *mort-de-chien*. But these two are really distortions of Portuguese words.

A few words from China have settled on the Indian shores and been adopted by Anglo-India, but most of them are, I think, names of fruits or other products which have been imported, such as *loquot*, *leechee*, *chow-chow*, *cumquat*, *ginseng*, &c. and (recently) *jinrickshaw*. For it must be noted that a considerable proportion of words much used in Chinese ports, and often ascribed to a Chinese origin, such as *mandarin*, *junk*, *chop*, *pagoda*, and (as I believe) *typhoon* (though this is a word much debated) are not Chinese at all, but words of Indian languages, or of Malay, which have been precipitated in Chinese waters during the flux and reflux of foreign trade.

Within my own earliest memory Spanish dollars were current in England at a specified value if they bore a stamp from the English mint. And similarly there are certain English words, often obsolete in Europe, which have received in India currency with a special stamp of meaning; whilst in other cases our language has formed in India new compounds applicable to new objects or shades of meaning. To one or other of these classes belong *outcry*, *buggy*, *home*, *interloper*, *rogue* (-elephant), *tiffin*, *furlough*, *elk*, *roundel* ('an umbrella,' obsolete), *pish-pash*, *earth-oil*, *hog-deer*, *flying-fox*, *garden-house*, *musk-rat*, *nor-wester*, *iron-wood*, *long-drawers*, *barking-deer*, *custard-apple*, *grasscutter*, &c.

Other terms again are corruptions, more or less violent, of Oriental words and phrases which have put on an English mask. Such are *maund*, *fool's rack*, *bearer*, *cot*, *boy*, *belly-band*, *Penang-lawyer*, *buckshaw*, *goddess* (in the Malay region, representing Malay *gādīs*, 'a maiden'), *compound*, *college*-pheasant, *chopper*, *summer-head*,[1] *eagle-wood*, *jackass*-copal, *bobbery*, *Upper Roger* (used in a correspondence given by Dalrymple, for *Yuva Raja*, the 'Young King,' or Caesar, of Indo-Chinese monarchies), *Isle-o'-Bats* (for Allahābād or *Ilahābāz* as the natives often call it), *hobson-jobson* (see Preface), *St. John's*. The last proper name has at least three applications. There is "St. John's" in Guzerat, viz. *Sanjān*, the landing-place of the Parsee immigration in the 8th century; there is another "St. John's" which is a corruption of *Shang-Chuang*, the name of that island off the southern coast of China whence the pure and ardent spirit of Francis Xavier fled to a better world: there is the group of "St. John's Islands" near Singapore, the chief of which is properly Pulo-*Sikajang*.

Yet again we have hybrids and corruptions of English fully accepted and adopted as Hindustani by the natives with whom we have to do, such as *simkin*, *port-shrāb*, *brandy-pānī*, *apīl*, *rasīd*, *tumlet* (a tumbler), *gilās* ('glass,' for drinking vessels of sorts), *rail-ghārī*, *lumber-dār*, *jail-khāna*, *bottle-khāna*, *buggy-khāna*, 'et omne quod exit in' *khāna*, including *gymkhāna*, a very modern concoction (q.v.), and many more.

Taking our subject as a whole, however considerable the philological interest attaching to it, there is no disputing the truth of a remark with which Burnell's fragment of intended introduction concludes, and the application of which goes beyond the limit of

1 This is in the Bombay ordnance nomenclature for a large umbrella. It represents the Port. *sombrero!*

those words which can be considered to have 'accrued as additions to the English language': "Considering the long intercourse with India, it is noteworthy that the additions which have thus accrued to the English language are, from the intellectual standpoint, of no intrinsic value. Nearly all the borrowed words refer to material facts, or to peculiar customs and stages of society, and, though a few of them furnish allusions to the penny-a-liner, they do not represent new ideas."

It is singular how often, in tracing to their origin words that come within the field of our research, we light upon an absolute dilemma, or bifurcation, *i.e.* on two or more sources of almost equal probability, and in themselves entirely diverse. In such cases it may be that, though the use of the word *originated* from one of the sources, the existence of the other has invigorated that use, and contributed to its eventual diffusion.

An example of this is *boy*, in its application to a native servant. To this application have contributed both the old English use of *boy* (analogous to that of *puer*, *garçon*, *Knabe*) for a camp-servant, or for a slave, and the Hindī-Marāṭhī *bhoi*, the name of a caste which has furnished palanquin and umbrella-bearers to many generations of Europeans in India. The habitual use of the word by the Portuguese, for many years before any English influence had touched the shores of India (*e.g.* *bóy de sombrero*, *bóy d'aguoa*, *bóy de palanquy*), shows that the earliest source was the Indian one.

Cooly, in its application to a carrier of burdens, or performer of inferior labour, is another example. The most probable origin of this is from a *nomen gentile*,* that of the *Kolīs*, a hill-people of Guzerat and the Western Ghats (compare the origin of *slave*). But the matter is perplexed by other facts which it is difficult to connect with this. Thus, in S. India, there is a Tamil word *kūli*, in common use, signifying 'daily hire or wages,' which H. H. Wilson regards as the true origin of the word which we call *cooly*. Again, both in Oriental and Osmali Turkish, *kol* is a word for a slave, and in the latter also there is *kūleh*, 'a male slave, a bondsman.' *Khol* is, in Tibetan also, a word for a slave or servant.

Tank, for a reservoir of water, we are apt to derive without hesitation, from *stagnum*, whence Sp. *estanc*, old Fr. *estang*, old Eng. and Lowland Scotch *stank*, Port. *tanque*, till we find that the word is regarded by the Portuguese themselves as Indian, and that there is excellent testimony to the existence of *tānkā* in Guzerat and Rajputana as an indigenous word, and with a plausible Sanskrit etymology.

Veranda has been confidently derived by some etymologists (among others by M. Defrémery, a distinguished scholar) from the Pers. *barāmada*, 'a projection,' a balcony; an etymology which is indeed hardly a possible one, but has been treated by Mr. Beames (who was evidently unacquainted with the facts that do make it hardly possible) with inappropriate derision, he giving as the unquestionable original a Sanskrit word *baraṇḍa*, 'a portico.' On this Burnell has observed that the word does not belong to the older Sanskrit, but is only found in comparatively modern works. Be that as it may, it need not be doubted that the word *veranda*, as used in England and France, was imported from India, *i.e.* from the usage of Europeans in India; but it is still more certain that either in the same sense, or in one closely allied, the word existed, quite independent of either Sanskrit or Persian, in Portuguese and Spanish, and the manner in which it occurs in the very earliest narrative of the Portuguese adventure to India (*Roteiro do Viagem de Vasco da Gama*, written by one of the expedition of 1497), confirmed by the Hispano-Arabic vocabulary of Pedro de Alcalà, printed in 1505, preclude the possibility of its having been adopted by the Portuguese from intercourse with India.

Mangrove, John Crawfurd tells us, has been adopted from the Malay *manggi-manggi*, applied to trees of the genus *Rhizophora*. But we learn from Oviedo, writing early in the sixteenth century, that the name *mangle* was applied by the natives of the Spanish Main to trees of the same, or a kindred genus, on the coast of S. America, which same *mangle* is undoubtedly the parent of the French *manglier*, and not improbably therefore of the English form *mangrove*.[1]

The words *bearer*, *mate*, *cotwal*, partake of this kind of dual or doubtful ancestry, as may be seen by reference to them in the Glossary.

Before concluding, a word should be said as to the orthography used in the Glossary.

My intention has been to give the headings of the articles under

1 Mr. Skeat's *Etym. Dict.* does not contain *mangrove*. [It will be found in his *Concise Etymological Dict.* ed. 1901.]

the most usual of the popular, or, if you will, vulgar quasi-English spellings, whilst the Oriental words, from which the headings are derived or corrupted, are set forth under precise transliteration, the system of which is given in a following "Nota Bene." When using the words and names in the course of discursive elucidation, I fear I have not been consistent in sticking either always to the popular or always to the scientific spelling, and I can the better understand why a German critic of a book of mine, once upon a time, remarked upon the *etwas schwankende yulische Orthographie.** Indeed it is difficult, it never will for me be possible, in a book for popular use, to adhere to one system in this matter without the assumption of an ill-fitting and repulsive pedantry. Even in regard to Indian proper names, in which I once advocated adhesion, with a small number of exceptions, to scientific precision in transliteration, I feel much more inclined than formerly to sympathise with my friends Sir William Muir and General Maclagan, who have always favoured a large and liberal recognition of popular spelling in such names. And when I see other good and able friends following the scientific Will-o'-the-Wisp into such bogs as the use in English composition of *sipáhí* and *jangal*, and *verandah*—nay, I have not only heard of *bagí*, but have recently seen it—instead of the good English words 'sepoy,' and 'jungle,' 'veranda,' and 'buggy,' my dread of pedantic usage becomes the greater.[1]

For the spelling of *Mahratta*, *Mahratti*, I suppose I must apologize (though something is to be said for it), *Marāthī* having established itself as orthodox.

1 'Buggy' of course is not an Oriental word at all, except as adopted from us by Orientals. I call *sepoy*, *jungle*, and *veranda*, good English words; and so I regard them, just as good as *alligator*, or *hurricane*, or *canoe*, or *Jerusalem* artichoke, or *cheroot*. What would my friends think of spelling these in English books as *alagarto*, and *huracan*, and *canoa*, and *girasole*, and *shuruṭṭu?*

NOTE A.—LIST OF GLOSSARIES.

1. Appended to the **Roteiro de Vasco da Gama** (see Book-list, p. 44) is a Vocabulary of 138 Portuguese words with their corresponding word in the *Lingua de Calicut, i.e.* in Malayālam.
2. Appended to the **Voyages**, &c., du Sieur **de la Boullaye-le-Gouz** (Book-list, p. 33), is an *Explication de plusieurs mots dont l'intelligence est nécessaire au Lecteur* (pp. 27).
3. **Fryer's New Account** (Book-list, p. 35) has an *Index Explanatory*, including *Proper Names, Names of Things*, and *Names of Persons* (12 pages).
4. "**Indian Vocabulary**, to which is prefixed the Forms of Impeachment." 12mo. Stockdale, 1788 (pp. 136).
5. "An **Indian Glossary**, consisting of some Thousand Words and Forms commonly used in the East Indies ... . extremely serviceable in assisting Strangers to acquire with Ease and Quickness the Language of that Country." By **T. T. Robarts**, Lieut., &c., of the 3rd Regt. Native Infantry, E.I. Printed for Murray & Highley, Fleet Street, 1800. 12mo. (not paged).
6. "**A Dictionary of Mohammedan Law**, Bengal Revenue Terms, Shanscrit, Hindoo, and other words used in the East Indies, with full explanations, the leading word used in each article being printed in a new Nustaluk Type," &c. By **S. Rousseau**. London, 1802. 12mo. (pp. lxiv.–287). Also 2nd ed. 1805.
7. **Glossary** prepared for the **Fifth Report** (see Book-list, p. 34), by Sir **Charles Wilkins**. This is dated in the preface "E. I. House, 1813." The copy used is a Parliamentary reprint, dated 1830.
8. The Folio compilation of the **Bengal Regulations**, published in 1828–29, contains in each volume a Glossarial Index, based chiefly upon the Glossary of Sir C. Wilkins.
9. In 1842 a preliminary "**Glossary of Indian Terms**," drawn up at the E. I. House by Prof. H. H. Wilson, 4to, unpublished, with a blank column on each page "for Suggestions and Additions," was circulated in India, intended as a basis for a comprehensive official Glossary. In this one the words are entered in the vulgar spelling, as they occur in the documents.
10. The only important result of the circulation of No. 9. was "**Supplement to the Glossary of Indian Terms, A–J.**" By **H. M. Elliot**, Esq., Bengal Civil Service. Agra, 1845. 8vo. (pp. 447).

    This remarkable work has been revised, re-arranged, and re-edited, with additions from Elliot's notes and other sources, by **Mr. John Beames**, of the Bengal Civil Service, under the title of "**Memoirs on the Folk-Lore and Distribution of the Races** of the North-Western Provinces of India, being an amplified edition of" (the above). 2 vols. 8vo. Trübner, 1869.
11. To "**Morley's Analytical Digest** of all the Reported Cases Decided in the Supreme Courts of Judicature in India," Vol. I., 1850, there is appended a "Glossary of Native Terms used in the Text" (pp. 20).
12. In "**Wanderings of a Pilgrim**" (Book-list, p. 47), there is a Glossary of some considerable extent (pp. 10 in double columns).
13. "The **Zillah Dictionary** in the Roman character, explaining the Various Words used in Business in India." By **Charles Philip Brown**, of the Madras Civil Service, &c. Madras, 1852. Imp. 8vo. (pp. 132).
14. "A **Glossary of Judicial and Revenue** Terms, and of Useful Words occurring in Official Documents, relating to the Administration of the Government of British India, from the Arabic, Persian, Hindústání, Sanskrit, Hindí, Bengálí, Uriyá, Maráṭhí, Guzaráthí, Telugu, Karnáta, Támil, Mayalálam, and other languages. By **H. H. Wilson**, M.A., F.R.S., Boden Professor, &c." London, 1855. 4to. (pp. 585, besides copious Index).
15. A useful folio Glossary published by Government at Calcutta between 1860 and 1870, has been used by me and is quoted in the present GLOSS. as "Calcutta Glossary." But I have not been able to trace it again so as to give the proper title.
16. **Ceylonese Vocabulary**. See Booklist, p. 31.
17. "**Kachahri Technicalities**, or A Glossary of Terms, Rural, Official, and General, in Daily Use in the Courts of Law, and in Illustration of the Tenures, Customs, Arts, and Manufactures of Hindustan." By **Patrick Carnegy**, Commissioner of Rai Bareli, Oudh. 8vo. 2nd ed. Allahabad, 1877 (pp. 361).
18. "A **Glossary of Indian Terms**, containing many of the most important and Useful Indian Words Designed for the

Use of Officers of Revenue and Judicial Practitioners and Students." Madras, 1877. 8vo. (pp. 255).

19. "**A Glossary of Reference** on Subjects connected with the Far East" (China and Japan). By **H. A. Giles**. Hong-Kong, 1878, 8vo. (pp. 182).

20. "**Glossary of Vernacular Terms** used in Official Correspondence in the Province of **Assam**." Shillong, 1879. (Pamphlet).

21. "**Anglo-Indian Dictionary**. A Glossary of such Indian Terms used in English, and such English or other non-Indian terms as have obtained special meanings in India." By **George Clifford Whitworth**, Bombay Civil Service. London, 8vo, 1885 (pp. xv.—350).

Also the following minor Glossaries contained in Books of Travel or History:—

22. In "**Cambridge's Account** of the War in India," 1761 (Book-list, p. 30); 23. In "**Grose's Voyage**," 1772 (Booklist, p. 35); 24. In **Carraccioli's** "**Life of Clive**" (Book-list, p. 30); 25. In "**Bp. Heber's Narrative**" (Book-list, p. 36); 26. In **Herklot's** "**Qanoon-e-Islam** (Book-list, p. 36); [27. In "**Verelst's View of Bengal**," 1772; 28. "**The Malayan Words in English**," by C. P. G. Scott, reprinted from the Journal of the American Oriental Society: New Haven, 1897; 29. "**Manual of the Administration of the Madras Presidency**," Vol. III. Glossary, Madras, 1893. The name of the author of this, the most valuable book of the kind recently published in India, does not appear upon the title-page. It is believed to be the work of C. D. Macleane; 30. A useful Glossary of Malayālam words will be found in **Logan**, "**Manual of Malabar**."]

NOTE B.—THE INDO-PORTUGUESE PATOIS

(By A. C. Burnell.)

The phonetic changes of Indo-Portuguese are few. *F* is substituted for *p;* whilst the accent varies according to the race of the speaker.[1] The vocabulary varies, as regards the introduction of native Indian terms, from the same cause.

Grammatically, this dialect is very singular:

1. All traces of genders are lost—*e.g.* we find *sua poro* (Mat. i. 21); *sua nome* (Id. i. 23); *sua filho* (Id. i. 25); *sua filhos* (Id. ii. 18); *sua olhos* (Acts, ix. 8); *o dias* (Mat. ii. 1); *o rey* (Id. ii. 2); *hum voz tinha ouvido* (Id. ii. 18).
2. In the plural, *s* is rarely added; generally, the plural is the same as the singular.
3. The genitive is expressed by *de*, which is not combined with the article—*e.g. conforme de o tempo* (Mat. ii. 16); *Depois de o morte* (Id. ii. 19).
4. The definite article is unchanged in the plural: *como o discipulos* (Acts, ix. 19).
5. The pronouns still preserve some inflexions: *Eu, mi; nos, nossotros; minha, nossos*, &c.; *tu, ti, vossotros; tua, vos-sos; Elle, ella, ellotros, elles, sua, suas, lo, la.*
6. The verb substantive is (present) *tem*, (past) *timha*, and (subjunctive) *seja.*
7. Verbs are conjugated by adding, for the present, *te* to the only form, viz., the infinitive, which loses its final *r*. Thus, *te falla; te faze; te vi.* The past is formed by adding *ja*—e.g. *ja falla; ja olha.* The future is formed by adding *ser*. To express the infinitive, *per* is added to the Portuguese infinitive deprived of its *r*.

1 Unfortunately, the translators of the Indo-Portuguese New Testament have, as much as possible, preserved the Portuguese orthography.

NOTA BENE

IN THE USE OF THE GLOSSARY

(A.) The dates attached to quotations are not always quite consistent. In beginning the compilation, the dates given were those of the *publication* quoted; but as the date of the *composition*, or of the use of the word in question, is often much earlier than the date of the book or the edition in which it appears, the system was changed, and, where possible, the date given is that of the actual use of the word. But obvious doubts may sometimes rise on this point.

The dates of *publication* of the works quoted will be found, if required, from the BOOK LIST, following this *Nota bene.*

(B.) The system of transliteration used is substantially the same as that modification of Sir William Jones's which is used in Shakespear's *Hindustani Dictionary*. But—

The first of the three Sanskrit sibilants is expressed by (*ś*), and, as in Wilson's Glossary, no distinction is marked between the Indian aspirated *k*, *g*, and the Arabic gutturals *kh*, *gh*. Also, in words transliterated from Arabic, the sixteenth letter of the Arabic alphabet is expressed by (*ṭ*). This is the same type that is used for the cerebral Indian (*ṭ*). Though it can hardly give rise to any confusion, it would have been better to mark them by distinct types. The fact is, that it was wished at first to make as few demands as possible for distinct types, and, having begun so, change could not be made.

The fourth letter of the Arabic alphabet is in several cases represented by (*th*) when Arabic use is in question. In Hindustani it is pronounced as (*s*).

Also, in some of Mr. Burnell's transliterations from S. Indian languages, he has used (R) for the peculiar Tamil hard (*r*), elsewhere (**r**), and (*γ*) for the Tamil and Malayālam (*k*) when preceded and followed by a vowel.

LIST OF FULLER TITLES OF BOOKS QUOTED IN THE GLOSSARY

Abdallatif. Relation de l'Egypte. *See* **De Sacy, Silvestre.**

Abel-Rémusat. Nouveaux Mélanges Asiatiques. 2 vols. 8vo. Paris, 1829.

Abreu, A. de. **Desc. de Malaca**, from the *Parnaso Portuguez.*

Abulghazi. H. des Mogols et des Tatares, par Aboul Ghazi, with French transl. by Baron Desmaisons. 2 vols. 8vo. St. Petersb., 1871.

Academy, The. A Weekly Review, &c. London.

Acosta, Christ. Tractado de las Drogas y Medecinas de las Indias Orientales. 4to. Burgos, 1578.

— E. Hist. Rerum a Soc. Jesu in Oriente gestarum. Paris, 1572.

— Joseph de. Natural and Moral History of the Indies, E.T. of Edward Grimstone, 1604. Edited for HAK. Soc. by C. Markham. 2 vols. 1880.

Adams, Francis. Names of all Minerals, Plants, and Animals described by the Greek authors, &c. (Being a Suppl. to Dunbar's Greek Lexicon.)

Aelian. Claudii Aeliani, De Natura Animalium, Libri XVII.

Āīn. Āīn-i-Akbarī, The, by Abul Fazl 'Allami, tr. from the orig. Persian by H. Blochmann, M.A. Calcutta. 1873. Vol. i.; [vols. ii. and iii. translated by Col. H. S. Jarrett; Calcutta, 1891–94].

The MS. of the remainder disappeared at Mr. Blochmann's lamented death in 1878; a deplorable loss to Oriental literature.

— (Orig.). The same. Edited in the **original** Persian by H. Blochmann, M.A. 2 vols. 4to. Calcutta, 1872. Both these were printed by the Asiatic Society of Bengal.

Aitchison, C. U. Collection of Treaties, Engagements, and Sunnuds relating to India and Neighbouring Countries, 8 vols. 8vo. Revised ed., Calcutta, 1876–78.

Ajaib-al-Hind. *See* **Merveilles.**

Albirûnî. Chronology of Ancient Nations E.T. by Dr. C. E. Sachau (Or. Transl. Fund). 4to. 1879.

Alcalà, Fray Pedro de. Vocabulista Arauigo en letra Castellana. Salamanca, 1505.

Ali Baba, Sir. Twenty-one Days in India, being the Tour of (by G. Aberigh Mackay). London, 1880.

[**Ali**, Mrs Meer Hassan, Observations on the Mussulmauns of India. 2 vols. London, 1832.

[**Allardyce**, A. The City of Sunshine. Edinburgh. 3 vols. 1877.

[**Allen**, B. C. Monograph on the Silk Cloths of Assam. Shillong, 1899.]

Amari. I Diplomi Arabi del R. Archivio Fiorentino. 4to. Firenze, 1863.

Anderson, Philip, A.M. The English in Western India, &c. 2nd ed. Revised. 1856.

Andriesz, G. Beschrijving der Reyzen. 4to. Amsterdam, 1670.

Angria Tulagee. Authentic and Faithful History of that Arch-Pyrate. London, 1756.

Annaes Maritimos. 4 vols. 8vo. Lisbon, 1840–44.

Anquetil du Perron. Le Zendavesta. 3 vols. Discours Preliminaire, &c. (in first vol.). 1771.

Aragor Chronicle of King James of. E.T. by the late John Forster, M.P. 2 vols. imp. 8vo. [London, 1883.]

Arbuthnot, Sir A. Memoir of Sir T. Munro, prefixed to ed. of his Minutes. 2 vols. 1881.

Arch. Port. Or. Archivo Portuguez Oriental. A valuable and interesting collection published at Nova Goa, 1857 *seqq.*

Archivio Storico Italiano.

The quotations are from two articles in the *Appendice* to the early volumes, viz.:

(1) Relazione di Leonardo da Ca' Masser sopra il Commercio dei Portoghesi nell' India (1506). App. Tom. II. 1845.

(2) Lettere di Giov. da Empoli, e la Vita di Esso, scritta da suo zio (1530). App. Tom. III, 1846.

Arnold, Edwin. The Light of Asia (as told in Verse by an Indian Buddhist). 1879.

Assemani, Joseph Simonius, Syrus Maronita. Bibliotheca Orientalis Clementino-Vaticana. 3 vols. in 4, folio. Romae, 1719–1728.

Ayeen Akbery. By this spelling are distinguished quotations from the tr. of Francis Gladwin, first published at Calcutta in 1783. Most of the quotations are from the London edition, 2 vols. 4to. 1800.

Baber. Memoirs of Zehir-ed-din Muhammed Baber, Emperor of Hindustan. ... Translated partly by the late John Leyden, Esq., M.D., partly by William Erskine, Esq., &c. London and Edinb., 4to. 1826.

Baboo and other Tales, descriptive of Society in India. Smith & Elder. London, 1834. (By Augustus Prinsep, B.C.S., a brother of James and H. Thoby Prinsep.)

Bacon, T. First Impressions of Hindustan. 2 vols. 1837.

Baden Powell. Punjab Handbook, vol. ii. Manufactures and Arts. Lahore, 1872.

Bailey, Nathan. *Diction. Britannicum*, or a more Compleat Universal Etymol. English Dict. &c. The whole Revis'd and Improv'd by N. B., *Φιλόλογος*. Folio. 1730.

Baillie, N. B. E. Digest of Moohummudan Law applied by British Courts in India. 2 vols. 1865–69.

Baker, Mem. of Gen. Sir W. E., R.E., K.C.B. Privately printed. 1882.

Balbi, Gasparo. Viaggio dell' Indie Orientali. 12mo. Venetia, 1590.

Baldaeus, P. Of this writer Burnell used the Dutch ed., Naauwkeurige Beschryvinge van Malabar en Choromandel, folio, 1672, and —— Ceylon, folio, 1672.

I have used the German ed., containing in one volume seriatim, Wahrhaftige Ausführliche Beschreibung der beruhmten Ost-Indischen Kusten Malabar und Coromandel, als auch der Insel Zeylon ... benebst einer ... Entdeckung der Abgöterey der Ost-Indischen Heyden. ... Folio. Amsterdam, 1672.

Baldelli-Boni. Storia del Milione. 2 vols. Firenze, 1827.

Baldwin, Capt. J. H. Large and Small Game of Bengal and the N.W. Provinces of India. 1876.

Balfour, Dr. E. **Cyclopaedia of India**. [3rd ed. London, 1885.]

[**Ball**, J. D. Things Chinese, being Notes on various Subjects connected with China. 3rd ed. London, 1900.

Ball, V. Jungle Life in India, or the Journeys and Journals of an Indian Geologist. London, 1880.]

Banarus, Narrative of Insurrection at, in 1781. 4to. Calcutta, 1782. Reprinted at Roorkee, 1853.

Bányan Tree, The. A Poem. Printed for private circulation. Calcutta, 1856. (The author was Lt.-Col. R. A. Yule, 9th Lancers, who fell before Delhi, June 19, 1857.)

Barbaro; Iosafa. Viaggio alla Tana, &c. In *Ramusio*, tom. ii. Also E.T. by W. Thomas, Clerk of Council to King Edward VI., embraced in Travels to Tana and Persia, Hak. Soc., 1873.

N.B.—It is impossible to discover from Lord Stanley of Alderley's Preface whether this was a reprint, or printed from an unpublished MS.

Barbier de Méynard, Dictionnaire Géogr. Hist. et Littér. de la Perse, &c. Extrait ... de Yaqout. Par C. B. de M. Large 8vo. Paris, 1861.

Barbosa. A Description of the Coasts of E. Africa and Malabar in the beginning of the 16th century. By Duarte Barbosa. Transl. &c., by Hon. H. E. J. Stanley. Hak. Soc., 1866.

—— **Lisbon Ed.** Livro de Duarte Barbosa. Being No. VII. in Collecção de Noticias para a Historia e Geografia, &c. Publ. pela Academia Real das Sciencias, tomo ii. Lisboa, 1812.

—— Also in tom. ii. of Ramusio.

Barretto. Relation de la Province de Malabar. Fr. tr. 8vo. Paris, 1646.

Originally pub. in Italian. Roma, 1645.

Barros, João de. Decadas de Asia, Dos feitos que os Portuguezes fizeram na Conquista e Descubrimento das Terras e Mares do Oriente.

Most of the quotations are taken from the edition in 12mo., Lisboa, 1778, issued along with Couto in 24 vols.

The first Decad was originally printed in 1552, the 2nd in 1553, the 3rd in 1563, the 4th as completed by Lavanha in 1613 (Barbosa-Machado, Bibl. Lusit. ii. pp. 606–607, as corrected by Figaniere, *Bibliogr. Hist. Port.* p. 169). A. B.

In some of Burnell's quotations he uses the 2nd ed. of Decs. i. to iii. (1628), and the 1st ed. of Dec. iv. (1613). In these there is apparently no division into chapters, and I have transferred the references to the edition of 1778, from which all my own quotations are made, whenever I could identify the passages, having myself no convenient access to the older editions.

Barth, A. Les Religions de l'Inde. Paris, 1879. Also English translation by Rev. T. Wood. Trübner's Or. Series. 1882.

Bastian, Adolf, Dr. Die Völker des Oestlichen Asien, Studien und Reisen. 8vo. Leipzig, 1866—Jena, 1871.

Beale, Rev. Samuel. Travels of **Fah-hian** and Sung-yun, Buddhist Pilgrims from China to India. Sm. 8vo. 1869.

Beames, John. **Comparative Grammar** of the Modern Aryan Languages of India &c. 3 vols. 8vo. 1872–79.

—— See also in *List of Glossaries*.

Beatson, Lt.-Col. A. View of the Origin and Conduct of the War with Tippoo Sultaun. 4to. London, 1800.

[**Belcher**, Capt. Sir E. Narrative of the Voyage of H.M.S. Samarang, during the years 1843–46, employed surveying the Islands of the Eastern Archipelago. 2 vols. London, 1846.]

Bellew, H. W. Journal of a Political Mission

to Afghanistan in 1857 under Major Lumsden. 8vo. 1862.

— [The Races of Afghanistan, being A Brief Account of the Principal Nations inhabiting that Country. Calcutta and London, 1880.]

Belon, Pierre, du Mans. Les **Observations** de Plvsievrs Singularités et Choses memorables, trouuées en Grece, Asie, Iudée, Egypte, Arabie, &c. Sm. 4to. Paris, 1554.

Bengal, Descriptive Ethnology of, by Col. E. T. Dalton. Folio. Calcutta, 1872.

Bengal Annual, or Literary Keepsake, 1831–32.

Bengal Obituary. Calcutta, 1848. This was I believe an extended edition of De Rozario's 'Complete Monumental Register,' Calcutta, 1815. But I have not been able to recover trace of the book.

Benzoni, Girolamo. The Travels of, (1542–56), orig. Venice, 1572. Tr. and ed. by Admiral W. H. Smyth, HAK. SOC. 1857.

[**Berncastle**, J. Voyage to China, including a Visit to the Bombay Presidency. 2 vols. London, 1850.]

Beschi, Padre. *See* **Gooroo Paramarttan.**

[**Beveridge**, H. The District of Bakarganj, its History and Statistics. London, 1876.]

Bhotan and the History of the Dooar War. By Surgeon **Rennie**, M.D. 1866.

Bird's Guzerat. The Political and Statistical History of Guzerat, transl. from the Persian of Ali Mohammed Khan. Or. Tr. Fund. 8vo. 1835.

Bird, Isabella (now Mrs. Bishop). The **Golden Chersonese**, and the Way Thither. 1883.

Bird's Japan. Unbeaten Tracks in J. by Isabella B. 2 vols. 1880.

Birdwood (Sir) George, C.S.I., M.D. The Industrial Arts of India. 1880.

[— Report on The Old Records of the India Office, with Supplementary Note and Appendices. Second Reprint. London, 1891.

[— and Foster, W. The First Letter Book of the East India Company, 1600–19. London, 1893.]

[**Blacker**, Lt.-Col. V. Memoir of the British Army in India in 1817–19. 2 vols. London, 1821.

[**Blanford**, W. T. The Fauna of British India: Mammalia. London, 1888–91.

Blumentritt, Ferd. **Vocabular** einzelner Ausdrücke und Redensarten, welche dem Spanischen der Philippinschen Inseln eigenthümlich sind. Druck von Dr. Karl Pickert in Leitmeritz. 1882.

Birteau, Padre D. Raphael. Vocabulario Portuguez Latino, Aulico, Anatomico, Architectonico, (and so on to Zoologico) … Lisboa, 1712–21. 8 vols. folio, with 2 vols. of Supplemento, 1727–28.

Bocarro. Decáda 13 da Historia da India, composta por Antonio B. (Published by the Royal Academy of Lisbon). 1876.

Bocarro. Detailed Report (Portuguese) upon the Portuguese Forts and Settlements in India, **MS.** transcript in India Office. Geog. Dept. from B.M. Sloane MSS. No. 197, fol. 172 *seqq.* Date 1644.

Bocharti Hierozoicon. In vol. i. of Opera Omnia, 3 vols. folio. Lugd. Bat. 1712.

Bock, Carl. Temples and Elephants. 1884.

Bogle. *See* **Markham's Tibet.**

Boileau, A. H. E. (Bengal Engineers). **Tour through** the Western States of **Rajwara** in 1835. 4to. Calcutta, 1837.

Boldensele, Gulielmus de. **Itinerarium** in the *Thesaurus* of *Canisius*, 1604. v. pt. ii. p. 95, also in ed. of same by *Basnage*, 1725, iv. 337; and by C. L. Grotefend in *Zeitschrift* des Histor. Vereins für Nieder Sachsen, Jahrgang 1852. Hannover, 1855.

Bole Pongis, by H. M. Parker. 2 vols. 8vo. 1851.

Bombay. A Description of the Port and Island of, and Hist. Account of the Transactions between the English and Portuguese concerning it, from the year 1661 to the present time. 12mo. Printed in the year 1724.

[**Bond**, E. A. Speeches of the Manager and Counsel in the Trial of Warren Hastings. 4 vols. London, 1859–61.]

Bongarsii, Gesta Dei der Francos. Folio. Hanovine, 1611.

Bontius, Jacobi B. Hist. Natural et Medic. Indiae Orientalis Libri Sex. Printed with **Piso**, q.v.

[**Bose**, S. C. The Hindoos as they are: A Description of the Manners, Customs, and Inner Life of Hindoo Society in Bengal. Calcutta, 1881.

Bosquejo das Possessões, &c. See p. 459*b*.

[**Boswell**, J. A. C. Manual of the Nellore District. Madras, 1887.]

Botelho, Simão. Tombo do Estado da India. 1554. Forming a part of the **Subsidios**, q.v.

Bourchier, Col. (Sir George). Eight Months' Campaign against the Bengal Sepoy Army. 8vo. London, 1858.

Bowring, Sir John. The Kingdom and People of **Siam**. 2 vols. 8vo. 1857.

Boyd, Hugh. The Indian Observer, with Life, Letters, &c. By L. D. Campbell. London, 1798.

Briggs, H. Cities of Gujarashtra; their Topography and History Illustrated. 4to. Bombay, 1849.

Brigg's Firishta. H. of the Rise of the Mahomedan Power in India. Translated from the Orig. Persian of Mahomed Kasim Firishta. By John Briggs, Lieut-Col. Madras Army. 4 vols. 8vo. 1829.

[**Brinckman**, A. The Rifle in Cashmere: A Narrative of Shooting Expeditions. London, 1862.]

Brooks, T. Weights, Measures, Exchanges, &c., in East India. Small 4to. 1752.

Broome, Capt. Arthur. Hist. of the Rise and Progress of the **Bengal Army**. 8vo. 1850. Only vol. i. published.

Broughton, T. D. Letters written in a Mahratta Camp during the year 1809. 4to. 1813. [New ed. London, 1892.]

Bruce's Annals. Annals of the Honourable E. India Company. (1600–1707–8.) By John Bruce, Esq., M.P., F.R.S. 3 vols. 4to. 1810.

Brugsch Bey (Dr. Henry). Hist. of Egypt under the Pharaohs from the Monuments. E.T. 2nd ed. 2 vols. 1881.

Buchanan, Claudius, D.D. **Christian Researches** in Asia. 11th ed. 1819. Originally pubd. 1811.

Buchanan Hamilton, Fr. The Fishes of the Ganges River and its Branches, Oblong folio. Edinburgh, 1822.

[—— Also *see* **Eastern India**.

[**Buchanan**, Dr. Francis (afterwards Hamilton). A Journey ... through ... Mysore, Canara and Malabar ... &c. 3 vols. 4to. 1807.]

Burckhardt, J. L.

Burke, The **Writings** and Correspondence of the Rt. Hon. Edmund. 8 vols. 8vo. London, 1852.

Burman, The: His Life and Notions. By Shway Yoe. 2 vols. 1882.

Burnes, Alexander. Travels into Bokhara. 3 vols. 2nd ed. 1835.

[**Burnes**, J. A Visit to the Court of Scinde. London, 1831.]

Burnouf, Eugène. Introduction à l'Histoire du **Bouddhisme Indien**. (Vol. i. alone published.) 4to. 1844.

Burton, Capt. R. F. **Pilgrimage** to El Medina and Mecca. 3 vols. 1855–56.

[—— Memorial Edition. 2 vols. London, 1893.]

—— **Scinde**, or the Unhappy Valley. 2 vols. 1851.

—— **Sind Revisited.** 2 vols. 1877.

—— **Camoens.** *Os Lusiadas*, Englished by R. F. Burton. 2 vols. 1880. And 2 vols. of Life and Commentary, 1881.

—— **Goa** and the Blue Mountains. 1851.

[—— The Book of the Thousand Nights and a Night, translated from the Arabic by Capt. Sir R. F. Burton, edited by L. C. Smithers. 12 vols. London, 1894.]

Busbequii, A. Gislenii. Omnia quae extant. Amstelod. Elzevir. 1660.

[**Busteed**, H. E. Echoes of Old Calcutta. 3rd ed. Calcutta, 1857.

[**Buyers**, Rev. W. Recollections of Northern India. London, 1848.]

Cadamosto, Luiz de. **Navegação Primeira.** In Collecção de Noticias of the Academia Real das Sciencias. Tomo II. Lisboa, 1812.

Caldwell, Rev. Dr. (afterwards Bishop). A **Comparative Grammar** of the Dravidian or South Indian Family of Languages. 2nd ed. Revd. and Enlarged, 1875.

Caldwell, Right Rev. Bishop. Pol. and Gen. History of the District of **Tinnevelly**. Madras, 1881.

——, Dr. R. (now Bishop). Lectures on **Tinnevelly Missions.** 12mo. London, 1857.

Ca' Masser. Relazione di Lionardo in **Archivio Storico Italiano,** q.v.

Cambridge, R. Owen. An Account of the **War in India** between the English and French, on the Coast of Coromandel (1750–1760). 4to. 1761.

Cameron, J. Our Tropical Possessions in Malayan India. 1865.

Camões, Luiz de. **Os Lusiadas**. Folio ed. of 1720, and Paris ed., 8vo., of 1847 are those used.

[**Campbell**, Maj.-Gen. John. A Personal Narrative of Thirteen Years' Service among the Wild Tribes of Khondistan. London, 1864.

[**Campbell**, Col. W. The Old Forest Ranger. London, 1853.]

Capmany, Ant. Memorias Hist. sobre la Marina, Comercio, y Artes de Barcelona. 4 vols. 4to. Madrid, 1779.

Cardim, T. Relation de la Province du **Japon.** du Malabar, &c. (trad. du Portug.). Tournay, 1645.

[**Carey**, W. H. The Good Old Days of Honble. John Company. 2 vols. Simla, 1882.]

Carletti, Francesco. Ragionamenti di— Fiorentino, sopra le cose da lui vedute ne' suoi Viaggi, &c. (1594–1606). First published in Firenze, 1701. 2 vols. in 12mo.

Carnegy, Patrick. See *List of Glossaries*.

Carpini, Joannes de Plano. Hist. Mongalorum, ed. by D'Avezac, in Recueil de Voyages et de Mémoires de la Soc. de Géographie, tom. iv. 1837.

Carraccioli, C. Life of Lord Clive. 4 vols. 8vo. No date (c. 1735).

It is not certain who wrote this ignoble book, but the author must have been in India.

Castanheda, Fernão Lopez de. Historia do descobrimento e conquista da India.

The original edition appeared at

Coimbra, 1551–1561 (in 8 vols. 4to and folio), and was reprinted at Lisbon in 1833 (8 vols. sm. 4to). This last ed. is used in quotations of the Port. text.

Castanheda was the first writer on Indian affairs (*Barbosa Machado, Bibl. Lusit.*, ii. p. 30. See also *Figanière, Bibliographia Hist. Port.*, pp. 165–167).

He went to Goa in 1528, and died in Portugal in 1559.

Castañeda. The First Booke of the Historie of the Discouerie and Conquest of the East Indias. ... Transld. into English by N. L.(itchfield), Gentleman. 4to. London, 1582.

The translator has often altered the spelling of the Indian words, and his version is very loose, comparing it with the printed text of the Port. in the ed. of 1833. It is possible, however, that Litchfield had the first ed. of the first book (1551) before him, whereas the ed. of 1833 is a reprint of 1554. (A.B.).

Cathay and the Way Thither. By H. Yule, HAK. SOC. 8vo. 2 vols. (Continuously paged.) 1866.

[**Catrou**, F. F. A History of the Mogul Dynasty in India. London, 1826.]

Cavenagh, Lt.-Gen. Sir Orfeur. **Reminiscences** of an Indian Official. 8vo. 1884.

Ceylonese Vocabulary. List of Native Words commonly occurring in Official Correspondence and other Documents. Printed by order of the Government. Columbo, June 1869.

[**Chamberlain**, B. H. Things Japanese, being Notes on Various Subjects connected with Japan. 3rd ed. London, 1898.]

Chardin, Voyages en Perse. Several editions are quoted, *e.g.* Amsterdam, 4 vols. 4to, 1735; by Langlès, 10 vols. 8vo. 1811.

Charnock's Hist. of **Marine Architecture.** 2 vols. 1801.

Charters, &c., of the **East India Company** (a vol. in India Office without date).

Chaudoir, Baron Stan. Aperçu sur les Monnaies Russes, &c. 4to. St. Pétersbourg, 1836–37.

[**Chevers**, N. A. A Manual of Medical Jurisprudence for India. Calcutta, 1870.]

Childers, R. A **Dictionary** of the **Pali** Language. 1875.

Chitty, S. C. The **Ceylon Gazetteer.** Ceylon, 1834.

Chow Chow, being Selections from a Journal kept in India, &c., by Viscountess Falkland. 2 vols. 1857.

Cieza de Leon, Travels of Pedro. Ed. by C. Markham. HAK. SOC. 1864.

Clarke, Capt. H. W., R.E. Translation of the **Sikandar Nāma** of Nizāmī. London, 1881.

Clavijo. Itineraire de l'Ambassade Espagnole à Samarcande, in 1403–1406 (original Spanish, with Russian version by I. Sreznevevsky). St. Petersburg, 1881.

—— Embassy of Ruy Gonzalez de, to the Court of Timour. E.T. by C. Markham. HAK. SOC. 1859.

Cleghorn, Dr. Hugh. Forests and Gardens of S. India. 8vo. 1861.

Coast of Coromandel: Regulations for the Hon. Comp.'s Black Troops on the. 1787.

Cobarruvias, Tesoro de la Lengua Castellana o Española, compvesto per el Licenciado Don Sebastian de. Folio. Madrid, 1611.

Cocks, Richard. Diary of ——, Cape-Merchant in the English Factory at Japan (first published from the original MS. in the B. M. and Admiralty). Edited by Edward Maunde Thompson, 2 vols. HAK. SOC. 1883.

Cogan. *See* **Pinto.**

Colebrooke, Life of, forming the first vol. of the collection of his Essays, by his son, Sir E. Colebrooke. 1873.

Collet, S. The Brahmo Year-Book. Brief Records of Work and Life in the Theistic Churches of India. London, 1876 *seqq.*

Collingwood, C. Rambles of a Naturalist on Shores and Waters of the China Sea. 8vo. 1868.

Colomb, Capt. R.N. Slave-catching in the Indian Ocean. 8vo. 1873.

Colonial Papers. *See* **Sainsbury.**

Competition-wallah, Letters of a (by G. O. Trevelyan). 1864.

Complete Hist. of the War in India (Tract). 1761.

Conti, Nicolo. *See* **Poggius**; also see **India in the XVth Century.**

[**Cooper**, T. T. The Mishmee Hills, an Account of a Journey made in an Attempt to penetrate Thibet from Assam, to open out new Routes for Commerce. London, 1873.]

Cordiner, Rev. J. A. Description of **Ceylon**, &c. 2 vols. 4to. 1807.

Cornwallis, Correspondence of Charles, First Marquis. Edited by C. Ross. 3 vols. 1859.

Correa, Gaspar, Lendas da India por. This most valuable, interesting, and detailed chronicle of Portuguese India was not published till in our own day it was issued by the Royal Academy of Lisbon—4 vols. in 7, in 4to, 1858–1864. The author went to India apparently with Jorge de Mello in 1512, and at an early date began to make notes for his history. The latest year that he mentions as having in it written a part of his history is 1561. The date of his death is not known.

Most of the quotations from Correa, begun by Burnell and continued by me, are from this work published in Lisbon. Some are, however, taken from "The **Three Voyages of Vasco da Gama** and his Viceroyalty, from the Lendas da India of Gaspar Correa," by the Hon. E. J. Stanley (now Lord Stanley of Alderley). HAK. SOC. 1869.

Coryat, T. **Crudities.** Reprinted from the ed. of 1611. 3 vols. 8vo. 1776.

Couto, Diogo de. The edition of the **Decadas** da Asia quoted habitually is that of 1778 (see **Barros**). The 4th Decade (Couto's first) was published first in 1602, fol.; the 5th, 1612; the 6th, 1614; the 7th, 1616; the 8th, 1673; 5 books of the 12th, Paris, 1645. The 9th was first published in an edition issued in 1736; and 120 pp. of the 10th (when, is not clear). But the whole of the 10th, in ten books, is included in the publication of 1778. The 11th was lost, and a substitute by the editor is given in the ed. of 1778. Couto died 10th Dec. 1616.

— **Dialogo** do Soldado Pratico (written in 1611, printed at Lisbon under the title Observações, &c., 1790).

Cowley, Abraham. His Six Books of **Plants.** In Works, folio ed. of 1700.

Crawfurd, John. **Descriptive Dict.** of the Indian Islands and adjacent countries. 8vo. 1856.

— **Malay Dictionary**, A Grammar and Dict. of the Malay Language. Vol. i. Dissertation and Grammar. Vol. ii. Dictionary. London, 1852.

— Journal of an Embassy to Siam and Cochin China. 2nd ed. 2 vols. 1838. (First ed. 4to, 1828.)

— Journal of an Embassy to the Court of **Ava** in 1827. 4to. 1829.

[**Crooke**, W. The Popular Religion and Folk-lore of Northern India. 1st ed. 1 vol. Allahabad, 1893; 2nd ed. 2 vols. London, 1896.

[— The Tribes and Castes of the North-Western Provinces and Oudh, 4 vols. Calcutta, 1896.]

Cunningham, Capt. Joseph Davy, B.E. History of the Sikhs, from the Rise of the Nation to the Battles of the Sutlej. 8vo. 2nd ed. 1853. (1st ed. 1849.)

Cunningham, Major Alex., B.E. **Ladak**, Physical, Statistical, and Historical. 8vo. 1854.

Cunningham, M.-Gen., R.E., C.S.I. (the same). Reports of the Archaeological Survey of India. Vol. i., Simla, 1871. Vol. xix., Calcutta, 1885.

Cyclades, The. By J. Theodore **Bent.** 8vo. 1885.

Dabistan, The; or, School of Manners. Transl. from the Persian by David Shea and Anthony Troyer. (Or. Tr. Fund.) 3 vols. Paris, 1843.

D'Acunha, Dr. Gerson. Contributions to the Hist. of Indo-**Portuguese Numismatics.** 4 fascic. Bombay, 1880 *seqq.*

Da Gama. *See* **Roteiro** and **Correa.**

D'Albuquerque, Afonso. Commentarios. Folio. Lisboa, 1557.

— **Commentaries**, transl. and edited by Walter de Grey Birch. HAK. SOC. 4 vols. 1875–1884.

Dalrymple, A. The **Oriental Repertory** (originally published in numbers, 1791–97), then at the expense of the E.I. Co. 2 vols. 4to. 1808.

Damiani a Göes, Diensis Oppugnatio. Ed. 1602.

— De Bello Cambaico.

— **Chronica.**

Dampier's Voyages. (Collection including sundry others). 4 vols. 8vo. London, 1729.

[**Danvers**, F. C., and Foster W. Letters received by the E.I. Co. from its Servants in the East. 4 vols. London, 1896–1900.]

D'Anville. Eclaircissemens sur la Carte de l'Inde. 4to. Paris, 1753.

Darmesteter, James. Ormazd et Ahriman. 1877.

— The Zendavesta. (Sacred Books of the East, vol. iv.) 1880.

Davidson, Col. C. J. (Bengal Engineers). Diary of Travels and Adventures in Upper India. 2 vols. 8vo. 1843.

Davies, T. Lewis O., M.A. **A Supplemental English Glossary.** 8vo. 1881.

Davis, Voyages and Works of John. Ed. by A. H. Markham. HAK. SOC. 1880.

[**Davy**, J. An Account of the Interior of Ceylon. London, 1821.]

Dawk Bungalow, The; or, Is his appointment pucka? (By G. O. Trevelyan). In Fraser's Mag., 1866, vol. lxiii. pp. 215–231 and pp. 382–391.

Day, Dr. Francis. The **Fishes of India.** 2 vols. 4to. 1876–1878.

De Bry, J. F. and J. "Indien Orientalis." 10 parts, 1599–1614.

The quotations from this are chiefly such as were derived through it by Mr. Burnell from Linschoten, before he had a copy of the latter. He notes from the *Biog. Univ.* that Linschoten's text is altered and re-arranged in De Bry, and that the Collection is remarkable for endless misprints.

De Bussy, Lettres de M., de Lally et autres. Paris, 1766.

De Candolle, Alphonse. **Origine** des Plantes Cultivées. 8vo. Paris, 1883.

De Castro, D. João de. Primeiro Roterio

da Costa da India, desde Goa até Dio. Segundo MS. Autografo. Porto, 1843.

De Castro. Roteiro de Dom Joam do Viagem que fizeram os Portuguezes ao Mar Roxo no Anno de 1541. Paris, 1883.

De Gubernatis, Angelo. Storia dei **Viaggiatori Italiani** nelle Indie Orientali. Livorno, 1875. 12mo. There was a previous issue containing much less matter.

De la Boullaye-le-Gous, **Voyages** et Observations du Seigneur Gentilhomme Angevin. Sm. 4to. Paris, 1653, and 2nd ed. 1657.

De la Loubère. Historical Relation of **Siam** by M. E.T. 2 vols. folio in one. 1693.

Della Tomba, Marco. Published by De Gubernatis. Florence, 1878.

Della Valle, Pietro. Viaggi de —, il Pellegrino, descritti, da lui medesimo in Lettere Familiari ... (1614–1626). Originally published at Rome, 1650–53.

The Edition quoted is that published at Brighton (but printed at Turin), 1843. 2 vols. in small 8vo.

[— From the O.E. Tr. of 1664, by G. Havers. 2 vols. ed. by E. Grey. HAK. Soc. 1891.]

Dellon. Relation de l'**Inquisition de Goa**. 1688. Also E.T., Hull, 1812.

De Monfart, H. An Exact and Curious Survey of all the East Indies, even to Canton, the chiefe citie of China. Folio. 1615. (A worthless book.)

De Morga, Antonio. **The Philippine Islands**, ed. by Hon. E. J. Stanley. HAK. Soc. 1868.

[**Dennys**, N. B. Descriptive Dictionary of British Malaya. London, 1894.]

De Orta, Garcia. *See* **Garcia**.

De Sacy, Silvestre. Chrestomathie Arabe. 2nd ed. 3 vols. Paris, 1826–27.

Desideri, P. Ipolito. MS. transcript of his Narrative of a residence in Tibet, belonging to the Hakluyt Society. 1714–1729.

Diccionario della Lengua **Castellana** compuesto por l'Academia Real. 6 vols. folio. Madrid, 1726–1739.

Dicty. of Words used in the **East Indies**. 2nd ed. 1805. (List of Glossaries, No. 6.).

Diez, Friedrich. **Etymologisches Wörterbuch** der Romanischen Sprachen. 2te. Ausgabe. 2 vols. 8vo. Bonn, 1861–62.

Dilemma, The. (A novel, by Col. G. Chesney, R.E.) 3 vols. 1875.

Dipavanso. The Dipavamso: edited and translated by H. Oldenberg. London, 1879.

Diplomi Arabi. *See* **Amari**.

Dirom. Narrative of the Campaign in India which terminated the War with Tippoo Sultan in 1792. 4to. 1793.

D'Ohsson, Baron C. Hist. des Mongols. La Haye et Amsterdam. 1834. 4 vols.

Dom Manuel of Portugal, **Letter of**. Reprint of old Italian version, by A. Burnell. 1881.

Also Latin in **Grynaeus**, Novus Orbis.

Dorn, Bernhard. **Hist. of the Afghans**, translated from the Persian of Neamet Allah. In Two Parts. 4to. (Or. Tr. Fund.) 1829–1836.

Dosabhai Framji. Hist. of the **Parsis**. 2 vols. 8vo. 1884.

Dostoyeffski. 1881. *See* p. 471*b*.

Douglas, Revd. Carstairs. Chinese-English Dictionary of the Vernacular or Spoken Language of Amoy Imp. 8vo. London, 1873.

[**Douglas**, J. Bombay and Western India. 2 vols. London, 1893.]

Dowson. *See* **Elliot**.

Dozy and Engelmann. Glossaire des Mots Espagnols et Portugais derivés de l'Arabe, par R. D. et W. H. F. 2nd ed. Leide, 1869.

— **Oosterlingen**. Verklarende Lijst der Nederlandsche Woorden die mit het Arabsch, Hebreeuwsch, Chaldeeuwsch, Perzisch, en Turksch afkomstig zijn, door R. Dozy. S' Gravenhage, 1867. (Tract.)

— Supplément aux Dictionnaires Arabes. 2 vols. 4to.

Drake, The World Encompassed by Sir Francis (orig. 1628). Edited by W. S. W. Vaux. HAK. Soc. 1856.

Drummond, R. **Illustrations** of the Grammatical parts of Guzarattee, Mahrattee, and English Languages. Folio. Bombay, 1808.

Dry Leaves from Young Egypt, by an ex-Political (E. B. Eastwick). 1849.

Dubois, Abbé J. Desc. of the Character, Manners, &c., of the People of India. E.T. from French MS. 4to. 1817.

[**Dufferin** and Ava, Marchioness of. Our Viceregal Life in India. New edition. London, 1890.]

Dunn. A New Directory for the East Indies. London, 1780.

Du Tertre, P. Hist. Générale des **Antilles** Habitées par les François. Paris, 1667.

Eastern India, The History, Antiquities, Topography and Statistics of. By Montgomery Martin (in reality compiled entirely from the papers of Dr. **Francis Buchanan**, whose name does not appear at all in a very diffuse title-page!) 3 vols. 8vo. 1838.

Echoes of Old Calcutta, by H. E. Busteed. Calcutta, 1882. [3rd ed. Calcutta, 1897.]

[**Eden**, Hon. **E**. Up the Country. 2 vols. London, 1866.]

Eden, R. A. **Hist. of Trauayle**, &c. R. Jugge. Small 4to. 1577.

Edrisi. Géographie. (Fr. Tr.) par Amedée

Jaubert. 2 vols. 4to. Paris, 1836. (Soc. de Géogr.)

[**Edwardes**, Major H. B. A Year on the Punjab Frontier. 2 vols. London, 1851.

[**Egerton**, Hon. W. An Illustrated Handbook of Indian Arms, being a Classified and Descriptive Catalogue of the Arms exhibited at the India Museum. London, 1880.]

Elgin, Lord. Letters and Journals of James Eighth Earl of E. Edited by T. Walrond. 1872.

Elliot. The Hist. of India as told by its own Historians. Edited from the Posth. Papers of Sir H. M. Elliot, R.C.B., by Prof. John **Dowson**. 8 vols. 8vo. 1867–1877.

Elliot, Sir Walter. Coins of S. India, belonging to the new ed. of Numismata Orientalia. Not yet issued (Nov. 1885).

Elphinstone, The Hon. **Mount-Stewart**, Life of, by Sir Edward Colebrooke, Bart. 2 vols. 8vo. 1884.

Elphinstone, The Hon. Mount-Stewart. Account of the Kingdom of **Caubool**. New edition. 2 vols. 8vo. 1839.

Emerson Tennent. An Account of the Island of **Ceylon**, by Sir James. 2 vols. 8vo. [3rd ed. 1859.] 4th ed. 1860.

Empoli, Giovanni da. Letters, in **Archivio** Storico Italiano, q.v.

Eredia. *See* **Godinho**.

Evelyn, John, Esq., F.R.S., The **Diary** of, from 1641 to 1705–6. (First published and edited by Mr. W. Bray in 1818.)

Fahian, or **Fah-hian**. *See* **Beale**.

Fallon, S. W. New Hindustani-English Dictionary. Banāras (Benares), 1879.

Fankwae, or Canton before Treaty Days: by an Old Resident. 1881.

Faria y Sousa (Manoel). **Asia Portuguesa**. 3 vols. folio. 1666–1675.

—— E.T. by Capt. J. Stevens. 3 vols. 8vo. 1695.

Favre, P. **Dictionnaire** Malais-Français et Français-Malais, 4 vols. Vienne, 1875–80.

Fayrer, (Sir) Joseph. **Thanatophidia** of India, being a Description of the Venomous Snakes of the Indian Peninsula. Folio. 1872.

Federici (or Fedrici). Viaggio de M. Cesare de F.— nell' India Orientale et oltra l'India. In Venetia, 1587. Also in vol. iii. of Ramusio, ed. 1606.

Ferguson. A Dictionary of the Hindostan Language. 4to. London, 1773.

Fergusson, James, D.C.L., F.R.S. Hist. of **Indian** and Eastern **Architecture**. 8vo. 1875.

[**Ferrier**, J. P. Caravan Journeys in Persia, Afghanistan, Turkestan, and Beloochistan. London, 1856.]

Fifth Report from the Select Committee of the House of Commons on the Affairs of the E.I. Company. Folio. 1812.

Filet, G. F. Plant-kundig Woordenboek voor Nederlandsch Indie. Leiden, 1876.

Firishta, **Scott's**. Ferishta's H. of the Dekkan from the great Mahommedan Conquests. Tr. by Capt. J. Scott. 2 vols. 4to. Shrewsbury, 1794.

—— **Briggs's**. *See* **Briggs**.

Flacourt, Hist. de la Grande isle **Madagascar**, composée par le Sieur de. 4to. 1658.

Flückiger. *See* **Hanbury**.

Fonseca, Dr. J. N. da. **Hist.** and Archæological Sketch of the City of **Goa**. 8vo. Bombay, 1878.

Forbes, A. Kinloch. *See* **Râs Mâlâ**.

[**Forbes**, Capt. C. J. F. S. British Burmah, and its People, being Sketches of Native Manners, Customs, and Religion. London, 1878.]

Forbes, Gordon S. Wild Life in Canara and Ganjam. 1885.

Forbes, James. Oriental Memoirs. 4 vols. 4to. 1813. [2nd ed. 2 vols. 1834.]

Forbes, H. O. A Naturalist's Wanderings in the Indian Archipelago. 1885.

Forbes Watson's Nomenclature. A List of Indian Products, &c., by J. F. W., M.A., M.D., &c. Part II., largest 8vo. 1872.

[—— The Textile Manufactures and the Costumes of the People of India. London, 1866.]

Forrest, Thomas. Voyage from Calcutta to the **Mergui** Archipelago, &c., by ——, Esq. 4to. London, 1792.

—— Voyage to **New Guinea** and the Moluccas from Balambangan, 1774–76. 4to. 1779.

Forster, George. **Journey** from Bengal to England. 2 vols. 8vo. London, 1808. Original ed., Calcutta, 1790.

Forsyth, Capt. J. Highlands of Central India, &c. 8vo. London, 1872. [2nd ed. London, 1899.]

Forsyth, Sir T. Douglas. Report of his **Mission** to Yarkund in 1873. 4to. Calcutta, 1875.

[**Foster**. *See* **Danvers**, F. C.

[**Francis**, E. B. Monograph on Cotton Manufacture in the Punjab. Lahore, 1884.

[**Francis**, Sir P. The Francis Letters, ed. by Beata Francis and Eliza Keary. 2 vols. London, 1901.]

Fraser, James Baillie. Journal of a Tour through Part of the Snowy Range of the Himālā Mountains. 4to. 1820.

[—— The Persian Adventurer. 3 vols. London, 1830.]

Frere, Miss M. **Deccan Days**, or Hindoo Fairy Legends current in S. India, 1868.

Frescobaldi, Lionardo. **Viaggi** in Terra

Santa di L. F. ed. altri. Firenze, 1862; very small.

Friar Jordanus. *See* **Jordanus.**

Fryer, John, M.D. A New Account of **East India** and Persia, in 8 Letters; being 9 years Travels. Begun 1672. And Finished 1681. Folio. London, 1698.

No work has been more serviceable in the compilation of the Glossary.

Fullarton, Col. View of English Interests in India. 1787.

Galland, Antoine. Journal pendant son Séjour à Constantinople, 1672–73. Annoté par Ch. Schefer. 2 vols. 8vo. Paris, 1881.

Galvano, A. Discoveries of the World, with E.T. by Vice-Admiral Bethune, C.B. HAK. Soc., 1863.

Garcia. Colloquios dos Simples e Drogas e Cousas Medecinaes da India, e assi de Algumas Fructas achadas nella ... compostos pelo Doutor **Garcia de Orta**. Physico del Rei João 3º. 2a edicão. Lisboa, 1872.

(Printed nearly page for page with the original edition, which was printed at Goa by João de Eredem in 1563.) A most valuable book, full of curious matter and good sense.

Garcin de Tassy. Particularités de la Religion Musulmane dans l'Inde. Paris, 1851.

Garden, In my Indian. By Phil. Robinson. 2nd ed. 1878.

Garnier, Francis. **Voyage d'Exploration** en Indo-Chine. 2 vols. 4to and two atlases. Paris, 1873.

Gildemeister. Scriptorum Arabum de Rebus Indicis Loci et Opuscula Inedita. Bonn, 1838.

Giles, Herbert A. Chinese Sketches. 1876.

——. See *List of Glossaries*.

Gill, Captain William. The **River of Golden Sand**, The Narrative of a Journey through China and Eastern Tibet to Burmah. 2 vols. 8vo. 1880. [Condensed ed., London, 1883.]

Gleig, Rev. G. R. Mem. of Warren Hastings. 3 vols. 8vo. 1841.

—— *See* **Munro**.

Glossographia, by T. B. (Blount). Folio ed. 1674.

Gmelin. Reise durch Siberien. 1773.

Godinho de Eredia, Malaca, L'Inde Meridionale et le Cathay, MS. orig. autographe de, reproduit et traduit par L. Janssen. 4to. Bruxelles, 1882.

Gooroo Pararmattan, written in Tamil by P. Beschi; E.T. by Babington. 4to. 1822.

Gouvea, A. de. Iornada do Arcebispo de Goa, D. Frey Aleixo de Menezes ... quando foy as Serras de Malabar, &c. Sm. folio. Coimbra, 1606.

[**Gover**, C. E. The Folk-Songs of Southern India. Madras, 1871.]

Govinda Sámanta, or the History of a Bengal Ráiyat. By the Rev. Lál Behári Day, Chinsurah, Bengal. 2 vols. London, 1874.

Graham, Maria. Journal of a Residence in India. 4to. Edinburgh, 1812.

An excellent book.

Grainger, James. The Sugar-Cane, a Poem in 4 books, with notes. 4to. 1764.

Gramatica Indostana. Roma, 1778.

See p. 260*a*.

Grand Master, The, or Adventures of Qui Hi, by Quiz. 1816.

One of those would-be funny mountains of doggerel, begotten by the success of Dr Syntax, and similarly illustrated.

Grant, Colesworthy. Rural Life in Bengal.

Letters from an artist in India to his Sisters in England. [The author died in Calcutta, 1883.] Large 8vo. 1860.

Grant, Gen. Sir Hope. Incidents in the Sepoy War, 1857–58. London, 1873.

Grant-Duff, Mount-Stewart Elph. Notes of an Indian Journey. 1876.

Greathed, Hervey. Letters written during the Siege of Delhi. 8vo. 1858.

[**Gribble**, J. D. B. Manual of Cuddapah. Madras, 1875.

[**Grierson**, G. A. Bihār Peasant Life. Calcutta, 1885.

[**Grigg**, H. B. Manual of the Nilagiri District. Madras, 1880.]

Groeneveldt. Notes on the Malay Archipelago, &c. From Chinese sources. Batavia, 1876.

Grose, Mr. A **Voyage** to the **East Indies**, &c. &c. In 2 vols. A new edition. 1772.

The first edition seems to have been pub. in 1766. I have never seen it. [The 1st ed., of which I possess a copy, is dated 1757.]

[**Growse**, F. S. Mathurá, a District Memoir. 3rd ed. Allahabad, 1883.]

Guerreiro, Fernan. **Relacion** Annual de las cosas que han hecho los Padres de la Comp. de J. ... en (1)600 y (1)601, traduzida de Portuguez par Colaco. Sq. 8vo. Valladolid, 1604.

Gundert, Dr. Malayālam and English Dictionary. Mangalore, 1872.

Haafner, M. J. **Voyages** dans la Péninsule Occid. de l'Inde et dans l'Ile de Ceilan. Trad. du Hollandois par M. J. 2 vols. 8vo. Paris, 1811.

[**Hadi**, S. M. A Monograph on Dyes and Dyeing in the North-Western Provinces and Oudh. Allahabad, 1896.]

Hadley. *See* under **Moors, The**, in the GLOSSARY.

Haeckel, Ernest. A Visit to Ceylon. E.T. by Clara Bell. 1883.

Haex, David. Dictionarium Malaico-Latinum et Latino-Malaicum. Romae, 1631.

Hajji Baba of Ispahan. Ed. 1835 and 1851. Originally pubd. 1824. 2 vols.

— in England. Ed. in 1 vol. 1835 and 1850. Originally pubd. 1828. 2 vols.

Hakluyt. The references to this name are, with a very few exceptions, to the reprint, with many additions, in 5 vols. 4to. 1807.

Several of the additions are from travellers subsequent to the time of Richard Hakluyt, which gives an odd aspect to some of the quotations.

Halhed, N. B. **Code** of Gentoo Laws. 4to. London, 1776.

Hall, Fitz Edward. Modern English, 1873.

Hamilton, Alexander, Captain. A New Account of the East Indies.

The original publication (2 vols. 8vo.) was at Edinburgh, 1727; again published, London, 1744. I fear the quotations are from both; they differ to a small extent in the pagination. [Many of the references have now been checked with the edition of 1744.]

Hamilton, Walter. **Hindustan**. Geographical, Statistical, and Historical Description of Hindustan and the Adjacent Countries. 2 vols. 4to. London, 1820.

Hammer-Purgstall, Joseph. Geschichte der Goldenen Horde. 8vo. Pesth, 1840.

Hanbury and Flückiger. Pharmacographia: A Hist. of the Principal Drugs of Vegetable Origin. Imp. 8vo. 1874. There has been a 2nd ed.

Hanway, Jonas. Hist. Acc. of the British Trade over the Caspian Sea, with a Journal of **Travels**, &c. 4 vols. 4to. 1753.

[**Harcourt**, Capt. A. F. P. The Himalayan Districts of Kooloo, Lahoul, and Spiti. London, 1871.]

Hardy, Revd. Spence. Manual of **Buddhism** in its Modern Development.

The title-page in my copy says 1860, but it was first published in 1853.

Harrington, J. H. Elementary **Analysis** of the Laws and Regulations enacted by the G.-G. in C. at Fort William. 3 vols. folio. 1805–1817.

Haug, Martin. **Essays** on the Sacred Language, Writings, and Religion of the Parsis. 8vo. 1878.

Havart, Daniel, M.D. Op- en Ondergang van Coromandel. 4to. Amsterdam, 1693.

Hawkins. The Hawkins' Voyages. HAK. SOC. Ed. by C. Markham. 1878.

Heber, Bp. Reginald. **Narrative** of a Journey through the Upper Provinces of India. 3rd ed. 3 vols. 1878.

But most of the quotations are from the edition of 1844 (Colonial and Home Library). 2 vols. Double columns.

Hedges, **Diary** of Mr. (afterwards Sir) William, in Bengal, &c., 1681–1688.

The earlier quotations are from a MS. transcription, by date; the later, paged, from its sheets printed by the HAK. SOC. (still unpublished). [Issued in 2 vols., HAK. SOC. 1886.]

Hehn, **V. Kulturpflanzen** und **Hausthiere** in ihren Uebergang aus Asien nach Griechenland und Italien so wie in das übrige Europa. 4th ed. Berlin, 1883.

Heiden, T. Vervaerlyke Schipbreuk, 1675.

Herbert, Sir Thomas. Some Yeares **Travels** into Divers Parts of Asia and Afrique. Revised and Enlarged by the Author. Folio, 1638. Also 3rd ed. 1665.

Herklots, G. B. **Qanoon-e-Islam**. 1832. 2nd ed. Madras, 1863.

Heylin, Peter. **Cosmographie**, in 4 Books (paged as sep. volumes), folio, 1652.

Heyne, Benjamin. **Tracts** on India. 4to 1814.

Hodges, William. Travels in India during the Years 1780–83. 4to. 1793.

[**Hoey**, W. A Monograph on Trade and Manufactures in Northern India, Lucknow. 1880.]

Hoffmeister. **Travels**. 1848.

Holland, Philemon. The Historie of the World, commonly called The Natvrall Historie of **C. Plinivs** Secvndvs. ... Tr. into English by P. H., Doctor in Physic. 2 vols. Folio. London, 1601.

Holwell, J. Z. Interesting **Historical Events** Relative to the Province of Bengal and the Empire of Indostan, &c. Part I. 2nd ed. 1766. Part II. 1767.

Hooker (Sir) Jos. Dalton. Himalayan Journals. Notes of a Naturalist, &c. 2 vols. Ed. 1855.

[**Hoole**, E. Madras, Mysore, and the South of India, or a Personal Narrative of a Mission to those Countries from 1820 to 1828. London, 1844.]

Horsburgh's India Directory. Various editions have been used.

Houtman. Voyage. *See* **Spielbergen**. I believe this is in the same collection.

Huc et Gabet. Souvenirs d'un Voyage dans la Tartarie, le Thibet, et la Chine pendant les Années 1844, 1845, et 1846. 2 vols. 8vo. Paris 1850. [E.T. by W. Hazlitt. 2 vols. London, 1852.]

[**Hügel**, Baron Charles. Travels in Kashmir and the Panjab, with notes by Major T. B. Jervis. London, 1845.

[**Hughes**, T. P. A Dictionary of Islam. London, 1885.]

Hulsius. Collection of Voyages, 1602–1623.

Humāyūn. Private **Mem.** of the Emperor. Tr. by Major C. Stewart. (Or. Tr. Fund.) 4to. 1832.

Humboldt, W. von. Die Kawi Sprache auf der Insel Java. 3 vols. 4to. Berlin, 1836–38.

Hunter, W. W. **Orissa.** 2 vols. 8vo. 1872.

Hyde, Thomas. Syntagma Dissertationum, 2 vols. 4to. Oxon., 1767.

Hydur Naik, Hist. of, by Meer Hussein Ali Khan Kirmani. Trd. by Col. W. Miles. (Or. Tr. Fund). 8vo. 1842.

[**Ibbetson**, D. C. J. Outlines of Panjab Ethnography. Calcutta, 1883.]

Ibn Baithar. Heil und Nahrungsmittel von Abu Mohammed Abdallah ... bekannt unter dem Namen Ebn Baithar. (Germ. Transl. by Dr. Jos. v. Sontheimer). 2 vols. large 8vo. Stuttgart, 1840.

Ibn Batuta. Voyages d'Ibn Batoutah, Texte Arabe, accompagné d'une Traduction par C. De Frémery et le Dr. B. R. Sanguinetti (Société Asiatique). 4 vols. Paris, 1853–58.

Ibn Khallikan's Biographical Dictionary. Tr. from the Arabic by Baron McGuckin de Slane. 4 vols. 4to. Paris, 1842–71.

India in the XVth Century. Being a Coll. of Narratives of Voyages to India, &c. Edited by R. H. Major, Esq., F.S.A. Hak. Soc. 1857.

Indian Administration of Lord Ellenborough. Ed. by Lord Colchester. 8vo. 1874.

Indian Antiquary, The, a Journal of Oriental Research. 4to. Bombay, 1872, and succeeding years till now.

Indian Vocabulary. See *List of Glossaries*.

Intrigues of a Nabob. By H. F. Thompson. *See* under **Nabob** in Glossary.

Isidori Hispalensis Opera. Folio. Paris, 1601.

Ives, Edward. A **Voyage** from England to India in the year 1754, &c. 4to. London, 1773.

Jacquemont Victor. **Correspondance** avec sa Famille, &c. (1828–32). 2 vols. Paris, 1832.

—— (English Translation.) 2 vols. 1834.

Jagor, F. Ost-Indische Handwerk und Gewerbe. 1878.

Jahanguier, Mem. of the Emperor, tr. by Major D. Price (Or. Tr. Fund). 4to. 1829.

Jal, A. **Archéologie Navale.** 2 vols. large 8vo. Paris, 1840.

Japan. A Collection of Documents on Japan, with comment. by Thomas Rundall, Esq. Hak. Soc. 1850.

Jarric, P. (S.J.). Rerum Indicarum **Thesaurus.** 3 vols. 12mo. Coloniae, 1615–16.

Jenkins, E. The Coolie. 1871.

Jerdon's Birds. The Birds of India, being a Natural Hist. of all the Birds known to inhabit Continental India, &c. Calcutta, 1862.

The quotations are from the Edition issued by Major Godwin Austen. 2 vols. (in 3). Calcutta, 1877.

—— **Mammals**. The Mammals of India, A Nat. Hist. of all the Animals known to inhabit Continental India. By T. C. Jerdon, Surgeon-Major Madras Army. London, 1874.

[**Johnson**, D. Sketches of Field Sports as followed by the Natives of India. London, 1822.]

Joinville, Jean Sire de. **Hist. de Saint Louis**, &c. Texte et Trad. par M. Natalis de Wailly. Large 8vo. Paris, 1874.

Jones, Mem. of the Life, Writings, and Correspondence of **Sir William**. By Lord Teignmouth. Orig. ed., 4to., 1804. That quoted is—2nd ed. 8vo., 1807.

Jordanus, Friar, Mirabilia Descripta (c. 1328). Hak. Soc. 1863.

J. Ind. Arch. Journal of the Indian Archipelago, edited by Logan. Singapore, 1847, *seqq.*

Julien, Stanislas. *See* **Pèlerins.**

Kaempfer Engelbert. Hist. Naturelle, Civile et Ecclesiastique du Japon. Folio. La Haye. 1729.

—— **Am. Exot.** Amœnitatum Exoticarum ... Fasciculi V. ... Auctore Engelberto Kæmpfero, D. Sm. 4to. Lemgoviæ, 1712.

Khozeh Abdulkurreem, Mem. of, tr. by **Gladwin**. Calcutta, 1788.

Kinloch, A. A. Large Game Shooting in Thibet and the N.W.P. 2nd Series. 4to. 1870.

Kinneir, John Macdonald. Geogr. Memoir of the **Persian Empire**. 4to. 1813.

[**Kipling**, J. L. Beast and Man in India, a Popular Sketch of Indian Animals in their Relations with the People. London, 1892.]

Kircher, Athan. **China** Monumentis, &c. **Illustrata**. Folio. Amstelod. 1667.

Kirkpatrick, Col. Account of **Nepaul**, 4to. 1811.

Klaproth, Jules. **Magasin Asiatique.** 2 vols. 8vo. 1825.

Knox, Robert. An Historical Relation of the Island of **Ceylon** in the East Indies, &c. Folio. London, 1681.

Kuzzilbash, The (By J. B. Fraser). 3 vols. 1828.

La Croze, M. V. **Hist. du Christianisme** des Indes. 12mo. A la Haye, 1724.

La Roque. Voyage to Arabia the Happy, &c. E.T. London, 1726. (French orig. London, 1715.)

La Rousse, **Dictionnaire Universel** du XIXe Siècle. 16 vols. 4to. 1864–1878.

Lane's Modern Egyptians, ed. 2 vols. 1856.

— Do., ed. 1 vol. 8vo. 1860.

— **Arabian Nights**, 3 vols. 8vo. 1841.

[**Le Fanu**, H. Manual of the Salem District. 2 vols. Madras, 1883.]

Leland, C. G. **Pidgin-English** Sing-song, 16mo. 1876.

[**Leman**, G. D. Manual of the Ganjam District. Madras, 1882.]

Lembrança de Cousas da India em 1525, forming the last part of **Subsidios**, q.v.

Letter to a Proprietor of the E. India Company. (Tract.) 1750.

Letters of Simpkin the Second on the Trial of Warren Hastings. London, 1791.

Letters from Madras during the years 1836–1839. By a Lady. [Julia Charlotte Maitland.] 1843.

Lettres Edifiantes et Curieuses. 1st issue in 34 Recueils. 12mo. 1717 to 1774. 2nd do. re-arranged, 26 vols. 1780–1783.

Leunclavius. Annales Sultanorum Othmanidarum. Folio ed. 1650.

An earlier ed. 4to. Francof. 1588, in the B. M., has autograph notes by Jos. Scaliger.

Lewin, Lt.-Col. T. A Fly on the Wheel, or How I helped to Govern India. 8vo. 1885. An excellent book.

[— The Wild Races of South-Eastern India. London, 1870.]

Leyden, John. Poetical Remains, with Memoirs of his Life, by Rev. **J. Morton**. London, 1819.

(Burnell has quoted from a reprint at Calcutta of the Life, 1823.)

Life in the Mofussil, by an Ex-Civilian. 2 vols. 8vo. 1878.

Light of Asia, or the Great Renunciation. As told in verse by an Indian Buddhist. By Edwin Arnold. 1879.

Lindsays, Lives of The, or a Mem. of the House of Crawford and Balcarres. By Lord Lindsay, 3 vols. 8vo. 1849.

Linschoten. Most of the quotations are from the old English version: Iohn Hvighen van Linschoten, his Discours of Voyages into Ye Easte and Weste Indies. Printed at London by Iohn Wolfe, 1598—either from the black-letter folio, or from the reprint for the Hak. Soc. (2 vols. 1885), edited by Mr. Burnell and Mr. P. Tiele. If not specified, they are from the former.

The original Dutch is: "Itinerarie Voyage ofter Schipvaert van Jan Huygen van Linschoten." To T'Amstelredam, 1596.

Littré, E. Dict. de la Langue Française. 4 vols. 4to., 1873–74, and 1 vol. Suppt., 1877.

Livros das Monções. (Collecçao de Monumentos Ineditos). Publd. by R. Academy of Lisbon. 4to. Lisbon, 1880.

[**Lloyd**, Sir W. **Gerard**. Capt. A. A Narrative of a Journey from Caunpoor to the Boorendo Pass in the Himalaya Mountains. 2 vols. London, 1840.]

Lockyer, Charles. An Account of the Trade in India, &c. London, 1711.

[**Logan**, W. Malabar. 3 vols. Madras, 1887–91.]

Long, Rev. James. Selections from Unpublished Records of Government (Fort William) for the years 1748–1767. Calcutta, 1869.

Lord. Display of two forraigne Sects in the East Indies. 1. A Discouerie of the Sect of the Banians. 2. The Religion of the Persees. Sm. 4to. 1630.

Lowe, Lieut. C. R. History of the Indian Navy. 2 vols. 8vo. 1877.

Lubbock, Sir John. Origin of Civilisation. 1870.

Lucena, P. João de. Hist da Vida do Padre F. de Xavier. Folio. Lisbon, 1600.

Ludolphus, Job. Historia Aethiopica Francof. ad Moenum. Folio. 1681.

Luillier. Voyage du Sieur, aux Grandes Indes. 12mo. Paris, 1705. Also E.T., 1715.

Lutfullah. Autobiog. of a Mahomedan Gentleman. Ed. by E. B. Eastwick. 1857.

Macarius. Travels of the Patriarch. E.T. by F. C. Belfour (Or. Trans. Fund). 4to. 1829.

McCrindle, J. W. Ancient India as described by Megasthenes and Arrian. 8vo. 1877.

— Transl. of the Periplus Maris Erythraei, and of Arrian's Voyage of Nearchus. 1879.

M'Crindle, J. W. Ancient India as described by Ktesias the Knidian. 1882.

— Ancient India as described by Ptolemy, 1885.

[— The Invasion of India by Alexander the Great. New ed. London, 1896.]

Macdonald, D., M.D. A Short Account of the Fisheries of the Bombay Presidency (prepared for the great Fisheries Exhibition of 1883).

Macgregor, Col. (now Sir Charles). A Journey through Khorassan. 2 vols. 1875.

Mackenzie. Storms and Sunshine of a Soldier's Life. By Mrs. Colin Mackenzie. 2 vols. 8vo. 1882.

[— Life in the Mission, the Camp, and the Zenáná, or Six Years in India. 2nd ed. London, 1854.]

Mackenzie Collection. Desc. Catalogue of.

By H. H. Wilson. 2 vols. 8vo. Calcutta, 1828.

Mackintosh, Capt. A. An Account of the Origin and Present Condition of the Tribe of Ramoosies, &c. Bombay, 1833.

[**Maclagan**, E. D. Monograph on the Gold and Silver Works of the Punjab. Lahore, 1890.]

MacLennan, J. F. An Inquiry into the origin of the form of Capture in Marriage Ceremonies. Edinburgh, 1865.

[**McMahon**, Lieut.-Col. A. R. The Karens of the Golden Chersonese. London, 1876.]

McNair, Major. Perak and the Malays. 1878.

Madras, or Fort St. George. Dialogues written originally in the Naruga or Gentou language. By B. S. V. Halle, 1750. (German).

Maffeus, Joannes Petrus, E. S. J. Historiarum Indicarum Libri XVI. Ed. Vienna, 1751.

—— also Selectarum Epistolarum ex India Libri IV. Folio. (Hist. first pubd. at Florence, 1588).

Maine, Sir Henry S. Village Communities. 3rd ed. 1876.

—— Early History of Institutions. 1875.

Makrizi. Hist. des Sultans Mamlouks de l'Egypte par ... trad. par M. Quatremère. (Or. Transl. Fund). 2 vols. 4to. 1837–1842.

Malaca Conquistada pelo Grande Af. de Alboquerque. A Poem by Fr. de Sa de Menezes. 4to. 1634.

Malcolm, Sir John. Hist. of Central India. 1st ed. 1823; 2nd, 1824; 3rd, 1832. 2 vols.

—— Hist. of Persia. 2 vols. 4to. 1815. [New ed. 2 vols. 1829.]

—— Life of Robert, Lord Clive. 3 vols. 1836.

Malcolm's Aneodotes of the Manners and Customs of London during the 18th Century. 4to. 1808.

Mandelslo, Voyages and Travels of J. A., into the E. Indies, E.T. 1669. Folio.

Manning. *See* **Markham's Tibet**.

Manual ou **Breue Instructção** que serue por Uso D'as Crianças, que Aprendem Ler, e comêçam rezar nas Escholas Portuguezas, que são em India Oriental; e especialmente na Costa dos Malabaros que se chama Coromandel. Anno 1713.

(In Br. Museum. No place or Printer. It is a Protestant work, no doubt of the first Danish missionaries of the S.P.G. It contains a prayer "A oração por a Illustrissima Companhia da India Oriental.")

Manual of the Geology of India. Large 8vo. 2 parts by Medlicott and Blanford. Calcutta, 1879. Part 3 by V. Ball, M.A. Economic Geology, 1881.

Marcel Devic. Dictionnaire Etymologique des Mots d'origine orientale. In the Supplemental Vol. of Littré. 1877.

Marini. Hist. Nouuelle et Cvrievse des Royaumes de Tunquin et de Lao. Tradde l'Italien. Paris, 1666.

Marino Sanudo. Secretorum Fidelium Crucis. *See* **Bongarsius**, of whose work it forms the 2nd part.

Markham, C. R., C. B. Travels in Peru and India. 1862.

—— Clavijo. Narr. of Embassy of Ruy Gonzalez de C. to the Court of Timour (1403–6). Tra. and Ed. by C. R. M. Hak. Soc. 1859.

——**'s Tibet**. Narrative of the Mission of G. Bogle to Tibet; and of the Journey of Thomas Manning to Lhasa. 8vo. 1876.

[—— A Memoir of the Indian Surveys. 2nd ed. London, 1878.]

Marmol, El Veedor Lvys de. Descripcion General de **Africa**; Libro Tercero, y Segundo Volumen de la Primera parte. En Granada, 1573.

Marre. Kata-Kata Malayou, ou Recueil des Mots Malais Françisés, par Avis-Marre (Ext. from Compte Rendu du Congrès Prov. des Orientalistes). Paris, 1875.

Marsden, W. Memoirs of a Malayan Family, transl. from the original by, (O. T. F.). 1830.

—— **History of Sumatra**. 2nd ed. 4to. 1784; 3rd ed. 4to. 1811.

—— **Dictionary** of the Malayan Language. In two Parts. 4to. 1812.

—— A Brief Mem. of his Life and Writings. Written by Himself. 4to. 1838.

Martinez de la Puente. Compendio de los Descubrimentos, Conquistas y Guerras de la India Oriental y sus Islas. Sq. 8vo. Madrid, 1681.

[**Mason**, F. Burmah, its People and Natural Productions. Rangoon, 1860.

[**Maspero**, G. The Dawn of Civilisation. Egypt and Chaldaea. Ed. by A. H. Sayce. London, 1894.]

Mas'udi. Maçoudi, Les Prairies d'Or, par Barbier de Meynar et Pavet de Courteille. 9 vols. 8vo. 1861–1877.

[**Mateer**, S. The Land of Charity: A Descriptive Account of Travancore and its People. London, 1871.]

Matthioli, P. A. Commentary on Dioscorides. The edition chiefly used is an old French transl. Folio. Lyon, 1560.

Maundeville, Sir John. Ed. by Halliwell. 8vo. 1866.

Max Havelaar door Multatuli (E. Douwes Dékker). 4th ed. Amsterdam, 1875.

This is a novel describing Society in Java, but especially the abuses of rural administration. It was originally published c. 1860, and made a great noise in Java and the mother country. It was translated into English a few years later.

[**Mayne**, J. D. A Treatise on Hindu Law and Custom. 2nd ed. Madras, 1880.]

Mehren, M. A. F. Manuel de la Cosmographie du Moyen Age (tr. de l'Arabe de Chemseddîn Dimichqi). Copenhague, &c. 1874.

Memoirs of the Revolution in Bengal. (Tract.) 1760.

Mendoza, Padre Juan Gonzales de. The work was first published at Rome in 1585: Historia de las cossas mas notables, Ritos y Costumbres del Gran Reyno de **la China** (&c.) ... hecho y ordenado por el mvy R. P. Maestro Fr. Joan Gonzalez de Mendoça, &c. The quotations are from the HAK. Soc.'s reprint, 2 vols. (1853) of R. Parke's E.T., entitled "The Historie of the Great and Mightie Kingdome of China" (&c). London, 1588.

Meninski, F. à M. Thesaurus Linguarum Orientalium. 4 vols. folio. Vienna, 1670. New ed. Vienna, 1780.

Merveilles de l'Inde, Livre des. Par MM. Van der Lith et Devic. 4to. Leide, 1883.

Middleton's Voyage, Sir H. Last East India V. to Bantam and the Maluco Islands, 1604. 4to. London, 1606; also reprint HAK. SOC. 1857.

Milburn, Wm. Oriental Commerce, &c. 2 vols. 4to. 1813. [New ed. 1 vol. 1825.]

Miles. *See* **Hydur Ali** and **Tipú**.

Mill, James. Hist. of **British India**. Originally published 3 vols. 4to. 1817. Edition used in 8vo, edited and completed by H. H. Wilson. 9 vols. 1840.

Milman, Bishop. Memoir of, by Frances Maria Milman. 8vo. 1879.

Millingen. Wild Life among the Koords. 1870.

Minsheu, John. The Guide into the Tongues, &c. The 2nd ed. folio. 1627.

Minto, Lord, in India. Life and Letters of Gilbert Elliot, first Earl of Minto from 1807 to 1814, while Governor-General of India. Edited by his great niece, the Countess of Minto. 8vo. 1880.

Minto Life of Gilbert Elliot, by Countess of Minto. 3 vols. 1874.

Mirat-i-Ahmedi. *See* **Bird's Guzerat**.

Miscellanea Curiosa (Norimbergae). *See* pp. 537*a*, and 63*a*.

Mission to Ava. Narrative of the M. sent to the Court of A. in 1855. By Capt. H. Yule, Secretary to the Envoy, Major Phayre. 1858.

Mocquet, Jean. Voyages en Afrique, Asie, Indes Orientales et Occidentales. Paris, 1617. The edition quoted is of 1645.

Mohit, The, by Sidi Ali Kapudan. Translated Extracts, &c., by Joseph v. Hammer-Purgstall, in J. A. S. Soc. Bengal. Vols. III. and V. [Also see **Sidi Ali**.]

Molesworth's Dicty. Maráthí and English. 2nd ed. 4to. Bombay 1857.

Money, William. **Java**, or How to Manage a Colony. 2 vols. 1860. (I believe Mr. Money was not responsible for the vulgar second title.)

Moor, Lieut. E. **Narrative** of the operations of Capt. Little's Detachment, &c. 4to. 1794.

Moore, Thomas. Lalla Bookh. 1817.

[**Morier**, J. A Journey through Persia, Armenia and Asia Minor, to Constantinople, in the years 1808 and 1809. London, 1812.]

Morton, Life of Leyden. *See* **Leyden**.

Mountain, Mem. and Letters of Col. Armine S. H. 1857.

Muir, Sir William. Annals of the Early **Caliphate**, from original sources. 1883.

[**Mukharji**, T. N. Art-Manufactures of India. Calcutta, 1888.]

Müller, Prof. Max. Lectures on the Science of Language. 1st Ser. 1861. 2nd Ser. 1864.

—— Hibbert Lectures on the Origin and Growth of Religion, as illustrated by the Religions of India. 1878.

[**Mundy**, Gen. G. C. Pen and Pencil Sketches in India. 3rd ed. London, 1858.]

Munro, Sir T. Life of M.-Gen., by the Rev. G. R. **Gleig**. 3 vols. 1830. (At first 2 vols., then a 3rd vol. of additional letters.)

—— His **Minutes**, &c., edited by Sir A. Arbuthnot, with a Memoir. 2 vols. 8vo. 1881.

Munro, Capt. Innes. **Narrative** of Military Operations against the French, Dutch, and Hyder Ally Cawn, 1780–84. 4to. 1789.

Munro, Surgeon Gen., C.B. **Reminiscences** of Military Service with the 93rd Highlanders. 1883. (An admirable book of its kind.)

Napier, General Sir Charles. Records of the Indian Command of, comprising all his General Orders, &c. Compiled by John Mawson. Calcutta, 1851.

[**Neale**, F. A. Narrative of a Residence at the Capital of the Kingdom of Siam, with a Description of the Manners, Customs, and Laws of the modern Siamese. London, 1852.

[**N.E.D**. A New English Dictionary on Historical Principles: founded mainly on the Materials collected by the Philological Society: edited by J. H. Murray and H. Bradley. 5 vols. Oxford. 1888–1902.]

Nelson, J. H., M.A. The **Madura** Country, a Manual. Madras, 1868.

Niebuhr, Carsten. **Voyage** en **Arabie**, &c. 2 vols. 4to. Amsterdam, 1774.

—**Desc. de l'Arabie**, 4to. Amsterdam, 1774.

Nieuhof, Joan. Zee-en Lant Reize. 2 vols. folio. 1682.

Norbert, Père (O.S.F.). **Mémoires** Historiques presentés au Souverain Pontife Benoit XIV. sur les Missions des Indes Orientales (A bitter enemy of the Jesuits). 2 vols. 4to. Luques (Avignon). 1744. A 3rd vol. London, 1750; also 4 pts. (4 vols.) 12mo. Luques, 1745.

Notes and Extracts from the Govt. Records in Fort St. George (1670–1681). Parts I., II., III. Madras, 1871–73.

N. & E. Notices et Extraits des Manuscrits de la Bibliothèque du Roi (and afterwards *Nationale, Impériale, Royale*, &c.). 4to. Paris, 1787, *et seqq.*

Notices of Madras and Cuddalore in the Last Century, from the Journals and Letters of the Earlier Missionaries (Germans) of the S.P.C.K. Small 8vo. 1858. A very interesting little work.

Novus orbis Regionum ac Insularum Veteribus Incognitarum, &c. Basiliae apud Io. Hervagium. 1555, folio. Orig. ed., 1537.

Nunes, A. Livro dos Pesos da Ymdia, e assy Medidas e Moedas. 1554. Contained in **Subsidios**, q.v.

Oakfield, or Fellowship in the East. By **W. D. Arnold**, late 58th Reg. B.N.I. 2 vols. 2nd ed. 1854. The 1st ed. was apparently of the same year.

Observer, The Indian. *See* **Boyd.**

[**Oliphant**, L. Narrative of the Earl of Elgin's Mission to China and Japan in the years 1857–8–9. 2 vols. Edinburgh, 1859.

[**Oppert**, G. The Original Inhabitants of Bharatavarsa or India. Westminster, 1893.

[**Oriental Sporting Magazine**, June 1828 to June 1833, reprint. 2 vols. London, 1873.]

Orme, Robert. **Historical Fragments** of the Mogul Empire, &c. This was first published by Mr. Orme in 1782. But a more complete ed. with sketch of his life, &c., was issued after his death. 4to. 1805.

Orme, Robert. **Hist. of the Military Transactions** of the British Nation in Indostan. 3 vols. 4to. The dates of editions are as follows: Vol. I., 1763; 2nd ed., 1773; 3rd ed., 1781. Vol. II. (in two Sections commonly called Vols. II. and III.), 1778. Posthumous edition of the complete work, 1805. These all in 4to. Reprint at Madras, large 8vo. 1861–62.

Osbeck. A Voyage to China and the E. Indies. Tr. by J. R. Forster. 2 vols. 1771.

Osborne, Hon. W. G. **Court and Camp of Runjeet Singh.** 8vo. 1840.

Ousely, Sir William. **Travels** in Various Countries of the East. 3 vols. 4to. 1819–23.

Ovington, Rev. F. A Voyage to Suratt in the year 1689. London, 1696.

[**Owen**, Capt. W. F. W. Narrative of Voyages to explore the Shores of Africa, Arabia, and Madagascar. 2 vols. London, 1833.]

Palgrave, W. Gifford. Narrative of a Year's Journey through Central and Western **Arabia.** 2 vols. 1865. [New ed. 1 vol. 1868.]

Pallegoix. Monseigneur. **Description** du Royaume Thai ou **Siam.** 2 vols. 1854.

[**Palmer**, Rev. A. S. Folk-etymology. London, 1882.]

Pandurang Hari, or Memoirs of a Hindoo, originally published by Whitaker. 3 vols. 1826. The author was Mr. Hockley of the Bo. C.S. of whom little is known. The quotations are partly from the reissue by H. S. King & Co. in 1873, with a preface by Sir Bartle Frere, 2 vols. small 8vo.; but Burnell's apparently from a 1-vol. issue in 1877. [See 4 Ser. N. & Q. xi. 439, 527. The quotations have now been given from the ed. of 1873.]

Panjab Notes and Queries, a monthly Periodical, ed. by Capt. R. C. Temple. 1883 *seqq.* [Continued as "**North Indian Notes and Queries**," ed. by W. Crooke. 5 vols. 1891–96.]

Paolino, Fra P. da S. Bartolomeo. **Viaggio** alle Indiè Orientali. 4to. Roma, 1796.

Paolino, E.T. by J. R. Forster. 8vo. 1800.

[**Pearce**, N. Life and Adventures in Abyssinia, ed. J. J. Halls. 2 vols. London, 1831.]

Pegolotti, Fr. Balducci. La Pratica di Mercatura, written c. 1343; publd. by Gian Francisco Pagnini del Ventura of Volterra in his work Della Decima, &c. Lisbone e Lucca (really Florence), 1765–66. 4 vols. 4to. Of this work it constitutes the 3rd volume. Extracts translated in Cathay and the Way Thither, q.v. The 5th volume is a similar work by **G. Uzzano**, written c. 1440.

Pèlerins Bouddhistes, by **Stanislas, Julien.** Vol. 1. Vie et Voyages de Hiouen Thsang. Vols. II. and III. Mémoires des Contrées Occidentales. Paris. 1857.

[**Pelly**, Col. Sir L. The Miracle Play of Hasan and Husain, collected from Oral Tradition, ed. A. N. Wollaston. 2 vols. London, 1879.]

Pemberton, Major R. B. **Report** on the Eastern Frontier of British India. 8vo. Calcutta, 1835.

Pennant's (T.) **View of Hindoostan**, India extra Gangem, China, and Japan. 4 vols. 4to. 1798–1800.

Percival, R. An Account of the Island of **Ceylon.** 2 vols. 1833.

Peregrinatoris Medii Aevi **Quatuor**. Recensuit J. C. M. Laurent. Lipsiae. 1864.

Peregrine Pultuney. A Novel. 3 vols. 1844. (Said to be written by the late Sir John Kaye.)

Periplus Maris Erythraei (I have used sometimes C. Müller in the Geog. Graeci Minores, and sometimes the edition of B. Fabricius, Leipzig, 1883).

Petis de la Croix. Hist. de **Timur-bec**, &c. 4 vols. 12mo. Delf. 1723.

Philalethes, The **Boscawen's Voyage** to Bombay, 1750.

Philippi, R.P.F., de Sanctma. Trinitate, **Itinerarium** Orientale, &c. 1652.

Phillips, Sir Richard. **A Million of Facts**. Ed. 1837. This Million of Facts contains innumerable absurdities.

Phillips, Mr. An Account of the Religion, Manners, and the Learning of the People of Malabar. 16mo. London, 1717.

Pictet, Adolphe. **Les Origines** Indo-Européenes. 2 vols. imp. 8vo. 1859–1863.

Pigafetta, and other contemporary Writers. The first Voyage round the World by **Magellan**, translated from the accounts of—. By Lord Stanley of Alderley. Hak. Soc. 1874.

Pilot, The English, by Thornton, Part III. Folio. 1711.

Pinto, Fernam **Mendez**. **Peregrinação** de — por elle escrita, &c. Folio. Originally published at Lisbon, 1614.

Pinto (**Cogan's**). The Voyages and Adventures of Fernand Mendez P., A Portugal, &c. Done into English by H. C. Gent. Folio. London, 1653.

Pioneer & Pioneer Mail. (Daily and Weekly Newspapers published at Allahabad.)

Piso, Gulielmus, de Indiae utriusque Re Naturali et Medicâ. Folio. Amsterdam, 1658. See *Bontius*, whose book is attached.

[**Platts**, J. T. A Dictionary of Urdū, Classical Hindī, and English. London, 1884.]

Playfair, G. **Taleef-i-Shereef**, or Indian Materia Medica. Tr. from the original by. Calcutta, 1883.

Poggius De Varietate Fortunae. The quotations under this reference are from the reprint of what pertains to the travels of Nicolo Conti in Dr. Friedr. Kuntsmann's *Die Kenntniss Indiens*. München. 1863.

Pollok, Lt.-Col. **Sport in British Burmah**, Assam, and the Jynteah Hills. 2 vols. 1879.

Polo, The Book of Ser Marco, the Venetian. Newly Tr. and Ed. by Colonel Henry Yule, C.B. In 2 vols. 1871. 2nd ed., revised, with new matter and many new Illustrations. 1875.

Price, Joseph. *Tracts*. 3 vols. 8vo. 1783.

Pridham, C. An Hist., Pol. and Stat. Ac. of Ceylon and its Dependencies. 2 vols. 8vo. 1849.

Primor e Honra da Vida Soldadesca no estado da India. Fr. A. Freyre (1580). Lisbon, 1630.

Pringle (Mrs.) M.A. A Journey in East Africa. 1880.

[**Pringle**, A. T. Selections from the Consultations of the Agent, Governor, and Council of Fort St. George, 1681. 4th Series. Madras, 1893.

—The Diary and Consultation Book of the Agent, Governor, and Council of Fort St. George. 1st Series, 1682–85. 4 vols. (in progress). Madras, 1894–95.]

Prinsep's Essays. Essays on Indian Antiquities of the late James Prinsep ... to which are added his **Useful Tables** ed. ... by **Edward Thomas**. 2 vols. 8vo. 1858.

Prinsep, H. T. Hist. of Political and Military Transactions in India, during the Adm. of the Marquess of Hastings. 2 vols. 1825.

Propagation of the Gospel in the East. In Three Parts. Ed. of 1718. An English Translation of the letters of the first Protestant Missionaries **Ziegenbalg** and **Plutscho**.

Prosper Alpinus. Hist. Aegypt. Naturalis et Rerum Aegyptiarum Libri. 3 vols. sm. 4to. Lugd. Bat. 1755.

Punjab Plants, comprising Botanical and Vernacular Names and Uses, by J. L. **Stewart**. Lahore, 1869.

Punjaub Trade Report. Report on the Trade and Resources of the Countries on the N.W. Boundary of British India. By **R. H. Davies**, Sec. to Govt. Punjab. Lahore, 1862.

Purchas, his **Pilgrimes**, &c. 4 vols. folio. 1625–26. The Pilgrimage is often bound as Vol. V. It is really a separate work.

—His Pilgrimage, or Relations of the World, &c. The 4th ed. folio. 1625. The 1st ed. is of 1614.

Pyrard de Laval, François. Discours du **Voyage** des Francais aux Indes Orientales, 1615–16. 2 pts. in 1 vol. 1619 in 2 vols. 12mo. Also published, 2 vols. 4to in 1679 as Voyage de Franc. Pyrard de Laval. This is most frequently quoted.

There is a smaller first sketch of 1611, under the name "Discours des Voyages des Francais aux Indes Orientales." [Ed. for Hak. Soc. by A. Gray and H. C. P. Bell, 1887–89.]

Qanoon-e-Islam. *See* **Herklots**.

Raffles' Hist. of Java. [2nd. ed. 2 vols. London, 1830.]

[**Raikes**, C. Notes on the North-Western Provinces of India. London, 1852.

[**Rájendralála Mitra**, Indo-Aryans. Contributions towards the Elucidation of their Ancient and Mediæval History. 2 vols. London, 1881.]

Raleigh, Sir W. The Discourse of the Empire of **Guiana**. Ed. by Sir R. Schomburgk. Hak. Soc. 1850.

Ramāyana of **Tulsi Dās**. Translated by F. **Growse**. 1878. [Revised ed. 1 vol. Allahabad, 1883.]

Ramusio, G. B. Delle **Navigationi** e Viaggi. 3 vols. folio, in Venetia. The editions used by me are Vol. I., 1613; Vol. II., 1606; Vol. III., 1556; except a few quotations from C. Federici, which are from Vol. III. of 1606, in the B. M.

Rashiduddin, in Quatremère, **Histoire des Mongols** de la Perse, par Raschid-el-din, trad. &c., par **M. Quatremère**. Atlas folio. 1836.

Râs Mâlâ, or Hindoo Annals of the Province of Goozerat. By Alex. Kinloch Forbes, H.E.I.C.C.S. 2 vols. 8vo. London, 1856.

Also a New Edition in one volume, 1878.

Rates and Valuatioun of Merchandize (**Scotland**). Published by the Treasury. Edinb. 1867.

Ravenshaw, J. H. Gaur, its Ruins and Inscriptions. 4to. 1878.

Raverty, Major H. G. **Tabakāt-i-Nāsiri**, E.T. 2 vols. 8vo. London, 1881.

Rawlinson's Herodotus. 4 vols. 8vo. 4th edition. 1880.

Ray, Mr. John. **A Collection** of Curious Travels and Voyages. In Two Parts (includes **Rauwolff**). The second edition. 2 vols. 1705.

— Historia Plantarum. Folio. *See* p. 957*a*.

— Synopsis Methodica Animalium Quadrupedum et Serpentini Generis, &c. Auctore Joanne Raio, F.R.S. Londini, 1693.

Raynal, Abbé W. F. **Histoire Philosophique** et Politique des Etablissements des Européens dans les deux Indes. (First published, Amsterdam, 1770. 4 vols. First English translation by J. Justamond, London, 1776.) There were an immense number of editions of the original, with modifications, and a second English version by the same Justamond in 6 vols. 1798.

Reformer, A True. (By Col. George **Chesney**, R.E.). 3 vols. 1873.

Regulations for the Hon. **Company's Troops** on the Coast of **Coromandel**, by M.-Gen. Sir A. Campbell, K.B., &c. &c. Madras, 1787.

Reinaud. Fragmens sur l'Inde, in *Journ. Asiatique*, Ser. IV. tom. iv.

— *See* **Relation**.

— **Mémoire** sur l'Inde. 4to. 1849.

Relation des **Voyages faites par les Arabes** et les Persans ... trad., &c., par M. Reinaud. 2 sm. vols. Paris, 1845.

Rennell, Major James. **Memoir** of a Map of Hindoostan, or the Mogul Empire. 3rd edition. 4to. 1793.

Resende, Garcia de. **Chron**. del Rey dom João II. Folio. Evora, 1554.

[**Revelations**, the, of an Orderly. By Paunchkouree Khan. Benares, 1866.]

Rhede, H., van Drakenstein. **Hortus Malabaricus.** 6 vols. folio. Amstelod. 1686.

Rhys Davids. Buddhism. S.P.C.K. *No date* (more shame to S.P.C.K.).

Ribeiro, J. Fadalidade Historica. (1685.) First published recently.

[**Rice**, B. L. Gazetteer of Mysore. 2 vols. London, 1897.

[**Riddell**, Dr. R. Indian Domestic Economy. 7th ed. Calcutta, 1871.

[**Risley**, H. H. The Tribes and Castes of Bengal. 2 vols. Calcutta, 1891.]

Ritter, Carl. **Erdkunde.** 19 vols. in 21. Berlin, 1822–1859.

Robinson Philip. *See* **Garden, in My Indian**.

Rochon, Abbé.

[**Roe**, Sir T. Embassy to the Court of the Great Mogul, 1615–19. Ed. by W. Foster. Hak. Soc. 2 vols. 1899.]

Roebuck, T. An English and Hindoostanee **Naval Dictionary**. 12mo. Calcutta, 1811. *See* **Small**.

Rogerius, Abr. **De open Deure** tot het Verborgen Hyedendom. 4to. Leyden, 1651.

Also sometimes quoted from the French version, viz.:—

Roger, Abraham. **La Porte Ouverte** ... ou la Vraye Representation, &c. 4to. Amsterdam, 1670.

The author was the first Chaplain at Pulicat (1631–1641), and then for some years at Batavia (see Havart, p. 132). He returned home in 1647 and died in 1649, at Gouda (Pref. p. 3). The book was brought out by his widow. Thus, at the time that the English Chaplain **Lord** (q.v.) was studying the religion of the Hindus at Surat, the Dutch Chaplain Roger was doing the same at Pulicat. The work of the last is in every way vastly superior to the former. It was written at Batavia (see p. 117), and, owing to its publication after his death, there are a few misprints of Indian words. The author had his information from a Brahman named Padmanaba (*Padmanābha*), who knew Dutch, and who gave him a Dutch translation of Bhartrihari's Satakas, which is printed at the end of the book. It is the first translation from Sanskrit into an European language (A.B.).

Roteiro da Viagem de **Vasco da Gama** em MCCCCXCVII. 2a edição. Lisboa, 1861. The 1st ed. was published in 1838. The work is inscribed to Alvaro Velho. See Figanière, *Bibliog. Hist. Port.* p. 159. (Note by A.B.).

— *See* **De Castro.**

Rousset Léon. A Travers la Chine. 8vo. Paris, 1878.

[**Row**, T. V. Manual of Tanjore District. Madras, 1883.]

Royle, J. F., M.D. An Essay on the Antiquity of **Hindoo Medicine.** 8vo. 1837.

— Illustrations of the **Botany** and other branches of Nat. History of the **Himalayas**, and of the Floras of Cashmere. 2 vols. folio. 1839.

Rubruk, Wilhelmus de. **Itinerarium** in **Recueil de Voyages** et de Mémoires de la Soc. de Géographie. Tom. iv. 1837.

Rumphius (Geo. Everard Rumphf.). Herbarium Amboinense. 7 vols. folio. Amstelod. 1741. (He died in 1693.)

Russell, Patrick. An Account of Indian **Snakes** collected on the coast of Coromandel. 2 vols. folio. 1803.

Rycaut, Sir Paul. Present State of the Ottoman Empire. Folio, 1687. Appended to ed. of **Knollys' Hist.** of the Turks.

Saar, Johann Jacob, Ost-Indianische **Fūnfzehn-Jāhrige Kriegs-Dienste** (&c.). (1644–1659.) Folio. Nurnberg, 1672.

Sacy, Silvestre de. Relation de l'Egypte. *See* **Abdallatif.**

— **Chrestomathie Arabe.** 2de Ed. 3 vols. 8vo. Paris, 1826–27.

Sadik Isfahani, The Geographical Works of. Translated by J. C. from original Persian MSS., &c. Oriental Translation Fund, 1832.

Sainsbury, W. Noel. **Calendar** of State Papers, **East Indies.** Vol. I., 1862 (1513–1616); Vol. II., 1870 (1617–1621); Vol. III., 1878 (1622–1624); Vol. IV., 1884 (1625–1629). An admirable work.

Sanang Setzen. Geschichte der Ost-Mongolen ... von Ssanang Ssetzen Chungtaidschi der Ordus. aus dem Mongol ... von Isaac Jacob Schmidt. 4to. St. Petersburg, 1829.

[**Sanderson**, G. P. Thirteen Years among the Wild Beasts of India, 3rd ed. London, 1882.]

Sangermano, Rev. Father. A description of the **Burmese Empire.** Translated by W. Tandy, D.D. (Or. Transl. Fund). 4to. Rome, 1833.

San Roman, Fray A. **Historia General** de la India Oriental. Folio. Valladolid, 1603.

Sassetti, Lettere, contained in **De Gubernatis**, q.v.

Saty. Rev. The Saturday Review, London weekly newspaper.

Schiltberger, Johann. The Bondage and **Travels** of. Tr. by Capt. J. Buchan Telfer, R.N. HAK. SOC. 1879.

Schouten, Wouter. Oost-Indische **Voyagie**, &c. t'Amsterdam, 1676.

This is the Dutch original rendered in German as **Walter Schulzen**, q.v.

[**Schrader**, O. Prehistoric Antiquities of the Aryan Peoples. Tr. by F. B. Jevons. London, 1890.]

Schulzen, Walter. Ost-Indische Reise-Beschreibung. Folio. Amsterdam, 1676. See **Schouten.**

Schuyler, Eugene. **Turkistan.** 2 vols. 8vo. 1876.

[**Scott**, J. G. and J. P. Hardiman. Gazetteer of Upper Burma and the Shan States. 5 vols. Rangoon, 1900.]

Scrafton, Luke. **Reflexions** on the Government of Hindostan, with a Sketch of the Hist. of Bengal. 1770.

Seely, Capt. J. B. The **Wonders of Ellora.** 8vo. 1824.

Seir Mutaqherin, or a View of Modern Times, being a History of India from the year 1118 to 1195 of the Hedjirah. From the Persian of Gholam Hussain Khan. 2 vols. in 3. 4to. Calcutta, 1789.

Seton-Karr, W. S., and Hugh Sandeman. **Selections** from Calcutta Gazettes (1784–1823). 5 vols. 8vo. (The 4th and 5th by H. S.) Calcutta, 1864–1869.

Shaw, Robert. Visits to **High Tartary**, Yarkand, and Kâshghâr, 1871.

Shaw, Dr. T. Travels or Observations relating to several Parts of **Barbary** and the Levant. 2nd ed. 1757. (Orig. ed. is of 1738).

Shelvocke's Voyage. A V. round the World, by the Way of the Great South Sea, Perform'd in the Years 1719, 20, 21, 22. By Capt. George S. London, 1726.

Sherring, Revd., M.A. Hindu Tribes and Castes. 3 vols. 4to. Calcutta, 1872–81.

Sherwood, Mrs. **Stories** from the Church Catechism. Ed. 1873. This work was originally published about 1817, but I cannot trace the exact date. It is almost unique as giving some view of the life of the non-commissioned ranks of a British regiment in India, though of course much is changed since its date.

Sherwood, Mrs., The Life of, chiefly Autobiographical. 1857.

Shipp, John. Memoirs of the Extraordinary Military Career of ... written by Himself. 2nd ed. (First ed., 1829). 3 vols. 8vo. 1830.

Sibree, Revd. J. **The Great African Island**. 1880.

Sidi 'Ali. The **Mohit**, by S. A. Kapudan. Exts. translated by Joseph v. Hammer, in *J. As. Soc. Bengal*, Vols. III. & V.

— **Relation** des **Voyages** de, nommé ordinairement Katibi Roumi, trad. sur la version allemande de M. Diez par M. Moris in *Journal Asiatique*, Ser. I. tom. ix.

[— The Travels and Adventures of the Turkish Admiral. Trans. by A. Vambéry. London, 1899.]

Sigoli, Simone. **Viaggio** al Monte Sinai. See **Frescobaldi**.

Simpkin. See *Letters*.

[**Skeat**, W. W. Malay Magic, being an Introduction to the Folklore and Popular Religion of the Malay Peninsula. 8vo. London, 1900.

[**Skinner**, Capt. T. Excursions in India, including a Walk over the Himalaya Mountains to the Sources of the Jumna and the Ganges, 2nd ed. 2 vols. London, 1833.]

Skinner, Lt.-Col. James, Military Memoirs of. Ed. by J. B. Fraser. 2 vols. 1851.

Sleeman, Lt.-Col. (Sir Wm.). **Ramaseeana** and Vocabulary of the Peculiar Language of the Thugs. 8vo. Calcutta, 1836.

— **Rambles and Recollections** of an Indian Official. 2 vols. large 8vo. 1844. An excellent book. [New ed. in 2 vols., by V. A. Smith, in Constable's Oriental Miscellany. London, 1893.]

[— A Journey through the Kingdom of Oudh in 1849–50. 2 vols. London, 1858.]

Small, Rev. G. A. **Laskari** Dictionary. 12mo., 1882 (being an enlarged ed. of **Roebuck**, q.v.).

Smith, **R. Bosworth**. **Life of Lord Lawrence**. 2 vols. 8vo. 1883.

Smith, Major L. F. Sketch of the **Regular Corps** in the service of Native Princes. 4to. Tract. Calcutta, N.D. London. 1805.

[**Society** in India, by an Indian Officer. 2 vols. London, 1841.

Society, Manners, Tales, and Fictions of India. 3 vols. London, 1844.]

Solvyns, F. B. **Les Hindous**. 4 vols. folio. Paris, 1808.

Sonnerat. **Voyages** aux Indes Orientales et à la Chine 2 vols. 4to. 1781. Also 3 vols. 8vo. 1782.

Sousa, P. Francesco de. **Oriente Conquistado** a Jesus Christo pelos Padres da Companha de Jesus. Folio. Lisbon. 1710. Reprint of Pt. I., at Bombay, 1881.

Southey, R. **Curse of Kehama**. 1810. In Collected Works.

Spielbergen van Waerwijck, **Voyage of**. (Four Voyages to the E. Indies from 1594 to 1604, in Dutch.) 1646.

Sprenger, Prof. Aloys. Die **Post und Reise-Routen** des Orients. 8vo. Leipzig, 1864.

[**Stanford** Dictionary, the, of Anglicised Words and Phrases, by C. A. M. Fennell. Cambridge, 1892.]

Stanley's Vasco da Gama. *See* **Correa**.

Staunton, Sir G. Authentic **Account** of Lord Macartney's Embassy to the Emperor of China. 2 vols. 4to. 1797.

Stavorinus. **Voyage** to the E. Indies. Tr. from Dutch by S. H. Wilcocke. 3 vols. 1798.

Stedman, J. G. Narrative of a Five Years' Expedition against the Revolted Negroes in Surinam. 2 vols. 4to. 1806.

Stephen, Sir James F. Story of **Nuncomar** and Impey. 2 vols. 1885.

Stokes, M. **Indian Fairy Tales**. Calcutta, 1879.

Strangford, Viscount, Select Writings of. 2 vols. 8vo. 1869.

St. Pierre, B. de. **La Chaumière Indienne**. 1791.

[**Stuart**, H. A. *See* **Sturrock**, J.

[**Sturrock**, J. and Stuart, H. A. Manual of S. Canara. 2 vols. Madras, 1891–95.]

Subsidios para a Historia da India Portugueza. (Published by the Royal Academy of Lisbon.) Lisbon, 1878.

Sulivan, Capt. G. L., R.A. **Dhow Chasing** in Zanzibar Waters, and on the Eastern Coast of Africa. 1873.

Surgeon's Daughter. By Sir **Walter Scott**. 1827. Reference by chapter.

Symes, Major Michael. Account of an **Embassy to** the Kingdom of **Ava**, in the year 1795. 4to. 1800.

Taranatha's Geschichte des Buddhismus in India. Germ. Tr. by A. Schiefner. St. Petersburg, 1869.

Tavernier, J. B. Les Six Voyages en Turquie, en Perse, et aux Indes. 2 vols. 4to. Paris, 1676.

— E.T., which is generally that quoted, being contained in Collections of Travels, &c.; being the Travels of Monsieur Tavernier, Bernier, and other great men. In 2 vols. folio. London, 1684. [Ed. by V. A. Ball. 2 vols. London, 1889.]

Taylor, Col. Meadows. **Story of My Life**. 8vo. (1877). 2nd ed. 1878.

[**Taylor**, J. A Descriptive and Historical Account of the Cotton Manufacture of Dacea, in Bengal. London, 1851.]

Teignmouth, Mem. of **Life** of John Lord, by his Son, Lord Teignmouth. 2 vols. 1843.

Teixeira, P. Pedro. Relaciones ... de los Reyes de Persia, de los Reyes de Harmuz, y de un Viage dende la India Oriental hasta

Italia por terra (all three separately paged). En Amberes, 1610.

Tennent, Sir Emerson. *See* **Emerson**.

Tenreiro, Antonio. **Itinerario** ... como da India veo por terra a estes Reynos. Orig. ed. Coimbra, 1560. Edition quoted (by Burnell) seems to be of Lisbon, 1762.

Terry. A **Voyage** to **East India**, &c. Observed by Edward Terry, then Chaplain to the Right Hon. Sir Thomas Row, Knt., Lord Ambassador to the Great Mogul. Reprint, 1777. Ed. 1655.

—An issue without the Author's name, printed at the end of the E.T. of the Travels of Sig. Pietro della Valle into East India, &c. 1665.

—Also a part in Parchas, Vol. II.

Thevenot, Melehizedek. (**Collection**). Relations de divers Voyages Curieux. 2nd ed. 2 vols. folio. 1696.

Thevenot, J. de. **Voyages** en Europe, Asie et Afrique. 2nd ed. 5 vols. 12mo. 1727.

Thevet, André. **Cosmographie** Universelle. Folio. Paris, 1575.

Thevet. **Les Singularitez** de la **France Antarticque**, autrement nommée Amerique. Paris, 1558.

Thomas, H. S. **The Rod in India**. 8vo. Mangalore, 1873.

Thomas, Edward. **Chronicles of the Pathán Kings of Dehli**. 8vo. 1871.

Thomson, Dr. T. **Western Himalaya and Tibet**. 8vo. London, 1852.

Thomson, J. The **Straits of Malacca**, Indo-China, and China. 8vo. 1875.

Thornhill, Mark. **Personal Adventures**, &c., in the Mutiny. 8vo. 1884.

[—Haunts and Hobbies of an Indian Official. London, 1899.]

Thunberg. C. P., M.D. **Travels** in Europe, Africa, and Asia, made between the years 1770 and 1779. E.T. 4 vols. 8vo. 1799.

Timour, **Institutes of**. E.T. by Joseph White. 4to. Oxford, 1783.

Timur, Autobiographical **Memoirs of**. E.T. by Major C. Stewart (Or. Tr. Fund). 4to. 1830.

Tippoo Sultan, Select **Letters** of. E.T. by Col. W. Kirkpatrick. 4to. 1811.

Tipú Sultán, Hist. of, by Hussein Ali Khan Kirmani. E.T. by Miles. (Or. Tr. Fund.) 8vo. 1864.

Tod, Lieut.-Col. James. **Annals** and Antiquities of Rajasthan. 2 vols. 4to. 1829. [Reprinted at Calcutta. 2 vols. 1884.]

Tohfut-ul-Mujahideen (Hist. of the Mahomedans in Malabar). Trd. by Lieut. M. J. Rowlandson. (Or. Tr. Fund.) 8vo. 1833. (Very badly edited.)

Tom Cringle's Log. Ed. 1863. (Originally published in Blackwood, c. 1830–31.)

Tombo do Estado da India. *See* **Subsidios** and **Botelho**.

Tr. Lit. Soc. Bo. Transactions of the Literary Society of Bombay. 3 vols. 4to. London, 1819–23.

Trevelyan, G. O. *See* **Competition-Wallah** and **Dawk-Bungalow**.

Tribes on My Frontier. Bombay, 1883.

Trigautius. De Christiana Expeditione apud Sinas. 4to. Lugduni, 1616.

Turnour's (Hon. George) **Mahawanso**. The M. in Roman characters with the translation subjoined, &c. (Only one vol. published.) 4to. Ceylon, 1837.

Tylor, E. B. **Primitive Culture**. 2 vols. 8vo. 1871.

[—Anahuac; or Mexico and the Mexicans, Ancient and Modern. London, 1861.]

Tyr, Guillaume de, et ses Continuateurs—Texte du XIII. Siècle—par M. Paulin. Paris. 2 vols. large 8vo. 1879–80.

[**Tytler**, A. F. Considerations on the Present Political State of India. 2 vols. London, 1815.]

Uzzano, G. A book of *Pratica della Mercatura* of 1440, which forms the 4th vol. of *Della Decima*. *See* **Pegolotti**.

Valentia, Lord. Voyages and Travels to India, &c. 1802–1806. 3 vols. 4to. 1809.

Valentijn. Oud en Niew **Oost-Indien**. 6 vols. folio—often bound in 8 or 9. Amsterdam, 1624–6.

[**Vámbéry**, A. Sketches of Central Asia. Additional Chapters on my Travels, Adventures, and on the Ethnology of Central Asia. London, 1868.]

Van Braam Houckgeist (**Embassy** to China), E.T. London, 1798.

Van den Broecke, Pieter. Reysen naer Oost Indien, &c. Amsterdam, edns. 1620? 1634, 1646, 1648.

Vander Lith. *See* **Merveilles**.

Vanity Fair, a Novel without a Hero, **Thackeray's**. This is usually quoted by chapter. If by page, it is from ed. 1867. 2 vols. 8vo.

Vansittart H. A **Narrative** of the Transactions in Bengal, 1760–1764. 3 vols. 8vo. 1766.

Van Twist, Jehan; Gewesen Overhooft van de Nederlandsche comtooren *Amadabat*, *Cambaya*, *Brodera*, en *Broitchia*, **Generall Beschrijvinge** van Indien, &c. t'Amsteledam, 1648.

Varthema, Lodovico di. The **Travels** of. Tr. from the orig. Italian Edition of 1510 by T. Winter Jones, F.S.A., and edited, &c., by George Percy Badger. HAK. SOC. 1863.

This is the edn. quoted with a few exceptions. Mr. Burnell writes:

"We have also used the second edition of the original (?) Italian text (12mo. Venice, 1517). A third edition appeared at Milan in 1523 (4to.), and a fourth at Venice in 1535. This interesting Journal was translated into English by Eden in 1576 (8vo.), and Purchas (ii. pp. 1483–1494) gives an abridgement; it is thus one of the most important sources."

Neither Mr. Winter Jones nor my friend Dr. Badger, in editing Varthema, seem to have been aware of the disparagement cast on his veracity in the famous Colloquios of Garcia de Orta (f. 29*v.* and f. 30). These affect his statements as to his voyages in the further East; and deny his ever having gone beyond Calicut and Cochin; a thesis which it would not be difficult to demonstrate out of his own narrative.

[**Verelst**, H. A View of the Rise, Progress, and Present State of the English Government in Bengal, including a Reply to the Misrepresentations of Mr. Bolts, and other Writers. London, 1772.]

Vermeulen, Genet. Oost Indische **Voyage**. 1677.

Vigne, G. **Travels** in Kashmir, Ladakh, &c. 2 vols. 8vo. 1842.

Vincenzo Maria. Il **Viaggio** all' Indie orientalí del P. ... Procuratore Generale de' Carmelitani Scalzi. Folio. Roma, 1672.

Vitriaci, Jacobi (Jacques de Vitry). Hist. Jherosolym. *See* **Bongars**.

Vocabulista in **Arabico**. (Edited by C. Schiaparelli.) Firenze, 1871.

Voigt. Hortus Suburbanus Calcuttensis. 8vo. Calcutta, 1845.

Von Harff, Arnold. **Pilgerfahrt** des Ritters (1496–1499). From MSS. Cöln, 1860.

Voyage to the East Indies in 1747 and 1748. ... Interspersed with many useful and curious Observations and Anecdotes. 8vo. London, 1762.

Vüllers, J. A. **Lexicon** Persico-Latinum. 2 vols. and Suppt. Bonnae ad Rhenum. 1855–67.

Wallace, A. R. The Malay Archipelago. 7th ed. 1880.

[**Wallace**, Lieut. Fifteen Years in India, or Sketches of a Soldier's Life. London, 1822.]

Wanderings of a Pilgrim in Search of the Picturesque (by Fanny Parkes). 2 vols. imp. 8vo. 1850.

Ward, W. A **View of the** History, Literature, and Religion of the **Hindoos**. 3rd ed. 4 vols. 8vo. London, 1817–1820.

In the titles of first 2 vols. publd. in 1817, this ed. is stated to be in 2 vols. In those of the 3rd and 4th, 1820, it is stated to be in 4 vols. This arose from some mistake, the author being absent in India when the first two were published.

The work originally appeared at Serampore, 1811, 4 vols. 4to, and an abridged ed. *ibid.* 1 vol. 4to. 1815.

Waring, E. J. The Tropical Resident at Home, &c. 8vo. 1866.

Wassaf, Geschichte Wassafs, Persisch herausgegeben, und Deutsch übersetzt, von Joseph **Hammer-Purgstall**. 4to. Wien, 1856.

Watreman, W. **The Fardle of Facions**. London, 1555. Also reprinted in the Hakluyt of 1807.

[**Watt**, G. A Dictionary of the Economic Products of India. 10 vols. Calcutta, 1889–93.]

Wellington Despatches. The Edn. quoted is usually that of 1837.

Welsh, Col. James. **Military Reminiscences** ... of nearly 40 years' Active Service in the E. Indies. 2 vols. 8vo. 1830. (An excellent book.)

Wheeler, J. T. Madras in the Olden Time ... compiled from Official Records. 3 vols. sm. sq. 8vo. 1861.

—— **Early Records** of British India. Calcutta, 1878. 2nd ed. 1879.

Wheler, Rev. **Sir George**. Journey into Greece. Folio. 1682.

Witney (Prof. W. D.) **Oriental and Linguistical Studies**. 2 vols. New York, 1873–74.

Widows, Hindoo. Papers relating to E.I. Affairs; printed by order of Parliament. Folio. 1821.

[**Wilkinson**, R. J. A Malay-English Dictionary. Part I. Singapore, 1901.]

Wilks, Col. Mark. **Historical Sketches** of the South of India in an Attempt to trace the Hist of Mysoor. 3 vols. 4to. 1810–17. 2nd ed., 2 vols. 8vo. Madras, 1869.

Williams, Monier. **Religious Thought** and Life in India. Part I., 1883.

[—— Brähmanism and Hindūism. 4th ed. London, 1891.]

Williams, S. Wells. **Chinese Commercial Guide**. 4th ed. Canton, 1856.

Williamson, V. M. The East India Vade Mecum, by Capt. Thomas Williamson (the author of *Oriental Field Sports*). 2 vols. 8vo. 1810.

Williamson, Capt. T. **Oriental Field Sports**. Atlas folio. 1807.

Wills, C. T. In the Land of the Lion and the Sun, or **Modern Persia**. 1883.

[**Wilson**, A. The Abode of Snow, Observations on a Journey from Chinese Tibet to the Indian Caucasus. Edinburgh, 1875.]

Wilson, John, D.D., Life of, by George **Smith**, LL.D. 1878.

[—— Indian Caste. 2 vols. Bombay, 1877.]

Wolff, J. Travels and Adventures. 2 vols. London, 1860.]

Wollaston, A. N. **English-Persian Dictionary**. 8vo. 1882.

Wright, T. **Early Travels** in Palestine, edited with Notes. (Bohn.) 1848.

Wright, T. Domestic Manners and Sentiments in England in the Middle Ages. 1862.

Wyllie, J. W. S. **Essays** on the External Policy of India. Edited by Dr. W. W. Hunter. 1875.

Wytfliet. Histoire des Indes. Fo., 3 pts. Douay. 1611.

Xaverii, Scti. Francisci. Indiarum Apostoli **Epistolarum** Libri Quinque. Pragae, 1667.

Xavier, St. Francis, Life and Letters of, by Rev. H. I. **Coleridge** (S.J.). 2 vols. 8vo. 1872.

[**Yusuf Ali**, A. A Monograph on Silk Fabrics produced in the North-Western Provinces and Oudh. Allahabad, 1900.]

Zedler, J. H. Grosses Vollständliges Universal Lexicon. 64 vols. folio. Leipzig, 1732–1750; and Supplement, 4 vols. 1751–1754.

Ziegenbalg. *See* **Propagation of the Gospel**.

A GLOSSARY

OF

ANGLO-INDIAN COLLOQUIAL TERMS AND PHRASES OF ANALOGOUS ORIGIN.

ABCÁREE, ABKÁRY. H. from P. *āb-kārī*, the business of distilling or selling (strong) waters, and hence elliptically the excise upon such business. This last is the sense in which it is used by Anglo-Indians. In every district of India the privilege of selling spirits is farmed to contractors, who manage the sale through retail shopkeepers. This is what is called the '**Abkary** System.' The system has often been attacked as promoting tippling, and there are strong opinions on both sides. We subjoin an extract from a note on the subject, too long for insertion in integrity, by one of much experience in Bengal—Sir G. U. Yule.

June, 1879.—"Natives who have expressed their views are, I believe, unanimous in ascribing the increase of drinking to our **Abkaree** system. I don't say that this is putting the cart before the horse, but they are certainly too forgetful of the increased means in the country, which, if not the sole cause of the increased consumption, has been at least a very large factor in that result. I myself believe that more people drink now than formerly; but I knew one gentleman of very long and intimate knowledge of Bengal, who held that there was as much drinking in 1820 as in 1860."

In any case exaggeration is abundant. All Sanskrit literature shows that tippling is no absolute novelty in India. [See the article on "Spirituous Drinks in Ancient India," by Rajendralala Mitra, *Indo-Aryans*, i. 389 *seqq.*]

1790.—"In respect to **Abkarry**, or Tax on Spirituous Liquors, which is reserved for Taxation ... it is evident that we cannot establish a general rate, since the quantity of consumption and expense of manufacture, etc., depends upon the vicinity of principal stations. For the amount leviable upon different Stills we must rely upon officers' local knowledge. The public, indeed, cannot suffer, since, if a few stills are suppressed by over-taxation, drunkenness is diminished."—In a *Letter from Board of Revenue* (Bengal) to Government, 12th July. MS. in *India Office*.

1797.—"The stamps are to have the words '**Abcaree** licenses' inscribed in the Persian and Hindu languages and character."—*Bengal Regulations*, x. 33.

A. C. (*i.e.* 'after compliments'). In official versions of native letters these letters stand for the omitted formalities of native compliments.

***ACHÁR**, s. P. *āchār*, Malay *ăchār*, adopted in nearly all the vernaculars of India for acid and salt relishes. By Europeans it is used as the equivalent of 'pickles,' and is applied to all the stores of Crosse and Blackwell in that kind. We have adopted the word through the Portuguese; but it is not impossible that Western Asiatics got it originally from the Latin *acetaria*.—(See *Plin. Hist. Nat.* xix. 19).

1563.—"And they prepare a conserve of it (*Anacardium*) with salt, and when it is green (and this they call **Achar**), and this is sold in the market just as olives are with us."—*Garcia*, f. 17.

1596.—Linschoten in the Dutch gives the word correctly, but in the English version (Hak. Soc. ii. 26) it is printed *Machar*.

[1612.—"**Achar** none to be had except one jar."—*Danvers, Letters*, i. 230.]

1616.—"Our *jurebasso's* wife came and brought me a small jarr of **Achar** for a present, desyring me to exskews her husband in that he abcented hymselfe to take phisik."—*Cocks*, i. 135.

1623.—"And all these preserved in a way that is really very good, which they call **acciao.**"—*P. della Valle*, ii. 708. [Hak. Soc. ii. 327.]

1653.—"**Achar** est vn nom Indistanni, ou Indien, que signifie des mangues, ou autres fruits confis avec de la moutarde, de l'ail, du sel, et du vinaigre à l'Indienne."—*De la Boullaye-le-Gouz*, 531.

1687.—"**Achar** I presume signifies sauce. They make in the *East Indies*, especially at *Siam* and *Pegu*, several sorts of **Achar**, as of the young tops of Bamboes, &c. Bambo-*Achar* and Mango-*Achar* are most used."—*Dampier*, i. 391.

1727.—"And the Soldiery, Fishers, Peasants,

and Handicrafts (of Goa) feed on a little Rice boiled in Water, with a little bit of Salt Fish, or **Atchaar**, which is pickled Fruits or Roots."—*A. Hamilton*, i. 252. [And see under KEDGEREE.]

1783.—We learn from Forrest that limes, salted for sea-use against scurvy, were used by the *Chulias* and were called **atchar** (*Voyage to Mergui*, 40). Thus the word passed to Java, as in next quotation:

1768–71.—"When green it (the mango) is made into **attjar**; for this the kernel is taken out, and the space filled in with ginger, pimento, and other spicy ingredients, after which it is pickled in vinegar."—*Stavorinus*, i. 237.

ADAWLUT, s. Ar.—H.—*'adālat*, 'a Court of Justice,' from *'adl*, 'doing justice.' Under the Mohammedan government there were 3 such courts, viz., *Nizāmat* **'Adālat**, *Dīwānī* **Adālat**, and *Faujdārī* **'Adālat**, so-called from the respective titles of the officials who nominally presided over them. The first was the chief Criminal Court, the second a Civil Court, the third a kind of Police Court. In 1793 regular Courts were established under the British Government, and then the *Sudder* **Adawlut** (*Sadr 'Adālat*) became the chief Court of Appeal for each Presidency, and its work was done by several European (Civilian) Judges. That Court was, on the criminal side, termed *Nizamut Adawlat*, and on the civil side *Dewanny Ad.* At Madras and Bombay, *Foujdarry* was the style adopted in lieu of *Nizamut*. This system ended in 1863, on the introduction of the Penal Code, and the institution of the High Courts on their present footing. (On the original history and constitution of the Courts see *Fifth Report*, 1812, p. 6.)

What follows applies only to the Bengal Presidency, and to the administration of justice under the Company's Courts beyond the limits of the Presidency town. Brief particulars regarding the history of the Supreme Courts and those Courts which preceded them will be found under SUPREME COURT.

The grant, by Shāh 'Ālam, in 1765, of the Dewanny of Bengal, Behar, and Orissa to the Company, transferred all power, civil and military, in those provinces, to that body. But no immediate attempt was made to undertake the direct detailed administration of either revenue or justice by the agency of the European servants of the Company. Such superintendence, indeed, of the administration was maintained in the prior acquisitions of the Company—viz., in the Zemindary of Calcutta, in the Twenty-four Pergunnas, and in the Chucklas or districts of Burdwan, Midnapoor, and Chittagong, which had been transferred by the Nawab, Kāsim 'Ali Khān, in 1760; but in the rest of the territory it was confined to the agency of a Resident at the Moorshedabad Durbar, and of a 'Chief' at Patna. Justice was administered by the Mohammedan courts under the native officials of the Dewanny.

In 1770, European officers were appointed in the districts, under the name of *Supervisors*, with powers of control over the natives employed in the collection of the Revenue and the administration of justice, whilst local councils, with superior authority in all branches, were established at Moorshedabad and Patna. It was not till two years later that, under express orders from the Court of Directors, the effective administration of the provinces was undertaken by the agency of the Company's covenanted servants. At this time (1772) Courts of Civil Justice (*Mofussil Dewanny Adawlut*) were established in each of the Districts then recognised. There were also District Criminal Courts (*Foujdary Adawlut*) held by **Cazee** or **Mufty** under the superintendence, like the Civil Court, of the Collectors, as the Supervisors were now styled; whilst Superior Courts (*Sudder Dewanny, Sudder Nizamut* **Adawlut**) were established at the Presidency, to be under the superintendence of three or four members of the Council of Fort William.

In 1774 the Collectors were recalled, and native 'Amils appointed in their stead. Provincial Councils were set up for the divisions of Calcutta, Burdwan, Dacca, Moorshedabad, Dinagepore, and Patna, in whose hands the superintendence, both of revenue collection and of the administration of civil justice, was vested, but exercised by the members in rotation.

The state of things that existed under this system was discreditable. As Courts of Justice the provincial Councils were only "colourable imitations of courts, which had abdicated their functions in favour of their own subordinate (native) officers, and though their decisions were nominally subject to the Governor-General in Council, the Appellate Court was even a more shadowy body than the Courts of first instance. The Court never sat at all, though there are some traces of its having at one time decided appeals on the report of the head of the **Khalsa**, or native exchequer, just as the Provincial Council decided them on the report of the Cazis and Muftis."[1]

In 1770 the Government resolved that Civil Courts, independent of the Provincial Councils, should be established in the six divisions named above,[2] each under a civilian judge with the title of Superintendent of the *Dewanny Adawlut*; whilst to the Councils should still pertain the trial of causes relating to the public revenue, to the demands of zemindars upon their tenants, and to boundary questions. The appeal from the District Courts still lay to the Governor-General and his Council, as forming the Court of *Sudder Dewanny*; but that this might be real, a judge was appointed its head in the person of Sir Elijah Impey, the Chief Justice of the Supreme Court, an appointment which became famous. For it was represented as a transaction intended to compromise the acute dissensions which had been going on between that Court and the Bengal Government, and in fact as a bribe to Impey. It led, by an address from the House of Commons, to the recall of Impey, and constituted one of the charges in the abortive impeachment of that personage. Hence his charge of the Sudder Dewanny ceased in November, 1782, and it was resumed in form by the Governor-General and Council.

In 1787, the first year of Lord Cornwallis's government, in consequence of instructions from the Court of Directors, it was resolved that, with an exception as to the Courts at Moorshedabad, Patna, and Dacca, which were to be maintained independently, the office of judge in the Mofussil Courts was to be attached to that of the collection of the revenue; in fact, the offices of Judge and Collector, which had been divorced since 1774, were to be reunited. The duties of Magistrate and Judge became mere appendages to that of Collector; the administration of justice became a subordinate function; and in fact all Regulations respecting that administration were passed in the Revenue Department of the Government.

Up to 1790 the criminal judiciary had remained in the hands of the native courts. But this was now altered; four Courts of Circuit were created, each to be superintended by two civil servants as judges; the *Sudder Nizamut Adawlut* at the Presidency being presided over by the Governor-General and the members of Council.

In 1793 the constant succession of revolutions in the judicial system came to something like a pause, with the entire reformation which was enacted by the Regulations of that year. The Collection of Revenue was now entirely separated from the administration of justice; Zillah Courts under European judges were established (Reg. iii.) in each of 23 Districts and 3 cities, in Bengal, Behar, and Orissa; whilst Provincial Courts of Appeal, each consisting of three judges (Reg. v.), were established at Moorshedabad, Patna, Dacca, and Calcutta. From these Courts, under certain conditions, further appeal lay to the Sudder Dewanny **Adawluts** at the Presidency.

As regarded criminal jurisdiction, the judges of the Provincial Courts were also (Reg. ix., 1793) constituted Circuit Courts, liable to review by the *Sudder Nizamut*. Strange to say, the impracticable idea of placing the duties of both of the higher Courts, civil and criminal, on the shoulders of the executive Government was still maintained, and the Governor-General and his Council were the constituted heads of the *Sudder Dewanny* and *Sudder Nizamut*. This of course continued as unworkable as it had been; and in Lord Wellesley's time, eight years later, the two *Sudder Adawluts* were reconstituted, with three regular judges to each, though it was still ruled (Reg. ii., 1801) that the chief judge in each Court was to be a member of the Supreme Council, not being either the Governor-General or the Commander-in-Chief. This rule was rescinded by Reg. x. of 1805.

The number of Provincial and Zillah Courts was augmented in after years with the extension of territory, and additional Sudder Courts, for the service of the Upper Provinces, were established at Allahabad in 1831 (Reg. vi.), a step which may be regarded as the inception of the separation of the N.W. Provinces into a distinct Lieutenant-Governorship, carried out five years later. But no change that can be considered at all organic occurred again in the judiciary system till 1862; for we can hardly consider as such the abolition of the Courts of Circuit

1 *Sir James Stephen*, in *Nuncomar and Impey*, ii. 221.

2 These six were increased in 1781 to eighteen.

in 1829 (Reg. i.), and that of the Provincial Courts of Appeal initiated by a section in Reg. v. of 1831, and completed in 1833.

1822.—"This refers to a traditional story which Mr. Elphinstone used to relate ... During the progress of our conquests in the North-West many of the inhabitants were encountered flying from the newly-occupied territory. 'Is Lord Lake coming?' was the enquiry. 'No,' was the reply, 'the **Adawlut** is coming.'"—*Life of Ephinstone*, ii. 131.

1826.—"The **adawlut** or Court-house was close by."—*Pandurang Hari*, 271 [ed. 1873, ii. 90].

ADJUTANT, s. A bird so called (no doubt) from its comical resemblance to a human figure in a stiff dress pacing slowly on a parade-ground. It is the H. *haṛgīlā*, or gigantic crane, and popular scavenger of Bengal, the *Leptoptilus argala* of Linnæus. The H. name is by some dictionaries derived from a supposed Skt. word *haḍḍa-gila*, 'bone-swallower.' The compound, however appropriate, is not to be found in Böhtlingk and Roth's great Dictionary. The bird is very well described by Aelian, under the name of *Κήλα*, which is perhaps a relic of the still preserved vernacular one. It is described by another name, as one of the peculiarities of India, by Sultan Baber. See PELICAN.

"The feathers known as Marabou or Comercolly feathers, and sold in Calcutta, are the tail-coverts of this, and the *Lept. Javanica*, another and smaller species" (*Jerdon*). The name *marabout* (from the Ar. *murābit*, 'quiet,' and thence 'a hermit,' through the Port. *marabuto*) seems to have been given to the bird in Africa on like reason to that of adjutant in India. [Comercolly, properly Kumārkhāli, is a town in the Nadiya District, Bengal. See *Balfour, Cycl.* i. 1082.]

c. A.D. 250.—"And I hear that there is in India a bird *Kēla*, which is 3 times as big as a bustard; it has a mouth of a frightful size, and long legs, and it carries a huge crop which looks like a leather bag: it has a most dissonant voice, and whilst the rest of the plumage is ash-coloured, the tail-feathers are of a pale (or greenish) colour."—*Aelian, de Nat. Anim.* xvi. 4.

c. 1530.—"One of these (fowls) is the *dīng*, which is a large bird. Each of its wings is the length of a man; on its head and neck there is no hair. Something like a bag hangs from its neck; its back is black, its breast white; it frequently visits Kābul. One year they caught and brought me a *dīng*, which became very tame. The flesh which they threw it, it never failed to catch in its beak, and swallowed without ceremony. On one occasion it swallowed a shoe well shod with iron; on another occasion it swallowed a good-sized fowl right down, with its wings and feathers."—*Baber*, 321.

1754.—"In the evening excursions ... we had often observed an extraordinary species of birds, called by the natives *Argill* or *Hargill*, a native of Bengal. They would majestically stalk along before us, and at first we took them for Indians naked. ... The following are the exact marks and dimensions. ... The wings extended 14 feet and 10 inches. From the tip of the bill to the extremity of the claw it measured 7 feet 6 inches. ... In the craw was a *Terapin* or land-tortoise, 10 inches long; and a large black male cat was found entire in its stomach."—*Ives*, 183–4.

1798.—"The next is the great Heron, the *Argali* or **Adjutant**, or Gigantic Crane of Latham. ... It is found also in Guinea."—*Pennant's View of Hindostan*, ii. 156.

1810.—"Every bird saving the vulture, the **Adjutant** (or *argeelah*) and kite, retires to some shady spot."—*Williamson, V. M.* ii. 3.

[1880.—Ball (*Jungle Life*, 82) describes the "snake-stone" said to be found in the head of the bird.]

***AFGHÁN**, n.p. P.—H—*Afghān*. The most general name of the predominant portion of the congeries of tribes beyond the N.W. frontier of India, whose country is called from them *Afghānistān*. In England one often hears the country called *Afgunist-un*, which is a mispronunciation painful to an Anglo-Indian ear, and even *Af'gann*, which is a still more excruciating solecism. [The common local pronunciation of the name is *Aoghān*, which accounts for some of the forms below. Bellew insists on the distinction between the Afghān and the Pathān (PUTTAN). "The Afghan is a Pathan merely because he inhabits a Pathan country, and has to a great extent mixed with its people and adopted their language" (*Races of Af.*, p. 25). The name represents Skt. *asvaka* in the sense of a 'cavalier,' and this reappears scarcely modified in the Assakani or Assakeni of the historians of the expedition of Alexander.]

c. 1020.—"... **Afgháns** and Khiljis ..."—*'Utbi* in *Elliot*, ii. 24; see also 50, 114.

c. 1265.—"He also repaired the fort of Jalálí, which he garrisoned with **Afgháns**."—*Táríkh-i-Firozsháhí* in do. iii. 106.

14th cent.—The **Afghans** are named by the continuator of Rashiduddin among the tribes in the vicinity of Herat (see *N. & E.* xiv. 494).

1504.—"The **Afghans**, when they are reduced to extremities in war, come into the presence of their enemy with grass between their teeth; being as much as to say, 'I am your ox.'"[1]—*Baber*, 159.

c. 1556.—"He was afraid of the **Afgháns**."—*Sidi 'Ali*, in *J. As.*, 1st S., ix. 201.

1609.—"**Agwans** and *Potans*."—*W. Finch*, in *Purchas*, i. 521.

c. 1665.—"Such are those petty Sovereigns, who are seated on the Frontiers of Persia, who almost never pay him anything, no more than they do to the King of Persia. As also the *Balouches* and **Augans**, and other Mountaineers, of whom the greatest part pay him but a small matter, and even care but little for him: witness the Affront they did him, when they stopped his whole Army by cutting off the Water ... when he passed from *Atek* on the River *Indus* to **Caboul** to lay siege to **Kandahar** ..."—*Bernier*, E. T. 64 [ed. *Constable*, 205].

1676.—"The people called **Augans** who inhabit from *Candahar* to *Caboul* ... a sturdy sort of people, and great robbers in the night-time."—*Tavernier*, E. T. ii. 44; [*ed. Ball*, i. 92].

1767.—"Our final sentiments are that we have no occasion to take any measures against the **Afghans**' King if it should appear he comes only to raise contributions, but if he proceeds to the eastward of Delhi to make an attack on your allies, or threatens the peace of Bengal, you will concert such measures with Sujah Dowla as may appear best adapted for your mutual defence."—*Court's Letter*, Nov. 20. In *Long*, 486; also see ROHILLA.

1838.—"Professor Dorn ... discusses severally the theories that have been maintained of the descent of the **Afghauns**: 1st, from the Copts; 2nd, the Jews; 3rd, the Georgians; 4th, the Toorks; 5th, the Moguls; 6th, the Armenians: and he mentions more cursorily the opinion that they are descended from the Indo-Scythians, Medians, Sogdians, Persians, and Indians: on considering all which, he comes to the rational conclusion, that they cannot be traced to any tribe or country beyond their present seats and the adjoining mountains."—*Elphinstone's Caubool*, ed. 1839, i. 209.

AGDAUN, s. A hybrid H. word from H. *āg* and P. *dān*, made in imitation of *pīk-dān*, *ḳalam-dān*, *shama-dān* ('spittoon, pencase, candlestick'). It means a small vessel for holding fire to light a cheroot.

ĀG-GĀRI, s. H. 'Fire carriage.' In native use for a railway train.

AGUN-BOAT, s. A hybrid word for a steamer, from H. *agan*, 'fire,' and Eng. *boat*. In Bombay *Ag-bōt* is used.

1853.—"... **Agin boat**."—*Oakfield*, i. 84.

***AKALEE**, or *Nihang* ('the naked one'), s. A member of a body of zealots among the Sikhs, who take this name 'from being worshippers of Him who is without time, eternal' (*Wilson*). Skt. *a* privative, and *kāl*, 'time.' The Akālis may be regarded as the Wahābis of Sikhism. They claim their body to have been instituted by Guru Govind himself, but this is very doubtful. Cunningham's view of the order is that it was the outcome of the struggle to reconcile warlike activity with the abandonment of the world; the founders of the Sikh doctrine rejecting the inert asceticism of the Hindu sects. The Akālis threw off all subjection to the earthly government, and acted as the censors of the Sikh community in every rank. Runjeet Singh found them very difficult to control. Since the annexation of the Panjab, however, they have ceased to give trouble. The **Akalee** is distinguished by blue clothing and steel armlets. Many of them also used to carry several steel *chakras* (CHUCKER) encircling their turbans. [See *Ibbetson, Panjab Ethnog.*, 286; *Maclagan*, in *Panjab Census Rep.*, 1891, i. 166.]

1832.—"We received a message from the **Acali** who had set fire to the village. ... These fanatics of the Seik creed acknowledge no superior, and the ruler of the country can only moderate their frenzy by intrigues and bribery. They go about everywhere with naked swords, and lavish their abuse on the nobles as well as the peaceable subjects. ... They have on several occasions attempted the life of Runjeet Singh."—*Burnes, Travels*, ii. 10–11.

1840.—"The **Akalis** being summoned to surrender, requested a conference with one of the attacking party. The young Khan bravely went forward, and was straightway shot through the head."—*Mrs Mackenzie, Storms and Sunshine*, i. 115.

ALA-BLAZE PAN, s. This name is given in the Bombay Presidency to a tinned-copper stew-pan, having a cover, and staples for straps, which is carried on the march by

---

1 This symbolical action was common among *beldars* (Bildar), or native *navvies*, employed on the Ganges Canal many years ago, where they came before the engineer to make a petition. But besides grass in mouth, the beldar stood *on one leg*, with hands joined before him.

European soldiers, for the purpose of cooking in, and eating out of. Out on picnics a larger kind is frequently used, and kept continually going, as a kind of *pot-au-feu*. [It has been suggested that the word may be a corr. of some French or Port. term—Fr. *braiser*; Port. *brazeiro*, 'a fire-pan,' *braza*, 'hot coals.']

ALBATROSS, s. The great seabird (*Diomedea exulans*, L.), from the Port. *alcatraz*, to which the forms used by Hawkins and Dampier, and by Flacourt (according to Marcel Devic) closely approach. [*Alcatras* 'in this sense altered to *albi-*, *albe-*, *albatross* (perhaps with etymological reference to *albus*, "white," the albatross being white, while the *alcatras* was black.') *N.E.D.* s.v.] The Port. word properly means 'a pelican.' A reference to the latter word in our Glossary will show another curious misapplication. Devic states that *alcatruz* in Port. means 'the bucket of a Persian wheel,'[1] representing the Ar. *al-kādūs*, which is again from κάδος. He supposes that the pelican may have got this name in the same way that it is called in ordinary Ar. *saḳḳa*, 'a water-carrier.' It has been pointed out by Dr Murray, that the *alcatruz* of some of the earlier voyagers, *e.g.*, of Davis below, is not the *Diomedea*, but the Man-of-War (or Frigate) Bird (*Fregatus aquilus*). Hawkins, at p. 187 of the work quoted, describes, without naming, a bird which is evidently the modern albatross. In the quotation from Mocquet again, *alcatruz* is applied to some smaller sea-bird. The passage from Shelvocke is that which suggested to Coleridge "The Ancient Mariner."

1564.—"The 8th December we ankered by a small Island called **Alcatrarsa**, wherein at our going a shoare, we found nothing but sea-birds, as we call them Ganets, but by the Portugals called **Alcatrarses**, who for that cause gave the said Island the same name."—*Hawkins* (Hak. Soc.), 15.

1593.—"The dolphins and bonitoes are the houndes, and the **alcatrarces** the hawkes, and the flying fishes the game."—*Ibid.* 152.

1604.—"The other foule called **Alcatrarzi** is a kind of Hawke that liueth by fishing. For when the Bonitos or Dolphines doe chase the flying fish vnder the water ... this **Alcatrarzi** flyeth after them like a Hawke after a Partridge."—*Davis* (Hak. Soc.), 158.

c. 1608–10.—"**Alcatraz** sont petis oiseaux ainsi comme estourneaux."—*Mocquet, Voyages*, 226.

1672.—"We met with those feathered Harbingers of the Cape ... **Albetrosses** ... they haue great Bodies, yet not proportionate to their Wings, which mete out twice their length."—*Fryer*, 12.

1690.—"They have several other Signs, whereby to know when they are near it, as by the Sea Fowl they meet at Sea, especially the **Algatrosses**, a very large long-winged Bird."—*Dampier*, i. 531.

1719.—"We had not had the sight of one fish of any kind, since we were come Southward of the Streights of *Le Mair*, nor one sea-bird, except a disconsolate black **Albitross**, who accompanied us for several days, hovering about us as if he had lost himself, till *Hatley* (my second Captain) observing, in one of his melancholy fits, that this bird was always hovering near us, imagin'd from his colour, that it might be some ill omen. ... But be that as it would, he after some fruitless attempts, at length shot the **Albitross**, not doubting (perhaps) that we should have a fair wind after it. ..."—*Shelvocke's Voyage*, 72, 73.

1740.—"... a vast variety of sea fowl, amongst which the most remarkable are the *Penguins*; they are in size and shape like a goose, but instead of wings they have short stumps like fins ... their bills are narrow like those of an **Albitross**, and they stand and walk in an erect posture. From this and their white bellies, *Sir John Narborough* has whimsically likened them to little children standing up in white aprons."—*Anson's Voyage*, 9th ed. (1756), p. 68.

1754.—"An **albatrose**, a sea-fowl, was shot off the Cape of Good Hope, which measured 17½ feet from wing to wing."—*Ives*, 5.

1803.—

"At length did cross an **Albatross**;
  Thorough the fog it came;
As if it had been a Christian soul
  We hailed it in God's name."

The Ancient Mariner.

c. 1861.—

"Souvent pour s'amuser, les hommes
  d'équipage
Prennent des **albatros**, vastes oiseaux des
  mers,
Qui suivent, indolents compagnons de
  voyage,
Le navire glissant sur les gouffres amers."

Baudelaire, L'Albatros.

ALCOVE, s. This English word comes to us

1 Also see Dozy, s. v. *alcadus*. *Alcadus*, according to Cobarruvias, is in Sp. one of the earthen pots of the *noria* or Persian wheel.

through the Span. *alcova* and Fr. *alcove* (old Fr. *aucube*), from Ar. *al-ḳubbah*, applied first to a kind of tent (so in Hebr. *Numbers* xxv. 8) and then to a vaulted building or recess. An edifice of Saracenic construction at Palermo is still known as *La Cuba*; and another, a domed tomb, as *La Cubola*. Whatever be the true formation of the last word, it seems to have given us, through the Italian, *Cupola*. [Not so in *N.E.D.*]

1738.—"**Cubba**, commonly used for the vaulted tomb of *marab-butts*" [**Adjutant**.]—*Shaw's Travels*, ed. 1757, p. 40.

ALLAHABAD, n.p. This name, which was given in the time of Akbar to the old Hindu Prayāg or Prāg has been subjected to a variety of corrupt pronunciations, both European and native. *Illahābāz* is a not uncommon native form, converted by Europeans into *Halabas*, and further by English soldiers formerly into *Isle o' bats*. And the *Illiabad*, which we find in the Hastings charges, survives in the *Elleeabad* still heard occasionally.

c. 1666.—"La Province de **Halabas** s'appelloit autrefois *Purop*."—*Thevenot*, v. 197.

["**Elabas** (where the Gemna (**Jumna**) falls into the Ganges."—*Bernier* (ed. *Constable*), p. 36.]

1726.—"This exceptionally great river (Ganges) ... comes so far from the N. to the S. ... and so further to the city **Halabas**."—*Valentijn*.

1753.—"Mais ce qui-interesse davantage dans la position de **Helabas**, c'est d'y retrouver celle de l'ancienne *Palibothra*. Aucune ville de l'Inde ne paroit égaler *Palibothra* ou *Palimbothra*, dans l'Antiquité ... C'est satisfaire une curiosité géographique bien placée, que de retrouver l'emplacement d'une ville de cette considération: mais j'ai lieu de croire qu'il faut employer quelque critique, dans l'examen des circonstances que l'Antiquité a fourni sur ce point. ... Je suis donc persuadé, qu'il ne faut point chercher d'autre emplacement à Palibothra que celui de la ville d'**Helabas**. ..."—*D'Anville*, *Eclaircissemens*, pp. 53–55.

(Here D'Anville is in error. But see Rennell's *Memoir*, pp. 50–54, which clearly identifies Palibothra with **Patna**.)

1786.—"... an attack and invasion of the Rohillas ... which nevertheless the said Warren Hastings undertook at the very time when, under the pretence of the difficulty of defending Corah and **Illiabad**, he sold these provinces to Sujah Dowla."—*Articles of Charge*, &c., in *Burke*, vi. 577.

"You will see in the letters from the Board ... a plan for obtaining **Illabad** from the Vizier, to which he had spirit enough to make a successful resistance."—*Cornwallis*, i. 238.

***ALLIGATOR**, s. This is the usual Anglo-Indian term for the great lacertine amphibia of the rivers. It was apparently in origin a corruption, imported from S. America, of the Spanish *el* or *al lagarto* (from Lat. *lacerta*), 'a lizard.' The "Summary of the Western Indies" by Pietro Martire d'Angheria, as given in Ramusio, recounting the last voyage of Columbus, says that, in a certain river, "they sometimes encountered those crocodiles which they call **Lagarti**; these make away when they see the Christians, and in making away they leave behind them an odour more fragrant than musk." (*Ram.* iii. f. 17*v.*). Oviedo, on another page of the same volume, calls them "**Lagarti** o dragoni" (f. 62).

Bluteau gives "**Lagarto**, *Crocodilo*" and adds: "In the Oriente Conquistado (Part I. f. 823) you will find a description of the Crocodile under the name of *Lagarto*."

One often, in Anglo-Indian conversation, used to meet with the endeavour to distinguish the two well-known species of the Ganges as *Crocodile* and **Alligator**, but this, like other applications of popular and general terms to mark scientific distinctions, involves fallacy, as in the cases of 'panther, leopard,' 'camel, dromedary,' 'attorney, solicitor,' and so forth. The two kinds of Gangetic crocodile were known to Aelian (c. 250 A.D.), who writes: "It (the Ganges) breeds two kinds of crocodiles; one of these is not at all hurtful, while the other is the most voracious and cruel eater of flesh; and these have a horny prominence on the top of the nostril. These latter are used as ministers of vengeance upon evil-doers; for those convicted of the greatest crimes are cast to them; and they require no executioner."

1493.—"In a small adjacent island ... our men saw an enormous kind of lizard (**lagarto** *muy grande*), which they said was as large round as a calf, and with a tail as long as a lance ... but bulky as it was, it got into the sea, so that they could not catch it."—*Letter of Dr. Chanca*, in *Select Letters of Columbus* by Major, Hak. Soc. 2nd ed., 43.

1539.—"All along this River, that was not very broad, there were a number of Lizards (**lagartos**), which might more properly be called Serpents ... with scales upon their backs, and mouths two foot wide ... there be of them that will sometimes get upon an **almadia** ... and overturn it with their tails, swallowing up the men whole, without dismembering of them."—*Pinto*, in Cogan's tr. 17 (*orig.* cap. xiv.).

1552.—"... aquatic animals such as ... very great lizards (**lagartos**), which in form and nature are just the crocodiles of the Nile."—*Barros*, I. iii. 8.

1568.—"In this River we killed a monstrous **Lagarto**, or Crocodile ... he was 23 foote by the rule, headed like a hogge. ..."—*Iob Hortop*, in *Hakl.* iii. 580.

1579.—"We found here many good commodities ... besides **alagartoes**, munckeyes, and the like."—*Drake, World Encompassed*, Hak. Soc. 112.

1591.—"In this place I have seen very great water **aligartos** (which we call in English crocodiles), seven yards long."—*Master Antonie Knivet*, in *Purchas*, iv. 1228.

1593.—"In this River (of Guayaquill) and all the Rivers of this Coast, are great abundance of **Alagartoes** ... persons of credit have certified to me that as small fishes in other Rivers abound in scoales, so the *Alagartoes* in this ..."—*Sir Richard Hawkins*, in *Purchas*, iv. 1400.

c. 1593.—
"And in his needy shop a tortoise hung,
An **alligator** stuff'd, and other skins
Of ill-shaped fishes... ."—
Romeo & Juliet, v. 1.

1595.—"Vpon this river there were great store of fowle ... but for **lagartos** it exceeded, for there were thousands of those vgly serpents; and the people called it for the abundance of them, the riuer of **Lagartos** in their language."—*Raleigh, The Discoverie of Guiana*, in *Hakl.* iv. 137.

1596.—"Once he would needs defend a rat to be *animal rationale* ... because she eate and gnawd his bookes ... And the more to confirme it, because everie one laught at him ... the next rat he seaz'd on hee made an anatomie of, and read a lecture of 3 dayes long upon everie artire or musckle, and after hanged her over his head in his studie in stead of an apothecarie's crocodile or dride **Alligatur**."—*T. Nashe's 'Have with you to Saffron Walden.'* Repr. in J. Payne Collier's *Misc. Tracts*, p. 72.

1610.—"These Blackes ... told me the River was full of **Aligatas**, and if I saw any I must fight with him, else he would kill me."—*D. Midleton*, in *Purchas*, i. 244.

1613.—"... mais avante ... por distancia de 2 legoas, esta o fermoso ryo de Cassam de **lagarthos** o crocodillos."—*Godinho de Eredia*, 10.

1673.—"The River was full of **Aligators** or Crocodiles, which lay basking in the Sun in the Mud on the River's side."—*Fryer*, 55.

1727.—"I was cleaning a vessel ... and had Stages fitted for my People to stand on ... and we were plagued with five or six **Allegators**, which wanted to be on the Stage."—*A. Hamilton*, ii. 133.

1761.—
"... else that sea-like Stream
(Whence Traffic pours her bounties on mankind)
Dread **Alligators** would alone possess."
Grainger, Bk. ii.

1881.—"The Hooghly alone has never been so full of sharks and **alligators** as now. We have it on undoubted authority that within the past two months over a hundred people have fallen victims to these brutes."—*Pioneer Mail*, July 10th.

***ALLIGATOR-PEAR**, s. The fruit of the *Laurus persea*, Lin., *Persea gratissima*, Gaertn. The name as here given is an extravagant, and that of *avocato* or *avogato* a more moderate, corruption of *aguacate* or *ahuacatl* (see below), which appears to have been the native name in Central America, still surviving there. The Quichua name is *palta*, which is used as well as *aguacaté* by Cieza de Leon, and also by Joseph de Acosta. Grainger (*Sugarcane*, Bk. I.) calls it "rich *sabbaca*," which he says is "the Indian name of the *avocato, avocado, avigato*, or as the English corruptly call it, *alligator pear*. The Spaniards in S. America call it *Aguacate*, and under that name it is described by Ulloa." In French it is called **avocat**. The praise which Grainger, as quoted below, "liberally bestows" on this fruit, is, if we might judge from the specimens occasionally met with in India, absurd. With liberal pepper and salt there may be a remote suggestion of marrow: but that is all. Indeed it is hardly a fruit in the ordinary sense. Its common sea name of 'midshipman's butter' [or 'subaltern's butter'] is suggestive of its merits, or demerits.

Though common and naturalised throughout the W. Indies and E. coasts of tropical S. America, its actual native country is unknown. Its introduction into the Eastern world is comparatively recent; not older than the middle of 18th century. Had it been worth eating it would have come long before.

1532–50.—"There are other fruits belonging to the country, such as fragrant pines and plantains, many excellent *guavas, caymitos*, **aguacates**, and other fruits."—*Cieza de Leon*, 16.

1608.—"The *Palta* is a great tree, and carries a faire leafe, which hath a fruite like to great peares; within it hath a great stone, and all the rest is soft meate, so as when they are full ripe, they are, as it were, butter, and have a delicate taste."—*Joseph de Acosta*, 250.

c. 1660.—

"The **Aguacat** no less is *Venus* Friend
(To th' *Indies Venus* Conquest doth extend)
A fragrant Leaf the **Aguacata** bears;
Her Fruit in fashion of an Egg appears,
With such a white and spermy Juice it swells
As represents moist Life's first Principles."

Cowley, *Of Plantes*, v.

1680.—"This Tavoga is an exceeding pleasant Island, abounding in all manner of fruits, such as Pine-apples ... **Albecatos**, Pears, Mammes."—*Capt. Sharpe*, in *Dampier*, iv.

1685.—"The **Avogato** Pear-tree is as big as most Pear-trees ... and the Fruit as big as a large Lemon. ... The Substance in the inside is green, or a little yellowish, and soft as Butter. ..."—*Dampier*, i. 203.

1736.—"**Avogato,** *Baum*. ... This fruit itself has no taste, but when mixt with sugar and lemon juice gives a wholesome and tasty flavour."—*Zeidler's Lexicon*, s.v.

1761.—

"And thou green **avocato**, charm of sense,
Thy ripen'd marrow liberally bestows't."

Grainger, Bk. I.

1830.—"The **avocada**, with its Brobdignag pear, as large as a purser's lantern."—*Tom Cringle*, ed. 1863, 40.

[1861.—"There is a well-known West Indian fruit which we call an **avocado** or **alligator pear**."—*Tylor, Anahuac*, 227.]

1870.—"The **aguacate** or **Alligator pear**."—*Squier, Honduras*, 142.

1873.—"Thus the fruit of the *Persea gratissima* was called **Ahucatl**' by the ancient Mexicans; the Spaniards corrupted it to **avocado**, and our sailors still further to '**Alligator pears**.'"—*Belt's Nicaragua*, 107.

ALMYRA, s. H. *almārī*. A wardrobe, chest of drawers, or like piece of (closed) furniture. The word is in general use, by masters and servants in Anglo-Indian households, in both N. and S. India. It has come to us from the Port. **almario**, but it is the same word as Fr. *armoire*, Old E. *ambry* [for which see *N.E.D.*] &c., and Sc. *awmry*, orginating in the Lat. *armarium*, or *-ria*, which occurs also in L. Gr. as ἀρμαρή, ἀρμάριον.

c. B.C. 200.—"Hoc est quod olim clanculum ex **armario** te surripuisse aiebas uxori tuae ..."—*Plautus, Men.* iii. 3.

A.D. 1450.—"Item, I will my chambre prestes haue ... the thone of thame the to **almer**, & the tothir of yame the tother **almar** whilk I ordnyd for kepyng of vestmentes."—*Will of Sir T. Cumberlege*, in *Academy*, Sept. 27, 1879, p. 231.

1589.—"——item ane langsettle, item ane **almarie**, ane Kist, ane sait burde ..."—*Ext. Records Burgh of Glasgow*, 1876, 130.

1878.—"Sahib, have you looked in Mr Morrison's **almirah**?"—*Life in Mofussil*, i. 34.

ALOO, s. Skt.—H. *ālū*. This word is now used in Hindustani and other dialects for the 'potato.' The original Skt. is said to mean the esculent root *Arum campanulatum*.

AMAH, s. A wet nurse; used in Madras, Bombay, China and Japan. It is Port. *ama* (comp. German and Swedish *amme*).

1839.—"... A sort of good-natured housekeeper-like bodies, who talk only of ayahs and **amahs**, and bad nights, and babies, and the advantages of Hodgson's ale while they are nursing: seeming in short devoted to 'suckling fools and chronicling small beer.'"—*Letters from Madras*, 294. See also p. 106.

AMBOYNA, n.p. A famous island in the Molucca Sea, belonging to the Dutch. The native form of the name is **Ambun** [which according to Marsden means 'dew'].

[1605.—"He hath sent hither his forces which hath expelled all the Portingalls out of the ffforts they here hould att **Ambweno** and Tydore."—*Birdwood, First Letter Book*, 68.]

AMEER, s. Ar. *Amīr* (root *amr*, 'commanding,' and so) 'a commander, chief, or lord,' and, in Ar. application, any kind of chief from the *Amīru' l-mūminīn*, 'the Amīr of the Faithful' *i.e.* the Caliph, downwards. The word in this form perhaps first became familiar as applied to the Princes of Sind, at the time of the conquest of that Province by Sir C. J. Napier. It is the title affected by many Musulman sovereigns of various calibres, as the Amīr of Kābul, the Amīr of Bokhārā, &c. But in sundry other forms the word has, more or less, taken root in European languages since the early Middle Ages. Thus it is the origin of the title 'Admiral,' now confined to generals of the sea service, but applied in varying forms by medieval Christian writers to the **Amīrs**, or lords, of the court and army of Egypt and other Mohammedan States. The word also came to us again, by a later importation from the Levant, in the French form, **Emir** or **Emer**.—See also OMRAH, which is in fact

Umarā, the pl. of *Amīr*. Byzantine writers use Ἀμὲρ, Ἀμηρᾶς, Ἀμυράς, Ἀμηραῖος, &c. (See *Ducange, Gloss. Græcit.*) It is the opinion of the best scholars that the forms *Amiral*, *Ammiraglio*, *Admiral* &c., originated in the application of a Low Latin termination *-alis* or *-alius*, though some doubt may still attach to this question. (See Marcel Devic, s.v. *Amiral*, and Dozy, Oosterlingen, s.v. *Admiraal* [and *N.E.D.* s.v. *Admiral*]. The *d* in admiral probably came from a false imagination of connection with *admirari*.

1250.—"Li grand **amiraus** des galies m'envoia querre, et me demanda si j'estoie cousins le roy; et je le di que nanin ..."—*Joinville*, p. 178. This passage illustrates the sort of way in which our modern use of the word **admiral** originated.

c. 1345.—"The Master of the Ship is like a great **amīr**; when he goes ashore the archers and the blackamoors march before him with javelins and swords, with drums and horns and trumpets."—*Ibn Batuta*, iv. 93.

Compare with this description of the Commander of a Chinese Junk in the 14th century, A. Hamilton's of an English Captain in Malabar in the end of the 17th:

"Captain Beawes, who commanded the *Albemarle*, accompanied us also, carrying a Drum and two Trumpets with us, so as to make our Compliment the more solemn."—i. 294.

And this again of an "interloper" skipper at Hooghly, in 1683:

1683.—"Alley went in a splendid Equipage, habitted in scarlet richly laced. Ten Englishmen in Blue Capps and Coats edged with Red, all armed with Blunderbusses, went before his pallankeen, 80 (? 8) *Peons* before them, and 4 Musicians playing on the Weights with 2 Flaggs, before him, like an Agent ..."—*Hedges*, Oct. 8 (Hak. Soc. i. 123).

1384.—"Il Soldano fu cristiano di Grecia, e fu venduto per schiavo quando era fanciullo a uno **ammiraglio**, come tu dicessi 'capitano di guerra.'"—*Frescobaldi*, p. 39.

1615.—"The inhabitants (of Sidon) are of sundry nations and religions; governed by a succession of Princes whom they call **Emers**; descended, as they say, from the Druses."—*Sandys, Iourney*, 210.

***A MUCK**, to run, v. There is we believe no room for doubt that, to us at least, this expression came from the Malay countries, where both the phrase and the practice are still familiar. Some valuable remarks on the phenomenon, as prevalent among the Malays, were contributed by Dr Oxley of Singapore to the *Journal of the Indian Archipelago*, vol. iii. p. 532; see a quotation below. [Mr W. W. Skeat writes—"The best explanation of the fact is perhaps that it was the Malay national method of committing suicide, especially as one never hears of Malays committing suicide in any other way. This form of suicide may arise from a wish to die fighting and thus avoid a 'straw death, a cow's death'; but it is curious that women and children are often among the victims, and especially members of the suicide's own family. The act of running **amuck** is probably due to causes over which the culprit has some amount of control, as the custom has now died out in the British Possessions in the Peninsula, the offenders probably objecting to being caught and tried in cold blood. I remember hearing of only about two cases (one by a Sikh soldier) in about six years. It has been suggested further that the extreme monotonous heat of the Peninsula may have conducted to such out-breaks as those of Running **amuck** and Latah.]

The word is by Crawfurd ascribed to the Javanese, and this is his explanation:

"*Amuk* (J.). An *a-muck*; to run *a-muck*; to tilt; to run furiously and desperately at any one; to make a furious onset or charge in combat."—(*Malay Dict.*) [The standard Malay, according to Mr Skeat, is rather *amok* (*mengāmok*).]

Marsden says that the word rarely occurs in any other than the verbal form *mengāmuk*, 'to make a furious attack' (*Mem. of a Malayan Family*, 96).

There is reason, however, to ascribe an Indian origin to the term; whilst the practice, apart from the term, is of no rare occurrence in Indian history. Thus Tod records some notable instances in the history of the Rājputs. In one of these (1634) the eldest son of the Raja of Mārwār ran *a-muck* at the court of Shāh Jahān, failing in his blow at the Emperor, but killing five courtiers of eminence before he fell himself. Again, in the 18th century, Bījai Singh, also of Mārwār, bore strong resentment against the Tālpura prince of Hyderabad, Bījar Khān, who had sent to demand from the Rājput tribute and a bride. A Bhattī and a Chondāwat offered their services for vengeance, and set out for Sind as envoys. Whilst Bījar Khān read their credentials, muttering, 'No mention of the bride!' the Chondāwat buried a dagger in his heart, exclaiming 'This for the bride!' 'And this for the tribute!' cried the Bhattī, repeating the blow. The pair then plied their daggers right and left, and 26 persons were slain before the envoys were hacked to pieces (*Tod*, ii. 45 & 315).

But it is in Malabar that we trace the apparent origin of the Malay term in the existence of certain desperadoes who are called by a variety of old travellers **amouchi** or **amuco**. The nearest approach to this that we have been able to discover is the Malayālam *amar-kkan*, 'a warrior' (from *amar*, 'fight, war'). [The proper Malayālam term for such men was *Chaver*, literally those who took up or devoted themselves to death.] One of the special applications of this word is remarkable in connection with a singular custom in Malabar. After the **Zamorin** had reigned 12 years, a great assembly was held at Tirunāvāyi, when that Prince took his seat surrounded by his dependants, fully armed. Any one might then attack him, and the assailant, if successful in killing the Zamorin, got the throne. This had often happened. [For a full discussion of this custom see *Frazer, Golden Bough*, 2nd ed., ii. 14 sq.] In 1600 thirty such assailants were killed in the enterprise. Now these men were called *amar-kkār* (pl. of *amar-kkan*, see *Gundert* s.v.). These men evidently ran *a-muck* in the true Malay sense; and quotations below will show other illustrations from Malabar which confirm the idea that both name and practice originated in Continental India. There is indeed a difficulty as to the derivation here indicated, in the fact that the *amuco* or *amouchi* of European writers on Malabar seems by no means close enough to *amarkkan*, whilst it is so close to the Malay *āmuk*; and on this further light may be hoped for. The identity between the **amoucos** of Malabar and the **amuck** runners of the Malay peninsula is clearly shown by the passage from *Correa* given below. [Mr Whiteway adds—"Gouvea (1606) in his *Iornada* (ch. 9, Bk. ii.) applies the word **amouques** to certain Hindus whom he saw in S. Malabar near Quilon, whose duty it was to defend the Syrian Christians with their lives. There are reasons for thinking that the worthy priest got hold of the story of a cock and a bull; but in any case the Hindus referred to were really Jangadas."]

De Gubernatis has indeed suggested that the word *amouchi* was derived from the Skt. *amokshya*, 'that cannot be loosed'; and this would be very consistent with several of the passages which we shall quote, in which the idea of being 'bound by a vow' underlies the conduct of the persons to whom the term was applicable both in Malabar and in the Archipelago. But *amokshya* is a word unknown to Malayālam, in such a sense at least.

We have seen *a-muck* derived from the Ar. *aḥmak*, 'fatuous' [(*e.g. Ball, Jungle Life*, 358).] But this is etymology of the kind which scorns history.

The phrase has been thoroughly naturalised in England since the days of Dryden and Pope. [The earliest quotation for "running *amuck*" in the N.E.D. is from Marvell (1672).]

c. 1430.—Nicolo Conti, speaking of the greater Islands of the Archipelago under the name of the Two Javas, does not use the word, but describes a form of the practice:—

"Homicide is here a jest, and goes without punishment. Debtors are made over to their creditors as slaves; and some of these, preferring death to slavery, will with drawn swords rush on, stabbing all whom they fall in with of less strength than themselves, until they meet death at the hands of some one more than a match for them. This man, the creditors then sue in Court for the dead man's debt."—In *India in the XVth C.* 45.

1516.—"There are some of them (Javanese) who if they fall ill of any severe illness vow to God that if they remain in health they will of their own accord seek another more honourable death for his service, and as soon as they get well they take a dagger in their hands, and go out into the streets and kill as many persons as they meet, both men, women, and children, in such wise that they go like mad dogs, killing until they are killed. These are called **Amuco.** And as soon as they see them begin this work, they cry out, saying **Amuco, Amuco,** in order that people may take care of themselves, and they kill them with dagger and spear thrusts."—*Barbosa*, Hak. Soc. 194. This passage seems to show that the word *amuk* must have been commonly used in Malay countries before the arrival of the Portuguese there, c. 1511.

1539.—"... The Tyrant (*o Rey Ache*) sallied forth in person, accompanied with 5000 resolute men (*cinco mil* **Amoucos**) and charged the *Bataes* very furiously."—*Pinto* (orig. cap. xvii.) in *Cogan*, p. 20.

1552.—De Barros, speaking of the capture of the Island of Beth (*Beyt*, off the N.W. point of Kāthiāwār) by Nuno da Cunha in 1531, says: "But the natives of Guzarat stood in such fear of Sultan Badur that they would not consent to the terms. And so, like people determined on death, all that night they shaved their heads (this is a superstitious practice of those who despise life, people whom they call in India **Amaucos**) and betook themselves to their mosque, and there devoted their persons to death ... and as an earnest of this vow, and an example of this resolution, the Captain ordered a great fire to be made, and cast into it his wife, and a little son that he had, and all his household and his goods, in fear lest anything of his should fall into our possession." Others did the like, and then they fell upon the Portuguese.—Dec. IV. iv. 13.

c. 1561.—In war between the Kings of Calicut and Cochin (1503) two princes of Cochin were killed. A number of these desperadoes who have been spoken of in the quotations were killed. ... "But some remained who were not killed, and these went in shame, not to have died avenging their lords ... these were more than 200, who all, according to their custom, shaved off all their hair, even to the eyebrows, and embraced each other and their friends and relations, as men about to suffer death. In this case they are as madmen—known as **amoucos**—and count themselves as already among the dead. These men dispersed, seeking wherever they might find men of Calicut, and among these they rushed fearless, killing and slaying till they were slain. And some of them, about twenty, reckoning more highly of their honour, desired to turn their death to better account; and these separated, and found their way secretly to Calicut, determined to slay the king. But as it became known that they were **amoucos**, the city gave the alarm, and the King sent his servants to slay them as they slew others. But they like desperate men played the devil (*fazião diabruras*) before they were slain, and killed many people, with women and children. And five of them got together to a wood near the city, which they haunted for a good while after, making robberies and doing much mischief, until the whole of them were killed."—*Correa*, i. 364–5.

1566.—"The King of *Cochin* ... hath a great number of gentlemen which he calleth **Amocchi**, and some are called *Nairi*: these two sorts of men esteem not their lives anything, so that it may be for the honour of their King."—*M. Cæsar Frederike* in *Purchas*, ii. 1708. [See *Logan, Man. Malabar*, i. 138.]

1584.—"Their forces (in Cochin) consist in a kind of soldiers whom they call **amocchi**, who are under obligation to die at the King's pleasure, and all soldiers who in war lose their King or their general lie under this obligation. And of such the King makes use in urgent cases, sending them to die fighting."—Letter of *F. Sassetti* to *Francesco I.*, Gd. D. of Tuscany, in *De Gubernatis*, 154.

c. 1584.—"There are some also who are called **Amocchi** ... who being weary of living, set themselves in the way with a weapon in their hands, which they call a *Crise*, and kill as many as they meete with, till somebody killeth them; and this they doe for the least anger they conceive, as desperate men."—*G. Balbi* in *Purchas*, ii. 1724.

1602.—De Couto, speaking of the Javanese: "They are chivalrous men, and of such determination that for whatever offence may be offered them they make themselves **amoucos** in order to get satisfaction thereof. And were a spear run into the stomach of such an one he would still press forward without fear till he got at his foe."—*Dec.* IV. iii. 1.

In another passage (*ib.* vii. 14) De Couto speaks of the **amoucos** of Malabar just as Della Valle does below. In *Dec.* VI. viii. 8 he describes how, on the death of the King of Pimenta, in action with the Portuguese, "nearly 4000 Nairs made themselves **amoucos** with the usual ceremonies, shaving their heads on one side, and swearing by their pagoda to avenge the King's death."

1603.—"Este es el genero de milicia de la India, y los Reyes señalan mas o menos **Amoyos** (ò **Amacos**, que todo es uno) para su guarda ordinaria."—*San Roman, Historia*, 48.

1604.—"Auia hecho vna junta de **Amocos**, con sus ceremonias para venir a morir adonde el Panical auia sedo muerto."—*Guerrero, Relacion*, 91.

1611.—"**Viceroy**. What is the meaning of **amoucos**? **Soldier**. It means men who have made up their mind to die in killing as many as they can, as is done in the parts about Malaca by those whom they call **amoucos** in the language of the country."—*Couto, Dialogo do Soldado Pratico*, 2nd part, p. 9.—(Printed at Lisbon in 1790).

1615.—"Hos inter Nairos genus est et ordo quem **Amocas** vocant quibus ob studium rei bellicae praecipua laus tribuitur, et omnium habentur validissimi."—*Jarric, Thesaurus*, i. 65.

1624.—"Though two kings may be at war, either enemy takes great heed not to kill the King of the opposite faction, nor yet to strike his umbrella, wherever it may go ... for the whole kingdom of the slain or wounded king would be bound to avenge him with the complete destruction of the enemy, or all, if needful, to perish in the attempt. The greater the king's dignity among these people, the longer period lasts this obligation to furious revenge ... this period or method of revenge is termed **Amoco**, and so they say that the **Amoco** of the Samori lasts one day; the **Amoco** of the king of Cochin lasts a life-time; and so of others."—*P. della Valle*, ii. 745 [Hak. Soc., ii. 380 *seq.*].

1648.—"Derrière ces palissades s'estoit caché

un coquin de Bantamois qui estoit revenu de la Mecque et jouoit à **Moqua** ... il court par les rues et tue tous ceux qu'il rencontre. ..."—*Tavernier, V. des Indes, liv.* iii. ch. 24 [Ed. *Ball,* ii. 361 seq.].

1659.—"I saw in this month of February at Batavia the breasts torn with red-hot tongs off a black Indian by the executioner; and after this he was broken on the wheel from below upwards. This was because through the evil habit of eating opium (according to the godless custom of the Indians) he had become mad and raised the cry of *Amocle* (misp. for **Amock**) ... in which mad state he had slain five persons. ... This was the third **Amock**-cryer whom I saw during that visit to Batavia (a few months) broken on the wheel for murder."

* * * * *

... "Such a murderer and **Amock**-runner has sometimes the fame of being an invincible hero because he has so manfully repulsed all who tried to seize him. ... So the Netherlands Government is compelled when such an **Amock**-runner is taken alive to punish him in a terrific manner."—*Walter Schulzens Ost-Indische Reise-Beschreibung* (German ed.), Amsterdam, 1676, pp. 19–20 and 227.

1672.—"Every community (of the Malabar Christians), every church has its own **Amouchi**, which ... are people who take an oath to protect with their own lives the persons and places put under their safeguard, from all and every harm."—*P. Vicenzo Maria,* 145.

"If the Prince is slain the **amouchi**, who are numerous, would avenge him desperately. If he be injured they put on festive raiment, take leave of their parents, and with fire and sword in hand invade the hostile territory, burning every dwelling, and slaying man, woman, and child, sparing none, until they themselves fall."—*Ibid.* 237-8.

1673.—"And they (the Mohammedans) are hardly restrained from running **a muck** (which is to kill whoever they meet, till they be slain themselves), especially if they have been at *Hodge* [**Hadgee**] a Pilgrimage to Mecca."—*Fryer,* 91.

1687.—Dryden assailing Burnet:—

"Prompt to assault, and careless of defence,
Invulnerable in his impudence,
He dares the World; and eager of a name,
He thrusts about and justles into fame.
Frontless and satire-proof, he scours the streets
And runs an **Indian Muck** at all he meets."

The Hind and the Panther, line 2477.

1689.—"Those that run these are called **Amouki**, and the doing of it *Running* **a Muck**."—*Ovington,* 237.

1712.—"**Amouco** (Termo da India) val o mesmo que homem determinado e apostado que despreza a vida e não teme a morte."—*Bluteau,* s.v.

1727.—"I answered him that I could no longer bear their Insults, and, if I had not Permission in three Days, I would **run a Muck** (which is a mad Custom among the *Mallayas* when they become desperate)."—*A. Hamilton,* ii. 231.

1737.—

"Satire's my weapon, but I'm too discreet
To **run a muck**, and tilt at all I meet."

Pope, Im. of Horace, B. ii. Sat. i. 69.

1768–71.—"These acts of indiscriminate murder are called by us **mucks**, because the perpetrators of them, during their frenzy, continually cry out **amok**, **amok**, which signifies *kill, kill* ..."—*Stavorinus,* i. 291.

1783.—At Bencoolen in this year (1760)—"the Count (d'Estaing) afraid of an insurrection among the Buggesses ... invited several to the Fort, and when these had entered the Wicket was shut upon them; in attempting to disarm them, they *mangamoed,* that is **ran a muck**; they drew their cresses, killed one or two Frenchmen, wounded others, and at last suffered themselves, for supporting this point of honour."—*Forrest's Voyage to Mergui,* 77.

1784.—"It is not to be controverted that these desperate acts of indiscriminate murder, called by us **mucks**, and by the natives *mongamo,* do actually take place, and frequently too, in some parts of the east (in Java in particular)."—*Marsden, H. of Sumatra,* 239.

1788.—"We are determined to **run a muck** rather than suffer ourselves to be forced away by these Hollanders."—*Mem. of a Malayan Family,* 66.

1798.—"At Batavia, if an officer take one of these **amoks**, or **mohawks**, as they have been called by an easy corruption, his reward is very considerable; but if he kill them, nothing is added to his usual pay ..."—*Translator of Stavorinus,* i. 294.

1803.—"We cannot help thinking, that one day or another, when they are more full of opium than usual, they (the Malays) will **run a muck** from Cape Comorin to the Caspian."—*Sydney Smith,* Works, 3rd ed., iii. 6.

1846.—"On the 8th July, 1846, Sunan, a respectable Malay house-builder in Penang, **ran amok** ... killed an old Hindu woman, a Kling, a Chinese boy, and a Kling girl about three years old ... and wounded two Hindus, three Klings, and two Chinese, of whom only two survived. ... On the trial Sunan declared he did not know what he was about, and persisted in this at the place of execution. ... The **amok** took place on the 8th, the trial on the 13th, and the execution on the 15th July,—all within 8 days."—*J. Ind. Arch.,* vol. iii. 460–61.

1849.—"A man sitting quietly among his friends and relatives, will without provocation suddenly start up, weapon in hand, and slay all within his reach. ... Next day when interrogated ... the answer has invariably been, "The Devil entered into me, my eyes were darkened, I did not know what I was about." I have received the same reply on at least 20 different occasions; on examination of these monomaniacs, I have generally found them labouring under some gastric disease, or troublesome ulcer. ... The Bugis, whether from revenge or disease, are by far the most addicted to run **amok**. I should think three-fourths of all the cases I have seen have been by persons of this nation."—*Dr T. Oxley*, in *J. Ind. Archip.*, iii. 532.

[1869.—"Macassar is the most celebrated place in the East for 'running **a muck**.'"—Wallace, *Malay Archip.* (ed. 1890), p. 134.]

[1870.—For a full account of many cases in India, see *Chevers, Med. Jurisprudence*, p. 781 seqq.]

1873.—"They (the English) ... crave governors who, not having bound themselves beforehand to '**run amuck**,' may give the land some chance of repose."—*Blackwood's Magazine*, June, p. 759.

1875.—"On being struck the Malay at once stabbed Arshad with a *kriss*; the blood of the people who had witnessed the deed was aroused, they ran **amok**, attacked Mr Birch, who was bathing in a floating bath close to the shore, stabbed and killed him."—*Sir W. D. Jervois* to the E. of Carnarvon, Nov. 16, 1875.

1876.—"Twice over, while we were wending our way up the steep hill in Galata, it was our luck to see a Turk '**run a muck**' ... nine times out of ten this frenzy is feigned, but not always, as for instance in the case where a priest took to running *a-muck* on an Austrian Lloyd's boat on the Black Sea, and after killing one or two passengers, and wounding others, was only stopped by repeated shots from the Captain's pistol."—*Barkley, Five Years in Bulgaria*, 240–41.

1877.—The *Times* of February 11th mentions a fatal **muck** run by a Spanish sailor, Manuel Alves, at the Sailors' Home, Liverpool; and the *Overland Times of India* (31st August) another run by a sepoy at Meerut.

1879.—"Running **a-muck** does not seem to be confined to the Malays. At Ravenna, on Monday, when the streets were full of people celebrating the festa of St John the Baptist, a maniac rushed out, snatched up a knife from a butcher's stall and fell upon everyone he came across ... before he was captured he wounded more or less seriously 11 persons, among whom was one little child."—*Pall Mall Gazette*, July 1.

"Captain Shaw mentioned ... that he had known as many as 40 people being injured by a single '**amok**' runner. When the cry '**amok! amok!**' is raised, people fly to the right and left for shelter, for after the blinded madman's *kris* has once 'drunk blood,' his fury becomes ungovernable, his sole desire is to kill; he strikes here and there; he stabs fugitives in the back, his *kris* drips blood, he rushes on yet more wildly, blood and murder in his course; there are shrieks and groans, his bloodshot eyes start from their sockets, his frenzy gives him unnatural strength; then all of a sudden he drops, shot through the heart, or from sudden exhaustion, clutching his bloody *kris*."—*Miss Bird, Golden Chersonese*, 356.

***ANACONDA**, s. This word for a great python, or boa, is of very obscure origin. It is now applied in scientific zoology as the specific name of a great S. American water-snake. Cuvier has "**L'Anacondo** (*Boa scytale et murina*, L.—*Boa aquatica*, Prince Max.)," (*Règne Animal*, 1829, ii. 78). Again, in the Official Report prepared by the Brazilian Government for the Philadelphia Exhibition of 1876, we find: "Of the genus Boa ... we may mention the ... *sucuriù* or *sucuriuba* (B. **anaconda**), whose skins are used for boots and shoes and other purposes." And as the subject was engaging our attention we read the following in the *St James' Gazette* of April 3, 1882:—"A very unpleasant account is given by a Brazilian paper, the *Voz do Povo* of Diamantino, of the proceedings of a huge water-snake called the *sucuruyu*, which is to be found in some of the rivers of Brazil. ... A slave, with some companions, was fishing with a net in the river, when he was suddenly seized by a *sucuruyu*, who made an effort with his hinder coils to carry off at the same time another of the fishing party." We had naturally supposed the name to be S. American, and its S. American character was rather corroborated by our finding in Ramusio's version of Pietro Martire d'Augheria such S. American names as *Anacauchoa* and *Anacaona*. Serious doubt was however thrown on the American origin of the word when we found that Mr H. W. Bates entirely disbelieved it, and when we failed to trace the name in any older books about S. America.

In fact the oldest authority that we have met with, the famous John Ray, distinctly assigns the name, and the serpent to which the name properly belonged, to Ceylon. This occurs in his *Synopsis Methodica*

Animalium Quadrupedum et Serpentini Generis, Lond. 1693. In this he gives a Catalogue of Indian Serpents, which he had received from his friend Dr Tancred Robinson, and which the latter had noted *e Museo Leydensi*. No. 8 in this list runs as follows:—

"8. *Serpens Indicus Bubalinus*, **Anacandaia** Zeylonensibus, id est Bubalorum aliorumque jumentorum membra conterens," p. 332.

The following passage from St Jerome, giving an etymology, right or wrong, of the word *boa*, which our naturalists now limit to certain great serpents of America, but which is often popularly applied to the pythons of E. Asia, shows a remarkable analogy to Ray's explanation of the name *Anacandaia*:—

c. A.D. 395–400.—"Si quidem draco mirae magnitudinis, quos gentili sermone *Boas* vocant, *ab eo quod tam grandes sint ut* boves *glutire soleant*, omnem late vastabat provinciam, et non solum armenta et pecudes sed agricolas quoque et pastores tractos ad so vi spiritus absorbebat."—In *Vita Scti. Hilarionis Eremitae*, Opera Scti. Eus. Hieron. Venetiis, 1767, ii. col. 35.

Ray adds that on this No. 8 should be read what D. Cleyerus has said in the *Ephem. German*. An 12. obser. 7, entitled: *De Serpente magno Indiae Orientalis Urobubalum deglutiente*. The serpent in question was 25 feet long. Ray quotes in abridgment the description of its treatment of the buffalo; how, if the resistance is great, the victim is dragged to a tree, and compressed against it; how the noise of the crashing bones is heard as far as a cannon: how the crushed carcass is covered with saliva, etc. It is added that the country people (apparently this is in Amboyna) regard this great serpent as most desirable food.

The following are extracts from Cleyer's paper, which is, more fully cited, *Miscellanea Curiosa, sive Ephimeridum Medico-Physicarum Germanicarum Academiae Naturae Curiosorum*, Dec. ii.—Annus Secundus, Anni MDCLXXXIII. Norimbergae. Anno MDCLXXXIV. pp. 18–20. It is illustrated by a formidable but inaccurate picture showing the serpent seizing an ox (not a buffalo) by the muzzle, with huge teeth. He tells how he dissected a great snake that he bought from a huntsman in which he found a whole stag of middle age, entire in skin and every part; and another which contained a wild goat with great horns, likewise quite entire; and a third which had swallowed a porcupine armed with all his "sagittiferis aculeis." In Amboyna a woman great with child had been swallowed by such a serpent... .

"Quod si animal quoddam robustius renitatur, ut spiris anguinis enecari non possit, serpens crebris cum animali convolutionibus caudâ suâ proximam arborem in auxilium et robur corporis arripit eamque circumdat, quo eo fortius et valentius gyris suis animal comprimere, suffocare, et demum enecaro possit... ."

"Factum est hoc modo, ut (quod ex fide dignissimis habeo) in Regno Aracan ... talis vasti corporis anguis prope flumen quoddam, cum Uro-bubalo, sive sylvestri bubalo aut uro ... immani spectaculo congredi visus fuerit, eumque dicto modo occiderit; quo conflictu et plusquam hostili amplexu fragor ossium in bubalo comminutorum ad distantiam tormenti bellici majoris ... a spectatoribus sat eminus stantibus exaudiri potuit... ."

The natives said these great snakes had poisonous fangs. These Cleyer could not find, but he believes the teeth to be in some degree venomous, for a servant of his scratched his hand on one of them. It swelled, greatly inflamed, and produced fever and delirium:

"Nec prius cessabant symptomata, quam Serpentinus lapis (see SNAKE-STONE) quam Patres Jesuitae hic componunt, vulneri adaptatus omne venenum extraheret, et ubique symptomata convenientibus antidotis essent profligata."

Again, in 1768, we find in the *Scots Magazine*, App. p. 673, but quoted from "London pap. Aug. 1768," and signed by *R. Edwin*, a professed eye-witness, a story with the following heading: "Description of the **Anaconda**, a monstrous species of serpent. In a letter from an English gentleman, many years resident in the Island of Ceylon in the East Indies. ... The Ceylonese seem to know the creature well; they call it **Anaconda**, and talked of eating its flesh when they caught it." He describes its seizing and disposing of an enormous "tyger." The serpent darts on the "tyger" from a tree, attacking first with a bite, then partially crushing and dragging it to the tree ... "winding his body round both the tyger and the tree with all his violence, till the ribs and other bones began to give way ... each giving a loud crack when it burst ... the poor creature all this time was living, and at every loud crash of its bones gave a houl, not loud, yet piteous enough to pierce the cruelest heart."

Then the serpent drags away its victim, covers it with slaver, swallows it, etc. The whole thing is very cleverly told, but is evidently a romance founded on the description by "D. Cleyerus," which is quoted by Ray. There are no tigers in Ceylon. In fact, "R. Edwin" has developed the Romance of the Anaconda out of the description of D. Cleyerus, exactly as "Mynheer Försch" some years later developed the Romance of the Upas out of the older stories of the poison tree of Macassar. Indeed, when we find "Dr Andrew Cleyer" mentioned among the early relators of these latter stories, the suspicion becomes strong that both romances had the same author, and that "R. Edwin" was also the true author of the wonderful story told under the name of Foersch. (See further under UPAS.)

In Percival's *Ceylon* (1803) we read: "Before I arrived in the island I had heard many stories of a monstrous snake, so vast in size as to devour tigers and buffaloes, and so daring as even to attack the elephant" (p. 303). Also, in Pridham's *Ceylon and its Dependencies* (1849, ii. 750–51): "Pimbera or **Anaconda** is of the genus Python, Cuvier, and is known in English as the rock-snake." Emerson Tennent (*Ceylon*, 4th ed., 1860, i. 196) says: "The great python (the 'boa' as it is commonly designated by Europeans, the '**anaconda**' of Eastern story) which is supposed to crush the bones of an elephant, and to swallow a tiger". ... It may be suspected that the letter of "R. Edwin" was the foundation of all or most of the stories alluded to in these passages. Still we have the authority of Ray's friend that Anaconda, or rather *Anacondaia*, was at Leyden applied as a Ceylonese name to a specimen of this python. The only interpretation of this that we can offer is Tamil *ānai-kondra* [*āṇaikkóṇḍa*], "which killed an elephant"; an appellative, but not a name. We have no authority for the application of this appellative to a snake, though the passages quoted from Percival, Pridham, and Tennent are all suggestive of such stories, and the interpretation of the name *anacondaia* given to Bay: "*Bubalorum* ... membra conterens," is at least quite analogous as an appellative. It may be added that in Malay **anakanda** signifies "one that is well-born," which does not help us ... [Mr Skeat is unable to trace the word in Malay, and rejects the derivation from *anakanda* given above. A more plausible explanation is that given by Mr D. Ferguson (8 Ser. *N. & Q.* xii. 123), who derives *anacandaia* from Singhalese *Henakandayâ* (*hena*, 'lightning'; *kanda*, 'stem, trunk,') which is a name for the whip-snake (*Passerita mycterizans*), the name of the smaller reptile being by a blunder transferred to the greater. It is at least a curious coincidence that Ogilvy (1670) in his "*Description of the African Isles*" (p. 690), gives: "*Anakandef*, a sort of small snakes," which is the Malagasy *Anakandîfy*, 'a snake.']

1859.—"The skins of **anacondas** offered at Bangkok come from the northern provinces."—*D. O. King*, in *J. R. G. Soc.*, xxx. 184.

***ANDAMAN**, n.p. The name of a group of islands in the Bay of Bengal, inhabited by tribes of a negrito race, and now partially occupied as a convict settlement under the Government of India. The name (though perhaps obscurely indicated by Ptolemy—see H. Y. in *P.R.G.S.* 1881, p. 665) first appears distinctly in the Ar. narratives of the 9th century. [The Ar. dual form is said to be from *Agamitae*, the Malay name of the aborigines.] The persistent charge of cannibalism seems to have been unfounded. [See E. H. Man, *On the Aboriginal Inhabitants of the Andaman Islands*, Intro. xiii. 45.]

A.D. 851.—"Beyond are two islands divided by a sea called **Andāmān**. The natives of these isles devour men alive; their hue is black, their hair woolly; their countenance and eyes have something frightful in them ... they go naked, and have no boats. ..."—*Relation des Voyages*, &c. par *Reinaud*, i. 8.

c. 1050.—These islands are mentioned in the great Tanjore temple-inscription (11th cent.) as *Tīmaittīvu*, 'Islands of Impurity,' inhabited by cannibals.

c. 1292.—"**Angamanain** is a very large Island. The people are without a King and are idolators, and are no better than wild beasts ... they are a most cruel generation, and eat everybody that they can catch if not of their own race."—*Marco Polo*, Bk. iii. c. 13.

c. 1430.—"... leaving on his right hand an island called **Andemania**, which means the island of Gold, the circumference of which is 800 miles. The inhabitants are cannibals. No travellers touch here unless driven to do so by bad weather, for when taken they are torn to pieces and devoured by these cruel savages."—*Conti*, in *India in XV. Cent.*, 8.

c. 1566.—"Da Nicubar sinò a Pegu é vna catena d'Isole infinite, delle quali molte sono habitate da gente seluaggia, e chiamansi **Isole**

d'Andeman ... e se per disgratia si perde in queste Isole qualche naue, come già se n'ha perso, non ne scampa alcuno, che tutti gli amazzano, e mangiano."—*Cesare de' Federici*, in *Ramusio*, iii. 391.

1727.—"The Islands opposite the Coast of *Tanacerin* are the **Andemans**. They lie about 80 leagues off, and are surrounded by many dangerous Banks and Rocks; they are all inhabited with *Canibals*, who are so fearless that they will swim off to a Boat if she approach near the shore, and attack her with their wooden Weapons ..."—*A. Hamilton*, ii. 65.

***ANGENGO**, n.p. A place on the Travancore coast, the site of an old English Factory; properly said to be *Añju-tengu*, *Añchutennu*, Malayāl; the trivial meaning of which would be "five cocoa-nuts." This name gives rise to the marvellous rhapsody of the once famous Abbé Raynal, regarding "Sterne's Eliza," of which we quote below a few sentences from the 3½ pages of close print which it fills.

1711.—"... **Anjengo** is a small Fort belonging to the *English East India Company*. There are about 40 Soldiers to defend it ... most of whom are *Topazes*, or mungrel Portuguese."—*Lockyer*, 199.

1782.—"Territoire d'**Anjinga**; tu n'es rien; mais tu as donné naissance à Eliza. Un jour, ces entrepôts ... ne subsisteront plus ... mais si mes écrits ont quelque durée, le nom d'**Anjinga** restera dans le mémoire des hommes ... **Anjinga**, c'est à l'influence de ton heureux climat qu'elle devoit, sans doute, cet accord presqu'incompatible de volupté et de décence qui accompagnoit toute sa personne, et qui se mêloit à tous ses mouvements, &c., &c."—*Hist. Philosophique des Deux Indes*, ii. 72–73.

***ANILE, NEEL**, s. An old name for indigo, borrowed from the Port. *anil*. They got it from the Ar. *al-nīl*, pron. *an-nīl*; *nīl* again being the common name of indigo in India, from the Skt. *nīla*, 'blue.' The vernacular (in this instance Bengali) word appears in the title of a native satirical drama *Nīl-Darpan*, 'The Mirror of Indigo (planting),' famous in Calcutta in 1861, in connection with a *cause célèbre*, and with a sentence which discredited the now extinct Supreme Court of Calcutta in a manner unknown since the days of Impey.

"Neel-walla" is a phrase for an Indigo-planter [and his Factory is *"Neelkothee"*].

1501.—Amerigo Vespucci, in his letter from the Id. of Cape Verde to Lorenzo di Piero Francesco de' Medici, reporting his meeting with the Portuguese Fleet from India, mentions among other things brought "**anib** and tuzia," the former a manifest transcriber's error for *anil*.—In *Baldelli Boni*, *'Il Milione,'* p. lvii.

1516.—In Barbosa's price list of Malabar we have:

"**Anil** nadador (i.e. floating; see *Garcia* below) very good,
per *farazola* ... *fanams* 30.
Anil loaded, with much sand,
per *farazola* ... *fanams* 18 to 20."
In *Lisbon Collection*, ii. 393.

1525.—"A load of **anyll** in cakes which weighs 3½ maunds, 353 tangas."—*Lembranca*, 52.

1563.—"**Anil** is not a medicinal substance but an article of trade, so we have no need to speak thereof. ... The best is pure and clear of earth, and the surest test is to burn it in a candle ... others put it in water, and if it floats then they reckon it good."—*Garcia*, f. 25 v.

1583.—"**Neel**, the churle 70 duckats, and a churle is 27 rottles and a half of Aleppo."—*Mr Iohn Newton*, in *Hakl.* ii. 378.

1583.—"They vse to pricke the skinne, and to put on it a kind of **anile**, or blacking which doth continue alwayes."—*Fitch*, in *Hakl.* ii. 395.

c. 1610.—"... l'**Anil** on Indique, qui est vne teinture bleüe violette, dont il ne s'en trouue qu'à Cambaye et Suratte."—*Pyrard de Laval*, ii. 158; [Hak. Soc. ii. 246].

[1614.—"I have 30 fardels **Anil** Geree." *Foster*, *Letters*, ii. 140. Here *Geree* is probably H. *jaṛi* (from *jaṛ*, 'the root'), the crop of indigo growing from the stumps of the plants left from the former year.]

1622.—"E conforme a dita pauta se despachará o dito **anil** e canella."—In *Archiv. Port. Orient.*, fasc. 2, 240.

1638.—"Les autres marchandises, que l'on y débite le plus, sont ... du sel ammoniac, et de l'indigo, que ceux de pais appellent **Anil**."—*Mandelslo*, Paris, 1659, 138.

1648.—"... and a good quantity of **Anil**, which, after the place where most of it is got, is called *Chirchees* Indigo."—*Van Twist*, 14. Sharkej or Sirkej, 5 m. from Ahmedabad. "Cirquez Indigo" (1624) occurs in *Sainsbury*, iii. 442. It is the *"Sercase"* of Forbes [*Or. Mem.* 2nd ed. ii. 204]. The Dutch, about 1620, established a factory there on account of the indigo. Many of the Sultans of Guzerat were buried there (*Stavorinus*, iii. 109). Some account of the "Sarkhej *Rozas*," or Mausolea, is given in H. Brigg's *Cities of Gujaráshtra* (Bombay, 1849, pp. 274, *seqq.*). ["Indigo of Bian (Biana) *Sicchese*" (1609), *Danvers*, *Letters*, i. 28; "Indico, of Laher, here worth viij[s] the pounde *Serchis*."—*Birdwood*, *Letter Book*, 287.]

1653.—"Indico est un mot Portugais, dont l'on appelle une teinture bleüe qui vient des Indes Orientales, qui est de contrabande en France, les Turqs et les Arabes la nomment **Nil**."—*De la Boullaye-le-Gouz*, 543.

[1670.—"The neighbourhood of Delhi produces **Anil** or Indigo."—*Bernier* (ed. *Constable*), 283.]

***ANNA**, s. Properly H. *āna, ānah*, the 16th part of a rupee. The term belongs to the Mohammedan monetary system (RUPEE). There is no coin of one *anna* only, so that it is a money of account only. The term *anna* is used in denoting a corresponding fraction of any kind of property, and especially in regard to coparcenary shares in land, or shares in a speculation. Thus a one-*anna* share is 1⁄16 of such right, or a share of 1⁄16 in the speculation; a four-*anna* is ¼, and so on. In some parts of India the term is used as subdivision (1⁄16) of the current land measure. Thus, in Saugor, the *anna* = 16 *rūsīs*, and is itself 1⁄16 of a *kancha* (*Elliot, Gloss.* s.v.). The term is also sometimes applied colloquially to persons of mixt parentage. 'Such a one has at least 2 *annas* of dark blood,' or 'coffee-colour.' This may be compared with the Scotch expression that a person of deficient intellect 'wants twopence in the shilling.'

1708.—"Provided ... that a debt due from Sir Edward Littleton ... of 80,407 Rupees and Eight **Annas** Money of *Bengal*, with Interest and Damages to the said English Company shall still remain to them ..."—*Earl of Godolphin's Award* between the Old and the New E. I. Co., in *Charters*, &c., p. 358.

1727.—"The current money in Surat:
Bitter Almonds go 32 to a *Pice*:
1 **Annoe** is . . . 4 Pice.
1 Rupee . . . 16 **Annoes**.
* * * * *
In Bengal their Accounts are kept in *Pice*:
12 to an Annoe.
16 **Annoes** to a Rupee."
A. Hamilton, ii. App. pp. 5, 8.

ANT, WHITE, s. The insect (*Termes bellicosus* of naturalists) not properly an ant, of whose destructive powers there are in India so many disagreeable experiences, and so many marvellous stories. The phrase was perhaps taken up by the English from the Port, *formigas branchas*, which is in Bluteau's Dict. (1713, iv. 175). But indeed exactly the same expression is used in the 14th century by our medieval authority. It is, we believe, a fact that these insects have been established at Rochelle in France, for a long period, and more recently at St. Helena. They exist also at the Convent of Mt. Sinai, and a species in Queensland.

A.D. c. 250.—It seems probable that Aelian speaks of White Ants.—"But the Indian ants construct a kind of heaped-up dwellings, and these not in depressed or flat positions easily liable to be flooded, but in lofty and elevated positions ..."—*De Nat. Animal.* xvi. cap. 15.

c. 1328.—"Est etiam unum genus parvissimarum *formicarum* sicut lana *albarum*, quarum durities dentium tanta est quod etiam ligna rodunt et venas lapidum; et quotquot breviter inveniunt siccum super terram, et pannos laneos, et bombycinos laniant; et faciunt ad modum muri crustam unam de arenâ minutissimâ, ita quod sol non possit eas tangere; et sic remanent coopertae; verum est quod si contingat illam crustam frangi, et solem eas tangere, quam citius moriuntur.—*Fr. Jordanus*, p. 53.

1679.—"But there is yet a far greater inconvenience in this Country, which proceeds from the infinite number of **white Emmets**, which though they are but little, have teeth so sharp, that they will eat down a wooden Post in a short time. And if great care be not taken in the places where you lock up your Bales of Silk, in four and twenty hours they will eat through a Bale, as if it had been saw'd in two in the middle."—*Tavernier's Tunquin*, E. T., p. 11.

1688.—"Here are also abundance of Ants of several sorts, and Wood-lice, called by the English in the East Indies, **White Ants**."—*Dampier*, ii. 127.

1713.—"On voit encore des fourmis de plusieurs espèces; la plus pernicieuse est celle que les Européens ont nommé **fourmi blanche**."—*Lettres Edifiantes*, xii. 98.

1727.—"He then began to form Projects how to clear Accounts with his Master's Creditors, without putting anything in their Pockets. The first was on 500 chests of *Japan* Copper ... and they were brought into Account of Profit and Loss, for so much eaten up by the **White Ants**."—*A. Hamilton*, ii. 169.

1751.—"... concerning the Organ, we sent for the Revd. Mr. Bellamy, who declared that when Mr. Frankland applied to him for it that he told him that it was not in his power to give it, but wished it was removed from thence, as Mr. Pearson informed him it was eaten up by the **White Ants**."—*Ft. Will. Cons.*, Aug. 12. In *Long*, 25.

1789.—"The **White Ant** is an insect greatly dreaded in every house; and this is not to be wondered at, as the devastation it occasions is almost incredible."—*Munro, Narrative*, 31.

1876.—"The metal cases of his baggage are disagreeably suggestive of **White Ants**, and such omnivorous vermin."—*Sat. Review*, No. 1057, p. 6.

APĪL, s. Transfer of Eng. 'Appeal'; in general native use, in connection with our Courts.

1872.—"There is no Sindi, however wild, that cannot now understand 'Rasíd' (receipt) [**Raseed**] and '**Apīl**' (appeal)."—*Burton, Sind Revisited*, i. 283.

***APOLLO BUNDER**, n.p. A well-known wharf at Bombay. A street near it is called Apollo Street, and a gate of the Fort leading to it 'the Apollo Gate.' The name is said to be a corruption, and probably is so, but of what it is a corruption is not clear. The quotations given afford different suggestions, and Dr Wilson's dictum is entitled to respect, though we do not know what *pālawā* here means. Sir G. Birdwood writes that it used to be said in Bombay, that *Apollo-bandar* was a corr. of *palwa*-bandar, because the pier was the place where the boats used to land *palwa* fish. But we know of no fish so called; it is however possible that the *palla* or *Sable-fish* (**Hilsa**) is meant, which is so called in Bombay, as well as in Sind. [The *Āīn* (ii. 338) speaks of "a kind of fish called *palwah* which comes up into the Indus from the sea, unrivalled for its fine and exquisite flavour," which is the **Hilsa**.] On the other hand we may observe that there was at Calcutta in 1748 a frequented tavern called the Apollo (see *Long*, p. 11). And it is not impossible that a house of the same name may have given its title to the Bombay street and wharf. But Sir Michael Westropp's quotation below shows that *Pallo* was at least the native representation of the name more than 150 years ago. [Mr. S. M. Edwardes, (*History of Bombay, Town and Island, Census Report*, 1901, p. 17) derives this name from 'Pallav Bandar,' 'The Harbour of Clustering Shoots.'] We may add that a native told Mr W. G. Pedder, of the Bombay C.S., from whom we have it, that the name was due to the site having been the place where the "*poli*" cake, eaten at the Holi festival, was baked. And so we leave the matter.

[1823.—"Lieut. Mudge had a tent on **Apollo**-green for astronomical observations."—*Owen, Narratice*, i. 327.]

1847.—"A little after sunset, on 2nd Jan. 1843, I left my domicile in Ambrolie, and drove to the **Pálawá bandar**, which receives from our accommodative countrymen the more classical name of *Apollo* pier."—*Wilson, Lands of the Bible*, p. 4.

1860.—"And atte what place ye Knyghte came to Londe, theyre ye ffolke ... worschyppen II Idolys in cheefe. Ye ffyrste is **Apollo**, wherefore yē cheefe londynge place of theyr Metropole is hyght **Apollo-Bundar** ..."—Ext. from a MS. of Sir John Mandeville, lately discovered. (A friend here queries: 'By Mr. Shapira?')

1877.—"This bunder is of comparatively recent date. Its name '**Apollo**' is an English corruption of the native word *Pallow* (fish), and it was probably not extended and brought into use for passenger traffic till about the year 1819 ..."—*Maclean, Guide to Bombay*, 167. The last work adds a note: "Sir Michael Westropp gives a different derivation. ...: *Polo*, a corruption of *Pálwa*, derived from *Pál*, which *inter alia* means a fighting vessel, by which kind of craft the locality was probably frequented. From *Pálwa* or *Pálwar*, the bunder now called Apollo is supposed to take its name. In the memorial of a grant of land, dated 5th Dec., 1743, the *pákhádé* in question is called *Pallo*."—*High Court Reports*, iv. pt. 3.

[1880.—"His mind is not prehensile like the tail of the **Apollo Bundar**."—*Aberigh-Mackay, Twenty-one Days in India*, p. 141.]

ARAB, s. This, it may be said, in Anglo-Indian always means 'an Arab horse.'

1298.—"Car il va du port d'Aden en Inde moult grant quantité de bons destriers **arrabins** et chevaus et grans roncins de ij selles."—*Marco Polo*, Bk. iii. ch. 36. [See *Sir H. Yule's* note, 1st ed., vol. ii. 375.]

1338.—"Alexandre descent du destrier **Arrabis**."—*Rommant d'Alexandre* (Bodl. MS.).

c. 1590.—"There are fine horses bred in every part of the country; but those of Cachh excell, being equal to **Arabs**."—*Āīn*, i. 133.

1825.—"**Arabs** are excessively scarce and dear; and one which was sent for me to look at, at a price of 800 rupees, was a skittish, cat-legged thing."—*Heber*, i. 189 (ed. 1844).

c. 1844.—A local magistrate at Simla had returned from an unsuccessful investigation. An acquaintance hailed him next day: 'So I hear you came back *re infectâ*?' 'No such thing,' was the reply; 'I came back on my grey **Arab**!'

1856.—

"... the true blood-royal of his race,
The silver **Arab** with his purple veins
Translucent, and his nostrils caverned wide,
And flaming eye... ." *The Banyan Tree.*

ARECA, s. The seed (in common parlance the nut) of the palm *Areca catechu*, L., commonly, though somewhat improperly, called 'betel-nut'; the term **Betel** belonging in reality to the leaf which is chewed along with the *areca*. Though so widely cultivated, the palm is unknown in a truly indigenous state. The word is Malayāl. *adakka* [according to Bp. Caldwell, from *adai* 'close arrangement of the cluster,' *kay*, 'nut' *N.E.D.*], and comes to us through the Port.

1510.—"When they eat the said leaves (betel), they eat with them a certain fruit which is called *coffolo*, and the tree of the said *coffolo* is called **Arecha**."—*Varthema*, Hak. Soc., 144.

1516.—"There arrived there many zambucos ... with **areca**."—*Barbosa*, Hak. Soc., 64.

1521.—"They are always chewing **Arecca**, a certaine Fruit like a Peare, cut in quarters and rolled up in leaves of a Tree called *Bettre* (or *Vettele*), like Bay leaves; which having chewed they spit forth. It makes the mouth red. They say they doe it to comfort the heart, nor could live without it."—*Pigafetta*, in *Purchas*, i. 38.

1548.—"In the *Renda do Betel*, or Betel duties at Goa are included Betel, **arequa**, jacks, green ginger, oranges, lemons, figs, coir, mangos, citrons."—*Botelho, Tombo*, 48. The Port. also formed a word *ariqueira* for the tree bearing the nuts.

1563.—"... and in Malabar they call it *pac* (Tam. *pāk*); and the Nairs (who are the gentlemen) call it **areca**."—*García D'O.*, f. 91 *b*.

c. 1566.—"Great quantitie of **Archa**, which is a fruite of the bignesse of nutmegs, which fruite they eate in all these parts of the Indies, with the leafe of an Herbe, which they call *Bettell*."—*C. Frederike*, transl. in *Hakl.* ii. 350.

1586.—"Their friends come and bring gifts, cocos, figges, **arrecaes**, and other fruits."—*Fitch*, in *Hakl.*, ii. 395.

[1624.—"And therewith they mix a little ashes of sea-shells and some small pieces of an Indian nut sufficiently common, which they here call *Foufel*, and in other places **Areca**; a very dry fruit, seeming within like perfect wood; and being of an astringent nature they hold it good to strengthen the Teeth."—*P. della Valle*, Hak. Soc. i. 36. Mr Grey says: "As to the Port. name, *Foufel* or *Fofel*, the origin is uncertain. In Sir J. Maundeville's Travels it is said that black pepper "is called *Fulful*," which is probably the same word as "*Foufel*." But the Ar. *Fawfal* or *Fufal* is 'betel-nut.']

1689.—"... the *Neri* which is drawn from the **Arequies** Tree in a fresh earthen vessel, is as sweet and pleasant as Milk"—*Ovington*, 237. [*Neri* = H. and Mahr. *nīr*, 'sap,' but *neri* is, we are told, Guzerati for toddy in some form.]

ARRACK, RACK, s. This word is the Ar. *'araḳ*, properly 'perspiration,' and then, first the exudation or sap drawn from the date palm (*'araḳ al-tamar*); secondly any strong drink, 'distilled spirit,' 'essence,' etc. But it has spread to very remote corners of Asia. Thus it is used in the forms *ariki* and *arki* in Mongolia and Manchuria, for spirit distilled from grain. In India it is applied to a variety of common spirits; in S. India to those distilled from the fermented sap of sundry palms; in E. and N. India to the spirit distilled from cane-molasses, and also to that from rice. The Turkish form of the word, *rāḳi*, is applied to a spirit made from grape-skins; and in Syria and Egypt to a spirit flavoured with aniseed, made in the Lebanon. There is a popular or slang Fr. word, *riquiqui*, for brandy, which appears also to be derived from *araḳī* (*Marcel Devic*). Humboldt (*Examen*, &c., ii. 300) says that the word first appears in Pigafetta's Voyage of Magellan; but this is not correct.

c. 1420.—"At every *yam* (post-house) they give the travellers a sheep, a goose, a fowl ... **'arak** ..."—*Shah Rukh's Embassy to China*, in N. & E., xiv. 396.

1516.—"And they bring cocoa-nuts, **hurraca** (which is something to drink) ..."—*Barbosa*, Hak. Soc. 59.

1518.—"—que todos os mantimentos asy de pão, como vinhos, **orracas**, arrozes, carnes, e pescados."—In *Archiv. Port. Orient.*, fasc. 2, 57.

1521.—"When these people saw the politeness of the captain, they presented some fish, and a vessel of palm-wine, which they call in their language **uraca**. ..."—*Pigafetta*, Hak. Soc. 72.

1544.—"Manueli a cruce ... commendo ut plurimum invigilet duobus illis Christianorum Carearum pagis, diligenter attendere ... nemo potu **Orracae** se inebriet ... si ex hoc deinceps tempore Punicali **Orracha** potetur, ipsos ad mihi suo gravi damno luituros."—*Scti. Fr. Xav. Epistt.*, p. 111.

1554.—"And the excise on the *orraquas* made from palm-trees, of which there are three kinds, viz., *çura*, which is as it is drawn; **orraqua**, which is *çura* once boiled (*cozida*, qu. distilled?); *sharab* (*xarao*) which is boiled two or three times and is stronger than *orraqua*."—*S. Botelho, Tombo*, 50.

1563.—"One kind (of coco palm) they keep to bear fruit, the other for the sake of the *çura*, which is *vino mosto*; and this when it has been distilled they call **orraca**."—*Garcia D'O.*, f. 67. (The word *surā*, used here, is a very ancient importation from India, for Cosmas

(6th century) in his account of the coco-nut, confounding (it would seem) the milk with the toddy of that palm, says: "The *Argellion* is at first full of a very sweet water, which the Indians drink from the nut, using it instead of wine. This drink is called *rhoncosura*, and is extremely pleasant." It is indeed possible that the **rhonco** here may already be the word *arrack*).

1605.—"A Chines borne, but now turned Iauan, who was our next neighbour ... and brewed **Aracke** which is a kind of hot drinke, that is vsed in most of these parts of the world, instead of Wine ..."—*E. Scot*, in *Purchas*, i. 173.

1631.—"... jecur ... a potu istius maledicti **Arac**, non tantum in temperamento immutatum, sed etiam in substantiâ suâ corrumpitur."—*Jac. Bontius*, lib. ii. cap. vii. p. 22.

1687.—"Two jars of **Arack** (made of rice as I judged) called by the Chinese *Samshu*."—*Dampier*, i. 419.

1719.—"We exchanged some of our wares for opium and some **arrack**. ..."—*Robinson Crusoe*, Pt. II.

1727.—"Mr Boucher had been 14 Months soliciting to procure his *Phirmaund*; but his repeated Petitions ... had no Effect. But he had an *Englishman*, one *Swan*, for his Interpreter, who often took a large Dose of **Arrack**. ... Swan got pretty near the King (Aurungzeb) ... and cried with a loud Voice in the Persian Language that his Master wanted Justice done him" (see DOAI.—*A. Hamilton*, i. 97.

Rack is a further corruption; and **rack-punch** is perhaps not quite obsolete.

1603.—"We taking the But-ends of Pikes and Halberts and Faggot-sticks, drave them into a **Racke**-house."—*E. Scot*, in *Purchas*, i. 184.

Purchas also has **Vraca** and other forms; and at i. 648 there is mention of a strong kind of spirit called **Rack**-*apee* (Malay *āpī* = 'fire'). See FOOL'S RACK.

1616.—"Some small quantitie of Wine, but not common, is made among them; they call it **Raack**, distilled from Sugar and a spicie Rinde of a Tree called *Iagru* [**Jaggery**]."—*Terry*, in *Purchas*, ii. 1470.

1622.—"We'll send him a jar of **rack** by next conveyance."—Letter in *Sainsbury*, iii. 40.

1627.—"Java hath been fatal to many of the English, but much through their own distemper with **Rack**."—*Purchas, Pilgrimage*, 693.

1848.—"Jos ... finally insisted upon having a bowl of **rack punch**. ... That bowl of **rack punch** was the cause of all this history."—*Vanity Fair*, ch. vi.

***ART, EUROPEAN.** We have heard much, and justly, of late years regarding the corruption of Indian art and artistic instinct by the employment of the artists in working for European patrons, and after European patterns. The copying of such patterns is no new thing, as we may see from this passage of the brightest of writers upon India whilst still under Asiatic government.

c. 1665.—"... not that the Indians have not wit enough to make them successful in Arts, they doing very well (as to some of them) in many parts of India, and it being found that they have inclination enough for them, and that some of them make (even without a Master) very pretty workmanship and imitate so well our work of Europe, that the difference thereof will hardly be discerned."—*Bernier*, E. T., 81–82 [ed. *Constable*, 254].

ARTICHOKE, s. The genealogy of this word appears to be somewhat as follows: The Ar. is **al-ḥarshūf** (perhaps connected with *ḥarash*, 'rough-skinned') or *al-kharshūf*; hence Sp. **alcarchofa** and It. *carcioffo* and *arciocco*, Fr. *artichaut*, Eng. *artichoke*.

c. 1348.—"The Incense (benzoin) tree is small ... its branches are like those of a thistle or an artichoke (**al-kharshaf**)."—*Ibn Batuta*, iv. 240. **Al-kharshaf** in the published text. The spelling with *h* instead of *kh* is believed to be correct (see *Dozy*, s.v. *Alcarchofa*); [also see *N.E.D.* s.v. *Artichoke*].

***ARYAN**, adj. Skt. *Ārya*, 'noble.' A term frequently used to include all the races (Indo-Persic, Greek, Roman, Celtic, Sclavonic, &c.) which speak languages belonging to the same family as Sanskrit. Much vogue was given to the term by Pictet's publication of *Les Origines Indo-Européennes, ou les Aryas Primitifs* (Paris, 1859), and this writer seems almost to claim the name in this sense as his own (see quotation below). But it was in use long before the date of his book. Our first quotation is from Ritter, and there it has hardly reached the full extent of application. Ritter seems to have derived the use in this passage from Lassen's *Pentapotamia*. The word has in great measure superseded the older term *Indo-Germanic*, proposed by F. Schlegel at the beginning of the last century. The latter is, however, still sometimes used, and M. Hovelacque, especially, prefers it. We may observe here that the connection which evidently exists between the several languages classed together as Aryan cannot be regarded, as it was formerly, as warranting an assumption of identity of race in all the peoples who speak them.

It may be noted as curious that among the Javanese (a people so remote in blood from what we understand by Aryan), the word *ārya* is commonly used as an honorary prefix to the names of men of rank; a survival of the ancient Hindu influence on the civilisation of the island.

The earliest use of *Aryan* in an ethnic sense is in the Inscription on the tomb of Darius, in which the king calls himself an Aryan, and of Aryan descent, whilst Ormuzd is in the Median version styled, 'God of the Aryans'

B.C. c. 486.—"*Adam Dáryavush Khsháyathiya vazarka ... Pársa, Pársahiyá putra,* **Ariya**, **Ariya** *chitra*." *i.e.* "I (am) Darius, the Great King, the King of Kings, the King of all inhabited countries, the King of this great Earth far and near, the son of Hystaspes, an Achaemenian, a Persian, an **Arian**, of *Arian* descent."—In *Rawlinson's Herodotus*, 3rd ed., iv. 250.

"These Medes were called anciently by all people **Arians**, but when Medêa, the Colchian, came to them from Athens, they changed their name."—*Herodot.*, vii. 62 (Rawlins).

1835.—"Those eastern and proper Indians, whose territory, however, Alexander never touched by a long way, call themselves in the most ancient period *Arians* (**Arier**) (*Manu*, ii. 22, x. 45), a name coinciding with that of the ancient Medes."—*Ritter*, v. 458.

1838.—See also *Ritter*, viii. 17 seqq.; and Potto's art. in *Ersch & Grueber's Encyc.*, ii. 18, 46.

1850.—"The **Aryan** tribes in conquering India, urged by the Brahmans, made war against the Turanian demon-worship, but not always with complete success."—*Dr. J. Wilson*, in *Life*, 450.

1851.—"We must request the patience of our readers whilst we give a short outline of the component members of the great **Arian** family. The first is the Sanskrit. ... The second branch of the Arian family is the Persian. ... There are other scions of the Arian stock which struck root in the soil of Asia, before the Arians reached the shores of Europe ..."—(*Prof. Max Müller*) *Edinburgh Review*, Oct. 1851, pp. 312–313.

1853.—"Sur les sept premières civilisations, qui sont celles de l'ancien monde, six appartiennent, en partie au moins, à la race **ariane**."—*Gobineau, De l'Inégalité des Races Humaines*, i. 364.

1855.—"I believe that all who have lived in India will bear testimony ... that to natives of India, of whatever class or caste, Mussulman, Hindoo, or Parsee, '**Aryan** or Tamulian,' unless they have had a special training, our European paintings, prints, drawings, and photographs, plain or coloured, if they are landscapes, are absolutely unintelligible."—*Yule, Mission to Ava*, 59 (publ. 1858).

1858.—"The **Aryan** tribes—for that is the name they gave themselves, both in their old and new homes—brought with them institutions of a simplicity almost primitive."—*Whitney, Or. & Ling. Studies*, ii. 5.

1861.—"Latin, again, with Greek, and the Celtic, the Teutonic, and Slavonic languages, together likewise with the ancient dialects of India and Persia, must have sprung from an earlier language, the mother of the whole Indo-European or **Aryan** family of speech."—*Prof. Max Müller, Lectures*, 1st Ser. 32.

We also find the verb *Aryanize:*

1858.—"Thus all India was brought under the sway, physical or intellectual and moral, of the alien race; it was thoroughly **Aryanized**."—*Whitney, u. s.* 7.

ATOLL, s. A group of coral islands forming a ring or chaplet, sometimes of many miles in diameter, inclosing a space of comparatively shallow water, each of the islands being on the same type as the *atoll*. We derive the expression from the Maldive islands, which are the typical examples of this structure, and where the form of the word is *atoḷu*. [P. de Laval (Hak. Soc. i. 93) states that the provinces in the Maldives were known as *Atollon*.] It is probably connected with the Singhalese *ätul*, 'inside'; [or *etula*, as Mr Gray (*P. de Laval*, Hak. Soc. i. 94) writes the word. The *Mad. Admin. Man.* in the *Glossary* gives Malayāl. *attālam*, 'a sinking reef']. The term was made a scientific one by Darwin in his publication on Coral Reefs (see below), but our second quotation shows that it had been generalised at an earlier date.

c. 1610.—"Estant au milieu d'vn **Atollon**, vous voyez autour de vous ce grand banc de pierre que jay dit, qui environne et qui defend les isles contre l'impetuosité de la mer."—*Pyrard de Laval*, i. 71 (ed. 1679); [Hak. Soc. i. 94].

1732.—"**Atollon**, a name applied to such a place in the sea as exhibits a heap of little islands lying close together, and almost hanging on to each other."—*Zeidler's* (German) *Universal Lexicon*, s.v.

1842.—"I have invariably used in this volume the term **atoll**, which is the name given to these circular groups of coral islets by their inhabitants in the Indian Ocean, and is synonymous with 'lagoon-island.'"—*Darwin, The Structure, &c., of Coral Reefs*, 2.

AURUNG, s. H. from P. *aurang*, 'a place where goods are manufactured, a depôt for such goods.' During the Company's trading days this term was applied to their factories for the purchase, on advances, of native piece-goods, &c.

1778.—"... Gentoo-factors in their own pay to provide the investments at the different **Aurungs** or cloth markets in the province."—*Orme*, ii. 51.

1789.—"I doubt, however, very much whether he has had sufficient experience in the commercial line to enable him to manage so difficult and so important an **aurung** as Luckipore, which is almost the only one of any magnitude which supplies the species of coarse cloths which do not interfere with the British manufacture."—*Cornwallis*. i. 435.

AVA, n.p. The name of the city which was for several centuries the capital of the Burmese Empire, and was applied often to that State itself. This name is borrowed, according to Crawfurd, from the form *Awa* or *Awak* used by the Malays. The proper Burmese form was *Eng-wa*, or 'the Lake-Mouth,' because the city was built near the opening of a lagoon into the Irawadi; but this was called, even by the Burmese, more popularly *A-wā*, 'The Mouth.' The city was founded A.D. 1364. The first European occurrence of the name, so far as we know, is (c. 1440) in the narrative of Nicolo Conti, and it appears again (no doubt from Conti's information) in the great World-Map of Fra Mauro at Venice (1459).

c. 1430.—"Having sailed up this river for the space of a month he arrived at a city more noble than all the others, called **Ava**, and the circumference of which is 15 miles."—*Conti*, in *India in the XVth Cent.* 11.

c. 1490.—"The country (Pegu) is distant 15 days' journey by land from another called **Ava** in which grow rubies and many other precious stones."—*Hier. di Sto. Stefano*, u. s. p. 6.

1516.—"Inland beyond this Kingdom of Pegu ... there is another Kingdom of Gentiles which has a King who resides in a very great and opulent city called **Ava**, 8 days' journey from the sea; a place of rich merchants, in which there is a great trade of jewels, rubies, and spinel-rubies, which are gathered in this Kingdom."—*Barbosa*, 186.

c. 1610.—"... The King of **Ová** having already sent much people, with cavalry, to relieve Porão (Prome), which marches with the Pozão (?) and city of **Ová** or **Anvá**, (which means 'surrounded on all sides with streams') ..."—*Antonio Bocarro*, *Decada*, 150.

1726.—"The city **Ava** is surpassing great. ... One may not travel by land to Ava, both because this is permitted by the Emperor to none but envoys, on account of the Rubies on the way, and also because it is a very perilous journey on account of the tigers."—*Valentijn*, *V.* (*Chorom.*) 127.

AVATAR, s. Skt. *Avatāra*, an incarnation on earth of a divine Being. This word first appears in Baldaeus (1672) in the form **Autaar** (*Afgoderye*, p. 52), which in the German version generally quoted in this book takes the corrupter shape of *Altar*.

[c. 1590.—"In the city of Sambal is a temple called Hari Mandal (the temple of Vishnu) belonging to a Brahman, from among whose descendants the tenth **avatar** will appear at this spot."—*Āīn*, tr. Jarrett, ii. 281.].

1672.—"Bey den Benjanen haben auch diese zehen Verwandlungen den Namen daas sie **Altare** heissen, und also hat Mats *Altar* als dieser erste, gewähret 2500 Jahr."—*Baldaeus*, 472.

1784.—"The ten **Avatárs** or descents of the deity, in his capacity of Preserver."—*Sir W. Jones*, in *Asiat. Res.* (reprint) i. 234.

1812.—"The **Awatars** of Vishnu, by which are meant his descents upon earth, are usually counted ten. ..."—*Maria Graham*, 49.

1821.—"The Irish **Avatar**."—*Byron*.

1845.—"In Vishnu-land what **Avatar**?"—*Browning*, *Dramatic Romances*, *Works*, ed. 1870, iv. pp. 209, 210.

1872.—"... all which cannot blind us to the fact that the Master is merely another **avatar** of Dr Holmes himself."—*Sat. Review*, Dec. 14, p. 768.

1873.—"He ... builds up a curious History of Spiritualism, according to which all matter is mediately or immediately the **avatar** of some Intelligence, not necessarily the highest."—*Academy*, May 15th, 172*b*.

1875.—"Balzac's **avatars** were a hundred-fold as numerous as those of Vishnu."—*Ibid.*, April 24th, p. 421.

AYAH, s. A native lady's-maid or nurse-maid. The word has been adopted into most of the Indian vernaculars in the forms *āya* or *āyā*, but it is really Portuguese (f. **aia**, 'a nurse, or governess'; m. *aio*, 'the governor of a young noble'). [These again have been connected with L. Latin *aidus*, Fr. *aide*, 'a helper.']

1779.—"I was sitting in my own house in the compound, when the **iya** came down and told me that her mistress wanted a candle."

—*Kitmutgar's evidence*, in the case of *Grand v. Francis*, Ext. in *Echoes of Old Calcutta*, 225.

1782.—(A Table of Wages):—
"*Consumah* ... 10 (rupees a month).
* * * * * *
Eyah ... 5."—*India Gazette*, Oct. 12.

1810.—"The female who attends a lady while she is dressing, etc., is called an **Ayah**."—*Williamson, V. M.* i. 337.

1826.—"The lieutenant's visits were now less frequent than usual; one day, however, he came ... and on leaving the house I observed him slip something, which I doubted not was money, into the hand of the **Ayah**, or serving woman, of Jane."—*Pandurang Hari*, 71; [ed. 1873, i. 99].

1842.—"Here (at Simla) there is a great preponderence of Mahometans. I am told that the guns produced absolute consternation, visible in their countenances. One **Ayah** threw herself upon the ground in an agony of despair. ... I fired 42 guns for Ghuzni and Cabul; the 22nd (42nd?) gun—which announced that all was finished—was what overcame the Mahometans."—*Lord Ellenborough*, in *Indian Administration* 295. This stuff was written to the great Duke of Wellington!

1873.—"The white-robed **ayah** flits in and out of the tents, finding a home for our various possessions, and thither we soon retire."—*Fraser's Mag.*, June, i. 99.

1879.—"He was exceedingly fond of his two children, and got for them servants; a man to cook their dinner, and an **ayah** to take care of them."—*Miss Stokes, Indian Fairy Tales*, 7.

B

BABA, s. This is the word usually applied in Anglo-Indian families, by both Europeans and natives, to the children—often in the plural form, *bābā lōg* (*lōg* = 'folk'). The word is not used by the natives among themselves in the same way, at least not habitually: and it would seem as if our word *baby* had influenced the use. The word *bābā* is properly Turki = 'father'; sometimes used to a child as a term of endearment (or forming part of such a term, as in the P. *Bābājān*, 'Life of your Father'). Compare the Russian use of *batushka*. [*Bābājī* is a common form of address to a Fakīr, usually a member of one of the Musulman sects. And hence it is used generally as a title of respect.]

[1685.—"A Letter from the Pettepolle **Bobba**."—*Pringle, Diary, Fort St. Geo.* iv. 92.]

1826.—"I reached the hut of a Gossein ... and reluctantly tapped at the wicket, calling, 'O **Baba**, O Maharaj.'"—*Pandurang Hari* [ed. 1873, i. 76].

[1880.—"While **Sunny Baba** is at large, and might at any time make a raid on Mamma, who is dozing over a novel on the spider chair near the mouth of the thermantidote, the Ayah and Bearer dare not leave their charge."—*Aberigh-Mackay, Twenty-one Days*, p. 94.]

***BABOO**, s. Beng. and H. *Bābū* [Skt. *vapra*, 'a father']. Properly a term of respect attached to a name, like *Master* or *Mr.*, and formerly in some parts of Hindustan applied to certain persons of distinction. Its application as a term of respect is now almost or altogether confined to Lower Bengal (though C. P. Brown states that it is also used in S. India for 'Sir, My lord, your Honour'). In Bengal and elsewhere, among Anglo-Indians, it is often used with a slight savour of disparagement, as characterizing a superficially cultivated, but too often effeminate, Bengali. And from the extensive employment of the class, to which the term was applied as a title, in the capacity of clerks in English offices, the word has come often to signify 'a native clerk who writes English.'

1781.—"I said ... From my youth to this day I am a servant to the English. I have never gone to any Rajahs or **Bauboos** nor will I go to them."—Depn. of *Dooud Sing*, Commandant. In *Narr. of Insurn. at Banaras* in 1781. Calc. 1782. Reprinted at Roorkee, 1853. App., p. 165.

1782.—"*Cantoo* **Baboo**" appears as a subscriber to a famine fund at Madras for 200 Sicca Rupees.—*India Gazette*, Oct. 12.

1791.
"Here Edmund was making a monstrous ado,
About some bloody Letter and Conta
Bah-Booh."[1]
Letters of Simkin the Second, 147.

1803.—"... Calling on Mr. Neave I found there **Baboo** Dheep Narrain, brother to Oodit Narrain, Rajah at Benares."—*Lord Valentia's Travels*, i. 112.

1824.—"... the immense convent-like mansion of some of the more wealthy **Baboos** ..."—*Heber*, i. 31, ed. 1844.

1834.—"The **Baboo** and other Tales, descriptive of Society in India."—Smith & Elder, London. (By Augustus Prinsep.)

1850.—"If instruction were sought for from them (the Mohammedan historians) we should no longer hear bombastic **Baboos**, enjoying under our Government the highest degree of

1 ["Mr Burke's method of pronouncing it."]

personal liberty ... rave about patriotism, and the degradation of their present position."—*Sir H. M. Elliot*, Orig. Preface to *Mahom. Historians of India*, in Dowson's ed., I. xxii.

c. 1866.

"But I'd sooner be robbed by a tall man who
showed me a yard of steel,
Than be fleeced by a sneaking **Baboo**, with a
peon and badge at his heel."

Sir A. C. Lyall, The Old Pindaree.

1873.—"The pliable, plastic, receptive **Baboo** of Bengal eagerly avails himself of this system (of English education) partly from a servile wish to please the *Sahib logue*, and partly from a desire to obtain a Government appointment."—*Fraser's Mag.*, August, 209.

[1880.—"English officers who have become de-Europeanised from long residence among undomesticated natives. ... Such officials are what Lord Lytton calls White **Baboos**."—*Aberigh-Mackay, Twenty-one Days*, p. 104.]

N.B.—In Java and the further East *bābū* means a nurse or female servant (Javanese word).

BAHAUDUR, s. H. *Bahādur*, 'a hero, or champion.' It is a title affixed commonly to the names of European officers in Indian documents, or when spoken of ceremoniously by natives (*e.g.* "Jones Sāhib *Bahādur*"), in which use it may be compared with "the gallant officer" of Parliamentary courtesy, or the *Illustrissimo Signore* of the Italians. It was conferred as a title of honour by the Great Mogul and by other native princes [while in Persia it was often applied to slaves (Burton, *Ar. Nights*, iii. 114)]. Thus it was particularly affected to the end of his life by Hyder Ali, to whom it had been given by the Raja of Mysore (see quotation from John Lindsay below [and Wilks, *Mysoor*, Madras reprint, i. 280]). *Bahādur* and *Sirdār Bahādur* are also the official titles of members of the 2nd and 1st classes respectively of the Order of British India, established for native officers of the army in 1837. [The title of *Rāē Bahādur* is also conferred upon Hindu civil officers.]

As conferred by the Court of Delhi the usual gradation of titles was (ascending):—1. *Bahādur*; 2. *Bahādur Jang*; 3. *Bahādur ud-Daulah*; 4. *Bahādur ul-mulk*. At Hyderabad they had also *Bahādur ul-Umrā* (*Kirkpatrick*, in *Tippoo's Letters*, 354). [Many such titles of Europeans will be found in *North Indian N. & Q.*, i. 35, 143, 179; iv. 17.]

In Anglo-Indian colloquial parlance the word denotes a haughty or pompous personage, exercising his brief authority with a strong sense of his own importance; a *don* rather than a swaggerer. Thackeray, who derived from his Indian birth and connections a humorous felicity in the use of Anglo-Indian expressions, has not omitted this serviceable word. In that brilliant burlesque, the *Memoirs of Major Gahagan*, we have the Mahratta traitor *Bobachee Bahauder*. It is said also that Mr Canning's malicious wit bestowed on Sir John Malcolm, who was not less great as a talker than as a soldier and statesman, the title, not included in the Great Mogul's repertory, of *Bahauder Jaw*.[1]

Bahādur is one of the terms which the hosts of Chingiz Khan brought with them from the Mongol Steppes. In the Mongol genealogies we find Yesugai *Bahādur*, the father of Chingiz, and many more. Subutai *Bahādur*, one of the great soldiers of the Mongol host, twice led it to the conquest of Southern Russia, twice to that of Northern China. In Sanang Setzen's poetical annals of the Mongols, as rendered by I. J. Schmidt, the word is written *Baghatur*, whence in Russian *Bogatir* still survives as a memento probably of the Tartar domination, meaning 'a hero or champion.' It occurs often in the old Russian epic ballads in this sense; and is also applied to Samson of the Bible. It occurs in a Russian chronicler as early as 1240, but in application to Mongol leaders. In Polish it is found as *Bohatyr*, and in Hungarian as *Bátor*,—this last being in fact the popular Mongol pronunciation of *Baghatur*. In Turki also this elision of the guttural extends to the spelling, and the word becomes *Bātur*, as we find it in the Dicts. of Vambéry and Pavet de Courteille. In Manchu also the word takes the form of *Baturu*, expressed in Chinese characters as *Pa-tu-lu*;[2] the Kirghiz has it as *Batyr*; the Altai-Tataric as *Paattyr*, and the other dialects even as *Magathyr*. But the singular history of the word is not yet entirely told. Benfey has suggested that the word

1 At Lord Wellesley's table, Major Malcolm mentioned as a notable fact that he and three of his brothers had once met together in India. "Impossible, Malcolm, quite impossible!" said the Governor-General. Malcolm persisted. "No, no," said Lord Wellesley, "if four Malcolms had met, we should have heard the noise all over India!"

2 See *Chinese Recorder*, 1876, vii. 324, and *Kovalafski's Mongol Dict.* No. 1058.

originated in Skt. *bhaga-dhara* ('happiness-possessing').[1] But the late lamented Prof. A. Schiefner, who favoured us with a note on the subject, was strongly of opinion that the word was rather a corruption "through dissimulation of the consonant," of the Zend *bagha-puthra* 'Son of God,' and thus but another form of the famous term **Faghfūr**, by which the old Persians rendered the Chinese *Tien-tsz* ('Son of Heaven'), applying it to the Emperor of China.

1280–90.—In an eccentric Persian poem purposely stuffed with Mongol expressions, written by Purbahā Jāmī in praise of Arghūn Khān of Persia, of which Hammer has given a German translation, we have the following:—

"The Great Kaan names thee his *Ulugh-Bitekchī* [Great Secretary],
Seeing thou art *bitekchi* and **Behādir** to boot;
O Well-beloved, the *yarlīgh* [rescript] that thou dost issue is obeyed
By Turk and Mongol, by Persian, Greek, and Barbarian!"

Gesch. der Gold. Horde, 461.

c. 1400.—"I ordained that every Ameer who should reduce a Kingdom, or defeat an army, should be exalted by three things: by a title of honour, by the *Tugh* [Yak's tail standard], and by the *Nakkára* [great kettle drum]; and should be dignified by the title of **Bahaudur**."—*Timour's Institutes*, 283; see also 291–293.

1404.—"E elles le dixeron q̃ aquel era uno de los valiẽtes e **Bahadures** q'en el linage del Señor auia."—*Clavijo*, § lxxxix.

"E el home q̃ este haze e mas vino beue dizen que es **Bahadur**, que dizen elles por homem rezio."—Do. § cxii.

1407.—"The Prince mounted, escorted by a troop of **Bahadurs**, who were always about his person."—*Abdurrazāk's Hist.* in *Not. et Ext.* xiv. 126.

1536.—(As a proper name.) "Itaq̃ ille potentissimus Rex **Badur**, Indiae universae terror, a quo nonulli regnũ Pori maximi quõdam regis teneri affirmant. ..."—Letter from *John III. of Portugal* to Pope Paul III.

Hardly any native name occurs more frequently in the Portuguese Hist. of India than this of *Badur*—viz. Bahādur Shāh, the warlike and powerful king of Guzerat (1526–37), killed in a fray which closed an interview with the Viceroy, Nuno da Cunha, at Diu.

1754.—"The *Kirgeese Tartars* ... are divided into three *Hordas*, under the Government of a *Khan*. That part which borders on the Russian dominions was under the authority of *Jean Beek*, whose name on all occasions was honoured with the title of **Bater**."—*Hanway*, i. 239. The name *Jean Beek* is probably *Janibek*, a name which one finds among the hordes as far back as the early part of the 14th century (see *Ibn Batuta*, ii. 397).

1759.—"From Shah Alum **Bahadre**, son of Alum Guire, the Great Mogul, and successor of the Empire, to Colonel Sabut Jung **Bahadre**" (*i.e.* Clive).—Letter in *Long*, p. 163.

We have said that the title *Behauder* (*Bahādur*) was one by which Hyder Ali of Mysore was commonly known in his day. Thus in the two next quotations:

1781.—"Sheikh Hussein upon the guard tells me that our army has beat the **Behauder** [*i.e.* Hyder Ali], and that peace was making. Another sepoy in the afternoon tells us that the **Behauder** had destroyed our army, and was besieging Madras."—*Captivity of Hon. John Lindsay*, in *Lives of the Lindsays*, iii. 296.

1800.—"One lac of **Behaudry** pagodas."—*Wellington*, i. 148.

1801.—"Thomas, who was much in liquor, now turned round to his *sowars*, and said—'Could any one have stopped Sahib **Bahaudoor** at this gate but one month ago?' 'No, no,' replied they; on which——"—*Skinner, Mil. Mem.* i. 236.

1872.—"... the word '**Bahádur**' ... (at the Mogul's Court) ... was only used as an epithet. Ahmed Shah used it as a title and ordered his name to be read in the Friday prayer as 'Mujahid ud dín Muhammad Abú naçr Ahmad Sháh **Bahádur**. Hence also '*Kampaní* **Bahadur**,' the name by which the E. I. Company is still known in India. The modern 'Khan **Bahádur**' is, in Bengal, by permission assumed by Muhammedan Deputy Magistrates, whilst Hindu Deputy Magistrates assume 'Rái **Bahádur**'; it stands, of course, for 'Khán-i-**Bahádur**,' 'the courageous Khán.' The compound, however, is a modern abnormal one; for 'Khán' was conferred by the Dihli Emperors, and so also 'Bahádur' and 'Bahádur Khán,' but not 'Khán Bahádur.'"—*Prof. Blochmann*, in *Ind. Antiquary*, i. 261.

1876.—"Reverencing at the same time bravery, dash, and boldness, and loving their freedom, they (the Kirghiz) were always ready to follow the standard of any **batyr**, or hero, ... who might appear on the stage."—*Schuyler's Turkistan*, i. 33.

1878.—"Peacock feathers for some of the subordinate officers, a yellow jacket for the successful general, and the bestowal of the Manchoo title of **Baturu**, or 'Brave,' on some of the most distinguished brigadiers, are probably all the honours which await the return of

1 *Orient und Occident*, i. 137.

a triumphal army. The reward which fell to the share of 'Chinese Gordon' for the part he took in the suppression of the Taiping rebellion was a yellow jacket, and the title of *Baturu* has lately been bestowed on Mr Mesny for years of faithful service against the rebels in the province of Kweichow."—*Saturday Rev.*, Aug. 10, p. 182.

"There is nothing of the great **bahawder** about him."—*Athenaeum*, No. 2670, p. 851.

1879.—"This strictly prohibitive Proclamation is issued by the Provincial Administrative Board of Likim ... and Chang, Brevet-Provincial Judge, chief of the Foochow Likim Central Office, Taot'ai for special service, and **Bat'uru** with the title of 'Awe-inspiring Brave'"—Transl. of *Proclamation against the cultivation of the Poppy* in Foochow, July 1879.

BALSORA, BUSSORA, &c., n.p. These old forms used to be familiar from their use in the popular version of the Arabian Nights after Galland. The place is the sea-port city of *Basra* at the mouth of the Shat-al-'Arab, or United Euphrates and Tigris. [Burton (*Ar. Nights*, x. 1) writes *Bassorah.*]

1298.—"There is also on the river as you go from Baudas to Kisi, a great city called **Bastra** surrounded by woods in which grow the best dates in the world."—*Marco Polo*, Bk. i. ch. 6.

c. 1580.—"**Balsara,** altrimente detta **Bassora,** è una città posta nell' Arabia, la quale al presente e signoreggiata dal Turco ... è città di gran negocio di spetiarie, di droghe, e altre merci che uengono di Ormus; è abondante di dattoli, risi, e grani."—*Balbi*, f. 32*f.*

[1598.—"The town of **Balsora**; also **Bassora.**"—*Linschoten*, Hak. Soc. i. 45.]

1671.—

"From Atropatia and the neighbouring plains
Of Adiabene, Media, and the south
Of Susiana to **Balsara's** Haven ..."
Paradise Regained, iii.

1747.—"He (the Prest. of Bombay) further advises us that they have wrote our Honble. Masters of the Loss of Madrass by way of **Bussero**, the 7th of November."—*Ft. St. David Consn.*, 8th January 1746–7. MS. in India Office.

BALTY, s. **H.** *bāltī*, 'a bucket,' [which Platts very improbably connects with Skt. *vāri*, 'water'], is the Port. *balde.*

BÁLWAR, s. This is the native servant's form of 'barber,' shaped by the 'striving after meaning' as *bālwār*, for *bālwālā*, *i.e.* 'capillarius,' 'hair-man.' It often takes the further form **bāl-būr**, another factitious hybrid, shaped by P. *būrīdan*, 'to cut,' quasi 'hair-cutter.' But though now obsolete, there was also (see both *Meninski* and *Vullers* s.v.) a Persian word *bărbăr*, for a barber or surgeon, from which came this Turkish term "Le *Berber*-bachi, qui fait la barbe au Pacha," which we find (c. 1674) in the Appendix to the journal of Antoine Galland, pubd. at Paris, 1881 (ii. 190). It looks as if this must have been an early loan from Europe.

***BAMBOO,** s. Applied to many gigantic grasses, of which *Bambusa arundinacea* and *B. vulgaris* are the most commonly cultivated; but there are many other species of the same and allied genera in use; natives of tropical Asia, Africa, and America. This word, one of the commonest in Anglo-Indian daily use, and thoroughly naturalised in English, is of exceedingly obscure origin. According to Wilson it is Canarese *bănbŭ* [or as the *Madras Admin. Man.* (*Gloss.* s.v.) writes it, *bombu*, which is said to be "onomatopaeic from the crackling and explosions when they burn"]. Marsden inserts it in his dictionary as good Malay. Crawfurd says it is certainly used on the west coast of Sumatra as a native word, but that it is elsewhere unknown to the Malay languages. The usual Malay word is *buluh*. He thinks it more likely to have found its way into English from Sumatra than from Canara. But there is evidence enough of its familiarity among the Portuguese before the end of the 16th century to indicate the probability that we adopted the word, like so many others, through them. We believe that the correct Canarese word is *baṇwu*. In the 16th century the form in the Concan appears to have been *mambu*, or at least it was so represented by the Portuguese. Rumphius seems to suggest a quaint *onomatopoeia:* "vehementissimos edunt ictus et sonitus, quum incendio comburuntur, quando notum ejus nomen *Bambu, Bambu*, facile exauditur."—(*Herb. Amb.* iv. 17.) [Mr. Skeat writes: "Although *buluh* is the standard Malay, and *bambu* apparently introduced, I think *bambu* is the form used in the low Javanese vernacular, which is quite a different language from high Javanese. Even in low Javanese, however, it may be a borrowed word. It looks curiously like a trade corruption of the common Malay word *samambu*, which means the well-known 'Malacca cane,' both the bamboo and the Malacca cane being articles of export. Klinkert says that the *samambu* is a kind of rattan, which was used as a walking-stick, and which was called the Malacca cane by the English. This Malacca cane and the rattan 'bamboo cane' referred to by Sir H. Yule must surely be identical. The fuller Malay name is actually *rotan samambu*, which is given as the equivalent of *Calamus Scipionum*, Lour. by Mr. Ridley in his Plant List (*J.R.A.S.*, July 1897).]

The term applied to *ṭābāshīr*, a siliceous concretion in the bamboo, in our first quotation seems to show that *bambu* or *mambu* was one of the words which the Portuguese inherited from an earlier use by Persian or Arab traders. But we have not been successful in finding other proof of this. With reference to *sakkar-mambu* Ritter says: "That this drug (*Tabashir*), as a product of the bamboo-cane, is to this day known in India by the name of *Sacar Mambu* is a thing which no one needs to be told" (ix. 334). But in fact the name seems now entirely unknown.

It is possible that the Canarese word is a vernacular corruption, or development, of the Skt. *vaṇśa* [or *vambha*], from the former of which comes the H. *bāṇs*. *Bamboo* does not occur, so far as we can find, in any of the *earlier* 16th-century books, which employ *canna* or the like.

In England the term *bamboo-cane* is habitually applied to a kind of walking-stick, which is formed not from any bamboo but from a species of *rattan*. It may be noted that some 30 to 35 years ago there existed along the high road between Putney Station and West Hill a garden fence of bamboos of considerable extent; it often attracted the attention of one of the present writers.

1563.—"The people from whom it (*tabashir*) is got call it *sacar*-**mambum** ... because the canes of that plant are called by the Indians **mambu**."—*Garcia*, f. 194.

1578.—"Some of these (canes), especially in Malabar, are found so large that the people make use of them as boats (*embarcaciones*) not opening them out, but cutting one of the canes right across and using the natural knots to stop the ends, and so a couple of naked blacks go upon it ... each of them at his own end of the **mambu** [in orig. *mãbu*] (so they call it), being provided with two paddles, one in each hand ... and so upon a cane of this kind the folk pass across, and sitting with their legs clinging naked."—*C. Acosta, Tructado*, 296.

Again:

"... and many people on that river (of Cranganor) make use of these canes in place of boats, to be safe from the numerous Crocodiles or *Caymoins* (as they call them) which are in the river (which are in fact great and ferocious lizards)" [*lagartos*].—*Ibid.* 297.

These passages are curious as explaining, if they hardly justify, Ctesias, in what we have regarded as one of his greatest bounces, viz. his story of Indian canes big enough to be used as boats.

1586.—"All the houses are made of canes, which they call **Bambos**, and bee covered with Strawe."—*Fitch*, in *Hakl.* ii. 391.

1598.—"... a thicke reede as big as a man's legge, which is called **Bambus**."—*Linschoten*, 56; [Hak. Soc. i. 195].

1608.—"Iava multas producit arundines grossas, quas **Manbu** vocant."—*Prima Pars Desc. Itin. Naralis in Indiam* (Houtman's *Voyage*), p. 36.

c. 1610.—"Les Portugais et les Indiens ne se seruent point d'autres bastons pour porter leurs palanquins ou litieres. Ils l'appellent partout **Bambou**."—*Pyrard*, i. 237; [Hak. Soc. i. 329].

1615.—"These two kings (of Camboja and Siam) have neyther Horses, nor any fiery Instruments: but make use only of bowes, and a certaine kind of pike, made of a knottie wood like Canes, called **Bambuc**, which is exceeding strong, though pliant and supple for vse."—*De Monfart*, 33.

1621.—"These Forts will better appeare by the Draught thereof, herewith sent to your Worships, inclosed in a **Bamboo**."—Letter in *Purchas*, i. 699.

1623.—"Among the other trees there was an immense quantity of **bambù**, or very large Indian canes, and all clothed and covered with pretty green foliage that went creeping up them."—*P. della Valle*, ii. 640; [Hak. Soc. ii. 220].

c. 1666.—"Cette machine est suspendue à une longue barre que l'on appelle **Pambou**."—*Thevenot*, v. 162. (This spelling recurs throughout a chapter describing palankins, though elsewhere the traveller writes *bambou*.)

1673.—"A **Bambo**, which is a long hollow cane."—*Fryer*, 34.

1727.—"The City (Ava) tho' great and populous, is only built of **Bambou** canes."—*A. Hamilton*, ii. 47.

1855.—"When I speak of bamboo huts, I mean to say that post and walls, wall-plates and rafters, floor and thatch and the withes that bind them, are all of bamboo. In fact it might almost be said that among the Indo-Chinese nations the staff of life is a **Bamboo**. Scaffolding and ladders, landing-jetties, fishing apparatus, irrigation-wheels and scoops, oars, masts and yards, spears and arrows, hats and helmets, bow, bow-string and quiver, oil-cans, water-stoups and cooking-pots, pipe-sticks, conduits, clothes-boxes, pan boxes, dinner trays, pickles, preserves, and melodious musical instruments, torches, footballs, cordage, bellows, mats, paper, these are but a few of the articles that are made from the bamboo."—*Yule, Mission to Ava*, p. 153. To these may be added, from a cursory inspection of a collection in one of the museums at Kew, combs, mugs, sun-blinds, cages, grotesque carvings, brushes, fans, shirts, sails, teapots, pipes and harps.

Bamboos are sometimes popularly distinguished (after a native idiom) as male and female; the latter embracing all the common species with hollow stems, the former title being applied to a certain kind (in fact, a sp. of a distinct genus, *Dendrocalamus strictus*), which has a solid or nearly solid core, and is much used for bludgeons (see LATTEE) and spearshafts. It is remarkable that this popular distinction by sex was known to Ctesias (c. B.C. 400) who says that the Indian reeds were divided into male and female, the male having no ἐντερώνην.

One of the present writers has seen (and partaken of) rice cooked in a joint of bamboo, among the Khyens, a hill-people of Arakan. And Mr Markham mentions the same practice as prevalent among the Chunchos and savage aborigines on the eastern slopes of the Andes (*J. R. Geog. Soc.* xxv. 155). An endeavour was made in Pegu in 1855 to procure the largest obtainable bamboo. It was a little over 10 inches in diameter. But Clusius states that he had seen two great specimens in the University at Leyden, 30 feet long and from 14 to 16 inches in diameter. And E. Haeckel, in his *Visit to Ceylon* (1882), speaks of bamboo-stems at Peridenia, "each from a foot to two feet thick." We can obtain no corroboration of anything approaching 2 feet.—[See Gray's note on *Pyrard*, Hak. Soc. i. 330.]

***BANCHOOT, BETEECHOOT**, ss. Terms of abuse, which we should hesitate to print if their odious meaning were not obscure "to the general." If it were known to the Englishmen who sometimes use the words, we believe there are few who would not shrink from such brutality. Somewhat similar in character seem the words which Saul in his rage flings at his noble son (1 Sam. xx. 30).

1638.—"L'on nous monstra à vne demy lieue de la ville vn sepulchre, qu'ils appellent **Bety-chuit**, c'est à dire la vergogne de la fille decouverte."—*Mandelslo*, Paris, 1659, 142. See also *Valentijn*, iv. 157.

There is a handsome tomb and mosque to the N. of Ahmedabad, erected by Hajji Malik Bahā-ud-dīn, a wazīr of Sultan Mohammed Bigara, in memory of his wife *Bībī Achut* or *Achhūt;* and probably the vile story to which the 17th-century travellers refer is founded only on a vulgar misrepresentation of this name.

1648.—"**Bety-chuit**; dat is (onder eerbredinge gesproocken) in onse tale te seggen, u Dochters Schaemelheyt."—*Van Twist*, 16.

1792.—"The officer (of Tippoo's troops) who led, on being challenged in Moors answered (*Agari que logue*), 'We belong to the advance'—the title of Lally's brigade, supposing the people he saw to be their own Europeans, whose uniform also is red; but soon discovering his mistake the commandant called out (*Feringhy* **Banchoot**!—*chelow*) 'they are the rascally English! Make off'; in which he set the corps a ready example."—*Dirom's Narrative*, 147.

BANCOCK, n.p. The modern capital of Siam, properly *Bang-kok;* see explanation by Bp. Pallegoix in quotation. It had been the site of forts erected on the ascent of the Menam to the old capital Ayuthia, by Constantine Phaulcon in 1675; here the modern city was established as the seat of government in 1767, after the capture of Ayuthia by the Burmese in that year. It is uncertain if the first quotation refer to **Bancock**.

1552.—"... and **Bamplacot**, which stands at the mouth of the Menam."—*Barros*, I. ix. 1.

1611.—"They had arrived in the Road of *Syam* the fifteenth of August, and cast Anchor at three fathome high water. ... The Towne lyeth some thirtie leagues vp along the Riuer, whither they sent newes of their arrivall. The Sabander (see SHAH-BUNDER) and the Governor of **Mancock** (a place scituated by the Riuer), came backe with the Messengers to receiue his Majesties Letters, but chiefly for the presents expected."—*P. Williamson Floris*, in *Purchas*, i. 321.

1727.—The Ship arrived at **Bencock**, a Castle about half-way up, where it is customary for all Ships to put their Guns ashore."—*A. Hamilton*, i. 363.

1850.—"Civitas regia tria habet nomina: ... *ban măkōk*, per contractionem **Bangkōk**, pagūs oleastrorum, est nomen primitivum quod hodie etiam vulgo usurpatur."—*Pallegoix, Gram. Linguae Thai.*, Bangkok, 1850, p. 167.

***BANDANNA**, s. This term is properly applied to the rich yellow or red silk handkerchief, with diamond spots left white by pressure applied to prevent their receiving the dye. The etymology may be gathered from Shakespear's Dict., which gives "*Bāndhnū:* 1. A mode of dyeing in which the cloth is tied in different places, to prevent the parts tied from receiving the dye; ... 3. A kind of silk cloth" A class or caste in Guzerat who do this kind of preparation for dyeing are called *Bandhārā* (*Drummond*). [Such handkerchiefs are known in S. India as **Pulicat** handkerchiefs. Cloth dyed in this way is in Upper India known as *Chūnrī*. A full account of the process will be found in *Journ. Ind. Art*, ii. 63, and *S. M. Hadi's Mon. on Dyes and Dyeing*, p. 35.]

c. 1590.—"His Majesty improved this department in four ways. ... *Thirdly*, in stuffs as ... **Bándhnún**, *Chhínt*, *Alchah*."—*Āīn*, i. 91.

1752.—"The Cossembazar merchants having fallen short in gurrahs, plain taffaties, ordinary **bandannoes**, and chappas."—In *Long*, 31.

1813.—"**Bandannoes** ... 800."—*Milburn* (List of Bengal Piece-goods, and no. to the ton), ii. 221.

1848.—"Mr Scape, lately admitted partner into the great Calcutta House of Fogle, Fake, and Cracksman ... taking Fake's place, who retired to a princely Park in Sussex (the Fogles have long been out of the firm, and Sir Horace Fogle is about to be raised to the peerage as Baron **Bandanna**), ... two years before it failed for a million, and plunged half the Indian public into misery and ruin."—*Vanity Fair*, ii. ch. 25.

1866.—"'Of course, said Toogood, wiping his eyes with a large red **bandana** handkerchief. 'By all means, come along, Major.' The major had turned his face away, and he also was weeping."—*Last Chronicle of Barset*, ii. 362.

1875.—"In Calcutta Tariff Valuations: 'Piece goods silk: **Bandanah** Choppahs, per piece of 7 handkerchiefs ... score ... 115 *Rs*."

BANDICOOT, s. Corr. from the Telegu *pandi-kokku*, lit. 'pig-rat.' The name has spread all over India, as applied to the great rat called by naturalists *Mus malabaricus* (Shaw), *Mus giganteus* (Hardwicke), *Mus bandicota* (Bechstein), [*Nesocia bandicota* (Blanford, p. 425)]. The word is now used also in Queensland, [and is the origin of the name of the famous *Bendigo* gold-field (3 ser. *N. & Q.* ix. 97)].

c. 1330.—"In Lesser India there be some rats as big as foxes, and venomous exceedingly."—*Friar Jordanus*, Hak. Soc. 29.

c. 1343.—"They imprison in the dungeons (of Dwaigīr, *i.e.* Daulatābād) those who have been guilty of great crimes. There are in those dungeons enormous rats, bigger than cats. In fact, these latter animals run away from them, and can't stand against them, for they would get the worst of it. So they are only caught by stratagem. I have seen these rats at Dwaigīr, and much amazed I was!"—*Ibn Batuta*, iv. 47.

Fryer seems to exaggerate worse than the Moor;

1673.—"For Vermin, the strongest huge Rats as big as our Pigs, which burrow under the Houses, and are bold enough to venture on Poultry."—*Fryer*, 116.

The following surprisingly confounds two entirely different animals:

1789.—"The **Bandicoot**, or musk rat, is another troublesome animal, more indeed from its offensive smell than anything else."—*Munro, Narrative*, 32. See MUSK-RAT.

[1828.—"They be called **Brandy-cutes**."—*Or. Sporting Mag.* i. 128.]

1879.—"I shall never forget my first night here (on the Cocos Islands). As soon as the Sun had gone down, and the moon risen, thousands upon thousands of rats, in size equal to a **bandicoot**, appeared."—*Pollok, Sport in B. Burmah*, &c., ii. 14.

1880.—"They (wild dogs in Queensland) hunted Kangaroo when in numbers ... but usually preferred smaller and more easily obtained prey, as rats, **bandicoots**, and 'possums.'"—*Blackwood's Mag.*, Jan., p. 65.

[1880.—"In England the Collector is to be found riding at anchor in the **Bandicoot** Club."—*Aberigh-Mackay, Twenty-one Days*, 87.]

BANDO! H. imperative *bāndho*, 'tie or make fast.' "This and probably other Indian words have been naturalised in the docks on the Thames frequented by Lascar crews. I have heard a London lighter-man, in the Victoria Docks, throw a rope ashore to another Londoner, calling out, **Bando**!"—(*M.-Gen. Keatinge.*)

BANG, BHANG, s. H. *bhāng*, the dried leaves and small stalks of hemp (*i.e. Cannabis indica*), used to cause intoxication, either by smoking, or when eaten mixed up into a sweetmeat (see MAJOON). *Hashīsh* of the Arabs is substantially the same; Birdwood says it "consists of the tender tops of the plants after flowering."

[*Bhang* is usually derived from Skt. *bhaṇga*, 'breaking,' but Burton derives both it and the Ar. *banj* from the old Coptic *Nibanj*, "meaning a preparation of hemp; and here it is easy to recognise the Homeric *Nepenthe*."

"On the other hand, not a few apply the word to the henbane (*hyoscyamus niger*) so much used in mediæval Europe. The Kámús evidently means henbane, distinguishing it from Hashísh *al haráfish*, 'rascal's grass,' *i.e.* the herb Pantagruelion ... The use of Bhang doubtless dates from the dawn of civilisation, whose earliest social pleasures would be inebriants. Herodotus (iv. c. 75) shows the Scythians burning the seeds (leaves and capsules) in worship and becoming drunk upon the fumes, as do the S. African Bushmen of the present day."—(*Arab. Nights*, i. 65.)]

1563.—"The great Sultan Badur told Martim Affonzo de Souza, for whom he had a great liking, and to whom he told all his secrets, that when in the night he had a desire to visit Portugal, and the Brazil, and Turkey, and Arabia, and Persia, all he had to do was to eat a little **bangue**. ..."—*Garcia*, f. 26.

1578.—"**Bangue** is a plant resembling hemp, or the Cannabis of the Latins ... the Arabs call this **Bangue** '*Axis*'" (*i.e.* Hashīsh).—*C. Acosta*, 360–61.

1598.—"They have ... also many kinds of Drogues, as Amfion, or Opium, Camfora, **Bangue** and Sandall Wood."—*Linschoten*, 19; [Hak. Soc. i. 61; also see ii. 115].

1606.—"O mais de tẽpo estava cheo de **bangue**."—*Gouvea*, 93.

1638.—"Il se fit apporter vn petit cabinet d'or ... dont il tira deux layettes, et prit dans l'vne de l'*offion*, ou opium, et dans l'autre du **bengi**, qui est vne certaine drogue ou poudre, dont ils se seruent pour s'exciter à la luxure."—*Mandelslo*, Paris, 1659, 150.

1685.—"I have two sorts of the **Bangue**, which were sent from two several places of the East Indies; they both differ much from our Hemp, although they seem to differ most as to their magnitude."—*Dr. Hans Sloane to Mr. Ray*, in *Ray's Correspondence*, 1848, p. 160.

1673.—"**Bang** (a pleasant intoxicating Seed mixed with Milk). ..."—*Fryer*, 91.

1711.—"**Bang** has likewise its Vertues attributed to it; for being used as Tea, it inebriates, or exhilarates them according to the Quantity they take."—*Lockyer*, 61.

1727.—"Before they engage in a Fight, they drink **Bang**, which is made of a Seed like Hempseed, that has an intoxicating Quality."—*A. Hamilton*, i. 131.

1763.—"Most of the troops, as is customary during the agitations of this festival, had eaten plentifully of **bang**. ..."—*Orme*, i. 194.

1784.—"... it does not appear that the use of **bank**, an intoxicating weed which resembles the hemp of Europe, ... is considered even by the most rigid (Hindoo) a breach of the law."—*G. Forster, Journey*, ed. 1808, ii. 291.

1789.—"A shop of **Bang** may be kept with a capital of no more than two shillings, or one rupee. It is only some mats stretched under some tree, where the *Bangeras* of the town, that is, the vilest of mankind, assemble to drink **Bang**."—Note on *Seir Mutaqherin*, iii. 308.

1868.—

"The Hemp—with which we used to hang
Our prison pets, yon felon gang,—
In Eastern climes produces **Bang**,
Esteemed a drug divine.
As Hashish dressed, its magic powers
Can lap us in Elysian bowers;
But sweeter far our social hours,
O'er a flask of rosy wine."

Lord Neaves.

BANGED—is also used as a participle, for 'stimulated by *bang*,' *e.g.* "*banged* up to the eyes."

BANGLE, s. H. *bangṛī* or *bangrī*. The original word properly means a ring of coloured glass worn on the wrist by women; [the *chūrī* of N. India;] but *bangle* is applied to any native ring-bracelet, and also to an *anklet* or ring of any kind worn on the ankle or leg. Indian silver bangles on the wrist have recently come into common use among English girls.

1803.—"To the *cutwahl* he gave a heavy pair of gold **bangles**, of which he considerably enhanced the value by putting them on his wrists with his own hands."—Journal of *Sir J. Nicholls*, in note to *Wellington Despatches*, ed. 1837, ii. 373.

1809.—"**Bangles**, or bracelets."—*Maria Graham*, 13.

1810.—"Some wear ... a stout silver ornament of the ring kind, called a **bangle**, or *karrah* [*kaṛā*] on either wrist."—*Williamson, V. M.* i. 305.

1826.—"I am paid with the silver **bangles** of my enemy, and his cash to boot."—*Pandurang Hari*, 27; [ed. 1873, i. 36].

1873.—"Year after year he found some excuse for coming up to Sirmoori—now a proposal for a tax on **bangles**, now a scheme for a new mode of Hindustani pronunciation."—*The True Reformer*, i. 24.

BANGY, BANGHY, &c. s. H. *bahaṅgī*, Mahr. *baṅgī;* Skt. *vihaṅgamā*, and *vihaṅgikā*.

a. A shoulder-yoke for carrying loads, the yoke or bangy resting on the shoulder, while the load is apportioned at either end in two equal weights, and generally hung by cords. The milkmaid's yoke is the nearest approach to a survival of the bangy-staff in England. Also such a yoke with its pair of baskets or boxes.—

b. Hence a parcel post, carried originally in this way, was called **bangy** or dawk-**bangy**, even when the primitive mode of transport had long become obsolete. "A **bangy** parcel" is a parcel received or sent by such post.

a.—

1789.—
"But I'll give them 2000, with **Bhanges** and
Coolies,
With elephants, camels, with hackeries and
doolies."
Letters of Simpkin the Second, p. 57.

1803.—"We take with us indeed, in six **banghys**, sufficient changes of linen."—*Ld. Valentia*, i. 67.

1810.—"The **bangy**-*wollah*, that is the bearer who carries the **bangy**, supports the bamboo on his shoulder, so as to equipoise the baskets suspended at each end."—*Williamson, V. M.* i. 323.

[1843.—"I engaged eight bearers to carry my palankeen. Besides these I had four **banghy**-*burdars*, men who are each obliged to carry forty pound weight, in small wooden or tin boxes, called *petarrahs*."—*Traveller's account, Carey, Good Old Days*, ii. 91.]

b.—

c. 1844.—"I will forward with this by **bhangy** *dâk* a copy of Capt. Moresby's Survey of the Red Sea."—*Sir G. Arthur*, in *Ind. Admin. of Lord Ellenborough*, p. 221.

1873.—"The officers of his regiment ... subscribed to buy the young people a set of crockery, and a plated tea and coffee service (got up by **dawk banghee** ... at not much more than 200 per cent. in advance of the English price."—*The True Reformer*, i. 57.

BANKSHALL, s. **a**. A warehouse. **b**. The office of a Harbour Master or other Port Authority. In the former sense the word is still used in S. India; in Bengal the latter is the only sense recognised, at least among Anglo-Indians; in Northern India the word is not in use. As the Calcutta office stands on the *banks* of the Hoogly, the name is, we believe, often accepted as having some indefinite reference to this position. And in a late work we find a positive and plausible, but entirely unfounded, explanation of this kind, which we quote below. In Java the word has a specific application to the open hall of audience, supported by wooden pillars without walls, which forms part of every princely residence. The word is used in Sea Hindustani, in the forms *bansār*, and *bangsāl* for a 'store-room' (*Roebuck*).

Bankshall is in fact one of the oldest of the words taken up by foreign traders in India. And its use not only by Correa (c. 1561) but by King John (1524), with the regularly-formed Portuguese plural of words in *-al*, shows how early it was adopted by the Portuguese. Indeed, Correa does not even explain it, as is his usual practice with Indian terms.

More than one serious etymology has been suggested:—(1). Crawfurd takes it to be the Malay word *bangsal*, defined by him in his Malay Dict. thus: "(J.) A shed; a storehouse; a workshop; a porch; a covered passage" (see *J. Ind. Archip.* iv. 182). [Mr Skeat adds that it also means in Malay 'half-husked paddy,' and 'fallen timber, of which the outer layer has rotted and only the core remains.'] But it is probable that the Malay word, though marked by Crawfurd ("J.") as Javanese in origin, is a corruption of one of the two following:

(2) Beng. *baṇkaśāla*, from Skt. *baṇik* or *vaṇik*, 'trade,' and *śāla*, 'a hall.' This is Wilson's etymology.

(3). Skt. *bhāṇḍaśāla*, Canar. *bhaṇḍaśāle*, Malayāl. *pāṇḍiśāla*, Tam. *paṇḍaśālai* or *paṇḍakaśālai*, 'a storehouse or magazine.'

It is difficult to decide which of the two last is the original word; the prevalence of the second in S. India is an argument in its favour; and the substitution of *g* for *ḍ* would be in accordance with a phonetic practice of not uncommon occurrence.

a.—

c. 1345.—"For the *bandar* there is in every island (of the Maldives) a wooden building, which they call **bajanṣār** [evidently for *banjasār*, *i.e.* Arabic spelling for *bangaṣār*] where the Governor ... collects all the goods, and there sells or barters them."—*Ibn Batuta*, iv. 120.

[1520.—"Collected in his **bamgasal**" (in the Maldives).—*Doc. da Torre do Tombo*, p. 452.]

1524.—A grant from K. John to the City of Goa, says: "that henceforward even if no market rent in the city is collected from the **bacacés**, viz. those at which are sold honey, oil, butter, *betre* (*i.e.* betel), spices, and cloths, for permission to sell such things in the said *bacacés*, it is our pleasure that they shall sell them freely." A note says: "Apparently the word should be *bacaçaes*, or **bancacaes**, or *bangaçaes*, which then signified any place to sell things, but now particularly a wooden house."—*Archiv. Portug. Or.*, Fasc. ii. 43.

1561.—"... in the **bengaçaes**, in which stand the goods ready for shipment."—*Correa, Lendas*, i. 2, 260.

1610.—The form and use of the word have led P. Teixeira into a curious confusion (as it would seem) when, speaking of foreigners at Ormus, he says: "hay muchos gentiles, Baneanes [see BANYAN], **Bangasalys**, y Cambayatys"—where the word in italics probably represents *Bangalys*, *i.e.* Bengālis (*Rel. de Harmuz*, 18).

c. 1610.—"Le facteur du Roy chrestien des Maldiues tenoit sa **banquesalle** ou plustost cellier, sur le bord de la mer en l'isle de Malé."—*Pyrard de Laval*, ed. 1679, i. 65; [Hak. Soc. i. 85; also see i. 267].

1613.—"The other settlement of Yler ... with houses of wood thatched extends ... to the fields of Tanjonpacer, where there is a **bangasal** or sentry's house without other defense."—*Godinho de Eredia*, 6.

1623.—"**Bangsal**, a shed (or barn), or often also a roof without walls to sit under, sheltered from the rain or sun."—*Gaspar Willens, Vocabularium*, &c., ins' Gravenhaage; repr. Batavia, 1706.

1734–5.—"Paid the **Bankshall** Merchants for the house poles, country **reapers**, &c., necessary for housebuilding."—In *Wheeler*, iii. 148.

1748.—"A little blow the town of Wampo ... These people (*compradores*) build a house for each ship. ... They are called by us **banksalls**. In these we deposit the rigging and yards of the vessel, chests, water-casks, and every thing that incommodes us aboard."—*A Voyage to the E. Indies* in 1747 and 1748 (1762), p. 294. It appears from this book (p. 118) that the place in Canton River was known as **Banksall** Island.

1750–52.—"One of the first things on arriving here (Canton River) is to procure a **bancshall**, that is, a great house, constructed of bamboo and mats ... in which the stores of the ship are laid up."—*A Voyage*, &c., by *Olof Toreen* ... in a series of letters to Dr Linnæus, Transl. by J. R. Forster (with Osbeck's Voyage), 1771.

1783.—"These people (*Chulias*, &c., from India, at Achin) ... on their arrival immediately build, by contract with the natives, houses of bamboo, like what in China at Wampo is called **bankshall**, very regular, on a convenient spot close to the river."—*Forrest, V. to Mergui*, 41.

1788.—"**Banksauls**—Storehouses for depositing ships' stores in, while the ships are unlading and refitting."—*Indian Vocab.* (Stockdale).

1813.—"The East India Company for seventy years had a large **banksaul**, or warehouse, at Mirzee, for the reception of the pepper and sandalwood purchased in the dominions of the Mysore Rajah."—*Forbes, Or. Mem.* iv. 109.

1817.—"The **bāngsal** or *mendōpo* is a large open hall, supported by a double row of pillars, and covered with shingles, the interior being richly decorated with paint and gilding."—*Raffles, Java* (2nd ed.), i. 93. The Javanese use, as in this passage, corresponds to the meaning given in Jansz, Javanese Dict.: "**Bangsal**, Vorstelijke Zitplaats" (Prince's Sitting-place).

b.—

[1614.—"The custom house or **banksall** at Masulpatam."—*Foster, Letters*, ii. 86.]

1623.—"And on the Place by the sea there was the Custom-house, which the Persians in their language call **Benksal**, a building of no great size, with some open outer porticoes."—*P. della Valle*, ii. 465.

1673.—"... Their **Bank Solls**, or Custom House Keys, where they land, are Two; but mean, and shut only with ordinary Gates at Night."—*Fryer*, 27.

1683.—"I came ashore in Capt. Goyer's Pinnace to ye **Bankshall**, about 7 miles from Ballasore."—*Hedges, Diary*, Feb. 2; [Hak. Soc. i. 65].

1687.—"The Mayor and Aldermen, etc., do humbly request the Honourable President and Council would please to grant and assign over to the Corporation the petty dues of **Banksall** Tolls."—In *Wheeler*, i. 207.

1727.—"Above it is the *Dutch* **Bankshall**, a Place where their Ships ride when they cannot get further up for the too swift Currents."—*A. Hamilton*, ii. 6.

1789.—"And that no one may plead ignorance of this order, it is hereby directed that it be placed constantly in view at the **Bankshall** in the English and country languages."—*Procl. against Slave-Trading* in *Seton-Karr*, ii. 5.

1878.—"The term '**Banksoll**' has always been a puzzle to the English in India. It is borrowed from the Dutch. The 'Soll' is the Dutch or Danish 'Zoll,' the English 'Toll.' The **Banksoll** was then the place on the 'bank' where all tolls or duties were levied on landing goods."—*Talboys Wheeler, Early Records of B. India*, 196. (Quite erroneous, as already said; and *Zoll* is not Dutch.)

(1) ***BANYAN**, s. **a.** A Hindu trader, and especially of the Province of Guzerat; many of which class have for ages been settled in

Arabian ports and known by this name; but the term is often applied by early travellers in Western India to persons of the Hindu religion generally. **b.** In Calcutta also it is (or perhaps rather was) specifically applied to the native brokers attached to houses of business, or to persons in the employment of a private gentleman doing analogous duties (now usually called **sircar**).

The word was adopted from *Vāṇiya*, a man of the trading caste (in Gujarāti *vāṇiyo*), and that comes from Skt. *vaṇij*, 'a merchant.' The terminal nasal may be a Portuguese addition (as in *palanquin, mandarin, Bassein*), or it may be taken from the plural form *vāṇiyān*. It is probable, however, that the Portuguese found the word already in use by the Arab traders. Sidi 'Ali, the Turkish Admiral, uses it in precisely the same form, applying it to the Hindus generally; and in the poem of Sassui and Panhu, the Sindian Romeo and Juliet, as given by Burton in his *Sindh* (p. 101), we have the form *Wāniyān*. P. F. Vincenzo Maria, who is quoted below absurdly alleges that the Portuguese called these Hindus of Guzerat **Bagnani**, because they were always washing themselves "... chiamati da Portughesi *Bagnani*, per la frequenza e superstitione, con quale si lauano piu volte il giorno" (251). See also Luillier below. The men of this class profess an extravagant respect for animal life; but after Stanley brought home Dr. Livingstone's letters they became notorious as chief promoters of slave-trade in Eastern Africa. A. K. Forbes speaks of the mediæval **Wānias** at the Court of Anhilwāra as "equally gallant in the field (with Rajputs), and wiser in council ... already in profession puritans of peace, but not yet drained enough of their fiery Kshatri blood."—(*Rās Māla*, i. 240; [ed. 1878, 184].)

Bunya is the form in which *vāṇiya* appears in the Anglo-Indian use of Bengal, with a different shade of meaning, and generally indicating a grain-dealer.

1516.—"There are three qualities of these Gentiles, that is to say, some are called Razbuts ... others are called **Banians**, and are merchants and traders."—*Barbosa*, 51.

1552.—"... Among whom came certain men who are called **Baneanes** of the same heathen of the Kingdom of Cambaia ... coming on board the ship of Vasco da Gama, and seeing in his cabin a pictorial image of Our Lady, to which our people did reverence, they also made adoration with much more fervency. ..."—*Barros*, Dec., I. liv. iv. cap. 6.

1555.—"We may mention that the inhabitants of Guzerat call the unbelievers **Banyāns**, whilst the inhabitants of Hindustan call them Hindū."—*Sidi 'Ali Kapudān*, in J. As., 1ère S. ix. 197–8.

1563.—"*R.* If the fruits were all as good as this (mango) it would be no such great matter in the **Baneanes**, as you tell me, not to eat flesh. And since I touch on this matter, tell me, prithee, who are these **Baneanes** ... who do not eat flesh? ..."—*Garcia*, f. 136.

1608.—"The Gouernour of the Towne of *Gandeuee* is a **Bannyan**, and one of those kind of people that obserue the Law of Pythagoras."—*Jones*, in *Purchas*, i. 231.

[1610.—"**Baneanes**." See quotation under BANKSHALL, **a.**]

1623.—"One of these races of Indians is that of those which call themselves *Vanià*, but who are called, somewhat corruptly by the Portuguese, and by all our other Franks, **Banians**; they are all, for the most part, traders and brokers."—*P. della Valle*, i. 486–7; [and see i. 78 Hak. Soc.].

1630.—"A people presented themselves to mine eyes, cloathed in linnen garments, somewhat low descending, of a gesture and garbe, as I may say, maidenly and well nigh effeminate; of a countenance shy, and somewhat estranged; yet smiling out a glosed and bashful familiarity. ... I asked what manner of people these were, so strangely notable, and notably strange. Reply was made that they were **Banians**."—*Lord, Preface*.

1665.—"In trade these **Banians** are a thousand times worse than the *Jews*; more expert in all sorts of cunning tricks, and more maliciously mischievous in their revenge."—*Tavernier*, E. T. ii. 58; [ed. *Ball*, i. 136, and see i. 91].

c. 1666.—"Aussi chacun a son **Banian** dans les Indes, et il y a des personnes de qualité qui leur confient tout ce qu'ils ont. ..."—*Thevenot*, v. 166. This passage shows in anticipation the transition to the Calcutta use (**b.**, below).

1672.—"The inhabitants are called Guizeratts and **Benyans**."—*Baldaeus*, 2.

"It is the custom to say that to make one **Bagnan** (so they call the Gentile Merchants) you need three Chinese, and to make one Chinese three Hebrews."—*P. F. Vincenzo di Maria*, 114.

1673.—"The **Banyan** follows the Soldier, though as contrary in Humour as the Antipodes in the same Meridian are opposite to one another. ... In Cases of Trade they are not so hide-bound, giving their Consciences more Scope, and boggle at no Villainy for an Emolument."—*Fryer*, 193.

1677.—"In their letter to Ft. St. George, 15th March, the Court offer £20 reward to any of our servants or soldiers as shall be able to speak, write, and translate the **Banian** language, and to learn their arithmetic."—In Madras *Notes and Exts.*, No. I. p. 18.

1705.—"... ceux des premieres castes, comme les **Baignans**."—*Luillier*, 106.

1813.—"... it will, I believe, be generally allowed by those who have dealt much with **Banians** and merchants in the larger trading towns of India, that their moral character cannot be held in high estimation."—*Forbes, Or. Mem.* ii. 456.

1877.—"Of the *Wani*, **Banyan**, or trader-caste there are five great families in this country."—*Burton, Sind Revisited*, ii. 281.

b.—

1761.—"We expect and positively direct that if our servants employ **Banians** or black people under them, they shall be accountable for their conduct."—*The Court of Directors*, in *Long*, 254.

1764.—"*Resolutions and Orders*. That no Moonshee, Linguist, **Banian**, or Writer, be allowed to any officer, excepting the Commander-in-Chief."—*Ft. William Proc.*, in *Long*, 382.

1775.—"We have reason to suspect that the intention was to make him (Nundcomar) **Banyan** to General Clavering, to surround the General and us with the Governor's creatures, and to keep us totally unacquainted with the real state of the Government."—*Minute by Clavering, Monson, and Francis, Ft. William*, 11th April. In *Price's Tracts*, ii. 138.

1780.—"We are informed that the Juty Wallahs or Makers and Vendors of Bengal Shoes in and about Calcutta ... intend sending a Joint Petition to the Supreme Council ... on account of the great decay of their Trade, entirely owing to the Luxury of the Bengalies, chiefly the **Bangans** (*sic*) and Sarcars, as there are scarce any of them to be found who does not keep a Chariot, Phaeton, Buggy or Pallanquin, and some all four ..."—In *Hicky's Bengal Gazette*, June 24th.

1783.—"Mr. Hastings' **bannian** was, after this auction, found possessed of territories yielding a rent of £140,000 a year."—*Burke, Speech on E. I. Bill*, in *Writings*, &c., iii. 490.

1786.—"The said Warren Hastings did permit and suffer his own **banyan** or principal black steward, named Canto Baboo, to hold farms ... to the amount of 13 lacs of rupees per annum."—*Art. agst. Hastings, Burke*, vii. 111.

"A practice has gradually crept in among the **Banians** and other rich men of Calcutta, of dressing some of their servants ... nearly in the uniform of the Honourable Company's Sepoys and Lascars. ..."—*Notification*, in *Seton Karr*, i. 122.

1788.—"**Banyan**—A Gentoo servant employed in the management of commercial affairs. Every English gentleman at Bengal has a **Banyan** who either acts of himself, or as the substitute of some great man or black merchant."—*Indian Vocabulary* (Stockdale).

1810.—"The same person frequently was **banian** to several European gentlemen; all of whose concerns were of course accurately known to him, and thus became the subject of conversation at those meetings the **banians** of Calcutta invariably held. ..."—*Williamson, V. M.* i. 189.

1817.—"The European functionary ... has first his **banyan** or native secretary."—*Mill, Hist.* (ed. 1840), iii. 14. Mr. Mill does not here accurately interpret the word.

(2) BANYAN, s. An undershirt, originally of muslin, and so called as resembling the body garment of the Hindus; but now commonly applied to under body-clothing of elastic cotton, woollen, or silk web. The following quotations illustrate the stages by which the word reached its present application. And they show that our predecessors in India used to adopt the native or **Banyan** costume in their hours of ease. C. P. Brown defines **Banyan** as "a *loose dressing-gown*, such as Hindu tradesmen wear." Probably this may have been the original use; but it is never so employed in Northern India.

1672.—"It is likewise ordered that both Officers and Souldiers in the Fort shall, both on every Sabbath Day, and on every day when they exercise, *weare English apparel*; in respect the garbe is most becoming as Souldiers, and correspondent to their profession."—*Sir W. Langhorne's Standing Order*, in *Wheeler*, iii. 426.

1731.—"The Ensign (as it proved, for his first appearance, being undressed and in his **banyon** coat, I did not know him) came off from his cot, and in a very haughty manner cried out, 'None of your disturbance, Gentlemen.'"—In *Wheeler*, iii. 109.

1781.—"I am an Old Stager in this Country, having arrived in Calcutta in the Year 1736. ... Those were the days, when Gentlemen studied *Ease* instead of *Fashion*; when even the Hon. Members of the Council met in **Banyan Shirts**, **Long Drawers** (q.v.), and Conjee (**Congee**) caps; with a Case Bottle of good old Arrack, and a Gouglet of Water placed on the Table, which the Secretary (a Skilful Hand) frequently converted into Punch ..."—Letter from *An Old Country Captain*, in *India Gazette*, Feb. 24th.

[1773.—In a letter from Horace Walpole to the Countess of Upper Ossory, dated April 30th, 1773 (*Cunningham's* ed., v. 459) he describes a ball at Lord Stanley's, at which two of the dancers, Mr. Storer and Miss Wrottesley, were dressed "in **banians** with furs, for winter, cock and hen." It would be interesting to have further details of these garments, which were, it may be hoped, different from the modern **Banyan**.]

1810.—"... an undershirt, commonly called **a banian**."—*Williamson, V.M.* i. 19.

(3) **BANYAN**, s. See BANYAN-TREE.

BANYAN-DAY, s. This is sea-slang for a *jour maigre*, or a day on which no ration of meat was allowed; when (as one of our quotations above expresses it) the crew had "to observe the Law of Pythagoras."

1690.—"Of this (*Kitchery* or **Kedgeree**, q.v.) the *European* Sailors feed in these parts once or twice a Week, and are forc'd at those times to a Pagan Abstinence from Flesh, which creates in them a perfect Dislike and utter Detestation to those **Bannian Days**, as they commonly call them."—*Ovington*, 310, 311.

BANYAN-FIGHT, s. Thus:

1690.—"This Tongue Tempest is termed there a **Bannian-Fight**, for it never rises to blows or bloodshed."—*Ovington*, 275. Sir G. Birdwood tells us that this is a phrase still current in Bombay.

***BANYAN-TREE**, also elliptically **Banyan**, s. The Indian Fig-Tree (*Ficus Indica*, or *Ficus bengalensis*, L.), called in H. *bar* [or *baṛgat*, the latter the "*Bourgade*" of Bernier (ed. *Constable*, p. 309).] The name appears to have been first bestowed popularly on a famous tree of this species growing near Gombroon, under which the *Banyans* or Hindu traders settled at that port, had built a little pagoda. So says Tavernier below. This original *Banyan-tree* is described by P. della Valle (ii. 453), and by Valentijn (v. 202). P. della Valle's account (1622) is extremely interesting, but too long for quotation. He calls it by the Persian name, *lūl*. The tree still stood, within half a mile of the English factory, in 1758, when it was visited by Ives, who quotes Tickell's verses given below.

c. A.D. 70.—"First and foremost, there is a Fig-tree there (in India) which beareth very small and slender figges. The propertie of this Tree, is to plant and set it selfe without mans helpe. For it spreadeth out with mightie armes, and the lowest water-boughes underneath, do bend so downeward to the very earth, that they touch it againe, and lie upon it: whereby, within one years space they will take fast root in the ground, and put foorth a new Spring round about the Mother-tree: so as these braunches, thus growing, seeme like & traile or border of arbours most curiously and artificially made," &c.—*Plinies Nat. Historie*, by *Philemon Holland*, i. 360.

1624.—

"... The goodly bole being got
To certain cubits' height, from every side
The boughs decline, which, taking root
afresh,
Spring up new boles, and these spring new,
and newer,
Till the whole tree become a porticus,
Or arched arbour, able to receive
A numerous troop."

Ben Jonson, Neptune's Triumph.

c. 1650.—"Cet Arbre estoit de même espece que celuy qui est a une lieue du Bander, et qui passe pour une merveille; mais dans les Indes il y en a quantité. Les Persans l'appellent *Lul*, les Portugais *Arber de Reys*, et les Francais **l'Arbre des Banianes**; parce que les Banianes ont fait bâtir dessous une Pagode avec un carvansera accompagné de plusieurs petits étangs pour se laver."—*Tavernier, V. de Perse*, liv. v. ch. 23. [Also see ed. *Ball*, ii. 198.]

c.1650.—"Near to the City of *Ormus* was a **Bannians tree**, being the only tree that grew in the Island."—*Tavernier*, Eng. Tr. i. 255.

c. 1666.—"Nous vimes à cent ou cent cinquante pas de ce jardin, l'arbre *War* dans toute son etenduë. On l'appelle aussi *Ber*, et **arbre des Banians**, et *arbre des racines*. ..."—*Thevenot* v. 76.

1667.—

"The fig-tree, not that kind for fruit renown'd;
But such as at this day, to Indians known,
In Malabar or Decan spreads her arms
Branching so broad and long, that in the
ground
The bended twigs take root, and daughters
grow
About the mother-tree, a pillar'd shade
High over-arch'd, and echoing walks
between."

Paradise Lost, ix. 1101.

[Warton points out that Milton must have had in view a description of the Banyan-tree in *Gerard's Herbal* under the heading "of the arched Indian fig-tree."]

1672.—"*Eastward of Surat* two *Courses*, *i.e.* a League, we pitched our Tent under a Tree that besides its Leafs, the Branches bear its own Roots, therefore called by the *Portugals*, *Arbor de Raiz*; For the Adoration the *Banyans* pay it, the **Banyan-Tree**."—*Fryer*, 105.

1691.—"About a (Dutch) mile from Gamron

... stands a tree, heretofore described by Mandelslo and others. ... Beside this tree is an idol temple where the **Banyans** do their worship."—*Valentijn*, v. 267–8.

1717.—

"The fair descendants of thy sacred bed
Wide-branching o'er the Western World shall spread,
Like the fam'd **Banian Tree**, whose pliant shoot
To earthward bending of itself takes root,
Till like their mother plant ten thousand stand
In verdant arches on the fertile land;
Beneath her shade the tawny Indians rove,
Or hunt at large through the wide-echoing grove."

Tickell, Epistle from a Lady in England to a Lady in Avignon.

1726.—"On the north side of the city (Surat) is there an uncommonly great Pichar or *Waringin*[1] tree ... The Portuguese call this tree Albero de laiz, *i.e.* Root-tree. ... Under it is a small chapel built by a *Benyan*. ... Day and night lamps are alight there, and **Benyans** constantly come in pilgrimage, to offer their prayers to this saint."—*Valentijn*, iv. 145.

1771.—"... being employed to construct a military work at the fort of Triplasore (afterwards called Marsden's Bastion) it was necessary to cut down a **banyan-tree** which so incensed the brahmans of that place, that they found means to poison him" (*i.e.* Thomas Marsden of the Madras Engineers).—*Mem. of W. Marsden*, 7–8.

1809.—"Their greatest enemy (*i.e.* of the buildings) is the **Banyan-Tree**."—*Ld. Valentia*, i. 396.

1810.—

"In the midst an aged **Banian** grew.
It was a goodly sight to see
That venerable tree,
For o'er the lawn, irregularly spread,
Fifty straight columns propt its lofty head;
And many a long depending shoot,
Seeking to strike its root,
Straight like a plummet grew towards the ground,
Some on the lower boughs which crost their way,
Fixing their bearded fibres, round and round,
With many a ring and wild contortion wound;
Some to the passing wind at times, with sway
Of gentle motion swung;
Others of younger growth, unmoved, were hung
Like stone-drops from the cavern's fretted height."

Southey, Curse of Kehama, xiii. 51.

[Southey takes his account from *Williamson, Orient. Field Sports*, ii. 113.]

1821.—

"Des **banians** touffus, par les brames adorés,
Depuis longtemps la langueur nous implore,
Courbés par le midi, dont l'ardeur les dévore,
Ils étendent vers nous leurs rameaux altérés."

Casimir Delavigne, Le Paria, iii. 6.

A note of the publishers on the preceding passage, in the edition of 1855, is diverting: "Un journaliste allemand a accusé M. Casimir Delavigne d'avoir pris pour un arbre une secte religieuse de l'Inde. ..." The German journalist was wrong here, but he might have found plenty of matter for ridicule in the play. Thus the Brahmins (men) are *Akebar* (!), *Idamore* (!!), and *Empsael* (!!!); their women *Néala* (?), *Zaide* (!), and *Mirza* (!!).

1825.—"Near this village was the finest **banyan-tree** which I had ever seen, literally a grove rising from a single primary stem, whose massive secondary trunks, with their straightness, orderly arrangement, and evident connexion with the parent stock, gave the general effect of a vast vegetable organ. The first impression which I felt on coming under its shade was, 'What a noble place of worship!'"—*Heber*, ii. 93 (ed. 1844).

1834.—"Cast forth thy word into the everliving, everworking universe; it is a seed-grain that cannot die; unnoticed today, it will be found flourishing as a **banyan-grove**—(perhaps alas! as a hemlock forest) after a thousand years."—*Sartor Resartus*.

1856.—

"... its pendant branches, rooting in the air,
Yearn to the parent earth and grappling fast,
Grow up huge stems again, which shooting forth
In massy branches, these again despatch
Their drooping heralds, till a labyrinth
Of root and stem and branch commingling, forms
A great cathedral, aisled and choired in wood."

The **Banyan Tree**, a Poem

1865.—"A family tends to multiply families around it, till it becomes the centre of a tribe, just as the **banyan** tends to surround itself with a forest of its own offspring."—*Maclennan, Primitive Marriage*, 269.

1878.—"... des **banyans** soutenus par des racines aëriennes et dont les branches tombantes engendrent en touchant terre des sujets nouveaux." *Rev. des Deux Mondes*, Oct. 15, p. 832.

BARBIERS, s. This is a term which was

1 *Waringin* is the Javanese name of a sp. kindred to the banyan, *Ficus benjamina*, L.

formerly very current in the East, as the name of a kind of paralysis, often occasioned by exposure to chills. It began with numbness and imperfect command of the power of movement, sometimes also affecting the muscles of the neck and power of articulation, and often followed by loss of appetite, emaciation, and death. It has often been identified with **Beriberi,** and medical opinion seems to have come back to the view that the two are *forms* of one disorder, though this was not admitted by some older authors of the last century. The allegation of Lind and others, that the most frequent subjects of *barbiers* were Europeans of the lower class who, when in drink, went to sleep in the open air, must be contrasted with the general experience that *beriberi* rarely attacks Europeans. The name now seems obsolete.

1673.—"Whence follows Fluxes, Dropsy, Scurvy, **Barbiers** (which is an enervating (*sic*) the whole Body, being neither able to use hands or Feet), Gout, Stone, Malignant and Putrid Fevers."—*Fryer*, 68.

1690.—"Another Distemper with which the Europeans are sometimes afflicted, is the **Barbeers**, or a deprivation of the Vse and Activity of their Limbs, whereby they are rendered unable to move either Hand or Foot."—*Ovington*, 350.

1755.—(If the land wind blow on a person sleeping) "the consequence of this is always dangerous, as it seldom fails to bring on a fit of the **Barbiers** (as it is called in this country), that is, a total deprivation of the use of the limbs."—*Ives*, 77.

[c. 1757.—"There was a disease common to the lower class of Europeans, called the **Barbers**, a species of palsy, owing to exposure to the land winds after a fit of intoxication."—In *Carey, Good Old Days*, ii. 266.]

1768.—"The **barbiers**, a species of palsy, is a disease most frequent in India. It distresses chiefly the lower class of Europeans, who when intoxicated with liquors frequently sleep in the open air, exposed to the land winds."—*Lind* on *Diseases of Hot Climates*, 260. (See BERIBERI.)

BARRACKPORE, n.p. The auxiliary Cantonment of Calcutta, from which it is 15 m. distant, established in 1772. Here also is the country residence of the Governor-General, built by Lord Minto, and much frequented in former days before the annual migration to Simla was established. The name is a hybrid.

BASHAW, s. The old form of what we now call *pasha*, the former being taken from *bāshā*, the Ar. form of the word, which is itself generally believed to be a corruption of the P. *pādishāh*. Of this the first part is Skt. *patis*, Zend. *paitis*, Old P. *pati*, 'a lord or master' (comp. Gr. *δεσπότης*). *Pechah*, indeed, for 'Governor' (but with the *ch* guttural) occurs in I. Kings x. 15, II. Chron. ix. 14, and in Daniel iii. 2, 3, 27. Prof. Max Müller notices this, but it would seem merely as a curious coincidence.—(See *Pusey on Daniel*, 567.)

1554.—"Hujusmodi **Bassarum** sermonibus reliquorum Turcarum sermones congruebant."—*Busbeq*. Epist. ii. (p. 124).

1584.—

"Great kings of Barbary and my portly
bassas."

Marlowe, Tamburlane the Great, 1st Part, iii. 1.

c. 1590.—"Filius alter Osmanis, Vrchanis frater, alium non habet in Annalibus titulum, quam Alis **bassa:** quod *bassae* vocabulum Turcis caput significat."—*Lennclavius, Annales Sultanorum Othmanidarum*, ed. 1650, p. 402. This etymology connecting *bāshā* with the Turkish *bāsh*, 'head,' must be rejected.

c. 1610.—"Un **Bascha** estoit venu en sa Cour pour luy rendre compte du tribut qu'il luy apportoit; mais il fut neuf mois entiers à attendre que celuy qui a la charge ... eut le temps et le loisir de le compter ..." *Pyrard de Laval* (of the Great Mogul), ii. 161.

1702.—"... The most notorious injustice we have suffered from the Arabs of Muscat, and the **Bashaw** of Judda."—In *Wheeler*, ii. 7.

1727.—"It (Bagdad) is now a prodigious large City, and the Seat of a *Beglerbeg*. ... The **Bashaws** of *Bassora*, *Comera*, and *Musol* (the ancient Nineveh) are subordinate to him."—*A. Hamilton*, i. 78.

BATAVIA, n.p. The famous capital of the Dutch possessions in the Indies; occupying the site of the old city of Jakatra, the seat of a Javanese kingdom which combined the present Dutch Provinces of Bantam, Buitenzorg, Krawang, and the Preanger Regencies.

1619.—"On the day of the capture of Jakatra, 30th May 1619, it was certainly time and place to speak of the Governor-General's dissatisfaction that the name of **Batavia** had been given to the Castle."—*Valentijn*, iv. 489.

The Governor-General, Jan Pietersen Coen, who had taken **Jakatra**, desired to have called the new fortress *New Hoorn*, from his own birth-place, Hoorn, on the Zuider Zee.

c. 1649.—"While I stay'd at **Batavia**, my Brother dy'd; and it was pretty to consider what the *Dutch* made me pay for his Funeral."—*Tavernier* (E.T.), i. 203.

***BATTA**, s. Two different words are thus expressed in Anglo-Indian colloquial, and in a manner confounded.

a. H. *bhata* or *bhātā*: an extra allowance made to officers, soldiers, or other public servants, when in the field, or on other special grounds; also subsistence money to witnesses, prisoners, and the like. Military **Batta**, originally an occasional allowance, as defined, grew to be a constant addition to the pay of officers in India, and constituted the chief part of the excess of Indian over English military emoluments. The question of the right to *batta* on several occasions created great agitation among the officers of the Indian army, and the measure of economy carried out by Lord William Bentinck when Governor-General (G. O. of the Gov.-Gen. in Council, 29th November 1828) in the reduction of full *batta* to half *batta*, in the allowances received by all regimental officers serving at stations within a certain distance of the Presidency in Bengal (viz. Barrackpore, Dumdum, Berhampore, and Dinapore) caused an enduring bitterness against that upright ruler.

It is difficult to arrive at the origin of this word. There are, however several Hindi words in rural use, such as *bhāt*, *bhantā*, 'advances made to ploughmen without interest,' and *bhaṭṭa*, *bhanṭā*, 'ploughmen's wages in kind,' with which it is possibly connected. It has also been suggested, without much probability, that it may be allied to *bahut*, 'much, excess,' an idea entering into the meaning of both **a** and **b**. It is just possible that the familiar military use of the term in India may have been influenced by the existence of the European military term *bât* or *bât-money*. The latter is from *bât*, 'a pack-saddle,' [Late Lat. *bastum*], and implies an allowance for carrying baggage in the field. It will be seen that one writer below seems to confound the two words.

b. H. *baṭṭā* and *bāṭṭā*: agio, or difference in exchange, discount on coins not current, or of short weight. We may notice that Sir H. Elliot does not recognize an absolute separation between the two senses of **Batta**. His definition runs thus: "Difference of exchange; anything extra; an extra allowance; discount on uncurrent, or short-weight coins; usually called **Batta**. The word has been supposed to be a corruption of *Bharta*, increase, but it is a pure Hindi vocable, and is more usually applied to discount than to premium."—(*Supp. Gloss.* ii. 41.) [Platts, on the other hand, distinguishes the two words—*Baṭṭa*, Skt. *vṛitta*, 'turned,' or *varta*, 'livelihood'—"Exchange, discount, difference of exchange, deduction, &c.," and *Bhaṭṭa*, Skt. *bhakta* 'allotted,'—"advances to ploughmen without interest; ploughman's wages in kind."] It will be seen that we have early Portuguese instances of the word apparently in both senses.

The most probable explanation is that the word (and I may add, the thing) originated in the Portuguese practice, and in the use of the Canarese word *bhatta*, Mahr, *bhāt*, 'rice' in 'the husk,' called by the Portuguese *bate* and *bata*, for a maintenance allowance.

The word *batty*, for what is more generally called *paddy*, is or was commonly used by the English also in S. and W. India (see *Linschoten*, *Lucena* and *Fryer* quoted s.v. **Paddy**, and *Wilson's Glossary*, s.v. *Bhatta*).

The practice of giving a special allowance for *mantimento* began from a very early date in the Indian history of the Portuguese, and it evidently became a recognised augmentation of pay, corresponding closely to our *batta*, whilst the quotation from Botelho below shows also that *bata* and *mantimento* were used, more or less interchangeably, for this allowance. The correspondence with our Anglo-Indian *batta* went very far, and a case singularly parallel to the discontent raised in the Indian army by the reduction of full-*batta* to half-*batta* is spoken of by Correa (iv. 256). The *mantimento* had been paid all the year round, but the Governor, Martin Afonso de Sousa, in 1542, "desiring," says the historian, "a way to curry favour for himself, whilst going against the people and sending his soul to hell," ordered that in future the *mantimento* should be paid only during the 6 months of **Winter** (*i.e.* of the rainy season), when the force was on shore, and not for the other 6 months when they were on board the cruisers, and received rations. This created great bitterness, perfectly analogous in depth and in expression to that entertained with regard to Lord W. Bentinck and Sir John Malcolm, in 1829. Correa's utterance, just quoted, illustrates this, and a little lower down he adds: "And thus he took away from the troops the half of their *mantimento* (*half their batta*, in fact), and whether he did well or ill in that, he'll find in the next world."—(See also *ibid.* p. 430).

The following quotations illustrate the Portuguese practice from an early date:

1502.—"The Captain-major ... between officers and men-at-arms, left 60 men (at Cochin), to whom the factor was to give their pay, and every month a *cruzádo* of *mantimento*, and to the officers when on service 2 *cruzados*. ..."—*Correā*, i. 328.

1507.—(In establishing the settlement at Mozambique) "And the Captains took counsel among themselves, and from the money in the chest, paid the force each a *cruzado* a month for *mantimento*, with which the men greatly refreshed themselves. ..."—*Ibid.* 786.

1511.—"All the people who served in Malaca, whether by sea or by land, were paid their pay for six months in advance, and also received monthly *two cruzados* of *mantimento*, cash in hand" (*i.e.* they had *double batta*).—*Ibid.* ii. 267.

a.—

1548.—"And for 2 *ffarazes* 2 pardaos a month for the two and 4 tangas for **bata**." ...—*S. Botelho, Tombo*, 233. The editor thinks this is for *bate, i.e. paddy*. But even if so it is used exactly like **batta** or maintenance money. A following entry has: "To the constable 38,920 reis a year, in which is comprised maintenance (*mantimento*)."

The following quotation shows *battee* (or *batty*) used at Madras in a way that also indicates the original identity of *batty*, 'rice,' and **batta**, 'extra allowance':—

1680.—"The *Peons* and *Tarryars* sent in quest of two soldiers who had deserted from the garrison returned with answer that they could not light of them, whereupon the Peons were turned out of service, but upon Verona's intercession were taken in again, and fined each one month's pay, and to repay the money paid them for **Battee**. ..."—*Ft. St. Geo. Consn.*, Feb. 10. In *Notes and Exts.* No. iii. p. 3.

1707.—"... that they would allow **Batta** or subsistence money to all that should desert us."—In *Wheeler*, ii. 63.

1765.—"... orders were accordingly issued ... that on the 1st January, 1766, the double **batta** should cease. ..."—*Caraccioli's Clive*, iv. 160.

1789.—"... **batta**, or as it is termed in England, *bât* and forage money, which is here, in the field, almost double the peace allowance."—*Munro's Narrative*, p. 97.

1799.—"He would rather live on halfpay, in a garrison that could boast of a fives court, than vegetate on *full* **batta**, where there was none."—*Life of Sir T. Munro*, i. 227.

The following shows Batty used for rice in Bombay:

[1813.—Rice, or **batty**, is sown in June."—*Forbes, Or. Mem.* 2nd ed. i. 23.]

1829.—"*To the Editor of the Bengal Hurkaru.*—Sir,—Is it understood that the Wives and daughters of officers on *half* **batta** are included in the order to mourn for the Queen of Wirtemberg; or will *half*-mourning be considered sufficient for them?"—Letter in above, dated 15th April 1829.

1857.—"They have made me a K.C.B. I may confess to you that I would much rather have got a year's **batta**, because the latter would enable me to leave this country a year sooner."—*Sir Hope Grant*, in *Incidents of the Sepoy War.*

b.—

1554.—"And gold, if of 10 *mates* or 24 carats, is worth 10 cruzados the tael ... if of 9 *mates*, 9 cruzados; and according to whatever the *mates* may be it is valued; but moreover it has its **batao**, *i.e.* its shroffage (*çarrafagem*) or agio (*caibo*) varying with the season."—*A. Nunes*, 40.

1680.—"The payment or receipt of **Batta** or **Vatum** upon the exchange of Pollicat for Madras pagodas prohibited, both coines being of the same **Matt** and weight, upon pain of forfeiture of 24 pagodas for every offence together with the loss of the **Batta**."—*Ft. St. Geo. Consn.*, Feb. 10. In *Notes and Exts.*, p. 17.

1760.—"The Nabob receives his revenues in the **siccas** of the current year only ... and all **siccas** of a lower date being esteemed, like the coin of foreign provinces, only a merchandize, are bought and sold at a certain discount called **batta**, which rises and falls like the price of other goods in the market. ..."—*Ft. Wm. Cons.*, June 30, in *Long*, 216.

1810.—"... he immediately tells master that the **batta**, *i.e.* the exchange, is altered."—*Williamson, V. M.* i. 203.

BAYA, s. H. *baiā* [*bayā*], the Weaver-bird, as it is called in books of Nat. Hist., *Ploceus baya*, Blyth (Fam. *Fringillidae*). This clever little bird is not only in its natural state the builder of those remarkable pendant nests which are such striking objects, hanging from eaves or palm-branches; but it is also docile to a singular degree in domestication, and is often exhibited by itinerant natives as the performer of the most delightful tricks, as we have seen, and as is detailed in a paper of Mr Blyth's quoted by Jerdon. "The usual procedure is, when ladies are present, for the bird on a sign from its master to take a cardamom or sweatmeat in its bill, and deposit it between a lady's lips. ... A miniature cannon is then brought, which the bird loads with coarse grains of powder one by one ... it next seizes and skilfully uses a small ramrod: and then takes a lighted match from its master, which it applies to the touch-hole." Another common performance is to scatter small beads on a sheet; the bird is provided with a needle and thread, and proceeds in the prettiest way to thread the beads successively. [The quotation from Abul Fazl shows that these performances are as old as the time of Akbar and probably older still.]

[c. 1590.—"The **baya** is like a wild sparrow but yellow. It is extremely intelligent, obedient and docile. It will take small coins from the hand and bring them to its master, and will come to a call from a long distance. Its nests are so ingeniously constructed as to defy the rivalry of clever artificers."—*Āīn* (trans. Jarrett), iii. 122.]

1790.—"The young Hindu women of Banáras ... wear very thin plates of gold, called *tíca's*, slightly fixed by way of ornament between the eyebrows; and when they pass through the streets, it is not uncommon for the youthful libertines, who amuse themselves with training **Bayā's**, to give them a sign, which they understand, and to send them to pluck the pieces of gold from the foreheads of their mistresses."—*Asiat. Researches*, ii. 110.

[1813.—Forbes gives a similar account of the nests and tricks of the **Baya**.—*Or. Mem.*, 2nd ed. i. 33.]

***BAYADÈRE**, s. A Hindu dancing-girl. The word is especially used by French writers, from whom it has been sometimes borrowed as if it were a genuine Indian word, particularly characteristic of the persons in question. The word is in fact only a Gallicized form of the Portuguese *bailadeira*, from *bailar*, to dance. Some 50 to 60 years ago there was a famous ballet called *Le dieu et la* **bayadère**, and under this title *Punch* made one of the most famous hits of his early days by presenting a cartoon of Lord Ellenborough as the **Bayadère** dancing before the idol of Somnāth; [also see DANCING-GIRL].

1513.—"There also came to the ground many dancing women (*molheres* **bailadeiras**) with their instruments of music, who make their living by that business, and these danced and sang all the time of the banquet ..."—*Correa*, ii. 364.

1526.—"XLVII. The dancers and danceresses (bayladores e **bayladeiras**) who come to perform at a village shall first go and perform at the house of the principal man of the village"—*Foral de usos costumes dos Gancares e Lavradores de esta Ilha de Goa*, in *Arch. Port. Or.*, fascic. 5, 132.

1598.—"The heathenish whore called **Balliadera**, who is a dancer."—*Linschoten*, 74; [Hak. Soc. i. 264].

1599.—"In hâc icone primum proponitur *Inda* **Balliadera**, id est saltatrix, quae in publicis ludis aliisque solennitatibus saltando spectaculum exhibet."—*De Bry*, Text to pl. xii. in vol. ii. (also see p. 90, and vol. vii. 26), etc.

[c. 1676.—"All the **Baladines** of Gombroon were present to dance in their own manner according to custom."—*Tavernier*, ed. *Ball*, ii. 335.]

1782.—"Surate est renommé par ses **Bayadères**, dont le véritable nom est *Décédassi*: celui de *Bayadères* que nous leur donnons, vient du mot **Balladeiras**, qui signifie en Portugais *Danseuses*."—*Sonnerat*, i. 7.

1794.—"The name of **Balliadere**, we never heard applied to the dancing girls; or saw but in Raynal, and 'War in Asia, by an Officer of Colonel Baillie's Detachment;' it is a corrupt Portuguese word."—*Moor's Narrative of Little's Detachment*, 356.

1825.—"This was the first specimen I had seen of the southern **Bayadère**, who differ considerably from the nâch girls of northern India, being all in the service of different temples, for which they are purchased young."—*Heber*, ii. 180.

c. 1836.—"On one occasion a rumour reached London that a great success had been achieved in Paris by the performance of a set of Hindoo dancers, called **Les Bayadères**, who were supposed to be priestesses of a certain sect, and the London theatrical managers were at once on the *qui vive* to secure the new attraction ... My father had concluded the arrangement with the Bayadères before his brother managers arrived in Paris. Shortly afterwards, the Hindoo priestesses appeared at the Adelphi. They were utterly uninteresting, wholly unattractive. My father lost £2000 by the speculation; and in the family they were known as the '**Buy-em-dears**' ever after."—*Edmund Yates, Recollections*, i. 29, 30 (1884).

BAYPARREE, BEOPARRY, s. H. *bepārī*, and *byopārī* (from Skt. *vyāpārin*); a trader, and especially a petty trader or dealer.

A friend long engaged in business in Calcutta (Mr J. F. Ogilvy, of Gillanders &

Co.) communicates a letter from an intelligent Bengalee gentleman, illustrating the course of trade in country produce before it reaches the hands of the European shipper:

1878.—"... the enhanced rates ... do not practically benefit the producer in a marked, or even in a corresponding degree; for the lion's share goes into the pockets of certain intermediate classes, who are the growth of the above system of business.

"Following the course of trade as it flows into Calcutta, we find that between the cultivators and the exporter these are: 1st. The **Bepparree**, or petty trader; 2nd. The *Aurut-dar*;[1] and 3rd. The **Mahajun**, interested in the Calcutta trade. As soon as the crops are cut, **Bepparree** appears upon the scene; he visits village after village, and goes from homestead to homestead, buying there, or at the village marts, from the **ryots**; he then takes his purchases to the *Aurut-dar*, who is stationed at a centre of trade, and to whom he is perhaps under advances, and from the *Aurut-dar* the Calcutta Mahajun obtains his supplies ... for eventual despatch to the capital. There is also a fourth class of dealers called *Phoreas*, who buy from the Mahajun and sell to the European exporter. Thus, between the cultivator and the shipper there are so many middlemen, whose participation in the trade involves a multiplication of profits, which goes a great way towards enhancing the price of commodities before they reach the shipper's hands."—*Letter from Baboo Nobokissin Ghose*. [Similar details for Northern India will be found in *Hoey, Mon. Trade and Manufactures of Lucknow*, 59 *seqq*.]

BAZAAR, s. H. &c. From P. *bāzār*, a permanent market or street of shops. The word has spread westward into Arabic, Turkish, and, in special senses, into European languages, and eastward into India, where it has generally been adopted into the vernaculars. The popular pronunciation is *băzár*. In S. India and Ceylon the word is used for a single shop or stall kept by a native. The word seems to have come to S. Europe very early. F. Balducci Pegolotti, in his Mercantile Handbook (c. 1340) gives **Bazarra** as a Genoese word for 'market-place' (*Cathay*, &c. ii. 286). The word is adopted into Malay as *pāsār*, [or in the poems *pasara*].

1474.—Ambrose Contarini writes of Kazan, that it is "walled like Como, and with **bazars** (*bazzari*) like it."—*Ramusio*, ii. f. 117.

1478.—Josafat Barbaro writes: "An Armenian Choza Mirech, a rich merchant in the **bazar**" (*bazarro*).—*Ibid.* f. 111*v*.

1563.—"... **bazar**, as much as to say the place where things are sold."—*Garcia*, f. 170.

1564.—A privilege by Don Sebastian of Portugal gives authority "to sell garden produce freely in the **bazars** (*bazares*), markets, and streets (of Goa) without necessity for consent or license from the farmers of the garden produce, or from any other person whatsoever."—*Arch. Port. Or.*, fasc. 2, 157.

c. 1566.—"La Pescaria delle Perle ... si fa ogn' anno ... e su la costa all' in contro piantano vna villa di case, e **bazarri** di paglia."—*Cesare de' Federici*, in *Ramusio*, iii. 390.

1606.—"... the Christians of the **Bazar**."—*Gouvea*, 29.

1610.—"En la Ville de Cananor il y a vn beau marché tous les jours, qu'ils appellent **Basare**."—*Pyrard de Laral*, i. 325; [Hak. Soc. i. 448].

[1615.—"To buy pepper as cheap as we could in the **busser**."—*Foster, Letters*, iii. 114.]

["He forbad all the **bezar** to sell us victuals or else ..."—*Ibid.* iv. 80.]

[1623.—"They call it **Bezari Kelan**, that is the Great Merkat ..."—*P. della Valle*, Hak. Soc. i. 96. (P. *Kalān*, 'great').]

1638.—"We came into a **Bussar**, or very faire Market place."—*W. Bruton*, in *Hakl.* v. 50.

1666.—"Les **Bazards** ou Marchés sont dans une grande rue qui est au pié de la montagne."—*Thevenot*, v. 18.

1672.—"... Let us now pass the Pale to the Heathen Town (of Madras) only parted by a wide Parrade, which is used for a **Buzzar** or Mercate-place."—*Fryer*, 38.

[1826.—"The Kotwall went to the **bazaar-master**."—*Pandurang Hari*, ed. 1873, p. 156.]

1837.—"Lord, there is a honey **bazar**, repair thither."—*Turnour's* transl. of *Mahawanso*, 24.

1873.—"This, remarked my handsome Greek friend from Vienna, is the finest wife-**bazaar** in this part of Europe. ... Go a little way east of this, say to Roumania, and you will find wife-**bazaar** completely undisguised, the ladies seated in their carriages, the youths filing by, and pausing before this or that beauty, to bargain with papa about the dower, under her very nose."—*Fraser's Mag. N. S.* vii. p. 617 (*Vienna*, by *M. D. Conway*).

BEARER, s. The word has two meanings in Anglo-Indian colloquial: **a.** A palanquin-carrier; **b.** (In the Bengal Presidency) a domestic servant who has charge of his master's clothes, household furniture, and (often) of his ready money. The word in the latter meaning has been regarded as

1 *Aurut-dar* is *āṛhat-dār*, from H. *ārhat*, 'agency'; *phorea* = H. *phaṛiyā*, 'a retailer.'

distinct in origin, and is stated by Wilson to be a corruption of the Bengali *vehārā* from Skt. *vyavahāri*, a domestic servant. There seems, however, to be no *historical* evidence for such an origin, *e.g.* in any habitual use of the term *vehārā*, whilst as a matter of fact the domestic bearer (or *sirdār-bearer*, as he is usually styled by his fellow-servants, often even when he has no one under him) was in Calcutta, in the penultimate generation when English gentlemen still kept palankins, usually just what this literally implies, viz. the head-man of a set of palankin-bearers. And throughout the Presidency the **bearer**, or valet, still, as a rule, belongs to the caste of *Kahārs*, or palki-bearers. [See BOY.]

a.—

c. 1760.—"... The poles which ... are carried by six, but most commonly four **bearers**."—*Grose*, i. 153.

1768–71.—"Every house has likewise ... one or two sets of **berras**, or palankeen-bearers."—*Stavorinus*, i. 523.

1771.—"Le bout le plus court du Palanquin est en devant, et porté par deux **Beras**, que l'on nomme **Boys** à la Côte (c'est a-dire *Garçons, Serviteurs*, en Anglois). Le long bout est par derrière et porte par trois **Beras**."—*Anquetil du Perron, Desc. Prelim.* p. xxiii. *note*.

1778.—"They came on foot, the town having neither horses nor palankin-**bearers** to carry them, and Colonel Coote received them at his headquarters. ..."—*Orme*, iii. 719.

1803.—"I was ... detained by the scarcity of **bearers**."—*Lord Valentia*, i. 372.

b.—

1782.—"... imposition ... that a gentleman should pay a rascal of a *Sirdar* **Bearer** monthly wages for 8 or 10 men ... out of whom he gives 4, or may perhaps indulge his master with 5, to carry his palankeen."—*India Gazette*, Sept. 2.

c. 1815.—"... *Henry and his* **Bearer**."—(Title of a well-known book of Mrs. Sherwood's.)

1824.—"... I called to my *sirdar*-**bearer** who was lying on the floor, outside the bedroom."—*Seely, Ellora*, ch. i.

1831.—"... le grand maître de ma garde-robe, *sirdar* **beehrah**."—*Jacquemont, Correspondance*, i. 114.

1876.—"My **bearer** who was to go with us (Eva's ayah had struck at the last moment and stopped behind) had literally girt up his loins, and was loading a diminutive mule with a miscellaneous assortment of brass pots and blankets."—*A True Reformer*, ch. iv.

***BEEBEE**, s. H. from P. *bībī*, a lady. [In its contracted form *bī*, it is added as a title of distinction to the names of Musulman ladies.] On the principle of degradation of titles which is so general, this word in application to European ladies has been superseded by the hybrids *Mem-Sāhib*, or *Madam-Sāhib*, though it is often applied to European maid-servants or other Englishwomen of that rank of life. [It retains its dignity as the title of the *Bībī* of Cananore, known as *Bībī Valiya*, Malayāl., 'great lady,' who rules in that neighbourhood and exercises authority over three of the islands of the Laccadives, and is by race a Moplah Mohammedan.] The word also is sometimes applied to a prostitute. It is originally, it would seem, Oriental Turki. In Pavet de Courteille's Dict. we have "*Bībī*, dame, épouse légitime" (p. 181). In W. India the word is said to be pronounced *bobo* (see *Burton's Sind*). It is curious that among the Sákaláva of Madagascar the wives of chiefs are termed *biby*; but there seems hardly a possibility of this having come from Persia or India. [But for Indian influence on the island, see *Encycl. Britt.* 9th ed. xv. 174.] The word in Hova means 'animal.'—(*Sibree's Madagascar*, p. 253.)

[c. 1610.—"Nobles in blood ... call their wives **Bybis**."—*Pyrard de Laval*, Hak. Soc. i. 217.]

1611.—"... the title **Bibi** ... is in Persian the same as among us, sennora, or doña."—*Teixeira, Relacion ... de Hormuz*. 19.

c. 1786.—"The word *Lowndika*, which means the son of a slave-girl, was also continually on the tongue of the Nawaub, and if he was angry with any one he called him by this name; but it was also used as an endearing fond appellation to which was attached great favour,[1] until one day, Ali Zumán Khan ... represented to him that the word was low, discreditable, and not fit for the use of men of knowledge and rank. The Nawaub smiled, and said, 'O friend, you and I are both the sons of slave women, and the two Husseins only (on whom be good wishes and Paradise!) are the sons of a **Bibi**."—*Hist. of Hydur Naik*, tr. by Miles, 486.

[1793.—"I, **Beebee Bulea**, the Princess of

1 The "Bahadur" could hardly have read Don Quixote! But what a curious parallel presents itself! When Sancho is bragging of his daughter to the "Squire of the Wood," and takes umbrage at the free epithet which the said Squire applies to her (= *laundikā* and more); the latter reminds him of the like term of apparent abuse (hardly reproduceable here) with which the mob were wont to greet a champion in the bull-ring after a deft spear-thrust, meaning only the highest fondness and applause!—Part ii. ch. 13.

Cannanore and of the Laccadives Islands, &c., do acknowledge and give in writing that I will pay to the Government of the English East India Company the moiety of whatever is the produce of my country. ..."—*Engagement* in *Logan, Malabar*, iii. 181.]

BEEGUM, BEGUM, &c. s. A Princess, a Mistress, a Lady of Rank; applied to Mahommedan ladies, and in the well-known case of the *Beegum Sumroo* to the professedly Christian (native) wife of a European. The word appears to be Or. Turki, *bīgam*, [which some connect with Skt. *bhaga*, 'lord,'] a feminine formation from *Beg*, 'chief, or lord,' like *Khānum* from *Khān*; hence P. *begam*. [*Beg* appears in the early travellers as *Beage*.]

[1614.—"Narranse saith he standeth bound before **Beage** for 4,800 and odd mamoodies."—*Foster, Letters*, ii. 282.]

[1617.—"Their Company that offered to rob the **Beagam's** junck."—*Sir T. Roe*, Hak. Soc. ii. 454.]

1619.—"Behind the girl came another **Begum**, also an old woman, but lean and feeble, holding on to life with her teeth, as one might say."—*P. della Valle*, Hak. Soc. ii. 6.

1653.—"**Begun**, Reine, on espouse du Schah."—*De la Boullaye le Gouz*, 127.

[1708.—"They are called for this reason '**Begom**,' which means Free from Care or Solicitude" (as if P. *be-gham*, 'without care'!)—*Catron, H. of the Mogul Dynasty in India*, E. T., 287.]

1787.—"Among the charges (against Hastings) there is but one engaged, two at most—the **Begum's** to Sheridan; the Rannee of Goheed (Gohud) to Sir James Erskine. So please your palate."—*Ed. Burke* to Sir G. Elliot. *L. of Ld. Minto*, i. 119.

BEER, s. This liquor, imported from England, [and now largely made in the country], has been a favourite in India from an early date. *Porter* seems to have been common in the 18th century, judging from the advertisements in the *Calcutta Gazette*; and the *Pale Ale* made, it is presumed, expressly for the India market, appears in the earliest years of that publication. That expression has long been disused in India, and *beer*, simply, has represented the thing. Hodgson's at the beginning of this century, was the beer in almost universal use, replaced by Bass, and Allsopp, and of late years by a variety of other brands. [Hodgson's ale is immortalised in *Bon Gualtier*.]

1638.—"... the Captain ... was well provided with ... excellent good Sack, *English* **Beer**, French Wines, *Arak*, and other refreshments."—*Mandelslo, E. T.*, p. 10.

1690.—(At Surat in the English Factory). ... *Europe* Wines and *English* **Beer**, because of their former acquaintance with our Palates, are most coveted and most desirable Liquors, and tho' sold at high Rates, are yet purchased and drunk with pleasure."—*Ovington*, 395.

1784.—"London Porter and *Pale Ale*, light and excellent ... 150 Sicca Rs. per hhd. ..."—In *Seton-Karr*, i. 39.

1810.—"Porter, pale-ale and table-**beer** of great strength, are often drank after meals."—*Williamson, V. M.* i. 122.

1814.—

"What are the luxuries they boast them here?
The lolling couch, the joys of bottled beer."

From '*The Cadet*, a Poem in 6 parts, &c. by a late resident in the East.' This is a most lugubrious production, the author finding nothing to his taste in India. In this respect it reads something like a caricature of "Oakfield," without the noble character and sentiment of that book. As the Rev. Hobart Caunter, the author seems to have come to a less doleful view of things Indian, and for some years he wrote the letterpress of the "Oriental Annual."

BEER, COUNTRY. At present, at least in Upper India, this expression simply indicates ale made in India (see COUNTRY) as at Masūri, Kasauli, and Ootacamund Breweries. But it formerly was (and in Madras perhaps still is) applied to ginger-beer, or to a beverage described in some of the quotations below, which must have become obsolete early in the last century. A drink of this nature called *Sugar-beer* was the ordinary drink at Batavia in the 17th century, and to its use some travellers ascribed the prevalent unhealthiness. This is probably what is described by Jacob Bontius in the first quotation:

1631.—There is a recipe given for a **beer** of this kind, "not at all less good than Dutch beer. ... Take a hooped cask of 30 *amphorae* (?), fill with pure river water; add 2lb. black Java sugar, 4oz. tamarinds, 3 lemons cut up, cork well and put in a cool place. After 14 hours it will boil as if on a fire," &c.—*Hist. Nat. et Med. Indiae Orient.*, p. 8. We doubt the result anticipated.

1789.—"They use a pleasant kind of drink, called **Country-beer**, with their victuals; which is composed of toddy ... porter, and brown-sugar; is of a brisk nature, but when cooled with saltpetre and water, becomes a very refreshing draught."—*Munro, Narrative*, 42.

1810.—"A temporary beverage, suited to the very hot weather, and called **Country-beer**, is in rather *general* use, though water artificially cooled is commonly drunk during the repasts."—*Williamson, V. M.* ii. 122.

BEER-DRINKING. Up to about 1850, and a little later, an ordinary exchange of courtesies at an Anglo-Indian dinner-table in the provinces, especially a mess-table, was to ask a guest, perhaps many yards distant, to "drink beer" with you; in imitation of the English custom of drinking wine together, which became obsolete somewhat earlier. In Western India, when such an invitation was given at a mess-table, two tumblers, holding half a bottle each, were brought to the inviter, who carefully divided the bottle between the two, and then sent one to the guest whom he invited to drink with him.

1848.—"'He aint got distangy manners, dammy,' Bragg observed to his first mate; 'he wouldn't do at Government House, Roper, where his Lordship and Lady William was as kind to me ... and asking me at dinner to **take beer** with him before the Commander-in-Chief himself ...'"—*Vanity Fair*, II. ch. xxii.

1853.—"First one officer, and then another, asked him to **drink beer** at mess, as a kind of tacit suspension of hostilities."—*Oakfield*, ii. 52.

BEGAR, BIGARRY, s. H. *begārī*, from P. *begār*, 'forced labour' [*be* 'without,' *gār* (for *kār*), 'one who works']; a person pressed to carry a load, or do other work really or professedly for public service. In some provinces *begār* is the forced labour, and *bigārī* the pressed man; whilst in Karnāta, *begārī* is the performance of the lowest village offices without money payment, but with remuneration in grain or land (*Wilson*). C. P. Brown says the word is Canarese; but the P. origin is hardly doubtful.

[1519.—"It happened that one day sixty **bigairis** went from the Comorin side towards the fort loaded with oyster-shells."—*Castanheda*, Bk. V. ch. 38.]

[1525.—"The inhabitants of the villages are bound to supply **begarins** who are workmen."—*Archiv. Port. Orient.* Fasc. V. p. 126.]

[1535.—"Telling him that they fought like heroes and worked (at building the fort) like **bygairys**."—*Correa*, iii. 625.]

1554.—"And to 4 **begguaryns**, who serve as water carriers to the Portuguese and others in the said intrenchment, 15 leals a day to each. ..."—*S. Botelho, Tombo*, 78.

1673.—"*Gocurn*, whither I took a Pilgrimage, with one other of the Factors, Four Peons, and Two **Biggereens**, or Porters only."—*Fryer*, 158.

1800.—"The **bygarry** system is not bearable: it must be abolished entirely."—*Wellington*, i. 244.

1815.—*Aitchison's Indian Treaties*, &c., contains under this year numerous *sunnuds* issued, in Nepāl War, to Hill Chiefs, stipulating for attendance when required with "**begarees** and sepoys."—ii. 339 *seqq*.

1882.—"The Malauna people were some time back ordered to make a practicable road, but they flatly refused to do anything of the kind, saying they had never done any **begâr** labour, and did not intend to do any."—(*ref. wanting*.)

BENARES, n.p. The famous and holy city on the Ganges. H. *Banāras* from Skt. *Vārānasī*. The popular Pundit etymology is from the names of the streams *Varaṇā* (mod. *Barnā*) and *Āsī*, the former a river of some size on the north and east of the city, the latter a rivulet now embraced within its area; [or from the mythical founder, *Rājā Banār*]. This origin is very questionable. The name, as that of a city, has been (according to Dr. F. Hall) familiar to Sanscrit literature since B.C. 120. The Buddhist legends would carry it much further back, the name being in them very familiar.

[c. 250 A.D.—"... and the **Errenysis** from the Mathai, an Indian tribe, unite with the Ganges."—*Aelian, Indika*, iv.]

c. 637.—"The Kingdom of *P'o-lo-nis-se* (**Vârânaçî** *Bénarès*) is 4000 *li* in compass. On the west the capital adjoins the Ganges. ..."—*Hiouen Thsang*, in *Pèl. Boudd.* ii. 354.

c. 1020.—"If you go from Bárí on the banks of the Ganges, in an easterly direction, you come to Ajodh, at the distance of 25 parasangs; thence to the great Benares (**Bānāras**) about 20."—*Al-Birūnī*, in *Elliot*, i. 56.

1665.—"**Banarou** is a large City, and handsomely built; the most part of the Houses being either of Brick or Stone ... but the inconveniency is that the Streets are very narrow."—*Tavernier*, E. T., ii. 52; [ed. *Ball*, i. 118. He also uses the forms **Benarez** and **Banarous**, *Ibid.* ii. 182, 225].

BENGAL, n.p. The region of the Ganges Delta and the districts immediately above it; but often in English use with a wide application to the whole territory garrisoned by the

Bengal army. This name does not appear, so far as we have been able to learn, in any Mahommedan or Western writing before the latter part of the 13th century. In the earlier part of that century the Mahommedan writers generally call the province *Lakhnaotī*, after the chief city, but we have also the old form *Bang*, from the indigenous *Vanga*. Already, however, in the 11th century we have it as *Vangālam* on the Inscription of the great Tanjore Pagoda. This is the oldest occurrence that we can cite.

The alleged *City of Bengala* of the Portuguese which has greatly perplexed geographers, probably originated with the Arab custom of giving an important foreign city or seaport the name of the country in which it lay (compare the city of *Solmandala*, under COROMANDEL). It long kept a place in maps. The last occurrence that we know of is in a chart of 1743, in Dalrymple's Collection, which identifies it with Chittagong, and it may be considered certain that Chittagong was the place intended by the older writers (see *Varthema* and *Ovington*). The former, as regards his visiting *Banghella*, deals in fiction—a thing clear from internal evidence, and expressly alleged, by the judicious Garcia de Orta: "As to what you say of Ludovico Vartomano, I have spoken, both here and in Portugal, with men who knew him here in India, and they told me that he went about here in the garb of a Moor, and then reverted to us, doing penance for his sins; and that the man never went further than Calecut and Cochin."—*Colloquios*, f. 30.

c. 1250.—"Muhammad Bakhtiyár ... returned to Behár. Great fear of him prevailed in the minds of the infidels of the territories of Lakhnauti, Behar, **Bang**, and Kámrúp."—*Tabakát-i-Násiri*, in *Elliot*, ii. 307.

1298.—"**Bangala** is a Province towards the south, which up to the year 1290 ... had not yet been conquered. ..." (&c.).—*Marco Polo*, Bk. ii. ch. 55.

c. 1300.—"... then to Bijalár (but better reading **Bangālā**), which from of old is subject to Delhi ..."—*Rashīduddīn*, in *Elliot*, i. 72.

c. 1345.—"... we were at sea 43 days and then arrived in the country of **Banjāla**, which is a vast region abounding in rice. I have seen no country in the world where provisions are cheaper than in this; but it is muggy, and those who come from Khorāsān call it 'a hell full of good things.'"—*Ibn Batuta*, iv. 211. (But the Emperor Aurungzebe is alleged to have "emphatically styled it the *Paradise of Nations*."—Note in *Stavorinus*, i. 291.)

c. 1350.—

"Shukr shikan shawand hama ṭūṭiān-i-Hind
Zīn ḳand-i-Pārsī kih ba **Bangāla** *mi rawad."*
Hāfiz.

i.e.,

"Sugar nibbling are all the parrots of Ind
From this Persian candy that travels to
Bengal" (viz. his own poems).

1498.—"**Bemgala**: in this Kingdom are many Moors, and few Christians, and the King is a Moor ... in this land are many cotton cloths, and silk cloths, and much silver; it is 40 days with a fair wind from Calicut."—*Roteiro de V. da Gama*, 2nd ed. p. 110.

1506.—"A **Banzelo**, el suo Re è Moro, e li se fa el forzo de' panni de gotton ..."—*Leonardo do Ca' Masser*, 28.

1510.—"We took the route towards the city of **Banghella** ... one of the best that I had hitherto seen."—*Varthema*, 210.

1516.—"... the Kingdom of **Bengals**, in which there are many towns. ... Those of the interior are inhabited by Gentiles subject to the King of Bengala, who is a Moor; and the seaports are inhabited by Moors and Gentiles, amongst whom there is much trade and much shipping to many parts, because this sea is a gulf ... and at its inner extremity there is a very great city inhabited by Moors, which is called **Bengala**, with a very good harbour."—*Barbosa*, 178–9.

c. 1590.—"**Bungaleh** originally was called **Bung**; it derived the additional *al* from that being the name given to the mounds of earth which the ancient Rajahs caused to be raised in the low lands, at the foot of the hills."—*Ayeen Akbery*, tr. *Gladwin*, ii. 4 (ed. 1800); [tr. *Jarrett*, ii. 120].

1690.—"Arracan ... is bounded on the *North-West* by the Kingdom of *Bengala*, some Authors making *Chatigam* to be its first Frontier City; but *Teixeira*, and generally the *Portuguese* Writers, reckon that as a City of **Bengala**; and not only so, but place the City of *Bengala* it self ... more South than *Chatigam*. Tho' I confess a late *French* Geographer has put *Bengala* into his Catalogue of imaginary Cities ..."—*Ovington*, 554.

BENGAL, s. This was also the designation of a kind of piece-goods exported from that country to England, in the 17th century. But long before, among the Moors of Spain, a fine muslin seems to have been known as *al-bangala*, surviving in Spanish *albengala*. (See *Dozy and Eng.* s. v.) [What were called "*Bengal* Stripes" were striped ginghams brought first from Bengal and first made in

Great Britain at Paisley. (*Draper's Dict.* s. v.). So a particular kind of silk was known as "*Bengal* wound," because it was "rolled in the rude and artless manner immemorially practised by the natives of that country." (*Milburn*, in *Watt, Econ. Dict.* vi. pt. 3, 185.) See *N.E.D.* for examples of the use of the word as late as Lord Macaulay.]

1696.—"Tis granted that **Bengals** and stain'd Callicoes, and other *East India* Goods, do hinder the Consumption of Norwich stuffs ..."—*Davenant, An Essay on the East India Trade*, 31.

BENGALEE, n.p. A native of Bengal [**Baboo**]. In the following early occurrence in Portuguese, *Bengala* is used:

1552.—"In the defence of the bridge died three of the King's captains and Tuam Bandam, to whose charge it was committed, a *Bengali* (**Bengala**) by nation, and a man sagacious and crafty in stratagems rather than a soldier (cavalheiro)."—*Barros*, II., vi. iii.

[1610.—"**Bangasalys.**" See quotation from Teixeira under BANKSHALL.]

A note to the *Seir Mutaqherin* quotes a Hindustani proverb: **Bangālī** *jangālī, Kashmīrī bepīrī, i.e.* 'The Bengalee is ever an entangler, the Cashmeeree without religion.'

[In modern Anglo-Indian parlance the title is often applied in provinces other than Bengal to officers from N. India. The following from Madras is a curious early instance of the same use of the word:—

[1699.—"Two **Bengalles** here of Council."—*Hedges, Diary*, Hak. Soc. ii. cclxvii.]

***BENIGHTED, THE**, adj. An epithet applied by the denizens of the other Presidencies, in facetious disparagement to Madras. At Madras itself "all Carnatic fashion" is an habitual expression among older English-speaking natives, which appears to convey a similar idea. (See MADRAS, MULL.)

1860.—"... to ye Londe of St Thomé. It ys ane darke Londe, & ther dwellen ye Cimmerians whereof speketh Homerus Poeta in hys Odysseia & to thys Daye thei clepen Tenebrosi, or Ye Benyhted ffolke."—*Fragments of Sir J. Maundevile, from a MS. lately discovered.*

BERIBERI, s. An acute disease, obscure in its nature and pathology, generally but not always presenting dropsical symptoms, as well as paralytic weakness and numbness of the lower extremities, with oppressed breathing. In cases where debility, oppression, anxiety and dyspnœa are extremely severe, the patient sometimes dies in 6 to 30 hours. Though recent reports seem to refer to this disease as almost confined to natives, it is on record that in 1795, in Trincomalee, 200 Europeans died of it.

The word has been alleged to be Singhalese *beri* [the *Mad. Admin. Man. Gloss.* s. v. gives *baribari*], 'debility.' This kind of reduplication is really a common Singhalese practice. It is also sometimes alleged to be a W. Indian Negro term; and other worthless guesses have been made at its origin. The Singhalese origin is on the whole most probable [and is accepted by the *N.E.D.*]. In the quotations from Bontius and Bluteau, the disease described seems to be that formerly known as **Barbiers**. Some authorities have considered these diseases as quite distinct, but Sir Joseph Fayrer, who has paid attention to *beriberi* and written upon it (see *The Practitioner*, January 1877), regards Barbiers as "the dry form of *beri-beri*," and Dr. Lodewijks, quoted below, says briefly that "the Barbiers of some French writers is incontestably the same disease." (On this it is necessary to remark that the use of the term *Barbiers* is by no means confined to French writers, as a glance at the quotations under that word will show). The disease prevails endemically in Ceylon, and in Peninsular India in the coast-tracts, and up to 40 or 60 m. inland; also in Burma and the Malay region, including all the islands, at least so far as New Guinea, and also Japan, where it is known as *kakké:* [see *Chamberlain, Things Japanese*, 3rd ed. p. 238 *seqq.*]. It is very prevalent in certain Madras Jails. The name has become somewhat old-fashioned, but it has recurred of late years, especially in hospital reports from Madras and Burma. It is frequently epidemic, and some of the Dutch physicians regard it as infectious. See a pamphlet, **Beri-Beri** *door J. A. Lodewijks, ond-officier van Gezondheit bij het Ned. Indische Leger*, Harderwijk, 1882. In this pamphlet it is stated that in 1879 the total number of *beri-beri* patients in the military hospitals of Netherlands-India, amounted to 9873, and the deaths among these to 1682. In the great military hospitals at Achin there died of *beri-beri* between 1st November 1879, and 1st April 1880, 574 persons, of whom the great majority were *dwangarbeiders, i.e.* 'forced labourers.' These statistics show the extraordinary prevalence and fatality of the disease in the Archipelago. Dutch literature on the subject is considerable.

Sir George Birdwood tells us that during the Persian Expedition of 1857 he witnessed *beri-beri* of extraordinary virulence, especially among the East African stokers on board the steamers. The sufferers became dropsically distended to a vast extent, and died in a few hours.

In the second quotation *scurvy* is evidently meant. This seems much allied by *causes* to *beriberi* though different in character.

[1568.—"Our people sickened of a disease called **berbere**, the belly and legs swell, and in a few days they die, as there died many, ten or twelve a day."—*Couto*, viii. ch. 25.]

c. 1610.—"Ce ne fut pas tout, car i'eus encor ceste fascheuse maladie de *louende* que les Portugais appellent autrement **berber** et les Hollandais *scurbut*."—*Mocquet*, 221.

1613.—"And under the orders of the said General André Furtado de Mendoça, the discoverer departed to the court of Goa, being ill with the malady of the **berebere**, in order to get himself treated."—*Godinho de Eredia*, f. 58.

1631.—"... Constat frequenti illorum usu, praesertim liquoris *saguier* dicti, non solum diarrhaeas ... sed et paralysin **Beriberi** dictam hinc natam esse."—*Jac. Bontii*, Dial. iv. See also Lib. ii. cap. iii., and Lib. iii. p. 40.

1659.—"There is also another sickness which prevails in Banda and Ceylon, and is called **Barberi**; it does not vex the natives so much as foreigners."—*Sarr*, 37.

1682.—"The Indian and Portuguese women draw from the green flowers and cloves, by means of firing with a still, a water or spirit of marvellous sweet smell ... especially is it good against a certain kind of paralysis called **Berebery**."—*Nieuhof, Zee en Lant-Reize*, ii. 33.

1685.—"The Portuguese in the Island suffer from another sickness which the natives call **béri-béri**."—*Ribeiro*, f. 55.

1720.—"**Berebere** (termo da India). Huma *Paralysia* bastarde, ou entorpecemento, com que fica o corpo como tolhido."—*Bluteau, Dict.* s. v.

1809.—"A complaint, as far as I have learnt, peculiar to the island (Ceylon), the **berri-berri**; it is in fact a dropsy that frequently destroys in a few days."—*Ld. Valentia*, i. 318.

1835.—(On the Maldives) "... the crew of the vessels during the survey ... suffered mostly from two diseases; the **Beri-beri** which attacked the Indians only, and generally proved fatal."—*Young and Christopher*, in *Tr. Ro. Geog. Soc.*, vol. i.

1837.—"Empyreumatic oil called *oleum nigrum*, from the seeds of *Celostrus nutans* (*Malkungnee*) described in Mr. Malcolmson's able prize Essay on the Hist. and Treatment of **Beriberi** ... the most efficacious remedy in that intractable complaint."—*Royle on Hindu Medicine*, 46.

1880.—"A malady much dreaded by the Japanese, called *Kakké*. ... It excites a most singular dread. It is considered to be the same disease as that which, under the name of **Beriberi**, makes such havoc at times on crowded jails and barracks."—*Miss Bird's Japan*, i. 288.

1882.—"**Berbá**, a disease which consists in great swelling of the abdomen."—*Blumentritt, Vocabular*, s. v.

1885.—"Dr. Wallace Taylor, of Osaka, Japan, reports important discoveries respecting the origin of the disease known as **beri-beri**. He has traced it to a microscopic spore largely developed in rice. He has finally detected the same organism in the earth of certain alluvial and damp localities."—*St. James's Gazette*, Aug. 9th.

Also see Report on Prison Admin. in Br. Burma, for 1878, p. 26.

***BERYL**, s. This word is perhaps a very ancient importation from India to the West, it having been supposed that its origin was the Skt. *vaidūrya*, Prak. *velūriya*, whence [Malay *baiduri* and *biduri*], P. *billaur*, and Greek *βήρωλλος*. Bochart points out the probable identity of the two last words by the transposition of *l* and *r*. Another transposition appears to have given Ptolemy his Ὀρούδια ὄρη (for the Western Ghats), representing probably the native *Vaidūrya* mountains. In Ezekiel xxvii. 13, the Sept. has *βηρύλλιον*, where the Hebrew now has *tarshīsh*, [another word with probably the same meaning being *shohsm* (see Professor Ridgeway in *Encycl. Bibl.* s.v. *Beryl*)]. Professor Max Müller has treated of the possible relation between *vaidūrya* and *vidāla*, 'a cat,' and in connection with this observes that "we should, at all events, have learnt the useful lesson that the chapter of accidents is sometimes larger than we suppose."—(*India, What can it Teach us?*" p. 267). This is a lesson which many articles in our book suggest; and in dealing with the same words, it may be indicated that the resemblance between the Greek *αἴλουρος*, *bilaur*, a common H. word for a cat, and the P. *billaur*, 'beryl,' are at least additional illustrations of the remark quoted.

c. A.D. 70.—"**Beryls** ... from India they come as from their native place, for seldom are they to be found elsewhere. ... Those are best accounted of which carrie a sea-water greene."—*Pliny*, Bk. XXXVII. cap. 20 (in *P. Holland*, ii. 613).

c. 150.—"Πυννάτα ἐν ᾗ βήρυλλος"—*Ptolemy*, l. vii.

BETEL, s. The leaf of the *Piper betel*, L., chewed with the dried **areca**-nut (which is thence improperly called *betel-nut*, a mistake as old as Fryer—1673,—see p. 40), *chunam*, etc., by the natives of India and the Indo-Chinese countries. The word is Malayāl. *veṭṭila, i.e. veru* + *ila* = 'simple or mere leaf,' and comes to us through the Port. *betre* and *betle*. **Pawn** (q.v.) is the term more generally used by modern Anglo-Indians. In former times the *betel-leaf* was in S. India the subject of a monopoly of the E. I. Co.

1298.—"All the people of this city (Cael) as well as of the rest of India, have a custom of perpetually keeping in the mouth a certain leaf called *Tembul* ... . the lords and gentlefolks and the King have these leaves prepared with camphor and other aromatic spices, and also mixt with quick-lime. ..."—*Marco Polo*, ii. 358. See also *Abdurrazzāk*, in *India in XV. Cent.*, p. 32.

1498.—In Vasco da Gama's *Roteiro*, p. 59, the word used is *atombor, i.e. al-tambūl* (Arab.) from the Skt. *tāmbūla*. See also *Acosta*, p. 139.

1510.—"This **betel** resembles the leaves of the sour orange, and they are constantly eating it."—*Varthema*, p. 144.

1516.—"We call this **betel** Indian leaf."[1]—*Barbosa*, 73.

[1521.—"**Bettre** (or **vettele**)." See under **ARECA.**]

1552.—"... at one side of the bed ... stood a man ... who held in his hand a gold plate with leaves of **betelle**. ..."—*De Barros*, Dec. I. liv. iv. cap. viii.

1563.—"We call it **betre**, because the first land known by the Portuguese was Malabar, and it comes to my remembrance that in Portugal they used to speak of their coming not to *India*, but to Calecut ... insomuch that in all the names that occur, which are not Portuguese, are Malabar, like **betre**."—*Garcia*, f. 37*g*.

1582.—The transl. of *Castañeda* by N. L. has **betele** (f. 35), and also **vitele** (f. 44).

1585.—A King's letter grants the revenue from betel (**betre**) to the bishop and clergy of Goa.—In *Arch. Port. Or.*, fasc. 3, p. 38.

1615.—"He sent for Coco-Nuts to give the Company, himselfe chewing **Bittle** and lime of Oyster-shels, with a Kernell of Nut called *Arracca*, like an Akorne, it bites in the mouth, accords rheume, cooles the head, strengthens the teeth, & is all their Phisicke."—*Sir T. Roe*, in *Purchas*, i. 537; [with some trifling variations in *Foster's* ed. (Hak. Soc.) i. 19].

1623.—"Celebratur in universo oriente radix quaedam vocata **Betel**, quam Indi et reliqui in ore habere et mandere consueverunt, atque ex eâ mansione mire recreantur, et ad labores tolerandos, et ad languores discutiendos ... . videtur autem esse ex *narcoticis*, quia magnopere denigrat dentes."—*Bacon, Historia Vitae et Mortis*, ed. Amst. 1673, p. 97.

1672.—"They pass the greater part of the day in indolence, occupied only with talk, and chewing **Betel** and Areca, by which means their lips and teeth are always stained."—*P. di Vincenzo Maria*, 232.

1677.—The Court of the E. I. Co. in a letter to Ft. St. George, Dec. 12, disapprove of allowing "Valentine Nurse 20 Rupees a month for diet, 7 Rs. for house-rent, 2 for a cook, 1 for **Beetle**, and 2 for a Porter, which is a most extravagant rate, which we shall not allow him or any other."—*Notes and Exts.*, No. i. p. 21.

1727.—"I presented the Officer that waited on me to the Sea-side (at Calicut) with 5 zequeens for a feast of **bettle** to him and his companions."—*A. Hamilton*, i. 306.

BHEEL, n.p. Skt. *Bhilla*; H. *Bhīl*. The name of a race inhabiting the hills and forests of the Vindhya, Malwa, and of the N.-Western Deccan, and believed to have been the aborigines of Rājputāna; some have supposed them to be the Φυλλῖται of Ptolemy. They are closely allied to the **Coolies** (q. v.) of Guzerat, and are believed to belong to the *Kolarian* division of Indian aborigines. But no distinct Bhīl language survives.

1785.—"A most infernal yell suddenly issued from the deep ravines. Our guides informed us that this was the noise always made by the **Bheels** previous to an attack."—*Forbes, Or. Mem.* iii. 480.

1825.—"All the **Bheels** whom we saw today were small, slender men, less broad-shouldered ... and with faces less Celtic than the Puharees of the Rajmahal. ... Two of them had rude swords and shields, the remainder had all bows and arrows."—*Heber*, ed. 1844, ii. 75.

***BHEESTY**, s. The universal word in the Anglo-Indian households of N. India for the domestic (corresponding to the *saḳḳā* of Egypt) who supplies the family with water, carrying it in a **mussuck**, (q.v.), or goatskin, slung on his back. The word is P. *bihishtī*,

1 *Folium indicum* of the druggist is, however, not *betel*, but the leaf of the wild cassia.

a person of *bihisht* or paradise, though the application appears to be peculiar to Hindustan. We have not been able to trace the history of this term, which does not apparently occur in the *Āīn*, even in the curious account of the way in which water was cooled and supplied in the Court of Akbar (*Blochmann*, tr. i. 55 *seqq.*), or in the old travellers, and is not given in Meninski's lexicon. Vullers gives it only as from Shakespear's Hindustani Dict. [The trade must be of ancient origin in India, as the leather bag is mentioned in the Veda and Manu (*Wilson*, *Rig Veda*, ii. 28; *Institutes*, ii. 79.) Hence Col. Temple (*Ind. Ant.*, xi. 117) suggests that the word is Indian, and connects it with the Skt. *vish*, 'to sprinkle.'] It is one of the fine titles which Indian servants rejoice to bestow on one another, like *Mehtar*, *Khalīfa*, &c. The title in this case has some justification. No class of men (as all Anglo-Indians will agree) is so diligent, so faithful, so unobtrusive, and uncomplaining as that of the *bihishtīs*. And often in battle they have shown their courage and fidelity in supplying water to the wounded in face of much personal danger.

[c. 1660.—"Even the menials and carriers of water belonging to that nation (the Pathāns) are high-spirited and war-like."—*Bernier*, ed. *Constable*, 207.]

1773.—"**Bheestee**, Waterman" (etc.)—*Fergusson*, *Dict. of the Hindostan Language*, &c.

1781.—"I have the happiness to inform you of the fall of Bijah Gurh on the 9th inst. with the loss of only 1 sepoy, 1 **beasty**, and a cossy (? Cossid) killed ..."—Letter in *India Gazette* of Nov. 24th.

1782.—(Table of Wages in Calcutta),

Consummah . . .	10 Rs.
Kistmutdar . . .	6 „
Beasty . . .	5 „

India Gazette, Oct. 12.

Five Rupees continued to be the standard wage of a *bikishtī* for full 80 years after the date given.

1810.—"... If he carries the water himself in the skin of a goat, prepared for that purpose, he then receives the designation of **Bheesty**."—*Williamson*, *V.M.* i. 229.

1829.—"Dressing in a hurry, find the drunken **bheesty** ... has mistaken your boot for the goglet in which you carry your water on the line of march."—*Camp Miseries*, in *John Shipp*, ii. 149. N.B.—We never knew a drunken *bheesty*.

1878.—"Here comes a seal carrying a porpoise on its back. No! it is only our friend the **bheesty**."—*In my Indian Garden*, 79.

[1898
"Of all them black-faced crew,
The finest man I knew
Was our regimental **bhisti**, Ganga Din."
R. Kipling, *Barrack-room Ballads*, p. 23.]

BILAYUT, BILLAIT, &c. n.p. Europe. The word is properly Ar. *Wilāyat*, 'a kingdom, a province,' variously used with specific denotation, as the Afghans term their own country often by this name; and in India again it has come to be employed for distant Europe. In Sicily *Il Regno* is used for the interior of the island, as we use *Mofussil* in India. *Wilāyat* is the usual form in Bombay.

BILAYUTEE PAWNEE, BILÁTEE PANEE. The adject. *bilāyatī* or *wilāyatī* is applied specifically to a variety of exotic articles, *e.g. bilāyatī baingan* (see BRINJAUL), to the tomato, and most especially *bilāyatī pānī*, 'European water,' the usual name for soda-water in Anglo-India.

1885.—"'But look at us English,' I urged, 'we are ordered thousands of miles away from home, and we go without a murmur.' 'It is true, *Khadawund*,' said Gunga Pursad, 'but you *sahebs* drink **English-water** (soda-water), and the strength of it enables you to bear up under all fatigues and sorrows.' His idea (adds Mr. Knighton) was that the effervescing force of the soda-water, and the strength of it which drove out the cork so violently, gave strength to the drinker of it."—*Times of India Mail*, Aug. 11, 1885.

***BILDAR**, s. H. from P. *beldār*, 'a spade-wielder,' an excavator or digging labourer. Term usual in the Public Works Department of Upper India for men employed in that way.

1847.—
"Ye Lyme is alle oute! Ye Masouns lounge aboute!
Ye **Beldars** have alle strucke, and are smoaking atte their Eese!
Ye Brickes are alle done! Ye Kyne are Skynne and Bone,
And ye Threasurour has bolted with xii thousand Rupeese!"
Ye Dreme of an Executive Engineere.

BIRDS' NESTS. The famous edible nests, formed with mucus, by certain swiftlets, *Collocalia nidifica*, and *C. linchi*. Both have long been known on the eastern coasts of the B. of Bengal, in the Malay Islands [and, according to Mr. Skeat in the islands of the Inland Sea (*Tale Sap*) at Singora]. The former is also now known to visit Darjeeling, the Assam Hills, the Western Ghats, &c., and to breed on the islets off Malabar and the Concan.

[**BISMILLAH**, intj., lit. "In the name of God"; a pious ejaculation used by Mahommedans at the commencement of any undertaking. The ordinary form runs—*Bi-'smi 'llāhi 'r-raḥmāni 'r-raḥīm, i.e.* "In the name of God, the Compassionate, the Merciful," is of Jewish origin, and is used at the commencement of meals, putting on new clothes, beginning any new work, &c. In the second form, used at the time of going into battle or slaughtering animals, the allusion to the attribute of mercy is omitted.

[1535.—"As they were killed after the Portuguese manner without the **bysmela**, which they did not say over them."—*Correa*, iii. 746.]

BLACK, s. Adj. and substantive denoting natives of India. Old-fashioned, and heard, if still heard, only from the lower class of Europeans; even in the last generation its habitual use was chiefly confined to these, and to old officers of the Queen's Army.

[1614.—"The 5th ditto came in a ship from Mollacco with 28 Portugals and 36 **Blacks**."—*Foster, Letters*, ii. 31.]

1676.—"We do not approve of your sending any persons to St. Helena against their wills. One of them you sent there makes a great complaint, and we have ordered his liberty to return again if he desires it; for we know not what effect it may have if complaints should be made to the King that we send away the natives; besides that it is against our inclination to buy any **blacks**, and to transport them from their wives and children without their own consent."—*Court's Letter to Ft. St. Geo.*, in *Notes and Exts.* No. i. p. 12.

1747.—"Vencatachlam, the Commanding Officer of the **Black** Military, having behaved very commendably on several occasions against the French; In consideration thereof *Agreed* that a Present be made him of Six hundred Rupees to buy a Horse, that it may encourage him to act in like manner."—*Ft. St. Darid Cons.*, Feb. 6. (MS. Record, in India Office).

1750.—"Having received information that some **Blacks** residing in this town were dealing with the French for goods proper for the Europe market, we told them if we found any proof against any residing under your Honors' protection, that such should suffer our utmost displeasure."—*Ft. Wm. Cons.*, Feb. 4, in *Long*, 24.

1753.—"John Wood, a free merchant, applies for a pass which, if refused him, he says 'it will reduce a free merchant to the condition of a foreigner, or indeed of the meanest **black** fellow.'"—*Ft. Wm. Cons.*, in *Long*, p. 41.

1761.—"You will also receive several private letters from Hastings and Sykes, which must convince me as Circumstances did me at the time, that the Dutch forces were not sent with a View only of defending their own Settlements, but absolutely with a Design of disputing our Influence and Possessions; certain Ruin must have been the Consequence to the East India Company. They were raising **black** Forces at Patna, Cossimbazar, Chinsura, &c., and were working Night and day to compleat a Field Artillery ... all these preparations previous to the commencement of Hostilities plainly prove the Dutch meant to act offensively not defensively."—*Holograph Letter from Clive* (unpublished) *in the* India Office Records. *Dated* Berkeley Square, and *indorsed* "27th Decr. 1761."

1762.—"The **Black** inhabitants send in a petition setting forth the great hardship they labour under in being required to sit as arbitrators in the Court of Cutcherry."—*Ft. Wm. Cons.*, in *Long*, 277.

1782.—See quotation under **Sepoy**, from *Price*.

"... the 35th Regiment, commanded by Major Popham, which had lately behaved in a mutinous manner ... was broke with infamy. ... The **black** officers with halters about their necks, and the sepoys stript of their coats and turbands were drummed out of the Cantonments."—*India Gazette*, March 30.

1787.—"As to yesterday's particular charge, the thing that has made me most inveterate and unrelenting in it is only that it related to cruelty or oppression inflicted on two **black** ladies. ..."—*Lord Minto*, in *Life, &c.*, i. 128.

1789.—"I have just learned from a Friend at the India House, y[t] the object of Treves' ambition at present is to be appointed to the *Adaulet* of Benares, w[h] is now held by a **Black** named Alii Caun. Understanding that most of the *Adaulets* are now held by Europeans, and as I am informed y[t] it is the intention y[t] the Europeans are to be so placed in future, I s[hd] be vastly happy if without committing any injustice you c[d] place young Treves in y[t] situation."—*George P. of Wales*, to Lord Cornwallis, in *C.'s Corresp.* ii. 29.

1832-3.—"And be it further enacted that ... in all captures which shall be made by H. M.'s Army, Royal Artillery, provincial, **black**, or other troops. ..."—*Act* 2 & 3 Will. IV., ch. 53, sec. 2.

The phrase is in use among natives, we know not whether originating with them, or adopted from the usage of the foreigner. But *Kālā ādmī* **'black man,'** is often used by them in speaking to Europeans of other natives. A case in point is perhaps worth recording. A statue of Lord William Bentinck, on foot, and in bronze, stands in front of the Calcutta Town Hall. Many years ago a native officer, returning from duty at Calcutta to Barrackpore, where his regiment was, reported himself to his adjutant (from whom we had the story in later days). 'Anything new, Sūbadār, Sāhib?' said the Adjutant. 'Yes,' said the Sūbadār, 'there is a figure of the former Lord Sahib arrived.' 'And what do you think of it?' '*Sāhib,*' said the Sūbadār, '*abhi hai* kālā ādmī *kā sā, jab potā ho jaegā jab achchhā hogā!*' ('It is now just like a native—'a **black man**'); when the whitewash is applied it will be excellent.'

In some few phrases the term has become crystallised and semi-official. Thus the native dressers in a hospital were, and possibly still are, called **Black Doctors.**

1787.—"The Surgeon's assistant and **Black Doctor** take their station 100 paces in the rear, or in any place of security to which the Doolies may readily carry the wounded."—*Regulations for the H. C.'s Troops on the Coast of Coromandel.*

In the following the meaning is special:

1788.—"*For Sale.* That small upper-roomed Garden House, with about 5 biggahs of ground, on the road leading from Cheringhee to the Burying Ground, which formerly belonged to the Moravians; it is very private, from the number of trees on the ground, and having lately received considerable additions and repairs, is well adapted for a **Black** *Family.* ☞ Apply to Mr. Camac."—*In Seton-Karr,* i. 282.

***BLACK ACT**. This was the name given in odium by the non-official Europeans in India to Act XI., 1836, of the Indian Legislature, which laid down that no person should by reason of his place of birth or of his descent be, in any civil proceeding, excepted from the jurisdiction of the Courts named, viz.: Sudder Dewanny Adawlut, Zillah and City Judge's Courts, Principal Sudder Ameens, Sudder Ameens, and Moonsiff's Court, or, in other words, it placed European subjects on a level with natives as to their subjection in civil causes to all the Company's Courts, including those under Native Judges. This Act was drafted by T. B. Macaulay, then Legislative Member of the Governor-General's Council, and brought great abuse on his head. Recent agitation caused by the "Ilbert Bill," proposing to make Europeans subject to native magistrates in regard to police and criminal charges, has been, by advocates of the latter measure, put on all fours with the agitation of 1836. But there is much that discriminates the two cases.

1876.—"The motive of the scurrility with which Macaulay was assailed by a handful of sorry scribblers was his advocacy of the Act, familiarly known as the **Black Act**, which withdrew from British subjects resident in the provinces their so called privilege of bringing civil appeals before the Supreme Court at Calcutta."—*Trevelyan's Life of Macaulay,* 2nd ed., i. 398.

BLACK LANGUAGE. An old-fashioned expression, for Hindustani and other vernaculars, which used to be common among officers and men of the Royal Army, but was almost confined to them.

BLACK PARTRIDGE, s. The popular Indian name of the common francolin of S.E. Europe and Western Asia (*Francolinus vulgaris,* Stephens), notable for its harsh quasi-articulate call, interpreted in various parts of the world into very different syllables. The rhythm of the call is fairly represented by two of the imitations which come nearest one another, viz. that given by Sultan Baber (Persian): '*Shīr dāram, shakrak*' ('I've got milk and sugar'!) and (Hind.) one given by Jerdon: '*Lahsan piyāz adrak*' ('Garlic, onion, and ginger'!) A more pious one is: *Khudā terī ḳudrat,* 'God is thy strength!' Another mentioned by Capt. Baldwin is very like the truth: 'Be quick, pay your debts!' But perhaps the Greek interpretation recorded by Athenaeus (ix. 39) is best of all: τρὶς τοῖς κακούργοις κακά 'Three-fold ills to the ill-doers!' see *Marco Polo,* Bk. i. ch. xviii. and note 1; [*Burton, Ar. Nights,* iii. 234, iv. 17].

BLACK TOWN; n.p. Still the popular name of the native city of Madras, as distinguished from the Fort and southern suburbs occupied by the English residents, and the bazars which supply their wants. The term is also used at Bombay.

1673.—Fryer calls the native town of Madras "the Heathen Town," and "the Indian Town."

1727.—"The **Black Town** (of Madras) is inhabited by *Gentows, Mahometans,* and *Indian Christians.* ... It was walled in towards the Land, when Governor *Pit* ruled it."—*A. Hamilton,* i. 367.

1780.—"Adjoining the glacis of Fort St. George, to the northward, is a large town commonly called the **Black Town**, and which is fortified sufficiently to prevent any surprise by a body of horse."—*Hodges,* p. 6.

1780.—"... Cadets upon their arrival in the country, many of whom ... are obliged to take up their residence in dirty punch-houses in the **Black Town** ..."—*Munro's Narrative,* 22.

1782.—"When Mr. Hastings came to the government he added some new regulations ... divided the **black** and white **town** (Calcutta) into 35 wards, and purchased the consent of the natives to go a little further off."—*Price, Some Observations, &c.,* p. 60. In *Tracts,* vol. i.

[1813.—"The large bazar, or the street in the **Black Town,** (Bombay) ... contained many good Asiatic houses."—*Forbes, Or. Mem.,* 2nd ed., i. 96. Also see quotation (1809) under BOMBAY.]

1827.—"Hartley hastened from the **Black Town,** more satisfied than before that some deceit was about to be practised towards Menie Gray."—*Walter Scott, The Surgeon's Daughter,* ch. xi.

BOBACHEE, s. A cook (male). This is an Anglo-Indian vulgarisation of *bāwarchī,* a term originally brought, according to Hammer, by the hordes of Chingiz Khan into Western Asia. At the Mongol Court the *Bāwarchī* was a high dignitary, 'Lord Sewer' or the like (see *Hammer's Golden Horde,* 235, 461). The late Prof. A. Schiefner, however, stated to us that he could not trace a Mongol origin for the word, which appears to be Or. Turki. [Platts derives it from P. *bāwar,* 'confidence.']

c. 1333.—"Chaque émir a un **bâwerdjy,** et lorsque la table a éte dressée, cet officier s'assied devant son maître ... le *bâwerdjy* coupe la viande en petits morceaux. Ces gens-là possèdent une grande habileté pour dépecer la viande."—*Ibn Batuta,* ii. 407.

c. 1590.—**Bāwarchī** is the word used for cook in the original of the *Āīn* (*Blochmann's* Eng. Tr. i. 58).

1810.—"... the dripping ... is returned to the meat by a bunch of feathers ... tied to the end of a short stick. This little neat, *cleanly,* and cheap dripping-ladle, answers admirably; it being in the power of the **babachy** to baste any part with great precision."—*Williamson, V. M.* i. 238.

1866.—

"And every night and morning
  The **bobachee** shall kill
The sempiternal *moorghee,*
  And we'll all have a grill."

The Dawk Bungalow, 223.

BOBACHEE CONNAH, s. H. *Bāwarchī-khāna,* 'Cook-house,' *i.e.* Kitchen; generally in a cottage detached from the residence of a European household.

[1829.—"In defiance of all **Bawurchee-khana** rules and regulations."—*Or. Sport Mag.,* i. 118.]

BOBBERY, s. For the origin see BOBBERY-BOB. A noise, a disturbance, a row.

[1710.—"And beat with their hand on the mouth, making a certain noise, which we Portuguese call **babare. Babare** is a word composed of *baba,* 'a child' and *are,* an adverb implying 'to call.'"—*Oriente Conquistado,* vol ii.; *Conquista,* i. div. i. sec. 8.]

1830.—"When the band struck up (my Arab) was much frightened, made **bobbery,** set his foot in a hole and nearly pitched me."—*Mem. of Col. Mountain,* 2nd ed., 106.

1866.—"But what is the meaning of all this **bobbery**?"—*The Dawk Bungalow,* p. 387.

Bobbery is used in 'pigeon English,' and of course a Chinese origin is found for it, viz. *pa-pi,* Cantonese, 'a noise.' [The idea that there is a similar English word (see 7 ser. *N. & Q.,* v. 205, 271, 338, 415, 513) is rejected by the *N.E.D.*]

BOBBERY-BOB! interj. The Anglo-Indian colloquial representation of a common exclamation of Hindus when in surprise or grief—'**Bāp-rē**! or **Bap-rē Bāp,**' 'O Father!' (we have known a friend from north of Tweed whose ordinary interjection was 'My great-grandmother!'). Blumenroth's *Philippine Vocabulary* gives *Nacú!* = *Madre mia,* as a vulgar exclamation of admiration.

1782.—"Captain Cowe being again examined ... if he had any opportunity to make any observations concerning the execution of Nundcomar! said, he had; that he saw the whole except the immediate act of execution ... there were 8 or 10,000 people assembled; who at the moment the Rajah was turned off, dispersed suddenly, crying **'Ah-bauparee!'** leaving nobody about the gallows but the Sheriff and his attendants, and a few European spectators. He explains the term **Ah-baup-aree,** to be an exclamation of the **black** people, upon the appearance of anything very alarming, and when they are in great pain."—*Price's 2nd Letter to E. Burke*, p. 5. In *Tracts*, vol. ii.

"If an Hindoo was to see a house on fire, to receive a smart slap on the face, break a china basin, cut his finger, see two Europeans boxing, or a sparrow shot, he would call out **Ah-baup-aree**!"—From *Report of Select Committee of H. of C., Ibid.* pp. 9–10.

1834.—"They both hastened to the spot, where the man lay senseless, and the syce by his side muttering **Bāpre bāpre**."—*The Baboo*, i. 48.

1863–64.—"My men soon became aware of the unwelcome visitor, and raised the cry, 'A bear, a bear!'

"**Ahi! bap-re-bap!** Oh, my father! go and drive him away,' said a timorous voice from under a blanket close by."—*Lt.-Col. Lewin, A Fly on the Wheel*, 142.

BOBBERY-PACK, s. A pack of hounds of different breeds, or (oftener) of no breed at all, wherewith young officers hunt jackals or the like; presumably so called from the noise and disturbance that such a pack are apt to raise. And hence a 'scratch pack' of any kind, as a 'scratch match' at cricket, &c. (See a quotation under BUNOW.)

1878.—"... on the mornings when the '**bobbera' pack** went out, of which Macpherson was 'master,' and I 'whip,' we used to be up by 4 A.M."—*Life in the Mofussil*, i. 142.

The following occurs in a letter received from an old Indian by one of the authors, some years ago:

"What a Cabinet—has put together!—a regular **bobbery-pack**."

BOMBAY, n.p. It has been alleged, often and positively (as in the quotations below from Fryer and Grose), that this name is an English corruption from the Portuguese *Bombahia*, 'good bay.' The grammar of the alleged etymon is bad, and the history is no better; for the name can be traced long before the Portuguese occupation, long before the arrival of the Portuguese in India. C. 1430, we find the islands of Mahim and *Mumba*-Devi, which united form the existing island of Bombay, held, along with Salsette, by a Hindu Rāī, who was tributary to the Mohammedan King of Guzerat. (See *Rās Mālā*, ii. 350); [ed. 1878, p. 270]. The same form reappears (1516) in Barbosa's Tana-*Mayambu* (p. 68), in the *Estado da India* under 1525, and (1563) in Garcia de Orta, who writes both *Mombaim* and *Bombaim*. The latter author, mentioning the excellence of the areca produced there, speaks of himself having had a grant of the island from the King of Portugal (see below). It is customarily called *Bombaim* on the earliest English Rupee coinage. (See under RUPEE.) The shrine of the goddess **Mumba-Devī** from whom the name is supposed to have been taken, stood on the Esplanade till the middle of the 17th century, when it was removed to its present site in the middle of what is now the most frequented part of the native town.

1507.—"Sultan Mahommed Bigarrah of Guzerat having carried an army against Chaiwal, in the year of the Hijra 913, in order to destroy the Europeans, he effected his designs against the towns of Bassai and **Manbai**, and returned to his own capital. ..."—*Mirat-i-Ahmedi* (Bird's transl.), 214–15.

1508.—"The Viceroy quitted Dabul, passing by Chaul, where he did not care to go in, to avoid delay, and anchored at **Bombaim**, whence the people fled when they saw the fleet, and our men carried off many cows, and caught some blacks whom they found hiding in the woods, and of these they took away those that were good, and killed the rest."—*Correa*, i. 926.

1516.—"... a fortress of the before-named King (of Guzerat), called Tana-**mayambu**, and near it is a Moorish town, very pleasant, with many gardens ... a town of very great Moorish mosques, and temples of worship of the Gentiles ... it is likewise a sea port, but of little trade."—*Barbosa*, 69. The name here appears to combine, in a common oriental fashion, the name of the adjoining town of Thana and Bombay.

1525.—"E a Ilha de **Mombayn**, que no forall velho estaua em catorze mill e quatro cento fedeas ... ĵ xii ij. iiii.[c] fedeas.

"E os anos otros estaua arrendada por mill trezentos setenta e cinque pardaos ... j iii.[c] lxxv. pardaos.

"Foy aforada a mestre Dioguo pelo dito governador, por mill quatro centos trinta dous pardaos méo ... ĵ iiij.[c] xxxij. pardaos méo."—*Tombo do Estada da India*, 160–161.

1531.—"The Governor at the island of **Bombaim** awaited the junction of the whole expedition, of which he made a muster, taking a roll from each captain, of the Portuguese soldiers and sailors and of the captive slaves who could fight and help, and of the number of musketeers, and of other people, such as servants. And all taken together he found in the whole fleet some 3560 soldiers (*homens d'armas*), counting captains and gentlemen; and some

1450 Portuguese seamen, with the pilots and masters; and some 2000 soldiers who were Malabars and Goa Canarines; and 8000 slaves fit to fight; and among these he found more than 3000 musketeers (*espingardeiros*), and 4000 country seamen who could row (*marinheiros de terra remeiros*), besides the mariners of the junks who were more than 800; and with married and single women, and people taking goods and provisions to sell, and menial servants, the whole together was more than 30,000 souls. ..."—*Correa*, iii. 392.

1538.—"The Isle of **Bombay** has on the south the waters of the bay which is called after it, and the island of Chaul; on the N. the island of **Salsete**; on the east Salsete also; and on the west the Indian Ocean. The land of this island is very low, and covered with great and beautiful groves of trees. There is much game, and abundance of meat and rice, and there is no memory of any scarcity. Nowadays it is called the island of **Boa-Vida**; a name given to it by Hector da Silveira, because when his fleet was cruising on this coast his soldiers had great refreshment and enjoyment there."—*J. de Castro, Primeiro Roteiro*, p. 81.

1552.—"... a small stream called *Bate* which runs into the Bay of **Bombain**, and which is regarded as the demarcation between the Kingdom of Guzurate and the Kingdom of Decan."—*Barros*, I. ix. 1.

1552.—"The Governor advanced against **Bombaym** on the 6th February, which was moreover the very day on which Ash Wednesday fell."—*Couto*, IV., v. 5.

1554.—"Item of Mazaguao 8500 *fedeas*.

"Item of **Monbaym**, 17,000 *fedeas*.

"Rents of the land surrendered by the King of Canbaya in 1543, from 1535 to 1548."—*S. Botelko, Tombo*, 139.

1563.—"... and better still is (that the **areca**) of **Mombaim**, an estate and island which the King our Lord has graciously granted me on perpetual lease."[1]—*Garcia De Orta*, f. 91*v*.

"SERVANT. Sir, here is Simon Toscano, your tenant at **Bombaim**, who has brought this basket of mangoes for you to make a present to the Governor; and he says that when he has moored his vessel he will come here to put up."—*Ibid.* f. 134*v*.

1644.—"*Description of the Port of* **Mombaym**. ... The Viceroy Conde de Linhares sent the 8 councillors to fortify this Bay, so that no European enemy should be able to enter. These Ministers visited the place, and were of opinion that the width (of the entrance) being so great, becoming even wider and more unobstructed further in, there was no place that you could fortify so as to defend the entrance. ..."—*Bocarro*, MS. f. 227.

1666.—"Ces Tchérons ... demeurent pour la plupart à Baroche, à **Bambaye** et à Amedabad."—*Thevenot*, v. 40.

"De Bacaim à **Bombaiim** il y a six lieues."—*Ibid.* 248.

1673.—"December the Eighth we paid our Homage to the Union-flag flying on the Fort of **Bombaim**."—*Fryer*, 59.

"Bombaim ... ventures furthest out" into the Sea, making the Mouth of a spacious Bay, whence it has its Etymology; **Bombaim**, quasi *Boon bay*."—*Ibid.* 62.

1676.—"Since the present King of *England* married the Princess of *Portugall*, who had in Portion the famous Port of **Bombeye** ... they coin both Silver, Copper, and Tinn."—*Tavernier*, E. T., ii. 6.

1677.—"Quod dicta Insula de **Bombaim**, una cum dependentiis suis, nobis ab origine bonâ fide ex pacto (sicut oportuit) tradita non fuerit."—*King Charles II.* to the Viceroy L. de Mendoza Furtado, in *Descn., &c. of the Port and Island of* **Bombay**, 1724, p. 77.

1690.—"This Island has its Denomination from the Harbour, which ... was originally called **Boon Bay**, *i.e.* in the *Portuguese* Language, a Good Bay or Harbour."—*Ovington*, 129.

1711.—Lockyer declares it to be impossible, with all the Company's Strength and Art, to make **Bombay** "a Mart of great Business."—P. 83.

c. 1760.—"... one of the most commodious bays perhaps in the world, from which distinction it received the denomination of **Bombay**, by corruption from the Portuguese *Buona-Bahia*, though now usually written by them **Bombaim**."—*Grose*, i. 29.

1770.—"No man chose to settle in a country so unhealthy as to give rise to the proverb *That at* **Bombay** *a man's life did not exceed two monsoons*."—*Raynal* (E. T., 1777), i. 389.

1809.—"The largest pagoda in **Bombay** is in the Black Town. ... It is dedicated to *Momba Devee* ... who by her images and attributes seems to be Parvati, the wife of Siva."—*Maria Graham*, 14.

BONZE, s. A term long applied by Europeans in China to the Buddhist clergy, but originating with early visitors to Japan.

1 "Terra e ilha de que El-Rei nosso senhor me fez mercé, aforada em fatiota." *Em fatiota* is a corruption apparently of *emphyteuta*, *i.e.* properly the person to whom land was granted on a lease such as the Civil Law called *emphyteusis*. "The emphyteuta was a perpetual lessee who paid a perpetual rent to the owner."—*English Cycl.* s.v. *Emphyteusis*.

Its origin is however not quite clear. The Chinese *Fán-sēng*, 'a religious person' is in Japanese *bonzi* or *bonzô;* but Köppen prefers *fă-sze*, 'Teacher of the Law,' pron. in Japanese *bo-zi* (*Die Rel. des Buddha*, i. 321, and also Schott's *Zur Litt. des Chin. Buddhismus*, 1873, p. 46). It will be seen that some of the old quotations favour one, and some the other, of these sources. On the other hand, *Bandhya* (for Skt. *vandya*, 'to whom worship or reverence is due, very reverend') seems to be applied in Nepal to the Buddhist clergy, and Hodgson considers the Japanese bonze (*bonzô ?*) traceable to this. (*Essays*, 1874, p. 63.) The same word, as *bandhe* or *bande*, is in Tibetan similarly applied.—(See *Jaeschke's Dict.*, p. 365.) The word first occurs in Jorge Alvarez's account of Japan, and next, a little later, in the letters of St. Francis Xavier. Cocks in his Diary uses forms approaching *boze*.

1549.—"I find the common secular people here less impure and more obedient to reason than their priests, whom they call **bonzos**."—*Letter of St. F. Xavier*, in *Coleridge's Life*, ii. 238.

1552.—"Erubescunt enim, et incredibiliter confunduntur **Bonxii**, ubi male cohaerere, ac pugnare inter sese ea, quae docent, palam ostenditur."—*Scti. Fr. Xaverii Epistt.* V. xvii., ed. 1667.

1572.—"... sacerdotes ... qui ipsorum linguâ. **Bonzii** appellantur."—*E. Acosta*, 58.

1585.—"They have amongst them (in Japan) many priests of their idols whom they call **Bonsos**, of the which there be great convents."—*Parkes's Tr. of Mendoza* (1589), ii. 300.

1590.—"This doctrine doe all they embrace, which are in China called *Cen*, but with us at Iapon are named **Bonzi**."—*An Exct. Treatise of the Kingd. of China, &c., Hakl.* ii. 580.

c. 1606.—"Capt. Saris has **Bonzees**."—*Purchas*, i. 374.

1618.—"And their is 300 **boze** (or pagon pristes) have alowance and mentaynance for eaver to pray for his sole, in the same sorte as munkes and fryres use to doe amongst the Roman papistes."—*Cocks's Diary*, ii. 75; [in i. 117, **bose**]; **bosses** (i. 143).

[1676.—"It is estimated that there are in this country (Siam) more than 200,000 priests called **Bonzes**."—*Tavernier*, ed. *Ball*, ii. 293.]

1727.—"... or perhaps make him fadge in a *China* **bonzee** in his Calendar, under the name of a Christian Saint."—*A. Hamilton*, i. 253.

1794–7.—

"Alike to me encas'd in Grecian bronze
Koran or Vulgate, Veda, Priest, or **Bonze**."

Pursuits of Literature, 6th ed., p. 335.

c. 1814.—

"While Fum deals in Mandarins, **Bonzes**, Bohea—
Peers, Bishops, and Punch, Hum—are sacred to thee."

T. Moore, Hum and Fum.

BORNEO, n.p. This name, as applied to the great Island in its entirety, is taken from that of the capital town of the chief Malay State existing on it when it became known to Europeans, *Bruné*, *Burné*, *Brunai*, or *Burnai*, still existing and known as *Brunei*.

1516.—"In this island much camphor for eating is gathered, and the Indians value it highly. ... This island is called **Borney**."—*Barbosa*, 203–4.

1521.—"The two ships departed thence, and running among many islands came on one which contained much cinnamon of the finest kind. And then again running among many islands they came to the Island of **Borneo**, where in the harbour they found many junks belonging to merchants from all the parts about Malacca, who make a great mart in that **Borneo**."—*Correa*, ii. 631.

1584.—"Camphora from **Brimeo** (misreading probably for **Bruneo**) neare to China."—*Barret*, in *Hakl.* ii. 412.

[1610.—"**Bornelaya** are with white and black quarls, like checkers, such as Poling-knytsy are."—*Danvers, Letters*, i. 72.]

The cloth called **Bornelaya** perhaps took its name from this island.

["There is brimstone, pepper, **Bournesh** camphor."—*Danvers, Letters*, i. 79.]

1614.—In *Sainsbury*, i. 313 [and in *Foster, Letters*, ii. 94], it is written **Burnea**.

1727.—"The great island of **Bornew** or **Borneo**, the largest except *California* in the known world."—*A. Hamilton*, ii. 44.

BOSH, s. and interj. This is alleged to be taken from the Turkish *bosh*, signifying "empty, vain, useless, void of sense, meaning or utility" (*Red-house's Dict.*). But we have not been able to trace its history or first appearance in English. [According to the *N.E.D.* the word seems to have come into use about 1834 under the influence of Morier's novels, *Ayesha*, *Hajji Baba*, &c. For various speculations on its origin see 5 ser. *N. & Q.* iii. 114, 173, 257.

[1843.—"The people flatter the Envoy into the belief that the tumult is **Bash** (nothing)."—*Lady Sale, Journal*, 47.]

BO TREE, s. The name given in Ceylon to

the Pipal tree (see PEEPUL) as reverenced by the Buddhists; Singh. *bo-gās*. See in *Emerson Tennent* (*Ceylon*, ii. 632 *seqq.*), a chronological series of notices of the Bo-tree from B.C. 288 to A.D. 1739.

1675.—"Of their (the Veddas') worship there is little to tell, except that like the Cingaleze, they set round the high trees **Bogas**, which our people call *Pagod-trees*, with a stone base and put lamps upon it."—*Ryklof Van Goens*, in *Valentijn* (Ceylon), 209.

1681.—"I shall mention but one Tree more as famous and highly set by as any of the rest, if not more so, tho' it bear no fruit, the benefit consisting chiefly in the Holiness of it. This tree they call **Bogahah**; we the *God-tree*."—*Knox*, 18.

BOXWALLAH, s. Hybrid H. *Bakas-* (*i.e.* box) *wālā*. A native itinerant pedlar, or *pack-man*, as he would be called in Scotland by an analogous term. The *Boxwālā* sells cutlery, cheap nick-nacks, and small wares of all kinds, chiefly European. In former days he was a welcome visitor to small stations and solitary bungalows. The **Borā** of Bombay is often a *boxwālā*, and the *boxwālā* in that region is commonly called *Borā*.

BOY, s.

a. A servant. In Southern India and in China a native personal servant is so termed, and is habitually summoned with the vocative '**Boy**!' The same was formerly common in Jamaica and other W. I. Islands. Similar uses are familiar of *puer* (*e.g.* in the Vulgate *Dixit Giezi* puer *Viri Dei*. II Kings v. 20), Ar. *walad*, *παιδάριον*, *garçon*, *knave* (Germ. *Knabe*); and this same word is used for a camp-servant in Shakespeare, where Fluelen says: "Kill the **Poys** and the luggage! 'tis expressly against the laws of arms."—See also *Grose's Mil. Antiquities*, i. 183, The word, however, came to be especially used for 'Slave-boy,' and applied to slaves of any age. The Portuguese used *moço* in the same way. In 'Pigeon English' also 'servant' is *Boy*, whilst 'boy' in our ordinary sense is discriminated as '*smallo-boy*!'

b. A Palankin-bearer. From the name of the caste, Telug. and Malayāl. *bōyi*, Tam. *bōvi*, &c. Wilson gives *bhoi* as H. and Mahr. also. The word is in use northward at least to the Nerbudda R. In the Konkan, people of this class are called *Kahār bhūī* (see *Ind. Ant.* ii. 154, iii. 77). P. Paolino is therefore in error, as he often is, when he says that the word *boy* as applied by the English and other Europeans to the coolies or *facchini* who carry the dooly, "has nothing to do with any Indian language." In the first and third quotations (under **b**), the use is more like **a**, but any connection with English at the dates seems impossible.

a.—

1609.—"I bought of them a *Portugall* **Boy** (which the Hollanders had given unto the King) ... hee cost mee fortie-five Dollers."—*Keeling*, in *Purchas*, i. 196.

"My **Boy** Stephen Grovenor."—*Hawkins*, in *Purchas*, 211. See also 267, 296.

1681.—"We had a *black* **boy** my Father brought from Porto Nova to attend upon him, who seeing his Master to be a Prisoner in the hands of the People of his own Complexion, would not now obey his Command."—*Knox*, 124.

1696.—"Being informed where the Chief man of the Choultry lived, he (Dr. Brown) took his sword and pistol, and being followed by his **boy** with another pistol, and his horse keeper. ..."—In *Wheeler*, i. 300.

1784.—"*Eloped*. From his master's House at Moidapore, a few days since, A Malay Slave **Boy**."—In *Seton-Karr*, i. 45; see also pp. 120, 179.

1836.—"The real Indian ladies lie on a sofa, and if they drop their handkerchief, they just lower their voices and say **Boy**! in a very gentle tone."—*Letters from Madras*, 38.

1866.—"Yes, Sahib, I Christian **Boy**. Plenty poojah do. Sunday time never no work do."—*Trevelyan, The Dawk Bungalow*, p. 226.

Also used by the French in the East:

1872.—"Mon **boy** m'accompagnait pour me servir à l'occasion de guide et d'interprète."—*Rev. des Deux Mondes*, xcviii. 957.

1875.—"He was a faithful servant, or **boy**, as they are here called, about forty years of age."—*Thomson's Malacca*, 228.

1876.—"A Portuguese **Boy** ... from Bombay."—*Blackwood's Mag.*, Nov., p. 578.

b.—

1554.—(At Goa) "also to a *naique*, with 6 *peons* (*piães*) and a *mocadam* with 6 torch-bearers (*tochās*), one umbrella **boy** (*hum* **bóy** *do sombreiro*), two washermen (*mainatos*), 6 water-carriers (**bóys** *d'aguoa*) all serving the governor ... in all 280 pardaos and 4 tangas annually, or 84,240 reis."—*S. Botelho, Tombo*, 57.

[1563.—"And there are men who carry this umbrella so dexterously to ward off the sun, that although their master trots on his horse, the sun does not touch any part of his body, and such men are called in India **boi**."—*Barros*, Dec. 3, Bk. x. ch. 9.]

1591.—A proclamation of the viceroy, Matthias d'Alboquerque, orders: "that no person, of what quality or condition soever, shall go in a *palanquim* without my express licence, save they be over 60 years of age, to be first proved before the Auditor-General of Police ... and those who contravene this shall pay a penalty of 200 cruzados, and persons of mean estate the half, the *palanquys* and their belongings to be forfeited, and the **bois** or mouços who carry such *palanquys* shall be condemned to his Majesty's galleys."—*Archiv. Port. Orient.*, fasc. 3, 324.

1608–10.—"... faisans les graues et obseruans le *Sossiego* à l'Espagnole, ayans tousiours leur **boay** qui porte leur parasol, sans lequel ils n'osent sortir de logis, ou autrement on les estimeroit *picaros* et miserables."—*Mocquet, Voyages*, 305.

1610.—"... autres Gentils qui sont comme Crocheteurs et Porte-faix, qu'ils appellent **Boye**, c'est a dire Bœuf pour porter quelque pesãt faix que ce soit."—*Pyrard de Laval*, ii. 27; [Hak. Soc. ii. 44. On this Mr. Gray notes: "Pyrard's fanciful interpretation 'ox,' Port. *boi*, may be due either to himself or to some Portuguese friend who would have his joke. It is repeated by Boullaye-de-Gouz (p. 211), who finds a parallel indignity in the use of the term *mulets* by the French gentry towards their chair-men."]

1673.—"We might recite the Coolies ... and *Palenkeen* **Boys**; by the very Heathens esteemed a degenerate Offspring of the *Holencores* (see HALALCORE)."—*Fryer*, 34.

1720.—"**Bois**. In Portuguese India are those who carry the *Andores*, and in Salsete there is a village of them which pays its dues from the fish which they sell, buying it from the fishermen of the shores."—*Bluteau, Dict.* s.v.

1755–60.—"... Palankin-**boys**."—*Ives*, 50.

1778.—"**Boys** *de palanquim*, Kàhàr."—*Gramatica Indostanà* (Port.), Roma, 86.

1782.—"... un bambou arqué dans le milieu, qui tient au palanquin, and sur les bouts duquel se mettent 5 ou 6 porteurs qu'on appelle **Bouéu**."—*Sonnerat, Voyage*, i. 58.

1785.—"The **boys** with Colonel Lawrence's palankeen having straggled a little out of the line of march, were picked up by the Morattas."—*Carraccioli, Life of Clive*, i. 207.

1804.—"My palanquin **boys** will be laid on the road on Monday."—*Wellington*, iii. 553.

1809.—"My **boys** were in high spirits, laughing and singing through the whole night."—*Ld. Valentia*, i. 326.

1810.—"The palankeen-bearers are called **Bhois**, and are remarkable for strength and swiftness."—*Maria Graham*, 128.

BRAHMIN, BRAHMAN, BRAMIN, s. In some parts of India called *Bahman*; Skt. *Brāhmaṇa*. This word now means a member of the priestly caste, but the original meaning and use were different. Haug. (*Brahma und die Brahmanen*, pp. 8–11) traces the word to the root *brih*, 'to increase,' and shows how it has come to have its present signification. The older English form is **Brachman**, which comes to us through the Greek and Latin authors.

c. B.C. 330.—" ... τῶν ἐν Ταξίλοις σοφιστῶν ἰδεῖν δύο φησί, Βραχμᾶνας ἀμφοτέρους, τὸν μὲν πρεσβύτερον ἐξυρημένον, τὸν δὲ νεώτερον κομήτην, ἀμφοτέροις δ' ἀκολουθεῖν μαθητάς ..."—*Aristobulus*, quoted in *Strabo*, xv. c. 61.

c. B.C. 300.—"Ἄλλην δὲ διαίρεσιν ποιεῖται περὶ τῶν φιλοσόφων δύο γένη φάσκων, ὧν τοὺς μὲν Βραχμᾶνας καλεῖ, τοὺς δὲ Γαρμάνας [Σαρμάνας?]"—From *Megasthenes*, in *Strabo*, xv. c. 59.

c. A.D. 150.—"But the evil stars have not forced the **Brahmins** to do evil and abominable things; nor have the good stars persuaded the rest of the (Indians) to abstain from evil things."—*Bardesanes*, in *Cureton's Spicilegium*, 18.

c. A.D. 500.—"Βραχμᾶνες; Ἰνδικὸν ἔθνος σοφώτατον οὓς καὶ βράχμας καλοῦσιν."—*Stephanus Byzantinus*.

1298.—Marco Polo writes (pl.) **Abraiaman** or *Abraiamin*, which seems to represent an incorrect Ar. plural (*e.g. Abrāhamīn*) picked up from Arab sailors; the correct Ar. plural is *Barāhima*.

1444.—Poggio taking down the reminiscences of Nicolo Conti writes **Brammones**.

1555.—"Among these is ther a people called **Brachmanes**, whiche (as Didimus their Kinge wrote unto Alexandre ...) live a pure and simple life, led with no likerous lustes of other mennes vanities."—*W. Watreman, Fardle of Faciouns*.

1572.—

"**Brahmenes** são os seus religiosos,
Nome antiguo, e de grande preeminencia:
Observam os preceitos tão famosos
D'hum, que primeiro poz nomo á sciencia."

Camões, vii. 40.

1578.—Acosta has **Bragmen**.

1582.—"Castañeda, tr. by N. L.," has **Bramane**.

1630.—"The **Bramanes** ... Origen, cap. 13 & 15, affirmeth to bee descended from Abraham by Cheturah, who seated themselves in India, and that so they were called **Abrahmanes**."—*Lord, Desc. of the Banian Rel.*, 71.

1676.—
"Comes he to upbraid us with his innocence?
Seize him, and take this preaching
Brachman hence."
Dryden, Aurungzebe, iii. 3.

1688.—"The public worship of the pagods was tolerated at Goa, and the sect of the **Brachmans** daily increased in power, because these Pagan priests had bribed the Portuguese officers."—*Dryden, Life of Xavier*.

1714.—"The Dervis at first made some scruple of violating his promise to the dying **brachman**."—*The Spectator*, No. 578.

BRAHMINY BULL, s. A bull devoted to Siva and let loose; generally found frequenting Hindu bazars, and fattened by the run of the Bunyas' shops. The term is sometimes used more generally (*Brahminy* bull, -ox, or -cow) to denote the humped Indian ox as a species.

1872.—"He could stop a huge **Bramini bull**, when running in fury, by catching hold of its horns."—*Govinda Samanta*, i. 85.

[1889.—"Herbert Edwards made his mark as a writer of the **Brahminee Bull Letters** in the Delhi Gazette."—*Calcutta Rec.*, app. xxii.]

BRAHMINY DUCK, s. The common Anglo-Indian name of the handsome bird *Casarca rutila* (Pallas), or 'Ruddy Shieldrake'; constantly seen on the sandy shores of the Gangetic rivers in single pairs, the pair almost always at some distance apart. The Hindi name is *chakwā*, and the *chakwā-chakwī* (male and female of the species) afford a commonplace comparison in Hindi literature for faithful lovers and spouses. "The Hindus have a legend that two lovers for their indiscretion were transformed into Brahminy Ducks, that they are condemned to pass the night apart from each other, on opposite banks of the river, and that all night long each, in its turn, asks its mate if it shall come across, but the question is always met by a negative—"Chakwa, shall I come?" "No, Chakwi." "Chakwi, shall I come?" "No, Chakwa."—(*Jerdon*.) The same author says the bird is occasionally killed in England.

BRAHMINY KITE, s. The *Milvus Pondicerianus* of Jerdon, *Haliastur Indus*, Boddaert. The name is given because the bird is regarded with some reverence by the Hindus as sacred to Vishnu. It is found throughout India.

c. 1328.—"There is also in this India a certain bird, big, like a **Kite**, having a white head and belly, but all red above, which boldly snatches fish out of the hands of fishermen and other people, and indeed [these birds] go on just like dogs."—*Friar Jordanus*, 36.

1673.—" ... 'tis Sacrilege with them to kill a Cow or Calf; but highly piacular to shoot a **Kite**, *dedicated to the* **Brachmins**, for which Money will hardly pacify."—*Fryer*, 33.

[1813.—"We had a still bolder and more ravenous enemy in the hawks and **brahminee kites**."—*Forbes, Or. Mem.*, 2nd ed., ii. 162.]

BRAHMO-SOMAJ, s. The Bengali pronunciation of Skt. *Brahma Samāja*, 'assembly of Brahmists'; Brahma being the Supreme Being according to the Indian philosophic systems. The reform of Hinduism so called was begun by Ram Mohun Roy (*Rāma Mohana Rāï*) in 1830. Professor A. Weber has shown that it does not constitute an independent Indian movement, but is derived from European Theism. [Also see *Monier-Williams, Brahmanism*, 486.]

1876.—"The **Brahmo Somaj**, or Theistic Church of India, is an experiment hitherto unique in religious history."—*Collet, Brahmo Year-book*, 5.

BRANDY COORTEE, -COATEE, s. Or sometimes simply *Brandy*. A corruption of *bārānī*, 'a cloak,' literally *pluviale*, from P. *bārdu*, 'rain.' **Bārānīkurtī** seems to be a kind of hybrid shaped by the English word *coat*, though *kurtā* and *kurtī* are true P. words for various forms of jacket or tunic.

[1754.—"Their women also being not less than 6000, were dressed with great-coats (these are called **baranni**) of crimson cloth, after the manner of the men, and not to be distinguished at a distance; so that the whole made a very formidable appearance."—*H. of Nadir Shah*, in *Hanway*, 367.]

1788.—"**Barrannee**—a cloak to cover one from the rain."—*Ind. Vocab.* (Stockdale).

[The word **Bārānī** is now commonly used to describe those crops which are dependent on the annual rains, not on artificial irrigation.

[1900.—"The recent rain has improved the **barani** crops."—*Pioneer Mail*, 19th Feb.]

BRANDYPAWNEE, s. Brandy and water; a specimen of genuine *Urdū*, *i.e.* Camp jargon, which hardly needs interpretation. H.

panī, 'water.' Williamson (1810) has *brandy-shraub-pauny* (*V. M.*. ii. 123).

[1854.—"I'm sorry to see you gentlemen drinking **brandy-pawnee**," says he; "it plays the deuce with our young men in India."—*Thackeray, Newcomes*, ch. i.]

1866.—"The **brandy pawnee** of the East, and the 'sangaree' of the West Indies, are happily now almost things of the past, or exist in a very modified form."—*Waring, Tropical Resident*, 177.

BRINJAUL, s. The name of a vegetable called in the W. Indies the *Egg-plant*, and more commonly known to the English in Bengal under that of *bangun* (prop. *baingan*). It is the *Solanum Melongena*, L., very commonly cultivated on the shores of the Mediterranean as well as in India and the East generally. Though not known in a wild state under this form, there is no reasonable doubt that *S. Melongena* is a derivative of the common Indian *S. insanum*, L. The word in the form *brinjaul* is from the Portuguese, as we shall see. But probably there is no word of the kind which has undergone such extraordinary variety of modifications, whilst retaining the same meaning, as this. The Skt. is *bhaṇṭākī*, H. *bhāṇṭā*, *baigan*, *baingan*, P. *badingān*, *badilgān*, Ar. *badinjān*, Span. *alberengena*, *berengena*, Port. *beringela*, *bringiela*, **bringella**, Low Latin *melangolus*, *merangolus*, Ital. *melangola*, *melanzana*, *mela insana*, &c. (see *P. della Valle*, below), French *aubergine* (from *alberengena*), *melongène*, *merangène*, and provincially *belingène*, *albergaine*, *albergine*, *albergame*. (See *Marcel Devic*, p. 46.) Littré, we may remark, explains (*dormitante Homero?*) *aubergine* as '*espèce de morelle*,' giving the etym. as "diminutif de *auberge*" (in the sense of a kind of peach). *Melongena* is no real Latin word, but a factitious rendering of *melanzana*, or, as Marcel Devic says, "Latin du botaniste." It looks as if the Skt. word were the original of all. The H. *baingan* again seems to have been modified from the P. *badingān*, [or, as Platts asserts, direct from the Skt. *vanga*, *vangana*, 'the plant of Bengal,'] and *baingan* also through the Ar. to have been the parent of the Span. *berengena*, and so of all the other European names except the English 'egg-plant.' The Ital. *mela insana* is the most curious of these corruptions, framed by the usual effort after meaning, and connecting itself with the somewhat indigestible reputation of the vegetable as it is eaten in Italy, which is a fact. When cholera is abroad it is considered (*e.g.* in Sicily) to be an act of folly to eat the *melanzana*. There is, however, behind this, some notion (exemplified in the quotation from *Lane's Mod. Egypt.* below) connecting the *badinjān* with madness. [*Burton, Ar. Nights*, iii. 417.] And it would seem that the old Arab medical writers give it a bad character as an article of diet. Thus Avicenna says the *badinjān* generates melancholy and obstructions. To the N. O. *Solanaceae* many poisonous plants belong.

The word has been carried, with the vegetable, to the Archipelago, probably by the Portuguese, for the Malays call it *berinjalā*. [On this Mr. Skeat writes: "The Malay form *brinjal*, from the Port., not *bérinjalā*, is given by Clifford and Swettenham, but it cannot be established as a Malay word, being almost certainly the Eng. *brinjaul* done into Malay. It finds no place in Klinkert, and the native Malay word, which is the only word used in pure Peninsular Malay, is *terong* or *trong*. The form *berinjalā*, I believe, must have come from the Islands if it really exists."]

1554.—(At Goa). "And the excise from garden stuff under which are comprised these things, viz.: Radishes, beetroot, garlick, onions green and dry, green tamarinds, lettuces, *conbalinguas*, ginger, oranges, dill, coriander, mint, cabbage, salted mangoes, **brinjelas**, lemons, gourds, citrons, cucumbers, which articles none may sell in retail except the Rendeiro of this excise, or some one who has got permission from him. ..."—*S. Botelho, Tombo*, 49.

c. 1580.—"Trifolium quoque virens comedunt *Arabes*, mentham *Judaei* crudam, ... **mala insana** ..."—*Prosper Alpinus*, i. 65.

1611.—"We had a market there kept upon the Strand of diuers sorts of prouisions, towit ... **Pallingenies**, cucumbers ..."—*N. Dounton*, in *Purchas*, i. 298.

1616.—"It seems to me to be one of those fruits which are called in good Tuscan *petronciani*, but which by the Lombards are called **melanzane**, and by the vulgar at Rome *marignani*; and if my memory does not deceive me, by the Neapolitans in their patois *molegnane*."—*P. della Valle*, i. 197.

1673.—"The Garden ... planted with Potatoes, Yawms, **Berenjaws**, both hot plants ..."—*Fryer*, 104.

1788.—"Then follow during the rest of the summer, *calabashas* ... **bedin-janas**, and tomatas."—*Shaw's Travels*, 2nd ed. 1757, p. 141.

c. 1740.—"This man (Balaji Rao), who had become absolute in Hindostan as well as in Decan, was fond of bread made of Badjrah ... he lived on raw **Bringelas**, on unripe mangoes, and on raw red pepper."—*Seir Mutaqherin*, iii. 229.

1782.—Sonnerat writes **Béringédes**.—i. 186.

1783.—Forrest spells **brinjalles** (*V. to Mergui*, 40); and (1810) Williamson **biringal** (*V. M.* i. 133). Forbes (1813), **bringal** and **berenjal** (*Or. Mem.* i. 32) [in 2nd ed. i. 22, **bungal**,] ii. 50; [in 2nd ed. i. 348].

1810.—"I saw last night at least two acres covered with **brinjaal**, a species of Solanum."—*Maria Graham*, 24.

1826.—"A plate of poached eggs, fried in sugar and butter; a dish of **badenjâns**, slit in the middle and boiled in grease."—*Hajji Baba*, ed. 1835, p. 150.

1835.—"The neighbours unanimously declared that the husband was mad, ... One exclaimed: 'There is no strength nor power but in God! God restore thee!' Another said: 'How sad! He was really a worthy man.' A third remarked: '**Badingâns** are very abundant just now.'"—*Lane, Mod. Egyptians*, ed. 1860, 299.

1860.—"Amongst other triumphs of the native cuisine were some singular, but by no means inelegant *chefs d'œuvre*, **brinjals** boiled and stuffed with savoury meats, but exhibiting ripe and undressed fruit growing on the same branch."—*Tennent's Ceylon*, ii. 161. This dish is mentioned in the Sanskrit Cookery Book, which passes as by King Nala. It is managed by wrapping part of the fruit in wet cloths whilst the rest is being cooked.

BUCK, v. To prate, to chatter, to talk much and egotistically. H. *baknā*. [A *buck-stick* is a chatterer.]

1880.—"And then ... he **bucks** with a quiet stubborn determination that would fill an American editor, or an Under Secretary of State with despair. He belongs to the 12-foot-tiger school, so perhaps he can't help it."—*Ali Baba*, 164.

BUCKSHEESH, BUXEES, s. P. through P.—H. *bakhshish*. Buonamano, Trinkgeld, pourboire; we don't seem to have in England any exact equivalent for the word, though the thing is so general; 'something for (the driver)' is a poor expression; *tip* is accurate, but is slang; gratuity is official or dictionary English.

[1625.—"**Bacsheese** (as they say in the Arabicke tongue) that is gratis freely."—*Purchas*, ii. 1340 [N.E.D.].

1759.—"To Presents:—

	R.	A.	P.
2 Pieces of flowered Velvet	532	7	0
1 ditto of Broad Cloth ...	50	0	0
Buxis to the Servants ...	50	0	0"

Cost of Entertainment to Jugget Set. In *Long*, 190.

c. 1760.—"... **Buxie** money."—*Ives*, 51.

1810.—"... each mile will cost full one rupee (*i.e.* 2*s.* 6*d.*), besides various little disbursements by way of **buxees**, or presents, to every set of bearers."—*Williamson, V. M.* ii. 235.

1823.—"These Christmas-boxes are said to be an ancient custom here, and I could almost fancy that our name of *box* for this particular kind of present ... is a corruption of **buckshish**, a gift or gratuity, in Turkish, Persian, and Hindoostanee."—*Heber*, i. 45.

1853.—"The relieved bearers opened the shutters, thrust in their torch, and their black heads, and most unceremoniously demanded **buxees**."—*W. Arnold, Oakfield*, i. 239.

BUDDHA, BUDDHISM, BUDDHIST. These words are often written with a quite erroneous assumption of precision *Bhudda*, &c. All that we shall do here is to collect some of the earlier mentions of Buddha and the religion called by his name.

c. 200.—"*Εἰσὶ δὲ τῶν Ἰνδῶν οἱ τοῖς Βούττα πειθόμενοι παραγγέλμασιν· ὃν δι' ὑπερβολὴν σεμνότητος εἰς θεὸν τετιμήκασι.*" *Clemens Alexandrinus*, Strōmatōn, Liber I. (Oxford ed., 1715, i. 359).

c. 240.—"Wisdom and deeds have always from time to time been brought to mankind by the messengers of God. So in one age they have been brought to mankind by the messenger called **Buddha** to India, in another by Zarâdusht to Persia, in another by Jesus to the West. Thereupon this revelation has come down, this prophecy in this last age, through me, Mânî, the messenger of the God of truth to Babylonia."—The Book of *Mānī*, called *Shābūrkān*, quoted by *Albirūnī*, in his *Chronology*, tr. by Sachau, p. 190.

c. 400.—"Apud Gymnosophistas Indiae quasi per manus hujus opinionis auctoritas traditur, quod **Buddam** principem dogmatis eorum, e latere suo virgo generaret. Nec hoc mirum de barbaris, quum Minervam quoque de capite Jovis, et Liberum patrem de femore ejus procreatos, docta finxit Graecia."—*St. Jerome, Adv. Jovinianum*, Lib. i. ed. Vallarsii, ii. 309.

c.440.—"... *Τηνικαῦτα γαρ τὸ Ἐμπεδοκλέους τοῦ παρ' Ἕλλησι φιλοσόφου δόγμα, διὰ τοῦ Μανιχαίου χριστιανισμὸν ὑπερκρίνατο ... τούτου δὲ τοῦ Σκυθιανοῦ μαθητὴς γίνεται Βούδδας, πρότερον Τερέβινθος καλούμενος* ... κ. τ. λ." (see the same matter from *Georgius Cedrenus* below).—*Socratis, Hist. Eccles*. Lib. I. cap. 22.

c. 840.—"An certè Bragmanorum sequemur opinionem, ut quemadmodum illi sectae suae auctorem **Bubdam**, per virginis latus narrant exortum, ita nos Christum fuisse praedicemus? Vel magis sic nascitur Dei sapientia de virginis cerebro, quomodo Minerva de Jovis vertice, tamquam Liber Pater de femore? Ut Christicolam de virginis partu non solennis natura, vel auctoritas sacrae lectionis, sed superstitio Gentilis, et commenta perdoceant fabulosa."—*Ratramni Corbeiensis L. de Nativitate Xti.*, cap. iii. in *L. D' Achery, Spicilegium*, tom. i. p. 54, Paris, 1723.

c. 870.—"The Indians give in general the name of **budd** to anything connected with their worship, or which forms the object of their veneration. So, an idol is called *budd*."—*Biláduri*, in *Elliot*, i. 123.

c. 904.—"**Budāsaf** was the founder of the Sabaean Religion ... he preached to mankind renunciation (of this world) and the intimate contemplation of the superior worlds. ... There was to be read on the gate of the Naobihar[1] at Balkh an inscription in the Persian tongue of which this is the interpretation: 'The words of **Budāsaf**: In the courts of kings three things are needed, Sense, Patience, Wealth.' Below had been written in Arabic: '**Budāsaf** lies. If a free man possesses any of the three, he will flee from the courts of Kings.'"—*Mas'ūdī*, iv. 45 and 49.

1000.—"... pseudo-prophets came forward, the number and history of whom it would be impossible to detail. ... The first mentioned is **Bûdhâsaf**, who came forward in India."—*Albirûnî, Chronology*, by Sachau, p. 186. This name given to Buddha is specially interesting as showing a step nearer the true *Bodhisattra*, the origin of the name *Ἰωάσαφ*, under which Buddha became a Saint of the Church, and as elucidating Prof. Max Müller's ingenious suggestion of that origin (see *Chips*, &c., iv. 184; see also *Academy*, Sept. 1, 1883, p. 146).

c. 1030.—"A stone was found there in the temple of the great **Budda** on which an inscription ... purporting that the temple had been founded 50,000 years ago. ..."—*Al 'Utbi*, in *Elliot*, ii. 39.

c. 1060.—"This madman then, Manēs (also called Soythianus) was by race a Brachman, and he had for his teacher **Budas**, formerly called Terebinthus, who having been brought up by Scythianus in the learning of the Greeks became a follower of the sect of Empedocles (who said there were two first principles opposed to one another), and when he entered Persia declared that he had been born of a virgin, and had been brought up among the hills ... and this **Budas** (alias Terebinthus) did perish, crushed by an unclean spirit."—*Georg. Cedrenus, Hist. Comp.*, Bonn ed., 455 (old ed. i. 259). This wonderful jumble, mainly copied, as we see, from Socrates (*supra*), seems to bring Buddha and Manes together. "Many of the ideas of Manicheism were but fragments of Buddhism."—*E. B. Cowell*, in *Smith's Dict. of Christ. Biog.*

c. 1190.—"Very grieved was Sārang Deva. Constantly he performed the worship of the Arihant; the **Buddhist** religion he adopted; he wore no sword."—*The Poem of Chand Bardai*, paraphr. by *Beames*, in *Ind. Ant.* i. 271.

1610.—"... This Prince is called in the histories of him by many names: his proper name was *Dramá Rajo*; but that by which he has been known since they have held him for a saint is the **Budao**, which is as much as to say 'Sage' ... and to this name the Gentiles throughout all India have dedicated great and superb Pagodas."—*Couto*, Dec. V., liv. vi. cap. 2.

[1615.—"The image of **Dibottes**, with the hudge collosso or bras imadg (or rather idoll) in it."—*Cock's Diary*, i. 200.]

c. 1666.—"There is indeed another, a seventh Sect, which is called **Bauté**, whence do proceed 12 other different sects; but this is not so common as the others, the Votaries of it being hated and despised as a company of irreligious and atheistical people, nor do they live like the rest."—*Bernier*, E. T., ii. 107; [ed. *Constable*, 336].

1685.—"Above all these they have one to whom they pay much veneration, whom they call **Bodu**; his figure is that of a man."—*Ribeiro*, f. 40*b*.

1728.—"Before Gautama **Budhum** there have been known 26 *Budhums*—viz.:. ..."—*Valentijn*, v. (Ceylon) 369.

1753.—"Edrisi nous instruit de cette circonstance, en disant que le *Balahar* est adorateur de **Bodda**. Les Brahmènes du Malabar disent que c'est le nom que Vishtnu a pris dans une de ses apparitions, et on connolt Vishtnu pour une des trois principales divinités Indiennes. Suivant St. Jerôme et St. Clément d'Alexandrie, **Budda** ou **Butta** est le legislateur des Gymno-Sophistes de l'Inde. La secte des **Shamans** ou Samanéens, qui est demeurée la dominante dans tous les royaumes d'au delà du Gange, a fait de **Budda** en cette qualité son objet d'adoration. C'est la première des divinités Chingulaises ou de Ceilan, selon Ribeiro. Samano-Codom (see GAUTAMA), la grande idole des Siamois, est par eux appelé Putti."—*D'Anville, Éclaircissemens*, 75. What knowledge and apprehension, on a subject then so obscure, is shown by this great Geographer! Compare the pretentious ignorance of the flashy Abbé Raynal in the quotations under 1770.

1 Naobihār = Nava-Vihāra ('New Buddhist Monastery') is still the name of a district adjoining Balkh.

1770.—"Among the deities of the second order, particular honours are paid to **Buddou**, who descended upon earth to take upon himself the office of mediator between God and mankind."—*Raynal* (tr. 1777), i. 91.

"The *Budzoists* are another sect of Japan, of which **Budzo** was the founder. ... The spirit of *Budzoism* is dreadful. It breathes nothing but penitence, excessive fear, and cruel severity."—*Ibid.* i. 138. Raynal in the two preceding passages shows that he was not aware that the religions alluded to in Ceylon and in Japan were the same.

1779.—"Il y avoit alors dans ces parties de l'Inde, et principalement à la Côte de Coromandel et à Ceylan, un Culte dont on ignore absolument les Dogmes; le Dieu **Baouth**, dont on ne connoit aujourd'hui, dans l'Inde que le Nom et l'objet de ce Culte; mais il est tout-à-fait aboli, si ce n'est, qu'il se trouve encore quelques familles d'Indiens séparées et méprisées des autres Castes, qui sont restées fidèles à **Baouth**, et qui ne reconnoissent pas la religion des Brames."—*Voyage de M. Gentil*, quoted by *W. Chambers*, in *As. Res.* i. 170.

1801.—"It is generally known that the religion of **Bouddhou** is the religion of the people of *Ceylon*, but no one is acquainted with its forms and precepts. I shall here relate what I have heard upon the subject."—*M. Joinville*, in *As. Res.* vii. 399.

1806.—"... The head is covered with the cone that ever adorns the head of the Chinese deity Fo, who has been often supposed to be the same as **Boudah**."—*Salt, Caves of Salsette*, in *Tr. Lit. Soc. Bo.* i. 50.

1810.—"Among the **Bhuddists** there are no distinct castes."—*Maria Graham*, 89.

It is remarkable how many poems on the subject of Buddha have appeared of late years. We have noted:

1. **Buddha**, *Epische Dichtung in Zwanzig Gesängen, i.e.* an Epic Poem in 20 cantos (in *ottava rima*). Von Joseph Vittor Widmann, Bern. 1869.

2. *The Story of* **Gautama Buddha** *and his Creed*: An Epic bv Richard Phillips, Longmans, 1871. This is also printed in octaves, but each octave consists of 4 heroic couplets.

3. *Vasadavatta*, a **Buddhist** *Idyll*; by Dean Plumtre. Republished in *Things New and Old*, 1884. The subject is the story of the Courtesan of Mathura ("Vāsavadattā and Upagupta"), which is given in Burnouf's *Introd. a l'Histoire du Buddhisme Indien*, 146–148; a touching story, even in its original crude form.

It opens:

"Where proud **Mathoura** rears her hundred towers... ."

The Skt. Dict. gives indeed as an alternative *Mathūra*, but *Mathŭra* is the usual name, whence Anglo-Ind. **Muttra**.

4. The brilliant Poem of Sir Edwin Arnold, called *The Light of Asia, or the Great Renunciation, being the Life and Teaching of* **Gautama**, *Prince of India, and Founder of* **Buddhism**, *as told in verse by an Indian* **Buddhist**, 1879.

BUDLEE, s. A substitute in public or domestic service. H. *badlī*, 'exchange; a person taken in exchange; a *locum tenens*'; from Ar. *badal*, 'he changed.' (See MUDDLE.)

BUDMÁSH, s. One following evil courses; Fr. *mauvais sujet*; It. *malandrino*. Properly *bad-ma'āsh*, from P. *bad*, 'evil,' and Ar. *ma'āsh*, 'means of livelihood.'

1844.—"... the reputation which John Lawrence acquired ... by the masterly manœuvring of a body of police with whom he descended on a nest of gamblers and cut-throats, '**budmashes**' of every description, and took them all prisoners."—*Bosworth Smith's Life of Ld. Lawrence*, i. 178.

1866.—"The truth of the matter is that I was foolish enough to pay these **budmashes** beforehand, and they have thrown me over."—*The Dawk Bungalow*, by *G. O. Trevelyan*, in *Fraser*, p. 385.

BUDZAT, s. H. from P. *badzāt*, 'evil race,' a low fellow, 'a bad lot,' a blackguard.

1866.—"*Cholmondeley.* Why the shaitan didn't you come before, you lazy old **budzart?**"—*The Dawk Bungalow*, p. 215.

BUFFALO, s. This is of course originally from the Latin *bubalus*, which we have in older English forms, *buffle* and *buff* and *bugle*, through the French. The present form probably came from India, as it seems to be the Port. *bufalo*. The proper meaning of *bubalus*, according to Pliny, was not an animal of the ox-kind (βούβαλις was a kind of African antelope); but in Martial, as quoted, it would seem to bear the vulgar sense, rejected by Pliny.

At an early period of our connection with India the name of *buffalo* appears to have been given erroneously to the common Indian ox, whence came the still surviving misnomer of London shops, '*buffalo* humps.'

(See also the quotation from *Ovington.*) The *buffalo* has no hump. Buffalo *tongues* are another matter, and an old luxury, as the third quotation shows. The ox having appropriated the name of the buffalo, the true Indian domestic buffalo was differentiated as the '*water buffalo*,' a phrase still maintained by the British soldier in India. This has probably misled Mr. Blochmann, who uses the term '*water buffalo*,' in his excellent English version of the *Āīn* (*e.g.* i. 219). We find the same phrase in *Barkley's Five Years in Bulgaria*, 1876: "Besides their bullocks every well-to-do Turk had a drove of *water-buffaloes*" (32). Also in *Collingwood's Rambles of a Naturalist* (1868), p. 43, and in *Miss Bird's Golden Chersonese* (1883), 60, 274. [The unscientific use of the word as applied to the American Bison is as old as the end of the 18th century (see *N.E.D.*).]

The domestic buffalo is apparently derived from the wild buffalo (*Bubalus arni*, Jerd.; *Bos bubalus*, Blanf.), whose favourite habitat is in the swampy sites of the Sunderbunds and Eastern Bengal, but whose haunts extend north-eastward to the head of the Assam valley, in the Terai west to Oudh, and south nearly to the Godavery; not beyond this in the Peninsula, though the animal is found in the north and north-east of Ceylon.

The domestic buffalo exists not only in India but in Java, Sumatra, and Manilla, in Mazanderan, Mesopotamia, Babylonia, Adherbijan, Egypt, Turkey, and Italy. It does not seem to be known how or when it was introduced into Italy.—(See *Hehn.*) [According to the *Encycl. Britt.* (9th ed. iv. 442), it was introduced into Greece and Italy towards the close of the 6th century.]

c. A.D. 70.—"Howbeit that country bringeth forth certain kinds of goodly great wild bœufes: to wit the Bisontes, mained with a collar, like Lions; and the Vri [Urus], a mightie strong beast, and a swift, which the ignorant people cali *Buffles* (**bubalos**), whereas indeed the *Buffle* is bred in Affrica, and carieth some resemblance of a calfe rather, or a Stag."—*Pliny*, by *Ph. Hollande*, i. 199–200.

c. A.D. 90.—

"Ille tulit geminos facili cervice juvencos
Illi cessit atrox **bubalus** atque bison."

Martial, De Spectaculis, xxiv.

c. 1580.—"Veneti mercatores linguas **Bubalorum**, tanquam mensis optimas, sale conditas, in magna copia Venetias mittunt."—*Prosperi Alpini, Hist. Nat. Aegypti*, P. I. p. 228.

1585.—"Here be many Tigers, wild **Bufs**, and great store of wilde Foule ..."—*R. Fitch*, in *Hakl.* ii. 389.

"Here are many wilde **buffes** and Elephants."—*Ibid.* 394.

"The King (Akbar) hath ... as they doe credibly report, 1000 Elephants, 30,000 horses, 1400 tame deere, 800 concubines; such store of ounces, tigers, **Buffles**, cocks and Haukes, that it is very strange to see."—*Ibid.* 386.

1589.—"They doo plough and till their ground with kine, **bufalos**, and bulles."—*Mendoza's China*, tr. by *Parkes*, ii. 56.

[c. 1590.—Two methods of snaring the **buffalo** are described in *Āīn, Blochmann*, tr. i. 293.]

1598.—"There is also an infinite number of wild **buffs** that go wandering about the desarts."—*Pigafetta, E. T.* in *Harleian Coll. of Voyages*, ii. 546.

[1623.—"The inhabitants (of Malabar) keep Cows, or **buffalls**."—*P. della Valle*, Hak. Soc. ii. 207.]

1630.—"As to Kine and **Buffaloes** ... they besmeare the floores of their houses with their dung, and thinke the ground sanctified by such pollution."—*Lord, Discoverie of the Banian Religion*, 60–61.

1644.—"We tooke coach to Livorno, thro' the Great Duke's new Parke, full of huge corke-trees; the underwood all myrtills, amongst which were many **buffalos** feeding, a kind of wild ox, short nos'd, horns reversed."—*Evelyn*, Oct. 21.

1666.—"... it produces Elephants in great number, oxen and **buffaloes**" (*bufarox*).—*Faria y Souza*, i. 189.

1689.—"... both of this kind (of Oxen), and the **Buffaloes**, are remarkable for a big piece of Flesh that rises above Six Inches high between their Shoulders, which is the choicest and delicatest piece of Meat upon them, especially put into a dish of Palau."—*Ovington*, 254.

1808.—"... the **Buffala** milk, and curd, and butter simply churned and clarified, is in common use among these Indians, whilst the dainties of the Cow Dairy is prescribed to valetudinarians, as Hectics, and preferred by vicicous (*sic*) appetites, or impotents alone, as that of the caprine and assine is at home."—*Drummond, Illus. of Guzerattee*, &c.

1810.—

"The tank which fed his fields was there ...
There from the intolerable heat
The **buffaloes** retreat;
Only their nostrils raised to meet the air,
Amid the shelt'ring element they rest."

Curse of Kehama ix. 7.

1878.—"I had in my possession a head of a cow **buffalo** that measures 13 feet 8 inches in circumference, and 6 feet 6 inches between the tips—the largest **buffalo** head in the world."—*Pollok, Sport in Br. Burmah,* &c., i. 107.

***BUGGY**, s. In India this is a (two-wheeled) gig with a hood, like the gentleman's cab that was in vogue in London about 1830–40, before broughams came in. Latham puts a (?) after the word, and the earliest examples that he gives are from the second quarter of this century (from Praed and I. D'Israeli). Though we trace the word much further back, we have not discovered its birthplace or etymology. The word, though used in England, has never been very common there; it is better known both in Ireland and in America. Littré gives *boghei* as French also. The American *buggy* is defined by Noah Webster as "a light, one-horse, four-wheel vehicle, usually with one seat, and with or without a calash-top." Cuthbert Bede shows (*N. & Q.* 5 ser. v. p. 445) that the adjective 'buggy' is used in the Eastern Midlands for 'conceited.' This suggests a possible origin. "When the Hunterian spelling-controversy raged in India, a learned Member of Council is said to have stated that he approved the change until —— —— began to spell *buggy as bagī*. Then he gave it up."—(*M.-G. Keatinge.*) I have recently seen this spelling in print. [The *N.E.D.* leaves the etymology unsettled, merely saying that it has been connected with *bogie* and *bug*. The earliest quotation given is that of 1773 below.]

1773.—"Thursday 3d (June). At the sessions at Hicks's Hall two boys were indicted for driving a post-coach and four against a single horse-chaise, throwing out the driver of it, and breaking the chaise to pieces. Justice Welch, the Chairman, took notice of the frequency of the brutish custom among the post drivers, and their insensibility in making it a matter of sport, ludicrously denominating mischief of this kind 'Running down the **Buggies**.'—The prisoners were sentenced to be confined in Newgate for 12 months."—*Gentleman's Magazine*, xliii. 297.

1780.—
"Shall D(*onal*)d come with Butts and tons
And knock down Epegrams and Puns?
With Chairs, old Cots, and **Buggies** trick ye?
Forbid it, Phœbus, and forbid it, Hicky!"
In *Hicky's Bengal Gazette*, May 13th.

"... go twice round the Race-Course as hard as we can set legs to ground, but we are beat hollow by Bob Crochet's Horses driven by Miss Fanny Hardheart, who in her career oversets Tim Capias the Attorney in his **Buggy**. ..."—In *India Gazette*, Dec. 23rd.

1782.—"Wanted, an excellent **Buggy** Horse about 15 Hands high, that will trot 15 miles an hour."—*India Gazette*, Sept. 14.

1784.—"For sale at Mr. Mann's, Rada Bazar. A Phaeton, a four-spring'd **Buggy**, and a two-spring'd ditto. ..."—*Calcutta Gazette*, in *Seton-Karr*, i. 41.

1793.—"For sale. A good **Buggy** and Horse. ..."—*Bombay Courier*, Jan. 20th.

1824.—"... the Archdeacon's **buggy** and horse had every appearance of issuing from the back-gate of a college in Cambridge on Sunday morning."—*Heber*, i. 192 (ed. 1844).

[1837.—"The vehicles of the place (Monghir), amounting to four **Buggies** (that is a foolish term for a cabriolet, but as it is the only vehicle in use in India, and as *buggy* is the only name for said vehicle, I give it up), ... were assembled for our use."—*Miss Eden, Up the Country*, i. 14.]

c. 1838.—"But substitute for him an average ordinary, uninteresting Minister; obese, dumpy ... with a second-rate wife—dusty, deliquescent— ... or let him be seen in one of those Shem-Ham-and-Japhet **buggies**, made on Mount Ararat soon after the subsidence of the waters. ..."—*Sydney Smith*, 3rd Letter to Archdeacon Singleton.

1848.—"'Joseph wants me to see if his—his **buggy** is at the door.'

"'What is a **buggy**, papa?'

"'It is a one-horse palanquin,' said the old gentleman, who was a wag in his way."—*Vanity Fair*, ch. iii.

1872.—"He drove his charger in his old **buggy**."—*A True Reformer*, ch. i.

1878.—"I don't like your new Bombay **buggy**. With much practice I have learned to get into it, I am hanged if I can ever get out."—*Overland Times of India*, 4th Feb.

1879.—"Driven by that hunger for news which impels special correspondents, he had actually ventured to drive in a 'spider,' apparently a kind of **buggy**, from the Tugela to Ginglihovo."—*Spectator*, May 24th.

BULBUL, s. The word *bulbul* is originally Persian (no doubt intended to imitate the bird's note), and applied to a bird which does duty with Persian poets for the nightingale. Whatever the Persian *bulbul* may be correctly, the application of the name to certain species in India "has led to many misconceptions about their powers of voice and song," says Jerdon. These species belong to the family *Brachipodidae*, or short-legged thrushes, and the true *bulbuls* to the sub-family *Pycnonotinae*, *e.g.* genera *Hypsipetes*, *Hemixos*, *Alcurus*, *Criniger*,

Ixos, *Kelaartia*, *Rubigula*, *Brachipodius*, *Otocompsa*, *Pycnonotus* (*P. pygaeus*, common Bengal Bulbul; *P. haemorhous*, common Madras Bulbul). Another sub-family, *Phyllornithinae*, contains various species which Jerdon calls *green Bulbuls*.

[A lady having asked the late Lord Robertson, a Judge of the Court of Session, "What sort of animal is the *bull-bull?*" he replied, "I suppose, Ma'am, it must be the mate of the *coo-coo*."—3rd ser., *N. & Q.* v. 81.]

1784.—"We are literally lulled to sleep by Persian nightingales, and cease to wonder that the **Bulbul**, with a thousand tales, makes such a figure in Persian poetry."—*Sir W. Jones*, in *Memoirs*, &c., ii. 37.

1813.—"The **bulbul** or Persian nightingale. ... I never heard one that possessed the charming variety of the English nightingale ... whether the Indian **bulbul** and that of Iran entirely correspond I have some doubts."—*Forbes, Oriental Memoirs*, i. 50; [2nd ed. i. 34].

1848.—"'It is one's nature to sing and the other's to hoot,' he said, laughing, 'and with such a sweet voice as you have yourself, you must belong to the **Bulbul** faction."—*Vanity Fair*, ii. ch. xxvii.

BULLUMTEER, s. Anglo-Sepoy dialect for '*Volunteer*.' This distinctive title was applied to certain regiments of the old Bengal Army, whose terms of enlistment embraced service beyond sea; and in the days of that army various ludicrous stories were current in connection with the name.

BUMMELO, s. A small fish, abounding on all the coasts of India and the Archipelago; *Harpodon nehereus* of Buch. Hamilton; the specific name being taken from the Bengali name *nehare*. The fish is a great delicacy when fresh caught and fried. When dried it becomes the famous Bombay Duck (see DUCKS, BOMBAY), which is now imported into England.

The origin of either name is obscure. Molesworth gives the word as Mahratti with the spelling *bombīl*, or *bombīla* (p. 595 *a*). *Bummelo* occurs in the Supp. (1727) to Bluteau's Dict. in the Portuguese form *bambulim*, as "the name of a very savoury fish in India." The same word *bambulim* is also explained to mean '*humas pregas na saya a moda*,' 'certain plaits in the fashionable ruff,' but we know not if there is any connection between the two. The form *Bombay Duck* has an analogy to *Digby Chicks* which are sold in the London shops, also a kind of dried fish, pilchards we believe, and the name may have originated in imitation of this or some similar English name. [The *Digby Chick* is said to be a small herring cured in a peculiar manner at *Digby*, in Lincolnshire: but the Americans derive them from *Digby* in Nova Scotia; see 8 ser. *N. & Q.* vii. 247.]

In an old chart of Chittagong River (by B. Plaisted, 1764, published by A. Dalrymple, 1785) we find a point called *Bumbello Point*.

1673.—"Up the Bay a Mile lies Massi-goung, a great Fishing-Town, peculiarly notable for a Fish called **Bumbelow**, the Sustenance of the Poorer sort."—*Fryer*, 67.

1785.—"My friend General Campbell, Governor of Madras, tells me that they make Speldings in the East Indies, particularly at Bombay, where they call them **Bumbaloes**."—Note by *Boswell* in his *Tour to the Hebrides*, under August 18th, 1773.

1810.—"The **bumbelo** is like a large sandeel; it is dried in the sun, and is usually eaten at breakfast with kedgeree."—*Maria Graham*, 25.

1813.—Forbes has **bumbalo**; *Or. Mem.*, i. 53; [2nd ed., i. 36].

1877.—"**Bummalow** or *Bobil*, the dried fish still called 'Bombay Duck.'"—*Burton, Sind Revisited*, i. 68.

BUND, s. Any artificial embankment, a dam, dyke, or causeway. H. *band*. The root is both Skt. (*bandh*) and P., but the common word, used as it is without aspirate, seems to have come from the latter. The word is common in Persia. It is also naturalised in the Anglo-Chinese ports. It is there applied especially to the embanked quay along the shore of the settlements. In Hong Kong alone this is called (not *bund*, but) *praia* (Port. 'shore'), probably adopted from Macao.

1810.—"The great **bund** or dyke."—*Williamson, V. M.* ii. 279.

1860.—"The natives have a tradition that the destruction of the **bund** was effected by a foreign enemy."—*Tennent's Ceylon*, ii. 504.

1875.—"... it is pleasant to see the Chinese ... being propelled along the **bund** in their hand carts."—*Thomson's Malacca*, &c., 408.

1876.—"... so I took a stroll on Tien-Tsin **bund**."—*Gill, River of Golden Sand*, i. 28.

BUNDER, s. P. *bandar*, a landing-place or quay; a seaport; a harbour; (and sometimes also a custom-house). The old Ital. *scala*, mod. *scalo*, is the nearest equivalent in most of the senses that occurs to us. We have (c. 1565) the *Mīr-bandar*, or Port Master, in Sind (*Elliot*, i. 277) [cf. **Shabunder**]. The Portuguese often wrote the word **bandel**. **Bunder** is in S. India the popular native name of Masulipatam, or *Machli-bandar*.

c. 1344.—"The profit of the treasury, which they call **bandar**, consists in the right of buying a certain portion of all sorts of cargo at a fixed price, whether the goods be only worth that or more; and this is called the *Law of the Bandar*."—*Ibn Batuta*, iv. 120.

c. 1346.—"So we landed at the **bandar**, which is a large collection of houses on the seashore."—*Ibid.* 228.

1552.—"Coga-atar sent word to Affonzo d'Alboquerque that on the coast of the main land opposite, at a port which is called **Bandar** Angon ... were arrived two ambassadors of the King of Shiraz."—*Barros*, II. ii. 4.

[1616.—"Besides the danger in intercepting our boats to and from the shore, &c., their firing from the **Banda** would be with much difficulty."—*Foster, Letters*, iv. 328.]

1673.—"We fortify our Houses, have **Bunders** or Docks for our Vessels, to which belong Yards for Seamen, Soldiers, and Stores."—*Fryer*, 115.

1809.—"On the new bunder or pier."—*Maria Graham*, 11.

[1847, 1860.—See quotations under APOLLO BUNDER.]

BUNDOBUST, s. P.-H.—*band-o-bast*, lit. 'tying and binding.' Any system or mode of regulation; discipline; a revenue settlement.

[1768.—"Mr. Rumbold advises us ... he proposes making a tour through that province ... and to settle the **Bandobust** for the ensuing year."—*Letter to the Court of Directors*, in *Verelst, View of Bengal*, App. 77.]

c. 1843.—"There must be *bahut achch'hā bandobast* (*i.e.* very good order or discipline) in your country," said an aged Khānsamā (in Hindustani) to one of the present writers. "When I have gone to the Sandheads to meet a young gentleman from *Bilāyat*, if I gave him a cup of tea, '*tānki tānki*,' said he. Three months afterwards this was all changed; bad language, violence, no more *tānki*."

1880.—"There is not a more fearful wild-fowl than your travelling M.P. This unhappy creature, whose mind is a perfect blank regarding *Faujdari* and **Bandobast**. ..."—*Ali Baba*, 181.

BUNGALOW, s. H. and Mahr. *banglā*. The most usual class of house occupied by Europeans in the interior of India; being on one story, and covered by a pyramidal roof, which in the normal bungalow is of thatch, but may be of tiles without impairing its title to be called a *bungalow*. Most of the houses of officers in Indian cantonments are of this character. In reference to the style of the house, *bungalow* is sometimes employed in contradistinction to the (usually more pretentious) *pucka house*; by which latter term is implied a masonry house with a terraced roof. A *bungalow* may also be a small building of the type which we have described, but of temporary material, in a garden, on a terraced roof for sleeping in, &c., &c. The word has also been adopted by the French in the East, and by Europeans generally in Ceylon, China, Japan, and the coast of Africa.

Wilson writes the word *bānglā*, giving it as a Bengālī word, and as probably derived from *Banga*, Bengal. This is fundamentally the etymology mentioned by Bp. Heber in his *Journal* (see below), and that etymology is corroborated by our first quotation, from a native historian, as well as by that from F. Buchanan. It is to be remembered that in Hindustan proper the adjective 'of or belonging to Bengal' is constantly pronounced as *bangălā* or *banglā*. Thus one of the eras used in E. India is distinguished as the *Banglā* era. The probability is that, when Europeans began to build houses of this character in Behar and Upper India, these were called *Banglā* or 'Bengal-fashion' houses; that the name was adopted by the Europeans themselves and their followers, and so was brought back to Bengal itself, as well as carried to other parts of India. ["In Bengal, and notably in the districts near Calcutta, native houses to this day are divided into *ath-chala*, *chau-chala*, and *Bangala*, or eight-roofed, four-roofed, and Bengali, or common huts. The first term does not imply that the house has eight coverings, but that the roof has four distinct sides with four more projections, so as to cover a verandah all round the house, which is square. The *Bangala*, or Bengali house, or *bungalow* has a sloping roof on two sides and two gable ends. Doubtless the term was taken up by the first settlers in Bengal from the native style of edifice, was materially improved, and was thence carried to other parts of India. It is not necessary to assume that the first bungalows were erected in Behar." (*Saturday Rev.*, 17th April 1886, in a review of the first ed. of this book).]

A.H. 1041 = A.D. 1633.—"Under the rule of

the Bengalis (*darahd-i-Bangālīyān*) a party of Frank merchants, who are inhabitants of Sundíp, came trading to Sátgánw. One kos above that place they occupied some ground on the banks of the estuary. Under the pretence that a building was necessary for their transactions in buying and selling, they erected several houses in the **Bengálí** style."—*Bādshāhnāma*, in *Elliot*, vii. 31.

c. 1680.—In the tracing of an old Dutch chart in the India Office, which may be assigned to about this date, as it has no indication of Calcutta, we find at Hoogly: "*Ougli ... Hollantze Logie* ... **Bangelaer** *of Speelhuys*," *i.e.* "Hoogly ... Dutch Factory ... **Bungalow**, or Pleasure-house."

1711.—"*Mr. Herring, the Pilot's, Directions for bringing of Ships down the River of Hughley.*

"From *Gull Gat* all along the *Hughley* Shore until below the *New Chaney* almost as far as the *Dutch* **Bungelow** lies a Sand. ..."—*Thornton, The English Pilot*, Pt. III. p. 54.

1711.—"*Natty* **Bungelo** or *Nedds* **Bangalla** River lies in this Reach (Tanna) on the Larboard side ..."—*Ibid.* 56. The place in the chart is *Nedds* **Bengalla**, and seems to have been near the present Akra on the Hoogly.

1747.—"Nabob's Camp near the Hedge of the Bounds, building a **Bangallaa**, raising Mudd Walls round the Camp, making Gun Carriages, &c. ... (Pagodas) 55 : 10 : 73."—*Acct. of Extraordinary Charges* ... January, at *Fort St. David, MS. Records in India Office.*

1758.—"I was talking with my friends in Dr. Fullerton's **bangla** when news came of Ram Narain's being defeated."—*Seir Mutaqherin*, ii. 103.

1780.—"To be Sold or Let, A Commodious **Bungalo** and out Houses ... situated on the Road leading from the Hospital to the Burying Ground, and directly opposite to the Avenue in front of Sir Elijah Impey's House. ..."—*The India Gazette*, Dec. 23.

1781–83.—"**Bungalows** are buildings in India, generally raised on a base of brick, one, two, or three feet from the ground, and consist of only one story: the plan of them usually is a large room in the center for an eating and sitting room, and rooms at each corner for sleeping; the whole is covered with one general thatch, which comes low to each side; the spaces between the angle rooms are *viranders* or open porticoes ... sometimes the center *viranders* at each end are converted into rooms."—*Hodges, Travels*, 146.

1784.—"To be let at Chinsurah ... That large and commodious House. ... The out-buildings are—a warehouse and two large *bottle-connahs*, 6 store-rooms, a cook-room, and a garden, with a **bungalow** near the house."—*Cal. Gazette*, in *Seton-Karr*, i. 40.

1787.—"At Barrackpore many of the **Bungalows** much damaged, though none entirely destroyed."—*Ibid.* p. 213.

1793.—"... the **bungalo**, or Summer-house. ..."—*Dirom*, 211.

"For Sale, a **Bungalo** situated between the two Tombstones, in the Island of Coulaba."—*Bombay Courier*, Jan. 12.

1794.—"The candid critic will not however expect the parched plains of India, or **bungaloes** in the land-winds, will hardly tempt the Aonian maids wont to disport on the banks of Tiber and Thames. ..."—*Hugh Boyd*, 170.

1809.—"We came to a small **bungalo** or garden-house, at the point of the hill, from which there is, I think, the finest view I ever saw."—*Maria Graham*, 10.

c. 1810.—"The style of private edifices that is proper and peculiar to Bengal consists of a hut with a pent roof constructed of two sloping sides which meet in a ridge forming the segment of a circle. ... This kind of hut, it is said, from being peculiar to Bengal, is called by the natives **Banggolo**, a name which has been somewhat altered by Europeans, and applied by them to all their buildings in the cottage style, although none of them have the proper shape, and many of them are excellent brick houses."—*Buchanan's Dinagepore* (in *Eastern India*, ii. 922).

1817.—"The *Yorŭ-bangala* is made like two thatched houses or **bangalas**, placed side by side. ... These temples are dedicated to different gods, but are not now frequently seen in Bengal."—*Ward's Hindoos*, Bk. II. ch. i.

c. 1818.—"As soon as the sun is down we will go over to the Captain's **bungalow**."—*Mrs Sherwood, Stories*, &c., ed. 1873, p. 1. The original editions of this book contain an engraving of "The Captain's Bungalow at Cawnpore" (c. 1811–12), which shows that no material change has occurred in the character of such dwellings down to the present time.

1824.—"The house itself of Barrackpore ... barely accommodates Lord Amherst's own family; and his aides-de-camp and visitors sleep in bungalows built at some little distance from it in the Park. **Bungalow**, a corruption of Bengalee, is the general name in this country for any structure in the cottage style, and only of one floor. Some of these are spacious and comfortable dwellings. ..."—*Heber*, ed. 1844, i. 33.

1872.—"L'emplacement du **bungalou** avait été choisi avec un soin tout particulier."—*Rev. des Deux Mondes*, tom., xcviii. 930.

1875.—"The little groups of officers dispersed to their respective **bungalows** to dress and breakfast."—*The Dilemma*, ch. i.

[In Oudh the name was specially applied to Fyzabad.

[1858.—"Fyzabad ... was founded by the first rulers of the reigning family, and called for some time **Bungalow**, from a bungalow which they built on the verge of the stream."—*Sleeman, Journey through the Kingdom of Oudh*, i. 137.].

BUNGALOW, DAWK-, s. A rest-house for the accommodation of travellers, formerly maintained (and still to a reduced extent) by the paternal care of the Government of India. The *matériel* of the accommodation was humble enough, but comprised the things essential for the weary traveller—shelter, a bed and table, a bathroom, and a servant furnishing food at a very moderate cost. On principal lines of thoroughfare these bungalows were at a distance of 10 to 15 miles apart, so that it was possible for a traveller to make his journey by marches without carrying a tent. On some less frequented roads they were 40 or 50 miles apart, adapted to a night's run in a palankin.

1853.—"**Dâk-bungalows** have been described by some Oriental travellers as the 'Inns of India.' Playful satirists!"—*Oakfield*, ii. 17.

1866.—"The **Dawk Bungalow**; or, Is his Appointment Pucka?"—By *G. O. Trevelyan*, in *Fraser's Magazine*, vol. 73, p. 215.

1878.—"I am inclined to think the value of life to a **dak bungalow** fowl must be very trifling."—*In my Indian Garden*, 11.

BUNGY, s. H. *bhangī*. The name of a low caste, habitually employed as sweepers, and in the lowest menial offices, the man being a house sweeper and dog-boy, [his wife an **Ayah**]. Its members are found throughout Northern and Western India, and every European household has a servant of this class. The colloquial application of the term *bungy* to such servants is however peculiar to Bombay, [but the word is commonly used in the N.W.P. but always with a contemptuous significance]. In the Bengal Pry. he is generally called **Mehtar** (q.v.), and by politer natives Halālkhor (see HALALCORE), &c. In Madras *totī* is the usual word; [in W. India *Dher* or *Dheḍ*]. Wilson suggests that the caste name may be derived from *bhang* (see BANG), and this is possible enough, as the class is generally given to strong drink and intoxicating drugs.

1826.—"The *Kalpa* or Skinner, and the **Bunghee**, or Sweeper, are yet one step below the *Dher*."—*Tr. Lit. Soc. Bombay*, iii. 362.

BUNOW, s. and v. H. *banāo*, used in the sense of 'preparation, fabrication,' &c., but properly the imperative of *banānā*, 'to make, prepare, fabricate.' The Anglo-Indian word is applied to anything fictitious or factitious, 'a cram, a shave, a sham'; or, as a verb, to the manufacture of the like. The following lines have been found among old papers belonging to an officer who was at the Court of the Nawāb Sa'ādat 'Ali at Lucknow, at the beginning of the last century:—

"Young Grant and Ford the other day
Would fain have had some Sport,
But Hound nor Beagle none had they,
Nor aught of Canine sort.
A luckless *Parry*[1] came most pat
When Ford—'we've Dogs enow!
Here *Maitre—Kawn aur Doom ko Kaut Juld!* Terrier **bunnow**!'[2]
"So Saadut with the like design
(I mean, to form a Pack)
To ***** t gave a Feather fine
And Red Coat to his Back;
A Persian Sword to clog his side,
And Boots Hussar *sub-nyah*,[3]
Then eyed his Handiwork with Pride,
Crying *Meejir myn* **bunnayah** ! ! !"[4]

"Appointed to be said or sung in all Mosques, Mutts, Tuckeahs, or Eedgahs within the Reserved Dominions."[5]

1853.—"You will see within a week if this is anything more than a **banau**."—*Oakfield*, ii. 58.

[1870.—"We shall be satisfied with choosing for illustration, out of many, one kind of **benowed** or prepared evidence."—*Chevers, Med. Jurisprud.*, 86.]

BURGHER. This word has three distinct applications.

a. s. This is only used in Ceylon. It is the Dutch word *burger*, 'citizen.' The Dutch admitted people of mixt descent to a kind

1 *I.e.* Pariah dog.

2 "Mehtar! cut his ears and tail, quick; *fabricate* a Terrier!"

3 All new.

4 "See, *I* have *fabricated* a Major!"

5 The writer of these lines is believed to have been Captain Robert Skirving, of Croys, Galloway, a brother of Archibald Skirving, a Scotch artist of repute, and the son of Archibald Skirving, of East Lothian, the author of a once famous ballad on the battle of Prestonpans. Captain Skirving served in the Bengal army from about 1780 to 1806, and died about 1840.

of citizenship, and these people were distinguished by this name from pure natives. The word now indicates any persons who claim to be of partly European descent, and is used in the same sense as '*half-caste*' and '*Eurasian*' in India Proper. [In its higher sense it is still used by the Boers of the Transvaal.]

1807.—"The greater part of them were admitted by the Dutch to all the privileges of citizens under the denomination of **Burghers**."—*Cordiner, Desc. of Ceylon.*

1877.—"About 60 years ago the **Burghers** of Ceylon occupied a position similar to that of the Eurasians of India at the present moment."—*Calcutta Review*, cxvii. 180–1.

b. n.p. People of the **Nilgherry** Hills, properly *Baḍagas*, or 'Northerners.'

c. s. A rafter, H. *bargā*.

BURMA, BURMAH (with **BURMESE**, &c.) n.p. The name by which we designate the ancient kingdom and nation occupying the central basin of the Irawadi River. "British Burma" is constituted of the provinces conquered from that kingdom in the two wars of 1824–26 and 1852–53, viz. (in the first) Arakan, Martaban, Tenasserim, and (in the second) Pegu. [Upper Burma and the Shan States were annexed after the third war of 1885.]

The name is taken from **Mran-mā**, the national name of the Burmese people, which they themselves generally pronounce *Bam-mā*, unless when speaking formally and emphatically. Sir Arthur Phayre considers that this name was in all probability adopted by the Mongoloid tribes of the Upper Irawadi, on their conversion to Buddhism by missionaries from Gangetic India, and is identical with that (*Brām-mā*) by which the first and holy inhabitants of the world are styled in the (Pali) Buddhist Scriptures. *Brahma-desa* was the term applied to the country by a Singhalese monk returning thence to Ceylon, in conversation with one of the present writers. It is however the view of Bp. Bigandet and of Prof. Forchhammer, supported by considerable arguments, that *Mran*, *Myan*, or *Myen* was the original name of the Burmese people, and is traceable in the names given to them by their neighbours; *e.g.* by Chinese *Mien* (and in Marco Polo); by Kakhyens, *Myen* or *Mren*; by Shans, *Mān*; by Sgaw Karens, *Payo*; by Pgaw Karens, *Payān*; by Paloungs, *Parān*, &c.[1] Prof. F. considers that Mran-*mā* (with this honorific suffix) does not date beyond the 14th century. [In *J. R A. Soc.* (1894, p. 152 *seqq.*), Mr. St John suggests that the word *Myamma* is derived from *myan*, 'swift,' and *ma*, 'strong,' and was taken as a soubriquet by the people at some early date, perhaps in the time of Anawrahta, A.D. 1150.]

1516.—"Having passed the Kingdom of Bengale, along the coast which turns to the South, there is another Kingdom of Gentiles, called **Berma**. ... They frequently are at war with the King of Peigu. We have no further information respecting this country, because it has no shipping."—*Barbosa*, 181.

[1538.—"But the war lasted on and the **Bramās** took all the kingdom."—*Correa*, iii. 851.]

1543.—"And folk coming to know of the secrecy with which the force was being despatched, a great desire took possession of all to know whither the Governor intended to send so large an armament, there being no Rumis to go after, and nothing being known of any other cause why ships should be despatched in secret at such a time. So some gentlemen spoke of it to the Governor, and much importuned him to tell them whither they were going, and the Governor, all the more bent on concealment of his intentions, told them that the expedition was going to Pegu to fight with the **Bramas** who had taken that Kingdom."—*Ibid.* iv. 298.

c. 1545.—"*How the King of* **Bramâ** *undertook the conquest of this kingdom of Sião* (Siam), *and of what happened till his arrival at the City of Odiâ.*"—*F. M. Pinto* (orig.) cap. 185.

1606.—"Although one's whole life were wasted in describing the superstitions of these Gentiles—the Pegus and the **Bramas**—one could not have done with the half, therefore I only treat of some, in passing, as I am now about to do."—*Couto*, viii. cap. xii.

[1639.—"His (King of Pegu's) Guard consists of a great number of Souldiers, with them called **Brahmans**, is kept at the second Port."—*Mandelslo, Travels*, E. T. ii. 118.]

1680.—"ARTICLES of COMMERCE to be proposed to the King of **Barma** and Pegu, in behalfe of the English Nation for the settling of a Trade in those countrys."—*Ft. St. Geo. Cons.*, in *Notes and Exts.*, iii. 7.

1727.—"The Dominions of **Barma** are at present very large, reaching from *Moravi* near *Tanacerin*, to the Province of *Yunan* in *China*."—*A. Hamilton*, ii. 41.

---

1 Forchhammer argues further that the original name was Ran or Yan, with *m'*, *mā*, or *pa* as a pronominal accent.

1759.—"The **Bûraghmahs** are much more numerous than the Peguese and more addicted to commerce; even in Pegu their numbers are 100 to 1."—Letter in *Dalrymple, O. R.*, i. 99. The writer appears desirous to convey by his unusual spelling some accurate reproduction of the name as he had heard it. His testimony as to the predominance of Burmese in Pegu, at that date even, is remarkable.

[1782.—"**Bahmans.**" See quotation under GAUTAMA.]

1793.—"**Burmah** borders on Pegu to the north, and occupies both banks of the river as far as the frontiers of China."—*Rennell's Memoir*, 297.

[c. 1819.—"In fact in their own language, their name is not **Burmese**, which we have borrowed from the Portuguese, but **Biamma.**"—*Sangermano*, 36.]

BURRA-BEEBEE, s. H. *barī bībī*, 'Grande dame.' This is a kind of slang word applied in Anglo-Indian society to the lady who claims precedence at a party. [Nowadays *Baṛī Mem* is the term applied to the chief lady in a Station.]

1807.—"At table I have hitherto been allowed but one dish, namely the **Burro Bebee**, or lady of the highest rank."—*Lord Minto in India*, 29.

1848.—"The ladies carry their **burrah-bibiship** into the steamers when they go to England. ... My friend endeavoured in vain to persuade them that whatever their social importance in the 'City of Palaces,' they would be but small folk in London."—*Chow Chow*, by *Viscountess Falkland*, i. 92.

[**BURRA-DIN**, s. H. *baṛā-din*. A 'great day,' the term applied by natives to a great festival of Europeans, particularly to Christmas Day.

[1880.—"This being the **Burra Din**, or great day, the fact of an animal being shot was interpreted by the men as a favourable augury."—*Ball; Jungle Life*, 279.]

BURRA-KHANA, s. H. *barā khāna*, 'big dinner'; a term of the same character as the two last, applied to a vast and solemn entertainment.

[1880.—"To go out to a **burra khana**, or big dinner, which is succeeded in the same or some other house by a larger evening party."—*Wilson, Abode of Snow*, 51.]

BURRA SAHIB. H. *baṛā*, 'great'; 'the great *Ṣāḥib* (or Master),' a term constantly occurring, whether in a family to distinguish the father or the elder brother, in a station to indicate the Collector, Commissioner, or whatever officer may be the recognised head of the society, or in a department to designate the head of that department, local or remote.

[1889.—"At any rate a few of the great lords and ladies (**Burra Sahib** and **Burra Mem Sahib**) did speak to me without being driven to it."—*Lady Dufferin*, 34.]

BUS, adv. P-H. *bas*, 'enough.' Used commonly as a kind of interjection: 'Enough! Stop! *Ohe jam satis! Basta, basta!*' Few Hindustani words stick closer by the returned Anglo-Indian. The Italian expression, though of obscure etymology, can hardly have any connection with *bas*. But in use it always feels like a mere expansion of it!

1853.—"'And if you pass,' say my dear good-natured friends, 'you may get an appointment. **Bus**! (you see my Hindostanee knowledge already carries me the length of that emphatic monosyllable). ...'"—*Oakfield*, 2nd ed. i. 42.

BUSTEE, s. An inhabited quarter, a village. H. *bastī*, from Skt. *vas* = 'dwell.' Many years ago a native in Upper India said to a European assistant in the Canal Department: "You Feringis talk much of your country and its power, but we know that the whole of you come from five villages" (*pānch* **basti**). The word is applied in Calcutta to the separate groups of huts in the humbler native quarters, the sanitary state of which has often been held up to reprobation.

[1889.—"There is a dreary **bustee** in the neighbourhood which is said to make the most of any cholera that may be going."—*R. Kipling, City of Dreadful Night*, 54.]

BUTLER, s. In the Madras and Bombay Presidencies this is the title usually applied to the head-servant of any English or quasi-English household. He generally makes the daily market, has charge of domestic stores, and superintends the table. As his profession is one which affords a large scope for feathering a nest at the expense of a foreign master, it is often followed at Madras by men of comparatively good caste. (See CONSUMAH.)

1616.—"Yosky the **butler**, being sick, asked lycense to goe to his howse to take phisick."—*Cocks*, i. 135.

1689.—"... the **Butlers** are enjoin'd to take an account of the Place each Night, before they depart home, that they (the Peons) might be examin'd before they stir, if ought be wanting."—*Ovington*, 393.

1782.—"Wanted a Person to act as Steward or **Butler** in a Gentleman's House, *he must understand Hairdressing*."—*India Gazette*, March 2.

1789.—"No person considers himself as comfortably accommodated without entertaining a *Dubash* at 4 pagodas per month, a **Butler** at 3, a Peon at 2, a Cook at 3, a Compradore at 2, and kitchen boy at 1 pagoda."—*Munro's Narrative of Operations*, p. 27.

1873.—"Glancing round, my eye fell on the pantry department ... and the **butler** trimming the reading lamps."—*Camp Life in India, Fraser's Mag.*, June, 696.

1879.—"... the moment when it occurred to him (*i.e.* the Nyoung-young Prince of Burma) that he ought really to assume the guise of a Madras **butler**, and be off to the Residency, was the happiest inspiration of his life."—*Standard*, July 11.

BUTLER-ENGLISH: The broken English spoken by native servants in the Madras Presidency; which is not very much better than the **Pigeon-English** of China. It is a singular dialect; the present participle (*e.g.*) being used for the future indicative, and the preterite indicative being formed by 'done'; thus *I telling* = 'I will tell'; *I done tell* = 'I have told'; *done come* = 'actually arrived.' Peculiar meanings are also attached to words; thus *family* = 'wife.' The oddest characteristic about this jargon is (or was) that masters used it in speaking to their servants as well as servants to their masters.

C

CABOB, s. Ar.-H. *kabāb*. This word is used in Anglo-Indian households generically for roast meat. [It usually follows the name of the dish, *e.g. murghī kabāb*, 'roast fowl'.] But specifically it is applied to the dish described in the quotations from Fryer and Ovington.

c. 1580.—"Altero modo ... ipsam (carnem) in parva frustra dissectam, et veruculis ferreis acuum modo infixam, super crates ferreas igne supposito positam torrefaciunt, quam succo limonum aspersam avidè esitant."—*Prosper Alpinus*, Pt. i. 229.

1673.—"**Cabob** is Rostmeat on Skewers, cut in little round pieces no bigger than a Sixpence, and Ginger and Garlick put between each."—*Fryer*, 404.

1689.—"**Cabob**, that is Beef or Mutton cut in small pieces, sprinkled with salt and pepper, and dipt with Oil and Garlick, which have been mixt together in a dish, and then roasted on a Spit, with sweet Herbs put between and stuff in them, and basted with Oil and Garlick all the while."—*Ovington*, 397.

1814.—"I often partook with my Arabs of a dish common in Arabia called **Kabob** or **Kab-ab**, which is meat cut into small pieces and placed on thin skewers, alternately between slices of onion and green ginger, seasoned with pepper, salt, and Kian, fried in ghee, to be ate with rice and dholl."—*Forbes, Or. Mem.* ii. 480; [2nd ed. ii. 82; in i. 315 he writes **Kebabs**].

[1876.—"... *kavap* (a name which is naturalised with us as **Cabobs**), small bits of meat roasted on a spit. ..."—*Schuyler*, *Turkistan*, i. 125.]

***CABUL, CAUBOOL**, &c., n.p. This name (*Kābul*) of the chief city of N. Afghanistan, now so familiar, is perhaps traceable in Ptolemy, who gives in that same region a people called *Καβολῖται*, and a city called *Κάβουρα*. Perhaps, however, one or both may be corroborated by the *νάρδος Καβαλίτη* of the Periplus. The accent of Kābul is most distinctly on the first and long syllable, but English mouths are very perverse in error here. Moore accents the last syllable:

"... pomegranates full
Of melting sweetness, and the pears
And sunniest apples that **Caubul**
In all its thousand gardens bears."
Light of the Harem.

Mr. Arnold does likewise in *Sohrab and Rustam:*

"But as a troop of pedlars from **Cabool**,
Cross underneath the Indian Caucasus... ."

It was told characteristically of the late Lord Ellenborough that, after his arrival in India, though for months he heard the name correctly spoken by his councillors and his staff, he persisted in calling it *Căbōōl* till he met Dost Mahommed Khan. After the interview the Governor-General announced as a new discovery, from the Amir's pronunciation, that *Cābŭl* was the correct form.

1552.—Barros calls it "a Cidade **Cabol**, Metropoli dos Mogoles."—IV. vi. 1.

[c. 1590.—"The territory of **Kábul** comprises twenty Tumáns."—*Āīn*, tr. *Jarrett*, ii. 410.]

1856.—

"Ah **Cabul**! word of woe and bitter shame;
Where proud old England's flag, dishonoured, sank
Beneath the Crescent; and the butcher knives

Beat down like reeds the bayonets that had flashed
From Plassey on to snow-capt Caucasus,
In triumph through a hundred years of war."
The Banyan Tree, a Poem.

CADDY, s. *i.e.* tea-caddy. This is possibly, as Crawfurd suggests, from **Catty** (q.v.), and may have been originally applied to a small box containing a *catty* or two of tea. The suggestion is confirmed by this advertisement:

1792.—"By R. Henderson ... A Quantity of Tea in Quarter Chests and **Caddies**, imported last season. ..."—*Madras Courier*, Dec. 2.

CAFFER, CAFFRE, COFFREE, &c., n.p. The word is properly the Ar. *Kāfir*, pl. *Kofra*, 'an infidel, an unbeliever in Islām.' As the Arabs applied this to Pagan negroes, among others, the Portuguese at an early date took it up in this sense, and our countrymen from them. A further appropriation in one direction has since made the name specifically that of the black tribes of South Africa, whom we now call, or till recently did call, **Caffres**. It was also applied in the Philippine Islands to the Papuas of N. Guinea, and the Alfuras of the Moluccas, brought into the slave-market.

In another direction the word has become a quasi-proper name of the (more or less) fair, and non-Mahommedan, tribes of Hindu-Kush, sometimes called more specifically the *Siāhposh* or 'black-robed' **Cafirs**.

The term is often applied malevolently by Mahommedans to Christians, and this is probably the origin of the mistake pervading some of the early Portuguese narratives, especially the *Roteiro of Vasco da Gama*, which described many of the Hindu and Indo-Chinese States as being Christian.[1]

[c. 1300.—"**Kāfir.**" See under LACK.]

c. 1404.—Of a people near China: "They were Christians after the manner of those of Cathay."—*Clavijo* by *Markham*, 141.

And of India: "The people of India are Christians, the Lord and most part of the people, after the manner of the Greeks; and among them also are other Christians who mark themselves with fire in the face, and their creed is different from that of the others; for those who thus mark themselves with fire are less esteemed than the others. And among them are Moors and Jews, but they are subject to the Christians."—*Clavijo*, (orig.) § cxxi.; comp. *Markham*, 153–4. Here we have (1) the confusion of **Caffer** and Christian; and (2) the confusion of Abyssinia (*India Tertia* or *Middle India* of some medieval writers) with India Proper.

c. 1470.—"The sea is infested with pirates, all of whom are **Kofars**, neither Christians nor Mussulmans; they pray to stone idols, and know not Christ."—*Athan. Nitikin*, in *India in the XVth Cent.*, p. 11.

1552.—"... he learned that the whole people of the Island of S. Lourenco ... were black **Cafres** with curly hair like those of Mozambique."—*Barros*, II. i. 1.

1563.—"In the year 1484 there came to Portugal the King of Benin, a **Caffre** by nation, and he became a Christian."—*Stanley's Correa* p. 8

1572.—
"Verão os **Cafres** asperos e avaros
Tirar a linda dama seus vestidos."
Camões, v. 47.

By Burton:
"shall see the **Caffres**, greedy race and fere
"strip the fair Ladye of her raiment torn."

1582.—"These men are called **Cafres** and are Gentiles."—*Castañeda* (by N.L.), f. 42*b*.

c. 1610.—"Il estoit fils d'vn **Cafre** d'Ethiopie, et d'vne femme de ces isles, ce qu'on appelle Mulastre."—*Pyrard de Laval*, i. 220; [Hak. Soc. i. 307].

[c. 1610.—"... a Christian whom they call **Caparou.**"—*Ibid.*, Hak. Soc. i. 261.]

1614:—"That knave Simon the **Caffro**, not what the writer took him for—he is a knave, and better lost than found."—*Sainsbury*, i. 356.

[1615.—"Odola and Gala are **Capharrs** which signifieth misbelievers:"—*Sir T. Roe*, Hak. Soc. i: 23.]

1653.—"... toy mesme qui passe pour vn **Kiaffer**, ou homme sans Dieu, parmi les Mausulmans."—*De la Boullaye-le-Gouz*, 310 (ed. 1657).

c. 1665.—"It will appear in the sequel of this History, that the pretence used by *Aureng-Zebe*, his third Brother, to cut off his (*Dara's*) head, was that he was turned **Kafer**, that is to say, an Infidel, of no Religion, an Idolater."—*Bernier*, E. T. p. 3; [ed. *Constable*, p. 7].

1673:—"They show their Greatness by their number of Sumbreeroes and **Cofferies**, whereby it is dangerous to walk late."—*Fryer*, 74.

"Beggars of the Musslemen Cast, that if they see a Christian in good Clothes ... are presently

1 Thus: "*Chomandarla* (i.e. Coromandel) he de Christãoos e o rey Christãoo." So also *Ceylam Camatarra*, *Melequa* (Malacca), *Peguo*, &c., are all described as Christian states with Christian kings. Also the so-called Indian Christians who came on board Da Gama at Melinde seem to have been Hindu banians.

upon their Punctilios with God Almighty, and interrogate him, Why he suffers him to go afoot and in Rags, and this **Coffery** (Unbeliever) to vaunt it thus!"—*Ibid.* 91.

1678.—"The Justices of the Choultry to turn Padry Pasquall, a Popish Priest, out of town, not to return again, and if it proves to be true that he attempted to seduce Mr. Mohun's **Coffre** Franck from the Protestant religion."—*Ft. St. Geo. Cons.* in *Notes and Exts.*, Pt. i. p. 72.

1759.—"Blacks, whites, **Coffries**, and even the natives of the country (Pegu) have not been exempted, but all universally have been subject to intermittent Fevers and Fluxes" (at Negrais).—In *Dalrymple, Or. Rep.* i. 124.

Among expenses of the Council at Calcutta in entertaining the Nabob we find "Purchasing a **Coffre** boy, Rs. 500."—In *Long*, 194.

1781.—"*To be sold by Private Sale*—Two **Coffree** Boys, who can play remarkably well on the French Horn, about 18 Years of Age: belonging to a Portuguese Paddrie lately deceased. For particulars apply to the Vicar of the Portuguese Church, Calcutta, March 17th, 1781."—*The India Gazette or Public Advertiser*, No. 19.

1781.—"Run away from his Master, a good-looking **Coffree** Boy, about 20 years old, and about 6 *feet* 7 *inches in height. ... When he went off he had a high toupie.*"—*Ibid.* Dec. 29.

1782.—"On Tuesday next will be sold three **Coffree** Boys, two of whom play the French Horn ... a three-wheel'd Buggy, and a variety of other articles."—*India Gazette*, June 15.

1799.—"He (Tippoo) had given himself out as a Champion of the Faith, who was to drive the English **Caffers** out of India."—Letter in *Life of Sir T. Munro*, i. 221.

1800.—"The **Caffre** slaves, who had been introduced for the purpose of cultivating the lands, rose upon their masters, and seizing on the boats belonging to the island, effected their escape."—*Symes, Embassy to Ava*, p. 10.

c. 1866.—

"And if I were forty years younger, and my life
 before me to choose,
I wouldn't be lectured by **Kafirs**, or swindled
 by fat Hindoos."

Sir A. C. Lyall, The Old Pindaree.

CAFIRISTAN, n.p. P. *Kāfiristān*, the country of *Kāfirs, i.e.* of the pagan tribes of the Hindu Kush noticed in the article **Caffer**.

c. 1514.—"In Cheghânserâi there are neither grapes nor vineyards; but they bring the wines down the river from **Kaferistân**. ... So prevalent is the use of wine among them that every **Kafer** has a *khig*, or leathern bottle of wine about his neck; they drink wine instead of water."—*Autobiog. of Baber*, p. 144.

[c. 1590.—The **Káfirs** in the Túmáns of Alishang and Najrao are mentioned in the *Āīn*, tr. *Jarrett*, ii. 406.]

1603.—"... they fell in with a certain pilgrim and devotee, from whom they learned that at a distance of 30 days' journey there was a city called **Capperstam**, into which no Mahomedan was allowed to enter ..."—*Journey of Bened. Goës*, in *Cathay*, &c. ii. 554.

CALCUTTA, n.p. B. *Kalikātā*, or *Kalikattā*, a name of uncertain etymology. The first mention that we are aware of occurs in the *Āīn-i-Akbari*. It is well to note that in some early charts, such as that in Valentijn, and the oldest in the *English Pilot*, though Calcutta is not entered, there is a place on the Hoogly *Calcula*, or *Calcuta*, which leads to mistake. It is far below, near the modern Fulta. [With reference to the quotations below from Luillier and Sonnerat, Sir H. Yule writes (*Hedges, Diary*, Hak. Soc. ii. xcvi.): "In Orme's *Historical Fragments*, Job Charnock is described as 'Governor of the Factory at Golgot near Hughley.' This name Golgot and the corresponding Golghāt in an extract from Muhabbat Khān indicate the name of the particular locality where the English Factory at Hugli was situated. And some confusion of this name with that of Calcutta may have led to the curious error of the Frenchman Luiller and Sonnerat, the former of whom calls Calcutta *Golgouthe*, while the latter says: 'Les Anglais prononcent et ecrivent *Golgota*.'"]

c. 1590.—"**Kalikatā**, *wa Bakoya wa Barbakpūr, 3 Mahal.*"—*Āīn.* (orig.) i. 408; [tr. *Jarrett*, ii. 141].

[1688.—"Soe myself accompanyed with Capt. Haddock and the 120 soldiers we carryed from hence embarked, and about the 20th September arrived at **Calcutta**."—*Hedges, Diary*, Hak. Soc. ii. lxxix.]

1698.—"This avaricious disposition the English plied with presents, which in 1698 obtained his permission to purchase from the Zemindar ... the towns of Sootanutty, **Calcutta**, and Goomopore, with their districts extending about 3 miles along the eastern bank of the river."—*Orme*, repr. ii. 71.

1702.—"The next Morning we pass'd by the *English* Factory belonging to the old Company, which they call **Golgotha**, and is a handsome Building, to which were adding stately Warehouses."—*Voyage to the E. Indies, by Le Sieur Luillier*, E. T. 1715, p. 259.

1726.—"The ships which sail thither (to Hugli) first pass by the English Lodge in

Collecatte, 9 miles (Dutch miles) lower down than ours, and after that the French one called *Chandarnagor*. ..."—*Valentijn*, v. 162.

1727.—"The Company has a pretty good Hospital at **Calcutta**, where many go in to undergo the Penance of Physic, but few come out to give an Account of its Operation. ... One Year I was there, and there were reckoned in August about 1200 *English*, some Military, some Servants to the Company, some private Merchants residing in the Town, and some Seamen belong to Shipping lying at the Town, and before the beginning of *January* there were 460 Burials registred in the Clerk's Books of Mortality."—*A. Hamilton*, ii. 9 and 6.

c. 1742.—"I had occasion to stop at the city of Firáshdánga (Chandernagore) which is inhabited by a tribe of Frenchmen. The city of **Calcutta**, which is on the other side of the water, and inhabited by a tribe of English who have settled there, is much more extensive and thickly populated. ..."—*'Abdul Karím Khán*, in *Elliot*, viii. 127.

1753.—"An dessous d'Ugli immédiatement, est l'établissement Hollandois de **Shinsura**, puis **Shandernagor**, établissement François, puis la loge Danoise (Serampore), et plus bas, sur la rivage opposé, qui est celui de la gauche en descendant, Banki-bazar, où les Ostendois n'ont pû se maintenir; enfin **Colicotta** aux Anglois, à quelques lieues de Banki-bazar, et du même côté."—*D'Anville, Eclaircissemens*, 64. With this compare: "Almost opposite to the *Danes* Factory is *Bankebanksal*, a Place where the Ostend Company settled a Factory, but, in *Anno* 1723, they quarrelled with the *Fouzdaar* or Governor of *Hughly*, and he forced the *Ostenders* to quit. ..."—*A. Hamilton*, ii. 18.

1782.—"Les Anglais pourroient retirer aujourd'hui des sommes immenses de l'Inde, s'ils avoient eu l'attention de mieux composer le conseil suprême de **Calecuta**."[1]—*Sonnerat, Voyage*, i. 14.

CALEEFA, s. Ar. *Khalīfa*, the Caliph or Vice-gerent, a word which we do not introduce here in its high Mahommedan use, but because of its quaint application in Anglo-Indian households, at least in Upper India, to two classes of domestic servants, the tailor and the cook, and sometimes to the barber and farrier. The first is *always* so addressed by his fellow-servants (*Khalīfa-jī*). In South India the cook is called **Maistry**, *i.e. artiste*. In Sicily, we may note, he is always called *Monsù* (!) an indication of what ought to be his nationality. The root of the word *Khalīfa*, according to Prof. Sayce, means 'to change,' and another derivative, *khālif*, 'exchange or agio' is the origin of the Greek κολλύβος (*Princ. of Philology*, 2nd ed., 213).

c. 1253.—"... vindrent marcheant en l'ost qui nous distrent et conterent que li roys des Tartarins avoit prise la citei de Baudas et l'apostole des Sarrazins ... lequel on appeloit le **calife** de Baudas. ..."—*Joinville*, cxiv.

1298.—"Baudas is a great city, which used to be the seat of the **Calif** of all the Saracens in the world, just as Rome is the seat of the Pope of all the Christians."—*Marco Polo*, Bk. I. ch. 6.

1552.—"To which the Sheikh replied that he was the vassal of the Soldan of Cairo, and that without his permission who was the sovereign **Califa** of the Prophet Mahamed, he could hold no communication with people who so persecuted his followers. ..."—*Barros*, II. i. 2.

1738.—"Muzeratty, the late **Kaleefa**, or lieutenant of this province, assured me that he saw a bone belonging to one of them (ancient stone coffins) which was near two of their *drass* (*i.e.* 36 inches) in length."—*Shaw's Travels in Barbary*, ed. 1757, p. 30.

1747.—'As to the house, and the patrimonial lands, together with the appendages of the murdered minister, they were presented by the **Qhalif** of the age, that is by the Emperor himself, to his own daughter."—*Seir Mutaqherin*, iii. 37.

c. 1760 (?).—

"I hate all Kings and the thrones they sit on,
From the King of France to the **Caliph** of Britain."

These lines were found among the papers of Pr. Charles Edward, and supposed to be his. But Lord Stanhope, in the 2nd ed. of his *Miscellanies*, says he finds that they are slightly altered from a poem by Lord Rochester. This we cannot find. [The original lines of Rochester (*Poems on State Affairs*, i. 171) run:

"I hate all Monarchs, and the thrones they sit on,
From the Hector of France to the Cully of Britain."]

[1813.—"The most skilful among them (the wrestlers) is appointed **khuleofu**, or superintendent for the season. ..."—*Broughton, Letters*, ed. 1892, p. 164.]

CALICO, s. Cotton cloth, ordinarily of tolerably fine texture. The word appears in the 17th century sometimes in the form of *Calicut*, but possibly this may have been a purism, for *calicoe* or *callico* occurs in English earlier, or at least more commonly

1 "Capitale des établissements Anglais dans le Bengale. *Les Anglais prononcent et écrivent* Golgota"(!)

in early voyages. [*Callaca* in 1578, *Draper's Dict.* p. 42.] The word may have come to us through the French *calicot*, which though retaining the *t* to the eye, does not do so to the ear. The quotations sufficiently illustrate the use of the word and its origin from Calicut. The fine cotton stuffs of Malabar are already mentioned by Marco Polo (ii. 379). Possibly they may have been all brought from beyond the Ghauts, as the Malabar cotton, ripening during the rains, is not usable, and the cotton stuffs now used in Malabar all come from Madura (see *Fryer* below). The Germans, we may note, call the turkey *Calecutische Hahn*, though it comes no more from Calicut than it does from Turkey.

1579.—"3 great and large Canowes, in each whereof were certaine of the greatest personages that were about him, attired all of them in white Lawne, or cloth of **Calecut**."—*Drake, World Encompassed*, Hak. Soc. 139.

1591.—"The commodities of the shippes that come from Bengala bee ... fine **Calicut** cloth, *Pintados*, and Rice."—*Barker's Lancaster*, in *Hakl.* ii. 592.

1592.—"The **calicos** were book-**calicos**, **calico** launes, broad white **calicos**, fine starched **calicos**, coarse white **calicos**, browne coarse **calicos**."—*Desc. of the Great Carrack Madre de Dios.*

1602.—"And at his departure gane a robe, and a Tucke of **Calico** wrought with gold."—*Lancaster's Voyage*, in *Purchas*, i. 153.

1604.—"It doth appear by the abbreviate of the Accounts sent home out of the Indies, that there remained in the hands of the Agent, Master Starkey, 482 fardels of **Calicos**."—In *Middleton's Voyage*, Hak. Soc. App. iii. 13.

"I can fit you, gentlemen, with fine **callicoes** too, for doublets; the only sweet fashion now, most delicate and courtly: a meek gentle **callico**, cut upon two double affable taffatas; all most neat, feat, and unmatchable."—*Dekker, The Honest Whore*, Act. II. Sc. v.

1605.—"... about their loynes they (the Javanese) weare a kind of **Callico**-cloth."—*Edm. Scot, ibid.* 165.

1608.—"They esteem not so much of money as of **Calecut** clothes, Pintados, and such like stuffs."—*Iohn Davis, ibid.* 136.

1612.—"**Calico** copboord claiths, the piece ... xls."—*Rates and Valuatiouns*, &c. (Scotland), p. 294.

1616.—"Angarezia ... inhabited by Moores trading with the Maine, and other three Easterne Ilands with their Cattell and fruits, for **Căllicoes** or other linnen to cover them."—*Sir T. Roe*, in *Purchas*; [with some verbal differences in Hak. Soc. i. 17].

1627.—"**Calicoe**, *tela delicata Indica.* H. **Calicúd**, *dicta* à Calecút, *Indiae regione ubi conficitur.*"—*Minsheu*, 2nd ed., s.v.

1673.—"Staple Commodities are **Calicuts**, white and painted."—*Fryer*, 34.

"Calecut for Spice ... and no Cloath, though it give the name of **Calecut** to all in India, it being the first Port from whence they are known to be brought into Europe."—*Ibid.* 86.

1707.—"The Governor lays before the Council the insolent action of Captain Leaton, who on Sunday last marched part of his company ... over the Company's **Calicoes** that lay a dyeing."—Minute in *Wheeler*, ii. 48.

1720.—Act 7 Geo. I. cap. vii. "An Act to preserve and encourage the woollen and silk manufacture of this kingdom, and for more effectual employing of the Poor, by prohibiting the Use and Wear of all printed, painted, stained or dyed **Callicoes** in Apparel, Houshold Stuff, Furniture, or otherwise. ..."—*Stat. at Large*, v. 229.

1812.—

"Like Iris' bow down darts the painted clue,
Starred, striped, and spotted, yellow, red, and blue,
Old **calico**, torn silk, and muslin new."
Rejected Addresses (*Crabbe*).

CAMBOJA, n.p. An ancient kingdom in the eastern part of Indo-China, once great and powerful: now fallen, and under the 'protectorate' of France, whose Saigon colony it adjoins. The name, like so many others of Indo-China since the days of Ptolemy, is of Skt. origin, being apparently a transfer of the name of a nation and country on the N.W. frontier of India, *Kamboja*, supposed to have been about the locality of Chitral or Kafiristan. Ignoring this, fantastic Chinese and other etymologies have been invented for the name. In the older Chinese annals (c. 1200 B.C.) this region had the name of *Fu-nan*; from the period after our era, when the kingdom of Camboja had become powerful, it was known to the Chinese as *Chin-la.* Its power seems to have extended at one time westward, perhaps to the shores of the B. of Bengal. Ruins of extraordinary vastness and architectural elaboration are numerous, and have attracted great attention since M. Mouhot's visit in 1859; though they had been mentioned by 16th century missionaries, and some of the buildings when standing in splendour were described by a Chinese visitor at the end of the 13th century. The Cambojans proper call themselves *Khmer*, a name which seems to have given rise to singular confusions (see COMAR). The gum **Gamboge** (*Cambodiam* in the early records [*Birdwood, Rep. on Old Rec.*, 27]) so familiar in use, derives its name from this country, the chief source of supply.

c. 1161.—"... although ... because the belief of the people of Rámánya (Pegu) was the same as that of the Buddha-believing men of Ceylon. ... Parakrama the king was living in peace with the king of Rámánya—yet the ruler of Rámánya ... forsook the old custom of providing maintenance for the ambassadors ... saying: 'These messengers are sent to go to **Kámboja**,' and so plundered all their goods and put them in prison in the Malaya country. ... Soon after this he seized some royal virgins sent by the King of Ceylon to the King of **Kámboja**. ..."—Ext. from *Ceylonese Annals*, by *T. Rhys Davids*, in *J.A.S.B.* xli. Pt. i. p. 198.

1295.—"Le pays de Tchin-la ... Les gens du pays le nomment **Kan-phou-tchi**. Sous la dynastie actuelle, les livres sacrés des Tibétains nomment ce pays **Kan-phou-tchi**. ..."—*Chinese Account of Chinla*, in *Abel Rémusat, Nouv. Mél.* i. 100.

c. 1535.—"Passing from Siam towards China by the coast we find the kingdom of Cambaia (read **Camboia**) ... the people are great warriors ... and the country of **Camboia** abounds in all sorts of victuals ... in this land the lords voluntarily burn themselves when the king dies. ..."—*Sommario de' Regni*, in *Ramusio*, i. f. 336.

1552.—"And the next State adjoining Siam is the kingdom of **Camboja**, through the middle of which flows that splendid river the Mecon, the source of which is in the regions of China. ..."—*Barros*, Dec. I. Liv. ix. cap. 1.

1572.—

"Vês, passa por **Camboja** Mecom rio,
Que capitão das aguas se interpreta... ."

Camões, x. 127.

[1616.—"22 cattes **camboja** (gamboge)."—*Foster, Letters*, iv. 188.]

CAMEEZE, s. This word (*ḳamīṣ*) is used in colloquial H. and Tamil for 'a shirt.' It comes from the Port *camisa*. But that word is directly from the Arab *ḳamīṣ*, 'a tunic.' Was St. Jerome's Latin word an earlier loan from the Arabic, or the source of the Arabic word? probably the latter; [so *N.E.D.* s.v. *Camise*]. The Mod. Greek Dict. of Sophocles has *καμίσιον*. *Camesa* is, according to the *Slang Dictionary*, used in the cant of English thieves; and in more ancient slang it was made into '*commission*.'

c. 400.—"Solent militantes habere lineas quas **Camisias** vocant, sic aptas membris et adstrictas corporibus, ut expediti sint vel ad cursum, vel ad praelia ... quocumque necessitas traxerit."—*Scti. Hieronymi Epist.* (lxiv.) *ad Fabiolam*, § 11.

1404.—"And to the said Ruy Gonzalez he gave a big horse, an ambler, for they prize a horse that ambles, furnished with saddle and bridle, very well according to their fashion; and besides he gave him a **camisa** and an umbrella" (see SOMBRERO).—*Clavijo*, § lxxxix.; *Markham*, 100.

1464.—"to William and Richard my sons, all my fair **camises**. ..."—*Will of Richard Strode*, of Newnham, Devon.

1498.—"That a very fine **camysa**, which in Portugal would be worth 300 *reis*, was given here for 2 *fanons*, which in that country is the equivalent of 30 *reis*, though the value of 30 *reis* is in that country no small matter."—*Roteiro de V. da Gama*, 77.

1573.—"The richest of all (the shops in Fez) are where they sell **camisas**. ..."—*Marmol. Desc. General de Affrica*, Pt. I. Bk. iii. f. 87*v*.

CAMP, s. In the Madras Presidency [as well as in N. India] an official not at his headquarters is always addressed as 'in Camp.'

***CANDAHAR**, n.p. *Kandahār*. The application of this name is now exclusively to (**a**) the well-known city of Western Afghanistan, which is the object of so much political interest. But by the Ar. geographers of the 9th to 11th centuries the name is applied to (**b**) the country about Peshāwar, as the equivalent of the ancient Indian *Gandhāra*, and the *Gandaritis* of Strabo. Some think the name was transferred to (**a**) in consequence of a migration of the people of Gandhāra carrying with them the begging-pot of Buddha, believed by Sir H. Rawlinson to be identical with a large sacred vessel of stone preserved in a mosque of Candahar. Others think that Candahar may represent *Alexandropolis* in Arachosia. We find a third application of the name (**c**) in Ibn Batuta, as well as in earlier and later writers, to a former port on the east shore of the Gulf of Cambay, Ghandhar in the Broach District.

a.—1552.—"Those who go from Persia, from the kingdom of Horaçam (Khoraṣan), from Bohára, and all the Western Regions, travel to the city which the natives corruptly call

Candar, instead of Scandar, the name by which the Persians call Alexander. ..."—*Barros*, IV. vi. 1.

1664.—"All these great preparations give us cause to apprehend that, instead of going to *Kachemire*, we be not led to besiege that important city of **Kandahar**, which is the Frontier to Persia, Indostan, and Usbeck, and the Capital of an excellent Country."—*Bernier*, E. T., p. 113; [ed. *Constable*, 352].

1671.—

"From Arachosia, from **Candaor** east,
And Margiana to the Hyrcanian cliffs
Of Caucasus... ."

Paradise Regained, iii. 316 *seqq.*

b.—c. 1030.—"... thence to the river Chandráha (Chináb) 12 (parasangs); thence to Jailam on the West of the Báyat (or Hydaspes) 18; thence to Waihind, capital of **Ḳandahár** ... 20; thence to Parsháwar 14. ..."—*Al-Birūni*, in *Elliot*, i. 63 (corrected).

c.—c. 1343.—"From Kinbāya (Cambay) we went to the town of Kāwi (*Kānvi*, opp. Cambay), on an estuary where the tide rises and falls ... thence to **Kandahār**, a considerable city belonging to the Infidels, and situated on an estuary from the sea."—*Ibn Batuta*, iv. 57-8.

1516.—"Further on ... there is another place, in the mouth of a small river, which is called **Guendari**. ... And it is a very good town, a seaport."—*Barbosa*, 64.

1814.—"**Candhar**, eighteen miles from the wells, is pleasantly situated on the banks of a river; and a place of considerable trade; being a great thoroughfare from the sea coast to the Gaut mountains."—*Forbes*, *Or. Mem.* i. 206; [2nd ed. i. 116].

(1) **CANDY**, n.p. A town in the hill country of Ceylon, which became the deposit of the sacred tooth of Buddha at the beginning of the 14th century, and was adopted as the native capital about 1592. Chitty says the name is unknown to the natives, who call the place *Mahā nuvera*, 'great city.' The name seems to have arisen out of some misapprehension by the Portuguese, which may be illustrated by the quotation from Valentijn.

c. 1530.—"And passing into the heart of the Island, there came to the Kingdom of **Candia**, a certain Friar Pascoal with two companions, who were well received by the King of the country Javira Bandar ... in so much that he gave them a great piece of ground, and everything needful to build a church, and houses for them to dwell in."—*Couto*, Dec. VI. liv. iv. cap. 7.

1552.—"... and at three or four places, like the passes of the Alps of Italy, one finds entrance within this circuit (of mountains) which forms a Kingdom called **Cande**."—*Barros*, Dec. III. Liv. ii. cap. 1.

1645.—"Now then as soon as the Emperor was come to his Castle in **Candi** he gave order that the 600 captive Hollanders should be distributed throughout his country among the peasants, and in the City."—*J. J. Saar's 15-Jäkrige Kriegs-Dienst*, 97.

1681.—"The First is the City of *Candy*, so generally called by the *Christians*, probably from *Conde*, which in the *Chingulays* Language signifies *Hills*, for among them *i.e.* is situated, but by the Inhabitants called *Hingodagul-neure*, as much as to say 'The City of the *Chingulay* people,' and *Mauneur*, signifying the 'Chief or Royal City.'"—*R. Knox*, p. 5.

1726.—"**Candi**, otherwise *Candia*, or named in Cingalees *Conde Ouda*, *i.e.* the high mountain country."—*Valentijn* (*Ceylon*), 19.

(2) **CANDY**, s. A weight used in S. India, which may be stated roughly at about 500 lbs., but varying much in different parts. It corresponds broadly with the Arabian **Bahar** and was generally equivalent to 20 **Maunds**, varying therefore with the maund. The word is Mahr. and Tel. *khaṇḍi*, written in Tam. and Mal. *kaṇḍi*, or Mal. *kaṇṭi*, [and comes from the Skt. *khaṇḍ*, 'to divide.' A **Candy** of land is supposed to be as much as will produce a *candy* of grain, approximately 75 acres]. The Portuguese write the word *candil*.

1563.—"A **candil** which amounts to 522 pounds" (*arrateis*).—*Garcia*, f. 55.

1598.—"One **candiel** (v.l. *candiil*) is little more or less than 14 bushels, wherewith they measure Rice, Corne, and all graine."—*Linschoten*, 69; [Hak. Soc. i. 245].

1618.—"The **Candee** at this place (Batecala) containeth neere 500 pounds."—*W. Hore*, in *Purchas*, i. 657.

1710.—"They advised that they have supplied Habib Khan with ten **candy** of country gunpowder."—In *Wheeler*, ii. 136.

c. 1760.—Grose gives the Bombay **candy** as 20 maunds of 28 lbs. each = 560 lbs.; the Surat ditto as 20 maunds of 37⅓ lbs. = 746⅔ lbs.; the Anjengo ditto 560 lbs.; the Carwar ditto 575 lbs.; the Coromandel ditto at 500 lbs. &c.

(3) **CANDY** (**SUGAR**-). This name of crystallized sugar, though it came no doubt to Europe from the P.-Ar. *ḳand* (P. also *shakar ḳand*; Sp. *azucar cande*; It. *candi* and *zucchero candito*; Fr. *sucre candi*) is of Indian origin. There is a Skt. root *khaṇḍ*, 'to break,' whence *khaṇḍa*, 'broken,' also applied

in various compounds to granulated and candied sugar. But there is also Tam. *kar-kaṇḍa, kala-kaṇḍa,* Mal. *kaṇḍi, kalkaṇḍi,* and *kalkaṇṭu,* which may have been the direct source of the P. and Ar. adoption of the word, and perhaps its original, from a Dravidian word = 'lump.' [The Dravidian terms mean 'stone-piece.']

A German writer, long within last century (as we learn from Mahn, quoted in Diez's Lexicon), appears to derive **candy** from Candia, "because most of the sugar which the Venetians imported was brought from that island"—a fact probably invented for the nonce. But the writer was the same wiseacre who (in the year 1829) characterised the book of Marco Polo as a "clumsily compiled ecclesiastical fiction disguised as a Book of Travels" (see *Introduction* to *Marco Polo,* 2nd ed. pp. 112–113).

c. 1343.—"A centinajo si vende giengiovo, cannella, lacca, incenso, indaco ... verzino scorzuto, zucchero ... **zucchero candi** ... porcellane ... costo ..."—*Pegolotti,* p. 134.

1461.—"... Un ampoletto di balsamo. Teriaca bossoletti 15. Zuccheri Moccari (?) panni 42. **Zuccheri canditi**, scattole 5. ..."—*List of Presents from Sultan of Egypt to the Doge.*

c. 1596.—"White sugar candy (**kandī** *safed*) ... 5½ *dams* per *ser.*"—*Āīn,* i. 63.

1627.—"**Sugar Candie**, or Stone Sugar."—*Minshew,* 2nd ed. s.v.

1727.—"The Trade they have to China is divided between them and *Surat* ... the Gross of their own Cargo, which consists in Sugar, **Sugar-candy**, Allom, and some Drugs ... are all for the *Suraí* Market."—*A. Hamilton,* i. 371.

CANTON, n.p. The great seaport of Southern China, the chief city of the Province of Kwang-tung, whence we take the name, through the Portuguese, whose older writers call it *Cantão.* The proper name of the city is *Kwang-chau-fu.* The Chin. name *Kwang-tung* (= 'Broad East') is an ellipsis for "capital of the E. Division of the Province *Liang-Kwang* (or 'Two Broad Realms')."—(*Bp. Moule*).

1516.—"So as this went on Fernão Peres arrived from Pacem with his cargo (of pepper), and having furnished himself with necessaries set off on his voyage in June 1516 ... they were 7 sail altogether, and they made their voyage with the aid of good pilots whom they had taken, and went without harming anybody touching at certain ports, most of which were subject to the King of China, who called himself the Son of God and Lord of the World. Fernão Peres arrived at the islands of China, and when he was seen there came an armed squadron of 12 junks, which in the season of navigation always cruized about, guarding the sea, to prevent the numerous pirates from attacking the ships. Fernão Peres knew about this from the pilots, and as it was late, and he could not double a certain island there, he anchored, sending word to his captains to have their guns ready for defence if the Chins desired to fight. Next day he made sail towards the island of Veniaga, which is 18 leagues from the city of **Cantão**. It is on that island that all the traders buy and sell, without licence from the rulers of the city. ... And 3 leagues from that island of Veniaga is another island, where is posted the Admiral or Captain-Major of the Sea, who immediately on the arrival of strangers at the island of Veniaga reports to the rulers of **Cantão**, who they are, and what goods they bring or wish to buy; that the rulers may send orders what course to take."—*Correa,* ii. 524.

c. 1535.—"... queste cose ... vanno alla China con li lor giunchi, e a **Camton**, che è Città grande. ..."—*Sommario de' Regni, Ramusio,* i. f. 337.

1585.—"The Chinos do vse in their pronunciation to terme their cities with this sylable, Fu, that is as much as to say, citie, as Taybin fu, **Canton** fu, and their townes with this syllable, Cheu."—*Mendoza,* Parke's old E. T. (1588) Hak. Soc. i. 24.

1727.—"**Canton** or *Quantung* (as the Chinese express it) is the next maritime Province."—*A. Hamilton,* ii. 217.

CANTONMENT, s. (Pron. *Cantoonment,* with accent on penult.). This English word has become almost appropriated as Anglo-Indian, being so constantly used in India, and so little used elsewhere. It is applied to military stations in India, built usually on a plan which is originally that of a standing camp or 'cantonment.'

1783.—"I know not the full meaning of the word **cantonment**, and a camp this singular place cannot well be termed; it more resembles a large town, very many miles in circumference. The officers' bungalos on the banks of the Tappee are large and convenient," &c.—*Forbes,* Letter in *Or. Mem.* describing the "Bengal Cantonments near Surat." iv. 239.

1825.—"The fact, however, is certain ... the **cantonments** at Lucknow, nay Calcutta itself, are abominably situated. I have heard the same of Madras; and now the lately-settled **cantonment** of Nusseerabad appears to be as objectionable as any of them."—*Heber,* ed. 1844, ii. 7.

1848.—"Her ladyship, our old acquaintance, is as much at home at Madras as at Brussels—in the **cantonment** as under the tents."—*Vanity Fair*, ii. ch. 8.

CARAT, s. Arab *ḳirrāt*, which is taken from the Gr. *κεράτιον*, a bean of the *κερατεία* or carob tree (*Ceratonia siliqua*, L.). This bean, like the Indian *rati* was used as a weight, and thence also it gave name to a coin of account, if not actual. To discuss the carat fully would be a task of extreme complexity, and would occupy several pages.

Under the name of *siliqua* it was the 24th part of the golden solidus of Constantine, which was again = 1/6 of an ounce. Hence this carat was = 1/144 of an ounce. In the passage from St. Isidore quoted below, the *cerates* is distinct from the *siliqua*, and = 1½ *siliquae*. This we cannot explain, but the *siliqua Graeca* was the *κεράτιον*; and the *siliqua* as 1/24 of a solidus is the parent of the *carat* in all its uses. [See Prof. Gardner, in Smith, *Dict. Ant.* 3rd ed. ii. 675.] Thus we find the *carat* at Constantinople in the 14th century = 1/24 of the *hyperpera* or Greek *bezant*, which was a debased representative of the solidus; and at Alexandria 1/24 of the Arabic *dīnār*, which was a purer representative of the solidus. And so, as the Roman *uncia* signified 1/12 of any unit (compare *ounce*, *inch*), so to a certain extent *carat* came to signify 1/24. Dictionaries give Arab. *ḳirrāṭ* as "1/24 of an ounce." Of this we do not know the evidence. The *English Cyclopaedia* (s.v.) again states that "the *carat* was originally the 24th part of the *marc*, or half-pound, among the French, from whom the word came." This sentence perhaps contains more than one error; but still both of these allegations exhibit the *carat* as 1/24th part. Among our goldsmiths the term is still used to measure the proportionate quality of gold; pure gold being put at 24 *carats*, gold with 1/12 alloy at 22 *carats*, with ¼ alloy at 18 *carats*, &c. And the word seems also (like **Anna**, q.v.) sometimes to have been used to express a proportionate scale in other matters, as is illustrated by a curious passage in Marco Polo, quoted below.

The *carat* is also used as a weight for diamonds. As 1/144 of an ounce troy this ought to make it 3⅓ grains. But these carats really run 151½ to the ounce troy, so that the diamond *carat* is 3⅙ grs. nearly. This we presume was adopted direct from some foreign system in which the carat *was* 1/144 of the local ounce. [See Ball, *Tavernier*, ii. 447.]

c. A.D. 636.—"Siliqua vigesima quarta pars solidi est, ab arboris semine vocabulum tenens. **Cerates** oboli pars media est siliquã habens unam semis. Hanc latinitas semiobulũ vocat; **Cerates** autem Graece, Latine siliqua cornuû interpretatur. Obulus siliquis tribus appenditur, habens *cerates* duos, calcos quatuor."—*Isidori Hispalensis Opera* (ed. Paris, 1601), p. 224.

1298.—"The Great Kaan sends his commissioners to the Province to select four or five hundred ... of the most beautiful young women, according to the scale of beauty enjoined upon them. The commissioners ... assemble all the girls of the province, in presence of appraisers appointed for the purpose. These carefully survey the points of each girl. ... They will then set down some as estimated at 16 **carats**, some at 17, 18, 20, or more or less, according to the sum of the beauties or defects of each. And whatever standard the Great Kaan may have fixed for those that are to be brought to him, whether it be 20 carats or 21, the commissioners select the required number from those who have attained to that standard."—*Marco Polo*, 2nd ed. i, 350–351.

1673.—"A stone of one **Carrack** is worth 10*l*."—*Fryer*, 214.

CARAVAN, s. P. *karwān*; a convoy of travellers. The Ar. *ḳāfila* is more generally used in India. The word is found in French as early as the 13th century (*Littré*). A quotation below shows that the English transfer of the word to a wheeled conveyance for travellers (now for goods also) dates from the 17th century. The abbreviation *van* in this sense seems to have acquired rights as an English word, though the altogether analogous *bus* is still looked on as slang.

c. 1270.—"Meanwhile the convoy (la **caravana**) from Tortosa ... armed seven vessels in such wise that any one of them could take a galley if it ran alongside."—*Chronicle of James of Aragon*, tr. by *Foster*, i. 379.

1330.—"De hac civitate recedens cum **caravanis** et cum quadam societate, ivi versus Indiam Superiorem."—*Friar Odoric*, in *Cathay*, &c., ii. App. iii.

1384.—"Rimonda che l'avemo, vedemo venire una grandissima **carovana** di cammelli e di Saracini, che recavano spezierie delle parti d' India."—*Frescobaldi*, 64.

c. 1420.—"Is adolescens ab Damasco Syriae, ubi mercaturae gratiâ erat, perceptâ prius Arabum linguâ, in coetu mercatorum—hi sexcenti erant—quam vulgo **caroanam** dicunt. ..."—*N. Conti*, in *Poggius de Varietate Fortunae.*

1627.—"A **Caravan** is a convoy of souldiers for the safety of merchants that trauell in the East Countreys."—*Minshew*, 2nd ed. s.v.

1674.—"**Caravan** or **Karavan** (Fr. *caravane*) a Convoy of Souldiers for the safety of Merchants that travel by Land. Also of late corruptly used with us for a kind of Waggon to carry passengers to and from London."—*Glossographia*, &c., by J. E.

CARAVANSERAY, s. P. *karwānsarāī*; a **Serai** (q.v.) for the reception of **Caravans** (q.v.).

1404.—"And the next day being Tuesday, they departed thence and going about 2 leagues arrived at a great house like an Inn, which they call **Carabansaca** (read *-sara*), and here were Chacatays looking after the Emperor's horses."—*Clavijo*, § xcviii. Comp. *Markham*, p. 114.

[1528.—"In the Persian language they call these houses **carvancaras**, which means resting-place for caravans and strangers."—*Tenreiro*, ii. p. 11.]

1554.—"I'ay à parler souuent de ce nom de **Carbachara**: ... Ie ne peux le nommer autrement en François, sinon vn **Carbachara**: et pour le sçauoir donner à entendre, il fault supposer qu'il n'y a point d'hostelleries es pays ou domaine le Turc, ne de lieux pour se loger, sinon dedens celles maisons publiques appellée **Carbachara**. ..."—*Observations* par *P. Belon*, f. 59.

1564.—"Hic diverti in diversorium publicum, **Caravasarai** Turcae vocant ... vastum est aedificium ... in cujus medio patet area ponendis sarcinis et camelis."—*Busbequii, Epist.* i. (p. 35).

1619.—"... a great bazar, enclosed and roofed in, where they sell stuffs, cloths, &c. with the House of the Mint, and the great **caravanserai**, which bears the name of *Lala Beig* (because Lala Beig the Treasurer gives audiences, and does his business there) and another little **caravanserai**, called that of the *Ghilac* or people of Ghilan."—*P. della Valle* (from Ispahan), ii. 8; [comp. Hak. Soc. i. 95].

1627.—"At *Band Ally* we found a neat **Carravansraw** or Inne ... built by mens charity, to give all civill passengers a resting place *gratis*; to keepe them from the injury of theeves, beasts, weather, &c."—*Herbert*, p. 124.

CARENS, n.p. Burm. *Ka-reng*, [a word of which the meaning is very uncertain. It is said to mean 'dirty-feeders,' or 'low-caste people,' and it has been connected with the *Kirāta* tribe (see the question discussed by *McMahon*, *The Karens of the Golden Chersonese*, 43 *seqq.*)]. A name applied to a group of non-Burmese tribes, settled in the forest and hill tracts of Pegu and the adjoining parts of Burma, from Mergui in the south, to beyond Toungoo in the north, and from Arakan to the Salwen, and beyond that river far into Siamese territory. They do not know the name *Kareng*, nor have they one name for their own race; distinguishing, among these whom we call Karens, three tribes, *Sgaw*, *Pwo*, and *Bghai*, which differ somewhat in customs and traditions, and especially in language. "The results of the labours among them of the American Baptist Mission have the appearance of being almost miraculous, and it is not going too far to state that the cessation of blood feuds, and the peaceable way in which the various tribes are living ... and have lived together since they came under British rule, is far more due to the influence exercised over them by the missionaries than to the measures adopted by the English Government, beneficial as these doubtless have been" (*Br. Burma Gazetteer*, [ii. 226]). The author of this excellent work should not, however, have admitted the quotation of Dr. Mason's fanciful notion about the identity of Marco Polo's *Carajan* with Karen, which is totally groundless.

1759.—"There is another people in this country called **Carianners**, whiter than either (Burmans or Peguans), distinguished into *Buraghmah* and *Pegu* **Carianners**; they live in the *woods*, in small Societies, of ten or twelve *houses*; are not wanting in industry, though it goes no further than to procure them an annual subsistence."—In *Dalrymple*, *Or. Rep.* i. 100.

1799—"From this reverend father (V. Sangermano) I received much useful information. He told me of a singular description of people called **Carayners** or **Carianers**, that inhabit different parts of the country, particularly the western provinces of Dalla and Bassein, several societies of whom also dwell in the district adjacent to Rangoon. He represented them as a simple, innocent race, speaking a language distinct from that of the Birmans, and entertaining rude notions of religion. ... They are timorous, honest, mild in their manners, and exceedingly hospitable to strangers."—*Symes*, 207.

c. 1819.—"We must not omit here the **Carian**, a good and peaceable people, who live dispersed through the forests of Pegù, in small villages consisting of 4 or 5 houses ... they are totally dependent upon the despotic government of the Burmese."—*Sangermano*, p. 34.

CARTMEEL, s. This is, at least in the

Punjab, the ordinary form that 'mail-cart' takes among the natives. Such inversions are not uncommon. Thus Sir David Ochterlony was always called by the Sepoys *Loni-okhtar*. In our memory an officer named *Holroyd* was always called by the Sepoys *Roydāl*, [and *Brownlow*, *Lobrūn*. By another curious corruption *Mackintosh* becomes *Makkhanī-tosh*, 'buttered toast'!]

CARTOOCE, s. A cartridge; *kārtūs*, Sepoy H.

CASH, s. A name applied by Europeans to sundry coins of low value in various parts of the Indies. The word in its original form is of extreme antiquity, "Skt. *karsha* ... a weight of silver or gold equal to 1/400 of a *Tulā*" (*Williams, Skt. Dict.;* and see also a Note on the *Kārsha*, or rather *kārshāpaṇa*, as a copper coin of great antiquity, in *E. Thomas's Pathân Kings of Delhi*, 361–362). From the Tam. form *kāsu*, or perhaps from some Konkani form which we have not traced, the Portuguese seem to have made *caixa*, whence the English *cash*. In Singalese also *kāsi* is used for 'coin' in general. The English term was appropriated in the monetary system which prevailed in S. India up to 1818; thus there was a copper coin for use in Madras struck in England in 1803, which bears on the reverse, "XX Cash." A figure of this coin is given in *Ruding*. Under this system 80 cash = 1 fanam, 42 fanams = 1 star pagoda. But from an early date the Portuguese had applied *caixa* to the small money of foreign systems, such as those of the Malay Islands, and especially to that of the Chinese. In China the word *cash* is used, by Europeans and their hangers-on, as the synonym of the Chinese *le* and *tsien*, which are those coins made of an alloy of copper and lead with a square hole in the middle, which in former days ran 1000 to the *liang* or **tael** and which are strung in certain numbers on cords. [This type of money, as was recently pointed out by Lord Avebury, is a survival of the primitive currency, which was in the shape of an axe.] Rouleaux of coin thus strung are represented on the surviving bank-notes of the Ming dynasty (A.D. 1368 onwards), and probably were also on the notes of their Mongol predecessors.

The existence of the distinct English word *cash* may probably have affected the form of the corruption before us. This word had a European origin from It. *cassa*, French *caisse*, 'the money-chest': this word in book-keeping having given name to the heading of account under which actual disbursements of coin were entered (see *Wedgwood* and *N.E.D.* s.v.). In Minsheu (2nd ed. 1627) the present sense of the word is not attained. He only gives "a tradesman's Cash, or Counter to keepe money in."

1510.—"They have also another coin called **cas**, 16 of which go to a *tare* of silver."—*Varthema*, 130.

"In this country (Calicut) a great number of apes are produced, one of which is worth 4 **casse**, and one **casse** is worth a *quattrino*."—*Ibid.* 172. (Why a monkey should be worth 4 *casse* is obscure.)

1598.—"You must understand that in *Sunda* there is also no other kind of money than certaine copper mynt called **Caixa**, of the bignes of a Hollãdes doite, but not half so thicke, in the middle whereof is a hole to hang it on a string, for that commonlie they put two hundreth or a thousand vpon one string."—*Linschoten*, 34; [Hak. Soc. i. 113].

1600.—"Those (coins) of Lead are called **caxas**, whereof 1600 make one mas."—*John Davis*, in *Purchas*, i. 117.

1609.—"Ils (les Chinois) apportent la monnoye qui a le cours en toute l'isle de Iava, et Isles circonvoisines, laquelle en lãgue Malaique est appellee **Cas**. ... Cette monnoye est jettée en moule en Chine, a la Ville de Chincheu."—*Houtman*, in *Nav. des Hollandois*, i. 30*b*.

[1621.—"In many places they threw abroad **Cashes** (or brasse money) in great quantety."—*Cocks, Diary*, ii. 202.]

1711.—"Doodoos and **Cash** are Copper Coins, eight of the former make one Fanham, and ten of the latter one Doodoo."—*Lockyer*, 8. [*Doodoo* is the Tel. *duddu*, Skt. *dvi*, 'two'; a more modern scale is: 2 *dooggaunies* = 1 *doody:* 3 *doodies* = 1 *anna*.—*Mad. Gloss.* s.v.]

1718.—"**Cass** (a very small coin, eighty whereof make one Fano)."—*Propagation of the Gospel in the East*, ii. 52.

1727.—"At Atcheen they have a small coin of leaden Money called Cash, from 12 to 1600 of them goes to one *Mace*, or *Masscie*."—*A. Hamilton*, ii. 109.

c. 1750–60.—"At Madras and other parts of the coast of Coromandel, 80 **casches** make a fanam, or 3d. sterling; and 36 fanams a silver pagoda, or 7s. 8d. sterling."—*Grose*, i. 282.

1790.—"So far am I from giving credit to the late Government (of Madras) for œconomy, in not making the necessary preparations for war, according to the positive orders of the Supreme Government, after having received the most gross insult that could be offered to any nation! I think it very possible that every **Cash** of that ill-judged saving may cost the company a crore of rupees."—Letter of *Lord Cornwallis* to E. J. Hollond, Esq., see the *Madras Courier*, 22nd Sept. 1791.

[1792.—"Whereas the sum of Raheties 1223, 6 fanams and 30 **khas** has been deducted."—Agreement in *Logan, Malabar*, iii. 226.]

1813.—"At Madras, according to Milburn, the coinage ran:

"10 **Cash** = 1 *doodee*; 2 *doodees* = 1 pice; 8 *doodees* = 1 single fanam," &c.

The following shows a singular corruption, probably of the Chinese *tsien*, and illustrates how the striving after meaning shapes such corruptions:—

1876.—"All money transactions (at Manwyne on the Burman-Chinese frontier) are effected in the copper coin of China called *'change'* of which about 400 or 500 go to the rupee. These coins are generally strung on cord," &c.—*Report on the Country through which the Force passed to meet the Governor*, by *W. J. Charlton, M.D.*

An intermediate step in this transformation is found in Cocks's *Japan Journal*, *passim*, *e.g.*, ii. 89:

"But that which I tooke most note of was of the liberalitee and devotion of these heathen people, who thronged into the Pagod in multetudes one after another to cast money into a little chapell before the idalles, most parte ... being *gins* or brass money, whereof 100 of them may vallie som 10d. str., and are about the bignes of a 3d. English money."

CASHMERE, n.p. The famous valley province of the Western Himālaya, H. and P. *Kashmīr*, from Skt. *Kaśmīra*, and sometimes *Kāśmīra*, alleged by Burnouf to be a contraction of *Kaśyapamīra*. [The name is more probably connected with the *Khasa* tribe.] Whether or not it be the *Kaspatyrus* or *Kaspapyrus* of Herodotus, we believe it undoubtedly to be the *Kaspeiria* (kingdom) of Ptolemy. Several of the old Arabian geographers write the name with the guttural *ḳ*, but this is not so used in modern times.

c. 630.—"The Kingdom of **Kia-shi-mi-lo** (*Kaśmīra*) has about 7000 *li* of circuit. On all sides its frontiers are surrounded by mountains; these are of prodigious height; and although there are paths affording access to it, these are extremely narrow."—*Hwen T'sang* (*Pèl. Bouddh.*) ii. 167.

c. 940.—"**Ḳashmīr** ... is a mountainous country, forming a large kingdom, containing not less than 60,000 or 70,000 towns or villages. It is inaccessible except on one side, and can only be entered by one gate."—*Mas'ūdi*, i. 373.

1275.—"**Ḳashmīr**, a province of India, adjoining the Turks; and its people of mixt Turk and Indian blood excel all others in beauty."—*Zakarīya Kazwīni*, in *Gildemeister*, 210.

1298.—"**Keshimur** also is a province inhabited by a people who are idolaters and have a language of their own ... this country is the very source from which idolatry has spread abroad."—*Marco Polo*, i. 175.

1552.—"The Mogols hold especially towards the N.E. the region Sogdiana, which they now call **Queximir**, and also Mount Caucasus which divides India from the other Provinces."—*Barros*, IV. vi. 1.

1615.—"**Chishmeere**, the chiefe Citie is called *Sirinkar*."—*Terry*, in *Purchas*, ii. 1467; [so in *Roe's* Map, vol. ii. Hak. Soc. ed.; **Chismer** in *Foster, Letters*, iii. 283].

1664.—"From all that hath been said, one may easily conjecture, that I am somewhat charmed with **Kachemire**, and that I pretend there is nothing in the world like it for so small a kingdom."—*Bernier*, E. T. 128; [ed. *Constable*, 400].

1676.—

"A trial of your kindness I must make;
Though not for mine, so much as virtue's sake,
The Queen of **Cassimere** ..."

Dryden's Aurungzebe, iii. 1.

1814.—"The shawls of **Cassimer** and the silks of Iran."—*Forbes, Or. Mem.* iii. 177; [2nd ed. ii. 232]. (See KERSEYMERE.)

***CASTE**, s. "The artificial divisions of society in India, first made known to us by the Portuguese, and described by them under their term *caste*, signifying 'breed, race, kind,' which has been retained in English under the supposition that it was the native name" (*Wedgwood*, s.v.). [See the extraordinary derivation of Hamilton below.] Mr. Elphinstone prefers to write "*Cast*."

We do not find that the early Portuguese writer Barbosa (1516) applies the word *casta* to the divisions of Hindu society. He calls these divisions in Narsinga and Malabar so many *leis de gentios*, *i.e.* 'laws' of the heathen, in the sense of sectarian rules of life. But he uses the word *casta* in a less technical way, which shows how it should easily have passed into the technical sense. Thus, speaking of the King of Calicut: "This King keeps 1000 women, to whom he gives regular maintenance, and they always go to his court to act as the sweepers of his palaces ... these are ladies, and of good family" (*estas saom fidalgas e de boa* **casta**.—In *Coll. of Lisbon Academy*, ii. 316). So also Castanheda: "There fled a knight who was called Fernão Lopez, *homem de boa* **casta**." (iii. 239). In the quotations from Barros, Correa, and Garcia de Orta, we have the word in what we may call the technical sense.

c. 1444.—"Whence I conclude that this race (**casta**) of men is the most agile and dexterous that there is in the world."—*Cadamosto, Navegação*, i. 14.

1552.—"The Admiral ... received these Naires with honour and joy, showing great contentment with the King for sending his message by such persons, saying that he expected this coming of theirs to prosper, as there did not enter into the business any man of the **caste** of the Moors."—*Barros*, I. vi. 5.

1561.—"Some of them asserted that they were of the **caste** (*casta*) of the Christians."—*Correa, Lendas*, i. 2, 685.

1563.—"One thing is to be noted ... that no one changes from his father's trade, and all those of the same **caste** (*casta*) of shoemakers are the same."—*Garcia*, f. 213*b*.

1567.—"In some parts of this Province (of Goa) the Gentoos divide themselves into distinct races or **castes** (*castas*) of greater or less dignity, holding the Christians as of lower degree, and keep these so superstitiously that no one of a higher caste can eat or drink with those of a lower. ..."—Decree 2nd of the *Sacred Council of Goa*, in *Archiv. Port. Orient.*, fasc. 4.

1572.—

"Dous modos ha de gente; porque a nobre
Nairos chamados são, e a menos dina
Poleas tem por nome, a quem obriga
A lei não misturar a **castà** antiga."—
Camões, vii. 37.

By Burton:

"Two modes of men are known; the nobles know
the name of Nayrs, who call the lower **Caste**
Poléas, whom their haughty laws contain
from intermingling with the higher strain."

1612.—"As regards the **castes** (*castas*) the great impediment to the conversion of the Gentoos is the superstition which they maintain in relation to their **castes**, and which prevents them from touching, communicating, or mingling with others, whether superior or inferior; these of one observance with those of another."—*Couto*, Dec. V. vi. 4. See also as regards the Portuguese use of the word, *Gouvea*, ff. 103, 104, 105, 106*b*, 129*b*; *Synodo*, 18*b*, &c.

1613.—"The Banians kill nothing; there are thirtie and odd severall **Casts** of these that differ something in Religion, and may not eat with each other."—*N. Withington*, in *Purchas*, i. 485; see also *Pilgrimage*, pp. 997, 1003.

1630.—"The common *Bramane* hath eighty two **Casts** or Tribes, assuming to themselves the name of that tribe. ..."—*Lord's Display of the Banians*, p. 72.

1673.—"The mixture of **Casts** or Tribes of all India are distinguished by the different modes of binding their Turbats."—*Fryer*, 115.

c. 1760.—"The distinction of the Gentoos into their tribes or **Casts**, forms another considerable object of their religion."—*Grose*, i. 201.

1763—"The **Casts** or tribes into which the Indians are divided, are reckoned by travellers to be eighty-four."—*Orme* (ed. 1803), i. 4.

[1820.—"The Kayasthas (pronounced Kaists, hence the word **caste**) follow next."—*W. Hamilton, Descr. of Hindostan*, i. 109.]

1878—"There are thousands and thousands of these so-called **Castes**; no man knows their number, no man can know it; for the conception is a very flexible one, and moreover new **castes** continually spring up and pass away."—*F. Jagor, Ost-Indische Handwerk und Gewerbe*, 13.

Castes are, according to Indian social views, either high or low.

1876.—"**Low-caste** Hindoos in their own land are, to all ordinary apprehension, slovenly, dirty, ungraceful, generally unacceptable in person and surroundings. ... Yet offensive as is the *low-caste* Indian, were I estate-owner, or colonial governor, I had rather see the lowest Pariahs of the low, than a single trim, smooth-faced, smooth-wayed, clever **high-caste** Hindoo, on my lands or in my colony."—*W. G. Palgrave*, in *Fortnightly Rev.*, cx. 226.

In the Madras Pres. *castes* are also '*Right-hand*' and '*Left-hand*.' This distinction represents the agricultural classes on the one hand, and the artizans, &c., on the other, as was pointed out by F. W. Ellis. In the old days of Ft. St. George, faction-fights between the two were very common, and the terms *right-hand* and *left-hand* castes occur early in the old records of that settlement, and frequently in Mr. Talboys Wheeler's extracts from them. They are mentioned by Couto. [See *Nelson, Madura*, Pt. ii. p. 4; *Oppert. Orig. Inhab.* p. 57.]

Sir Walter Elliot considers this feud to be "nothing else than the occasional outbreak of the smouldering antagonism between Brahmanism and Buddhism, although in the lapse of ages both parties have lost sight of the fact. The points on which they split now are mere trifles, such as parading on horse-back or in a palankeen in procession, erecting a pandal or marriage-shed on a given number of pillars, and claiming to carry certain flags, &c. The right-hand party is headed by the Brahmans, and includes the Parias, who assume the van, beating their tom-toms when they come to blows. The chief of the left-hand are the Panchalars [*i.e.* the Five Classes, workers in metal and stone, &c.], followed by the Pallars and workers in leather, who sound their long trumpets and engage the Parias." (In *Journ. Ethnol. Soc.* N.S. 1869, p. 112.)

1612.—"From these four **castes** are derived 196; and those again are divided into two parties, which they call *Valanga* and *Elange* [Tam. *valangai, idangai*], which is as much as to say 'the right hand' and 'the left hand' ..."—*Couto*, u. s.

The word is current in French:

1842.—"Il est clair que les **castes** n'ont jamais pu exister solidement sans une veritable conservation religieuse."—*Comte, Cours de Phil. Positive*, vi. 505.

1877.—"Nous avons aboli les **castes** et les privilèges, nous avons inscrit partout le principe de l'égalité devant la loi, nous avons donné le suffrage à tous, mais voilà qu'on réclame maintenant l'égalité des conditions."—*E. de Laveleye, De la Propriété*, p. iv.

Caste is also applied to breeds of animals, as 'a **high-caste** Arab.' In such cases the usage may possibly have come directly from the Port. *alta casta, casta baixa*, in the sense of breed or strain.

CATAMARÁN, s. Also **CUTMURRAM**, **CUTMURAL**. Tam. *kàṭṭu*, 'binding,' *maram*, 'wood.' A raft formed of three or four logs of wood lashed together. The Anglo-Indian accentuation of the last syllable is not correct.

1583.—"Seven round timbers lashed together for each of the said boats, and of the said seven timbers five form the bottom; one in the middle longer than the rest makes a cutwater, and another makes a poop which is under water, and on which a man sits ... These boats are called **Gatameroni**."—*Balbi, Viaggio*, f. 82.

1673.—"Coasting along some **Cattamarans** (Logs lashed to that advantage that they waft off all their Goods, only having a Sail in the midst and Paddles to guide them) made after us. ..."—*Fryer*, 24.

1698.—"Some time after the **Cattamaran** brought a letter. ..."—In *Wheeler*, i. 334.

1700.—"Un pecheur assis sur un **catimaron**, c'est à dire sur quelques grosses pièces de bois liées ensemble en manière de radeau."—*Lett. Edif.* x. 58.

c. 1780.—"The wind was high, and the ship had but two anchors, and in the next forenoon parted from that by which she was riding, before that one who was coming from the shore on a **Catamaran** could reach her."—*Orme*, iii. 300.

1810.—Williamson (*V. M.* i. 65) applies the term to the rafts of the Brazilian fishermen.

1836.—"None can compare to the **Catamarans** and the wonderful people that manage them ... each **catamaran** has one, two, or three men ... they sit crouched upon their heels, throwing their paddles about very dexterously, but very unlike rowing."—*Letters from Madras*, 34.

1860.—"The **Cattamaran** is common to Ceylon and Coromandel."—*Tennent, Ceylon*, i. 442.

[During the war with Napoleon, the word came to be applied to a sort of fire-ship. "Great hopes have been formed at the Admiralty (in 1804) of certain vessels which were filled with combustibles and called **catamarans**."—(*Ld. Stanhope, Life of Pitt*, iv. 218.) This may have introduced the word in English and led to its use as 'old cat' for a shrewish hag.]

CATHAY, n.p. China; originally Northern China. The origin of the name is given in the quotation below from the Introduction to Marco Polo. In the 16th century, and even later, from a misunderstanding of the medieval travellers, Cathay was supposed to be a country north of China, and is so represented in many maps. Its identity with China was fully recognised by P. Martin Martini in his *Atlas Sinensis*; also by Valentijn, iv. *China*, 2.

1247.—"**Kitai** autem ... homines sunt pagani, qui habent literam specialem ... homines benigni et humani satis esse videantur. Barbam non habent, et in dispositione faciei satis concordant cum Mongalis, non tamen sunt in facie ita lati ... meliores artifices non inveniuntur in toto mundo ... terra eorum est opulenta valde."—*J. de Plano Carpini, Hist. Mongalorum*, 653–4.

1253.—"Ultra est magna **Cataya**, qui antiquitus, ut credo, dicebantur Seres. ... Isti Catai sunt parvi homines, loquendo multum aspirantes per nares et ... habent parvam aperturam oculorum," &c.—*Itin. Wilhelmi de Rubruk*, 291–2.

c. 1330.—"**Cathay** is a very great Empire, which extendeth over more than c. days' journey, and it hath only one lord. ..."—*Friar Jordanus*, p. 54.

1404.—"E lo mas alxofar que en el mundo se ha, se pesia e falla en aq̃l mar del **Catay**."—*Clavijo*, f. 32.

1555.—"The Yndians called **Catheies** have eche man many wiues."—*Watreman, Fardle of Faciouns*, M. ii.

1598.—"In the lande lying westward from China, they say there are white people, and the land called **Cathaia**, where (as it is thought) are many Christians, and that it should confine and border upon *Persia*."—*Linschoten*, 57; [Hak. Soc. i. 126].

[1602.—"... and arriued at any porte within the dominions of the kingdomes of **Cataya**, China, or Japan."—*Birdwood, First Letter Book*, 24. Here *China* and *Cataya* are spoken of as different countries. Comp. *Birdwood, Rep. on Old Rec.*, 168 note.]

Before 1633.—
"I'll wish you in the Indies or **Cataia**... ."
Beaum. & Fletch., The Woman's Prize, iv. 5.

1634.—
"Domadores das terras e dos mares
Não so im Malaca, Indo e Perseu streito
Mas na China, **Catai**, Japão estranho
Lei nova introduzindo em sacro banho."
Malaca Conquistada.

1664.—"'Tis not yet twenty years, that there went caravans every year from *Kachemire*, which crossed all those mountains of the great *Tibet*, entred into Tartary, and arrived in about three months at **Cataja**. ..."—*Bernier*, E. T., 136; [ed. *Constable*, 425].

1842.—
"Better fifty years of Europe
than a cycle of **Cathay**."
Tennyson, Locksley Hall.

1871.—"For about three centuries the Northern Provinces of China had been detached from native rule, and subject to foreign dynasties; first to the *Khitan* ... whose rule subsisted for 200 years, and originated the name of *Khitai*, Khata, or **Cathay**, by which for nearly 1000 years China has been known to the nations of Inner Asia, and to those whose acquaintance with it was got by that channel."—*Marco Polo*, *Introd.* ch. ii.

CATUR, s. A light rowing vessel used on the coast of Malabar in the early days of the Portuguese. We have not been able to trace the name to any Indian source, [unless possibly Skt. *chatura*, 'swift']. Is it not probably the origin of our '*cutter*'? We see that Sir R. Burton in his Commentary on Camoens (vol. iv. 391) says: "*Catur* is the Arab. *katīreh*, a small craft, our 'cutter.'" [This view is rejected by the *N.E.D.*, which regards it as an English word from 'to cut.'] We cannot say when *cutter* was introduced in marine use. We cannot find it in Dampier, nor in *Robinson Crusoe*; the first instance we have found is that quoted below from *Anson's Voyage*. [The *N.E.D.* has nothing earlier than 1745.]

Bluteau gives *catur* as an Indian term indicating a small war vessel, which in a calm can be aided by oars. Jal (*Archéologie Navale*, ii. 259) quotes Witsen as saying that the *Caturi* or **Almadias** were Calicut vessels, having a length of 12 to 13 paces (60 to 65 feet), sharp at both ends, and curving back, using both sails and oars. But there was a larger kind, 80 feet long, with only 7 or 8 feet beam.

1510.—"There is also another kind of vessel. ... These are all made of one piece ... sharp at both ends. These ships are called **Chaturi**, and go either with a sail or oars more swiftly than any galley, *fusta*, or brigantine."—*Varthema*, 154.

1544.—"... navigium majus quod vocant **caturem**."—*Scti. Franc. Xav. Epistolae*, 121.

1549.—"Naves item duas (quas Indi **catures** vocant) summâ celeritate armari jussit, vt oram maritimam legentes, hostes commeatu prohiberent."—*Goës, de Bello Cambaico*, 1331.

1552.—"And this winter the Governor sent to have built in Cochin thirty **Catures**, which are vessels with oars, but smaller than brigantines."—*Castanheda*, iii. 271.

1588.—"Cambaicam oram Jacobus Lacteus duobos **caturibus** tueri jussus. ..."—*Maffei*, lib. xiii. ed. 1752, p. 283.

1601.—"Biremes, seu **Cathuris** quam plurimae conduntur in Lassaon, Javae civitate. ..."—*De Bry*, iii. 109 (where there is a plate, iii, No. xxxvii.).

1688.—"No man was so bold to contradict the man of God; and they all went to the Arsenal. There they found a good and sufficient bark of those they call **Catur**, besides seven old foysts."—*Dryden, Life of Xavier*, in *Works*, 1821, xvi. 200.

1742.—"... to prevent even the possibility of the galeons escaping us in the night, the two **Cutters** belonging to the *Centurion* and the *Gloucester* were both manned and sent in shore. ..."—*Anson's Voyage*, 9th ed. 1756, p. 251. **Cutter** also occurs pp. 111, 129, 150, and other places.

CAWNPORE, n.p. The correct name is *Kānhpur*, 'the town of Kānh, Kanhaiya or Krishna.' The city of the Doab so called, having in 1891 a population of 188,712, has grown up entirely under British rule, at first as the bazar and dependence of the cantonment established here under a treaty made with the Nabob of Oudh in 1766, and afterwards as a great mart of trade.

CAZEE, KAJEE, &c., s. Arab. *ḳāḍi*, 'a judge,' the letter *zwād* with which it is spelt being always pronounced in India like a *z*. The form *Cadi*, familiar from its use in the old version of the Arabian Nights, comes to us from the Levant. The word with the article, *al-ḳāḍi*, becomes in Spanish *alcalde*;[1] not *alcaide*, which is from *ḳā'īd*, 'a chief'; nor *alguacil*, which is from *wazīr*. So Dozy and Engelmann, no doubt correctly. But in Pinto, cap. 8, we find "ao *guazil* da justica q̃ em elles he como corregedor entre nos"; where *guazil* seems to stand for *ḳāẓī*.

It is not easy to give an accurate account of the position of the *Ḳāẓī* in British India, which has gone through variations of which a distinct record cannot be found. But the following outline is believed to be substantially correct.

Under **Adawlut** I have given a brief sketch of the history of the judiciary under the Company in the Bengal Presidency. Down to 1790 the greater part of the administration of criminal justice was still in the hands of native judges, and other native officials of various kinds, though under European supervision in varying forms. But the native judiciary, except in positions of a quite subordinate character, then ceased. It was, however, still in substance Mahommedan law that was administered in criminal cases, and also in civil cases between Mahommedans as affecting succession, &c. And a *Ḳāẓī* and a *Muftī* were retained in the Provincial Courts of Appeal and Circuit as the exponents of Mahommedan law, and the deliverers of a formal **Futwa**. There was also a *Ḳāẓī-al-Ḳoẓāt*, or chief *Ḳāẓī* of Bengal, Behar and Orissa, attached to the Sudder Courts of Dewanny and Nizamut, assisted by two *Muftis*, and these also gave written *futwas* on references from the District Courts.

The style of *Ḳāẓī* and *Muftī* presumably continued in formal existence in connection with the Sudder Courts till the abolition of these in 1862; but with the earlier abolition of the Provincial Courts in 1829–31 it had quite ceased, in this sense, to be familiar. In the District Courts the corresponding exponents were in English officially designated **Law-officers**, and, I believe, in official vernacular, as well as commonly among Anglo-Indians, **Moolvees** (q.v.).

Under the article LAW-OFFICER, it will be seen that certain trivial cases were, at the discretion of the magistrate, referred for disposal by the Law-officer of the district. And the latter, from this fact, as well as, perhaps, from the tradition of the elders, was in some parts of Bengal popularly known as 'the *Ḳāẓī*.' "In the Magistrate's office," writes my friend Mr. Seton-Karr, "it was quite common to speak of this case as referred to the joint magistrate, and that to the *Chhoṭā Ṣāḥib* (the Assistant), and that again to the *Ḳāẓī*."

But the duties of the *Ḳāẓī* popularly so styled and officially recognised, had, almost from the beginning of the century, become limited to certain notarial functions, to the performance and registration of Mahommedan marriages, and some other matters connected with the social life of their co-religionists. To these functions must also be added as regards the 18th century and the earlier years of the 19th, duties in connection with distraint for rent on behalf of Zemindars. There were such *Ḳāẓīs* nominated by Government in towns and pergunnas, with great variation in the area of the localities over which they officiated. The Act XI. of 1864, which repealed the laws relating to law-officers, put an end also to the appointment by Government of *Ḳāẓīs*. But this seems to have led to inconveniences which were complained of by Mahommedans in some parts of India, and it was enacted in 1880 (Act XII., styled "The *Ḳāẓīs* Act") that with reference to any particular locality, and after consultation with the chief Musulman residents therein, the Local Government might select and nominate a *Ḳāẓī* or *Ḳāẓīs* for that local area (see FUTWA, LAW-OFFICER, MUFTY).

1338.—"They treated me civilly and set me in front of their mosque during their Easter; at which mosque, on account of its being their Easter, there were assembled from divers quarters a number of their **Cadini**, *i.e.* of their bishops."—Letter of *Friar Pascal*, in *Cathay, &c.*, 235.

1 Dr. R. Rost observes to us that the Arabic letter *ẓwād* is pronounced by the Malays like *ll* (see also *Crawfurd's Malay Grammar*, p. 7). And it is curious to find a transfer of the same letter into Spanish as *ld*. In Malay *ḳāḍī* becomes *ḳāllī*.

c. 1461.—
"Au tems que Alexandre regna
Ung hom, nommé Diomedès
Devant luy, on luy amena
Engrilloné poulces et detz
Comme ung larron; car il fut des
Escumeurs que voyons courir
Si fut mys devant le **cadès**,
Pour estre jugé à mourir."
Gd. Testament de Fr. Villon.

[c. 1610.—"The Pandiare is called **Cady** in the Arabic tongue."—*Pyrard de Laval*, Hak. Soc. i. 199.]

1648.—"The Government of the city (Ahmedabad) and surrounding villages rests with the Governor *Coutewael*, and the Judge (whom they call **Casgy**)."—*Van Twist*, 15.

[1670.—"The Shawbunder, **Cozzy**."—*Hedges, Diary*, Hak. Soc. ii. ccxxix.]

1673.—"Their Law-Disputes, they are soon ended; the Governor hearing; and the **Cadi** or Judge determining every Morning."—*Fryer*, 32.

"The **Cazy** or Judge ... marries them."—*Ibid.* 94.

1683.—"... more than that 3000 poor men gathered together, complaining with full mouths of his exaction and injustice towards them: some demanding Rupees 10, others Rupees 20 per man, which Bulchund very generously paid them in the **Cazee's** presence. ..."—*Hedges*, Nov. 5; [Hak. Soc. i. 134; **Cazze** in i. 85].

1684.—"*January* 12.—From Cassumbasar 'tis advised ye Merchants and Picars appeal again to ye **Cazee** for Justice against Mr. Charnock. Ye **Cazee** cites Mr. Charnock to appear. ..."—*Ibid.* i. 147.

1689.—"A **Cogee** ... who is a Person skilled in their Law."—*Ovington*, 206.

Here there is perhaps a confusion with **Coja**.

1727.—"When the Man sees his Spouse, and likes her, they agree on the Price and Term of Weeks, Months, or Years, and then appear before the **Cadjee** or Judge."—*A. Hamilton*, i. 52.

1763.—"The **Cadi** holds court in which are tried all disputes of property."—*Orme*, i. 26 (ed. 1803).

1773.—"That they should be mean, weak, ignorant, and corrupt, is not surprising, when the salary of the principal judge, the **Cazi**, does not exceed Rs. 100 per month."—*From* Impey's *Judgment in the Patna Cause*, quoted by *Stephen*, ii. 176.

1790.—"*Regulations for the Court of Circuit.*

"24. That each of the Courts of Circuit be superintended by two covenanted civil servants of the Company, to be denominated Judges of the Courts of Circuit ... assisted by a **Kazi** and a Mufti."—*Regns. for the Adm. of Justice in the Foujdarry or Criminal Courts in Bengal, Bahar, and Orissa.* Passed by the G.-G. in C., Dec. 3, 1790.

"32. ... The charge against the prisoner, his confession, which is always to be received with circumspection and tenderness ... &c. ... being all heard and gone through in his presence and that of the **Kazi** and Mufti of the Court, the **Kazi** and Mufti are then to write at the bottom of the record of the proceedings held in the trial, the *futwa* or law as applicable to the circumstances of the case. ... The Judges of the Court shall attentively consider such *futwa*, &c."—*Ibid.*

1791.—"The Judges of the Courts of Circuit shall refer to the **Kazi** and Mufti of their respective Courts all questions on points of law ... regarding which they may not have been furnished with specific instructions from the G.-G. in C. or the *Nizamut Adawlut.* ..."—*Regn. No. XXXV.*

1792.—Revenue Regulation of July 20, No. lxxv., empowers Landholders and Farmers of Land to distrain for Arrears of Rent or Revenue. The "**Kazi** of the Pegunnah" is the official under the Collector, repeatedly referred to as regulating and carrying out the distraint. So, again, in *Regn.* XVII. of 1793.

1793.—"lxvi. The Nizamut Adaulat shall continue to be held at Calcutta.

"lxvii. The Court shall consist of the Governor-General, and the members of the Supreme Council, assisted by the head **Cauzy** of Bengal, Behar, and Orissa, and two Muftis." (This was already in the Regulations of 1791.)—*Regn. IX. of* 1793. See also quotation under MUFTY.

1793.—"I. **Cauzies** are stationed at the Cities of Patna, Dacca, and Moorahedabad, and the principal towns, and in the pergunnahs, for the purpose of preparing and attesting deeds of transfer, and other law papers, celebrating marriages, and performing such religious duties or ceremonies prescribed by the Mahommedan law, as have been hitherto discharged by them under the British Government."—*Reg. XXXIX. of* 1793.

1803.—Regulation XLVI. regulates the appointment of **Cauzy** in towns and pergunnahs, "for the purpose of preparing and attesting deeds of transfer, and other law papers, celebrating marriages," &c., but makes no allusion to judicial duties.

1824.—"Have you not learned this common saying—'Every one's teeth are blunted by acids except the **cadi's**, which are by sweets.'"—*Hajji Baba*, ed. 1885, p. 316.

1864.—"Whereas it is unnecessary to continue the offices of Hindoo and Mahomedan **Law-Officers**, and is inexpedient that the appointment of **Cazee**-*ool-Cozaat*, or of City,

Town, or Pergunnah **Cazees** should be made by Government, it is enacted as follows:—

* * *

"II. Nothing contained in this Act shall be construed so as to prevent a **Cazee**-*ool-Cozaat* or other **Cazee** from performing, when required to do so, any duties or ceremonies prescribed by the Mahomedan Law."—*Act No. XI. of* 1864.

1880.—"... whereas by the usage of the Muhammadan community in some parts of India the presence of **Kázís** appointed by the Government is required at the celebration of marriages. ..."—*Bill introduced into the Council of Gov.-Gen.*, January 30, 1880.

"An Act for the appointment of persons to the office of **Kází**.

"Whereas by the preamble to Act No. XI. of 1864 ... it was (among other things declared inexpedient, &c.) ... and whereas by the usage of the Muhammadan community in some parts of India the presence of **Kázís** appointed by the Government is required at the celebration of marriages and the performance of certain other rites and ceremonies, and it is therefore expedient that the Government should again be empowered to appoint such persons to the office of **Kází**; It is hereby enacted ..."—*Act No. XII. of* 1880.

1885.—"To come to something more specific. 'There were instances in which men of the most venerable dignity, persecuted without a cause by extortioners, died of rage and shame in the gripe of the vile alguazils of Impey' [**Macaulay's** *Essay on Hastings*].

"Here we see one **Cazi** turned into an indefinite number of 'men of the most venerable dignity'; a man found guilty by legal process of corruptly oppressing a helpless widow into 'men of the most venerable dignity' persecuted by extortioners without a cause; and a guard of sepoys, with which the Supreme Court had nothing to do, into 'vile alguazils of Impey.'"—*Stephen, Story of Nuncomar*, ii. 250–251.

Cazee also is a title used in Nepal for Ministers of State.

1848.—"**Kajees**, Counsellors, and mitred Lamas were there, to the number of twenty, all planted with their backs to the wall, mute and motionless as statues."—*Hooker's Himalayan Journals*, ed. 1855, i. 286.

1868.—"The Durbar (of Nepal) have written to the four **Kajees** of Thibet enquiring the reason."—Letter from *Col. R. Lawrence*, dated 1st April, regarding persecution of R. C. Missions in Tibet.

1873.—

"Ho, lamas, get ye ready,
 Ho, **Kazis**, clear the way;
The chief will ride in all his pride
 To the Rungeet Stream to-day."

Wilfrid Heeley, A Lay of Modern Darjeeling.

CEYLON, n.p. This name, as applied to the great island which hangs from India like a dependent jewel, becomes usual about the 13th century. But it can be traced much earlier. For it appears undoubtedly to be formed from *Sinhala* or *Sihala*, 'lions' abode,' the name adopted in the island itself at an early date. This, with the addition of 'Island,' *Sihala-dvīpa*, comes down to us in Cosmas as *Σιελεδίβα*. There was a Pali form *Sihalan*, which, at an early date, must have been colloquially shortened to *Silan*, as appears from the old Tamil name *Ilam* (the Tamil having no proper sibilant), and probably from this was formed the *Sarandīp* and *Sarandīb* which was long the name in use by mariners of the Persian Gulf.

It has been suggested by Mr. Van der Tuuk, that the name *Sailan* or *Silan* was really of Javanese origin, as *sela* (from Skt. *śilā*, 'a rock, a stone') in Javanese (and in Malay) means 'a precious stone,' hence *Pulo Selan* would be 'Isle of Gems.' ["This," writes Mr. Skeat, "is possible, but it remains to be proved that the gem was not named after the island (*i.e.* 'Ceylon stone'). The full phrase in standard Malay is *batu Sēlan*, where *batu* means 'stone.' Klinkert merely marks *Sailan* (Ceylon) as Persian."] The island was really called anciently *Ratnadvīpa*, 'Isle of Gems,' and is termed by an Arab historian of the 9th century *Jazīrat-al yaḳūt*, 'Isle of Rubies.' So that there is considerable plausibility in Van der Tuuk's suggestion. But the genealogy of the name from *Sihala* is so legitimate that the utmost that can be conceded is the possibility that the Malay form *Selan* may have been shaped by the consideration suggested, and may have influenced the general adoption of the form *Sailān*, through the predominance of Malay navigation in the Middle Ages.

c. 362.—"Unde nationibus Indicis certatim cum donis optimates mittentibus ante tempus, ab usque Divis et **Serendivis**."—*Ammianus Marcellinus*, XXI. vii.

c. 430.—"The island of Lanka was called **Sihala** after the Lion; listen ye to the narration of the island which I (am going to) tell: 'The daughter of the Vanga King cohabited in the forest with a lion.'"—*Dipavanso*, IX. i. 2.

c. 545.—"This is the great island in the

ocean, lying in the Indian Sea. By the Indians it is called **Sielediba**, but by the Greeks Taprobane."—*Cosmas*, Bk. xi.

851.—"Near **Sarandīb** is the pearl-fishery. *Sarandīb* is entirely surrounded by the sea."—*Relation des Voyages*, i. p. 5.

c. 940.—"Mas'ūdi proceeds: In the Island **Sarandīb**, I myself witnessed that when the King was dead, he was placed on a chariot with low wheels so that his hair dragged upon the ground."—In *Gildemeister*, 154.

c. 1020.—"There you enter the country of Lárán, where is Jaimúr, then Malia, then Kánji, then Darúd, where there is a great gulf in which is **Sinkaldíp** (*Sinhala dvīpa*), or the island of **Sarandíp**."—*Al Birūnī*, as given by *Rashíduddín*, in *Elliot*, i. 66.

1275.—"The island **Sailan** is a vast island between China and India, 80 parasangs in circuit. ... It produces wonderful things, sandalwood, spikenard, cinnamon, cloves, brazil, and various spices. ..."—*Kazvīnī*, in *Gildemeister*, 203.

1298.—"You come to the island of **Seilan**, which is in good sooth the best island of its size in the world."—*Marco Polo*, Bk. iii. ch. 14.

c. 1300.—"There are two courses ... from this place (Ma'bar); one leads by sea to Chín and Máchín, passing by the island of **Sílán**."—*Rashíduddín*, in *Elliot*, i. 70.

1330.—"There is another island called **Sillan**. ... In this ... there is an exceeding great mountain, of which the folk relate that it was upon it that Adam mourned for his son one hundred years."—*Fr. Odoric*, in *Cathay*, i. 98.

c. 1337.—"I met in this city (Brussa) the pious sheikh 'Abd-Allah-al-Miṣrī, the Traveller. He was a worthy man. He made the circuit of the earth, except he never entered China, nor the island of **Sarandīb**, nor Andalusia, nor the Sūdān. I have excelled him, for I have visited those regions."—*Ibn Batuta*, ii. 321.

c. 1350.—"... I proceeded to sea by **Seyllan**, a glorious mountain opposite to Paradise. ... 'Tis said the sound of the waters falling from the fountain of Paradise is heard there."—*Marignolli*, in *Cathay*, ii. 346.

c. 1420.—"In the middle of the Gulf there is a very noble island called **Zeilam**, which is 3000 miles in circumference, and on which they find by digging, rubies, saffires, garnets, and those stones which are called cats'-eyes."—*N. Conti*, in *India in the XVth Century*, 7.

1498.—"... much ginger, and pepper, and cinnamon, but this is not so fine as that which comes from an island which is called **Cillam**, and which is 8 days distant from Calicut."—*Roteiro de V. da Gama*, 88.

1514.—"Passando avanti intra la terra e il mare si truova l'isola di **Zolan** dove nasce la cannella. ..."—*Giov. da Empoli*, in *Archiv. Stor. Ital.*, Append. 79.

1516.—"Leaving these islands of Mahaldiva ... there is a very large and beautiful island which the Moors, Arabs, and Persians call **Ceylam**, and the Indians call it Ylinarim."—*Barbosa*, 166.

1586.—"This **Ceylon** is a brave Iland, very fruitful and fair."—*Hakl.* ii. 397.

[1605.—"Heare you shall buie theis Comodities followinge of the Inhabitants of **Selland**."—*Birdwood, First Letter Book*, 84.

[1615.—"40 tons of cinnamon of **Celand**."—*Foster, Letters*, iii. 277.

["Here is arrived a ship out of Holland ... at present turning under **Silon**."—*Ibid.* iv. 34.]

1682.—"... having run 35 miles North without seeing **Zeilon**."—*Hedges, Diary*, July 7; [Hak. Soc. i. 28].

1727.—A. Hamilton writes **Zeloan** (i. 340, &c.), and as late as 1780, in *Dunn's Naval Directory*, we find **Zeloan** throughout.

1781.—"We explored the whole coast of **Zelone**, from Pt. Pedro to the Little Basses, looked into every port and spoke to every vessel we saw, without hearing of French vessels."—*Price's Letter to Ph. Francis*, in *Tracts*, i. 9.

1830.—

"For dearer to him are the shells that sleep
By his own sweet native stream,
Than all the pearls of **Serendeep**,
Or the Ava ruby's gleam!
Home! Home! Friends—health—repose,
What are Golconda's gems to those?"
Bengal Annual.

CHABEE, s. H. *chābī*, *chābhī*, 'a key,' from Port. *chave*. In Bengali it becomes *sābī*, and in Tam. *sāvī*. In Sea-H. 'a fid.'

CHACKUR, s. P.—H. *chākar*, 'a servant.' The word is hardly ever now used in Anglo-Indian households except as a sort of rhyming amplification to *Naukar* (see NOKUR: "*Naukar-chākar*," the whole following. But in a past generation there was a distinction made between *naukar*, the superior servant, such as a *munshī*, a *gomāshta*, a *chobdār*, a *khānsama*, &c., and *chākar*, a menial servant. Williamson gives a curious list of both classes, showing what a large Calcutta household embraced at the beginning of last century (*V. M.* i. 185–187).

1810.—"Such is the superiority claimed by the *nokers*, that to ask one of them 'whose **chauker** he is?' would be considered a gross insult."—*Williamson*, i. 187.

CHARPOY, s. H. *chārpāī*, from P. *chihār-pāī* (*i.e.* four-feet), the common Indian bedstead, sometimes of very rude materials, but in other cases handsomely wrought and painted. It is correctly described in the quotation from Ibn Batuta.

c. 1350.—"The beds in India are very light. A single man can carry one, and every traveller should have his own bed, which his slave carries about on his head. The bed consists of four conical legs, on which four staves are laid; between they plait a sort of ribbon of silk or cotton. When you lie on it you need nothing else to render the bed sufficiently elastic."—iii. 380.

c. 1540.—"Husain Khan Tashtdár was sent on some business from Bengal. He went on travelling night and day. Whenever sleep came over him he placed himself on a bed (**chahār-pāī**) and the villagers carried him along on their shoulders."—MS. quoted in *Elliot*, iv. 418.

1662.—"Turbans, long coats, trowsers, shoes, and sleeping on **chárpáis**, are quite unusual."—*H. of Mir Jumla's Invasion of Assam*, transl. by *Blochmann*, *J.A.S.B.* xli. pt. i. 80.

1876.—"A syce at Mozuffernuggar, lying asleep on a **charpoy** ... was killed by a tame buck goring him in the side ... it was supposed in play."—*Baldwin*, *Large and Small Game of Bengal*, 195.

1883.—"After a gallop across country, he would rest on a **charpoy**, or country bed, and hold an impromptu *levee* of all the village folk."—*C. Raikes*, in *L. of L. Lawrence*, i. 57.

CHAWBUCK, s. and v. A whip; to whip. An obsolete vulgarism from P. *chābuk*, 'alert'; in H. 'a horsewhip.' It seems to be the same as the *sjambok* in use at the Cape, and apparently carried from India (see the quotation from Van Twist). [Mr. Skeat points out that Klinkert gives *chambok* or *sambok*, as Javanese forms, the standard Malay being *chabok* or *chabuk*; and this perhaps suggests that the word may have been introduced by Malay grooms once largely employed at the Cape.]

1648. "... Poor and little thieves are flogged with a great whip (called **Siamback**) several days in succession."—*Van Twist*, 29.

1673.—"Upon any suspicion of default he has a Black Guard that by a **Chawbuck**, a great Whip, extorts Confession."—*Fryer*, 98.

1673.—"The one was of an Armenian, **Chawbucked** through the City for selling of Wine."—*Ibid.* 97.

1682.—"... Ramgivan, our *Vekeel* there (at Hugly) was sent for by Permesuradass, Bulchund's servant, who immediately clapt him in prison. Ye same day was brought forth and slippered; the next day he was beat on ye soles of his feet, ye third day **Chawbuckt**, and ye 4th drub'd till he could not speak, and all to force a writing in our names to pay Rupees 50,000 for custome of ye Silver brought out this year."—*Hedges*, *Diary*, Nov. 2; [Hak. Soc. i. 45].

[1684-5.—"Notwithstanding his being a great person was soon stripped and **chawbuckt**."—*Pringle*, *Madras Consns.* iv. 4.]

1688.—"Small offenders are only whipt on the Back, which sort of Punishment they call **Chawbuck**."—*Dampier*, ii. 138.

1699.—"The Governor of Surrat ordered the cloth Broker to be tyed up and **chawbucked**."—*Letter from General and Council at Bombay to E. I. C.* (in Record Office), 23rd March, 1698-9.

1726.—"Another Pariah he **chawbucked** 25 blows, put him in the Stocks, and kept him there an hour."—*Wheeler*, ii. 410.

1756.—"... a letter from Mr. Hastings ... says that the Nabob to engage the Dutch and French to purchase also, had put peons upon their Factories and threatened their *Vaquills* with the **Chaubac**."—In *Long*, 79.

1760.—"Mr. Barton, laying in wait, seized Benautrom Chattogee opposite to the door of the Council, and with the assistance of his bearer and his peons tied his hands and his feet, swung him upon a bamboo like a hog, carried him to his own house, there with his own hand **chawbooked** him in the most cruel manner, almost to the deprivation of life; endeavoured to force beef into his mouth, to the irreparable loss of his Bramin's caste, and all this without giving ear to, or suffering the man to speak in his own defence. ..."—*Fort Wm. Consn.*, in *Long*, 214-215.

1784.—

"The sentinels placed at the door
  Are for our security bail;
With Muskets and **Chaubucks** secure,
  They guard us in Bangalore Jail."

Song, by a *Gentleman of the Navy* (prisoner with Hyder) in *Seton-Karr*, i. 18.

1817.—"... ready to prescribe his favourite regimen of the **Chabuk** for every man, woman, or child who dared to think otherwise."—*Lalla Rookh*.

CHEECHEE, adj. A disparaging term applied to half-castes or **Eurasians** (q.v.) (corresponding to the **Lip-lap** of the Dutch in Java) and also to their manner of speech. The word is said to be taken from *chī* (Fie!), a common native (S. Indian) interjection of remonstrance or reproof, supposed to be much used by the class in question. The term is, however, perhaps also a kind of onomatopœia, indicating the mincing pronunciation which often characterises them (see below). It should, however, be added that there are many well-educated East Indians who are quite free from this mincing accent.

1781.—
"Pretty little Looking-Glasses,
Good and cheap for **Chee-chee** Misses."
Hicky's Bengal Gazette, March 17.

1873.—"He is no favourite with the pure native, whose language he speaks as his own in addition to the hybrid minced English (known as **chee-chee**), which he also employs."—*Fraser's Magazine*, Oct., 437.

1880.—"The Eurasian girl is often pretty and graceful. ... 'What though upon her lips there hung The accents of her **tchi-tchi** tongue.'"—*Sir Ali Baba*, 122.

1881.—"There is no doubt that the '**Chee Chee** twang,' which becomes so objectionable to every Englishman before he has been long in the East, was originally learned in the convent and the Brothers' school, and will be clung to as firmly as the queer turns of speech learned in the same place."—*St. James's Gazette*, Aug. 26.

CHEESE, s. This word is well known to be used in modern English slang for "anything good, first-rate in quality, genuine, pleasant, or advantageous" (*Slang Dict.*). And the most probable source of the term is P. and H. *chīz*, 'thing.' For the expression used to be common among Anglo-Indians, *e.g.*, "My new Arab is the real *chīz*"; "These cheroots are the real *chīz*," *i.e.* the real thing. The word may have been an Anglo-Indian importation, and it is difficult otherwise to account for it. [This view is accepted by the *N.E.D.*; for other explanations see 1 ser. *N. & Q.* viii. 89; 3 ser. vii. 465, 505.]

CHEETA, s. H. *chītā*, the *Felis jubata*, Schreber, [*Cynaelurus jubatus*, Blanford], or 'Hunting Leopard,' so called from its being commonly trained to use in the chase. From Skt. *chitraka*, or *chitrakāya*, lit. 'having a speckled body.'

1563.—"... and when they wish to pay him much honour they call him *Ráo*; as for example Chita-Ráo, whom I am acquainted with; and this is a proud name, for **Chita** signifies 'Ounce' (or panther) and this *Chita*-Rao means 'King as strong as a Panther.'"—*Garcia*, f. 36.

c. 1596.—"Once a leopard (**chīta**) had been caught, and without previous training, on a mere hint by His Majesty, it brought in the prey, like trained leopards."—*Āīn-i-Akbarī*, ed. *Blochmann*, i. 286.

1610.—Hawkins calls the **Cheetas** at Akbar's Court 'ounces for game.'—In *Purchas*, i. 218.

[1785.—"The **Cheetah**-connah, the place where the Nabob's panthers and other animals for hunting are kept."—*Forbes, Or. Mem.* 2nd ed. ii. 450.]

1862.—"The true **Cheetah**, the Hunting Leopard of India, does not exist in Ceylon."—*Tennent*, i. 140.

1879.—"Two young **cheetahs** had just come in from Bombay; one of these was as tame as a house-cat, and like the puma, purred beautifully when stroked."—*"Jamrack's,"* in *Sat. Review*, May 17, p. 612.

It has been ingeniously suggested by Mr. Aldis Wright that the word *cheater*, as used by Shakspere, in the following passage, refers to this animal:—

Falstaff: "He's no swaggerer, Hostess; a *tame* **cheater** i' faith; you may stroke him gently as a puppy greyhound; he'll not swagger."—2nd Part *King Henry IV.* ii. 4.

Compare this with the passage just quoted from the *Saturday Review*! And the interpretation would rather derive confirmation from a parallel passage from Beaumont & Fletcher:

"... if you give any credit to the juggling rascal, you are worse than simple widgeons, and will be drawn into the net by this decoy-duck, this *tame* **cheater**."—*The Fair Maid of the Inn*, iv. 2.

But we have not been able to trace any possible source from which Shakspere could have derived the name of the animal at all, to say nothing of the familiar use of it. [The *N.E.D.* gives no support to the suggestion.]

CHEROOT, s. A cigar; but the term has been appropriated specially to cigars truncated at both ends, as the Indian and Manilla cigars always were in former days. The word is Tam. *shuruṭṭu*, [Mal. *churuṭṭu*,] 'a roll (of tobacco).' In the South cheroots are chiefly made at Trichinopoly and in the Godavery Delta, the produce being known respectively as **Trichies** and **Lunkas**. The earliest occurrence of the word that we know is in Father Beschi's Tamil story of Parmartta Guru (c. 1725). On p. 1 one of the characters is described as carrying a firebrand to light his *pugaiyailai shshuruṭṭu*, 'roll (cheroot) of tobacco.' [The *N.E.D.* quotes **cheroota** in 1669.] Grose (1750–60), speaking of Bombay, whilst describing the cheroot does not use that word, but another which is, as far as we know, entirely obsolete in British India, viz. **Buncus** (q.v.).

1759.—In the expenses of the Nabob's entertainment at Calcutta in this year we find:

"60 lbs. of Masulipatam **cheroots**, Rs. 500."—In *Long*, 194.

1781.—"... am tormented every day by a parcel of gentlemen coming to the end of my berth to talk politics and smoke **cheroots**—advise them rather to think of mending the holes in their old shirts, like me."—*Hon. J. Lindsay* (in *Lives of the Lindsays*), iii. 297.

"Our evening amusements instead of your stupid Harmonics, was playing Cards and Backgammon, chewing Beetle and smoking **Cherutes**."—*Old Country Captain*, in *India Gazette*, Feby. 24.

1782.—"Le tabac y réussit très bien; les **chiroutes** de Manille sont renommées dans toute l'Inde par leur goût agréable; aussi les Dames dans ce pays fument-elles toute la journée."—*Sonnerat, Voyage*, iii. 43.

1792.—"At that time (c. 1757) I have seen the officers mount guard many's the time and oft ... neither did they at that time carry your fusees, but had a long Pole with an iron head to it. ... With this in one Hand and a **Chiroot** in the other you saw them saluting away at the Main Guard."—*Madras Courier*, April 3.

1810.—"The lowest classes of Europeans, as also of the natives ... frequently smoke **cheroots**, exactly corresponding with the Spanish *segar*, though usually made rather more bulky."—*Williamson, V. M.* i. 499.

1811.—"Dire que le **T'cherout** est la cigarre, c'est me dispenser d'en faire la description."—*Solvyns*, iii.

[1823.—"He amused himself by smoking several **carrotes**."—*Owen, Narr.* ii. 50.]

1875.—"The meal despatched, all who were not on duty lay down ... almost too tired to smoke their **cheroots** before falling asleep."—*The Dilemma*, ch. xxxvii.

[**CHEYLA**, s. "Originally a H. word (*chelā*, Skt. *cheṭaka, cheḍaka*) meaning 'a servant,' many changes have been rung upon it in Hindu life, so that it has meant a slave, a household slave, a family retainer, an adopted member of a great family, a dependant relative and a soldier in its secular senses; a follower, a pupil, a disciple and a convert in its ecclesiastical senses. It has passed out of Hindu usage into Muhammadan usage with much the same meanings and ideas attached to it, and has even meant a convert from Hinduism to Islam." (*Col. Temple*, in *Ind. Ant.*, July, 1896, pp. 200 *seqq.*). In Anglo-Indian usage it came to mean a special battalion made up of prisoners and converts.

[c. 1596.—"The **Chelahs** or Slaves. His Majesty from religious motives dislikes the name *bandah* or slave. ... He therefore calls this class of men **Chelahs**, which Hindi term signifies a faithful disciple."—*Āīn, Blochmann*, i. 253 *seqq.*

[1791.—"(The Europeans) all were bound on the parade and rings (*boly*) the badge of slavery were put into their ears. They were then incorporated into a battalion of **Cheylas**."—In *Seton-Karr*, ii. 311.

[1795.—"... a Havildar ... compelled to serve in one of his **Chela** Corps."—*Ibid.* ii. 407.]

CHICANE, CHICANERY, ss. These English words, signifying pettifogging, captious contention, taking every possible advantage in a contest, have been referred to Spanish *chico*, 'little,' and to Fr. *chic*, *chicquet*, 'a little bit,' as by Mr. Wedgwood in his *Dict. of Eng. Etymology*. See also quotation from *Saturday Review* below. But there can be little doubt that the words are really traceable to the game of *chaugān*, or horse-golf. This game is now well known in England under the name of **Polo** (q.v.). But the recent introduction under that name is its second importation into Western Europe. For in the Middle Ages it came from Persia to Byzantium, where it was popular under a modification of its Persian name (verb τζυκανίζειν, playing ground τζυκανιστήριον), and from Byzantium it passed, as a pedestrian game, to Languedoc, where it was called, by a further modification, *chicane* (see *Ducange, Dissertations sur l'Histoire de St. Louis*, viii., and his *Glossarium Graecitatis*, s.v. τζυκανίζειν; also *Ouseley's Travels*, i. 345). The analogy of certain periods of the game of golf suggests how the figurative meaning of *chicaner* might arise in taking advantage of the petty accidents of the surface. And this is the strict meaning of *chicaner*, as used by military writers.

Ducange's idea was that the Greeks had borrowed both the game and the name from France, but this is evidently erroneous. He was not aware of the Persian *chaugān*. But he explains well how the tactics of the game would have led to the application of its name to "those tortuous proceedings of pleaders which we old practitioners call *barres*." The indication of the Persian origin of both the Greek and French words is due to W. Ouseley and to Quatremère. The latter has an interesting note, full of his usual wealth of Oriental reading, in his translation of Makrizi's *Mameluke Sultans*, tom. i. pt. i. pp. 121 *seqq.*

The preceding etymology was put forward again in Notes upon Mr. Wedgwood's Dictionary published by one of the present writers in *Ocean Highways*, Sept. 1872, p. 186. The same etymology has since been given by Littré (s.v.), who says: "Dès lors, la série des sens est: jeu de mail, puis action de disputer la partie, et enfin manœuvres processives"; [and is accepted by the *N.E.D.* with the reservation that "evidence actually connecting the French with the Greek word appears not to be known"].

The P. forms of the name are *chaugān* and *chauigān*; but according to the *Bahāri 'Ajam* (a great Persian dictionary compiled in India, 1768) the primitive form of the word is *chulgān* from *chūl*, 'bent,' which (as to the form) is corroborated by the Arabic *sawljān*. On the other hand, a probable origin of *chaugān* would be an Indian (Prakrit) word, meaning 'four corners' [Platts gives *chaugāna*, 'four-fold'], viz. as a name for the polo-ground. The *chulgān* is possibly a 'striving after meaning.' The meanings are according to Vüllers (1) any stick with a crook; (2) such a stick used as a drumstick; (3) a crook from which a steel ball is suspended, which was one of the royal insignia, otherwise called *kaukaba* [see *Blochmann*, *Āīn*, vol. i. plate ix. No. 2.]; (4) (The golf-stick, and) the game of horse-golf.

The game is now quite extinct in Persia and Western Asia, surviving only in certain regions adjoining India, as is specified under **Polo**. But for many centuries it was the game of kings and courts over all Mahommedan Asia. The earliest Mahommedan historians represent the game of *chaugān* as familiar to the Sassanian kings; Ferdusi puts the *chaugān*-stick into the hands of Siāwūsh, the father of Kai Khusrū or Cyrus; many famous kings were devoted to the game, among whom may be mentioned Nūruddīn the Just, Atābek of Syria and the great enemy of the Crusaders. He was so fond of the game that he used (like Akbar in after days) to play it by lamp-light, and was severely rebuked by a devout Mussulman for being so devoted to a mere amusement. Other zealous *chaugān*-players were the great Saladin, Jalāluddīn Mankbarni of Khwārizm, and Malik Bībars, Marco Polo's "Bendocquedar Soldan of Babylon," who was said more than once to have played *chaugān* at Damascus and at Cairo within the same week. Many illustrious persons also are mentioned in Asiatic history as having met their death by accidents in the *maidān*, as the *chaugān*-field was especially called; *e.g.* Kutbuddīn Ibak of Delhi, who was killed by such a fall at Lahore in (or about) 1207. In Makrizi (I. i. 121) we read of an Amīr at the Mameluke Court called Husāmuddīn Lajīn 'Azīzī the *Jukāndār* (or Lord High Polo-stick).

It is not known when the game was conveyed to Constantinople, but it must have been not later than the beginning of the 8th century.[1] The fullest description of the game as played there is given by Johannes Cinnamus (c. 1190), who does not however give the barbarian name:

"The winter now being over and the gloom cleared away, he (the Emperor Manuel Comnenus) devoted himself to a certain sober exercise which from the first had been the custom of the Emperors and their sons to practise. This is the manner thereof. A party of young men divide into two equal bands, and in a flat space which has been measured out purposely they cast a leather ball in size somewhat like an apple; and setting this in the middle as if it were a prize to be contended for they rush into the contest at full speed, each grasping in his right hand a stick of moderate length which comes suddenly to a broad rounded end, the middle of which is closed by a network of dried catgut. Then each party strives who shall first send the ball beyond the goal planted conspicuously on the opposite side, for whenever the ball is struck by the netted sticks through the goal at either side, that gives the victory to the other side. This is the kind of game, evidently a slippery and dangerous one. For a player must be continually throwing himself right back, or bending to one side or the other, as he turns his horse short, or suddenly dashes off at speed, with such strokes and twists as are needed to follow up the ball. ... And thus as the Emperor was rushing round in furious fashion in this game, it so happened that the horse which he rode came violently to the ground. He was prostrate below the horse, and as he struggled vainly to extricate himself from its incumbent weight his thigh and hand were

---

1 The court for *chaugān* is ascribed by Codinus (see below) to Theodosius Parvus. This could hardly be the son of Arcadius (A.D. 408–450), but rather Theodosius III. (716–718).

crushed beneath the saddle and much injured. ..."—In Bonn ed. pp. 263–264.

We see from this passage that at Byzantium the game was played with a kind of racket, and not with a polostick.

We have not been able to find an instance of the medieval French *chicane* in this sense, nor does Littré's Dictionary give any. But Ducange states positively that in his time the word in this sense survived in Languedoc, and there could be no better evidence. From Henschel's *Ducange* also we borrow a quotation which shows *chuca*, used for some game of ball, in French-Latin, surely a form of *chaugān* or *chicane*.

The game of *chaugān*, the ball (*gū* or *gavī*) and the playing-ground (*maidān*) afford constant metaphors in Persian literature.

c. 820.—"If a man dream that he is on horseback along with the King himself, or some great personage, and that he strikes the ball home, or wins the **chukān** (*ἤτοι τζυκανίζει*) he shall find grace and favour thereupon, conformable to the success of his ball and the dexterity of his horse." Again: "If the King dream that he has won in the **chukān** (*ὅτι ἐτζυκανίζεν*) he shall find things prosper with him."—*The Dream Judgments of Achmet Ibn Seirim*, from a MS. Greek version quoted by *Ducange* in *Gloss. Graecitatis*.

c. 940.—Constantine Porphyrogenitus, speaking of the rapids of the *Danapris* or Dnieper, says: "*ὁ δὲ τούτο φραγμὸς τοσοῦτον ἐστι στενὸς ὅσον τὸ πλάτος τοῦ τζυκανιστηρίου*" ("The defile in this case is as narrow as the width of the *chukan*-ground.")—*De Adm. Imp.*, cap. ix. (Bonn ed. iii. 75).

969.—"Cumque inquisitionis sedicio non modica petit pro Constantino ... ex ea parte qua **Zucanistri** magnitudo portenditur, Constantinus crines solutus per cancellos caput exposuit, suaque ostensione populi mox tumultum sedavit."—*Liudprandus*, in *Pertz, Mon. Germ.*, iii. 333.

"... he selected certain of his medicines and drugs, and made a *goff-stick* (**jaukan**?) [Burton, 'a bat'] with a hollow handle, into which he introduced them; after which ... he went again to the King ... and directed him to repair to the horse-course, and to play with the ball and *goff-stick*. ..."—*Lane's Arabian Nights*, i. 85–86; [*Burton*, i. 43].

c. 1030–40.—"Whenever you march ... you must take these people with you, and you must ... not allow them to drink wine or to play at **chaughān**."—*Baihaki*, in *Elliot*, ii. 120.

1416.—"Bernardus de Castro novo et nonnulli alii in studio Tholosano studentes, ad ludum lignobolini sive **Chucarum** luderunt pro vino et volema, qui ludus est quasi ludus billardi," &c.—MS. quoted in *Henschel's Ducange*.

c. 1420.—"The *Τζυκανιστήριον* was founded by Theodosius the Less ... Basilius the Macedonian extended and levelled the *Τζυκανιστήριον*."—*Georgius Codinus de Antiq. Constant.*, Bonn ed. 81–82.

1516.—Barbosa, speaking of the Mahommedans of Cambay, says: "Saom tam ligeiros e manhosos na sela que a cavalo jogaom ha **choqua**, ho qual joguo eles tem antre sy na conta em que nos temos ho das canas"—(Lisbon ed. 271); *i.e.* "They are so swift and dexterous in the saddle that they play **choca** on horseback, a game which they hold in as high esteem as we do that of the canes" (*i.e.* the *jereed*).

1560.—"They (the Arabs) are such great riders that they play tennis on horseback" (*que jogão a* **choca** *a cavallo*).—*Tenreiro, Itinerario*, ed. 1762, p. 359.

c. 1590.—"His Majesty also plays at **chaugán** in dark nights ... the balls which are used at night are set on fire. ... For the sake of adding splendour to the games ... His Majesty has knobs of gold and silver fixed to the tops of the *chaugán* sticks. If one of them breaks, any player that gets hold of the pieces may keep them."—*Āīn-i-Akbarī*, i. 298; [ii. 303].

1837.—"The game of **choughan** mentioned by Baber is still played everywhere in Tibet; it is nothing but 'hockey on horseback,' and is excellent fun."—*Vigne*, in *J. A. S. Bengal*, vi. 774.

In the following I would say, in justice to the great man whose words are quoted, that *chicane* is used in the quasi-military sense of taking every possible advantage of the ground in a contest:

1761.—"I do suspect that some of the great Ones have had hopes given to them that the Dutch may be induced to join us in this war against the Spaniards,—if such an Event should take place I fear some sacrifices will be made in the East Indies—I pray God my suspicions may be without foundation. I think Delays and **Chicanery** is allowable against those who take Advantage of the times, our Distresses, and situation."—*Unpublished Holograph Letter from Lord Clive*, in India Office Records. *Dated* Berkeley Square, and indorsed 27th Decr. 1761.

1881.—"One would at first sight be inclined to derive the French *chic* from the English 'cheek'; but it appears that the English is itself the derived word, *chic* being an old Romance word signifying *finesse*, or subtlety, and forming the root of our own word **chicanery**."—*Sat. Rev.*, Sept. 10, p. 326 (Essay on French Slang).

CHICK, s.

a. H.—P. *chik;* a kind of screen-blind made

of finely-split bamboo, laced with twine, and often painted on the outer side. It is hung or framed in doorways or windows, both in houses and in tents. The thing [which is described by Roe,] may possibly have come in with the Mongols, for we find in Kovalefski's Mongol Dict. (2174) "*Tchik* = *Natte.*" The Āīn (i. 226) has *chigh. Chicks* are now made in London, as well as imported from China and Japan. *Chicks* are described by Clavijo in the tents of Timour's chief wife:

1404.—"And this tent had two doors, one in front of the other, and the first doors were of certain thin coloured wands, joined one to another like in a hurdle, and covered on the outside with a texture of rose-coloured silk, and finely woven; and these doors were made in this fashion, in order that when shut the air might yet enter, whilst those within could see those outside, but those outside could not see those who were within."—§ cxxvi.

[1616.—His wives "whose Curiositye made them breake little holes in a grate of reede that hung before it to gaze on mee."—*Sir T. Roe*, Hak. Soc. ii. 321.]

1673.—"Glass is dear, and scarcely purchase-able ... therefore their Windows are usually folding doors, screened with **Cheeks** or latises."—*Fryer*, 92.

The pron. *cheek* is still not uncommon among English people:—"The Coach where the Women were was covered with **cheeks**, a sort of hanging Curtain, made with Bents variously coloured with Lacker, and Checquered with Packthred so artificially that you see all without, and yourself within unperceived."—*Fryer*, 83.

1810.—"**Cheeks** or Screens to keep out the glare."—*Williamson, V. M.* ii. 43.

1825.—"The **check** cf the tent prevents effectually any person from seeing what passes within. ..."—*Heber* (ed. 1844), i. 192.

b. Short for *chickeen*, a sum of four rupees. This is the Venetian *zecchino*, *cecchino*, or *sequin*, a gold coin long current on the shores of India, and which still frequently turns up in treasure-trove, and in hoards. In the early part of the 15th century Nicolo Conti mentions that in some parts of India, Venetian ducats, *i.e.* sequins, were current (p. 30). And recently, in fact in our own day, *chick* was a term in frequent Anglo-Indian use, *e.g.* "I'll bet you a **chick**."

The word *zecchino* is from the *Zecca*, or Mint at Venice, and that name is of Arabic origin, from *sikka*, 'a coining die.' The double history of this word is curious. We have just seen how in one form, and by what circuitous secular journey, through Egypt, Venice, India, it has gained a place in the Anglo-Indian Vocabulary. By a directer route it has also found a distinct place in the same repository under the form **Sicca** (q.v.), and in this shape it still retains a ghostly kind of existence at the India Office. It is remarkable how first the spread of Saracenic power and civilisation, then the spread of Venetian commerce and coinage, and lastly the spread of English commerce and power, should thus have brought together two words identical in origin, after so widely divergent a career.

The sequin is sometimes called in the South *shānārcash*, because the Doge with his sceptre is taken for the *Shānār*, or toddy-drawer climbing the palm-tree! [See *Burnell, Linschoten*, i. 243.]

We apprehend that the gambling phrases '*chicken*-stakes' and '*chicken*-nazard' originate in the same word.

1583.—"**Chickinos** which be pieces of Golde woorth seuen shillings a piece sterling."—*Caesar Frederici*, in *Hakl.* ii. 343.

1608.—"When I was there (at Venice) a **chiquiney** was worth eleven livers and twelve sols."—*Coryat's Crudities*, ii. 68.

1609.—"Three or four thousand **chequins** were as pretty a proportion to live quietly on, and so give over."—*Pericles, P. of Tyre*, iv. 2.

1612.—"The Grand Signiors Custome of this Port Moha is worth yearly unto him 1500 **chicquenes**."—*Saris*, in *Purchas*, i. 348.

[1616.—"Shee tooke **chickenes** and royalls for her goods."—*Sir T. Roe*, Hak. Soc. i. 228.]

1623.—"Shall not be worth a **chequin**, if it were knock'd at an outcry."—*Beaum. & Flet.*, *The Maid in the Mill*, v. 2.

1689.—"Four Thousand **Checkins** he privately tied to the flooks of an Anchor under Water."—*Ovington*, 418.

1711.—"He (the Broker) will charge 32 *Shahees per* **Chequeen** when they are not worth 31½ in the Bazar."—*Lockyer*, 227.

1727.—"When my Barge landed him, he gave the Cockswain five **Zequeens**, and loaded her back with Poultry and Fruit."—*A. Hamilton*, i. 301; ed. 1744, i. 303.

1767.—"Received ...

* * * * *

"**Chequins** 5 at 5. Arcot Rs. 25 0 0"

* * * * *

Lord Clive's Account of his Voyage to India, in *Long*, 497.

1866.—
"Whenever master spends a **chick**,
I keep back two rupees, Sir."
Trevelyan, The Dawk Bungalow.

1875.—"'Can't do much harm by losing twenty **chicks**,' observed the Colonel in Anglo-Indian *argot*."—*The Dilemma*, ch. x.

CHILLUM, s. H. *chilam*; "the part of the *huḳḳa* (see HOOKA) which contains the tobacco and charcoal balls, whence it is sometimes loosely used for the pipe itself, or the act of smoking it" (*Wilson*). It is also applied to the replenishment of the bowl, in the same way as a man asks for "another glass." The tobacco, as used by the masses in the hubble-bubble, is cut small and kneaded into a pulp with *goor*, *i.e.* molasses, and a little water. Hence actual contact with glowing charcoal is needed to keep it alight.

1781.—"Dressing a hubble-bubble, per week at 3 **chillums** a day.
fan 0, *dubs* 3, *cash* 0."
—*Prison Experiences in Captivity of Hon. J. Lindsay*, in *Lives of Lindsays*, iii.

1811.—"They have not the same scruples for the **Chillum** as for the rest of the Hooka, and it is often lent ... whereas the very proposition for the Hooka gives rise frequently to the most ridiculous quarrels."—*Solvyns*, iii.

1828.—"Every sound was hushed but the noise of that wind ... and the occasional bubbling of my *hookah*, which had just been furnished with another **chillum**."—*The Kuzzilbash*, i. 2.

1829.—"Tugging away at your hookah, find no smoke; a thief having purloined your silver **chelam** and **surpoose**."—*John Shipp*, ii. 159.

1848.—"Jos however ... could not think of moving till his baggage was cleared, or of travelling until he could do so with his **chillum**."—*Vanity Fair*, ii. ch. xxiii.

CHILLUMCHEE, s. H. *chilamchī*, also *silfchī*, and *silpchī*, of which *chilamchī* is probably a corruption. A basin of brass (as in Bengal), or tinned copper (as usually in the West and South) for washing hands. The form of the word seems Turkish, but we cannot trace it.

1715.—"We prepared for our first present, viz., 1000 gold mohurs ... the unicorn's horn ... the astoa (?) and **chelumgie** of Manilla work. ..."—In *Wheeler*, ii. 246.

1833.—"Our supper was a *peelaw* ... when it was removed a **chillumchee** and goblet of warm water was handed round, and each washed his hands and mouth."—*P. Gordon, Fragment of the Journal of a Tour*, &c.

1851.—"When a **chillumchee** of water *sans* soap was provided, 'Have you no soap?' Sir C. Napier asked——"—*Mawson, Indian Command of Sir C. Napier*.

1857.—"I went alone to the Fort Adjutant, to report my arrival, and inquire to what regiment of the Bengal army I was likely to be posted.

"Army!—regiment!' was the reply. 'There is *no* Bengal Army; it is all in revolt. ... Provide yourself with a campbedstead, and a **chillumchee**, and wait for orders.'

"I saluted and left the presence of my superior officer, deeply pondering as to the possible nature and qualities of a **chillumchee**, but not venturing to enquire further."—*Lt.-Col. Lewin, A Fly on the Wheel*, p. 3.

There is an Anglo-Indian tradition, which we would not vouch for, that one of the orators on the great Hastings trial depicted the oppressor on some occasion, as "grasping his *chillum* in one hand and his **chillumchee** in the other."

The latter word is used chiefly by Anglo-Indians of the Bengal Presidency and their servants. In Bombay the article has another name. And it is told of a gallant veteran of the old Bengal Artillery, who was full of "Presidential" prejudices, that on hearing the Bombay army commended by a brother officer, he broke out in just wrath: "The Bombay Army! Don't talk to me of the Bombay Army! They call a **chillumchee** a *gindy!*—THE BEASTS!"

CHILLY, s. The popular Anglo-Indian name of the pod of red pepper (*Capsicum fruticosum* and *C. annuum*, Nat. Ord. *Solanaceae*). There can be little doubt that the name, as stated by Bontius in the quotation, was taken from *Chili* in S. America, whence the plant was carried to the Indian Archipelago, and thence to India.

[1604.—"Indian pepper. ... In the language of Cusco, it is called Vchu, and in that of Mexico, **chili**."—*Grimston*, tr. *D'Acosta, H. W. Indies*, I. Bk. iv. 239 (*Stanf. Dict.*)]

1631.—"... eos addere fructum Ricini Americani, quod **lada Chili** Malaii vocant, quasi dicas Piper e **Chile**, Brasiliae contermina regione."—*Jac. Bontii*, Dial. V. p. 10.

Again (lib. vi. cap. 40, p. 131) Bontius calls it '*piper Chilensis*,' and also 'Ricinus Braziliensis.' But his commentator, Piso, observes that Ricinus is quite improper; "vera Piperis sive Capsici Braziliensis species apparet." Bontius says it was a common custom of natives, and even of certain Dutchmen, to keep a piece of **chilly** continually chewed, but he found it intolerable.

1848.—"'Try a **chili** with it, Miss Sharp,' said Joseph, really interested. '**A chili?**' said Rebecca, gasping. 'Oh yes!' ... 'How fresh and green they look,' she said, and put one into her mouth. It was hotter than the curry; flesh and blood could bear it no longer."—*Vanity Fair*, ch. iii.

CHINA, n.p. The European knowledge of this name in the forms *Thinae* and *Sinae* goes back nearly to the Christian era. The famous mention of the *Sinim* by the prophet Isaiah would carry us much further back, but we fear the possibility of that referring to the Chinese must be abandoned, as must be likewise, perhaps, the similar application of the name *Chinas* in ancient Sanskrit works. The most probable origin of the name—which is essentially a name applied by *foreigners* to the country—as yet suggested, is that put forward by Baron F. von Richthofen, that it comes from *Jih-nan*, an old name of Tongking, seeing that in Jih-nan lay the only port which was open for foreign trade with China at the beginning of our era, and that that province was then included administratively. within the limits of China Proper (see *Richthofen*, *China*, i. 504–510; the same author's papers in the *Trans. of the Berlin Geog. Soc.* for 1876; and a paper by one of the present writers in *Proc. R. Geog. Soc.*, November 1882.)

Another theory has been suggested by our friend M. Terrien de la Couperie in an elaborate note, of which we can but state the general gist. Whilst he quite accepts the suggestion that Kiao-chi or Tongking, anciently called *Kiao-ti*, was the *Kattigara* of Ptolemy's authority, he denies that *Jih-nan* can have been the origin of Sinae. This he does on two chief grounds: (1) That Jih-nan was not Kiao-chi, but a province a good deal further south, corresponding to the modern province of *An* (*Nghé Ane*, in the map of M. Dutreuil de Rhins, the capital of which is about 2° 17′ in lat. S. of Hanoi). This is distinctly stated in the Official Geography of Annam. *An* was one of the twelve provinces of Cochin China proper till 1820–41, when, with two others, it was transferred to Tongking. Also, in the Chinese Historical Atlas, Jih-nan lies in Chen-Ching, *i.e.* Cochin-China. (2) That the ancient pronunciation of Jih-nan, as indicated by the Chinese authorities of the Han period, was *Nit-nam*. It is still pronounced in Sinico-Annamite (the most archaic of the Chinese dialects) *Nhut-nam*, and in Cantonese *Yat-nam*. M. Terrien further points out that the export of Chinese goods, and the traffic with the south and west, was for several centuries B.C. monopolised by the State of *Tsen* (now pronounced in Sinico-Annamite *Chen*, and in Mandarin *Tien*), which corresponded to the centre and west of modern Yun-nan. The *She-ki* of Sze-ma Tsien (B.C. 91), and the Annals of the Han Dynasty afford interesting information on this subject. When the Emperor Wu-ti, in consequence of Chang-Kien's information brought back from Bactria, sent envoys to find the route followed by the traders of Shuh (*i.e.* Sze-chuen) to India, these envoys were detained by Tang-Kiang, King of Tsen, who objected to their exploring trade-routes through his territory, saying haughtily: "Has the Han a greater dominion than ours?"

M. Terrien conceives that as the only communication of this Tsen State with the Sea would be by the Song-Koi R., the emporium of sea-trade with that State would be at its mouth, viz. at Kiaoti or Kattigara. Thus, he considers, the name of *Tsen*, this powerful and arrogant State, the monopoliser of trade-routes, is in all probability that which spread far and wide the name of *Chīn*, *Sīn*, *Sinae*, *Thinae*, and preserved its predominance in the mouths of foreigners, even when, as in the 2nd century of our era, the great Empire of the Han has extended over the Delta of the Song-Koi.

This theory needs more consideration than we can now give it. But it will doubtless have discussion elsewhere, and it does not disturb Richthofen's identification of Kattigara.

[Prof. Giles regards the suggestions of Richthofen and T. de la Couperie as mere guesses. From a recent reconsideration of the subject he has come to the conclusion that the name may possibly be derived from the name of a dynasty, *Ch'in* or *Ts'in*, which flourished B.C. 255–207, and became widely known in India, Persia, and other Asiatic countries, the final *a* being added by the Portuguese.]

c. A.D. 80–89.—"Behind this country (*Chrysē*) the sea comes to a termination somewhere in **Thin**, and in the interior of that country, quite to the north, there is a very great city called

Thinae, from which raw silk and silk thread and silk stuffs are brought overland through Bactria to Barygaza, as they are on the other hand by the Ganges River to Limyricē. It is not easy, however, to get to this **Thin**, and few and far between are those who come from it. ..."—*Periplus Maris Erythraei;* see Müller, *Geog. Gr. Min.* i. 303.

c. 150—"The inhabited part of our earth is bounded on the east by the Unknown Land which lies along the region occupied by the easternmost races of Asia Minor, the **Sinae** and the natives of Sericē. ..."—*Claudius Ptolemy*, Bk. vii. ch. 5.

c. 545.—"The country of silk, I may mention, is the remotest of all the Indies, lying towards the left when you enter the Indian Sea, but a vast distance further off than the Persian Gulf or that island which the Indians call Selediba, and the Greeks Taprobane. **Tzinitza** (elsewhere **Tzinista**) is the name of the Country, and the Ocean compasses it round to the left, just as the same Ocean compasses Barbari (*i.e.* the Somāli Country) round to the right. And the Indian philosophers called Brachmans tell you that if you were to stretch a straight cord from **Txinitza** through Persia to the Roman territory, you would just divide the world in halves."—*Cosmas, Topog. Christ.*, Bk. II.

c. 641.—"In 641 the King of Magadha (Behar, &c.) sent an ambassador with a letter to the Chinese Court. The emperor ... in return directed one of his officers to go to the King ... and to invite his submission. The King Shiloyto (Siladitya) was all astonishment. 'Since time immemorial,' he asked his officer, 'did ever an ambassador come from *Mohochintan?*' ... The Chinese author remarks that in the tongue of the barbarians the Middle Kingdom is called *Moho***chin***tan* (Mahā-**Chīna**-sthāna)."—From *Cathay*, &c., lxviii.

781.—"Adam Priest and Bishop and Pope of **Tzinesthan.** ... The preachings of our Fathers to the King of **Tzinia.**"—*Syriac Part* of the *Inscription of Singanfu.*

11th Century.—The "King of China" (**Shina**-*ttarashan*) appears in the list of provinces and monarchies in the great Inscription of the Tanjore Pagoda.

1128.—"**Chīna** and *Mahā***chīna** appear in a list of places producing silk and other cloths, in the *Abhilashitārthachintāmani* of the Chālukya King."—*Somesvaradiva* (*MS.*)[1] Bk. III. ch. 6.

1298.—"You must know the Sea in which lie the Islands of those parts is called the Sea of **Chin**. ... For, in the language in those Isles, when they say **Chin**, 'tis Manzi they mean."—*Marco Polo*, Bk. III. ch. iv.

c. 1300.—"Large ships, called in the language of **Chin** 'junks,' bring various sorts of choice merchandize and cloths. ..."—*Rashíduddín*, in *Elliot.* i. 69.

1516.—"... there is the Kingdom of **China**, which they say is a very extensive dominion, both along the coast of the sea, and in the interior. ..."—*Barbosa*, 204.

1563.—"*R.* Then Ruelius and Mathiolus of Siena say that the best camphor is from **China**, and that the best of all Camphors is that purified by a certain barbarian King whom they call King (of) **China**.

"*O.* Then you may tell Ruelius and Mathiolus of Siena that though they are so well acquainted with Greek and Latin, there's no need to make such a show of it as to call every body 'barbarians' who is not of their own race, and that besides this they are quite wrong in the fact ... that the King of China does not occupy himself with making camphor, and is in fact one of the greatest Kings known in the world."—*Garcia De Orta*, f. 45*b*.

c. 1590.—"Near to this is Pegu, which former writers called **Cheen**, accounting this to be the capital city."—*Ayeen*, ed. 1800, ii. 4; [tr. *Jarrett*, ii. 119].

CHINA, s. In the sense of porcelain this word (*Chīnī*, &c.) is used in Asiatic languages as well as in English. In English it does not occur in Minshew (2nd ed. 1627), though it does in some earlier publications. [The earliest quotation in *N.E.D.* is from *Cogan's Pinto*, 1653.] The phrase *China-dishes* as occurring in Drake and in Shakspere, shows how the word took the sense of porcelain in our own and other languages. The phrase *China-dishes* as first used was analogous to *Turkey-carpets.* But in the latter we have never lost the geographical sense of the adjective. In the word *turquoises*, again, the phrase was no doubt originally *pierres turquoises*, or the like, and here, as in *china dishes*, the specific has superseded the generic sense. The use of *arab* in India for an Arab horse is analogous to *china*. The word is used in the sense of a

1 It may be well to append here the whole list which I find on a scrap of paper in Dr. Burnell's handwriting (Y):

Pohālapura.	Aṇitavāta (*Anhilvād*).
Chīnavallī.	Sunāpura.
Avantikshetra (*Ujjain*).	*Mūlasthāna* (*Multan*).
Nāgapaṭṭaṇa (*Negapatam?*)	Toṭṭideśa.
Pāṇḍyadeśa (*Madura*).	Pañchapaṭṭaṇa.
Allikākara.	Chīna.
Simhaladvīpa (*Ceylon*).	Mahāchīna.
*Gopāka*sthāna (! ?).	Kalingadeśa (*Telugu Country*).
Gujaṇasthāna.	
Thānaka (*Thana?*)	Vaṅgadeśa (*Bengal*).

china dish in *Lane's Arabian Nights*, iii. 492; [Burton, I. 375].

851.—"There is in China a very fine clay with which they make vases transparent like bottles; water can be seen inside of them. These vases are made of clay."—*Reinaud, Relations*, i. 34.

c. 1350.—"**China**-ware (*al-fakhkhār al-* **Sīnīy**) is not made except in the cities of Zaītūn and of Sīn Kalān. ..."—*Ibn Batuta*, iv. 256.

c. 1530.—"I was passing one day along a street in Damascus, when I saw a slave-boy let fall from his hands a great China dish (*ṣaḥfat min al-bakhkhār al-* **Sīnīy**) which they call in that country *sahn*. It broke, and a crowd gathered round the little Mameluke."—*Ibn Batuta*, i. 238.

c. 1567.—"Le mercantie ch'andauano ogn' anno da Goa a Bezeneger erano molti caualli Arabi ... e anche *pezze di* **China**, zafaran, e scarlatti."—*Cesare de' Federici*, in *Ramusio*, iii. 389.

1579.—"... we met with one ship more loaden with linnen, China silke, and **China dishes**. ..."—*Drake, World Encompassed*, in Hak. Soc. 112.

c. 1580.—"Usum vasorum aureorum et argenteorum Aegyptii rejecerunt, ubi murrhina vasa adinvenere; quae ex India afferuntur, et ex ea regione quam **Sini** vocant, ubi conficiuntur ex variis lapidibus, praecipueque ex jaspide."—*Prosp. Alpinus*, Pt. I. p. 55.

c. 1590.—"The gold and silver dishes are tied up in red cloths, and those in Copper and **China** (*chīnī*) in white ones."—*Āīn*, i. 58.

c. 1603.—"... as it were in a fruit-dish, a dish of some threepence, your honours have seen such dishes; they are not **China** dishes, but very good dishes."—*Measure for Measure*, ii. 1.

1608–9.—"A faire **China** dish (which cost ninetie Rupias, or forty-five Reals of eight) was broken."—*Hawkins*, in *Purchas*, i. 220.

1609.—"He has a lodging in the Strand for the purpose, or to watch when ladies are gone to the **China**-house, or the Exchange, that he may meet them by chance and give them presents... ."

"Ay, sir: his wife was the rich **China**-woman, that the courtiers visited so often."—*Ben Jonson, Silent Woman*, i. 1.

1615.—

"... Oh had I now my Wishes,
Sure you should learn to make their **China**
Dishes."

Doggrel prefixed to *Coryat's Crudities*.

c. 1690.—Kaempfer in his account of the Persian Court mentions that the department where porcelain and plate dishes, &c., were kept and cleaned was called **Chīn-khāna**, 'the China-closet'; and those servants who carried in the dishes were called **Chīnīkash**.—*Amoen. Exot.*, p. 125.

1711.—"Purselaine, or **China**-ware is so tender a Commodity that good Instructions are as necessary for Package as Purchase."—*Lockyer*, 126.

1747.—"The Art of Cookery made Plain and Easy; which far Exceeds any Thing of the Kind yet Published. By a Lady. London. Printed for the Author, and Sold by Mrs. Asburn a **China** Shop Woman, Corner of Fleet Ditch, MDCCXLVII." This the title of the original edition of Mrs. Glass's Cookery, as given by G. A. Sala, in *Illd. News*, May 12, 1883.

1876.—"Schuyler mentions that the best native earthenware in Turkistan is called **Chīnī**, and bears a clumsy imitation of a Chinese mark"—(see *Turkistan*, i. 187.)

For the following interesting note on the Arabic use we are indebted to Professor Robertson Smith:—

Ṣīnīya is spoken of thus in the Latāifo'l-ma'ārif of al-Th'ālibī, ed. De Jong, Leyden, 1867, a book written in A.D. 990. "The Arabs were wont to call all elegant vessels and the like **Sīnīya** (*i.e.* Chinese), whatever they really were, because of the specialty of the Chinese in objects of vertu; and this usage remains in the common word *ṣawānā* (pl. of *ṣīnīya*) to the present day."

So in the *Tajāribo'l-Omam* of Ibn Maskowaih (Fr. Hist. Ar. ii. 457), it is said that at the wedding of Mamūn with Būrān "her grandmother strewed over her 1000 pearls from a **sīnīya** of gold." In Egypt the familiar round brass trays used to dine off, are now called *ṣīnīya* (vulgo *ṣanīya*), [the *ṣīnī*, *ṣenī* of N. India] and so is a European saucer.

The expression *ṣīnīyat al ṣīn*, "A Chinese *ṣīnīya*," is quoted again by De Goeje from a poem of Abul-shibl Agānī, xiii. 27.

CHIN-CHIN. In the "pigeon English" of Chinese ports this signifies 'salutation, compliments,' or 'to salute,' and is much used by Englishmen as slang in such senses. It is a corruption of the Chinese phrase *ts'ing-ts'ing*, Pekingese *ch'ing-ch'ing*, a term of salutation answering to 'thank-you,' 'adieu.' In the same vulgar dialect *chin-chin joss* means religious worship of any kind (see **JOSS**). It is curious that the phrase occurs in a quaint story told to William of Rubruck by a Chinese priest whom he met at the Court of the Great Kaan (see below). And it is equally remarkable to find the same story related with singular closeness of correspondence out of "the Chinese books of

Geography" by Francesco Carletti, 350 years later (in 1600). He calls the creatures **Zinzin** (*Ragionamenti di F. C.*, pp. 138–9).

1253.—"One day there sate by me a certain priest of Cathay, dressed in a red cloth of exquisite colour, and when I asked him whence they got such a dye, he told me how in the eastern parts of Cathay there were lofty cliffs on which dwelt certain creatures in all things partaking of human form, except that their knees did not bend. ... The huntsmen go thither, taking very strong beer with them, and make holes in the rocks which they fill with this beer. ... Then they hide themselves and these creatures come out of their holes and taste the liquor, and call out '**Chin Chin**.'"—*Itinerarium*, in *Rec. de Voyaqes*, &c., iv. 328.

Probably some form of this phrase is intended in the word used by Pinto in the following passage, which Cogan leaves untranslated:—

c. 1540.—"So after we had saluted one another after the manner of the Country, they went and anchored by the shore" (in orig. "*despois de se fazerem as suas e as nossas salvas a* **Charachina** *como entre este gente se custuma.*")—In *Cogan*, p. 56; in orig. ch. xlvii.

1795.—"The two junior members of the Chinese deputation came at the appointed hour. ... On entering the door of the marquee they both made an abrupt stop, and resisted all solicitation to advance to chairs that had been prepared for them, until I should first be seated; in this dilemma, Dr. Buchanan, who had visited China, advised me what was to be done; I immediately seized on the foremost, whilst the Doctor himself grappled with the second; thus we soon fixed them in their seats, both parties during the struggle, repeating **Chin Chin, Chin Chin**, the Chinese term of salutation."—*Symes, Embassy to Ava*, 295.

1829.—"One of the Chinese servants came to me and said, 'Mr. Talbot **chin-chin** you come down.'"—*The Fankwae at Canton*, p. 20.

1880.—"But far from thinking it any shame to deface our beautiful language, the English seem to glory in its distortion, and will often ask one another to come to 'chow-chow' instead of dinner; and send their '**chin-chin**,' even in letters, rather than their compliments; most of them ignorant of the fact that '*chow-chow*' is no more Chinese than it is Hebrew; that '*chin-chin*,' though an expression used by the Chinese, does not in its true meaning come near to the 'good-bye, old fellow,' for which it is often used, or the compliments for which it is frequently substituted."—*W. Gill*, *River of Golden Sand*, i. 156; [ed. 1883, p. 41].

CHINTZ, s. A printed or spotted cotton cloth; Port. *chita*; Mahr. *chīt*, and H. *chīṇt*. The word in this last form occurs (c. 1590) in the *Āīn-i-Akbari* (i. 95). It comes apparently from the Skt. *chitra*, 'variegated, speckled.' The best *chintzes* were bought on the Madras coast, at Masulipatam and Sadras. The French form of the word is *chite*, which has suggested the possibility of our *sheet* being of the same origin. But *chite* is apparently of Indian origin, through the Portuguese, whilst *sheet* is much older than the Portuguese communication with India. Thus (1450) in Sir T. Cumberworth's will he directs his "wreched body to be beryd in a *chitte* with owte any kyste" (*Academy*, Sept. 27, 1879, p. 230). The resemblance to the Indian forms in this is very curious.

1614.—"... **chintz** and chadors. ..."—*Peyton*, in *Purchas*, i. 530.

[1616.—"3 per **Chint** bramport."—*Cocks's Diary*, i. 171.

[1623.—"Linnen stamp'd with works of sundry colours (which they call **cit**)."—*P. della Valle*, Hak. Soc. i. 45.]

1653.—"**Chites** en Indou signifie des toilles imprimeés."—*De la Boullaye-le-Gouz*, ed. 1647, p. 536.

c. 1666.—"Le principal trafic des Hollandois à Amedabad, est de **chites**, qui sont de toiles peintes."—*Thecenot*, v. 35. In the English version (1687) this is written **schites** (iv. ch. v.).

1676.—"**Chites** or Painted Calicuts, which they call *Calmendar*, that is done with a pencil, are made in the Kingdom of Golconda, and particularly about *Masulipatam*."—*Tavernier*, E.T., p. 126; [ed. *Ball*, ii. 4].

1725.—"The returns that are injurious to our manufactures, or growth of our own country, are printed calicoes, **chintz**, wrought silks, stuffs, of herba, and barks."—*Defoe, New Voyage round the World. Works*, Oxford, 1840, p. 161.

1726.—"The Warehouse Keeper reported to the Board, that the **chintzes**, being brought from painting, had been examined at the sorting godown, and that it was the general opinion that both the cloth and the paintings were worse than the musters."—In *Wheeler*, ii. 407.

c. 1733.—

"No, let a charming **chintz** and Brussels lace
Wrap my cold limbs, and shade my lifeless face."

Pope, Moral Essays, i. 248.

"And, when she sees her friend in deep despair,
Observes how much a **Chintz** exceeds Mohair... ."

Ibid. ii. 170.

1817.—"Blue cloths, and **chintzes** in particular have always formed an extensive article of import from Western India."—*Raffles, H. of Java*, i. 86; [2nd ed. i. 95, and comp. i. 190].

In the earlier books about India some kind of *chintz* is often termed **pintado**. See the phraseology in the quotation from Wheeler above.

This export from India to Europe has long ceased. When one of the present writers was Sub-Collector of the Madras District (1866–67), chintzes were still figured by an old man at Sadras, who had been taught by the Dutch, the cambric being furnished to him by a Madras **Chetty**. He is now dead, and the business has ceased; in fact the colours for the process are no longer to be had.[1] The former *chintz* manufactures of Pulicat are mentioned by *Correa, Lendas*, ii. 2, p. 567. Havart (1693) mentions the manufacture at Sadras (i. 92), and gives a good description of the process of painting these cloths, which he calls **chitsen** (iii. 13). There is also a very complete account in the *Lettres Édifiantes*, xiv. 116 *seqq.*

In Java and Sumatra *chintzes* of a very peculiar kind of marbled pattern are still manufactured by women, under the name of *bātik*.

CHIT, CHITTY, s. A letter or note; also a certificate given to a servant, or the like; a pass. H. *chiṭṭhī;* Mahr. *chiṭṭī*. [Skt. *chitra*, 'marked.'] The Indian Portuguese also use *chito* for *escrito* (*Bluteau*, Supplement). The Tamil people use *shīt* for a ticket, or for a playing-card.

1673.—"I sent one of our Guides, with his Master's **Chitty**, or Pass, to the Governor, who received it kindly."—*Fryer*, 126.

[1757.—"If Mr. Ives is not too busie to honour this **chitt** which nothing but the greatest uneasiness could draw from me."—*Ives*, 134.]

1785.—"... Those Ladies and Gentlemen who wish to be taught that polite Art (drawing) by Mr. Hone, may know his terms by sending a **Chit**. ..."—In *Seton-Karr*, i. 114.

1786.—"You are to sell rice, &c., to every merchant from Muscat who brings you a **chitty** from Meer Kâzim."—*Tippoo's Letters*, 284.

1787.—"Mrs. Arend ... will wait upon any Lady at her own house on the shortest notice, by addressing a **chit** to her in Chattawala Gully, opposite Mr. Motte's old house, Tiretta's bazar."—Advt. in *Seton-Karr*, i. 226.

1794.—"The petty but constant and universal manufacture of **chits** which prevails here."—*Hugh Boyd*, 147.

1829.—"He wanted a **chithee** or note, for this is the most note-writing country under heaven; the very Drum-major writes me a note to tell me about the mails."—*Mem. of Col. Mountain*, 2nd ed., 80.

1839.—"A thorough Madras lady ... receives a number of morning visitors, takes up a little worsted work; goes to tiffin with Mrs. C., unless Mrs. D. comes to tiffin with her, and writes some dozens of **chits**. ... These incessant **chits** are an immense trouble and interruption, but the ladies seem to like them."—*Letters from Madras*, 284.

---

1 I leave this passage as Dr. Burnell wrote it. But though limited to a specific locality, of which I doubt not it was true, it conveys an idea of the entire extinction of the ancient chintz production which I find is not justified by the facts, as shown in a most interesting letter from Mr. Purdon Clarke, C.S.I., of the India Museum. One kind is still made at Masulipatam, under the superintendence of Persian merchants, to supply the Ispahan market and the "Moghul" traders at Bombay. At Pulicat very peculiar chintzes are made, which are entirely *Ḳalam Kārī* work, or hand-painted (apparently the word now used instead of the *Calmendār* of Tavernier,—see above. This is a work of infinite labour, as the ground has to be stopped off with wax almost as many times as there are colours used. At Combaconum **Sarongs** (q.v.) are printed for the Straits. Very bold printing is done at Wālājāpet in N. Arcot, for sale to the Moslem at Hyderabad and Bangalore.

An anecdote is told me by Mr. Clarke which indicates a caution as to more things than chintz printing. One particular kind of chintz met with in S. India, he was assured by the vendor, was printed at W——; but he did not recognize the locality. Shortly afterwards, visiting for the second time the city of X. (we will call it), where he had already been assured by the collector's native aids that there was no such manufacture, and showing the stuff, with the statement of its being made at W——, 'Why,' said the collector, 'that is where I live!' Immediately behind his bungalow was a small bazar, and in this the work was found going on, though on a small scale.

Just so we shall often find persons "who have been in India, and on the spot"—asseverating that at such and such a place there are no missions or no converts; whilst those who have cared to know, know better.—(H. Y.)

[For Indian chintzes, see Forbes Watson, *Textile Manufactures*, 90 *seqq.*; Mukharji, *Art Manufactures of India*, 348 *seqq.*; S. H. Hadi, *Mon. on Dyes and Dyeing in the N.W.P. and Oudh*, 44 *seqq.*; Francis, *Mon. on Punjab Cotton Industry*, 6.]

CHOBDAR, s. H. from P. *chobdār*, 'a stick-bearer.' A frequent attendant of Indian nobles, and in former days of Anglo-Indian officials of rank. They are still a part of the state of the Viceroy, Governors, and Judges of the High Courts. The *chobdārs* carry a staff overlaid with silver.

1442.—"At the end of the hall stand **tchobdars** ... drawn up in line."—*Abdur-Razzāk*, in *India in the XV. Cent.* 25.

1673.—"If he (the President) move out of his Chamber, the *Silver Staves* wait on him."—*Fryer*, 68.

1701.—"... Yesterday, of his own accord, he told our Linguists that he had sent four **Chobdars** and 25 men, as a safe-guard."—In *Wheeler*, i. 371.

1788.—"**Chubdár** ... Among the Nabobs he proclaims their praises aloud, as he runs before their palankeens."—*Indian Vocabulary* (Stockdale's).

1793.—"They said a **Chubdar**, with a silver-stick, one of the Sultan's messengers of justice, had taken them from the place, where they were confined, to the public Bazar, where their hands were cut off."—*Dirom, Narrative*, 235.

1798.—"The chief's **Chobedar** ... also endeavoured to impress me with an ill opinion of these messengers."—*G. Forster's Travels*, i. 222.

1810.—"While we were seated at breakfast, we were surprised by the entrance of a **Choabdar**, that is, a servant who attends on persons of consequence, runs before them with a silver stick, and keeps silence at the doors of their apartments, from which last office he derives his name."—*Maria Graham*, 57.

This usually accurate lady has been here misled, as if the word were *chup-dār*, 'silence-keeper,' a hardly possible hybrid.

CHOKIDAR, s. A watchman. Derivative in Persian form from **Choky**. The word is usually applied to a private watchman; in some parts of India he is generally of a thieving tribe, and his employment may be regarded as a sort of blackmail to ensure one's property. [In N. India the village *Chaukīdār* is the rural policeman, and he is also employed for watch and ward in the smaller towns.]

1689.—"And the Day following the **Chocadars**, or Souldiers were remov'd from before our Gates."—*Ovington*, 416.

1810.—"The **chokey-dar** attends during the day, often performing many little offices, ... at night parading about with his spear, shield, and sword, and assuming a most terrific aspect, until all the family are asleep; when HE GOES TO SLEEP TOO."—*Williamson, V. M.* i. 295.

c. 1817.—"The birds were scarcely beginning to move in the branches of the trees, and there was not a servant excepting the **chockedaurs**, stirring about any house in the neighbourhood, it was so early."—*Mrs. Sherwood's Stories*, &c. (ed. 1873), 243.

1837.—"Every village is under a *potail*, and there is a *pursau* or priest, and **choukeednop** (sic!) or watchman."—*Phillips, Million of Facts*, 320.

1864.—The church book at Peshawar records the death there of "The Revd. I—— L——l, who on the night of the —th ——, 1864, when walking in his veranda was shot by his own **chokidar**"—to which record the hand of an injudicious friend has added: "Well done, thou good and faithful servant!" (The exact words will now be found in the late Mr. E. B. Eastwick's *Panjáb Handbook*, p. 279).

CHOKRA, s. Hind. *chhokrā*, 'a boy, a youngster'; and hence, more specifically, a boy employed about a household, or a regiment. Its chief use in S. India is with the latter. (See CHUCKAROO.)

[1875.—"He was dubbed 'the **chokra**, or simply 'boy.'"—*Wilson, Abode of Snow*, 136.]

CHOKY, s. H. *chaukī*, which in all its senses is probably connected with Skt. *chatur*, 'four'; whence *chatushka*, 'of four,' 'four-sided,' &c.

a. (Perhaps first a shed resting on four posts); a station of police; a lockup; also a station of palankin bearers, horses, &c., when a post is laid; a customs or toll-station, and hence, as in the first quotation, the dues levied at such a place; the act of watching or guarding.

[1535.—"They only pay the **choqueis** coming in ships from the Moluccas to Malacca, which amounts to 3 parts in 10 for the owner of the ship for *choque*, which is freight; that which belongs to His Highness pays nothing when it comes in ships. This *choque* is as far as Malacca, from thence to India is another freight as arranged between the parties. Thus when cloves are brought in His Highness's ships, paying the third and the *choquies*, there goes from every 30 bahars 16 to the King, our Lord."—*Arrangement made by Nuno da Cunha*, quoted in *Botelho Tombo*, p. 113. On this Mr. Whiteway remarks: "By this arrangement the King of Portugal did not ship any cloves of his own at the Moluccas, but he took one-third of every shipment free, and on the balance he took one-third as **Choky**, which is, I imagine, in lieu of customs."]

c. 1590.—"Mounting guard is called in Hindi **Chauki**."—*Āīn*, i. 257.

1608.—"The Kings Custome called **Chukey**, is eight bagges upon the hundred bagges."—*Saris*, in *Purchas*, i. 391.

1664.—"Near this Tent there is another great one, which is called **Tchaukykane**, because it is the place where the Omrahs keep guard, every one in his turn, once a week twenty-four hours together."—*Bernier*, E.T., 117; [ed. *Constable*, 363].

1673.—"We went out of the Walls by Broach, Gate ... where, as at every gate, stands a **Chocky**, or Watch to receive Toll for the Emperor. ..."—*Fryer*, 100.

"And when they must rest, if they have no Tents, they must shelter themselves under Trees ... unless they happen on a **Chowkie**, *i.e.*, a Shed where the Customer keeps a Watch to take Custom."—*Ibid*. 410.

1682.—"About 12 o'clock Noon we got to ye **Chowkee**, where after we had shown our *Dustick* and given our present, we were dismissed immediately."—*Hedges, Diary*, Dec. 17; [Hak. Soc. i. 58].

1774.—"Il più difficile per viaggiare nell' Indostan sono certi posti. di guardie chiamate **Cioki** ... questi **Cioki** sono insolentissimi."—*Della Tomba*, 33.

1810.—"... **Chokies**, or patrol stations."—*Williamson, V. M.*, i. 297.

This word has passed into the English slang vocabulary in the sense of 'prison.'

b. A chair. This use is almost peculiar to the Bengal Presidency. Dr. John Muir [*Orig. Skt. Texts*, ii. 5] cites it in this sense, as a Hindi word which has no resemblance to any Skt. vocable. Mr. Growse, however, connects it with *chatar*, 'four' (*Ind. Antiq.*, i. 105). See also beginning of this article. *Chau* is the common form of 'four' in composition, *e.g. chaubandi*, (*i.e.* 'four fastening') the complete shoeing of a horse; *chaupahra* ('four watches') all night long; *chaupār*, 'a quadruped'; *chaukaṭ* and *chaukhaṭ* ('four timber'), a frame (of a door, &c.). So *chaukī* seems to have been used for a square-framed stool, and thence a chair.

1772.—"Don't throw yourself back in your *barra* **chokey**, and tell me it won't do. ..."—*W. Hastings to G. Vansittart*, in *Gleig*, i. 238.

c. 1782.—"As soon as morning appeared he (Haidar) sat down on his chair (**chaukī**) and washed his face."—*H. of Hydur Naik*, 505.

***CHOLERA**, and **CHOLERA MORBUS**, s. The Disease. The term 'cholera,' though employed by the old medical writers, no doubt came, as regards its familiar use, from India. Littré alleges that it is a mistake to suppose that the word *cholera* (*χολέρα*) is a derivative from *χολή*, 'bile,' and that it really means 'a gutter,' the disease being so called from the symptoms. This should, however, rather be *ἀπὸ τῶν χολάδων*, the latter word being anciently used for the intestines (the etym. given by the medical writer, Alex. Trallianus). But there is a discussion on the subject in the modern ed. of *Stephani Thesaurus*, which indicates a conclusion that the derivation from *χολή* is probably right; it is that of Celsus (see below). [The *N.E.D.* takes the same view, but admits that there is some doubt.] For quotations and some particulars in reference to the history of this terrible disease, see under MORT-DE-CHIEN.

c. A.D. 20.—"Primoque facienda mentio est **cholerae**; quia commune id stomachi atque intestinorum vitium videri potest ... intestina torquentur, bilis supra infraque erumpit, primum aquae similis: deinde ut in eâ recens caro tota esse videatur, interdum alba, nonnunquam nigra vel varia. Ergo eo nomine morbum hunc *χολέραν* Graeci nominârunt. ..." &c.—*A. C. Celsi Med. Libri* VIII. iv. xi.

c. A.D. 100.—"*ΠΕΡΊ ΧΟΛΈΡΗΣ* ... *θάνατος ἐπώδυνος καὶ οἴκτιστος σπασμῷ καὶ πνιγὶ καὶ ἐμέσῳ κενῷ*"—*Aretaeus, De Causis et signis acutorum morborum*, ii. 5.

Also *Θεραπεία Χολερῆς, in De Curatione Morb. Ac.* ii. 4.

1563.—"*R*. Is this disease the one which kills so quickly, and from which so few recover? Tell me how it is called among us, and among them, and its symptoms, and the treatment of it in use?

"*O*. Among us it is called **Collerica passio**. ..."—*Garcia*, f. 74*v*.

[1611.—"As those ill of **Colera**."—*Couto, Dialogo de Soldado Pratico*, p. 5.]

1673.—"The Diseases reign according to the Seasons. ... In the extreme Heats, **Cholera Morbus**."—*Fryer*, 113–114.

1832.—"Le **Choléra Morbus**, dont vous me parlez, n'est pas inconnu à Cachemire."—*Jacquemont, Corresp*. ii. 109.

CHOP, s. Properly a seal-impression, stamp, or brand; H. *chhāp*; the verb (*chhāpnā*) being that which is now used in Hindustani to express the art of printing (books).

The word *chhāp* seems not to have been traced back with any accuracy beyond the modern vernaculars. It has been thought possible (at least till the history should be more accurately traced) that it might be of Portuguese origin. For there is a Port. word *chapa*, 'a thin plate of metal,' which is no doubt the original of the Old English *chape* for the metal plate on the sheath of a sword or dagger[1] The word in this sense is not in the Portuguese Dictionaries; but we find 'homem *chapado*,' explained as 'a man of notable worth or excellence,' and Bluteau considers this a metaphor 'taken from the *chapas* or plates of metal on which the kings of India caused their letters patent to be engraven.' Thus he would seem to have regarded, though perhaps erroneously, the *chhāpā* and the Portuguese *chapa* as identical. On the other hand, Mr. Beames entertains no doubt that the word is genuine Hindi, and connects it with a variety of other words signifying *striking*, or *pressing*. And Thompson in his *Hindi Dictionary* says that *chhāppā* is a technical term used by the Vaishnavas to denote the sectarial marks (lotus, trident, &c.), which they delineate on their bodies. Fallon gives the same meaning, and quotes a Hindi verse, using it in this sense. We may add that while *chhāpā* is used all over the N.W.P. and Punjab for printed cloths, Drummond (1808) gives *chhāpānīya*, *chhapārā*, as words for 'Stampers or Printers of Cloth' in Guzerati, and that the passage quoted below from a Treaty made with an ambassador from Guzerat by the Portuguese in 1537, uses the word *chapada* for struck or coined, exactly as the modern Hindi verb *chhāpnā* might be used.[2] *Chop*, in writers prior to the last century, is often used for the seal itself. "Owen Cambridge says the *Mohr* was the great seal, but the small or privy seal was called a '**chop**' or 'stamp.'" (*C. P. Brown*).

The word *chop* is hardly used now among Anglo-Indians in the sense of seal or stamp. But it got a permanent footing in the 'Pigeon English' of the Chinese ports, and thence has come back to England and India, in the phrase "*first*-**chop**," *i.e.* of the first *brand* or quality.

The word **chop** (*chāp*) is adopted in Malay [with the meanings of seal-impression, stamp, to seal or stamp, though there is, as Mr. Skeat points out, a pure native word *tera* or *tra*, which is used in all these senses;] and **chop** has acquired the specific sense of a passport or licence. The word has also obtained a variety of applications, including that just mentioned, in the *lingua franca* of foreigners in the China seas. Van Braam applies it to a tablet bearing the Emperor's name, to which he and his fellow envoys made **kotow** on their first landing in China (*Voyage*, &c., Paris, An vi., 1798, i. 20–21). Again, in the same jargon, a **chop** of tea means a certain number of chests of tea, all bearing the same brand. **Chop**-*houses* are customs stations on the Canton River, so called from the chops, or seals, used there (*Giles, Glossary*). **Chop**-*dollar* is a dollar *chopped*, or stamped with a private mark, as a guarantee of its genuineness (*ibid.*). (Dollars similarly marked had currency in England in the first quarter of last century, and one of the present writers can recollect their occasional occurrence in Scotland in his childhood). The *grand* **chop** is the port clearance granted by the Chinese customs when all dues have been paid (*ibid.*). All these have obviously the same origin; but there are other uses of the word in China not so easily explained, *e.g. chop*, for 'a hulk'; *chop-boat* for a lighter or cargo-boat.

In Captain Forrest's work, quoted below, a golden badge or decoration, conferred on him by the King of Achin, is called a **chapp** (p. 55). The portrait of Forrest, engraved by Sharp, shows this badge, and gives the inscription, translated: "Capt. Thomas Forrest, Orancayo of the Golden Sword. This **chapp** was conferred as a mark of honour in the city of Atcheen, belonging to the Faithful, by the hands of the Shabander [see SHAHBUNDER] of Atcheen, on Capt. Thomas Forrest."

[1534.—"The Governor said that he would receive nothing save under his **chapa**." "Until he returned from Badur with his reply and the **chapa** required."—*Correa*, iii. 585.]

1537.—"And the said Nizamamede Zamom was present and then before me signed, and swore on his Koran (*moçafo*) to keep and

1 Thus, in Shakspeare, "This is Monsieur Parolles, the gallant militarist ... that had the whole theorie of war in the knot of his scarf, the practice in the *chape* of his dagger."—*All's Well that Ends Well*, iv. 3. And, in the Scottish *Rates and Valuatiouns*, under 1612:

"Lockattis and *Chapes* for daggers."

2 "... e quanto á moeda, ser *chapada de sua sica* (by error printed *sita*), pois já lhe concedea, que todo o proveyto serya del Rey de Portuguall, como soya a ser dos Reis dos Guzarates, e ysto nas terras que nos tiuermos em Canbaya, e a nos quisermos bater."—Treaty (1537) in *S. Botelho, Tombo*, 226.

maintain and fulfil this agreement entirely ... and he sealed it with his seal" (*e o* **chapo** *de sua* **chapa**).—Treaty above quoted, in *S. Botelho, Tombo*, 228.

1552.—"... ordered ... that they should allow no person to enter or to leave the island without taking away his **chapa**. ... And this **chapa** was, as it were, a seal."—*Castanheda*, iii. 32.

1614.—"The King (of Achen) sent us his **Chop**."—*Milward*, in *Purchas*, i. 526.

1615.—"Sailed to Acheen; the King sent his **Chope** for them to go ashore, without which it was unlawful for any one to do so."—*Sainsbury*, i. 445.

["2 chistes plate ... with the rendadors **chape** upon it."—*Cocks's Diary*, i. 219.]

1618.—"Signed with my **chop**, the 14th day of May (*sic*), in the Yeare of our Prophet Mahomet 1027."—Letter from Gov. of Mocha, in *Purchas*, i. 625.

1673.—"The Custom-house has a good Front, where the chief Customer appears certain Hours to **chop**, that is to mark Goods outward-bound."—*Fryer*, 98.

1678.—"... sending of our *Vuckeel* this day to Compare the Coppys with those sent, in order to y^e^ **Chaup**, he refused it, alledging that they came without ye Visiers **Chaup** to him. ..."—*Letter* (in India Office) *from Dacca Factory* to Mr. Matthias Vincent (Ft. St. George?).

1682.—"To Rajemaul I sent ye old Duan ...'s Perwanna, **Chopt** both by the Nabob and new Duan, for its confirmation."—*Hedges, Diary*, Hak. Soc. i. 37.

1689.—"Upon their **Chops** as they call them in India, or Seals engraven, are only Characters, generally those of their Name."—*Ovington*, 251.

1711.—"This (Oath at Acheen) is administered by the Shabander ... lifting, very respectfully, a short Dagger in a Gold Case, like a Scepter, three times to their Heads; and it is called receiving the **Chop** for Trade."—*Lockyer*, 35.

1715.—"It would be very proper also to put our **chop** on the said Books."—In *Wheeler*, ii. 224.

c. 1720.—"Here they demanded tax and toll; felt us all over, not excepting our mouths, and when they found nothing, stamped a **chop** upon our arms in red paint; which was to serve for a pass."—*Zesteen Jaarige Reize* ... door *Jacob de Bucquoy*, Haarlem, 1757.

1727.—"On my Arrival (at Acheen) I took the **Chap** at the great River's Mouth, according to Custom. This *Chap* is a Piece of Silver about 8 ounces Weight, made in Form of a Cross, but the cross Part is very short, that we ... put to our Fore-head, and declare to the Officer that brings the *Chap*, that we come on an honest Design to trade."—*A. Hamilton*, ii. 103.

1771.—"... with **Tiapp** or passports."—*Osbeck*, i. 181.

1782.—"... le Pilote ... apporte avec lui leur **chappe**, ensuite il adore et consulte son Poussa, puis il fait lever l'ancre."—*Sonnerat*, ii. 233.

1783.—"The bales (at Acheen) are immediately opened; 12 in the hundred are taken for the king's duty, and the remainder being marked with a certain mark (**chapp**) may be carried where the owner pleases."—*Forrest, V. to Mergui*, 41.

1785.—"The only pretended original produced was a manifest forgery, for it had not the **chop** or smaller seal, on which is engraved the name of the Mogul."—*Carraccioli's Clive*, i. 214.

1817.—"... and so great reluctance did he (the Nabob) show to the ratification of the Treaty, that Mr. Pigot is said to have seized his **chop**, or seal, and applied it to the paper."—*Mill's Hist.* iii. 340.

1876.—"'*First* **chop**! tremendously pretty too,' said the elegant Grecian, who had been paying her assiduous attention."—*Daniel Deronda*, Bk. I. ch. x.

1882.—"On the edge of the river facing the 'Pow-shan' and the Creek Hongs, were **Chop** *houses*, or branches of the Hoppo's department, whose *duty* it was to prevent smuggling, but whose *interest* it was to aid and facilitate the shipping of silks ... at a considerable reduction on the Imperial tariff."—*The Fankwae at Canton*, p. 25.

The writer last quoted, and others before him, have imagined a Chinese origin for **chop**, *e.g.*, as "from *chah*, 'an official note from a superior,' or *chah*, 'a contract, a diploma, &c.,' both having at Canton the sound *chăp*, and between them covering most of the 'pigeon' uses of *chop*" (Note by *Bishop Moule*). But few of the words used by Europeans in Chinese trade are really Chinese, and we think it has been made clear that *chop* comes from India.

CHOP-CHOP. Pigeon-English (or -Chinese) for 'Make haste! look sharp!' This is supposed to be from the Cantonese, pron. *kăp-kăp*, of what is in the Mandarin dialect *kip-kip*. In the Northern dialects *kwai-kwai*, 'quick-quick' is more usual (*Bishop Moule*). [Mr. Skeat compares the Malay *chepat-chepat*, 'quick-quick.']

CHOPPER-COT, a. Much as this looks like a European concoction, it is a genuine

H. term, *chappar khāṭ*, 'a bedstead with curtains.'

1778.—"Leito com armação. **Châpâr cátt.**"—*Grammatica Indostana*, 128.

c. 1809.—"Bedsteads are much more common than in Puraniya. The best are called *Palang*, or **Chhapar Khat** ... they have curtains, mattrasses, pillows, and a sheet. ..."—*Buchanan, Eastern India*, ii. 92.

c. 1817.—"My husband chanced to light upon a very pretty **chopper-cot**, with curtains and everything complete."—*Mrs. Sherwood's Stories*, ed. 1873, 161. (See COT.)

CHOPSTICKS, s. The sticks used in pairs by the Chinese in feeding themselves ... The Chinese name of the article is *'kwai-tsz,'* 'speedy-ones.'" Possibly the inventor of the present word, hearing that the Chinese name had this meaning, and accustomed to the phrase *chop-chop* for 'speedily,' used *chop* as a translation" (*Bishop Moule*). [Prof. Giles writes: "The *N.E.D.* gives incorrectly *kwai-tze, i.e.* 'nimble boys,' 'nimble ones.' Even Sir H. Yule is not without blemish. He leaves the aspirate out of *kwai*, of which the official orthography is now *k'uai-k'uai-tzŭ*, 'hasteners,' the termination *-ers* bringing out the value of *tzŭ*, an enclitic particle, better than 'ones.' Bishop Moule's suggestion is on the right track. I think, however, that **chopstick** came from a Chinaman, who of course knew the meaning of *k'uai* and applied it accordingly, using the 'pidgin' word **chop** as the, to him, natural equivalent."]

c. 1540.—"... his young daughters, with their brother, did nothing but laugh to see us feed ourselves with our hands, for that is contrary to the custome which is observed throughout the whole empire of *China*, where the Inhabitants at their meat carry it to their mouthes with two little sticks made like a pair of Cizers" (this is the translator's folly; it is really *com duos paos feitos como fusos*—"like spindles)."—*Pinto*, orig. cap. lxxxiii., in *Cogan*, p. 103.

[1598.—"Two little peeces of blacke woode made round ... these they use instead of forkes."—*Linschoten*, Hak. Soc. i. 144.]

c. 1610.—"... ont comme deux petites spatules de bois fort bien faites, qu'ils tiennent entre leurs doigts, et prennent avec cela ce qu'ils veulent manger, si dextrement, que rien plus."—*Mocquet*, 346.

1711—"They take it very dexterously with a couple of small **Chopsticks**, which serve them instead of Forks."—*Lockyer*, 174.

1876.—"Before each there will be found a pair of **chopsticks**, a wine-cup, a small saucer for soy ... and a pile of small pieces of paper for cleaning these articles as required."—*Giles, Chinese Sketches*, 153–4.

CHOTA-HAZRY, s. H. *chhoṭī hāzirī*, vulg. *hāẓrī*, 'little breakfast'; refreshment taken in the early morning, before or after the morning exercise. The term (see HAZREE) was originally peculiar to the Bengal Presidency. In Madras the meal is called 'early tea.' Among the Dutch in Java, this meal consists (or did consist in 1860) of a large cup of tea, and a large piece of cheese, presented by the servant who calls one in the morning.

1853.—"After a bath, and hasty ante-breakfast (which is called in India '**a little breakfast**') at the Euston Hotel, he proceeded to the private residence of a man of law."—*Oakfield*, ii. 179.

1866.—"There is one small meal ... it is that commonly known in India by the Hindustani name of **chota-hāziri**, and in our English colonies as 'Early Tea.' ..."—*Waring, Tropical Resident*, 172.

1875.—"We took **early tea** with him this morning."—*The Dilemma*, ch. iii.

CHOUSE, s. and v. This word is originally Turk. *chāush*, in former days a sergeant-at-arms, herald, or the like. [Vambéry (*Sketches*, 17) speaks of the *Tchaush* as the leader of a party of pilgrims.] Its meaning as 'a cheat,' or 'to swindle' is, apparently beyond doubt, derived from the anecdote thus related in a note of W. Gifford's upon the passage in Ben Jonson's *Alchemist*, which is quoted below. "In 1609 Sir Robert Shirley sent a messenger or *chiaus* (as our old writers call him) to this country, as his agent, from the Grand Signor and the Sophy, to transact some preparatory business. Sir Robert followed him, at his leisure, as ambassador from both these princes; but before he reached England, his agent had *chiaused* the Turkish and Persian merchants here of 4000*l.*, and taken his flight, unconscious perhaps that he had enriched the language with a word of which the etymology would mislead Upton and puzzle Dr. Johnson."—Ed. of *Ben Jonson*, iv. 27. "In Kattywar, where the native chiefs employ Arab mercenaries, the **Chaus** still flourishes as an officer of a company. When I joined the Political Agency in that Province, there was a company of Arabs attached to the Residency under a *Chaus*." (*M.-Gen. Keatinge*). [The *N.E.D.* thinks that "Gifford's note must be taken with reserve." The *Stanf.*

Dict. adds that Gifford's note asserts that two other *Chiauses* arrived in 1618–1625. One of the above quotations proves his accuracy as to 1618. Perhaps, however, the particular fraud had little to do with the modern use of the word. As Jonson suggests, *chiaus* may have been used for 'Turk' in the sense of 'cheat'; just as *Cataian* stood for 'thief' or 'rogue.' For a further discussion of the word see *N. & Q.*, 7 ser. vi. 387; 8 ser. iv. 129.]

1560.—"Cum vero me taederet inclusionis in eodem diversorio, ago cum meo **Chiauso** (genus id est, ut tibi scripsi alias, multiplicis apud Turcas officii, quod etiam ad oratorum custodiam extenditur) ut mihi liceat aere meo domum conducere. ..."—*Busbeq. Epist.* iii. p. 149.

1610.—"*Dapper.* ... What do you think of me, that I am a **chiaus**?
Face. What's that?
Dapper. The Turk was here.
As one would say, do you think I am a Turk?

* * * * *

Face. Come, noble doctor, pray thee let's prevail;
This is the gentleman, and he's no **chiaus**."
Ben. Jonson, The Alchemist, Act I. sc. i.

1638.—
"*Fulgoso.* Gulls or Moguls,
Tag, rag, or other, hogen-mogen, vanden,
Ship-jack or **chouses**. Whoo! the brace are flinched.
The pair of shavers are sneak'd from us, Don... ."
Ford, The Lady's Trial, Act II. sc. i.

1619.—"Con gli ambasciatori stranieri che seco conduceva, cioè l'Indiano, di Sciah Selim, un **ciausc** Turco ed i Moscoviti. ..."—*P. della Valle,* ii. 6.

1653.—"**Chiaoux** en Turq est vn Sergent du Diuan, et dans la campagne la garde d'vne Karauane, qui fait le guet, se nomme aussi **Chiaoux**, et cet employ n'est pas autrement honeste."—*Le Gouz,* ed. 1657, p. 536.

1659.—
"*Conquest.* We are
In a fair way to be ridiculous.
What think you? **Chiaus'd** by a scholar."
Shirley, Honoria & Mammon, Act II. sc. iii.

1663.—"The Portugals have **choused** us, it seems, in the Island of Bombay in the East Indys; for after a great charge of our fleets being sent thither with full commission from the King of Portugal to receive it, the Governour by some pretence or other will not deliver it to Sir Abraham Shipman."—*Pepys, Diary,* May 15; [ed. *Wheatley* iii. 125].

1674.—
"When geese and pullen are seduc'd
And sows of sucking pigs are **chows'd.**"
Hudibras, Pt. II. canto 3.

1674.—
"Transform'd to a Frenchman by my art;
He stole your cloak, and pick'd your pocket,
Chows'd and caldes'd ye like a block-head."
Ibid.

1754.—"900 **chiaux**: they carried in their hand a baton with a double silver crook on the end of it; ... these frequently chanted moral sentences and encomiums on the SHAH, occasionally proclaiming also his victories as he passed along."—*Hanway,* i. 170.

1762.—"Le 27e d'Août 1762 nous entendîmes un coup de canon du chateau de Kâhira, c'étoit signe qu'un **Tsjaus** (courier) étoit arrivé de la grande caravane."—*Niebuhr, Voyage,* i. 171.

1826.—"We started at break of day from the northern suburb of Ispahan, led by the **chaoushes** of the pilgrimage. ..."—*Hajji Baba,* ed. 1835, p. 6.

CHOW-CHOW, s. A common application of the *Pigeon*-English term in China is to mixed preserves; but, as the quotation shows, it has many uses; the idea of mixture seems to prevail. It is the name given to a book by Viscountess Falkland, whose husband was Governor of Bombay. There it seems to mean 'a medley of trifles.' **Chow** is in 'pigeon' applied to food of any kind. ["From the erroneous impression that dogs form one of the principal items of a Chinaman's diet, the common variety has been dubbed the '**chow** dog'" (*Ball, Things Chinese,* p. 179).] We find the word **chow-chow** in Blumentritt's *Vocabular* of Manilla terms: "*Chau-chau,* a Tagal dish so called."

1858.—"The word **chow-chow** is suggestive, especially to the Indian reader, of a mixture of things, 'good, bad, and indifferent,' of sweet little oranges and bits of bamboo stick, slices of sugar-cane and rinds of unripe fruit, all concocted together, and made upon the whole into a very tolerable confection... .

"Lady Falkland, by her happy selection of a name, to a certain extent deprecates and disarms criticism. We cannot complain that her work is without plan, unconnected, and sometimes trashy, for these are exactly the conditions implied in the word **chow-chow**."—*Bombay Quarterly Review,* January, p. 100.

1882.—"The variety of uses to which the compound word '**chow-chow**' is put is almost endless. ... A 'No. 1 *chow-chow*' thing signifies utterly worthless, but when applied to a breakfast or dinner it means 'unexceptionably good.' A '*chow-chow*' cargo is an assorted cargo; a 'general shop' is a '*chow-chow*' shop ... one (factory) was called the '*chow-chow*,' from its being inhabited by divers Parsees, Moormen, or other natives of India."—*The Fankwae*, p. 63.

CHOWDRY, s. H. *chaudharī*, lit. 'a holder of four'; the explanation of which is obscure: [rather Skt. *chakra-dharin*, 'the bearer of the discus as an ensign of authority']. The usual application of the term is to the headman of a craft in a town, and more particularly to the person who is selected by Government as the agent through whom supplies, workmen, &c., are supplied for public purposes. [Thus the *Chaudharī* of carters provides carriage, the *Chaudharī* of Kahārs bearers, and so on.] Formerly, in places, to the headman of a village; to certain holders of lands; and in Cuttack it was, under native rule, applied to a district Revenue officer. In a paper of 'Explanations of Terms' furnished to the Council at Fort William by Warren Hastings, then Resident at Moradbagh (1759), **chowdrees** are defined as "Landholders in the next rank to Zemindars." (In *Long*, p. 176.) It is also an honorific title given by servants to one of their number, usually, we believe, to the *mālī* [see MOLLY], or gardener—as *khalīfa* to the cook and tailor, *jama'dār* to the *bhishtī*, *mehtar* to the sweeper, *sirdār* to the bearer.

c. 1300.—"... The people were brought to such a state of obedience that one revenue officer would string twenty ... **chaudharis** together by the neck, and enforce payment by blows."—*Ziā-ud-dīn Barnī*, in *Elliot*, iii. 183.

c. 1343.—"The territories dependent on the capital (Delhi) are divided into hundreds, each of which has a **Jautharī**, who is the Sheikh or chief man of the Hindus."—*Ibn Batuta*, iii. 388.

[1772.—"**Chowdrahs**, land-holders, in the next rank to Zemeendars."—*Verelst, View of Bengal*, Gloss. s.v.]

1788.—"**Chowdry**.—A Landholder or Farmer. Properly he is above the Zemindar in rank; but, according to the present custom of Bengal, he is deemed the next to the Zemindar. Most commonly used as the principal purveyor of the markets in towns or camps."—*Indian Vocabulary* (Stockdale's).

CHOWK, s. H. *chauk*. An open place or wide street in the middle of a city where the market is held, [as, for example, the *Chāndnī Chauk* of Delhi]. It seems to be adopted in Persian, and there is an Arabic form *Sūḳ*, which, it is just possible, may have been borrowed and Arabized from the present word. The radical idea of *chauk* seems to be "four ways" [Skt. *chatushka*], the crossing of streets at the centre of business. Compare *Carfax*, and the *Quattro Cantoni* of Palermo. In the latter city there is a market place called Piazza Ballarò, which in the 16th century a chronicler calls *Seggeballarath*, or as Amari interprets, *Sūḳ*-Balharā.

[1833.—"The Chandy **Choke**, in Delhi ... is perhaps the broadest street in any city in the East."—*Skinner, Excursions in India*, i. 49.]

CHOWRINGHEE, n.p. The name of a road and quarter of Calcutta, in which most of the best European houses stand; *Chaurangī*.

1789.—"The houses ... at **Chowringee** also will be much more healthy."—*Seton-Karr*, ii. 205.

1790.—"To dig a large tank opposite to the **Cheringhee** Buildings."—*Ibid.* 13.

1791.—"Whereas a robbery was committed on Tuesday night, the first instant, on the **Chowringhy** Road."—*Ibid.* 54.

1792.—"*For Private Sale.* A neat, compact and new built garden house, pleasantly situated at **Chouringy**, and from its contiguity to Fort William, peculiarly well calculated for an officer; it would likewise be a handsome provision for a native lady, or a child. The price is 1500 sicca rupees."—*Ibid.* ii. 541.

1803.—"**Chouringhee**, an entire village of palaces, runs for a considerable length at right angles with it, and altogether forms the finest view I ever beheld in any city."—*Ld. Valentia*, i. 236.

1810.—"As I enjoyed Calcutta much less this time ... I left it with less regret. Still, when passing the **Chowringhee** road the last day, I—

'Looked on stream and sea and plain
As what I ne'er might see again.'"

Elphinstone, in *Life*, i. 231.

1848.—"He wished all Cheltenham, all **Chowringhee**, all Calcutta, could see him in that position, waving his hand to such a beauty, and in company with such a famous buck as Rawdon Crawley, of the Guards."—*Vanity Fair*, ed. 1867, i. 237.

CHOWRY, s.

H. *chaṅwar, chauṅrī*; from Skt. *chamara, chāmara*. The bushy tail of the Tibetan **Yak** (q.v.), often set in a costly decorated handle to use as a fly-flapper, in which form it was one of the insignia of ancient Asiatic royalty. The tail was also often attached to the horse-trappings of native warriors; whilst it formed from remote times the standard of nations and nomad tribes of Central Asia. The Yak-tails and their uses are mentioned by Aelian, and by Cosmas (see under **YAK**). Allusions to the *chāmara*, as a sign of royalty, are frequent in Skt. books and inscriptions, *e.g.* in the Poet Kalidāsa (see transl. by Dr. Mill in *J. As. Soc. Beng.* i. 342; the *Amarakosha*, ii. 7, 31, &c.). The common Anglo-Indian expression in the 18th century appears to have been "**Cow-tails**" (q.v.). And hence Bogle in his Journal, as published by Mr. Markham, calls *Yaks* by the absurd name of "*cow-tailed cows*," though "horse-tailed cows" would have been more germane!

c. A.D. 250.—"*Βοῶν δε γένη δύο, δρομικούς τε καὶ ἄλλους ἀγρίους δεινῶς· ἐκ τουτῶν γε τῶν βοῶν καὶ τὰς μυιοσόβας ποιοῦνται, καὶ τὸ μὲν σῶμα παμμέλανες εἴσιν οἵδε· τὰς δὲ οὐρὰς ἔχουσι λευκὰς ἰσχυρῶς.*"—*Aelian. de Nat. An.* xv. 14.

A.D. 634–5.—"... with his armies which were darkened by the spotless **chāmaras** that were waved over them."—*Aihole Inscription.*

c. 940.—"They export from this country the hair named *al-zamar* (or **al-chamar**) of which those fly-flaps are made, with handles of silver or ivory, which attendants held over the heads of kings when giving audience."—*Maṣ'ūdī*, i. 385. The expressions of *Maṣ'ūdī* are aptly illustrated by the Assyrian and Persepolitan sculptures. (See also *Marco Polo*, bk. iii. ch. 18; *Nic. Conti*, p. 14, in *India in the XVth Century*).

1623.—"For adornment of their horses they carried, hung to the cantles of their saddles, great tufts of a certain white hair, long and fine, which they told me were the tails of certain wild oxen found in India."—*P. della Valle*, ii. 662; [Hak. Soc. ii. 260].

1809.—"He also presented me in trays, which were as usual laid at my feet, two beautiful **chowries**."—*Lord Valentia*, i. 428.

1810.—"Near Brahma are Indra and Indranee on their elephant, and below is a female figure holding a *chamara* or **chowree**."—*Maria Graham*, 56.

1827.—"A black female slave, richly dressed, stood behind him with a **chowry**, or cow's tail, having a silver handle, which she used to keep off the flies."—*Sir W. Scott, The Surgeon's Daughter*, ch. x.

CHUCKAROO, s. English soldier's lingo for **Chokra** (q.v.)

CHUCKER. From H. *chakar*, *chakkar*, *chakrā*, Skt. *chakra*, 'a wheel or circle.'

(**a.**) s. A quoit for playing the English game; but more properly the sharp quoit or discus which constituted an ancient Hindu missile weapon, and is, or was till recently, carried by the Sikh fanatics called *Akālī* (see **AKALEE**), generally encircling their peaked turbans. The thing is described by Tavernier (E. T. ii. 41: [ed. *Ball*, i. 82]) as carried by a company of Mahommedan Fakīrs whom he met at Sherpūr in Guzerat. See also *Lt.-Col. T. Lewin, A Fly*, &c., p. 47 : [*Egerton, Handbook*, Pl. 15, No. 64].

1516.—"In the Kingdom of Dely ... they have some steel wheels which they call **chacarani**, two fingers broad, sharp outside like knives, and without edge inside; and the surface of these is the size of a small plate. And they carry seven or eight of these each, put on the left arm; and they take one and put it on the finger of the right hand, and make it spin round many times, and so they hurl it at their enemies."—*Barbosa*, 100–101.

1630.—"In her right hand shee bare a **chuckerey**, which is an instrument of a round forme, and sharp-edged in the superficies thereof ... and slung off, in the quickness of his motion, it is able to deliuer or conuey death to a farre remote enemy."—*Lord, Disc. of the Banian Religion*, 12.

(**b**) v. and s. To lunge a horse. H. *chakarnā* or *chakar karnā*. Also 'the lunge.'

1829.—"It was truly tantalizing to see those fellows **chūckering** their horses, not more than a quarter of a mile from our post."—*John Shipp*, i. 153.

[(**c.**) In Polo, a 'period.'

[1900.—"Two bouts were played to-day ... In the opening **chūkker** Capt. —— carried the ball in."—*Overland Mail*, Aug. 13.]

CHUDDER, s. H. *chādar*, a sheet, or square piece of cloth of any kind; the ample sheet commonly worn as a mantle by women in N. India. It is also applied to the cloths spread over Mahommedan tombs. Barbosa (1516) and Linschoten (1598) have *chautars*, *chautares*, as a kind of cotton piece-goods, but it is certain that this is not the same word. *Chowtars* occur among Bengal piece-goods in *Milburn*, ii. 221. [The word is *chautár*, 'anything with four threads,' and it occurs in the list of cotton cloths in the *Āīn* (i. 94). In a letter of 1610 we have "*Chautares* are white and well requested" (*Danvers, Letters*, i. 75); "*Chauters* of Agra" (*Foster, Letters*, ii. 45); Cocks has "fine *Casho* or *Chowter*" (*Diary*, i. 86); and in 1615 they are called "*Cowter*" (*Foster*, iv. 51).]

1525.—"**Chader** of Cambaya."—*Lembranca*, 56.

[c. 1610.—"From Bengal comes another sort of hanging, of fine linen painted and ornamented with colours in a very agreeable fashion; these they call **iader**."—*Pyrard de Laval*, Hak. Soc. i. 222.]

1614.—"Pintados, chints and **chadors**."—*Peyton*, in *Purchas*, i. 530.

1673.—"The habit of these waternymphs was fine **Shudders** of lawn embroidered on the neck, wrist, and skirt with a border of several coloured silks or threads of gold."—*Herbert*, 3rd ed. 191.

1832.—"**Chuddur** ... a large piece of cloth or sheet, of one and a half or two breadths, thrown over the head, so as to cover the whole body. Men usually sleep rolled up in it."—*Herklots*, *Qanoon-e-Islam*, xii.-xiii.

1878.—"Two or three women, who had been chattering away till we appeared, but who, on seeing us, drew their '**chadders**' ... round their faces, and retired to the further end of the boat."—*Life in the Mofussil*, i. 79.

The **Rampore Chudder** is a kind of shawl, of the Tibetan shawl-wool, of uniform colour without pattern, made originally at Rāmpur on the Sutlej; and of late years largely imported into England: [(see the *Panjab Mono. on Wool*, p. 9). Curiously enough a claim to the derivation of the title from Rāmpur, in Rohilkhand, N.W.P. is made in the *Imperial Gazetteer*, 1st ed. (s.v.).]

CHUL! CHULLO! v. m imperative; 'Go on! Be quick.' H. *chalo!* imper. of *chalnā*, to go, go speedily. [Another common use of the word in Anglo-Indian slang is—"It won't **chul**," 'it won't answer, succeed.']

c. 1790.—"Je montai de très-bonne heure dans mon palanquin.—**Tschollo** (c'est-à-dire, marche), crièrent mes **coulis**, et aussitôt le voyage commença."—*Haafuer*, ii. 5.

[**CHUMAR**, s. H. *Chamār*, Skt. *charmakāra*, 'one who works in leather,' and thus answering to the **Chuckler** of S. India; an important caste found all through N. India, whose primary occupation is tanning, but a large number are agriculturists and day labourers of various kinds.

[1823.—"From this abomination, beef-eating ... they [the Bheels] only rank above the **Choomars**, or shoemakers, who feast on dead carcases, and are in Central India, as elsewhere, deemed so unclean that they are not allowed to dwell within the precincts of the village."—*Malcolm*, *Central India*, 2nd ed. ii. 179.]

CHUMPUK, s. A highly ornamental and sacred tree (*Michelia champaca*, L., also *M. Rheedii*), a kind of magnolia, whose odorous yellow blossoms are much prized by Hindus, offered at shrines, and rubbed on the body at marriages, &c. H. *champak*, Skt. *champaka*. Drury strangely says that the name is "derived from *Ciampa*, an island between Cambogia and Cochin China, where the tree grows." *Champa* is *not* an island, and certainly derives its Sanskrit name from India, and did *not* give a name to an Indian tree. The tree is found wild in the Himālaya from Nepāl, eastward; also in Pegu and Tenasserim, and along the Ghauts to Travancore. The use of the term *champaka* extends to the Philippine Islands. [Mr. Skeat notes that it is highly prized by Malay women, who put it in their hair.]

1623.—"Among others they showed me a flower, in size and form not unlike our lily, but of a yellowish white colour, with a sweet and powerful scent, and which they call **champà** [**ciampá**]."—*P. della Valle*, ii. 517; [Hak. Soc. i. 40].

1786.—"The walks are scented with blossoms of the **champac** and nagisar, and the plantations of pepper and coffee are equally new and pleasing."—*Sir W. Jones*, in *Mem.*, &c., ii. 81.

1810.—"Some of these (birds) build in the sweet-scented **champaka** and the mango."—*Maria Graham*, 22.

1819.—

"The wandering airs they faint
On the dark, the silent stream;
And the **chumpak's** odours fail
Like sweet thoughts in a dream."
Shelley, *Lines to an Indian Air*.

1821.—

"Some **chumpak** flowers proclaim it yet divine."
Mediwin, *Sketches in Hindoostan*, 73.

CHUPATTY, s. H. *chapātī*, an unleavened cake of bread (generally of coarse wheaten meal), patted flat with the hand, and baked upon a griddle; the usual form of native bread, and the staple food of Upper India.

1615.—Parson Terry well describes the thing, but names it not: "The ordinary sort of people eat bread made of a coarse grain, but both toothsome and wholesome and hearty. They make it up in broad cakes, thick like our oaten cakes; and then bake it upon small round iron hearths which they carry with them."—In *Purchas*, ii. 1468.

1810.—"**Chow-patties**, or bannocks."—*Williamson*, *V. M.* ii. 348.

1857.—"From village to village brought by one messenger and sent forward by another passed a mysterious token in the shape of one of those flat cakes made from flour and water, and forming the common bread of the people, which in their language, are called **chupatties.**"—*Kaye's Sepoy War*, i. 570. [The original account of this by the Correspondent of the '*Times*,' dated "Bombay, March 3, 1857," is quoted in 2 ser. *N. & Q.* iii.365.]

There is a tradition of a noble and gallant Governor-General who, when compelled to rough it for a day or two, acknowledged that "*chuprassies* and *masaulchies* were not such bad diet," meaning **Chupatties** and **Mussalla.**

CHUPRASSY, s. H. *chaprāsī*, the bearer of a *chaprās*, *i.e.* a badge-plate inscribed with the name of the office to which the bearer is attached. The *chaprāsī* is an office-messenger, or henchman, bearing such a badge on a cloth or leather belt. The term belongs to the Bengal Presidency. In Madras **Peon** is the usual term; in Bombay **Puttywalla**, (H. *paṭṭīwālā*), or "man of the belt." The etymology of *chaprās* is obscure; [the popular account is that it is a corr. of P. *chap-o-rāst*, 'left and right']; but see *Beames* (*Comp. Gram.* i. 212), who gives *buckle* as the original meaning.

1865.—"I remember the days when every servant in my house was a **chuprassee**, with the exception of the Khansaumaun and a Portuguese Ayah."—*The Dawk Bungalow*, p. 389.

c. 1866.—

"The big Sahib's tent has gone from under the
Peepul tree,
With his horde of hungry **chuprassees**, and
oily sons of the quill—
I paid them the bribe they wanted, and
Sheitan will settle the bill."

Sir A. C. Lyall, The Old Pindaree.

1877.—"One of my **chuprassies** or messengers ... was badly wounded."—*Meadows Taylor, Life*, i. 227.

1880.—"Through this refractory medium the people of India see their rulers. The **Chuprassie** paints his master in colours drawn from his own black heart. Every lie he tells, every insinuation he throws out, every demand he makes, is endorsed with his master's name. He is the arch-slanderer of our name in India."—*Ali Baba*, 102–3.

CHURRUCK, s. A wheel or any rotating machine; particularly applied to simple machines for cleaning cotton. Pers. *charkh*, 'the celestial sphere,' 'a wheel of any kind,' &c. Beng. *charak* is apparently a corruption of the Persian word, facilitated by the nearness of the Skt. *chakra*, &c.

—— **POOJAH**. Beng. *charak-pūjā* (see POOJA). The Swinging Festival of the Hindus, held on the sun's entrance into Aries. The performer is suspended from a long yard, traversing round on a mast, by hooks passed through the muscle over the blade-bones, and then whirled round so as to fly out centrifugally. The chief seat of this barbarous display is, or latterly was, in Bengal, but it was formerly prevalent in many parts of India. [It is the Shirry (Ca. and Tel. *sidi*, Tam. *shedil*, Tel. *sidi*, 'a hook') of S. India.] There is an old description in Purchas's *Pilgrimage*, p. 1000; also (in Malabar) in *A. Hamilton*, i. 270; [at Ikkeri, *P. della Valle*, Hak. Soc. ii. 259]; and (at Calcutta) in Heber's *Journal*, quoted below.

c. 1430.—"Alii ad ornandos currus perforato latere, fune per corpus immisso se ad currum suspendunt, pendentesque et ipsi exanimati idolum comitantur; id optimum sacrificium putant et acceptissimum deo."—*Conti*, in *Poggius, De Var. Fortunae*, iv.

[1754.—See a long account of the Bengal rite in *Ives*, 27 *seqq.*].

1824.—"The Hindoo Festival of '**Churruck Poojah**' commenced to-day, of which, as my wife has given an account in her journal, I shall only add a few particulars."—*Heber*, ed. 1844, i. 57.

CHUTNY, s. H. *chatnī*. A kind of strong relish, made of a number of condiments and fruits, &c., used in India, and more especially by Mahommedans, and the merits of which are now well known in England. For native *chutny* recipes, see *Herklots, Qanoon-e-Islam*, 2nd ed. xlvii. *seqq.*

1813.—"The **Chatna** is sometimes made with cocoa-nut, lime-juice, garlic, and chillies, and with the pickles is placed in deep leaves round the large cover, to the number of 30 or 40."—*Forbes, Or. Mem.* ii. 50 *seq.*; [2nd ed. i. 348].

1820.—"**Chitnee, Chatnee**, some of the hot spices made into a paste, by being bruised with water, the 'kitchen' of an Indian peasant."—*Acc. of Township of Loony*, in *Tr. Lit. Soc. Bombay*, ii. 194.

CINDERELLA'S SLIPPER. A. Hindu story on the like theme appears among the Hala Kanara MSS. of the Mackenzie Collection:—

"*Suvarṇadevi* having dropped her slipper in a reservoir, it was found by a fisherman of *Kusumakesari*, who sold it to a shopkeeper, by whom it was presented to the King *Ugrabáhu.* The Prince, on seeing the beauty of the slipper, fell in love with the wearer, and offered large rewards to any person who should find and bring her to him. An old woman undertook the task, and succeeded in tracing the shoe to its owner. ..."—*Mackenzie Collection*, by *H. H. Wilson*, ii. 52. [The tale is not uncommon in Indian folk-lore. See *Miss Cox*, *Cinderella* (Folk-lore Soc.), ii. 91, 183, 465, &c.]

CIVILIAN, s. A term which came into use about 1750–1770, as a designation of the covenanted European servants of the E. I. Company, not in military employ. It is not used by Grose, c. 1760, who was himself of such service at Bombay. [The earliest quotation in the *N.E.D.* is of 1766 from *Malcolm's L. of Clive*, 54.] In Anglo-Indian parlance it is still appropriated to members of the covenanted Civil Service [see COVENANTED SERVANTS]. The *Civil* Service is mentioned in *Carraccioli's L. of Clive*, (c. 1785), iii. 164. From an early date in the Company's history up to 1833, the members of the Civil Service were classified during the first five years as **Writers** (q.v.), then to the 8th year as **Factors** (q.v.); in the 9th and 11th as *Junior Merchants*; and thenceforward as *Senior Merchants*. These names were relics of the original commercial character of the E. I. Company's transactions, and had long ceased to have any practical meaning at the time of their abolition in 1833, when the Charter Act (3 & 4 Will. IV. c. 85), removed the last traces of the Company's commercial existence.

1848.—(Lady O'Dowd's) "quarrel with Lady Smith, wife of Minos Smith the puisne Judge, is still remembered by some at Madras, when the Colonel's lady snapped her fingers in the Judge's lady's face, and said *she'd* never walk behind ever a beggarly civilian."—*Vanity Fair*, ed. 1867, ii. 85.

1872.—"You bloated **civilians** are never satisfied, retorted the other."—*A True Reformer*, i. 4.

CLOVE, s. The flower-bud of *Caryophyllum aromaticum*, L., a tree of the Moluccas. The modern English name of this spice is a kind of ellipsis from the French *clous de girofles*, 'Nails of Girofles,' *i.e.* of *garofala*, *caryophylla*, &c., the name by which this spice was known to the ancients; the full old English name was similar, 'clove gillofloure,' a name which, cut in two like a polypus, has formed two different creatures, the clove (or *nail*) being assigned to the spice, and the 'gilly-flower' to a familiar clove-smelling flower. The comparison to nails runs through many languages. In Chinese the thing is called *ting-hiang*, or 'nail-spice'; in Persian *mekhak*, 'little nails,' or 'nailkins,' like the German *Nelken*, *Nägelchen*, and *Gewürtz-nagel* (spice nail).

[1602–3.—"Alsoe be carefull to gett together all the **cloues** you can."—*Birdwood, First Letter Book*, 36.]

COCKATOO, s. This word is taken from the Malay *kākātūwa*. According to Crawfurd the word means properly 'a vice,' or 'gripe,' but is applied to the bird. It seems probable, however, that the name, which is asserted to be the natural cry of the bird, may have come with the latter from some remoter region of the Archipelago, and the name of the tool may have been taken from the bird. This would be more in accordance with usual analogy. [Mr. Skeat writes: "There is no doubt that Sir H. Yule is right here and Crawfurd wrong. *Kakak tuwa* (or *tua*) means in Malay, if the words are thus separated, 'old sister,' or 'old lady.' 'I think it is possible that it may be a familiar Malay name for the bird, like our 'Polly.' The final *k* in *kakak* is a mere click, which would easily drop out."]

1638.—"Il y en a qui sont blancs ... et sont coeffés d'vne houpe incarnate ... l'on les appelle **kakatou**, à cause de ce mot qu'ils prononcent en leur chant assez distinctement."—*Mandelslo* (Paris, 1669), 144.

1654.—"Some rarities of naturall things, but nothing extraordinary save the skin of a *jaccall*, a rarely colour'd **jacatoo** or prodigious parrot. ..."—*Evelyn's Diary*, July 11.

1673.—"... **Cockatooas** and **Newries** (see LORY) from Bantem."—*Fryer*, 116.

1705.—"The **Crockadore** is a Bird of various Sizes, some being as big as a Hen, and others no bigger than a Pidgeon. They are in all Parts exactly of the shape of a Parrot. ... When they fly wild up and down the Woods they will call **Crockadore**, **Crockadore**; for which reason they go by that name."—*Funnel*, in *Dampier*, iv. 265–6.

1719.—"Maccaws, **Cokatoes**, plovers, and a

great variety of other birds of curious colours."—*Shelvocke's Voyage*, 54–55.

1775.—"At Sooloo there are no Loories, but the **Cocatores** have yellow tufts."—*Forrest, V. to N. Guinea*, 295.

[1843.—"... saucy **Krocotoas**, and gaudy-coloured Loris."—*Belcher, Narr. of Voyage of Samarang*, i. 15.]

COCKROACH, s. This objectionable insect (*Blatta orientalis*) is called by the Portuguese *cacalacca*, for the reason given by Bontius below; a name adopted by the Dutch as *kakerlak*, and by the French as *cancrelat*. The Dutch also apply their term as a slang name to half-castes. But our word seems to have come from the Spanish *cucaracha*. The original application of this Spanish name appears to have been to a common insect found under water-vessels standing on the ground, &c. (apparently *Oniscus*, or woodlouse); but as *cucaracha de Indias* it was applied to the insect now in question (see *Dicc. de la Lengua Castellana*, 1729).

1577.—"We were likewise annoyed not a little by the biting of an Indian fly called **Cacaroch**, a name agreeable to its bad condition; for living it vext our flesh; and being kill'd smelt as loathsomely as the French punaise, whose smell is odious."—*Herbert's Travels*, 3rd ed., 332–33.

[1598.—"There is a kind of beast that flyeth, twice as big as a Bee, and is called *Baratta* (Blatta)."—*Linschoten*, Hak. Soc. i. 304.]

1631.—"Scarabaeos autem hos Lusitani *Caca-laccas* vocant, quod ova quae excludunt, colorem et laevorem Laccae factitiae (*i.e.* of sealing-wax) referant."—*Jac. Bontii*, lib. v. cap 4.

1764.—

"... from their retreats
Cockroaches crawl displeasingly abroad."
Grainger, Bk. i.

c. 1775.—"Most of my shirts, books, &c., were gnawed to dust by the *blatta* or **cockroach**, called *cackerlakke* in Surinam."—*Stedman*, i. 203.

COCO, **COCOA**, **COCOA-NUT**, and (vulg.) **COKER-NUT**, s. The tree and nut *Cocos nucifera*, L.; a palm found in all tropical countries, and the only one common to the Old and New Worlds.

The etymology of this name is very obscure. Some conjectural origins are given in the passages quoted below. Ritter supposes, from a passage in Pigafetta's *Voyage of Magellan*, which we cite, that the name may have been indigenous in the Ladrone Islands, to which that passage refers, and that it was first introduced into Europe by Magellan's crew. On the other hand, the late Mr. C. W. Goodwin found in ancient Egyptian the word *kuku* used as "the name of the fruit of a palm 60 cubits high, which fruit contained water." (*Chabas, Mélanges Égyptologiques*, ii. 239.) It is hard, however, to conceive how this name should have survived, to reappear in Europe in the later Middle Ages, without being known in any intermediate literature.[1]

The more common etymology is that which is given by Barros, Garcia de Orta, Linschoten, &c., as from a Spanish word *coco* applied to a monkey's or other grotesque face, with reference to the appearance of the base of the shell with its three holes. But after all may the term not have originated in the old Span. *coca*, 'a shell' (presumably Lat. *concha*), which we have also in French *coque*? properly an egg-shell, but used also for the shell of any nut. (See a remark under **COPRAH**.)

The Skt. *narikila* [*nārikera*, *nārikela*] has originated the Pers. *nārgīl*, which Cosmas grecizes into ἀργελλίον, [and H. *nāriyal*].

Medieval writers generally (such as *Marco Polo*, *Fr. Jordanus*, &c.) call the fruit the *Indian Nut*, the name by which it was known to the Arabs (*al jauz-al-Hindī*). There is no evidence of its having been known to classical writers, nor are we aware of any Greek or Latin mention of it before Cosmas. But Brugsch, describing from the Egyptian wall-paintings of c. B.C. 1600, on the temple of Queen Hashop, representing the expeditions by sea which she sent to the Incense Land of Punt, says: "Men never seen before, the inhabitants of this divine land, showed themselves on the coast, not less astonished than the Egyptians. They lived on pile-buildings, in little dome-shaped huts, the entrance to which was effected by a ladder, under the shade of cocoa-palms laden with fruit, and splendid incense-trees, on whose boughs strange fowls rocked themselves, and at whose feet herds of cattle

1 It may be noted that Theophrastus describes under the names of κύκας and κόϊξ a palm of Ethiopia, which was perhaps the *Doom* palm of Upper Egypt (*Theoph. H. P.* ii. 6, 10). Schneider, the editor of Theoph, states that Sprengel identified this with the coco-palm. See the quotation from Pliny below.

peacefully reposed." (*H. of Egypt*, 2nd ed. i. 353; [*Maspero, Struggle of the Nations*, 248].)

c. A.D. 70.—"In ipsâ quidem Aethiopiâ fricatur haec, tanta est siccitas, et farinae modo spissatur in panem. Gignitur autem in frutice ramis cubitalibus, folio latiore, pomo rotundo majore quam mali amplitudine, **coicas** vocant."—*Pliny*, xiii. § 9.

A.D. 545.—"Another tree is that which bears the *Argell*, *i.e.* the great *Indian Nut*."—*Cosmas*, in *Cathay*, &c., clxxvi.

1292.—"The *Indian Nuts* are as big as melons, and in colour green, like gourds. Their leaves and branches are like those of the date-tree."—*John of Monte Corvino*, in do., p. 213.

c. 1328.—"First of these is a certain tree called *Nargil*; which tree every month in the year sends out a beautiful frond like [that of] a [date-] palm tree, which frond or branch produces very large fruit, as big as a man's head. ... And both flowers and fruit are produced at the same time, beginning with the first month, and going up gradually to the twelfth. ... The fruit is that which we call *nuts of India*."—*Friar Jordanus*, 15 *seq*. The wonder of the coco-palm is so often noticed in this form by medieval writers, that doubtless in their minds they referred it to that "tree of life, which bare twelve manner of fruit, and yielded her fruit every month" (*Apocal.* xxii. 2).

c. 1340.—"Le *nargîl*, appelé autrement *noix d'Inde*, auquel on ne peut comparer aucun autre fruit, est vert et rempli d'huile."—*Shihâbbuddîn Dimishkî*, in *Not. et Exts.* xiii. 175.

c. 1350.—"Wonderful fruits there are, which we never see in these parts, such as the *Nargil*. Now the Nargil is the *Indian Nut*."—*John Marignolli*, in *Cathay*, p. 352.

1498–99.—"And we who were nearest boarded the vessel, and found nothing in her but provisions and arms; and the provisions consisted of **coquos** and of four jars of certain cakes of palm-sugar, and there was nothing else but sand for ballast."—*Roteiro de Vasco da Gama*, 94.

1510.—Varthema gives an excellent account of the tree; but he uses only the Malayāl. name *tenga*. [Tam. *tennai*, *ten*, 'south' as it was supposed to have been brought from Ceylon.]

1516.—"These trees have clean smooth stems, without any branch, only a tuft of leaves at the top, amongst which grows a large fruit which they call *tenga* ... We call these fruits **quoquos**."—*Barbosa*, 154 (collating Portuguese of *Lisbon Academy*, p. 346).

1519.—"**Cocas** (*coche*) are the fruits of palm-trees, and as we have bread, wine, oil, and vinegar, so in that country they extract all these things from this one tree."—*Pigafetta, Viaggio intorno il Mondo*, in *Ramusio*, i. f. 356.

1553.—"Our people have given it the name of **coco**, a word applied by women to anything with which they try to frighten children; and this name has stuck, because nobody knew any other, though the proper name was, as the Malabars call it, *tenga*, or as the Canarins call it, *narle*."—*Barros*, Dec. III. liv. iii. cap. 7.

c. 1561.—Correa writes **coquos**.—I. i. 115.

1563.—"... We have given it the name of **coco**, because it looks like the face of a monkey, or of some other animal."—*Garcia*, 66*b*.

"That which we call **coco**, and the Malabars *Temga*."—*Ibid.* 67*b*.

1578.—"The Portuguese call it **coco** (because of those three holes that it has)."—*Acosta*, 98.

1598.—"Another that bears the Indian nuts called **Coecos**, because they have within them a certain shell that is like an ape; and on this account they use in Spain to show their children a **Coecota** when they would make them afraid."—English trans. of *Pigafetta's Congo*, in *Harleian Coll.* ii. 553.

The parallel passage in De Bry runs: "Illas quoque quae nuces Indicas **coceas**, id est *Simias* (intus enim simiae caput referunt) dictas palmas appellant."—i. 29.

Purchas has various forms in different narratives: **Cocus** (i. 37); **Cokers**, a form which still holds its ground among London stall-keepers and costermongers (i. 461, 502); **coquer**-nuts (*Terry*, in ii. 1466); **coco** (ii. 1008); **coquo** (*Pilgrimage*, 567), &c.

[c. 1610.—"None, however, is more useful than the **coco** or Indian nut, which they (in the Maldives) call roul (Malē, *rū*)."—*Pyrard de Laval*, Hak. Soc. i. 113.]

c. 1690.—Rumphius, who has **cocus** in Latin, and **cocos** in Dutch, mentions the derivation already given as that of Linschoten and many others, but proceeds:—

"Meo vero judicio verior et certior vocis origo invenienda est, plures enim nationes, quibus hic fructus est notus, *nucem* appellant. Sic dicitur Arabicè *Gauzos-Indi* vel *Geuzos-Indi*, h. e. Nux Indica. ... Turcis *Cock-Indi* eadem significatione, unde sine dubio Æthiopes, Africani, eorumque vicini Hispani ac Portugalli **coquo** deflexerunt. Omnia vero ista nomina, originem suam debent Hebraicae voci *Egoz* quae nucem significat."—*Herb. Amboin.* i. p. 7.

"... in India Occidentali **Kokernoot** vocatus. ..."—*Ibid.* p. 47.

One would like to know where Rumphius got the term *Cock-Indi*, of which we can find no trace.

1810.—

"What if he felt no wind! The air was still.

That was the general will
Of Nature ...
Yon rows of rice erect and silent stand,
The shadow of the **Cocoa's** lightest plume
Is steady on the sand."

Curse of Kehama, iv. 4.

1881.—"Among the popular French slang words for 'head' we may notice the term '**coco**,' given—like our own 'nut'—on account of the similarity in shape between a cocoa-nut and a human skull:—

"'Mais de ce franc picton de table
Qui rend spirituel, aimable,
Sans vous alourdir le **coco**,
Je m'en fourre à gogo.'—H. Valère."

Sat. Review, Sept. 10, p. 326.

The *Dict. Hist. d'Argot* of Lorédan Larchey, from which this seems taken, explains *picton* as 'vin supérieur.'

COFFEE, s. Arab. *kahwa*, a word which appears to have been originally a term for wine.[1] [So in the *Arab. Nights*, ii. 158, where Burton gives the derivation as *akhá*, fastidire fecit, causing disinclination for food. In old days the scrupulous called coffee *ḳihwah* to distinguish it from *ḳahwah*, wine.] It is probable, therefore, that a somewhat similar word was twisted into this form by the usual propensity to strive after meaning. Indeed, the derivation of the name has been plausibly traced to *Kaffa*, one of those districts of the S. Abyssinian highlands (Enarea and Kaffa) which appear to have been the original habitat of the Coffee plant (*Coffea arabica*, L.); and if this is correct, then *Coffee* is nearer the original than *Ḳahwa*. On the other hand, *Ḳahwa*, or some form thereof, is in the earliest mentions appropriated to the drink, whilst some form of the word *Bunn* is that given to the plant, and *Būn* is the existing name of the plant in Shoa. This name is also that applied in Yemen to the coffee-berry. There is very fair evidence in Arabic literature that the use of coffee was introduced into Aden by a certain Sheikh Shihābuddīn Dhabḥānī, who had made acquaintance with it on the African coast, and who died in the year H. 875, *i.e.* A.D. 1470, so that the introduction may be put about the middle of the 15th century, a time consistent with the other negative and positive data.[2] From Yemen it spread to Mecca (where there arose after some years, in 1511, a crusade against its use as unlawful), to Cairo, to Damascus and Aleppo, and to Constantinople, where the first coffee-house was established in 1554. [It is said to have been introduced into S. India some two centuries ago by a Mahommedan pilgrim, named Bābā Būdan, who brought a few seeds with him from Mecca: see *Grigg, Nilagiri Man.* 483; *Rice, Mysore*, i. 162.] The first European mention of coffee seems to be by Rauwolff, who knew it in Aleppo in 1573. [See 1 ser. *N. & Q.* I. 25 *seqq.*] It is singular that in the *Observations* of Pierre Belon, who was in Egypt, 1546–49, full of intelligence and curious matter as they are, there is no indication of a knowledge of coffee.

1558.—Extrait du Livre intitulé: "Les Preuves le plus fortes en faveur de la legitimité de l'usage du Café (**Kahwa**); par le Scheikh Abd-Alkader Ansari Djézéri Hanbali, fils de Mohammed."—In *De Sacy, Chrest. Arabe*, 2nd ed. i. 412.

1573.—"Among the rest they have a very good Drink, by them called **Chaube**, that is almost black as Ink, and very good in Illness, chiefly that of the Stomach; of this they drink in the Morning early in open places before everybody, without any fear or regard, out of *China* cups, as hot as they can; they put it often to their Lips, but drink but little at a Time, and let it go round as they sit. In the same water they take a Fruit called *Bunru*, which in its Bigness, Shape, and Colour, is almost like unto a Bay-berry, with two thin Shells ... they agree in the Virtue, Figure, Looks, and Name with the *Buncho* of Avicen, and *Bancha* of *Rasis ad Almans.* exactly; therefore I take them to be the same."—*Rauwolff*, 92.

c. 1580.—"Arborem vidi in viridario Halydei Turcae, cujus tu iconem nuno spectabis, ex qua semina illa ibi vulgatissima, *Bon* vel *Ban* appellata, producuntur; ex his tum Aegyptii tum Arabes parant decoctum vulgatissimum, quod vini loco ipsi potant, venditurque in publicis œnopoliis, non secus quod apud nos vinum: illique ipsum vocant **Caova**. ... Avicenna de his seminibus meminit."[3]—*Prosper Alpinus*, ii. 36.

1598.—In a note on the use of tea in Japan, Dr. Paludanus says: "The Turkes holde almost the same mañer of drinking of their *Chaona* (read **Chaoua**), which they make of a certaine fruit, which is like unto the *Bakelaer*,[4] and by the Egyptians called *Bon* or *Ban*; they take of

1 It is curious that Ducange has a L. Latin word *cahua*, 'vinum album et debile.'

2 See the extract in De Sacy's *Chrestomathie Arabe* cited below. Playfair, in his history of Yemen, says coffee was first introduced from Abyssinia by Jamāluddīn Ibn Abdalla, Kāḍī of Aden, in the middle of the 15th century: the person differs, but the time coincides.

3 There seems no foundation for this.

4 *i.e. Bacca Lauri*; laurel berry.

this fruite one pound and a halfe, and roast them a little in the fire, and then sieth them in twentie poundes of water, till the half be consumed away; this drinke they take everie morning fasting in their chambers, out of an earthen pot, being verie hote, as we doe here drinke *aqua composita* in the morning; and they say that it strengtheneth them and maketh them warm, breaketh wind, and openeth any stopping."—In *Linschoten*, 46; [Hak. Soc. i. 157].

c. 1610.—"La boisson la plus commune c'est de l'eau, ou bien du vin de Cocos tiré le mesme iour. On en fait de deux autres sortes plus delicates; l'vne est chaude, composée de l'eau et de mièl de Cocos, avec quantité de poivre (dont ils vsent beaucoup en toutes leurs viandes, et ils le nomment *Pasme*) et d'vne autre graine appellée **Cahoa**. ..."—*Pyrard de Laval*, i. 128; [Hak. Soc. i. 172].

[1611.—"Buy some **coho** pots and send me."—*Danvers, Letters*, i. 122; "**coffao** pots."—*Ibid.* i. 124.]

1615.—"They have in steed of it (wine) a certaine drinke called **Cashiete** as black as Inke, which they make with the barke of a tree (!) and drinke as hot as they can endure it."—*Monfart*, 28.

"... passano tutto il resto della notte con mille feste e bagordi; e particolarmente in certi luoghi pubblici ... bevendo di quando in quando a sorsi (per chè è calda che cuoce) più d'uno scodellino di certa loro acqua nera, che chiamano **cahue**; la quale, nelle conversazioni serve a loro, appunto come a noi il giuoco dello sbaraglino" (*i.e.* backgammon).—*P. della Valle* (from Constant.), i. 51. See also pp. 74–76.

["**Cohu**, blake liquor taken as hotte as may be endured."—*Sir T. Roe*, Hak. Soc. i. 32.]

1616.—"Many of the people there (in India), who are strict in their Religion, drink no Wine at all; but they use a Liquor more wholesome than pleasant, they call **Coffee**; made by a black Seed boyld in water, which turnes it almost into the same colour, but doth very little alter the taste of the water (!): notwithstanding it is very good to help Digestion, to quicken the Spirits, and to cleanse the Blood."—*Terry*, ed. of 1665, p. 365.

1623.—"Turcae habent etiam in usu herbae genus quam vocant **Caphe** ... quam dicunt haud parvum praestans illis vigorem, et in animas (*sic*) et in ingenio; quae tamen largius sumpta mentem movet et turbat. ..."—*F. Bacon, Hist. Vitae et Mortis*, 25.

c. 1628.—"They drink (in Persia) ... above all the rest, **Coho** or **Copha**: by Turk and Arab called **Caphe** and **Cahua**: a drink imitating that in the Stigian lake, black, thick, and bitter: destrain'd from Bunchy, Bunnu, or Bay berries; wholsome they say, if hot, for it expels melancholy ... but not so much regarded for those good properties, as from a Romance that it was invented and brew'd by Gabriel ... to restore the decayed radical Moysture of kind hearted *Mahomet*. ..."—*Sir T. Herbert, Travels*, ed. 1638, p. 241.

[1631.—"**Caveah**." See quotation under TEA.]

c. 1637.—"There came in my time to the Coll: (Balliol) one Nathaniel Conopios out of Greece, from Cyril the Patriarch of Constantinople. ... He was the first I ever saw drink **coffee**, which custom came not into England till 30 years after."—*Evelyn's Diary*, [May 10].

1673.—"Every one pays him their congratulations, and after a dish of **Coho** or Tea, mounting, accompany him to the Palace."—*Fryer*, 225.

"Cependant on l'apporta le **cavé**, le parfum, et le sorbet."—*Journal d'Antoine Galland*, ii. 124.

[1677.—"**Cave**." See quotation under TEA.]

1690.—"For Tea and **Coffee** which are judg'd the privileg'd Liquors of all the *Mahometans*, as well *Turks*, as those of *Persia*, *India*, and other parts of *Arabia*, are condemn'd by them (the Arabs of Muscatt) as unlawful Refreshments, and abominated as Bug-bear Liquors, as well as Wine."—*Ovington*, 427.

1726.—"A certain gentleman, M. Paschius, maintains in his Latin work published at Leipzig in 1700, that the parched corn (1 Sam. xxv. 18) which Abigail presented with other things to David, to appease his wrath, was nought else but **Coffi**-beans."—*Valentijn*, v. 192.

COIR, s. The fibre of the coco-nut husk, from which rope is made. But properly the word, which is Tam. *kayiru*, Malayāl. *kāyar*, from v. *kāyāṛu*. 'to be twisted,' means 'cord' itself (see the accurate *Al-Birūnī* below). The former use among Europeans is very early. And both the fibre and the rope made from it appear to have been exported to Europe in the middle of the 16th century. The word appears in early Arabic writers in the forms *ḳānbar* and *ḳanbār*, arising probably from some misreading of the diacritical points (for *ḳāiyar*, and *ḳaiyār*). The Portuguese adopted the word in the form *cairo*. The form *coir* seems to have been introduced by the English in the 18th century. [The *N.E.D.* gives *coire* in 1697; *coir* in 1779.] It was less likely to be used by the Portuguese because *coiro* in their language is 'leather.' And Barros (where quoted below) says allusively of the rope: "*parece feito de coiro* (leather) encolhendo e estendendo a vontade do mar," contracting and stretching with the movement of the sea.

c. 1030.—"The other islands are called *Dīva Ḳanbār* from the word **Ḳanbār** signifying the cord plaited from the fibre of the coco-tree with which they stitch their ships together."—*Al-Birūnī*, in *J. As.*, Ser. iv. tom. viii. 266.

c. 1346.—"They export ... cowries and **kanbar**; the latter is the name which they give to the fibrous husk of the coco-nut. ... They make of it twine to stitch together the planks of their ships, and the cordage is also exported to China, India, and Yemen. This *ḳanbar* is better than hemp."—*Ibn Batuta*, iv. 121.

1510.—"The Governor (Alboquerque) ... in Cananor devoted much care to the preparation of cables and rigging for the whole fleet, for what they had was all rotten from the rains in Goa River; ordering that all should be made of **coir** (*cairo*), of which there was great abundance in Cananor; because a Moor called Mamalle, a chief trader there, held the whole trade of the Maldive islands by a contract with the kings of the isles ... so that this Moor came to be called the Lord of the Maldives, and that all the **coir** that was used throughout India had to be bought from the hands of this Moor. ... The Governor, learning this, sent for the said Moor, and ordered him to abandon this island trade and to recall his factors. ... The Moor, not to lose such a profitable business, ... finally arranged with the Governor that the Isles should not be taken from him, and that he in return would furnish for the king 1000 *bakars* (*barés*) of coarse **coir**, and 1000 more of fine **coir**, each *bahar* weighing 4½ *quintals*; and this every year, and laid down at his own charges in Cananor and Cochym, gratis and free of all charge to the King (not being able to endure that the Portuguese should frequent the Isles at their pleasure)."—*Correa*, ii. 129–30.

1516.—"These islands make much cordage of palm-trees, which they call **cayro**."—*Barbosa*, 164.

c. 1530.—"They made ropes of **coir**, which is a thread which the people of the country make of the husks which the coco-nuts have outside."—*Correa*, by *Stanley*, 133.

1553.—"They make much use of this **cairo** in place of nails; for as it has this quality of recovering its freshness and swelling in the sea-water, they stitch with it the planking of a ship's sides, and reckon them then very secure."—*De Barros*, Dec. III. liv. iii. cap. 7.

1563.—"The first rind is very tough, and from it is made **cairo**, so called by the Malabars and by us, from which is made the cord for the rigging of all kinds of vessels."—*Garcia*, f. 67*v*.

1582.—"The Dwellers therein are Moores; which trade to Sofala in great Ships that have no Decks, nor nailes, but are sowed with **Cayro**."—*Castañeda* (by N. L.), f. 14*b*.

c. 1610.—"This revenue consists in ... **Cairo**, which is the cord made of the cocotree."—*Pyrard de Laval*, i. 172; [Hak. Soc. i. 250].

1673.—"They (the Surat people) have not only the **Cair**-yarn made of the Cocoe for cordage, but good Flax and Hemp."—*Fryer*, 121.

c. 1690.—"Externus nucis cortex putamen ambiens, quum exsiccatus, et stupae similis ... dicitur ... Malabarice **Cairo**, quod nomen ubique usurpatur ubi lingua Portugallica est in usu. ..."—*Rumphius*, i. 7.

1727.—"Of the Rind of the Nut they make **Cayar**, which are the Fibres of the Cask that environs the Nut spun fit to make Cordage and Cables for Shipping."—*A. Hamilton*, i. 296; [ed. 1744, i. 298].

[1773.—"... these they call **Kiar** Yarns."—*Ives*, 457.]

COLLECTOR, s. The chief administrative official of an Indian Zillah or District. The special duty of the office is, as the name intimates, the Collection of Revenue; but in India generally, with the exception of Bengal Proper, the Collector, also holding controlling magisterial powers, has been a small pro-consul, or kind of *préfet*. This is, however, much modified of late years by the greater definition of powers, and subdivision of duties everywhere. The title was originally no doubt a translation of *taḥṣīldār*. It was introduced, with the office, under Warren Hastings, but the Collector's duties were not formally settled till 1793, when these appointments were reserved to members of the covenanted Civil Service.

1772.—"The Company having determined to stand forth as *dewan*, the Supervisors, should now be designated **Collectors**."—Reg. of 14th May, 1772.

1773.—"Do not laugh at the formality with which we have made a law to change their name from *supervisors* to **collectors**. You know full well how much the world's opinion is governed by names."—*W. Hastings* to *Josias Dupre*, in *Gleig*, i. 267.

1785.—"The numerous **Collectors** with their assistants had hitherto enjoyed very moderate allowances from their employers."—*Letter in Colebrooke's Life*, p. 16.

1838.—"As soon as three or four of them get together they speak about nothing but 'employment' and 'promotion' ... and if left to themselves, they sit and conjugate the verb 'to collect': 'I am a **Collector**—He was a *Collector*—We shall be *Collectors*—You ought to be a *Collector*—They would have been *Collectors*.'"—*Letters from Madras*, 146.

1848.—"Yet she could not bring herself to suppose that the little grateful gentle governess would dare to look up to such a magnificent personage as the **Collector** of Boggleywallah."—*Thackeray, Vanity Fair*, ch. iv.

1871.—"There is no doubt a decay of discretionary administration throughout India ... it may be taken for granted that in earlier days **Collectors** and Commissioners changed their rules far oftener than does the Legislature at present."—*Maine, Village Communities*, 214.

1876.—"These 'distinguished visitors' are becoming a frightful nuisance; they think that **Collectors** and Judges have nothing to do but to act as their guides, and that Indian officials have so little work, and suffer so much from *ennui*, that even ordinary thanks for hospitality are unnecessary; they take it all as their right."—Ext. of a *Letter from India*.

COLLEGE-PHEASANT, s. An absurd enough corruption of *kālij*; the name in the Himālaya about Simla and Mussooree for the birds of the genus *Gallophasis* of Hodgson, intermediate between the pheasants and the Jungle-fowls. "The group is composed of at least three species, two being found in the Himalayas, and one in Assam, Chittagong and Arakan." (*Jerdon*).

[1880.—"These, with **kalege** pheasants, afforded me some very fair sport."—*Ball, Jungle Life* 538.

[1882.—"Jungle-fowl were plentiful, as well as the black **Khalege** pheasant."—*Sanderson, Thirteen Years among Wild Beasts*, 147.]

COLLERY, n.p. The name given to a non-Aryan race inhabiting part of the country east of Madura. Tam. *kallar*, 'thieves.' They are called in Nelson's *Madura*, [Pt. ii. 44 *seqq.*] *Kallans*; *Kallan* being the singular, *Kallar* plural.

1763.—"The Polygar Tondiman ... likewise sent 3000 **Colleries**; these are a people who, under several petty chiefs, inhabit the woods between Trichinopoly and Cape Comorin; their name in their own language signifies Thieves, and justly describes their general character."—*Orme*, i. 208.

c. 1785.—"**Colleries**, inhabitants of the woods under the Government of the Tondiman."—*Carraccioli, Life of Clive*, iv. 561.

1790.—"The country of the **Colleries** ... extends from the sea coast to the confines of Madura, in a range of sixty miles by fifty-five."—*Cal. Monthly Register* or *India Repository*, i. 7.

COLLERY-HORN, s. This is a long brass horn of hideous sound, which is often used at native funerals in the Peninsula, and has come to be called, absurdly enough, *Cholera-horn!*

[1832.—"*Toorree* or *Toorrtooree*, commonly designated by Europeans **collery horn**, consists of three pieces fixed into one another, of a semicircular shape."—*Herklots, Qanoon-e-Islam*, ed. 1863, p. liv. App.]

1879.—"... an early start being necessary, a happy thought struck the Chief Commissioner, to have the Amildar's **Cholera-horn** men out at that hour to sound the reveillé, making the round of the camp."—*Madras Mail*, Oct. 7.

COMPETITION-WALLAH, s. A hybrid of English and Hindustani, applied in modern Anglo-Indian colloquial to members of the Civil Service who have entered it by the competitive system first introduced in 1856. The phrase was probably the invention of one of the older or Haileybury members of the same service. These latter, whose nominations were due to interest, and who were bound together by the intimacies and *esprit de corps* of a common college, looked with some disfavour upon the children of Innovation. The name was readily taken up in India, but its familiarity in England is probably due in great part to the "Letters of a **Competition-wala**," written by one who had no real claim to the title, Sir G. O. Trevelyan, who was later on member for Hawick Burghs, Chief Secretary for Ireland, and author of the excellent *Life* of his uncle, Lord Macaulay.

The second portion of the word, *wālā*, is properly a Hindi adjectival affix, corresponding in a general way to the Latin *-arius*. Its usual employment as affix to a substantive makes it frequently denote "agent, doer, keeper, man, inhabitant, master, lord, possessor, owner," as Shakespear vainly tries to define it, and as in Anglo-Indian usage is popularly assumed to be its meaning. But this kind of denotation is incidental; there is no real limitation to such meaning. This is demonstrable from such phrases as *Kābul-wālā ghoṛā*, 'the Kabulian horse,' and from the common form of village nomenclature in the Panjāb, *e.g.* *Mīr-Khān-wālā*, *Ganda-Singh-wālā*, and so forth, implying the village established by Mir-Khan or Ganda-Singh. In the three immediately following quotations, the second and third exhibit a strictly idiomatic use of *wālā*, the first an incorrect English use of it.

1785.—

"Tho' then the Bostonians made such a fuss,
Their example ought not to be followed by us,
But I wish that a band of good Patriot-**wallahs** ..."—In *Seton-Karr*, i. 93.

In this year Tippoo Sahib addresses a rude letter to the Nawāb of Shānūr (or Savanūr) as "The Shahnoor**wâlah**."—*Select Letters of Tippoo*, 184.

1814.—"Gungadhur Shastree is a person of great shrewdness and talent. ... Though a very learned shastree, he affects to be quite an Englishman, walks fast, talks fast, interrupts and contradicts, and calls the Peshwa and his ministers 'old fools' and ... 'dam rascals.' He mixes English words with everything he says, and will say of some one (Holkar for instance): *Bkot tricks***walla** *tha, laiken barra akulkund*, Kukhye *tha*, ('He was very tricky, but very sagacious; he was cock-eyed')."—*Elphinstone*, in *Life*, i. 276.

1853.—"'No, I'm a Suffolk-**walla**.'"—*Oakfield*, i. 66.

1864.—"The stories against the **Competition-wallahs**, which are told and fondly believed by the Haileybury men, are all founded more or less on the want of *savoir faire*. A collection of these stories would by a curious proof of the credulity of the human mind on a question of class against class."—*Trevelyan*, p. 9.

1867.—"From a deficiency of civil servants ... it became necessary to seek reinforcements, not alone from Haileybury, ... but from new recruiting fields whence volunteers might be obtained ... under the pressure of necessity, such an exceptional measure was sanctioned by Parliament. Mr. Elliot, having been nominated as a candidate by Campbell Marjoribanks, was the first of the since celebrated list of the **Competition-wallahs**."—Biog. Notice prefixed to vol. i. of *Dowson's Ed. of Elliot's Historians of India*, p. xxviii.

The exceptional arrangement alluded to in the preceding quotation was authorised by 7 Geo. IV. cap. 56. But it did not involve competition; it only authorised a system by which writerships could be given to young men who had not been at Haileybury College, on their passing certain test examinations, and they were ranked according to their merit in passing such examinations, but below the writers who had left Haileybury at the preceding half-yearly examination. The first examination under this system was held 29th March, 1827, and Sir H. M. Elliot headed the list. The system continued in force for live years, the last examination being held in April, 1832. In all 83 civilians were nominated in this way, and, among other well-known names, the list included H. Torrens, Sir H. B. Harington, Sir R. Montgomery, Sir J. Cracroft Wilson, Sir T. Pycroft, W. Tayler, the Hon. E. Drummond.

1878—"The **Competition-Wallah**, at home on leave or retirement, dins perpetually into our ears the greatness of India. ... We are asked to feel awestruck and humbled at the fact that Bengal alone has 66 millions of inhabitants. We are invited to experience an awful thrill of sublimity when we learn that the area of Madras far exceeds that of the United Kingdom."—*Sat. Rev.*, June 15, p. 750.

***COMPOUND**, s. The enclosed ground, whether garden or waste, which surrounds an Anglo-Indian house. Various derivations have been suggested for this word, but its history is very obscure. The following are the principal suggestions that have been made:—[1]

(*a.*) That it is a corruption of some supposed Portuguese word.

(*b.*) That it is a corruption of the French *campagne*.

(*c.*) That it is a corruption of the Malay word *kampung*, as first (we believe) indicated by Mr. John Crawfurd.

(**a.**) The Portuguese origin is assumed by Bishop Heber in passages quoted below. In one he derives it from *campaña* (for which, in modern Portuguese at least, we should read *campanha*); but *campanha* is not used in such a sense. It seems to be used only for 'a campaign,' or for the Roman *Campagna*. In the other passage he derives it from *campao* (*sic*), but there is no such word.

It is also alleged by Sir Emerson Tennent (*infra*), who suggests *campinho*; but this, meaning 'a small plain,' is not used for compound. Neither is the latter word, nor

1 On the origin of this word for a long time different opinious were held by my lamented friend Burnell and by me. And when we printed a few speciments in the *Indian Antiquary*, our different arguments were given in brief (see *I. A.*, July 1879, pp. 202, 203). But at a later date he was much disposed to come round to the other view, insomuch that in a letter of Sept. 21, 1881, he says: "*Compound* can, I think, after all, be Malay *Kampong*; take these lines from a Malay poem"—then giving the lines which I have transcribed on the following page. I have therefore had no scruple in giving the same unity to this article that had been unbroken in almost all other cases.—H. Y.

any word suggestive of it, used among the Indo-Portuguese.

In the early Portuguese histories of India (*e.g. Castanheda*, iii. 436, 442; vi. 3) the words used for what we term *compound*, are *jardim, patio, horta*. An examination of all the passages of the Indo-Portuguese Bible, where the word might be expected to occur, affords only *horta*.

There is a use of *campo* by the Italian Capuchin P. Vincenzo Maria (Roma, 1672), which we thought at first to be analogous: "Gionti alla porta della città (Aleppo) ... arrivatial *Campo* de' Francesi; doue è la Dogana ..." (p. 475). We find also in Rauwolff's *Travels* (c. 1573), as published in English by the famous John Ray: "Each of these nations (at Aleppo) have their peculiar *Champ* to themselves, commonly named after the Master that built it ..."; and again: "When ... the *Turks* have washed and cleansed themselves, they go into their Chappells, which are in the Middle of their great *Camps* or *Carvatschars* ..." (p. 84 and p. 259 of Ray's 2nd edition). This use of *Campo*, and *Champ*, has a curious kind of analogy to *compound*, but it is probably only a translation of *Maidān* or some such Oriental word.

(**b.**) As regards *campagne*, which once commended itself as probable, it must be observed that nothing like the required sense is found among the seven or eight classes of meaning assigned to the word in *Littré*.

The word *campo* again in the Portuguese of the 16th century seems to mean always, or nearly always, a *camp*. We have found only one instance in those writers of its use with a meaning in the least suggestive of *compound*, but in this its real meaning is 'site': "queymou a cidade toda ate não ficar mais que ho *campo* em que estevera." ("They burned the whole city till nothing remained but the site on which it stood"—*Castanheda*, vi. 130). There is a special use of *campo* by the Portuguese in the Further East, alluded to in the quotation from Pallegoix's *Siam*, but that we shall see to be only a representation of the Malay *Kampung*. We shall come back upon it. [See quotation from *Correa*, with note, under FACTORY.]

(**c.**) The objection raised to *kampung* as the origin of *compound* is chiefly that the former word is not so used in Java by either Dutch or natives, and the author of *Max Havelaar* expresses doubt if *compound* is a Malay or Javanese word at all (pp. 360–361). *Erf.* is the usual word among the Dutch. In Java *kampung* seems to be used only for a native village, or for a particular ward or quarter of a town.

But it is impossible to doubt that among the English in our Malay settlements **compound** is used in this sense in speaking English, and *kampung* in speaking Malay. *Kampung* is also used by the Malays themselves, in our settlements, in this sense. All the modern dictionaries that we have consulted give this sense among others. The old *Dictionarium Malaico-Latinum* of David Haex (Romae, 1631) is a little vague:

"**Campon**, coniunctio, vel conuentus. Hinc viciniae et parua loca, *campon* etiam appellantur."

Crawfurd (1852): "**Kampung** ... an enclosure, a space fenced in; a village; a quarter or subdivision of a town."

Favre (1875): "Maison avec **un** terrain qui l'entoure."

Pijnappel (1875), *Maleisch-Hollandisch Woordenboek*: "**Kampoeng**—Omheind Erf, Wijk, Buurt, Kamp," *i.e.* "Ground hedged round, village, hamlet, *camp*."

And also, let it be noted, the Javanese Dict. of *P. Jansz* (*Javaansch-Nederlandsch Woordenboek*, Samarang, 1876): "**Kampoeng**—Omheind erf van Woningen; wijk die onder een hoofd staat," *i.e.* "Enclosed ground of dwellings: village which is under one Headman."

Marre, in his *Kata-Kata Malayou* (Paris, 1875), gives the following expanded definition: "Village palissadé, ou, dans une ville, quartier séparé et généralement clos, occupé par des gens de même nation, Malays, Siamois, Chinois, Bouguis, &c. Ce mot signifie proprement un enclos, une enciente, et par extension quartier clos, faubourg, ou village palissadé. Le mot *Kampong* désigne parfois aussi une maison d'une certaine importance avec le terrain clos qui en depend, et qui l'entoure" (p. 95).

We take Marsden last (*Malay Dictionary*, 1812) because he gives an illustration: "**Kampong**, an enclosure, a place surrounded with a paling; a fenced or fortified village; a quarter, district, or suburb of a city; a collection of buildings. *Membûat* [to make] *rumah* [house] *serta dañgan* [together with] **kampong**-*nia* [compound thereof], to erect a house with its enclosure ... *Ber-Kampong*, to assemble, come together; *meñgampong*, to collect, to bring together." The Reverse Dictionary gives: "YARD, *alaman*, **Kampong**." [See also many further references much to the same effect in Scott, *Malayan Words*, p. 123 *seqq.*]

In a Malay poem given in the *Journal of the Ind. Archipelago*, vol i. p. 44, we have these words:—

"*Trúsláh ka* **kampong** *s'orange Saudágar.*"
["Passed to the *kampong* of a Merchant."]

and

"*Titáh bágindú rajá sultáni*
Kámpong *śiápá garángun íní.*"
["Thus said the Prince, the Raja Sultani,
Whose *kampong* may this be?"]

These explanations and illustrations render it almost unnecessary to add in corroboration that a friend who held office in the Straits for twenty years assures us that the word **kampung** is habitually used, in the Malay there spoken, as the equivalent of the Indian **compound**. If this was the case 150 years ago in the English settlements at Bencoolen and elsewhere (and we know from Marsden that it *was* so 100 years ago), it does not matter whether such a use of *kampung* was correct or not, *compound* will have been a natural corruption of it. Mr. E. C. Baber, who lately spent some time in our Malay settlements on his way from China, tells me (H. Y.) that the frequency with which he heard *kampung* applied to the 'compound,' convinced him of this etymology, which he had before doubted greatly.

It is not difficult to suppose that the word, if its use originated in our Malay factories and settlements, should have spread to the continental Presidencies, and so over India.

Our factories in the Archipelago were older than any of our settlements in India Proper. The factors and writers were frequently moved about, and it is conceivable that a word so much wanted (for no English word now in use *does* express the idea satisfactorily) should have found ready acceptance. In fact the word, from like causes, *has* spread to the ports of China and to the missionary and mercantile stations in tropical Africa, East and West, and in Madagascar.

But it may be observed that it was possible that the word *kampung* was itself originally a corruption of the Port. *campo*, taking the meaning first of *camp*, and thence of an enclosed area, or rather that in some less definable way the two words reacted on each other. The Chinese quarter at Batavia—*Kampong Tzina*—is commonly called in Dutch '*het Chinesche* Kamp' or '*het* Kamp *der Chinezen*.' *Kampung* was used at Portuguese Malacca in this way at least 270 years ago, as the quotation from Godinho de Eredia shows. The earliest Anglo-Indian example of the word **compound** is that of 1679 (below). In a quotation from Dampier (1688) under **Cot**, where *compound* would come in naturally, he says '*yard*.'

1613.—(At Malacca). "And this settlement is divided into 2 parishes, S. Thomé and S. Stephen, and that part of S. Thomé called **Campon** *Chelim* extends from the shore of the *Jaos* bazar to N.W., terminating at the Stone Bastion; and in this dwell the *Chelis* of Coromandel. ... And the other part of S. Stephen's, called **Campon** *China*, extends from the said shore of the *Jaos* Bazar, and mouth of the river to the N.E., ... and in this part, called **Campon** *China*, dwell the *Chincheos* ... and foreign traders, and native fishermen."—*Godinho, de Eredia*, **i. 6.** In the plans given by this writer, we find different parts of the city marked accordingly, as **Campon** *Chelim*, **Campon** *China*, **Campon** *Bendara* (the quarter where the native magistrate, the **Bendāra** lived).

1679.—(At Pollicull near Madapollam), "There the Dutch have a Factory of a large **Compounde**, where they dye much blew cloth, having above 300 jars set in the ground for that work; also they make many of their best paintings there."—*Fort St. Geo. Consns.* (on Tour), April 14. In *Notes and Extracts*, Madras 1871.

1696.—"The 27th we began to unlade, and come to their custom-houses, of which there are *three*, in a *square* **Compound** of about 100 paces over each way. ... The goods being brought and set in *two Rows* in the middle of the *square* are one by one opened before the *Mandareens*."—*Mr. Bowyear's Journal at Cochin China*, dated Foy-Foe, April 30. *Dalrymple, Or. Rep.* i. 79.

1772.—"YARD (before or behind a house), Aungâun. Commonly called a **Compound**."—Vocabulary in *Hadley's Grammar*, 129. (See under MOORS.)

1781.—

"In common usage here a *chit*
Serves for our business or our wit.
Bankshal's a place to lodge our ropes,
And Mango orchards all are *Topes*.
Godown usurps the ware-house place,
Compound denotes each walled space.
To *Dufterkhanna*, *Ottor*, *Tanks*,
The English language owes no thanks;
Since Office, Essence, Fish-pond shew
We need not words so harsh and new.

Much more I could such words expose,
But *Ghauts* and *Dawks* the list shall close;
Which in plain English is no more
Than Wharf and Post expressed before."
India Gazette, March 3.

"... will be sold by Public Auction ... all that Brick Dwelling-house, Godowns, and **Compound**."—*Ibid.*, April 21.

1788.—"**Compound**—The court-yard belonging to a house. A corrupt word."—The *Indian Vocabulary*, London, Stockdale.

1793.—"To be sold by Public Outcry ... the House, Out Houses, and **Compound**," &c.—*Bombay Courier*, Nov. 2.

1810.—"The houses (at Madras) are usually surrounded by a field or **compound**, with a few trees or shrubs, but it is with incredible pains that flowers or fruit are raised."—*Maria Graham*, 124.

"When I entered the great gates, and looked around for my palankeen ... and when I beheld the beauty and extent of the **compound** ... I thought that I was no longer in the world that I had left in the East."—*An Account of Bengal, and of a Visit to Government House* (at Calcutta) *by Ibrahim the son of Candu the Merchant, ibid.*, p. 198. This is a Malay narrative translated by Dr. Leyden. Very probably the word translated **compound** was *kampung*, but that cannot be ascertained.

1811.—"Major Yule's attack was equally spirited, but after routing the enemy's force at **Campong** Malayo, and killing many of them, he found the bridge on fire, and was unable to penetrate further."—*Sir S. Auchmuty's Report of the Capture of Fort Cornelis.*

c. 1817.—"When they got into the **compound**, they saw all the ladies and gentlemen in the verandah waiting."—*Mrs. Sherwood's Stories*, ed. 1863, p. 6.

1824.—"He then proceeded to the rear **compound** of the house, returned, and said, 'It is a tiger, sir.'"—*Seely, Wonders of Ellora*, ch. i.

"... The large and handsome edifices of Garden Reach, each standing by itself in a little woody lawn (a '**compound**' they call it here, by an easy corruption from the Portuguese word *campaña* ...)."—*Heber*, ed. 1844, i. 28.

1848.—"Lady O'Dowd, too, had gone to her bed in the nuptial chamber, on the ground floor, and had tucked her mosquito curtains round her fair form, when the guard at the gates of the commanding officer's **compound** beheld Major Dobbin, in the moonlight, rushing towards the house with a swift step."—*Vanity Fair*, ed. 1867, ii. 93.

1860.—"Even amongst the English, the number of Portuguese terms in daily use is remarkable. The grounds attached to a house are its '**compound**,' *campinko*."—*Emerson Tennent, Ceylon*, ii. 70.

[1869.—"I obtained the use of a good-sized house in the **Campong** Sirani (or Christian village)."—*Wallace, Malay Archip.*, ed. 1890, p. 256.]

We have found this word singularly transformed in a passage extracted from a modern novel:

1877.—"When the Rebellion broke out at other stations in India, I left our own **compost**."—*Sat. Review*, Feb. 3, p. 148.

A little learning is a dangerous thing!

The following shows the adoption of the word in West Africa.

1880.—From West Afr. Mission, Port Lokkoh, Mr. A. Burchaell writes: "Every evening we go out visiting and preaching the Gospel to our Timneh friends in their **compounds**."—*Proceedings of C. M. Society* for 1878–9, p. 14.

***CONGEE**, s. In use all over India for the water in which rice has been boiled. The article being used as one of invalid diet, the word is sometimes applied to such slops generally. *Congee* also forms the usual starch of Indian washermen. [A *conjee*-cap was a sort of starched night-cap, and Mr. Draper, the husband of Sterne's Eliza, had it put on by Mrs. Draper's rival when he took his afternoon nap. (*Douglas, Glimpses of Old Bombay*, pp. 86, 201.)] It is from the Tamil *kanjī*, 'boilings.' *Congee* is known to Horace, though reckoned, it would seem, so costly a remedy that the miser patient would as life die as be plundered to the extent implied in its use:

"... Hunc medicus multum celer atque fidelis
Excitat hoc pacto ...
... 'Agedum; sume hoc *ptisanarium Oryzae*.'
'Quanti emptae?' 'Parvo.' '*Quanti* ergo.'
'Octussibus.' 'Eheu!
Quid refert, morbo, an furtis pereamve
rapinis?'"
Sat. II. iii. 147 *seqq.*

c. A.D. 70.—(Indi) "maxime quidem **oryza** gaudent, ex qua **tisanam** conficiunt quam reliqui mortales ex hordeo."—*Pliny*, xviii. § 13.

1563.—"They give him to drink the water squeezed out of rice with pepper and cummin (which they call **canje**)."—*Garcia*, f. 76*b*

1578.—"... **Canju**, which is the water from the boiling of rice, keeping it first for some hours till it becomes acid. ..."—*Acosta, Tractado*, 56.

1631.—"Potus quotidianus itaque sit decoctum oryzae quod **Candgie** Indi vocant."—*Jac. Bontii*, Lib. II. cap. iii.

1672.—"... la **cangia**, ordinaria colatione degl' Indiani ... quale colano del riso mal cotto."—*P. Vinc. Maria*, 3rd ed., 379.

1673.—"They have ... a great smooth Stone on which they beat their Cloaths till clean; and if for Family use, starch them with **Congee**."—*Fryer*, 200.

1680.—"Le dejeûné des noirs est ordinairement du **Cangé**, qui est une eau de ris epaisse."—*Dellon, Inquisition at Goa*, 136.

1796.—"**Cagni**, boiled rice water, which the Europeans call **Cangi**, is given free of all expenses, in order that the traveller may quench his thirst with a cooling and wholesome beverage."—*P. Paulinus, Voyage*, p. 70.

"Can't drink as it is hot, and can't throw away as it is **Kanji**."—*Ceylon Proverb, Ind. Ant.* i. 59.

CONGEE-HOUSE, CONJEEHOUSE, s. The 'cells' (or temporary lock-up) of a regiment in India; so called from the traditionary regimen of the inmates; [in N. India commonly applied to a cattle-pound].

1835.—"All men confined for drunkenness should, if possible, be confined by themselves in the **Congee-House**, till sober."—G. O., quoted in *Mawson's Records of the Indian Command of Sir C. Napier*, 101 note.

CONSOO-HOUSE, n.p. At Canton this was a range of buildings adjoining the foreign Factories, called also the 'Council Hall' of the foreign Factories. It was the property of the body of Hong merchants, and was the place of meeting of these merchants among themselves, or with the chiefs of the Foreign houses, when there was need for such conference (see *Fankwae*, p. 23). The name is probably a corruption of 'Council.' Bp. Moule, however, says: "The name is likely to have come from *kung-su*, the public hall, where a *kung-sz'*, a 'public company,' or guild, meets."

CONSUMAH, KHANSAMA, s. P. *Khānsāmān*; 'a house-steward.' In Anglo-Indian households in the Bengal Presidency, this is the title of the chief table servant and provider, now always a Mahommedan. [See BUTLER.] The literal meaning of the word is 'Master of the household gear'; it is not connected with *khwān*, 'a tray,' as Wilson suggests. The analogous word *Mīr-sāmān* occurs in *Elliot*, vii. 153. The Anglo-Indian form **Consumer** seems to have been not uncommon in the 18th century, probably with a spice of intention. From tables quoted in *Long*, 182, and in *Seton-Karr*, i. 95, 107, we see that the wages of a "**Consumah**, Christian, Moor, or Gentoo," were at Calcutta, in 1759, 5 rupees a month, and in 1785, 8 to 10 rupees.

[1609.—"Emersee Nooherdee being called by the **Cauncamma**."—*Danvers, Letters*, i. 24.]

c. 1664.—"Some time after ... she chose for her **Kane-saman**, that is, her Steward, a certain *Persian* called *Nazerkan*, who was a young Omrah, the handsomest and most accomplished of the whole Court."—*Bernier*, E.T., p. 4; [ed. *Constable*, p. 13].

1712.—"They were brought by a great circuit on the River to the **Chansamma** or Steward (Dispenser) of the aforesaid *Mahal*."—*Valentijn*, iv. (*Suratte*) 288.

1759.—"DUSTUCK *or* ORDER, *under the* **Chan Sumaun**, *or* Steward's *Seal, for the Honourable Company's holding the King's* [*i.e.* the Great Mogul's] *fleet*."

* * * * *

"At the back of this is the seal of Zecah al Doulat Tidaudin Caun Bahadour, who is **Caun Samaun**, or Steward to his Majesty, whose prerogative it is to grant this Order."—*R. Owen Cambridge*, pp. 231 *seq.*

1788.—"After some deliberation I asked the **Khansaman**, what quantity was remaining of the clothes that had been brought from Iran to camp for sale, who answered that there were 15,000 jackets, and 12,000 pairs of long drawers."—*Mem. of Khojeh Abdulkurreem*, tr. by *Gladwin*, 55.

1810.—"The **Kansamah** may be classed with the house-steward, and butler; both of which offices appear to unite in this servant."—*Williamson, V. M.*, i. 199.

1831.—"I have taught my **khansama** to make very light iced punch."—*Jacquemont, Letters*, E.T., ii. 104.

COOK-ROOM, s. Kitchen; in Anglo-Indian establishments always detached from the house.

1758.—"We will not in future admit of any expenses being defrayed by the Company either under the head of **cook-rooms**, gardens, or other expenses whatever."—*The Court's Letter*, March 3, in *Long*, 130.

1878.—"I was one day watching an old female monkey who had a young one by her side to whom she was giving small bits of a piece of bread which she had evidently just received from my **cook-room**."—*Life in the Mofussil*, ii. 44.

***COOLY**, s. A hired labourer, or burden-carrier; and, in modern days especially, a labourer induced to emigrate from India, or from China, to labour in the plantations of Mauritius, Réunion, or the West Indies, sometimes under circumstances, especially in French colonies, which have brought the cooly's condition very near to slavery. In Upper India the term has frequently a specific application to the lower class of labourer who carries earth, bricks, &c., as distinguished from the skilled workman, and even from the digger.

The original of the word appears to have been a *nomen gentile*, the name (**Kolī**) of a race or caste in Western India, who have long performed such offices as have been mentioned, and whose savagery, filth, and general degradation attracted much attention in former times, [see *Hamilton, Descr. of Hindostan* (1820), i. 609]. The application of the word would thus be analogous to that which has rendered the name of a *Slav*, captured and made a bondservant, the word for such a bondservant in many European tongues. According to Dr. H. V. Carter the *Kolīs* proper are a true hill-people, whose especial locality lies in the Western Ghāts, and in the northern extension of that range, between 18° and 24° N. lat. They exist in large numbers in Guzerat, and in the Konkan, and in the adjoining districts of the Deccan, but not beyond these limits (see *Ind. Antiquary*, ii. 154). [But they are possibly kinsfolk of the *Kols*, an important Dravidian race in Bengal and the N.W.P. (see *Risley, T. and C. of Bengal*, ii. 101; *Crooke, T. C. of N.W.P.* iii. 294).] In the *Rās Mālā* [ed. 1878, p. 78 *seqq.*] the *Koolies* are spoken of as a tribe who lived long near the Indus, but who were removed to the country of the Null (the Nal, a brackish lake some 40 m. S.W. of Ahmedabad) by the goddess Hinglāj.

Though this explanation of the general use of the term *Cooly* is the most probable, the matter is perplexed by other facts which it is difficult to trace to the same origin. Thus in S. India there is a Tamil and Can. word *kūli* in common use, signifying 'hire' or 'wages,' which Wilson indeed regards as the true origin of *Cooly*. [Oppert (*Orig. Inhab. of Bharatavarsa*, p. 131) adopts the same view, and disputing the connection of *Cooly* with *Koli* or *Kol*, regards the word as equivalent to 'hired servant' and originating in the English Factories on the E. coast.] Also in both Oriental and Osmanli Turkish *kol* is a word for a slave, whilst in the latter also *kūleh* means 'a male slave, a bondsman' (*Redhouse*). *Khol* is in Tibetan also a word for a servant or slave (Note from A. Schiefner; see also Jäschke's *Tibetan Dict.*, 1881, p. 59). But with this the Indian term seems to have no connection. The familiar use of *Cooly* has extended to the Straits Settlements, Java, and China, as well as to all tropical and sub-tropical colonies, whether English or foreign.

In the quotations following, those in which the race is distinctly intended are marked with an *.

*1548.—"And for the duty from the **Colés** who fish at the sea-stakes and on the river of Bacaim. ..."—*S. Botelho, Tombo*, 155.

*1553.—"Soltan Badur ... ordered those pagans to be seized, and if they would not become Moors, to be flayed alive, saying that was all the black-mail the **Collijs** should get from Champanel."—*Barros*, Dec. IV. liv. v. cap. 7.

*1563.—"These **Colles** ... live by robbing and thieving at this day."—*Garcia*, f. 34.

*1584.—"I attacked and laid waste nearly fifty villages of the **Kolís** and Grassias, and I built forts in seven different places to keep these people in check."—*Ṭabaḳāt-i-Akbarī*, in *Elliot*, v. 447.

*1598.—"Others that yet dwell within the countrie called **Colles**: which *Colles* ... doe yet live by robbing and stealing. ..."—*Linschoten*, ch. xxvii.; [Hak. Soc. i. 166].

*1616.—"Those who inhabit the country villages are called **Coolees**; these till the ground and breed up cattle."—*Terry*, in *Purchas*; [ed. 1777, p. 180].

*"The people called **Collees** or **Quillees**."—In *Purchas*, i. 436.

1630.—"The husbandmen or inferior sort of people called the **Coulies**."—*Lord's Display*, &c., ch. xiii.

1638.—"He lent us horses to ride on, and **Cowlers** (which are Porters) to carry our goods."—*W. Bruton*, in Hakl. v. 49.

In this form there was perhaps an indefinite suggestion of the *cowl-staff* used in carrying heavy loads.

1644.—"In these lands of Damam the people who dwell there as His Majesty's Vassals are heathen, whom they call **Collis**, and all the *Padres* make great complaints that the owners of the *aldeas* do not look with favour on the conversion of these heathen **Collis**, nor do they consent to their being made Christians, lest there thus may be hindrance to the greater service which is rendered by them when they remain heathen."—*Bocarro* (*Port. MS.*).

*1659.—"To relate how I got away from those Robbers, the **Koullis** ... how we became good Friends by the means of my Profession of Physick ... I must not insist upon to describe."—*Bernier*, E.T., p. 30; [ed. *Constable*, 91].

*c. 1666.—"Nous rencontrâmes quantité de **Colys**, qui sont gens d'une Caste ou tribut des Gentils, qui n'ont point d'habitation arrêtée, mais qui vont de village en village et portent avec eux tout leur ménage."—*Thevenot*, v. 21.

*1673.—"The Inhabitants of Ramnagur are the Salvages called **Coolies**. ..."—*Fryer*, 161.

"**Coolies**, Frasses, and Holencores, are the Dregs of the People."—*Ibid*. 194.

1680.—"... It is therefore ordered forthwith that the drum be beat to call all **coolies**, carpenters. ..."—*Official Memo*. in *Wheeler*, i. 129.

*c. 1703.—"The Imperial officers ... sent ... ten or twelve *sardārs*, with 13,000 or 14,000 horse, and 7,000 or 8,000 trained **Kolís** of that country."—*Khāfi Khān*, in *Elliot*, vii. 375.

1711.—"The better sort of people travel in Palankeens, carry'd by six or eight **Cooleys**, whose Hire, if they go not far from Town, is threepence a Day each."—*Lockyer*, 26.

1726.—"**Coeli's**. Bearers of all sorts of Burdens, goods, Andols and Palankins. ..."—*Valentijn*, vol. v., *Names*, &c., 2.

*1727.—"Goga ... has had some Mud Wall Fortifications, which still defend them from the Insults of their Neighbours the **Coulies**."—*A. Hamilton*, i: 141; [ed. 1744, i. 142].

1755.—"The Families of the **Coolies** sent to the Negrais complain that Mr. Brook has paid to the Head **Cooley** what money those who died there left behind them."—In *Long*, 54.

1785.—"... the officers were obliged to have their baggage transported upon men's heads over an extent of upwards of 800 miles, at the rate of *5l.* per month for every **couley** or porter employed."—*Carraccioli's L. of Clive*, i. 243 *seq*.

1789.—"If you should ask a common **cooly** or porter, what cast he is of, he will answer, the same as Master, *pariar-cast*."—*Munro's Narrative*, 29.

1791.—"... deux relais de vigoreux **coulis**, ou porteurs, de quatre hommes chacun. ..."—*B. de St. Pierre, La Chaumière Indienne*, 15.

[1798.—"The Resident hopes all distinctions between the **Cooley** and Portuguese inhabitants will be laid aside."—*Procl*. in *Logan, Malabar*, iii. 302.]

*1813.—"Gudgerah, a large populous town surrounded by a wall, to protect it from the depredations of the **Coolees**, who are a very insolent set among the numerous and probably indigenous tribes of free-booters, and robbers in this part of India."—*Forbes, Orient. Mem*. iii. 63; [2nd ed. ii. 160; also see i. 146].

1817.—"These (Chinese) emigrants are usually employed as **coolees** or labourers on their first arrival (in Java)."—*Raffles, H. of Jaca*, i. 205.

*1820.—"In the profession of thieving the **Koolees** may be said to act *con amore*. A **Koolee** of this order, meeting a defenceless person in a lane about dusk, would no more think of allowing him to pass unplundered than a Frenchman would a woman without bowing to her; it may be considered a point of honour of the caste."—*Tr. Lit. Soc. Bo*. iii. 335.

*1825.—"The head man of the village said he was a *Kholee*, the name of a degenerate race of Rajpoots in Guzerat, who from the low occupations in which they are generally employed have (under the corrupt name of **Coolie**) given a name, probably through the medium of the Portuguese, to bearers of burdens all over India."—*Heber*, ed. 1844, ii. 92.

1867.—"Bien que de race différente les **Coolies** et les Chinois sont comportés à peu-près de même."—*Quatrefages, Rapport sur le Progrès de l'Anthropologie*, 219.

1871.—"I have hopes for the **Coolies** in British Guiana, but it will be more sure and certain when the immigration system is based on better laws."—*Jenkins, The Coolie*.

1873.—"The appellant, the Hon. Julian Pauncefote, is the Attorney-General for the Colony (Hong Kong) and the respondent Hwoka-Sing is a **Coolie** or labourer, and a native of China."—*Report of Case before Jud. Com. of Privy Council*.

"A man (Col. Gordon) who had wrought such wonders with means so modest as a levy of **Coolies** ... needed, we may be sure, only to be put to the highest test to show how just those were who had marked him out in his Crimean days as a youth whose extraordinary genius for war could not be surpassed in the army that lay before Sebastopol."—*Sat. Review*, Aug. 16, 203.

1875.—"A long row of cottages, evidently pattern-built ... announced the presence of **Coolies**, Indian or Chinese."—*Palgrave, Dutch Guiana*, ch. i.

The word **Cooly** has passed into English thieves' jargon in the sense of 'a soldier' (v. *Slang Dict*.).

COPRAH, s. The dried kernel of the coconut, much used for the expression of its oil, and exported largely from the Malabar ports. The Portuguese probably took the word from the Malayāl. *koppara*, which is, however, apparently borrowed from the H. *khoprā*, of the same meaning. The latter is connected by some with *khapnā*, 'to dry up.' Shakespear however, more probably, connects *khoprā*, as well as *khoprī*, 'a skull, a shell,' and *khappar*, 'a skull,' with Skt. *kharpara*, having also the meaning of 'skull.' Compare with this a derivation which we have suggested (s.v.) as possible of **coco** from old Fr. and Span. *coque, coco*, 'a shell'; and with the slang use of *coco* there mentioned.

1563.—"And they also dry these cocos ... and these dried ones they call **copra**, and they carry them to Ormuz, and to the Balaghat."—*Garcia, Colloq.* f. 68*b*.

1578.—"The kernel of these cocos is dried in the sun, and is called **copra**. ... From this same *copra* oil is made in presses, as we make it from olives."—*Acosta*, 104.

1584.—"**Chopra**, from Cochin and Malabar. ..."—*Barret*, in *Hakl.* ii. 413.

1598.—"The other Oyle is prest out of the dried Cocus, which is called **Copra**. ..."—*Linschoten*, 101. See also (1602), *Couto*, Dec. I. liv. iv. cap. 8; (1606) *Gouvea*, f. 62*b*; [(1610) *Pyrard de Lacal*, Hak. Soc. ii. 384 (reading *kuppara* for *suppara*);] (c. 1690) *Rumphius, Herb. Amb.* i. 7.

1727.—"That tree (coco-nut) produceth ... **Copera**, or the Kernels of the Nut dried, and out of these Kernels there is a very clear Oil exprest."—*A. Hamilton*, i. 307; [ed. 1744, i. 308].

1860.—"The ordinary estimate is that one thousand full-grown nuts of Jaffna will yield 525 pounds of **Copra** when dried, which in turn will produce 25 gallons of cocoa-nut oil."—*Tennent, Ceylon*, ii. 531.

1878.—It appears from Lady Brassey's *Voyage in the Sunbeam* (5th ed. 248) that this word is naturalised in Tahiti.

1883.—"I suppose there are but few English people outside the trade who know what **copra** is; I will therefore explain:—it is the white pith of the ripe cocoa-nut cut into strips and dried in the sun. This is brought to the trader (at New Britain) in baskets varying from 3 to 20 lbs. in weight; the payment ... was a thimbleful of beads for each pound of copra. ... The nut is full of oil, and on reaching Europe the copra is crushed in mills, and the oil pressed from it ... half the oil sold as 'olive-oil' is really from the cocoa-nut."—*Wilfred Powell, Wanderings in a Wild Country*, p. 37.

COROMANDEL, n.p. A name which has been long applied by Europeans to the Northern Tamil Country, or (more comprehensively) to the eastern coast of the Peninsula of India from Pt. Calimere northward to the mouth of the Kistna, sometimes to Orissa. It corresponds pretty nearly to the *Maabar* of Marco Polo and the Mahommedan writers of his age, though that is defined more accurately as from C. Comorin to Nellore.

Much that is fanciful has been written on the origin of this name. Tod makes it *Kūrū-mandala*, the Realm of the Kūrūs (*Trans. R. As. Soc.* iii. 157). Bp. Caldwell, in the first edition of his *Dravidian Grammar*, suggested that European traders might have taken this familiar name from that of *Karumaṇal* ('black sand'), the name of a small village on the coast north of Madras, which is habitually pronounced and written *Coromandel* by European residents at Madras. [The same suggestion was made earlier (see. *Wilks, Hist. Sketches*, ed. 1869, i. 5, note)]. The learned author, in his second edition, has given up this suggestion, and has accepted that to which we adhere. But Mr. C. P. Brown, the eminent Telugu scholar, in repeating the former suggestion, ventures positively to assert: "The earliest Portuguese sailors pronounced this *Coromandel*, and called the whole coast by this name, which was unknown to the Hindus";[1] a passage containing in three lines several errors. Again, a writer in the *Ind. Antiquary* (i. 380) speaks of this supposed origin of the name as "pretty generally accepted," and proceeds to give an imaginative explanation of how it was propagated. These etymologies are founded on a corrupted form of the name, and the same remark would apply to *Kharamaṇḍalam*, the 'hot country,' which Bp. Caldwell mentions as one of the names given, in Telugu, to the eastern coast. Padre Paolino gives the name more accurately as *Ciola* (*i.e. Chola*) *maṇḍalam*, but his explanation of it as meaning the Country of *Cholam* (or *iuwārī—Sorghum vulgare*, Pers.) is erroneous. An absurd etymology is given by Teixeira (*Relacion de Harmuz*, 28; 1610). He writes: "*Choromãdel* or Choro Bãdel, *i.e.* Rice Fort, because of the great export of rice from thence." He apparently compounds H. *chaul, chāwal*, 'cooked rice' (!) and **bandel**, *i.e.* **bandar** 'harbour.' This is a very good type of the way etymologies are made by some people, and then confidently repeated.

The name is in fact **Chôṛamaṇḍala**, the

1 *J.R.A.S.*, N.S. v. 148. He had said the same in earlier writings, and was apparently the original author of this suggestion. [But see above.]

Realm of *Chôṛa*; this being the Tamil form of the very ancient title of the Tamil Kings who reigned at Tanjore. This correct explanation of the name was already given by D'Anville (see *Éclaircissemens*, p. 117), and by W. Hamilton in 1820 (ii. 405), by Ritter, quoting him in 1836 (*Erdkunde*, vi. 296); by the late M. Reinaud in 1845 (*Relation*, &c., i. lxxxvi.); and by Sir Walter Elliot in 1869 (*J. Ethnol. Soc.* N.S. i. 117). And the name occurs in the forms **Cholamaṇḍalam** or **Solamaṇḍalam** on the great Temple inscription of Tanjore (11th century), and in an inscription of A.D. 1101 at a temple dedicated to Varāhasvāmi near the Seven Pagodas. We have other quite analogous names in early inscriptions, *e.g.* *Ilamaṇḍalam* (Ceylon), *Cheramaṇḍalam*, *Tondaimaṇḍalam*, &c.

Chola, as the name of a Tamil people and of their royal dynasty appears as *Choda* in one of Asoka's inscriptions, and in the Telugu inscriptions of the Chālukya dynasty. Nor can we doubt that the same name is represented by *Σῶρα* of Ptolemy who reigned at Ἀρκατοῦ (Arcot), *Σώρ-ναζ* who regined at Ὄρθουρα (Wariūr), and the *Σῶραι νομάδες* who dwelt inland from the site of Madras.[1]

The word *Soli*, as applied to the Tanjore country, occurs in Marco Polo (Bk. iii. ch. 20), showing that *Chola* in some form was used in his day. Indeed *Soli* is used in Ceylon.[2] And although the *Choromandel* of Baldaeus and other Dutch writers is, as pronounced in their language, ambiguous or erroneous, Valentijn (1726) calls the country *Sjola*, and defines it as extending from Negapatam to Orissa, saying that it derived its name from a certain kingdom, and adding that *mandalam* is 'kingdom.'[3] So that this respectable writer had already distinctly indicated the true etymology of *Coromandel*.

Some old documents in Valentijn speak of the 'old city of Coromandel.' It is not absolutely clear what place was so called (probably by the Arabs in their fashion of calling a chief town by the name of the country), but the indications point almost certainly to Negapatam.[4]

The oldest European mention of the name is, we believe, in the *Roteiro de Vasco da Gama*, where it appears as **Chomandarla**. The short Italian narrative of Hieronymo da Sto. Stefano is, however, perhaps earlier still, and he curiously enough gives the name in exactly the modern form "Coromandel," though perhaps his *C* had originally a *cedilla* (*Ramusio*, i. f. 345*v.*). These instances suffice to show that the name was not given by the Portuguese. Da Gama and his companions knew the east coast only by hearsay, and no doubt derived their information chiefly from Mahommedan traders, through their "Moorish" interpreter. That the name was in familiar Mahommedan use at a later date may be seen from Rowlandson's Translation of the *Tohfat-ul-Mujāhidīn*, where we find it stated that the Franks had built fortresses "at Meelapoor (*i.e. Mailapur* or San Tomé) and Nagapatam, and other ports of **Solmundul**," showing that the name was used by them just as we use it (p. 153). Again (p. 154) this writer says that the Mahommedans of Malabar were cut off from extra-Indian trade, and limited "to the ports of Guzerat, the Concan, *Solmondul*, and the countries about Kaeel." At page 160 of the same work we have mention of "**Coromandel** and other parts," but we do not know how this is written in the original Arabic. Varthema (1510) has **Ciormandel**, *i.e. Chormandel*, but which Eden in his translation (1577, which probably affords the earliest English occurrence of the name) deforms into **Cyromandel** (f. 396*b*). [Albuquerque in his *Cartas* (see p. 135 for a letter of 1513) has **Choromandell** *passim*.] Barbosa has in the Portuguese edition of the Lisbon Academy, **Charamandel**; in the Span. MS. translated by Lord Stanley of Alderley, **Cholmendel** and *Cholmender*. D'Alboquerque's *Commentaries* (1557), Mendez Pinto (c. 1550) and Barros (1553) have **Choromandel**, and Garcia De Orta (1563) **Charamandel**. The ambiguity of the *ch*, soft in Portuguese and Spanish, but hard in Italian, seems to have led early

1 See Bp. Caldwell's *Comp. Gram.*, 18, 95, &c.

2 See *Tennent*, i. 395.

3 "This coast bears commonly the corrupted name of *Choromandel*, and is now called only thus; but the right name is *Sjola-mandalam*, after *Sjola*, a certain kingdom of that name, and *mandalam*, 'a kingdom,' one that used in the old times to be an independent and mighty empire."—*Val.* v. 2.

4 *e.g.* 1675.—"Hence the country ... has become very rich, wherefore the Portuguese were induced to build a town on the site of the old Gentoo (*Jentiefze*) city *Chiormandelan*."—Report on the Dutch Conquests in Ceylon and S. India, by *Rykloof Van Goens* in *Valentijn*, v. (Ceylon) 234.

to the corrupt form *Coromandel*, which we find in Parkes's *Mendoza* (1589), and **Coromandyll**, among other spellings, in the English version of Castanheda (1582). Cesare Federici has in the Italian (1587) **Chiaramandel** (probably pronounced soft in the Venetian manner), and the translation of 1599 has **Coromandel**. This form thenceforward generally prevails in English books, but not without exceptions. A Madras document of 1672 in Wheeler has **Cormandell**, and so have the early Bengal records in the India Office; Dampier (1689) has **Coromondel** (i. 509); Lockyer (1711) has "the Coast of **Cormandel**"; A. Hamilton (1727) **Chormondel** (i. 349); ed. 1744, i. 351; and a paper of about 1759, published by Dalrymple, has "**Choromandel** Coast" (*Orient. Repert.* i. 120–121). The poet Thomson has **Cormandel**:

"all that from the tract
Of woody mountains stretch'd through
gorgeous Ind
Fall on *Cormandel's* Coast or Malabar."
Summer.

The Portuguese appear to have adhered in the main to the correcter form **Choromandel**: *e.g. Archivio Port. Oriental*, fase. 3, p. 480, and *passim*. A Protestant Missionary Catechism, printed at Tranquebar in 1713 for the use of Portuguese schools in India has: "na costa dos Malabaros que se chama **Cormandel**." Bernier has "la côte de **Koromandel**" (Amst. ed. ii. 322). W. Hamilton says it is written *Choramandel* in the Madras Records until 1779, which is substantially correct. In the MS. "List of Persons in the Service of the Rt. Honble. E. I. Company in Fort St. George and other places on the Coast of **Choromandell**," preserved in the Indian Office, that spelling continues down to 1778. In that year it is changed to **Coromandel**. In the French translation of Ibn Batuta (iv. 142) we find *Coromandel*, but this is only the perverse and misleading manner of Frenchmen, who make Julius Caesar cross from "France" to "England." The word is *Ma'bar* in the original. [Alboquerque (*Comm.* Hak. Soc. i. 41) speaks of a violent squall under the name of *vara de Coromandel.*]

CORPORAL FORBES, s. A soldier's grimly jesting name for *Cholera Morbus*.

1829.—"We are all pretty well, only the regiment is sickly, and a great quantity are in hospital with the **Corporal Forbes**, which carries them away before they have time to die, or say who comes there."—In *Shipp's Memoirs*, ii. 218.

CORRAL, s. An enclosure as used in Ceylon for the capture of wild elephants, corresponding to the **Keddah** of Bengal. The word is Sp. *corral*, 'a court,' &c., Port. *curral*, 'a cattle-pen, a paddock.' The Americans have the same word, direct from the Spanish, in common use for a cattle-pen; and they have formed a verb 'to *corral*,' *i.e.* to enclose in a pen, to pen. The word *kraal* applied to native camps and villages at the Cape of Good Hope appears to be the same word introduced there by the Dutch. The word *corral* is explained by Bluteau: "A receptacle for any kind of cattle, with railings round it and no roof, in which respect it differs from *Corte*, which is a building with a roof." Also he states that the word is used especially in churches for *septum nobilium feminarum*, a pen for ladies.

c. 1270.—"When morning came, and I rose and had heard mass, I proclaimed a council to be held in the open space (**corral**) between my house and that of Montaragon."—*Chron. of James of Aragon*, tr. by *Foster*, i. 65.

1404.—"And this mosque and these chapels were very rich, and very finely wrought with gold and azure, and enamelled tiles (*azulejos*); and within there was a great **corral**, with trees and tanks of water."—*Clarijo*, § cv. Comp. *Markham*, 123.

1672.—"About Mature they catch the Elephants with **Coraals**" (*Coralen*, but sing. *Coraal*).—*Baldaeus, Ceylon*, 168.

1860.—In Emerson Tennent's *Ceylon*, Bk. VIII. ch. iv. the **corral** is fully described.

1880.—"A few hundred pounds expended in houses, and the erection of **coralls** in the neighbourhood of a permanent stream will form a basis of operations." (In Colorado.)—*Fortnightly Rev.*, Jan., 125.

COSS, s. The most usual popular measure of distance in India, but like the *mile* in Europe, and indeed like the mile within the British Islands up to a recent date, varying much in different localities.

The Skt. word is *krośa*, which also is a measure of distance, but originally signified 'a call,' hence the distance at which a man's call can be heard.[1]

1 "It is characteristic of this region (central forests of Ceylon) that in traversing the forest

In the Pali vocabulary called *Abhidhānappadīpikā*, which is of the 12th century, the word appears in the form *koss*; and nearly this, *kos*, is the ordinary Hindi. *Kuroh* is a Persian form of the word, which is often found in Mahommedan authors and in early travellers. These latter (English) often write **course.** It is a notable circumstance that, according to Wrangell, the Yakuts of N. Siberia reckon distance by *kiosses* (a word which, considering the Russian way of writing Turkish and Persian words, must be identical with *kos*). With them this measure is "indicated by the time necessary to cook a piece of meat." *Kioss* is = to about 5 *versts*, or 1⅔ miles, in hilly or marshy country, but on plain ground to 7 *versts*, or 2⅓ miles.[1] The Yakuts are a Turk people, and their language is a Turki dialect. The suggestion arises whether the form *kos* may not have come with the Mongols into India, and modified the previous *krośa*? But this is met by the existence of the word *kos* in Pali, as mentioned above.

In ancient Indian measurement, or estimation, 4 *krośas* went to the *yojana*. Sir H. M. Elliot deduced from distances in the route of the Chinese pilgrim Fa-hian that the *yojana* of his age was as nearly as possible 7 miles. Cunningham makes it 7½ or 8, Fergusson 6; but taking Elliot's estimate as a mean, the ancient *kos* would be 1¾ miles.

The *kos* as laid down in the *Āīn* [ed. *Jarrett*, iii. 414] was of 5000 *gaz*. The official decision of the British Government has assigned the length of Akbar's *Ilāhī gaz* as 33 inches, and this would make Akbar's *kos* = 2 m. 4 f. 183⅓ yards. Actual measurement of road distances between 5 pair of Akbar's *kos-minārs*,[2] near Delhi, gave a mean of 2 m. 4 f. 158 yards.

they calculate their march, not by the eye, or by measures of distance, but by sounds. Thus a '*dog's cry*' indicates a quarter of a mile; a '*cock's crow*,' something more; and a '*hoo*' implies the space over which a man can be heard when shouting that particular monosyllable at the pitch of his voice.—*Tennent's Ceylon*, ii. 582. In S. Canara also to this day such expressions as "a horn's blow," "a man's call," are used in the estimation of distances.

1 *Le Nord de la Sibérie*, i. 82.

2 "... that Royal Alley of Trees planted by the command of *Jehan-Guire*, and continued by the same order for 150 leagues, with little Pyramids or Turrets erected every half league."—*Bernier*, E.T. 91; (ed. *Constable*, 284).

In the greater part of the Bengal Presidency the estimated *kos* is about 2 miles, but it is much less as you approach the N.W. In the upper part of the Doab, it is, with fair accuracy, 1¼ miles. In Bundelkhand again it is nearly 3 m. (*Carnegy*), or, according to Beames, even 4 m. [In Madras it is 2¼ m., and in Mysore the *Sultānī kos* is about 4 m.] Reference may be made on this subject to Mr. Thomas's ed. of *Prinsep's Essays*, ii. 129; and to Mr. Beames's ed. of Elliot's *Glossary* ("*The Races of the N.-W. Provinces*," ii. 194). The latter editor remarks that in several parts of the country there are two kinds of *kos*, a *pakkā* and a *kachchā kos*, a double system which pervades all the weights and measures of India; and which has prevailed also in many other parts of the world [see PUCKA].

c. 500.—"A *gavyūtih* (or league) is two **krosas.**"—*Amarakosha*, ii. 2, 18.

c. 600.—"The descendant of Kukulstha (*i.e.* Rāma) having gone half a **krośa.** ..."—*Raghuvamsā*, xiii. 79.

c. 1340.—"As for the mile it is called among the Indians al-**Kurūh.**"—*Ibn Batuta*, iii. 95.

"The Sultan gave orders to assign me a certain number of villages. ... They were at a distance of 16 **Kurūhs** from Dihli."—*Ibn Batuta*, 388.

c. 1470.—"The Sultan sent ten viziers to encounter him at a distance of ten **Kors** (a *kor* is equal to 10 versts). ..."—*Atk. Nikitin*, 26, in *India in the XVth Cent.*

"From Chivil to Jooneer it is 20 **Kors**; from Jooneer to Beder 40; from Beder to Kulongher, 9 **Kors**; from Beder to Koluberg, 9."—*Ibid.* p. 12.

1528.—"I directed Chikmâk Beg, by a writing under the royal hand and seal, to measure the distance from Agra to Kâbul; that at every nine **kos** he should raise a minâr or turret, twelve *gez* in height, on the top of which he was to construct a pavilion. ..."—*Baber*, 393.

1537.—"... that the King of Portugal should hold for himself and all his descendants, from this day forth for aye, the Port of the City of Mangualor (in Guzerat) with all its privileges, revenues, and jurisdiction, with 2½ **coucees** round about. ..."—*Treaty in S. Botelho, Tombo*, 225.

c. 1550.—"Being all unmanned by their love of Raghoba, they had gone but two **Kos** by the close of day, then scanning land and water they halted."—*Rāmāyana* of *Tulsī Dās*, by *Growse*, 1878, p. 119.

[1604.—"At the rate of four *coss* (**Coces**) the league by the calculation of the Moors."—*Couto*, Dec. XII., Bk. I. cap. 4.]

1616.—"The three and twentieth arrived at

Adsmeere, 219 **Courses** from Brampoore, 418 English miles, the **Courses** being longer than towards the Sea."—*Sir T. Roe*, in *Purchas*, i. 541; [Hak. Soc. i. 105].

"The length of these forenamed Provinces is North-West to South-East, at the least 1000 **Courses**, every Indian **Course** being two English miles."—*Terry*, in *Purchas*, ii. 1468.

1623.—"The distance by road to the said city they called seven **cos**, or **corū**, which is all one; and every *cos* or *corū* is half a *ferseng* or league of Persia, so that it will answer to a little less than two Italian [English] miles."—*P. della Valle*, ii. 504; [Hak. Soc.i. 23].

1648.—"... which two **Coss** are equivalent to a Dutch mile."—*Van Twist, Gen. Beschrijv.* 2.

1666.—"... une **cosse** qui est la mesure des Indes pour l'espace des lieux, est environ d'une demi-lieue."—*Thevenot*, v. 12.

COT, s. A light bedstead. There is a little difficulty about the true origin of this word. It is universal as a sea-term, and in the South of India. In Northern India its place has been very generally taken by **charpoy** (q.v.), and *cot*, though well understood, is not in such prevalent European use as it formerly was, except as applied to barrack furniture, and among soldiers and their families. Words with this last characteristic have very frequently been introduced from the south. There are, however, both in north and south, vernacular words which may have led to the adoption of the term *cot* in their respective localities. In the north we have H. *khāṭ* and *khaṭwā*, both used in this sense, the latter also in Sanskrit; in the south, Tam. and Malayāl. *kaṭṭil*, a form adopted by the Portuguese. The quotations show, however, no *Anglo*-Indian use of the word in any form but *cot*.

The question of origin is perhaps further perplexed by the use of *quatre* as a Spanish term in the West Indies (see *Tom Cringle* below). A Spanish lady tells us that *catre*, or *catre de tigera* ("scissors-cot") is applied to a bedstead with X-trestles. *Catre* is also common Portuguese for a wooden bedstead, and is found as such in a dictionary of 1611. These forms, however, we shall hold to be of Indian origin; unless it can be shown that they are older in Spain and Portugal than the 16th century. The form *quatre* has a curious analogy (probably accidental) to *chārpāī*.

1553.—"The Camarij (Zamorin) who was at the end of a house, placed on a bedstead, which they call **catle**. ..."—*De Barros*, Dec. I. liv. iv. cap. viii.

1557.—"The king commanded his men to furnish a tent on that spot, where the interview was to take place, all carpeted inside with very rich tapestries, and fitted with a sofa (**catle**) covered over with a silken cloth."—*Alboquerque*, Hak. Soc. ii. 204.

1566.—"The king was set on a **catel** (the name of a kind of field bedstead) covered with a cloth of white silk and gold. ..."—*Damian de Goës, Chron. del R. Dom Emanuel*, 48.

1600.—"He retired to the hospital of the sick and poor, and there had his cell, the walls of which were of coarse palm-mats. Inside there was a little table, and on it a crucifix of the wood of St. Thomé, covered with a cloth, and a breviary. There was also a **catre** of coir, with a stone for pillow; and this completes the inventory of the furniture of that house."—*Lucena, V. do P. F. Xavier*, 199.

[1613.—"Here hired a **catele** and 4 men to have carried me to Agra."—*Danvers, Letters*, i. 277.

[1634.—"The better sort sleepe upon **cots**, or Beds two foot high, matted or done with girth-web."—*Sir T. Herbert, Trav.* 149. N.E.D.]

1648.—"Indian bedsteads or **Cadels**."—*Van Twist*, 64.

1673.—"... where did sit the King in State on a **Cott** or Bed."—*Fryer*, 18.

1678.—"Upon being thus abused the said Serjeant Waterhouse commanded the corporal Edward Short, to tie Savage down on his **cot**."—In *Wheeler*, i. 106.

1685.—"I hired 12 stout fellows ... to carry me as far as Lar in my **cott** (Palankeen fashion). ..."—*Hedges, Diary*, July 29; [Hak Soc. i. 203].

1688.—"In the East Indies, at Fort St. George, also Men take their **Cotts** or little Field-Beds and put them into the Yards, and go to sleep in the Air."—*Dampier's Voyages*, ii. Pt. iii.

1690.—"... the **Cot** or Bed that was by ..."—*Ovington*, 211.

1711.—In Canton Price Current: "Bamboo **Cotts** for Servants each ... 1 mace."—*Lockyer*, 150.

1768–71.—"We here found the **body** of the deceased, lying upon a **kadel**, or couch."—*Stavorinus*, E.T., i. 442.

1794.—"Notice is hereby given that sealed proposals will be received ... for supplying ... the different General Hospitals with clothing, **cotts**, and bedding."—In *Seton-Karr*, ii. 115.

1824.—"I found three of the party insisted upon accompanying me the first stage, and had despatched their camp-**cots**."—*Seely, Ellora*, ch. iii.

c. 1830.—"After being ... furnished with food

and raiment, we retired to our **quatres**, a most primitive sort of couch, with a piece of canvas stretched over it."—*Tom Cringle's Log*, ed. 1863, p. 100.

1872.—"As Badan was too poor to have a **khāt**, that is, a wooden bedstead with tester frames and mosquito curtains."—*Govinda Samanta*, i. 140.

***COTWAL, CUTWAUL**, s. A police-officer; superintendent of police; native town magistrate. P. *kotwāl*, 'a seneschal, a commandant of a castle or fort.' This looks as if it had been first taken from an Indian word, *koṭwālā*; [Skt. *koṭha-* or *koshṭha pālā* 'castle-porter']; but some doubt arises whether it may not have been a Turki term. In Turki it is written *kotāul, kotāwal*, and seems to be regarded by both Vambéry and Pavet de Courteille as a genuine Turki word. V. defines it as: "*Ketaul*, garde de forteresse, chef de la garnison; nom d'un tribu d'Ozbegs;" P. "*kotāwal, kotāwāl*, gardien d'une citadelle." There are many Turki words of analogous form, as *ḳarāwal*, 'a vidette,' *baḳāwal*, 'a table-steward,' *yasāwal*, 'a chamberlain,' *tangāwal*, 'a patrol,' &c. In modern Bokhara *Kataul* is a title conferred on a person who superintends the Amir's buildings (*Khanikoff*, 241). On the whole it seems probable that the title was originally Turki, but was shaped by Indian associations.

[The duties of the *Kotwāl*, as head of the police, are exhaustively laid down in the *Āīn* (*Jarrett*, ii. 41). Amongst other rules: "He shall amputate the hand of any who is the pot-companion of an executioner, and the finger of such as converse with his family."] The office of *Kotwāl* in Western and Southern India, technically speaking, ceased about 1862, when the new police system (under Act, India, V. of 1861, and corresponding local Acts) was introduced. In Bengal the term has been long obsolete. [It is still in use in the N.W.P. to designate the chief police officer of one of the larger cities or cantonments.]

c. 1040.—"Bu-Ali **Kotwal** (of Ghazni) returned from the Khilj expedition, having adjusted matters."—*Baihaki*, in *Elliot*, ii. 151.

1406-7.—"They fortified the city of Astarābād, where Abul Leïth was placed with the rank of **Kotwal**."—*Abdurrazāk*, in *Not. et Extr.* xiv. 123.

1553.—"The message of the Camorij arriving, Vasco da Gama landed with a dozen followers, and was received by a noble person whom they called **Catual**. ..."—*Barros*, Dec. I. liv. iv. ch. viii.

1572.—

"Nã praya hum regedor do Regno estava
Que na sua lingua **Catual** se chama."
Camões, vii. 44.

By Burton:

"There stood a Regent of the Realm ashore, a chief, in native parlance **'Cat'ual'** hight."

also the plural:

"Mas aquelles avaros **Catuais**
Que o Gentilico povo governavam."
Ibid. viii. 56.

1616.—Roe has **Cutwall** *passim*; [*e.g.* Hak. Soc. i. 90. &c.].

1727.—"Mr. Boucher being bred a Druggist in his youth, presently knew the Poison, and carried it to the **Cautwaul** or Sheriff, and showed it."—*A. Hamilton*, ii. 199. [In ed. 1744, ii. 199, **cautwal**].

1763.—"The **Catwal** is the judge and executor of justice in criminal cases."—*Orme* (ed. 1803), i. 26.

1812.—"... an officer retained from the former system, denominated **cutwal**, to whom the general police of the city and regulation of the market was entrusted."—*Fifth Report*, 44.

1847.—"The **Kutwal** ... seems to have done his duty resolutely and to the best of his judgment."—*G. O.* by *Sir C. Napier*, 121.

[1880.—"The son of the Raja's **Kotwal** was the prince's great friend."—*Miss Stokes, Indian Fairy Tales*, 209.]

COUNSILLEE, s. This is the title by which the natives in Calcutta generally designate English barristers. It is the same use as the Irish one of *Counsellor*, and a corruption of that word.

***COUNTRY**, adj. This term is used colloquially, and in trade, as an adjective to distinguish articles produced in India (generally with a sub-indication of disparagement), from such as are imported, and especially imported from Europe. Indeed **Europe** (q.v.) was, and still occasionally is, used as the contrary adjective. Thus, **'country** harness' is opposed to **'Europe** harness'; '*country*-born' people are persons of European descent, but born in India; '*country* horses' are Indian-bred in distinction from **Arabs, Walers** English horses, and even from 'stud-breds,' which are horses reared in India, but from foreign sires; '*country* ships' are those which are owned in Indian ports, though often officered by Europeans; *country* bottled beer is beer imported from England in cask and bottled in India; ['*country*-wound' silk is that reeled in the crude native fashion]. The term, as well as the H. *desī*, of which *country* is a translation, is also especially used for things grown or made in India as substitutes for certain foreign articles. Thus the *Cicca disticha* in Bombay gardens is called '*Country* gooseberry'; *Convolvulus batatas*, or sweet potato, is sometimes called the '*country* potato.' It was, equally with our quotidian root which has stolen its name, a foreigner in India, but was introduced and familiarised at a much earlier date. Thus again *desī bādām*, or '*country* almond,' is applied in Bengal to the nut of the *Terminalia Catappa*. On *desī*, which is applied, among other things, to silk, the great Ritter (*dormitans Homerus*) makes the odd remark that *desī* is just *Seide* reversed! But it would be equally apposite to remark that *Trigon*-ometry is just *Country*-ometry reversed!

Possibly the idiom may have been taken up from the Portuguese, who also use it, *e.g.* '*açafrao da* terra,' '*country* saffron,' *i.e.* **safflower**, otherwise called bastard saffron, the term being sometimes applied to turmeric. But the source of the idiom is general, as the use of *desī* shows. Moreover the Arabic *baladī*, having the same literal meaning, is applied in a manner strictly analogous, including the note of disparagement, insomuch that it has been naturalised in Spanish as indicating 'of little or no value.' Illustrations of the mercantile use of *beledi* (*i.e. baladī*) will be found in a note to *Marco Polo*, 2nd ed. ii. 370. For the Spanish use we may quote the Dict. of Cobarruvias (1611): "*Baladi*, the thing which is produced at less cost, and is of small duration and profit." (See also *Dozy* and *Engelmann*, 232 *seq.*)

1516.—"*Beledyn* ginger grows at a distance of two or three leagues all round the city of Calicut. ... In Bengal there is also much ginger of the **country** (*Gengivre Beledi*)."—*Barbosa*, 221 *seq.*

[1530.—"I at once sent some of these **country** men (*homeens raladis*) to the Thanas."—*Alboquerque, Cartas*, p. 148.]

1582.—"The Nayres maye not take anye **Countrie** women, and they also doe not marrie."—*Castañeda*, (by N. L.), f. 36.

[1608.—"The **Country** here are at dissension among themselves."—*Danvers, Letters*, i. 20.]

1619.—"The twelfth in the morning Master *Methwold* came from *Messalipatam* in one of the **Countrey** Boats."—*Pring*, in *Purchas*, i. 638.

1685.—"The inhabitants of the Gentoo Town, all in arms, bringing with them also elephants, kettle-drums, and all the **Country** music."—*Wheeler*, i. 140.

1747.—"It is resolved and ordered that a Serjeant with two Troopers and a Party of **Country** Horse, to be sent to Markisnah Puram to patroll. ..."—*Ft. St. David Council of War*, Dec. 25. *MS. Records* in India Office.

1752.—"Captain Clive did not despair ... and at ten at night sent one Shawlum, a serjeant who spoke the **country** languages, with a few sepoys to reconnoitre."—*Orme*, i. 211 (ed. 1803).

1769.—"I supped last night at a **Country** Captain's; where I saw for the first time a specimen of the Indian taste."—*Teignmouth, Mem.* i. 15.

1775.—"The Moors in what is called **Country** ships in East India, have also their chearing songs; at work in hoisting, or in their boats a rowing."—*Forrest, V. to N. Guinea*, 305.

1793.—"The jolting springs of **country**-made carriages, or the grunts of **country**-made carriers, commonly called *palankeen-boys*."—*Hugh Boyd*, 146.

1809.—"The Rajah had a drawing of it made for me, on a scale, by a **country** Draftsman of great merit."—*Ld. Valentia*, i. 356.

"... split **country** peas ..."—*Maria Graham*, 25.

1817.—"Since the conquest (of Java) a very extensive trade has been carried on by the English in **country** ships."—*Raffles, H. of Java*, i. 210.

[1882.—"There was a **country**-born European living in a room in the bungalow."—*Sanderson, Thirteen Years*, 256.]

COUNTRY-CAPTAIN, s. This is in Bengal the name of a peculiar dry kind of curry, often served as a breakfast dish. We can only conjecture that it was a favourite dish at the table of the skippers of '*country* ships,' who were themselves called '*country* captains,' as in our first quotation. In Madras the term is applied to a *spatch-cock* dressed with onions and curry stuff, which is probably the original form. [Riddell says: "**Country-captain.**—Cut a fowl in pieces; shred an onion small and fry it brown in butter; sprinkle the fowl with fine salt and curry powder and fry it brown; then put it into a stewpan with a pint of soup; stew it slowly down to a half and serve it with rice" (*Ind. Dom. Econ.* 176).]

1792.—"But now, Sir, a **Country Captain** is

not to be known from an ordinary man, or a Christian, by any certain mark whatever."—*Madras Courier*, April 26.

c. 1825.—"The local name for their business was the 'Country Trade,' the ships were '**Country** Ships,' and the masters of them '**Country Captains**.' Some of my readers may recall a dish which was often placed before us when dining on board these vessels at Whampoa, viz. '**Country Captain**.'"—*The Fankwae at Canton* (1882), p. 33.

COURSE, s. The drive usually frequented by European gentlemen and ladies at an Indian station.

1853.—"It was curious to Oakfield to be back on the Ferozepore **course**, after a six months' interval, which seemed like years. How much had happened in these six months!"—*Oakfield*, ii. 124.

COVENANTED SERVANTS. This term is specially applied to the regular Civil Service of India, whose members used to enter into a formal covenant with the East India Company, and do now with the Secretary of State for India. Many other classes of servants now go out to India under a variety of contracts and covenants, but the term in question continues to be appropriated as before. [See CIVILIAN.]

1757.—"There being a great scarcity of **covenanted servants** in Calcutta, we have entertained Mr. Hewitt as a monthly writer ... and beg to recommend him to be covenanted upon this Establishment."—Letter in *Long*, 112.

COW-ITCH, s. The irritating hairs on the pod of the common Indian climbing herb *Mucuna pruriens*, D.C., N. O. *Leguminosae*, and the plant itself. Both pods and roots are used in native practice. The name is doubtless the Hind. *kewānch* (Skt. *kapikachchhu*), modified in Hobson-Jobson fashion, by the 'striving after meaning.'

[1773.—"**Cow-itch**. This is the down found on the outside of a pod, which is about the size and thickness of a man's little finger, and of the shape of an Italian S."—*Ives*, 494.]

***COWLE**, s. A lease, or grant in writing; a safe-conduct, amnesty, or in fact any written engagement. The Emperor Sigismund gave *Cowle* to John Huss—and broke it. The word is Ar. *kaul*, 'word, promise, agreement,' and it has become technical in the Indian vernaculars, owing to the prevalence of Mahommedan Law.

[1611.—"We desired to have a **cowl** of the Shah bunder to send some persons aland."—*Danvers, Letters*, i. 133.

[1613.—"Procured a **cowl** for such ships as should come."—*Foster, Letters*, ii. 17.]

1680.—"A **Cowle** granted by the Right Worshipful Streynsham Master, Esq., Agent and Governour for affairs of the Honorable East India Company in ffort St. George at Chinapatnam, by and with the advice of his Councell to all the Pegu Ruby Marchants. ..."—*Fort St. George Cons*. Feb. 23, in *Notes and Extracts*, No. iii. p. 10.

1688.—"The President has by private correspondence procured a **Cowle** for renting the Town and customs of S. Thomé."—*Wheeler*, i. 176.

1758.—"The Nawaub ... having mounted some large guns on that hill ... sent to the Killadar a **Kowl-nama**, or a summons and terms for his surrender."—*H. of Hydur Naik*, 123.

1780.—"This **Caoul** was confirmed by another King of Gingy ... of the Bramin Caste."—*Dunn, New Directory*, 140.

Sir A. Wellesley often uses the word in his Indian letters. Thus:

1800.—"One tandah of brinjarries ... has sent to me for **cowle**. ..."—*Wellington Desp*. (ed. 1837), i. 59.

1804.—"On my arrival in the neighbourhood of the *pettah* I offered **cowle** to the inhabitants."—*Ibid*. ii. 193.

COWRY, s. Hind. *kauṛī* (*kauḍī*), Mahr. *kavaḍī*, Skt. *kaparda, kapardika*. The small white shell, *Cypraea moneta*, current as money extensively in parts of S. Asia and of Africa.

By far the most ancient mention of shell currency comes from Chinese literature. It is mentioned in the famous "Tribute of Yü" (or *Yü-Kung*); in the *Shu-King* (about the 14th cent. B.C.); and in the "Book of Poetry" (*Shi-King*), in an ode of the 10th cent. B.C. The Chinese seem to have adopted the use from the aborigines in the East and South; and they extended the system to tortoise-shell, and to other shells, the cowry remaining the unit. In 338 B.C., the King of Tsin, the supply of shells failing, suppressed the cowry currency, and issued copper coin, already adopted in other States of China. The usurper Wang Mang, who ruled A.D. 9–23, tried to revive the old systems, and issued rules instituting, in addition to the metallic money, ten classes of tortoise-shell and five of smaller shells, the value of all based on the *cowry*, which was worth 3 cash.[1] [Cowries were part of the tribute paid by the aborigines of Puanit to Metesouphis I. (*Maspero, Dawn of Civ.*, p. 427).]

The currency of cowries in India does not seem to be alluded to by any Greek or Latin author. It is mentioned by Mas'ūdī (c. 943), and their use for small change in the Indo-Chinese countries is repeatedly spoken of by Marco Polo, who calls them *pourcelaines*, the name by which this kind of shell was known in Italy (*porcellane*) and France. When the Mahommedans conquered Bengal, early in the 13th century, they found the ordinary currency composed exclusively of cowries, and in some remote districts this continued to the beginning of the last century. Thus, up to 1801, the whole revenue of the Silhet District, amounting then to Rs. 250,000, was collected in these shells, but by 1813 the whole was realised in specie. Interesting details in connection with this subject are given by the Hon. Robert Lindsay, who was one of the early Collectors of Silhet (*Lives of the Lindsays*, iii. 170).

The Sanskrit vocabulary called *Trikāṇḍaśesha* (iii. 3, 206) makes 20 *kapardika* (or *kauṛīs*) = ¼ *paṇa*; and this value seems to have been pretty constant. The cowry table given by Mr. Lindsay at Silhet, circa 1778, exactly agrees with that given by Milburn as in Calcutta use in the beginning of last century, and up to 1854 or thereabouts it continued to be the same:

4 *kauṛis* = 1 *ganda*
20 *gandas* = 1 *paṇ*
4 *paṇ* = 1 *āna*
4 *ānas* = 1 *kāhan*, or about ¼ rupee.

This gives about 5120 cowries to the Rupee. We have not met with any denomination of currency in actual use below the cowry, but it will be seen that, in a quotation from Mrs. Parkes, two such are indicated. It is, however, Hindu idiosyncracy to indulge in imaginary submultiples as well as imaginary multiples. (See a parallel under LACK).

In Bastar, a secluded inland State between Orissa and the Godavery, in 1870, the following was the prevailing table of cowry currency, according to Sir W. Hunter's *Gazetteer*:

28 *kauṛis* = 1 *borī*
12 *boris* = 1 *dugānī*
12 *dugānīs* = 1 Rupee, *i.e.* 2880 cowries.

Here we may remark that both the *paṇ* in Bengal, and the *dugānī* in this secluded Bastar, were originally the names of pieces of money, though now in the respective localities they represent only certain quantities of cowries. ["Up to 1865 *bee-a* or cowries were in use in Siam; the value of these was so small that from 800 to 1500 went to a *fuang* (7½ cents.)."—*Hallett, A Thousand Miles on an Elephant*, p. 164. Mr. Gray has an interesting note on cowries in his ed. of *Pyrard de Laval*, Hak. Soc. i. 236 *seqq.*]

Cowries were at one time imported into England in considerable quantities for use in the African slave-trade. "For this purpose," says Milburn, "they should be small, clean, and white, with a beautiful gloss" (i. 273). The duty on this importation was £53, 16*s.* 3*d.* per cent. on the sale value, with ⅓ added for war-tax. In 1803, 1418 cwt. were sold at the E. I. auctions, fetching £3,626; but after that few were sold at all. In the height of slave-trade, the great mart for cowries was at Amsterdam, where there were spacious warehouses for them (see the *Voyage*, &c., quoted 1747).

c. A.D. 943.—"Trading affairs are carried on with *cowries* (*al-wada'*), which are the money of the country."—*Maṣ'ūdī*, i. 385.

c. 1020.—"These isles are divided into two classes, according to the nature of their chief products. The one are called *Dewa-Kauḍha*, 'the Isles of the **Cowries**,' because of the **Cowries** that they collect on the branches of coco-trees planted in the sea."—*Albírūnī*, in *J. As.*, Ser. IV. tom. iv. 266.

c. 1240.—"It has been narrated on this wise that as in that country (Bengal), the **kauṛi** [shell] is current in place of silver, the least gift he used to bestow was a *lak* of **kauṛis**. The Almighty mitigate his punishment [in hell]!"—*Ṭabaḳāt-t-Nāṣiri*, by *Raverty*, 555 *seq.*

c. 1350.—"The money of the Islanders (of the Maldives) consists of *cowries* (*al-wada'*). They so style creatures which they collect in the sea, and bury in holes dug on the shore. The flesh wastes away, and only a white shell remains. 100 of these shells are called *siyāh*, and 700 *fāl*; 12,000 they call *kutta*; and 100,000 *bustū*. Bargains are made with these cowries at the rate of 4 *bustū* for a gold dīnār. [This would be about 40,000 for a rupee.] Sometimes the

---

1 Note communicated by Professor Terrien de la Couperie.

rate falls, and 12 *bustū* are exchanged for a gold dīnār. The islanders barter them to the people of Bengal for rice, for they also form the currency in use in that country. ... These cowries serve also for barter with the negroes in their own land. I have seen them sold at Mālī and Gūgū [on the Niger] at the rate of 1150 for a gold dīnār."—*Ibn Batuta*, iv. 122.

c. 1420.—"A man on whom I could rely assured me that he saw the people of one of the chief towns of the Said employ as currency, in the purchase of low-priced articles of provision, **kaudas**, which in Egypt are known as *wada*, just as people in Egypt use *fals*."—*Makrizi, S. de Sacy, Chrest. Arabe*, 2nd ed. i. 252.

[1510.—Mr. Whiteway writes: "In an abstract of an unpublished letter of Alboquerque which was written about 1510, and abstracted in the following year, occurs this sentence:—'The merchandize which they carry from Cairo consists of snails (*caracoes*) of the Twelve Thousand Islands.' He is speaking of the internal caravan-trade of Africa, and these snails must be **cowries**."]

1554.—At the Maldives: "**Cowries** 12,000 make one *cota*; and 4½ *cotas* of average size weigh one *quintal*; the big ones something more."—*A. Nunes*, 35.

"In these isles ... are certain white little shells which they call **cauris**."—*Castanheda*, iv. 7.

1561.—"Which vessels (*Gundras*, or palm-wood boats from the Maldives) come loaded with coir and **caury**, which are certain little white shells found among the Islands in such abundance that whole vessels are laden with them, and which make a great trade in Bengala, where they are current as money."—*Correa*, I. i. 341.

1586.—"In Bengal are current those little shells that are found in the islands of Maldiva, called here **courim**, and in Portugal *Buzio*."—*Sassetti*, in *De Gubernatis*, 205.

[c. 1590.—"Four kos from this is a well, into which if the bone of any animal be thrown it petrifies, like a **cowrie** shell, only smaller."—*Āīn*, ed. *Jarrett*, ii. 229.]

c. 1610.—"Les marchandises qu'ils portent le plus souvent sont ces petites coquilles des Maldives, dont ils chargent tous les ans grand nombre de nauires. Ceux des Maldives les appellent *Boly*, et les autres Indiens **Caury**."—*Pyrard de Laval*, i. 517; see also p. 165; [Hak. Soc. i. 438; also comp. i. 78, 157, 228, 236, 240, 250, 299; *Boly* is Singh. *bella*, a cowry].

c. 1664.—"... lastly, it (Indostan) wants those little *Sea-cockles* of the Maldives, which serve for common Coyne in *Bengale*, and in some other places. ..."—*Bernier*, E.T. 63; [ed. *Constable*, 204].

[c. 1665.—"The other small money consists of shells called **Cowries**, which have the edges inverted, and they are not found in any other part of the world save only the Maldive Islands. ... Close to the sea they give up to 80 for the *paisa*, and that diminishes as you leave the sea, on account of carriage; so that at Agra you receive but 50 or 55 for the *paisa*."—*Tavernier*, ed. *Ball*, i. 27 *seq*.]

1672.—"**Cowreys**, like sea-shells, come from Siam, and the Philippine Islands."—*Fryer*, 86.

1683.—"The Ship Britannia—from the Maldiva Islands, arrived before the Factory ... at their first going ashore, their first salutation from the natives was a shower of Stones and Arrows, whereby 6 of their Men were wounded, which made them immediately return on board, and by ye mouths of their Guns forced them to a complyance, and permission to load what **Cowries** they would at Markett Price; so that in a few days time they sett sayle from thence for Surrat with above 60 Tunn of **Cowryes**."—*Hedges, Diary*, July 1; [Hak. Soc. i. 96].

1705.—"... **Coris**, qui sont des petits coquillages."—*Luillier*, 245.

1727.—"The **Couries** are caught by putting Branches of Cocoa-nut trees with their Leaves on, into the Sea, and in five or six Months the little Shell-fish stick to those leaves in Clusters, which they take off, and digging Pits in the Sand, put them in and cover them up, and leave them two or three Years in the Pit, that the Fish may putrefy, and then they take them out of the Pit, and barter them for Rice, Butter, and Cloth, which Shipping bring from *Ballasore* in *Orisa* near *Bengal*, in which Countries **Couries** pass for Money from 2500 to 3000 for a Rupee, or half a Crown *English*."—*A. Hamilton* [ed. 1744], i. 349.

1747.—"Formerly 12,000 weight of these **cowries** would purchase a cargo of five or six hundred Negroes: but those lucrative times are now no more; and the Negroes now set such a value on their countrymen, that there is no such thing as having a cargo under 12 or 14 tuns of cowries.

"As payments of this kind of specie are attended with some intricacy, the Negroes, though so simple as to sell one another for shells, have contrived a kind of copper vessel, holding exactly 108 pounds, which is a great dispatch to business."—*A Voyage to the Id. of Ceylon on board a Dutch Indiaman in the year* 1747, &c. &c. Written by a Dutch Gentleman. Transl. &c. London, 1754, pp .21 *seq*.

1749.—"The only Trade they deal in is **Cowries** (or Blackamoor's Teeth as they call them in England), the King's sole Property, which the sea throws up in great abundance."—*The*

Boscawen's Voyage to Bombay, by *Philalethes* (1750), p. 52.

1753.—"Our Hon'ble Masters having expressly directed ten tons of **couries** to be laden in each of their ships homeward bound, we ordered the Secretary to prepare a protest against Captain Cooke for refusing to take any on board the Admiral Vernon."—In *Long*, 41.

1762.—"The trade of the salt and *butty wood* in the Chucla of Sillett, has for a long time been granted to me, in consideration of which I pay a yearly rent of 40,000 *caouns*[1] of **cowries**. ..."—Native Letter to Nabob, in *Van Sittart*, i. 203.

1770.—"... millions of millions of lires, pounds, rupees, and **cowries**."—*H. Walpole's Letters*, v. 421.

1780.—"We are informed that a Copper Coinage is now on the Carpet ... it will be of the greatest utility to the Public, and will totally abolish the trade of **Cowries**, which for a long time has formed so extensive a field for deception and fraud. A greviance (*sic*) the poor has long groan'd under."—*Hicky's Bengal Gazette*, April 29.

1786.—In a Calcutta Gazette the rates of payment at Pultah Ferry are stated in Rupees, Annas, *Puns*, and *Gundas* (*i.e.* of *Cowries*, see above).—In *Seton-Karr*, i. 140.

1791.—"Notice is hereby given, that on or before the 1st November next, sealed proposals of Contract for the remittance in Dacca of the cowries received on account of the Revenues of Sylhet ... will be received at the Office of the Secretary to the Board of Revenue. ... All persons who may deliver in proposals, are desired to specify the rates per cowan or *cowans* of **cowries** (see *kāhan* above) at which they will engage to make the remittance proposed."—In *Seton-Karr*, ii. 53.

1803.—"I will continue to pay, without demur, to the said Government, as my annual *peshkush* or tribute, 12,000 *kahuns* of **cowries** in three instalments, as specified herein below."—*Treaty Engagement* by the Rajah of Kitta Keonghur, a Tributary subordinate to Cuttack, 16th December, 1803.

1833.—"May 1st. Notice was given in the Supreme Court that Messrs. Gould and Campbell would pay a dividend at the rate of nine *gundahs*, one **cowrie**, one *cawg*, and eighteen *teel*, in every sicca rupee, on and after the 1st of June. A curious dividend, not quite a farthing in the rupee!"[2]—*The Pilgrim* (by Fanny Parkes), i. 273.

c. 1865.—"Strip him stark naked, and cast him upon a desert island, and he would manage to play heads and tails for **cowries** with the sea-gulls, if land-gulls were not to be found."—*Zelda's Fortune*, ch. iv.

1883.—"Johnnie found a lovely **cowrie** two inches long, like mottled tortoise-shell, walking on a rock, with its red fleshy body covering half its shell, like a jacket trimmed with chenille fringe."—*Letter* (of Miss North's) *from Seychelle Islands*, in *Pall Mall Gazette*, Jan. 21, 1884.

CRANCHEE, s. Beng. H. *karānchī*. This appears peculiar to Calcutta, [but the word is also used in N. India]. A kind of ricketty and sordid carriage resembling, as Bp. Heber says below, the skeleton of an old English hackney-coach of 1800–35 (which no doubt was the model), drawn by wretched ponies, harnessed with rope, and standing for native hire in various parts of the city.

1823.—"... a considerable number of '**caranchies**,' or native carriages, each drawn by two horses, and looking like the skeletons of hackney coaches in our own country."—*Heber*, i. 28 (ed. 1844).

1834.—"As Lady Wroughton guided her horse through the crowd to the right, a **kuranchy**, or hackney-coach, suddenly passed her at full speed."—*The Baboo*, i. 228.

CRANNY, s. In Bengal commonly used for a clerk writing English, and thence vulgarly applied generically to the East Indians, or half-caste class, from among whom English copyists are chiefly recruited. The original is Hind. *karānī*, *kirānī*, which Wilson derives from Skt. *karan*, 'a doer.' *Karaṇa* is also the name of one of the (so-called) mixt castes of the Hindus, sprung from a Sudra mother and Vaisya father, or (according to some) from a pure Kshatriya mother by a father of degraded Kshatriya origin. The occupation of the members of this mixt caste is that of writers and accountants; [see *Risley*, *Tribes and Castes of Bengal*, i. 424 *seqq.*].

The word was probably at one time applied by natives to the junior members of the Covenanted Civil Service—"Writers," as they were designated. See the quotations from the "*Seir Mutaqherin*" and from Hugh Boyd. And in our own remembrance the

1 *Kāhan*, see above = 1280 cowries.

2 A *Kāg* would seem here to be equivalent to ¼ of a cowry. Wilson, with (?) as to its origin [perhaps P. *kāk*, 'minute'], explains it as "a small division of money of account, less than a *gaṇḍa* of Kauris." *Til* is properly the sesamum seed, applied in Bengal, Wilson says, "in account to 1/80 of a kauri." The Table would probably thus run: 20 *til* = 1 *kāg*, 4 *kāg* = 1 *kauri*, and so forth. And 1 rupee = 409,600 til!

"Writers' Buildings" in Calcutta, where those young gentlemen were at one time quartered (a range of apartments which has now been transfigured into a splendid series of public offices, but, wisely, has been kept to its old name), was known to the natives as *Karānī kī Bārik*.

c. 1350.—"They have the custom that when a ship arrives from India or elsewhere, the slaves of the Sultan ... carry with them complete suits ... for the *Rabban* or skipper, and for the **kirānī**, who is the ship's clerk."—*Ibn Batuta*, ii. 198.

"The second day after our arrival at the port of Kailūkari, the princess escorted the *nakhodāh* (or skipper), the **kirānī**, or clerk. ..."—*Ibid.* iv. 250.

c. 1590.—"The **Karrání** is a writer who keeps the accounts of the ship, and serves out the water to the passengers."—*Āīn* (*Blochmann*), i. 280.

c. 1610.—"Le Secretaire s'apelle **carans** ..."—*Pyrard de Laval*, i. 152; [Hak. Soc. i. 214].

[1611.—"Doubt you not but it is too true, howsoever the **Cranny** flatters you with better hopes."—*Danvers, Letters*, i. 117, and see also i. 190.

[1684.—"Ye Noceda and **Cranee**."—*Pringle, Diary of Ft. St. George*, iii. 111.]

c. 1781.—"The gentlemen likewise, other than the Military, who are in high offices and employments, have amongst themselves degrees of service and work, which have not come minutely to my knowledge; but the whole of them collectively are called **Carranis**."—*Seir Mutaqherin*, ii. 543.

1793.—"But, as Gay has it, example gains where precept fails. As an encouragement therefore to my brother **crannies**, I will offer an instance or two, which are remembered as good Company's jokes."—*Hugh Boyd, The Indian Observer*, 42.

1810.—"The **Cranny**, or clerk, may be either a native Armenian, a native Portuguese, or a Bengallee."—*Williamson, V. M.* i. 209.

1834.—"Nazir, see bail taken for 2000 rupees. The **Crany** will write your evidence, Captain Forrester."—*The Baboo*, i. 311

It is curious to find this word explained by an old French writer, in almost the modern application to East Indians. This shows that the word was used at Goa in something of its Hindu sense of one of mixt blood.

1653.—"Les **karanes** sont engendrez d'vn Mestis, et d'vne Indienne, lesquels sont oliaustres. Ce mot de **Karanes** vient a mon advis de *Kara*, qui signifie en Turq la terre, ou bien la couleur noire, comme si l'on vouloit dire par **karanes** les enfans du païs, ou bien les noirs: ils ont les mesmes aduantages dans leur professions que les autres Mestis."—*De la Boullaye-le-Gouz*, ed. 1657, p. 226. Compare in *M. Polo*, Bk. I., ch. 18, his statement about the **Caraonas**, and note thereon.

CREASE, CRIS, &c., s. A kind of dagger, which is the characteristic weapon of the Malay nations; from the Javanese name of the weapon, adopted in Malay, *krīs, kirīs*, or *kres* (see *Favre, Dict. Javanais-Français*, 137*b*, *Crawfurd's Malay Dict.* s.v., *Jansz, Javaansch-Nederl. Woordenboek*, 202). The word has been generalised, and is often applied to analogous weapons of other nations, as 'an Arab *crease*,' &c. It seems probable that the H. word *kirich*, applied to a straight sword, and now almost specifically to a sword of European make, is identical with the Malay word *krīs*. See the form of the latter word in Barbosa, almost exactly *kirich*. Perhaps Turki *kīlīch* is the original. [Platts gives Skt. *kṛiti*, 'a sort of knife or dagger.'] If Reinaud is right in his translation of the Arab *Relations* of the 9th and 10th centuries, in correcting a reading, otherwise unintelligible, to *khrī*, we shall have a very early adoption of this word by Western travellers. It occurs, however, in a passage relating to Ceylon.

c. 910.—"Formerly it was common enough to see in this island a man of the country walk into the market grasping in his hand a **khrī**, *i.e.* a dagger peculiar to the country, of admirable make, and sharpened to the finest edge. The man would lay hands on the wealthiest of the merchants that he found, take him by the throat, brandish his dagger before his eyes, and finally drag him outside of the town. ..."—*Relation*, &c., *par Reinaud*, p. 156; and see Arabic text, p. 120, near bottom.

It is curious to find the **cris** adopted by Alboquerque as a piece of state costume. When he received the ambassadors of Sheikh Ismael, *i.e.* the Shāh of Persia, Ismael Sūfi, at Ormuz, we read:

1515.—"For their reception there was prepared a dais of three steps ... which was covered with carpets, and the Governor seated thereon in a decorated chair, arrayed in a tunic and surcoat of black damask, with his collar, and his golden **cris**, as I described before, and with his big, long snow-white beard; and at the back of the dais the captains and gentlemen, handsomely attired, with their swords girt, and behind them their pages with lances and targets, and all uncovered."—*Correa*, ii. 423.

The portrait of Alboquerque in the 1st vol. of Mr. Birch's Translation of the Commentaries, realises the snow-white beard, tunic, and black surcoat, but the *cris* is missing. [The Malay **Creese** is referred to in iii. 85.]

1516.—"They are girt with belts, and carry daggers in their waists, wrought with rich inlaid work, these they call **querix**."—*Barbosa*, 193.

1552.—"And the quartermaster ran up to the top, and thence beheld the son of Timuta raja to be standing over the Captain Major with a cris half drawn."—*Castanheda*, ii. 363.

1572.—

"... assentada
Lá no gremio da Aurora, onde nasceste,
Opulenta Malaca nomeada!
As settas venenosas que fizeste!
Os **crises**, com que já te vejo armáda ..."
Camões, x. 44.

By Burton:

"... so strong thy site
there on Aurora's bosom, whence they rise,
thou Home of Opulence, Malacca hight!
The poysoned arrows which thine art supplies,
the **krises** thirsting, as I see, for fight ..."

1580.—A vocabulary of "Wordes of the naturall language of Iaua" in the voyage of Sir Fr. Drake, has **Cricke**, 'a dagger.'—*Hakl.* iv. 246.

[1584.—"**Crise.**" See quotation under A MUCK.]

1586-98.—"The custom is that whenever the King (of Java) doth die ... the wives of the said King ... every one with a daggor in her hand (which daggor they call a **crese**, and is as sharp as a razor) stab themselves to the heart."—*Carendish*, in *Hakl.* iv. 337.

1591.—"Furthermore I enjoin and order in the name of our said Lord ... that no servant go armed whether it be with staves or daggers, or **crisses**."—Procl. of *Viceroy Mathias d'Alboquerque* in *Archiv. Port. Oriental*, fasc. 3, p. 325.

1598.—"In the Western part of the Island (Sumatra) is Manancabo where they make Poinyards, which in India are called **Cryses**, which are very well accounted and esteemed of."—*Linschoten*, 33; [with some slight differences of reading, Hak. Soc. i. 110].

1602.—"... Chinesische Dolchen, so sie **Cris** nennen."—*Hulsius*, i. 33.

c. 1610.—"Ceux-là ont d'ordinaire à leur costé vn poignard ondé qui s'apelle **cris**, et qui vient d'Achen en Sumatra, de Iaua, et de la Chine."—*Pyrard de Laval*, i. 121; [Hak. Soc. i. 164]; also see ii. 101; [ii. 162, 170].

1634.—"Malayos **crises**, Arabes alfanges."—*Malaca Conquistada*, ix. 32.

1686.—"The **Cresset** is a small thing like a Baggonet which they always wear in War or Peace, at Work or Play, from the greatest of them to the poorest or meanest person."—*Dampier*, i. 337.

1690.—"And as the Japanners ... rip up their Bowels with a **Cric**. ..."—*Ovington*, 173.

1727.—"A Page of twelve Years of Age ... (said) that he would shew him the Way to die, and with that he took a **Cress**, and ran himself through the body."—*A. Hamilton*, ii. 99; [ed. 1744, ii. 98].

1770.—"The people never go without a poniard which they call **cris**."—*Raynal* (tr. 1777), i. 97.

c. 1850-60.—"They (the English) chew hashish, cut themselves with poisoned **creases** ... taste every poison, buy every secret."—*Emerson, English Traits* [ed. 1866, ii. 59].

The Portuguese also formed a word **crisada**, a blow with a **cris** (see *Castanheda*, iii. 379). And in English we find a verb to '*crease*'; see in *Purchas*, i. 532, and this:

1604.—"This Boyhog we tortured not, because of his confession, but **crysed** him."—*Scot's Discourse of Iava*, in *Purchas*, i. 175.

[1704.—"At which our people ... were most of them **creezed**."—*Yule, Hedges' Diary*, Hak. Soc. ii. cccxxxvii.]

1817.—"the Portuguese commander requested permission to see the **Cross** which Janiere wore ..."—*Rev. R. Fellowes, History of Ceylon*, chap. v. quoted in 9 ser. *N. & Q.* I. 85.

Also in *Braddel's Abstract of the Sijara Malayu*:

"He was in consequence **creased** at the shop of a sweetmeat seller, his blood flowed on the ground, but his body disappeared miraculously."—*Sijara Malayu*, in *J. Ind. Arch.* v. 318.

CREOLE, s. This word is never used by the English in India, though the mistake is sometimes made in England of supposing it to be an Anglo-Indian term. The original, so far as we can learn, is Span, *criollo*, a word of uncertain etymology, whence the French *créole*, a person of European blood but colonial birth. See *Skeat*, who concludes that *criollo* is a negro corruption of *criadillo*, dim. of *criado*, and is = 'little nursling.' *Criados, criadas*, according to Pyrard de Laval, [Hak. Soc. ii. 89 *seq.*] were used at Goa for male and female servants. And see the passage quoted under NEELAM from Correa, where the words 'apparel and servants' are in the original '*todo o fato e* criados.'

1782.—"Mr. Macintosh being the son of a Scotch Planter by a French **Creole**, of one of the

West India Islands, is as swarthy and ill-looking a man as is to be seen on the Portugueze Walk on the Royal Exchange."—*Price's Observations*, &c. in *Price's Tracts*, i. 9.

CRORE, s. One hundred *lakhs*, *i.e.* 10,000,000. Thus a crore of rupees was for many years almost the exact equivalent of a million sterling. It had once been a good deal more, and has now been for some years a good deal less. The H. is *karoṛ*, Skt. *koṭi*.

c. 1315.—"Kales Dewar, the ruler of Ma'bar, enjoyed a highly prosperous life. ... His coffers were replete with wealth, insomuch that in the city of Mardī (Madura) there were 1200 **crores** of gold deposited, every *crore* being equal to a thousand laks, and every lak to one hundred thousand dinārs."—*Wassāf*, in *Elliot*, iii. 52. N.B.—The reading of the word *crore* is however doubtful here (see note by Elliot *in loco*). In any case the value of *crore* is misstated by Wassāf.

c. 1343.—"They told me that a certain Hindu farmed the revenue of the city and its territories (Daulatābād) for 17 **karōr** ... as for the **karōr** it is equivalent to 100 *laks*, and the *lak* to 100,000 dīnārs."—*Ibn Batuta*, iv. 49.

c. 1350.—"In the course of three years he had misappropriated about a **kror** of *tankas* from the revenue."—*Ziā-uddīn-Barnī*, in *Elliot*, iii. 247.

c. 1590.—"Zealous and upright men were put in charge of the revenues, each over one **Krōr** of dams." (These, it appears, were called **krōris**.)—*Āīn-i-Akbari*, i. 13.

1609.—"The King's yeerely Income of his Crowne Land is fiftie **Crou** of *Rupias*, every **Crou** is an hundred *Leckes*, and every *Lecke* is an hundred thousand *Rupias*."—*Hawkins*, in *Purchas*, i. 216.

1628.—"The revenue of all the territories under the Emperors of Delhi amounts, according to the Royal registers, to six *arbs* and thirty **krors** of *dāms*. One *arb* is equal to a hundred **krors** (a *kror* being ten millions) and a hundred *Krors* of *dāms* are equivalent to two *krors* and fifty *lacs* of rupees."—*Muhammad Sharīf Hanafi*, in *Elliot*, vii. 138.

1690.—"The *Nabob* or Governour of *Bengal* was reputed to have left behind him at his Death, twenty **Courous** of Roupies: A **kourou** is an hundred thousand lacks."—*Ovington*, 189.

1757.—"In consideration of the losses which the English Company have sustained ... I will give them one **crore** of rupees."—*Orme*, ii. 162 (ed. 1803).

c. 1785.—"The revenues of the city of Decca, once the capital of Bengal, at a low estimation amount annually to two **kherore**."—*Carraccioli's Life of Clive*, i. 172.

1797.—"An Englishman, for H. E.'s amusement, introduced the elegant European diversion of a race in sacks by old women: the Nabob was delighted beyond measure, and declared that though he had spent a crore of rupees ... in procuring amusement, he had never found one so pleasing to him."—*Teignmouth, Mem.* i. 407.

1879.—

"'Tell me what lies beyond our brazen gates.'
Then one replied, 'The city first, fair Prince!
* * * * * *
And next King Bimbasâra's realm, and then
The vast flat world with **crores** on **crores**
of folk.'"

Sir E. Arnold, The Light of Asia, iii.

CUMMERBUND, s. A girdle. H. from P. *kamar-band*, *i.e.* 'loin-band.' Such an article of dress is habitually worn by domestic servants, peons, and irregular troops; but any waist-belt is so termed.

[1534.—"And tying on a **cummerbund** (*camarabando*) of yellow silk."—*Correa*, iii. 588. *Camarabandes* in *Dalboquerque, Comm.*, Hak. Soc. iv. 104.]

1552.—"The Governor arriving at Goa received there a present of a rich cloth of Persia which is called **comarbãdos**, being of gold and silk."—*Castanheda*, iii. 396.

1616.—"The nobleman of Xaxma sent to have a sample of gallie pottes, jugges, podingers, lookinglasses, table bookes, chint bramport, and **combarbands**, with the prices."—*Cocks's Diary*, i. 147.

1638.—"Ils serrent la veste d'vne ceinture, qu'ils appellent **Commerbant**."—*Mandelslo*, 223.

1648.—"In the middle they have a well adjusted girdle, called a **Commerbant**."—*Van Twist*, 55.

1727.—"They have also a fine Turband, embroidered Shoes, and a Dagger of Value, stuck into a fine **Cummerband**, or Sash."—*A. Hamilton*, i. 229; [ed. 1744, ii. 233].

1810.—"They generally have the turbans and **cummer-bunds** of the same colour, by way of livery."—*Williamson, V. M.* i. 274.

[1826.—"My white coat was loose, for want of a **kumberbund**."—*Pandurang Hari*, ed. 1873, i. 275.]

1880.—"... The Punjab seems to have found out Manchester. A meeting of native merchants at Umritsur ... describes the effects of a shower of rain on the English-made turbans and **Kummerbunds** as if their heads and loins were enveloped by layers of starch."—*Pioneer Mail*, June 17.

CUMSHAW, s. Chin. Pigeon-English for

bucksheesh (q.v.), or a present of any kind. According to Giles it is the Amoy pron. (*kam-siā*) of two characters signifying 'grateful thanks.' Bp. Moule suggests *kan-siu* (or Cantonese) *kăm-sau*, 'thank-gift.'

1879.—"... they pressed upon us, blocking out the light, uttering discordant cries, and clamouring with one voice, **Kum-sha**, *i.e.* backsheesh, looking more like demons than living men."—*Miss Bird's Golden Chersonese*, 70.

1882.—"As the ship got under weigh, the Compradore's **cumshas**, according to 'olo custom,' were brought on board ... dried lychee, Nankin dates ... baskets of oranges, and preserved ginger."—*The Fankwae*, 103.

CUNCHUNEE, s. H. *kanchanī*. A dancing-girl. According to Shakespear, this is the feminine of a caste, *Kanchan*, whose women are dancers. But there is doubt as to this: [see Crooke, *Tribes and Castes, N.W.P.* iv. 364, for the *Kanchan* caste.] *Kanchan* is 'gold'; also a yellow pigment, which the women may have used; see quot. from Bernier. [See DANCING-GIRL.]

[c. 1590.—"The Kanjari; the men of this class play the Pakhāwaj, the Rabāb, and the Tāla, while the women sing and dance. His Majesty calls them **Kanchanis**."—*Āīn*, ed. *Jarrett*, iii. 257.]

c. 1660.—"But there is one thing which seems to me a little too extravagant ... the publick Women, I mean not those of the Bazar, but those more retired and considerable ones that go to the great marriages at the houses of the *Omrahs* and Mansebdars to sing and dance, those that are called **Kenchen**, as if you should say the *guilded* the *blossoming* ones. ..."—*Bernier*, E.T. 88; [ed. *Constable*, 273 *seq.*].

c. 1661.—"On regala dans le Serrail, toutes ces Dames Etrangères, de festins et des dances des **Quenchenies**, qui sont dea femmes et des filles d'une Caste de ce nom, qui n'ont point d'autre profession que celle de la danse."—*Thevenot*, v. 151.

1689.—"And here the Dancing Wenches, or **Quenchenies**, entertain you, if you please."—*Ovington*, 257.

1799.—"In the evening the **Canchanis** ... have exhibited before the Prince and court."—Diary in *Life of Colebrooke*, 153.

1810.—"The dancing-women are of different kinds ... the *Meeraseens* never perform before assemblies of men. ... The **Kunchenee** are of an opposite stamp; they dance and sing for the amusement of the male sex."—*Williamson, V. M.* i. 386.

CURRY, s. In the East the staple food consists of some cereal, either (as in N. India) in the form of flour baked into unleavened cakes, or boiled in the grain, as rice is. Such food having little taste, some small quantity of a much more savoury preparation is added as a relish, or 'kitchen,' to use the phrase of our forefathers. And this is in fact the proper office of *curry* in native diet. It consists of meat, fish, fruit, or vegetables, cooked with a quantity of bruised spices and turmeric [see MUSSALLA]; and a little of this gives a flavour to a large mess of rice. The word is Tam. *kari, i.e.* 'sauce'; [*kari*, v. 'to eat by biting']. The Canarese from *karil* was that adopted by the Portuguese, and is still in use at Goa. It is remarkable in how many countries a similar dish is habitual; *pilāo* [see PILLAU] is the analogous mess in Persia, and *kuskussu* in Algeria; in Egypt a dish well known as *ruzz mufalfal* [Lane, *Mod. Egypt*, ed. 1871, i. 185], or "peppered rice." In England the proportions of rice and "kitchen" are usually reversed, so that the latter is made to constitute the bulk of the dish.

The oldest indication of the Indian cuisine in this kind, though not a very precise one, is cited by Athenaeus from Megasthenes: "Among the Indians, at a banquet, a table is set before each individual ... and on the table is placed a golden dish on which they throw, first of all, boiled rice ... and then they add many sorts of meat dressed after the Indian fashion" (*Athen.*, by *Yonge*, iv. 39). The earliest precise mention of *curry* is in the Mahavanso (c. A.D. 477), where it is said of Kassapo that "he partook of rice dressed in butter, with its full accompaniment of *curries*." This is Turnour's translation, the original Pali being *sūpa*.

It is possible, however, that the kind of *curry* used by Europeans and Mahommedans is not of purely Indian origin, but has come down from the spiced cookery of medieval Europe and Western Asia. The medieval spiced dishes in question were even coloured like curry. Turmeric, indeed, called by Garcia de Orta, *Indian saffron*, was yet unknown in Europe, but it was represented by saffron and sandalwood. A notable incident occurs in the old English poem of King Richard, wherein the Lion-heart feasts on the head of a Saracen—

"soden full hastily
With powder and with spysory,
And with saffron of good colour."

Moreover, there is hardly room for doubt that *capsicum* or red pepper (see **CHILLY**) was introduced into India by the Portuguese (see *Hanbury and Flückiger*, 407); and this spice constitutes the most important ingredient in modern curries. The Sanskrit books of cookery, which cannot be of any considerable antiquity, contain many recipes for curry without this ingredient. A recipe for curry (*caril*) is given, according to Bluteau, in the Portuguese *Arte de Cozinha*, p. 101. This must be of the 17th century.

It should be added that *kari* was, among the people of S. India, the name of only one form of 'kitchen' for rice, viz. of that in consistency resembling broth, as several of the earlier quotations indicate. Europeans have applied it to all the savoury concoctions of analogous spicy character eaten with rice. These may be divided into three classes—viz. (1), that just noticed; (2), that in the form of a stew of meat, fish or vegetables; (3), that called by Europeans 'dry curry.' These form the successive courses of a Hindu meal in S. India, and have in the vernaculars several discriminating names.

In Java the Dutch, in their employment of curry, keep much nearer to the original Hindu practice. At a breakfast, it is common to hand round with the rice a dish divided into many sectoral spaces, each of which contains a different kind of curry, more or less liquid.

According to the *Fankwae at Canton* (1882), the word is used at the Chinese ports (we presume in talking with Chinese servants) in the form **kāārle** (p. 62).

1502.—"Then the Captain-major commanded them to cut off the hands and ears of all the crews, and put all that into one of the small vessels, into which he ordered them to put the friar, also without ears or nose or hands, which he ordered to be strung round his neck with a palm-leaf for the King, on which he told him to have a curry (**caril**) made to eat of what his friar brought him."—*Correa, Three Voyages*, Hak. Soc. 331. The "Friar" was a Brahman, in the dress of a friar, to whom the odious ruffian Vasco da Gama had given a safe-conduct.

1563.—"They made dishes of fowl and flesh, which they call **caril**."—*Garcia*, f. 68.

c. 1580.—"The victual of these (renegade soldiers) is like that of the barbarous people; that of Moors all *bringe* [*birinj*, 'rice']; that of Gentoos rice-**carril**."—*Primor e Honra*, &c., f. 9*v*.

1598.—"Most of their fish is eaten with rice, which they seeth in broth, which they put upon the rice, and is somewhat soure, as if it were sodden in gooseberries, or unripe grapes, but it tasteth well, and is called **Carriel** [v.l. **Carriil**], which is their daily meat."—*Linschoten*, 88; [Hak. Soc. ii. 11]. This is a good description of the ordinary tamarind curry of S. India.

1606.—"Their ordinary food is boiled rice with many varieties of certain soups which they pour upon it, and which in those parts are commonly called **caril**."—*Gouvea*, 61*b*.

1608–1610.—"... me disoit qu'il y auoit plus de 40 ans, qu'il estoit esclaue, et auoit gagné bon argent à celuy qui le possedoit; et toute fois qu'il ne luy donnoit pour tout viure qu'vne mesure de riz cru par iour sans autre chose ... et quelquefois deux *baseruques*, qui sont quelque deux deniers pour auoir du **Caril** à mettre auec le riz."—*Mocquet, Voyages*, 337.

1623.—"In India they give the name of **caril** to certain messes made with butter, with the kernel of the coco-nut (in place of which might be used in our part of the world milk of almonds) ... with spiceries of every kind, among the rest cardamom and ginger ... with vegetables, fruits, and a thousand other condiments of sorts; ... and the Christians, who eat everything, put in also flesh or fish of every kind, and sometimes eggs ... with all which things they make a kind of broth in the fashion of our *guazzetti* (or hotch-potches) ... and this broth with all the said condiments in it they pour over a good quantity of rice boiled simply with water and salt, and the whole makes a most savoury and substantial mess."—*P. della Valle*, ii. 709; [Hak. Soc. ii. 328.]

1681.—"Most sorts of these delicious Fruits they gather before they be ripe, and boyl them to make **Carrees**, to use the Portuguese word, that is somewhat to eat with and relish their Rice."—*Knox*, p. 12. This perhaps indicates that the English *curry* is formed from the Port. *caris*, plural of *caril*.

c. 1690.—"Curcuma in Indiâ tam ad cibum quam ad medecinam adhibetur, Indi enin ... adeo ipsi adsueti sunt ut cum cunctis ádmiscent condimentis et piscibus, praesertim autem isti quod **karri** ipsis vocatur."—*Rumphius*, Pars Vta. p. 166.

c. 1759–60.—"The **currees** are infinitely various, being a sort of fricacees to eat with rice, made of any animals or vegetables."—*Grose*, i. 150.

1781.—"To-day have **curry** and rice for my dinner, and plenty of it as C——, my messmate, has got the gripes, and cannot eat his share."—*Hon. J. Lindsay's Imprisonment*, in *Lives of Lindsays*, iii. 296.

1794–97.—

"The Bengal squad he fed so wondrous nice,
Baring his **currie** took, and Scott his rice."

Pursuits of Literature, 5th ed., p. 287.

This shows that **curry** was not a domesticated dish in England at the date of publication. It also is a sample of what the wit was that ran through so many editions!

c. 1830.—"J'ai substitué le lait à l'eau pour boisson ... c'est une sorte de contrepoison pour l'essence de feu que forme la sauce enragée de mon sempiternel **cari.**"—*Jacquemont, Correspondance*, i. 196.

1848.—"Now we have seen how Mrs. Sedley had prepared a fine **curry** for her son."—*Vanity Fair*, ch. iv.

1860.—"... Vegetables, and especially farinaceous food, are especially to be commended. The latter is indeed rendered attractive by the unrivalled excellence of the Singhalese in the preparation of innumerable **curries**, each tempered by the delicate creamy juice expressed from the flesh of the cocoa-nut, after it has been reduced to a pulp."—*Tennent's Ceylon*, i. 77. N.B. Tennent is misled in supposing (i. 437) that chillies are mentioned in the Mahavanso. The word is *maricha*, which simply means "pepper," and which Turnour has translated erroneously (p. 158).

1874.—"The craving of the day is for quasi-intellectual food, not less highly peppered than the **curries** which gratify the faded stomach of a returned Nabob."—*Blackwood's Magazine*, Oct. 434.

The Dutch use the word as **Kerrie** or **Karrie**; and **Kari** *à l'Indienne* has a place in French cartes.

CURRY-STUFF, s. Onions, chillies, &c.; the usual material for preparing curry, otherwise **mussalla** (q.v.), represented in England by the preparations called *curry-powder* and *curry-paste*.

1860.—"... with plots of esculents and **curry-stuffs** of every variety, onions, chillies, yams, cassavas, and sweet potatoes."—*Tennent's Ceylon*, i. 463.

CUTCHA, KUTCHA, adj. Hind. *kachchā*, 'raw, crude, unripe, uncooked.' This word is with its opposite *pakkā* (see PUCKA) among the most constantly recurring Anglo-Indian colloquial terms, owing to the great variety of metaphorical applications of which both are susceptible. The following are a few examples only, but they will indicate the manner of use better than any attempt at comprehensive definition [*see table below*].

1763.—"Il parait que les **catcha** cosses sont plus en usage que les autres cosses dans le gouvernement du Decan."—*Lettres Edifiantes*, xv. 190.

1863.—"In short, in America, where they cannot get a *pucka* railway they take a **kutcha** one instead. This, I think, is what we must do in India."—*Lord Elgin*, in *Letters and Journals*, 432.

Captain Burton, in a letter dated Aug. 26, 1879, and printed in the "*Academy*" (p. 177), explains the gypsy word *gorgio*, for a Gentile or non-Rommany, as being **kachhā** or **cutcha**. This may be, but it does not carry conviction.

A **cutcha** *Brick* is a sun-dried brick.	A **pucka** *Brick* is a properly kiln-burnt brick.
„ *House* is built of mud, or of sun-dried brick.	„ *House* is of burnt brick or stone with lime, and generally with a terraced plaster roof.
„ *Road* is earthwork only.	„ *Road* is a Macadamised one.
„ *Appointment* is acting or temporary.	„ *Appointment* is permanent.
„ *Settlement* is one where the land is held without lease.	„ *Settlement* is one fixed for a term of years.
„ *Account* or *Estimate*, is one which is rough, superficial, and untrustworthy.	„ *Account*, or *Estimate*, is carefully made, and claiming to be relied on.
„ *Maund*, or *Seer*, is the smaller, where two weights are in use, as often happens.	„ *Maund*, or *Seer*, is the larger of two in use.
„ *Major* is a brevet or local Major	„ *Major*, is a regimental Major.
„ *Colour* is one that won't wash.	„ *Colour*, is one that will wash.
„ *Fever* is a simple ague or a light attack.	„ *Fever*, is a dangerous remittent or the like (what the Italians call *pernizziosa*).
„ *Pice* generally means one of those amorphous coppers, current in up-country bazars at varying rates of value.	„ *Pice*; a double copper coin formerly in use; also a proper pice (= ¼ anna) from the Govt. mints.
„ *Coss*—see analogy under *Maund* above.	„ *Coss*—see under *Maund* above.
„ *Roof*. A roof of mud laid on beams; or of thatch, &c.	„ *Roof*; a terraced roof made with cement.
„ *Scoundrel*, a limp and fatuous knave.	„ *Scoundrel*, one whose motto is "Thorough."
„ *Seam* (*silāī*) is the tailor's tack for trying on.	„ *Seam* is the definite stitch of the garment.

CUTCHA-PUCKA, adj. This term is applied in Bengal to a mixt kind of building in which burnt brick is used, but which is cemented with mud instead of lime-mortar.

CUTCHERRY, and in Madras **CUTCHERY**, s. An office of administration, a court-house. Hind. *kachahrī*; used also in Ceylon. The word is not usually now, in Bengal, applied to a merchant's counting-house, which is called **dufter**, but it *is* applied to the office of an Indigo-Planter or a Zemindar, the business in which is more like that of a Magistrate's or Collector's Office. In the service of Tippoo Sahib **cutcherry** was used in peculiar senses besides the ordinary one. In the civil administration it seems to have been used for something like what we should now call *Department* (see *e.g. Tippoo's Letters*, 292); and in the army for a division or large brigade (*e.g. ibid.* 332; and quotation from *Wilks* below).

1610.—"Over against this seat is the **Cichery** or Court of Rolls, where the King's Viseer sits every morning some three houres, by whose hands passe all matters of Rents, Grants, Lands, Firmans, Debts, &c."—*Hawkins*, in *Purchas*, i. 439.

1673.—"At the lower End the Royal Exchange or **Queshery** ... opens its folding doors."—*Fryer*, 261.

[1702.—"But not makeing an early escape themselves were carried into the **Cacherra** or publick Gaol."—*Hedges, Diary*, Hak. Soc. ii. cvi.]

1763.—"The Secretary acquaints the Board that agreeably to their orders of the 9th May, he last Saturday attended the Court of **Cutcherry**, and acquainted the Members with the charge the President of the Court had laid against them for non-attendance."—In *Long*, 316.

"The protection of our Gomastahs and servants from the oppression and jurisdiction of the Zemindars and their **Cutcherries** has been ever found to be a liberty highly essential both to the honour and interest of our nation."—From the Chief and Council at Dacca, in *Van Sittart*, i. 247.

c. 1765.—"We can truly aver that during almost five years that we presided in the **Cutchery** Court of *Calcutta*, never any murder or atrocious crime came before us but it was proved in the end a *Bramin* was at the bottom of it."—*Holwell, Interesting Historical Events*, Pt. II. 152.

1783.—"The moment they find it true that the English Government shall remain as it is, they will divide sugar and sweetmeats among all the people in the **Cutcheree**; then every body will speak sweet words."—*Native Letter*, in *Forbes, Or. Mem.* iv. 227.

1786.—"You must not suffer any one to come to your house; and whatever business you may have to do, let it be transacted in our **Kuchurry**."—*Tippoo's Letters*, 303.

1791.—"At Seringapatam General Matthews was in confinement. James Skurry was sent for one day to the **Kutcherry** there, and some pewter plates with marks on them were shown to him to explain; he saw on them words to this purport, 'I am indebted to the Malabar Christians on account of the Public Service 40,000 Rs.; the Company owes me (about) 30,000 Rs.; I have taken *Poison* and am now within a short time of *Death*; whoever communicates this to the Bombay Govt. or to my wife will be amply rewarded. (Signed) Richard Matthews.'"—*Narrative* of *Mr. William Drake, and other Prisoners* (in Mysore), in *Madras Courier*, 17th Nov.

c. 1796.—" ... the other Asof Mirán Hussein, was a low fellow and a debauchee, ... who in different ... towns was carried in his pálkí on the shoulders of dancing girls as ugly as demons to his **Kutcheri** or hall of audience."—*H. of Tipú Sultán*, E.T. by *Miles*, 246.

"... the favour of the Sultan towards that worthy man (Dundia Wágh) still continued to increase ... but although, after a time, a **Kutcheri**, or brigade, was named after him, and orders were issued for his release, it was to no purpose."—*Ibid.* 248.

[c. 1810.—"Four appears to have been the fortunate number (with Tippoo; four companies (*yeaz*), one battalion (*teep*), four *teeps* one *cushoon*: ... four *cushoons*, one **Cutcherry**. The establishment ... of a *cutcherry* ... 5,688, but these numbers fluctuated with the Sultaun's caprices, and at one time a *cushoon*, with its cavalry attached, was a legion of about 3,000."—*Wilks, Mysore*, ed. 1869, ii. 132.]

1834.—"I mean, my dear Lady Wroughton, that the man to whom Sir Charles is most heavily indebted, is an officer of his own **Kucheree**, the very sircar who cringes to you every morning for orders."—*The Baboo*, ii. 126.

1860.—"I was told that many years ago, what remained of the Dutch records were removed from the record-room of the Colonial Office to the **Cutcherry** of the Government Agent."—*Tennent's Ceylon*, i. xxviii.

1873.—"I'd rather be out here in a tent any time ... than be stewing all day in a stuffy **Kutcherry** listening to Ram Buksh and Co. perjuring themselves till they are nearly white in the face."—*The True Reformer*, i. 4.

1883.—"Surrounded by what seemed to me a mob of natives, with two or three dogs at his feet, talking, writing, dictating,—in short doing **Cutcherry**."—*C. Raikes*, in *Bosworth Smith's Lord Lawrence*, i. 59.

D

DACCA, n.p. Properly *Dhākā*, ['the wood of *ḍhāk* trees'; the *Imp. Gaz.* suggests Dhakeswarī, 'the concealed goddess']. A city in the east of Bengal, once of great importance, especially in the later Mahommedan history; famous also for the "*Dacca* muslins" woven there, the annual advances for which, prior to 1801, are said to have amounted to £250,000. [*Taylor, Descr. and Hist. Account of the Cotton Manufacture of Dacca in Bengal*]. **Dāka** is throughout Central Asia applied to all muslins imported through Kabul.

c. 1612.—"... liberos Osmanis assecutus vivos cepit, eosque cum elephantis et omnibus thesauris defuncti, post quam **Daeck** Bengalae metropolim est reversus, misit ad regem."—*De Laet*, quoted by *Blochmann, Āīn*, i. 521.

[c. 1617.—"**Dekaka**" in *Sir T. Roe's* List, Hak. Soc. ii. 538.]

c. 1660.—"The same Robbers took *Sultan-Sujah* at **Daka**, to carry him away in their Galeasses to *Rakan*. ..."—*Bernier*, E.T. 55; [ed. *Constable*, 109].

1665.—"**Daca** is a great Town, that extends itself only in length; every one coveting to have an House by the Ganges side. The length ... is above two leagues. ... These Houses are properly no more than paltry Huts built up with *Bambouc's*, and daub'd over with fat Earth."—*Tavernier*, E.T. ii. 55; [ed. *Ball*, i. 128].

1682.—"The only expedient left was for the Agent to go himself in person to the *Nabob* and *Duan* at **Decca**."—*Hedges, Diary*, Oct. 9; [Hak. Soc. i. 33].

***DACOIT**, **DACOO**, s. Hind. *ḍakait*, *ḍākāyat*, *ḍākū*; a robber belonging to an armed gang. The term, being current in Bengal, got into the Penal Code. By law, to constitute *dacoity*, there must be five or more in the gang committing the crime. Beames derives the word from *ḍāknā*, 'to shout,' a sense not in Shakespear's Dict. [It is to be found in Platts, and Fallon gives it as used in E. H. It appears to be connected with Skt. *dashṭa*, 'pressed together.']

1810.—"**Decoits**, or water-robbers."—*Williamson, V. M.* ii. 396.

1812.—"**Dacoits**, a species of depredators who infest the country in gangs."—*Fifth Report*, p. 9.

1817.—"The crime of **dacoity**" (that is, robbery by gangs), says Sir Henry Strachey, "... has, I believe, increased greatly since the British administration of justice."—*Mill, H. of B. I.*, v. 466.

1834.—"It is a conspiracy! a false warrant!—they are **Dakoos! Dakoos!!**"—*The Baboo*, ii. 202.

1872.—"Daroga! Why, what has he come here for? I have not heard of any **dacoity** or murder in the Village."—*Govinda Samanta*, i. 264.

DAM, s. H. *dām*. Originally an actual copper coin, regarding which we find the following in the *Āīn*, i. 31, ed. *Blochmann*:—"1. The *Dám* weighs 5 *tánks*, *i.e.* 1 *tolah*, 8 *māshas*, and 7 *surkhs*; it is the fortieth part of a rupee. At first this coin was called *Paisah*, and also *Bahloli*; now it is known under this name (*dám*). On one side the place is given where it was struck, on the other the date. For the purpose of calculation, the *dám* is divided into 25 parts, each of which is called a *jétal*. This imaginary division is only used by accountants.

"2. The *adhelah* is half of a *dám*. 3. The *Páulah* is a quarter of a *dám*. 4. The *damrí* is an eighth of a *dám*."

It is curious that Akbar's revenues were registered in this small currency, viz. in *laks* of *dáms*. We may compare the Portuguese use of *reis*.

The tendency of denominations of coins is always to sink in value. The *jetal*, which had become an imaginary money of account in Akbar's time, was, in the 14th century, a real coin, which Mr. E. Thomas, chief of Indian numismatologists, has unearthed [see *Chron. Pathan Kings*, 231]. And now the *dām* itself is imaginary. According to Elliot the people of the N.W.P. not long ago calculated 25 *dāms* to the *paisā*, which would be 1600 to a rupee. Carnegy gives the Oudh popular currency table as:

26 *kauris*	=	1 *damrī*
1 *damrī*	=	3 dām
20 „	=	1 *ānā*
25 *dām*	=	1 pice.

But the Calcutta Glossary says the *dām* is in Bengal reckoned 1/20 of an *ānā*, *i.e.* 320 to the rupee. ["Most things of little value, here as well as in Bhagalpur (writing of Behar) are sold by an imaginary money called *Takā*, which is here reckoned equal to two *Paysas*.

There are also imaginary monies called *Chadām* and *Damrī*; the former is equal to 1 *Paysa* or 25 cowries, the latter is equal to one-eighth of a *Paysa*" (*Buchanan, Eastern Ind.* i. 382 *seq.*)]. We have not in our own experience met with any reckoning of *dāms*. In the case of the *damrī* the denomination has increased instead of sinking in relation to the *dām*. For above we have the *damrī* = 3 *dāms*, or according to Elliot (*Beames*, ii. 296) = 3¼ *dāms*, instead of ⅛ of a *dām* as in Akbar's time. But in reality the *damrī's* absolute value has remained the same. For by Carnegy's table 1 rupee or 16 anas would be equal to 320 *damrīs*, and by the *Āīn*, 1 rupee = 40 × 8 *damrīs* = 320 *damrīs*. *Damrī* is a common enough expression for the infinitesimal in coin, and one has often heard a Briton in India say: "No, I won't give a *dumree!*" with but a vague notion what a *damrī* meant, as in Scotland we have heard, "I won't give a *plack*," though certainly the speaker could not have stated the value of that ancient coin. And this leads to the suggestion that a like expression, often heard from coarse talkers in England as well as in India, originated in the latter country, and that whatever profanity there may be in the animus, there is none in the etymology, when such an one blurts out "I don't care a ***dām!***" *i.e.* in other words, "I don't care a brass farthing!"

If the Gentle Reader deems this a far-fetched suggestion, let us back it by a second. We find in Chaucer (*The Miller's Tale*);

"——ne raught he not a *kers*,"

which means, "he recked not a *cress*" (*ne flocci quidem*); an expression which is also found in Piers Plowman:

"Wisdom and witte is nowe not worthe a *kerse*."

And this we doubt not has given rise to that other vulgar expression, "I don't care a curse";—curiously parallel in its corruption to that in illustration of which we quote it.

[This suggestion about *dām* was made by a writer in *Asiat. Res.*, ed. 1803, vii. 461: "This word was perhaps in use even among our forefathers, and may innocently account for the expression '*not worth a fig*,' or a *dam*, especially if we recollect that *ba-dam*, an *almond*, is to-day current in some parts of India as small money. Might not dried figs have been employed anciently in the same way, since the Arabic word *fooloos*, a *halfpenny*, also denotes a *cassia bean*, and the root *fuls* means the scale of a fish. Mankind are so apt, from a natural depravity, that 'flesh is heir to,' in their use of words, to pervert them from their original sense, that it is not a convincing argument against the present conjecture our using the word *curse* in vulgar language in lieu of *dam*." The *N.E.D.* disposes of the matter: "The suggestion is ingenious, but has no basis in fact." In a letter to Mr. Ellis, Macaulay writes: "How they settle the matter I care not, as the Duke says, one *twopenny damn*"; and Sir G. Trevelyan notes: "It was the Duke of Wellington who invented this oath, so disproportioned to the greatness of its author." (*Life*, ed. 1878, ii. 257.)]

1628.—"The revenue of all the territories under the Emperors of Delhi amounts, according to the Royal registers, to 6 *arbs* and 30 *krors* of **dáms**. One *arb* is equal to 100 *krors* (a *kror* being 10,000,000), and a hundred *krors* of **dams** are equal to 2 *krors* and 50 *lacs* of rupees."—*Muhammad Sharīf Hanijī*, in *Elliot*, vii. 138.

c. 1840.—"Charles Greville saw the Duke soon after, and expressing the pleasure he had felt in reading his speech (commending the conduct of Capt. Charles Elliot in China), added that, however, many of the party were angry with it; to which the Duke replied,—'I know they are, and I don't care a **damn**. I have no time to do what is right.'

"A *twopenny damn* was, I believe, the form usually employed by the Duke, as an expression of value: but on the present occasion he seems to have been less precise."—*Autobiography of Sir Henry Taylor*, i. 296. The term referred to seems curiously to preserve an unconscious tradition of the pecuniary, or what the idiotical jargon of our time calls the 'monetary,' estimation contained in the expression.

1881.—"A Bavarian printer, jealous of the influence of capital, said that 'Cladstone baid millions of money to the beeble to fote for him, and Beegonsfeel would not bay them a **tam**, so they fote for Cladstone.'"—*A Socialistic Picnic*, in *St. James's Gazette*, July 6.

[1900.—"There is not, I dare wager, a single bishop who cares one 'twopenny-halfpenny **dime**' for any of that plenteousness for himself."—*H. Bell*, Vicar of Muncaster, in *Times*, Aug. 31.]

DANCING-GIRL, s. This, or among the older Anglo-Indians, *Dancing-Wench*, was the representative of the (Portuguese *Bailadeira*) **Bayadère**, or **Nautch**-girl (q.v.), also **Cunchunee**. In S. India dancing-girls are all Hindus, [and known as *Devadāsī* or *Bhogam-dāsī*;] in N. India they are both Hindu, called *Rāmjanī* (see RUM-JOHNNY), and Mussulman, called *Kanchanī* (see CUNCHUNEE). In Dutch the phrase takes a very plain-spoken form, see quotation from Valentijn; [others are equally explicit, *e.g.* Sir T. Roe (Hak. Soc. i. 145) and P. della Valle, ii. 282.]

1606.—See description by *Gouvea*, f. 39.

1673.—"After supper they treated us with the **Dancing Wenches**, and good soops of Brandy and Delf Beer, till it was late enough."—*Fryer*, 152.

1701.—"The Governor conducted the Nabob into the Consultation Room ... after dinner they were diverted with the **Dancing Wenches**."—In *Wheeler*, i. 377.

1726.—"Wat de **dans-Hoeren** (anders *Dewataschi* (**Deva-dāsī**) ... genaamd, en an de Goden hunner Pagoden als getrouwd) belangd."—*Valentijn, Chor*. 54.

1763–78.—"Mandelslow tells a story of a Nabob who cut off the heads of a set of **dancing girls** ... because they did not come to his palace on the first summons."—*Orme*, i. 28 (ed. 1803).

1789.—"... **dancing girls** who display amazing agility and grace in all their motions."—*Munro, Narrative*, 73.

c. 1812.—"I often sat by the open window, and there, night after night, I used to hear the songs of the unhappy **dancing girls**, accompanied by the sweet yet melancholy music of the *cithára*."—*Mrs. Sherwood's Autobiog*. 423.

[1813.—Forbes gives an account of the two classes of **dancing girls**, those who sing and dance in private houses, and those attached to temples.—*Or. Mem.* 2nd ed. i. 61.]

1815.—"**dancing girls** were once numerous in Persia; and the first poets of that country have celebrated the beauty of their persons and the melody of their voices."—*Malcolm, H. of Persia*, ii. 587.

1838.—"The Maharajah sent us in the evening a new set of **dancing girls**, as they were called, though they turned out to be twelve of the ugliest old women I ever saw."—*Osborne, Court and Camp of Runjeet Singh*, 154.

1843.—'We decorated the Temples of the false gods. We provided the **dancing girls**. We gilded and painted the images to which our ignorant subjects bowed down."—*Macaulay's Speech on the Somnauth Proclamation.*

DANDY, s.

(**a**). A boatman. The term is peculiar to the Gangetic rivers. H. and Beng. *ḍānḍi*, from *ḍānḍ* or *ḍanḍ*, 'a staff, an oar.'

1685.—"Our **Dandees** (or boatmen) boyled their rice, and we supped here."—*Hedges, Diary*, Jan. 6; [Hak. Soc. i. 175].

1763.—"The oppressions of your officers were carried to such a length that they put a stop to all business, and plundered and seized the **Dandies** and Mangies' vessel."—*W. Hastings* to the Nawab, in *Long*, 347.

1809.—"Two naked **dandys** paddling at the head of the vessel."—*Ld. Valentia*, i. 67.

1824.—"I am indeed often surprised to observe the difference between my **dandees** (who are nearly the colour of a black tea-pot) and the generality of the peasants whom we meet."—*Bp. Heber* i. 149 (ed. 1844).

—— (**b**). A kind of ascetic who carries a staff. Same etymology. See *Solvyns*, who gives a plate of such an one.

[1828.—"... the **Dandi** is distinguished by carrying a small *Dand*, or wand, with several processes or projections from it, and a piece of cloth dyed with red ochre, in which the Brahmanical cord is supposed to be enshrined, attached to it."—*H. H. Wilson, Sketch of the Religious Sects of the Hindus*, ed. 1861, i. 193.]

—— (**c**). H. same spelling, and same etymology. A kind of vehicle used in the Himālaya, consisting of a strong cloth slung like a hammock to a bamboo staff, and carried by two (or more) men. The traveller can either sit side-ways, or lie on his back. It is much the same as the Malabar **muncheel** (q.v.), [and P. della Valle describes a similar vehicle which he says the Portuguese call *Rete* (Hak. Soc. i. 183)].

[1875.—"The nearest approach to travelling in a **dandi** I can think of, is sitting in a half-reefed top-sail in a storm, with the head and shoulders above the yard."—*Wilson, Abode of Snow*, 103.]

1876.—"In the lower hills when she did not walk she travelled in a **dandy**."—*Kinloch, Large Game Shooting in Thibet*, 2nd S., p. vii.

***DARJEELING, DĀRJĪLING**, n.p. A famous sanitarium in the Eastern Himālaya, the cession of which was purchased from the Raja of Sikkim in 1835; a tract largely added to by annexation in 1849, following on an outrage committed by the Sikkim Minister in imprisoning Dr. (afterwards Sir) Joseph Hooker and the late Dr. A. Campbell, Superintendent of Darjeeling. The sanitarium stands at 6500 to 7500 feet above the sea. The popular Tibetan spelling of the name is, according to Jaeshcke, *rDorrje-glin*, 'Land of the *Dorje*,' *i.e.* 'of the Adamant or thunderbolt,' the ritual sceptre of the Lamas. But 'according to several titles of books in the Petersburg list of MSS. it ought properly to be spelt *Dar-rgyas-glin*' (*Tib. Eng. Dict.* p. 287).

DARÓGA, s. P. and H. *dāroghā*. This word seems to be originally Mongol (see *Kovalevsky's Dict.* No. 1672). In any case it is one of those terms brought by the Mongol hosts from the far East. In their nomenclature it was applied to a Governor of a province or city, and in this sense it continued to be used under Timur and his immediate successors. But it is the tendency of official titles, as of denominations of coin, to descend in value; and that of *dāroghā* has in later days been bestowed on a variety of humbler persons. Wilson defines the word thus: "The chief native officer in various departments under the native government, a superintendent, a manager: but in later times he is especially the head of a police, customs, or excise station." Under the British Police system, from 1793 to 1862–63, the *Darogha* was a local Chief of Police, or Head Constable, [and this is still the popular title in the N.W.P. for the officer in charge of a Police Station.] The word occurs in the sense of a Governor in a Mongol inscription, of the year 1314, found in the Chinese Province of Shensi, which is given by Pauthier in his *Marc. Pol.*, p. 773. The Mongol Governor of Moscow, during a part of the Tartar domination in Russia, is called in the old Russian Chronicles *Doroga* (see *Hammer*, *Golden Horde*, 384). And according to the same writer the word appears in a Byzantine writer (unnamed) as *Δάρηγας* (*ibid.* 238–9). The Byzantine form and the passages below of 1404 and 1665 seem to imply some former variation in pronunciation. But Clavijo has also **derroga** in § clii.

c. 1220.—"Tuli Khan named as **Darugha** at Merv one called Barmas, and himself marched upon Nishapur."—*Abulghāzi*, by *Desmaisons*, 135.

1404.—"And in this city (Tauris) there was a kinsman of the Emperor as Magistrate thereof, whom they call **Derrega**, and he treated the said Ambassadors with much respect."—*Clarijo*, § lxxxii. Comp. *Markham*, 90.

1441.—"... I reached the city of Kerman. ... The **deroghah** (governor) the Emir Hadji Mohamed Kaiaschirin, being then absent. ..."—*Abdurrazzāk*, in *India in the XVth Cent.*, p. 5.

c. 1590.—"The officers and servants attached to the Imperial Stables. 1. The *Atbegi*. ... 2. The **Dāroghah**. There is one appointed for each stable. ..."—*Āīn*, tr. *Blochmann*, i. 137.

1621.—"The 10th of October, the **darogā**, or Governor of Ispahan, Mir Abdulaazim, the King's son-in-law, who, as was afterwards seen in that charge of his, was a downright madman. ..."—*P. della Valle*, ii. 166.

1665.—"There stands a **Derega**, upon each side of the River, who will not suffer any person to pass without leave."—*Tavernier*, E.T., ii. 52; [ed. *Ball*, i. 117].

1673.—"The **Droger**, or Mayor of the City, or Captain of the Watch, or the Rounds; It is his duty to preside with the Main Guard a-nights before the Palace-gates."—*Fryer*, 339.

1673.—"The **Droger** being Master of his Science, persists; what comfort can I reap from your Disturbance?"—*Fryer*, 389.

1682.—"I received a letter from Mr. Hill at Rajemaul advising ye **Droga** of ye Mint would not obey a Copy, but required at least a sight of ye Originall."—*Hedges*, *Diary*, Dec. 14; [Hak. Soc. i. 57].

c. 1781.—"About this time, however, one day being very angry, the **Darogha**, or master of the mint, presented himself, and asked the Nawaub what device he would have struck on his new copper coinage. Hydur, in a violent passion, told him to stamp an obscene figure on it."—*Hydur Naik*, tr. by *Miles*, 488.

1812.—"Each division is guarded by a **Darogha**, with an establishment of armed men."—*Fifth Report*, 44.

***DATURA**, s. This Latin-like name is really Skt. *dhattūra*, and so has passed into the derived vernaculars. The widely-spread *Datura Stramonium*, or Thorn-apple, is well known over Europe, but is not regarded as indigenous to India; though it appears to be wild in the Himālaya from Kashmīr to Sikkim. The Indian species, from which our generic name has been borrowed, is *Datura alba*, Nees (see *Hanbury and Flückiger*, 415) (*D. fastuosa*, L.). Garcia de Orta mentions the common use of this by thieves in India. Its effect on the victim was to produce temporary alienation of mind, and violent laughter, permitting the thief to act unopposed. He describes his own practice in dealing with such cases, which he had always found successful. *Datura* was also often given as a practical joke, whence the Portuguese called it *Buriadora* ('Joker'). De

Orta strongly disapproves of such pranks. The criminal use of *datura* by a class of Thugs is rife in our own time. One of the present writers has judicially convicted many. Coolies returning with fortunes from the colonies often become the victims of such crimes. [See details in *Chevers, Ind. Med. Jurispr.* 179 *seqq.*]

1563.—"*Maidservant.* A black woman of the house has been giving **datura** to my mistress; she stole the keys, and the jewels that my mistress had on her neck and in her jewel box, and has made off with a black man. It would be a kindness to come to her help."—*Garcia, Colloquios*, f. 83.

1578.—"They call this plant in the Malabar tongue *unmata caya* [*ummata-kāya*] ... in Canarese **Datyro**. ..."—*Acosta*, 87.

c. 1580.—"Nascitur et ... **Datura** Indorum, quarum ex seminibus Latrones bellaria parant, quae in caravanis mercatoribus exhibentes largumque somnum, profundumque inducentes aurum gemmasque surripiunt et abeunt."—*Prosper Alpinus*, Pt. I. 190–1.

1598.—"They name [have] likewise an hearbe called **Deutroa**, which beareth a seede, whereof bruising out the sap, they put it into a cup, or other vessell, and give it to their husbands, eyther in meate or drinke, and presently therewith the Man is as though hee were half out of his wits."—*Linschoten*, 60; [Hak. Soc. i. 209].

1608–10.—"Mais ainsi de mesme les femmes quand elles sçauent que leurs maris en entretiennent quelqu'autre, elles s'en desfont par poison ou autrement, et se seruent fort à cela de la semence de **Datura**, qui est d'vne estrange vertu. Ce *Datura* ou **Duroa**, espece de *Stramonium*, est vne plante grande et haute qui porte des fleurs blanches en Campane, comme le *Cisampelo*, mais plus grande."—*Mocquet, Voyages*, 312.

[1610.—"In other parts of the Indies it is called **Dutroa**."—*Pyrard de Laval*, Hak. Soc. ii. 114.

[1621.—"Garcias ab Horto ... makes mention of an hearb called **Datura**, which, if it be eaten, for 24 hours following, takes away all sense of grief, makes them incline to laughter and mirth."—*Burton, Anatomy of Mel.*, Pt. 2, Sec. 5 Mem. I. Subs. 5.]

1673.—"**Dutry**, the deadliest sort of *Solarium* (*Solanum*) or *Nightshade*."—*Fryer*, 32.

1676.—

"Make lechers and their punks with **dewtry**
Commit fantastical advowtry."
Hudibras, Pt. iii. Canto 1.

1690.—"And many of them (the Moors) take the liberty of mixing **Dutra** and Water together to drink ... which will intoxicate almost to Madness."—*Ovington*, 235.

1810.—"The **datura** that grows in every part of India."—*Williamson, V. M.* ii. 135.

1874.—"**Datura.** This plant, a native of the East Indies, and of Abyssinia, more than a century ago had spread as a naturalized plant through every country in Europe except Sweden, Lapland, and Norway, through the aid of gipsy quacks, who used the seed as anti-spasmodics, or for more questionable purposes."—*R. Brown* in *Geog. Magazine*, i. 371. *Note.*—The statements derived from *Hanbury and Flückiger* in the beginning of this article disagree with this view, both as to the origin of the European *Datura* and the identity of the Indian plant. The doubts about the birthplace of the various species of the genus remain in fact undetermined. [See the discussion in *Watt, Econ. Dict.* iii. 29 *seqq.*]

DAWK, s. H. and Mahr. *ḍāk*, 'Post,' *i.e.* properly transport by relays of men and horses, and thence 'the mail' or letter-post, as well as any arrangement for travelling, or for transmitting articles by such relays. The institution was no doubt imitated from the *barīd*, or post, established throughout the empire of the Caliphs by Mo'āwia. The *barīd* is itself connected with the Latin *verēdus*, and *verēdius*.

1310.—"It was the practice of the Sultan (Aláuddín) when he sent an army on an expedition to establish posts on the road, wherever posts could be maintained. ... At every half or quarter *kos* runners were posted ... the securing of accurate intelligence from the court on one side and the army on the other was a great public benefit."—*Ziā-uddīn Barnī*, in *Elliot*, iii. 203.

c. 1340.—"The foot-post (in India) is thus arranged: every mile is divided into three equal intervals which are called **Dāwah**, which is as much as to say 'the third part of a mile' (the mile itself being called in India *Koruh*). At every third of a mile there is a village well inhabited, outside of which are three tents where men are seated ready to start. ..."—*Ibn Batuta*, iii. 95.

c. 1340.—"So he wrote to the Sultan to announce our arrival, and sent his letter by the **dāwah**, which is the foot post, as we have told you. ..."—*Ibid.* 145.

"At every mile (*i.e. Korūh* or *coss*) from Delhi to Daulatabād there are three **dāwah** or posts."—*Ibid.* 191–2. It seems probable that this **dāwah** is some misunderstanding of **ḍāk.**

"There are established, between the capital and the chief cities of the different territories, posts placed at certain distances from each other; which are like the post-relays in Egypt and Syria ... but the distance between them is not more than four bowshots or even less. At each of these posts ten swift runners are stationed ... as soon as one of these men receives a letter he runs off as rapidly as possible. ... At each of these post stations there are mosques, where prayers are said, and where the traveller can find shelter, reservoirs full of good water, and markets ... so that there is very little necessity for carrying water, or food, or tents."—*Shahābuddīn Dimishkā*, in *Elliot*, iii. 581.

1528.—"... that every ten *kos* he should erect a *yam*, or post-house, which they call a **dâk-choki**, for six horses. ..."—*Baber*, 393.

c. 1612.—"He (Akbar) established posts throughout his dominions, having two horses and a set of footmen stationed at every five coss. The Indians call this establishment '**Dak** *chowky*.'"—*Firishta*, by *Briggs*, ii. 280–1.

1657.—"But when the intelligence of his (Dara-Shekoh's) officious meddling had spread abroad through the provinces by the **dák** *chauki*. ..."—*Khāfi Khān*, in *Elliot*, vii. 214.

1727.—"The Post in the Mogul's Dominions goes very swift, for at every Caravanseray, which are built on the High-roads, about ten miles distant from one another, Men, very swift of Foot, are kept ready. ... And these Curriers are called **Dog** *Chouckies*."—*A. Hamilton*, i. 149; [ed. 1744, i. 150].

1771.—"I wrote to the Governor for permission to visit Calcutta by the **Dawks**. ..."—Letter in the *Intrigues of a Nabob*, &c., 76.

1781.—"I mean the absurd, unfair, irregular and dangerous Mode, of suffering People to paw over their Neighbours' Letters at the **Dock**. ..."—Letter in *Hicky's Bengal Gazette*, Mar. 24.

1796.—"The Honble. the Governor-General in Council has been pleased to order the re-establishment of **Dawk** *Bearers* upon the new road from Calcutta to Benares and Patna. ... The following are the rates fixed ...

"From Calcutta to Benares. ... Sicca Rupees 500." In *Seton-Karr*, ii. 185.

1809.—"He advised me to proceed immediately by **Dawk**. ..."—*Ld. Valentia*, i. 62.

1824.—"The **dāk** or post carrier having passed me on the preceding day, I dropped a letter into his leathern bag, requesting a friend to send his horse on for me."—*Seely*, *Wonders of Ellora*, ch. iv. A letter so sent by the post-runner, in the absence of any receiving office, was said to go "*by outside* **dawk**."

1843.—"Jam: You have received the money of the British for taking charge of the **dawk**; you have betrayed your trust, and stopped the **dawks**. ... If you come in and make your salám, and promise fidelity to the British Government, I will restore to you your lands ... and the superintendence of the **dawks**. If you refuse I will wait till the hot weather has gone past, and then I will carry fire and sword into your territory ... and if I catch you, I will hang you as a rebel."—*Sir C. Napier* to the Jam of the Jokees (in *Life of Dr. J. Wilson*, p. 440).

1873.—"... the true reason being, Mr, Barton declared, that he was too stingy to pay her **dawk**."—*The True Reformer*, i. 63.

DAWK, To lay a, v. To cause relays of bearers, or horses, to be posted on a road. As regards palankin bearers this used to be done either through the post-office, or through local **chowdries** (q.v.) of bearers. During the mutiny of 1857–58, when several young surgeons had arrived in India, whose services were urgently wanted at the front, it is said that the Head of the Department to which they had reported themselves, directed them immediately to '**lay a dawk**.' One of them turned back from the door, saying: 'Would you explain, Sir; for you might just as well tell me to lay an egg!'

DAWK BUNGALOW See under BUNGALOW.

DAYE, DHYE, s. A wet-nurse; used in Bengal and N. India, where this is the sense now attached to the word. Hind. *dāī*, Skt. *dātrikā*; conf. Pers. *dāyah*, a nurse, a midwife. The word also in the earlier English Regulations is applied, Wilson states, to "a female commissioner employed to interrogate and swear native women of condition, who could not appear to give evidence in a Court."

[1568.—"No Christian shall call an infidel **Daya** at the time of her labour."—*Archiv. Port. Orient.* fasc. iv. p. 25.]

1578.—"The whole plant is commonly known and used by the **Dayas**, or as we call them *comadres*" ("gossips," midwives).—*Acosta*, *Tractado*, 282.

1613.—"The medicines of the Malays ... ordinarily are roots of plants ... horns and claws and stones, which are used by their leeches, and for the most part by **Dayas**, which are women physicians, excellent herbalists, apprentices of the schools of Java Major."—*Godinho de Eredia*, f. 37.

1782.—In a Table of monthly Wages at Calcutta, we have:—

"**Dy** (Wet-nurse) 10 Rs."

India Gazette, Oct. 12.

1808.—"If the bearer hath not strength what

can the **Daee** (midwife) do?"—**Guzerati** Proverb, in *Drummond's Illustrations*, 1803.

1810.—"The **Dhye** is more generally an attendant upon native ladies."—*Williamson, V.M.* i. 341.

1883.—"... the '**dyah**' or wet-nurse is looked on as a second mother, and usually provided for for life."—*Wills, Modern Persia*, 326.

[1887.—"I was much interested in the **Dhais** ('midwives') class."—*Lady Dufferin, Viceregal Life in India*, 337.]

DEANER, s. This is not Anglo-Indian, but it is a curious word of English Thieves' cant, signifying 'a shilling.' It seems doubtful whether it comes from the Italian *danaro* or the Arabic **dīnār** (q.v.); both eventually derived from the Latin *denarius*.

DECCAN, n.p. and adj. Hind. *Dakhin, Dakkhin, Dakhan, Dakkhan*; *dakkhiṇa*, the Prakr. form of Skt. *dakshiṇa*, 'the South'; originally 'on the right hand'; compare *dexter*, δεξίος. The Southern part of India, the Peninsula, and especially the Tableland between the Eastern and Western Ghauts. It has been often applied also, politically, to specific States in that part of India, *e.g.* by the Portuguese in the 16th century to the Mahommedan Kingdom of Bījapur, and in more recent times by ourselves to the State of Hyderabad. In Western India the **Deccan** stands opposed to the **Concan**, *i.e.* the tableland of the interior to the maritime plain; in Upper India the **Deccan** stands opposed to **Hindūstān**, *i.e.* roundly speaking, the country south of the Nerbudda to that north of it. The term frequently occurs in the Skt. books in the form *dakshiṇāpatha* ('Southern region,' whence the Greek form in our first quotation), and *dakshīṇātya* ('Southern'—qualifying some word for 'country'). So, in the *Pañchatantra*: "There is in the Southern region (*dakshīṇātya janapada*) a town called Mihilāropya."

c. A.D. 80–90.—"But immediately after Barygaza the adjoining continent extends from the North to the South, wherefore the region is called **Dachinabadēs** (Δαχιναβάδης), for the South is called in their tongue **Dachanos** (Δάχανος)."—*Periplus M.E., Geog. Gr. Min.* i. 254.

1510.—"In the said city of **Decan** there reigns a King, who is a Mahommedan."—*Varthema*, 117. (Here the term is applied to the city and kingdom of Bījapur).

1517.—"On coming out of this Kingdom of Guzarat and Cambay towards the South, and the inner parts of India, is the Kingdom of **Dacani**, which the Indians call **Decan**."—*Barbosa*, 69.

1552.—"Of **Decani** or **Daquē** as we now call it."—*Castanheda*, ii. 50.

"He (Mahmūd Shāh) was so powerful that he now presumed to style himself King of Canara, giving it the name of **Decan**. And the name is said to have been given to it from the combination of different nations contained in it, because **Decanij** in their language signifies 'mongrel.'"—*De Barros*, Dec. II. liv. v. cap. 2. (It is difficult to discover what has led astray here the usually well-informed De Barros).

1608.—"For the *Portugals* of *Daman* had wrought with an ancient friend of theirs a *Raga*, who was absolute Lord of a Prouince (betweene *Daman, Guzerat*, and **Decan**) called Cruly, to be readie with 200 Horsemen to stay my passage."—*Capt. W. Hawkins*, in *Purchas*, i. 209.

[1612.—"The **Desanins**, a people bordering on them (Portuguese) have besieged six of their port towns."—*Danvers, Letters*, i. 258.]

1616.—"... his son Sultan Coron, who he designed, should command in **Deccan**."—*Sir T. Roe.*

["There is a resolution taken that Sultan Caronne shall go to the **Decan** Warres."—*Ibid.* Hak. Soc. i. 192.

[1623.—"A Moor of **Dacàn**."—*P. della Valle*, Hak. Soc. ii. 225.]

1667.—

"But such as at this day, to Indians known,
In Malabar or **Decan** spreads her arms."
Paradise Lost, ix. [1102–3].

1726.—"**Decan** [as a division] includes **Decan**, *Cunkam*, and *Balagatta*."—*Valentijn*, v. 1.

c. 1750.—"... alors le Nababe d'Arcate, tout petit Seigneur qu'il étoit, comparé au Souba du **Dekam** dont il n'étoit que le Fermier traiter (*sic*) avec nous comme un Souverain avec ses sujets."—Letter of M. Bussy, in *Cambridge's War in India*, p. xxix.

1870.—"In the **Deccan** and in Ceylon trees and bushes near springs, may often be seen covered with votive flowers."—*Lubbock, Origin of Civilization*, 200. N.B.—This is a questionable statement as regards the Deccan.

DECK, s. A look, a peep. Imp. of Hind. *dekh-nā*, 'to look.'

[1830.—"When on a sudden, coming to a check, Thompson's mahout called out, '**Dekh!** Sahib, **Dekh!**'"—*Or. Sporting Mag.*, ed. 1873, i. 350.]

1854.—"... these formed the whole assemblage, with the occasional exception of some officer, stopping as he passed by, returning from his morning ride 'just to have a **dekh** at the steamer.' ..."—*W. Arnold, Oakfield*, i. 85.

DELHI, n.p. The famous capital of the great Moghuls, in the latter years of that family; and the seat under various names of many preceding dynasties, going back into ages of which we have no distinct record. *Dillī* is, according to Cunningham, the old Hindu form of the name; *Dihlī* is that used by Mahommedans. According to *Panjab Notes and Queries* (ii. 117 *seq.*), *Dilpat* is traditionally the name of the Dillī of Prithvī Rāj. *Dil* is an old Hindi word for an eminence; and this is probably the etymology of *Dilpat* and *Dilli*. The second quotation from Correa curiously illustrates the looseness of his geography. [The name has become unpleasantly familiar in connection with the so-called '*Delhi boil*,' a form of Oriental sore, similar to Biskra Button, Aleppo Evil, Lahore or Multan Sore (see *Delhi Gazetteer*, 15, note).]

1205.—(Muhammad Ghori marched) "towards **Dehli** (may God preserve its prosperity, and perpetuate its splendour!), which is among the chief (mother) cities of Hind."—*Hasan Nizāmi*, in *Elliot*, ii. 216.

c. 1321.—"Hanc terram (Tana, near Bombay) regunt Sarraceni, nunc subjacentes dal **dili**. ... Audiens ipse imperator dol **Dali** ... misit et ordinavit ut ipse Lomelic penitus caperetur. ..."—*Fr. Odoric*. See *Cathay*, &c., App., pp. v. and x.

c. 1330.—"**Dillī** ... a certain traveller relates that the brick-built walls of this great city are loftier than the walls of Hamath; it stands in a plain on a soil of mingled stones and sand. At the distance of a parasang runs a great river, not so big, however, as Euphrates."—*Abulfeda*, in *Gildemeister*, 189 *seq.*

c. 1334.—"The wall that surrounds **Dihlī** has no equal. ... The city of **Dihlī** has 28 gates ..." &c.—*Ibn Batuta*, iii. 147 *seqq.*

c. 1375.—The *Carta Catalana* of the French Library shows *ciutat de* **Dilli** and also *Lo Rey Dilli*, with 'this rubric below it: "*Avi esta un soldã gran e podaros molt rich. Aquest soldã ha* DCC *orifans e* C *millia homens à cavall sot lo seu imperi. Ha encora paons sens nombre* ..."

1459.—Fra Mauro's great map at Venice shows **Deli** *cittade grandissima*, and the rubrick *Questa cittade nobilissima zà dominava tuto el paese del* **Deli** *over India Prima.*

1516.—"This king of **Dely** confines with Tatars, and has taken many lands from the King of Cambay; and from the King of Decan, his servants and captains with many of his people, took much, and afterwards in time they revolted, and set themselves up as kings."—*Barbosa*, p. 100.

1533.—"And this kingdom to which the Badur proceeded was called the **Dely**; it was very great, but it was all disturbed by wars and the risings of one party against another, because the King was dead, and the sons were fighting with each other for the sovereignty."—*Correa*, iii. 506.

"This Kingdom of **Dely** is the greatest that is to be seen in those parts, for one point that it holds is in Persia, and the other is in contact with the Loochoos (*os Lequios*) beyond China."—*Ibid.* iii. 572.

c. 1568.—"About sixteen yeeres past this King (of Cuttack), with his Kingdome, were destroyed by the King of Pattane, which was also King of the greatest part of Bengala ... but this tyrant enjoyed his Kingdome but a small time, but was conquered by another tyrant, which was the great Mogol King of Agra, **Delly**, and of all Cambaia."—*Caesar Frederike* in *Hakl.* ii. 358.

1611.—"On the left hand is seene the carkasse of old **Dely**, called the nine castles and fiftie-two gates, now inhabited onely by *Googers*. ... The city is 2e betweene Gate and Gate, begirt with a strong wall, but much ruinate. ..."—*W. Finch*, in *Purchas*, i. 430.

DEODAR, s. The *Cedrus deodara*, Loud., of the Himālaya, now known as an ornamental tree in England for some seventy-five years past. The finest specimens in the Himālaya are often found in clumps shadowing a small temple. The **Deodar** is now regarded by botanists as a variety of *Cedrus Libani*. It is confined to the W. Himālaya from Nepāl to Afghanistan; it reappears as the Cedar of Lebanon in Syria, and on through Cyprus and Asia Minor; and emerges once more in Algeria, and thence westwards to the Riff Mountains in Morocco, under the name of *C. Atlantica*. The word occurs in Avicenna, who speaks of the *Deiudar* as yielding a kind of turpentine (see below). We may note that an article called *Deodarwood Oil* appears in Dr. Forbes Watson's "List of Indian Products" (No. 2941) [and see *Watt, Econ. Dict.* ii. 235].

Deodar is by no means the universal name of the great Cedar in the Himālay. It is called so (*Dewdār*, *Diār*, or *Dyār* [*Drew, Jummoo*, 100]) in Kashmīr, where the *deodār* pillars of the great mosque of Srinagar date from A.D. 1401. The name, indeed (*devadāru*, 'timber of the gods'), is applied in different parts of India to different trees, and even in the Himālaya to more than one. The list just referred to (which however has not been revised critically) gives this name in different modifications as applied also to the pencil Cedar (*Juniperus excelsa*), to *Guatteria* (or *Uvaria*) *longifolia*, to *Sethia Indica*, to *Erythroxylon areolatum*, and (on the Rāvī and Sutlej) to *Cupressus torulosa*.

The **Deodār** first became known to Europeans in the beginning of the last century, when specimens were sent to Dr. Roxburgh, who called it a *Pinus*. Seeds were sent to Europe by Capt. Gerard in 1819; but the first that grew were those sent by the Hon. W. Leslie Melville in 1822.

c. 1030.—"**Deiudar** (or rather **Diudar**) est ex genere abhel (*i.e.* juniper) quae dicitur pinus Inda, et *Syr deiudar* (Milk of Deodar) est ejus lac (turpentine)."—*Avicenna*, Lat. Transl. p. 297.

c. 1220.—"He sent for two trees, one of which was a ... white poplar, and the other a **deodár**, that is a fir. He planted them both on the boundary of Kashmir."—*Chach Námah* in *Elliot*, i. 144.

DERVISH, s. P. *darvesh*; a member of a Mahommedan religious order. The word is hardly used now among Anglo-Indians, *fakīr* [see FAKEER] having taken its place. On the Mahommedan confraternities of this class, see *Herklots*, 179 *seqq.*; *Lane, Mod. Egyptians, Brown's Dervishes*, or *Oriental Spiritualism*; *Capt. E. de Neven, Les Khouan, Ordres Religieux chez les Musulmans* (Paris, 1846).

c. 1540.—"The dog *Coia Acem* ... crying out with a loud voyce, that every one might hear him. ... *To them, To them, for as we are assured by the Book of Flowers, wherein the Prophet* Noby *doth promise eternal delights to the* **Daroezes** *of the House of* Mecqua, *that he will keep his word both with you and me, provided that we bathe ourselves in the blood of these dogs without Law!*"—*Pinto* (cap. lix.), in *Cogan*, 72.

1554.—"Hic multa didicimus à monachis Turcicis, quos **Dervis** vocant."—*Busbeq. Epist.* I. p. 93.

1616.—"Among the *Mahometans* are many called **Dervises**, which relinquish the World, and spend their days in Solitude."—*Terry*, in *Purchas*, ii. 1477.

1653.—"Il estoit **Dervische** ou Fakir et menoit une vie solitaire dans les bois."—*De la Boullaye-le-Gouz*, ed. 1657, p. 182.

1670.—"Aureng-Zebe ... was reserved, crafty, and exceedingly versed in dissembling, insomuch that for a long time he made profession to be a *Fakire*, that is, Poor, **Dervich**, or Devout, renouncing the World." *Bernier*, E.T. 3; [ed. *Constable*, 10].

1673.—"The **Dervises** professing Poverty, assume this Garb here (*i.e.* in Persia), but not with that state they ramble up and down in India."—*Fryer*, 392.

DEVA-DĀSĪ, s. H. 'Slave-girl of the gods'; the official name of the poor girls who are devoted to dancing and prostitution in the idol-temples, of Southern India especially. "The like existed at ancient Corinth under the name of ἱερόδουλοι, which is nearly a translation of the Hindi name ... (see *Strabo*, viii. 6)."—*Marco Polo*, 2nd ed. ii. 338. These appendages of Aphrodite worship, borrowed from Phœnicia, were the same thing as the *ḳĕdēshōth* repeatedly mentioned in the Old Testament, *e.g. Deut.* xxiii. 18: "Thou shalt not bring the wages of a *kĕdēsha* ... into the House of Jehovah." [See *Cheyne*, in *Encycl. Bibl.* ii. 1964 *seq.*] Both male and female ἱερόδουλοι are mentioned in the famous inscription of Citium in Cyprus (*Corp. Inscr. Semit.* No. 86); the latter under the name of *'alma*, curiously near that of the modern Egyptian *'ālima*. (See DANCING-GIRL.)

1702.—"Peu de temps après je baptisai une **Deva-Dachi**, ou *Esclave Divine*, c'est ainsi qu'on appelle les femmes dont les Prêtres des idoles abusent, sous prétexte que leurs dieux les demandent."—*Lettres Edifiantes*, x. 245.

c. 1790.—"La principale occupation des **devedaschies**, est de danser devant l'image de la divinité qu'elles servent, et de chanter ses louanges, soit dans son temple, soit dans les rues, lorsqu'on porte l'idole dans des processions. ..."—*Haafner* ii. 105.

1868.—"The **Dâsis**, the dancing girls attached to Pagodas. They are each of them married to an idol when quite young. Their male children ... have no difficulty in acquiring a decent position in society. The female children are generally brought up to the trade of their mothers. ... It is customary with a few castes to present their superfluous daughters to the Pagodas. ..."—*Nelson's Madura*, Pt. 2, p. 79.

DEVIL, s. A petty whirlwind, or circular storm, is often so called. (See SHAITAN, TYPHOON.)

[1608–10.—"Often you see coming from afar great whirlwinds which the sailors call **dragons**."—*Pyrard de Laval*, Hak. Soc. i. 11.

[1813.—"... we were often surrounded by the

little whirlwinds called *bugulas*, or **Devils**."—*Forbes, Or. Mem.* 2nd ed. i. 118.]

DEVIL WORSHIP. This phrase is a literal translation of *bhūta-pūjā*, *i.e.* worship of *bhūtas*, a word which appears in slightly differing forms in various languages of India, including the Tamil country. A *bhūta*, or as in Tamil more usually, *pēy*, is a malignant being which is conceived to arise from the person of anyone who has come to a violent death. This superstition, in one form or another, seems to have formed the religion of the Dravidian tribes of S. India before the introduction of Brahmanism, and is still the real religion of nearly all the low castes in that region, whilst it is often patronized also by the higher castes. These superstitions, and especially the demonolatrous rites called 'devil-dancing,' are identical in character with those commonly known as *Shamanism* [see SHAMAN], and which are spread all over Northern Asia, among the red races of America, and among a vast variety of tribes in Ceylon and in Indo-China, not excluding the Burmese. A full account of the demonworship of Tinnevelly was given by Bp. Caldwell in a small pamphlet on the "Tinnevelly Shanars" (Madras 1849), and interesting evidence of its identity with the Shamanism of other regions will be found in his *Comparative Grammar* (2nd ed. 579 *seqq.*); see also *Marco Polo*, 2nd ed. ii. 79 *seq.*; [Oppert. *Orig. Inhabit. of Bharatavarśa*, 554 *seqq.*]

DEWALLY, s. H. *diwālī*, from Skt. *dīpa-ālikā*, 'a row of lamps,' *i.e.* an illumination. An autumnal feast attributed to the celebration of various divinities, as of Lakshmī and of Bhavānī, and also in honour of Krishna's slaying of the demon Naraka, and the release of 16,000 maidens, his prisoners. It is held on the last two days of the dark half of the month *Aśvina* or *Aśan*, and on the new moon and four following days of *Karttika*, *i.e.* usually some time in October. But there are variations of Calendar in different parts of India, and feasts will not always coincide, *e.g.* at the three Presidency towns, nor will any curt expression define the dates. In Bengal the name *Diwālī* is not used; it is *Kālī Pūjā*, the feast of that grim goddess, a midnight festival on the most moonless nights of the month, celebrated by illuminations and fireworks, on land and river, by feasting, carousing, gambling, and sacrifice of goats, sheep, and buffaloes.

1613.—"... no equinoctio da entrada de libra, dià chamado **Divâly**, tem tal privilegio e vertude que obriga falar as arvores, plantas e ervas. ..."—*Godinho de Eredia*, f. 38*v*.

[1623.—"October the four and twentieth was the **Davàli**, or Feast of the Indian Gentiles."—*P. della Valle*, Hak. Soc. ii. 206.]

1651.—"In the month of *October*, eight days after the full moon, there is a feast held in honour of Vistnou, which is called **Dipáwali**."—*A. Rogerius, De Open-Deure*.

[1671.—"In October they begin their yeare with great feasting, Jollity, Sending Presents to all they have any busynes with, which time is called **Dually**."—*Hedges, Diary*, Hak. Soc. ii. cccxiv.]

1673.—"The first New Moon in October is the Banyan's **Dually**."—*Fryer*, 110.

1690.—"... their Grand Festival Season, called the **Dually** Time."—*Ovington*, 401.

1820.—"The **Dewalee**, **Deepaullee**, or Time of Lights, takes place 20 days after the **Dussera**, and lasts three days; during which there is feasting, illumination, and fireworks."—*T. Coats*, in *Tr. Lit. Soc. Bo.*, ii. 211.

1843.—"Nov. 5. The **Dīwālī**, happening to fall on this day, the whole river was bright with lamps. ... Ever and anon some votary would offer up his prayers to Lakshmi the *Fortuna*, and launch a tiny raft bearing a cluster of lamps into the water,—then watch it with fixed and anxious gaze. If it floats on till the far distance hides it, thrice happy he ... but if, caught in some wild eddy of the stream, it disappears at once, so will the bark of his fortunes be engulphed in the whirlpool of adversity."—*Dry Leaves from Young Egypt*, 84.

1883.—"The **Dīvālī** is celebrated with splendid effect at Benares. ... At the approach of night small earthen lamps, fed with oil, are prepared by millions, and placed quite close together, so as to mark out every line of mansion, palace, temple, minaret, and dome in streaks of fire."—*Monier Williams, Religious Thought and Life in India*, 432.

***DEWAUN**, s. The chief meanings of this word in Anglo-Indian usage are:

(1) Under the Mahommedan Governments which preceded us, "the head financial minister, whether of the state or a province ... charged, in the latter, with the collection of the revenue, the remittance of it to the imperial treasury, and invested with extensive judicial powers in all civil and financial causes" (*Wilson*). It was in this sense that

the grant of the **Dewauny** (q.v.) to the E. I. Company in 1765 became the foundation of the British Empire in India. (2) The prime minister of a native State. (3) The chief native officer of certain Government establishments, such as the Mint; or the native manager of a Zemindary. (4) (In Bengal) a native servant in confidential charge of the dealings of a house of business with natives, or of the affairs of a large domestic establishment. These meanings are perhaps all reducible to one conception, of which 'Steward' would be an appropriate expression. But the word has had many other ramifications of meaning, and has travelled far.

The Arabian *dīwān* is, according to Lane, an Arabicized word of Persian origin (though some hold it for pure Arabic), and is in original meaning nearly equivalent to Persian *daftar* (see DUFTER), *i.e.* a collection of written leaves or sheets (forming a book for registration); hence 'a register of accounts'; a 'register of soldiers or pensioners'; a 'register of the rights or dues of the State, or relating to the acts of government, the finances and the administration'; also any book, and especially a collection of the poems of some particular poet. It was also applied to signify 'an account'; then a 'writer of accounts'; a 'place of such writers of accounts'; also a 'council, court, or tribunal'; and in the present day, a 'long seat formed of a mattress laid along the wall of a room, with cushions, raised or on the floor'; or 'two or more of such seats.' Thus far (in this paragraph) we abstract from Lane.

The Arabian historian Bilāduri (c. 860) relates as to the first introduction of the *dīwān* that, when 'Omar was discussing with the people how to divide the enormous wealth derived from the conquests in his time, Walīd bin Hishām bin Moghaira said to the caliph, 'I have been in Syria, and saw that its kings make a **dīwān**; do thou the like.' So 'Omar accepted his advice, and sent for two men of the Persian tongue, and said to them: 'Write down the people according to their rank' (and corresponding pensions).[1]

We must observe that in the Mahommedan States of the Mediterranean the word *dīwān* became especially applied to the Custom-house, and thus passed into the Romance languages as *aduana, douane, dogana*, &c. Littré indeed avoids any decision as to the etymology of *douane*, &c. And Hyde (Note on Abr. Peritsol, in *Syntagma Dissertt.* i. 101) derives *dogana* from *docân* (*i.e.* P. *dukān*, '*officina*, a shop'). But such passages as that below from Ibn Jubair, and the fact that, in the medieval Florentine treaties with the Mahommedan powers of Barbary and Egypt, the word *dīwān* in the Arabic texts constantly represents the *dogana* of the Italian, seem sufficient to settle the question (see *Amari, Diplomi Arabi del Real Archivio*, &c.; *e.g.* p. 104, and (Latin) p. 305, and in many other places).[2] The Spanish Dict. of Cobarruvias (1611) quotes Urrea as saying that "from the Arabic noun **Diuanum**, which signifies the house where the duties are collected, we form *diuana*, and thence *adiuana*, and lastly *aduana*."

At a later date the word was re-imported into Europe in the sense of a hall furnished with Turkish couches and cushions, as well as of a couch of this kind. Hence we get *cigar-***divans**, *et hoc genus omne*. The application to certain collections of poems is noticed above. It seems to be especially applied to assemblages of short poems of homogeneous character. Thus the *Odes* of Horace, the *Sonnets* of Petrarch, the *In Memoriam* of Tennyson, answer to the character of **Dīwān** so used. Hence also Goethe took the title of his *West-Östliche Diwan*.

c. A.D. 636.—"... in the Caliphate of Omar the spoil of Syria and Persia began in ever-increasing volume to pour into the treasury of Medina, where it was distributed almost as soon as received. What was easy in small beginnings by equal sharing or discretionary preference, became now a heavy task. ... At length, in the 2nd or 3rd year of his Caliphate, Omar determined that the distribution should be regulated on a fixed and systematic scale. ... To carry out this vast design, a Register had to be drawn and kept up of every man, woman, and child, entitled to a stipend from the State. ... The Register itself, as well as the office for

1 We owe this quotation, as well as that below from Ibn Jubair, to the kindness of Prof. Robertson Smith. On the proceedings of 'Omar see also Sir Wm. Muir's *Annals of the Early Caliphate* in the chapter quoted below.

2 At p. 6 there is an Arabic letter, dated A.D. 1200, from Abdurrahmān ibn 'Ali Tāhir, '*al-nązir ba-dīwān Ifriķiya*,' inspector of the dogana of Africa. But in the Latin version this appears as *Rector omnium Christianorum qui veniunt in totam provinciam de Africa* (p. 276). In another letter, without date, from Yusuf ibu Mahommed *Sāhib diwān Tunis wal-Mahdia*, Amari renders 'prepoato della dogana di Tunis,' &c. (p. 311).

its maintenance and for pensionary account, was called the **Dewân** or Department of the Exchequer."—*Muir's Annals*, &c., pp. 225–9.

As Minister, &c.

[1610.—"We propose to send you the copy hereof by the old scrivano of the **Aduano**."—*Danvers, Letters*, i. 51.

[1616.—"Sheak Isuph **Dyvon** of Amadavaz."—*Foster, Letters*, iv. 311.]

1690.—"Fearing miscarriage of ye Originall *ffarcuttee* [*fārigh-khaṭṭī*, Ar. 'a deed of release,' variously corrupted in Indian technical use] we have herewi^th^ Sent you a Coppy Attested by Hugly Cazee, hoping y^e^ **Duan** may be Sattisfied therewi^th^."—MS. Letter in India Office, from *Job Charnock* and others at Chuttanutte to Mr. Ch. Eyre at Ballasore.

c. 1718.—"Even the **Divan** of the Qhalissah Office, who is, properly speaking, the Minister of the finances, or at least the accomptant general, was become a mere cypher, or a body without a soul."—*Seir Mutaqherin*, i. 110.

1762.—"A letter from Dacca states that the Hon'ble Company's **Dewan** (Manikchand) died on the morning of this letter. ... As they apprehend he has died worth a large sum of money which the Government's people (*i.e.* of the Nawāb) may be desirous to possess to the injury of his lawful heirs, they request the protection of the flag ... to the family of a man who has served the Company for upwards of 30 years with care and fidelity."—*Ft. Wm. Cons.*, Nov. 29. In *Long*, 283.

1766.—"There then resided at his Court a *Gentoo* named *Allum Chund*, who had been many years **Dewan** to Soujah Khan, by whom he was much revered for his great age, wisdom, and faithful services."—*Holwell, Hist. Events*, i. 74.

1771.—"By our general address you will be informed that we have to be dissatisfied with the administration of Mahomet Reza Cawn, and will perceive the expediency of our divesting him of the rank and influence he holds as Naib **Duan** of the Kingdom of Bengal."—*Court of Directors to W. Hastings*, in *Gleig*, i. 121.

1783.—"The Committee, with the best intentions, best abilities, and steadiest of application, must after all be a tool in the hands of their **Duan**."—*Teignmouth, Mem.* i. 74.

1834.—"His (Raja of Ulwar's) **Dewanjee**, Balmochun, who chanced to be in the neighbourhood, with 6 Risalas of horse ... was further ordered to go out and meet me."—*Mem. of Col. Mountain*, 132.

In the following quotations the identity of *dīwān* and *douane* or *dogana* is shown more or less clearly.

A.D. 1178.—"The Moslem were ordered to disembark their goods (at Alexandria), and what remained of their stock of provisions; and on the shore were officers who took them in charge, and carried all that was landed to the **Dīwān**. They were called forward one by one; the property of each was brought out, and the **Dīwān** was straitened with the crowd. The search fell on every article, small or great; one thing got mixt up with another, and hands were thrust into the midst of the packages to discover if anything were concealed in them. Then, after this, an oath was administered to the owners that they had nothing more than had been found. Amid all this, in the confusion of hands and the greatness of the crowd many things went amissing. At length the passengers were dismissed after a scene of humiliation and great ignominy, for which we pray God to grant an ample recompense. But this, past doubt, is one of the things kept hidden from the great Sultan Salāh-ud-dīn, whose well-known justice and benevolence are such that, if he knew it, he would certainly abolish the practice" [*viz.* as regards Mecca pilgrims].[1]—*Ibn Jubair*, orig. in *Wright's* ed., p. 36.

c. 1340.—"**Doana** *in all the cities of the Saracens*, in Sicily, in Naples, and throughout the Kingdom of Apulia ... *Dazio* at Venice; *Gabella* throughout Tuscany; ... *Costuma* throughout the Island of England. ... All these names mean *duties* which have to be paid for goods and wares and other things, imported to, or exported from, or passed through the countries and places detailed."—*Francesco Balducci Pegolotti*, see *Cuthay*, &c., ii. 285–6.

c. 1348.—"They then order the skipper to state in detail all the goods that the vessel contains. ... Then everybody lands, and the keepers of the custom-house (*al*-**dīwān**) sit and pass in review whatever one has."—*Ibn Batuta*, iv. 265.

The following medieval passage in one of our note-books remains a fragment without date or source:

(?).—"Multi quoque Saracenorum, qui vel in apothecis suis mercibus vendendis praeerunt, vel in **Duanis** fiscales ..."

1440.—The Handbook of Giovanni da Uzzano, published along with Pegolotti by Pagnini (1765–66) has for custom-house **Dovana**,

1 The present generation in England can have no conception how closely this description applies to what took place at many an English port before Sir Robert Peel's great changes in the import tariff. The present writer, in landing from a P. & O. steamer at Portsmouth in 1845, after four or five days' quarantine in the Solent, had to go through *five to six hours* of such treatment as Ibn Jubair describes, and his feelings were very much the same as the Moor's.—[H. Y.]

which corroborates the identity of *Dogana* with *Dīwān*.

A Council Hall:

1367.—"Hussyn, fearing for his life, came down and hid himself under the tower, but his enemies ... surrounded the mosque, and having found him, brought him to the (**Dyvan**-*Khane*) Council Chamber."—*Mem. of Timūr*, tr. by *Stewart*, p. 130.

1554.—"Utcunque sit, cum mane in **Divanum** (is concilii vt alias dixi locus est) imprudens omnium venisset. ..."—*Busbequii Epistolae*, ii. p. 138.

A place, fitted with mattresses, &c., to sit in:

1676.—"On the side that looks towards the River, there is a **Divan**, or a kind of out-jutting Balcony, where the King sits."—*Tavernier*, E.T. ii. 49; [ed. *Ball*, i. 108].

[1785.—"It seems to have been intended for a **Duan Konna**, or eating room."—*Forbes, Or. Mem.* 2nd ed. ii. 393.]

A Collection of Poems:

1783.—"One (writer) died a few years ago at Benares, of the name of Souda, who composed a **Dewan** in Moors."—*Teignmouth, Mem.* i. 105.

DEWAUNY, DEWANNY, &c., s. Properly, *dīwānī*; popularly, *dewānī*. The office of *dīwān* (**Dewaun**); and especially the right of receiving as *dīwān* the revenue of Bengal, Behar, and Orissa, conferred upon the E. I. Company by the Great Mogul Shāh 'Ālam in 1765. Also used sometimes for the territory which was the subject of that grant.

1765.—(Lord Clive) "visited the Vezir, and having exchanged with him some sumptuous entertainments and curious and magnificent presents, he explained the project he had in his mind, and asked that the Company should be invested with the *Divanship* (no doubt in orig. **Dīwānī**) of the three provinces. ..."—*Seir Mutaqherin*, ii. 384.

1783.—(The opium monopoly) "is stated to have begun at Patna so early as the year 1761, but it received no considerable degree of strength until the year 1765; when the acquisition of the **Duanne** opened a wide field for all projects of this nature."—*Report of a Committee on Affairs of India*, in *Burke's Life and Works*, vi. 447.

***DEWAUNY, DEWANNY**, adj. Civil, as distinguished from Criminal; *e.g. Dīwānī 'Adālat* as opposite to *Faujdāri Adālat*. (See ADAWLUT). The use of *Diwāni* for civil as opposed to criminal is probably modern and Indian. For Kaempfer in his account of the Persian administration at the end of the 17th century, has: "**Diwaen** *begì*, id est, *Supremus* criminalis *Judicii Dominus* ... de latrociniis et homicidiis non modo in hâc Regiâ metropoli, verùm etiam in toto Regno disponendi facultatem habet."—*Amoenit. Exot.* 80.

DHALL, DOLL, s. Hind. *dāl*, a kind of pulse much used in India, both by natives as a kind of porridge, and by Europeans as an ingredient in **kedgeree** (q.v.), or to mix with rice as a breakfast dish. It is best represented in England by what are called 'split pease.' The proper *dāl*, which Wilson derives from the Skt. root *dal*, 'to divide' (and which thus corresponds in meaning also to 'split pease'), is, according to the same authority, *Phaseolus aureus*: but, be that as it may, the *dāls* most commonly in use are varieties of the shrubby plant *Cajanus Indicus*, Spreng., called in Hind. *arhar*, *rahar*, &c. It is not known where this is indigenous; [De Candolle thinks it probably a native of tropical Africa, introduced perhaps 3,000 years ago into India;] it is cultivated throughout India. The term is also applied occasionally to other pulses, such as *mūng*, *urd*, &c. (See MOONG, OORD.) It should also be noted that in its original sense *dāl* is not the name of a particular pea, but the generic name of pulses prepared for use by being broken in a hand-mill; though the peas named are those commonly used in Upper India in this way.

1673.—"At their coming up out of the Water they bestow the largess of Rice or **Doll** (an Indian Bean)."—*Fryer*, 101.

1690.—"*Kitcheree* ... made of **Dol**, that is, a small round Pea, and Rice boiled together, and is very strengthening, tho' not very savoury."—*Ovington*, 310.

1727.—"They have several species of Legumen, but those of **Doll** are most in use, for some **Doll** and Rice being mingled together and boiled, make *Kitcheree*."—*A. Hamilton*, i. 162; [ed. 1744].

1776.—"If a person hath bought the seeds of ... **doll** ... or such kinds of Grain, without Inspection, and in ten Days discovers any Defect in that Grain, he may return such Grain."—*Halhed, Code*, 178.

1778.—"... the essential articles of a Sepoy's diet, rice, **doll** (a species of pea), ghee (an indifferent kind of butter), &c., were not to be purchased."—*Acc. of the Gallant Defence made at Mangalore*.

1809.—"... **dol**, split country peas."—*Maria Graham*, 25.

[1813.—"Tuar (*cytisus cajan*, Lin.) ... is called **Dohll**. ..."—*Forbes, Or. Mem.* 2nd ed. ii. 35.]

DHOBY, DOBIE, s. A washerman; H. *dhobī*, [from *dhonā*, Skt. *dhāv*, 'to wash.'] In colloquial Anglo-Indian use all over India. A common H. proverb runs: *Dhobī kā kuttā kā sā, na ghar kā na ghāṭ kā, i.e.* "Like a **Dhoby's** dog belonging neither to the house nor to the river side." [**Dhoby's** itch is a troublesome cutaneous disease supposed to be communicated by clothes from the wash, and **Dhoby's** earth is a whitish-grey sandy efflorescence, found in many places, from which by boiling and the addition of quicklime an alkali of considerable strength is obtained.

[c. 1804.—"**Dobes.**" See under DIRZEE].

DHOOLY, DOOLIE, s. A covered litter; Hind. *ḍolī*. It consists of a cot *or frame*, suspended by the four corners from a bamboo pole, and is carried by two or four men (see figure in *Herklots, Qanoon-e-Islam*, pl. vii. fig. 4). *Ḍoli* is from *ḍolnā*, 'to swing.' The word is also applied to the meat- (or milk-) safe, which is usually slung to a tree, or to a hook in the verandah. As it is lighter and cheaper than a palankin it costs less both to buy or hire and to carry, and is used by the poorer classes. It also forms the usual ambulance of the Indian army. Hence the familiar story of the orator in Parliament who, in celebrating a battle in India, spoke of the "ferocious *Doolies* rushing down from the mountain and carrying off the wounded"; a story which, to our regret, we have not been able to verify. [According to one account the words were used by Burke: "After a sanguinary engagement, the said Warren Hastings had actually ordered ferocious *Doolys* to seize upon the wounded" (2nd ser. *Notes & Queries*, iv. 367).

[But Burke knew too much of India to make this mistake. In the *Calcutta Review* (Dec. 1846, p. 286, footnote) Herbert Edwardes, writing on the first Sikh War, says: "It is not long since a member of the British Legislature, recounting the incidents of one of our Indian fights, informed his countrymen that 'the ferocious *Dūlī*' rushed from the hills and carried off the wounded soldiers."] *Dūla* occurs in *Ibn Batuta*, but the translators render '*palankin*,' and do not notice the word.

c. 1343.—"The principal vehicle of the people (of Malabar) is a **dūla**, carried on the shoulders of slaves and hired men. Those who do not ride in a *dūla*, whoever they may be, go on foot."—*Ibn Batuta*, iv. 73.

c. 1590.—"The *Kahárs* or *Pálkí-bearers*. They form a class of foot servants peculiar to India. With their *pálkís* ... and **dúlís**, they walk so evenly that the man inside is not inconvenienced by any jolting."—*Āīn*, i. 254; [and see the account of the *sukhāsan, ibid.* ii. 122].

1609.—"He turned *Moore*, and bereaved his elder Brother of this holde by this stratageme. He invited him and his women to a Banket, which his Brother requiting with like inuitation of him and his, in steed of women he sends choice Souldiers well appointed, and close couered, two and two in a **Dowle**."—*Hawkins*, in *Purchas*, i. 435.

1662.—"The Rájah and the Phúkans travel in singhásans, and chiefs and rich people in **dúlís**, made in a most ridiculous way."—*Mir Jumlah's Invasion of Asam*, tr. by *Blochmann*, in *J. As. Soc. Ben.*, xli., pt. I. 80.

1702.—"... un **Douli**, e'est unc voiture moins honorable que le palanquin."—*Lettres Edif.* xi. 143.

c. 1760.—"**Doolies** are much of the same material as the *andolas*; but made of the meanest materials."—*Grose*, i. 155.

c. 1768.—"... leaving all his wounded ... on the field of battle, telling them to be of good cheer, for that he would send **Doolies** for them from Astara. ..."—*H. of Hydur Naik*, 226.

1774.—"If by a **dooley**, chairs, or any other contrivance they can be secured from the fatigues and hazards of the way, the expense is to be no objection."—*Letter of W. Hastings*, in *Markham's Tibet*, 18.

1785.—"You must despatch **Doolies** to Dhârwâr to bring back the wounded men."—*Letters of Tippoo*, 133.

1789.—"... **doolies**, or sick beds, which are a mean representation of a palanquin: the number attached to a corps is in the proportion of one to every ten men, with four bearers to each."—*Munro, Narrative*, 184.

1845.—"Head Qrs., Kurrachee, 27 Decr., 1845.

"The Governor desires that it may be made known to the **Doolee**-*wallas* and Camel-men, that no increase of wages shall be given to them. They are very highly paid. If any man deserts, the Governor will have him pursued by the police, and if caught he shall be hanged."—*G. O. by Sir Charles Napier*, 113.

1872.—"At last ... a woman arrived from

Dargánagar with a **dúlí** and two bearers, for carrying Máláti."—*Govinda Samanta*, ii. 7.

1880.—"The consequence of holding that this would be a Trust enforceable in a Court of Law would be so monstrous that persons would be probably startled ... if it be a Trust, then every one of those persons in England or in India—from persons of the highest rank down to the lowest **dhoolie**-*bearer*, might file a bill for the administration of the Trust."—*Ld. Justice James*, Judgment on the Kirwee and Banda Prize Appeal, 13th April.

1883.—"I have great pleasure here in bearing my testimony to the courage and devotion of the Indian **dhooly**-bearers. I ... never knew them shrink from the dangers of the battle-field, or neglect or forsake a wounded European. I have several times seen one of these bearers killed and many of them disabled while carrying a wounded soldier out of action."—*Surgeon-General Munro, C.B., Reminiscences of Mil. Service with the 93rd Sutherland Highlanders*, p. 193.

DHOTY, s. Hind. *dhotī*. The loin-cloth worn by all the respectable Hindu castes of Upper India, wrapt round the body, the end being then passed between the legs and tucked in at the waist, so that a festoon of calico hangs down to either knee. [It is mentioned, not by name, by Arrian (*Indika*, 16) as "an under garment of cotton which reaches below the knee, half way to the ankle"; and the Orissa *dhotī* of 1200 years ago, as shown on the monuments, does not differ from the mode of the present time, save that men of rank wore a jewelled girdle with a pendant in front. (*Rajendralala Mitra, Indo-Aryans*, i. 187).] The word *duttee* in old trade lists of cotton goods is possibly the same; [but at the present time a coarse cotton cloth woven by Dhers in Surat is known as *Doti*.]

[1609.—"Here is also a strong sort of cloth called **Dhootie**."—*Danvers, Letters*, i. 29.

[1614.—"20 corge of strong **Dutties**, such as may be fit for making and mending sails."—*Forster, Letters*, ii. 219.

[1615.—"200 peeces **Dutts**."—*Cocks's Diary*, i. 83.]

1622.—"Price of calicoes, **duttees** fixed."

* * * * *

"List of goods sold, including diamonds, pepper, bastas, (read *baftas*), **duttees**, and silks from Persia."—*Court Minutes*, &c., in *Sainsbury*, iii. 24.

1810.—"... a **dotee** or waist-cloth."—*Williamson, V. M.* i. 247.

1872.—"The human figure which was moving with rapid strides had no other clothing than a **dhuti** wrapped round the waist, and descending to the knee-joints."—*Govinda Samanta*, i. 8.

DHURNA, TO SIT, v. In H. *dharnā denā* or *baithnā*, Skt. *dhṛi*, 'to hold.' A mode of extorting payment or compliance with a demand, effected by the complainant or creditor sitting at the debtor's door, and there remaining without tasting food till his demand shall be complied with, or (sometimes) by threatening to do himself some mortal violence if it be not complied with. Traces of this custom in some form are found in many parts of the world, and Sir H. Maine (see below) has quoted a remarkable example from the Irish Brehon Laws. There was a curious variety of the practice, in arrest for debt, current in S. India, which is described by Marco Polo and many later travellers (see *M. P.*, 2nd ed., ii. 327, 335, [and for N. India, *Crooke, Pop. Rel. and Folklore*, ii. 42, *seq.*]). The practice of *dharnā* is made an offence under the Indian Penal Code. There is a systematic kind of *dharnā* practised by classes of beggars, *e.g.* in the Punjab by a class called *Tasmīwālās*, or 'strap-riggers,' who twist a leather strap round the neck, and throw themselves on the ground before a shop, until alms are given; [*Dorīwālās*, who threaten to hang themselves: *Dandīwālās*, who rattle sticks, and stand cursing till they get alms; *Urimārs*, who simply stand before a shop all day, and *Gurzmārs* and *Chharimārs*, who cut themselves with knives and spiked clubs] (see *Ind. Antiq.* i. 162, [*Herklots, Qanoon-e-Islam*, ed. 1863, p. 193 *seq*]. It appears from Elphinstone (below) that the custom sometimes received the Ar. Pers. name of *takāẓa*, 'dunning' or 'importunity.'

c. 1747.—"While Nundi Raj, the Dulwai was encamped at Sutti Mangul, his troops, for want of pay, placed him in **Dhurna**. ... Hurree Singh, forgetting the ties of salt or gratitude to his master, in order to obtain his arrears of pay, forbade the sleeping and eating of the Dulwai, by placing him in **Dhurna** ... and that in so great a degree as even to stop the water used in his kitchen. The Dulwai, losing heart from this rigour, with his clothes and the vessels of silver and gold used in travelling, and a small sum of money, paid him off and discharged him."—*H. of Hydur Naik*, 41 *seq.*

c. 1794.—"The practice called **dharna**, which

may be translated caption, or arrest."—*Sir J. Shore*, in *As. Res.* iv. 144.

1808.—"A remarkable circumstance took place yesterday. Some Sirdars put the Maharaja (Sindia) in **dhurna**. He was angry, and threatened to put them to death. Bhugwunt Ras Byse, their head, said, 'Sit still; put us to death.' Sindia was enraged, and ordered him to be paid and driven from camp. He refused to go. ... The bazaars were shut the whole day; troops were posted to guard them and defend the tents. ... At last the mutineers marched off, and all was settled."—*Elphinstone's Diary*, in *Life*, i. 179 *seq.*

1809.—"Seendhiya (*i.e.* Sindia), who has been lately plagued by repeated **D'hurnas**, seems now resolved to partake also in the active part of the amusement: he had permitted this same Patunkur, as a signal mark of favour, to borrow 50,000 rupees from the *Khasgee*, or private treasury. ... The time elapsed without the agreement having been fulfilled; and Seendhiya immediately dispatched the treasurer to sit **D'hurna** on his behalf at Patunkur's tents."—*Broughton, Letters from a Mahratta Camp*, 169 *seq.*; [ed. 1892, 127].

[1812.—Morier (*Journey through Persia*, 32) describes similar proceedings by a Dervish at Bushire.]

1819.—"It is this which is called *tukaza*[1] by the Mahrattas. ... If a man have demand from (? upon) his inferior or equal, he places him under restraint, prevents his leaving his house or eating, and even compels him to sit in the sun until he comes to some accommodation. If the debtor were a superior, the creditor had first recourse to supplications and appeals to the honour and sense of shame of the other party; he laid himself on his threshold, threw himself in his road, clamoured before his door, or he employed others to do this for him; he would even sit down and fast before the debtor's door, during which time the other was compelled to fast also; or he would appeal to the gods, and invoke their curses upon the person by whom he was injured."—*Elphinstone*, in *Life*, ii. 37.

1837.[2]—"Whoever voluntarily causes or attempts to cause any person to do anything which that person is not legally bound to do ... by inducing ... that person to believe that he ... will become ... by some act of the offender, an object of the divine displeasure if he does not do the thing ... shall be punished with imprisonment of either description for a term which may extend to one year, or with fine, or with both.

Illustrations.

"(*a*) A. sits **dhurna** at Z.'s door with the intention of causing it to be believed that by so sitting he renders Z. an object of divine displeasure. A. has committed the offence defined in this section.

"(*b*) A. threatens Z. that unless Z. performs a certain act A. will kill one of A.'s own children, under such circumstances that the killing would be believed to render Z. an object of the divine displeasure. A. has committed the offence described in this section."—*Indian Penal Code*, 508, in Chap. XXII., *Criminal Intimidation, Insult, and Annoyance.*

1875.—"If you have a legal claim against a man of a certain rank and you are desirous of compelling him to discharge it, the Senchus Mor tells you 'to fast upon him.' ... The institution is unquestionably identical with one widely diffused throughout the East, which is called by the Hindoos 'sitting **dharna**.' It consists in sitting at the debtor's door and starving yourself till he pays. From the English point of view the practice has always been considered barbarous and immoral, and the Indian Penal Code expressly forbids it. It suggests, however, the question—what would follow if the debtor simply allowed the creditor to starve? Undoubtedly the Hindoo supposes that some supernatural penalty would follow; indeed, he generally gives definiteness to it by retaining a Brahmin to starve himself vicariously, and no Hindoo doubts what would come of causing a Brahmin's death."—*Maine, Hist. of Early Institutions*, 40. See also 297–304.

1885.—"One of the most curious practices in India is that still followed in the native states by a Brahman creditor to compel payment of his debt, and called in Hindi **dharná**, and in Sanskrit *ācharita*, 'customary proceeding,' or *Prāyopaveçana*, 'sitting down to die by hunger.' This procedure has long since been identified with the practice of 'fasting upon' (*troscud for*) a debtor to God or man, which is so frequently mentioned in the Irish so-called Brehon Laws. ... In a MS. in the Bodleian ... there is a Middle-Irish legend which tells how St. Patrick 'fasted upon' Loegaire, the unbelieving over-king of Ireland. Loegaire's pious queen declares that she will not eat anything while Patrick is fasting. Her son Enna seeks for food. 'It is not fitting for thee,' says his mother, 'to eat food while Patrick is fasting upon you.' ... It would seem from this story that in Ireland the wife and children of the debtor, and, *a fortiori*, the debtor himself, had to fast so long as the creditor fasted."—*Letter from Mr. Whitley Stokes*, in *Academy*, Sept. 12th.

A striking story is told in Forbes's *Rās Māla* (ii. 393 *seq.*; [ed. 1878, p. 657]) of a

---

1 Ar. *takāsā*, dunning or importunity.

2 This is the date of the Penal Code, as originally submitted to Lord Auckland, by T. B. Macaulay and his colleagues; and in that original form this passage is found as § 283, and in chap. xv. of *Offences relating to Religion and Caste.*

farther proceeding following upon an unsuccessful **dharnā**, put in practice by a company of Chārans, or bards, in Kathiawāṛ, to enforce payment of a debt by a chief of Jailā to one of their number. After fasting three days in vain, they proceeded from **dharnā** to the further rite of **trāgā** (q.v.). Some hacked their own arms; others decapitated three old women of their party, and hung their heads up as a garland at the gate. Certain of the women cut off their own breasts. The bards also pierced the throats of four of the older men with spikes, and took two young girls and dashed their brains out against the town-gate. Finally the Chāran creditor soaked his quilted clothes in oil, and set fire to himself. As he burned to death he cried out, 'I am now dying, but I will become a headless ghost (*Kavīs*) in the Palace, and will take the chief's life, and cut off his posterity!'

DIGGORY, DIGRĪ, DEGREE, s. Anglo-Hindustani of law-court jargon for 'decree.'

[1866.—"This is grand, thought bold Bhuwanee Singh, **diggree** *to pāh, lekin roopyea to morpāss bah*, 'He has got his decree, but I have the money.'"—*Confessions of an Orderly*, 138.]

DIKK, s. Worry, trouble, botheration; what the Italians call *seccatura*. This is the Anglo-Indian use. But the word is more properly adjective, Ar.-P.-H. *dik*, *dikk*, 'vexed, worried,' and so *dikk-honā*, 'to be worried.' [The noun *dikk-dārī*, 'worry,' in vulgar usage, has become an adjective.]

1873.—
"And Beaufort learned in the law,
And Atkinson the Sage,
And if his locks are white as snow,
'Tis more from **dikk** than age!"
Wilfrid Heeley, A Lay of Modern Darjeeling.

[1889.—"Were the Company's pumps to be beaten by the vagaries of that **dikhdari**, Tarachunda nuddee?"—*R. Kipling, In Black and White*, 52.]

DINGY, DINGHY, s. Beng. *diṅgī*; [H. *dingī*, *dengī*, another form of *dongī*, Skt. *droṇa*, 'a trough.'] A small boat or skiff; sometimes also 'a canoe,' *i.e.* dug out of a single trunk. This word is not merely Anglo-Indian; it has become legitimately incorporated in the vocabulary of the British navy, as the name of the smallest ship's boat; [in this sense, according to the *N.E.D.*, first in *Midshipman Easy* (1836)]. *Dingā* occurs as the name of some kind of war-boat used by the Portuguese in the defence of Hugli in 1631 ("Sixty-four large **díngas**"; *Elliot*, vii. 34). The word *dingī* is also used for vessels of size in the quotation from Tippoo. Sir J. Campbell, in the *Bombay Gazetteer*, says that *dhangī* is a large vessel belonging to the Mekrān coast; the word is said to mean 'a log' in Bilūchī. In Guzerat the larger vessel seems to be called *dangā*; and besides this there is *dhangī*, like a canoe, but *built*, not dug out.

[1610.—"I have brought with me the pinnace and her **ginge** for better performance."—*Danvers, Letters*, i. 61.]

1705.—"... pour aller à terre on est obligé de se servir d'un petit Bateau dont les bords sont très hauts, qu'on appelle **Dingues**. ..."—*Luiller*, 39.

1785.—"Propose to the merchants of *Muscat* ... to bring hither, on the **Dingies**, such horses as they may have for sale; which, being sold to us, the owner can carry back the produce in rice."—*Letters of Tippoo*, 6.

1810.—"On these larger pieces of water there are usually canoes, or **dingies**."—*Williamson, V. M.* ii. 59.

[1813.—"The Indian pomegranates ... are by no means equal to those brought from Arabia by the Muscat **dingeys**."—*Forbes, Or. Mem.* 2nd ed. i. 468.]

1878.—"I observed among a crowd of **dinghies**, one contained a number of native commercial agents."—*Life in the Mofussil*, i. 18.

DITCH, DITCHER. Disparaging sobriquets for Calcutta and its European citizens, for the rationale of which see MAHRATTA DITCH.

***DOAI! DWYE!** Interj. Properly H. *dohāī*, or *dūhāī*, Gujarātī *dawāhī*, an exclamation (hitherto of obscure etymology) shouted aloud by a petitioner for redress at a Court of Justice, or as any one passes who is supposed to have it in his power to aid in rendering the justice sought. It has a kind of analogy, as Thevenot pointed out over 200 years ago, to the old Norman *Haro! Haro! viens à mon aide, mon Prince!*[1] but does not now carry the privilege of the Norman cry; though one

1 It will be seen that the Indian cry also appeals to the Prince expressly. It was the good fortune of one of the present writers (A. B.) to have witnessed the call of Haro! brought into serious operation at Jersey.

may conjecture, both from Indian analogies and from the statement of Ibn Batuta quoted below, that it once did. Every Englishman in Upper India has often been saluted by the calls of, '**Dohāi** *Khudāwand kī!* **Dohāi** *Mahārāj!* **Dohāi** *Kompanī Bahādur!*' 'Justice, my Lord! Justice, O King! Justice, O Company!'—perhaps in consequence of some oppression by his followers, perhaps in reference to some grievance with which he has no power to interfere. "Until 1860 no one dared to ignore the appeal of **dohāī** to a native Prince within his territory. I have heard a serious charge made against a person for calling the **dohāī** needlessly" (*M.-Gen. Keatinge*).

Wilson derives the exclamation from *do*, 'two' or repeatedly, and *hāi* 'alas' illustrating this by the phrase '*dohāī tīhāī karnā*,' 'to make exclamation (or invocation of justice) twice and thrice.' [Platts says, *do-hāy*, Skt. *hrī-hāhā*,' a crying twice "alas!"] This phrase, however, we take to be merely an example of the 'striving after meaning,' usual in cases where the real origin of the phrase is forgotten. We cannot doubt that the word is really a form of the Skt. *droha*, 'injury, wrong.' And this is confirmed by the form in Ibn Batuta, and the Mahr. *durāhi*; "an exclamation or expression used in prohibiting in the name of the Raja ... implying an imprecation of his vengeance in case of disobedience" (*Molesworth's Dict.*); also Tel. and Canar. *durāi*, 'protest, prohibition, caveat, or veto in arrest of proceedings' (*Wilson and C. P. B., MS.*)

c. 1340.—"It is a custom in India that when money is due from any person who is favoured by the Sultan, and the creditor wants his debt settled, he lies in wait at the Palace gate for the debtor, and when the latter is about to enter he assails him with the exclamation **Darōhai** *us-Sultan!* 'O Enemy of the Sultan.—I swear by the head of the King thou shalt not enter till thou hast paid me what thou owest.' The debtor cannot then stir from the spot, until he has satisfied the creditor, or has obtained his consent to the respite."—*Ibn Batuta*, iii. 412. The signification assigned to the words by the Moorish traveller probably only shows that the real meaning was unknown to his Musulman friends at Delhi, whilst its form strongly corroborates our etymology, and shows that it still kept close to the Sanskrit.

1609.—"He is severe enough, but all helpeth not; for his poore Riats or clownes complaine of Iniustice done them, and cry for justice at the King's hands."—*Hawkins*, in *Purchas*, i. 223.

c. 1666.—"Quand on y veut arrêter une personne, on crie seulement **Doa** *padecha*; cette clameur a autant de force que celle de haro en Normandie; et si on defend à quel-qu'un de sortir, du lieu où il est, en disant **Doa** *padecha*, il ne peut partir sans se rendre criminel, et il est obligé de se presentir à la Justice."—*Thevenot*, v. 61.

1834.—"The servant woman began to make a great outcry, and wanted to leave the ship, and cried **Dohaee** to the Company, for she was murdered and kidnapped."—*The Baboo*, ii. 242.

DOLLY, s. Hind. *ḍālī*. A complimentary offering of fruit, flowers, vegetables, sweetmeats and the like, presented usually on one or more trays; also the daily basket of garden produce laid before the owner by the *Mālī* or gardener ("The *Molly* with his *dolly*"). The proper meaning of *ḍālī* is a 'branch' or 'twig' (Skt. *dār*); then a 'basket,' a 'tray,' or a 'pair of trays slung to a yoke,' as used in making the offerings. Twenty years ago the custom of presenting *ḍālīs* was innocent and merely complimentary; but, if the letter quoted under 1882 is correct, it must have grown into a gross abuse, especially in the Punjab. [The custom has now been in most Provinces regulated by Government orders.]

[1832.—"A **Dhaullie** is a flat basket, on which is arranged in neat order whatever fruit, vegetables, or herbs are at the time in season."—*Mrs. Meer Hassan Ali, Observations*, i. 333.]

1880.—"Brass dishes filled with pistachio nuts are displayed here and there; they are the oblations of the would-be visitors. The English call these offerings **dollies**; the natives **dáli**. They represent in the profuse East the visiting cards of the meagre West."—*Ali Baba*, 84.

1882.—"I learn that in Madras **dallies** are restricted to a single gilded orange or lime, or a tiny sugar pagoda, and Madras officers who have seen the *bushels* of fruit, nuts, almonds, sugar-candy ... &c., received by single officials in a single day in the N.W. Provinces, and in addition the number of bottles of brandy, champagne, liquors, &c., received along with all the preceding in the Punjab, have been ... astounded that such a practice should be countenanced by Government."—*Letter in Pioneer Mail*, March 15.

DOME, DHOME; in S. India commonly **Dombaree**, **Dombar**, s. Hind. *Ḍōm* or *Ḍōmrā*. The name of a very low caste, representing some old aboriginal race, spread all over India. In many places they perform such offices as carrying dead bodies, removing carrion, &c. They are often musicians; in Oudh sweepers; in Champāran professional thieves (see *Elliot's Races of the N.W.P.*, [*Risley, Tribes and Castes of Bengal*, s.v.]). It is possible, as has been suggested by some one, that the Gypsy *Romany* is this word.

c. 1328.—"There be also certain others which be called **Dumbri** who eat carrion and carcases; who have absolutely no object of worship; and who have to do the drudgeries of other people, and carry loads."—*Friar Jordanus*, Hak. Soc. p. 21.

1817.—"There is yet another tribe of vagrants, who are also a separate sect. They are the class of mountebanks, buffoons, posture-masters, tumblers, dancers, and the like. ... The most dissolute body is that of the **Dumbars** or **Dumbaru.**"—*Abbé Dubois*, 468.

DOOMBUR, s. The name commonly given in India to the fat-tailed sheep, breeds of which are spread over West Asia and East Africa. The word is properly Pers. *dunba, dumba*; *dumb*, 'tail,' or especially this fat tail. The old story of little carts being attached to the quarters of these sheep to bear their tails is found in many books, but it is difficult to trace any modern evidence of the fact. We quote some passages bearing on it:

c. A.D. 250.—"The tails of the sheep (of India) reach to their feet. ... The shepherds ... cut open the tails and take out the tallow, and then sew it up again. ..."—*Aelian, De Nat. Animal.* iv. 32.

1298.—"Then there are sheep here as big as asses; and their tails are so large and fat, that one tail shall weigh some 30 lbs. They are fine fat beasts, and afford capital mutton."—*Marco Polo*, Bk. i. ch. 18.

1436.—"Their iiijth kinde of beasts are sheepe, which be unreasonable great, longe legged, longe woll, and great tayles, that waie about xij*l*. a piece. And some such I have seene as have drawen a wheele aftre them, their tailes being holden vp."—*Jos. Barbaro*, Hak. Soc. 21.

c. 1520.—"These sheep are not different from others, except as regards the tail, which is very large, and the fatter the sheep is the bigger is his tail. Some of them have tails weighing 10 and 20 pounds, and that will happen when they get fat of their own accord. But in Egypt many persons make a business of fattening sheep, and feed them on bran and wheat, and then the tail gets so big that the sheep can't stir. But those who keep them tie the tail on a kind of little cart, and in this way they move about. I saw one sheep's tail of this kind at Asiot, a city of Egypt 150 miles from Cairo, on the Nile, which weighed 80 lbs., and many people asserted that they have seen such tails that weighed 150 lbs."—*Leo Africanus*, in *Ramusio*, i. f. 92*v*.

[c. 1610.—"The tails of rams and ewes are wondrous big and heavy; one we weighed (in the Island of St. Lawrence) turned 28 pounds."—*Pyrard de Laval*, i. 36.

[1612.—"Goodly Barbary sheep with great rumps."—*Danvers, Letters*, i. 178.]

1828.—"We had a **Doomba** ram at Prag. The *Doomba* sheep are difficult to keep alive in this climate."—*Wanderings of a Pilgrim*, i. 28.

1846.—"I was informed by a person who possessed large flocks, and who had no reason to deceive me, that sometimes the tail of the Tymunnee **doombas** increased to such a size, that a cart or small truck on wheels was necessary to support the weight, and that without it the animal could not wander about; he declared also that he had produced tails in his flock which weighed 12 *Tabreezi munds*, or 48 *seers puckah*, equal to about 96 *lbs.*"—*Cāptain Hutton*, in *Jour. As. Soc. Beng.* xv. 160.

DOOPUTTY, s. Hind. *do-paṭṭah, dupaṭṭā*, &c. A piece of stuff of 'two breadths,' a sheet. "The principal or only garment of women of the lower orders" (in Bengal—*Wilson*). ["Formerly these pieces were woven narrow, and joined alongside of one another to produce the proper width; now, however, the *dupatta* is all woven in one piece. This is a piece of cloth worn entire as it comes from the loom. It is worn either round the head or over the shoulders, and is used by both men and women, Hindu and Muhammadan" (*Yusuf Ali, Mon. on Silk*, 71).] Applied in S. India by native servants, when speaking their own language, to European bed-sheets.

[1615.—"... **dubeties** gouzerams."—*Foster, Letters*, iii. 156.]

DOORGA POOJA, s. Skt. *Durgāpūjā*, 'Worship of Durga.' The chief Hindu festival in Bengal, lasting for 10 days in September—October, and forming the principal holiday-time of all the Calcutta offices. [The common term for these holidays nowadays is 'the **Poojahs**.']

c. 1835.—

"And every **Doorga Pooja** would good Mr. Simms explore
The famous river Hoogly up as high as Barrackpore."

Lines in honour of the late Mr. Simms, Bole Ponjis, 1857, ii. 220.

[1900.—"Calcutta has been in the throes of

the **Pujahs** since yesterday."—*Pioneer Mail*, Oct. 5.]

DORAY, DURAI, s. This is a South Indian equivalent of **Sāhib** (q.v.); Tel. *dora*, Tam. *turai*, 'Master.' *Sinnaturai*, 'small gentleman' is the equivalent of *Chhoṭa Sāhib*, a junior officer; and Tel. *dorasāni*, Tam. *turaisāni* (corruptly *doresáni*) of 'Lady' or 'Madam.'

1680.—"The delivery of three Iron guns to the **Deura** of Ramacole at the rate of 15 *Pagodas* per *candy* is ordered ... which is much more than what they cost."—*Fort St. Geo. Cons.*, Aug. 5. In *Notes and Extracts*, No. iii. p. 31.

1837.—"The Vakeels stand behind their masters during all the visit, and discuss with them all that A—— says. Sometimes they tell him some barefaced lie, and when they find he does not believe it, they turn to me grinning, and say, 'Ma'am, the **Doory** plenty cunning gentlyman.'"—*Letters from Madras*, 86.

1882.—"The appellation by which Sir T. Munro was most commonly known in the Ceded Districts was that of 'Colonel **Dora**.' And to this day it is considered a sufficient answer to inquiries regarding the reason for any Revenue Rule, that it was laid down by the Colonel **Dora**."—*Arbuthnot's Memoir of Sir T. M.*, p. xcviii.

"A village up the Godavery, on the left bank, is inhabited by a race of people known as **Doraylu**, or 'gentlemen.' That this is the understood meaning is shown by the fact that their women are called **Doresandlu**, *i.e.* 'ladies.' These people rifle their arrow feathers, *i.e.* give them a spiral." (Reference lost.) [These are perhaps the Keis, who are called by the Telingas *Koidhoras*, "the word *dhora* meaning 'gentleman' or Sahib."—(*Central Prov. Gaz.* 500; also see *Ind. Ant.* viii. 34)].

***DRAVIDIAN**, adj. The Skt. term *Drāviḍa* seems to have been originally the name of the Conjevaram Kingdom (4th to 11th cent. A.D.), but in recent times it has been used as equivalent to 'Tamil.' About A.D. 700 Kumārila Bhaṭṭa calls the language of the South *Andhradrāviḍa-bhāshā*, meaning probably, as Bishop Caldwell suggests, what we should now describe as '*Telegu-Tamil*-language.' Indeed he has shown reason for believing that *Tamil* and *Drāviḍa*, of which *Dramiḍa* (written *Tiramiḍa*), and *Dramila* are old forms, are really the same word. [Also see *Oppert, Orig. Inhab.* 25 *seq.*, and *Dravira*, in a quotation from Al-biruni under MALABAR.] It may be suggested as possible that the *Tropina* of Pliny is also the same (see below). Dr. Caldwell proposed *Dravidian* as a convenient name for the S. Indian languages which belong to the Tamil family, and the cultivated members of which are Tamil, Malayālam, Canarese, Tulu, Kudagu (or Coorg), and Telegu; the uncultivated Tuḍa, Kōta, Gōṇḍ, Khoṇḍ, Orāon, Rājmahāli. [It has also been adopted as an ethnological term to designate the non-**Aryan** races of India (see *Risley, Tribes and Castes of Bengal*, i. Intro. xxxi.).]

c. A.D. 70.—"From the mouth of Ganges where he entereth into the sea unto the cape Calingon, and the town Dandagula, are counted 725 miles; from thence to **Tropina** where standeth the chief mart or towne of merchandise in all India, 1225 miles. Then to the promontorie of Perimula they reckon 750 miles, from which to the towne abovesaid Patale ... 620."—*Pliny*, by *Phil. Holland*, vi. chap. xx.

A.D. 404.—In a south-western direction are the following tracts ... Surashtrians, Bâdaras, and **Drâviḍas**.—*Varâha-mihira*, in *J.R.A.S.*, 2nd ser. v. 84.

"The eastern half of the Narbadda district ... the Pulindas, the eastern half of the **Drâviḍas** ... of all these the Sun is the Lord."—*Ibid.* p. 231.

c. 1045.—"Moreover, chief of the sons of Bharata, there are, the nations of the South, the **Dráviḍas** ... the Karnátakas, Máhishakas. ..."—*Vishnu Purána*, by *H. H. Wilson*, 1865, ii. 177 *seq.*

1856.—"The idioms which are included in this work under the general term '**Dravidian**' constitute the vernacular speech of the great majority of the inhabitants of S. India."—*Caldwell, Comp. Grammar of the Dravidian Languages*, 1st ed.

1869.—"The people themselves arrange their countrymen under two heads; five termed *Panch-gaura*, belonging to the Hindi, or as it is now generally called, the Aryan group, and the remaining five, or *Panch*-**Dravida**, to the Tamil type."—*Sir W. Elliot*, in *J. Ethn. Soc.* N.S. i. 94.

DRAWERS, LONG, s. An old-fashioned term, probably obsolete except in Madras, equivalent to **pyjāmas** (q.v.).

1794.—"The contractor shall engage to supply ... every patient ... with ... a clean gown, cap, shirt, and **long drawers**."—In *Seton-Karr*, ii. 115.

DRUGGERMAN, s. Neither this word for an 'interpreter,' nor the Levantine *dragoman*, of which it was a quaint old English corruption, is used in Anglo-Indian colloquial; nor is the Arab *tarjumān*, which is the correct form, a word usual in Hindustānī. But the character of the two former words seems to entitle them not to be passed over in this Glossary. The Arabic is a loan-word from Aramaic *targĕmān*, *metargĕmān*, 'an interpreter'; the Jewish *Targums*, or Chaldee paraphrases of the Scriptures, being named from the same root. The original force of the Aramaic root is seen in the Assyrian *ragāmu*, 'to speak,' *rigmu*, 'the word.' See *Proc. Soc. Bibl. Arch.*, 1883, p. 73, and *Delitsch*, *The Hebrew Lang. viewed in the Light of Assyrian Research*, p. 50. In old Italian we find a form somewhat nearer to the Arabic. (See quotation from Pegolotti below.)

c. 1150?.—"Quorum lingua cum praenominato Iohanni, Indorum patriarchae, nimis esset obscura, quod neque ipse quod Romani dicerent, neque Romani quod ipse diceret intelligerent, interprete interposito, quem Achivi **drogomanum** vocant, de mutuo statu Romanorum et Indicae regionis ad invicem querere coeperunt."—*De Adventu Patriarchae Indorum*, printed in *Zarncke*, *Der Priester Johannes*, i. 12. Leipzig, 1879.

[1252.—"Quia meus **Turgemanus** non erat sufficiens."—*W. de Rubruk*, p. 154.]

c. 1270.—"After this my address to the assembly, I sent my message to Elx by a dragoman (**trujaman**) of mine."—*Chron. of James of Aragon*, tr. by *Foster*, ii. 538.

Villehardouin, early in the 13th century, uses **drughement**, [and for other early forms see *N.E.D.* s.v. *Dragoman*.]

c. 1309.—"Il avoit gens illec qui savoient le Sarrazinnois et le françois que l'on apelle **drugemens**, qui enromancoient le Sarrazinnois au Conte Perron."—*Joinville*, ed. *de Wailly*, 182.

c. 1343.—"And at Tana you should furnish yourself with dragomans (**turcimanni**)."—*Pegolotti's Handbook*, in *Cathay*, &c., ii. 291, and App. iii.

1404.—"... el maestro en Theologia dixo por su **Truximan** que dixesse al Señor q̃ aquella carta que su fijo el rey le embiara non la sabia otro leer, salvo el. ..."—*Clavijo*, 446.

1585.—"... e dopo m'esservi prouisto di vn buonissimo **dràgomano**, et interprete, fu inteso il suono delle trombette le quali annuntiauano l'udienza del Rè" (di Pegù).—*Gasparo Balbi*, f. 102*v*.

1613.—"To the *Trojan* Shoare, where I landed Feb. 22 with fourteene *English* men more, and a Iew or **Druggerman**."—*T. Coryat*, in *Purchas*, ii. 1813.

1615.—"E dietro, a cavallo, i **dragomanni**, cioè interpreti della repubblica e con loro tutti i **dragomanni** degli altri ambasciatori ai loro luoghi."—*P. della Valle*, i. 89.

1738.—

"Till I cried out, you prove yourself so able,
Pity! you was not **Druggerman** at Babel!
For had they found a linguist half so good,
I make no question that the Tower had
stood."—*Pope*, after *Donne*, *Sat.* iv. 81.

Other forms of the word are (from Span. *trujaman*) the old French *truchement*, Low Latin *drocmandus*, *turchimannus*, Low Greek δραγούμανος, &c.

DUB, s. Telugu *dabbu*, Tam. *idappu*; a small copper coin, the same as the *doody* (see **CASH**), value 20 *cash*; whence it comes to stand for money in general. It is curious that we have also an English *provincial* word, "*Dubs* = money, E. Sussex" (*Holloway*, *Gen. Dict. of Provincialisms*, Lewes, 1838). And the slang 'to dub up,' for to pay up, is common (see *Slang Dict.*).

1781.—"In "Table of Prison Expenses and articles of luxury only to be attained by the opulent, after a length of saving" (*i.e.* in captivity in Mysore), we have—

"Eight cheroots ... 0 1 0.

"The prices are in *fanams*, **dubs**, and cash. The fanam changes for 11 *dubs* and 4 cash."—In *Lives of the Lindsays*, iii.

c. 1790.—"J'eus pour quatre **dabous**, qui font environ cinq sous de France, d'excellent poisson pour notre souper."—*Haafner*, ii. 75.

DUBASH, DOBASH, DEBASH, s. H. *dubhāshiyā*, *dobāshī* (lit. 'man of two languages'), Tam. *tupāshi*. An interpreter; obsolete except at Madras, and perhaps there also now, at least in its original sense; [now it is applied to a dressing-boy or other servant with a European.] The *Dubash* was at Madras formerly a usual servant in every household; and there is still one attached to each mercantile house, as the broker transacting business with natives, and corresponding to the Calcutta **banyan** (q.v.). According to Drummond the word has a peculiar meaning in Guzerat: "A *Doobasheeo* in Guzerat is viewed as an evil spirit, who by telling lies, sets people by the ears." This illustrates the original meaning of *dubash*, which might be rendered in Bunyan's fashion as Mr. Two-Tongues.

[1566.—"Bring **toopaz** and interpreter, Antonio Fernandes."—*India Office MSS.* Gaveta's agreement with the jangadas of the fort of Quilon, Aug. 13.

[1664.—"Per nossa conta a ambos por manilha 400 fanoim e ao **tupay** 50 fanoim."—*Letter of Zamorin*, in *Logan, Malabar*, iii. 1.]

1673.—"The Moors are very grave and haughty in their Demeanor, not vouchsafing to return an Answer by a slave, but by a **Deubash**."—*Fryer*, 30.

[1679.—"The **Dubass** of this Factory having to regaine his freedom."—*S. Master*, in *Man. of Kistna Dist.* 133.]

1693.—"The chief **Dubash** was ordered to treat ... for putting a stop to their proceedings."—*Wheeler*, i. 279.

1780.—"He ordered his **Dubash** to give the messenger two pagodas (sixteen shillings);—it was poor reward for having received two wounds, and risked his life in bringing him intelligence."—Letter of *Sir T. Munro*, in *Life*, i. 26.

1800.—"The **Dubash** there ought to be hanged for having made difficulties in collecting the rice."—Letter of *Sir A. Wellesley*, in *do.* 259.

c. 1804.—"I could neither understand them nor they me; but they would not give me up until a **Debash**, whom Mrs. Sherwood had hired ... came to my relief with a palanquin."—*Autobiog. of Mrs. Sherwood*, 272.

1809.—"He (Mr. North) drove at once from the coast the tribe of Aumils and **Debashes**."—*Ld. Valentia*, i. 315.

1810.—"In this first boat a number of **debashes** are sure to arrive."—*Williamson, V. M.* i. 133.

"The **Dubashes**, then all powerful at Madras, threatened loss o caste, and absolute destruction to any Bramin who should dare to unveil the mysteries of their sacred language."—*Morton's Life of Leyden*, 30.

1860.—"The moodliars and native officers ... were superseded by Malabar **Dubashes**, men aptly described as enemies to the religion of the Singhalese, strangers to their habits, and animated by no impulse but extortion."—*Tennent's Ceylon*, ii. 72.

***DUCKS**, s. The slang distinctive name for gentlemen belonging to the Bombay service; the correlative of the **Mulls** of Madras and of the **Qui-His** of Bengal. It seems to have been taken from the term next following.

1803.—"I think they manage it here famously. They have neither the comforts of a Bengal army, nor do they rough it, like the **Ducks**."—*Elphinstone*, in *Life*, i. 53.

1860.—"Then came Sire Jhone by Waye of Baldagh and Hormuz to yẽ Costys of Ynde ... And atte what Place yẽ Knyghte came to Londe, theyre yẽ ffolke clepen **Duckys** (quasi DUCES INDIAE)."—Extract from a MS. of the *Travels of Sir John Maundevill* in the E. Indies, lately discovered (Calcutta).

[In the following the word is a corruption of the Tam. *tūkku*, a weight equal to 1¼ viss, about 3 lbs. 13 oz.

[1787.—"We have fixed the produce of each vine at 4 **ducks** of wet pepper."—*Purwannah of Tippoo Sultan*, in *Logan, Malabar*, iii. 125.]

DUCKS, BOMBAY. See **BUMMELO**.

1860.—"A fish nearly related to the salmon is dried and exported in large quantities from Bombay, and has acquired the name of **Bombay Ducks**."—*Mason, Burmah*, 273.

DUFTER, s. Ar.—H. *daftar*. Colloquially 'the office,' and interchangeable with **cutcherry**, except that the latter generally implies an office of the nature of a Court. *Daftarkhāna* is more accurate, [but this usually means rather a record-room where documents are stored]. The original Arab. *daftar* is from the Greek διφθέρα = *membranum*, 'a parchment,' and thin 'paper' (whence also *diphtheria*), and was applied to loose sheets filed on a string, which formed the record of accounts; hence *daftar* becomes 'a register,' a public record. In Arab. any account-book is still a *daftar*, and in S. India *daftar* means a bundle of connected papers tied up in a cloth, [the *basta* of Upper India].

c. 1590.—"Honest experienced officers upon whose forehead the stamp of correctness shines, write the agreement upon loose pages and sheets, so that the transaction cannot be forgotten. These loose sheets, into which all *sanads* are entered, are called the **daftar**."—*Āīn*, i. 260, and see *Blochmann's* note there.

[1757.—"... that after the expiration of the year they take a discharge according to custom, and that they deliver the accounts of their Zemindarry agreeable to the stated forms every year into the **Dufter** Cana of the Sircar. ..."—*Sunnud for the Company's Zemindarry*, in *Verelst, View of Bengal*, App. 147.]

DUMBCOW, v., and **DUMBCOWED**, participle. To brow-beat, to cow; and cowed, brow-beaten, set-down. This is a capital specimen of Anglo-Indian dialect. *Dam khānā*, 'to eat one's breath,' is a Hind. idiom for 'to be silent.' Hobson-Jobson converts this into a transitive verb, to *damkhāo*, and both spelling and meaning being affected by English suggestions of sound, this comes in Anglo-Indian use to imply *cowing* and *silencing*. [A more probable derivation is from Hind. *dhamkānā*,' 'to chide, scold, threaten, to repress by threats or reproof' (*Platts, H. Dict.*).]

DUMPOKE, s. A name given in the Anglo-Indian kitchen to a baked dish, consisting usually of a duck, boned and stuffed. The word is Pers. *dampukht*, 'air-cooked,' *i.e.* baked. A recipe for a dish so called, as used in Akbar's kitchen, is in the first quotation:

c. 1590.—"**Dampukht**. 10 sers meat; 2 s. ghi; 1 s. onions; 11 m. fresh ginger; 10 m. pepper; 2 d. cardamoms."—*Āīn*, i. 61.

1673.—"These eat highly of all Flesh **Dumpoked**, which is baked with Spice in Butter."—*Fryer*, 93.

"Baked Meat they call **Dumpoke** which is dressed with sweet Herbs and Butter, with whose Gravy they swallow Rice dry Boiled."—*Ibid*. 404.

1689.—"... and a **dumpoked** Fowl, that is boil'd with Butter in any small Vessel, and stuft with Raisins and Almonds is another (Dish)."—*Ovington*, 397.

DUNGAREE, s. A kind of coarse and inferior cotton cloth; the word is not in any dictionary that we know. [Platts gives H. *dungrī*, 'a coarse kind of cloth.' The *Madras Gloss*. gives Tel. *dangidi*, which is derived from Dāngidi, a village near Bombay. Molesworth in his *Mahr. Dict*. gives: "*Dongarī Kāpaṛ*, a term originally for the common country cloth sold in the quarter contiguous to the *Ḍongarī Ḳilla* (Fort George, Bombay), applied now to poor and low-priced cotton cloth. Hence in the corruption *Dungarie*." He traces the word to *ḍongarī*, "a little hill". Dungaree is woven with two or more threads together in the web and woof. The finer kinds are used for clothing by poor people; the coarser for sails for native boats and tents. The same word seems to be used of silk (see below).]

1613.—"We traded with the *Naturalls* for Cloves ... by bartering and exchanging cotton cloth of *Cambay* and *Coromandell* for Cloves. The sorts requested, and prices that they yeelded. *Candakeens* of *Barochie*, 6 Cattees of Cloves. ... **Dongerijns**, the finest, twelve."—*Capt. Saris*, in *Purchas*, i. 363.

1673.—"Along the Coasts are Bombaim ... Carwar for **Dungarees** and the weightiest pepper."—*Fryer*, 86.

[1812.—"The Prince's Messenger ... told him, 'Come, now is the time to open your purse-strings; you are no longer a merchant or in prison; you are no longer to sell **Dungaree**' (a species of coarse linen)."—*Morier, Journey through Persia*, 26.]

1813.—"**Dungarees** (pieces to a ton) 400."—*Milburn*, ii. 221.

[1859.—"In addition to those which were real ... were long lines of sham batteries, known to sailors as **Dungaree** forts, and which were made simply of coarse cloth or canvas, stretched and painted so as to resemble batteries."—*L. Oliphant, Narr. of Ld. Elgin's Mission*, ii. 6.]

1868.—"Such **dungeree** as you now pay half a rupee a yard for, you could then buy from 20 to 40 yards per rupee."—*Miss Frere's Old Deccan Days*, p. xxiv.

[1900.—"From this thread the **Dongari** Tasar is prepared, which may be compared to the organzine of silk, being both twisted and doubled."—*Yusuf Ali, Mem. on Silk*, 35.]

DURBAR, s. A Court or Levee. Pers. *darbār*. Also the Executive Government of a Native State (*Carnegie*). "In Kattywar, by a curious idiom, the chief himself is so addressed: 'Yes, **Durbar**'; 'no, **Durbar**,' being common replies to him."—(*M.-Gen. Keatinge*).

1609.—"On the left hand, thorow another gate you enter into an inner court where the King keepes his **Darbar**."—*Hawkins*, in *Purchas*, i. 432.

1616.—"The tenth of Ianuary, I went to Court at foure in the euening to the **Durbar**, which is the place where the *Mogoll* sits out daily, to entertaine strangers, to receiue Petitions and Presents, to giue commands, to see and to be seene."—*Sir T. Roe*, in *Purchas*, i. 541; [with some slight differences of reading, in Hak. Soc. i. 106].

1633.—"This place they call the **Derba** (or place of Councill) where Law and Justice was administered according to the Custome of the Countrey."—*W. Bruton*, in *Hakl*. v. 51.

c. 1750.—"... il faut se rappeller ces tems d'humiliations où le Francois étoient forcés pour le bien de leur commerce, d'aller timidement porter leurs presens et leurs hommages à de petis chefs de Bourgades que nous n'admetons aujourd'hui à nos **Dorbards** que lorsque nos intérêts l'exigent."—Letter of *M. de Bussy*, in *Cambridge's Account*, p. xxix.

1793.—"At my **durbar** yesterday I had proof of the affection entertained by the natives for Sir William Jones. The Professors of the Hindu Law, who were in the habit of attendance upon him, burst into unrestrained tears when they spoke to me."—*Teignmouth, Mem*. i. 289.

1809.—"It was the **durbar** of the native Gentoo Princes."—*Ld. Valentia*, i. 362.

[1826.—"... a **Durbar**, or police-officer, should have men in waiting. ..."—*Pandurang Hari*, ed. 1873, i. 126.]

1875.—"Sitting there in the centre of the **durbar**, we assisted at our first nautch."—*Sir M. E. Grant Duff*, in *Contemp. Rev.*, July.

[1881.—"Near the centre (at Amritsar) lies the sacred tank, from whose midst rises the **Darbar** Sahib, or great temple of the Sikh faith."—*Imperial Gazetteer*, i. 186.]

DURIAN, DORIAN, s. Malay *duren*, Molucca form *duriyān*, from *durī*, 'a thorn or prickle, [and *ān*, the common substantival ending; Mr. Skeat gives the standard Malay as *duriyan* or *durian*]; the great fruit of the tree (N. O. *Bombaceae*) called by botanists *Durio zibethinus*, D. C. The tree appears to be a native of the Malay Peninsula, and the nearest islands; from which it has been carried to Tenasserim on one side and to Mindanao on the other.

The earliest European mention of this fruit is that by Nicolo Conti. The passage is thus rendered by Winter Jones: "In this island (Sumatra) there also grows a green fruit which they call *duriano*, of the size of a cucumber. When opened five fruits are found within, resembling oblong oranges. The taste varies like that of cheese." (In *India in the XVth Cent.*, p. 9.) We give the original Latin of Poggio below, which must be more correctly rendered thus: "They have a green fruit which they call *durian*, as big as a water-melon. Inside there are five things like elongated oranges, and resembling thick butter, with a combination of flavours." (See *Carletti*, below).

The *dorian* in Sumatra often forms a staple article of food, as the **jack** (q.v.) does in Malabar. By natives and old European residents in the Malay regions in which it is produced the *dorian* is regarded as incomparable, but novices have a difficulty in getting over the peculiar, strong, and offensive odour of the fruit, on account of which it is usual to open it away from the house, and which procured for it the inelegant Dutch nickname of *stancker*. "When that aversion, however, is conquered, many fall into the taste of the natives, and become passionately fond of it." (*Crawfurd, H. of Ind. Arch.* i. 419.) [Wallace (*Malay Arch.* 57) says that he could not bear the smell when he "first tried it in Malacca, but in Borneo I found a ripe fruit on the ground, and, eating it out of doors, I at once became a confirmed Durian eater ... the more you eat of it the less you feel inclined to stop. In fact to eat Durians is a new sensation, worth a voyage to the East to experience."] Our forefathers had not such delicate noses, as may be gathered from some of the older notices. A Governor of the Straits, some forty-five years ago, used to compare the *Dorian* to 'carrion in custard.'

c. 1440.—"Fructum viridem habent nomine **durianum**, magnitudine cucumeris, in quo sunt quinque veluti malarancia oblonga, varii saporis, instar butyri coagulati."—*Poggii, de Varietate Fortunae*, Lib. iv.

1552.—"**Durions**, which are fashioned like artichokes" (!)—*Castanheda*, ii. 355.

1553.—"Among these fruits was one kind now known by the name of **durions**, a thing greatly esteemed, and so luscious that the Malacca merchants tell how a certain trader came to that port with a ship load of great value, and he consumed the whole of it in guzzling **durions** and in gallantries among the Malay girls."—*Barros*, II. vi. i.

1563.—"A gentleman in this country (Portuguese India) tells me that he remembers to have read in a Tuscan version of Pliny, '*nobiles* **durianes**.' I have since asked him to find the passage in order that I might trace it in the Latin, but up to this time he says he has not found it."—*Garcia*, f. 85.

1588.—"There is one that is called in the Malacca tongue **durion**, and is so good that I have heard it affirmed by manie that have gone about the worlde, that it doth exceede in savour all others that ever they had seene or tasted. ... Some do say that have seene it that it seemeth to be that wherewith Adam did transgresse, being carried away by the singular savour."—*Parke's Mendoza*, ii. 318.

1598.—"**Duryoen** is a fruit ỹt only groweth in Malacca, and is so much comẽded by those which have proued ye same, that there is no fruite in the world to bee compared with it."—*Linschoten*, 102; [Hak. Soc. i. 51].

1599.—The **Dorian**, Carletti thought, had a smell of onions, and he did not at first much like it, but when at last he got used to this he liked the fruit greatly, and thought nothing of a simple and natural kind could be tasted which possessed a more complex and elaborate variety of odours and flavours than this did.—See *Viaggi*, Florence, 1701; Pt. II. p. 211.

1601.—"**Duryoen** ... ad apertionem primam ... putridum coepe redolet, sed dotem tamen divinam iilam omnem gustui profundit."—*Debry*, iv. 33.

[1610.—"The **Darion** tree nearly resembles a

pear tree in size."—*Pyrard de Laval*, Hak. Soc. ii. 366.]

1615.—"There groweth a certaine fruit, prickled like a ches-nut, and as big as one's fist, the best in the world to eate, these are somewhat costly, all other fruits being at an easie rate. It must be broken with force and therein is contained a white liquor like vnto creame, never the lesse it yields a very vnsauory sent like to a rotten oynion, and it is called **Esturion**" (probably a misprint).—*De Monfart*, 27.

1727.—"The **Durean** is another excellent Fruit, but offensive to some People's Noses, for it smells very like ... but when once tasted the smell vanishes."—*A. Hamilton*, ii. 81; [ed. 1744, ii. 80].

1855.—"The fetid **Dorian**, prince of fruits to those who like it, but chief of abominations to all strangers and novices, does not grow within the present territories of Ava, but the King makes great efforts to obtain a supply in eatable condition from the Tenasserim Coast. King Tharawadi used to lay post-horses from Martaban to Ava, to bring his odoriferous delicacy."—*Yule, Mission to Ava*, 161.

1878.—"The **Durian** will grow as large as a man's head, is covered closely with terribly sharp spines, set hexagonally upon its hard skin, and when ripe it falls; if it should strike any one under the tree, severe injury or death may be the result."—*M'Nair, Perak*, 60.

1885.—"I proceeded ... under a continuous shade of tall **Durian** trees from 35 to 40 feet high. ... In the flowering time it was a most pleasant shady wood; but later in the season the chance of a fruit now and then descending on one's head would be less agreeable." *Note.*—"Of this fruit the natives are passionately fond; ... and the elephants flock to its shade in the fruiting time; but, more singular still, the tiger is said to devour it with avidity."—*Forbes, A Naturalist's Wanderings*, p. 240.

DURJUN, s. H. *darjan*, a corr. of the English *dozen*.

DURWAUN, s. H. from P. *darwān*, *darbān*. A doorkeeper. A domestic servant so called is usual in the larger houses of Calcutta. He is porter at the gate of the **compound** (q.v.).

[c. 1590.—"The **Darbáns**, or Porters. A thousand of these active men are employed to guard the palace."—*Āīn*, i. 258.]

c. 1755.—"**Derwan**."—List of servants in *Ives*, 50.

1781.—(After an account of an alleged attempt to seize Mr. Hicky's *Darwān*). "Mr. Hicky begs leave to make the following remarks. That he is clearly of opinion that these horrid Assassins wanted to dispatch him whilst he lay a sleep, as a **Door-van** is well known to be the alarm of the House, to prevent which the Villians wanted to carry him off,—and their precipitate flight the moment they heard Mr. Hicky's Voice puts it past a Doubt."—Reflections on the consequence of the late attempt made to Assassinate the Printer of the original *Bengal Gazette* (in the same, April 14).

1784.—"Yesterday at daybreak, a most extraordinary and horrid murder was committed upon the **Dirwan** of Thomas Martin, Esq."—In *Seton-Karr*, i. 12.

"In the entrance passage, often on both sides of it, is a raised floor with one or two open cells, in which the **Darwans** (or doorkeepers) sit, lie, and sleep—in fact dwell."—*Calc. Review*, vol. lix. p. 207.

DURWAUZA-BUND. The formula by which a native servant in an Anglo-Indian household intimates that his master or mistress cannot receive a visitor—'Not at home'—without the untruth. It is elliptical for *darwāza band hai*, 'the door is closed.'

[1877.—"When they did not find him there, it was **Darwaza** bund."—*Allardyce, The City of Sunshine*, i. 125.]

DUSTOOR, **DUSTOORY**, s. P.—H. *dastūr*, 'custom' *dastūrī*, 'that which is customary. That commission or percentage on the money passing in any cash transaction which, with or without acknowledgment or permission, sticks to the fingers of the agent of payment. Such 'customary' appropriations are, we believe, very nearly as common in England as in India; a fact of which newspaper correspondence from time to time makes us aware, though Europeans in India, in condemning the natives, often forget, or are ignorant of this. In India the practice is perhaps more distinctly recognised, as the word denotes. Ibn Batuta tells us that at the Court of Delhi, in his time (c. 1340), the custom was for the officials to deduct 1/10 of every sum which the Sultan ordered to be paid from the treasury (see *I. B.* pp. 408, 426, &c.).

[1616.—"The **dusturia** in all bought goodes ... is a great matter."—*Sir T. Roe*, Hak. Soc. ii. 350.]

1638.—"Ces vallets ne sont point nourris au logis, mais ont leurs gages, dont ils s'entretiennent, quoy qu'ils ne montent qu'à trois ou quatre Ropias par moys ... mais ils ont leur tour du baston, qu'ils appellent **Testury**, qu'ils prennent du consentement du Maistre de celuy dont ils achettent quelque chose."—*Mandelslo*, Paris, 1659, 224.

[1679.—"The usuall **Dustoore** shall be equally divided."—*S. Master*, in *Kistna Man.* 136.]

1680.—"It is also ordered that in future the *Vakils* (see VAKEEL), *Mutsuddees* or Writers of the *Tagadgeers*,[1] *Dumiers*, (?)[2] or overseers of the Weavers, and the Picars and Podars shall not receive any monthly wages, but shall be content with the **Dustoor** ... of a quarter anna in the rupee, which the merchants and weavers are to allow them. The **Dustoor** may be divided twice a year or oftener by the Chief and Council among the said employers."—*Ft. St. Geo. Cons.*, Dec. 2. In *Notes and Extracts*, No. II. p. 61.

1681.—"For the farme of **Dustoory** on cooley hire at Pagodas 20 per annum received a part ... (Pag.) 13 00 0."—*Ibid.* Jan. 10; *Ibid.* No. III. p. 45.

[1684.—"The Honble. Comp. having order'd ... that the **Dustore** upon their Investment ... be brought into the Generall Books."—*Pringle, Diary, Ft. St. Geo.* 1st ser. iii. 69.]

1780.—"It never can be in the power of a superintendent of Police to reform the numberless abuses which servants of every Denomination have introduced, and now support on the Broad Basis of **Dustoor**."—*Hicky's Bengal Gazette*, April 29.

1785.—"The Public are hereby informed that no Commission, Brokerage, or **Dustoor** is charged by the Bank, or permitted to be taken by any Agent or Servant employed by them."—In *Seton-Karr*, i. 130.

1795.—"All servants belonging to the Company's Shed have been strictly prohibited from demanding or receiving any fees or **dastoors** on any pretence whatever."—*Ibid.* ii. 16.

1824.—"The profits however he made during the voyage, and by a **dustoory** on all the alms given or received ... were so considerable that on his return some of his confidential disciples and a quarrel with him."—*Heber*, ed. 1844, i. 198.

1866.—"... of all taxes small and great the heaviest is **dustooree**."—*Trevelyan, Dawk Bungalow*, 217.

DUSTUCK, s. P. *dastak*, ['a little hand, hand-clapping to attract attention, a notice']. A pass or permit. The *dustucks* granted by the Company's covenanted servants in the early half of the 18th century seems to have been a constant instrument of abuse, or bone of contention, with the native authorities in Bengal. [The modern sense of the word in N. India is a notice of the revenue demand served on a defaulter.]

1716.—"A passport or **dustuck**, signed by the President of Calcutta, should exempt the goods specified from being visited or stopped."—*Orme*, ed. 1803, ii. 21.

1748.—"The Zemindar near Pultah having stopped several boats with English **Dusticks** and taken money from them, and disregarding the Phousdar's orders to clear them. ..."—In *Long*, 6.

[1762.—"**Dusticks.**" See WRITER.]

1763.—"The dignity and benefit of our **Dustucks** are the chief badges of honour, or at least interest, we enjoy from our *Phirmaund*."—From the Chief and Council at Dacca, in *Van Sittart*, i. 210.

[1866.—"It is a practice of the Revenue Courts of the **sircar** to issue **Dustuck** for the malgoozaree the very day the **kist** (instalment) became due."—*Confessions of an Orderly*, 132.]

E

EARTH-OIL, s. Petroleum, such as that exported from Burma ... The term is a literal translation of that used in nearly all the Indian vernaculars. The chief sources are at *Ye-nan-gyoung* on the Irawadi, lat. c. 20° 22′.

1755.—"Raynan-Goung ... at this Place there are about 200 Families, who are chiefly employed in getting **Earth-oil** out of Pitts, some five miles in the Country."—*Baker*, in *Dalrymple's Or. Rep.* i. 172.

1810.—"Petroleum, called by the natives **earth-oil** ... which is imported from Pegu, Ava, and the Arvean (read Aracan) Coast."—*Williamson, V.M.* ii. 21–23.

ECKA, s. A small one-horse carriage used by natives. It is Hind. *ekkā*, from *ek*, 'one.' But we have seen it written *acre*, and punned upon as quasi-*acher*, by those who have travelled by it! [Something of the kind was perhaps known in very early times, for

---

1 *Tagādāgīr*, under the Mahrattas, was an officer who enforced the State demands against defaulting cultivators (*Wilson*); and no doubt it was here an officer similarly employed to enforce the execution of contracts by weavers and others who had received advances. It is a corruption of Pers. *takāẓagīr*, from Ar. *takāẓā*, importunity (see quotation of 1819, under DHURNA).

2 [Mr. F. Brandt suggests that this word may be Telegu *Thumiar*, *túmu*, being a measure of grain, and possibly the "Dumiers" may have been those entitled to receive the *dustooree* in grain.]

Arrian (*Indika*, xvii.) says: "To be drawn by a single horse is considered no distinction." For a good description with drawing of the *ekka*, see *Kipling, Beast and Man in India*, 190 *seq.*]

1811.—"... perhaps the simplest carriage that can be imagined, being nothing more than a chair covered with red cloth, and fixed upon an axle-tree between two small wheels. The **Ekka** is drawn by one horse, who has no other harness than a girt, to which the shaft of the carriage is fastened."—*Solvyns*, iii.

1834.—"One of those native carriages called **ekkas** was in waiting. This vehicle resembles in shape a meat-safe, placed upon the axletree of two wheels, but the sides are composed of hanging curtains instead of wire pannels."—*The Baboo*, ii. 4.

[1843.—"**Ekhees**, a species of single horse carriage, with cloth hoods, drawn by one pony, were by no means uncommon."—*Davidson, Travels in Upper India*, i. 116.]

EED, s. Arab. *'Īd*. A Mahommedan holy festival, but in common application in India restricted to two such, called there the *barī* and *chhoṭī* (or Great and Little) *'Id*. The former is the commemoration of Abraham's sacrifice, the victim of which was, according to the Mahommedans, Ishmael. [See Hughes, *Dict. of Islam*, 192 *seqq.*] This is called among other names, *Baḳr-'Īd*, the 'Bull *'Īd*,' *Baḳarah' 'Īd*, 'the cow festival,' but this is usually corrupted by ignorant natives as well as Europeans into *Bakrī-'Id* (Hind. *bakrā*, f. *bakrī*, 'a goat'). The other is the *'Īd* of the *Ramazān*, *viz.* the termination of the annual fast; the festival called in Turkey *Bairam*, and by old travellers sometimes the "Mahommedan Easter."

c. 1610.—"Le temps du ieusne finy on celebre vne grande feste, et des plus solennelles qu'ils ayent, qui s'appelle **ydu**."—*Pyrard de Laval*, i. 104; [Hak. Soc. i. 140].

[1671.—"They have allsoe a great **feast**, which they call **Buckery Eed**."—In *Yule, Hedges' Diary*, Hak. Soc. ii. cccx.]

1673.—"The New Moon before the New Year (which commences at the *Vernal Equinox*), is the Moors **Æde**, when the Governor in no less Pomp than before, goes to sacrifice a Ram or He-Goat, in remembrance of that offered for *Isaac* (by them called *Ishauh*); the like does every one in his own House, that is able to purchase one, and sprinkle their blood on the sides of their Doors."—*Fryer*, 108. (The passage is full of errors.)

1860.—"By the Nazim's invitation we took out a party to the palace at the *Bakri* **Eed** (or Feast of the Goat), in memory of the sacrifice of Isaac, or, as the Moslems say, of Ishmael."—*Mrs. Mackenzie, Storms and Sunshine*, &c., ii. 255 *seq.*

1869.—"Il n'y a proprement que deux fêtes parmi les Musulmans sunnites, celle de la rupture du jeûne de *Ramazan*, **'Id** *fito*, et celle des victimes **'Id** *curbân*, nommée aussi dans l'Inde *Bacr* **'Id**, fête du *Taureau*, ou simplement **'Id**, la fête par excellence, laquelle est établie en mémoire du sacrifice d'Ismael."—*Garcin de Tassy, Rel. Mus. dans l'Inde*, 9 *seq.*

***EKTENG**, adj. The native representation of the official designation '*acting*' applied to a substitute, especially in the Civil Service. The manner in which the natives used to explain the expression to themselves is shown in the quotation.

1883.—"Lawrence had been only 'acting' there; a term which has suggested to the minds of the natives, in accordance with their pronunciation of it, and with that striving after meaning in syllables which leads to so many etymological fallacies, the interpretation **ek-tang**, 'one-leg,' as if the temporary incumbent had but one leg in the official stirrup."—H. Y. in *Quarterly Review* (on *Bosworth Smith's Life of Lord Lawrence*), April, p. 297.

***ELEPHANT**, s. This article will be confined to notes connected with the various suggestions which have been put forward as to the origin of the word—a sufficiently ample subject.

The oldest occurrence of the word (ἐλέφας—φαντος) is in Homer. With him, and so with Hesiod and Pindar, the word means 'ivory.' Herodotus first uses it as the name of the animal (iv. 191). Hence an occasional, probably an erroneous, assumption that the word ἐλέφας originally meant only the material, and not the beast that bears it.

In Persian the usual term for the beast is *pīl*, with which agree the Aramaic *pīl* (already found in the Chaldee and Syriac versions of the O. T.), and the Arabic *fīl*. Old etymologists tried to develop *elephant* out of *fīl*; and it is natural to connect with it the Spanish for 'ivory' (*marfil*, Port. *marfim*), but no satisfactory explanation has yet been given of the first syllable of that word. More certain is the fact that in early Swedish and Danish the word for 'elephant' is *fil*, in Icelandic *fill*; a term supposed to have been introduced by old traders from the East *viâ* Russia. The old Swedish for 'ivory' is *filsben*.[1]

The oldest Hebrew mention of ivory is in the notice of the products brought to Solomon from Ophir, or India. Among these are ivory tusks—*shenhabbim*, *i.e.* 'teeth of *habbīm*,' a word which has been interpreted as from Skt. *ibha*, elephant.[2] But it is entirely doubtful what this *habbīm*, occurring here only, really means.[3] We know from other evidence that ivory was known in Egypt and Western Asia for ages before Solomon. And in other cases the Hebrew word for ivory is simply *shen*, corresponding to *dens Indus* in Ovid and other Latin writers. In Ezekiel (xxvii. 15) we find *karnoth shen* = 'cornua dentis.' The use of the word '*horns*' does not necessarily imply a confusion of these great curved tusks with horns; it has many parallels, as in Pliny's, "*cum arbore exacuant limentque* cornua *elephanti*" (xviii. 7); in Martial's "*Indicoque* cornu" (i. 73); in Aelian's story, as alleged by the Mauritanians, that the elephants there shed their *horns* every ten years ("*δεκάτῳ ἔτει πάντως τὰ κέρατα ἐκπεσεῖν*"—xiv. 5; whilst Cleasby quotes from an Icelandic saga '*olifant*-horni' for 'ivory.'

We have mentioned Skt. *ibha*, from which Lassen assumes a compound *ibhadantā* for ivory, suggesting that this, combined by early traders with the Arabic article, formed *al-ibhadantā*, and so originated *ἐλέφαντος*. Pott, besides other doubts, objects that *ibhadantā*, though the name of a plant (*Tiaridium indicum*, Lehm.), is never actually a name of ivory.

Pott's own etymology is *alaf-hindi*, 'Indian ox,' from a word existing in sundry resembling forms, in Hebrew and in Assyrian (*alif*, *alap*).[4] This has met with favour; though it is a little hard to accept any form like *Hindī* as earlier than Homer.

Other suggested origins are Pictet's from *airāvata* (lit. 'proceeding from water'), the proper name of the elephant of Indra, or Elephant of the Eastern Quarter in the Hindu Cosmology.[5] This is felt to be only too ingenious, but as improbable. It is, however, suggested, it would seem independently, by Mr. Kittel (*Indian Antiquary*, i. 128), who supposes the first part of the word to be Dravidian, a transformation from *āne*, 'elephant.'

Pictet, finding his first suggestion not accepted, has called up a Singhalese word *aliya*, used for 'elephant,' which he takes to be from *āla*, 'great'; thence *aliya*, 'great creature'; and proceeding further, presents a combination of *āla*, 'great,' with Skt. *phaṭa*, sometimes signifying 'a tooth,' thus *aliphaṭa*, 'great tooth' = *elephantus*.[6]

Hodgson, in *Notes on Northern Africa* (p. 19, quoted by Pott), gives *elef ameqran* ('Great Boar,' *elef* being 'boar') as the name of the animal among the Kabyles of that region, and appears to present it as the origin of the Greek and Latin words.

Again we have the Gothic *ulbandus*, 'a camel,' which has been regarded by some as the same word with *elephantus*. To this we shall recur.

Pott, in his elaborate paper already quoted, comes to the conclusion that the choice of etymologies must lie between his own *alaf-hindī* and Lassen's *al-ibha-dantā*. His paper is 50 years old, but he repeats this conclusion in his *Wurzel-Wörterbüch der Indo-Germanische Sprachen*, published in 1871,[7] nor can I ascertain that there has been any later advance towards a true etymology. Yet it can hardly be said that either of the alternatives carries conviction.

Both, let it be observed, apart from other difficulties, rest on the assumption that the knowledge of *ἐλέφας*, whether as fine material or as monstrous animal, came

1 *Pīlu*, for elephant, occurs in certain Sanskrit books, but it is regarded as a foreign word.

2 See *Lassen*, i. 313; *Max Müller's Lectures on Sc. of Language*, 1st S. p. 189.

3 "As regards the interpretation of *habbim*, a *ἅπαξ λεγ.*, in the passage where the state of the text, as shown by comparison with the LXX, is very unsatisfactory, it seems impossible to say anything that can be of the least use in clearing up the origin of *elephant*. The O. T. speaks so often of ivory, and never again by this name, that *habbim* must be either a corruption or some trade-name, presumably for some special kind of ivory. Personally, I believe it far more likely that *habbim* is at bottom the same as *hobnim* (ebony?) associated with *shen* in Ezekiel xxvii. 15, and that the passage once ran 'ivory and ebony'" (*W. Robertson Smith*); [also see *Encycl. Bibl.* ii. 2297 *seq.*].

4 See *Zeitschr. für die Kie Kunds des Morgs*, iv. 12 *seqq.*; also *Ebehr. Schrader* in *Zeitsch. d. M. Gesellsch.* xxvii. 706 *seqq.*; [*Encycl. Bibl.* ii. 1262].

5 In *Journ. As.*, ser. iv. tom. ii.

6 In *Kuhn's Zeitschr. für Vergleichende Sprachkunst*, iv. 128–131.

7 Detmold, pp. 950–952.

from India, whilst nearly all the other or less-favoured suggestions point to the same assumption.

But knowledge acquired, or at least taken cognizance of, since Pott's latest reference to the subject, puts us in possession of the new and surprising fact that, even in times which we are entitled to call historic, the elephant existed wild, far to the westward of India, and not very far from the eastern extremity of the Mediterranean. Though the fact was indicated from the wall-paintings by Wilkinson some 65 years ago,[1] and has more recently been amply displayed in historical works which have circulated by scores in popular libraries, it is singular how little attention or interest it seems to have elicited.[2]

The document which gives precise Egyptian testimony to this fact is an inscription (first interpreted by Ebers in 1873)[3] from the tomb of Amenemhib, a captain under the great conqueror Thotmes III. [Thūtmosis], who reigned B.C. c. 1600. This warrior, speaking from his tomb of the great deeds of his master, and of his own right arm, tells how the king, in the neighbourhood of *Ni*, hunted 120 elephants for the sake of their tusks; and how he himself (Amenemhib) encountered the biggest of them, which had attacked the sacred person of the king, and cut through its trunk. The elephant chased him into the water, where he saved himself between two rocks; and the king bestowed on him rich rewards.

The position of *Ni* is uncertain, though some have identified it with Nineveh.[4] [Maspero writes: 'Nīi, long confounded with Nineveh, after Champolion (*Gram. égyptienne*, p. 150), was identified by Lenormant (*Les Origines*, vol. iii. p. 316 *et seq.*) with Ninus Vetus, Membidj, and by Max Müller (*Asien und Europa*, p. 267) with Balis on the Euphrates: I am inclined to make it Kefer-Naya, between Aleppo and Turmanīn" (*Struggle of the Nations*, 144, note).] It is named in another inscription between *Arinath* and *Akerith*, as, all three, cities of *Naharain* or Northern Mesopotamia, captured by Amenhotep II., the son of Thotmes III. Might not *Ni* be Nisibis? We shall find that Assyrian inscriptions of later date have been interpreted as placing elephant-hunts in the land of Harran and in the vicinity of the Chaboras.

If then these elephant-hunts may be located on the southern skirts of Taurus, we shall more easily understand how a tribute of elephant-tusks should have been offered at the court of Egypt by the people of *Rutennu* or Northern Syria, and also by the people of the adjacent *Asebi* or Cyprus, as we find repeatedly recorded on the Egyptian monuments, both in hieroglyphic writing and pictorially.[5]

What the stones of Egypt allege in the 17th cent. B.C., the stones of Assyria 500 years afterwards have been alleged to corroborate. The great inscription of Tighlath-Pileser I., who is calculated to have reigned about B.C. 1120–1100, as rendered by Lotz, relates:

"Ten mighty Elephants
Slew I in Harran, and on the banks of the Haboras.
Four Elephants I took alive;
Their hides,
Their teeth, and the live Elephants
I brought to my city Assur."[6]

The same facts are recorded in a later inscription, on the broken obelisk of Assurnazirpal from Kouyunjik, now in the Br. Museum, which commemorates the deeds of the king's ancestor, Tighlath Pileser.[7]

In the case of these Assyrian inscriptions, however, *elephant* is by no means an undisputed interpretation. In the famous quadruple *test* exercise on this inscription in 1857, which gave the death-blow to the doubts which some sceptics had emitted as to the genuine character of the Assyrian

1 See *Topography of Thebes, with a General View of Egypt*, 1835, p. 153.

2 See *e.g. Brugsch's Hist. of the Pharaohs*, 2d ed. i. 396–400; and *Canon Rawlinson's Egypt*, ii. 235–6.

3 In *Z. für Aegypt. Spr. und Aetferth.* 1873, pp. 1–9, 63, 64; also tr. by Dr. Birch in *Records of the Past*, vol. ii. p. 59 (*no date*, more shame to S. Bagster & Sons); and again by Ebers, revised in Z.D.M.G., 1876, pp. 391 *seqq.*

4 See Canon Rawlinson's *Egypt*, u.s.

5 For the painting see *Wilkinson's Ancient Egyptians*, edited by Birch, vol. i. pl. 11 b, which shows the Rutennu bringing a chariot and horses, a bear, an elephant, and ivory tusks, as tribute to Thotmes III. For other records see *Brugsch*, E.T., 2nd ed. i. 381, 384, 404.

6 *Die Inschriften Tightathpileser's I., ... mit Übersetsung und Kommentar von Dr. Wilhelm Lotz*, Leipzig, 1880, p. 53; [and see Maspero, *op. cit.* 661 *seq.*].

7 *Lotz, loc. cit.* p. 197.

interpretations, Sir H. Rawlinson, in this passage, rendered the animals slain and taken alive as *wild buffaloes*. The ideogram given as *teeth* he had not interpreted. The question is argued at length by Lotz in the work already quoted, but it is a question for cuneiform experts, dealing, as it does, with the interpretation of more than one *ideogram*, and enveloped as yet in uncertainties. It is to be observed, that in 1857 Dr. Hincks, one of the four test-translators,[1] had rendered the passage almost exactly as Lotz has done 23 years later, though I cannot see that Lotz makes any allusion to this fact. [See *Encycl. Bibl.* ii. 1262.] Apart from arguments as to decipherment and ideograms, it is certain that probabilities are much affected by the publication of the Egyptian inscription of Amenhoteb, which gives a greater plausibility to the rendering 'elephant' than could be ascribed to it in 1857. And should it eventually be upheld, it will be all the more remarkable that the sagacity of Dr. Hincks should then have ventured on that rendering.

In various suggestions, including Pott's, besides others that we have omitted, the etymology has been based on a transfer of the name of the ox, or some other familiar quadruped. There would be nothing extraordinary in such a transfer of meaning. The reference to the *bos Luca*[2] is trite; the Tibetan word for ox (*glan*) is also the word for 'elephant'; we have seen how the name 'Great Boar' is alleged to be given to the elephant among the Kabyles; we have heard of an elephant in a menagerie being described by a Scotch rustic as 'a muckle sow'; Pausanias, according to Bochart, calls rhinoceroses 'Aethiopic bulls' [Bk. ix. 21, 2]. And let me finally illustrate the matter by a circumstance related to me by a brother officer who accompanied Sir Neville Chamberlain on an expedition among the turbulent Pathan tribes *c.* 1860. The women of the villages gathered to gaze on the elephants that accompanied the force, a stranger sight to them than it would have been to the women of the most secluded village in Scotland. 'Do you see these?' said a soldier of the Frontier Horse; 'do you know what they are? These are the Queen of England's buffaloes that give 5 maunds (about 160 quarts) of milk a day!'

Now it is an obvious suggestion, that if there were elephants on the skirts of Taurus down to B.C. 1100, or even (taking the less questionable evidence) down only to B.C. 1600, it is highly improbable that the Greeks would have had to seek a name for the animal, or its tusk, from Indian trade. And if the Greeks had a vernacular name for the elephant, there is also a probability, if not a presumption, that some tradition of this name would be found, *mutatis mutandis*, among other Aryan nations of Europe.

Now may it not be that *ἐλέφας—φαντος* in Greek, and *ulbandus* in Moeso-Gothic, represent this vernacular name? The latter form is exactly the modification of the former which Grimm's law demands. Nor is the word confined to Gothic. It is found in the Old H. German (*olpentâ*); in Anglo-Saxon (*olfend, oluend*, &c.); in Old Swedish (*aelpand, alwandyr, ulfwald*); in Icelandic (*ulfaldi*). All these Northern words, it is true, are used in the sense of *camel*, not of *elephant*. But instances already given may illustrate that there is nothing surprising in this transfer, all the less where the animal originally indicated had long been lost sight of. Further, Jülg, who has published a paper on the Gothic word, points out its resemblance to the Slav forms *welbond, welblond*, or *wielblad*, also meaning 'camel' (compare also Russian *verbliud*). This, in the last form (*wielblad*), may, he says, be regarded as resolvable into 'Great beast.' Herr Jülg ends his paper with a hint that in this meaning may perhaps be found a solution of the origin of *elephant* (an idea at which Pictet also transiently pointed in a paper referred to above), and half promises to follow up this hint; but in thirty years he has not done so, so far as I can discover. Nevertheless it is one which may yet be pregnant.

Nor is it inconsistent with this suggestion that we find also in some of the Northern languages a second series of names designating the elephant—not, as we suppose

---

1 See *J.R. As. Soc.* vol. xviii.

2 "Inde *boves Lucas* turrito corpore tetros,
Anguimanos, belli docuerunt volnera Pœnei
Sufferre, et magnas Martis turbars catervas."
Lucretius, v. 1301–3.

Here is the origin of Tennyson's 'serpent-hands.' The title *bos Luca* is explained by St. Isidore:

"Hos *boves Lucanos* vocabant antiqui Romani: *boves* quia nullum animal grandius videbant: *Lucanos* quia in Lucania illos primus Pyrrhus in prœlio objecit Romanis."—*Isid. Hispal.* lib. xii. *Originum*, cap. 2.

ulbandus and its kin to be, common vocables descending from a remote age in parallel development—but adoptions from Latin at a much more recent period. Thus, we have in Old and Middle German *Elefant* and *Helfant*, with *elfendein* and *helfenbein* for ivory; in Anglo-Saxon, *ylpend*, *elpend*, with shortened forms *ylp* and *elp*, and *ylpenban* for ivory; whilst the Scandinavian tongues adopt and retain *fil*. [The *N.E.D.* regards the derivation as doubtful, but considers the theory of Indian origin improbable.

[A curious instance of misapprehension is the use of the term '*Chain elephants*.' This is a misunderstanding of the ordinary locution *zanjīr-i-fīl* when speaking of elephants. *Zanjīr* is literally a 'chain,' but is here akin to our expressions, a 'pair,' 'couple,' 'brace' of anything. It was used, no doubt, with reference to the iron chain by which an elephant is hobbled. In an account 100 elephants would be entered thus; *Fīl, Zanjīr*, 100. (See NUMERICAL AFFIXES.)]

[1826.—"Very frequent mention is made in Asiatic histories of *chain*-**elephants**; which always mean elephants trained for war; but it is not very clear why they are so denominated."—*Ranking, Hist. Res. on the Wars and Sports of the Mongols and Romans*, 1826, Intro. p. 12.]

ELEPHANTA.

a. n.p. An island in Bombay Harbour, the native name of which is *Ghārāpurī* (or sometimes, it would seem, shortly, *Purī*), famous for its magnificent excavated temple, considered by Burgess to date after the middle of the 8th cent. The name was given by the Portuguese from the life-size figure of an elephant, hewn from an isolated mass of trap-rock, which formerly stood in the lower part of the island, not far from the usual landing-place. This figure fell down many years ago, and was often said to have disappeared. But it actually lay *in situ* till 1864–5, when (on the suggestion of the late Mr. W. E. Frere) it was removed by Dr. (now Sir) George Birdwood to the Victoria Gardens at Bombay, in order to save the relic from destruction. The elephant had originally a smaller figure on its back, which several of the earlier authorities speak of as a young elephant, but which Mr. Erskine and Capt. Basil Hall regarded as a tiger. The horse mentioned by Fryer remained in 1712; it had disappeared apparently before Niebuhr's visit in 1764. [Compare the recovery of a similar pair of elephant figures at Delhi, *Cunningham, Archaeol. Rep.* i. 225 *seqq.*]

c. 1321.—"In quod dum sic ascendissem, in xxviii. dietis me transtuli usque ad Tanam ... haec terra multum bene est situata. ... Haec terra antiquitus fuit valde magna. Nam ipsa fuit terra regis Pori, qui cum rege Alexandro praelium maximum commisit."—*Friar Odoric*, in *Cathay*, &c., App. p. v.

We quote this because of its relation to the passages following. It seems probable that the alleged connection with Porus and Alexander may have grown out of the name *Puri* or *Pori*.

[1539.—Mr. Whiteway notes that in João de Crastro's Log of his voyage to Diu will be found a very interesting account with measurements of the **Elephanta** Caves.]

1548.—"And the Isle of Pory, which is that of the **Elephant** (*do Alyfante*), is leased to João Pirez by arrangements of the said Governor (dom João de Crastro) for 150 pardaos."—*S. Botelko, Tombo*, 158.

1580.—"At 3 hours of the day we found ourselves abreast of a cape called Bombain, where is to be seen an ancient Roman temple, hollowed in the living rock. And above the said temple are many tamarind-trees, and below it a living spring, in which they have never been able to find bottom. The said temple is called **Alefante**, and is adorned with many figures, and inhabited by a great multitude of bats; and here they say that Alexander Magnus arrived, and for memorial thereof caused this temple to be made, and further than this he advanced not."—*Gasparo Balbi*, f. 62*v.*-63.

1598.—"There is yet an other Pagode, which they hold and esteem for the highest and chiefest Pagode of all the rest, which standeth in a little Iland called *Pory*; this Pagode by the Portingalls is called the Pagode of the **Elephant**. In that Iland standeth an high hill, and on the top thereof there is a hole, that goeth down into the hill, digged and carved out of the hard rock or stones as big as a great cloyster ... round about the wals are cut and formed, the shapes of Elephants, Lions, tigers, & a thousand such like wilde and cruel beasts. ..."—*Linschoten*, ch. xliv.; [Hak. Soc. i. 291].

1616.—Diogo de Couto devotes a chapter of 11 pp. to his detailed account "*do muito notavel e espantoso Pagode do* **Elefante**." We extract a few paragraphs:

"This notable and above all others astonishing Pagoda of the **Elephant** stands on a small islet, less than half a league in compass, which is formed by the river of Bombain, where it is about to discharge itself southward into the sea. It is so called because of a great **elephant** of stone, which one sees in entering the river. They say that it was made by the orders of a heathen king called Banasur, who ruled the whole country inland from the Ganges. ... On the left side of this chapel is a doorway 6 palms in depth and 5 in width, by which one enters a chamber which is nearly square and very dark, so that there is nothing to be seen there; and with this ends the fabric of this great pagoda. It has been in many parts demolished; and what the soldiers have left is so maltreated that it is grievous to see destroyed in such fashion one of the Wonders of the World. It is now 50 years since I went to see this marvellous Pagoda; and as I did not then visit it with such curiosity as I should now feel in doing so, I failed to remark many particulars which exist no longer. But I do remember me to have seen a certain Chapel, not to be seen now, open on the whole façade (which was more than 40 feet in length), and which along the rock formed a plinth the whole length of the edifice, fashioned like our altars both as to breadth and height; and on this plinth were many remarkable things to be seen. Among others I remember to have noticed the story of Queen Pasiphae and the bull; also the Angel with naked sword thrusting forth from below a tree two beautiful figures of a man and a woman, who were naked, as the Holy Scripture paints for us the appearance of our first parents Adam and Eve."—*Couto*, Dec. VII. liv. iii. cap. xi.

1644.—"... an islet which they call **Ilheo do Ellefanté**. ... In the highest part of this Islet is an eminence on which there is a mast from which a flag is unfurled when there are prows (*paros*) about, as often happens, to warn the small unarmed vessels to look out. ... There is on this island a pagoda called that of the Elephant, a work of extraordinary magnitude, being cut out of the solid rock," &c.—*Bocarro, MS.*

1673.—"... We steered by the south side of the Bay, purposely to touch at **Elephanto**, so called from a monstrous Elephant cut out of the main Rock, bearing a young one on its Back; not far from it the Effigies of a Horse stuck up to the Belly in the Earth in the Valley; from thence we clambered up the highest Mountain on the Island, on whose summit was a miraculous Piece hewed out of solid Stone: It is supported with 42 *Corinthian* Pillars," &c.—*Fryer*, 75.

1690.—"At 3 Leagues distance from *Bombay* is a small Island called **Elephanta**, from the Statue of an Elephant cut in Stone. ... Here likewise are the just dimensions of a Horse Carved in Stone, so lively ... that many have rather Fancyed it, at a distance, a living Animal. ... But that which adds the most Remarkable Charactor to this Island, is the fam'd *Pagode* at the top of it; so much spoke of by the *Portuguese*, and at present admir'd by the present Queen Dowager, that she cannot think any one has seen this part of India, who comes not Freighted home with some Account of it."—*Ovington*, 158–9.

1712.—"The island of **Elephanta** ... takes its name from an elephant in stone, with another on its back, which stands on a small hill, and serves as a sea mark. ... As they advanced towards the pagoda through a smooth narrow pass cut in the rock, they observed another hewn figure which was called Alexander's horse."—From an account written by *Captain Pyke*, on board the Stringer East Indiaman, and illd. by drawings. *Read by A. Dalrymple to the Soc. of Antiquaries*, 10th Feb. 1780, and pubd. in *Archaeologia*, vii. 323 *seqq*. One of the plates (xxi.) shows the elephant having on its back distinctly a small elephant, whose proboscis comes down into contact with the head of the large one.

1727.—"A league from thence is another larger, called **Elephanto**, belonging to the *Portugueze*, and serves only to feed some Cattle. I believe it took its name from an Elephant carved out of a great black Stone, about Seven Foot in Height."—*A. Hamilton*, i. 240; [ed. 1744, i. 241].

1760.—"Le lendemain, 7 Decembre, des que le jour parut, je me transportai au bas de la seconde montagne, en face de Bombaye, dans un coin de l'Isle, où est l'Elephant qui a fait donner à Galipouri le nom d'**Elephante**. L'animal est de grandeur naturelle, d'une pierre noire, et detachée du sol, et paroit porter son petit sur son dos."—*Anquetil du Perron*, I. ccccxxiii.

1761.—"... The work I mention is an artificial cave cut out of a solid Rock, and decorated with a number of pillars, and gigantic statues, some of which discover ye work of a skilful artist; and I am inform'd by an acquaintance who is well read in ye antient history, and has minutely considered ye figures, that it appears to be ye work of King Sesostris after his Indian Expedition."—MS. Letter of *James Rennell.*

1764.—"Plusieurs Voyageurs font bien mention du vieux temple Payen sur la petite Isle **Elephanta** près de Bombay, mais ils n'en parlent qu'en passant. Je le trouvois si curieux et si digne de l'attention des Amateurs d'Antiquités, que j'y fis trois fois le Voyage, et que j'y dessinois tout ce que s'y trouve de plus remarquable. ..."—*Carsten Niebuhr, Voyaye*, ii. 25.

"Pas loin du Rivage de la Mer, et en pleine Campagne, on voit encore un Elephant d'une pierre dure et noiratre ... La Statue ... porte quelque chose sur le dos, mais que le tems a rendu entièrement meconnoissable. ... Quant au Cheval dont Ovington et Hamilton font mention je ne l'ai pas vu."—*Ibid*. 33.

1780.—"That which has principally attracted the attention of travellers is the small island of **Elephanta**, situated in the east side of the harbour of Bombay. ... Near the south end is the figure of an elephant rudely cut in stone, from which the island has its name. ... On the back are the remains of something that is said to have formerly represented a young elephant, though no traces of such a resemblance are now to be found."—*Account*, &c. By *Mr. William Hunter*, Surgeon in the E. Indies, *Archaeologia*, vii. 286.

1783.—In vol. viii. of the *Archaeologia*, p. 251, is another account in a letter from Hector Macneil, Esq. He mentions "the elephant cut out of stone," but not the small elephant, nor the horse.

1795.—"*Some Account of the Caves in the Island of* **Elephanta.** By *J. Goldingham*, Esq." (No date of paper). In *As. Researches*, iv. 409 *seqq.*

1813.—*Account of the Cave Temple of* **Elephanta** ... by *Wm. Erskine*, *Trans. Bombay Lit. Soc.* i. 198 *seqq.* Mr. Erskine says in regard to the figure on the back of the large elephant: "The remains of its paws, and also the junction of its belly with the larger animal, were perfectly distinct; and the appearance it offered is represented on the annexed drawing made by Captain Hall (Pl. II.),[1] who from its appearance conjectured that it must have been a tiger rather than an elephant; an idea in which I feel disposed to agree."—*Ibid.* 208.

b. s. A name given, originally by the Portuguese, to violent storms occurring at the termination, though some travellers describe it as at the setting-in, of the Monsoon. [The Portuguese, however, took the name from the H. *hathiyā*, Skt. *hastā*, the 13th lunar Asterism, connected with *hastin*, an elephant, and hence sometimes called 'the sign of the elephant.' The *hathiyā* is at the close of the Rains.]

1554.—"The *Damani*, that is to say a violent storm arose; the kind of storm is known under the name of the **Elephant**; it blows from the west."—*Sidi 'Ali*, p. 75.

[1611.—"The storm of **Ofante** doth begin."—*Danvers, Letters*, i. 126.]

c. 1616.—"The 20th day (August), the night past fell a storme of raine called the **Oliphant**, vsuall at going out of the raines."—*Sir T. Roe*, in *Purchas*, i. 549; [Hak. Soc. i. 247].

1659.—"The boldest among us became dismayed; and the more when the whole culminated in such a terrific storm that we were compelled to believe that it must be that yearly raging tempest which is called the **Elephant**. This storm, annually, in September and October, makes itself heard in a frightful manner, in the Sea of Bengal."—*Walter Schulze*, 67.

c. 1665.—"Il y fait si mauvais pour le Vaisseaux au commencement de ce mois à cause d'un Vent d'Orient qui y souffle en ce tems-là avec violence, et qui est toujours accompagnè de gros nuages qu'on appelle **Elephans**, parcequ'ils en ont la figure. ..."—*Thevenot*, v. 38.

1673.—"Not to deviate any longer, we are now winding about the *South-West* part of Ceilon; where we have the **Tail of the Elephant** full in our mouth; a constellation by the *Portugals* called **Rabo del Elephanto**, known for the breaking up of the *Munsoons*, which is the last Flory this season makes."—*Fryer*, 48.

[1690.—"The Mussoans (**Monsoon**) are rude and Boisterous in their departure, as well as at their coming in, which two seasons are called the **Elephant** in India, and just before their breaking up, take their farewell for the most part in very rugged puffing weather."—*Ovington*, 137].

1756.—"9th (October). We had what they call here an **Elephanta**, which is an excessive hard gale, with very severe thunder, lightning and rain, but it was of short continuance. In about 4 hours there fell ... 2 (inches)."—*Ives*, 42.

c. 1760.—"The setting in of the rains is commonly ushered in by a violent thunderstorm, generally called the **Elephanta**."—*Grose*, i. 33.

ELL'ORA, (though very commonly called **Ellóra**), n.p. Properly *Elurā*, [Tel. *elu*, 'rule,' *ūru*, 'village,'] otherwise *Vērulē*, a village in the Nizam's territory, 7 m. from Daulatābād, which gives its name to the famous and wonderful rock-caves and temples in its vicinity, excavated in the crescent-shaped scarp of a plateau, about 1½ m. in length. These works are Buddhist (ranging from A.D. 450 to 700), Brahminical (c. 650 to 700), and Jain (c. 800–1000).

c. 1665.—"On m'avoit fait a Sourat grande estime des Pagodes **d'Elora** ... (and after describing them) ... Quoiqu'il en soit, si l'on considère cette quantité de Temples spacieux, remplis de pilastres et de colonnes, et tant de milliers de figures, et le tout taillé dans le roc vif, on peut dire avec verité que ces ouvrages surpassent la force humaine; et qu'au moins les gens du siècle dans lequel ils ont été faits, n'étoient pas tout-à-fait barbares."—*Thevenot*, v. p. 222.

1684.—"Muhammad Sháh Malik Júná, son of Tughlik, selected the fort of Deogir as a central point whereat to establish the seat of government, and gave it the name of Daulatábád. He removed the inhabitants of Delhí thither. ... Ellora is only a short distance from this place.

1 It is not easy to understand the bearing of the drawing in question.

At some very remote period a race of men, as if by magic, excavated caves high up among the defiles of the mountains. These rooms extended over a breadth of one *kos*. Carvings of various designs and of correct execution adorned all the walls and ceilings; but the outside of the mountain is perfectly level, and there is no sign of any dwelling. From the long period of time these Pagans remained masters of this territory, it is reasonable to conclude, although historians differ, that to them is to be attributed the construction of these places."—*Sākī Musta'idd Khān, Ma-āṣir-i-'Ālamgīrī*, in *Elliot*, vii. 189 *seq.*

1760.—"Je descendis ensuite par un sentier frayé dans le roc, et après m'être muni de deux Brahmes que l'on me donna pour fort instruits je commencai la visite de ce que j'appelle les Pagodes d'**Eloura.**"—*Anquetil du Perron*, I. ccxxxiii.

1794.—"*Description of the Caves ... on the Mountain, about a Mile to the Eastward of the town of* **Ellora**, *or as called on the spot, Verrool.*" (By Sir C. W. Malet.) In *As. Researches*, vi. 38 *seqq.*

1803.—"*Hindoo Excavations in the Mountain of ...* **Ellora** *in Twenty-four Views. ... Engraved from the Drawings of* James Wales, *by and under the direction of* Thomas Daniell.

EURASIAN, a. A modern name for persons of mixt European and Indian blood, devised as being more euphemistic than **Half-caste** and more precise than *East-Indian*. ["No name has yet been found or coined which correctly represents this section. **Eurasian** certainly does not. When the European and Anglo-Indian Defence Association was established 17 years ago, the term *Anglo-Indian*, after much consideration, was adopted as best designating this community."—(*Procs. Imperial Anglo-Indian Ass.*, in *Pioneer Mail*, April 13, 1900.)]

[1844.—"*The* **Eurasian Belle**," *in a few Local Sketches by J. M.*, Calcutta.—6th ser. *Notes and Queries*, xii. 177.

[1866.—See quotation under KHUDD.]

1880.—"The shovel-hats are surprised that the **Eurasian** does not become a missionary or a schoolmaster, or a policeman, or something of that sort. The native papers say, 'Deport him'; the white prints say, 'Make him a soldier'; and the *Eurasian* himself says, 'Make me a Commissioner, give me a pension.'"—*Ali Baba*, 123.

EUROPE, adj. Commonly used in India for "European," in contradistinction to **country** (q.v.) as qualifying goods, viz. those imported from Europe. The phrase is probably obsolescent, but still in common use. "Europe shop" is a shop where European goods of sorts are sold in an up-country station. The first quotation applies the word to a *man*. [A "*Europe* morning" is lying late in bed, as opposed to the Anglo-Indian's habit of early rising.]

1673.—"The Enemies, by the help of an **Europe** Engineer, had sprung a Mine to blow up the Castle."—*Fryer*, 87.

[1682-3.—"Ordered that a sloop be sent to Conimero with **Europe** goods. ..."—*Pringle, Diary, Ft. St. Geo.*, 1st ser. ii. 14.]

1711.—"On the arrival of a **Europe** ship, the Sea-Gate is always throng'd with People."—*Lockyer*, 27.

1781.—"Guthrie and Wordie take this method of acquainting the Public that they intend quitting the **Europe** Shop Business."—*India Gazette*, May 26.

1782.—"To be Sold, a magnificent **Europe** Chariot, finished in a most elegant manner, and peculiarly adapted to this Country."—*Ibid.* May 11.

c. 1817.—"Now the **Europe** shop into which Mrs. Browne and Mary went was a very large one, and full of all sorts of things. One side was set out with **Europe** caps and bonnets, ribbons, feathers, sashes, and what not."—*Mrs. Sherwood's Stories*, ed. 1873, 23.

1866.—"*Mrs. Smart.* Ah, Mr. Cholmondeley, I was called the **Europe** Angel."—*The Dawk Bungalow*, 219.

[1888.—"I took a '**European** morning' after having had three days of going out before breakfast. ..."—*Lady Dufferin, Vice-regal Life*, 371.]

F

***FACTOR**, s. Originally a commercial agent; the executive head of a **factory**. Till some 55 years ago the *Factors* formed the third of the four classes into which the covenanted civil servants of the Company were theoretically divided, viz. Senior Merchants, Junior Merchants, **factors** and **writers**. But these terms had long ceased to have any relation to the occupation of these officials, and even to have any application at all except in the nominal lists of the service. The titles, however, continue (through *vis inertiae* of administration in such matters) in the classified lists of the Civil Service for years after the abolition of the last vestige of the Company's trading character, and it is not till the publication of the E. I. Register for the first half of 1842 that they disappear from that official publication. In this the whole body appears without any classification; and in that for the second half of 1842 they are divided into six classes, first class, second class, &c., an arrangement which, with the omission of the 6th class, still continues. Possibly the expressions *Factor*, *Factory*, may have been adopted from the Portuguese *Feitor*, *Feitoria*. The formal authority for the classification of the civilians is quoted under 1675.

1501.—"With which answer night came on, and there came aboard the Captain Mór that Christian of Calecut sent by the **Factor** (*feitor*) to say that Cojebequi assured him, and he knew it to be the case, that the King of Calecut was arming a great fleet."—*Correa*, i. 250.

1582.—"The **Factor** and the Catuall having seen these parcels began to laugh thereat."—*Castañeda*, tr. by N. L., f. 46*b*.

1600.—"Capt. Middleton, John Havard, and Francis Barne, elected the three principal **Factors**. John Havard, being present, willingly accepted."—*Sainsbury*, i. 111.

c. 1610.—"Les Portugais de Malaca ont des commis et **facteurs** par toutes ces Isles pour le trafic."—*Pyrard de Laval*, ii. 106. [Hak. Soc. ii. 170].

1653.—"**Feitor** est vn terme Portugais signifiant vn Consul aux Indes."—*De la Boullaye-le-Gouz*, ed. 1657, p. 538.

1666.—"The Viceroy came to Cochin, and there received the news that Antonio de Sà, **Factor** (*Fator*) of Coulam, with all his officers, had been slain by the Moors."—*Faria y Sousa*, i. 35.

1675-6.—"For the advancement of our Apprentices, we direct that, after they have served the first five yeares, they shall have £10 per annum, for the last two yeares; and having served these two yeares, to be entertayned one year longer, as **Writers**, and have Writers' Sallary: and having served that yeare, to enter into ye degree of **Factor**, which otherwise would have been ten yeares. And knowing that a distinction of titles is, in many respects necessary, we do order that when the Apprentices have served their times, they be stiled *Writers*; and when the Writers have served their times, they be stiled **Factors**, and Factors having served their times to be stiled *Merchants*; and Merchants having served their times to be stiled *Senior Merchants*."—*Ext. of Court's Letter* in *Bruce's Annals of the E.I. Co.*, ii. 374-5.

1689.—"These are the chief Places of Note and Trade where their Presidents and Agents reside, for the support of whom, with their Writers and **Factors**, large Privileges and Salaries are allowed."—*Ovington*, 386. (The same writer tells us that *Factors* got £40 a year; junior Factors, £15; Writers, £7. Peons got 4 rupees a month. P. 392.)

1711.—Lockyer gives the salaries at Madras as follows: "The Governor, £200 and £100 gratuity; 6 Councillors, of whom the chief (2nd ?) had £100, 3d. £70, 4th. £50, the others £40, which was the salary of 6 Senior Merchants. 2 Junior Merchants £30 per annum; 5 **Factors**, £15; 10 Writers, £5; 2 Ministers, £100; 1 Surgeon, £36.

* * * * * * *

"Attorney-General has 50 Pagodas per *Annum* gratuity.

"Scavenger 100 do."

* * * * * * *

(p. 14.)

c. 1748.—"He was appointed to be a Writer in the Company's Civil Service, becoming ... after the first five (years) a **factor**."—*Orme*, *Fragments*, viii.

1781.—"Why we should have a Council and Senior and Junior Merchants, **factors** and writers, to load one ship in the year (at Penang), and to collect a very small revenue, appears to me perfectly incomprehensible."—*Corresp. of Ld. Cornwallis*, i. 390.

1786.—In a notification of Aug. 10th, the subsistence of civil servants out of employ is fixed thus:—

A Senior Merchant—£400 sterling per ann.
A Junior Merchant—£300 " "
Factors and Writers-£200 " "

In *Seton-Karr*, i. 131.

***FACTORY**, s. A trading establishment at a foreign port or mart (see preceding).

1500.—"And then he sent ashore the Factor Ayres Correa with the ship's carpenters ... and sent to ask the King for timber ... all which the King sent in great sufficiency, and he sent orders also for him to have many carpenters and labourers to assist in making the houses; and they brought much plank and wood, and palm-trees which they cut down at the Point, so that they made a great Campo,[1] in which they made houses for the Captain Mór, and for each of the Captains, and houses for the people, and they made also a separate large house for the **factory** (*feitoria*)."—*Correa*, i. 168.

1582.—"... he sent a Nayre ... to the intent hee might remaine in the **Factorye**."—*Castañeda* (by N. L.), ff. 54*b*.

1606.—"In which time the *Portingall* and

1 This use of *campo* is more like the sense of Compound (q.v.) than in any instance we had found when completing that article.

Tydoryan Slaves had sacked the towne, setting fire to the **factory**."—*Middleton's Voyage*, G. (4).

1615.—"The King of Acheen desiring that the Hector should leave a merchant in his country ... it has been thought fit to settle a **factory** at Acheen, and leave Juxon and Nicolls in charge of it."—*Sainsbury*, i. 415.

1809.—"The **factory**-house (at Cuddalore) is a chaste piece of architecture, built by my relative Diamond Pitt, when this was the chief station of the British on the Coromandel Coast."—*Ld. Valentia*, i. 372.

***FAILSOOF**, s. Ar.—H. *failsūf*, from φιλόσοφος. But its popular sense is a 'crafty schemer,' an 'artful dodger.' **Filosofo**, in Manilla, is applied to a native who has been at college, and returns to his birthplace in the provinces, with all the importance of his acquisitions, and the affection of European habits (*Blumentritt*, *Vocabular.*).

***FAKEER**, s. Hind. from Arab. *faḳīr* ('poor'). Properly an indigent person, but specially 'one poor in the sight of God,' applied to a Mahommedan religious mendicant, and then, loosely and inaccurately, to Hindu devotees and naked ascetics. And this last is the most ordinary Anglo-Indian use.

1604.—"**Fokers** are men of good life, which are only given to peace. Leo calls them Hermites; others call them *Talbies* and Saints."—*Collection of things ... of Barbarie*, in *Purchas*, ii. 857.

"*Muley Boferes* sent certaine **Fokers**, held of great estimation amongst the *Moores*, to his brother *Muley Sidan*, to treate conditions of Peace."—*Ibid.*

1633.—"Also they are called **Fackeeres**, which are religious names."—*W. Bruton*, in *Hakl.* v. 56.

1653.—"**Fakir** signifie pauure en Turq et Persan, mais en Indien signifie ... vne espece de Religieux Indou, qui foullent le monde aux pieds, et ne s'habillent que de haillons qu'ils ramassent dans les ruës."—*De la Boullaye-le-Gouz*, ed. 1657, 538.

c. 1660.—"I have often met in the Field, especially upon the Lands of the Rajas, whole squadrons of these **Faquires**, altogether naked, dreadful to behold. Some held their Arms lifted up ...; others had their terrible Hair hanging about them ...; some had a kind of *Hercules's* Club; others had dry and stiff Tiger-skins over their Shoulders. ..."—*Bernier*, E.T. p. 102; [ed. *Constable*, 317].

1673.—"**Fakiers** or Holy Men, abstracted from the World, and resigned to God."—*Fryer*, 95.

[1684.—"The **Ffuckeer** that Killed ye Boy at Ennore with severall others ... were brought to their tryalls. ..."—*Pringle, Diary, Ft. St. Geo.* 1st ser. iii. 111.]

1690.—"They are called **Faquirs** by the Natives, but *Ashmen* commonly by us, because of the abundance of Ashes with which they powder their Heads."—*Ovington*, 350.

1727.—"Being now settled in Peace, he invited his holy Brethren the **Fakires**, who are very numerous in India, to come to Agra and receive a new Suit of Clothes."—*A. Hamilton*, i. 175; [ed. 1744, ii. 177].

1763.—"Received a letter from Dacca dated 29th Novr., desiring our orders with regard to the **Fakirs** who were taken prisoners at the retaking of Dacoa."—*Ft. William Cons.* Dec. 5, in *Long*, 342. On these latter *Fakirs*, see under SUNYASEE.

1770.—"Singular expedients have been tried by men jealous of superiority to share with the Bramins the veneration of the multitude; this has given rise to a race of monks known in India by the name of **Fakirs**."—*Raynal* (tr. 1777), i. 49.

1774.—"The character of a **fakir** is held in great estimation in this country."—*Bogle*, in *Markham's Tibet*, 23.

1856.—

"There stalks a row of Hindoo devotees,
Bedaubed with ashes, their foul matted hair
Down to their heels; their blear eyes fiercely scowl
Beneath their painted brows. On this side struts
A Mussulman **Fakeer**, who tells his beads,
By way of prayer, but cursing all the while
The heathen."—*The Banyan Tree*.

1878.—"Les mains abandonnées sur les genoux, dans une immobilité de **fakir**."—*Alph. Daudet*, *Le Nabob*, ch. vi.

FANQUI, s. Chin. *fan-kwei*, 'foreign demon'; sometimes with the affix *tsz* or *tsŭ*, 'son'; the popular Chinese name for Europeans. ["During the 15th and 16th centuries large numbers of black slaves of both sexes from the E. I. Archipelago were purchased by the great houses of Canton to serve as gate-keepers. They were called 'devil slaves,' and it is not improbable that the term 'foreign devil,' so freely used by the Chinese for foreigners, may have had this origin."—*Ball, Things Chinese*, 535.]

***FIREFLY**, s. Called in South Indian vernaculars by names signifying 'Lightning Insect.'

A curious question has been discussed

among entomologists, &c., of late years, viz. as to the truth of the alleged rhythmical or synchronous flashing of fireflies when visible in great numbers. Both the present writers can testify to the fact of a distinct effect of this kind. One of them can never forget an instance in which he witnessed it, twenty years or more before he was aware that any one had published, or questioned, the fact. It was in descending the Chāndor Ghāt, in Nāsik District of the Bombay Presidency, in the end of May or beginning of June 1843, during a fine night preceding the rains. There was a large amphitheatre of forest-covered hills, and every leaf of every tree seemed to bear a firefly. They flashed and intermitted throughout the whole area in apparent rhythm and sympathy. It is, we suppose, possible that this may have been a deceptive impression, though it is difficult to see how it could originate. The suggestions made at the meetings of the Entomological Society are utterly unsatisfactory to those who have observed the phenomenon. In fact it may be said that those suggested explanations only assume that the *soidisant* observers did not observe what they alleged. We quote several independent testimonies to the phenomenon.

1579.—"Among these trees, night by night, did show themselues an infinite swarme of fierie seeming wormes flying in the aire, whose bodies (no bigger than an ordinarie flie) did make a shew, and giue such light as euery twigge on euery tree had beene a lighted candle, or as if that place had beene the starry spheare."—*Drake's Voyage*, by *F. Fletcher*, Hak. Soc. 149.

1675.—"We ... left our Burnt Wood on the Right-hand, but entred another made us better Sport, deluding us with false Flashes, that you would have thought the Trees on a Flame, and presently, as if untouch'd by **Fire**, they retained their wonted Verdure. The Coolies beheld the Sight with Horror and Amazement ... where we found an Host of **Flies**, the Subject both of our Fear and Wonder. ... This gave my Thoughts the Contemplation of that Miraculous Bush crowned with Innocent Flames, ... the Fire that consumes everything seeming rather to dress than offend it."—*Fryer*, 141–142.

1682.—"**Fireflies** (*de vuur-vliegen*) are so called by us because at eventide, whenever they fly they burn so like fire, that from a distance one fancies to see so many lanterns; in fact they give light enough to write by. ... They gather in the rainy season in great multitudes in the bushes and trees, and live on the flowers of the trees. There are various kinds."—*Nieuhoff*, ii. 291.

1764.—
"Ere **fireflies** trimmed their vital lamps, and ere
Dun Evening trod on rapid Twilight's heel,
His knell was rung."—*Grainger*, Bk. I.

1824.—
"Yet mark! as fade the upper skies,
Each thicket opes ten thousand eyes.
Before, behind us, and above,
The **fire-fly** lights his lamp of love,
Retreating, chasing, sinking, soaring,
The darkness of the copse exploring."
Heber, ed. 1844, i. 258.

1865.—"The bushes literally swarm with **fireflies**, which flash out their intermittent light almost contemporaneously; the effect being that for an instant the exact outline of all the bushes stands prominently forward, as if lit up with electric sparks, and next moment all is jetty dark—darker from the momentary illumination that preceded. These flashes succeed one another every 3 or 4 seconds for about 10 minutes, when an interval of similar duration takes place; as if to allow the insects to regain their electric or phosphoric vigour."—*Cameron, Our Tropical Possessions in Malayan India*, 80–81.

The passage quoted from Mr. Cameron's book was read at the Entom. Soc. of London in May 1865, by the Rev. Hamlet Clarke, who added that:

"Though he was utterly unable to give an explanation of the phenomenon, he could so far corroborate Mr. Cameron as to say that he had himself witnessed this simultaneous flashing; he had a vivid recollection of a particular glen in the Organ Mountains where he had on several occasions noticed the contemporaneous exhibition of their light by numerous individuals, as if they were acting in concert."

Mr. McLachlan then suggested that this might be caused by currents of wind, which by inducing a number of the insects simultaneously to change the direction of their flight, might occasion a momentary concealment of their light.

Mr. Bates had never in his experience received the impression of any simultaneous flashing ... he regarded the contemporaneous flashing as an illusion produced probably by the swarms of insects flying among foliage, and being continually, but only momentarily, hidden behind the leaves.—*Proc. Entom. Soc. of London*, 1865, pp. 94–95.

Fifteen years later at the same Society:

"Sir Sidney Saunders stated that in the South of Europe (Corfu and Albania) the simultaneous flashing of *Luciola italica*, with intervals of complete darkness for some seconds, was constantly witnessed in the dark summer nights, when swarming myriads were to be seen. ... He did not concur in the hypothesis propounded by Mr. McLachlan ... the flashes are certainly intermittent ... the simultaneous character of these coruscations among vast swarms would seem to depend upon an instinctive impulse to emit their light at certain intervals as a protective influence, which intervals became assimilated to each other by imitative emulation. But whatever be the causes ... the fact itself was incontestable."—*Ibid.* for 1880, Feby. 24, p. ii.; see also p. vii.

1868.—"At Singapore ... the little luminous beetle commonly known as the **firefly** (Lampyris, sp. ign.) is common ... clustered in the foliage of the trees, instead of keeping up an irregular twinkle, every individual shines simultaneously at regular intervals, as though by a common impulse; so that their light pulsates, as it were, and the tree is for one moment illuminated by a hundred brilliant points, and the next is almost in total darkness. The intervals have about the duration of a second, and during the intermission only one or two remain luminous."—*Collingwood, Rambles of a Naturalist*, p. 255.

1880.—"Harbingers of the Monsoon.—One of the surest indications of the approach of the monsoon is the spectacle 'presented nightly in the Mawul taluka, that is, at Khandalla and Lanoli, where the trees are filled with myriads of **fireflies**, which flash their phosphoric light simultaneously. Each tree suddenly flashes from bottom to top. Thousands of trees presenting this appearance simultaneously, afford a spectacle beautiful, if not grand, beyond conception. This little insect, the female of its kind, only appears and displays its brilliant light immediately before the monsoon."—*Deccan Herald*. (From *Pioneer Mail*, June 17).

FIRINGHEE, s. Pers. *Farangī*, *Firingī*; Ar. *Al-Faranj*, *Ifranjī*, *Firanjī*, *i.e.* a Frank. This term for a European is very old in Asia, but when now employed by natives in India is either applied (especially in the South) specifically to the Indian-born Portuguese, or, when used more generally, for 'European,' implies something of hostility or disparagement. (See *Sonnerat* and *Elphinstone* below.) In South India the Tamil *P'arangi*, the Singhalese *Parangi*, mean only 'Portuguese,' [or natives converted by the Portuguese, or by Mahommedans, any European (*Madras Gloss.* s.v.). St. Thomas's Mount is called in Tam. *Parangi Malai*, from the original Portuguese settlement]. *Piringi* is in Tel. = 'cannon,' (C. B. P.), just as in the medieval Mahommedan historians we find certain mangonels for sieges called *maghribī* or 'Westerns.' [And so *Farhangī* or *Phirangī* is used for the straight cut and thrust swords introduced by the Portuguese into India, or made there in imitation of the foreign weapon (*Sir W. Elliot, Ind. Antiq.* xv. 30)]. And it may be added that Baber, in describing the battle of Pānipat (1526) calls his artillery *Farangīha* (see *Autob.* by Leyden and Erskine, p. 306, note. See also paper by Gen. R. Maclagan, R.E., on early Asiatic fire-weapons, in *J.A.S. Beng.* xlv. Pt. i. pp. 66–67).

c. 930.—"The **Afranjah** are of all those nations the most warlike ... the best organised, the most submissive to the authority of their rulers."—*Maṣ'ūdī*, iii. 66.

c. 1340.—"They call **Franchi** all the Christians of these parts from Romania westward."—*Pegolotti*, in *Cathay*, &c., 292.

c. 1350.—"——**Franks**. For so they term us, not indeed from France, but from Frank-land (non a *Franciâ* sed a *Franquiâ*)."—*Marignolli*, *ibid.* 336.

In a Chinese notice of the same age the horses carried by Marignolli as a present from the Pope to the Great Khan are called "horses of the kingdom of **Fulang**," *i.e.* of *Farang* or Europe.

1384.—"E quello nominare **Franchi** procede da' Franceschi, che tutti ci appellano Franceschi."—*Frescobaldi, Viaggio*, p. 23.

1436.—"At which time, talking of *Cataio*, he told me howe the chief of that Princes corte knewe well enough what the **Franchi** were. ... Thou knowest, said he, how neere wee bee unto Capha, and that we practise thither continually ... adding this further, We Cataini have twoo eyes, and yow **Franchi** one, whereas yow (torneng him towards the Tartares that were wth him) have neuer a one. ..."—*Barbaro*, Hak. Soc. 58.

c. 1440.—"Hi nos **Francos** appellant, aiuntque cum ceteras gentes coecas vocent, se duobis oculis, nos unico esse, superiores existimates se esse prudentiâ."—*Conti*, in *Poggius, de Var. Fortunae*, iv.

1498.—"And when he heard this he said that such people could be none other than **Francos**, for so they call us in those parts."—*Roteiro de V. da Gama*, 97.

1560.—"Habitão aqui (Tabriz) duas nações de Christãos ... e huns delles a qui chamão **Franques**, estes tem o costume e fé, como nos ...

e outros são Armenos."—*A. Tenreiro, Itinerario*, ch. xv.

1565.—"Suddenly news came from Tuatta that the **Firingis** had passed Lahori Bandar, and attacked the city."—*Táríkh-i-Táhirí* in *Elliot*, i. 276.

c. 1610.—"La renommée des François a esté telle par leur conquestes en Orient, que leur nom y est demeuré pour memoire éternelle, en ce qu'encore aujourd'huy par toute l'Asie et Afrique on appelle du nom de **Franghi** tous ceux qui viennent d'Occident."—*Mocquet*, 24.

[1614.—"... including us within the word **Franqueis**."—*Foster, Letters*, ii. 299.]

1616.—"... alii *Cafres* et *Cafaros* eos dicunt, alii **Francos**, quo nomine omnes passim Christiani ... dicuntur."—*Jarric, Thesaurus*, iii. 217.

[1623.—"**Franchi**, or Christians."—*P. della Valle*, Hak. Soc. ii. 251.]

1632.—"... he shew'd two Passes from the Portugals which they call by the name of **Fringes**."—*W. Bruton*, in *Hakluyt*, v. 32.

1648.—"Mais en ce repas-là tout fut bien accommodé, et il y a apparence qu'un cuisinier **Frangui** s'en estoit mélé."—*Tavernier, V. des Indes*, iii. ch. 22; [ed. *Ball*, ii. 335].

1653.—"**Frenk** signifie en Turq vn Europpeen, ou plustost vn Chrestien ayant des cheueux et vn chapeau comme les François, Anglois. ..."—*De la Boullaye-le-Gouz*, ed. 1657, 538.

c. 1660.—"The same Fathers say that this King (Jehan-Guire), to begin in good earnest to countenance the Christian Religion, designed to put the whole Court into the habit of the **Franqui**, and that after he had ... even dressed himself in that fashion, he called to him one of the chief Omrahs ... this Omrah ... having answered him very seriously, that it was a very dangerous thing, he thought himself obliged to change his mind, and turned all to raillery."—*Bernier*, E.T. 92; [ed. *Constable*, 287; also see p. 3].

1673.—"The Artillery in which the **Fringis** are Listed; formerly for good Pay, now very ordinary, having not above 30 or 40 Rupees a month."—*Fryer*, 195.

1682.—"... whether I had been in Turky and Arabia (as he was informed) and could speak those languages ... with which they were pleased, and admired to hear from a **Frenge** (as they call us)."—*Hedges, Diary*, Oct. 29; [Hak. Soc. i. 44].

1712.—"*Johan Whelo, Serdaar* **Frengiaan**, or Captain of the Europeans in the Emperor's service. ..."—*Valentijn*, iv. (Suratte) 295.

1755.—"By **Feringy** I mean all the black *mustee* (see MUSTEES) Portuguese Christians residing in the settlement as a people distinct from the natural and proper subjects of Portugal; and as a people who sprung originally from Hindoos or Mussulmen."—*Holwell*, in *Long*, 59.

1774.—"He said it was true, but everybody was afraid of the **Firingies**."—*Bogle*, in *Markham's Tibet*, 176.

1782.—"Ainsi un Européen est tout ce que les Indiens connoissent de plus méprisable; ils le nomment **Parangui**, nom qu'ils donnèrent aux Portugais, lorsque ceux-ci abordèrent dans leur pays, et c'est un terme qui marque le souverain mépris qu'ils ont pour toutes les nations de l'Europe."—*Sonnerat*, i. 102.

1791.—"... il demande à la passer (la nuit) dans un des logemens de la pagoda; mais on lui refusa d'y coucher, à cause qu'il étoit **frangui**."—*B. de St. Pierre, Chaumière Indienne*, 21.

1794.—"**Feringee**. The name given by the natives of the Decan to Europeans in general, but generally understood by the English to be confined to the Portuguese."—*Moor's Narrative*, 504.

[1820.—"In the southern quarter (of Backergunje) there still exist several original Portuguese colonies. ... They are a meagre, puny, imbecile race, blacker than the natives, who hold them in the utmost contempt, and designate them by the appellation of *Caula* **Ferenghies**, or black Europeans."—*Hamilton, Descr. of Hindostan*, i. 133; for an account of the Feringhis of Sibpur, see *Beveridge, Bākarganj*, 110.]

1824.—"'Now Hajji,' said the ambassador. ... 'The **Franks** are composed of many, many nations. As fast as I hear of one hog, another begins to grunt, and then another and another, until I find that there is a whole herd of them.'"—*Hajji Baba*, ed. 1835, p. 432.

1825.—"Europeans, too, are very little known here, and I heard the children continually calling out to us, as we passed through the villages, '**Feringhee**, *ue* **Feringhee**!'"—*Heber*, ii. 43.

1828.—"Mr. Elphinstone adds in a note that in India it is a positive affront to call an Englishman a **Feringhee**."—*Life of E.* ii. 207.

c. 1861.—

"There goes my lord the **Feringhee**, who
 talks so civil and bland,
But raves like a soul in Jehannum if I don't
 quite understand—
He begins by calling me Sahib, and ends by
 calling me fool ..."

Sir A. C. Lyall, The Old Pindaree.

The Tibetans are said to have corrupted **Firinghee** into **Pelong** (or *Philin*). But Jaeschke disputes this origin of *Pelong*.

FIRMAUN, s. Pers. *farmān*, 'an order, patent, or passport,' der. from *farmūdan*, 'to order.' Sir T. Roe below calls it *firma*, as if suggestive of the Italian for 'signature.'

[1561.—"... wrote him a letter called **Firmao**. ..."—*Castanheda*, Bk. viii. ch. 99.

[1602.—"They said that he had a **Firmao** of the Grand Turk to go overland to the Kingdom of (Portugal). ..."—*Couto*, Dec. viii. ch. 15.]

1606.—"We made our journey having a **Firman** (*Firmão*) of safe conduct from the same Soltan of Shiraz."—*Gouvea*, f. 140*b*.

[1614.—"But if possible, bring their chaps, their **Firms**, for what they say or promise."—*Foster, Letters*, ii. 28.]

1616.—"Then I moued him for his favour for an *English* Factory to be resident in the Towne, which hee willingly granted, and gave present order to the Buxy to draw a **Firma**. ... for their residence."—*Sir T. Roe*, in *Purchas*, i. 541; [Hak. Soc. i. 93; also see i. 47].

1648.—"The 21st April the Bassa sent me a **Firman** or Letter of credentials to all his lords and Governors."—*T. Van den Broecke*, 32.

1673.—"Our Usage by the **Pharmaund** (or charters) granted successively from their Emperors, is kind enough, but the better because our Naval Power curbs them."—*Fryer*, 115.

1683.—"They (the English) complain, and not without a Cause; they having a **Phirmaund**, and Hodgee Sophee Caun's *Perwannas* thereon, in their hands, which cleared them thereof; and to pay Custome now they will not consent, but will rather withdraw their trading. Wherefore their desire is that for 3,000 rup. *Piscash* (as they paid formerly at Hugly) and 2,000 r. more yearly on account of *Jidgea*, which they are willing to pay, they may on that condition have a grant to be Custome Free."—*Nabob's Letter to Vizier* (MS.), in *Hedges' Diary*, July 18; [Hak. Soc. i. 101].

1689.—"... by her came Bengal Peons who brought in several letters and a **firmaun** from the new Nabob of Bengal."—*Wheeler*, i. 213.

c. 1690.—"Now we may see the Mogul's Stile in his **Phirmaund** to be sent to Surat, as it stands translated by the Company's Interpreter."—*A. Hamilton*, i. 227; [ed. 1744, i. 230].

FOOL'S RACK, s. (For *Rack* see **ARRACK**.) *Fool Rack* is originally, as will be seen from Garcia and Acosta, the name of the strongest distillation from *toddy* or *sura*, the 'flower' (*p'hūl*, in H. and Mahr.) of the spirit. But the 'striving after meaning' caused the English corruption of this name to be applied to a peculiarly abominable and pernicious spirit, in which, according to the statement of various old writers, the stinging sea-blubber was mixed, or even a distillation of the same, with a view of making it more ardent.

1563.—"... this çura they distil like brandy (*agua ardente*): and the result is a liquor like brandy; and a rag steeped in this will burn as in the case of brandy; and this fine spirit they call **fula**, which means 'flower'; and the other quality that remains they call **orraca**, mixing with it a small quantity of the first kind. ..."—*Garcia*, f. 67.

1578.—"... la qual (*sura*) en vasos despues distilan, para hazer agua ardiente, de la qual una, a que ellos llaman **Fula**, que quiere dezir 'flor,' es mas fina ... y la segunda, que llaman **Orraca**, no tanto."—*Acosta*, p. 101.

1598.—"This *Sura* being [beeing] distilled, is called **Fula** or Nipe [see **NIPA**], and is as excellent *aqua vitae* as any is made in *Dort* of their best renish [rennish] wine, but this is of the finest kinde of distillation."—*Linschoten*, 101; [Hak. Soc. ii. 49].

1631.—"DURAEUS ... Apparet te etiam a vino adusto, nec Arac Chinensi, abhorrere? BONTIUS. Usum commendo, abusum abominor ... at cane pejus et angue vitandum est quod Chinenses avarissimi simul et astutissimi bipedum, mixtis Holothuriis in mari fluctuantibus, parant ... eaque tam exurentis sunt caloris ut solo attactu vesicas in cute excitent. ..."—*Jac. Bontii, Hist. Nat. et Med. Ind., Dial.* iii.

1673.—"Among the worst of these (causes of disease) **Fool Rack** (Brandy made of *Blubber*, or *Carvil*, by the *Portugals*, because it swims always in a Blubber, as if nothing else were in it; but touch it, and it stings like nettles; the latter, because sailing on the Waves it bears up like a *Portuguese Carvil*: It is, being taken, a Gelly, and distilled causes those that take it to be **Fools**. ..."—*Fryer*, 68–69.

[1753.—"... that fiery, single and simple distilled spirit, called **Fool**, with which our seamen were too frequently intoxicated."—*Ives*, 457.

[1868.—"The first spirit that passes over is called '**phúl**.'"—*B. H. Powell, Handbook, Econ. Prod. of Punjab*, 311.]

FOOZILOW, TO, v. The imperative *p'huslāo* of the H. verb *p'huslānā*, 'to flatter or cajole,' used, in a common Anglo-Indian fashion (see **BUNNOW**, **PUCKAROW**, **LUGOW**), as a verbal infinitive.

FULEETA, s. Properly P. *palīta* or *fatīla*, 'a slow-match,' as of a matchlock, but its usual colloquial Anglo-Indian application is to a cotton slow-match used to light cigars, and often furnished with a neat or decorated silver tube. This kind of cigar-light is called at Madras **Ramasammy** (q.v.).

FULEETA-PUP, s. This, in Bengal, is a well-known dish in the repertory of the ordinary native cook. It is a corruption of '*fritter-puff*'!

FURLOUGH, s. This word for a soldier's leave has acquired a peculiar citizenship in Anglo-Indian colloquial, from the importance of the matter to those employed in Indian service. It appears to have been first made the subject of systematic regulation in 1796. The word seems to have come to England from the Dutch *Verlof*, 'leave of absence,' in the early part of the 17th century, through those of our countrymen who had been engaged in the wars of the Netherlands. It is used by Ben Jonson, who had himself served in those wars:

1625.—
"*Pennyboy, Jun.* Where is the deed? hast
 thou it with thee?
Picklock. No.
It is a thing of greater consequence
Than to be borne about in a black box
Like a Low-Country **vorloffe**, or Welsh brief."
The Staple of News, Act v. sc. 1.

FUTWA, s. Ar. *fatwā*. The decision of a council of men learned in Mahommedan law, on any point of Moslem law or morals. But technically and specifically, the deliverance of a Mahommedan law-officer on a case put before him. Such a deliverance was, as a rule, given officially and in writing, by such an officer, who was attached to the Courts of British India up to a little later than the middle of last century, and it was more or less a basis of the judge's decision. (See more particularly under ADAWLUT, CAZEE and LAW-OFFICER.)

1796.—"In all instances wherein the **Futwah** of the **Law-officers** of the *Nizamut-Adaulat* shall declare the prisoners liable to more severe punishment than under the evidence, and all the circumstances of the case shall appear to the Court to be just and equitable. ..."—*Regn. VI.* of 1796, § ii.

1836.—"And it is hereby enacted that no Court shall, on a Trial of any person accused of the offence made punishable by this Act require any **Futwa** from any Law-Officer. ..."—*Act XXX. of* 1836, *regarding Thuggee*, § iii.

G

GALEE, s. H. *gālī*, abuse; bad language.

[1813.—"... the grossest **galee**, or abuse, resounded throughout the camp."—*Broughton, Letters from a Mahr. Camp.*, ed. 1892, p. 205.

[1877.—"You provoke me to give you **gali** (abuse), and then you cry out like a neglected wife."—*Allardyce, The City of Sunshine*, ii. 2.]

GALLEECE, s. Domestic Hindustani *gālīs*, 'a pair of braces,' from the old-fashioned *gallows*, now obsolete, except in Scotland, [S. Ireland and U.S.,] where the form is *gallowses*.

***GALLEVAT**, s. The name applied to a kind of galley, or war-boat with oars, of small draught of water, which continued to be employed on the west coast of India down to the latter half of the 18th century. The work quoted below under 1717 explains the *galleywatts* to be "large boats like Gravesend Tilt-boats; they carry about 6 Carvel-Guns and 60 men at small arms, and Oars; They sail with a Peak Sail like the Mizen of a Man-of-War, and row with 30 or 40 Oars. ... They are principally used for landing Troops for a Descent. ..." (p. 22). The word is highly interesting from its genealogical tree; it is a descendant of the great historical and numerous family of the *Galley* (galley, galiot, galleon, galeass, galleida, galeoncino, &c.), and it is almost certainly the immediate parent of the hardly less historical *Jolly-boat*, which plays so important a part in British naval annals. [Prof. Skeat takes *jolly-boat* to be an English adaptation of Danish *jolle*, 'a yawl'; Mr. Foster remarks that *jollyvatt* as an English word, is at least as old as 1495–97 (*Oppenheim, Naval Accounts and Inventories, Navy Rec. Soc.* viii. 193) (*Letters*, iii. 296).] If this be true, which we can hardly doubt, we shall have three of the boats of the British man-of-war owing their names (*quod minime reris!*) to Indian originals, viz. the *Cutter*, the *Dingy*, and the *Jolly-boat* to **catur**, **dingy** and **gallevat**. This last derivation we take from Sir J. Campbell's *Bombay Gazetteer* (xiii. 417), a work that one can hardly mention without admiration. This writer, who states that a form of the same word, *galbat*, is now generally used by the natives in Bombay waters for large foreign vessels, such as English ships and steamers, is inclined to refer it to *jalba*, a word for a small boat used on the shores of the Red Sea (see *Dozy and Eng.*, p. 276), which appears below in a quotation from Ibn Batuta, and which vessels were called by the early Portuguese *geluas*. Whether this word is the parent of *galley* and its derivatives, as Sir J. Campbell thinks, must be very doubtful, for *galley* is much older in European use than he seems to think, as the quotation from Asser shows. The word also occurs in Byzantine writers of the 9th century, such as the Continuator of Theophanes quoted below, and the Emperor Leo. We shall find below the occurrence of *galley* as an Oriental word in the form *jalia*, which looks like an Arabized adoption from a Mediterranean tongue. The Turkish, too, still has *ḳālyūn* for a ship of the line, which is certainly an adoption from *galeone*. The origin of *galley* is a very obscure question. Amongst other suggestions mentioned by Diez (*Etym. Worterb.*, 2nd ed. i. 198–199) is one from γαλεός, a shark, or from γαλεώτης, a sword-fish—the latter very suggestive of a galley with its aggressive beak; another is from γάλη, a word in Hesychius, which is the apparent origin of '*gallery*.' It is possible that *galeota*, *galiote*, may have been taken directly from the shark or sword-fish, though in imitation of the *galea* already in use. For we shall see below that *galiot* was used for a pirate. [The *N.E.D.* gives the European synonymous words, and regards the ultimate etymology of *galley* as unknown.]

The word *gallevat* seems to come directly from the *galeota* of the Portuguese and other S. European nations, a kind of inferior galley with only one bank of oars, which appears under the form *galion* in Joinville, *infra* (not to be confounded with the *galleons* of a later period, which were larger vessels), and often in the 13th and 14th centuries as *galeota*, *galiotes*, &c. It is constantly mentioned as forming part of the Portuguese fleets in India. Bluteau defines *galeota* as "a small galley with one mast, and with 15 or 20 benches a side, and one oar to each bench."

a. *Galley.*

c. 865.—"And then the incursion of the Russians (τῶν Ῥῶς) afflicted the Roman territory (these are a Scythian nation of rude and savage character), devastating Pontus ... and investing the City itself when Michael was away engaged in war with the Ishmaelites. ... So this incursion of these people afflicted the empire on the one hand, and on the other the advance of the fleet on Crete, which with some 20 cymbaria, and 7 **galleys** (γαλέας), and taking with it cargo-vessels also, went about, descending sometimes on the Cyclades Islands, and sometimes on the whole coast (of the main) right up to Proconnesus."—*Theophanis Continuatio*, Lib. iv. 33–34.

A.D. 877.—"Crescebat insuper diebus singulis perversorum numerus; adeo quidem, ut si triginta ex eis millia una die necarentur, alii succedebant numero duplicato. Tunc rex Aelfredus jussit cymbas et **galeas**, id est longas naves, fabricari per regnum, ut navali proelio hostibus adventantibus obviaret."—*Asser*, *Annales Rer. Gest. Aelfredi Magni*, ed. *West*, 1722, p. 29.

c. 1232.—"En cele navie de Genevois avoit soissante et dis **galeis**, mout bien armées; cheuetaine en estoient dui grant home de Gene. ..."—*Guillaume de Tyr*, Texte Français, ed. *Paulin Paris*, i. 393.

1243.—Under this year Matthew Paris puts into the mouth of the Archbishop of York a punning couplet which shows the difference of accent with which **galea** in its two senses was pronounced:

"In terris galeas, in aquis formido **galeias**:
Inter eas et eas consulo cautus eas."

1249.—"Lors s'esmut notre **galie**, et alames bien une grant lieue avant que li uns ne parlast à l'autre. ... Lors vint messires Phelippes de Monfort en un **galion**,[1] et escria au roy: 'Sires, sires, parlés à vostre frere le conte de Poitiers, qui est en cel autre vessel.' Lors escria li roys: 'Alume, alume!'"—*Joinville*, ed. *de Wailly*, p. 212.

1517.—"At the Archinale ther (at Venice) we saw in makyng iiii^{xx} (*i.e.* 80) new **galyes** and **galye** Bastards, and **galye** Sotyltes, besyd they that be in viage in the haven."—*Torkington's Pilgrimage*, p. 8.

1542.—"They said that the Turk had sent orders to certain lords at Alexandria to make him up **galleys** (*galés*) in wrought timber, to be sent on camels to Suez; and this they did with great diligence ... insomuch that every day a **galley** was put together at Suez ... where they were making up 50 **galleys**, and 12 **galeons**, and also small rowing-vessels, such as **caturs**, much swifter than ours."—*Correa*, iv. 237.

b. *Jalia.*

1612.—"... and coming to Malaca and consulting with the General they made the best arrangements that they could for the enterprise, adding a flotilla ... sufficient for any need, for it consisted of seven **Galeots**, a *calamute* (?),

1 *Galeon* is here the galliot of later days. See above.

a **sanguicel**, five *bantins*,[1] and one **jalia**."—*Bocarro*, 101.

1615.—"You must know that in 1605 there had come from the Reino (*i.e.* Portugal) one Sebastian Gonçalves Tibau ... of humble parentage, who betook himself to Bengal and commenced life as a soldier; and afterwards became a factor in cargoes of salt (which forms the chief traffic in those parts), and acquiring some capital in this business, with that he bought a **jalia**, a kind of vessel that is there used for fighting and trading at once."—*Ibid.* 431.

1634.—"Many others (of the Firingis) who were on board the *ghrábs*, set fire to their vessels, and turned their faces towards hell. Out of the 64 large *dingas*, *57 ghrábs*, and 200 **jaliyas**, one *ghráb* and two **jaliyas** escaped."—Capture of Hoogly in 1634, *Bādshāh Nāma*, in *Elliot*, vii. 34.

c. *Jalba, Jeloa*, &c.

c. 1330.—"We embarked at this town (Jedda) on a vessel called **jalba** which belonged to Rashīd-eddīn al-alfī al-Yamanī, a native of Ḥabsh."—*Ibn Batuta*, ii. 158. The Translators comment: "A large boat or gondola made of planks stitched together with coco-nut fibre."

1518.—"And Merocem, Captain of the fleet of the Grand Sultan, who was in Cambaya ... no sooner learned that Goa was taken ... than he gave up all hopes of bringing his mission to a fortunate termination, and obtained permission from the King of Cambaya to go to Judá ... and from that port set out for Suez in a shallop" (**gelua**).—*Alboquerque*, Hak. Soc. iii. 19.

1538.—"... before we arrived at the Island of Rocks, we discerned three vessels on the other side, that seemed to us to be **Geloas**, or *Terradas*, which are the names of the vessels of that country."—*Pinto*, in *Cogan*, p. 7.

[1611.—"Messengers will be sent along the coast to give warning of any **jelba** or ship approaching."—*Danvers, Letters*, i. 94.]

1690.—"In this is a Creek very convenient for building Grabbs or **Geloas**."—*Ovington*, 467.

d. *Galliot.*

In the first quotation we have *galiot* in the sense of "pirate."

c. 1232.—"L'en leur demanda de quel terre; il respondirent de Flandres, de Hollande et de Frise; et ce estoit voirs que il avoient esté **galiot** et ulague de mer, bien huit anz; or s'estoient repenti et pour penitence venoient en pelerinage en Jerusalem."—*Guill. de Tyr*, as above, p. 117.

1337.—"... que elles doivent partir pour uenir au seruice du roy le jer J. de may l'an 337 au plus tart e doiuent couster les d. 40 galées pour quatre mois 144000 florins d'or, payez en partie par la compagnie des Bardes ... et 2000 autres florins pour viretons et 2 **galiotes**."—*Contract with Genoese for Service of Philip of Valois*, quoted by *Jal*, ii. 337.

1518.—"The Governor put on great pressure to embark the force, and started from Cochin the 20th September, 1518, with 17 sail, besides the Goa foists, taking 3 **galleys** (*galés*) and one **galeota**, two brigantines (*bargantys*), four caravels, and the rest round ships of small size."—*Correa*, ii. 539.

1548.—"... pera a **gualveta** em que ha d'andar o alcaide do maar."—*S. Botelho, Tombo*, 239.

1552.—"As soon as this news reached the Sublime Porte the Sandjak of Katif was ordered to send Murad-Beg to take command of the fleet, enjoining him to leave in the port of Bassora one or two ships, five galleys, and a **galiot**."—*Sidi 'Ali*, p. 48.

"They (the Portuguese) had 4 ships as big as carracks, 3 *ghurābs* or great (rowing) vessels, 6 Portuguese caravels and 12 smaller ghurabs, *i.e.* **galiots** with oars."—*Ibid.* 67–68. Unfortunately the translator does not give the original Turkish word for *galiot*.

c. 1610.—"Es grandes Galeres il y peut deux et trois cens hommes de guerre, et en d'autres grandes **Galiotes**, qu'ils nomment *Fregates*, il y en peut cent. ..."—*Pyrard de Laval*, ii. 72; [Hak. Soc. ii. 118].

[1665.—"He gave a sufficient number of **galiotes** to escort them to sea."—*Tavernier*, ed. *Ball*, i. 193.]

1689.—"He embarked about the middle of October in the year 1542, in a **galiot**, which carried the new Captain of Comorin."—*Dryden, Life of Xavier*. (In *Works*, ed. 1821, xvi. 87.)

e. *Gallevat.*

1613.—"Assoone as I anchored I sent Master *Molineux* in his Pinnasse, and Master *Spooner*, and *Samuell Squire* in my **Gellywatte** to sound the depths within the sands."—*Capt. N. Downton*, in *Purchas*, i. 501. This illustrates the origin of *Jolly-boat*.

[1679.—"I know not how many **Galwets**."—In *Hedges, Diary*, Hak. Soc. ii. clxxxiv.]

1717.—"Besides the Salamander Fireship, Terrible Bomb, six **Galleywatts** of 8 guns, and 60 men each, and 4 of 6 guns and 50 men each."—*Authentic and Faithful History of that Arch-Pyrate Tulajee Angria* (1756), p. 47.

c. 1760.—"Of these armed boats called **Gallevats**, the Company maintains also a competent number, for the service of their marine."—*Grose*, ii. 62.

---

1 "A kind of boat," is all that Crawfurd tells.—*Malay Dict.* s.v. ["*Banting*, a native sailing-vessel with two masts"—Williamson, *Malay Dict.*: "*Bantieng*, soort van boot met twee masten"—Var. Eysinga, *Malay-Dutch Dict.*]

1763.—"The **Gallevats** are large row-boats, built like the grab, but of smaller dimensions, the largest rarely exceeding 70 tons; they have two masts ... they have 40 or 50 stout oars, and may be rowed four miles an hour."—*Orme*, i. 409.

[1813.—"... here they build vessels of all sizes, from a ship of the line to the smallest grabs and **gallivats**, employed in the Company's services."—*Forbes. Or Mem.* 2nd ed. i. 94–5.]

GARDENS, GARDEN-HOUSE, s. In the 18th century suburban villas at Madras and Calcutta were so called. 'Garden Reach' below Fort William took its name from these.

1682.—"Early in the morning I was met by Mr. Littleton and most of the Factory, near Hugly, and about 9 or 10 o'clock by Mr. Vincent near the Dutch **Garden**, who came attended by severall Boats and Budge-rows guarded by 35 Firelocks, and about 50 Rashpoots and Peons well armed."—*Hedges, Diary*, July 24; [Hak. Soc. i. 32].

1685.—"The whole Council ... came to attend the President at the **garden-house**. ..."—*Pringle, Diary, Fort St. Geo.* 1st ser. iv. 115; in *Wheeler*, i. 139.

1747.—"In case of an Attack at the **Garden House**, if by a superior Force they should be oblig'd to retire, according to the orders and send a Horseman before them to advise of the Approach. ..."—*Report of Council of War at Fort St. David*, in *India Office MS. Records*.

1758.—"The guard of the redoubt retreated before them to the **garden-house**."—*Orme*, ii. 303.

"Mahomed Isoof ... rode with a party of horse as far as Maskelyne's **garden**."—*Ibid.* iii. 425.

1772.—"The place of my residence at present is a **garden-house** of the Nabob, about 4 miles distant from Moorshedabad."—*Teignmouth, Mem.* i. 34.

1782.—"A body of Hyder's horse were at St. Thomas's Mount on the 29th ult. and Gen. Munro and Mr. Brodie with great difficulty escaped from the General's **Gardens**. They were pursued by Hyder's horse within a mile of the Black Town."—*India Gazette*, May 11.

1809.—"The gentlemen of the settlement live entirely in their **garden-houses**, as they very properly call them."—*Ld. Valentia*, i. 389.

1810.—"... Rural retreats called **Garden-houses**."—*Williamson, V. M.* i: 137.

1873.—"To let, or for sale, Serle's **Gardens** at Adyar.—For particulars apply," &c.—*Madras Mail*, July 3.

GARRY, GHARRY, s. H. *gāṛī*, a cart or carriage. The word is used by Anglo-Indians, at least on the Bengal side, in both senses. Frequently the species is discriminated by a distinctive prefix, as *palkee-garry* (palankin carriage), *sej-garry* (chaise), *rel-garry* (railway carriage), &c. [The modern *dawk-garry* was in its original form called the "Equirotal Carriage," from the four wheels being of equal dimensions. The design is said to have been suggested by Lord Ellenborough. (See the account and drawing in *Grant, Rural Life in Bengal*, 3 *seq.*).]

1810.—"The common **g'horry** ... is rarely, if ever, kept by any European, but may be seen plying for hire in various parts of Calcutta."—*Williamson, V. M.* i. 329.

1811.—The **Gary** is represented in Solvyns's engravings as a two-wheeled *rath* [see RUT] (*i.e.* the primitive native carriage, built like a light hackery) with two ponies.

1866.—"My husband was to have met us with a two-horse **gharee**."—*Trevelyan, Dawk Bungalow*, 384.

[1892.—"The *brūm* **gārī**, brougham; the *fitton* **gārī**, phaeton or barouche; the *vāgnīt*, waggonette, are now built in most large towns. ... The *vāgnīt* seems likely to be the carriage of the future, because of its capacity."—*R. Kipling, Beast and Man in India*, 193.]

GAURIAN, adj. This is a convenient name which has been adopted of late years as a generic name for the existing Aryan languages of India, *i.e.* those which are radically sprung from, or cognate to, the Sanskrit. The name (according to Mr. E. L. Brandreth) was given by Prof. Hoernle; but it is in fact an adoption and adaptation of a term used by the Pundits of Northern India. They divide the colloquial languages of (civilised) India into the 5 *Gauṛas* and 5 *Drāviras* [see DRAVIDIAN]. The *Gauṛas* of the Pundits appear to be (1) Bengalee (*Bangālī*) which is the proper language of *Gauḍa*, or Northern Bengal, from which the name is taken (see GOUR c.), (2) Oriya, the language of Orissa, (3) Hindī, (4) Panjābī, (5) Sindhī; their *Drāvira* languages are (1) Telinga, (2) Karṇāṭaka (Canarese), (3) Marāthī, (4) Gurjara (Gujarātī), (5) Drāvira (Tamil). But of these last (3) and (4) are really to be classed with the Gaurian group, so that the latter is to be considered as embracing 7 principal languages. Kashmīrī, Singhalese, and the languages or dialects of Assam, of Nepaul, and some others, have also been added to the list of this class.

The extraordinary analogies between the changes in grammar and phonology from Sanskrit in passing into those Gaurian languages, and the changes of Latin in passing into the Romance languages, analogies extending into minute details, have been treated by several scholars; and a very interesting view of the subject is given by Mr. Brandreth in vols. xi. and xii. of the *J.R.A.S.*, N.S.

GAUTAMA, n.p. The surname, according to Buddhist legend, of the Sakya tribe from which the Buddha Sakya Muni sprang. It is a derivative from *Gotama*, a name of "one of the ancient Vedic bard-families" (*Oldenberg*). It is one of the most common names for Buddha among the Indo-Chinese nations. The *Sommona*-**codom** of many old narratives represents the Pali form of *S'ramaṇa Gautama*, "The Ascetic Gautama."

1545.—"I will pass by them of the sect of **Godomem**, who spend their whole life in crying day and night on those mountains, **Godomem**, **Godomem**, and desist not from it until they fall down stark dead to the ground."—*F. M. Pinto*, in *Cogan*, p. 222.

c. 1590.—See under **Godavery** passage from *Āīs*, where **Gotam** occurs.

1686.—"J'ai cru devoir expliquer toutes ces choses avant que de parler de *Sommono*-**khodom** (c'est ainsi que les Siamois appellent le Dieu qu'ils adorent à present)."—*Voy. de Siam, Des Pères Jesuites*, Paris, 1686, p. 397.

1687-88.—"Now tho' they say that several have attained to this Felicity (*Nireupan, i.e.* Nirvana) ... yet they honour only one alone, whom they esteem to have surpassed all the rest in Vertue. They call him *Sommona*-**Codom**; and they say that **Codom** was his Name, and that Sommona signifies in the *Balie* Tongue a *Talapoin* of the Woods."—*Hist. Rel. of Siam*, by *De La Laubere*, E.T. i. 130.

[1727.—"... inferior Gods, such as *Somma* **Cuddom**. ..."—*A. Hamilton*, ed. 1744, ii. 54.]

1782.—"Les Pegonins et les Bahmans. ... Quant à leurs Dieux, ils en comptent sept principaux. ... Cependant ils n'en adorent qu'un seul, qu'ils appellent **Godeman**. ..."—*Sonnerat*, ii. 299.

1800.—"**Gotma**, or **Goutum**, according to the Hindoos of India, or **Gaudma** among the inhabitants of the more eastern parts, is said to have been a philosopher ... he taught in the Indian schools, the heterodox religion and philosophy of Boodh. The image that represents Boodh is called Gautama, or **Goutum**. ..."—*Symes, Embassy*, 299.

1828.—"The titles or synonymes of Buddha, as they were given to me, are as follow: "**Kotamo** (*Gautama*) ... *Somana* **kotamo**, agreeably to the interpretation given me, means in the Pali language, the priest **Gautama**."—*Crawfurd, Emb. to Siam*, p. 367.

GAZAT, s. This is domestic Hind. for 'dessert.' (*Panjab N. & Q.* ii. 184).

GECKO, s. A kind of house lizard. The word is not now in Anglo-Indian use; it is a naturalist's word; and also is French. It was no doubt originally an onomatopoeia from the creature's reiterated utterance. Marcel Devic says the word is adopted from Malay *gekok* [*gēkoq*]. This we do not find in Crawfurd, who has *tăké*, *tăkék*, and *goké*, all evidently attempts to represent the utterance. In Burma the same, or a kindred lizard, is called *tokté*, in like imitation.

1631.—Bontius seems to identify this lizard with the **Guana** (q.v.), and says its bite is so venomous as to be fatal unless the part be immediately cut out, or cauterized. This is no doubt a fable. "Nostratis ipsum animal apposito vocabulo **gecco** vocant; quippe non secus ac *Coccyx* apud nos suum cantum iterat, etiam *gecko* assiduo sonat, prius edito stridore qualem Picus emittit."—Lib. V. cap. 5, p. 57.

1711.—"**Chaccos**, as Cuckoos receive their Names from the Noise they make. ... They are much iike lizards, but larger. 'Tis said their Dung is so venomous," &c.—*Lockyer*, 84.

1727.—"They have one dangerous little Animal called a **Jackoa**, in shape almost like a Lizard. It is very malicious ... and wherever the Liquor lights on an Animal Body, it presently cankers the Flesh."—*A. Hamilton*, ii. 131; [ed. 1744, ii. 136].

This is still a common belief.

1883.—"This was one of those little house lizards called **geckos**, which have pellets at the ends of their toes. They are not repulsive brutes like the garden lizard, and I am always on good terms with them. They have full liberty to make use of my house, for which they seem grateful, and say chuck, chuck, chuck."—*Tribes on My Frontier*, 38.

GENTOO, s. and adj. This word is a corruption of the Portuguese *Gentio*, 'a gentile' or heathen, which they applied to the Hindus in contradistinction to the Moros or 'Moors,' *i.e.* Mahommedans. [See MOOR.] Both terms are now obsolete among English people, except perhaps that *Gentoo* still lingers at

Madras in the sense **b**; for the terms *Gentio* and *Gentoo* were applied in two senses:

a. To the Hindūs generally.

b. To the Telugu-speaking Hindūs of the Peninsula specially, and to their language.

The reason why the term became thus specifically applied to the Telugu people is probably because, when the Portuguese arrived, the Telugu monarchy of Vijayanagara, or Bijanagar was dominant over great part of the Peninsula. The officials were chiefly of Telugu race, and thus the people of this race, as the most important section of the Hindūs, were *par excellence* the *Gentiles*, and their language the Gentile language. Besides these two specific senses, *Gentio* was sometimes used for *heathen* in general. Thus in F. M. Pinto: "A very famous Corsair who was called Hinimilau, a Chinese by nation, and who from a *Gentio* as he was, had a little time since turned Moor. ..."—Ch. L.

a.—

1548.—"The *Religiosos* of this territory spend so largely, and give such great alms at the cost of your Highness's administration that it disposes of a good part of the funds. ... I believe indeed they do all this in real zeal and sincerity ... but I think it might be reduced a half, and all for the better; for there are some of them who often try to make Christians by force, and worry the **Gentoos** (*jentios*) to such a degree that it drives the population away."—*Simao Botelho Cartas*, 35.

1563.—"... Among the *Gentiles* (**Gentios**) Rão is as much as to say 'King.'"—*Garcia*, f. 35*b*.

"This ambergris is not so highly valued among the Moors, but it is highly prized among the **Gentiles**."—*Ibid.* f. 14.

1582.—"A **gentile** ... whose name was Canaca."—*Castañala*, trans. by N. L., f. 31.

1588.—In a letter of this year to the Viceroy, the King (Philip II.) says he "understands the **Gentios** are much the best persons to whom to farm the *alfandegas* (customs, &c.), paying well and regularly, and it does not seem contrary to canon-law to farm to them, but on this he will consult the learned."—In *Arch. Port. Orient.* fasc. 3, 135.

c. 1610.—"Ils (les Portugais) exercent ordinairement de semblables cruautes lors qu'ils sortent en trouppe le long des costes, bruslans et saccageans ces pauures **Gentils** qui ne desirent que leur bonne grace, et leur amitié mais ils n'en ont pas plus de pitié pour cela."—*Mocquet*, 349.

1630.—"... which **Gentiles** are of two sorts ... first the purer **Gentiles** ... or else the impure or vncleane *Gentiles* ... such are the husbandmen or inferior sort of people called the *Coulees*."—*H. Lord, Display*, &c., 85.

1673.—"The finest Dames of the **Gentues** disdained not to carry Water on their Heads."—*Fryer*, 116.

"**Gentues**, the Portuguese idiom for *Gentiles*, are the Aborigines."—*Ibid.* 27.

1679.—In Fort St. Geo. Cons. of 29th January, the **Black Town** of Madras is called "the **Gentue** Town."—*Notes and Exts.*, No. ii. 3.

1682.—"This morning a **Gentoo** sent by Bulchund, Governour of Hugly and Cassumbazar, made complaint to me that Mr. Charnock did shamefully—to y[e] great scandal of our Nation—keep a **Gentoo** woman of his kindred, which he has had these 19 years."—*Hedges, Diary*, Dec. 1.; [Hak. Soc. i. 52].

1683.—"The ceremony used by these **Gentu's** in their sicknesse is very strange; they bring y[e] sick person ... to y[e] brinke of y[e] River Ganges, on a *Cott.* ..."—*Ibid.* May 10; [Hak. Soc. i. 86].

In Stevens's Trans. of *Faria y Sousa* (1695) the Hindus are still called *Gentiles*. And it would seem that the English form **Gentoo** did not come into general use till late in the 17th century.

1767.—"In order to transact Business of any kind in this Countrey you must at least have a Smattering of the Language. ... The original Language of this Countrey (or at least the earliest we know of) is the Bengala or **Gentoo**; this is commonly spoken in all parts of the Countrey. But the politest Language is the Moors or Mussulmans, and Persian."—*MS. Letter of James Rennell.*

1772.—"It is customary with the **Gentoos**, as soon as they have acquired a moderate fortune, to dig a pond."—*Teignmouth, Mem.* i. 36.

1774.—"When I landed (on Island of Bali) the natives, who are **Gentoos**, came on board in little canoes, with outriggers on each side."—*Forrest, V. to N. Guinea*, 169.

1776.—"A Code of **Gentoo** Laws or Ordinations of the Pundits. From a Persian Translation, made from the original written in the Shanskrit Language. London, Printed in the Year 1776."—(Title of Work by Nathaniel Brassey Halhed.)

1778.—"The peculiar patience of the **Gentoos** in Bengal, their affection to business, and the peculiar cheapness of all productions either of commerce or of necessity, had concurred to render the details of the revenue the most minute, voluminous, and complicated system of accounts which exist in the universe."—*Orme*, ii. 7 (Reprint).

1781.—"They (Syrian Christians of Travancore) acknowledged a **Gentoo** Sovereign, but they were governed even in temporal concerns by the bishop of Angamala."—*Gibbon*, ch. xlvii.

1784.—"Captain Francis Swain Ward, of the Madras Establishment, whose paintings and drawings of **Gentoo** Architecture, &c., are well known."—In *Seton-Karr*, i. 31.

1785.—"I found this large concourse (at Chandernagore) of people were gathered to see a **Gentoo** woman burn herself with her husband."—*Ibid.* i. 90.

"The original inhabitants of India are called **Gentoos**."—*Carraccioli's Life of Clive*, i. 122.

1803.—"*Peregrine.* O mine is an accommodating palate, hostess. I have swallowed burgundy with the French, hollands with the Dutch, sherbet with a Turk, sloe-juice with an Englishman, and water with a simple **Gentoo**."—*Colman's John Bull*, i. sc. 1.

1807.—"I was not prepared for the entire nakedness of the **Gentoo** inhabitants."—*Lord Minto in India*, 17.

b.—

1648.—"The Heathen who inhabit the kingdom of *Golconda*, and are spread all over India, are called **Jentives**."—*Van Twist*, 59.

1673.—"Their Language they call generally **Gentu** ... the peculiar Name of their Speech is *Telinga*."—*Fryer*, 33.

1674.—"50 Pagodas gratuity to John Thomas ordered for good progress in the **Gentu** tongue, both speaking and writing."—*Fort St. Geo. Cons.*, in *Notes and Exts.* No. i. 32.

[1681.—"He hath the **Gentue** language."—In *Yule, Hedges' Diary*, Hak. Soc. ii. cclxxxiv.]

1683.—"Thursday, 21st June. ... The Hon. Company having sent us a Law with reference to the Natives ... it is ordered that the first be translated into Portuguese, **Gentoo**, Malabar, and Moors, and proclaimed solemnly by beat of drum."—*Madras Consultation*, in *Wheeler*, i. 314.

1719.—"Bills of sale wrote in **Gentoo** on Cajan leaves, which are entered in the Register kept by the Town Conicoply for that purpose."—*Ibid.* ii. 314.

1726.—"The proper vernacular here (Golconda) is the **Gentoos** (*Jentiefs*) or Telingaas."—*Valentijn, Chor.* 37.

1801.—"The **Gentoo** translation of the Regulations will answer for the Ceded Districts, for even ... the most Canarino part of them understand **Gentoo**."—*Munro*, in *Life*, i. 321.

1807.—"A Grammar of the **Gentoo** language, as it is understood and spoken by the **Gentoo** People, residing north and north-westward of Madras. By a Civil Servant under the Presidency of Fort St. George, many years resident in the Northern Circars. **Madras.** 1807."

1817.—The third grammar of the Telugu language, published in this year, is called a '**Gentoo** Grammar.'

1837.—"I mean to amuse myself with learning **Gentoo**, and have brought a Moonshee with me. **Gentoo** is the language of this part of the country [Godavery delta], and one of the prettiest of all the dialects."—*Letters from Madras*, 189.

GHAUT, s. Hind. *ghāt*.

a. A landing-place; a path of descent to a river; the place of a ferry, &c. Also a quay or the like.

b. A path of descent from a mountain; a mountain pass; and hence

c., n.p. The mountain ranges parallel to the western and eastern coasts of the Peninsula, through which the *ghāts* or passes lead from the table-lands above down to the coast and lowlands. It is probable that foreigners hearing these tracts spoken of respectively as the country above and the country below the *Ghāts* were led to regard the word *Ghāts* as a proper name of the mountain range itself, or (like De Barros below) as a word signifying *range*. And this is in analogy with many other cases of mountain nomenclature, where the name of a pass has been transferred to a mountain chain, or where the word for 'a pass' has been mistaken for a word for 'mountain range.' The proper sense of the word is well illustrated from Sir A. Wellesley, under **b.**

a.—

1809.—"The *dandys* there took to their paddles, and keeping the beam to the current the whole way, contrived to land us at the destined **gaut**."—*Ld. Valentia*, i. 185.

1824.—"It is really a very large place, and rises from the river in an amphitheatral form ... with many very fine **ghâts** descending to the water's edge."—*Heber*, i. 167.

b.—

c. 1315.—"In 17 more days they arrived at Gurganw. During these 17 days the **Ghâts** were passed, and great heights and depths were seen amongst the hills, where even the elephants became nearly invisible."—*Amīr Khusrū*, in *Elliot*, iii. 86.

This passage illustrates how the transition from **b** to **c** occurred. The *Ghāts* here meant are not a range of mountains so called, but, as the context shows, the passes among the Vindhya and Sātpūra hills. Compare the two following, in which 'down the *ghauts*' and 'down the *passes*' mean exactly the same thing, though to many people the former expression will suggest 'down through a range of mountains called the Ghauts.'

1803.—"The enemy are down the **ghauts** in great consternation."—*Wellington*, ii. 333.

"The enemy have fled northward, and are getting down the *passes* as fast as they can."—*M. Elphinstone*, in *Life* by *Colebrooke*, i. 71.

1826.—"Though it was still raining, I walked up the Bohr **Ghât**, four miles and a half, to Candaulah."—*Heber*, ii. 136, ed. 1844. That is, up one of the Passes, from which Europeans called the mountains themselves "the **Ghauts**."

The following passage indicates that the great Sir Walter, with his usual sagacity, saw the true sense of the word in its geographical use, though misled by books to attribute to the (so-called) 'Eastern Ghauts' the character that belongs to the Western only.

1827.—"... they approached the **Ghauts**, those tremendous mountain passes which descend from the table-land of Mysore, and through which the mighty streams that arise in the centre of the Indian Peninsula find their way to the ocean."—*The Surgeon's Daughter*, ch. xiii.

c.—

1553.—"The most notable division which Nature hath planted in this land is a chain of mountains, which the natives, by a generic appellation, because it has no proper name, call **Gate**, which is as much as to say *Serra*."—*De Barros*, Dec. I. liv. iv. cap. vii.

1561.—"This *Serra* is called **Gate**."—*Correa, Lendas*, ii. 2, 56.

1563.—"The *Cuncam*, which is the land skirting the sea, up to a lofty range which they call **Guate**."—*Garcia*, f. 34*b*.

1572.—

"Da terra os Naturaes lhe chamam **Gate**,
Do pe do qual pequena quantidade
Se estende hũa fralda estreita, que combate
Do mar a natural ferocidade ..."
Camões, vii. 22.

Englished by Burton:

"The country-people call this range the **Ghaut**,
and from its foot-hills scanty breadth there be,
whose seaward-sloping coast-plain long hath fought
'gainst Ocean's natural ferocity ..."

1623.—"We commenced then to ascend the mountain-(range) which the people of the country call **Gat**, and which traverses in the middle the whole length of that part of India which projects into the sea, bathed on the east side by the Gulf of Bengal, and on the west by the Ocean, or Sea of Goa."—*P. della Valle*, ii. 32; [Hak. Soc. ii. 222].

1673.—"The Mountains here are one continued ridge ... and are all along called **Gaot**."—*Fryer*, 187.

1685.—"On les appelle, *montagnes de* **Gatte**, c'est comme qui diroit montagnes de montagnes, *Gatte* en langue du pays ne signifiant autre chose que montagne" (quite wrong).—*Ribeyro, Ceylan*, (Fr. Transl.), p. 4.

1727.—"The great Rains and Dews that fall from the Mountains of **Gatti**, which ly 25 or 30 leagues up in the Country."—*A. Hamilton*, i. 282; [ed. 1744, ii. 285].

1762.—"All the South part of India save the Mountains of **Gate** (a string of Hills in ye country) is level Land the Mould scarce so deep as in England. ... As you make use of every expedient to drain the water from your tilled ground, so the Indians take care to keep it in theirs, and for this reason sow only in the level grounds."—*MS. Letter of James Rennell*, March 21.

1826.—"The mountains are nearly the same height ... with the average of Welsh mountains. ... In one respect, and only one, the **Ghâts** have the advantage,—their precipices are higher, and the outlines of the hills consequently bolder."—*Heber*, ed. 1844, ii. 136.

GHEE, s. Boiled butter; the universal medium of cookery throughout India, supplying the place occupied by oil in Southern Europe, and more; [the *samn* of Arabia, the *raughan* of Persia]. The word is Hind. *ghī*, Skt. *ghṛita*. A short but explicit account of the mode of preparation will be found in the *English Cyclopaedia* (Arts and Sciences), s.v.; [and in fuller detail in *Watt, Econ. Dict.* iii. 491 *seqq.*].

c. 1590.—"Most of them (Akbar's elephants) get 5 s. (ers) of sugar, 4 s. of ghí, and half a *man* of rice mixed with chillies, cloves, &c."—*Āīn-i-Akbarī*, i. 130.

1673.—"They will drink milk, and boil'd butter, which they call **Ghe**."—*Fryer*, 33.

1783.—"In most of the prisons [of Hyder 'Ali] it was the custom to celebrate particular days, when the funds admitted, with the luxury of plantain fritters, a draught of sherbet, and a convivial song. On one occasion the old Scotch ballad, 'My wife has ta'en the gee,' was admirably sung, and loudly encored. ... It was reported to the Kelledar that the prisoners said and sung throughout the night of nothing but ghee. ... The Kelledar, certain that discoveries had been made regarding his malversations in that article of garrison store, determined to conciliate their secrecy by causing an abundant supply of this unaccustomed luxury to be thenceforth placed within the reach of their farthing purchases."—*Wilks, Hist. Sketches*, ii. 154.

1785.—"The revenues of the city of Decca ... amount annually to two kherore (see CRORE), proceeding from the customs and duties levied on **ghee**."—*Carraccioli L. of Clive*, i. 172.

1817.—"The great luxury of the Hindu is butter, prepared in a manner peculiar to himself, and called by him **ghee**."—*Mill, Hist.* i. 410.

GHOUL, s. Ar. *ghūl*, P. *ghōl*. A goblin, ἔμπουσα, or man-devouring demon, especially haunting wildernesses.

c. 70.—"In the deserts of Affricke yee shall meet oftentimes with fairies,[1] appearing in the shape of men and women; but they vanish soone away, like fantasticall illusions."—*Pliny*, by *Ph. Holland*, vii. 2.

c. 940.—"The Arabs relate many strange stories about the **Ghūl** and their transformations. ... The Arabs allege that the two feet of the **Ghūl** are ass's feet. ... These Ghūl appeared to travellers in the night, and at hours when one meets with no one on the road; the traveller taking them for some of their companions followed them, but the Ghūl led them astray, and caused them to lose their way."—*Maṣ'ūdī*, iii. 314 *seqq.* (There is much more after the copious and higgledy-piggledy Plinian fashion of this writer.)

c. 1420.—"In exitu deserti ... rem mirandam dicit contigisse. Nam cum circiter mediam noctem quiescentes magno murmure strepituque audito suspicarentur omnes, Arabes praedones ad se spoliandos venire ... viderunt plurimas equitum turmas transeuntium. ... Plures qui id antea viderant, daemones (**ghūls**, no doubt) esse per desertum vagantes asseruere."—*Nic. Conti*, in *Poggio*, iv.

1814.—"The Afghauns believe each of the numerous solitudes in the mountains and desarts of their country to be inhabited by a lonely daemon, whom they call *Ghoolee Beeabaun* (the **Goule** or Spirit of the Waste); they represent him as a gigantic and frightful spectre (who devours any passenger whom chance may bring within his haunts."—*Elphinstone's Caubul*, ed. 1839, i. 291.

GINGER, s. The root of *Zingiber officinale*, Roxb. We get this word from the Arabic *zānjabīl*, Sp. *agengibre* (*al-zānjabīl*), Port. *gingibre*, Latin *zingiber*, Ital. *zenzero*, *gengiovo*, and many other old forms.

The Skt. name is *sṛiñgavera*, professedly connected with *sṛiñga*, 'a horn,' from the antler-like form of the root. But this is probably an introduced word shaped by this imaginary etymology. Though ginger is cultivated all over India, from the Himālaya to the extreme south,[2] the best is grown in Malabar, and in the language of that province (Malayālam) green ginger is called *inchi* and *inchi-ver*, from *inchi*, 'root.' *Inchi* was probably in an earlier form of the language *siñchi* or *chiñchi*, as we find it in Canarese still *sūnti*, which is perhaps the true origin of the H. *sūnth* for 'dry ginger,' [more usually connected with Skt. *sunṭhi*, *sunṭh*, 'to dry'].

It would appear that the Arabs, misled by the form of the name, attributed *zānjabīl* or *zinjabīl*, or ginger, to the coast of *Zinj* or Zanzibar; for it would seem to be ginger which some Arabic writers speak of as 'the plant of Zinj.' Thus a poet quoted by Kazwīnī enumerates among the products of India the *shajr al-Zānij* or *Arbor Zingitana*, along with shishamwood, pepper, steel, &c. (see *Gildemeister*, 218). And Abulfeda says also: "At Melinda is found the plant of Zinj" (*Geog.* by *Reinaud*, i. 257). In Marino Sanudo's map of the world also (c. 1320) we find a rubric connecting *Zinziber* with *Zinj*. We do not indeed find ginger spoken of as a product of eastern continental Africa, though Barbosa says a large quantity was produced in Madagascar, and Varthema says the like of the Comoro Islands.

c. A.D. 65.—"Ginger (Ζιγγίβερις) is a special kind of plant produced for the most part in Troglodytic Arabia, where they use the green plant in many ways, as we do rue (πήγανον), boiling it and mixing it with drinks and stews. The roots are small, like those of *cyperus*, whitish, and peppery to the taste and smell. ..."—*Dioscorides*, ii. cap. 189.

c. A.D. 70.—"This pepper of all kinds is most biting and sharpe. ... The blacke is more kindly and pleasant. ... Many have taken Ginger (which some call Zimbiperi and others **Zingiberi**) for the root of that tree; but it is not so, although in tast it somewhat resembleth pepper. ... A pound of **Ginger** is commonly sold at Rome for 6 deniers. ..."—*Pliny*, by *Ph. Holland*, xii. 7.

c. 620-30.—"And therein shall they be given to drink a cup of wine, mixed with the water of **Zenjebil**. ..."—*The Koran*, ch. lxxvi. (by *Sale*).

c. 940.—"Andalusia possesses considerable silver and quicksilver mines. ... They export from it also saffron, and roots of ginger (?'*arūḳ al-***zanjabīl**)."—*Maṣ'ūdi*, i. 367.

1 There is no justification for this word in the Latin.

2 "Rheede says: 'Etiam in sylvis et desertis reperitur' (*Hort. Mal.* xi. 10). But I am not aware of any botanist having found it wild. I suspect that no one has looked for it,"—*Sir. J. D. Hooker.*'

1298.—"Good ginger (**gengibre**) also grows here, and it is known by the same name of *Coilumin*, after the country."—*Marco Polo*, Bk. III. ch. 22.

c. 1343.—"**Giengiovo** si è di piu maniere, cioe *belledi* (see COUNTRY), e *colombino*, e *micchino*, e detti nomi portano per le contrade, onde sono nati ispezialmente il *colombino* e il *micchino*, che primieramente il belledi nasce in molte contrade dell' India, e il colombino nasce nel Isola del Colombo d' India, ed ha la scorza sua piana, e delicata, e cenerognola; e il micchino viene dalle contrade del Mecca ... e ragiona che il buono giengiovo dura buono 10 anni," &c.—*Pegolotti*, in *Della Decima*, iii. 361.

c. 1420.—"His in regionibus (Malabar) gingiber oritur, quod *belledi* (see COUNTRY), *gebeli* et *neli*[1] vulgo appellatur. Radices sunt arborum duorum cubitorum altitudine, foliis magnis instar enulae (elecampane), duro cortice, veluti arundinum radices, quae fructum tegunt; ex eis extrahitur gingiber, quod immistum cineri, ad solemque expositum, triduo exsiccatur."—*N. Conti*, in *Poggio*.

1580.—In a list of drugs sold at Ormuz we find
Zenzeri da buli (presumably from **Dabul.**)
„ mordaci
„ Mecchini
„ beledi
Zenzero condito in giaga
(preserved in **Jaggery**?)
—*Gasparo Balbi*, f. 54.

***GINGHAM**, s. A kind of stuff, defined in the *Draper's Dictionary* as made from cotton yarn dyed before being woven. The Indian ginghams were apparently sometimes of cotton mixt with some other material. The origin of this word is obscure, and has been the subject of many suggestions. Though it has long passed into the English language, it is on the whole most probable that, like **chintz** and **calico**, the term was one originating in the Indian trade.

We find it hardly possible to accept the derivation, given by Littré, from "*Guingamp*, ville de Bretagne, où il y a des fabriques de tissus." This is also alleged, indeed, in the *Encycl. Britannica*, 8th ed., which states, under the name of Guingamp, that there are in that town manufactures of *ginghams*, to which the town gives its name. [So also in 9th ed.] We may observe that the productions of Guingamp, and of the Côtes-du-Nord generally, are of *linen*, a manufacture dating from the 15th century. If it could be shown that *gingham* was either originally applied to linen fabrics, or that the word occurs before the Indian trade began, we should be more willing to admit the French etymology as possible.

The *Penny Cyclopaedia* suggests a derivation from *guingois*, 'awry.' "The variegated, striped, and crossed patterns may have suggested the name."

'Civilis,' a correspondent of *Notes and Queries* (5 ser. ii. 366, iii. 30) assigns the word to an Indian term, *ginghām*, a stuff which he alleges to be in universal use by Hindu women, and a name which he constantly found, when in judicial employment in Upper India, to be used in inventories of stolen property and the like. He mentions also that in Sir G. Wilkinson's *Egypt*, the word is assigned to an Egyptian origin. The alleged Hind. word is unknown to us and to the dictionaries; if used as 'Civilis' believes, it was almost certainly borrowed from the English term.

It is likely enough that the word came from the Archipelago. Jansz's *Javanese Dict.* gives "*ginggang*, a sort of striped or chequered East Indian *lijnwand*," the last word being applied to cotton as well as linen stuffs, equivalent to French *toile*. The verb *ginggang* in Javanese is given as meaning 'to separate, to go away,' but this seems to throw no light on the matter; nor can we connect the name with that of a place on the northern coast of Sumatra, a little E. of Acheen, which we have seen written *Gingham* (see *Bennett's Wanderings*, ii. 5, 6; also *Elmore, Directory to India and China Seas*, 1802, pp. 63–64). This place appears prominently as *Gingion* in a chart by W. Herbert, 1752. Finally, Bluteau gives the following:—"**Guingam**. So in some parts of the kingdom (Portugal) they call the excrement of the Silkworm, *Bombicis excrementum*. **Guingão**. A certain stuff which is made in the territories of the Mogul. *Beirames*, **guingoens**, *Canequis*, &c. (*Godinho, Viagam da India*, 44)." Wilson gives *kiṇḍan* as the Tamil equivalent of *gingham*, and perhaps intends to suggest that it is the original of this word. The *Tamil Dict.* gives "*kiṇḍan*, a kind of coarse cotton cloth, striped or chequered." [The *Madras Gloss.* gives Can. *ginta*, Tel. *gintena*, Tam. *kiṇḍan*, with the meaning of "double-thread texture." The *N.E.D.*, following Scott, *Malayan Words in English*, 142 *seq.*, accepts the

1 *Gebeli*, Ar. "of the hills." *Neli* is also read *dely*, probably for *d'Ely* (see DELY, MOUNT). The Ely ginger is mentioned by Barbosa (p. 220).

Javanese derivation as given above: "Malay *ginggang* ... a striped or checkered cotton fabric known to Europeans in the East as '*gingham*.' As an adjective, the word means, both in Malay and Javanese, where it seems to be original, 'striped.' The full expression is *kāin ginggang*, 'striped cloth' (*Grashuis*). The Tamil '*kindan*, a kind of coarse cotton cloth, striped or chequered' (quoted in *Yule*), cannot be the source of the European forms, nor, I think, of the Malayan forms. It must be an independent word, or a perversion of the Malayan term." On the other hand, Prof. Skeat rejects the Eastern derivation on the ground that "no one explains the spelling. The right explanation is simply that *gingham* is an old English spelling of *Guingamp*. See the account of the 'towne of Gyngham' in the *Paston Letters*, ed. *Gairdner*, iii. 357." (8th ser. *Notes and Queries*, iv. 386.)]

c. 1567.—Cesare Federici says there were at Tana many weavers who made "*ormesini* e **gingani** di lana e di bombaso"—ginghams of wool and cotton.—*Ramusio*, iii. 387 *v.*

1602.—"With these toils they got to Arakan, and took possession of two islets which stood at the entrance, where they immediately found on the beach two sacks of mouldy biscuit, and a box with some **ginghams** (*guingões*) in it."—*De Couto*, Dec. IV. liv. iv. cap. 10.

1615.—"Captain Cock is of opinion that the **ginghams**, both white and browne, which yow sent will prove a good commodity in the Kinge of Shashmahis cuntry, who is a Kinge of certaine of the most westermost ilandes of Japon ... and hath conquered the ilandes called The Leques."—*Letter appd. to Cock's Diary*, ii. 272.

1648.—"The principal names (of the stuffs) are these: **Gamiguins**, *Baftas, Chelas, Assamanis* (*asmānīs*? sky-blues), *Madafoene, Beronis, Tricandias, Chittes* (see CHINTZ), *Langans* (see LUNGOOTY?), *Toffochillen* (*Tafṣīla*, a gold stuff from Mecca), *Dotias* (see DHOTY)."—*Van Twist*, 63.

1726.—In a list of cloths at Pulicat:

"*Gekeperde* **Ginggangs** (Twilled ginghams)
Ditto *Chialones* (shaloons?)"—*Valentijn*, *Chor.* 14.

Also

"Bore (?) **Gingganes** driedraad."—v. 128.

1770.—"Une centaine de balles de mouchoirs, de pagnes, et de **guingans**, d'un très beau rouge, que les Malabares fabriquent à Gaffanapatam, où ils sont établis depuis très longtemps."—*Raynal, Hist. Philos.*, ii. 15, quoted by *Littré*.

1781.—"The trade of Fort St. David's consists in longcloths of different colours, sallamporees, morees, dimities, **Ginghams**, and succatoons."—*Carraccioli's L. of Clive*, i. 5. [Mr. Whiteway points out that this is taken word for word from *Hamilton, New Account* (i. 355), who wrote 40 years before.]

"*Sadras* est renommé par ses **guingans**, ses toiles peintes; et *Paliacate* par ses mouchoirs."—*Sonnerat*, i. 41.

1793.—"Even the **gingham** waistcoats, which striped or plain have so long stood their ground, must, I hear, ultimately give way to the stronger **kerseymere** (q.v.)."—*Hugh Boyd, Indian Observer*, 77.

1796.—"**Guingani** are cotton stuffs of Bengal and the Coromandel coast, in which the cotton is interwoven with thread made from certain barks of trees."—*Fra Paolino, Viaggio*, p. 35.

GINSENG, s. A medical root which has an extraordinary reputation in China as a restorative, and sells there at prices ranging from 6 to 400 dollars an ounce. The plant is *Aralia Ginseng*, Benth. (N.O. *Araliaceae*). The second word represents the Chinese name *Jên-Shên*. In the literary style the drug is called simply *Shên*. And possibly *Jên*, or 'Man,' has been prefixed on account of the forked radish, man-like aspect of the root. European practitioners do not recognise its alleged virtues. That which is most valued comes from Corea, but it grows also in Mongolia and Manchuria. A kind much less esteemed, the root of *Panax quinquefolium*, L., is imported into China from America. A very closely-allied plant occurs in the Himālaya, *A. Pseudo-Ginseng*, Benth. *Ginseng* is first mentioned by Alv. Semedo (Madrid, 1642). [See *Ball, Things Chinese*, 268 *seq.*, where Dr. P. Smith seems to believe that it has some medicinal value.]

GOA, n.p. Properly *Gowa, Gova*, Mahr. *Goven*, [which the *Madras Gloss.* connects with Skt. *go*, 'a cow,' in the sense of the 'cowherd country']. The famous capital of the Portuguese dominions in India since its capture by Albuquerque in 1510. In earlier history and geography the place appears under the name of **Sindābūr** or **Sandābūr** (Sundāpūr?) *Govā* or *Kuva* was an ancient name of the southern Konkan (see in *H. H. Wilson's Works, Vishnu Purana*, ii. 164, note 20). We find the place called by the Turkish admiral Sidi 'Ali **Gowai**-*Sandābūr*, which may mean "Sandābūr of Gova."

1391.—In a copper grant of this date (S. 1313) we have mention of a chief city of Kankan called **Gowa** and **Gowāpūra**. See the grant as published by Major Legrand Jacob in *J. Bo. Br. R. As. Soc.* iv. 107. The translation is too loose to make it worth while to transcribe a quotation; but it is interesting as mentioning the reconquest of Goa from the *Turushkas, i.e.* Turks or foreign Mahommedans. We know from Ibn Batuta that Mahommedan settlers at Hunāwar had taken the place about 1344.

1510 (but referring to some years earlier). "I departed from the city of Dabuli aforesaid, and went to another island which is about a mile distant from the mainland and is called **Goga**. ... In this island there is a fortress near the sea, walled round after our manner, in which there is sometimes a captain who is called Savaiu, who has 400 mamelukes, he himself being also a mameluke."—*Varthema*, 115–116.

c. 1520.—"In the Island of *Tissoury*, in which is situated the city of **Goa**, there are 31 **aldeas**, and these are as follows. ..."—In *Archiv. Port. Orient.*, fasc. 5.

c. 1554.—"At these words (addressed by the Vizir of Guzerat to a Portuguese Envoy) my wrath broke out, and I said: 'Malediction! You have found me with my fleet gone to wreck, but please God in his mercy, before long, under favour of the Pādshāh, you shall be driven not only from Hormuz, but from Diu and **Gowa** too!'"—*Sidī'Ali Kapudān*, in *J. Asiat.* Ser. I. tom. ix. 70.

1602.—"The island of **Goa** is so old a place that one finds nothing in the writings of the Canaras (to whom it always belonged) about the beginning of its population. But we find that it was always so frequented by strangers that they used to have a proverbial saying: 'Let us go and take our ease among the cool shades of **Goe** *moat*,' which in the old language of the country means 'the cool fertile land.'"—*Couto*, IV. x. cap. 4.

1648.—"All those that have seen *Europe* and *Asia* agree with me that the Port of **Goa**, the Port of *Constantinople*, and the Port of *Toulon*, are three of the fairest Ports of all our vast continent."—*Tavernier*, E.T. ii. 74; [ed. *Ball*, i. 186].

GODDESS, s. An absurd corruption which used to be applied by our countrymen in the old settlements in the Malay countries to the young women of the land. It is Malay *gādīs*, 'a virgin.'

c.1772.—

"And then how strange, at night opprest
By toils, with songs you're lulled to rest;
Of rural **goddesses** the guest, Delightful!"
W. Marsden, in *Memoirs*, 14.

1784.—"A lad at one of these entertainments, asked another his opinion of a **gaddees** who was then dancing. 'If she were plated with gold,' replied he, 'I would not take her for my concubine, much less for my wife.'"—*Marsden's H. of Sumatra*, 2nd ed., 230.

GODOWN, s. A warehouse for goods and stores; an outbuilding used for stores; a store-room. The word is in constant use in the Chinese ports as well as in India. The H. and Beng. *gudām* is apparently an adoption of the Anglo-Indian word, not its original. The word appears to have passed to the continent of India from the eastern settlements, where the Malay word **gadong** is used in the same sense of 'store-room,' but also in that of 'a house built of brick or stone.' Still the word appears to have come primarily from the South of India, where in Telugu *giḍaṅgi, giḍḍangi*, in Tamil *kiḍaṅgu*, signify 'a place where goods lie,' from *kiḍu*, 'to lie.' It appears in Singhalese also as *gudāma*. It is a fact that many common Malay and Javanese words are Tamil, or only to be explained by Tamil. Free intercourse between the Coromandel Coast and the Archipelago is very ancient, and when the Portuguese first appeared at Malacca they found there numerous settlers from S. India. Bluteau gives the word as *palavra da India*, and explains it as a "logea quasi debaixo de chão" ("almost under ground"), but this is seldom the case.

[1513.—"... in which all his rice and a **Gudam** full of mace was burned."—*Letter of F. P. Andrade to Albuquerque*, Feb. 22, India Office, MSS. *Corpo Chronologico*, vol. I.

[1552.—"At night secretly they cleared their **Gudams**, which are rooms almost under ground, for fear of fire."—*Barros*, Dec. II. Bk. vi. ch. 3.]

1552.—"... and ordered them to plunder many **godowns** (*gudoes*) in which there was such abundance of clove, nutmeg, mace, and sandal wood, that our people could not transport it all till they had called in the people of Malacca to complete its removal."—*Castanheda*, iii. 276–7.

1561.—"... **Godowns** (*Gudões*), which are strong houses of stone having the lower part built with lime."—*Correa*, II. i. 236. (The last two quotations refer to events in 1511.)

1570.—"... but the merchants have all one house or *Magazon*, which house they call **Godon**, which is made of brickes."—*Caesar Frederike*, in *Hakl.*

1585.—"In the Palace of the King (at Pegu) are many magazines both of gold and of silver. ... Sandalwood, and lign-aloes, and all such things, have their *gottons* (**gottoni**), which is as much as to say separate chambers."—*Gasparo Balbi*, f. III.

[c. 1612.—"... if I did not he would take away from me the key of the **gadong**."—*Danvers, Letters*, i. 195.]

1613.—"As fortelezas e fortificações de Malayos ordinariamente erão aedifficios de matte entaypado, de que havia muytas casas e armenyas ou **godoens** que são aedifficios sobterraneos, em que os mercadores recolhem as roupas de Choromandel per il perigo de fogo."—*Godinho de Eredia*, 22.

1615.—"We paid Jno. Dono 70 *taies* or plate of bars in full payment of the fee symple of the **gadonge** over the way, to westward of English howse, whereof 100 *taies* was paid before."—*Cocks's Diary*, i. 39; [in i. 15 **gedonge**].

["An old ruined brick house or **godung**."—*Foster, Letters*, iii. 109.

["The same goods to be locked up in the **gaddones**."—*Ibid.* iii. 159.]

1634.—

"Virão das ruas as secretas minas

* * * * *

Das abrazadas casas as ruinas,

E das riquezas os **gudões** desertos."

Malacca Conquistada, x. 61.

1680.—"Rent Rowle of Dwelling Houses, **Goedowns**, etc., within the Garrison in Christian Town."—In *Wheeler*, i. 253–4.

1683.—"I went to ye Bankshall to mark out and appoint a Plat of ground to build a **Godown** for ye Honble. Company's Salt Petre."—*Hedges, Diary*, March 5; [Hak. Soc. i. 67].

1696.—"Monday, 3rd August. The Choultry Justices having produced examinations taken by them concerning the murder of a child in the Black town, and the robbing of a **godown** within the walls:—it is ordered that the Judge-Advocate do cause a session to be held on Tuesday the 11th for the trial of the criminals."—*Official Memorandum*, in *Wheeler*, i. 303.

[1800.—"The cook-room and **Zodoun** at the Laul Baug are covered in."—*Wellington*, 1. 66.]

1809.—"The Black Hole is now part of a **godown** or warehouse: it was filled with goods, and I could not see it."—*Ld. Valentia*, i. 237.

1880.—"These '**Godowns**' ... are one of the most marked features of a Japanese town, both because they are white where all else is gray, and because they are solid where all else is perishable."—*Miss Bird's Japan*, i. 264.

GOMASTA, GOMASHTAH, s. Hind. from Pers. *gumāshtah*, part. 'appointed, delegated.' A native agent or factor. In Madras the modern application is to a clerk for vernacular correspondence.

1747.—"As for the Salem Cloth they beg leave to defer settling any Price for that sort till they can be advised from the **Goa Masters** (!) in that Province."—*Ft. St. David Cousn.*, May 11. MS. Records in India Office.

1762.—"You will direct the gentleman, **Gomastahs**, *Muttasuddies* and *Moonshies*, and other officers of the English Company to relinquish their farms, *taalucs*, **gunges**, and **golahs**."—*The Nabob to the Governor*, in *Van Sittart*, i. 229.

1776.—"The Magistrate shall appoint some one person his **gomastah** or Agent in each Town."—*Halhed's Code*, 55.

1778.—"The Company determining if possible to restore their investment to the former condition ... sent **gomastahs**, or Gentoo factors in their own pay."—*Orme*, ed. 1803, ii. 57.

c. 1785.—"I wrote an order to my **gomastah** in the factory of Hughly."—*Carraccioli's Life of Clive*, iii. 448.

1817.—"The banyan hires a species of broker, called a **Gomastah**, at so much a month."—*Mill's Hist.* iii. 13.

1837.—"... (The Rajah) sent us a very good breakfast; when we had eaten it, his **gomashta** (a sort of secretary, at least more like that than anything else) came to say ..."—*Letters from Madras*, 128.

GONG, s. This word appears to be Malay (or, according to Crawfurd, originally Javanese), *gong* or *agong*. ["The word *gong* is often said to be Chinese. Clifford and Swettenham so mark it; but no one seems to be able to point out the Chinese original" (*Scott, Malayan Words in English*, 53).] Its well-known application is to a disk of thin bell-metal, which when struck with a mallet, yields musical notes, and is used in the further east as a substitute for a bell. ["The name *gong*, *agong*, is considered to be imitative or suggestive of the sound which the instrument produces" (*Scott, loc. cit.* 51).] Marcel Devic says that the word exists in all the languages of the Archipelago; [for the variants see *Scott, loc. cit.*]. He defines it as meaning "instrument de musique aussi appele *tam-tam*"; but see under TOM-TOM. The great drum, to which Dampier applies the name, was used like the metallic *gong* for striking the hour. Systems of *gongs* variously arranged form harmonious musical instruments among the Burmese, and still more elaborately among the Javanese.

The word is commonly applied by Anglo-Indians also to the H. *ghanṭā* (*ganṭa*, Dec.) or *ghaṛī*, a thicker metal disc, not musical, used in India for striking the hour. The *gong* being used to strike the hour, we find the word applied by Fryer (like *gurry*) to the hour itself, or interval denoted.

c. 1590.—"In the morning before day the Generall did strike his **Gongo**, which is an instrument of War that soundeth like a Bell."—(This was in Africa, near Benguela). *Advent. of Andrew Battel*, in *Purchas*, ii. 970.

1673.—"They have no Watches nor Hour-Glasses, but measure Time by the dropping of Water out of a Brass Bason, which holds a **Ghong**, or less than half an Hour; when they strike once distinctly, to tell them it's the First **Ghong**, which is renewed at the Second **Ghong** for Two, and so Three at the End of it till they come to Eight; when they strike on the Brass Vessel at their liberty to give notice the *Pore* is out, and at last strike One leisurely to tell them it is the First *Pore*."—*Fryer*, 186.

1686.—"In the Sultan's Mosque (at Mindanao) there is a great Drum with but one Head, called a **Gong**; which is instead of a Clock. This **Gong** is beaten at 12 a Clock, at 3, 6, and 9."—*Dampier*, i. 333.

1726.—"These **gongs** (gongen) are beaten very gently at the time when the Prince is going to make his appearance."—*Valentijn*, iv. 58.

1750–52.—"Besides these (in China) they have little drums, great and small kettle drums, **gungungs** or round brass basons like frying pans."—*Olof Toreen*, 248.

1817.—

"War music bursting out from time to time
With **gong** and tymbalon' tremendous
chime."—*Lalla Rookh, Makanna.*

Tremendous sham poetry!

1878.—"... le nom plébéien ... sonna dans les salons. ... Comme un coup de cymbale, un de ces **gongs** qui sur les théâtres de féerie annoncent les apparitions fantastiques."—*Alph. Daudet, Le Nabab*, ch. 4.

***GOOJUR**, n.p. H. *Gūjar*, Skt. *Gurjjara*. The name of a great Hindu clan, very numerous in tribes and in population over nearly the whole of Northern India, from the Indus to Rohilkhand. In the Delhi territory and the Doab they were formerly notorious for thieving propensities, and are still much addicted to cattle-theft; and they are never such steady and industrious cultivators as the *Jāts*, among whose villages they are so largely interspersed. In the Punjab they are Mahommedans. Their extensive diffusion is illustrated by their having given name to Gujarāt (see GOOZERAT) as well as to *Gujrāt* and *Gujrānwāla* in the Punjab. And during the 18th century a great part of Sahāranpūr District in the Northern Doab was also called *Gujrāt* (see *Elliot's Races*, by *Beames*, i. 99 *seqq*.).

1519.—"In the hill-country between Nilâb and Behreh ... and adjoining to the hill-country of Kashmīr, are the Jats, **Gujers**, and many other men of similar tribes."—*Memoirs of Baber*, 259.

[1785.—"The road is infested by tribes of banditti called **googurs** and mewatties."—In *Forbes, Or. Mem.* 2nd ed. II. 426.]

***GOORKA, GOORKALLY**, n.p. H. *Gurkhā*, *Gurkhālī*. The name of the race now dominant in Nepāl, and taking their name from a town so called 53 miles W. of Khatmandu. [The name is usually derived from the Skt. *go-raksha*, 'cow-keeper.' For the early history see *Wright, H. of Nepāl*, 147]. They are probably the best soldiers of modern India, and several regiments of the Anglo-Indian army are recruited from the tribe.

1767.—"I believe, Sir, you have before been acquainted with the situation of Nipal, which has long been besieged by the **Goorcully** Rajah."—*Letter from Chief at Patna*, in *Long*, 526.

["The Rajah being now dispossessed of his country, and shut up in his capital by the Rajah of **Goercullah**, the usual channel of commerce has been obstructed."—*Letter from Council to E.I. Co.*, in *Verelst, View of Bengal*, App. 36.]

GOOROO, s. H. *gurū*, Skt. *guru* a spiritual teacher, a (Hindu) priest.

(Ancient).—"That brahman is called **guru** who performs according to rule the rites on conception and the like, and feeds (the child) with rice (for the first time)."—*Manu*, ii. 142.

c. 1550.—"You should do as you are told by your parents and your **Guru**."—*Rāmāyana* of Tulsī Dās, by *Growse* (1878), 43.

[1567.—"**Grous**." See quotation under CASIS.]

1626.—"There was a famous Prophet of the Ethnikes, named **Goru**."—*Purchas, Pilgrimage*, 520.

1700.—"... je suis fort surpris de voir à la porte ... le Pénitent au colier, qui demandoit à parler au **Gourou**."—*Lettres Edif.*, x. 95.

1810.—"Persons of this class often keep little schools ... and then are designated **gooroos**; a term implying that kind of respect we entertain for pastors in general."—*Williamson, V. M.* ii. 317.

1822.—"The Adventures of the **Gooroo** Paramartan; a tale in the Tamul Language" (translated by B. Babington from the original of Padre Beschi, written about 1720–1730), London.

1867.—"Except the **guru** of Bombay, no priest on earth has so large a power of acting on every weakness of the female heart as a Mormon bishop at Salt Lake."—*Dixon's New America*, 330.

GOOZERAT, GUZERAT, n.p. The name of a famous province in Western India, Skt. *Gurjjara, Gurjjara-rāshtra*, Prakrit passing into H. and Mahr. *Gujarāt, Gujrāt*, taking its name from the Gūjar (see **GOOJUR**) tribe. The name covers the British Districts of Surat, Broach, Kaira, Panch Mahals, and Ahmedābād, besides the territories of the Gaekwar of Baroda, and a multitude of native States. It is also often used as including the peninsula of Kāthiāwāṛ or Surāshtra, which alone embraces 180 petty States.

c. 640.—Hwen T'sang passes through *Kiuchi-lo, i.e.* **Gurjjara**, but there is some difficulty as to the position which he assigns to it.—*Pèlerins Bouddh.*, iii. 166; [*Cunningham, Arch. Rep.* ii. 70 *seqq.*].

1298.—"**Gozurat** is a great Kingdom. ... The people are the most desperate pirates in existence. ..."—*Marco Polo*, Bk. iii. ch. 26.

c. 1300.—"**Guzerat**, which is a large country, within which are Kambáy, Somnát, Kanken-Tána, and several other cities and towns."—*Rashiduddin*, in *Elliot*, i. 67.

1300.—"The Sultan despatched Ulugh Khán to Ma'bar and **Gujarát** for the destruction of the idol-temple of Somnát, on the 20th of Jumádá'-l awwal, 698 H. ..."—*Amīr Khusrū*, in *Elliot*, iii. 74.

[c. 1330.—"**Juzrat**."]

1554.—"At last we made the land of **Guchrát** in Hindustan."—*Sidi' Ali*, p. 79.

The name is sometimes used by the old writers for the people, and especially for the Hindu merchants or **banyans** (q.v.). of Guzerat. See *Sainsbury*, i. 445 and *passim*.

[c. 1605.—"And alsoe the **Guzatts** do saile in the Portugalls shipps in euery porte of the East Indies ..."—*Birdwood, First Letter Book*, 85.]

***GORA**, s. H. *gorā*, 'fair-complexioned.' A white man; a European soldier; any European who is not a **sahib** (q.v.). Plural *gorā-lōg*, 'white people.'

[1861.—"The cavalry ... rushed into the lines ... declaring that the **Gora Log** (the European soldiers) were coming down upon them."—*Cave Browne, Punjab and Delhi*, i. 243.]

GOSAIN, GOSSYNE, &c. s. H. and Mahr. *Gosāīn, Gosāī, Gosāvī, Gusā'īn*, &c., from Skt. *Goswāmī*, 'Lord of Passions' (lit. 'Lord of cows'), *i.e.* one who is supposed to have subdued his passions and renounced the world. Applied in various parts of India to different kinds of persons not necessarily celibates, but professing a life of religious mendicancy, and including some who dwell together in convents under a superior, and others who engage in trade and hardly pretend to lead a religious life.

1774.—"My hopes of seeing Teshu Lama were chiefly founded on the **Gosain**."—*Bogle*, in *Markham's Tibet*, 46.

c. 1781.—"It was at this time in the hands of a **Gosine**, or Hindoo Religious."—*Hodges*, 112. (The use of this barbarism by Hodges is remarkable, common as it has become of late years.)

[1813.—"Unlike the generality of Hindoos, these **Gosaings** do not burn their dead ..."

Forbes, Or. Mem. 2nd ed. i. 312–3; in i. 544 he writes **Gosannee**.]

1826.—"I found a lonely cottage with a light in the window, and being attired in the habit of a **gossein**, I did not hesitate to request a lodging for the night."—*Pandurang Hari*, 399; [ed. 1873, ii. 275].

GRAM, s. This word is properly the Portuguese *grão, i.e.* 'grain,' but it has been specially appropriated to that kind of vetch (*Cicer arietinum*, L.) which is the most general grain- (rather pulse-) food of horses all over India, called in H. *chanā*. It is the Ital. *cece*, Fr. *pois chiche*, Eng. *chick-pea* or *Egypt. pea*, much used in France and S. Europe. This specific application of *grão* is also Portuguese, as appears from Bluteau. The word *gram* is in some parts of India applied to other kinds of pulse, and then this application of it is recognised by qualifying it as *Bengal gram*. The plant exudes oxalate of potash, and to walk through a gram-field in a wet morning is destructive to shoe-leather. The natives collect the acid.

[1513.—"And for the food of these horses (exported from the Persian Gulf) the factor supplied **grãos**."—*Albuquerque, Cartas*, p. 200, Letter of Dec. 4.

[1554.—(Describing Vijayanagar.) "There the food of horses and elephants consists of **grãos**, rice and other vegetables, cooked with *jagra*, which is palm-tree sugar, as there is no barley in that country."—*Castanheda*, Bk. ii. ch. 16.

[c. 1610.—"They give them also a certain

grain like lentils."—*Pyrard de Laval*, Hak. Soc. ii. 79.]

1702.—"... he confessing before us that their allowance three times a week is but a quart of rice and **gram** together for five men a day, but promises that for the future it shall be rectified."—In *Wheeler*, ii. 10.

1776.—"... Lentils, **gram** ... mustard seed."—*Halhed's Code*, p. 8 (pt. ii.).

1789.—"... **Gram**, a small kind of pulse, universally used instead of oats."—*Munro's Narrative*, 85.

1793.—"... **gram**, which it is not customary to give to bullocks in the Carnatic."—*Dirom's Narrative*, 97.

1804.—"The **gram** alone, for the four regiments with me, has in some months cost 50,000 pagodas."—*Wellington*, iii. 71.

1865.—"But they had come at a wrong season, **gram** was dear, and prices low, and the sale concluded in a dead loss."—*Palgrave's Arabia*, 290.

GRAM-FED, adj. Properly the distinctive description of mutton and beef fattened upon gram, which used to be the pride of Bengal. But applied figuratively to any 'pampered creature.'

c. 1849.—"By an old Indian I mean a man full of curry and of bad Hindustani, with a fat liver and no brains, but with a self-sufficient idea that no one can know India except through long experience of brandy, champagne, **gram-fed** mutton, cheroots and hookahs."—*Sir C. Napier*, quoted in *Bos. Smith's Life of Ld. Lawrence*, i. 338.

1880.—"I missed two persons at the Delhi assemblage in 1877. All the **gram-fed** secretaries and most of the alcoholic chiefs were there; but the famine-haunted villagers and the delirium-shattered opium-eating Chinaman, who had to pay the bill, were not present."—*Ali Baba*, 127.

GRASS-WIDOW, s. This slang phrase is applied in India, with a shade of malignity, to ladies living apart from their husbands, especially as recreating at the Hill stations, whilst the husbands are at their duties in the plains.

We do not know the origin of the phrase. In the *Slang Dictionary* it is explained: "An unmarried mother; a deserted mistress." But no such opprobrious meanings attach to the Indian use. In *Notes and Queries*, 6th ser. viii. 414, will be found several communications on this phrase. [Also see *ibid.* x. 436, 526; xi. 178; 8th ser. iv. 37, 75.] We learn from these that in *Moor's Suffolk Words and Phrases*, **Grace-Widow** occurs with the meaning of an unmarried mother. Corresponding to this, it is stated also, is the N.S. (?) or Low German *gras-wedewe*. The Swedish *Gräsänka* or *-enka* also is used for 'a low dissolute married woman living by herself.' In Belgium a woman of this description is called *haecke-wedewe*, from *haecken*, 'to feel strong desire' (to 'hanker'). And so it is suggested *gräsenka* is contracted from *grädesenka*, from *gradig*, 'esuriens' (greedy, in fact). In Danish Dict. *graesenka* is interpreted as a woman whose betrothed lover is dead. But the German *Stroh-Wittwe*, 'straw-widow' (which Flügel interprets as 'mock widow'), seems rather inconsistent with the suggestion that *grass-widow* is a corruption of the kind suggested. A friend mentions that the masc. *Stroh-Wittwer* is used in Germany for a man whose wife is absent, and who therefore dines at the eating-house with the young fellows. [The *N.E.D.* gives the two meanings: 1. An unmarried woman who has cohabited with one or more men; a discarded mistress; 2. A married woman whose husband is absent from her. "The etymological notion is obscure, but the parallel forms disprove the notion that the word is a 'corruption' of *grace-widow*. It has been suggested that in sense 1. *grass* (and G. *stroh*) may have been used with opposition to bed. Sense 2. may have arisen as an etymologizing interpretation of the compound after it had ceased to be generally understood; in Eng. it seems to have first appeared as Anglo-Indian." The French equivalent, *Veuve de Malabar*, was in allusion to Lemierre's tragedy, produced in 1770.]

1878.—"In the evening my wife and I went out house-hunting; and we pitched upon one which the newly incorporated body of Municipal Commissioners and the Clergyman (who was a **Grass-widower**, his wife being at home) had taken between them."—*Life in the Mofussil*, ii. 99–100.

1879.—The Indian newspaper's "typical official rises to a late breakfast—probably on herrings and soda-water—and dresses tastefully for his round of morning calls, the last on a **grass-widow**, with whom he has a *tête-à-tête* tiffin, where 'pegs' alternate with champagne."—*Simla Letter* in *Times*, Aug. 16.

1880.—"The **Grass-widow** in Nephelococcygia."—*Sir Ali Baba*, 169.

"Pleasant times have these Indian **grass-widows!**"—*The World*, Jan. 21, 13.

***GRIFFIN, GRIFF**, s.; **GRIFFISH**, adj. One newly arrived in India, and unaccustomed to Indian ways and peculiarities; a Johnny Newcome. The origin of the phrase is unknown to us. There was an Admiral *Griffin* who commanded in the Indian seas from Nov. 1746 to June 1748, and was not very fortunate. Had his name to do with the origin of the term? The word seems to have been first used at Madras (see *Boyd*, below). [But also see the quotation from *Beaumont & Fletcher*, below.] Three references below indicate the parallel terms formerly used by the Portuguese at Goa, by the Dutch in the Archipelago, and by the English in Ceylon.

[c. 1624.—"Doves beget doves, and eagles eagles, Madam: a citizen's heir, though never so rich, seldom at the best proves a gentleman."—*Beaumont & Fletcher, Honest Man's Fortune*, Act III. sc. 1, vol. iii. p. 389, ed. *Dyce*. Mr. B. Nicolson (3 ser. *Notes and Queries*, xi. 439) points out that Dyce's MS. copy, licensed by Sir Henry Herbert in 1624, reads "proves but a **griffin** gentleman." Prof. Skeat (*ibid.* xi. 504) quoting from *Piers Plowman*, ed. *Wright*, p. 96, "*Gryffyn* the Walshe," shows that *Griffin* was an early name for a Welshman, apparently a corruption of *Griffith*. The word may have been used abroad to designate a raw Welshman, and thus acquired its present sense.]

1794.—"As I am little better than an unfledged **Griffin**, according to the fashionable phrase here" (Madras).—*Hugh Boyd*, 177.

1807.—"It seems really strange to a **griffin**—the cant word for a European just arrived."—*Ld. Minto, in India*, 17.

1808.—"At the Inn I was tormented to death by the impertinent persevering of the black people; for every one is a beggar, as long as you are reckoned a **griffin**, or a new-comer."—*Life of Leyden*, 107.

1836.—"I often tire myself ... rather than wait for their dawdling; but Mrs. Staunton laughs at me and calls me a '**Griffin**,' and says I must learn to have patience and save my strength."—*Letters from Madras*, 38.

"... he was living with bad men, and saw that they thought him no better than themselves, but only more **griffish** ..."—*Ibid.* 53.

1853.—"There were three more cadets on the same steamer, going up to that great **griff** depot, Oudapoor."—*Oakfield*, i. 38.

1853.—

"'Like drill?'

"'I don't dislike it much now: the goose-step was not lively.'

"'Ah, they don't give **griffs** half enough of it now-a-days; by Jove, Sir, when I was a **griff**—and thereupon ...'"—*Ibid.* i. 62.

[1900.—"Ten Rangoon sportsmen have joined to import ponies from Australia on the **griffin** system, and have submitted a proposal to the Stewards to frame their events to be confined to **griffins** at the forthcoming autumn meeting."—*Pioneer Mail*, May 18.]

The **griffin** at Goa also in the old days was called by a peculiar name.

1631.—"Haec exanthemata (prickly heat-spots) magis afficiunt recenter advenientes ut et Mosquitarum puncturae ... ita ut deridiculum ergo hic inter nostrates dicterium enatum sit, eum qui hoc modo affectus sit, esse **Orang Barou**, quod novitium hominem significat."—*Jac. Bontii, Hist. Nat.*, &c., ii. cap. xviii. p. 33.

Here **orang barou** is Malay **orang-baharu**, *i.e.* 'new man'; whilst *Oranglama*, 'man of long since,' is applied to old colonials. In connection with these terms we extract the following:—

c. 1790.—"Si je n'avois pas été un *oorlam*, et si un long séjour dans l'Inde ne m'avoit pas accoutumé à cette espèce de fleau, j'aurois certainement souffert l'impossible durant cette nuit."—*Haafner*, ii. 26–27.

On this his editor notes:

"*Oorlam* est un mot Malais corrumpu; il faut dire *Orang-lama*, ce qui signifie une personne qui a déjà été long-temps dans un endroit, ou dans un pays, et c'est par ce nom qu'on designe les Européens qui ont habité depuis un certain temps dans l'Inde-Ceux qui ne font qu'y arriver, sont appelés *Baar*; denomination qui vient du mot Malais **Orang-Baru** ... un homme nouvellement arrivé."

[1894.—"In the *Standard*, Jan. 1, there appears a letter entitled 'Ceylon Tea-Planting—a Warning,' and signed 'An **Ex-creeper**.' The correspondent sends a cutting from a recent issue of a Ceylon daily paper—a paragraph headed '**Creepers** Galore.' From this extract it appears that **Creeper** is the name given in Ceylon to paying pupils who go out there to learn tea-planting."—*Mr. A. L. Mayhew*, in 8 ser. *Notes and Queries*, v. 124.]

***GRUNTH**, s. Panjābī *Granth*, from Skt. *grantha*, lit. 'a knot,' leaves tied together by a string. 'The Book,' *i.e.* the Scripture of the Sikhs, containing the hymns composed or compiled by their leaders from Nānak (1469–1539) onwards. The *Granth* has been translated by Dr. Trumpp, and published, at the expense of the Indian Government.

1770.—"As the young man (Nānk) was early introduced to the knowledge of the most esteemed writings of the Mussulmen ... he made it a practice in his leisure hours to translate literally or virtually, as his mind prompted him, such of their maxims as made the deepest impression on his heart. This was in the idiom of Pendjab, his maternal language. Little by little he strung together those loose sentences, reduced them into some order, and put them in verses. ... His collection became numerous; it took the form of a book which was entitled **Grenth**."—*Seir Mutaqherin*, i. 89.

1798.—"A book entitled the **Grunth** ... is the only typical object which the Sicques have admitted into their places of worship."—*G. Forster's Travels*, i. 255.

1817.—"The fame of Nannak's book was diffused. He gave it a new name, **Kirrunt**."—*Mill's Hist.* ii. 377.

c. 1831.—"... Au centre du quel est le temple d'or où est gardé le **Grant** ou livre sacré des Sikes."—*Jacquemont, Correspondance*, ii. 166.

[1838.—"There was a large collection of priests, sitting in a circle, with the **Grooht**, their holy book, in the centre ..."—*Miss Eden, Up the Country*, ii. 7.]

GUBBROW, v. To bully, to dumbfound, and perturb a person. Made from *ghabrāo*, the imperative of *ghabrānā*. The latter, though sometimes used transitively, is more usually neuter, 'to be dumbfounded and perturbed.'

GUDDA, s. A donkey, literal and metaphorical. H. *gadhā:* [Skt. *gardabha*, 'the roarer']. The coincidence of the Scotch *cuddy* has been attributed to a loan from H. through the gypsies, who were the chief owners of the animal in Scotland, where it is not common. On the other hand, this is ascribed to a nickname *Cuddy* (for Cuthbert), like the English *Neddy*, similarly applied. [So the *N.E.D.* with hesitation.] A Punjab proverbial phrase is *gadōn khurkī*, "Donkeys' rubbing" their sides together, a sort of 'claw me and I'll claw thee.'

GUDDY, GUDDEE, s. H. *gaddī*, Mahr. *gādī*. 'The Throne.' Properly it is a cushion, a throne in the Oriental sense, *i.e.* the seat of royalty, "a simple sheet, or mat, or carpet on the floor, with a large cushion or pillow at the head, against which the great man reclines" (*Wilson*). "To be placed on the **guddee**" is to succeed to the kingdom. The word is also used for the pad placed on an elephant's back.

[1809.—"Seendhiya was seated nearly in the centre, on a large square cushion covered with gold brocade; his back supported by a round bolster, and his arms resting upon two flat cushions; all covered with the same costly material, and forming together a kind of throne, called a **musnud**, or **guddee**."—*Broughton, Letters from a Mahratta Camp*, ed. 1892, p. 28.]

***GUINEA-CLOTHS, GUINEA-STUFFS**, s. Apparently these were piece-goods bought in India to be used in the West African trade. [On the other hand, Sir G. Birdwood identifies them with **gunny** (*Report on old Recs.*, 224). The manufacture still goes on at Pondicherry.] These are presumably the *Negros-tücher* of Baldaeus (1672), p. 154.

[1675.—"**Guinea-stuffs**," in *Birdwood, ut supra.*]

1726.—We find in a list of cloths purchased by the Dutch Factory at Porto Novo, **Guinees Lywaat**, and *Negros-Kleederen* ('Guinea linens and Negro's clothing').—See *Valentijn, Chorom.* 9.

1813.—"The demand for Surat piece-goods has been much decreased in Europe ... and from the abolition of the slave trade, the demand for the African market has been much reduced ... **Guinea stuffs**, 4½ yards each (per ton) 1200 (pieces)."—*Milburn*, i. 289.

[1878.—"The chief trades of Pondicherry are, spinning, weaving and dyeing the cotton stuffs known by the name of **Guinees**."—*Garstin, Man. of S. Arcot*, 426.]

GUM-GUM, s. We had supposed this word to be an invention of the late Charles Dickens, but it seems to be a real Indian, or Anglo-Indian, word. The nearest approximation in Shakespear's Dict. is *gamak*, 'sound of the kettledrum.' But the word is perhaps a Malay plural of *gong* originally; see the quotation from *Osbeck*. [The quotations from *Bowdich* and *Medley* (from *Scott, Malay Words*, p. 53) perhaps indicate an African origin.]

[1659.—"... The roar of great guns, the sounding of trumpets, the beating of drums, and the noise of the **gomgommen** of the Indians."—From the account of the Dutch attack (1659) on a village in Ceram, given in *Wouter Schouten, Reistogt nadr en door Oostindiën*, 4th ed. 1775, i. 55. In the Dutch version, "en het geraas van de **gomgommen** der Indiäanen." The French of 1707 (i. 92) has "au bruit du canon, des trompettes, des tambour et des **gomgommes** Indiennes."

[1731.—"One of the Hottentot Instruments of Musick is common to several Negro Nations, and is called both by Negroes and Hottentots, **gom-gom** ... is a Bow of Iron, or Olive Wood, strung with twisted Sheep-Gut or Sinews."—*Medley*, tr. *Kolben's Cape of Good Hope*, i. 271.]

c. 1750–60.—"A music far from delightful, consisting of little drums they call **Gum-gums**, cymbals, and a sort of fife."—*Grose*, i. 139.

1768–71.—"They have a certain kind of musical instruments called **gom-goms**, consisting in hollow iron bowls, of various sizes and tones, upon which a man strikes with an iron or wooden stick ... not unlike a set of bells."—*Stavorinus*, E.T. i. 215. See also p. 65.

1771.—"At night we heard a sort of music, partly made by insects, and partly by the noise of the **Gungung**."—*Osbeck*, i. 185.

[1819.—"The **gong-gongs** and drums were beat all around us."—*Bowdich*, *Mission to Ashantee*, i. 7, 136.]

1836.—"'Did you ever hear a tom-tom, Sir?' sternly enquired the Captain ...

'A what?' asked Hardy, rather taken aback.

'A tom-tom.'

'Never!'

'Nor a **gum-gum**?'

'Never!'

'What *is* a **gum-gum**?' eagerly enquired several young ladies."—*Sketches by Boz, The Steam Excursion.*

[**GUNGE**, s. Hind. *ganj*, 'a store, storehouse, market.'

[1762.—See under GOMASTA.

[1772.—"**Gunge**, a market principally for grain."—*Verelst*, *View of Bengal*, Gloss. s.v.

[1858.—"The term **Gunge** signifies a range of buildings at a place of traffic, for the accommodation of merchants and all persons engaged in the purchase and sale of goods, and for that of their goods and of the shopkeepers who supply them."—*Sleeman, Journey through Oudh*, i. 278.]

GUNJA, s. Hind. *gānjhā*, *gānjā*. The flowering or fruiting shoots of the female plant of Indian hemp (*Cannabis sativa*, L., formerly distinguished as *C. indica*), used as an intoxicant. (See BANG.)

[c. 1813.—"The natives have two proper names for the hemp (*Cannabis satira*), and call it **Gangja** when young, and *Siddhi* when the flowers have fully expanded."—*Buchanan*, *Eastera India*, ii. 865.]

1874.—"In odour and the absence of taste, **ganjá** resembles *bhang*. It is said that after the leaves which constitute *bhang* have been gathered, little shoots sprout from the stem, and that these, picked off and dried, form what is called **ganjá**."—*Hanbury & Flückiger*, 493.

GUNNY, GUNNY-BAG, s. From Skt. *goṇi*, 'a sack'; Hind. and Mahr. *goṇ*, *goṇī*, 'a sack, sacking.' The popular and trading name of the coarse sacking and sacks made from the fibre of **jute**, much used in all Indian trade. *Ṭāṭ* is a common Hind. name for the stuff. [With this word Sir G. Birdwood identifies the forms found in the old records—"*Guiny* Stuffes (1671)," "*Guynie* stuffs," "*Guinea* stuffs," "*Gunnys*" (*Rep. on Old Records*, 26, 38, 39, 224); but see under GUINEA-CLOTHS.]

c. 1590.—"Sircar Ghoraghat produces raw silk, **gunneys**, and plenty of *Tanghion* horses."—*Gladwin's Ayeen*, ed. 1800, ii. 9; [ed. *Jarrett*, ii. 123]. (But here, in the original, the term is *pārchah-i-ṭāṭband*.)

1693.—"Besides the aforenamed articles **Goeny-sacks** are collected at Palicol."—*Hacart* (3), 14.

1711.—"When Sugar is pack'd in double **Goneys**, the outer Bag is always valued in Contract at 1 or 1½ *Shahee*."—*Lockyer*, 244.

1726.—In a list of goods procurable at *Dạatzerom*: "**Goeni-zakken** (Gunny bags)."—*Valentijn*, *Chor.* 40.

1727.—"Sheldon ... put on board some rotten long Pepper, that he could dispose of in no other Way, and some damaged **Gunnies**, which are much used in Persia for embaling Goods, when they are good in their kind."—*A. Hamilton*, ii. 15; [ed. 1744].

1764.—"Baskets, **Gunny bags**, and *dubbers* ... Rs. 24."—In *Long*, 384.

1785.—"We enclose two *parwanehs* ... directing them each to despatch 1000 **goonies** of grain to that person of mighty degree."—*Tippoo's Letters*, 171.

1885.—"The land was so covered with them (plover) that the hunters shot them with all kind of arms. We counted 80 birds in the **gunny**-sack that three of the soldiers brought in."—*Boots and Saddles*, by *Mrs. Custer*, p. 37. (American work.)

GUP, s. Idle gossip. P.—H. *gap*, 'prattle, tattle.' The word is perhaps an importation from Tūrān. Vámbéry gives Orient. Turki *gep*, *geb*, 'word, saying, talk'; which, however, Pavet de Courteille suggests to be a corruption from the Pers. *guftan*, 'to say'; of which, indeed, there is a form *guptan*. [So Platts, who also compares Skt. *jalpa*, which is the Bengali *golpo*, 'babble.'] See quotation from Schuyler showing the use in Turkistan. The word is perhaps best known in England through an unamiable account of society in S. India, published under the name of "**Gup**," in 1868.

1809–10.—"They (native ladies) sit on their cushions from day to day, with no other ... amusement than hearing the '**gup-gup**,' or gossip of the place."—*Mrs. Sherwood's Autobiog.* 357.

1876.—"The first day of mourning goes by the name of **gup**, *i.e.* commemorative talk."—*Schuyler's Turkistan*, i. 151.

GUREEBPURWUR, GURREEBNUWAUZ, ss. Ar.—P. *Gharībpārwar*, *Gharībnawāz*, used in Hind. as respectful terms of address, meaning respectively 'Provider of the Poor!' 'Cherisher of the Poor!'

1726.—"Those who are of equal condition bend the body somewhat towards each other, and lay hold of each other by the beard, saying **Grab-anemoas**, *i.e.* I wish you the prayers of the poor."—*Valentijn, Chor.* 109, who copies from *Van Twist* (1648), p. 55.

1824.—"I was appealed to loudly by both parties, the soldiers calling on me as '**Ghureeb purwur**,' the Goomashta, not to be outdone, exclaiming 'Donai, Lord Sahib! Donai! Rajah!'" (Read *Dohāī* and see DOAI).—*Heber*, i. 266. See also p. 279.

1867.—"'**Protector of the poor!**' he cried, prostrating himself at my feet, 'help thy most unworthy and wretched slave! An unblest and evil-minded alligator has this day devoured my little daughter. She went down to the river to fill her earthen jar with water, and the evil one dragged her down, and has devoured her. Alas! she had on her gold bangles. Great is my misfortune!'"—*Lt-Col. Lewin, A Fly on the Wheel*, p. 99.

***GUTTA PERCHA**, s. This is the Malay name *Gatah Pertja*, *i.e.* 'Sap of the Percha,' *Dichopsis Gutta*, Benth. (*Isonandra Gutta*, Hooker; N.O. *Sapotaceae*). Dr. Oxley writes (*J. Ind. Archip.* i. 22) that *percha* is properly the name of a tree which produces a spurious article; the real *gutta p.* is produced by the *túbau.* [Mr. Maxwell (*Ind. Ant.* xvii. 358) points out that the proper reading is *taban.*] The product was first brought to notice in 1843 by Dr. Montgomery. It is collected by first ringing the tree and then felling it, and no doubt by this process the article will speedily become extinct. The history of G. P. is, however, far from well known. Several trees are known to contribute to the exported article; their juices being mixed together. [Mr. Scott (*Malay Words*, 55 *seqq.*) writes the word *getah percha*, or *getah perchah*, 'gum of percha,' and remarks that it has been otherwise explained as meaning 'gum of Sumatra,'" there being another word *percha*, a name of Sumatra, as well as a third word *percha*, 'a rag, a remnant.'" Mr. Maxwell (*loc. cit.*) writes: "It is still uncertain whether there is a gutta-producing tree called *Percha* by the Malays. My experience is that they give the name of *Perchah* to that kind of *getah taban* which hardens into strips in boiling. These are stuck together and made into balls for export."]

[1847.—"**Gutta Percha** is a remarkable example of the rapidity with which a really useful invention becomes of importance to the English public. A year ago it was almost unknown, but now its peculiar properties are daily being made more available in some new branch of the useful or ornamental arts."—*Mundy, Journal*, in *Narrative of Events in Borneo and Celebes*, ii. 342 *seq.* (quoted by *Scott, loc. cit.*).]

1868.—"The late Mr. d'Almeida was the first to call the attention of the public to the substance now so well known as **gutta-percha**. At that time the *Isonandra Gutta* was an abundant tree in the forests of Singapore, and was first known to the Malays, who made use of the juice which they obtained by cutting down the trees. ... Mr. d'Almeida ... acting under the advice of a friend, forwarded some of the substance to the Society of Arts. There it met with no immediate attention, and was put away uncared for. A year or two afterwards Dr. Montgomery sent specimens to England, and bringing it under the notice of competent persons, its value was at once acknowledged. ... The sudden and great demand for it soon resulted in the disappearance of all the **gutta-percha** trees on Singapore Island."—*Collingwood, Rambles of a Naturalist*, pp. 268–9.

GYELONG, s. A Buddhist priest in Tibet. Tib. *dGe-sLong*, *i.e.* 'beggar of virtue,' *i.e.* a *bhikshu* or mendicant friar (see under BUXEE); but latterly a priest who has received the highest orders. See *Jaeschke*, p. 86.

1784.—"He was dressed in the festival habit of a **gylong** or priest, being covered with a scarlet satin cloak, and a gilded mitre on his head."—*Bogle*, in *Markham's Tibet*, 25.

***GYM-KHANA**, s. This word is quite modern, and was unknown 40 years ago. The first use that we can trace is (on the authority of Major John Trotter) at Rūrkī in 1861, when a *gymkhana* was instituted there. It is a factitious word, invented, we believe, in the Bombay Presidency, and probably based upon *gend-khāna* ('ball-house'), the name usually given in Hind. to an English racket-court. It is applied to a place of public resort at a station, where the needful facilities for athletics and games of sorts are provided, including (when that was in fashion) a skating-rink, a lawn-tennis ground, and so forth. The *gym* may have been simply a corruption of *gend* shaped by *gym*nastics, [of which the English public school short form *gym* passed into Anglo-Indian jargon]. The word is also applied to a meeting for such sports; and in this sense it has travelled already as far as Malta, and has since become common among Englishmen abroad. [The suggestion that the word originated in the P.—H. *jamā'at-khana*, 'a place of assemblage,' is not probable.]

1877.—"Their proposals are that the Cricket Club should include in their programme the games, &c., proposed by the promoters of a **gymkhana** Club, so far as not to interfere with cricket, and should join in making a rink and lawn-tennis, and badminton courts, within the cricket-ground enclosure."—*Pioneer Mail*, Nov. 3.

1879.—"Mr. A—— F—— can always he depended on for epigram, but not for accuracy. In his letters from Burma he talks of the **Gymkhana** at Rangoon as a sort of *establissement* [*sic*] where people have pleasant little dinners. In the 'Oriental Arcadia,' which Mr. F—— tells us is flavoured with naughtiness, people may do strange things, but they do *not* dine at **Gymkhanas**."—*Ibid*. July 2.

1881.—"R. E. **Gymkhana** at Malta, for Polo and other Ponies, 20th June, 1881."—Heading in *Royal Engineer Journal*, Aug. 1, p. 159.

1883.—"I am not speaking of Bombay people with their clubs and **gymkhanas** and other devices for oiling the wheels of existence. ..."—*Tribes on My Frontier*, 9.

H

HACKERY, s. In the Bengal Presidency this word is now applied only to the common native bullock-cart used in the slow draught of goods and materials. But formerly in Bengal, as still in Western India and Ceylon, the word was applied to lighter carriages (drawn by bullocks) for personal transport. In Broughton's *Letters from a Mahratta Camp* (p. 156; [ed. 1892, p. 117]) the word is used for what in Upper India is commonly called an ekka or light native pony-carriage; but this is an exceptional application. Though the word is used by Englishmen almost universally in India, it is unknown to natives, or if known is regarded as an English term; and its origin is exceedingly obscure. The word seems to have originated on the west side of India, where we find it in our earliest quotations. It is probably one of those numerous words which were long in use, and undergoing corruption by illiterate soldiers and sailors, before they appeared in any kind of literature. Wilson suggests a probable Portuguese origin, *e.g.* from *acarretar*, 'to convey in a cart.' It is possible that the mere Portuguese article and noun '*a carreta*' might have produced the Anglo-Indian *hackery*. Thus in Correa, under 1513, we have a description of the Surat hackeries; "and the carriages (*as carretas*) in which he and the Portuguese travelled, were elaborately wrought, and furnished with silk hangings, covering them from the sun; and these carriages (*as carretas*) run so smoothly (the country consisting of level plains) that the people travelling in them sleep as tranquilly as on the ground" (ii. 369).

But it is almost certain that the origin of the word is the H. *chhakra*, 'a two-wheeled cart'; and it may be noted that in old Singhalese *chakka*, 'a cart-wheel,' takes the forms *haka* and *saka* (see *Kuhn, On Oldest Aryan Elements of Singhalese*, translated by D. Ferguson in *Indian Ant.* xii. 64). [But this can have no connection with *chhakra*, which represents Skt. *śakaṭa*, 'a waggon.']

1673.—"The Coach wherein I was breaking, we were forced to mount the Indian **Hackery**, a Two-wheeled Chariot, drawn by swift little Oxen."—*Fryer*, 83.

1690.—"Their **Hackeries** likewise, which are a kind of Coach, with two Wheels, are all drawn by Oxen."—*Ovington*, 254.

1711.—"The Streets (at Surat) are wide and commodious; otherwise the **Hackerys**, which are very common, would be an Inconveniency. These are a sort of Coaches drawn by a Pair of Oxen."—*Lockyer*, 259.

1742.—"The bridges are much worn, and out of repair, by the number of **Hackaries** and other carriages which are continually passing over them."—In *Wheeler*, iii. 262.

1756.—"The 11th of July the Nawab arrived in the city, and with him Bundoo Sing, to whose house we were removed that afternoon in a

hackery."—*Holwell*, in *Wheeler's Early Records*, 249.

c. 1760.—"The **hackrees** are a conveyance drawn by oxen, which would at first give an idea of slowness that they do not deserve ... they are open on three sides, covered a-top, and are made to hold two people sitting cross-legged."—*Grose*, i. 155–156.

1780.—"A **hackery** is a small covered carriage upon two wheels drawn by bullocks, and used generally for the female part of the family."—*Hodges, Travels*, 5.

c. 1790.—"Quant aux palankins et **hakkaries** (voitures à deux roues), on les passe sur une double sangaria"—*Haafner*, ii. 173.

1793.—"To be sold by Public Auction ... a new Fashioned **Hackery**."—*Bombay Courier*, April 13.

1798.—"At half-past six o'clock we each got into a **hackeray**."—*Stavorinus*, tr. by *Wilcocks*, iii. 295.

1811.—Solvyns draws and describes the **Hackery** in the modern Bengal sense.

"Il y a cependant quelques endroits où l'on se sert de charettes couvertes à deux roues, appelées **hickeris**, devant lesquelles on attèle des bœufs, et qui servent à voyager."—Editor of *Haafner, Voyages*, ii. 3.

1813.—"Travelling in a light **hackaree**, at the rate of five miles an hour."—*Forbes, Or. Mem.* iii. 376; [2nd ed. ii. 352; in i. 150, **hackeries**, ii. 253, **hackarees**]. Forbes's engraving represents such an ox-carriage as would be called in Bengal a *bailī*.

1829.—"The genuine vehicle of the country is the **hackery**. This is a sort of wee tent, covered more or less with tinsel and scarlet, and bells and gilding, and placed upon a clumsy two-wheeled carriage with a pole that seems to be also a kind of boot, as it is at least a foot deep. This is drawn by a pair of white bullocks."—*Mem. of Col. Mountain*, 2nd ed., 84.

1860.—"Native gentlemen, driving fast trotting oxen in little **hackery** carts, hastened home from it."—*Tennent's Ceylon*, ii. 140.

HADGEE, s. Ar. *Ḥājj*, a pilgrim to Mecca; from *ḥajj*, the pilgrimage, or visit to a venerated spot. Hence *Hājjī* and *Hājī* used colloquially in Persian and Turkish. Prof. Robertson Smith writes: "There is current confusion about the word *ḥājj*. It is originally the participle of *ḥajj*, 'he went on the *ḥajj*.' But in modern use *ḥājij* is used as part, and *ḥājj* is the title given to one who has made the pilgrimage. When this is prefixed to a name, the double *j* cannot be pronounced without inserting a short vowel and the *a* is shortened; thus you say '*el-Hajjĕ* Soleimān,' or the like. The incorrect form *Hājjī* is however used by Turks and Persians."

[1609.—"Upon your order, if **Hoghee** Careen so please, I purpose to delve him 25 pigs of lead."—*Danvers, Letters*, i. 26.

[c. 1610.—"Those who have been to Arabia ... are called **Agy**."—*Pyrard de Laval*, Hak. Soc. i. 165.

[c. 1665.—"*Aureng-Zebe* once observed perhaps by way of joke, that *Sultan Sujah* was become at last an **Agy** or pilgrim."—*Bernier*, ed. *Constable*, 113.

[1673.—"**Hodge**, a Pilgrimage to Mecca." (See under A MUCK.)

[1683.—"**Hodgee** Sophee Caun." See under FIRMAUN.]

1765.—"**Hodgee** acquired this title from his having in his early years made a pilgrimage to **Hodge** (or the tomb of *Mahommed* at *Mecca*)."—*Holwell, Hist. Events*, &c., i. 59.

[c. 1833.—"The very word in Hebrew *Khog*, which means 'festival,' originally meant 'pilgrimage,' and corresponds with what the Arabs call **hatch**. ..."—*Travels of Dr. Wolff*, ii. 155.]

HÁKIM, s. H. from Ar. *ḥākim*, 'a judge, a ruler, a master'; 'the authority.' The same Ar. root *ḥakm*, 'bridling, restraining, judging,' supplies a variety of words occurring in this Glossary, viz. *Ḥākim* (as here); *Ḥakīm*; *Ḥukm*; *Ḥikmat*

[1611.—"Not standing with his greatness to answer every **Haccam**, which is as a Governor or petty King."—*Danvers, Letters*, i. 158. In *ibid.* i. 175, **Hackum** is used in the same way.]

1698.—"**Hackum**, a Governor."—*Fryer's Index Explanatory*.

c. 1861.—

"Then comes a settlement **Hakim**, to teach
me to plough and weed—
I sowed the cotton he gave me—but first I
boiled the seed ..."
Sir A. C. Lyall, The Old Pindaree.

HALÁLCORE, s. Lit. Ar.—P. *ḥalāl-khor*, 'one who eats what is lawful,' [*ḥalāl* being the technical Mahommedan phrase for the slaying of an animal to be used for food according to the proper ritual], applied euphemistically to a person of very low caste, a sweeper or scavenger, implying 'to whom all is lawful food.' Generally used as synonymous with **bungy** (q.v.). [According to Prof. Blochmann, "*Ḥalālkhūr, i.e.* one who eats that which the ceremonial law allows, is a euphemism for *ḥarāmkhūr*, one who eats forbidden things, as pork, &c. The word *ḥalālkhūr* is still in use among educated Muhammadans; but it is doubtful whether (as stated in the *Āīn*) it was Akbar's invention." (*Āīn*, i. 139 note.)]

1623.—"Schiah Selim nel principio ... si sdegnò tanto, che poco mancò che per dispetto non la desse per forza in matrimonio ad uno della razza che chiamano **halal chor**, quasi dica 'mangia lecito,' cioè che ha per lecito di mangiare ogni cosa. ..." (See other quotation under HAREM).—*P. della Valle*, ii. 525; [Hak. Soc. i. 54].

1638.—"... sont obligez de se purifier depuis la teste i'usqu'aux pieds si quelqu'vn de ces gens qu'ils appellent **Alchores**, leur a touché."—*Mandelslo*, Paris, 1659, 219.

1665.—"Ceux qui ne parlent que Persan dans les Indes, les appellent **Halalcour**, c'est à dire celui qui se donne la liberté de manger de tout ce qu'il lui plait, ou, selon quelques uns, celui qui mange ce qu'il a légitimement gagné. Et ceux qui approuvent cette dernière explication, disent qu'autrefois **Halalcours** s'appellent *Haramcours*, mangeurs de Viande defenduës."—*Thevenot*, v. 190.

1673.—"That they should be accounted the Offscum of the People, and as base as the **Holencores** (whom they account so, because they defile themselves by eating anything)."—*Fryer*, 28; [and see under BOY, **b**].

1690.—"The **Halalchors** ... are another Sort of Indians at Suratt, the most contemptible, but extremely necessary to be there."—*Ovington*, 382.

1763.—"And now I must mention the **Hallachores**, whom I cannot call a Tribe, being rather the refuse of all the Tribes. These are a set of poor unhappy wretches, destined to misery from their birth. ..."—*Reflexions*, &c., by *Luke Scrafton*, Esq., 7–8. It was probably in this passage that Burns (see below) picked up the word.

1783.—"That no **Hollocore**, Derah, or Chandala caste, shall upon any consideration come out of their houses after 9 o'clock in the morning, lest they should taint the air, or touch the superior Hindoos in the streets."—*Mahratta Proclamation at Baroch*, in *Forbes, Or. Mem.* iv. 232.

1786.—"When all my schoolfellows and youthful compeers (those misguided few excepted who joined, to use a Gentoo phrase, the **hallachores** of the human race) were striking off with eager hope and earnest intent, in some one or other of the many paths of a busy life, I was 'standing idle in the market-place.'"—*Letter of Robert Burns*, in A. Cunningham's ed. of *Works and Life*, vi. 63.

1788.—The *Indian Vocabulary* also gives **Hallachore**.

1810.—"For the meaner offices we have a **Hallalcor** or Chandela (one of the most wretched Pariahs)."—*Maria Graham*, 31.

HALÁLLCUR. V. used in the imperative for infinitive, as is common in the Anglo-Indian use of H. verbs, being Ar.—H. *ḥalāl-kar*, 'make lawful,' *i.e.* put (an animal) to death in the manner prescribed to Mahommedans, when it is to be used for food.

[1855.—"Before breakfast I bought a moderately sized sheep for a dollar. Shaykh Hamid '**halaled**' (butchered) it according to rule. ..."—*Burton, Pilgrimage*, ed. 1893, i. 255.]

1883.—"The diving powers of the poor duck are exhausted. ... I have only ... to seize my booty, which has just enough of life left to allow Peer Khan to **make it halal**, by cutting its throat in the name of Allah, and dividing the webs of its feet."—*Tribes on My Frontier*, 167.

HALF-CASTE, s. A person of mixt European and Indian blood. (See MUSTEES; EURASIAN.)

1789.—"Mulattoes, or as they are called in the East Indies, **half-casts**."—*Munro's Narrative*, 51.

1793.—"They (the Mahratta Infantry) are commanded by **half-cast** people of Portuguese and French extraction, who draw off the attention of the spectators from the bad clothing of their men, by the profusion of antiquated lace bestowed on their own."—*Dirom, Narrative*, ii.

1809.—"The Padre, who is a **half-cast** Portuguese, informed me that he had three districts under him."—*Ld. Valentia*, i. 329.

1828.—"An invalid sergeant ... came, attended by his wife, a very pretty young **half-caste**."—*Heber*, i. 298.

1875.—"Othello is black—the very tragedy lies there; the whole force of the contrast, the whole pathos and extenuation of his doubts of Desdemona, depend on this blackness. Fechter makes him a **half-caste**."—*G. H. Lewes, On Actors and the Art of Acting*.

HANSALERI, s. Table-servant's Hind. for 'horse-radish'! "A curious corruption, and apparently influenced by *saleri*, 'celery'"; (*Mr. M. L. Dames*, in *Panjab N. and Q.* ii. 184).

HARAKIRI, s. This, the native name of the Japanese rite of suicide committed as a point of honour or substitute for judicial execution, has long been interpreted as "happy despatch," but what the origin of this curious error is we do not know. [The *N.E.D.* s.v. *dispatch*, says that it is humorous.] The real meaning is realistic in the extreme, viz., *hara*, 'belly,' *kiri*, 'to cut.'

[1598.—"And it is often seene that they rip their own **bellies** open."—*Linschoten*, Hak. Soc. i. 158.

[1615.—"His mother **cut** her own **belly**."—*Foster, Letters*, iv. 45.]

1616.—"Here we had news how Galsa Same was to' passe this way to morrow to goe to a church near Miaco, called Coye; som say to **cut his bellie**, others say to be shaved a prist and to remeane theare the rest of his dais."—*Cocks's Diary*, i. 164.

1617.—"The King demanded 800 *tais* from Shosque Dono, or else to **cut his belly**, whoe, not having it to pay, did it."—*Ibid.* 337, see also ii. 202.

[1874.—See the elaborate account of the rite in *Mitford, Tales of Old Japan*, 2nd ed. 329 *seqq.* For a similar custom among the Karens, see *M'Mahon, Karens of the Golden Chersonese*, 294.]

***HARAMZADA**, s. A scoundrel; literally 'misbegotten'; a common term of abuse. It is Ar.—P. *ḥarāmzāda*, 'son of the unlawful.' *Ḥarām* is from a root signifying *sacer* (see under HAREM), and which appears as Hebrew in the sense of 'devoting to destruction,' and of 'a ban.' Thus in Numbers xxi. 3: "They utterly destroyed them and their cities; and he called the name of the place *Hormah*." [See *Encycl. Bibl.* i. 468; ii. 2110.]

[1857.—"I am no advocate for slaying Shahzadas or any such-like **Haramzadas** without trial."—*Bosworth Smith, L. of Ld. Lawrence*, ii. 251.]

HAREM, s. Ar. *ḥaram*, *ḥarīm*, *i.e. sacer*, applied to the women of the family and their apartment. This word is not now commonly used in India, **zenana** (q.v.) being the common word for 'the women of the family,' or their apartments.

1298.—"... car maintes homes emorurent e mantes dames en furent veves ... e maintes autres dames ne furent à toz jorz mès en plores et en lermes: ce furent les meres et les **araines** de homes qe hi morurent."—*Marco Polo*, in Old Text of *Soc. de Géographie*, 251.

1623.—"Non so come sciah Selim ebbe notizia di lei e s'innamorò. Volle condurla nel suo **haram** o *gynaeceo*, e tenerla quivi appresso di sè come una delle altre concubine; ma questa donna (Nurmahal) che era sopra modo astuta ... ricusò."—*P. della Valle*, ii. 525; [Hak. Soc. i. 53].

1630.—"This Duke here and in other seralios (or **Harams** as the Persians term them) has above 300 concubines."—*Herbert*, 139.

1676.—"In the midst of the large Gallery is a Nich in the Wall, into which the King descends out of his **Haram** by a private pair of Stairs."—*Tavernier*, E.T. ii. 49; [ed. *Ball*, i. 101].

1726.—"On the Ganges also lies a noble fortress, with the Palace of the old Emperor of Hindostan, with his **Hharaam** or women's apartment. ..."—*Valentijn*, v. 168.

[1727.—"The King ... took his Wife into his own **Harran** or Seraglio. ..."—*A. Hamilton*, ed. 1744, i. 171.

[1812.—"Adjoining to the Chel Sitoon is the **Harem**; the term in Persia is applied to the establishments of the great, *zenana* is confined to those of inferior people."—*Morier, Journey through Persia*, &c., 166.]

HATTYCHOOK, s. Hind. *hāthīchak*, servant's and gardener's Hind. for the globe artichoke; [the Jerusalem artichoke is *hāthīpīch*]. This is worth producing, because our word (**artichoke**) is itself the corruption of an Oriental word thus carried back to the East in a mangled form.

HAVILDAR, s. Hind. *ḥavildār*. A sepoy non-commissioned officer, corresponding to a sergeant, and wearing the chevrons of a sergeant. This dating from about the middle of the 18th century is the only modern use of the term in that form. It is a corruption of Pers. *ḥawāladār*, or *ḥawāldār*, 'one holding an office of trust'; and in this form it had, in other times, a variety of applications to different charges and subordinate officers. Thus among the Mahrattas the commandant of a fort was so styled; whilst in Eastern Bengal the term was, and perhaps still is, applied to the holder of a *ḥawāla*, an intermediate tenure between those of zemindar and ryot.

1672.—Regarding the **Cowle** obtained from the Nabob of Golcondah for the Fort and Town of Chinapatnam. 11,000 Pagodas to be paid in full of all demands for the past, and in future Pagodas 1200 per annum rent, "and so to hold the Fort and Town free from any **Avildar** or **Divan's** People, or any other imposition for ever."—*Fort St. George Consn.*, April 11, in *Notes and Exts.*, No. i. 25.

1673.—"We landed at about Nine in the Morning, and were civilly treated by the Customer in his *Choultry*, till the **Havildar** could be acquainted of my arrival."—*Fryer*, 123.

[1680.—"**Avaldar.**" See under JUNCAMEER.]

1696.—"... the **havildar** of St. Thomé and Pulecat."—*Wheeler*, i. 308.

[1763.—"Three *avaldars* (**avaldares**) or receivers."—India Office MSS. *Conselho, Ultramarino*, vol. i.

[1773.—"One or two Hircars, one **Havildah**, and a company of sepoys. ..."—*Ives*, 67.]

1824.—"Curreem Musseeh was, I believe, a **havildar** in the Company's army, and his sword and sash were still hung up, with a not unpleasing vanity, over the desk where he now presided as catechist."—*Heber*, i. 149.

HAVILDAR'S GUARD, s. There is a common way of cooking the fry of fresh-water fish (a little larger than whitebait) as a breakfast dish, by frying them in rows of a dozen or so, spitted on a small skewer. On the Bombay side this dish is known by the whimsical name in question.

HAZREE, s. This word is commonly used in Anglo-Indian households in the Bengal Presidency for 'breakfast.' It is not clear how it got this meaning. [The earlier sense was religious, as below.] It is properly *ḥāẓirī*, 'muster,' from the Ar. *ḥāẓir*, 'ready or present.' (See CHOTA-HAZRY.)

[1832.—"The Sheeahs prepare **hazree** (breakfast) in the name of his holiness Abbas Allee Ullum-burdar, Hosein's step-brother; *i.e.* they cook *polaoo, rotee*, curries, &c., and distribute them."—*Herklots, Qanoon-e-Islam*, ed. 1863, p. 183.]

***HIMALY̆A**, n.p. This is the common pronunciation of the name of the great range

"Whose snowy ridge the roving Tartar bounds,"

properly *Himālăya*, 'the Abode of Snow'; also called *Himavat*, 'the Snowy'; *Himagiri* and *Himaśaila*; *Himādri*, *Himakūta*, &c., from various forms of which the ancients made *Imaus*, *Emōdus*, &c. Pliny had got somewhere the true meaning of the name: "... a montibus Hemodis, quorum promontorium Imaus vocatur *nivosum* significante ..." (vi. 17). We do not know how far back the use of the modern name is to be found. [The references in early Hindu literature are collected by *Atkinson* (*Himalayan Gazetteer*, ii. 273 *seqq.*).] We do not find it in Baber, who gives *Siwālak* as the Indian name of the mountains. The oldest occurrence we know of is in the *Āīn*, which gives in the Geographical Tables, under the Third Climate, *Koh-i-***Himālah** (orig. ii. 36); [ed. *Jarrett*, iii. 69]). This is disguised in Gladwin's version by a wrong reading into *Kerdehmaleh* (ed. 1800, ii. 367).[1] This form (**Himmaleh**) is used by Major Rennell, but hardly as if it was yet a familiar term. In Elphinstone's Letters **Himāleh** or some other spelling of that form is always used (see below). When we get to Bishop Heber we find **Himalaya**, the established English form.

1822.—"What pleases me most is the contrast between your present enjoyment, and your former sickness and despondency. Depend upon it England will turn out as well as **Hemaleh**."—*Elphinstone* to Major Close, in *Life*, ii. 139; see also i. 336, where it is written **Himalleh**.

HINDEE, s. This is the Pers. adjective form from *Hind*, 'India,' and illustration of its use for a native of India will be found under HINDOO. By Europeans it is most commonly used for those dialects of Hindustani speech which are less modified by P. vocables than the usual Hindustani, and which are spoken by the rural population of the N.W. Provinces and its outskirts. The earliest literary work in Hindi is the great poem of Chand Bardai (c. 1200), which records the deeds of Prithirāja, the last Hindu sovereign of Delhi. [On this literature see Dr. G. A. Grierson, The *Modern Vernacular Literature of Hindustān*, in *J.A.S.B.* Part I., 1888.] The term **Hinduwī** appears to have been formerly used, in the Madras Presidency, for the Marāṭhī language. (See a note in *Sir A. Arbuthnot's* ed. of *Munro's Minutes*, i. 133.)

HINDOO, n.p. P. *Hindū*. A person of Indian religion and race. This is a term derived from the use of the Mahommedan

1 *Hemāchal* and *Hemakūt* also occur in the Āīn (see *Gladwin*, ii. 342, 343; [ed. *Jarrett*, iii. 30, 31]). *Karāchal* is the name used by Ibn Batuta in the 14th century, and by Al-Birūni 300 years earlier. 17th century writers often call the Himālaya the "Mountains of **Nuggur-Cote**" [Mr. Tawney writes: "We have in Ṛig Veda (x. 121) *ime himavanto parvatāh*, 'these snowy mountains,' spoken of as abiding by the might of Prajāpati. In the Bhagavadgītā, an episode of the Mahābhārata, Kṛishṇa says that he is 'the *Himālaya* among stable things,' and the word *Himālaya* is found in the Kumāra Sambhava of Kālidāsa, about the date of which opinions differ. Perhaps the Greek Ιμαος is *himavat*; Ἠμωδὸς, *himādri*."]

conquerors (see under INDIA). The word in this form is Persian; *Hindī* is that used in Arabic, *e.g.*

c. 940.—"An inhabitant of Mansūra in Sind, among the most illustrious and powerful of that city ... had brought up a young Indian or Sindian slave (**Hindī** aw Sindī)."—*Maṣ'ūdī*, vi. 264.

In the following quotation from a writer in Persian observe the distinction made between **Hindū** and *Hindī*:

c. 1290.—"Whatever live **Hindú** fell into the King's hands was pounded into bits under the feet of elephants. The Musalmáns, who were *Hindís* (country born), had their lives spared."—*Amīr Khosrū*, in *Elliot*, iii. 539.

1563.—"... moreover if people of Arabia or Persia would ask of the men of this country whether they are Moors or Gentoos, they ask in these words: 'Art thou Mosalman or **Indu**?'"—*Garcia*, f. 137*b*.

1653.—"Les **Indous** gardent soigneusement dans leurs Pagodes les Reliques de Ram, Schita (Sita), et les autres personnes illustres de l'antiquité."—*De la Boullaye-le-Gouz*, ed. 1657, 191.

Hindu is often used on the Peshawar frontier as synonymous with *bunya* (see under BANYAN). A soldier (of the tribes) will say: 'I am going to the **Hindu**,' *i.e.* to the *bunya* of the company.

HINDOO KOOSH, n.p. *Hindū-Kūsh*; a term applied by our geographers to the whole of the Alpine range which separates the basins of the Kabul River and the Helmand from that of the Oxus. It is, as Rennell points out, properly that part of the range immediately north of Kabul, the *Caucasus* of the historians of Alexander, who crossed and re-crossed it somewhere not far from the longitude of that city. The real origin of the name is not known; [the most plausible explanation is perhaps that it is a corruption of *Indicus Caucasus*]. It is, as far as we know, first used in literature by Ibn Batuta, and the explanation of the name which he gives, however doubtful, is still popular. The name has been by some later writers modified into Hindu *Koh* (mountain), but this is factitious, and throws no light on the origin of the name.

c. 1334.—"Another motive for our stoppage was the fear of snow; for there is midway on the road a mountain called **Hindū-Kūsh**, *i.e.* 'the Hindu-Killer,' because so many of the slaves, male and female, brought from India, die in the passage of this mountain, owing to the severe cold and quantity of snow."—*Ibn Batuta*, iii. 84.

1504.—"The country of Kâbul is very strong, and of difficult access. ... Between Balkh, Kundez, and Badakshân on the one side, and Kâbul on the other, is interposed the mountain of **Hindû-kûsh**, the passes over which are seven in number."—*Baber*, p. 139.

1548.—"From this place marched, and entered the mountains called **Hindû-Kush**."—*Mem. of Emp. Humayun*, 89.

"It was therefore determined to invade Badakhshan ... The Emperor, passing over the heel of the **Hindū-Kush**, encamped at Shergirán."—*Tabakāt-i-Akbarī*, in *Elliot*, v. 223.

1753.—"Les montagnes qui donnent naissance à l'Indus, et à plusieurs des rivières qu'il reçoit, se nomment **Hendou Kesh**, et c'est l'histoire de Timur qui m'instruit de cette denomination. Elle est composée du nom d'*Hendou* ou *Hind*, qui désigne l'Inde ... et de *kush* ou *kesh* ... que je remarque être propre à diverses montagnes."—*D'Anville*, p. 16.

1793.—"The term Hindoo-Kho, or **Hindoo-Kush**, is not applied to the ridge throughout its full extent; but seems confined to that part of it which forms the N.W. boundary of Cabul; and this is the INDIAN CAUCASUS of Alexander."—*Rennell, Mem.* 3rd ed. 150.

1817.— "... those
Who dwell beyond the everlasting snows
Of **Hindoo Koosh**, in stormy freedom
bred."—*Mokanna*.

HINDOSTAN, n.p. Pers. *Hindūstān*. (**a**) 'The country of the Hindūs,' India. In modern native parlance this word indicates distinctively (**b**) India north of the Nerbudda, and exclusive of Bengal and Behar. The latter provinces are regarded as *pūrb* and all south of the Nerbudda as *Dakhan*. But the word is used in older Mahommedan authors just as it is used in English school-books and atlases, viz. as (**a**) the equivalent of India Proper. Thus Baber says of Hindustān: "On the East, the South, and the West it is bounded by the Ocean" (310).

a.—

1553.—"... and so the Persian nation adjacent to it give it as at present its proper name that of **Indostān**."—*Barros*, I. iv. 7.

1563.—"... and common usage in Persia, and Coraçone, and Arabia, and Turkey, calls this country **Industam** ... for *istām* is as much as to say 'region,' and *indu* 'India.'"—*Garcia*, f. 137*b*.

1663.—"And thus it came to pass that the Persians called it **Indostan**."—*Faria y Sousa*, i. 33.

1665.—"La derniere parti est la plus connüe: c'est celle que l'on appelle **Indostan**, et dont les bornes naturelles au Couchant et au Levant, sont le Gange et l'Indus."—*Thevenot*, v. 9.

1672.—"It has been from old time divided into two parts, *i.e.* the Eastern, which is India beyond the Ganges, and the Western India within the Ganges, now called **Indostan.**"—*Baldaeus*, 1.

1770.—"By **Indostan** is properly meant a country lying between two celebrated rivers, the Indus and the Ganges. ... A ridge of mountains runs across this long tract from north to south, and dividing it into two equal parts, extends as far as Cape Comorin."—*Raynal* (tr.), i. 34.

1783.—"In Macassar **Indostan** is called *Neegree Telinga.*"—*Forrest, V. to Mergui*, 82.

b.—

1803.—"I feared that the dawk direct through **Hindostan** would have been stopped."—*Wellington*, ed. 1837, ii. 209.

1824.—"One of my servants called out to them,—'Aha! dandee folk, take care! You are now in **Hindostan!** The people of this country know well how to fight, and are not afraid."—*Heber*, i. 124. See also pp. 268, 269.

In the following stanza of the good bishop's the application is apparently the same; but the accentuation is excruciating—'Hindóstan,' as if rhyming to 'Boston.'

1824.—

"Then on! then on! where duty leads,
My course be onward still,
O'er broad **Hindostan's** sultry meads,
Or bleak Almora's hill."—*Ibid*, 113.

1884.—"It may be as well to state that Mr. H. G. Keene's forthcoming *History of Hindustan* ... will be limited in its scope to the strict meaning of the word '**Hindustan**' = India north of the Deccan."—*Academy*, April 26, p. 294.

HINDOSTANEE, s. *Hindūstānī*, properly an adjective, but used substantively in two senses, viz. (**a**) a native of Hindustān, and (**b**) (*Hindūstānī zabān*) 'the language of that country,' but in fact the language of the Mahommedans of Upper India, and eventually of the Mahommedans of the Deccan, developed out of the Hindi dialect of the Doab chiefly, and of the territory round Agra and Delhi, with a mixture of Persian vocables and phrases, and a readiness to adopt other foreign words. It is also called **Oordoo**, *i.e.* the language of the Urdū ('Horde') or Camp. This language was for a long time a kind of Mahommedan *lingua franca* over all India, and still possesses that character over a large part of the country, and among certain classes. Even in Madras, where it least prevails, it is still recognised in native regiments as the language of intercourse between officers and men. Old-fashioned Anglo-Indians used to call it the **Moors** (q.v.).

a.—

1653.—(applied to a native.) "**Indistanni** est vn Mahometan noir des Indes, ce nom est composé de *Indou*, Indien, et *stan*, habitation."—*De la Boullaye-le-Gouz*, ed. 1657, 543.

b.—

1616.—"After this he (Tom Coryate) got a great mastery in the **Indostan**, or more vulgar language; there was a woman, a landress, belonging to my Lord Embassador's house, who had such a freedom and liberty of speech, that she would sometimes scould, brawl, and rail from the sun-rising to the sun-set; one day he undertook her in her own language. And by eight of the clock he so silenced her, that she had not one word more to speak."—*Terry, Extracts relating to T. C.*

1673.—"The Language at Court is *Persian*, that commonly spoke is **Indostan** (for which they have no proper Character, the written Language being called *Banyan*), which is a mixture of *Persian* and *Sclavonian*, as are all the dialects of India."—*Fryer*, 201. This intelligent traveller's reference to Sclavonian is remarkable, and shows a notable perspicacity, which would have delighted the late Lord Strangford, had he noticed the passage.

1677.—In Court's letter of 12th Dec. to Ft. St. Geo. they renew the offer of a reward of £20, for proficiency in the Gentoo or **Indostan** languages, and sanction a reward of £10 each for proficiency in the Persian language, "and that fit persons to teach the said language be entertained."—*Notes and Exts.*, No. i. 22.

1685.—"... so applyed myself to a Portuguese mariner who spoke **Indostan** (ye current language of all these Islands)" [Maldives]."—*Hedges, Diary*, March 9; [Hak. Soc. i. 191].

1697.—"Questions addressed to Khodja Movaad, Ambassador from Abyssinia.

* * * * * *

4.—"What language he, in his audience made use of?

"The **Hindustani** language (*Hindoestanze taal*), which the late Hon. Paulus de Roo, then Secretary of their Excellencies the High Government of Batavia, interpreted."—*Valentijn*, iv. 327.

[1699.—"He is expert in the **Hindorstand** or Moores Language."—In *Yule, Hedges' Diary*, Hak. Soc. ii. cclxvii.]

1726.—"The language here is **Hindustans** or **Moors** (so 'tis called there), though he who can't speak any Arabic and Persian passes for an ignoramus."—*Valentijn, Chor.* i. 37.

1727.—"This Persian ... and I, were discoursing one Day of my Affairs in the **Industan** Language, which is the established Language spoken in the Mogul's large Dominions."—*A. Hamilton*, ii. 183; [ed. 1744, ii. 182].

1745.—"Benjamini Schulzii Missionarii Evangelici, Grammatica **Hindostanica** ... Edidit, et de suscipiendâ barbaricarum linguarum culturâ praefatus est D. Jo. Henr. Callenberg, Halae Saxoniae."—Title from Catalogue of M. Garcin de Tassy's Books, 1879. This is the earliest we have heard of.

1763.—"Two of the Council of Pondicherry went to the camp, one of them was well versed in the **Indostan** and Persic languages, which are the only tongues used in the Courts of the Mahomedan Princes."—*Orme*, i. 144 (ed. 1803).

1772.—"Manuscripts have indeed been handed about, ill spelt, with a confused mixture of Persian, **Indostans**, and Bengals."—Preface to *Hadley's Grammar*, xi. (See under MOORS.)

1777.—"Alphabetum Brammhanicum seu **Indostanum.**"—*Romae.*

1778.—"Grammatica **Indostana**—A mais Vulgar—Que se practica no Imperio do gram Mogol—Offerecida—Aos muitos Reverendos—Padres Missionarios—Do dito Imperio. Em Roma MDCCLXXVIII—Na Estamperia da Sagrada Congregação—de Propaganda Fide."—(Title transcribed.) There is a reprint of this (apparently) of 1865, in the Catalogue of Garcin de Tassy's books.

c. 1830.—"Cet ignoble patois d'**Hindoustani**, qui ne servira jamais à rien quand je serai retourné en Europe, est difficile."—*V. Jacquemont, Correspondance*, i. 95.

1844.—"Hd. Quarters, Kurrachee, 12th February, 1844. The Governor unfortunately does not understand **Hindoostanee**, nor Persian, nor Mahratta, nor any other eastern dialect. He therefore will feel particularly obliged to Collectors, sub-Collectors, and officers writing the proceedings of Courts-Martial, and all Staff Officers, to indite their various papers in English, larded with as small a portion of the to him unknown tongues as they conveniently can, instead of those he generally receives—namely, papers written in **Hindostanee** larded with occasional words in English.

"Any Indent made for English Dictionaries shall be duly attended to, if such be in the stores at Kurrachee; if not, gentlemen who have forgotten the vulgar tongue are requested to procure the requisite assistance from England."—*GG. OO.*, by *Sir Charles Napier*, 85.

[Compare the following:

[1617.—(In answer to a letter from the Court not now extant). "Wee have forbidden the severall Factoryes from wrighting words in this languadge and refrayned itt our selues, though in bookes of Coppies wee feare there are many which by wante of tyme for perusall wee cannot rectifie or expresse."—*Surat Factors* to *Court*, February 26, 1617. (*I.O. Records*: O. C., No. 450.)]

1856.—

"... they sound strange
As **Hindostanee** to an Ind-born man
Accustomed many years to English speech."
E. B. Browning, Aurora Leigh.

***HING**, s. Asafoetida. Skt. *hingu*, Hind. *hīng*, Dakh. *hīngu*. A repulsively smelling gum-resin which forms a favourite Hindu condiment, and is used also by Europeans in Western and Southern India as an ingredient in certain cakes eaten with curry. (See POPPER-CAKE). This product affords a curious example of the uncertainty which sometimes besets the origin of drugs which are the objects even of a large traffic. Hanbury and Flückiger, whilst describing Falconer's *Narthex Asafoetida* (*Ferula Narthex*, Boiss.) and *Scorodosma foetidum*, Bunge; (*F. asafoetida*, Boiss.) two umbelliferous plants, both cited as the source of this drug, say that neither has been proved to furnish the *asafoetida* of commerce. Yet the plant producing it has been described and drawn by Kaempfer, who saw the gum-resin collected in the Persian Province of Lāristān (near the eastern shore of the P. Gulf); and in recent years (1857) Surgeon-Major Bellew has described the collection of the drug near Kandahar. Asafoetida has been identified with the σίλφιον or *laserpitium* of the ancients. The substance is probably yielded not only by the species mentioned above, but by other allied plants, *e.g. Ferula Jaeschkiana*, Vatke, of Kashmīr and Turkistan. The *hing* of the Bombay market is the produce of F. *alliacea*, Boiss. [See *Watt, Econ. Dict.* iii. 328 *seqq.*]

c. 645.—"This kingdom of Tsao-kiu-tcha (Tsāukūta ?) has about 7000 *li* of compass,—the compass of the capital called *Ho-sí-na* (Ghazna) is 30 *li* ... The soil is favourable to the plant *Yo-Kin* (Curcuma, or turmeric) and to that called **Hing-kiu.**"—*Pèlerins Boudd.*, iii. 187.

1563.—"A Portuguese in Bisnagar had a horse of great value, but which exhibited a deal of flatulence, and on that account the King would not buy it. The Portuguese cured it by giving it this **ymgu** mixt with flour: the King then bought it, finding it thoroughly well, and asked him how he had cured it. When the man said it was with **ymgu**, the King replied: ' 'Tis nothing then to marvel at, for you have given it to eat the food of the gods' (or, as the poets say, nectar). Whereupon the Portuguese made answer *sotto voce* and in Portuguese: 'Better call it the food of the devils!'"—*Garcia*, f. 21*b*.. The Germans do worse than this Portuguese, for they call the drug *Teufels dreck, i.e. diaboli non cibus sed stercus!*

1586.—"I went from *Agra* to *Satagam* in *Bengale* in the companie of one hundred and four score Boates, laden with Salt, *Opium*, **Hinge**, Lead, Carpets, and divers other commodities down the River Jemena."—*R. Fitch*, in *Hakl.* ii. 386.

1611.—"In the Kingdom of Gujarat and Cambaya, the natives put in all their food **Ingu**, which is Assafetida."—*Teixeira, Relaciones*, 29.

1631.—"... ut totas aedas foetore replerent, qui insuetis vix tolerandus esset. Quod Javani et Malaii et caeteri Indiarum incolae negabant se quicquam odoratius naribus unquam percepisse. Apud hos **Hin** hic succus nominatur."—*Jac. Bontii*, lib. iv. p. 41.

1638.—"Le **Hingh**, que nos droguistes et apoticaires appellent *Assa foetida*, vient la plus part de Perse, mais celle que la Province d'Vtrad (?) produit dans les Indes est bien meilleur."—*Mandelslo*, 230.

1673.—"In this Country *Assa Foetida* is gathered at a place called *Descoon*; some deliver it to be the Juice of a Cane or Reed inspissated; others, of a Tree wounded: It differs much from the stinking Stuff called **Hing**, it being of the Province of *Carmania*; this latter is that the *Indians* perfume themselves with, mixing it in all their Pulse, and make it up in Wafers to correct the Windiness of their Food."—*Fryer*, 239.

1689.—"The Natives at Suratt are much taken with *Assa Foetida*, which they call **Hin**, and mix a little with the Cakes that they eat."—*Ovington*, 397.

1712.—"... substantiam obtinet ponderosam, instar rapae solidam candidissimamque, plenam succi pinguis, albissimi, foetidissimi, porraceo odore nares horridè ferientis; qui ex eâ collectus, Persis Indisque **Hingh**, Europaeis Asa foetida appellatur."—*Eng. Kaempfer Amoen. Exotic.* 537.

1726.—"**Hing** or *Assa Foetida*, otherwise called Devil's-dung (*Duivelsdrek*)."—*Valentijn*, iv. 146.

1857.—"Whilst riding in the plain to the N.E. of the city (Candahar) we noticed several assafœtida plants. The assafœtida, called **hang** or **hing** by the natives, grows wild in the sandy or gravelly plains that form the western part of Afghanistan. It is never cultivated, but its peculiar gum-resin is collected from the plants on the deserts where they grow. The produce is for the most part exported to Hindustan."—*Bellew, Journal of a Pol. Mission*, &c., p. 270.

HOBSON-JOBSON, s. A native festal excitement; a *tamāsha* (see TUMASHA); but especially the **Moharram** ceremonies. This phrase may be taken as a typical one of the most highly assimilated class of Anglo-Indian *argot*, and we have ventured to borrow from it a concise alternative title for this Glossary. It is peculiar to the British soldier and his surroundings, with whom it probably originated, and with whom it is by no means obsolete, as we once supposed. My friend Major John Trotter tells me that he has repeatedly heard it used by British soldiers in the Punjab; and has heard it also from a regimental Moonshee. It is in fact an Anglo-Saxon version of the wailings of the Mahommedans as they beat their breasts in the procession of the *Moharram*—'**Yā Hassan! Yā Hosain!**' It is to be remembered that these observances are *in India* by no means confined to Shīʻas. Except at Lucknow and Murshīdābād, the great majority of Mahommedans in that country are professed Sunnis. Yet here is a statement of the facts from an unexceptionable authority:

"The commonalty of the Mussalmans, and especially the women, have more regard for the memory of Hasan and Husein, than for that of Muhammad and his khalifs. The heresy of making Ta'ziyas (see TAZEEA) on the anniversary of the two latter imáms, is most common throughout India: so much so that opposition to it is ascribed by the ignorant to blasphemy. This example is followed by many of the Hindus, especially the Mahrattas. The Muharram is celebrated throughout the Dekhan and Malwa, with greater enthusiasm than in other parts of India. Grand preparations are made in every town on the occasion, as if for a festival of rejoicing, rather than of observing the rites of mourning, as they ought. The observance of this custom has so strong a hold on the mind of the commonalty of the Mussulmans that they believe Muhammadanism to depend merely on keeping the memory of the imáms in the above manner."—*Mīr Shahāmat 'Ali*, in *J.R. As. Soc.* xiii. 369.

We find no literary quotation to exemplify the phrase as it stands. [But see those from the *Orient. Sporting Mag.* and *Nineteenth*

Century below.] Those which follow show it in the process of evolution:

1618.—"... e particolarmente delle donne che, battendosi il petto e facendo gesti di grandissima compassione replicano spesso con gran dolore quegli ultimi versi di certi loro cantici: **Vah Hussein! sciah Hussein!**"—*P. della Valle*, i. 552.

c. 1630.—"Nine dayes they wander up and downe (shaving all that while neither head nor beard, nor seeming joyfull), incessantly calling out **Hussan, Hussan!** in a melancholy note, so long, so fiercely, that many can neither howle longer, nor for a month's space recover their voices."—*Sir T. Herbert*, 261.

1653.—"... ils dressent dans les rues des Sepulchres de pierres, qu'ils couronnent de Lampes ardentes, et les soirs ils y vont dancer et sauter crians **Hussan, Houssain, Houssain, Hassan**. ..."—*De la Boullaye-le-Gouz*, ed. 1657, p. 144.

c. 1665.—"... ainsi j'eus tout le loisir dont j'eus besoin pour y voir celebrer la Fête de Hussein Fils d'Aly. ... Les Mores de Golconde le celebrent avec encore beaucoup plus de folies qu'en Perse ... d'autres font des dances en rond, tenant des épées nües la pointe en haut, qu'ils touchent les unes contre les autres, en criant de toute leur force **Hussein**."—*Thevenot*, v. 320.

1673.—"About this time the Moors solemnize the Exequies of **Hosseen Gosseen**, a time of ten days Mourning for two Unfortunate Champions of theirs."—*Fryer*, p. 108.

"On the Days of their Feasts and Jubilees, Gladiators were approved and licensed; but feeling afterwards the Evils that attended that Liberty, which was chiefly used in their **Hossy Gossy**, any private Grudge being then openly revenged: it never was forbid, but it passed into an Edict by the following King, that it should be lawfull to Kill any found with Naked Swords in that Solemnity."—*Ibid.* 357.

[1710.—"And they sing around them **Saucem Saucem**."—*Oriente Conquistado*, vol. ii.; *Conquista*, i. Div. 2, sec. 59.]

1720.—"Under these promising circumstances the time came round for the Mussulman feast called **Hossein Jossen** ... better known as the Mohurrum."—In *Wheeler*, ii. 347.

1726.—"In their month Moharram they have a season of mourning for the two brothers Hassan and Hossein. ... They name this mourning-time in Arabic *Ashur*, or the 10 days; but the Hollanders call it **Jaksom Baksom**."—*Valentijn*, *Choro*. 107.

1763.—"It was the 14th of November, and the festival which commemorates the murder of the brothers **Hassein** and **Jassein** happened to fall out at this time."—*Orme*, i. 193.

[1773.—"The Moors likewise are not without their feasts and processions ... particularly of their **Hassan Hassan**. ..."—*Ives*, 28.

[1829.—"Them paper boxes are purty looking consarns, but then the folks makes sich a noise, firing and troompeting and shouting **Hobson Jobson, Hobson Jobson**."—*Oriental Sporting Mag.*, reprint 1873, i. 129.

[1830.—"The ceremony of **Husen Hasen** ... here passes by almost without notice."—*Raffles*, *Hist. Java*, 2nd ed. ii. 4.]

1832.—"... they kindle fires in these pits every evening during the festival; and the ignorant, old as well as young, amuse themselves in fencing across them with sticks or swords; or only in running and playing round them, calling out, *Ya Allee! Ya Allee!* ... **Shah Hussun! Shah Hussun!** ... **Shah Hosein! Shah Hosein!** ... *Doolha! Doolha!* (bridegroom! ...); *Haee dost! Haee dost!* (alas, friend! ...); *Ruheeo! Ruheeo!* (Stay! Stay!). Every two of these words are repeated probably a hundred times over as loud as they can bawl out."—*Jaffur Shureef*, *Qanoon-e-Islam*, tr. by *Herklots*, p. 173.

1883.—"... a long procession ... followed and preceded by the volunteer mourners and breast-beaters shouting their cry of **Hous-s-e-i-n H-as-san Houss-e-i-n H-a-s-san**, and a simultaneous blow is struck vigorously by hundreds of heavy hands on the bare breasts at the last syllable of each name."—*Wills' Modern Persia*, 282.

[1902.—"The **Hobson-Jobson**." By Miss A. Goodrich-Freer, in *The Nineteenth Century and After*, April 1902.]

***HOME**. In Anglo-Indian and colonial speech this means England.

1837.—"**Home** always means England; nobody calls India *home*—not even those who have been here thirty years or more, and are never likely to return to Europe."—*Letters from Madras*, 92.

1885.—"You may perhaps remember how often in times past we debated, with a seriousness becoming the gravity of the subject, what article of food we should each of us respectively indulge in, on our first arrival at **home**."—*Waring*, *Tropical Resident*, 154.

So also in the West Indies:

c. 1830.—"... 'Oh, your cousin Mary, I forgot—fine girl, Tom—may do for you at **home** yonder' (all Creoles speak of England as **home**, although they may never have seen it)."—*Tom Cringle*, ed. 1863, 238.

HONG, s. The Chinese word is *hang*, meaning 'a row or rank'; a house of business; at Canton a warehouse, a factory, and particularly applied to the establishments of the European nations ("Foreign Hongs"), and to those of the so-called "**Hong-Merchants**." These were a body of merchants who had the monopoly of trade with foreigners, in return for which privilege they became security for the good behaviour of the foreigners, and for their payment of dues. The guild of these merchants was called 'The **Hong**.' The monopoly seems to have been first established about 1720–30, and it was terminated under the Treaty of Nanking, in 1842. The *Hong* merchants are of course not mentioned in Lockyer (1711), nor by A. Hamilton (in China previous to and after 1700, pubd. 1727). The latter uses the word, however, and the rudiments of the institution may be traced not only in this narrative, but in that of Ibn Batuta.

c. 1346.—"When a Musulman trader arrives in a Chinese city, he is allowed to choose whether he will take up his quarters with one of the merchants of his own faith settled in the country, or will go to an inn. If he prefers to go and lodge with a merchant, they count all his money and confide it to the merchant of his choice; the latter then takes charge of all expenditure on account of the stranger's wants, but acts with perfect integrity. ..."—*Ibn Batuta*, iv. 265–6.

1727.—"When I arrived at *Canton* the *Hapoa* (see HOPPO) ordered me lodgings for myself, my Men, and Cargo, in (a) **Haung** or Inn belonging to one of his Merchants ... and when I went abroad, I had always some Servants belonging to the **Haung** to follow me at a Distance."—*A. Hamilton*, ii. 227; [ed. 1744].

1782.—"... *l'Opeou* (see HOPPO) ... s'embarque en grande ceremonie dans une galère pavoisée, emmenant ordinairement avec lui trois ou quatre **Hanistes**."—*Sonnerat*, ii. 236.

"... Les loges Européennes s'appellent **hams**."—*Ibid.* 245.

1783.—"It is stated indeed that a monopolizing Company in Canton, called the **Cohong**, had reduced commerce there to a desperate state."—*Report of Com. on Affairs of India, Burke*, vi. 461.

1797.—"A Society of **Hong**, or united merchants, who are answerable for one another, both to the Government and the foreign nations."—*Sir G. Staunton, Embassy to China*, ii. 565.

1882.—"The **Hong** merchants (collectively the **Co-hong**) of a body corporate, date from 1720."—*The Fankwae at Canton*, p. 34.

Cohong is, we believe, though speaking with diffidence, an exogamous union between the Latin *co-* and the Chinese *hong*. [Mr. G. T. Gardner confirms this explanation, and writes: "The term used in Canton itself is invariable: 'The Thirteen *Hong*,' or 'The Thirteen Firms'; and as these thirteen firms formed an association that had at one time the monopoly of the foreign trade, and as they were collectively responsible to the Chinese Government for the conduct of the trade, and to the foreign merchants for goods supplied to any one of the firms, some collective expression was required to denote the co-operation of the Thirteen Firms, and the word **Cohang**, I presume, was found most expressive."]

HONG-BOAT, s. A kind of **sampan** (q.v.) or boat, with a small wooden house in the middle, used by foreigners at Canton. "A public passenger-boat (all over China, I believe) is called **Hang-chwen**, where *chwen* is generically 'vessel,' and *hang* is perhaps used in the sense of '*plying* regularly.' Boats built for this purpose, used as private boats by merchants and others, probably gave the English name **Hong-boat** to those used by our countrymen at Canton" (Note by *Bp. Moule*).

[1878.—"The *Koong-Sze Teng*, or *Hong-Mee-Teng*, or **hong boats** are from thirty to forty feet in length, and are somewhat like the gondolas of Venice. They are in many instances carved and gilded, and the saloon is so spacious as to afford sitting room for eight or ten persons. Abaft the saloon there is a cabin for the boatmen. The boats are propelled by a large scull, which works on a pivot made fast in the stern post."—*Gray, China*, ii. 273.]

HONG KONG, n.p. The name of this flourishing settlement is *hiang-kiang*, 'fragrant waterway' (*Bp. Moule*).

HOOGLY, HOOGHLEY, n.p. Properly *Hūglī*, [and said to take its name from Beng. *hoglā*, 'the elephant grass' (*Typha angustifolia*)]: a town on the right bank of the Western Delta Branch of the Ganges, that which has long been known from this place as the **Hoogly River**, and on which Calcutta also stands, on the other bank, and 25 miles nearer the sea. Hoogly was one of the first places occupied by Europeans in the interior of Bengal; first by the Portuguese in the first half of the 16th century. An English factory was established here in 1640; and it was for some time their chief settlement in Bengal. In 1688 a quarrel with the Nawab led to armed action, and the English abandoned Hoogly; but on the arrangement of peace they settled at Chatānatī, now **Calcutta**.

[c. 1590.—"In the Sarkár of Satgáon, there are two ports at a distance of half a *kos* from each other; the one is Sátgáon, the other **Húglí**: the latter the chief; both are in possession of the Europeans."—*Āīn*, ed. *Jarrett*, ii. 125.]

1616.—"After the force of dom Francisco de Menezes arrived at Sundiva as we have related, there came a few days later to the same island 3 *sanguicels*, right well equipped with arms and soldiers, at the charges of Manuel Viegas, a householder and resident of **Ogolim**, or Porto Pequeno, where dwelt in Bengala many Portuguese, 80 leagues up the Ganges, in the territory of the Mogor, under his ill faith that every hour threatened their destruction."—*Bocarro, Decada*, 476.

c. 1632.—"Under the rule of the Bengális a party of Frank merchants ... came trading to Sátgánw; one *kos* above that place they occupied some ground on the bank of the estuary. ... In course of time, through the ignorance and negligence of the rulers of Bengal, these Europeans increased in number, and erected substantial buildings, which they fortified. ... In due course a considerable place grew up, which was known by the name of the Port of **Húglí**. ... These proceedings had come to the notice of the Emperor (Sháh Jehán), and he resolved to put an end to them," &c.—*'Abdul Ḥamīd Lāhorī*, in *Elliot*, vii. 31–32.

1644.—"The other important voyage which used to be made from Cochim was that to Bengalla, when the port and town of **Ugolim** were still standing, and much more when we had the Porto Grande and the town of *Diangâ*; this used to be made by so many ships that often in one monsoon there came 30 or more from Bengalla to Cochim, all laden with rice, sugar, lac, iron, salt-petre, and many kinds of cloths both of grass and cotton, ghee (*manteyga*), long pepper, a great quantity of wax, besides wheat and many things besides, such as quilts and rich bedding; so that every ship brought a capital of more than 20,000 xerafins. But since these two possessions were lost, and the two ports were closed, there go barely one or two vessels to *Orixa*."—*Bocarro, MS.*, f. 315.

1665.—"O Rey de Arracão nos tomou a fortaleza de Sirião em Pegù; O grão Mogor a cidade do **Golim** em Bengala."—*P. Manoel Godinho, Relação*, &c.

c. 1666.—"The rest they kept for their service to make Rowers of them; and such Christians as they were themselves, bringing them up to robbing and killing; or else they sold them to the Portugueses of *Goa, Ceilan, St. Thomas*, and others, and even to those that were remaining in *Bengall* at **Ogouli**, who were come thither to settle themselves there by favour of *Jehan-Guyre*, the Grandfather of *Aureng-Zebe*. ..."—*Bernier*, E.T. 54; [ed. *Constable*, 176].

1727.—"**Hughly** is a Town of large Extent, but ill built. It reaches about 2 Miles along the River's Side, from the *Chinchura* before mentioned to the **Bandel**, a Colony formerly settled by the *Portuguese*, but the *Mogul's Fouzdaar* governs both at present."—*A. Hamilton*, ii. 19; [ed. 1744].

1753.—"**Ugli** est une forteresse des Maures. ... Ce lieu étant le plus considérable de la contrée, des Européens qui remontent le Gange, lui ont donné le nom de **rivière d'Ugli** dans sa partie inférieure. ..."—*D'Anville*, p. 64.

HOOKA, s. Hind. from Arab-*ḥuḳḳah*, properly 'a round casket.' The Indian pipe for smoking through water, the elaborated **hubble-bubble** (q.v.). That which is smoked in the *hooka* is a curious compound of tobacco, spice, molasses, fruit, &c. [See *Baden-Powell, Panjab Products*, i. 290.] In 1840 the *hooka* was still very common at Calcutta dinner-tables, as well as regimental mess-tables, and its *bubble-bubble-bubble* was heard from various quarters before the cloth was removed—as was customary in those days. Going back further some twelve or fifteen years it was not very uncommon to see the use of the *hooka* kept up by old Indians after their return to Europe; one such at least, in the recollection of the elder of the present writers in his childhood, being a lady who continued its use in Scotland for several years. When the second of the present writers landed first at Madras, in 1860, there were perhaps half-a-dozen Europeans at the Presidency who still used the *hooka*; there is not one now (c. 1878). A few gentlemen at Hyderabad are said still to keep it up. [Mrs. Mackenzie writing in 1850 says: "There was a dinner party in the evening (at Agra), mostly civilians, as I quickly discovered by their *huqas*. I have never seen the *huqa* smoked save at Delhi and Agra, except by a very old general officer at Calcutta." (*Life in the Mission*, ii. 196). In 1837 Miss Eden says: "the aides-de-camp and doctor get their newspapers and *hookahs* in a cluster on their side of the street." (*Up the Country*, i. 70). The rules for the Calcutta Subscription Dances in 1792 provide: "That *hookers* be not admitted to the ball room during any part of the night. But *hookers* might be admitted to the supper rooms, to the card rooms, to the boxes in the theatre, and to each side of the assembly room, between the large pillars and the walls."—*Carey, Good Old Days*, i. 98.] "In former days it was a dire offence to step over another person's *hooka*-carpet and *hooka*-snake. Men who did so intentionally were called out." (*M.- Gen. Keatinge*).

1768.—"This last Season I have been without Company (except that of my Pipe or **Hooker**), and when employed in the innocent diversion of smoaking it, have often thought of you, and Old England."—*MS. Letter of James Rennell*, July 1.

1782.—"When he observes that the gentlemen introduce their **hookas** and smoak in the company of ladies, why did he not add that the mixture of sweet-scented Persian tobacco, sweet herbs, coarse sugar, spice, etc., which they inhale ... comes through clean water, and is so very pleasant, that many ladies take the tube, and draw a little of the smoak into their mouths."—*Price's Tracts*, vol. i. p. 78.

1783.—"For my part, in thirty years' residence, I never could find out one single luxury of the East, so much talked of here, except sitting in an arm-chair, smoaking a **hooka**, drinking cool water (when I could get it), and wearing clean linen."—(*Jos. Price*), *Some Observations on a late Publication*, &c., 79.

1789.—"When the cloth is removed, all the servants except the **hookerbedar** retire, and make way for the sea breeze to circulate, which is very refreshing to the Company, whilst they drink their wine, and smoke the **hooker**, a machine not easily described. ..."—*Munro's Narrative*, 53.

1828.—"Every one was hushed, but the noise of that wind ... and the occasional bubbling of my own **hookah**, which had just been furnished with another chillum."—*The Kuzzilbash*, i. 2.

c. 1849.—See Sir C. Napier, quoted under GRAM-FED.

c. 1858.—

"Son **houka** bigarré d'arabesques fleuries."

Leconte de Lisle, Poèmes Barbares.

1872.—"... in the background the carcase of a boar with a cluster of villagers sitting by it, passing a **hookah** of primitive form round, for each to take a pull in turn."—*A True Reformer*, ch. i.

1874.—"... des **houkas** d'argent emaillé et ciselé. ..."—*Franz, Souvenir d'une Cosaque*, ch. iv.

HOOKA-BURDAR, s. Hind, from Pers. *huḳḳa-bardār*, 'hooka-bearer'; the servant whose duty it was to attend to his master's hooka, and who considered that duty sufficient to occupy his time. See *Williamson, V.M.* i. 220.

[1779.—"Mr. and Mrs. Hastings present their compliments to Mr. —— and request the favour of his company to a concert and supper on Thursday next. Mr. —— is requested to bring no servants except his **Houccaburdar**."—In *Carey, Good Old Days*, i. 71.]

1789.—"**Hookerbedar**." (See under HOOKA.)

1801.—"The Resident ... tells a strange story how his **hookah-burdar**, after cheating and robbing him, proceeded to England, and set up as the Prince of Sylhet, took in everybody, was waited upon by Pitt, dined with the Duke of York, and was presented to the King."—*Elphinstone*, in *Life*, i. 34.

HOOLY, s. Hind. *holī* (Skt. *holākā*), [perhaps from the sound made in singing]. The spring festival, held at the approach of the vernal equinox, during the 10 days preceding the full moon of the month *P'hālguṇa*. It is a sort of carnival in honour of Krishna and the milkmaids. Passers-by are chaffed, and pelted with red powder, or drenched with yellow liquids from squirts. Songs, mostly obscene, are sung in praise of Kṛishna, and dances performed round fires. In Bengal the feast is called *ḍol jātrā*, or 'Swing-cradle festival.' [On the idea underlying the rite, see *Frazer, Golden Bough*, 2nd ed. iii. 306 *seq.*]

c. 1590.—"Here is also a place called Cheramutty, where, during the feast of the **Hooly**, flames issue out of the ground in a most astonishing manner."—*Gladwin's Ayeen Akbery*, ii. 34; [ed. *Jarrett*, ii. 173].

[1671.—"In Feb. or March they have a feast the Romanists call Carnival, the Indians **Whoolye**."—In *Yule, Hedges' Diary*, Hak. Soc. ii. cccxiv.]

1673.—"... their **Hooly**, which is at their other Seed-Time."—*Fryer*, 180.

1727.—"One (Feast) they kept on Sight of a New Moon in February, exceeded the rest in ridiculous Actions and Expense; and this they called the Feast of **Wooly**, who was ... a fierce fellow in a War with some Giants that infested Sindy. ..."—*A. Hamilton*, i. 128; [ed. 1744, i. 129].

1808.—"I have delivered your message to Mr. H. about April day, but he says he understands the learned to place the **Hooly** as according with May day, and he believes they have no occasion in India to set apart a particular day in the year for the manufacture. ..."—Letter from *Mrs. Halhed* to *W. Hastings*, in *Cal. Review*, xxvi. 93.

1809.—"... We paid the Muha Raj (Sindhia)

the customary visit at the **Hohlee**. Everything was prepared for playing; but at Captain C.'s particular request, that part of the ceremony was dispensed with. Playing the **Hohlee** consists in throwing about a quantity of flour, made from a water-nut called singara, and dyed with red sanders; it is called *abeer*; and the principal sport is to cast it into the eyes, mouth, and nose of the players, and to splash them all over with water tinged of an orange colour with the flowers of the *dak* tree."—*Broughton's Letters*, p. 87.; [ed. 1892, p. 65 *seq.*].

HOPPO, s. The Chinese Superintendent of Customs at Canton. Giles says: "The term is said to be a corruption of *Hoo poo*, the Board of Revenue, with which office the *Hoppo*, or Collector of duties, is in direct communication." Dr. Williams gives a different account (see below). Neither affords much satisfaction. [The *N.E.D.* accepts the account given in the quotation from Williams.]

1711.—"The **Hoppos**, who look on Europe Ships as a great Branch of their Profits, will give you all the fair words imaginable."—*Lockyer*, 101.

1727.—"I have staid about a Week, and found no Merchants come near me, which made me suspect, that there were some underhand dealings between the **Hapoa** and his Chaps, to my Prejudice."—*A. Hamilton*, ii. 228; [ed. 1744, ii. 227]. (See also under HONG.)

1743.—"... just as he (Mr. Anson) was ready to embark, the **Hoppo** or *Chinese* Custom-house officer of *Macao* refused to grant a permit to the boat."—*Anson's Voyage*, 9th ed. 1756, p. 355.

1750-52.—"The **hoppo**, **happa**, or first inspector of customs ... came to see us to-day."—*Osbeck*, i. 359.

1782.—"La charge d'**Opeou** répond à celle d'intendant de province."—*Sonnerat*, ii. 236.

1797.—"... the **Hoppo** or mandarine more immediately connected with Europeans."—*Sir G. Staunton*, i. 239.

1842 (?).—"The term **hoppo** is confined to Canton, and is a corruption of the term *hoi-po-sho*, the name of the officer who has control over the boats on the river, strangely applied to the Collector of Customs by foreigners."—*Wells Williams*, *Chinese Commercial Guide*, 221.

[1878.—"The second board or tribunal is named **hoopoo**, and to it is entrusted the care and keeping of the imperial revenue."—*Gray*, *China*, i. 19.]

1882.—"It may be as well to mention here that the '**Hoppo**' (as he was incorrectly styled) filled an office especially created for the foreign trade at Canton. ... The Board of Revenue is in Chinese 'Hoo-poo,' and the office was locally misapplied to the officer in question."—*The Fankwae at Canton*, p. 36.

HOWDAH, vulg. **HOWDER**, &c., s. Hind. modified from Ar. *haudaj*. A great chair or framed seat carried by an elephant. The original Arabic word *haudaj* is applied to litters carried by camels.

c. 1663.—"At other times he rideth on an Elephant in a *Mik-dember* or **Hauze** ... the *Mik-dember* being a little square House or Turret of Wood, is always painted and gilded; and the **Hauze**, which is an Oval seat, having a Canopy with Pillars over it, is so likewise."—*Bernier*, E.T. 119; [ed. *Constable*, 370].

c. 1785.—"Colonel Smith ... reviewed his troops from the **houdar** of his elephant."—*Carraccioli's L. of Clive*, iii. 133.

A popular rhyme which was applied in India successively to Warren Hastings' escape from Benares in 1781, and to Col. Monson's retreat from Malwa in 1804, and which was perhaps much older than either, runs:

"Ghore par **hauda**, hāthī par jīn
Jaldī bhāg-gāyā { Warren Hastīn! / Kornail Munsīn!"

which may be rendered with some anachronism in expression:

"Horses with **howdahs**, and elephants saddled
Off helter skelter the Sahibs skedaddled."

1831.—
"And when they talked of Elephants,
And riding in my **Howder**,
(So it was called by all my aunts)
I prouder grew and prouder."
H. M. Parker, in *Bengal Annual*, 119.

1856.—
"But she, the gallant lady, holding fast
With one soft arm the jewelled **howdah's** side,
Still with the other circles tight the babe
Sore smitten by a cruel shaft ..."
The Banyan Tree, a Poem.

1863.—"Elephants are also liable to be disabled ... ulcers arise from neglect or carelessness in fitting on the **howdah**."—*Sat. Review*, Sept. 6, 312.

HUBBLE-BUBBLE, s. An onomatopoeia applied to the *hooka* in its rudimentary form, as used by the masses in India. Tobacco, or a mixture containing tobacco amongst other things, is placed with embers in a terra-cotta **chillum** (q.v.), from which a reed carries the smoke into a coconut shell half full of water, and the smoke is drawn through a hole in the side, generally without any kind of mouthpiece, making a bubbling or gurgling sound. An elaborate description is given in Terry's *Voyage* (see below), and another in *Govinda Samanta*, i. 29 (1872).

1616.—"... they have little Earthen Pots ... having a narrow neck and an open round top, out of the belly of which comes a small spout, to the lower part of which spout they fill the Pot with water: then putting their *Tobacco* loose in the top, and a burning coal upon it, they having first fastned a very small strait hollow Cane or Reed ... within that spout ... the Pot standing on the ground, draw that smoak into their mouths, which first falls upon the Superficies of the water, and much discolours it. And this way of taking their *Tobacco*, they believe makes it much more cool and wholsom."—*Terry*, ed. 1665, p. 363.

c. 1630.—"Tobacco is of great account here; not strong (as our men love), but weake and leafie; suckt out of long canes call'd **hubble-bubbles** ..."—*Sir. T. Herbert*, 28.

1673.—"Coming back I found my troublesome Comrade very merry, and packing up his Household Stuff, his *Bang* bowl, and **Hubble-bubble**, to go along with me."—*Fryer*, 127.

1673.—"... bolstered up with embroidered Cushions, smoking out of a silver **Hubble-bubble**."—*Fryer*, 131.

1697.—"... Yesterday the King's Dewan, and this day the King's Buxee ... arrived ... to each of whom sent two bottles of Rose-water, and a glass **Hubble-bubble**, with a compliment."—In *Wheeler*, i. 318.

c. 1760.—See *Grose*, i. 146.

1811.—"Cette manière de fumer est extrêmement commune ... on la nomme **Hubbel de Bubbel**."—*Solvyns*, tom. iii.

1868.—"His (the Dyak's) favourite pipe is a huge **Hubble-bubble**."—*Wallace, Mal. Archip.*, ed. 1880, p. 80.

HULWA, s. Ar. *ḥalwā* and *ḥalāwa* is generic for sweetmeat, and the word is in use from Constantinople to Calcutta. In H. the word represents a particular class, of which the ingredients are milk, sugar, almond paste, and ghee flavoured with cardamom. "The best at Bombay is imported from Muskat" (*Birdwood*).

1672.—"Ce qui estoit plus le plaisant, c'estoit un homme qui précédoit le corps des confituriers, lequel avoit une chemise qui luy descendoit aux talons, toute couverte **d'alva**, c'est à dire, de confiture."—*Journ. d'Ant. Galland*, i. 118.

1673.—"... the Widow once a Moon (to) go to the Grave with her Acquaintance to repeat the doleful Dirge, after which she bestows **Holway**, a kind of Sacramental Wafer; and entreats their Prayers for the Soul of the Departed."—*Fryer*, 94.

1836.—"A curious cry of the seller of a kind of sweetmeat ('**haláweh**'), composed of treacle fried with some other ingredients, is 'For a nail! O sweetmeat! ...' children and servants often steal implements of iron, &c., from the house ... and give them to him in exchange. ..."—*Lane, Mod. Egypt.*, ed. 1371, ii. 15.

HURCARRA, **HIRCARA**, &c., s. Hind. *harkārā*, 'a messenger, a courier; an emissary, a spy' (*Wilson*). The etymology, according to the same authority, is *har*, 'every,' *kār*, 'business.' The word became very familiar in the Gilchristian spelling *Hurkaru*, from the existence of a Calcutta newspaper bearing that title (*Bengal Hurkaru*, generally enunciated by non-Indians as *Hurkĕroó*), for the first 60 years of last century, or thereabouts.

1747.—"Given to the **Ircaras** for bringing news of the Engagement. (Pag.) 4 3 0."—*Fort St David, Expenses of the Paymaster*, under January. MS. Records in India Office.

1748.—"The city of Dacca is in the utmost confusion on account of ... advices of a large force of Mahrattas coming by way of the Sunderbunds, and that they were advanced as far as Sundra Col, when first descried by their **Hurcurrahs**."—In *Long*, 4.

1757.—"I beg you to send me a good **alcara** who understands the Portuguese language."—Letter in *Ives*, 159.

"**Hircars** or Spies."—*Ibid.* 161; [and comp. 67].

1761.—"The head **Harcar** returned, and told me this as well as several other secrets very useful to me, which I got from him by dint of money and some rum."—Letter of *Capt. Martin White*, in *Long*, 260.

1780.—"One day upon the march a **Hircarrah** came up and delivered him a letter from Colonel Baillie."—Letter of *T. Munro*, in *Life*, i. 26.

1803.—"The **hircarras** reported the enemy to be at Bokerdun."—Letter of *A. Wellesley, ibid.* 348.

c. 1810.—"We were met at the entrance of Tippoo's dominions by four **hircarrahs**, or soldiers, whom the Sultan sent as a guard to conduct us safely."—*Miss Edgeworth, Lame Jervas*. Miss Edgeworth has oddly misused the word here.

1813.—"The contrivances of the native **halcarrahs** and spies to conceal a letter are extremely clever, and the measures they frequently adopt to elude the vigilance of an enemy are equally extraordinary."—*Forbes, Or. Mem.* iv. 129; [compare 2nd ed. i. 64; ii. 201].

HUZOOR, s. Ar. *ḥuẓūr*, 'the presence'; used by natives as a respectful way of talking of or to exalted personages, to or of their master, or occasionally of any European gentleman in presence of another European. [The allied words *ḥaẓrat* and *ḥuẓūrī* are used in kindred senses as in the examples.]

[1787.—"You will send to the **Huzzoor** an account particular of the assessment payable by each ryot."—*Parwana of Tippoo*, in *Logan, Malabar*, iii. 125.

[1813.—"The Mahratta cavalry are divided into several classes: the **Husserat**, or household troops called the *kassey-pagah*, are reckoned very superior to the ordinary horse. ..."—*Forbes, Or. Mem.* 2nd ed. i. 344.

[1824.—"The employment of that singular description of officers called **Huzooriah**, or servants of the presence, by the Mahratta princes of Central India, has been borrowed from the usages of the Poona court. *Huzooriahs* are personal attendants of the chief, generally of his own tribe, and are usually of respectable parentage; a great proportion are hereditary followers of the family of the prince they serve. ... They are the usual envoys to subjects on occasions of importance. ... Their appearance supersedes all other authority, and disobedience to the orders they convey is termed an act of rebellion."—*Malcolm, Central India*, 2nd ed. i. 536 *seq.*

[1826.—"These men of authority being aware that I was a **Hoogorie**, or one attached to the suite of a great man, received me with due respect."—*Pandurang Hari*, ed. 1873, i. 40.]

I

IMAUM, s. Ar. *Imām*, 'an exemplar, a leader' (from a root signifying 'to aim at, to follow after'), a title technically applied to the Caliph (*Khalīfa*) or 'Vicegerent,' or Successor, who is the head of Islām. The title "is also given—in its religious import only—to the heads of the four orthodox sects ... and in a more restricted sense still, to the ordinary functionary of a mosque who leads in the daily prayers of the congregation" (*Dr. Badger, Omân*, App. A.). The title has been perhaps most familiar to Anglo-Indians as that of the Princes of 'Omān; or "**Imaums** of Muscat," as they were commonly termed. This title they derived from being the heads of a sect (*Ibādhiya*) holding peculiar doctrine as to the Imamate, and rejecting the Caliphate of Ali or his successors. It has not been assumed by the Princes themselves since Sa'īd bin Ahmad who died in the early part of last century, but was always applied by the English to Saiyid Sa'īd, who reigned for 52 years, dying in 1856. Since then, and since the separation of the dominions of the dynasty in Omān and in Africa, the title **Imām** has no longer been used.

It is a singular thing that in an article on Zanzibar in the *J. R. Geog. Soc.* vol. xxiii. by the late Col. Sykes, the Sultan is always called the *Imaun*, [of which other examples will be found below].

1673.—"At night we saw *Muschat*, whose vast and horrid Mountains no Shade but Heaven does hide. ... The Prince of this country is called **Imaum**, who is guardian at *Mahomet's* Tomb, and on whom is devolved the right of *Caliphship* according to the Ottoman belief."—*Fryer*, 220.

[1753.—"These people are Mahommedans of a particular sect ... they are subject to an **Iman**, who has absolute authority over them."—*Hanway*, iii. 67.

[1901.—Of the Bombay Kojas, "there were only 12 **Imans**, the last of the number ... having disappeared without issue."—*Times*, April 12.]

IMAUMBARRA, s. This is a hybrid word *Imām-bāṛā*, in which the last part is the Hindī *bāṛā*, 'an enclosure,' &c. It is applied to a building maintained by Shī'a communities in India for the express purpose of celebrating the **mohurrum** ceremonies (see HOBSON-JOBSON). The sepulchre of the Founder and his family is often combined with this object. The Imāmbāṛā of the Nawāb Asaf-ud-daula at Lucknow is, or was till the siege of 1858, probably the most magnificent modern Oriental structure in India. It united with the objects already mentioned a mosque, a college, and apartments for the members of the religious establishment. The great hall is "conceived on so grand a scale," says Fergusson, "as to entitle it to rank with the buildings of an earlier age." The central part of it forms a vaulted apartment of 162 feet long by 53½ wide.

[1837.—"In the afternoon we went to see the **Emaunberra**."—*Miss Eden, Up the Country*, i. 87.]

IMPALE, v. It is startling to find an injunction to impale criminals given by an English governor (Vansittart, apparently) little more than a century ago.

1764.—"I request that you will give orders to the Naib of Dacca to send some of the Factory Sepoys along with some of his own people, to apprehend the said murderers and to **impale** them, which will be very serviceable to traders."—*The Governor of Fort William* to the Nawab; in *Long*, 389.

1768–71.—"The punishments inflicted at Batavia are excessively severe, especially such as fall upon the Indians. **Impalement** is the chief and most terrible."—*Stavorinus*, i. 288. This writer proceeds to give a description of the horrible process, which he witnessed.

INAUM, ENAUM, s. Ar. *in'ām*, 'a gift' (from a superior), 'a favour,' but especially in India a gift of rent-free land: also land so held. **In'āmdār**, the holder of such lands. A full detail of the different kinds of *in'ām*, especially among the Mahrattas, will be found in *Wilson*, s.v. The word is also used in Western India for **bucksheesh** (q.v.). This use is said to have given rise to a little mistake on the part of an English political traveller some 30 or 40 years ago, when there had been some agitation regarding the **in'am** lands and the alleged harshness of the Government in dealing with such claims. The traveller reported that the public feeling in the west of India was so strong on this subject that his very palankin-bearers at the end of their stage invariably joined their hands in supplication, shouting, "**In'am! In'am!** Sahib!"

***INDIA, INDIES**, n.p. A book might be written on this name. We can only notice a few points in connection with it.

It is not easy, if it be possible, to find a truly native (*i.e.* Hindu) name for the whole country which we call India; but the *conception* certainly existed from an early date. *Bhāratavarsha* is used apparently in the Purānas with something like this conception. *Jambudwīpa*, a term belonging to the mythical cosmography, is used in the Buddhist books, and sometimes, by the natives of the south, even now. The accuracy of the definitions of India in some of the Greek and Roman authors shows the existence of the same conception of the country that we have now; a conception also obvious in the modes of speech of Hwen T'sang and the other Chinese pilgrims. The Aśoka inscriptions, c. B.C. 250, had enumerated Indian kingdoms covering a considerable part of the conception, and in the great inscription at Tanjore, of the 11th century A.D., which incidentally mentions the conquest (real or imaginary) of a great part of India, by the king of Tanjore, Vīra-Chola, the same system is followed. In a copperplate of the 11th century, by the Chalukya dynasty of Kalyāna, we find the expression "from the Himālaya to the Bridge" (*Ind. Antiq.* i. 81), *i.e.* the Bridge of Rāma, or 'Adam's Bridge,' as our maps have it. And Mahommedan definitions as old, and with the name, will be found below. Under the Hindu kings of Vijayanagara also (from the 14th century) inscriptions indicate all India by like expressions.

The origin of the name is without doubt (Skt.) *Sindhu*, 'the sea,' and thence the Great River on the West, and the country on its banks, which we still call *Sindh*.[1] By a change common in many parts of the world, and in various parts of India itself, this name exchanged the initial sibilant for an aspirate, and became (eventually) in Persia *Hindū*, and so passed on to the Greeks and Latins, viz. Ἰνδοί for the people, Ἰνδός for the river, Ἰνδική and India for the country on its banks. Given this name for the western tract, and the conception of the country as a whole to which we have alluded, the name in the mouths of foreigners naturally but gradually spread to the whole.

Some have imagined that the name of the land of *Nod* ('wandering'), to which Cain is said to have migrated, and which has the same consonants, is but a form of this; which is worth noting, as this idea may have had to do with the curious statement in some medieval writers (*e.g.* John Marignolli) that certain eastern races were "the descendants of Cain." In the form *Hidhu* [*Hindus*, see *Encycl. Bibl.* ii. 2169] India appears in the great cuneiform inscription on the tomb of Darius Hystaspes near Persepolis, coupled with *Gadāra* (*i.e. Gandhāra*, or the Peshawar country), and no doubt still in some degree

1 In most of the important Asiatic languages the same word indicates the Sea or a River of the first class; *e.g. Sindhu* as here; in Western Tibet *Gyamtso* and *Samandrang* (corr. of Skt. *samundra*) 'the Sea,' which are applied to the Indus and Sutlej (see *J. R. Geog. Soc.* xxiii. 34–35); Hebrew *yam*, applied both to the sea and to the Nile; Ar. *bahr*; Pers. *daryā*; Mongol. *dalai*, &c. Compare the Homeric Ὠκεανός.

restricted in its application. In the Hebrew of Esther i. 1, and viii. 9, the form is *Hōd(d)ū*, or perhaps rather *Hiddū* (see also *Peritsol* below). The first Greek writers to speak of India and the Indians were Hecataeus of Miletus, Herodotus, and Ctesias (B.C. c. 500, c. 440, c. 400). The last, though repeating more fables than Herodotus, shows a truer conception of what India was.

Before going further, we ought to point out that **India** itself is a Latin form, and does not appear in a Greek writer, we believe, before Lucian and Polyænus, both writers of the middle of the 2nd century. The Greek form is ἡ Ἰνδική, or else 'The Land of the Indians.'

The name of 'India' spread not only from its original application, as denoting the country on the banks of the Indus, to the whole peninsula between (and including) the valleys of Indus and Ganges; but also in a vaguer way to all the regions beyond. The compromise between the vaguer and the more precise use of the term is seen in Ptolemy, where the boundaries of the true India are defined, on the whole, with surprising exactness, as 'India within the Ganges,' whilst the darker regions beyond appear as 'India beyond the Ganges.' And this double conception of India, as 'India Proper' (as we may call it), and India in the vaguer sense, has descended to our own time.

So vague became the conception in the 'dark ages' that the name is sometimes found to be used as synonymous with Asia, 'Europe, Africa, and India,' forming the three parts of the world. Earlier than this, however, we find a tendency to discriminate different Indias, in a form distinct from Ptolemy's *Intra et extra Gangem*; and the terms *India Major, India Minor* can be traced back to the 4th century. As was natural where there was so little knowledge, the application of these terms was various and oscillating, but they continued to hold their ground for 1000 years, and in the later centuries of that period we generally find a third India also, and a tendency (of which the roots go back, as far at least as Virgil's time) to place one of the three in Africa.

It is this conception of a twofold or threefold India that has given us and the other nations of Europe the vernacular expressions in plural form which hold their ground to this day: the *Indies*, les *Indes*, (It.) le *Indie*, &c.

And we may add further, that China is called by Friar Odoric Upper India (*India Superior*), whilst Marignolli calls it *India Magna* and *Maxima*, and calls Malabar *India Parva*, and *India Inferior*.

There was yet another, and an Oriental, application of the term India to the country at the mouth of the Tigris and Euphrates, which the people of Basra still call *Hind*; and which Sir H. Rawlinson connects with the fact that the Talmudic writers confounded Obillah in that region with the *Havila* of Genesis. (See *Cathay*, &c., 55, note.)

In the work of the Chinese traveller Hwen T'sang again we find that by him and his co-religionists a plurality of Indias was recognised, *i.e.* five, viz. North, Central, East, South, and West.

Here we may remark how two names grew out of the original *Sindhu*. The aspirated and Persianised form *Hind*, as applied to the great country beyond the Indus, passed to the Arabs. But when they invaded the valley of the Indus and found it called *Sindhu*, they adopted that name in the form *Sind*, and thenceforward '*Hind* and *Sind*' were habitually distinguished, though generally coupled, and conceived as two parts of a great whole.

Of the application of *India* to an Ethiopian region, an application of which indications extend over 1500 years, we have not space to speak here. On this and on the medieval plurality of Indias reference may be made to two notes on *Marco Polo*, 2nd ed. vol. ii. pp. 419 and 425.

The vague extension of the term India to which we have referred, survives in another form besides that in the use of '*Indies*.' *India*, to each European nation which has possessions in the East, may be said, without much inaccuracy, to mean in colloquial use that part of the East in which their own possessions lie. Thus to the Portuguese, *India* was, and probably still is, the West Coast only. In their writers of the 16th and 17th century a distinction is made between *India*, the territory of the Portuguese and their immediate neighbours on the West Coast, and *Mogor*, the dominions of the Great Mogul. To the Dutchman *India* means Java and its dependencies. To the Spaniard, if we mistake not, *India* is Manilla. To the Gaul are not *les Indes* Pondicherry, Chandernagore, and Réunion?

As regards the **West Indies**, this expression originates in the misconception of the great Admiral himself, who in his memorable enterprise was seeking, and thought he had found, a new route to the 'Indias' by sailing west instead of east. His discoveries were to Spain *the* Indies, until it gradually became manifest that they were not identical with the ancient lands of the east, and then they became the *West-Indies*.

Indian is a name which has been carried still further abroad; from being applied, as a matter of course, to the natives of the islands, supposed of India, discovered by Columbus, it naturally passed to the natives of the adjoining continent, till it came to be the familiar name of all the tribes between (and sometimes even including) the Esquimaux of the North and the Patagonians of the South.

This abuse no doubt has led to our hesitation in applying the term to a native of India itself. We use the adjective *Indian*, but no modern Englishman who has had to do with India ever speaks of a man of that country as 'an Indian.' Forrest, in his *Voyage to Mergui*, uses the inelegant word *Indostaners*; but in India itself a **Hindustani** means, as has been indicated under that word, a native of the upper Gangetic valley and adjoining districts. Among the Greeks 'an Indian' (Ἰνδὸς) acquired a notable specific application. viz. to an elephant driver or **mahout** (q.v.).

B.C. c. 486.—"Says Darius the King: By the grace of Ormazd these (are) the countries which I have acquired besides Persia. I have established my power over them. They have brought tribute to me. That which has been said to them by me they have done. They have obeyed my law. Medea ... Arachotia (*Harauvatish*), Sattagydia (*Thatagush*), Gandaria (*Gadára*), India (**Hidush**). ..."—On the Tomb of Darius at Nakhsh-i-Rustam, see *Rawlinson's Herod.* iv. 250.

B.C. c. 440.—"Eastward of **India** lies a tract which is entirely sand. Indeed, of all the inhabitants of Asia, concerning whom anything is known, the **Indians** dwell nearest to the east, and the rising of the Sun."—*Herodotus*, iii. c. 98 (*Rawlinson*).

B.C. c. 300.—"**India** then (ἡ τοίνυν Ἰνδικὴ) being four-sided in plan, the side which looks to the Orient and that to the South, the Great Sea compasseth; that towards the Arctic is divided by the mountain chain of Hēmōdus from Scythia, inhabited by that tribe of Scythians who are called Sakai; and on the fourth side, turned towards the West, the Indus marks the boundary, the biggest or nearly so of all rivers after the Nile."—*Megasthenes*, in *Diodorus*, ii. 35. (From Müller's *Fragm. Hist. Graec.*, ii. 402.)

A.D. c. 140.—"*Τὰ δὲ ἀπὸ τοῦ Ἰνδοῦ πρὸς ἕω, τοῦτό μοι ἔστω ἡ τῶν Ἰνδῶν γῆ, καὶ Ἰνδοὶ οὗτοι ἔστωσαν.*"—*Arrian, Indica*, ch. ii.

c. 590.—"As for the land of the Hind it is bounded on the East by the Persian Sea (*i.e.* the Indian Ocean), on the W. and S. by the countries of Islām, and on the N. by the Chinese Empire. ... The length of the land of the Hind from the government of Mokrān, the country of Manṣūra and Bodha and the rest of Sind, till thou comest to Ḳannūj and thence passest on to Tobbat (see TIBET), is about 4 months, and its breadth from the Indian Ocean to the country of Ḳannūj about three months."—*Istakhri*, pp. 6 and 11.

c. 650.—"The name of *T'ien-chu* (India) has gone through various and confused forms. ... Anciently they said *Shin-tu*; whilst some authors called it *Hien-teou*. Now conforming to the true pronunciation one should say **In-tu**."—*Hwen T'sang*, in *Pèl. Bouddh.*, ii. 57.

c. 944.—"For the nonce let us confine ourselves to summary notices concerning the kings of **Sind** and **Hind**. The language of Sind is different from that of **Hind**. ..." *Maṣ'ūdī*, i. 381.

c. 1020.—"**India** (**Al-Hind**) is one of those plains bounded on the south by the Sea of the Indians. Lofty mountains bound it on all the other quarters. Through this plain the waters descending from the mountains are discharged. Moreover, if thou wilt examine this country with thine eyes, if thou wilt regard the rounded and worn stones that are found in the soil, however deep thou mayest dig,—stones which near the mountains, where the rivers roll down violently, are large; but small at a distance from the mountains, where the current slackens; and which become mere sand where the currents are at rest, where the waters sink into the soil, and where the sea is at hand—then thou wilt be tempted to believe that this country was at a former period only a sea which the debris washed down by the torrents hath filled up. ..."—*Al-Birūnī*, in *Reinaud's Extracts, Journ. As.* ser. 4. 1844.

"**Hind** is surrounded on the East by Chín and Máchín, on the West by Sind and Kábul, and on the South by the Sea."—*Ibid.* in *Elliot*, i. 45.

1205.—"The whole country of **Hind**, from Pershaur to the shores of the Ocean, and in the other direction, from Siwistán to the hills of Chín. ..."—*Hasan Nizámī*, in *Elliot*, ii. 236. That is, from Peshawar in the north, to the Indian Ocean in the south; from Sehwan (on the west bank of the Indus) to the mountains on the east dividing from China.

c. 1500.—"**Hodu** quae est **India** extra et intra Gangem."—*Itinera Mundi* (in Hebrew), by *Abr. Peritsol*, in *Hyde, Syntagma Dissertt.*, Oxon, 1767, i. 75.

1553.—"And had Vasco da Gama belonged to a nation so glorious as the Romans he would perchance have added to the style of his family, noble as that is, the surname 'Of India,' since we know that those symbols of honour that a man wins are more glorious than those that he inherits, and that Scipio gloried more in the achievement which gave him the surname of '*Africanus*,' than in the name of Cornelius, which was that of his family."—*Barros*, I. iv. 12.

1572.—Defined, without being named, by Camoens:

"Alem do Indo faz, e aquem do Gange
Hu terreno muy grãde, e assaz famoso,
Que pela parte Austral o mar abrange,
E para o Norte o Emodio cavernoso."
Lusiadas, vii. 17.

Englished by Burton:

"Outside of Indus, inside Ganges, lies
a wide-spread country, famed enough of yore;
northward the peaks of caved Emódus rise,
and southward Ocean doth confine the shore."

1577.—"India is properly called that great Province of Asia, in the whiche great Alexander kepte his warres, and was so named of the ryuer Indus."—*Eden, Hist. of Trauayle*, f. 3*v*.

The *distinct* **Indias**.

c. 650.—"The circumference of the Five Indies is about 90,000 *li*; on three sides it is bounded by a great sea; on the north it is backed by snowy mountains. It is wide at the north and narrow at the south; its figure is that of a half-moon."—*Hwen T'sang*, in *Pèl. Bouddh.*, ii. 58.

1298.—"**India the Greater** is that which extends from Maabar to Kesmacoran (*i.e.* from Coromandel to Mekran), and it contains 13 great kingdoms. ... **India the Lesser** extends from the Province of Champa to Mutfili (*i.e.* from Cochin-China to the Kistna Delta), and contains 8 great Kingdoms. ... Abash (Abyssinia) is a very great province, and you must know that it constitutes the **Middle India**."—*Marco Polo*, Bk. iii. ch. 34, 35.

c. 1328.—"What shall I say? The greatness of this **India** is beyond description. But let this much suffice concerning **India the Greater** and **the Less**. Of **India Tertia** I will say this, that I have not indeed seen its many marvels, not having been there. ..."—*Friar Jordanus*, p. 41.

India Minor, in *Clavijo*, looks as if it were applied to Afghanistan:

1404.—"And this same Thursday that the said Ambassadors arrived at this great River (the Oxus) they crossed to the other side. And the same day ... came in the evening to a great city which is called *Tenmit* (Termedh), and this used to belong to **India Minor**, but now belongs to the empire of Samarkand, having been conquered by Tamurbec."—*Clavijo*, § ciii. (*Markham*, 119).

Indies.

c. 1601.—"He does smile his face into more lines than are in the new map with the augmentation of the **Indiaes**."—*Twelfth Night*, Act iii. sc. 2.

1653.—"I was thirteen times captive and seventeen times sold in the **Indies**."—*Trans. of Pinto*, by *H. Cogan*, p. 1.

1826.—"... Like a French lady of my acquaintance, who had so general a notion of the East, that upon taking leave of her, she enjoined me to get acquainted with a friend of hers, living as she said *quetque part dans* **les Indes**, and whom, to my astonishment, I found residing at the Cape of Good Hope."—*Hajji Baba*, Introd. Epistle, ed. 1835, p. ix.

India of the **Portuguese**.

c. 1567.—"Di qui (Coilan) a Cao Comeri si fanno settanta due miglia, *e qui si finisse la costa* **dell' India**."—*Ces. Federici*, in *Ramusio*, iii. 390.

1598.—"At the ende of the countrey of *Cambaia* beginneth **India** and the lands of Decam and Cuncam ... from the island called Das Vaguas (read *Vaquas*) ... which is the righte coast that in all the East Countries is called **India**. ... Now you must vnderstande that this coast of **India** beginneth at *Daman*, or the Island Das Vaguas, and stretched South and by East, to the Cape of *Comorin*, where it endeth."—*Linschoten*, ch. ix.-x.; [Hak. Soc. i. 62].

c. 1610.—"Il y a grand nombre des Portugais qui demeurent ès ports du cette coste de Bengale ... ils n'osoient retourner en **l'Inde**, pour quelques fautes qu'ils y ont commis."—*Pyrard de Laval*, i. 239; [Hak. Soc. i. 334].

1615.—"Sociorum literis, qui Mogoris Regiam incolunt auditum est in **India** de celeberrimo Regno illo quod Saraceni Cataium vocant."—*Trigautius, De Christianâ Expeditione apud Sinas*, p. 544.

1644.—(Speaking of the Daman district above Bombay.—"The fruits are nearly all the same as those that you get in **India**, and especially many *Mangas* and *Cassaras* (?), which are like chestnuts."—*Bocarro, MS.*

It is remarkable to find the term used, in a similar restricted sense, by the Court of the E.I.C. in writing to Fort St. George. They certainly mean some part of the west coast.

1670.—They desire that **dungarees** may be supplied thence if possible, as "they were not procurable on the **Coast of India**, by reason of the disturbances of Sevajee."—*Notes and Exts.*, Pt. i. 2.

1673.—"The Portugals ... might have subdued **India** by this time, had not we fallen out with them, and given them the first Blow at Ormuz ... they have added some Christians to those formerly converted by St. Thomas, but it is a loud Report to say all **India**."—*Fryer*, 137.

1881.—In a correspondence with Sir R. Morier, we observe the Portuguese Minister of Foreign Affairs calls their Goa Viceroy "The Governor General of **India**."

India of the **Dutch**.

1876.—The Dorian "is common throughout all **India**."—*Filet, Plant-Kunding Woordenboek*, 196.

Indies applied to **America**.

1563.—"And please to tell me ... which is better, this (*Radix Chinae*) or the *guiacão* of our **Indies** as we call them. ..."—*Garcia*, f. 177.

INDIAN. This word in English first occurs, according to Dr. Guest, in the following passage:—

A.D. 433–440.
"Mid israelum ic waes
Mid ebreum and **indeum**, and mid egyptum."
In *Guest's English Rhythms*, ii. 86–87.

But it may be queried whether *indeum* is not here an error for *iudeum*; the converse error to that supposed to have been made in the printing of Othello's death-speech—

"of one whose hand
Like the base *Judean* threw a pearl away."

Indian *used for* **Mahout**.

B.C. ? 116–105.—"And upon the beasts (the elephants) there were strong towers of wood, which covered every one of them, and were girt fast unto them with devices: there were also upon every one two and thirty strong men, that fought upon them, beside the **Indian** that ruled them."—*I. Maccabees*, vi. 37.

B.C. c. 150.—"Of Beasts (*i.e.* elephants) taken with all their **Indians** there were ten; and of all the rest, which had thrown their **Indians**, he got possession after the battle by driving them together."—*Polybius*, Bk. i. ch. 40; see also iii. 46, and xi. 1. It is very curious to see the drivers of *Carthaginian* elephants thus called *Indians*, though it may be presumed that this is only a Greek application of the term, not a Carthaginian use.

B.C. c. 20.—"Tertio die ... ad Thabusion castellum imminens fluvio Indo ventum est; cui fecerat nomen **Indus** ab elephanto dejectus."—*Livy*, Bk. xxxviii. 14. This Indus or "Indian" river, named after the Mahout thrown into it by his elephant, was somewhere on the borders of Phrygia.

A.D: c. 210.—"Along with this elephant was brought up a female one called Nikaia. And the wife of their **Indian** being near death placed her child of 30 days old beside this one. And when the woman died a certain marvellous attachment grew up of the Beast towards the child. ..."—*Athenaeus*, xiii. ch. 8.

Indian, for *Anglo-Indian*.

1816.—"... our best **Indians**. In the idleness and obscurity of home they look back with fondness to the country where they have been useful and distinguished, like the ghosts of Homer's heroes, who prefer the exertions of a labourer on the earth to all the listless enjoyments of Elysium."—*Elphinstone*, in *Life*, i. 367.

***INDIGO**, s. The plant *Indigofera tinctoria*, L. (N.O. *Leguminosae*), and the dark blue dye made from it. Greek Ἰνδικὸν. This word appears from Hippocrates to have been applied in his time to *pepper*. It is also applied by Dioscorides to the mineral substance (a variety of the red oxide of iron) called Indian red (*F. Adams*, Appendix to *Dunbar's Lexicon*). [*Liddell & Scott* call it "a dark-blue dye, indigo." The dye was used in Egyptian mummy-cloths (*Wilkinson*, *Ancient Egypt*, ed. 1878, ii. 163).]

A.D. c. 60.—"Of that which is called Ἰνδικὸν one kind is produced spontaneously, being as it were a scum thrown out by the Indian reeds; but that used for dyeing is a purple efflorescence which floats on the brazen cauldrons, which the craftsmen skim off and dry. That is deemed best which is blue in colour, succulent, and smooth to the touch."—*Dioscorides*, v. cap. 107.

c. 70.—"After this ... **Indico** (*Indicum*) is a colour most esteemed; out of India it commeth; whereupon it tooke the name; and it is nothing els but a slimie mud cleaving to the foame that gathereth about canes and reeds: whiles it is punned or ground, it looketh blacke; but being dissolved it yeeldeth a woonderfull lovely mixture of purple and azur ... **Indico** is valued at 20 denarii the pound. In physicke there is use of this **Indico**; for it doth assuage swellings that doe stretch the skin."—*Plinie*, by *Ph. Holland*, ii. 531.

c. 80–90.—"This river (*Sinthus, i.e.* Indus) has 7 mouths ... and it has none of them navigable except the middle one only, on which there is a coast mart called Barbaricon. ... The articles imported into this mart are. ... On the other hand there are exported *Costus, Bdellium* ... and *Indian Black* (Ἰνδικὸν μέλαν, *i.e.* **Indigo**)."—*Periplus*, 38, 39.

1298.—(At Coilum) "They have also abundance of very fine **indigo** (*ynde*). This is made of a certain herb which is gathered and [after the roots have been removed] is put into great vessels upon which they pour water, and then leave it till the whole of the plant is decomposed. ..."—*Marco Polo*, Bk. iii. ch. 22.

1584.—"**Indico** from Zindi and Cambaia."—*Barrett*, in *Hakl.* ii. 413.

[1605-6.—"... for all which we shall buie Ryse, **Indico**, Lapes Bezar which theare in aboundance are to be hadd."—*Birdwood, First Letter Book*, 77.

[1609.—"... to buy such Comodities as they shall finde there as **Indico**, of Laher (Lahore), here worth viijs the pounde *Serchis* and the best *Belondri*. ..."—*Ibid.* 287. *Serchis* is Sarkhej, the *Sercaze* of Forbes (*Or. Mem.*, 2nd ed. ii. 204) near Ahmadābād: Sir G. Birdwood with some hesitation identifies *Belondri* with Valabhi, 20 m. N.W. of Bhāvnagar.

[1610.—"*Anil* or **Indigue**, which is a violet-blue dye."—*Pyrard de Laval*, Hak. Soc. ii. 246.]

1610.—"In the country thereabouts is made some **Indigo**."—*Sir H. Middleton*, in *Purchas*, i. 259.

[1616.—"**Indigo** is made thus. In the prime June they sow it, which the rains bring up about the prime September: this they cut and it is called the *Newty* (H. *naudhā*, 'a young plant'), formerly mentioned, and is a good sort. Next year it sprouts again in the prime August, which they cut and is the best **Indigo**, called *Jerry* (H. *jaṛī*, 'growing from the root (*jaṛ*).'"—*Foster, Letters*, iv. 241.]

c. 1670.—Tavernier gives a detailed account of the manufacture as it was in his time. "They that sift this **Indigo** must be careful to keep a Linnen-cloath before their faces, and that their nostrils be well stopt. ... Yet ... they that have sifted **Indigo** for 9 or 10 days shall spit nothing but blew for a good while together. Once I laid an egg in the morning among the sifters, and when I came to break it in the evening it was all blew within."—*E.T.* ii. 128-9; [ed. *Ball*, ii. 11].

We have no conception what is meant by the following singular (apparently sarcastic) entry in the *Indian Vocabulary*:—

1788.—"**Indergo**—a drug of no estimation that grows wild in the woods." [This is H. *indarjau*, Skt. *indra-yava*, "barley of Indra," the *Wrightia tinctoria*, from the leaves of which a sort of indigo is made. See *Watt, Econ. Dict.* VI. pt. iv. 316. "**Inderjò** of the species of warm bitters."—*Halhed, Code*, ed. 1781, p. 9.]

1881.—"Découvertes et Inventions.—Décidément le cabinet Gladstone est poursuivi par la malechance. Voici un savant chimiste de Munich qui vient de trouver le moyen se préparer artificiellement et à très bon marché le bleu **Indigo**. Cette découverte peut amener la ruine du gouvernement des Indes anglaises, qui est déjà menacé de la banqueroute. **L'indigo**, en effet, est le principal article de commerce des Indes (!); dans l'Allemagne, seulement, on en importe par an pour plus de cent cinquante millions de francs."—*Havre Commercial Paper*, quoted in *Pioneer Mail*, Feb. 3.

INTERLOPER, s. One in former days who traded without the license, or outside the service, of a company (such as the E.I.C.) which had a charter of monopoly. The etymology of the word remains obscure. It *looks* like Dutch, but intelligent Dutch friends have sought in vain for a Dutch original. *Onderloopen*, the nearest word we can find, means 'to be inundated.' The hybrid etymology given by Bailey, though allowed by Skeat, seems hardly possible. Perhaps it is an English corruption from *ontloopen*, 'to evade, escape, run away from.' [The *N.E.D.* without hesitation gives *interlope*, a form of *leap*. Skeat, in his *Concise Dict.*, 2nd ed., agrees, and quotes Low Germ. and Dutch *enterloper*, 'a runner between.']

1627.—"**Interlopers** in trade, ¶ Attur Acad. pa. 54."—*Minsheu.* (What is the meaning of the reference?) [It refers to "The *Atturneyes Academie*" by Thomas Powell or Powel, for which see 9 ser. *Notes and Queries*, vii. 198, 392].

1680.—"The commissions relating to the **Interloper**, or private trader, being considered, it is resolved that a notice be fixed up warning all the Inhabitants of the Towne, not, directly or indirectly, to trade, negotiate, aid, assist, countenance, or hold any correspondence, with Captain William Alley or any person belonging to him or his ship without the license of the Honorable Company. Whoever shall offend herein shall answeare it at their Perill."—*Notes and Exts.*, Pt. iii. 29.

1681.—"The Shippe Expectation, Capt. Ally Coñandr, an **Interloper**, arrived in ye Downes from Porto Novo."—*Hedges, Diary*, Jan. 4; [Hak. Soc. i. 15].

[1682.—"The Agent having notice of an **Interloper** lying in Titticorin Bay, immediately sent for ye Councell to consult about it. ..."—*Pringle, Diary of Ft. St. Geo.* 1st ser. i. 69.]

"The Spirit of Commerce, which sees its drifts with eagle's eyes, formed associations at the risque of trying the consequence at law ... since the statutes did not authorize the Company to seize or stop the ships of these adventurers, whom they called **Interlopers**."—*Orme's Fragments*, 127.

1683.—"If God gives me life to get this *Phirmaund* into my possession, ye Honble. Compy. shall never more be much troubled with **Interlopers**."—*Hedges, Diary*, Jan. 6; [Hak. Soc. i. 62].

"*May* 28. About 9 this morning Mr. Littleton, Mr. Nedham, and Mr. Douglass came to y[e] factory, and being sent for, were asked 'Whether they did now, or ever intended, directly or indirectly, to trade with any **Interlopers** that shall arrive in the Bay of Bengall?'

"Mr. Littleton answered that, 'he did not, nor ever intended to trade with any **Interloper**.'

"Mr. Nedham answered, 'that at present he did not, and that he came to gett money, and if any such offer should happen, he would not refuse it.'

"Mr. Douglass answered, he did not, nor ever intended to trade with them; but he said 'what Estate he should gett here he would not scruple to send it home upon any **Interloper**.'

"And having given their respective answers they were dismist."—*Ibid*. Hak. Soc. i. 90–91.

1694.—"Whether y[e] souldiers lately sent up hath created any jealousye in y[e] **Interlop**[rs]: or their own Actions or guilt I know not, but they are so cautious y[t] every 2 or 3 bales y[t] are packt they immediately send on board."—MS. Letter from *Edwd. Hern* at *Hugley* to the Rt. Worship[ll] *Charles Eyre Esq. Agent for Affaires* of the *Rt. Honble. East India Comp*[a]. in *Bengall*, &c[a]. (9th Sept.). *MS. Record in India Office*.

1719.—"... their business in the *South Seas* was to sweep those coasts clear of the *French* **interlopers**, which they did very effectually."—*Shelvocke's Voyage*, 29.

"I wish you would explain yourself; I cannot imagine what reason I have to be afraid of any of the Company's ships, or Dutch ships, I am no **interloper**."—*Robinson Crusoe*, Pt. ii.

1730.—"To **Interlope** [of *inter*, L. between, and loopen, *Du.* to run, q. d. to run in between, and intercept the Commerce of others], to trade without proper Authority, or interfere with a Company in Commerce."—*Bailey's English Dict.* s.v.

1760.—"**Enterlooper**. Terme de Commerce de Mer, fort en usage parmi les Compagnies des Pays du Nord, comme l'Angleterre, la Hollande, Hambourg, le Danemark, &c. Il signifie un vaisseau d'un particulier qui pratique et fréquente les Côtes, et les Havres ou Ports de Mer éloignés, pour y faire un commerce clandestin, au préjudice des Compagnies qui sont autorisées elles seules à le faire dans ces mêmes lieux. ... Ce mot se prononce comme s'il étoit écrit **Eintrelopre**. Il est emprunté de l'Anglois, de *enter* qui signifie entrer et entreprendre, et de *Looper*, Courreur."—*Savary des Bruslons, Dict. Univ. de Commerce*, Nouv. ed., Copenhague, a.v.

c. 1812.—"The fault lies in the clause which gives the Company power to send home **interlopers** ... and is just as reasonable as one which should forbid all the people of England, except a select few, to look at the moon."—*Letter of Dr. Carey*, in *William Carey*, by James Culross, D.D., 1881, p. 165.

I-SAY. The Chinese mob used to call the English soldiers *A'says* or *Isays*, from the frequency of this apostrophe in their mouths. (The French gamins, it is said, do the same at Boulogne.) At Amoy the Chinese used to call out after foreigners **Akee! Akee!** a tradition from the Portuguese *Aqui!* 'Here!' In Java the French are called by the natives *Orang* **deedong**, *i.e.* the *dîtes-donc* people. (See *Fortune's Two Visits to the Tea Countries*, 1853, p. 52; and *Notes and Queries in China and Japan*, ii. 175.)

[1863.—"The Sepoys were ... invariably called '**Achas**.' *Acka* or good is the constantly recurring answer of a Sepoy when spoken to. ..."—*Fisher, Three Years in China*, 146.]

[**ISLAM**, s. Infn. of Ar. *salm*, 'to be or become safe'; the word generally used by Mahommedans for their religion.

[1616.—"Dated in Achen 1025 according to the rate of **Slam**."—*Foster, Letters*, iv. 125.

[1617.—"I demanded the debts ... one [of the debtors] for the valew of 110 r[ials] is termed Slam."—*Letter of E. Young*, from Jacatra, Oct. 3, I.O. Records: O.C. No. 541.]

ISTUBBUL, s. This usual Hind. word for 'stable' may naturally be imagined to be a corruption of the English word. But it is really Ar. *iṣṭabl*, though that no doubt came in old times from the Latin *stabulum* through some Byzantine Greek form.

J

JACK, s. Short for **Jack-Sepoy**; in former days a familiar style for the native soldier; kindly, rather than otherwise.

1853.—"... he should be leading the **Jacks**."—*Oakfield*, ii. 66.

JACK, s. The tree called by botanists *Artocarpus integrifolia*, L. fil., and its fruit. The name, says Drury, is "a corruption of the

Skt. word *Tchackka*, which means the fruit of the tree" (*Useful Plants*, p. 55). There is, however, no such Skt. word; the Skt. names are *Kantaka*, *Phala*, *Panasa*, and *Phalasa*. [But the Malayāl. *chakka* is from the Skt. *chakra*, 'round.'] Rheede rightly gives *Tsjaka* (*chăkka*) as the Malayālam name, and from this no doubt the Portuguese took *jaca* and handed it on to us. "They call it," says Garcia Orta, "in Malavar *jacas*, in Canarese and Guzerati *panas*" (f. 111). "The Tamil form is *sākkei*, the meaning of which, as may be adduced from various uses to which the word is put in Tamil, is 'the fruit abounding in rind and refuse.'" (*Letter from Bp. Caldwell*.)

We can hardly doubt that this is the fruit of which Pliny writes: "Major alia pomo et suavitate praecellentior; quo sapientiores Indorum vivunt. (Folium alas avium imitatur longitudine trium cubitorum, latitudine duum). *Fructum e cortice mittit admirabilem succi dulcedine; ut uno quaternos satiet*. Arbori nomen *palae*, pomo *arienae*; plurima est in Sydracis, expeditionum Alexandri termino. Est et alia similis huic; dulcior pomo; sed interaneorum valetudini infesta" (*Hist. Nat.* xii. 12). Thus rendered, not too faithfully, by Philemon Holland: "Another tree there is in India, greater yet than the former; bearing a fruit much fairer, bigger, and sweeter than the figs aforesaid; and whereof the Indian Sages and Philosophers do ordinarily live. The leaf resembleth birds' wings, carrying three cubits in length, and two in breadth. The fruit it putteth forth at the bark, having within it a wonderfull pleasant juice: insomuch as one of them is sufficient to give four men a competent and full refection. The tree's name is *Pala*, and the fruit is called *Ariena*. Great plenty of them is in the country of the Sydraci, the utmost limit of *Alexander* the Great his expeditions and voyages. And yet there is another tree much like to this, and beareth a fruit more delectable than this *Ariena*, albeit the guts in a man's belly it wringeth and breeds the bloudie flix" (i. 361).

Strange to say, the fruit thus described has been generally identified with the plantain: so generally that (we presume) the Linnaean name of the plantain *Musa sapientum*, was founded upon the interpretation of this passage. (It was, I find, the excellent Rumphius who originated the erroneous identification of the *ariena* with the plantain). Lassen, at first hesitatingly (i. 262), and then more positively (ii. 678), adopts this interpretation, and seeks *ariena* in the Skt. *vāraṇa*. The shrewder Gildemeister does the like, for he, *sans phrase*, uses *arienae* as Latin for 'plantains.' Ritter, too, accepts it, and is not staggered even by the *uno quaternos satiet*. Humboldt, quoth he, often saw Indians make their meal with a very little manioc and three bananas of the big kind (*Platano-arton*). Still less sufficed the Indian Brahmins (*sapientes*), when one fruit was enough for four of them (v. 876, 877). Bless the venerable Prince of Geographers! Would one *Kartoffel*, even "of the big kind," make a dinner for four German Professors? Just as little would one plantain suffice four Indian Sages.

The words which we have italicised in the passage from Pliny are quite enough to show that the *jack* is intended; the fruit growing *e cortice* (*i.e.* piercing the bark of the stem, not pendent from twigs like other fruit), the sweetness, the monstrous size, are in combination infallible. And as regards its being the fruit of the sages, we may observe that the *jack* fruit is at this day in Travancore one of the staples of life. But that Pliny, after his manner, has jumbled things, is also manifest. The first two clauses of his description (*Major alia*, &c.; *Folium alas*, &c.) are found in Theophrastus, but apply to *two different trees*. Hence we get rid of the puzzle about the big leaves, which led scholars astray after plantains, and originated *Musa sapientum*. And it is clear from Theophrastus that the fruit which caused dysentery in the Macedonian army was yet another. So Pliny has rolled three plants into one. Here are the passages of Theophrastus:—

"(1) And there is another tree which is both itself a tree of great size, and produces a fruit that is wonderfully big and sweet. This is used for food by the Indian Sages, who wear no clothes. (2) And there is yet another which has the leaf of a very long shape, and resembling the wings of birds, and this they set upon helmets; the length is about two cubits. ... (3) There is another tree the fruit of which is long, and not straight but crooked, and sweet to the taste. But this gives rise to colic and dysentery ("*Ἄλλο τέ ἐστιν οὗ ὁ καρπὸς μακρὸς καὶ οὐκ εὐθὺς ἀλλὰ σκολιὸς, ἐσθιόμενος δὲ γλυκύς. Οὗτος ἐν τῇ κοιλίᾳ δηγμὸν ποιεῖ καὶ δυσεντέριαν* ...") wherefore Alexander published a general order against eating it."—(*Hist. Plant.* iv. 4–5).

It is plain that Pliny and Theophrastus

were using the same authority, but neither copying the whole of what he found in it.

The second tree, whose leaves were like birds' wings and were used to fix upon helmets, is hard to identify. The first was, when we combine the additional characters quoted by Pliny but omitted by Theophrastus, certainly the *jack*; the third was, we suspect, the **mango** (q.v.). The terms long and crooked would, perhaps, answer better to the plantain, but hardly the unwholesome effect. As regards the *uno quaternos satiet*, compare Friar Jordanus below, on the *jack*: "Sufficiet circiter pro quinque personis." Indeed the whole of the Friar's account is worth comparing with Pliny's. Pliny says that it took four men *to eat* a *jack*, Jordanus says five. But an Englishman who had a plantation in Central Java told one of the present writers that he once cut a *jack* on his ground which took three men—not to eat—but to carry!

As regards the names given by Pliny it is hard to say anything to the purpose, because we do not know to which of the three trees jumbled together the names really applied. If *pala* really applied to the *jack*, possibly it may be the Skt. *phalasa*, or *panasa*. Or it may be merely *p'hala*, 'a fruit,' and the passage would then be a comical illustration of the persistence of Indian habits of mind. For a stranger in India, on asking the question, 'What on earth is that?' as he well might on his first sight of a *jack*-tree with its fruit, would at the present day almost certainly receive for answer: *'Phal hai khudāwand!'*—'It is a fruit, my lord!' *Ariena* looks like *hiraṇya*, 'golden,' which *might* be an epithet of the *jack*, but we find no such specific application of the word.

Omitting Theophrastus and Pliny, the oldest foreign description of the *jack* that we find is that by Hwen T'sang, who met with it in Bengal:

c. A.D. 650.—"Although the fruit of the *pan-wa-so* (*panasa*) is gathered in great quantities, it is held in high esteem. These fruits are as big as a pumpkin; when ripe they are of a reddish yellow. Split in two they disclose inside a quantity of little fruits as big as crane's eggs; and when these are broken there exudes a juice of reddish-yellow colour and delicious flavour. Sometimes the fruit hangs on the branches, as with other trees; but sometimes it grows from the roots, like the *fo-ling* (*Radix Chinae*), which is found under the ground."—*Julien*, iii. 75.

c. 1328.—"There are some trees that bear a very big fruit called **chaqui**; and the fruit is of such size that one is enough for about five persons. There is another tree that has a fruit like that just named, and it is called *Bloqui* [a corruption of *Malayāl. varikka*, 'superior fruit'], quite as big and as sweet, but not of the same species. These fruits never grow upon the twigs, for these are not able to bear their weight, but only from the main branches, and even from the trunk of the tree itself, down to the very roots."—*Friar Jordanus*, 13–14.

A unique MS. of the travels of Friar Odoric, in the Palatine Library at Florence, contains the following curious passage:—

c. 1330.—"And there be also trees which produce fruits so big that two will be a load for a strong man. And when they are eaten you must oil your hands and your mouth; they are of a fragrant odour and very savoury; the fruit is called *chabassi*." The name is probably corrupt (perhaps *chacassi*?). But the passage about oiling the hands and lips is aptly elucidated by the description in Baber's *Memoirs* (see below), a description matchless in its way, and which falls off sadly in the new translation by M. Pavet de Courteille, which quite omits the "haggises."

c. 1335.—"The **Shakī** and *Barkī*. This name is given to certain trees which live to a great age. Their leaves are like those of the walnut, and the fruit grows direct out of the stem of the tree. The fruits borne nearest to the ground are the *barkī*; they are sweeter and better-flavoured than the **Shakī** ..." etc. (much to the same effect as before).—*Ibn Batuta*, iii. 127; see also iv. 228.

c. 1350.—"There is again another wonderful tree called **Chake**-*Baruke*, as big as an oak. Its fruit is produced from the trunk, and not from the branches, and is something marvellous to see, being as big as a great lamb, or a child of three years old. It has a hard rind like that of our pine-cones, so that you have to cut it open with a hatchet; inside it has a pulp of surpassing flavour, with the sweetness of honey, and of the best Italian melon; and this also contains some 500 chestnuts of like flavour, which are capital eating when roasted."—*John de' Marignolli*, in *Cathay*, &c., 363.

c. 1440.—"There is a tree commonly found, the trunk of which bears a fruit resembling a pine-cone, but so big that a man can hardly lift it; the rind is green and hard, but still yields to the pressure of the finger. Inside there are some 250 or 300 pippins, as big as figs, very sweet in taste, and contained in separate membranes. These have each a kernel within, of a windy quality, of the consistence and taste of chestnuts, and which are roasted like chestnuts. And when cast among embers (to roast), unless you make a cut in them they will explode and jump out. The outer rind of the fruit is given to cattle. Sometimes the fruit is also found growing from the roots of the tree underground, and these fruits excel the others in flavour, wherefore they are sent as presents to kings and petty princes. These (moreover) have no kernels inside them. The tree itself resembles a large fig-tree, and the leaves are cut into fingers like the hand. The wood resembles box, and so it is esteemed for many uses. The name of the tree is **Cachi**" (*i.e.* *Çachi* or **Tzacchi**).—*Nicolo de' Conti.*

The description of the leaves ... "*foliis da modum palmi intercisis*"—is the only slip in this admirable description. Conti must, in memory, have confounded the Jack with its congener the bread-fruit (*Artocarpus incisa* or *incisifolia*). We have translated from Poggio's Latin, as the version by Mr. Winter Jones in *India in the XVth Century* is far from accurate.

1530.—"Another is the *kadhil.* This has a very bad look and flavour (odour?). It looks like a sheep's stomach stuffed and made into a haggis. It has a sweet sickly taste. Within it are stones like a filbert. ... The fruit is very adhesive, and on account of this adhesive quality many rub their mouths with oil before eating them. They grow not only from the branches and trunk, but from its root. You would say that the tree was all hung round with haggises!"—*Leyden and Erskine's Baber*, 325. Here *kadhil* represents the Hind. name *kaṭhal.* The practice of oiling the lips on account of the "adhesive quality" (or as modern mortals would call it, 'stickiness') of the jack, is still usual among natives, and is the cause of a proverb on premature precautions: *Gāch'h meṅ Kaṭhal, honṭh meṅ tel!* "You have oiled your lips while the jack still hangs on the tree!" We may observe that the call of the Indian cuckoo is in some of the Gangetic districts rendered by the natives as *Kaṭhal pakkā! Kaṭhal pakkā! i.e.* "Jack's ripe," the bird appearing at that season.

[1547.—"I consider it right to make over to them in perpetuity ... one palm grove and an area for planting certain mango trees and **jack** trees (mangueiras e **jaqueiras**) situate in the village of Calangute. ..."—*Archiv. Port. Orient.*, fasc. 5, No. 88.]

c. 1590.—"In Sircar Hajypoor there are plenty of the fruits called *Kathul* and *Budhul*; some of the first are so large as to be too heavy for one man to carry."—*Gladwin's Ayeen*, ii. 25. In Blochmann's ed. of the Persian text he reads *barhal*, [and so in Jarrett's trans. (ii. 152),] which is a Hind. name for the *Artocarpus Lakoocha* of Roxb.

1563.—"*R.* What fruit is that which is as big as the largest (coco) nuts?

"*O.* You just now ate the *chestnuts* from inside of it, and you said that roasted they were like real chestnuts. Now you shall eat the envelopes of these ...,

"*R.* They taste like a melon; but not so good as the better melons.

"*O.* True. And owing to their viscous nature they are ill to digest; or say rather they are not digested at all, and often issue from the body quite unchanged. I don't much use them. They are called in Malavar **jacas**; in Canarin and Guzerati *panás*. ... The tree is a great and tall one; and the fruits grow from the wood of the stem, right up to it, and not on the branches like other fruits."—*Garcia*, f. 111.

[1598.—"A certain fruit that in Malabar is called **iaca**, in Canara and Gusurate *Panar* and *Panasa*, by the Arabians *Panax*, by the Persians *Fanax*."—*Linschoten*, Hak. Soc. ii. 20.

[c. 1610.—"The **Jaques** is a tree of the height of a chestnut."—*Pyrard de Laval*, Hak. Soc. ii. 366.

[1623.—"We had **Ziacche**, a fruit very rare at this time."—*P. della Valle*, Hak. Soc. ii. 264.]

1673.—"Without the town (Madras) grows their Rice ... **Jawks**, a Coat of Armour over it, like an Hedg-hog's, guards its weighty Fruit."—*Fryer*, 40.

1810.—"The **jack**-wood ... at first yellow, becomes on exposure to the air of the colour of mahogany, and is of as fine a grain."—*Maria Graham*, 101.

1878.—"The monstrous **jack** that in its eccentric bulk contains a whole magazine of tastes and smells."—*Ph. Robinson, In My Indian Garden*, 49–50.

It will be observed that the older authorities mention two varieties of the fruit by the names of *shakī* and *barkī*, or modifications of these, different kinds according to Jordanus, only from different parts of the tree according to Ibn Batuta. P. Vincenzo Maria (1672) also distinguishes two kinds, one of which he calls **Giacha** *Barca*, the other **Giacha** *papa* or *girasole*. And Rheede, the great authority on Malabar plants, says (iii. 9):

"Of this tree, however, they reckon more than 30 varieties, distinguished by the quality of their fruit, but all may be reduced to two kinds; the fruit of one kind distinguished by plump and succulent pulp of delicious honey flavour, being the *varaka;* that of the other, filled with softer and more flabby pulp of inferior flavour, being the *Tsjakapa.*"

More modern writers seem to have less perception in such matters than the old travellers, who entered more fully and sympathetically into native tastes. Drury says, however, "There are several varieties, but what is called the Honey-jack is by far the sweetest and best."

"He that desireth to see more hereof let him reade Ludovicus Romanus, in his fifth Booke and fifteene Chapter of his Navigaciouns, and Christopherus a Costa in his cap. of **Iaca**, and Gracia ab Horto, in the Second Booke and fourth Chapter," saith the learned Paludanus ... And if there be any-body so unreasonable, so say we too—by all means let him do so! [A part of this article is derived from the notes to Jordanus by one of the present writers. We may also add, in aid of such further investigation, that Paludanus is the Latinised name of v.d. Broecke, the commentator on Linschoten. "Ludovicus Romanus" is our old friend Varthema, and "Gracia ab Horto" is Garcia De Orta.]

JACKAL, s. The *Canis aureus*, L., seldom seen in the daytime, unless it be fighting with the vultures for carrion, but in shrieking multitudes, or rather what seem multitudes from the noise they make, entering the precincts of villages, towns, of Calcutta itself, after dark, and startling the newcomer with their hideous yells. Our word is not apparently Anglo-Indian, being taken from the Turkish *chaḳāl*. But the Pers. *shaghāl* is close, and Skt. *srigāla*, 'the howler,' is probably the first form. The common Hind. word is *gīdar*, ['the greedy one,' Skt. *gṛidh*]. The jackal takes the place of the fox as the object of hunting 'meets' in India; the indigenous fox being too small for sport.

1554.—"Non procul inde audio magnum clamorem et velut hominum irridentium insultantiumque voces. Interrogo quid sit; ... narrant mihi ululatum esse bestiarum, quas Turcao **Ciacales** vocant. ..."—*Busbeq. Epist.* i. p. 78.

1615.—"The inhabitants do nightly house their goates and sheepe for feare of **Iaccals** (in my opinion no other than Foxes), whereof an infinite number do lurke in the obscure vaults."—*Sandys, Relation*, &c., 205.

1616.—"... those **jackalls** seem to be wild Doggs, who in great companies run up and down in the silent night, much disquieting the peace thereof, by their most hideous noyse."—*Terry*, ed. 1665, p. 371.

1653.—"Le **schekal** est vn espèce de chien sauvage, lequel demeure tout le jour en terre, et sort la nuit criant trois ou quatre fois à certaines heures."—*De la Boullaye-le-Gouz*, ed. 1657, p. 254.

1672:—"There is yet another kind of beast which they call **Jackhalz**; they are horribly greedy of man's flesh, so the inhabitants beset the graves of their dead with heavy stones."—*Baldaeus* (Germ. ed.), 422.

1673.—"An Hellish concert of **Jackals** (a kind of Fox)."—*Fryer*, 53.

1681.—"For here are many **Jackalls**, which catch their Henes, some *Tigres* that destroy their Cattle; but the greatest of all is the King; whose endeavour is to keep them poor and in want."—*Knox, Ceylon*, 87. On p. 20 he writes *Jacols*.

1711.—"**Jackcalls** are remarkable for Howling in the Night; one alone making as much noise as three or four Cur Dogs, and in different Notes, as if there were half a Dozen of them got together."—*Lockyer*, 382.

1810.—Colebrooke (*Essays*, ii. 109, [*Life*, 155]) spells **shakal**. But *Jackal* was already English.

c. 1816.—

"The **jackal's** troop, in gather'd cry,
Bayed from afar, complainingly."
Siege of Corinth, xxxiii.

1880.—"The mention of **Jackal**-hunting in one of the letters (of Lord Minto) may remind some Anglo-Indians still living, of the days when the Calcutta hounds used to throw off at gun-fire."—*Sat. Rev.* Feb. 14.

JADOO, s. Hind. from Pers. *jādū*, Skt. *yātu*; conjuring, magic, hocus-pocus.

[1826.—"'Pray, sir,' said the barber, 'is that Sanscrit, or what language?' 'May be it is **jadoo**,' I replied, in a solemn and deep voice."—*Pandurang Hari*, ed. 1873, i. 127.]

***JADOOGUR**, s. Properly Hind. *jādū-ghar*, 'conjuring-house' (see the last). The term commonly applied by natives to a Freemasons' Lodge, when there is one, at an English station. On the Bombay side it is also called *Shaitān khāna* (see Burton's *Sind Revisited*), a name consonant to the ideas of an Italian priest who intimated to one of the present writers that he had heard the raising of the devil was practised at Masonic meetings, and asked his friend's opinion as to the fact. In S. India the Lodge is called *Talai-vĕṭṭa-Kovil*, 'Cut-head Temple,' because part of the rite of initiation is supposed to consist in the candidate's head being cut off and put on again.

JAGGERY, s. Coarse brown (or almost black) sugar, made from the sap of various palms. The wild date tree (*Phoenix sylvestris*, Roxb.), Hind. *khajūr*, is that which chiefly supplies palm-sugar in Guzerat and

Coromandel, and almost alone in Bengal. But the palmyra, the caryota, and the cocopalm all give it; the first as the staple of Tinnevelly and northern Ceylon; the second chiefly in southern Ceylon, where it is known to Europeans as the **Jaggery** *Palm* (*kitūl* of natives); the third is much drawn for **toddy** (q.v.) in the coast districts of Western India, and this is occasionally boiled for sugar. Jaggery is usually made in the form of small round cakes. Great quantities are produced in Tinnevelly, where the cakes used to pass as a kind of currency (as cakes of salt used to pass in parts of Africa, and in Western China), and do even yet to some small extent. In Bombay all rough unrefined sugar-stuff is known by this name; and it is the title under which all kinds of half-prepared sugar is classified in the tariff of the Railways there. The word *jaggery* is only another form of **sugar** (q.v.), being like it a corr. of the Skt. *śarkarā*, Konkani *sakkarā*, [Malayāl. *chakkarā*, whence it passed into Port. *jagara*, *jagra*].

1516.—"Sugar of palms, which they call **xagara**."—*Barbosa*, 59.

1553.—Exports from the Maldives "also of fish-oil, coco-nuts, and **jágara**, which is made from these after the manner of sugar."—*Barros*, Dec. III. liv. iii. cap. 7.

1561.—"**Jagre**, which is sugar of palm-trees."—*Correa*, *Lendas*, i. 2, 592.

1563.—"And after they have drawn this pot of *çura*, if the tree gives much they draw another, of which they make sugar, prepared either by sun or fire, and this they call **jagra**."—*Garcia*, f. 67.

c. 1567.—"There come every yeere from Cochin and from Cananor tenne or fifteene great Shippes (to Chaul) laden with great nuts ... and with sugar made of the selfe same nuts called **Giagra**."—*Caesar Frederike*, in *Hakl.* ii. 344.

1598.—"Of the aforesaid *sura* they likewise make sugar, which is called **Iagra**; they seeth the water, and set it in the sun, whereof it becometh sugar, but it is little esteemed, because it is of a browne colour."—*Linschoten*, 102; [Hak. Soc. ii. 49].

1616.—"Some small quantity of wine, but not common, is made among them; they call it *Raak* (see ARRACK), distilled from Sugar, and a spicy rinde of a tree called **Jagra**."—*Terry*, ed. 1665, p. 365.

1727.—"The Produce of the Samorin's Country is ... Cocoa-Nut, and that tree produceth **Jaggery**, a kind of sugar, and Copera (see COPRAH), or the kernels of the Nut dried."—*A. Hamilton*, i. 306; [ed. 1744, i. 308].

c. 1750-60.—"Arrack, a coarse sort of sugar called **Jagree**, and vinegar are also extracted from it" (coco-palm).—*Grose*, i. 47.

1807.—"The *Tari* or fermented juice, and the **Jagory** or inspissated juice of the Palmira tree ... are in this country more esteemed than those of the wild date, which is contrary to the opinion of the Bengalese."—*F. Buchanan*, *Mysore*, &c., i. 5.

1860.—"In this state it is sold as **jaggery** in the bazaars, at about three farthings per pound."—*Tennent's Ceylon*, iii. 524.

***JAGHEER, JAGHIRE**, s. Pers. *jāgīr*, lit. 'place-holding.' A hereditary assignment of land and of its rent as annuity.

[c. 1590.—"*Farmán-i-zabíts* are issued for ... appointments to **jágírs**, without military service."—*Āīn*, i. 261.

[1617.—"Hee quittes diuers small **Jaggers** to the King."—*Sir T. Roe*, Hak. Soc. ii. 449.]

c. 1666.—"... Not to speak of what they finger out of the Pay of every Horse-man, and of the number of the Horses; which certainly amounts to very considerable Pensions, especially if they can obtain good **Jah-ghirs**, that is, good Lands for their Pensions."—*Bernier*, E.T. 66; [ed. *Constable*, 213].

1673.—"It (Surat) has for its Maintenance the Income of six Villages; over which the Governor sometimes presides, sometimes not, being in the **Jaggea**, or diocese of another."—*Fryer*, 120.

"**Jageah**, an Annuity."—*Ibid. Index*, vi.

1768.—"I say, Madam, I know nothing of books; and yet I believe upon a land-carriage fishery, a stamp act, or a **jaghire**, I can talk my two hours without feeling the want of them."—Mr. Lofty, in *The Good-Natured Man*, Act ii.

1778.—"Should it be more agreeable to the parties, Sir Matthew will settle upon Sir John and his Lady, for their joint lives, a **jagghire**.

"*Sir John*.—A **Jagghire**?

"*Thomas*.—The term is Indian, and means an annual Income."—*Foote*, *The Nabob*, i. 1.

We believe the traditional stage pronunciation in these passages is **Jag Hire** (assonant in both syllables to *Quag Mire*); and this is also the pronunciation given in some dictionaries.

1778.—"...**Jaghires**, which were always rents arising from lands."—*Orme*, ed. 1803, ii. 52.

1809.—"He was nominally in possession of a larger **jaghire**."—*Ld. Valentia*, i. 401.

A territory adjoining Fort St. George was long known as the **Jaghire**, or *the Company's* **Jaghire**, and is often so mentioned in histories of the 18th century. This territory, granted to the Company by the Nabob of Arcot in 1750 and

1763, nearly answers to the former Collectorate of Chengalput and present Collectorate of Madras.

[In the following the reference is to the *Jirgah* or tribal council of the Pathan tribes on the N.W. frontier.

[1900.—"No doubt upon the occasion of Lord Curzon's introduction to the Waziris and the Mohmunds, he will inform their **Jagirs** that he has long since written a book about them."—*Contemporary Rev.* Aug. p. 282.]

JAGHEERDAR, s. P.—H. *jāgīrdār*, the holder of a **jagheer**.

[1813.—"... in the Mahratta empire the principal **Jaghiredars**, or nobles, appear in the field. ..."—*Forbes, Or. Mem.* 2nd ed. i. 328.]

1826.—"The Resident, many officers, men of rank ... **jagheerdars**, Brahmins, and Pundits, were present, assembled round my father."—*Pandurang Hari*, 389; [ed. 1873, ii. 259].

1883.—"The Sikhs administered the country by means of **jagheerdars**, and paid them by their **jagheers**: the English administered it by highly paid British officers, at the same time that they endeavoured to lower the land-tax, and to introduce grand material reforms."—*Bosworth Smith, L. of Ld. Lawrence*, i. 378.

JAIL-KHANA, s. A hybrid word for 'a gaol,' commonly used in the Bengal Presidency.

JAIN, s. and adj. The non-Brahmanical sect so called; believed to represent the earliest heretics of Buddhism, at present chiefly to be found in the Bombay Presidency. There are a few in Mysore, Canara, and in some parts of the Madras Presidency, but in the Middle Ages they appear to have been numerous on the coast of the Peninsula generally. They are also found in various parts of Central and Northern India and Behar. The Jains are generally merchants, and some have been men of enormous wealth (see *Colebrooke's Essays*, i. 378 *seqq.*; [Lassen, in *Ind. Antiq.* ii. 193 *seqq.*, 258 *seqq.*]). The name is Skt. **jaina**, meaning a follower of **jina**. The latter word is a title applied to certain saints worshipped by the sect in the place of gods; it is also a name of the Buddhas. An older name for the followers of the sect appears to have been *Nirgrantha*, 'without bond,' properly the title of Jain *ascetics* only (otherwise *Yatis*), [and in particular of the *Digambara* or 'sky-clad,' naked branch]. (*Burnell, S. Indian Palaeography*, p. 47, note.)

[c. 1590.—"**Jaina**. The founder of this wonderful system was Jina, also called Arhat, or Arhant."—*Āīn*, ed. *Jarrett*, iii. 188.]

JAMES AND MARY, n.p. The name of a famous sand-bank in the Hoogly R. below Calcutta, which has been fatal to many a ship. It is mentioned under 1748, in the record of a survey of the river quoted in *Long*, p. 10. It is a common allegation that the name is a corruption of the Hind. words *jal mari*, with the supposed meaning of 'dead water.' But the real origin of the name dates, as Sir G. Birdwood has shown, out of India Office records, from the wreck of a vessel called the "*Royal James and Mary*," in September 1694, on that sand-bank (*Letter to the Court, from Chuttanuttee*, Dec. 19, 1694). [*Report on Old Records*, 90.] This shoal appears by name in a chart belonging to the *English Pilot*, 1711.

JAMMA, s. P.—H. *jāma*, a piece of native clothing. Thus, in composition, see PYJAMMAS. Also stuff for clothing, &c., *e.g. mom-***jama**, wax-cloth. ["The **jama** may have been brought by the Aryans from Central Asia, but as it is still now seen it is thoroughly Indian and of ancient date" (*Rajendralala Mitra, Indo-Aryans*, i. 187 *seq.*]

[1813.—"The better sort (of Hindus) wear ... a **jama**, or long gown of white calico, which is tied round the middle with a fringed or embroidered sash."—*Forbes, Or. Mem.* 2nd ed. i. 52].

JAPAN, n.p. Mr. Giles says: "Our word is from *Jeh-pun*, the Dutch orthography of the Japanese *Ni-pon*." What the Dutch have to do with the matter is hard to see. ["Our word '*Japan*' and the Japanese *Nihon* or *Nippon*, are alike corruptions of *Jihpen*, the Chinese pronunciation of the characters (meaning) literally 'sun-origin.'" (*Chamberlain, Things Japanese*, 3rd ed. 221).] A form closely resembling *Japán*, as we pronounce it, must have prevailed, among foreigners at least, in China as early as the 13th century; for Marco Polo calls it *Chipan*-gu or *Jipan*-ku, a name representing the Chinese *Zhi-pǎn-Kwe* ('Sun-origin-Kingdom'), the Kingdom of the Sunrise or Extreme Orient, of which the word *Nipon* or *Niphon*, used in Japan, is said to be a dialectic variation. But as there was a distinct gap in Western tradition between the 14th century and the 16th, no doubt we, or rather the Portuguese, acquired the name from the traders at Malacca, in the Malay forms, which Crawfurd gives as *Jăpung* and *Jăpang*.

1298.—"**Chipangu** is an Island towards the east in the high seas, 1,500 miles distant from the Continent; and a very great Island it is. The people are white, civilized, and well-favoured. They are Idolaters, and dependent on nobody. ..."—*Marco Polo*, bk. iii. ch. 2.

1505.—"... and not far off they took a ship belonging to the King of Calichut; out of which they have brought me certain jewels of good value; including Mccccc. pearls worth 8,000 ducats; also three astrological instruments of silver, such as are not used by our astrologers, large and well-wrought, which I hold in the highest estimation. They say that the King of Calichut had sent the said ship to an island called **Saponin** to obtain the said instruments. ..."—*Letter from the K. of Portugal* (Dom Manuel) *to the K. of Castille* (Ferdinand). Reprint by *A. Burnell*, 1881, p. 8.

1521.—"In going by this course we passed near two very rich islands; one is in twenty degrees latitude in the antarctic pole, and is called **Cipanghu**."—*Pigafetta, Magellan's Voyage*, Hak. Soc., 67. Here the name appears to be taken from the chart or Mappe-Monde which was carried on the voyage. **Cipanghu** appears by that name on the globe of Martin Behaim (1492), but 20 degrees *north*, not south, of the equator.

1545.—"Now as for us three *Portugals*, having nothing to sell, we employed our time either in fishing, hunting, or seeing the Temples of these *Gentiles*, which were very sumptuous and rich, whereinto the *Bonzes*, who are their priests, received us very courteously, for indeed it is the custom of those of **Jappon** (*do Japão*) to be exceeding kind and courteous."—*Pinto* (orig. cap. cxxxiv.), in *Cogan*, E.T. p. 173.

1553.—"After leaving to the eastward the isles of the Lequios and of the **Japons** (*dos Japões*), and the great province of Meaco, which for its great size we know not whether to call it Island or Continent, the coast of China still runs on, and those parts pass beyond the antipodes of the meridian of Lisbon."—*Barros*, I. ix. 1.

1572.—
"Esta meia escondida, que responde
De longe a China, donde vem buscar-se,
He **Japão**, onde nasce la prata fina,
Que illustrada será co' a Lei divina."
Camões, x. 131.

By Burton:
"This Realm, half-shadowed, China's empery
afar reflecting, whither ships are bound,
is the **Japan**, whose virgin silver mine
shall shine still sheenier with the Law
Divine."

1727.—"**Japon**, with the neighbouring Islands under its Dominions, is about the magnitude of Great Britain."—*A. Hamilton*, ii. 306; [ed. 1744, ii. 305].

JAVA, n.p. This is a geographical name of great antiquity, and occurs, as our first quotation shows, in Ptolemy's Tables. His Ἰαβαδίου represents with singular correctness what was probably the Prakrit or popular form of *Yava-dvīpa* (see under **MALDIVES**), and his interpretation of the Sanskrit is perfectly correct. It will still remain a question whether *Yava* was not applied to some cereal more congenial to the latitude than barley,[1] or was (as is possible) an attempt to give an Indian meaning to some aboriginal name of similar sound. But the sixth of our quotations, the transcript and translation of a Sanskrit inscription in the Museum at Batavia by Mr. Holle, which we owe to the kindness of Prof. Kern, indicates that a signification of wealth in cereals was attached to the name in the early days of its Indian civilization. This inscription is most interesting, as it is the oldest *dated* inscription yet discovered upon Javanese soil. Till a recent time it was not known that there was any mention of Java in Sanskrit literature, and this was so when Lassen published the 2nd vol. of his *Indian Antiquities* (1849). But in fact Java was mentioned in the *Rāmāyana*, though a perverted reading disguised the fact until the publication of the Bombay edition in 1863. The passage is given in our second quotation; and we also give passages from two later astronomical works whose date is approximately known. The *Yava-Koṭi*, or *Java Point* of these writers is understood by Prof. Kern to be the eastern extremity of the island.

We have already alluded to the fact that the terms *Jāwa, Jāwi* were applied by the Arabs to the Archipelago generally, and often with specific reference to Sumatra. Prof. Kern, in a paper to which we are largely indebted, has indicated that this larger application of the term was originally Indian. He has discussed it in connection with the terms "Golden and Silver Islands" (*Suvarṇa dvīpa* and *Rūpya dvīpa*), which occur in the quotation from

1 The Teutonic word *Corn* affords a handy instance of the varying application of the name of a cereal to that which is, or has been, the staple grain of each country. *Corn* in England familiarly means 'wheat'; in Scotland 'oats'; in Germany 'rye'; in America 'maize.'

the *Rāmāyana*, and elsewhere in Sanskrit literature, and which evidently were the basis of the Chryse and Argyrē, which take various forms in the writings of the Greek and Roman geographers. We cannot give the details of his discussion, but his condensed conclusions are as follows:—(1.) *Suvarṇa-dvīpa* and *Yava-dvīpa* were according to the prevalent representations the same; (2.) Two names of islands originally distinct were confounded with one another; (3.) *Suvarṇa-dvīpa* in its proper meaning is Sumatra, *Yava-dvīpa* in its proper meaning is Java; (4.) Sumatra, or a part of it, and Java were regarded as one whole, doubtless because they were politically united; (5.) By *Yava-koṭi* was indicated the east point of Java.

This Indian (and also insular) identification, in whole or in part, of Sumatra with Java explains a variety of puzzles, *e.g.* not merely the Arab application of *Java*, but also the ascription, in so many passages, of great wealth of gold to Java, though the island, to which that name properly belongs, produces no gold. This tradition of gold-produce we find in the passages quoted from Ptolemy, from the *Rāmāyana*, from the Holle inscription, and from Marco Polo. It becomes quite intelligible when we are taught that Java and Sumatra were at one time both embraced under the former name, for Sumatra has always been famous for its gold-production. [Mr. Skeat notes as an interesting fact that the standard Malay name *Jāwă* and the Javanese *Jāwa* preserve the original form of the word.]

(*Ancient*).—"Search carefully **Yava dvīpa**, adorned by seven Kingdoms, the Gold and Silver Island, rich in mines of gold. Beyond **Yava dvīpa** is the Mountain called Sisira, whose top touches the sky, and which is visited by gods and demons."—*Rāmāyana*, IV. xl. 30 (from Kern).

A.D. c. 150.—"**Iabadiu** (*Ἰαβαδίου*), which means 'Island of Barley,' most fruitful the island is said to be, and also to produce much gold; also the metropolis is said to have the name Argyrē (Silver), and to stand at the western end of the island."—*Ptolemy*, VII. ii. 29.

414.—"Thus they voyaged for about ninety days, when they arrived at a country called **Ya-va-di** [*i.e. Yava-dvīpa*]. In this country heretics and Brahmans flourish, but the Law of Buddha hardly deserves mentioning."—*Fahian*, ext. in *Groeneveldt's Notes from Chinese Sources*.

A.D. c. 500.—"When the sun rises in Ceylon it is sunset in the City of the Blessed (*Siddha-pura, i.e.* The Fortunate Islands), noon at **Yava-koti**, and midnight in the Land of the Romans."—*Aryabhata*, IV. v. 13 (from Kern).

A.D. c. 650.—"Eastward by a fourth part of the earth's circumference, in the world-quarter of the Bhadrāśvas lies the City famous under the name of **Yava koti** whose walls and gates are of gold."—*Suryā-Siddhānta*, XII. v. 38 (from Kern).

Saka, 654, *i.e.* A.D. 762.—"Dvīpavara*m* **Yavăkhyam** atulan dhân-yādivājâîhikam sam-panna*m* kanakākaraih" ... *i.e.* the incomparable splendid island called **Java**, excessively rich in grain and other seeds, and well provided with gold-mines."—*Inscription in Batavia Museum* (see above).

943.—"Eager ... to study with my own eyes the peculiarities of each country, I have with this object visited Sind and Zanj, and Sanf and Sīn (China), and **Zābaj**."—*Maṣ'ūdī*, i. 5.

"This Kingdom (India) borders upon that of **Zābaj**, which is the empire of the *Mahrāj*, King of the Isles."—*Ibid.* 163.

992.—"**Djava** is situated in the Southern Ocean. ... In the 12th month of the year (992) their King *Maradja* sent an embassy ... to go to court and bring tribute."—*Groeneveldt's Notes from Chinese Sources*, pp. 15–17.

1298.—"When you sail from Ziamba (Chamba) 1500 miles in a course between south and south-east, you come to a very great island called **Java**, which, according to the statement of some good mariners, is the greatest Island that there is in the world, seeing that it has a compass of more than 3000 miles, and is under the dominion of a great king. ... Pepper, nutmegs, spike, galanga, cubebs, cloves, and all the other good spices are produced in this island, and it is visited by many ships with quantities of merchandise from which they make great profits and gain, for such an amount of gold is found there that no one would believe it or venture to tell it."—*Marco Polo*, in *Ramusio*, ii. 51.

c. 1330.—"In the neighbourhood of that realm is a great island, **Java** by name, which hath a compass of a good 3000 miles. Now this island is populous exceedingly, and is the second best of all islands that exist. ... The King of this island hath a palace which is truly marvellous. ... Now the great Khan of Cathay many a time engaged in war with this King; but this King always vanquished and got the better of him."—*Friar Odoric*, in *Cathay*, &c., 87–89.

c. 1349.—"She clandestinely gave birth to a daughter, whom she made when grown up Queen of the finest island in the world, **Saba** by name. ..."—*John de' Marignolli, ibid.* 391.

c. 1444.—"Sunt insulae duae in interiori India, e pene extremis orbis finibus, ambae **Java** nomine, quarum altera tribus, altera duobus millibus milliarum protenditur orientem versus; sed Majoris, Minorisque cognomine discernuntur."—*N. Conti*, in *Poggius, De Var. Fortunae*.

1503.—The Syrian Bishops Thomas, Jaballaha, Jacob, and Denha, sent on a mission to India in 1503 by the (Nestorian) Patriarch Elias, were ordained to go "to the land of the Indians and the islands of the seas which are between **Dabag** and Sin and Masin."—*Assemani*, III. Pt. i. 592. This *Dabag* is probably a relic of the *Zābaj* of the *Relation*, of Maṣ'ūdī, and of Al-birūnī.

1516.—"Further on ... there are many islands, small and great, amongst which is one very large which they call *Java* the Great. ... They say that this island is the most abundant country in the world. ... There grow pepper, cinnamon, ginger, bamboos, cubebs, and gold. ..."—*Barbosa*, 197.

Referring to Sumatra, or the Archipelago in general.

Saka, 578, *i.e.* A.D. 656.—"The Prince Adityadharma is the Deva of the First **Java** Land (*prathama* **Yava**-*bhū*). May he be great! Written in the year of Saka, 578. May it be great!"—From a *Sanskrit Inscription from* Pager-Ruyong, *in* Menang Karbau (Sumatra), publd. by *Friedrich*, in the *Batavian Transactions*, vol. xxiii.

1224.—"**Ma'bar** (q.v.) is the last part of India; then comes the country of China (*Sín*), the first part of which is **Jāwa**, reached by a difficult and fatal sea."—*Yāḳūt*, i. 516.

"This is some account of remotest *Sín*, which I record without vouching for its truth ... for in sooth it is a far off land. I have seen no one who had gone to it and penetrated far into it; only the merchants seek its outlying parts, to wit the country known as **Jāwa** on the sea-coast, like to India; from it are brought Aloeswood (*'ūd*), camphor, and nard (*sunbul*), and clove, and mace (*basbāsa*), and China drugs, and vessels of china-ware."—*Ibid*. iii. 445.

Kazwīnī speaks in almost the same words of **Jāwa**. He often copies Yāḳūt, but perhaps he really means his own time (for he uses different words) when he says: "Up to this time the merchants came no further into China than to this country (**Jāwa**) on account of the distance and difference of religion"—ii. 18.

1298.—"When you leave this Island of Pentam and sail about 100 miles, you reach the Island of **Java** the Less. For all its name 'tis none so small but that it has a compass of 2000 miles or more. ..." &c.—*Marco Polo*, bk. iii. ch. 9.

c. 1300.—"... In the mountains of **Jáva** scented woods grow. ... The mountains of **Jáva** are very high. It is the custom of the people to puncture their hands and entire body with needles, and then rub in some black substance."—*Rashīd-uddīn*, in *Elliot*, i. 71.

1328.—"There is also another exceeding great island, which is called **Jaua**, which is in circuit more than seven [thousand?] miles as I have heard, and where are many world's wonders. Among which, besides the finest aromatic spices, this is one, to wit, that there be found pygmy men. ... There are also trees producing cloves, which when they are in flower emit an odour so pungent that they kill every man who cometh among them, unless he shut his mouth and nostrils. ... In a certain part of that island they delight to eat white and fat men when they can get them. ..."—*Friar Jordanus*, 30–31.

c. 1330.—"Parmi les isles de la Mer de l'Inde il faut citer celle de **Djâwah**, grande isle célèbre par l'abondance de ses drogues ... au sud de l'isle de **Djâwah** on remarque la ville de Fansour, d'où le camphre Fansoûri tire son nom."—*Geog. d'Aboulfeda*, II. pt. ii. 127.

c. 1346.—"After a passage of 25 days we arrived at the Island of **Jāwa**, which gives its name to the *lubān jāwiy*. ... We thus made our entrance into the capital, that is to say the city of Sumatra; a fine large town with a wall of wood and towers also of wood."—*Ibn Batuta*, iv. 228–230.

1553.—"And so these, as well as those of the interior of the Island (Sumatra), are all dark, with lank hair, of good nature and countenance, and not resembling the Javanese, although such near neighbours, indeed it is very notable that at so small a distance from each other their nature should vary so much, all the more because all the people of this Island call themselves by the common name of **Jawis** (*Jaüijs*), because they hold it for certain that the Javanese (*os* **Jãos**) were formerly lords of this great Island. ..."—*Barros*, III. v. 1.

1555.—"Beyond the Island of **Iaua** they sailed along by another called Bali; and then came also vnto other called Aujaue, Cambaba, Solor. ... The course by these Islands is about 500 leagues. The ancient cosmographers call all these Islands by the name **Iauos**; but late experience hath found the names to be very diuers as you see."—*Antonio Galvano*, old E.T. in *Hakl*. iv. 423.

1856.—

"It is a saying in Goozerat,—
'Who goes to **Java**
Never returns.
If by chance he return,
Then for two generations to live upon,
Money enough he brings back.'"

Râs Mâlâ, ii. 82; [ed. 1878, p. 418].

***JAWAUB**, s. Hind. from Ar. *jawāb*, 'an

answer.' In India it has, besides this ordinary meaning, that of 'dismissal.' And in Anglo-Indian colloquial it is especially used for a lady's refusal of an offer; whence the verb passive '*to be jawaub'd.*' [The **Jawaub** Club consisted of men who had been at least half a dozen times '*jawaub'd.*'

1830.—"'The **Juwawb'd Club**,' asked Elsmere, with surprise, 'what is that?'

"''Tis a fanciful association of those melancholy candidates for wedlock who have fallen in their pursuit, and are smarting under the sting of rejection.'"—*Orient. Sport. Mag.*, reprint 1873, i. 424.]

Jawāb among the natives is often applied to anything erected or planted for a symmetrical double, where

"Grove nods at grove, each alley has a brother,
And half the platform just reflects the other."

"In the houses of many chiefs every picture on the walls has its **jawab** (or duplicate). The portrait of Scindiah now in my dining-room was the **jawab** (copy in fact) of Mr. C. Landseer's picture, and hung opposite to the original in the Darbar room" (*M.-Gen. Keatinge*). ["The masjid with three domes of white marble occupies the left wing and has a counterpart (**jawāb**) in a precisely similar building on the right hand side of the Tāj. This last is sometimes called the false masjid; but it is in no sense dedicated to religious purposes."—*Führer*, *Monumental Antiquities, N.W.P.*, p. 64.]

JEHAUD, s. Ar. *jihād*, ['an effort, a striving']; then a sacred war of Musulmans against the infidel; which Sir Herbert Edwardes called, not very neatly, 'a crescentade.'

[c. 630 A.D.—"Make war upon such of those to whom the Scriptures have been given who believe not in God, or in the last day, and who forbid not that which God and his Prophet have forbidden, and who profess not the profession of the truth, until they pay tribute (*jizyah*) out of hand, and they be humbled."—*Korān*, Surah ix. 29.]

1880.—"When the Athenians invaded Ephesus, towards the end of the Peloponnesian War, Tissaphernes offered a mighty sacrifice at Artemis, and raised the people in a sort of **Jehad**, or holy war, for her defence."—*Sat. Review*, July 17, 84*b*.

[1901.—"The matter has now assumed the aspect of a '**Schad**,' or holy war against Christianity."—*Times*, April 4.]

JELAUBEE, s. Hind. *jalebī*, [which is apparently a corruption of the Ar. *zalābiya*, P. *zalībiya*]. A rich sweetmeat made of sugar and ghee, with a little flour, melted and trickled into a pan so as to form a kind of interlaced work, when baked.

[1870.—"The poison is said to have been given once in sweetmeats, **Jelabees**."—*Chevers, Med. Jurisp.* 178.]

JEMADAR, JEMAUTDAR, &c. Hind. from Ar.—P. *jama'dar*, *jama'* meaning 'an aggregate,' the word indicates generally, a leader of a body of individuals. [Some of the forms are as if from Ar.—P. *jamā'at*, 'an assemblage.'] Technically, in the Indian army, it is the title of the second rank of native officer in a company of sepoys, the Sūbadār (see SOUBADAR) being the first. In this sense the word dates from the reorganisation of the army in 1768. It is also applied to certain officers of police (under the *dārogha*), of the customs, and of other civil departments. And in larger domestic establishments there is often a *jemadār*, who is over the servants generally, or over the stables, camp service and orderlies. It is also an honorific title often used by the other household servants in addressing the *bihishtī* (see BHEESTY).

1752.—"The English battalion no sooner quitted Tritchinopoly than the regent set about accomplishing his scheme of surprising the City, and ... endeavoured to gain 500 of the Nabob's best peons with firelocks. The **jemautdars**, or captains of these troops, received his bribes and promised to join."—*Orme*, ed. 1803, i. 257.

1817.—"... Calliaud had commenced an intrigue with some of the **jematdars**, or captains of the enemy's troops, when he received intelligence that the French had arrived at Trichinopoly."—*Mill*, iii. 175.

1824.—"'Abdullah' was a Mussulman convert of Mr. Corrie's, who had travelled in Persia with Sir Gore Ouseley, and accompanied him to England, from whence he was returning ... when the Bishop took him into his service as a '**jemautdar**,' or head officer of the peons."—Editor's note to *Heber*, ed. 1844, i. 65.

[1826.—"The principal officers are called **Jummahdars**, some of whom command five thousand horse."—*Pandurang Hari*, ed. 1873, i. 56.]

JENNYRICKSHAW, s. Read Capt. Gill's description below. Giles states the word to be taken from the Japanese pronunciation of three characters, reading *jin-riki-sha*, signifying '*Man—Strength—Cart*.' The term is therefore, observes our friend E. C. Baber, an exact equivalent of "*Pullman-Car*"! The article has been introduced into India, and is now in use at Simla and other hill-stations. [The invention of the vehicle is attributed to various people—to an Englishman known as "Public-spirited Smith" (8 ser. *Notes and Queries*, viii. 325); to native Japanese about 1868–70, or to an American named Goble, "half-cobbler and half-missionary." See *Chamberlain, Things Japanese*, 3rd ed. 236 *seq.*]

1876.—"A machine called a **jinnyrickshaw** is the usual public conveyance of Shanghai. This is an importation from Japan, and is admirably adapted for the flat country, where the roads are good, and coolie hire cheap. ... In shape they are like a buggy, but very much smaller, with room inside for one person only. One coolie goes into the shafts and runs along at the rate of 6 miles an hour; if the distance is long, he is usually accompanied by a companion who runs behind, and they take it in turn to draw the vehicle."—*W. Gill, River of Golden Sand*, i. 10. See also p. 163.

1880.—"The Kuruma or **jin-ri-ki-sha** consists of a light perambulator body, an adjustable hood of oiled paper, a velvet or cloth lining and cushion, a well for parcels under the seat, two high slim wheels, and a pair of shafts connected by a bar at the ends."—*Miss Bird, Japan*, i. 18.

[1885.—"We ... got into **rickshaws** to make an otherwise impossible descent to the theatre."—*Lady Dufferin, Viceregal Life*, 89.]

JIGGY-JIGGY, adv. Japanese equivalent for 'make haste!' The Chinese syllables *chih-chih*, given as the origin, mean 'straight, straight!' Qu. 'right ahead'? (*Bp. Moule*).

***JOGEE**, s. Hind. *jogī*. A Hindu ascetic; and sometimes a 'conjuror.' From Skt. *yogīn*, one who practises the *yoga*, a system of meditation combined with austerities, which is supposed to induce miraculous power over elementary matter. In fact the stuff which has of late been propagated in India by certain persons, under the names of theosophy and esoteric Buddhism, is essentially the doctrine of the Jogis.

1298.—"There is another class of people called **Chughi** who ... form a religious order devoted to the Idols. They are extremely long-lived, every man of them living to 150 or 200 years ... there are certain members of the Order who lead the most ascetic life in the world, going stark naked."—*Marco Polo*, 2nd ed. ii. 351.

1343.—"We cast anchor by a little island near the main, **Anchediva** where there was a temple, a grove, and a tank of water. ... We found a **jogī** leaning against the wall of a *budkhāna* or temple of idols" (respecting whom he tells remarkable stories).—*Ibn Batuta*, iv. 62–63, and see p. 275.

c. 1442.—"The Infidels are divided into a great number of classes, such as the Bramins, the **Joghis** and others."—*Abdurrazzāk*, in *India in the XVth Cent.*, 17.

1498.—"They went and put in at Angediva ... there were good water-springs, and there was in the upper part of the island a tank built with stone, with very good water and much wood ... there were no inhabitants, only a beggar-man whom they call **joguedes**."—*Correa*, by *Lord Stanley*, 239. Compare Ibn Batuta above. After 150 years, tank, grove, and **jogi** just as they were!

1510.—"The King of the **Ioghe** is a man of great dignity, and has about 30,000 people, and he is a pagan, he and all his subjects; and by the pagan Kings he and his people are considered to be saints, on account of their lives, which you shall hear ..."—*Varthema*, p. 111. Perhaps the chief of the *Gorakhnātha* Gosains, who were once very numerous on the West Coast, and have still a settlement at Kadri, near Mangalore. See *P. della Valle's* notice below.

1516.—"And many of them noble and respectable people, not to be subject to the Moors, go out of the Kingdom, and take the habit of poverty, wandering the world ... they carry very heavy chains round their necks and waists, and legs; and they smear all their bodies and faces with ashes. ... These people are commonly called **jogues**, and in their own speech they are called *Zoame* (see SWAMY) which means Servant of God. ... These **jogues** eat all meats, and do not observe any idolatry."—*Barbosa*, 99–100.

1553.—"Much of the general fear that affected the inhabitants of that city (Goa before its capture) proceeded from a Gentoo, of Bengal by nation, who went about in the habit of a **Jogue**, which is the straitest sect of their Religion ... saying that the City would speedily have a new Lord, and would be inhabited by a strange people, contrary to the will of the natives."—*De Barros*, Dec. II. liv. v. cap. 3.

"For this reason the place (Adam's Peak) is so famous among all the Gentiledom of the East yonder, that they resort thither as pilgrims from more than 1000 leagues off, and chiefly those whom they call **Jógues**, who are as men who have abandoned the world and dedicated themselves to God, and make great pilgrimages to visit the Temples consecrated to him."—*Ibid.* Dec. III. liv. ii. cap. 1.

1563.—"... to make them fight, like the *cobras*

de capello which the **jogues** carry about asking alms of the people, and these **Jogues** are certain heathen (*Gentios*) who go begging all about the country, powdered all over with ashes, and venerated by all the poor heathen, and by some of the Moors also. ..."—*Garcia*, f. 156*v*, 157.

[c. 1610.—"The Gentiles have also their Abedalles (*Abd-Allah*), which are like to our hermits, and are called **Joguies**."—*Pyrard de Laval*, Hak. Soc. i. 343.]

1624.—"Finally I went to see the King of the **Jogis** (Gioghi) where he dwelt at that time, under the shade of a cottage, and I found him roughly occupied in his affairs as a man of the field and husbandman ... they told me his name was *Batinata*, and that the hermitage and the place generally was called Cadira (*Kadri*)."—*P. della Valle*, ii. 724; [Hak. Soc. ii. 350, and see i. 37, 75].

[1667.—"I allude particularly to the people called **Jauguis**, a name which signifies 'united to God.'"—*Bernier*, ed. *Constable*, 316.]

1673.—"Near the Gate in a Choultry sate more than Forty naked **Jougies**, or men united to God, covered with Ashes and pleited Turbats of their own Hair."—*Fryer*, 160.

1727.—"There is another sort called **Jougies**, who ... go naked except a bit of Cloth about their Loyns, and some deny themselves even that, delighting in Nastiness, and an holy Obscenity, with a great Show of Sanctity."—*A. Hamilton*, i. 152; [ed. 1744, i. 153].

1809.—

"Fate work'd its own the while. A band
Of **Yoguees**, as they roamed the land
Seeking a spouse for Jaga-Naut their God,
Stray'd to this solitary glade."
Curse of Kehama, xiii. 16.

c. 1812.—"Scarcely ... were we seated when behold, there poured into the space before us, not only all the **Yogees**, Fakeers, and rogues of that description ... but the King of the Beggars himself, wearing his peculiar badge."—*Mrs. Sherwood*, (describing a visit to Henry Martyn at Cawnpore), *Autobiog.*, 415.

"*Apnē gāṅw kā* **jogī** *ān gānw kā sidh.*" Hind. proverb: "The man who is a **jogi** in his own village is a deity in another."—Quoted by *Elliot*, ii. 207.

JOHN COMPANY, n.p. An old personification of the East India Company, by the natives often taken seriously, and so used, in former days. The term **Company** is still applied in Sumatra by natives to the existing (Dutch) Government (see *H. O. Forbes, Naturalist's Wanderings*, 1885, p. 204). [*Dohāī* **Company** *Bahādur kī* is still a common form of native appeal for justice, and **Company** *Bāgh* is the usual phrase for the public garden of a station. It has been suggested, but apparently without real reason, that the phrase is a corruption of **Company Jahān**, "which has a fine sounding smack about it, recalling Shāh Jehān and Jehāngīr, and the golden age of the Moguls" (*G. A. Sala*, quoted in *Notes and Queries*, 8 ser. ii. 37). And Sir G. Birdwood writes: "The earliest coins minted by the English in India were of copper, stamped with a figure of an irradiated *lingam*, the phallic 'Roi Soleil.' The mintage of this coin is unknown (? Madras), but without doubt it must have served to ingratiate us with the natives of the country, and may have given origin to their personification of the Company under the potent title of **Kumpani Jehan**, which, in English mouths, became 'John Company'" (*Report on Old Records*, 222, note).]

[1784.—"Further, I knew that as simple Hottentots and Indians could form no idea of the Dutch Company and its government and constitution, the Dutch in India had given out that this was one mighty ruling prince who was called **Jan** or **John**, with the surname Company, which also procured for them more reverence than if they could have actually made the people understand that they were, in fact, ruled by a company of merchants."—*Andreas Spurrmann, Travels to the Cape of Good Hope, the South-Polar Lands, and round the World*, p. 347; see 9 ser. *Notes and Queries*, vii. 34.]

1803.—(The Nawab) "much amused me by the account he gave of the manner in which my arrival was announced to him. ... '*Lord Sahab Ka bhànja, Company ki nawasa teshrìf laià*'; literally translated, 'The Lord's sister's son, and the grandson of the **Company**, has arrived."—*Lord Valentia*, i. 137.

1808.—"However the business is pleasant now, consisting principally of orders to countermand military operations, and preparations to save **Johnny Company's** cash."—*Lord Minto in India*, 184.

1818-19.—"In England the ruling power is possessed by two parties, one the King, who is Lord of the State, and the other the Honourable **Company**. The former governs his own country; and the latter, though only subjects, exceed the King in power, and are the directors of mercantile affairs."—*Sadāsukh*, in *Elliot*, viii. 411.

1826.—"He said that according to some accounts, he had heard the Company was an old Englishwoman ... then again he told me that some of the Topee wallas say '**John Company**,' and he knew that *John* was a man's name, for his master was called John Brice, but he could not say to a certainty whether '*Company*' was a man's or a woman's name."—*Pandurang Hari*, 60; [ed. 1873, i. 83, in a note to which the phrase is said to be a corruption of *Joint Company*].

1836.—"The jargon that the English speak to the natives is most absurd. I call it '**John Company's** English,' which rather affronts Mrs. Staunton."—*Letters from Madras*, 42.

1852.—"**John Company**, whatever may be his faults, is infinitely better than Downing Street. If India were made over to the Colonial Office, I should not think it worth three years' purchase."—*Mem. Col. Mountain*, 293.

1888.—"It fares with them as with the sceptics once mentioned by a South-Indian villager to a Government official. Some men had been now and then known, he said, to express doubt if there were any such person as **John Company**; but of such it was observed that something bad soon happened to them."—*Sat. Review*, Feb. 14, p. 220.

JOSS, s. An idol. This is a corruption of the Portuguese *Deos*, 'God,' first taken up in the 'Pidgin' language of the Chinese ports from the Portuguese, and then adopted from that jargon by Europeans as if they had got hold of a Chinese word. [See CHIN-CHIN.]

1659.—"But the Devil (whom the Chinese commonly called **Joosje**) is a mighty and powerful Prince of the World."—*Walter Schulz*, 17.

"In a four-cornered cabinet in their dwelling-rooms, they have, as it were, an altar, and thereon an image ... this they call **Josin**."—*Saar*, ed. 1672, p. 27:

1677.—"All the Sinese keep a limning of the Devil in their houses. ... They paint him with two horns on his head, and commonly call him **Josie** (Joosje)."—*Gerret Vermeulen, Oost Indische Voyagie*, 33.

1711.—"I know but little of their Religion, more than that every Man has a small **Joss** or God in his own House."—*Lockyer*, 181.

1727.—"Their **Josses** or Demi-gods some of human shape, some of monstrous Figure."—*A. Hamilton*, ii. 266; [ed. 1744, ii. 265].

c. 1790.—

"Down with dukes, earls, and lords, those
pagan **Josses**,
False gods! away with stars and strings and
crosses." *Peter Pindar*, Ode to Kien Long.

1798.—"The images which the Chinese worship are called **joostje** by the Dutch, and **joss** by the English seamen. The latter is evidently a corruption of the former, which being a Dutch nickname for the devil, was probably given to these idols by the Dutch who first saw them."—*Stavorinus*, E.T. i. 173.

This is of course quite wrong.

JOSS-HOUSE, s. An idol temple in China or Japan. From **joss**, as explained in the last article.

1750–52.—"The sailors, and even some books of voyages ... call the pagodas **Yoss-houses**, for on enquiring of a Chinese for the name of the idol, he answers *Grande* **Yoss**, instead of *Gran Dios*."—*Olof. Toreen*, 232.

1760–1810.—"On the 8th, 18th, and 28th day of the Moon those foreign barbarians may visit the Flower Gardens, and the Honam **Joss-house**, but not in *droves* of over ten at a time."—'8 Regulations' at Canton, from *The Fankwae at Canton* (1882), p. 29.

1840.—"Every town, every village, it is true, abounds with **Joss-houses**, upon which large sums of money have been spent."—*Mem. Col. Mountain*, 186.

1876.—"... the fantastic gables and tawdry ornaments of a large **joss-house**, or temple."—*Fortnightly Review*, No. cliii. 222.

1876:—

"One Tim Wang he makee-tlavel,
Makee stop one night in **Joss-house**."
Leland, Pidgin-English Sing-Song, p. 42.

Thus also in "pidgin," **Joss-house**-*man* or **Joss**-*pidgin-man* is a priest, or a missionary.

JOSTICK, JOSS-STICK, s. A stick of fragrant tinder (powdered *costus*, sandalwood, &c.) used by the Chinese as incense in their temples, and formerly exported for use as cigar-lights. The name appears to be from the temple use.

1876.—"Burnee **joss-stick**, talkee plitty."—*Leland, Pidgin-English Sing-Song*, p. 43.

1879.—"There is a recess outside each shop, and at dusk the **joss-sticks** burning in these fill the city with the fragrance of incense."—*Miss Bird, Golden Chersonese*, 49.

***JUGGURNAUT**, n.p. A corruption of the Skt. *Jagannātha*, 'Lord of the Universe,' a name of Krishna worshipped as Vishṇu at the famous shrine of Pūrī in Orissa. The image so called is an amorphous idol, much like those worshipped in some of the South Sea Islands, and it has been plausibly suggested (we believe first by Gen. Cunningham) that it was in reality a Buddhist symbol, which has been adopted as an object of Brahmanical worship, and made to serve as the image of a god. The idol was, and is, annually dragged forth in procession on a monstrous car, and as masses of excited pilgrims crowded round to drag or accompany it, accidents occurred. Occasionally also persons, sometimes sufferers from painful disease, cast themselves before the advancing wheels. The testimony of Mr. Stirling, who was for some years Collector of Orissa in the second decade of the last century, and that of Sir W. W. Hunter, who states that he had gone through the MS. archives of the province since it became British, show that the popular impression in regard to the continued frequency of immolations on these occasions—a belief that has made *Juggurnaut* a standing metaphor—was greatly exaggerated. The belief indeed in the custom of such immolation had existed for centuries, and the rehearsal of these or other cognate religious suicides at one or other of the great temples of the Peninsula, founded partly on fact, and partly on popular report, finds a place in almost every old narrative relating to India. The really great mortality from hardship, exhaustion, and epidemic disease which frequently ravaged the crowds of pilgrims on such occasions, doubtless aided in keeping up the popular impressions in connection with the Juggurnaut festival.

c. 1321.—"Annually on the recurrence of the day when that idol was made, the folk of the country come and take it down, and put it on a fine chariot; and then the King and Queen, and the whole body of the people, join together and draw it forth from the church with loud singing of songs, and all kinds of music ... and many pilgrims who have come to this feast cast themselves under the chariot, so that its wheels may go over them, saying that they desire to die for their god. And the car passes over them, and crushes them, and cuts them in sunder, and so they perish on the spot."—*Friar Odoric*, in *Cathay*, &c. i. 83.

c. 1430.—"In Bizenegalia also, at a certain time of the year, this idol is carried through the city, placed between two chariots ... accompanied by a great concourse of people. Many, carried away by the fervour of their faith, cast themselves on the ground before the wheels, in order that they may be crushed to death,—mode of death which they say is very acceptable to their god."—*N. Conti*, in *India in XVth Cent.*, 28.

c. 1581.—"All for devotion attach themselves to the trace of the car, which is drawn in this manner by a vast number of people ... and on the annual feast day of the Pagod this car is dragged by crowds of people through certain parts of the city (Negapatam), some of whom from devotion, or the desire to be thought to make a devoted end, cast themselves down under the wheels of the cars, and so perish, remaining all ground and crushed by the said cars."—*Gasparo Balbi*, f. 84. The preceding passages refer to scenes in the south of the Peninsula.

c. 1590.—"In the town of Pursotem on the banks of the sea stands the temple of **Jagnaut**, near to which are the images of Kishen, his brother, and their sister, made of Sandal-wood, which are said to be 4,000 years old. ... The Brahmins ... at certain times carry the image in procession upon a carriage of sixteen wheels, which in the Hindooee language is called *Rahth* (see RUT); and they believe that whoever assists in drawing it along obtains remission of all his sins."—*Gladwin's Ayeen*, ii. 13–15; [ed. *Jarrett*, ii. 127].

[1616.—"The chief city called **Jekanat**."—*Sir T. Roe*, Hak. Soc. ii. 538.]

1632.—"Vnto this Pagod or house of Sathen ... doe belong 9,000 Brammines or Priests, which doe dayly offer sacrifice vnto their great God **Iaggarnat**, from which Idoll the City is so called. ... And when it (the chariot of *Iaggarnat*) is going along the city, there are many that will offer themselves a sacrifice to this Idoll, and desperately lye downe on the ground, that the Chariott wheeles may runne over them, whereby they are killed outright; some get broken armes, some broken legges, so that many of them are destroyed, and by this meanes they thinke to merit Heauen."—*W. Bruton*, in *Hakl.* v. 57.

1667.—"In the town of **Jagannat**, which is seated upon the Gulf of *Bengala*, and where is that famous Temple of the Idol of the same name, there is yearly celebrated a certain Feast. ... The first day that they shew this Idol with Ceremony in the Temple, the Crowd is usually so great to see it, that there is not a year, but some of those poor Pilgrims, that come afar off, tired and harassed, are suffocated there; all the people blessing them for having been so happy. ... And when this Hellish Triumphant Chariot marcheth, there are found (which is no Fable) persons so foolishly credulous and superstitious as to throw themselves with their bellies under those large and heavy wheels, which bruise them to death. ..."—*Bernier, a Letter to Mr. Chapelain*, in Eng. ed. 1684, 97; [ed. *Constable*, 304 *seq.*].

[1669–79.—"In that great and Sumptuous Diabolicall Pagod, there Standeth theere gretest God **Jno. Gernaet**, whence ye Pagod receued that name alsoe."—*MS. Asia*, &c., by *T. B.* f. 12. Col. Temple adds: "Throughout the whole MS. *Jagannāth* is repeatedly called *Jno. Gernaet*, which obviously stands for the common transposition *Janganāth*..]

1682.—"... We lay by last night till 10 o'clock this morning, ye Captain being desirous to see ye **Jagernot** Pagodas for his better satisfaction. ..."—*Hedges, Diary*, July 16; [Hak. Soc. i. 30].

1727.—"His (**Jagarynat's**) Effigy is often carried abroad in Procession, mounted on a Coach four stories high ... they fasten small Ropes to the Cable, two or three Fathoms long, so that upwards of 2,000 People have room enough to draw the Coach, and some old Zealots, as it passes through the Street, fall flat on the Ground, to have the Honour to be crushed to Pieces by the Coach Wheels."—*A. Hamilton*, i. 387; [ed. 1744].

1809.—

"A thousand pilgrims strain
Arm, shoulder, breast, and thigh, with might and main,
To drag that sacred wain,
And scarce can draw along the enormous load.
Prone fall the frantic votaries on the road,
And calling on the God
Their self-devoted bodies there they lay
To pave his chariot way.
On **Jaga-Naut** they call,
The ponderous car rolls on, and crushes all,
Through flesh and bones it ploughs its dreadful path.
Groans rise unheard; the dying cry.
And death, and agony
Are trodden under foot by yon mad throng,
Who follow close and thrust the deadly wheels along."

Curse of Kehama, xiv. 5.

1814.—"The sight here beggars all description. Though **Juggernaut** made some progress on the 19th, and has travelled daily ever since, he has not yet reached the place of his destination. His brother is ahead of him, and the lady in the rear. One woman has devoted herself under the wheels, and a shocking sight it was. Another also intended to devote herself, missed the wheels with her body, and had her arm broken. Three people lost their lives in the crowd."—In *Asiatic Journal*—quoted in *Beveridge, Hist. of India*, ii. 54, without exacter reference.

c. 1818.—"That excess of fanaticism which formerly prompted the pilgrims to court death by throwing themselves in crowds under the wheels of the car of **Jagannáth** has happily long ceased to actuate the worshippers of the present day. During 4 years that I have witnessed the ceremony, three cases only of this revolting species of immolation have occurred, one of which I may observe is doubtful, and should probably be ascribed to accident; in the others the victims had long been suffering from some excruciating complaints, and chose this method of ridding themselves of the burthen of life in preference to other modes of suicide so prevalent with the lower orders under similar circumstances."—*A. Stirling*, in *As. Res.* xv. 324.

1827.—March 28th in this year, Mr. Poynder, in the E. I. Court of Proprietors, stated that "about the year 1790 no fewer than 28 Hindus were crushed to death at Ishera on the Ganges, under the wheels of **Juggurnaut**."—*As. Journal*, 1821, vol. xxiii. 702.

[1864.—"On the 7th July 1864, the editor of the Friend of India mentions that, a few days previously, he had seen, near Serampore, two persons crushed to death, and another frightfully lacerated, having thrown themselves under the wheels of a car during the Rath Jatra festival. It was afterwards stated that this occurrence was accidental."—*Chevers, Ind. Med. Jurispr.* 665.]

1871.—"... poor Johnny Tetterby staggering under his Moloch of an infant, the **Juggernaut** that crushed all his enjoyments."—*Forster's Life of Dickens*, ii. 415.

1876.—"Le monde en marchant n'a pas beaucoup plus de souci de ce qu'il écrase que le char de l'idole de **Jagarnata**."—*E. Renan*, in *Revue des Deux Mondes*, 3e Série, xviii. p. 504.

JUNGLE, s. Hind. and Mahr. *jangal*, from Skt. *jaṅgala* (a word which occurs chiefly in medical treatises). The native word means in strictness only waste, uncultivated ground; then, such ground covered with shrubs, trees or long grass; and thence again the Anglo-Indian application is to forest, or other wild growth, rather than to the fact that it is not cultivated. A forest; a thicket; a tangled wilderness. The word seems to have passed at a rather early date into Persian, and also into use in Turkistan. From Anglo-Indian it has been adopted into French as well as in English. The word does not seem to occur in *Fryer*, which rather indicates that its use was not so extremely common among foreigners as it is now.

c. 1200.—"... Now the land is humid, **jungle** (*jangalah*), or of the ordinary kind."—*Susruta*, i. ch. 35.

c. 1370.—"Elephants were numerous as sheep in the **jangal** round the Ráí's dwelling."—*Táríkh-i-Fíroz-Sháhí*, in *Elliot*, iii. 314.

c. 1450.—"The Kings of India hunt the elephant. They will stay a whole month or more in the wilderness, and in the **jungle** (*Jangal*)."—*Abdurrazāk*, in *Not. et Ext.* xiv. 51.

1474.—"... Bicheneger. The vast city is surrounded by three ravines, and intersected by a river, bordering on one side on a dreadful **Jungel**."—*Ath. Nikitin*, in *India in XVth Cent.*, 29.

1776.—"Land waste for five years ... is called **Jungle**."—*Halhed's Gentoo Code*, 190.

1809.—"The air of Calcutta is much affected by the closeness of the **jungle** around it."—*Ld. Valentia*, i. 207.

1809.—

"They built them here a bower of jointed cane,
Strong for the needful use, and light and long
Was the slight framework rear'd, with little pain;
Lithe creepers then the wicker sides supply,
And the tall **jungle** grass fit roofing gave
Beneath the genial sky."

Curse of Kehama, xiii. 7.

c. 1830.—"C'est là que je rencontrai les **jungles** ... j'avoue que je fus très désappointé."—*Jacquemont, Correspond.* i. 134.

c. 1833–38.—

"L'Hippotame au large ventre
Habite aux **Jungles** de Java,
Où grondent, au fond de chaque antre
Plus de monstres qu'on ne rêva."

Theoph. Gautier, in *Poésies Complètes*, ed. 1876, i. 325.

1848.—"But he was as lonely here as in his **jungle** at Boggleywala."—*Thackeray, Vanity Fair*, ch. iii.

"'Was there ever a battle won like Salamanca? Hey, Dobbin? But where was it he learnt his art? In India, my boy. The **jungle** is the school for a general, mark me that.'"—*Ibid.*, ed. 1863, i. 312.

c. 1858.—

"La bête formidable, habitante des **jungles**
S'endort, le ventre en l'air, et dilate ses ongles."—*Leconte de Lisle.*

"Des **djungles** du Pendj-Ab
Aux sables du Karnate."—*Ibid.*

1865.—"To an eye accustomed for years to the wild wastes of the **jungle**, the whole country presents the appearance of one continuous well-ordered garden."—*Waring, Tropical Resident at Home*, 7.

1867.—"... here are no cobwebs of plea and counterplea, no **jungles** of argument and brakes of analysis."—*Swinburne, Essays and Studies*, 133.

1873.—"**Jungle**, derived to us, through the living language of India, from the Sanskrit, may now be regarded as good English."—*Fitz-Edward Hall, Modern English*, 306.

1878.—"Cet animal est commun dans les forêts, et dans les **djengles**."—*Marre, Kata-Kata-Malayou*, 83.

1879.—"The owls of metaphysics hooted from the gloom of their various **jungles**."—*Fortnightly Rev.* No. clxv., N.S., 19.

JUNGLE-FEVER, s. A dangerous remittent fever arising from the malaria of forest or jungle tracts.

1808.—"I was one day sent to a great distance, to take charge of an officer who had been seized by **jungle-fever**."—Letter in *Morton's L. of Leyden*, 43.

JUNGLE-TERRY, n.p. Hind. *Jangal-tarāi*. A name formerly applied to a border-tract between Bengal and Behar, including the inland parts of Monghyr and Bhāgalpūr, and what are now termed the *Santāl Parganās*. Hodges, below, calls it to the "westward" of Bhāgalpūr; but Barkope, which he describes as near the centre of the tract, lies, according to Rennell's map, about 35 m. S.E. of Bhāgalpūr town; and the Cleveland inscription shows that the term included the tract occupied by the Rājmahāl hill-people. The Map No. 2 in Rennell's Bengal Atlas (1779) is entitled "the **Jungle-terry** District, with the adjacent provinces of Birbhoom, Rajemal, Boglipour, &c., comprehending the countries situated between Moorshedabad and Bahar." But the map itself does not show the name *Jungle Terry* anywhere.

1781.—"Early in February we set out on a tour through a part of the country called the **Jungle-Terry**, to the westward of Bauglepore ... after leaving the village of Barkope, which is nearly in the centre of the **Jungle Terry**, we entered the hills. ... In the great famine which raged through Indostan in the year 1770 ... the Jungle Terry is said to have suffered greatly."—*Hodges*, pp. 90–95.

1784.—"To be sold ... that capital collection of Paintings, late the property of A. Cleveland, Esq., deceased, consisting of the most capital views in the districts of Monghyr, Rajemehal, Boglipoor, and the **Jungleterry**, by Mr. Hodges. ..."—In *Seton-Karr*, i. 64.

c. 1788.—

"To the Memory of
Augustus Cleveland, Esq.,
Late Collector of the Districts of Bhaugulpore
and Rajamahall,
Who without Bloodshed or the Terror of
Authority,
Employing only the Means of Conciliation,
Confidence, and Benevolence,
Attempted and Accomplished
The entire Subjection of the Lawless and
Savage Inhabitants of the
Jungleterry of Rajamahall. ..." (etc.)

Inscription on the Monument *erected by* Government *to* Cleveland, *who died in* 1784.

1817.—"These hills are principally covered with wood, excepting where it has been cleared away for the natives to build their villages, and cultivate *janaira* (**Jowaur**), plantains and yams, which together with some of the small grains mentioned in the account of the **Jungleterry**, constitute almost the whole of the productions of these hills."—*Sutherland's Report on the Hill People* (in App. to *Long*, 560).

1824.—"This part, I find (he is writing at Monghyr), is not reckoned either in Bengal or Bahar, having been, under the name of the **Jungleterry** district, always regarded, till its pacification and settlement, as a sort of border or debateable land."—*Heber*, i. 131.

JUNGLO, s. Guz. *Janglo*. This term, we are told by R. Drummond, was used in his time (the beginning of the 19th century), by the less polite, to distinguish Europeans; "wild men of the woods," that is, who did not understand Guzerati!

1808.—"Joseph Maria, a well-known scribe of the order of Topeewallas ... was actually mobbed, on the first circuit of 1806, in the town of Pitland, by parties of curious old women and young, some of whom gazing upon him put the question, *Aré* **Jungla**, *too munne pirrneesh?* 'O wild one, wilt thou marry me?' He knew not what they asked, and made no answer, whereupon they declared that he was indeed a very *Jungla*, and it required all the address of Kripram (the worthy Brahmin who related this anecdote to the writer, uncontradicted in the presence of the said Senhor) to draw off the dames and damsels from the astonished Joseph."—*R. Drummond, Illus.* (s.v.).

JUNK, s. A large Eastern ship; especially (and in later use exclusively) a Chinese ship. This indeed is the earliest application also; any more general application belongs to an intermediate period. This is one of the oldest words in the Europeo-Indian vocabulary. It occurs in the travels of Friar Odorico, written down in 1331, and a few years later in the rambling reminiscences of John de' Marignolli. The great Catalan World-map of 1375 gives a sketch of one of those ships with their sails of bamboo matting and calls them Inchi, no doubt a clerical error for Iüchi. Dobner, the original editor of Marignolli, in the 18th century, says of the word (*junkos*): "This word I cannot find in any medieval glossary. Most probably we are to understand vessels of platted reeds (*a* juncis *texta*) which several authors relate to be used in India." It is notable that the same erroneous suggestion is made by Amerigo Vespucci in his curious letter to one of the Medici, giving an account of the voyage of Da Gama, whose squadron he had met at C. Verde on its way home.

The French translators of Ibn Batuta derive the word from the Chinese *tchouen* (*chwen*), and Littré gives the same etymology (s.v. *jonque*). It is possible that the word may be eventually traced to a Chinese original, but not very probable. The old Arab traders must have learned the word from Malay pilots, for it is certainly the Javanese and Malay *jong* and *ajong*, 'a ship or large vessel.' In Javanese the Great Bear is called *Lintang jong*, 'The Constellation *Junk*,' [which is in Malay *Bintang Jong*. The various forms in Malay and cognate languages, with the Chinese words which have been suggested as the origin, are very fully given by *Scott*, *Malayan Words in English*, p. 59 *seq.*].

c. 1300.—"Large ships called in the language of China '**Junks**' bring various sorts of choice merchandize and cloths from Chín and Máchín, and the countries of Hind and Sind."—*Rashíduddín*, in *Elliot*, i. 69.

1331.—"And when we were there in harbour at Polumbum, we embarked in another ship called a **Junk** (*aliam navim nomine* **Zuncum**). ... Now on board that ship were good 700 souls, 'what with sailors and with merchants. ..."—*Friar Odoric*, in *Cathay*, &c., 73.

c. 1343.—"They make no voyages on the China Sea except with Chinese vessels ... of these there are three kinds; the big ones which are called **junk**, in the plural *junūk*. ... Each of these big ships carries from three up to twelve sails. The sails are made of bamboo slips, woven like mats; they are never hauled down, but are shifted round as the wind blows from one quarter or another."—*Ibn Batuta*, iv. 91. The French translators write the words as *gonk* (and *gonoûk*). Ibn Batuta really indicates *chunk* (and *chunūk*); but both must have been quite wrong.

c. 1348.—"Wishing them to visit the shrine of St. Thomas the Apostle ... we embarked on certain *Junks* (*ascendentes* **Junkos**) from Lower India, which is called Minubar."—*Marignolli*, in *Cathay*, &c., 356.

1459.—"About the year of Our Lord 1420, a Ship or **Junk** of India, in crossing the Indian Sea, was driven ... in a westerly and south-westerly direction for 40 days, without seeing anything but sky and sea. ... The ship having touched on the coast to supply its wants, the mariners beheld there the egg of a certain bird called *chrocho*, which egg was as big as a butt. ..."—*Rubric* on *Fra Mauro's Great Map at Venice*.

"The Ships or *junks* (**Zonchi**) which navigate

this sea, carry 4 masts, and others besides that they can set up or strike (at will); and they have 40 to 60 little chambers for the merchants, and they have only one rudder. ..."—*Ibid.*

1516.—"Many Moorish merchants reside in it (Malacca), and also Gentiles, particularly *Chetis*, who are natives of Cholmendel; and they are all very rich, and have many large ships which they call **jungos**."—*Barbosa*, 191.

1549.—"Exclusus isto concilio, applicavit animum ad navem Sinensis formae, quam **Iuncum** vocant."—*Scti. Franc. Xaverii Epist.* 337.

[1554.—"... in the many ships and *junks* (**Jugos**) which certainly passed that way."—*Castanheda*, ii. c. 20.]

1563.—"**Juncos** are certain long ships that have stern and prow fashioned in the same way."—*Garcia*, f. 58*b*.

1591.—"By this Negro we were advertised of a small Barke of some thirtie tunnes (which the Moors call a **Iunco**)."—*Barker's Acc. of Lancaster's Voyage*, in *Hakl.* ii. 589.

1616.—"And doubtless they had made havock of them all, had they not presently been relieved by two Arabian **Junks** (for so their small ill-built ships are named. ...)"—*Terry*, ed. 1665, p. 342.

[1625.—"An hundred Prawes and **Iunkes**."—*Purchas, Pilgrimage*, i. 2, 43.

[1627.—"China also, and the great Atlantis (that you call America), which have now but **Iunks** and Canoas, abounded then in tall Ships."—*Bacon, New Atlantis*, p. 12.]

1630.—"So repairing to *Iasques*, a place in the *Persian* Gulph, they obtained a fleete of Seaven **Iuncks**, to convey them and theirs as Merchantmen bound for the Shoares of India."—*Lord, Religion of the Persees*, 3.

1673.—Fryer also speaks of "Portugal **Junks**." The word had thus come to mean any large vessel in the Indian Seas. Barker's use for a small vessel (above) is exceptional.

***JUNKAMEER**, s. This word occurs in *Wheeler*, i. 300, where it should certainly have been written **Juncaneer**. It was long a perplexity, and as it was the subject of one of Dr. Burnell's latest, if not the very last, of his contributions to this work, I transcribe the words of his communication:

"Working at improving the notes to v. Linschoten, I have accidentally cleared up the meaning of a word you asked me about long ago, but which I was then obliged to give up—'Jonkamīr.' It = 'a collector of customs.'

"(1745).—Notre Supérieur qui sçavoit qu'à moitié chemin certains **Jonquaniers**[1] mettoient les passans à contribution, nous avoit donné un ou deux *fanons* pour les payer en allant et en revenant, au cas qu'ils l'exigeassent de nous."—*P. Norbert, Memoires*, pp. 159–160.

"The original word is in Malayālam *chungakāran*, and do. in Tamil, though it does not occur in the Dictionaries of that language; but *chungam* (= 'Customs') does.

"I was much pleased to settle this curious word; but I should never have thought of the origin of it, had it not been for that rascally old Capuchin P. Norbert's note."

My friend's letter (from West Stratton) has no date, but it must have been written in July or August 1882.—[H.Y.]

1680.—"The *Didwan* (see DEWAUN) returned with Lingapas *Ruccas* upon the *Avaldar* (see HAVILDAR) at St. Thoma, and upon the two chief **Juncaneers** in this part of the country, ordering them not to stop goods or provisions coming into the town."—*Fort St. Geo. Consn.*, Nov. 22, *Notes and Exts.*, iii. 39.

1746.—"Given to the Governor's Servants, **Juncaneers**, &c., as usual at Christmas, *Salampores* 18Ps. P. 13."—*Acct. of Extra Charges at Fort St. David*, to Dec. 31. *MS. Report*, in India Office.

***JUTE**, s. The fibre (**gunny**-fibre) of the bark of *Corchorus capsularis*, L., and *Corchorus olitorius*, L., which in the last 45 years has become so important an export from India, and a material for manufacture in Great Britain as well as in India. "At the last meeting of the Cambridge Philosophical Society, Professor Skeat commented on various English words. *Jute*, a fibrous substance, he explained from the Sanskrit *jūṭa*, a less usual form of *jata*, meaning, 1st, the matted hair of an ascetic; 2ndly, the fibrous roots of a tree such as the banyan; 3rdly, any fibrous substance" (*Academy*, Dec. 27, 1879). The secondary meanings attributed here to *jaṭa* are very doubtful.[2] The term *jute* appears to have been first used by Dr. Roxburgh in a letter dated 1795, in which he drew the attention of the Court of Directors to the value of the fibre "called *jute* by the natives."

1 "Ce sont des Maures qui exigent de l'argent sur les grands chemins, de ceux qui passent avec quelques merchandises; souvent ils en demandent à ceux mêmes qui n'en portent point. On regarde ces gens-là à peu pres comme des voleurs."

2 This remark is from a letter of Dr. Burnell's dd. Tanjore, March 16, 1880.

[It appears, however, as early as 1746 in the Log of a voyage quoted by Col. Temple in *J.R.A.S.*, Jan. 1900, p. 158.] The name in fact appears to be taken from the vernacular name in Orissa. This is stated to be properly *jhōṭŏ*, but *jhŭṭŏ* is used by the uneducated. See *Report of the Jute Commission*, by Babu Hemchundra Kerr, Calcutta, 1874; also a letter from Mr. J. S. Cotton in the *Academy*, Jan. 17, 1880.

JUTKA, s. From Dak.—Hind. *jhaṭkā*, 'quick.' The native cab of Madras, and of Mofussil towns in that Presidency; a conveyance only to be characterised by the epithet *ramshackle*, though in that respect equalled by the Calcutta **cranchee** (q.v.). It consists of a sort of box with venetian windows, on two wheels, and drawn by a miserable pony. It is entered by a door at the back.

JUZAIL, s. This word *jazāil* is generally applied to the heavy Afghan rifle, fired with a forked rest. If it is Ar. it must be *jazā'il*, the plural of *jazīl*, 'big,' used as a substantive. *Jazīl* is often used for a big, thick thing, so it looks probable. Hence *jazā'ilchī*, one armed with such a weapon.

[1812.—"The **jezaerchi** also, the men who use blunderbusses, were to wear the new Russian dress."—*Morier, Journey through Persia*, 30.

[1898.—
"All night the cressets glimmered pale
On Ulwur sabre and Tonk **jezail**."
R. Kipling, Barrack-room Ballads, 84.

[1900.—"Two companies of Khyber **Jezailchies**."—*Warburton, Eighteen Years in the Khyber*, 78.]

K

[**KALA JUGGAH**, s. Anglo-H. *kālā jagah* for a 'dark place,' arranged near a ball-room for the purpose of flirtation.

[1885.—"At night it was rather cold, and the frequenters of the **Kala Jagah** (or dark places) were unable to enjoy it as much as I hoped they would."—*Lady Dufferin, Viceregal Life*, 91.

KEDGEREE, KITCHERY, s. Hind. *khichṛī*, a mess of rice, cooked with butter and *dāl* (see DHALL), and flavoured with a little spice, shred onion, and the like; a common dish all over India, and often served at Anglo-Indian breakfast tables, in which very old precedent is followed, as the first quotation shows. The word appears to have been applied metaphorically to mixtures of sundry kinds (see *Fryer*, below), and also to mixt jargon or *lingua franca*. In England we find the word is often applied to a mess of re-cooked fish, served for breakfast; but this is inaccurate. Fish is frequently eaten *with kedgeree*, but is no part of it. ["Fish *Kitcherie*" is an old Anglo-Indian dish, see the recipe in *Riddell, Indian Domestic Economy*, p. 437.]

c. 1340.—"The munj (**Moong**) is boiled with rice, and then buttered and eaten. This is what they call **Kishrī**, and on this dish they breakfast every day."—*Ibn Batuta*, iii. 131.

c. 1443.—"The elephants of the palace are fed upon **Kitchri**."—*Abdurrazzāk*, in *India in XVth Cent.* 27.

c. 1475.—"Horses are fed on pease; also on **Kichiris**, boiled with sugar and oil; and early in the morning they get *shishenivo*" (?).—*Athan. Nikitin*, in *do.*, p. 10.

The following recipe for **Kedgeree** is by Abu'l Fazl:—

c. 1590.—"**Khichri**, Rice, split *dál*, and *ghí*, 5 *ser* of each; ⅓ *ser* salt; this gives 7 dishes."—*Āīn*, i. 59.

1648.—"Their daily gains are very small, ... and with these they fill their hungry bellies with a certain food called **Kitserye**."—*Van Twist*, 57.

1653.—"**Kicheri** est vne sorte de legume dont les Indiens se nourissent ordinairement."—*De la Boullaye-le-Gouz*, ed. 1657, p. 545.

1672.—Baldaeus has **Kitzery**, Tavernier **Quicheri** [ed. *Ball*, i. 282, 391].

1673.—"The Diet of this Sort of People admits not of great Variety or Cost, their delightfullest Food being only **Cutcherry** a sort of Pulse and Rice mixed together, and boiled in Butter, with which they grow fat."—*Fryer*, 81.

Again, speaking of pearls in the Persian Gulf, he says: "Whatever is of any Value is very dear. Here is a great Plenty of what they call **Ketchery**, a mixture of all together, or Refuse of Rough, Yellow, and Unequal, which they sell by Bushels to the Russians."—*Ibid.* 320.

1727.—"Some Doll and Rice, being mingled together and boiled make **Kitcheree**, the common Food of the Country. They eat it with Butter and Atchar (see ACHAR)."—*A. Hamilton*, i. 161; [ed. 1744, i. 162].

1750–60.—"**Kitcharee** is only rice stewed, with a certain pulse they call Dholl, and is generally eaten with salt-fish, butter, and pickles of various sorts, to which they give the general name of *Atchar*."—*Grose*, i. 150.

[1813.—"He was always a welcome guest ... and ate as much of their rice and **Cutcheree** as he chose."—*Forbes, Or. Mem.* 2nd ed. i. 502.]

1880.—"A correspondent of the *Indian Mirror*, writing of the annual religious fair at Ajmere, thus describes a feature in the proceedings: "There are two tremendous copper pots, one of which is said to contain about eighty maunds of rice and the other forty maunds. To fill these pots with rice, sugar, and dried fruits requires a round sum of money, and it is only the rich who can afford to do so. This year His Highness the Nawab of Tonk paid Rs. 3,000 to fill up the pots. ... After the pots filled with **khichri** had been inspected by the Nawab, who was accompanied by the Commissioner of Ajmere and several Civil Officers, the distribution, or more properly the plunder, of **khichri** commenced, and men well wrapped up with clothes, stuffed with cotton, were seen leaping down into the boiling pot to secure their share of the booty."—*Pioneer Mail*, July 8. [See the reference to this custom in *Sir T. Roe*, Hak. Soc. ii. 314, and a full account in *Rajputana Gazetteer*, ii. 63.]

KERSEYMERE, s. This is an English draper's term, and not Anglo-Indian. But it is through forms like *cassimere* (also in English use), a corruption of *cashmere*, though the corruption has been shaped by the previously existing English word *kersey* for a kind of woollen cloth, as if *kersey* were one kind and *kerseymere* another, of similar goods. *Kersey* is given by Minsheu (2nd ed. 1627), without definition, thus: "Kersie *cloth*, G. (*i.e.* French) *carizé*." The only word like the last given by Littré is "*Carisil*, sorte de canevas." ... This does not apply to *kersey*, which appears to be represented by "*Creseau*—Terme de Commerce; étoffe de laine croissée à deux envers; etym. *croiser*." Both words are probably connected with *croiser* or with *carré*. Planché indeed (whose etymologies are generally worthless) says: "made originally at Kersey, in Suffolk, whence its name." And he adds, equal to the occasion, "*Kerseymere*, so named from the position of the original factory on the *mere*, or water which runs through the village of Kersey" (!) Mr. Skeat, however, we see, thinks that Kersey, in Suffolk, is perhaps the origin of the word *Kersey*: [and this he repeats in the new ed. (1901) of his *Concise Etym. Dict.*, adding, "Not from Jersey, which is also used as the name of a material." *Kerseymere*, he says, is "a corruption of *Cashmere* or *Cassimere*, by confusion with *kersey*"].

1495.—"Item the xv day of Februar, bocht fra Jhonne Andersoun x ellis of quhit **Caresay**, to be tua coitis, ane to the King, and ane to the Lard of Balgony; price of ellne vjs.; summa ... iij. *li.*"—*Accts. of the Ld. H. Treasurer of Scotland*, 1877, p. 225.

1583.—"I think cloth, **Kerseys** and tinne have never bene here at so lowe prices as they are now."—*Mr. John Newton*, from Babylon (*i.e.* Bagdad) July 20, in *Hakl.* 378.

1603.—"I had as lief be a list of an English **kersey**, as be pil'd as thou art pil'd, for a French velvet."—*Measure for Measure*, i. 2.

1625.—"Ordanet the thesaurer to tak aff to ilk ane of the officeris and to the drummer and pyper, ilk ane of thame, fyve elne of reid **Kairsie** claithe."—*Exts. from Recds. of Glasgow*, 1876, p. 347.

1626.—In a contract between the Factor of the King of Persia and a Dutch "Opper Koopman" for goods we find: "2000 Persian ells of **Carsay** at 1 *eocri* (?) the ell."—*Valentijn*, v. 295.

1784.—"For sale—superfine cambrics and edgings ... scarlet and blue **Kassimeres**."—In *Seton-Karr*, i. 47.

c. 1880.—(no date given) "**Kerseymere**. *Cassimere*. A finer description of kersey ... (then follows the absurd etymology as given by Planché). ... It is principally a manufacture of the west of England, and except in being tweeled (*sic*) and of narrow width it in no respect differs from superfine cloth."—*Draper's Dict.* s.v.

KHAKEE, vulgarly **KHARKI**, **KHARKEE**, s. or adj. Hind. *khākī*, 'dusty or dust-coloured,' from Pers. *khāk*, 'earth,' or 'dust'; applied to a light drab or chocolate-coloured cloth. This was the colour of the uniform worn by some of the Punjab regiments at the siege of Delhi, and became very popular in the army generally during the campaigns of 1857–58, being adopted as a convenient material by many other corps. [Gubbins (*Mutinies in Oudh*, 296) describes how the soldiers at Lucknow dyed their uniforms a light brown or dust colour with a mixture of black and red office inks, and Cave Brown (*Punjab and Delhi*, ii. 211) speaks of its introduction in place of the red uniform which gave the British soldier the name of "*Lal Coortee Wallahs*."]

[1858.—A book appeared called "Service and Adventures with the **Khakee** Ressalah, or Meerut Volunteer Horse during the Mutinies in 1857–8," by *R. H. W. Dunlop*.

[1859.—"It has been decided that the full dress will be of dark blue cloth, made up, not like the tunic, but as the native ungreekah (*angarkha*), and set off with red piping. The undress clothing will be entirely of **Khakee.**"—*Madras Govt. Order*, Feb. 18, quoted in *Calcutta Rev.* ciii. 407.

[1862.—"**Kharkee** does not catch in brambles so much as other stuffs."—*Brinckman, Rifle in Cashmere*, 136.]

1878.—"The Amir, we may mention, wore a **khaki** suit, edged with gold, and the well-known Herati cap."—*Sat. Review*, Nov. 30, 683.

[1899.—"The batteries to be painted with the **Kirkee** colour, which being similar to the roads of the country, will render the vehicles invisible."—*Times*, July 12.

[1890-91.—The newspapers have constant references to a **khaki** election, that is an election started on a war policy, and the War Loan for the Transvaal Campaign has been known as "**khakis.**"]

Recent military operations have led to the general introduction of **khaki** as the service uniform. Something like this has been used in the East for clothing from a very early time:—

[1611.—"See if you can get me a piece of very fine brown calico to make me clothes."—*Danvers, Letters*, i. 109.]

KHALSA, s. and adj. Hind. from Ar. *khālṣa* (properly *khāliṣa*) 'pure, genuine.' It has various technical meanings, but, as we introduce the word, it is applied by the Sikhs to their community and church (so to call it) collectively.

1783.—"The *Sicques* salute each other by the expression *Wah Gooroo*, without any inclination of the body, or motion of the hand. The Government at large, and their armies, are denominated **Khalsa**, and **Khalsajee.**"—*Forster's Journey*, ed. 1808, i. 307.

1881.—

"And all the Punjab knows me, for my father's
name was known
In the days of the conquering **Khalsa**, when
I was a boy half-grown."

Attar Singh loquitur, by *Sowar*, in an Indian paper; name and date lost.

KHAN, s. **a.** Turki through Pers. *Khān*. Originally this was a title, equivalent to Lord or Prince, used among the Mongol and Turk nomad hordes. Besides this sense, and an application to various other chiefs and nobles, it has still become in Persia, and still more in Afghanistan, a sort of vague title like "Esq.," whilst in India it has become a common affix to, or in fact part of, the name of Hindustānis out of every rank, properly, however of those claiming a Pathān descent. The tendency of swelling titles is always thus to degenerate, and when the value of *Khān* had sunk, a new form, *Khān-Khānān* (Khān of Khāns) was devised at the Court of Delhi, and applied to one of the high officers of State.

[c. 1610.—The "*Assant* **Caounas**" of Pyrard de Laval, which Mr. Gray fails to identify, is probably *Hasan-Khan*, Hak. Soc. i. 69.

[1616.—"All the Captayens, as **Channa Chana** (Khān-Khānān), Mahobet **Chan, Chan** John (Khān Jahān)."—*Sir T. Roe*, Hak. Soc. i. 192.

b. Pers. *khān*. A public building for the accommodation of travellers, a caravanserai. [The word appears in English as early as about 1400; see *Stanf. Dict.* s.v.]

1653.—"**Han** est vn Serrail ou enclos que les Arabes appellent *fondoux* ou se retirent les Carauanes, ou les Marchands Estrangers, ... ce mot de **Han** est Turq, et est le mesme que *Kiarauansarai* ou *Karbasara* (see CARAVANSERAY) dont parle Belon. ..."—*De la Boullaye-le-Gouz*, ed. 1657, p. 540.

1827.—"He lost all hope, being informed by his late fellow-traveller, whom he found at the **Khan**, that the Nuwaub was absent on a secret expedition."—*W. Scott, The Surgeon's Daughter*, ch. xiii.

KHANNA, CONNAH, &c. s. This term (Pers. *khāna*, 'a house, a compartment, apartment, department, receptacle,' &c.) is used almost *ad libitum* in India in composition, sometimes with most incongruous words, as *bobachee* (for *bāwarchī*) **connah**, 'cook-house,' **buggy-connah**, 'buggy, or coach-house,' **bottle-khanna**, tosha-khana, &c. &c.

1784.—"The house, cook-room, **bottle-connah**, godown, &c., are all pucka built."—In *Seton-Karr*, i. 41.

KHASS, KAUSS, &c., adj. Hind. from Ar. *khāṣṣ*, 'special, particular, Royal.' It has many particular applications, one of the most common being to estates retained in the hands of Government, which are said to be held *khāṣṣ*. The *khāṣṣ-maḥal* again, in a native house, is the women's apartment. Many years ago a white-bearded *khānsamān* (see CONSUMAH), in the service of one of the present writers, indulging in reminiscences of the days when he had been attached to Lord Lake's camp, in the beginning of the last century, extolled the *sāhibs* of those times above their successors, observing (in his native Hindustani): "In those days I think the Sahibs all came from London *khāṣṣ*; now a great lot of *Liverpoolwālās* come to the country!"

There were in the Palaces of the Great Mogul and other Mahommedan Princes of India always two Halls of Audience, or Durbar, the *Dewān-i-'Ām*, or Hall of the Public, and the *Dewān-i-Khāṣṣ*, the Special or Royal Hall, for those who had the *entrée*, as we say.

In the *Indian Vocabulary*, 1788, the word is written *Coss*.

KHUDD, KUDD, s. This is a term chiefly employed in the Himālaya, *khadd*, meaning a precipitous hill-side, also a deep valley. It is not in the dictionaries, but is probably allied to the Hind. *khāt*, 'a pit,' Dakh.—Hind. *khaḍḍā*. [Platts gives Hind. *khaḍ*. This is from Skt. *khaṇḍa*, 'a gap, a chasm,' while *khāt* comes from Skt. *khāta*, 'an excavation.'] The word is in constant Anglo-Indian colloquial use at Simla and other Himālayan stations.

1837.—"The steeps about Mussoori are so very perpendicular in many places, that a person of the strongest nerve would scarcely be able to look over the edge of the narrow footpath into the **Khud**, without a shudder."—*Bacon, First Impressions*, ii. 146.

1838.—"On my arrival I found one of the ponies at the estate had been killed by a fall over the precipice, when bringing up water from the **khud**."—*Wanderings of a Pilgrim*, ii. 240.

1866.—"When the men of the 43d Regt. refused to carry the guns any longer, the **Eurasian** gunners, about 20 in number, accompanying them, made an attempt to bring them on, but were unequal to doing so, and under the direction of this officer (Capt. Cockburn, R.A.) threw them down a **Khud**, as the ravines in the Himalaya are called. ..."—*Bhotan and the H. of the Dooar War*, by *Surgeon Rennie*, M.D. p. 199.

1879.—"The commander-in-chief ... is perhaps alive now because his horse so judiciously chose the spot on which suddenly to swerve round that its hind hoofs were only half over the **chud**" (*sic*.).—*Times Letter*, from Simla, Aug. 15.

***KHUTPUT**, s. This is a native slang term in Western India for a prevalent system of intrigue and corruption. The general meaning of *khaṭpaṭ* in Hind. and Mahr. is rather 'wrangling' and 'worry,' but it is in the former sense that the word became famous (1850–54) in consequence of Sir James Outram's struggles with the rascality, during his tenure of the Residency of Baroda.

[1881.—"**Khutput**, or court intrigue, rules more or less in every native State, to an extent incredible among the more civilised nations of Europe."—*Frazer, Records of Sport*, 204.]

KHUTTRY, KHETTRY, CUTTRY, s. Hind. *Khattrī*, *Khatrī*, Skt. *Kshatriya*. The second, or military caste, in the theoretical or fourfold division of the Hindus. [But the word is more commonly applied to a mercantile caste, which has its origin in the Punjab, but is found in considerable numbers in other parts of India. Whether they are really of Kshatriya descent is a matter on which there is much difference of opinion. See *Crooke, Tribes and Castes of N.W.P.*, iii. 264 *seqq.*] The *Χατριαῖοι* whom Ptolemy locates apparently towards Rājputānā are probably *Kshatriyas*.

[1623.—"They told me **Ciautru** was a title of honour."—*P. della Valle*, Hak. Soc. ii. 312.

1630.—"And because **Cuttery** was of a martiall temper God gave him power to sway Kingdomes with the scepter."—*Lord, Banians*, 5.

1638.—"Les habitans ... sont la pluspart *Benyans* et **Ketteris**, tisserans, teinturiers, et autres ouuriers en coton."—*Mandelslo*, ed. 1659, 130.

[1671.—"There are also **Cuttarees**, another Sect Principally about Agra and those parts up the Country, who are as the Banian Gentoos here."—In *Yule, Hedges' Diary*, Hak. Soc. ii. cccxi.]

1673.—"Opium is frequently eaten in great quantities by the Rashpoots, **Queteries**, and Patans."—*Fryer*, 193.

1726.—"The second generation in rank among these heathen is that of the **Settre'as**."—*Valentijn, Chorom.* 87.

1782.—"The **Chittery** occasionally betakes himself to traffic, and the Sooder has become the inheritor of principalities."—*G. Forster's Journey*, ed. 1808, i. 64.

1836.—"The Banians are the mercantile caste of the original Hindoos. ... They call themselves **Shudderies**, which signifies innocent or harmless (!)"—*Sir R. Phillips, Million of Facts*, 322.

KHYBER PASS, n.p. The famous gorge which forms the chief gate of Afghanistan from Peshawar, properly *Khaibar*. [The place of the same name near Al-Madinah is mentioned in the *Āīn* (iii. 57), and Sir R. Burton writes: "Khaybar in Hebrew is supposed to mean a castle. D'Herbelot makes it to mean a pact or association of the Jews against the Moslems." (*Pilgrimage*, ed. 1893, i. 346, note).]

1519.—"Early next morning we set out on our march, and crossing the **Kheiber Pass**, halted at the foot of it. The Khizer-Khail had been extremely licentious in their conduct. Both on the coming and going of our army they had shot upon the stragglers, and such of our people as lagged behind, or separated from the rest, and carried off their horses. It was clearly expedient that they should meet with a suitable chastisement."—*Baber*, p. 277.

1603.—

"On Thursday Jamrúd was our encamping ground.

"On Friday we went through the **Khaibar Pass**, and encamped at 'Alí Musjid."—*Jahángír*, in *Elliot*, vi. 314.

1783.—"The stage from Timrood (read *Jimrood*) to Dickah, usually called the **Hyber-pass**, being the only one in which much danger is to be apprehended from banditti, the officer of the escort gave orders to his party to ... march early on the next morning. ... Timur Shah, who used to pass the winter at Peshour ... never passed through the territory of the **Hybers**, without their attacking his advanced or rear guard."—*Forster's Travels*, ed. 1808, ii. 65–66.

1856.—

"... See the booted Moguls, like a pack
Of hungry wolves, burst from their desert lair,
And crowding through the **Khyber's** rocky strait,
Sweep like a bloody harrow o'er the land."
The Banyan Tree, p. 6.

KIDDERPORE, n.p. This is the name of a suburb of Calcutta, on the left bank of the Hoogly, a little way south of Fort William, and is the seat of the Government Dockyard. This establishment was formed in the 18th century by Gen. Kyd, "after whom," says the *Imperial Gazetteer*, "the village is named." This is the general belief, and was mine [H.Y.] till recently, when I found from the chart and directions in the *English Pilot* of 1711 that the village of Kidderpore (called in the same chart *Kitherepore*) then occupied the same position, *i.e.* immediately below "*Gobarnapore*" and that immediately below "*Chittanutte*" (*i.e.* Govindpūr and Chatānatī

1711.—"... then keep Rounding *Chitti Poe* (Chitpore) Bite down to *Chitty Nutty* Point. ... The Bite below *Gover Napore* (*Govindpūr*) is Shoal, and below the Shoal is an Eddy; therefore from Gover Napore, you must stand over to the Starboard-Shore, and keep it aboard till you come up almost with the Point opposite to **Kiddery-pore**, but no longer. ..."—*The English Pilot*, p. 65.

KILLUT, KILLAUT, &c., s. Ar.—H. *khil'at*. A dress of honour presented by a superior on ceremonial occasions; but the meaning is often extended to the whole of a ceremonial present of that nature, of whatever it may consist. [The Ar. *khil-a'h* properly means 'what a man strips from his person.' "There were (among the later Moguls) five degrees of *khila't*, those of three, five, six, or seven pieces; or they might as a special mark of favour consist of clothes that the emperor had actually worn." (See for further details Mr. Irvine in *J.R.A.S.*, N.S., July 1896, p. 533).] The word has in Russian been degraded to mean the long loose gown which forms the most common dress in Turkistan, called generally by Schuyler 'a dressing-gown' (Germ. *Schlafrock*). See *Fraehn, Wolga Bulgaren*, p. 43.

1411.—"Several days passed in sumptuous feasts. **Khil'ats** and girdles of royal magnificence were distributed."—*Abdurazzāk*, in *Not. et Exts.* xiv. 209.

1673.—"Sir George Oxenden held it. ... He defended himself and the Merchants so bravely, that he had a **Collat** or **Seerpaw**, (q.v.) a Robe of Honour from Head to Foot, offered him from the *Great Mogul*."—*Fryer*, 87.

1676.—"This is the Wardrobe, where the Royal Garments are kept; and from whence the King sends for the **Calaat**, or a whole Habit for a Man, when he would honour any Stranger. ..."—*Tavernier*, E.T. ii. 46; [ed. *Ball*, ii. 98].

1774.—"A flowered satin gown was brought me, and I was dressed in it as a **khilat**."—*Bogle*, in *Markham's Tibet*, 25.

1786.—"And he the said Warren Hastings did send **kellauts**, or robes of honour (the most public and distinguished mode of acknowledging merit known in India) to the said ministers in testimony of his approbation of their services."—*Articles of Charge against Hastings*, in *Burke's Works*, vii. 25.

1809.—"On paying a visit to any Asiatic Prince, an inferior receives from him a complete dress of honour, consisting of a **khelaut**, a robe, a turban, a shield and sword, with a string of pearls to go round the neck."—*Ld. Valentia*, i. 99.

1813.—"On examining the **khelauts** ... from

the great Maharajah Madajee Sindia, the ser-peych ... presented to Sir Charles Malet, was found to be composed of false stones."—*Forbes, Or. Mem.* iii. 50; [2nd ed. ii. 418].

KINCOB, s. Gold brocade. P.—H. *kamkhāb*, *kamkhwāb*, vulgarly *kimkhwāb*. The English is perhaps from the Gujarātī, as in that language the last syllable is short.

This word has been twice imported from the East. For it is only another form of the medieval name of an Eastern damask or brocade, **cammocca**. This was taken from the medieval Persian and Arabic forms *kamkhā* or *kīmkhwā*, 'damasked silk,' and seems to have come to Europe in the 13th century. F. Johnson's Dict. distinguishes between *kamkhā*, 'damask silk of one colour,' and *kimkhā*, 'damask silk of different colours.' And this again, according to Dozy, quoting Hoffmann, is originally a Chinese word *kin-kha*; in which doubtless *kin*, 'gold,' is the first element. *Kim* is the Fuhkien form of the word; qu. *kim-hoa*, 'gold-flower'? We have seen *kimkhwāb* derived from Pers. *kam-khwāb*, 'less sleep,' because such cloth is rough and prevents sleep! This is a type of many etymologies. ["The ordinary derivation of the word supposes that a man could not even dream of it who had not seen it (*kam*, 'little,' *khwāb*, 'dream')" (*Yusuf Ali, Mono. on Silk*, 86). Platts and the *Madras Gloss.* take it from *kam*, 'little,' *khwāb*, 'nap.'] Ducange appears to think the word survived in the French *mocade* (or *moquette*); but if so the application of the term must have degenerated in England. (See in *Draper's Dict. mockado*, the form of which has suggested a sham stuff.)

c. 1300.—"*Παιδὸς γὰρ εὐδαιμονοῦντος, καὶ τὸν πάτερα δεῖ συνευδαιμονεῖν· κατὰ τὴν ὑμνουμένην ἀντιπελάργωσιν. Ἐσθῆτα πηνοϋφῆ πεπομφῶς ἣν καμχᾶν ἡ Περσῶν φησι γλῶττα, δράσων εὖ ἴσθι, οὐ δίπλακα μὲν οὐδὲ μαρμαρέην οἵαν Ἑλένη ἐξύφαινεν, ἀλλ' ἠερειδῆ καὶ ποικίλην*,"—Letter of *Theodorus the Hyrtacenian* to *Lucites*, Protonotary and Protovestiary of the Trapezuntians. In *Notices et Extraits*, vi. 38.

1330.—"Their clothes are of Tartary cloth, and **camocas**, and other rich stuffs ofttimes adorned with gold and silver and precious stones."—*Book of the Estate of the Great Kaan*, in *Cathay*, 246.

c. 1340.—"You may reckon also that in Cathay you get three or three and a half pieces of damasked silk (**cammocca**) for a *sommo*."—*Pegolotti, ibid.* 295.

1342.—"The King of China had sent to the Sultan 100 slaves of both sexes for 500 pieces of **kamkhā**, of which 100 were made in the City of Zaitūn. ..."—*Ibn Batuta*, iv. 1.

c. 1375.—"Thei setten this Ydole upon a Chare with gret reverence, wel arrayed with Clothes of Gold, of riche Clothes of Tartarye, of **Camacaa**, and other precious Clothes."—*Sir John Maundevill*, ed. 1866, p. 175.

c. 1400.—"In kyrtle of **Cammaka** kynge am I cladde."—*Coventry Mystery*, 163.

1404.—"... é quando se del quisieron partir los Embajadores, fizo vestir al dicho Ruy Gonzalez una ropa de **camocan**, e dióle un sombrero, e dixole, que aquello tomase en señal del amor que el Tamurbec tenia al Señor Rey."—*Clavijo*, § lxxxviii.

1411.—"We have sent an ambassador who carries you from us **kīmkhā**."—Letter from *Emp. of Chian* to Shah Rukh, in *Not. et Ext.* xiv. 214.

1474.—"And the King gave a signe to him that wayted, comaunding him to give to the dauncer a peece of **Camocato**. And he taking this peece threwe it about the heade of the dauncer, and of the men and women: and useing certain wordes in praiseng the King, threwe it before the mynstrells."—*Josafa Barbaro, Travels in Persia*, E.T. Hak. Soc. p. 62.

1688.—"*Καμουχᾶς, Χαμουχᾶς*, Pannus sericus, sive ex bombyce confectus, et more Damasceno contextus, Italis *Damasco*, nostris olim Camocas, de quâ voce diximus in Gloss. Mediæ Latinit. hodie etiamnum *Mocade*." This is followed by several quotations from Medieval Greek MSS.—*Du Cange, Gloss. Med. et Inf. Graecitatis*, s.v.

1712.—In the *Spectator* under this year see an advertisement of an 'Isabella-coloured **Kincob** gown flowered with green and gold."—Cited in *Malcolm's Anecdotes of Manners*, &c., 1808, p. 429.

1733.—"Dieser mal waren von Seiten des Bräutigams ein Stück rother **Kamka** ... und eine rothe Pferdehaut; von Seiten der Braut aber ein Stück violet **Kamka**."—u. s. w.—*Gmelin, Reise durch Siberien*, i. 137–138.

1781.—"My holiday suit, consisting of a flowered Velvet Coat of the Carpet Pattern, with two rows of broad Gold Lace, a rich **Kingcob** Waistcoat, and Crimson Velvet Breeches with Gold Garters, is now a butt to the shafts of Macaroni ridicule."—Letter from *An Old Country Captain*, in *India Gazette*, Feb. 24.

1786—"... but not until the nabob's mother aforesaid had engaged to pay for the said change of prison, a sum of £10,000 ... and that she would ransack the *zenanah* ... for **Kincobs**, muslins, cloths, &c. &c. &c. ..."—*Articles of*

Charge against Hastings, in *Burke's Works*, 1852, vii. 23.

1809.—"Twenty trays of shawls, **kheenkaubs** ... were tendered to me."—*Ld. Valentia*, i. 117.

[1813.—Forbes writes **keemcob, keemcab**, *Or. Mem.* 2nd i. 311; ii. 418.]

1829.—"Tired of this service we took possession of the town of Muttra, driving them out. Here we had glorious plunder—shawls, silks, satins, **khemkaubs**, money, &c."—*Mem. of John Shipp*, i. 124.

KIOSQUE, s. From the Turki and Pers. *kūshk* or *kushk*, 'a pavilion, a villa,' &c. The word is not Anglo-Indian, nor is it a word, we think, at all common in modern native use.

c. 1350.—"When he was returned from his expedition, and drawing near to the capital, he ordered his son to build him a palace, or as those people call it a **kushk**, by the side of a river which runs at that place, which is called Afghanpūr."—*Ibn Batuta*, iii. 212.

1623.—"There is (in the garden) running water which issues from the entrance of a great **kiosck**, or covered place, where one may stay to take the air, which is built at the end of the garden over a great pond which adjoins the outside of the garden, so that, like the one at Surat, it serves also for the public use of the city."—*P. della Valle*, i. 535; [Hak. Soc. i. 68].

KISSMISS, s. Native servant's word for *Christmas*. But that festival is usually called *Baṛā din*, 'the great day.' (See BURRA DIN.)

KITMUTGAR, s. Hind. *khidmatgār*, from Ar.—P. *khidmat*, 'service,' therefore 'one rendering service.' The Anglo-Indian use is peculiar to the Bengal Presidency, where the word is habitually applied to a Musulman servant, whose duties are connected with serving meals and waiting at table under the **Consumah**, if there be one. *Kismutgar* is a vulgarism, now perhaps obsolete. The word is spelt by Hadley in his *Grammar* (see under MOORS) *khuzmutgâr*. In the word *khidmat*, as in *khil'at*, the terminal *t* in uninflected *Arabic* has long been dropt, though retained in the form in which these words have got into foreign tongues.

1759.—The wages of a **Khedmutgar** appear as 3 Rupees a month.—In *Long*, p. 182.

1765.—"... they were taken into the service of *Soujah Dowlah* as immediate attendants on his person; *Hodjee* (see HADJEE) in capacity of his first **Kistmutgar** (or valet)."—*Holwell, Hist. Events*, &c., i. 60.

1782.—"I therefore beg to caution strangers against those race of vagabonds who ply about them under the denomination of **Consumahs** and **Kismutdars**."—*Letter in India Gazette*, Sept. 28.

1784.—"The Bearer ... perceiving a quantity of blood ... called to the Hookaburdar and a **Kistmutgar**."—In *Seton-Karr*, i. 13.

1810.—"The **Khedmutgar**, or as he is often termed, the *Kismutgar*, is with very few exceptions, a Mussulman; his business is to ... wait at table."—*Williamson, V. M.* i. 212.

c. 1810.—"The **Kitmutgaur**, who had attended us from Calcutta, had done his work, and made his harvests, though in no very large way, of the '*Tazee Willaut*' or white people."—*Mrs. Sherwood, Autobiog.* 283. The phrase in italics stands for *tāzī Wilāyatī* (see BILAYUT), "fresh or green Europeans."—**Griffins** (q.v.).

1813.—"We ... saw nothing remarkable on the way but a **Khidmutgar** of Chimnagie Appa, who was rolling from Poona to Punderpoor, in performance of a vow which he made for a child. He had been a month at it, and had become so expert that he went on smoothly and without pausing, and kept rolling evenly along the middle of the road, over stones and everything. He travelled at the rate of two coss a day."—*Elphinstone*, in *Life*, i. 257–8.

1878.—"We had each our own ... **Kitmutgar** or table servant. It is the custom in India for each person to have his own table servant, and when dining out to take him with him to wait behind his chair."—*Life in the Mofussil*, i. 32.

[1889.—"Here's the **Khit** coming for the late change."—*R. Kipling, The Gadsbys*, 24.]

KITTYSOL, KITSOL, s. This word survived till lately in the Indian Tariff, but it is otherwise long obsolete. It was formerly in common use for 'an umbrella,' and especially for the kind, made of bamboo and paper, imported from China, such as the English fashion of to-day has adopted to screen fire-places in summer. The word is Portuguese, *quita-sol*, 'bar-sun.' Also *tirasole* occurs in Scot's *Discourse of Java*, quoted below from *Purchas*. See also *Hulsius, Coll. of Voyages*, in German, 1602, i. 27. [Mr. Skeat points out that in Howison's *Malay Dict.* (1801) we have, s.v. *Payong*; "A **kittasol**, sombrera," which is nearer to the Port. original than any of the examples given since 1611. This may be due to the strong Portuguese influence at Malacca.]

1588.—"The present was fortie peeces of silke

... a litter chaire and guilt, and two **quitasoles** of silke."—*Parkes's Mendoza*, ii. 105.

1605.—"... Before the shewes came, the King was brought out vpon a man's shoulders, bestriding his necke, and the man holding his legs before him, and had many rich **tyrasoles** carried ouer and round about him."—*E. Scot*, in *Purchas*, i. 181.

1611.—"Of **Kittasoles** of State for to shaddow him, there bee twentie" (in the Treasury of Akbar).—*Hawkins*, in *Purchas*, i. 215.

[1614.—"**Quitta solls** (or sombreros)."—*Foster, Letters*, ii. 207.]

1615.—"The China Capt., Andrea Dittis, retorned from Langasaque and brought me a present from his brother, viz., 1 faire **Kitesoll**. ..."—*Cocks's Diary*, i. 28.

1648.—"... above his head was borne two **Kippe-soles**, or Sun-skreens, made of Paper."—*Van Twist*, 51.

1673.—"Little but rich **Kitsolls** (which are the names of several Countries for Umbrelloes)."—*Fryer*, 160.

1687.—"They (the Aldermen of Madras) may be allowed to have **Kettysols** over them."—*Letter of Court of Directors*, in *Wheeler*, i. 200.

1690.—"nomen ... vulgo effertur *Peritsol* ... aliquando paulo aliter scribitur ... et utrumque rectius pronuntiandum est *Paresol* vel potius *Parasol* cujus significatio Appellativa est, *i. q.* **Quittesol** seu *une Ombrelle*, quâ in calidioribus regionibus utuntur homines ad caput a sole tuendum."—*Hyde's* Preface to *Travels of Abraham Peritsol*, p. vii., in *Syntag. Dissertt.* i.

"No Man in India, no not the *Mogul's* Son, is permitted the Privilege of wearing a **Kittisal** or Umbrella. ... The use of the Umbrella is sacred to the Prince, appropriated only to his use."—*Ovington*, 315.

1755.—"He carries a *Roundell*, or **Quit de Soleil** over your head."—*Ives*, 50.

1759.—In Expenses of Nawab's entertainment at Calcutta, we find: "A China **Kitysol** ... Rs. 3½."—*Long*, 194.

1761.—A chart of Chittagong, by Barth. Plaisted, marks on S. side of Chittagong R., an umbrella-like tree, called "**Kittysoll** Tree."

[1785.—"To finish the whole, a **Kittesaw** (a kind of umbrella) is suspended not infrequently over the lady's head."—*Diary*, in *Busteed, Echoes*, 3rd ed. 112.]

1792.—"In those days the **Ketesal**, which is now sported by our very Cooks and Boatswains, was prohibited, as I have heard, d'you see, to any one below the rank of field officer."—*Letter*, in *Madras Courier*, May 3.

1813.—In the table of exports from Macao, we find:—

"**Kittisolls**, large, 2,000 to 3,000,
do. small, 8,000 to 10,000,"
Milburn, ii. 464.

1875.—"Umbrellas, Chinese, of paper, or **Kettysolls**."—*Indian Tariff*.

In another table of the same year "Chinese paper **Kettisols**, valuation Rs. 30 for a box of 110, duty 5 per cent." (See UMBRELLA.)

KITTYSOL-BOY, s. A servant who carried an umbrella over his master. See *Milburn*, ii. 62.

KOËL, s. This is the common name in northern India of *Eudynamys orientalis*, L. (Fam. of *Cuckoos*), also called *kokilā* and *koklā*. The name *koīl* is taken from its cry during the breeding season, "*ku-il, ku-il*, increasing in vigour and intensity as it goes on. The male bird has also another note, which Blyth syllables as *Ho-whee-ho*, or *Ho-a-o*, or *Ho-y-o*. When it takes flight it has yet another somewhat melodious and rich liquid call; all thoroughly cuculine." (*Jerdon*.)

c. 1526.—"Another is the **Koel**, which in length may be equal to the crow, but is much thinner. It has a kind of song, and is the nightingale of Hindustan. It is respected by the natives of Hindustan as much as the nightingale is by us. It inhabits gardens where the trees are close planted."—*Baber*, p. 323.

c. 1590.—"The **Koyil** resembles the myneh (see MYNA), but is blacker, and has red eyes and a long tail. It is fabled to be enamoured of the rose, in the same manner as the nightingale."—*Ayeen*, ed. *Gladwin*, ii. 381; [ed. *Jarrett*, iii. 121].

c. 1790.—"Le plaisir que cause la fraîcheur dont on jouit sous cette belle verdure est augmenté encore par le gazouillement des oiseaux et les cris clairs et perçans du **Koewil**. ..."—*Haafner*, ii. 9.

1810.—"The **Kokeela** and a few other birds of song."—*Maria Graham*, 22.

1883.—"This same crow-pheasant has a second or third cousin called the **Koel**, which deposits its eggs in the nest of the crow, and has its young brought up by that discreditable foster-parent. Now this bird supposes that it has a musical voice, and devotes the best part of the night to vocal exercise, after the manner of the nightingale. You may call it the Indian nightingale if you like. There is a difference however in its song ... when it gets to the very top of its pitch, its voice cracks and there is an end of it, or rather there is not, for the persevering musician begins again. ... Does not the Maratha novelist, dwelling on the delights of a spring morning in an Indian village, tell how the air was filled with the dulcet melody of the **Koel**, the green parrot, and the peacock?"—*Tribes on My Frontier*, 156.

KOHINOR, n.p. Pers. *Koh-i-nūr*, 'Mountain of Light'; the name of one of the most famous diamonds in the world. It was an item in the Deccan booty of Alāuddīn Khiljī (dd. 1316), and was surrendered to Baber (or more precisely to his son Humāyūn) on the capture of Agra (1526). It remained in the possession of the Moghul dynasty till Nādir extorted it at Delhi from the conquered Mahommed Shāh (1739). After Nādir's death it came into the hands of Ahmed Shāh, the founder of the Afghān monarchy. Shāh Shujā', Ahmed's grandson, had in turn to give it up to Ranjīt Singh when a fugitive in his dominions. On the annexation of the Punjab in 1849 it passed to the English, and is now among the Crown jewels of England. Before it reached that position it ran through strange risks, as may be read in a most diverting story told by Bosworth Smith in his *Life of Lord Lawrence* (i. 327–8). In 1850–51, before being shown at the Great Exhibition in Hyde Park, it went through a process of cutting which, for reasons unintelligible to ordinary mortals, reduced its weight from 186¹⁄₁₆ carats to 106¹⁄₁₆. [See an interesting note in *Ball's Tavernier*, ii. 431 *seqq.*]

1526.—"In the battle in which Ibrâhim was defeated, Bikermâjit (Raja of Gwalior) was sent to hell. Bikermâjit's family ... were at this moment in Agra. When Hûmâiûn arrived ... (he) did not permit them to be plundered. Of their own free will they presented to Hûmâiûn a *peshkesh* (see PESHCUSH), consisting of a quantity of jewels and precious stones. Among these was one famous diamond which had been acquired by Sultân Alâeddîn. It is so valuable that a judge of diamonds valued it at half the daily expense of the whole world. It is about eight mishkals. ..."—*Baber*, p. 308.

1676.—(With an engraving of the stone.) "This diamond belongs to the Great Mogul ... and it weighs 319 *Ratis* and a half, which make 279 and nine 16ths of our Carats; when it was rough it weigh'd 907 *Ratis*, which make 793 carats."—*Tavernier*, E.T. ii. 148; [ed. *Ball*, ii. 123].

[1842.—"In one of the bracelets was the **Cohi Noor**, known to be one of the largest diamonds in the world."—*Elphinstone, Caubul*, i. 68.]

1856.—
"He (Akbar) bears no weapon, save his
dagger, hid
Up to the ivory haft in muslin swathes;
No ornament but that one famous gem,
Mountain of Light! bound with a silken
thread
Upon his nervous wrist; more used, I ween,
To feel the rough strap of his buckler there."
The Banyan Tree.

See also (1876) Browning, Epilogue to *Pacchiarotto*, &c.

***KOTOW, KOWTOW**, s. From the Chinese *k'o-t'ou*, lit. 'knock-head'; the salutation used in China before the Emperor, his representatives, or his symbols, made by prostrations repeated a fixed number of times, the forehead touching the ground at each prostration. It is also used as the most respectful form of salutation from children to parents, and from servants to masters on formal occasions, &c.

This mode of homage belongs to old Pan-Asiatic practice. It was not, however, according to M. Pauthier, of indigenous antiquity at the Court of China, for it is not found in the ancient Book of Rites of the Cheu Dynasty, and he supposes it to have been introduced by the great destroyer and reorganiser, Tsin shi Hwangti, the Builder of the Wall. It had certainly become established by the 8th century of our era, for it is mentioned that the Ambassadors who came to Court from the famous Hārūn-al-Rashīd (A.D. 798) had to perform it. Its nature is mentioned by Marco Polo, and by the ambassadors of Shāh Rukh (see below). It was also the established ceremonial in the presence of the Mongol Khāns, and is described by Baber under the name of *kornish*. It was probably introduced into Persia in the time of the Mongol Princes of the house of Hulākū, and it continued to be in use in the time of Shāh 'Abbās. The custom indeed in Persia may possibly have come down from time immemorial, for, as the classical quotations show, it was of very ancient prevalence in that country. But the interruptions to Persian monarchy are perhaps against this. In English the term, which was made familiar by Lord Amherst's refusal to perform it at Pekin in 1816, is frequently used for servile acquiescence or adulation.

K'o-tou-k'o-tou! is often colloquially used for 'Thank you' (*E. C. Baber*).

c. B.C. 484.—"And afterwards when they were come to Susa in the king's presence, and the guards ordered them to fall down and do obeisance, and went so far as to use force to compel them, they refused, and said they would never do any such thing, even were their heads thrust down to the ground, for it was not their custom to worship men, and they had not come to Persia for that purpose."—*Herodotus*, by *Rawlinson*, vii. 136.

c. B.C. 464.—"Themistocles ... first meets with Artabanus the Chiliarch, and tells him that he was a Greek, and wished to have an interview with the king. ... But quoth he; 'Stranger, the laws of men are various. ... You Greeks, 'tis said, most admire liberty and equality, but to us of our many and good laws the best is to honour the king, and adore him by prostration, as the Image of God, the Preserver of all things.' ... Themistocles, on hearing these things, says to him: 'But I, O Artabanus, ... will myself obey your laws.' ..."—*Plutarch, Themistoc.*, xxvii.

c. B.C. 390.—"Conon, being sent by Pharnabazus to the king, on his arrival, in accordance with Persian custom, first presented himself to the Chiliarch Tithraustes who held the second rank in the empire, and stated that he desired an interview with the king; for no one is admitted without this. The officer replied: 'It can be at once; but consider whether you think it best to have an interview, or to write the business on which you come. For if you come into the presence you must needs worship the king (what they call προσκυνεῖν). If this is disagreeable to you you may commit your wishes to me, without doubt of their being as well accomplished.' Then Conon says: 'Indeed it is not disagreeable to me to pay the king any honour whatever. But I fear lest I bring discredit upon my city, if belonging to a state which is wont to rule over other nations I adopt manners which are not her own, but those of foreigners.' Hence he delivered his wishes in writing to the officer."—*Corn. Nepos, Conon*, c. iv.

B.C. 324.—"But he (Alexander) was now downhearted, and beginning to be despairing towards the divinity, and suspicious towards his friends. Especially he dreaded Antipater and his sons. Of these Iolas was the Chief Cupbearer, whilst Kasander had come but lately. So the latter, seeing certain Barbarians prostrating themselves (προσκυνοῦντας), a sort of thing which he, having been brought up in Greek fashion, had never witnessed before, broke into fits of laughter. But Alexander in a rage gript him fast by the hair with both hands, and knocked his head against the wall."—*Plutarch, Alexander*, lxxiv.

A.D. 798.—"In the 14th year of Tchinyuan, the Khalif Galun (*Hārūn*) sent three ambassadors to the Emperor; they performed the ceremony of kneeling and beating the forehead on the ground, to salute the Emperor. The earlier ambassadors from the Khalifs who came to China had at first made difficulties about performing this ceremony. The Chinese history relates that the Mahomedans declared that they knelt only to worship Heaven. But eventually, being better informed, they made scruple no longer."—*Gaubil, Abrégé de l'Histoire des Thangs*, in *Amyot, Mémoires conc. les Chinois*, xvi. 144.

c. 1245.—"Tartari de mandato ipsius principes suos Baiochonoy et Bato violenter ab omnibus nunciis ad ipsos venientibus faciunt adorari cum triplici genuum flexione, triplici quoque capitum suorum in terram allisione."—*Vincent Bellovacensis, Spec. Historiale*, l. xxix. cap. 74.

1298.—"And when they are all seated, each in his proper place, then a great prelate rises and says with a loud voice: 'Bow and adore!' And as soon as he has said this, the company bow down until their foreheads touch the earth in adoration towards the Emperor as if he were a god. And this adoration they repeat four times."—*Marco Polo*, Bk. ii. ch. 15.

1404.—"E ficieronle vestir dos ropas de *camocan* (see KINCOB), é la usanza era, quando estas roupat ponian por el Señor, de facer un gran yantar, é despues de comer de les vestir de las ropas, é entonces de fincar los finojos tres yeces in tierra por reverencia del gran Señor."—*Clavijo*, § xcii.

"And the custom was, when these robes were presented as from the Emperor, to make a great feast, and after eating to clothe them with the robes, and then that they should touch the ground three times with the knees to show great reverence for the Lord."—See *Markham*, p. 104.

1421.—"His worship Hajji Yusuf the Kazi, who was ... chief of one of the twelve imperial Councils, came forward accompanied by several Mussulmans acquainted with the languages. They said to the ambassadors: 'First prostrate yourselves, and then touch the ground three times with your heads.'"—*Embassy from Shāh Rukh*, in *Cathay*, p. ccvi.

1502.—"My uncle the elder Khan came three or four farsangs out from Tashkend, and having erected an awning, seated himself under it. The younger Khan advanced ... and when he came to the distance at which the *kornish* is to be performed, he knelt nine times. ..."—*Baber*, 106.

c. 1590.—The *kornish* under Akbar had been greatly modified:

"His Majesty has commanded the palm of the right hand to be placed upon the forehead, and the head to be bent downwards. This mode of salutation, in the language of the present age, is called *Kornish*."—*Āīn*, ed. *Blochmann*, i. 158.

But for his position as the head of religion, in his new faith he permitted, or claimed prostration (*sijda*) before him:

"As some perverse and dark-minded men look upon prostration as blasphemous man-worship, His Majesty, from practical wisdom, has ordered it to be discontinued by the ignorant, and remitted it to all ranks. ... However, in the private assembly, when any of those are in waiting, upon whom the star of good fortune shines, and they receive the order of seating themselves, they certainly perform the prostration of gratitude by bowing down their foreheads to the earth."—*Ibid.* p. 159.

[1615.—"... Whereatt some officers called me to *size-da* (*sij-dah*), but the King answered no, no, in Persian."—*Sir T. Roe,* Hak. Soc. i. 244; and see ii. 296.]

1618.—"The King (Shāh 'Abbās) halted and looked at the Sultan, the latter on both knees, as is their fashion, near him, and advanced his right foot towards him to be kissed. The Sultan having kissed it, and touched it with his forehead ... made a circuit round the king, passing behind him, and making way for his companions to do the like. This done the Sultan came and kissed a second time, as did the other, and this they did three times."—*P. della Valle,* i. 646.

[c. 1686.—"Job (Charnock) made a salam *Koornis*, or low obeisance, every second step he advanced."—*Orme, Fragments,* quoted in *Yule, Hedges' Diary,* Hak. Soc. ii. xcvii.]

1816.—"Lord Amherst put into my hands ... a translation ... by Mr. Morrison of a document received at Tongchow with some others from Chang, containing an official description of the ceremonies to be observed at the public audience of the Embassador. ... The Embassador was then to have been conducted by the Mandarins to the level area, where kneeling ... he was next to have been conducted to the lower end of the hall, where facing the upper part ... he was to have performed the **ko-tou** with 9 prostrations; afterwards he was to have been led out of the hall, and having prostrated himself once behind the row of Mandarins, he was to have been allowed to sit down; he was further to have prostrated himself with the attendant Princes and Mandarins when the Emperor drank. Two other prostrations were to have been made, the first when the milk-tea was presented to him, and the other when he had finished drinking."—*Ellis's Journal of* (Lord Amherst's) *Embassy to China,* 213–214.

1824.—"The first ambassador, with all his following, shall then perform the ceremonial of the three kneelings and the nine prostrations; they shall then rise and be led away in proper order."—*Ceremonial observed at the Court of Peking for the Reception of Ambassadors,* ed. 1824, in *Pauthier,* 192.

1855.—"... The spectacle of one after another of the aristocracy of nature making the **kotow** to the aristocracy of the accident."—*H. Martineau, Autobiog.* ii. 377.

1860.—"Some Seiks, and a private in the Buffs having remained behind with the grog-carts, fell into the hands of the Chinese. On the next morning they were brought before the authorities, and commanded to perform the **kotou**. The Seiks obeyed; but Moyse, the English soldier, declaring that he would not prostrate himself before any Chinaman alive, was immediately knocked upon the head, and his body thrown upon a dunghill" (see China Correspondent of the *Times*). This passage prefaces some noble lines by Sir F. Doyle, ending:

"Vain mightiest fleets, of iron framed;
  Vain those all-shattering guns;
Unless proud England keep, untamed,
  The strong heart of her sons.
So let his name through Europe ring—
  A man of mean estate,
Who died, as firm as Sparta's king,
  Because his soul was great."
Macmillan's Mag. iii. 130.

1876.—"Nebba more **kowtow** big people."—*Leland,* 46.

1879.—"We know that John Bull adores a lord, but a man of Major L'Estrange's social standing would scarcely **kowtow** to every shabby little title to be found in stuffy little rooms in Mayfair."—*Sat. Review,* April 19, p. 505.

KUBBER, KHUBBER, s. Ar.—P.—H. *khabar,* 'news,' and especially as a sporting term, news of game, *e.g.* "There is **pucka khubber** of a tiger this morning."

[1828.—"... the servant informed us that there were some gongwalas, or villagers, in waiting, who had some **khubber** (news about tigers) to give us."—*Mundy, Pen and Pencil Sketches,* ed. 1858, p. 53.]

1878.—"**Khabar** of innumerable black partridges had been received."—*Life in the Mofussil,* i. 159.

1879.—"He will not tell me what **khabbar** has been received."—*'Vanity Fair,'* Nov. 29, p. 299.

***KUBBERDAUB.** An interjectional exclamation, 'Take care!' Pers. *khabar-dār!* 'take heed!' (see KUBBER). It is the usual cry of chokidārs to show that they are awake. [As a substantive it has the sense of a 'scout' or 'spy.']

c. 1664.—"Each *omrah* causeth a guard to be kept all the night long, in his particular camp, of such men that perpetually go the round, and cry **Kaber-dar**, have a care."—*Bernier,* E.T. 119; [ed. *Constable,* 369].

c. 1665.—"Les archers crient ensuite a pleine tête, **Caberdar**, c'est à dire prends garde."—*Thevenot*, v. 58.

[1813.—"There is a strange custom which prevails at all Indian courts, of having a servant called a **khubur-dar**, or newsman, who is an admitted spy upon the chief, about whose person he is employed."—*Broughton, Letters from a Mahratta Camp*, ed. 1892, p. 25.]

KUMPÁSS, s. Hind. *kampās*, corruption of English *compass*, and hence applied not only to a marine or a surveying compass, but also to theodolites, levelling instruments, and other elaborate instruments of observation, and even to the shaft of a carriage. Thus the sextant used to be called *tikunta kampāss*, "the 3-cornered compass."

[1866.—"Many an amusing story did I hear of this wonderful **kumpass**. It possessed the power of reversing everything observed. Hence if you looked through the *doorbeen* at a fort, everything inside was revealed. Thus the Feringhees so readily took forts, not by skill or by valour, but by means of the wonderful power of the *doorbeen*."—*Confess. of an Orderly*, 175.]

KUTTAUR, s. Hind. *kaṭār*, Skt. *kaṭṭāra*, 'a dagger,' especially a kind of dagger peculiar to India, having a solid blade of diamond-section, the handle of which consists of two parallel bars with a cross-piece joining them. The hand grips the cross-piece, and the bars pass along each side of the wrist. [See a drawing in *Egerton, Handbook, Indian Arms*, pl. ix.] Ibn Batuta's account is vivid, and perhaps in the matter of size there may be no exaggeration. Through the kindness of Col. Waterhouse I have a phototype of some Travancore weapons shown at the Calcutta Exhibition of 1883–4; among them two great *kaṭārs*, with sheaths made from the snouts of two sawfishes (with the teeth remaining in). They are done to scale, and one of the blades is 20 inches long, the other 26. There is also a plate in the *Ind. Antiq.* (vii. 193) representing some curious weapons from the Tanjore Palace Armoury, among which are *kaṭār*-hilted daggers evidently of great length, though the entire length is not shown. The plate accompanies interesting notes by Mr. M. J. Walhouse, who states the curious fact that many of the blades mounted *kaṭār*-fashion were of European manufacture, and that one of these bore the famous name of Andrea Ferara. I add an extract. Mr. Walhouse accounts for the adoption of these blades in a country possessing the far-famed Indian steel, in that the latter was excessively brittle. The passage from Stavorinus describes the weapon, without giving a native name. We do not know what name is indicated by 'belly piercer.'

c. 1343.—"The villagers gathered round him, and one of them stabbed him with a **kattāra**. This is the name given to an iron weapon resembling a plough-share; the hand is inserted into it so that the forearm is shielded; but the blade beyond is two cubits in length, and a blow with it is mortal."—*Ibn Batuta*, iv. 31–32.

1442.—"The blacks of this country have the body nearly naked. ... In one hand they hold an Indian poignard (**katārah**-*i-Hindī*), and in the other a buckler of oxhide ... this costume is common to the king and the beggar."—*Abdurrazzāk*, in *India in the XVth Cent.*, p. 17.

c. 1526.—"On the whole there were given one tipchâk horse with the saddle, two pairs of swords with the belts, 25 sets of enamelled daggers, 16 enamelled **kitârehs**, two daggers set with precious stones."—*Baber*, 338.

[c. 1590.—In the list of the Moghul arms we have: "10. **Katárah**, price ½ R. to 1 Muhur."—*Āīn*, ed. *Blochmann*, i. 110, with an engraving, No. 9, pl. xii.]

1638.—"Les personnes de qualité portẽt dans la ceinture vne sorte d'armes, ou de poignards, courte et large, qu'ils appellent *ginda* (?) ou **Catarre**, dont la garde et la gaine sont d'or."—*Mandelslo*, Paris, 1659, 223.

1673.—"They go rich in Attire, with a Poniard, or **Catarre**, at their girdle."—*Fryer*, 93.

1690.—"... which chafes and ferments him to such a pitch; that with a **Catarry** or Bagonet in his hands he first falls upon those that are near him ... killing and stabbing as he goes. ..."—*Ovington*, 237.

1754.—"To these were added an enamelled dagger (which the Indians call **cuttarri**) and two swords. ..."—*H. of Nadir*, in *Hanway's Travels*, ii. 386.

1768–71.—"They (the Moguls) on the left side ... wear a weapon which they call by a name that may be translated *belly-piercer*; it is about 14 inches long; broad near the hilt, and tapering away to a sharp point; it is made of fine steel; the handle has, on each side of it, a catch, which, when the weapon is griped by the hand, shuts round the wrist, and secures it from being dropped."—*Stavorinus*, E.T. i. 457.

1813.—"After a short silent prayer, Lullabhy, in the presence of all the company, waved his **catarra**, or short dagger, over the bed of the expiring man. ... The patient continued for some time motionless: in half an hour his heart appeared to beat, circulation quickened, ... at the expiration of the third hour Lullabhy had effected his cure."—*Forbes, Or. Mem.* iii. 249; [2nd ed. ii. 272, and see i. 69].

1856.—"The manners of the bardic tribe are very similar to those of their Rajpoot clients; their dress is nearly the same, but the bard seldom appears without the '**Kutâr**,' or dagger, a representation of which is scrawled beside his signature, and often rudely engraved upon his monumental stone, in evidence of his death in the sacred duty of **Trâgâ**" (q.v.).—*Forbes, Râs Mâlâ*, ed. 1878, pp. 559–560.

1878.—"The ancient Indian smiths seem to have had a difficulty in hitting on a medium between this highly refined brittle steel and a too soft metal. In ancient sculptures, as in Srirangam near Trichinapalli, life-sized figures of armed men are represented, bearing **Kuttars** or long daggers of a peculiar shape; the handles, not so broad as in the later **Kuttars**, are covered with a long narrow guard, and the blades 2¼ inches broad at bottom, taper very gradually to a point through a length of 18 inches, more than ¾ of which is deeply channelled on both sides with 6 converging grooves. There were many of these in the Tanjor armoury, perfectly corresponding ... and all were so soft as to be easily bent."—*Ind. Antiq.* vii.

***KYFE**, n. One often meets with this word (Ar. *kaif*) in books about the Levant, to indicate the absolute enjoyment of the *dolce far niente*. Though it is in the Hindustāni dictionaries, we never remember to have heard it used in India; but the first quotation below shows that it is, or has been, in use in Western India, in something like the Turkish sense. The proper meaning of the Ar. word is 'how?' 'in what manner?' the secondary is 'partial intoxication.' This looks almost like a parallel to the English vulgar slang of 'how comed you so?' But in fact a man's *kaif* is his 'howness,' *i.e.* what pleases him, his humour; and this passes into the sense of gaiety caused by *ḥashīsh*, &c.

1808.—"... a kind of *confectio Japonica* loaded with opium, *Gānja* or *Bang*, and causing **keif**, or the first degree of intoxication, lulling the senses and disposing to sleep."—*R. Drummond.*

L

LAC, s. Hind. *lākh*, from Skt. *lākshā*, for *rākshā*. The resinous incrustation produced on certain trees (of which the *dhāk* is one, but chiefly **Peepul**, and *khossum* [*kusum, kusumb*], *i.e. Schleichera bijuga, trijuga*) by the puncture of the Lac insect (*Coccus Lacca*, L.). See *Roxburgh*, in Vol. III. *As. Res.*, 384 *seqq*; [and a full list of the trees on which the insect feeds, in *Watt, Econ. Dict.* ii. 410 *seq.*]. The incrustation contains 60 to 70 per cent. of resinous *lac*, and 10 per cent. of dark red colouring matter from which is manufactured *lac-dye*. The material in its original crude form is called *stick-lac;* when boiled in water it loses its red colour, and is then termed *seed-lac;* the melted clarified substance, after the extraction of the dye, is turned out in thin irregular laminae called *shell-lac*. This is used to make sealing-wax, in the fabrication of varnishes, and very largely as a stiffening for men's hats.

Though *lāk* bears the same sense in Persian, and *lak* or *luk* are used in modern Arabic for sealing-wax, it would appear from Dozy (*Glos.*, pp. 295–6, and *Oosterlingen*, 57), that identical or approximate forms are used in various Arabic-speaking regions for a variety of substances giving a red dye, including the *coccus ilicis* or Kermes. Still, we have seen no evidence that in India the word was applied otherwise than to the *lac* of our heading. (Garcia says that the Arabs called it *loc-sumutri*, 'lac of Sumatra'; probably because the Pegu lac was brought to the ports of Sumatra, and purchased there.) And this the term in the *Periplus* seems unquestionably to indicate; whilst it is probable that the passage quoted from Aelian is a much misconceived account of the product. It is not nearly so absurd as De Monfart's account below. The English word *lake* for a certain red colour is from this. So also are *lacquer* and *lackered* ware, because *lac* is used in some of the varnishes with which such ware is prepared.

c. A.D. 80–90.—These articles are imported (to the ports of *Barbaricē*, on the W. of the Red Sea) from the interior parts of Ariakē:—

"Σίδηρος Ἰνδικὸς καὶ στόμωμα (Indian iron and steel)

* * * * *

Λάκκος χρωμάτινος (**Lac**-*dye*)."

Periplus, § 6.

c. 250.—"There are produced in India animals of the size of a beetle, of a red colour, and if you saw them for the first time you would compare them to cinnabar. They have very long legs, and are soft to the touch; they are produced on the trees that bear *electrum*, and they feed on the fruit of these. The Indians catch them and crush them, and with these dye their red cloaks, and the tunics under these, and everything else that they wish to turn to this colour, and to dye. And this kind of clothing is carried also to the King of Persia."—*Aelian, de Nat. Animal.* iv. 46.

c. 1343.—The notice of *lacca* in Pegolotti is in parts very difficult to translate, and we do not feel absolutely certain that it refers to the Indian product, though we believe it to be so. Thus, after explaining that there are two classes of *lacca*, the *matura* and *acerba*, or ripe and unripe, he goes on: "It is produced attached to stalks, *i.e.* to the branches of shrubs, but it ought to be clear from stalks, and earthy dust, and sand, and from *costiere* (?). The stalks are the twigs of the wood on which it is produced, the *costiere* or *figs*, as the Catalans call them, are composed of the dust of the thing, which when it is fresh heaps together and hardens like pitch; only that pitch is black, and those *costiere* or figs are red and of the colour of unripe **lacca.** And more of these *costiere* is found in the unripe than the ripe **lacca,**" and so on.—*Della Decima*, iii. 365.

1510.—"There also grows a very large quantity of **lacca** (or *lacra*) for making red colour, and the tree of this is formed like our trees which produce walnuts."—*Varthema*, 238.

1516.—"Here (in Pegu) they load much fine **laquar**, which grows in the country."—*Barbosa, Lisbon Acad.*, 366.

1519.—"And because he had it much in charge to get all the *lac* (**alacre**) that he could, the governor knowing through information of the merchants that much came to the Coast of Choromandel by the ships of Pegu and Martaban that frequented that coast. ..."—*Correa*, ii. 567.

1563.—"Now it is time to speak of the **lacre**, of which so much is consumed in this country in closing letters, and for other seals, in the place of wax."—*Garcia*, f. 112*v*.

1582.—"**Laker** is a kinde of gum that proceedeth of the ant."—*Castañeda*, tr. by N.L., f. 33.

c. 1590.—(Recipe for *Lac* varnish). "**Lac** is used for *chighs* (see CHICK, **a**). If red, 4 *ser* of **lac**, and 1 *s.* of vermilion; if yellow, 4 *s.* of **lac**, and 1 *s. zarnīkh.*"—*Āīn*, ed. *Blochmann*, i. 226.

1615.—"In this Iland (Goa) is the hard Waxe made (which we call Spanish Waxe), and is made in the manner following. They inclose a large plotte of ground, with a little trench filled with water; then they sticke up a great number of small staues vpon the sayd plot, that being done they bring thither a sort of pismires, farre biggar than ours, which beeing debar'd by the water to issue out, are constrained to retire themselves vppon the said staues, where they are kil'd with the Heate of the Sunne, and thereof it is that **Lacka** is made."—*De Monfart*, 35–36.

c. 1610.—"... Vne manière de boëte ronde, vernie, et **lacrèe**, qui est vne ouurage de ces isles."—*Pyrard de Laval*, i. 127; [Hak. Soc. i. 170].

1627.—"**Lac** is a strange drugge, made by certain winged Pismires of the gumme of Trees."—*Purchas, Pilgrimage*; 569.

1644.—"There are in the territories of the *Mogor*, besides those things mentioned, other articles of trade, such as **Lacre**, both the insect lacre and the cake" (*de formiga e de pasta*).—*Bocarro, MS.*

1663.—"In one of these Halls you shall find Embroiderers ... in another you shall see Goldsmiths ... in a fourth Workmen in **Lacca.**"—*Bernier* E.T. 83; [ed. *Constable*, 259].

1727.—"Their **lackt** or *japon'd* Ware is without any Doubt the best in the World."—*A. Hamilton*, ii. 305; [ed. 1744].

***LACK**, s. One hundred thousand, and especially in the Anglo-Indian colloquial 100,000 Rupees, in the days of better exchange the equivalent of £10,000. Hind. *lākh*, *lak*, &c., from Skt. *laksha*, used (see below) in the same sense, but which appears to have originally meant "a mark." It is necessary to explain that the term does not occur in the earlier Skt. works. Thus in the *Talavakāra Brāhmaṇā*, a complete series of the higher numerical terms is given. After *śata* (10), *sahasra* (1000), comes *ayuta* (10,000), *prayuta* (*now* a million), *niyuta* (*now* also a million), *arbuda* (100 millions), *nyarbuda* (not now used), *nikharṇa* (do.), and *padma* (now 10,000 millions). *Laksha* is therefore a modern substitute for *prayuta*, and the series has been expanded. This was probably done by the Indian astronomers between the 5th and 10th centuries A.D.

The word has been adopted in the Malay and Javanese, and other languages of the Archipelago. But it is remarkable that in all of this class of languages which have adopted the word it is used in the sense of 10,000 instead of 100,000 with the sole exception of the Lampungs of Sumatra, who use it correctly. (*Crawfurd*). (See CRORE.)

We should observe that though a *lack*, used absolutely for a sum of money, in modern times always implies rupees, this has not always been the case. Thus in the time of Akbar and his immediate successors the revenue was settled and reckoned in *laks* of **dams** (q.v.). Thus:

c. 1594.—"In the 40th year of his majesty's reign (Akbar's), his dominions consisted of 105 *Sircars*, subdivided into 2737 *Kusbahs* the revenue of which he settled for ten years, at the annual rent of 3 *Arribs*, 62 *Crore*, 97 **Lacks**, 55,246 *Dams*. ..."—*Ayeen*, ed. *Gladwin*, ii. 1; [ed. *Jarrett*, ii. 115].

At Ormuz again we find another **lack** in vogue, of which the unit was apparently the *dīnār*, not the old gold coin, but a degenerate *dīnār*, of small value. Thus:

1554.—"(Money of Ormuz).—A **leque** is equivalent to 50 pardaos of *çadis*, which is called 'bad money,' (and this *leque* is not a coin but a number by which they reckon at Ormuz): and each of these pardaos is equal to 2 *azares*, and each *azar* to 10 *çadis*, each *çadi* to 100 *dinars*, and after this fashion they calculate in the books of the Custom-house. ..."—*Nunez, Lyvro dos Pesos*, &c., in *Subsidios*, 25.

Here the *azar* is the Persian *hazār* or 1000 (*dīnārs*); the *çadi* Pers. *sad* or 100 (*dīnārs*); the **leque** or **lak**, 100,000 (*dīnārs*); and the *tomān*, which does not appear here, is 10,000 (*dīnārs*).

c. 1300.—"They went to the *Kāfir's* tent, killed him, and came back into the town, whence they carried off money belonging to the Sultan amounting to 12 **laks**. The **lak** is a sum of 100,000 (silver) *dīnārs*, equivalent to 10,000 Indian gold *dīnārs*."—*Ibn Batuta*, iii. 106.

c. 1340.—"The Sultan distributes daily two **lāks** in alms, never less; a sum of which the equivalent in money of Egypt and Syria would be 160,000 pieces of silver."—*Shihābuddīn Dimishki*, in *Notes and Exts.*, xiii. 192.

In these examples from Pinto the word is used apart from money, in the Malay form, but not in the Malay sense of 10,000:

c. 1540.—"The old man desiring to satisfie *Antonio de Faria's* demand, *Sir*, said he ... *the chronicles of those times affirm, how in only four yeares and an half sixteen* **Lacazaas** (*lacasá*) *of men were slain, every* **Lacazaa** *containing an hundred thousand*."—*Pinto* (orig. cap. xlv.) in *Cogan*, p. 53.

c. 1546.—"... he ruined in 4 months space all the enemies countries, with such a destruction of people as, if credit may be given to our histories ... there died fifty **Laquesaas** of persons."—*Ibid.* p. 224.

1615.—"And the whole present was worth ten of their **Leakes**, as they call them; a **Leake** being 10,000 pounds sterling; the whole 100,000 pounds sterling."—*Coryat's Letters from India* (*Crudities*, iii. f. 25*v*).

1616.—"He received twenty **lecks** of roupies towards his charge (two hundred thousand pounds sterling)."—*Sir T. Roe*, reprint, p. 35; [Hak. Soc. i. 201, and see i. 95, 183, 238].

1651.—"Yeder **Lac** is hondert duysend."—*Rogerius*, 77.

c. 1665.—"Il faut cent mille roupies pour faire un **lek**, cent mille **leks** pour faire un *courou*, cent mille *courous* pour faire un *padan*, et cent mille *padan* pour faire un *nil*."—*Thevenot*, v. 54.

1673.—"In these great Solemnities, it is usual for them to set it around with Lamps to the number of two or three **Leaques**, which is so many hundred thousand in our account."—*Fryer*, [p. 104, reading **Lecques**].

1684.—"They have by information of the servants dug in severall places of the house, where they have found great summes of money. Under his bed were found **Lacks** 4½. In the House of Office two **Lacks**. They in all found Ten **Lacks** already, and make no doubt but to find more."—*Hedges, Diary*, Jan. 2; [Hak. Soc. i. 145].

1692.—"... a **lack** of Pagodas. ..."—In *Wheeler*, i. 262.

1747.—"The Nabob and other Principal Persons of this Country are of such an extreme lacrative (*sic*) Disposition, and ... are so exceedingly avaritious, occasioned by the large Proffers they have received from the French, that nothing less than **Lacks** will go near to satisfie them."—*Letter from Ft. St. David to the Court*, May 2 (MS. Records in India Office).

1778.—"Sir Matthew Mite will make up the money already advanced in another name, by way of future mortgage upon his estate, for the entire purchase, 5 **lacks** of roupees."—*Foote, The Nabob*, Act I. sc. i.

1785.—"Your servants have no Trade in this country; neither do you pay them high wages, yet in a few years they return to England with many **lacs** of pagodas."—*Nabob of Arcot*, in Burke's Speech on his Debts, *Works*, iv. 18.

1833.—"Tout le reste (et dans le reste il y a des intendants riches de plus de vingt **laks**) s'assied par terre."—*Jacquemont, Correspond.* ii. 120.

1879.—"In modern times the only numbers in practical use above 'thousands' are *laksa* ('**lac**' or '**lakh**') and *koṭi* ('crore'); an an Indian sum is wont to be pointed thus: 123, 45, 67, 890, to signify 123 crores, 45 **lakhs**, + 67 thousand, eight hundred and ninety."—*Whitney, Sansk. Grammar*, 161.

The older writers, it will be observed (c. 1600–1620), put the **lakh** at £10,000; Hamilton (c. 1700) puts it at £12,500; Williamson (c. 1810) at the same; then for many years it stood again as the equivalent of £10,000; now (1880) it is little more than £8000; [now (1901) about £6666].

LALL-SHRAUB, s. Englishman's Hind. *lāl-sharāb*, 'red wine.' The universal name of claret in India.

[c. 1780.—"To every plate are set down two glasses; one pyramidal (like hobnob glasses in

England) for **Loll Shrub** (*scilicet*, claret); the other a common sized wineglass for whatever beverage is most agreeable."—*Diary of Mrs. Fay*, in *Busteed, Echoes*, 123.]

LAMA, s. A Tibetan Buddhist monk. Tibet. *bLama* (*b* being silent). The word is sometimes found written *Llama*; but this is nonsense. In fact it seems to be a popular confusion, arising from the name of the S. American quadruped which is so spelt. See quotation from *Times* below.

c. 1590.—"Fawning Court doctors ... said it was mentioned in some holy books that men used to live up to the age of 1000 years ... and in Thibet there were even now a class of **Lāmahs** or Mongolian devotees, and recluses, and hermits that live 200 years and more. ..."—*Badāonī*, quoted by *Blochmann*, *Āīn*, i. 201.

1664.—"This Ambassador had in his suit a Physician, which was said to be of the Kingdom of Lassa, and of the Tribe *Lamy* or **Lama**, which is that of the men of the Law in that country, as the *Brahmans* are in the Indies ... he related of his great **Lama** that when he was old, and ready to die, he assembled his council, and declared to them that now he was passing into the Body of a little child lately born. ..."—*Bernier*, E.T. 135; [ed. *Constable*, 424].

1716.—"Les Thibetaines ont des Religieux nommés **Lamas**."—In *Lettres Edif.* xii. 438.

1774.—"... ma questo primo figlio ... rinunziò la corona al secondo e lui difatti si fece religioso o **lama** del paese."—*Della Tomba*, 61.

c. 1818.—

"The Parliament of Thibet met—
 The little **Lama**, called before it,
 Did there and then his whipping get,
 And, as the Nursery Gazette
  Assures us, like a hero bore it."

T. Moore, *The Little Grand Lama*.

1876.—"... Hastings ... touches on the analogy between Tibet and the high valley of Quito, as described by De la Condamine, an analogy which Mr. Markham brings out in interesting detail. ... But when he enlarges on the wool which is a staple of both countries, and on the animals producing it, he risks confirming in careless readers that popular impression which might be expressed in the phraseology of Fluelen—''Tis all one; 'tis alike as my fingers is to my fingers, and there is **Llamas** in both."—*Rev. of Markham's Tibet*, in *Times*, May 15.

The passage last quoted is in jesting vein, but the following is serious and delightful:—

1879.—"The landlord prostrated himself as reverently, if not as lowly, as a Peruvian before his *Grand* **Llama**."—*Patty's Dream*, a novel reviewed in the *Academy*, May 17.

LAMASERY, LAMASERIE, s. This is a word, introduced apparently by the French R. C. Missionaries, for a **lama** convent. Without being positive, I would say that it does not represent any Oriental word (*e.g.* compound of *lami* and **serai**), but is a factitious French word analogous to *nonnerie*, *vacherie*, *laiterie*, &c.

[c. 1844.—"According to the Tartars, the **Lamasery** of the Five Towers is the best place you can be buried in."—*Huc*, *Travels in Tartary*, i. 78.]

LAOS, n.p. A name applied by the Portuguese to the civilised people who occupied the inland frontier of Burma and Siam, between those countries on the one hand and China and Tongking on the other; a people called by the Burmese **Shans**, a name which we have in recent years adopted. They are of the same race of *Thai* to which the Siamese belong, and which extends with singular identity of manners and language, though broken into many separate communities, from Assam to the Malay Peninsula. The name has since been frequently used as a singular, and applied as a territorial name to the region occupied by this people immediately to the North of Siam. There have been a great number of separate principalities in this region, of which now one and now another predominated and conquered its neighbours. Before the rise of Siam the most important was that of which Sakotai was the capital, afterwards represented by Xieng-mai, the Zimmé of the Burmese and the **Jangomay** of some old English documents. In later times the chief States were *Muang Luang Praban* and *Vien-shan*, both upon the Mekong. It would appear from Lieut. Macleod's narrative, and from Garnier, that the name of **Lao** is that by which the branch of these people on the Lower Mekong, *i.e.* of those two States, used to designate themselves. Muang Praban is still quasi independent; Vien-Shan was annexed with great cruelties by Siam, c. 1828.

1553.—"Of silver of 11 dinheiros alloy he (Alboquerque) made only a kind of money called *Malaquezes*, which silver came thither from Pegu, whilst from Siam came a very pure silver of 12 dinheiros assay, procured from certain people called **Laos**, lying to the north of these two kingdoms."—*Barros*, II. vi. 6.

1553.—"... certain very rugged mountain ranges, like the Alps, inhabited by the people called Gueos who fight on horseback, and with whom the King of Siam is continually at war. They are near him only on the north, leaving between the two the people called **Laos**, who encompass this Kingdom of Siam, both on the North, and on the East along the river Mecon ... and on the south adjoin these **Laos** the two Kingdoms of **Camboja** and Choampa, which are on the sea-board. These **Laos** ... though they are lords of so great territories, are all subject to this King of Siam, though often in rebellion against him."—*Ibid.* III. ii. 5.

"Three Kingdoms at the upper part of these, are those of the **Laos**, who (as we have said) obey Siam through fear: the first of these is called *Jangoma*, the chief city of which is called Chiamay ... the second *Chaneray Cheneran*: the third Lanchaa which is below the others, and adjoins the Kingdom of Cacho, or Cauchichina. ..." *Ibid.*

c. 1560.—"Those **Laos** came to Camboia, downe a River many daies Iournie, which they say to have his beginning in *China* as many others which runne into the Sea of India; it hath eight, fifteene, and twentie fathome water, as myselfe saw by experience in a great part of it; it passeth through manie vnknowne and desart Countries of great Woods and Forests where there are innumerable Elephants, and many Buffes ... and certayne beastes which in that Countrie they call *Badas.*"—*Gaspar da Cruz*, in *Purchas*, iii. 169.

c. 1598.—"... I offered to go to the **Laos** by land, at my expense, in search of the King of Cambodia, as I knew that that was the road to go by. ..."—*Blas de Herman Gonzalez*, in *De Morga* (E.T. by Hon. H. Stanley, Hak. Soc.), p. 97.

1641.—"*Concerning the Land of the* **Louwen**, *and a Journey made thereunto by our Folk in Anno* 1641" (&c.).—*Valentijn*, III. Pt. ii. pp. 50 *seqq.*

1663.—"*Relation Nouvele et Curieuse du Royaume de* **Lao**.—Traduite de l'Italien du P. de Marini, Romain. Paris, 1666."

1766.—"Les peuples de **Lao**, nos voisins, n'admittent ni la question ni les peines arbitraires ... ni les horribles supplices qui sont parmi nous en usage; mais aussi nous les regardons comme de barbares. ... Toute l'Asie convient que nous dansons beaucoup mieux qu'eux."—*Voltaire, Dialogue XXI., André des Couches à Siam.*

LASCAR, s. The word is originally from Pers. *lashkar*, 'an army,' 'a camp.' This is usually derived from Ar. *al'askar*, but it would rather seem that Ar. *'askar*, 'an army' is taken from this Pers. word: whence *lashkarī*, 'one belonging to an army, a soldier.' The word *lascár* or *láscár* (both these pronunciations are in vogue) appears to have been corrupted, through the Portuguese use of *lashkarī* in the forms *lasquarin*, *lascari*, &c., either by the Portuguese themselves, or by the Dutch and English who took up the word from them, and from these *laskār* has passed back again into native use in this corrupt shape. The early Portuguese writers have the forms we have just named in the sense of 'soldier'; but *lascar* is never so used now. It is in general the equivalent of *khalāsī*, in the various senses of that word viz. (1) an inferior class of artilleryman ('*gun-lascar*'); (2) a tent-pitcher, doing other work which the class are accustomed to do; (3) a sailor. The last is the most common Anglo-Indian use, and has passed into the English language. The use of *lascar* in the modern sense by Pyrard de Laval shows that this use was already general on the west coast at the beginning of the 17th century, [also see quotation from Pringle below]; whilst the curious distinction which Pyrard makes between *Lascar* and *Lascari*; and Dr. Fryer makes between *Luscar* and *Lascar* (accenting probably *Lúscar* and *Lascár*) shows that *lashkarī* for a soldier was still in use. In Ceylon the use of the word *lascareen* for a local or civil soldier long survived; perhaps is not yet extinct. The word *lashkari* does not seem to occur in the *Āīn*.

[1523.—"Fighting men called **Lascaryns.**"—*Alguns documentes, Tombo*, p. 479.

[1538.—"My mother only bore me to be a Captain, and not your **Lascar** (**lascarin**)."—Letter of *Nuno da Cunha*, in *Barros*, Dec. IV. bk. 10, ch. 21.]

1541.—"It is a proverbial saying all over **India** (*i.e. Portuguese India*, see s.v.) that the good **Lasquarim**, or 'soldier' as we should call him, must be an Abyssinian."—*Castro, Roteiro*, 73.

1546.—"Besides these there were others (who fell at Diu) whose names are unknown, being men of the lower rank, among whom I knew a **lascarym** (a man getting only 500 reis of pay!) who was the first man to lay his hand on the Moorish wall, and shouted aloud that they might see him, as many have told me. And he was immediately thrown down wounded in five places with stones and bullets, but still lived; and a noble gentleman sent and had him rescued and carried away by his slaves. And he survived, but being a common man he did not even get his pay!"—*Correa*, iv. 567.

1552.—"... eles os reparte polos **lascarins** do suas capitanias, q̃ assi chamão soldados."—

Castanheda, ii. 67. [Mr. Whiteway notes that in the orig. *repartem* for *reparte*, and the reference should be ii. 16.]

1554.—"Moreover the Senhor Governor conceded to the said ambassador that if in the territories of Idalshaa or in those of our Lord the King there shall be any differences or quarrels between any Portuguese **lascarins** or **peons** (*piães*) of ours, and **lascarins** of the territories of Idalshaa and peons of his, that the said Idalshaa shall order the delivery up of the Portuguese and peons that they may be punished if culpable. And in like manner ..."—*S. Botelho, Tombo*, 44.

1572.—"Erant in eo praesidio **Lasquarini** circiter septingenti artis scolopettariae peritissimi."—*E. Acosta*, f. 236*v*.

1598.—"The soldier of *Ballagate*, which is called **Lascarin**. ..."—*Linschoten*, 74; [in Hak. Soc. i. 264, **Lascariin**].

1600.—"Todo a mais churma e meneyo das naos são Mouros que chamão **Laschãres**. ..."—*Lucena, Life of St. Franc. Xav.*, liv. iv. p. 223.

[1602.—"... because the **Lascars** (**lascaris**), for so they call the Arab sailors."—*Couto*, Dec. X. bk. 3, ch. 13.]

c. 1610.—"Mesmes tous les mariniers et les pilotes sont Indiens, tant Gentils que Mahometans. Tous ces gens de mer les appellent **Lascars**, et les soldats **Lascarits**."—*Pyrard de Laval*, i. 317; [Hak. Soc. i. 438; also see ii. 3, 17].

[1615.—"... two horses with six **Lasceras** and two caffres (see CAFFER)."—*Foster, Letters*, iv. 112.]

1644.—"... The *aldeas* of the jurisdiction of Damam, in which district there are 4 fortified posts defended by *Lascars* (**Lascarīs**) who are mostly native Christian soldiers, though they may be heathen as some of them are."—*Bocarro*, MS.

1673.—"The Seamen and Soldiers differ only in a Vowel, the one being pronounced with an *u*, the other with an *a*, as **Luscar**, a soldier, **Lascar**, a seaman."—*Fryer*, 107.

[1683-84.—"The Warehousekeeper having Seaverall dayes advised the Council of Ship Welfares tardynesse in receiving & stowing away the Goods, ... alledging that they have not hands Sufficient to dispatch them, though we have spared them tenn **Laskars** for that purpose. ..."—*Pringle, Diary Ft. St. Geo.*, 1st ser. iii. 7 *seq.*; also see p. 43.]

1685.—"They sent also from Sofragan D. Antonio da Motta Galvaon with 6 companies, which made 190 men; the Dissava of the adjoining provinces joined him with 4000 **Lascarins**."—*Ribeyro, H. of the I. of Ceylan* (from French Tr., p. 241).

1690.—"For when the *English* Sailers at that time perceiv'd the softness of the Indian **Lascarrs**; how tame they were ... they embark'd again upon a new Design ... to ... rob these harmless Traffickers in the *Red Sea*."—*Ovington*, 464.

1726.—"**Lascaryns**, or Loopers, are native soldiers, who have some regular maintenance, and in return must always be ready."—*Valentijn, Ceylon*, Names of Offices, &c., 10.

1755.—"Some **Lascars** and Sepoys were now sent forward to clear the road."—*Orme*, ed. 1803, i. 394.

1787.—"The Field Pieces attached to the Cavalry draw up on the Right and Left Flank of the Regiment; the Artillery **Lascars** forming in a line with the Front Rank the full Extent of the Drag Ropes, which they hold in their hands."—*Regns. for the Hon. Company's Troops or the Coast of Coromandel*, by *M.-Gen. Sir Archibald Campbell*, K.B. Govr. & C. in C. Madras, p. 9.

1803.—"In those parts (of the low country of Ceylon) where it is not thought requisite to quarter a body of troops, there is a police corps of the natives appointed to enforce the commands of Government in each district; they are composed of *Conganies*, or sergeants, *Aratjies*, or corporals, and **Lascarines**, or common soldiers, and perform the same office as our Sheriff's men or constables."—*Percival's Ceylon*, 222.

1807.—"A large open boat formed the van, containing his excellency's guard of **lascoreens**, with their spears raised perpendicularly, the union colours flying, and Ceylon drums called **tomtoms** beating."—*Cordiner's Ceylon*, 170.

1872.—"The **lascars** on board the steamers were insignificant looking people."—*The Dilemma*, ch. ii.

In the following passages the original word *lashkar* is used in its proper sense for 'a camp.'

[1614.—"He said he bought it of a banyan in the **Lasker**."—*Foster, Letters*, ii. 142.

[1615.—"We came to the **Lasker** the 7th of February in the evening."—*Ibid.* iii. 85.]

1616.—"I tooke horse to auoyd presse, and other inconvenience, and crossed out of the **Leskar**, before him."—*Sir T. Roe*, in *Purchas*, i. 559; see also 560; [Hak. Soc. ii. 324].

[1682.—"... presents to the Seir **Lascarr** (*sar-i-lashkar*, 'head of the army') this day received."—*Pringle, Diary Ft. St. Geo.*, 1st ser. i. 84.]

LĀT, LĀT SĀHIB, s. This, a popular corruption of *Lord Sahib*, or *Lārd Sāhib*, as it is written in Hind., is the usual form from native lips, at least in the Bengal Presidency, of the title by which the Governor-General has long been known in the vernaculars. The term also extends nowadays to Lieutenant-Governors, who in contact with the higher anthority become *Chhoṭā* ('Little') **Lāt**, whilst the Governor-General and the Commander-in-Chief are sometimes discriminated as the *Mulkī* **Lāt Sāhib** [or **Barē Lāt**], and the *Jangī* **Lāt Sāhib** ('territorial' and 'military'), the Bishop as the **Lāt Pādrē Sāhib**, and the Chief Justice as the **Lāt Justy Sāhib**. The title is also sometimes, but very incorrectly, applied to minor dignitaries of the supreme Government, [whilst the common form of blessing addressed to a civil officer is "*Huzūr* **Lāt Guvnar, Lāt Sikritar** *ho-jāeṅ*."

1824.—"He seemed, however, much puzzled to make out my rank, never having heard (he said) of any **'Lord Sahib'** except the Governor-General, while he was still more perplexed by the exposition of **'Lord** *Bishop* **Sahib**,' which for some reason or other my servants always prefer to that of **Lord Padre**."—*Heber*, i. 69.

1837.—"The Arab, thinking I had purposely stolen his kitten, ran after the buggy at full speed, shouting as he passed Lord Auckland's tents, 'Dohā'ī, dohā'ī, Sāhib! dohā'ī, **Lord Sāhib**!' (see DOAI). 'Mercy, mercy, sir! mercy, Governor-General!' The faster the horse rushed on, the faster followed the shouting Arab."—*Wanderings of a Pilgrim*, ii. 142.

1868.—"The old barber at Roorkee, after telling me that he had known Strachey when he first began, added, 'Ab **Lāt-Sekretur** hai! Ah! hum bhi boodda hogya!' ('Now he is *Lord Secretary*! Ah! I too have become old!')"—*Letter from the late M.-Gen. W. W. H. Greathed.*

1877.—"... in a rare but most valuable book (*Galloway's Observations on India*, 1825, pp. 254–8), in which the author reports, with much quiet humour, an aged native's account of the awful consequences of contempt of an order of the (as he called the Supreme Court) '*Shubreem Koorut*,' the order of Impey being **'Lord Justey Sahib**-*ka-hookm*,' the instruments of whose will were '*abidabis*' or affidavits."—Letter from *Sir J. F. Stephen*, in *Times*, May 31.

LATTEE, s. A stick; a bludgeon, often made of the male bamboo (*Dendrocalamus strictus*), and sometimes bound at short intervals with iron rings, forming a formidable weapon. The word is Hind. *lāṭhī* and *laṭhī*, Mahr. *laṭhṭha*. This is from Prakrit *laṭṭhī*, for Skt. *yashṭi*, 'a stick,' according to the Prakrit grammar of Vavaruchi (ed. *Cowell*, ii. 32); see also *Lassen, Institutiones, Ling. Prakrit*, 195. *Jiskī lāṭhī, us kī bhaiṇs*, is a Hind. proverb (*cujus baculum ejus bubalus*), equivalent to the "good old rule, the simple plan."

1830.—"The natives use a very dangerous weapon, which they have been forbidden by Government to carry. I took one as a curiosity, which had been seized on a man in a fight in a village. It is a very heavy **lāthi**, a solid male bamboo, 5 feet 5 inches long, headed with iron in a most formidable manner. There are 6 jagged semicircular irons at the top, each 2 inches in length, 1 in height, and it is shod with iron bands 16 inches deep from the top."—*Wanderings of a Pilgrim*, i. 133.

1878.—"After driving some 6 miles, we came upon about 100 men seated in rows on the roadside, all with **latties**."—*Life in the Mofussil*, i. 114.

***LATTEEAL**, s. Hind. *lāṭhīyāl*, or, more cumbrously, *lāṭhīwālā*, 'a clubman,' a hired ruffian. Such gentry were not many years ago entertained in scores by planters in some parts of Bengal, to maintain by force their claims to lands for sowing indigo on.

1878.—"Doubtless there were hired **lattials** ... on both sides."—*Life in the Mofussil*, ii. 6.

LAW-OFFICER. This was the official designation of a Mahommedan officer learned in the (Mahommedan) law, who was for many years of our Indian administration an essential functionary of the judges' Courts in the districts, as well as of the Sudder or Courts of Review at the Presidency.

It is to be remembered that the law administered in Courts under the Company's government, from the assumption of the Dewanny of Bengal, Bahar, and Orissa, was the Mahommedan law; at first by the hands of native **Cazees** and **Mufties**, with some superintendence from the higher European servants of the Company; a superintendence which, while undergoing sundry vicissitudes of system during the next 30 years, developed gradually into a European judiciary, which again was set on an extended and quasi-permanent footing by Lord Cornwallis's Government, in Regulation IX. of 1793 (see ADAWLUT). The Mahommedan law continued, however, to be the professed basis of criminal jurisprudence, though modified more and more, as years went on, by new **Regulations**, and by the recorded constructions and circular orders of the superior Courts, until the accomplishment of the great changes which followed the Mutiny, and the assumption of the direct government of India by the Crown (1858). The landmarks of change were (*a*) the enactment of the Penal Code (Act XLV. of 1860), and (*b*) that of the Code of Criminal Procedure (Act. XXV. of 1861), followed by (*c*) the establishment of the High Court (July 1, 1862), in which became merged both the **Supreme Court** with its peculiar jurisdiction, and the (quondam-Company's) Sudder Courts of Review and Appeal, civil and criminal (*Dewanny* **Adawlat**, and *Nizamat* **Adawlut**).

The authoritative exposition of the Mahommedan Law, in aid and guidance of the English judges, was the function of the Mahommedan **Law-officer**. He sat with the judge on the bench at Sessions, *i.e.* in the hearing of criminal cases committed by the magistrate for trial; and at the end of the trial he gave in his written record of the proceedings with his **Futwa** (q.v.) (see Regn. IX. 1793, sect. 47), which was his judgment as to the guilt of the accused, as to the definition of the crime, and as to its appropriate punishment according to Mahommedan Law. The judge was bound attentively to consider the *futwa*, and if it seemed to him to be consonant with natural justice, and also in conformity with the Mahommedan Law, he passed sentence (save in certain excepted cases) in its terms, and issued his warrant to the magistrate for execution of the sentence, unless it were one of death, in which case the proceedings had to be referred to the Sudder Nizamut for confirmation. In cases also where there was disagreement between the civilian judge and the Law-officer, either as to finding or sentence, the matter was referred to the Sudder Court for ultimate decision.

In 1832, certain modifications were introduced by law (*Regn.* VI. of that year), which declared that the *futwa* might be dispensed with either by referring the case for report to a **punchayet** (q.v.), which sat apart from the Court; or by constituting assessors in the trial (generally three in number). The frequent adoption of the latter alternative rendered the appearance of the Law-officer and his *futwa* much less universal as time went on. The post of **Law-officer** was indeed not actually abolished till 1864. But it would appear from enquiry that I have made, among friends of old standing in the Civil Service, that for some years before the issue of the Penal Code and the other reforms already mentioned, the **Moolvee** (*maulavī*) or Mahommedan **Law-officer** had, in some at least of the Bengal districts, practically ceased to sit with the judge, even in cases where no assessors were summoned.[1] I cannot trace any legislative authority for this, nor any Circular of the Sudder Nizamut; and it is not easy, at this time of day, to obtain much personal testimony. But Sir George Yule (who was Judge of Rungpore and Bogra about 1855–56) writes thus:

"The **Moulvee**-ship ... must have been abolished before I became a judge (I think), which was 2 or 3 years before the Mutiny; for I have *no* recollection of *ever* sitting with a *Moulvee*, and I had a great number of heavy criminal cases to try in Rungpore and Bogra. Assessors were substituted for the *Moulvee* in some cases, but I have no recollection of employing these either."

Mr. Seton-Karr, again, who was Civil and Sessions Judge of Jessore (1857–1860), writes:

"I am quite certain of my own practice ... and I made deliberate choice of native assessors, whenever the law required me to have such functionaries. I determined *never* to sit with a *Maulavi*, as, even before the Penal Code was passed, and came into operation, I wished to get rid of **futwas** and differences of opinion.

The office of Law-officer was formally abolished by Act XI. of 1864.

In respect of civil litigation, it had been especially laid down (*Regn.* of April 11, 1780, quoted below) that in suits regarding successions, inheritance, marriage, caste, and all religious usages and institutions, the Mahommedan laws with respect to Mahommedans, and the Hindū laws with respect to Hindūs, were to be considered as the general rules by which the judges were to form their decisions. In the respective cases, it was laid down, the *Mahommedan and Hindū* **law-officers** of the court were to attend and expound the law.

In this note I have dealt only with the

---

1 Reg. I. of 1810 had empowered the Executive Government, by an official communication from its Secretary in the Judicial Department, to dispense with the attendance and futwa of the **Law officers** of the courts of circuit, when it seemed advisable. But in such case the judge of the court passed no sentence, but referred the proceedings with an opinion to the *Nizamut Adawlut*.

Mahommedan law-officer, whose presence and co-operation was so long (it has been seen) essential in a criminal trial. In civil cases he did not sit with the judge (at least in memory of man now living), but the judge could and did, in case of need, refer to him on any point of Mahommedan Law. The Hindū **law-officer** (**Pundit**) is found in the legislation of 1793, and is distinctly traceable in the Regulations down at least to 1821. In fact he is named in the Act XI. of 1864 (see quotation under CAZEE) abolishing Law-officers. But in many of the districts it would seem that he had very long before 1860 practically ceased to exist, under what circumstances exactly I have failed to discover. He had nothing to do with criminal justice, and the occasions for reference to him were presumably not frequent enough to justify his maintenance in every district. A *Pundit* continued to be attached to the Sudder Dewanny, and to him questions were referred by the District Courts when requisite. Neither *Pundit* nor *Moolvee* is attached to the High Court, but native judges sit on its Bench. It need only be added that under Regulation III. of 1821, a magistrate was authorized to refer for trial to the Law-officer of his district a variety of complaints and charges of a trivial character. The designation of the Law-officer was *Maulavi*. (See ADAWLUT, CAZEE, FUTWA, MOOLVEE, MUFTY.)

1780.—"That in all suits regarding inheritance, marriage, and caste, and other religious usages or institutions, the laws of the Koran with respect to Mahommedans, and those of the Shaster with respect to Gentoos, shall be invariably adhered to. On all such occasions the **Molavies** or Brahmins shall respectively attend to expound the law; and they shall sign the report and assist in passing the decree."—*Regulation passed by the G.-G. and Council*, April 11, 1780.

1793.—"II. The **Law Officers** of the Sudder Dewanny Adawlut, the Nizamut Adawlut, the provincial Courts of Appeal, the courts of circuit, and the zillah and city courts ... shall not be removed but for incapacity or misconduct. ..."—*Reg. XII.* of 1793.

In §§ iv., v., vi. **Cauxy** and **Mufty** are substituted for **Law-Officer**, but referring to the same persons.

1799.—"IV. If the **futwa** of the **law officers** of the Nizamut Adawlut declare any person convicted of wilful murder not liable to suffer death under the Mahomedan law on the ground of ... the Court of *Nizamut Adawlut* shall notwithstanding sentence the prisoner to suffer death. ...—*Reg. VIII.* of 1799.

LEECHEE, LYCHEE, s. Chin. *li-chi*, and in S. China (its native region) *lai-chi*; the beautiful and delicate fruit of the *Nephelium litchi*, Cambessèdes (N. O. *Sapindaceae*), a tree which has been for nearly a century introduced into Bengal with success. The dried fruit, usually ticketed as *lychee*, is now common in London shops.

c. 1540.—"... outra verdura muito mais fresca, e de melhor cheiro, que esta, a que os naturaes da terra chamão **lechias**. ..."—*Pinto*, ch. lxviii.

1563.—"*R.* Of the things of China you have not said a word; though there they have many fruits highly praised, such as are **lalichias** (*lalixias*) and other excellent fruits.

"*O.* I did not speak of the things of China, because China is a region of which there is so much to tell that it never comes to an end. ..."—*Garcia*, f. 157.

1585.—"Also they have a kinde of plummes that they doo call **lechias**, that are of an exceeding gallant tast, and never hurteth anybody, although they should eate a great number of them."—*Parke's Mendoza*, i. 14.

1598.—"There is a kind of fruit called **Lechyas**, which are like Plums, but of another taste, and are very good, and much esteemed, whereof I have eaten."—*Linschoten*, 38; [Hak. Soc. i. 131].

1631.—"Adfertur ad nos præterea fructus quidam *Lances* (read **Laices**) vocatus, qui racematim, ut uvæ, crescit."—*Jac. Bontii*, Dial. vi. p. 11.

1684.—"**Latsea**, or Chinese Chestnuts."—*Valentijn*, iv. (China) 12.

1750–52.—"**Leicki** is a species of trees which they seem to reckon equal to the sweet orange trees. ... It seems hardly credible that the country about Canton (in which place only the fruit grows) annually makes 100,000 *tel* of dried **leickis**."—*Olof Toreen*, 302–3.

1824.—"Of the fruits which this season offers, the finest are **leeches** (*sic*) and mangoes; the first is really very fine, being a sort of plum, with the flavour of a Frontignac grape."—*Heber*, i. 60.

c. 1858.—

"Et tandis que ton pied, sorti de la babouche,
Pendait, rose, au bord du **manchy** (see MUNCHEEL)
À l'ombre des bois noirs touffus, et du **Letchi**,
Aux fruits moins pourpres que ta bouche."
Leconte de Lisle.

1878.—"... and the lichi hiding under a shell of ruddy brown its globes of translucent and delicately fragrant flesh."—*Ph. Robinson, In My Indian Garden*, 49.

1879.—"... Here are a hundred and sixty **lichi** fruits for you. ..."—*M. Stokes, Indian Fairy Tales* (Calc. ed.) 51.

LEMON, s. *Citrus medica*, var. *Limonum*, Hooker. This is of course not an Anglo-Indian word. But it has come into European languages through the Ar. *leimūn*, and is, according to Hehn, of Indian origin. In Hind. we have both *līmū* and *nīmbū*, which last, at least, seems to be an indigenous form. The Skt. dictionaries give *nimbūka*. In England we get the word through the Romance languages, Fr. *limon*, It. *limone*, Sp. *limon*, &c., perhaps both from the Crusades and from the Moors of Spain. [Mr. Skeat writes: "The Malay form is *limau*, 'a lime, lemon, or orange.' The Port. *limão* may possibly come from this Malay form. I feel sure that *limau*, which in some dialects is *limar*, is an indigenous word which was transferred to Europe."] (See LIME.)

c. 1200.—"Sunt praeterea aliae arbores fructus acidos, pontici videlicet saporis, ex se procreantes, quos appellant **limones**."—*Jacobi de Vitriaco, Hist. Iherosolym*, cap. lxxxv. in *Bongars*.

c. 1328.—"I will only say this much, that this India, as regards fruit and other things, is entirely different from Christendom; except, indeed, that there be **lemons** in some places, as sweet as sugar, whilst there be other **lemons** sour like ours."—*Friar Jordanus*, 15.

1331.—"Profunditas hujus aquae plena est lapidibus preciosis. Quae aqua multum est yrudinibus et sanguisugis plena. Hos lapides non accipit rex, sed pro animâ suâ semel vel bis in anno sub aquas ipsos pauperes ire permittit. ... Et ut ipsi pauperes ire sub aquam possint accipiunt **limonem** et quemdam fructum quem bene pistant, et illo bene se ungunt. ... Et cum sic sint uncti yrudines et sanguisugæ illos offendere non valent."—*Fr. Odoric*, in *Cathay*, &c., App., p. xxi.

c. 1333.—"The fruit of the mango-tree (*al-'anba*) is the size of a great pear. When yet green they take the fallen fruit and powder it with salt and preserve it, as is done with the sweet citron and the *lemon* (*al*-**leimūn**) in our country."—*Ibn Batuta*, iii. 126.

LIKIN, LEKIN, s. We borrow from Mr. Giles "An arbitrary tax, originally of one cash per tael on all kinds of produce, imposed with a view of making up the deficiency in the land-tax of China caused by the Taiping and Nienfei troubles. It was to be set aside for military purposes only—hence its common name of 'war tax' ... The Chefoo Agreement makes the area of the Foreign concessions at the various Treaty Ports exempt from the tax of Lekin" (*Gloss. of Reference*, s.v.). The same authority explains the term as "*li* (*le, i.e.* a cash or 1/1000 of a tael)-money," because of the original rate of levy. The **likin** is professedly not an imperial customs-duty, but a provincial tax levied by the governors of the provinces, and at their discretion as to amount; hence varying in local rate, and from time to time changeable. This has been a chief difficulty in carrying out the Chefoo Agreement, which as yet has never been authoritatively interpreted or finally ratified by England. [It was ratified in 1886. For the conditions of the Agreement see *Ball, Things Chinese*, 3rd ed. 629 *seqq.*] We quote the article of the Agreement which deals with opium, which has involved the chief difficulties, as leaving not only the amount to be paid, but the line at which this is to be paid, undefined.

1876.—"Sect. III. ... (iii). On Opium Sir Thomas Wade will move his Government to sanction an arrangement different from that affecting other imports. British merchants, when opium is brought into port, will be obliged to have it taken cognizance of by the Customs, and deposited in Bond ... until such time as there is a sale for it. The importer will then pay the tariff duty upon it, and the purchasers the **likin**: in order to the prevention of the evasion of the duty. The amount of **likin** to be collected will be decided by the different Provincial Governments, according to the circumstances of each."—*Agreement of Chefoo*.

1878.—"La Chine est parsemée d'une infinité de petits bureaux d'octroi échelonnés le long des voies commerciales; les Chinois les nomment **Li-kin**. C'est la source la plus sure, et la plus productive des revenus."—*Rousset, A Travers la Chine*, 221.

LIME, s. The fruit of the small *Citrus medica*, var. *acida*, Hooker, is that generally called *lime* in India, approaching as it does very nearly to the fruit of the West India Lime. It is often not much bigger than a pigeon's egg, and one well-known miniature lime of this kind is called by the natives from its thin skin *kāghazī nīmbū*, or 'paper lime.' This seems to bear much the same relation to the lemon that the miniature thin-skinned orange, which in London shops is called *Tangerine*, bears to the "China orange." But lime is also used with the characterising adjective for the *Citrus medica*, var. *Limetta*, Hooker, or Sweet Lime, an insipid fruit.

The word no doubt comes from the Sp. and Port. *lima*, which is from the Ar. *līma*; Fr. *lime*, Pers. *līmū*, *līmūn* (see LEMON). But probably it came into English from the Portuguese in India. It is not in Minsheu (2nd ed. 1727).

1404.—"And in this land of Guilan snow never falls, so hot is it; and it produces abundance of citrons and **limes** and oranges (*cidrus é* **limas** *é naranjas*)."—*Clavijo*, § lxxxvi.

c. 1526.—"Another is the **lime** (*līmū*), which is very plentiful. Its size is about that of a hen's egg, which it resembles in shape. If one who is poisoned boils and eats its fibres, the injury done by the poison is averted."—*Baber*, 328.

1563.—"It is a fact that there are some Portuguese so pig-headed that they would rather die than acknowledge that we have here any fruit equal to that of Portugal; but there are many fruits here that bear the bell, as for instance all the *fructas de espinho*. For the **lemons** of those parts are so big that they look like citrons, besides being very tender and full of flavour, especially those of *Baçaim*; whilst the citrons themselves are much better and more tender (than those of Portugal); and the **limes** (*limas*) vastly better. ..."—*Garcia*, f. 133.

c. 1630.—"The Ile inricht us with many good things; Buffolls, Goats, Turtle, Hens, huge Batts ... also with Oranges, **Lemons**, **Lymes** ..."—*Sir T. Herbert*, 28.

1673.—"Here Asparagus flourish, as do **Limes**, Pomegranates, Genetins. ..."—*Fryer*, 110. ("Jenneting" from Fr. *genétin*, [or, according to Prof. Skeat, for *jeanneton*, a dimin. from Fr. *pomme de S. Jean*.]

1690.—"The Island (Johanna) abounds with Fowls and Rice, with Pepper, Yams, Plantens, Bonanoes, Potatoes, Oranges, **Lemons**, **Limes**, Pine-apples, &c. ..."—*Ovington*, 109.

LINGAIT, LINGAYET, LINGUIT, LINGAVANT, LINGADHARI, s. Mahr. *Liñgā-īt*, Can. *Lingāyata*, a member of a Sivaite sect in W. and S. India, whose members wear the *liñga* (see LINGAM) in a small gold or silver box suspended round the neck. The sect was founded in the 12th century by Bāsava. They are also called *Jangama*, or *Vīra Saiva*, and have various subdivisions. [See *Nelson*, *Madura*, pt. iii. 48 *seq.*; *Monier Williams*, *Brahmanism*, 88.]

1673.—"At *Hubly* in this Kingdom are a caste called **Linguits**, who are buried upright."—*Fryer*, 153. This is still their practice.

Lingua is given as the name or title of the King of Columbum in the 14th century, by Friar Jordanus (p. 41), which might have been taken to denote that he belonged to this sect; but this seems never to have had followers in Malabar.

***LINGAM**, s. This is taken from the S. Indian form of the word, which in N. India is Skt. and Hind. *liñga*, 'a token, badge,' &c., thence the symbol of Śiva which is so extensively an object of worship among the Hindus, in the form of a cylinder of stone. The great idol of Somnāth, destroyed by Mahmūd of Ghazni, and the object of so much romantic narrative, was a colossal symbol of this kind. In the quotation of 1838 below, the word is used simply for a badge of caste, which is certainly the original Skt. meaning, but is probably a mistake as attributed in that sense to modern vernacular use. The man may have been a **lingait** (q.v.), so that his badge was actually a figure of the lingam. But this clever authoress often gets out of her depth.

1311.—"The stone idols called **Ling** Mahádeo, which had been a long time established at that place ... these, up to this time, the kick of the horse of Islam had not attempted to break. ... Deo Narain fell down, and the other gods who had seats there raised their feet, and jumped so high, that at one leap they reached the foot of Lanka, and in that affright the **lings** themselves would have fled, had they had any legs to stand on."—*Amír Khusrú*, in *Elliot*, iv. 91.

1616.—"... above this there is elevated the figure of an idol, which in decency I abstain from naming, but which is called by the heathen **Linga**, and which they worship with many superstitions; and indeed they regard it to such a degree that the heathen of Canara carry well-wrought images of the kind round their necks. This abominable custom was abolished by a certain Canara King, a man of reason and righteousness."—*Couto*, Dec. VII. iii. 11.

1726.—"There are also some of them who wear a certain stone idol called **Lingam** ... round the neck, or else in the hair of the head. ..."—*Valentijn*, *Choro.* 74.

1781.—"These Pagodas have each a small chamber in the center of twelve feet square, with a lamp hanging over the **Lingham**."—*Hodges*, 94.

1799.—"I had often remarked near the banks of the rivulet a number of little altars, with a **linga** of Mahádeva upon them. It seems they are placed over the ashes of Hindus who have been burnt near the spot."—*Colebrooke*, in *Life*, p. 152.

1809.—"Without was an immense **lingam** of black stone."—*Ld. Valentia*, i. 371.

1814.—"... two respectable Brahmuns, a man and his wife, of the secular order; who, having no children, had made several religious pilgrimages, performed the accustomed ceremonies to the **linga**, and consulted the divines."—*Forbes, Or. Mem.* ii. 364; [2nd ed. ii. 4; in ii. 164, **lingam**].

1838.—"In addition to the preaching, Mr. G. got hold of a man's **Lingum**, or badge of caste, and took it away."—*Letters from Madras*, 156.

1843.—"The homage was paid to **Lingamism**. The insult was offered to Mahometanism. *Lingamism* is not merely idolatry, but idolatry in its most pernicious form."—*Macaulay, Speech on Gates of Somnauth.*

LINGUIST, s. An old word for an interpreter, formerly much used in the East. It long survived in China, and is there perhaps not yet obsolete. Probably adopted from the Port. *lingua*, used for an interpreter.

1554.—"To a **llingua** of the factory (at Goa) 2 pardaos monthly. ..."—*S. Botelho, Tombo*, 63.

"To the **linguoa** of this kingdom (Ormuz) a Portuguese ... To the **linguoa** of the custom-house, a bramen."—*Ibid.* 104.

[1612.—"Did Captain Saris' **Linguist** attend?"—*Danvers, Letters*, i. 68.]

1700.—"I carried the **Linguist** into a Merchant's House that was my Acquaintance to consult with that Merchant about removing that *Remora*, that stop'd the Man of War from entring into the Harbour."—*A. Hamilton*, iii. 254; [ed. 1744].

1711.—"**Linguists** require not too much haste, having always five or six to make choice of, never a Barrel the better Herring."—*Lockyer*, 102.

1760.—"I am sorry to think your Honour should have reason to think, that I have been anyway concerned in that unlucky affair that happened at the *Negrais*, in the month of October 1759; but give me leave to assure your Honour that I was no further concerned, than as a **Linguister** for the *King's Officer* who commanded the Party."—Letter to the Gov. of Fort St. George, from *Antonio the Linguist*, in *Dalrymple*, i. 396.

1760–1810.—"If the ten should presume to enter villages, public places, or bazaars, punishment will be inflicted on the **linguist** who accompanies them."—*Regulations at Canton*, from *The Fankwae at Canton*, p. 29.

1882.—"As up to treaty days, neither Consul nor Vice-Consul of a foreign nation was acknowledged, whenever either of these officers made a communication to the Hoppo, it had to be done through the Hong merchants, to whom the dispatch was taken by a **Linguist**."—*The Fankwae at Canton*, p. 50.

LIP-LAP, s. A vulgar and disparaging nickname given in the Dutch Indies to Eurasians, and corresponding to Anglo-Indian **chee-chee** (q.v.). The proper meaning of *lip-lap* seems to be the uncoagulated pulp of the coco-nut (see *Rumphius*, bk. i. ch. 1). [Mr. Skeat notes that the word is not in the dicts., but Klinkert gives Jav. *lap-lap*, 'a dish-clout.']

1768–71.—"Children born in the Indies are nicknamed **liplaps** by the Europeans, although both parents may have come from Europe."—*Stavorinus*, E.T. i. 315.

LISHTEE, LISTEE, s. Hind. *lishtī*, English word, 'a *list*.'

LONG-CLOTH, s. The usual name in India for (white) cotton shirtings, or Lancashire calico; but first applied to the Indian cloth of like kind exported to England, probably because it was made of length unusual in India; cloth for native use being ordinarily made in pieces sufficient only to clothe one person. Or it is just possible that it may have been a corruption or misapprehension of *lungi* (see LOONGHEE). [This latter view is accepted without question by Sir G. Birdwood (*Rep. on Old Rec.*, 224), who dates its introduction to Europe about 1675.]

1670.—"We have continued to supply you ... in reguard the Dutch do so fully fall in with the Calicoe trade that they had the last year 50,000 pieces of **Long-cloth**."—*Letter from Court of E.I.C.* to Madras, Nov. 9th. In *Notes and Exts.*, No. i. p. 2.

[1682.—"... for **Long cloth** brown English 72: Coveds long & 2¼ broad No. I. ..."—*Pringle, Diary, Ft. St. Geo.* 1st ser. i. 40.]

1727.—"*Saderass*, or *Saderass Patam*, a small Factory belonging to the *Dutch*, to buy up **long cloth**."—*A. Hamilton*, i. 358; [ed. 1744].

1785.—"The trade of Fort St. David's consists in **long cloths** of different colours."—*Carraccioli's Life of Clive*, i. 5.

1865.—"**Long-cloth**, as it is termed, is the material principally worn in the Tropics."—*Waring, Tropical Resident*, p. 111.

1880.—"A Chinaman is probably the last man in the world to be taken in twice with a fraudulent piece of **long-cloth**."—*Pall Mall Budget*, Jan. 9, p. 9.

LONG-DRAWERS, s. This is an old-fashioned equivalent for **pyjamas** (q.v.). Of late it is confined to the Madras Presidency, and to outfitters' lists. [*Mosquito drawers* were probably like these.]

[1623.—"They wear a pair of **long Drawers** of the same Cloth, which cover not only their Thighs, but legs also to the Feet."—*P. della Valle*, Hak. Soc. i. 43.]

1711.—"The better sort wear **long Drawers**, and a piece of Silk, or wrought Callico, thrown loose over the Shoulders."—*Lockyer*, 57.

1774.—"... gave each private man a frock and **long drawers** of chintz."—*Forrest, V. to N. Guinea*, 100.

1780.—"Leroy, one of the French hussars, who had saved me from being cut down by Hyder's horse, gave me some soup, and a shirt, and **long-drawers**, which I had great want of."—*Hon. John Lindsay* in *Lives of the Lindsays*, iv. 266.

1789.—"It is true that they (the *Sycs*) wear only a short blue jacket, and blue **long draws**."—Note by Translator of *Seir Mutaqherin*, i. 87.

1810.—"For wear on board ship, pantaloons ... together with as many pair of wove cotton **long-drawers**, to wear under them."—*Williamson, V. M.* i. 9.

[1853.—"The Doctor, his gaunt figure very scantily clad in a dirty shirt and a pair of **mosquito drawers**."—*Campbell, Old Forest Ranger*, 3rd ed. 108.]

(See PYJAMAS, MOGUL BREECHES, SHULWAURS, SIRDRARS.)

LOOCHER, s. This is often used in Anglo-Ind. colloquial for a blackguard libertine, a lewd loafer. It is properly Hind. *luchchā*, having that sense. Orme seems to have confounded the word, more or less, with *lūṭiya* (see under LOOTY). [A rogue in *Pandurang Hari* (ed. 1873, ii. 168) is *Loochajee.* The place at Matheran originally called "*Louisa* Point" has become "*Loocha* Point!"]

[1829.—"... nothing-to-do **lootchas** of every sect in Camp. ..."—*Or. Sport. Mag.* ed. 1873, i. 121.]

LOONGHEE, s. Hind. *lungī*, perhaps originally Pers. *lung* and *lunggī*; [but Platts connects it with *linga*]. A scarf or web of cloth to wrap round the body, whether applied as what the French call *pagne*, *i.e.* a cloth simply wrapped once or twice round the hips and tucked in at the upper edge, which is the proper Mussulman mode of wearing it; or as a cloth tucked between the legs like a **dhoty** (q.v.), which is the Hindu mode, and often followed also by Mahommedans in India. The *Qanoon-e-Islam* further distinguishes between the *lunggí* and *dhotī* that the former is a coloured cloth worn as described, and the latter a cloth with only a coloured border, worn by Hindus alone. This explanation must belong to S. India. ["The *lungi* is really meant to be worn round the waist, and is very generally of a checked pattern, but it is often used as a *paggri* (see PUGGRY), more especially that known as the Kohat *lungi*" (*Cookson, Mon. on Punjab Silk*, 4). For illustrations of various modes of wearing the garment, see *Forbes Watson, Textile Manufactures and Costumes*, pl. iii. iv.]

1653.—"**Longui** est vne petite pièce de linge, dont les Indiens se servent à cacher les parties naturelles."—*De la Boullaye-le-Gouz*, 529. But in the edition of 1657 it is given: "**Longui** est vn morceau de linge dont l'on se sert an bain en Turquie" (p. 547).

1673.—"The Elder sat in a Row, where the Men and Women came down together to wash, having **Lungies** about their Wastes only."—*Fryer*, 101. In the Index, Fryer explains as a "Waste-Clout."

1726.—"Silk **Longis** with red borders, 160 pieces in a pack, 14 *cobidos* long and 2 broad."—*Valentijn*, v. 178.

1727.—"... For some coarse chequered Cloth, called *Cambaya*, **Lungies**, made of Cotton-Yarn, the Natives would bring Elephant's Teeth."—*A. Hamilton*, i. 9; [ed. 1744].

(In Pegu) "Under the Frock they have a Scarf or **Lungee** doubled fourfold, made fast about the Middle. ..."—*Ibid.* ii. 49.

c. 1760.—"Instead of petticoats they wear what they call a **loongee**, which is simply a long piece of silk or cotton stuff."—*Grose*, i. 143.

c. 1809–10.—"Many use the **Lunggi**, a piece of blue cotton cloth, from 5 to 7 cubits long and 2 wide. It is wrapped simply two or three times round the waist, and hangs down to the knee."—*F. Buchanan*, in *Eastern India*, iii. 102.

LOOT, s. & v. Plunder; Hind. *lūt*, and that from Skt. *lotra*, for *loptra*, root *lup*, 'rob, plunder'; [rather *lunṭ*, 'to rob']. The word appears in Stockdale's *Vocabulary*, of 1788, as "**Loot**—plunder, pillage." It has thus long been a familiar item in the Anglo-Indian colloquial. But between the Chinese War of 1841, the Crimean War (1854–5), and the Indian Mutiny (1857–8), it gradually found acceptance in England also, and is now a recognised constituent of the English *Slang Dictionary*. Admiral Smyth has it in his *Nautical Glossary* (1867) thus: "**Loot**, plunder, or pillage, a term adopted from China."

1545.—St. Francis Xavier in a letter to a friend in Portugal admonishing him from encouraging any friend of his to go to India seems to have the thing *Loot* in his mind, though of course he does not use the word: "Neminem patiaris amicorum tuorum in Indiam cum Praefectura mitti, ad regias pecunias, et negotia tractanda. Nam de illis vere illud scriptum capere licet: 'Deleantur de libro viventium et cum justis non scribantur.' ... Invidiam tantum non culpam usus publicus detrahit, dum vix dubitatur fieri non malè quod impunè fit. Ubique, semper, rapitur, congeritur, aufertur. Semel captum nunquam redditur. Quis enumeret artes et nomina, praedarum? Equidem mirari satis nequeo, quot, praeter usitatos modos, insolitis flexionibus inauspicatum illud rapiendi verbum quaedam avaritiae barbaria conjuget!"—*Epistolae, Prague*, 1667, Lib. V. Ep. vii.

1842.—"I believe I have already told you that I did not take any **loot**—the Indian word for plunder—so that I have nothing of that kind, to which so many in this expedition helped themselves so bountifully."—*Colin Campbell* to his Sister, in *L. of Ld. Clyde*, i. 120.

"In the Saugor district the plunderers are beaten whenever they are caught, but there is a good deal of burning and '**looting**,' as they call it."—*Indian Administration of Ld. Ellenborough. To the D. of Wellington*, May 17, p. 194.

1847.—"Went to see Marshal Soult's pictures which he **looted** in Spain. There are many Murillos, all beautiful."—*Ld. Malmesbury, Mem. of an Ex-Minister*, i. 192.

1858.—"There is a word called '**loot**,' which gives, unfortunately, a venial character to what would in common English be styled robbery."—*Ld. Elgin, Letters and Journals*, 215.

1860.—"**Loot**, swag or plunder."—*Slang Dict.* s.v.

1864.—"When I mentioned the '**looting**' of villages in 1845, the word was printed in italics as little known. Unhappily it requires no distinction now, custom having rendered it rather common of late."—*Admiral W. H. Smyth, Synopsis*, p. 52.

1875.—"It was the Colonel Sahib who carried off the **loot**."—*The Dilemma*, ch. xxxvii.

1876.—"Public servants (in Turkey) have vied with one another in a system of universal **loot**."—*Blackwood's Mag.* No. cxix. p. 115.

1878.—"The city (Hongkong) is now patrolled night and day by strong parties of marines and Sikhs, for both the disposition to **loot** and the facilities for **looting** are very great."—*Miss Bird, Golden Chersonese*, 34.

1883.—"'**Loot**' is a word of Eastern origin, and for a couple of centuries past ... the **looting** of Delhi has been the day-dream of the most patriotic among the Sikh race."—*Bos. Smith's Life of Ld. Lawrence*, ii. 245.

"At Ta li fu ... a year or two ago, a fire, supposed to be an act of incendiarism, broke out among the Tibetan encampments which were then **looted** by the Chinese."—*Official Memo. on Chinese Trade with Tibet*, 1883.

LOOTY, LOOTIEWALLA, s.

a. A plunderer. Hind. *lūṭī, lūṭīyā, lūṭī-wālā*.

1757.—"A body of their **Louchees** (see LOOCHER) or plunderers, who are armed with clubs, passed into the Company's territory."—*Orme*, ed. 1803, ii. 129.

1782.—"Even the rascally **Leoty wallahs**, or Mysorean hussars, who had just before been meditating a general desertion to us, now pressed upon our flanks and rear."—*Munro's Narrative*, 295.

1792.—"The Colonel found him as much dismayed as if he had been surrounded by the whole Austrian army, and busy in placing an ambuscade to catch about six **looties**."—*Letter of T. Munro*, in *Life*.

"This body (horse plunderers round Madras) had been branded generally by the name of **Looties**, but they had some little title to a better appellation, for they were ... not guilty of those sanguinary and inhuman deeds. ..."—*Madras Courier*, Jan. 26.

1793.—"A party was immediately sent, who released 27 half-starved wretches in heavy irons; among them was Mr. Randal Cadman, a midshipman taken 10 years before by Suffrein. The remainder were private soldiers; some of whom had been taken by the **Looties**; others were deserters. ..."—*Dirom's Narrative*, p. 157.

b. A different word is the Ar.—Pers. *lūṭīy*, bearing a worse meaning, 'one of the people of Lot,' and more generally 'a blackguard.'

[1824.—"They were singing, dancing, and making the **luti** all the livelong day."—*Hajji Baba*, ed. 1851, p. 444.

[1858.—"The **Loutis**, who wandered from town to town with monkeys and other animals, taught them to cast earth upon their heads (a sign of the deepest grief among Asiatics) when they were asked whether they would be governors of Balkh or Akhcheh."—*Ferrier, H. of the Afghans*, 101.

[1883.—"Monkeys and baboons are kept and trained by the **Lūtis**, or professional buffoons."—*Will's Modern Persia*, ed. 1891, p. 306.]

The people of Shiraz are noted for a fondness for jingling phrases, common enough among many Asiatics, including the people of India, where one constantly hears one's servants speak of *chaukī-aukī* (for chairs and tables), *naukar-chākar* (where both are however real words), 'servants,' *lakṛī-akṛī*, 'sticks and staves,' and so forth. Regarding this Mr. Wills tells a story (*Modern Persia*, p. 239). The late Minister, Kawām-ud-Daulat, a Shirāzi, was asked by the Shāh:

"Why is it, Ḳawām, that you Shīrāzīs always talk of *Kabob-mabob* and so on? You always add a nonsense-word; is it for euphony?"

"Oh, Asylum of the Universe, may I be your sacrifice! No respectable person in Shīrāz does so, only the **lūtī-pūtī** says it!"

LORY, s. A name given to various brilliantly-coloured varieties of parrot, which are found in the Moluccas and other islands of the Archipelago. The word is a corruption of the Malay *nūri*, 'a parrot'; but the corruption seems not to be very old, as Fryer retains the correct form. Perhaps it came through the French (see *Luillier* below). [Mr. Skeat writes: "*Lūri* is hardly a corruption of *nūri*; it is rather a parallel form. The two forms appear in different dialects. *Nūri* may have been first introduced, and *lūri* may be some dialectic form of it."] The first quotation shows that *lories* were imported into S. India as early as the 14th century. They are still imported thither, where they are called in the vernacular by a name signifying 'Five-coloured parrots.' [Can. *panchavarnagini*.]

c. 1330.—"Parrots also, or popinjays, after their kind, of every possible colour, except black, for black ones are never found; but white all over, and green, and red, and also of mixed colours. The birds of this India seem really like the creatures of Paradise."—*Friar Jordanus*, 29.

c. 1430.—"In Bandan three kinds of parrot are found, some with red feathers and a yellow beak, and some parti-coloured which are called **Nori**, that is brilliant."—*Conti*, in *India in the XVth Cent.*, 17. The last words, in Poggio's original Latin, are: "quos *Noros* appellant hoc est *lucidos*," showing that Conti connected the word with the Pers. *nār* = "*lux*."

1516.—"In these islands there are many coloured parrots, of very splendid colours; they are tame, and the Moors call them **nure**, and they are much valued."—*Barbosa*, 202.

1555.—"There are hogs also with hornes and parats which prattle much, which they call **Noris**."—*Galvano*, E.T. in *Hakl.* iv. 424.

[1598.—"There cometh into India out of the Island of Molucas beyond Malacca a kind of birdes called **Noyras**; they are like Parrattes. ..."—*Linschoten*, Hak. Soc. i. 307.]

1601.—"Psittacorum passim in sylvis multae turmae obvolitant. Sed in Moluccanis Insulis per Malaccam avis alia, **Noyra** dicta, in Indiam importatur, quae psittaci faciem universim exprimit, quem cantu quoque adamussim aemulatur, nisi quod pennis rubicundis crebrioribus vestitur."—*De Bry*, v. 4.

1673.—"... Cockatooas and **Newries** from Bantam."—*Fryer*, 116.

1682.—"The **Lorys** are about as big as the parrots that one sees in the Netherlands. ... There are no birds that the Indians value more: and they will sometimes pay 30 rix dollars for one. ..."—*Nieuhof*, *Zee en Lant-Reize*, ii. 287.

1698.—"Brought ashore from the Resolution ... a **Newry** and four yards of broad cloth for a present to the Havildar."—In *Wheeler*, i. 333.

1705.—"On y trouve de quatre sortes de perroquets, sçavoir, perroquets, **lauris**, perruches, & cacatoris."—*Luillier*, 72.

1809.—

"'Twas Camdeo riding on his **lory**,
'Twas the immortal Youth of Love."
Kehama, x. 19.

1817.—

"Gay sparkling **loories**, such as gleam
between
The crimson blossoms of the coral-tree
In the warm isles of India's summer sea."
Mokanna.

LOTA, s. Hind. *loṭā*. The small spheroidal brass pot which Hindus use for drinking, and sometimes for cooking. This is the exclusive Anglo-Indian application; but natives also extend it to the spherical pipkins of earthenware.

1810.—"... a **lootah**, or brass water vessel."—*Williamson*, *V. M.* ii. 284.

LOTE, s. Mod. Hind. *lōṭ*, being a corruption of Eng. '*note*.' A bank-note; sometimes called *bănklōṭ*.

LOVE-BIRD, s. The bird to which this name is applied in Bengal is the pretty little lorikeet, *Loriculus vernalis*, Sparrman, called in Hind. *laṭkan* or 'pendant,' because of its quaint habit of sleeping suspended by the claws, head downwards.

LUDDOO, s. H. *laḍḍū*. A common native sweetmeat, consisting of balls of sugar and ghee, mixt with wheat and gram flour, and with cocoanut kernel rasped.

[1826.—"My friends ... called me *boor ke* **luddoo**, or the great man's sport."—*Pandurang Hari*, ed. 1873, i. 197.

[1828.—"When at large we cannot even get *rabri* (porridge), but in prison we eat **ladoo** (a sweetmeat)."—*Tod, Annals*, Calcutta reprint, ii. 185.]

LUGOW, TO, v. This is one of those imperatives transformed, in Anglo-Indian jargon, into infinitives, which are referred to under **BUNOW, PUCKEROW**. H. inf. *lagā-nā*, imperative *lagā-o*. The meanings of *lagānā*, as given by Shakespear, are: "to apply, close, attach, join, fix, affix, ascribe, impose, lay, add, place, put, plant, set, shut, spread, fasten, connect, plaster, put to work, employ, engage, use, impute, report anything in the way of scandal or malice"—in which long list he has omitted one of the most common uses of the verb, in its Anglo-Indian form *lugow*, which is "to lay a boat alongside the shore or wharf, to moor." The fact is that *lagānā* is the active form of the neuter verb *lag-nā*, 'to touch, lie, to be in contact with,' and used in all the neuter senses of which *lagānā* expresses the transitive senses. Besides neuter *lagnā*, active *lagānā*, we have a secondary casual verb, *lagwānā*, 'to cause to apply,' &c. *Lagnā, lagānā* are presumably the same words as our *lie*, and *lay*, A.-S. *licgan*, and *lecgan*, mod. Germ. *liegen* and *legen*. And the meaning 'lay' underlies all the senses which Shakespear gives of *lagā-nā*. [See *Skeat, Concise Etym. Dict.* s.v. *lie*.]

[1839.—"They **lugāoed**, or were fastened, about a quarter of a mile below us. ..."—*Davidson, Travels in Upper India*, ii. 20.]

LUMBERDAR, s. Hind. *lambardār*, a word formed from the English word '*number*' with the Pers. termination-*dār*, and meaning properly 'the man who is registered by a number.' "The registered representative of a coparcenary community, who is responsible for Government revenue." (*Carnegy*). "The cultivator who, either on his own account or as the representative of other members of the village, pays the Government dues and is registered in the Collector's Roll according to his number; as the representative of the rest he may hold the office by descent or by election." (*Wilson*).

[1875.—"... Chota Khan ... was exceedingly useful, and really frightened the astonished **Lambadars**."—*Wilson, Abode of Snow*, 97.]

LUNGOOR, s. Hind. *langūr*, from Skt. *lāngūlin*, 'caudatus.' The great white-bearded ape, much patronized by Hindus, and identified with the monkey-god Hanumān. The genus is *Presbytes*, Illiger, of which several species are now discriminated, but the differences are small. [See *Blanford, Mammalia*, 27, who classes the *Langūr* as *Semnopithecus entellus*.] The animal is well described by Aelian in the following quotation, which will recall to many what they have witnessed in the suburbs of Benares and other great Hindu cities. The *Langūr* of the *Prasii* is *P. Entellus*.

c. 250.—"Among the Prasii of India they say that there exists a kind of ape with human intelligence. These animals seem to be about the size of Hyrcanian dogs. Their front hair looks all grown together, and any one ignorant of the truth would say that it was dressed artificially. The beard is like that of a satyr, and the tail strong like that of a lion. All the rest of the body is white, but the head and the tail are red. These creatures are tame and gentle in character, but by race and manner of life they are wild. They go about in crowds in the suburbs of *Latagē* (now Latagē is a city of the Indians) and eat the boiled rice that is put out for them by the King's order. Every day their dinner is elegantly set out. Having eaten their fill it is said that they return to their parents in the woods in an orderly manner, and never hurt anybody that they meet by the way."—*Aelian, De Nat. Animal.* xvi. 10.

1825.—"An alarm was given by one of the sentries in consequence of a baboon drawing near his post. The character of the intruder was, however, soon detected by one of the Suwarrs, who on the Sepoy's repeating his exclamation of the broken English 'Who goes 'ere?' said with a laugh, 'Why do you challenge the **lungoor**? he cannot answer you.'"—*Heber*, ii. 85.

1859.—"I found myself in immediate proximity to a sort of parliament or general assembly of the largest and most humanlike monkeys I had over seen. There were at least 200 of them, great **lungoors**, some quite four feet high, the jetty black of their faces enhanced by a fringe of snowy whisker."—*Lewin, A Fly on the Wheel*, 49.

1884.—"Less interesting personally than the gibbon, but an animal of very developed social instincts, is *Semnopithecus entellus*, otherwise the Bengal **langur**. (He) fights for his wives according to a custom not unheard of in other cases; but what is peculiar to him is that the vanquished males 'receive charge of all the young ones of their own sex, with whom they retire to some neighbouring jungle.' Schoolmasters and private tutors will read this with interest, as showing the origin and early disabilities of their profession."—*Saturday Rev.*, May 31, on *Sterndale's Nat. Hist. of Mammalia of India, &c.*

LUNGOOTY, s. Hind. *langoṭī*. The original application of this word seems to be the scantiest modicum of covering worn for decency by some of the lower classes when at work, and tied before and behind by a string round the waist; but it is sometimes applied to the more ample *dhotī* (see DHOTY). According to R. Drummond, in Guzerat the "**Langoth** or **Lungota**" (as he writes) is "a pretty broad piece of cotton cloth, tied round the breech by men and boys bathing. ... The diminutive is **Langotee**, a long slip of cloth, stitched to a loin band of the same stuff, and forming exactly the T bandage of English Surgeons. ..." This distinction is probably originally correct, and the use of *langūta* by Abdurrazzāk would agree with it. The use of the word has spread to some of the Indo-Chinese countries. In the quotation from Mocquet it is applied in speaking of an American Indian near the R. Amazon. But the writer had been in India.

c. 1422.—"The blacks of this country have the body nearly naked; they wear only bandages round the middle called **lankoutah**, which descend from the navel to above the knee."—*Abdurrazzāk*, in *India in XV. Cent.* 17.

1526.—"Their peasants and the lower classes all go about naked. They tie on a thing which they call a **langoti**, which is a piece of clout that hangs down two spans from the navel, as a cover to their nakedness. Below this pendant modesty-clout is another slip of cloth, one end of which they fasten before to a string that ties on the **langoti**, and then passing the slip of cloth between the two legs, bring it up and fix it to the string of the **langoti** behind."—*Baber*, 333.

c. 1609.—"Leur capitaine auoit fort bonne façon, encore qu'il fust tout nud et luy seul auoit vn **langoutin**, qui est vne petite pièce de coton peinte."—*Mocquet*, 77.

1653.—"**Langouti** est une pièce de linge dont les Indou se seruent à cacher les parties naturelles."—*De la Boullaye-le-Gouz*, ed. 1657, p. 547.

[1822.—"The boatmen go nearly naked, seldom wearing more than a **langutty**. ..."—*Wallace, Fifteen Years in India*, 410.]

1869.—"Son costume se compose, comme celui de tous les Cambodgiens, d'une veste courte et d'un **langouti**."—*Rev. des Deux Mondes*, lxxix. 854.

"They wear nothing but the **langoty**, which is a string round the loins, and a piece of cloth about a hand's breadth fastened to it in front."—(*Ref. lost*), p. 26.

LUNKA, n.p. Skt. *Lañka*. The oldest name of Ceylon in the literature both of Buddhism and Brahmanism. Also 'an island' in general.

——, s. A kind of strong cheroot much prized in the Madras Presidency, and so called from being made of tobacco grown in the 'islands' (the local term for which is *lañka*) of the Godavery Delta.

M

MĀ-BĀP, s. '*Āp* mā-bāp *hai khudāwand!*' 'You, my Lord, are my mother and father!' This is an address from a native, seeking assistance, or begging release from a penalty, or reluctant to obey an order, which the young *ṣāhib* hears at first with astonishment, but soon as a matter of course.

MACAO, n.p.

a. The name applied by the Portuguese to the small peninsula and the city built on it, near the mouth of Canton River, which they have occupied since 1557. The place is called by the Chinese *Ngao-măn* (*Ngao*, 'bay or inlet,' *Măn*, 'gate'). The Portuguese name is alleged to be taken from *A-mā-ngao*, 'the Bay of Ama,' *i.e.* of the Mother, the so-called 'Queen of Heaven,' a patroness of seamen. And indeed *Amacao* is an old form often met with.

c. 1567.—"Hanno i Portoghesi fatta vna picciola cittáde in vna Isola vicina a' i liti della China chiamato **Machao** ... ma i datii sono del Rè della China, e vanno a pagarli a Canton, bellissima cittáde, e di grande importanza, distante da *Machao* due giorni e mezzo."—*Cesare de' Federici*, in *Ramusio*, iii. 391.

c. 1570.—"On the fifth day of our voyage it pleased God that we arrived at ... Lampacau, where at that time the *Portugals* exercised their commerce with the *Chineses*, which continued till the year 1557, when the *Mandarins* of *Canton*, at the request of the Merchants of that Country, gave us the port of **Macao**, where the trade now is; of which place (that was but a desart Iland before) our countrymen made a very goodly plantation, wherein there were houses worth three or four thousand Duckats, together with a Cathedral Church. ..."—*Pinto*, in *Cogan*, p. 315.

1584.—"There was in **Machao** a religious man of the order of the barefoote friars of S. Francis, who vnderstanding the great and good desire of this king, did sende him by certaine Portugal merchants ... a cloth whereon was painted the day of judgement and hell, and that by an excellent workman."—*Mendoza*, ii. 394.

1585.—"They came to **Amacao**, in Iuly, 1585. At the same time it seasonably hapned that *Linsilan* was commanded from the court to procure of the Strangers at **Amacao**, certaine goodly feathers for the King."—From the *Jesuit Accounts*, in *Purchas*, iii. 330.

1599 ...—"**Amacao.**" See under MONSOON.

1602.—"Being come, as heretofore I wrote your Worship, to **Macao** a city of the Portugals, adjoyning to the firme Land of China, where there is a Colledge of our Company."—Letter from *Diego de Pantoia*, in *Purchas*, iii. 350.

[1611.—"There came a Jesuit from a place called Langasack which place the Carrack of **Amakau** yearly was wont to come."—*Danvers, Letters*, i. 146.]

1615.—"He adviseth me that 4 juncks are arrived at **Langasaque** from Chanchew, which with this ship from **Amacau**, will cause all matters to be sould chepe."—*Cocks's Diary*, i. 35.

["... carried them prisoners a-board the great ship of **Amacan.**"—*Foster, Letters*, iv. 46.]

1625.—"That course continued divers yeeres till the *Chinois* growing lesse fearefull, granted them in the greater Iland a little *Peninsula* to dwell in. In that place was an Idoll, which still remained to be seene, called *Ama*, whence the Peninsula was called **Amacao**, that is Amas Bay."—*Purchas*, iii. 319.

b. MACAO, MACCAO, was also the name of a place on the Pegu River which was the port of the city so called in the day of its greatness. A village of the name still exists at the spot.

1554.—"The *baar* of **Macao** contains 120 biças, each biça 100 ticals ..."—*A. Nunes*, p. 39.

1568.—"Si fa commodamente il viaggio sino a **Maccao** distante da Pegu dodeci miglia, e qui si sbarca."—*Ces. Federici*, in *Ramusio*, iii. 395.

1587.—"From Cirion we went to **Macao**, &c."—*R. Fitch*, in *Hakl.* ii. 391.

1599.—"The King of *Arracan* is now ending his business at the Town of **Macao**, carrying thence the Silver which the King of *Tangu* had left, exceeding three millions."—*N. Pimenta*, in *Purchas*, iii. 1748.

MACAREO, s. A term applied by old voyagers to the phenomenon of the *bore*, or great tidal wave as seen especially in the Gulf of Cambay, and in the Sitang Estuary in Pegu. The word is used by them as if it were an Oriental word. At one time we were disposed to think it might be the Skt. word *makara*, which is applied to a mythological sea-monster, and to the Zodiacal sign Capricorn. This might easily have had a mythological association with the furious phenomenon in question, and several of the names given to it in various parts of the world seem due to associations of a similar kind. Thus the old English word *Oegir* or *Eagre* for the bore on the Severn, which occurs in Drayton, "seems to be a reminiscence of the old Scandinavian deity *Oegir*, the god of the stormy sea."[1] [This theory is rejected by *N.E.D.* s.v. *Eagre.*] One of the Hindi names for the phenomenon is *Meṇḍhā*, 'The Ram'; whilst in modern Guzerat, according to R. Drummond, the natives call it *ghoṛā*, "likening it to the war horse, or a squadron of them."[2] But nothing could illustrate the *naturalness* of such a figure as *makara*, applied to the bore, better than the following paragraph in the review-article just quoted (p. 401), which was evidently penned without any allusion to or suggestion of such an origin of the name, and which indeed makes no reference to the Indian name, but only to the French names of which we shall presently speak:

"Compared with what it used to be, if old descriptions may be trusted, the Mascaret is now stripped of its terrors. It resembles the great nature-force which used to ravage the valley of the Seine, *like one of the mythical dragons which, as legends tell, laid whole districts waste*, about as much as a lion confined in a cage resembles the free monarch of the African wilderness."

Take also the following:

1885.—"Here at his mouth Father Meghna is 20 miles broad, with islands on his breast as large as English counties, and a great tidal bore which made a daily and ever-varying excitement. ... In deep water, it passed merely as a large rolling billow; but in the shallows it rushed along, roaring like a crested and devouring monster, before which no small craft could live."—*Lt.-Col. T. Lewin, A Fly on the Wheel*, 161–162.

But unfortunately we can find no evidence of the designation of the phenomenon in

1 See an interesting paper in the *Saturday Review* of Sept. 29, 1883, on *Le Mascaret.*

2 Other names for the bore in India are: Hind. *hummā*, and in Bengal *bān*.

India by the name of *makara* or the like; whilst both *mascaret* (as indicated in the quotation just made) and *macrée* are found in French as terms for the bore. Both terms appear to belong properly to the Garonne, though *mascaret* has of late began on the Seine to supplant the old term *barre*, which is evidently the same as our *bore*. [The *N.E.D.* suggests O. N. *bára*, 'wave.'] Littré can suggest no etymology for *mascaret*; he mentions a whimsical one which connects the word with a place on the Garrone called St. *Macaire*, but only to reject it. There would be no impossibility in the transfer of an Indian word of this kind to France, any more than in the other alternative of the transfer of a French term to India in such a way that in the 16th century visitors to that country should have regarded it as an indigenous word, if we had but evidence of its Indian existence. The date of Littré's earliest quotation, which we borrow below, is also unfavourable to the probability of transplantation from India. There remains the possibility that the word is *Basque*. The Saturday Reviewer already quoted says that he could find nothing approaching to *Mascaret* in a Basque French Dict., but this hardly seems final.

The vast rapidity of the flood-tide in the Gulf of Cambay is mentioned by Maṣ'ūdī, who witnessed it in the year H. 303 (A.D. 915) i. 255; also less precisely by Ibn Batuta (iv. 60). There is a paper on it in the *Bo. Govt. Selections*, N.S. No: xxvi., from which it appears that the bore wave reaches a velocity of 10½ knots. [See also *Forbes, Or. Mem.* 2nd. ed. i. 313.]

1553.—"In which time there came hither (to Diu) a concourse of many vessels from the Red Sea, the Persian Gulf, and all the coast of Arabia and India, so that the places within the Gulf of Cambaya, which had become rich and noble by trade, were by this port undone. And this because it stood outside of the **Macareos** of the Gulf of Cambaya, which were the cause of the loss of many ships."—*Barros*, II. ii. cap 9.

1568.—"These Sholds (G. of Cambay) are an hundred and foure-score miles about in a straight or gulfe, which they call **Macareo** (*Maccareo* in orig.) which is as much as to say a race of a Tide."—*Master C. Frederick, Hakl.* ii. 342; [and comp. ii. 362].

1583.—"And having sailed until the 23d of the said month, we found ourselves in the neighbourhood of the **Macareo** (of Martaban) which is the most marvellous thing that ever was heard of in the way of tides, and high waters. ... The water in the channel rises to the height of a high tree, and then the boat is set to face it, waiting for the fury of the tide, which comes on with such violence that the noise is that of a great earthquake, insomuch that the boat is soused from stem to stern, and carried by that impulse swiftly up the channel."—*Gasparo Balbi*, ff. 91*v*, 92.

1613.—"The **Macareo** of waves is a disturbance of the sea, like water boiling, in which the sea casts up its waves in foam. For the space of an Italian mile, and within that distance only, this boiling and foaming occurs, whilst all the rest of the sea is smooth and waveless as a pond. ... And the stories of the Malays assert that it is caused by souls that are passing the Ocean from one region to another, or going in *cafilas* from the Golden Chersonesus ... to the river Ganges."—*Godinho de Eredia*, f. 41*v*. [See *Skeat, Malay Magic*, 10 *seq.*]

1644.—"... thence to the Gulf of Cambaya with the impetuosity of the currents which are called **Macareo**, of whose fury strange things are told, insomuch that a stone thrown with force from the hand even in the first speed of its projection does not move more swiftly than those waters run."—*Bocarro, MS.*

1727.—"A Body of Waters comes rolling in on the Sand, whose Front is above two Fathoms high, and whatever Body lies in its Way it overturns, and no Ship can evade its Force, but in a Moment is overturned, this violent Boer the Natives called a **Mackrea**."—*A. Hamilton*, ii. 33; [ed. 1744, ii. 32].

1811.—Solvyns uses the word **Macrée** as French for 'Bore,' and in English describes his print as "... the representation of a phenomenon of Nature, the **Macrée** or tide, at the mouth of the river Ougly."—*Les Hindous*, iii.

MACE, s.

a. The crimson net-like mantle, which envelops the hard outer shell of the nutmeg, when separated and dried constitutes the *mace* of commerce. Hanbury and Flückiger are satisfied that the attempt to identify the *Macir*, *Macer*, &c., of Pliny and other ancients with mace is a mistake, as indeed the sagacious Garcia also pointed out, and Chr. Acosta still more precisely. The name does not seem to be mentioned by Maṣ'ūdī; it is not in the list of aromatics, 25 in number, which he details (i. 367). It is mentioned by Edrisi, who wrote c. 1150, and whose information generally was of much older date, though we do not know what word he uses. The fact that nutmeg and mace are the product of one plant seems to have led to the fiction that clove and cinnamon also came from that same plant. It is, however, true that a kind of aromatic bark was known in the Arab pharmacopœia of the Middle Ages under the name of *ḳirfat-al-ḳaranful* or 'bark of clove,' which may have been either a cause of the mistake or a part of it. The mistake in question, in one form or another, prevailed for centuries. One of the authors of this book was asked many years ago by a respectable Mahommedan of Delhi if it were not the case that cinnamon, clove, and nutmeg were the produce of one tree. The prevalence of the mistake in Europe is shown by the fact that it is contradicted in a work of the 16th century (*Bodaei, Comment. in Theophrastum*, 992); and by the quotation from Funnel.

The name mace may have come from the Ar. *basbāsa*, possibly in some confusion with the ancient *macir*. [See Skeat, *Concise Dict.* who gives F. *macis*, which was confused with M. F. *macer*, probably Lat. *macer*, *macir*, doubtless of Eastern origin.]

c. 1150.—"On its shores (*i.e.* of the sea of Sanf or **Champa**), are the dominions of a King called Mihrāj, who possesses a great number of populous and fertile islands, covered with fields and pastures, and producing ivory, camphor, nutmeg, **mace**, clove, aloeswood, cardamom, cubeb, &c."—*Edrisi*, i. 89; see also 51.

c. 1347.—"The fruit of the clove is the nutmeg, which we know as the scented nut. The flower which grows upon it is the **mace** (*basbāsa*). And this is what I have seen with my own eyes."—*Ibn Batuta*, iv. 243.

c. 1370.—"A gret Yle and great Contree, that men clepen Java. ... There growen alle manere of Spicerie more plentyfous liche than in any other contree, as of Gyngevere, Clowegylofres, Canelle, Zedewalle, Notemuges, and **Maces**. And wytethe wel, that the Notemuge bereth the **Maces**. For righte as the Note of the Haselle hath an Husk withouten, that the Note is closed in, til it be ripe, and after falleth out; righte so it is of the Notemuge and of the **Maces**."—*Sir John Maundeville*, ed. 1866, p. 187-188. This is a remarkable passage for it is interpolated by Maundeville, from superior information, in what he is borrowing from Odoric. The comparison to the hazel-nut husk is just that used by Hanbury & Flückiger (*Pharmacographia*, 1st ed. 456).

c. 1430.—"Has (insulas Java) ultra xv dierum cursu duae reperiuntur insulae, orientem versus. Altera Sandai appellata, in quâ nuces muscatae et **maces**, altera Bandam nomine, in quâ solâ gariofali producuntur."—*Conti*, in *Poggius, De Var Fortunae.*

1514.—"The tree that produces the nut (meg) and **macis** is all one. By this ship I send you a sample of them in the green state."—*Letter of Giov. da Empoli*, in *Archiv. Stor. Ital.* 81.

1563.—"It is a very beautiful fruit, and pleasant to the taste; and you must know that when the nut is ripe it swells, and the first cover bursts as do the husks of our chestnuts, and shows the **maca**, of a bright vermilion like fine grain (*i.e. coccus*); it is the most beautiful sight in the world when the trees are loaded with it, and sometimes the mace splits off, and that is why the nutmegs often come without the **mace**."—*Garcia*, f. 129*v*–130.

[1602-3.—"In yor Provision you shall make in Nutmeggs and **Mace** haue you a greate care to receiue such as be good."—*Birdwood, First Letter Book*, 36; also see 67.]

1705.—"It is the commonly received opinion that Cloves, Nutmegs, **Mace**, and Cinnamon all grow upon one tree; but it is a great mistake."—*Funnel*, in *Dampier*, iv. 179.

MACE, s.

b. Jav. and Malay *mās*. [Mr. Skeat writes: "*Mās* is really short for *amās* or *emās*, one of those curious forms with prefixed *a*, as in the case of **abada**, which are probably native, but may have been influenced by Portuguese."] A weight used in Sumatra, being, according to Crawfurd, 1-16th of a Malay tael or about 40 grains (but see below). *Mace* is also the name of a small gold coin of Achīn, weighing 9 grs. and worth about 1*s*. 1*d*. And *mace* was adopted in the language of European traders in China to denominate the tenth part of the Chinese *liang* or *tael* of silver; the 100th part of the same value being denominated in like manner **candareen**. The word is originally Skt. *māsha*, 'a bean,' and then 'a particular weight of gold' (comp. CARAT).

1539.—"... by intervention of this thirdsman whom the Moor employed as broker they agreed on my price with the merchant at seven **mazes** of gold, which in our money makes a 1400 reys, at the rate of a half cruzado the **maz**."—*Pinto*, cap. xxv. Cogan has, "the fishermen sold me to the merchant for seven *mazes* of gold, which amounts in our money to seventeen shillings and sixpence."—p. 31.

1554.—"The weight with which they weigh (at Malaca) gold, musk, seed-pearl, coral, calambuco ... consists of *cates* which contain 20 *tael*, each *tael* 16 **mazes**, each **maz** 20 *cumduryns*. Also one *paual* 4 **mazes**, one **maz** 4 *cupões*, one *cupão* 5 *cumduryns*."—*A. Nunez*, 39.

1598.—"Likewise a Tael of Malacca is 16 **Mases.**"—*Linschoten*, 44; [Hak. Soc. i. 149].

1599.—"*Bezar* sive *Bazar* (*i.e.* **Bezoar**, per **Masas** venditur."—*De Bry*, ii. 64.

1625.—"I have also sent by Master Tomkins of their coine (Achin) ... that is of gold named a **Mas**, and is ninepence halfpenie neerest."—*Capt. T. Davis*, in *Purchas*, i. 117.

1813.—"Milburn gives the following table of weights used at Achin, but it is quite inconsistent with the statements of Crawfurd and Linschoten above.

4 copangs	=	1 **mace**
5 **mace**	=	1 mayam
16 mayam	=	1 tale
5 tales	=	1 bancal
20 bancals	=	1 catty.
200 catties	=	1 bahar."

Milburn, ii. 329. [Mr. Skeat notes that here "copang" is Malay *kupang*; tale, *tali*; bancal, *bongkal.*]

MĀCHIS, s. This is recent Hind. for 'lucifer matches.' An older and purer phrase for sulphur-matches is *dīwā-*, *dīyā-salāī*.

***MADRAS**, n.p. This alternative name of the place, officially called by its founders Fort St. George, first appears about the middle of the 17th century. Its origin has been much debated, but with little result. One derivation, backed by a fictitious legend, derives the name from an imaginary Christian fisherman called *Madarasen*; but this may be pronounced philologically impossible, as well as otherwise unworthy of serious regard.[1] Lassen makes the name to be a corruption of *Manda-rājya*, 'Realm of the Stupid!' No one will suspect the illustrious author of the *Indische Alterthumskunde* to be guilty of a joke; but it does look as if some malign Bengalee had suggested to him this gibe against the "Benighted"! It is indeed curious and true that, in Bengal, sepoys and the like always speak of the Southern Presidency as *Mandrāj*. In fact, however, all the earlier mentions of the name are in the form of *Madraspatanam*, 'the city of the *Madras*,' whatever the *Madras* may have been. The earliest maps show *Madraspatanam* as the Mahommedan settlement corresponding to the present Triplicane and Royapettah. The word is therefore probably of Mahommedan origin; and having got so far we need not hesitate to identify it with *Madrasa*, 'a college.' The Portuguese wrote this *Madaraza* (see *Faria y Sousa, Africa Portuguesa*, 1681, p. 6); and the European name probably came from them, close neighbours as they were to Fort St. George, at Mylapore or San Thomé. That there was such a *Madrasa* in existence is established by the quotation from Hamilton, who was there about the end of the 17th century.[2] Fryer's Map (1698, but illustrating 1672–73) represents the Governor's House as a building of Mahommedan architecture, with a dome. This may have been the *Madrasa* itself. Lockyer also (1711) speaks of a "College," of which the building was "very ancient"; formerly a hospital, and then used apparently as a residence for young writers. But it is not clear whether the name "College" was not given on this last account. [The *Madras Admin. Man.* says: "The origin of this name has been much discussed. *Madrissa*, a Mahommedan school, has been suggested, which considering the date at which the name is first found seems fanciful. *Manda* is in Sanscrit 'slow.' *Mandarāz* was a king of the lunar race. The place was probably called after this king" (ii. 91). The *Madras Gloss.* again writes: "Hind. *Madrās*, Can. *Madarāsu*, from Tel. *Mandaradzu*, name of a local Telegu Royer," or ruler. The whole question has been discussed by Mr. Pringle (*Diary Ft. St. Geo.*, 1st ser. i. 106 *seqq.*). He points out that while the earliest quotation given below is dated 1653, the name, in the form *Madrazpatam*, is used by the President and Council of Surat in a letter dated 29th December, 1640 (*I. O. Records*, O. C. No. 1764); "and the context makes it pretty certain that Francis Day or some other of the factors at the new Settlement must have previously made use of it in reference to the place, or 'rather,' as the Surat letter says, 'plot of ground' offered to him. It is no doubt just possible that in the course of the negotiations Day heard or caught up the name from the Portuguese, who were at the time in friendly relations with the English; but the probabilities are certainly in the opposite direction. The *nayak* from whom the plot was obtained must almost certainly

1 It is given in No. II. of *Selections from the Records of S. Arcot District*, p. 107.

2 In a letter from poor Arthur Burnell, on which this paragraph is founded, he adds: "It is sad that the most Philistine town (in the German sense) in all the East should have such a name."

have supplied the name, or what Francis Day conceived to be the name. Again, as regards Hamilton's mention of a 'college,' Sir H. Yule's remark certainly goes too far. Hamilton writes, 'There is a very Good Hospital in the Town, and the Company's Horse-stables are neat, but the old College where a good many Gentlemen Factors are obliged to lodge, is ill-kept in repair.' This remark taken together with that made by Lockyer ... affords proof, indeed, that there was a building known to the English as the 'College.' But it does not follow that this, or any, building was distinctively known to Musulmans as the '*madrasa*.' The 'old College' of Hamilton may have been the successor of a Musulman '*madrasa*' of some size and consequence, and if this was so the argument for the derivation would be strengthened. It is however equally possible that some old buildings within the plot of territory acquired by Day, which had never been a '*madrasa*,' was turned to use as a College or place where the young writers should live and receive instruction; and in this case the argument, so far as it rests on a mention of 'a College' by Hamilton and Lockyer, is entirely destroyed. Next as regards the probability that the first part of '*Madraspatanam*' is 'of Mahommedan origin.' Sir H. Yule does not mention that date of the maps in which *Madraspatanam* is shown 'as the Mahommedan settlement corresponding to the present Triplicane and Royapettah'; but in Fryer's map, which represents the fort as he saw it in 1672, the name '*Madirass*'—to which is added 'the Indian Town with flat houses'—is entered as the designation of the collection of houses on the north side of the English town, and the next makes it evident that in the year in question the name of *Madras* was applied chiefly to the crowded collection of houses styled in turn the 'Heathen,' the '**Malabar**,' and the 'Black' town. This consideration does not necessarily disprove the supposed Musulman origin of '**Madras**,' but it undoubtedly weakens the chain of Sir H. Yule's argument." Mr. Pringle ends by saying: "On the whole it is not unfair to say that the chief argument in favour of the derivation adopted by Sir H. Yule is of a negative kind. There are fatal objections to whatever other derivations have been suggested, but if the mongrel character of the compound '*Madrasapatanam*' is disregarded, there is no fatal objection to the derivation from '*madrasa*.' ... If however that derivation is to stand, it must not rest upon such accidental coincidences as the use of the word 'College' by writers whose knowledge of Madras was derived from visits made from 30 to 50 years after the foundation of the colony."]

1653.—"Estant desbarquez le R. P. Zenon reçut lettres de **Madraspatan** de la detention du Rev. P. Ephraim de Neuers par l'Inquisition de Portugal, pour avoir presché a **Madraspatan** que les Catholiques qui foüetoient et trampoient dans des puys les images de Sainct Antoine de Pade, et de la Vierge Marie, estoient impies, et que les Indous à tout le moins honorent ce qu'ils estiment Sainct. ..."—*De la Boullaye-le-Gouz*, ed. 1657, 244.

c. 1665.—"Le Roi de Golconde a de grands Revenus. ... Les Douanes des marchandises qui passent sur ses Terres, et celles des Ports de Masulipatan et de **Madrespatan**, lui rapportent beaucoup."—*Thevenot*, v. 306.

1672.—"... following upon **Madraspatan**, otherwise called *Chinnepatan*, where the English have a Fort called St. George, chiefly garrisoned by *Toepasses* and *Mistices*; from this place they annually send forth their ships, as also from Suratte."—*Baldaeus*, Germ. ed. 152.

1673.—"Let us now pass the Pale to the Heathen Town, only parted by a wide Parrade, which is used for a *Buzzar*, or Mercate-place. **Maderas** then divides itself into divers long streets, and they are checquered by as many transverse. It enjoys some *Choultries* for Places of Justice; one Exchange; one *Pagod*. ..."—*Fryer*, 38-39.

1726.—"The Town or Place, anciently called *Chinapatnam*, now called **Madraspatnam**, and Fort St. George."—*Letters Patent*, in *Charters of E.I. Company*, 368-9.

1727.—"Fort St. George or **Maderass**, or as the Natives call it, *China Patam*, is a Colony and City belonging to the *English East India Company*, situated in one of the most incommodious Places I ever saw. ... There is a very good Hospital in the Town, and the Company's Horse-Stables are neat, but the Old College, where a great many Gentlemen Factors are obliged to lodge, is kept in ill Repair."—*A. Hamilton*, i. 364, [ed. 1744, ii. 182].

MADRAS, s. This name is applied to large bright-coloured handkerchiefs, of silk warp and cotton woof, which were formerly exported from Madras, and much used by the negroes in the W. Indies as head-dresses. The word is preserved in French, but is now obsolete in England.

c. 1830.—"... We found President Petion, the black Washington, sitting on a very old ragged sofa, amidst a confused mass of papers, dressed in a blue military undress frock, white trowsers, and the everlasting **Madras** handkerchief bound round his brows."—*Tom Cringle*, ed. 1863, p. 425.

1846.—"Et Madame se manifesta! C'était une de ces vieilles dévinées par Adrien Brauwer dans ses sorcières pour le Sabbat ... coiffée d'un **Madras**, faisant encore papillottes avec les imprimés, que recevait gratuitement son maître."—*Balzac, Le Cousin Pons*, ch. xviii.

MAGAZINE, s. This word is, of course, not Anglo-Indian, but may find a place here because of its origin from Ar. *makhāzin*, plur. of *al-makhzan*, whence Sp. *almacen, almagacen, magacen*, Port. *almazem, armazem*, Ital. *magazzino*, Fr. *magazin*.

c. 1340.—"The Sultan ... made him a grant of the whole city of Sīrī and all its houses with the gardens and fields of the treasury (**makhzan**) adjacent to the city (of Delhi)."—*Ibn Batuta*, iii. 262.

1539.—"A que Pero de Faria respondea, que lhe desse elle commissão per mandar nos **almazẽs**, et que logo proveria no socorro que entendia ser necessario."—*Pinto*, cap. xxi.

MAHÁJUN, s. Hind. from Skt. *mahā-jan*, 'great person.' A banker and merchant. In Southern and Western India the vernacular word has various other applications which are given in *Wilson*.

[1813.—"**Mahajen, Mahajanum**, a great person, a merchant."—*Gloss. to 5th Rep.* s.v.]

c. 1861.—

"Down there lives a **Mahajun**—my father gave him a bill,
I have paid the knave thrice over, and here I'm paying him still.
He shows me a long stamp paper, and must have my land—must he?
If I were twenty years younger, he should get six feet by three."

Sir A. C. Lyall, The Old Pindaree.

1885.—"The **Mahajun** hospitably entertains his victim, and speeds his homeward departure, giving no word or sign of his business till the time for appeal has gone by, and the decree is made absolute. Then the storm bursts on the head of the luckless hill-man, who finds himself loaded with an overwhelming debt, which he has never incurred, and can never hope to discharge; and so he practically becomes the **Mahajun's** slave for the rest of his natural life."—*Lt.-Col. T. Lewin, A Fly on the Wheel*, 339.

***MAHOUT**, s. The driver and tender of an elephant. Hind. *mahāwat*, from Skt. *mahā-mātra*, 'great in measure,' a high officer, &c., so applied. The Skt. term occurs in this sense in the *Mahābhārata* (*e.g.* iv. 1761, &c.). The *Mahout* is mentioned in the 1st Book of Maccabees as 'the **Indian**.' It is remarkable that we find what is apparently *mahā-mātra*, in the sense of a high officer in Hesychius:

"*Μαμάτραι, οἱ στρατηγοὶ παρ' Ἰνδοῖς*."—*Hesych.* s.v.

c. 1590.—"*Mast* elephants. There are five and a half servants to each, viz., first a **Mahawat**, who sits on the neck of the animal and directs its movements. ... He gets 200 *dáms* per month. ... Secondly a *Bhói*, who sits behind, upon the rump of the elephant, and assists in battle, and in quickening the speed of the animal; but he often performs the duties of the **Mahawat**. ... Thirdly the *Met'hs* (see MATE). ... A *Met'h* fetches fodder, and assists in caparisoning the elephant. ..."—*Āīn*, ed. *Blochmann*, i. 125.

1648.—"... and **Mahouts** for the elephants. ..."—*Van Twist*, 56.

1826.—"I will now pass over the term of my infancy, which was employed in learning to read and write—my preceptor being a **mahouhut**, or elephant-driver—and will take up my adventures."—*Pandurang Hari*, 21; [ed. 1873, i. 28].

1848.—"Then he described a tiger hunt, and the manner in which the **Mahout** of his elephant had been pulled off his seat by one of the infuriate animals."—*Thackeray, Vanity Fair*, ch. iv.

MAHRATTA, n.p. Hind. *Marhaṭā, Marhaṭṭā, Marhāṭā* (*Marhaṭī, Marahṭī, Marhaiṭī*), and *Marāṭhā*. The name of a famous Hindu race, from the old Skt. name of their country, *Mahā-rāshṭra*, 'Magna Regio.' [On the other hand H. A. Acworth (*Ballads of the Marathas*, Intro. vi.) derives the word from a tribal name *Rathī* or *Raṭhā*, 'chariot fighters,' from *raṭh*, 'a chariot,' thus *Mahā-Raṭhā* means 'Great Warrior.' This was transferred to the country and finally Sanskritised into *Mahā-rāshṭra*. Again some authorities (Wilson, *Indian Caste*, ii. 48; Baden-Powell, *J. R. As. Soc.*, 1897, p. 249, note) prefer to derive the word from the *Mhār* or *Mahār*, a once numerous and dominant race. And see the discussion in the *Bombay Gazetteer*, I. pt. ii. 143 *seq.*]

c. 550.—"The planet (Saturn's) motion in Açleshâ causes affliction to aquatic animals or products, and snakes ... in Pûrva Phalguni to vendors of liquors, women of the town, damsels, and the **Mahrattas**. ..."—*Bṛhat Saṇhitā*, tr. by *Kern, J. R. As. Soc.* 2nd ser. v. 64.

640.—"De là il prit la direction du Nord-Ouest, traversa une vaste forêt, et ... il arriva au royaume de *Mo-ho-la-to* (**Mahārāshtra**). ..."—*Pèl. Bouddh.* i. 202; [*Bombay Gazetteer*, I. pt. ii. 353].

c. 1030.—"De Dhar, en se dirigeant vers le midi, jusqu'à la rivière de Nymyah on comte 7 parasanges; de là à **Mahrat-dessa** 18 paras."—*Albirúni*, in *Reinaud's Fragmens*, 109.

c. 1294–5:—"Alá-ud-dín marched to Elichpúr, and thence to Ghati-lajaura ... the people of that country had never heard of the Mussulmans; the **Mahratta** land had never been punished by their armies; no Mussulman King or Prince had penetrated so far."—*Ziá-ud-dín Barní*, in *Elliot*, iii. 150.

c. 1328.—"In this Greater India are twelve idolatrous Kings, and more. ... There is also the Kingdom of **Maratha** which is very great."—*Friar Jordanus*, 41.

1673.—"They tell their tale in **Moratty**; by Profession they are Gentues."—*Fryer*, 174.

1747.—"Agreed on the arrival of these Ships that We take Five Hundred (500) Peons more into our Service, that the 50 **Moratta** Horses be augmented to 100 as We found them very usefull in the last Skirmish. ..."—*Consn. at Ft. St. David*, Jan. 6 (MS. Record in India Office).

1748.—"That upon his hearing the **Mirattoes** had taken Tanner's Fort ..."—In *Long*, p. 5.

c. 1760.—"... those dangerous and powerful neighbors the **Morattoes**; who being now masters of the contiguous island of Salsette ..."—*Grose*, ii. 44.

"The name of **Morattoes**, or **Marattas**, is, I have reason to think, a derivation in their country-language, or by corruption, from *Mar-Rajah*."—*Ibid.* ii. 75.

1765.—"These united princes and people are those which are known by the general name of **Maharattors**; a word compounded of *Rattor* and *Maahah*; the first being the name of a particular *Raazpoot* (or *Rajpoot*) tribe; and the latter, signifying great or mighty (as explained by Mr. Fraser). ..."—*Holwell, Hist. Events*, &c., i. 105.

c. 1769.—Under a mezzotint portrait: "*The Right Honble* George Lord Pigot, *Baron* Pigot *of* Patshul *in the Kingdom of* Ireland, *President and Governor of and for all the Affairs of the United Company of Merchants of* England *trading to the* East Indies, *on the Coast of* Choromandel, *and* Orixa, *and of the* Chingee *and* **Moratta** *Countries*, &c., &c., &c."

c. 1842.—

"... Ah, for some retreat
Deep in yonder shining Orient, where my life began to beat;
Where in wild **Mahratta** battle fell my father evil starr'd."
—*Tennyson, Locksley Hall.*

The following is in the true **Hobson-Jobson** manner:

[1859.—"This term **Marhatta** or **Mârhutta**, is derived from the mode of warfare adopted by these men. *Mar* means to strike, and *hutna*, to get out of the way, *i.e.* those who struck a blow suddenly and at once retreated out of harm's way."—*H. Dundas Robertson, District Duties during the Revolt in* 1857, p. 104, note.]

MAHRATTA DITCH, n.p. An excavation made in 1742, as described in the extract from Orme, on the landward sides of Calcutta, to protect the settlement from the Mahratta bands. Hence the term, or for shortness 'The *Ditch*' simply, as a disparaging name for Calcutta. The line of the Ditch corresponded nearly with the outside of the existing Circular Road, except at the S.E. and S., where the work was never executed. [There is an excavation known by the same name at Madras excavated in 1780. (*Murray, Handbook*, 1859, p. 43).]

1742.—"In the year 1742 the Indian inhabitants of the Colony requested and obtained permission to dig a ditch at their own expense, round the Company's bounds, from the northern parts of Sootanatty to the southern part of Govindpore. In six months three miles were finished: when the inhabitants ... discontinued the work, which from the occasion was called the **Morattoe ditch**."—*Orme*, ed. 1803, ii. 45.

1757.—"That the Bounds of *Calcutta* are to extend the whole Circle of *Ditch* dug upon the Invasion of the **Marattes**; also 600 yards without it, for an Esplanade."—*Articles of Agreement sent by Colonel Clive* (previous to the Treaty with the Nabob of May 14). In *Memoirs of the Revolution in Bengal*, 1760, p. 89.

1782.—"To the Proprietors and Occupiers of Houses and other Tenements within the **Mahratta Entrenchment**."—*India Gazette*, Aug. 10.

[1840.—"Less than a hundred years ago, it was thought necessary to fortify Calcutta against the horsemen of Berar, and the name of the **Mahratta Ditch** still preserves the memory of the danger."—*Macaulay, Essay on Clive.*]

1872.—"The Calcutta cockney, who glories in the **Mahratta Ditch**. ..."—*Govinda Samanta*, i. 25.

MAISTRY, **MISTRY**, sometimes even **MYSTERY**, a. Hind. *mistrī*. This word, a corruption of the Portuguese *mestre*, has spread into the vernaculars all over India, and is in constant Anglo-Indian use. Properly 'a foreman,' 'a master-workman'; but used also, at least in Upper India, for any artizan, as *rāj-mistrī* (properly Pers. *rāz*), 'a mason or bricklayer,' *lohār-mistrī*, 'a blacksmith,' &c. The proper use of the word, as noted above, corresponds precisely to the definition of the Portuguese word, as applied to artizans in Bluteau: "Artifice que sabe bem o seu officio. *Peritus artifex ... Opifex, alienorum operum inspector.*" In W. and S. India **maistry**, as used in the household, generally means the cook, or the tailor. (See CALEEFA.)

Mastèr (Мастеръ) is also the Russian term for a skilled workman, and has given rise to several derived adjectives. There is too a similar word in modern Greek, μαγίστωρ.

1404.—"And in these (chambers) there were works of gold and azure and of many other colours, made in the most marvellous way; insomuch that even in Paris whence come the subtle **maestros**, it would be reckoned beautiful to see."—*Clavijo*, § cv. (Comp. *Markham*, p. 125).

1524.—"And the Viceroy (D. Vasco da Gama) sent to seize in the river of the Culymutys four newly-built **caturs**, and fetched them to Cochin. These were built very light for fast rowing, and were greatly admired. But he ordered them to be burned, saying that he intended to show the Moors that we knew how to build better **caturs** than they did; and he sent for **Mestre** Vyne the Genoese, whom he had brought to build galleys, and asked him if he could build boats that would row faster than the Malabar paraos. He answered: 'Sir, I'll build you brigantines fast enough to catch a mosquito. ...'"—*Correa*, ii. 830.

[1548.—"He ordered to be collected in the smithies of the dockyard as many smiths as could be had, for he had many misteres."—*Ibid.* iv. 663.]

1554.—"To the **mestrè** of the smith's shop (*ferraria*) 30,000 reis of salary and 600 reis for maintenance" (see BATTA).—*S. Botelho, Tombo*, 65.

1800.—"... I have not yet been able to remedy the mischief done in my absence, as we have the advantage here of the assistance of some Madras **dubashes** and **maistries**" (ironical).—*Wellington*, i. 67.

1883.—"... My mind goes back to my ancient Goanese cook. He was only a **maistry**, or more vulgarly a *bobberjee* (see BOBACHEE), yet his sonorous name recalled the conquest of Mexico, or the doubling of the Cape."—*Tribes on My Frontier*, 35.

[1900.—"**Mystery** very sick, Mem Sahib, very sick all the night."—*Temple Bar*, April.]

MAJOON, s. Hind. from Ar. *ma'jūn*, lit. 'kneaded,' and thence what old medical books call 'an electuary' (*i.e.* a compound of medicines kneaded with syrup into a soft mass), but especially applied to an intoxicating confection of hemp leaves, &c., sold in the bazar. [*Burton, Ar. Nights*, iii. 159.] In the Deccan the form is *ma'jūm*. Moodeen Sheriff, in his Suppt. to the *Pharmac. of India*, writes *maghjūn*. "The chief ingredients in making it are *ganja* (or hemp) leaves, milk, *ghee*, poppy-seeds, flowers of the thorn-apple (see DATURA), the powder of nux vomica, and sugar" (*Qanoon-e-Islam*, Gloss. lxxxiii).

1519.—"Next morning I halted ... and indulging myself with a **maajûn**, made them throw into the water the liquor used for 'intoxicating fishes, and caught a few fish."—*Baber*, 272.

1563.—"And this they make up into an electuary, with sugar, and with the things above mentioned, and this they call **maju**."—*Garcia*, f. 27 *v.*

1781.—"Our ill-favoured guard brought in a dose of **majum** each, and obliged us to eat it ... a little after sunset the surgeon came, and with him 30 or 40 Caffres, who seized us, and held us fast till the operation (circumcision) was performed."—*Soldier's letter* quoted in *Hon. John Lindsay's Journal of Captivity in Mysore, Lives of Lindsays*, iii. 293.

1874.—"... it (Bhang) is made up with flour and various additions into a sweetmeat or **majum** of a green colour."—*Hanbury and Flückiger*, 493.

MALABAR, n.p.

a. The name of the sea-board country which the Arabs called the 'Pepper-Coast,' the ancient *Kerala* of the Hindus, the Λιμύρικη, or rather Δυμύρικη, of the Greeks, is not in form indigenous, but was applied, apparently, first by the Arab or Arabo-Persian mariners of the Gulf. The substantive part of the name, *Malai*, or the like, is doubtless indigenous; it is the Dravadian term for 'mountain' in the Sanskritized form *Malaya*, which is applied specifically to the southern portion of the Western Ghauts, and from which is taken the indigenous term *Malayālam*, distinguishing that branch of the Dravidian language in the tract which we call *Malabar*. This name—*Male* or *Malai, Malīah*, &c.,—we find in the earlier post-classic notices of India; whilst in the great Temple-Inscription of Tanjore (11th century) we find the region in question called *Malai-nāḍu* (*nāḍu*, 'country'). The affix *bār* appears attached to it first (so far as we are aware) in the Geography of Edrisi (c. 1150). This (Persian ?) termination, *bār*, whatever be its origin, and whether or no it be connected either with the Ar. *barr*, 'a continent,' on the one hand, or with the Skt. *vāra*, 'a region, a slope,' on the other, was most assuredly applied by the navigators of the Gulf to other regions which they visited besides Western India. Thus we have *Zangī-bār* (mod. **Zanzibar**), 'the country of the Blacks'; *Kalāh-bār*, denoting apparently the coast of the Malay Peninsula; and even according to the dictionaries, *Hindū-bār* for India. In the Arabic work which affords the second of these examples (*Relation*, &c., tr. by *Reinaud*, i. 17) it is expressly explained: "The word *bār* serves to indicate that which is both a coast and a kingdom." It will be seen from the quotations below that in the Middle Ages, even after the establishment of the use of this termination, the exact form of the name as given by foreign travellers and writers, varies considerably. But, from the time of the Portuguese discovery of the Cape route, *Malavar*, or *Malabar*, as we have it now, is the persistent form. [Mr. Logan (*Manual*, i. 1) remarks that the name is not in use in the district itself except among foreigners and English-speaking natives; the ordinary name is *Malayālam* or *Malāyam*, 'the Hill Country.']

c. 545.—"The imports to Taprobane are silk, aloeswood, cloves, sandalwood. ... These again are passed on from Sielediba to the marts on this side, such as Μαλὲ, where the pepper is grown. ... And the most notable places of trade are these, Sindu ... and then the five marts of Μαλὲ, from which the pepper is exported, viz., *Parti*, *Mangaruth*, *Salopatana*, *Nalopatana*, and *Pudopatana*."—*Cosmas*, Bk. xi. In *Cathay*, &c., p. clxxviii.

c. 645.—"To the south this kingdom is near the sea. There rise the mountains called **Mo-la-ye** (*Malaya*), with their precipitous sides, and their lofty summits, their dark valleys and their deep ravines. On these mountains grows the white sandalwood."—*Hwen T'sang*, in *Julien*, iii. 122.

851.—"From this place (Maskat) ships sail for India, and run for Kaulam-**Malai**; the distance from Maskat to Kaulam-**Malai** is a month's sail with a moderate wind."—*Relation*, &c., tr. by *Reinaud*, i. 15. The same work at p. 15 uses the expression "Country of Pepper" (*Balad-ul-falfal*).

890.—"From Sindán to **Malí** is five days' journey; in the latter pepper is to be found, also the bamboo."—*Ibn Khurdádba*, in *Elliot*, i. 15.

c. 1030.—"You enter then on the country of Lárán, in which is Jaimúr, then **Maliah**, then Kánchí, then Dravira (see DRAVIDIAN)."—*Al-Birúni*, in *Reinaud*, *Fragmens*, 121.

c. 1150.—"Fandarina is a town built at the mouth of a river which comes from **Manibár**, where vessels from India and Sind cast anchor."—*Idrisi*, in *Elliot*, i. 90.

c. 1200.—"Hari sports here in the delightful spring ... when the breeze from **Malaya** is fragrant from passing over the charming *lavanga*" (cloves).—*Gīta Govinda.*

1270.—"**Malibar** is a large country of India, with many cities, in which pepper is produced."—*Kazwīnī*, in *Gildemeister*, 214.

1293.—"You can sail (upon that sea) between these islands and Ormes, and (from Ormes) to those parts which are called (**Minibar**), is a distance of 2,000 miles, in a direction between south and south-east; then 300 miles between east and south-east from **Minibar** to Maabar"—Letter of *Fr. John of Montecorvino*, in *Cathay*, i. 215.

1298.—"**Melibar** is a great kingdom lying towards the west. ... There is in this kingdom a great quantity of pepper."—*Marco Polo*, Bk. iii. ch. 25.

c. 1300.—"Beyond Guzerat are Kankan and **Tāna**; beyond them the country of **Malíbár**, which from the boundary of Karoha to Kúlam (probably from *Gheriah* to **Quilon**) is 300 parasangs in length."—*Rashíduddín*, in *Elliot*, i. 68.

c. 1320.—"A certain traveller states that India is divided into three parts, of which the first, which is also the most westerly, is that on the confines of Kerman and Sind, and is called Gūzerāt; the second **Manībār**, or the Land of Pepper, east of Gūzerāt."—*Abulfeda*, in *Gildemeister*, 184.

c. 1322.—"And now that ye may know how pepper is got, let me tell you that it groweth in a certain empire, whereunto I came to land, the name whereof is **Minibar**."—*Friar Odoric*, in *Cathay*, &c., 74.

c. 1343.—"After 3 days we arrived in the country of the **Mulaibār**, which is the country of Pepper. It stretches in length a distance of two months' march along the sea-shore."—*Ibn Batuta*, iv. 71.

c. 1348–49.—"We embarked on board certain junks from Lower India, which is called **Minubar**."—*John de' Marignolli*, in *Cathay*, 356.

c. 1420–30.—"... Departing thence he ...

arrived at a noble city called Coloen. ... This province is called **Melibaria**, and they collect in it the ginger called by the natives *colombi*, pepper, brazil-wood, and the cinnamon, called *canella grossa*."—*Conti*, corrected from Jones's tr. in *India in XVth Cent.* 17–18.

c. 1442.—"The coast which includes Calicut with some neighbouring ports, and which extends as far as (Kael), a place situated opposite to the Island of Serendib ... bears the general name of **Melībār**."—*Abdurrazzāk, ibid.* 19.

1459.—Fra Mauro's great Map has **Milibar**.

1514.—"In the region of India called **Melibar**, which province begins at Goa, and extends to Cape Comedis (**Comorin**). ..."—Letter of *Giov. da Empoli*, 79. It is remarkable to find this Florentine using this old form in 1514.

1516.—"And after that the Moors of Meca discovered India, and began to navigate near it, which was 610 years ago, they used to touch at this country of **Malabar** on account of the pepper which is found there."—*Barbosa*, 102.

1553.—"We shall hereafter describe particularly the position of this city of Calecut, and of the country of **Malauar** in which it stands."—*Barros*, Dec. I. iv. c. 6. In the following chapter he writes **Malabar**.

1554.—"*From Diu to the Islands of Dib*-Steer first S.S.E., the pole being made by five inches, side towards the land in the direction of E.S.E. and S.E. by E. till you see the mountains of **Moníbár**."—*The Mohit*, in *J. As. Soc. Ben.* v. 461.

1572.—

"Esta provincia cuja porto agora
Tomado tendes, **Malabar** se chama:
Do culto antiguo os idolos adora,
Que cà por estas partes se derrama."
Camões, vii. 32.

By Burton:

"This province, in whose Ports your ships have tane
refuge, the **Malabar** by name is known;
its ántique rite adoreth idols vain,
Idol-religion being broadest sown."

Since De Barros **Malabar** occurs almost universally.

[1623.—"... **Mahabar** Pirates. ..."—*P. della Valle*, Hak. Soc. i. 121.]

1877.—The form **Malibar** is used in a letter from Athanasius Peter III., "Patriarch of the Syrians of Antioch" to the Marquis of Salisbury, dated Cairo, July 18.

MALABAR, n.p.

b. This word, through circumstances which have been fully elucidated by Bishop Caldwell in his *Comparative Grammar* (2nd ed. 10–12), from which we give an extract below,[1] was applied by the Portuguese not only to the language and people of the country thus called, but also to the *Tamil* language and the people speaking Tamil. In the quotations following, those under *A* apply, or may apply, to the proper people or language of Malabar (see MALAYALAM); those under *B* are instances of the misapplication to Tamil, a misapplication which was general (see *e.g.* in *Orme, passim*) down to the beginning of the last century, and which still holds among the more ignorant Europeans and Eurasians in S. India and Ceylon.

(*A.*)

1552.—"A lingua dos Gentios de Canara e **Malabar**."—*Castanheda*, ii. 78.

1572.—

"Leva alguns **Malabares**, que tomou
Por força, dos que o Samorim mandara."
Camões, ix. 14.

[By Aubertin:

"He takes some **Malabars** he kept on board
By force, of those whom Samorin had
sent ..."]

1582.—"They asked of the **Malabars** which went with him what he was?"—*Castañeda*, (tr. by N. L.) f. 37*v*.

1602.—"We came to anchor in the Roade of Achen ... where we found sixteene or eighteene saile of shippes of diuers Nations, some *Goserats*, some of *Bengala*, some of *Calecut*, called **Malabares**, some *Pegues*, and some *Patanyes*."—*Sir J. Lancaster*, in *Purchas*, i. 153.

1606.—In *Gonvea* (*Synodo*, ff. 2*v*, 3, &c.) **Malavar** means the *Malayālam* language.

(*B.*)

1549.—"Enrico Enriques, a Portuguese priest of our Society, a man of excellent virtue and good example, who is now in the Promontory of Comorin, writes and speaks the **Malabar**

1 "The Portuguese ... sailing from Malabar on voyages of exploration ... made their acquaintance with various places on the eastern or Coromandel Coast ... and finding the language spoken by the fishing and sea-faring classes on the eastern coast similar to that spoken on the western, they came to the conclusion that it was identical with it, and called it in consequence by the same name—viz. **Malabar**. ... A circumstance which naturally confirmed the Portuguese in their notion of the identity of the people and language of the Coromandel Coast with those of Malabar was that when they arrived at Cael, in Tinnevelly, on the Coromandel Coast ... they found the King of Quilon (one of the most important places on the Malabar Coast) residing there."—*Bp. Caldwell*, u.a.

tongue very well indeed."—Letter of *Xavier*, in Coleridge's *Life*, ii. 73.

1680.—"Whereas it hath been hitherto accustomary at this place to make sales and alienations of houses in writing in the Portuguese, Gentue, and **Mallabar** languages, from which some inconveniences have arisen. ..."—*Ft. St. Geo. Consn.*, Sept 9, in *Notes and Extracts*, No. iii. 33.

[1682.—"An order in English Portuguez Gentue & **Mallabar** for the preventing the transportation of this Countrey People and makeing them slaves in other Strange Countreys. ..."—*Pringle, Diary Ft. St. Geo.*, 1st ser. i. 87.]

1718.—"This place (Tranquebar) is altogether inhabited by **Malabarian** Heathens."—*Propn. of the Gospel in the East*, Pt. i. (3rd ed.), p. 18.

"Two distinct languages are necessarily required; one is the *Damulian*, commonly called **Malabarick**."—*Ibid.* Pt. iii. 33.

1734.—"Magnopere commendantes zelum, ae studium Missionariorum, qui libros sacram Ecclesiae Catholicae doctrinam, rerumque sacrarum monumenta continentes, pro Indorum Christi fidelium eruditione in linguam **Malabaricam** seu Tamulicam transtulere."—*Brief of Pope Clement XII.*, in *Norbert*, ii. 432–3. These words are adopted from Card. Tournon's decree of 1704 (see *ibid.* i. 173).

c. 1760.—"Such was the ardent zeal of M. Ziegenbalg that in less than a year he attained a perfect knowledge of the **Malabarian** tongue. ... He composed also a **Malabarian** dictionary of 20,000 words."—*Grose*, i. 261.

1782.—"Les habitans de la côte de Coromandel sont appellés *Tamouls;* les Européens les nomment improprement **Malabars**."—*Sonnerat*, i. 47.

1801.—"From Niliseram to the Chandergerry River no language is understood but the **Malabars** of the Coast."—*Sir T. Munro*, in *Life*, i. 322.

In the following passage the word **Malabars** is misapplied still further, though by a writer usually most accurate and intelligent:

1810.—"The language spoken at Madras is the *Talinga*, here called **Malabars**."—*Maria Graham*, 128.

1860.—"The term '**Malabar**' is used throughout the following pages in the comprehensive sense in which it is applied in the Singhalese Chronicles to the continental invaders of Ceylon; but it must be observed that the adventurers in these expeditions, who are styled in the *Mahawanso 'damilos,'* or Tamils, came not only from ... 'Malabar,' but also from all parts of the Peninsula as far north as Cuttack and Orissa."—*Tennent's Ceylon*, i. 353.

MALABAR RITES. This was a name given to certain heathen and superstitious practices which the Jesuits of the Madura, Carnatic, and Mysore Missions permitted to their converts, in spite of repeated prohibitions by the Popes. And though these practices were finally condemned by the Legate Cardinal de Tournon in 1704, they still subsist, more or less, among native Catholic Christians, and especially those belonging to the (so-called) Goa Churches. These practices are generally alleged to have arisen under Father de' Nobili ("Robertus de Nobilibus"), who came to Madura about 1606. There can be no doubt that the aim of this famous Jesuit was to present Christianity to the people under the form, as it were, of a Hindu translation!

The nature of the practices of which we speak may be gathered from the following particulars of their prohibition. In 1623 Pope Gregory XV., by a constitution dated 31st January, condemned the following:—1. The investiture of Brahmans and certain other castes with the sacred thread, through the agency of Hindu priests, and with Hindu ceremonies. For these Christian ceremonies were to be substituted; and the thread was to be regarded as only a civil badge. 2. The ornamental use of sandalwood paste was permitted, but not its superstitious use, *e.g.*, in mixture with cowdung ashes, &c., for ceremonial purification. 3. Bathing as a ceremonial purification. 4. The observance of caste, and the refusal of high-caste Christians to mix with low-caste Christians in the churches was disapproved.

The quarrels between Capuchins and Jesuits later in the 17th century again brought the Malabar Rites into notice, and Cardinal de Tournon was sent on his unlucky mission to determine these matters finally. His decree (June 23, 1704) prohibited:—1. A mutilated form of baptism, in which were omitted certain ceremonies offensive to Hindus, specifically the use of '*saliva, sal, et insufflatio.*' 2. The use of Pagan names. 3. The Hinduizing of Christian terms by translation. 4. Deferring the baptism of children. 5. Infant marriages. 6. The use of the Hindu *tali* (see TALEE). 7. Hindu usages at marriages. 8. Augury at marriages, by means of a coco-nut. 9. The exclusion of women from churches during certain periods. 10. Ceremonies on a girl's attainment of puberty. 11. The making distinctions between Pariahs and others. 12. The assistance of Christian musicians at heathen ceremonies. 13. The use of ceremonial washing and bathings. 14. The use of cowdung-ashes. 15. The reading and use of Hindu books.

With regard to No. 11 it may be observed that in South India the distinction of castes still subsists, and the only Christian Mission in that quarter which has really succeeded in abolishing caste is that of the Basel Society.

MALAY, n.p. This is in the Malay language an adjective, *Malāyu*; thus *orang Malāyu*, 'a Malay'; *tāna* [*tānah*] *Malāyu*, 'the Malay country'; *bahāsa* [*bhāsa*] *Malāyu*, 'the Malay language.'

In Javanese the word *malāyu* signifies 'to run away,' and the proper name has traditionally been derived from this, in reference to the alleged foundation of **Malacca** by Javanese fugitives; but we can hardly attach importance to this. It may be worthy at least of consideration whether the name was not of foreign, *i.e.* of S. Indian origin, and connected with the *Malāya* of the Peninsula (see under MALABAR). [Mr. Skeat writes: "The tradition given me by Javanese in the Malay States was that the name was applied to Javanese refugees, who peopled the S. of Sumatra. Whatever be the original meaning of the word, it is probable that it started its life-history as a river-name in the S. of Sumatra, and thence became applied to the district through which the river ran, and so to the people who lived there; after which it spread with the Malay dialect until it included not only many allied, but also many foreign, tribes; all Malay-speaking tribes being eventually called Malays without regard to racial origin. A most important passage in this connection is to be found in Leyden's Tr. of the '*Malay Annals*' (1821), p. 20, in which direct reference to such a river is made: 'There is a country in the land of Andalás named Paralembang, which is at present denominated Palembang, the raja of which was denominated Damang Lebar Dawn (chieftain Broad-leaf), who derived his origin from Raja Sulan (Chulan?), whose great-grandson he was. The name of its river Muartatang, into which falls another river named Sungey **Malayu**, near the source of which is a mountain named the mountain Sagantang Maha Miru.' Here Palembang is the name of a well-known Sumatran State, often described as the original home of the Malay race. In standard Malay '*Damang Lebar Dawn*' would be '*Dĕmang Lebar Daun*.' Raja Chulan is probably some mythical Indian king, the story being evidently derived from Indian traditions. 'Muartatang' may be a mistake for *Muar Tenang*, which is a place one heard of in the Peninsula, though I do not know for certain where it is. 'Sungey Malayu' simply means 'River Malayu.' 'Sagantang Maha Miru' is, I think, a mistake for *Sa-gantang Maha Miru*, which is the name used in the Peninsula for the sacred central mountain of the world on which the episode related in the *Annals* occurred" (see Skeat, *Malay Magic*, p. 2).]

It is a remarkable circumstance, which has been noted by Crawfurd, that a name which appears on Ptolemy's Tables as on the coast of the Golden Chersonese, and which must be located somewhere about Maulmain, is *Μαλεοῦ Κῶλον*, words which in Javanese (*Malāyu-Kulon*) would signify "Malays of the West." After this the next (possible) occurrence of the name in literature is in the *Geography* of Edrisi, who describes *Malai* as a great island in the eastern seas, or rather as occupying the position of the *Lemuria* of Mr. Sclater, for (in partial accommodation to the Ptolemaic theory of the Indian Sea) it stretched eastward nearly from the coast of Zinj, *i.e.* of Eastern Africa, to the vicinity of China. Thus it must be uncertain without further accounts whether it is an adumbration of the great Malay islands (as is on the whole probable) or of the Island of the Malagashes (Madagascar), if it is either. We then come to Marco Polo, and after him there is, we believe, no mention of the Malay name till the Portuguese entered the seas of the Archipelago.

[A.D. 690.—Mr. Skeat notes: "I Tsing speaks of the '**Molo-yu** country,' *i.e.* the district W. or N.W. of Palembang in Sumatra."]

c. 1150.—"The Isle of **Malai** is very great. ... The people devote themselves to very profitable trade; aud there are found here elephants, rhinoceroses, and various aromatics and spices, such as clove, cinnamon, nard ... and nutmeg. In the mountains are mines of gold, of excellent quality ... the people also have windmills."—*Edrisi*, by *Jaubert*, i. 945.

c. 1273.—A Chinese notice records under this year that tribute was sent from Siam to the

Emperor. "The Siamese had long been at war with the **Maliyi**, or **Maliurh**, but both nations laid aside their feud and submitted to China."—Notice by Sir T. Wade, in *Bowring's Siam*, i. 72.

c. 1292.—"You come to an Island which forms a kingdom, and is called **Malaiur**. The people have a king of their own, and a peculiar language. The city is a fine and noble one, and there is a great trade carried on there. All kinds of spicery are to be found there."—*Marco Polo*, Bk. iii. ch. 8.

c. 1539.—"... as soon as he had delivered to him the letter, it was translated into the *Portugal* out of the **Malayan** tongue wherein it was written."—*Pinto*, E.T. p. 15.

1548.—"... having made a breach in the wall twelve fathom wide, he assaulted it with 10,000 strangers, *Turks*, *Abyssins*, *Moors*, *Malauares*, *Achems*, *Jaos*, and **Malayos**."—*Ibid*. p. 279.

1553:—"And so these Gentiles like the Moors who inhabit the sea-coasts of the Island (Sumatra), although they have each their peculiar language, almost all can speak the **Malay** of Malacca as being the most general language of those parts."—*Barros*, III. v. 1.

"Everything with them is to be a gentleman; and this has such prevalence in those parts that you will never find a native **Malay**, however poor he may be, who will set his hand to lift a thing of his own or anybody else's; every service must be done by slaves."—*Ibid*. II. vi. 1.

1610.—"I cannot imagine what the *Hollanders* meane, to suffer these **Malaysians**, *Chinesians*, and *Moores* of these countries, and to assist them in their free trade thorow all the *Indies*, and forbid it their owne seruants, countrymen, and Brethern, upon paine of death and losse of goods."—*Peter Williamson Floris*, in *Purchas*, i. 321.

[Mr. Skeat writes: "The word *Malaya* is now often applied by English writers to the Peninsula as a whole, and from this the term **Malaysia** as a term of wider application (*i.e.* to the Archipelago) has been coined (see quotation of 1610 above). The former is very frequently mis-written by English writers as '*Malay*,' a barbarism which has even found place on the title-page of a book—'Travel and Sport in Burma, Siam and **Malay**, by John Bradley, London, 1876.'"]

MALAYĀLAM. This is the name applied to one of the cultivated Dravidian languages, the closest in its relation to the Tamil. It is spoken along the Malabar coast, on the Western side of the **Ghauts** (or *Malāya* mountains), from the Chandragiri River on the North, near Mangalore (entering the sea in 12° 29′), beyond which the language is, for a limited distance, *Tulu*, and then Canarese, to Trevandrum on the South (lat. 8° 29′), where Tamil begins to supersede it. Tamil, however, also intertwines with Malayālam all along Malabar. The term *Malayālam* properly applies to territory, not language, and might be rendered "Mountain region" [See under MALABAR, and *Logan*, *Man. of Malabar*, i. 90.]

MALDIVES, MALDIVE ISLDS., n.p. The proper form of this name appears to be *Male-dīva*; not, as the estimable Garcia de Orta says, *Nale*-dīva; whilst the etymology which he gives is certainly wrong, hard as it may be to say what is the right one. The people of the islands formerly designated themselves and their country by a form of the word for 'island' which we have in the Skt. *dvīpa* and the Pali *dīpo*. We find this reflected in the *Divi* of Ammianus, and in the *Dīva* and *Dība*-jāt (Pers. plural) of old Arab geographers, whilst it survives in letters of the 18th century addressed to the Ceylon Government (Dutch) by the Sultan of the Isles, who calls his kingdom *Divehi Rajjé*, and his people *Divehe mīhun*. Something like the modern form first appears in Ibn Batuta. He, it will be seen, in his admirable account of these islands, calls them, as it were, *Mahal*-dives, and says they were so called from the chief group *Mahal*, which was the residence of the Sultan, indicating a connection with *Mahal*, 'a palace.' This form of the name looks like a foreign 'striving after meaning.' But Pyrard de Laval, the author of the most complete account in existence, also says that the name of the islands was taken from *Malé*, that on which the King resided. Bishop Caldwell has suggested that these islands were the *dives*, or islands, of *Malé*, as *Malebār* (see MALABAR) was the coast-tract or continent, of *Malé*. It is, however, not impossible that the true etymology was from *mālā*, 'a garland or necklace,' of which their configuration is highly suggestive. [The *Madras Gloss*. gives Malayāl. *māl*,' 'black,' and *dvīpa*, 'island,' from the dark soil. For a full account of early notices of the Maldives, see Mr. Gray's note on *Pyrard de Laval*, Hak. Soc. ii. 423 *seqq*.] Milburn (*Or. Commerce*, i. 335) says: "This island was (these islands were) discovered by the Portuguese in 1507." Let us see!

A.D. 362.—"Legationes undique solito ocius

concurrebant; hinc Transtigritanis pacem obsecrantibus et Armeniis, inde nationibus Indicis certatim cum donis optimates mittentibus ante tempus, ab usque **Divis** et Serendivis."—*Ammian. Marcellinus*, xxii. 3.

c. 545.—"And round about it (*Sielediba* or *Taprobane, i.e.* Ceylon) there are a number of small islands, in all of which you find fresh water and coco-nuts. And these are almost all set close to one another."—*Cosmas, in Cathay,* &c., clxxvii.

851.—"Between this Sea (of Horkand) and the Sea called Lāravi there is a great number of isles; their number, indeed, it is said, amounts to 1,900; ... the distance from island to island is 2, 3, or 4 parasangs. They are all inhabited, and all produce coco-palms. ... The last of these islands is Serendīb, in the Sea of Horkand; it is the chief of all; they give the islands the name of **Dībajāt**" (*i.e. Dības*).—*Relation*, &c., tr. by *Reinaud*, i. 4–5.

c. 1030.—"The special name of **Dīva** is given to islands which are formed in the sea, and which appear above water in the form of accumulations of sand; these sands continually augment, spread, and unite, till they present a firm aspect ... these islands are divided into two classes, according to the nature of their staple product. Those of one class are called **Dīva-***Kūzah* (or the Cowry Divahs), because of the cowries which are gathered from coco-branches planted in the sea. The others are called **Dīva-***Kanbar*, from the word *kanbar* (see COIR), which is the name of the twine made from coco-fibres, with which vessels are stitched."—*Al-Birūnī*, in *Reinaud, Fragmens*, 124.

1150.—See also *Edrisi*, in Jaubert's Transl. i. 68. But the translator prints a bad reading, *Raibiḥāt*, for **Dībajāt**.

c. 1343.—"Ten days after embarking at Calecut we arrived at the Islands called **Dhībat-al-Mahal**. ... These islands are reckoned among the wonders of the World; there are some 2000 of them. Groups of a hundred, or not quite so many, of these islands are found clustered into a ring, and each cluster has an entrance like a harbour-mouth, and it is only there that ships can enter. ... Most of the trees that grow on these islands are coco-palms. ... They are divided into regions or groups ... among which are distinguished ... 3° **Mahal**, the group which gives a name to the whole, and which is the residence of the Sultans."—*Ibn Batuta*, iv. 110 *seqq*.

1442.—Abdurrazzak also calls them "the isles of **Dīva-Mahal**."—In *Not. et Exts.* xiv. 429.

1503.—"But Dom Vasco ... said that things must go on as they were to India, and there he would inquire into the truth. And so arriving in the Gulf (*golfão*) where the storm befel them, all were separated, and that vessel which steered badly, parted company with the fleet, and found itself at one of the first islands of **Maldiva**, at which they stopped some days enjoying themselves. For the island abounded in provisions, and the men indulged to excess in eating cocos, and fish, and in drinking bad stagnant water, and in disorders with women; so that many died."—*Correa*, i. 347.

[1512.—"Mafamede Maçay with two ships put into the **Maldive** islands (ilhas de **Maldiva**)."—*Albuquerque, Cartas*, p. 30.]

1563.—"*R.* Though it be somewhat to interrupt the business in hand,—why is that chain of islands called 'Islands of **Maldiva**'?

"*O.* In this matter of the nomenclature of lands and seas and kingdoms, many of our people make great mistakes even in regard to our own lands; how then can you expect that one can give you the rationale of etymologies of names in foreign tongues? But, nevertheless, I will tell you what I have heard say. And that is that the right name is not **Maldiva**, but *Naledīva*; for *nale* in Malabar means 'four,' and *diva* 'island,' so that in the Malabar tongue the name is as much as to say 'Four Isles.' ... And in the same way we call a certain island that is 12 leagues from Goa *Angediva*, because there are five in the group, and so the name in Malabar means 'Five Isles,' for *ange* is 'five.' But these derivations rest on common report, I don't detail them to you as demonstrable facts."—*Garcia, Colloquios*, f. 11.

1572.—"Nas ilhas de **Maldiva**."

c. 1610.—"Ce Royaume en leur langage s'appelle Malé-*ragné*, Royaume de **Malé**, et des autres peuples de l'Inde il s'appelle **Malé-divar**, et les peuples **diues** ... L'Isle principale, comme j'ay dit, s'appelle **Malé**, qui donne le nom à tout le reste des autres; car le mot **Diues** signifie vn nombre de petites isles amassées."—*Pyrard de Laval*, i. 63, 68, ed. 1679. [Hak. Soc. i. 83, 177.]

1683.—"Mr. Beard sent up his Couries, which he had received from ye **Mauldivas**, to be put off and passed by Mr. Charnock at Cassumbazar."—*Hedges, Diary*, Oct. 2; [Hak. Soc. i. 122].

MALUM, s. In a ship with English officers and native crew, the mate is called *mālum sāhib*. The word is Ar. *mu'allim*, literally 'the Instructor,' and is properly applied to the pilot or sailing-master. The word may be compared, thus used, with our 'master' in the Navy. In regard to the first quotation we may observe that *Nākhuda* is, rather than *Mu'allim*, 'the captain'; though its proper meaning is the owner of the ship; the two capacities of owner and skipper being doubtless often combined. The distinction of *Mu'allim* from *Nākhuda* accounts for the former title being assigned to the mate.

1497.—"And he sent 20 cruzados in gold, and 20 testoons in silver for the **Malemos**, who were the pilots; for of these coins he would give each month whatever he (the Sheikh) should direct."—*Correa*, i. 38 (E.T. by *Ld. Stanley of Alderley*, 88). On this passage the Translator says: "The word is perhaps the Arabic for an instructor, a word in general use all over Africa." It is curious that his varied experience should have failed to recognise the habitual marine use of the term.

1541.—"Meanwhile he sent three **caturs** (q.v.) to the Port of the **Malems** (*Porto dos Malemos*) in order to get some pilot. ... In this Port of the *Bandel of the* **Malems** the ships of the Moors take pilots when they enter the Straits, and when they return they leave them here again."[1]—*Correa*, iv. 168.

1553.—"... among whom (at Melinda) came a Moor, a Guzarate by nation, called **Malem** Cana, who, as much for the satisfaction he had in conversing with our people, as to please the King, who was inquiring for a pilot to give them, agreed to accompany them."—*Barros*, I. iv. 6.

c. 1590.—"**Mu'allim** or Captain. He must be acquainted with the depths and shallow places of the Ocean, and must know astronomy. It is he who guides the ship to her destination, and prevents her falling into dangers."—*Āīn*, ed. *Blochmann*, i. 280.

[1887.—"The second class, or **Malumis**, are sailors."—*Logan, Malabar*, ii. ccxcv.]

MANDADORE, s. Port. *mandador*, 'one who commands.'

1673.—"Each of which Tribes have a **Mandadore** or Superintendent."—*Fryer*, 67.

MANDALAY, MANDALÉ, n.p. The capital of the King of Burmah, founded in 1860, 7 miles north of the preceding capital Amarapura, and between 2 and 3 miles from the left bank of the Irawadi. The name was taken from that of a conical isolated hill, rising high above the alluvial plain of the Irawadi, and crowned by a gilt pagoda. The name of the hill (and now of the city at its base) probably represents *Mandara*, the sacred mountain which in Hindu mythology served the gods as a churning-staff at the churning of the sea. The hill appears as *Mandiye-taung* in Major Grant Allan's Map of the Environs of Amarapura (1855), published in the Narrative of Major Phayre's Mission, but the name does not occur in the Narrative itself.

[1860.—See the account of **Mandelay** in *Mason, Burmah*, 14 *seqq.*]

1861.—"Next morning the son of my friendly host accompanied me to the **Mandalay** Hill, on which there stands in a gilt chapel the image of Shwesayatta, pointing down with outstretched finger to the Palace of **Mandalay**, interpreted as the divine command there to build a city ... on the other side where the hill falls in an abrupt precipice, sits a gigantic Buddha gazing in motionless meditation on the mountains opposite. There are here some caves in the hard rock, built up with bricks and white-washed, which are inhabited by eremites. ..."—*Bastian's Travels* (German), ii. 89–90.

MANDARIN, s. Port. *Mandarij, Mandarim*. Wedgwood explains and derives the word thus: "A Chinese officer, a name first made known to us by the Portuguese, and like the Indian *caste*, erroneously supposed to be a native term. From Portuguese *mandar*, to hold authority, command, govern, &c." So also T. Hyde in the quotation below. Except as regards the word having been first made known to us by the Portuguese, this is an old and persistent mistake. What sort of form would *mandarij* be as a derivative from *mandar*? The Portuguese might have applied to Eastern officials some such word as *mandador*, which a preceding article (see MANDADORE) shows that they did apply in certain cases. But the parallel to the assumed origin of *mandarin* from *mandar* would be that English voyagers on visiting China, or some other country in the far East, should have invented, as a title for the officials of that country, a new and abnormal derivation from 'order,' and called them *orderumbos*.

The word is really a slight corruption of Hind. (from Skt.) *mantri*, 'a counsellor, a

---

1 This Port was immediately outside the Straits, as appears from the description of Dom João de Castro (1541): "Now turning to the 'Gates' of the Strait, which are the chief object of our description, we remark that here the land of Arabia juts out into the sea, forming a prominent Point, and very prolonged. ... This is the point or promontory which Ptolemy calls *Possidium*. ... In front of it, a little more than a gunshot off, is an islet called the *Ilheo dos Roboeens*; because *Roboão* in Arabic means a pilot; and the pilots living here go aboard the ships which come from outside, and conduct them," &c.—*Roteiro do Mar Roxo*, &c., 35.

The Island retains its name, and is mentioned as *Pilot Island* by Capt. Haines in *J. R. Geog. Soc.* ix. 126. It lies about 1½ m. due east of Perim.

Minister of State,' for which it was indeed the proper old pre-Mahommedan term in India. It has been adopted, and specially affected in various Indo-Chinese countries, and particularly by the Malays, among whom it is habitually applied to the highest class of public officers (see *Crawfurd's Malay Dict.* s.v. [and Klinkert, who writes *manteri*, colloquially *mentri*]). Yet Crawfurd himself, strange to say, adopts the current explanation as from the Portuguese (see *J. Ind. Archip.* iv. 189). [Klinkert adopts the Skt. derivation.] It is, no doubt, probable that the instinctive "striving after meaning" may have shaped the corruption of *mantri* into a semblance of *mandar*. Marsden is still more oddly perverse, *videns meliora, deteriora secutus*, when he says: "The officers next in rank to the Sultan are *Mantree*, which some apprehend to be a corruption of the word *Mandarin*, a title of distinction among the Chinese" (*H. of Sumatra*, 2nd ed. 285). Ritter adopts the etymology from *mandar*, apparently after A. W. Schlegel.[1] The true etymon is pointed out in *Notes and Queries in China and Japan*, iii. 12, and by one of the present writers in *Ocean Highways* for Sept. 1872, p. 186. Several of the quotations below will show that the earlier applications of the title have no reference to China at all, but to officers of state, not only in the Malay countries, but in Continental India. We may add that *mantri* is still much in vogue among the less barbarous Hill Races on the Eastern frontier of Bengal (*e.g.* among the *Kasias* as a denomination for their petty dignitaries under the chief. Gibbon was perhaps aware of the true origin of *mandarin*; see below.

c. A.D. 400 (?).—"The King desirous of trying cases must enter the assembly composed in manner, together with Brahmans who know the Vedas, and **mantrins** (or counsellors)."—*Manu*, viii. 1.

[1522.—"... and for this purpose he sent one of his chief **mandarins** (*mandarim*)."—India Office MSS. in an Agreement made by the Portuguese with the "*Rey de Sunda*," this Sunda being that of the Straits.]

1524.—(At the Moluccas) "and they cut off the heads of all the dead Moors, and indeed fought with one another for these, because whoever brought in seven heads of enemies, they made him a knight, and called him **manderym**, which is their name for Knight."—*Correa*, ii. 808.

c. 1540.—"... the which corsairs had their own dealings with the **Mandarins** of those ports, to whom they used to give many and heavy bribes to allow them to sell on shore what they plundered on the sea."—*Pinto*, cap. 1.

1552.—(At Malacca) "whence subsist the King and the Prince with their **mandarins**, who are the gentlemen."—*Castanheda*, iii. 207.

(In China). "There are among them degrees of honour, and according to their degrees of honour is their service; gentlemen (*fidalgos*) whom they call **mandarins** ride on horseback, and when they pass along the streets the common people make way for them."—*Ibid.* iv. 57.

1553.—"Proceeding ashore in two or three boats dressed with flags and with a grand blare of trumpets (this was at **Malacca** in 1508–9). ... Jeronymo Teixeira was received by many **Mandarijs** of the King, these being the most noble class of the city."—*De Barros*, Dec. II. liv. iv. cap. 3.

"And he being already known to the **Mandarijs** (at Chittagong, in Bengal), and held to be a man profitable to the country, because of the heavy amounts of duty that he paid, he was regarded like a native."—*Ibid.* Dec. IV. liv. ix. cap. 2.

"And from these *Cellates* and native Malays come all the **Mandarins**, who are now the gentlemen (*fidalgos*) of Malaca."—*Ibid.* II. vi. 1.

1598.—"They are called ... **Mandorijns**, and are always borne in the streetes, sitting in chariots which are hanged about with Curtaines of Silke, covered with Clothes of Gold and Silver, and are much given to banketing, eating and drinking, and making good cheare, as also the whole land of China."—*Linschoten*, 39; [Hak. Soc. i. 135].

1610.—"The **Mandorins** (officious officers) would have interverted the king's command for their own covetousnesse" (at Siam).—*Peter Williamson Floris*, in *Purchas*, i. 322.

1612.—"Shah Indra Brama fled in like manner to Malacca, where they were graciously received by the King, Mansur Shah, who had the Prince converted to Islamism, and appointed him to be a **Mantor**."—*Sijara Malayu*, in *J. Ind. Arch.* v. 730.

c. 1663.—"Domandò il Signor Carlo se **mandarino** è voce Chinese. Disse esser Portoghese, e che in Chinese si chiamano *Quoan*, che significa signoreggiare, comandare, gobernare."—*Viaggio del P. Gio. Grueber*, in *Thevenot, Divers Voyages*.

1682.—In the Kingdome of Patane (on E. coast of Malay Peninsula) "The King's

---

1 See *Erdkunde*, v. 647. The Index to Ritter gives a reference to *A. W. Schott, Mag. für die Literat. des Ausl.*, 1837, No. 123. This we have not been able to see.

counsellors are called **Mentary**."—*Nieuhof, Zee en Lant-Reize*, ii. 64.

c. 1690.—"**Mandarinorum** autem nomine intelliguntur omnis generis officiarii, qui a *mandando* appellantur *mandarini* linguâ Lusitanicâ, quae unica Europaea est in oris Chinensibus obtinens."—*T. Hyde, De Ludis Orientalibus*, in *Syntagmata*, Oxon. 1767, ii. 266.

1719.—"... one of the **Mandarins**, a kind of viceroy or principal magistrate in the province where they reside."—*Robinson Crusoe*, Pt. ii.

1726.—"**Mantrís**. Councillors. These give rede and deed in things of moment, and otherwise are in the Government next to the King. ..." (in Ceylon).—*Valentijn, Names*, &c., 6.

1727.—"Every province or city (Burma) has a **Mandereen** or Deputy residing at Court, which is generally in the City of Ava, the present Metropolis."—*A. Hamilton*, ii. 43, [ed. 1744, ii. 42].

1774.—"... presented to each of the Batchian **Manteries** as well as the two officers a scarlet coat."—*Forrest, V. to N. Guinea*, p. 100.

1788.—"... Some words notoriously corrupt are fixed, and as it were naturalized in the vulgar tongue ... and we are pleased to blend the three Chinese monosyllables *Con-fû-tzee* in the respectable name of Confucius, or even to adopt the Portuguese corruption of **Mandarin**."—*Gibbon*, Preface to his 4th volume.

1879.—"The **Mentrí**, the Malay Governor of Larut ... was powerless to restore order."—*Miss Bird, Golden Chersonese*, 267.

Used as an adjective:

[c. 1848.—"The **mandarin**-boat, or 'Smug-boat,' as it is often called by the natives, is the most elegant thing that floats."—*Berncastle, Voyage to China*, ii. 71.

[1878.—"The Cho-Ka-Shun, or boats in which the **Mandarins** travel, are not unlike large floating caravans."—*Gray, China*, ii. 270.]

MANDARIN LANGUAGE, s. The language spoken by the official and literary class in China, as opposed to local dialects. In Chinese it is called *Kuan-Hua*. It is substantially the language of the people of the northern and middle zones of China, extending to Yun-nan. It is not to be confounded with the literary style which is used in books. [See *Ball, Things Chinese*, 169 *seq.*]

1674.—"The Language ... is called *Quenhra* (*hua*), or the **Language of Mandarines**, because as they spread their command they introduced it, and it is used throughout all the Empire, as Latin in Europe. It is very barren, and as it has more Letters far than any other, so it has fewer words."—*Faria y Sousa*, E.T. ii. 468.

MANGO, s. The royal fruit of the *Mangifera indica*, when of good quality is one of the richest and best fruits in the world. The original of the word is Tamil *mān-kāy* or *mān-gāy*, *i.e. mān* fruit (the tree being *māmarum*, '*mān*-tree'). The Portuguese formed from this *manga*, which we have adopted as *mango*. The tree is wild in the forests of various parts of India; but the fruit of the wild tree is uneatable.

The word has sometimes been supposed to be Malay; but it was in fact introduced into the Archipelago, along with the fruit itself, from S. India. Rumphius (*Herb. Amboyn.* i. 95) traces its then recent introduction into the islands, and says that it is called (*Malaicè*) "*mangka*, vel vulgo *Manga* et *Mapelaam*." This last word is only the Tamil *Māpaḷam*, *i.e.* '*mān* fruit' again. The close approximation of the Malay *mangka* to the Portuguese form might suggest that the latter name was derived from Malacca. But we see *manga* already used by Varthema, who, according to Garcia, never really went beyond Malabar. [Mr. Skeat. writes: "The modern standard Malay word is *mangga*, from which the Port form was probably taken. The other Malay form quoted from Rumphius is in standard Malay *mapĕlam*, with *mĕpĕlam*, *hĕmpĕlam*, *ampĕlam*, and *'pĕlam* or *'plam* as variants. The Javanese is *pĕlĕm*."]

The word has been taken to Madagascar, apparently by the Malayan colonists, whose language has left so large an impression there, in the precise shape *mangka*. Had the fruit been an Arab importation it is improbable that the name would have been introduced in that form.

The N. Indian names are *Ām* and *Amba*, and variations of these we find in several of the older European writers. Thus Fr. Jordanus, who had been in the Konkan, and appreciated the progenitors of the Goa and Bombay Mango (c. 1328), calls the fruit *Aniba*. Some 30 years later John de' Marignolli calls the tree "*amburan*, having a fruit of excellent fragrance and flavour, somewhat like a peach" (*Cathay*, &c., ii. 362). Garcia de Orta shows how early the Bombay fruit was prized. He seems to have been the owner of the parent tree. The Skt. name is *Amra*, and this we find in Hwen T'sang (c. 645) phoneticised as *'An-mo-lo*.

The mango is probably the fruit alluded to by Theophrastus as having caused dysentery in the army of Alexander. (See the passage s.v. **JACK**).

c. 1328.—"Est etiam alia arbor quae fructus facit ad modum pruni, grosissimos, qui vocantur *Aniba*. Hi sunt fructus ita dulces et amabiles, quod ore tenus exprimi hoc minimè possit."—*Fr. Jordanus*, in *Rec. de Voyages*, &c., iv. 42.

c. 1334.—"The mango tree (*'anba*) resembles an orange-tree, but is larger and more leafy; no other tree gives so much shade, but this shade is unwholesome, and whoever sleeps under it gets fever."—*Ibn Batuta*, iii. 125. At ii. 185 he writes *'anbā*. [The same charge is made against the tamarind; see *Burton, Ar. Nights*, iii. 81.]

c. 1349.—"They have also another tree called *Amburan*, having a fruit of excellent fragrance and flavour, somewhat like a peach."—*John de' Marignolli*, in *Cathay*, &c., 362.

1510.—"Another fruit is also found here, which is called *Amba*, the stem of which is called **Manga**," &c.—*Varthema*, 160–161.

c. 1526.—"Of the vegetable productions peculiar to Hindustân one is the mango (*ambeh*). ... Such mangoes as are good are excellent. ..." &c.—*Baber*, 324.

1563.—"*O.* Boy! go and see what two vessels those are coming in—you see them from the varanda here—and they seem but small ones.

"*Servant.* I will bring you word presently.

* * * * *

"*S.* Sir! it is Simon Toscano, your tenant in Bombay, and he brings this hamper of **mangas** for you to make a present to the Governor, and says that when he has moored the boat he will come here to stop.

"*O.* He couldn't have come more à propos. I have a **manga**-tree (*mangueira*) in that island of mine which is remarkable for both its two crops, one at this time of year, the other at the end of May, and much as the other crop excels this in quality for fragrance and flavour, this is just as remarkable for coming out of season. But come, let us taste them before His Excellency. Boy! take out six **mangas**."—*Garcia*, ff. 134*v*, 135. This author also mentions that the **mangas** of Ormuz were the most celebrated; also certain **mangas** of Guzerat, not large, but of surpassing fragrance and flavour, and having a very small stone. Those of Balaghat were both excellent and big; the Doctor had seen two that weighed 4 *arratel* and a half (4⅕ lbs.); and those of Bengal, Pegu, and Malacca were also good.

[1569.—"There is much fruit that comes from Arabia and Persia, which they call mangoes (**mangas**), which is very good fruit."—*Cronica dos Reys Dormuz*, translated from the Arabic in 1569.]

c. 1590.—"The Mangoe (*Anba*). ... This fruit is unrivalled in colour, smell, and taste; and some of the *gourmands* of Túrán and Irán place it above musk melons and grapes. ... If a half-ripe mango, together with its stalk to a length of about two fingers, be taken from the tree, and the broken end of its stalk be closed with warm wax, and kept in butter or honey, the fruit will retain its taste for two or three months."—*Āīn*, ed. *Blochmann*, i. 67–68.

[1614.—"Two jars of **Manges** at rupees 4½."—*Foster, Letters*, iii. 41.

[1615.—"George Durois sent in a present of two pottes of **Mangeas**."—*Cocks's Diary*, Hak. Soc. i. 79.]

"There is another very licquorish fruit called **Amangues** growing on trees, and it is as bigge as a great quince, with a very great stone in it."—*De Monfart*, 20.

1622.—P. della Valle describes the tree and fruit at Miná (*Minao*) near Hormuz, under the name of *Amba*, as an exotic introduced from India. Afterwards at Goa he speaks of it as "**manga** or *amba*."—ii. pp. 313–14, and 581; [Hak. Soc. i. 40].

1631.—"Alibi vero commemorat **mangae** speciem fortis admodum odoris, Terebinthinam scilicet, et Piceae arboris lacrymam redolentes, quas propterea nostri *stinkers* appellant."—*Piso* on *Bontius, Hist. Nat.* p. 95.

[1663.—"*Ambas*, or **Mangues**, are in season during two months in summer, and are plentiful and cheap; but those grown at Delhi are indifferent. The best come from *Bengale*, Golkonda, and Goa, and these are indeed excellent. I do not know any sweet-meat more agreeable."—*Bernier*, ed. *Constable*, 249.]

1673.—Of the Goa **Mango**,[1] Fryer says justly: "When ripe, the Apples of the *Hesperides* are but Fables to them; for Taste, the Nectarine, Peach, and Apricot fall short. ..."—p. 182.

1679.—"**Mango** and **saio** (see **SOY**), two sorts of sauces brought from the East Indies."—*Locke's Journal*, in *Ld. King's Life*, 1830, i. 249.

1727.—"The *Goa* **mango** is reckoned the largest and most delicious to the taste of any in the world, and I may add, the wholesomest and best tasted of any Fruit in the World."—*A. Hamilton*, i. 255, [ed. 1744, i. 258].

1883.—"... the unsophisticated ryot ... conceives that cultivation could only emasculate the pronounced flavour and firm fibrous texture

---

1 The excellence of the Goa Mangoes is stated to be due to the care and skill of the Jesuits (*Annaes Maritimos*, ii. 270). In S. India all good kinds have Portuguese or Mahommedan names. The author of *Tribes on My Frontier*, 1883, p. 148, mentions the luscious *peirie* and the delicate *afoos* as two fine varieties, supposed to bear the names of a certain *Peres* and a certain *Affonso*.

of that prince of fruits, the wild **mango**, likest a ball of tow soaked in turpentine."—*Tribes on My Frontier*, 149.

The name has been carried with the fruit to Mauritius and the West Indies. Among many greater services to India the late Sir Proby Cautley diffused largely in Upper India the delicious fruit of the Bombay mango, previously rare there, by creating and encouraging groves of grafts on the banks of the Ganges and Jumma canals. It is especially true of this fruit (as Sultan Baber indicates) that excellence depends on the variety. The common mango is coarse and strong of turpentine. Of this only an evanescent suggestion remains to give peculiarity to the finer varieties. [A useful account of these varieties, by Mr. Maries, will be found in *Watt, Econ. Dict.* v. 148 *seqq.*]

MANGO-TRICK. One of the most famous tricks of Indian jugglers, in which they plant a mango-stone, and show at brief intervals the tree shooting above ground, and successively producing leaves, flowers, and fruit. It has often been described, but the description given by the Emperor Jahāngīr in his *Autobiography* certainly surpasses all in its demand on our belief.

c. 1610.—"... Khaun-e-Jehaun, one of the nobles present, observed that if they spoke truly he should wish them to produce for his conviction a mulberry-tree. The men arose without hesitation, and having in ten separate spots set some seed in the ground, they recited among themselves ... when instantly a plant was seen springing from each of the ten places, and each proved the tree required by Khaun-e-Jehaun. In the same manner they produced a mango, an apple-tree, a cypress, a pine-apple, a fig-tree, an almond, a walnut ... open to the observation of all present, the trees were perceived gradually and slowly springing from the earth, to the height of one or perhaps of two cubits. ... Then making a sort of procession round the trees as they stood ... in a moment there appeared on the respective trees a sweet mango without the rind, an almond fresh and ripe, a large fig of the most delicious kind ... the fruit being pulled in my presence, and every one present was allowed to taste it. This, however, was not all; before the trees were removed there appeared among the foliage birds of such surpassing beauty, in colour and shape, and melody and song, as the world never saw before. ... At the close of the operation, the foliage, as in autumn, was seen to put on its variegated tints, and the trees gradually disappeared into the earth. ..."—*Mem. of the Emp. Jehanguier*, tr. by *Major D. Price*, pp. 96–97.

c. 1650.—"Then they thrust a piece of stick into the ground, and ask'd the Company what Fruit they would have. One told them he would have *Mengues*; then one of the Mountebanks hiding himself in the middle of a Sheet, stoopt to the ground five or six times one after another. I was so curious to go upstairs, and look out of a window, to see if I could spy what the Mountebank did, and perceived that after he had cut himself under the armpits with a Razor, he rubb'd the stick with his Blood. After the two first times that he rais'd himself, the stick seemed to the very eye to grow. The third time there sprung out branches with young buds. The fourth time the tree was covered with leaves; and the fifth time it bore flowers. ... The English Minister protested that he could not give his consent that any Christian should be Spectator of such delusions. So that as soon as he saw that these Mountebanks had of a dry stick, in less than half-an-hour, made a Tree four or five foot high, that bare leaves and flowers as in the Spring-time: he went about to break it, protesting that he would not give the Communion to any person that should stay any longer to see those things."—*Tavernier*, *Travels made English*, by J.P., ii. 36; [ed. *Ball*, i. 67, *seq.*].

1667.—"When two of these *Jauguis* (see JOGEE) that are eminent, do meet, and you stir them up on the point and power of their knowledge or *Jauguisme*, you shall see them do such tricks out of spight to one another, that I know not if *Simon Magus* could have outdone them. For they divine what one thinketh, make the Branch of a Tree blossome and bear fruit in less than an hour, hatch eggs in their bosome in less than half a quarter of an hour, and bring forth such birds as you demand. ... *I mean, if what is said of them is true.* ... For, as for me, I am with all my curiosity none of those happy Men, that are present at, and see these great feats."—*Bernier*, E.T. 103; [ed. *Constable*, 321].

1673.—"Others presented a Mock-Creation of a Mango-Tree, arising from the Stone in a short space (which they did in Hugger-Mugger, being very careful to avoid being discovered) with Fruit Green and Ripe; so that a Man must stretch his Fancy, to imagine it Witchcraft; though the common Sort think no less."—*Fryer*, 192.

1690.—"Others are said to raise a Mango-Tree, with ripe Fruit upon its Branches, in the space of one or two Hours. To confirm which Relation, it was affirmed confidently to me, that a Gentleman who had pluckt one of these Mangoes, fell sick upon it, and was never well as long as he kept it 'till he consulted a *Bramin* for his Health, who prescrib'd his only Remedy would be the restoring of the Mango, by which he was restor'd to his Health again."—*Ovington*, 258–259.

1726.—"They have some also who will show you the kernel of a mango-fruit, or may be only a twig, and ask if you will see the fruit or this stick planted, and in a short time see a tree grow from it and bear fruit: after they have got their answer the jugglers (*Koorde-danssers*) wrap themselves in a blanket, stick the twig into the ground, and then put a basket over them (&c. &c.).

"There are some who have prevailed on these jugglers by much money to let them see how they have accomplished this.

"These have revealed that the jugglers made a hole in their bodies under the armpits, and rubbed the twig with the blood from it, and every time that they stuck it in the ground they wetted it, and in this way they clearly saw it to grow and to come to the perfection before described.

"This is asserted by a certain writer who has seen it. But this can't move me to believe it!"—*Valentijn*, v. (*Chorom.*) 53.

Our own experience does not go beyond Dr. Fryer's, and the hugger-mugger performance that he disparages. But many others have testified to more remarkable skill. We once heard a traveller of note relate with much spirit such an exhibition as witnessed in the Deccan. The narrator, then a young officer, determined with a comrade, at all hazards of fair play or foul, to solve the mystery. In the middle of the trick one suddenly seized the conjuror, whilst the other uncovered and snatched at the mango-plant. But lo! it came from the earth *with a root*, and the mystery was darker than ever! We tell the tale as it was told.

It would seem that the trick was not unknown in European conjuring of the 16th or 17th centuries, *e.g.*

1657.—"... trium horarum spatio arbusculam veram spitamae longitudine e mensâ facere enasci, ut et alias arbores frondiferas et fructiferas."—*Magia Universalis*, of *P. Gaspar Schottus e Soc. Jes.*, Herbipoli, 1657, i. 32.

MARAMUT, MURRUMUT, s. Hind. from Ar. *maramma(t)*, 'repair.' In this sense the use is general in Hindustani (in which the terminal *t* is always pronounced, though not by the Arabs), whether as applied to a stocking, a fortress, or a ship. But in Madras Presidency the word had formerly a very specialised sense as the recognised title of that branch of the Executive which included the conservation of irrigation tanks and the like, and which was worked under the District Civil Officers, there being then no separate department of the State in charge of Civil Public Works. It is a curious illustration of the wide spread at one time of Musulman power that the same Arabic word, in the form **Marama**, is still applied in Sicily to a standing committee charged with repairs to the Duomo or Cathedral of Palermo. An analogous instance of the wide grasp of the Saracenic power is mentioned by one of the Musulman authors whom Amari quotes in his History of the Mahommedan rule in Sicily. It is that the Caliph Al-Māmūn, under whom conquest was advancing in India and in Sicily simultaneously, ordered that the idols taken from the infidels in India should be sent for sale to the infidels in Sicily!

[1757.—"On the 6th the Major (Eyre Coote) left *Muxadabad* with ... 10 **Marmutty** men, or pioneers to clear the road."—*Ives*, 156.

[1873.—"For the actual execution of works there was a **Maramat** Department constituted under the Collector."—*Boswell, Man. of Nellore*, 642.]

MARWÁREE, n.p. and s. This word *Mārwāṛī*, properly a man of the Mārwār [Skt. *maru*, 'desert'], or Jodhpur country in Rājputāna, is used in many parts of India as synonymous with Banya (see BANYAN) or **Sowcar**, from the fact that many of the traders and money-lenders have come originally from Mārwār, most frequently Jains in religion. Compare the Lombard of medieval England, and the *caorsino* of Dante's time.

[1819.—"Miseries seem to follow the footsteps of the **Marwarees**."—*Tr. Lit. Soc. Bo.* i. 297.

[1826—"One of my master's under-shopmen, Sewchund, a **Marwarry**."—*Pandurang Hari*, ed. 1873, i. 233.]

MASKEE. This is a term in Chinese "pigeon," meaning 'never mind,' '*n'importe*,' which is constantly in the mouths of Europeans in China. It is supposed that it may be the corruption or ellipsis of a Portuguese expression, but nothing satisfactory has been suggested. [Mr. Skeat writes: "Surely this is simply Port. *mas que*, probably imported direct through Macao, in the sense of 'although, even, in spite of,' like French *malgre*. And this seems to be its meaning in 'pigeon':

"That nightey tim begin chop-chop,
One young man walkee—no can stop.
Maskee snow, **maskee** ice!
He cally flag with chop so nice—
Topside Galow!
'Excelsior,' in 'pigeon.'"]

MATE, MATY, s. An assistant under a head servant; in which sense or something near it, but also sometimes in the sense of a 'head-man,' the word is in use almost all over India. In the Bengal Presidency we have a *mate-bearer* for the assistant body-servant (see **BEARER**); the *mate* attendant on an elephant under the mahout; a *mate* (head) of **coolies** or **jomponnies** &c. And in Madras the *maty* is an under-servant, whose business it is to clean crockery, knives, &c., to attend to lamps, and so forth.

The origin of the word is obscure, if indeed it has not more than one origin. Some have supposed it to be taken from the English word in the sense of comrade, &c.; whilst Wilson gives *meṭṭi* as a distinct **Malayālam** word for an inferior domestic servant, [which the *Madras Gloss.* derives from Tamil *mel*, 'high']. The last word is of very doubtful genuineness. Neither derivation will explain the fact that the word occurs in the *Āīn*, in which the three classes of attendants on an elephant in Akbar's establishment are styled respectively *Mahāwa*, *Bhoī*, and *Meth*; two of which terms would, under other circumstances, probably be regarded as corruptions of English words. This use of the word we find in Skt. dictionaries as *meṭha*, *menṭha*, and *meṇḍa*, 'an elephant-keeper or feeder.' But for the more general use we would query whether it may not be a genuine Prakrit form from Skt. *mitra*, 'associate, friend'? We have in Pali *metta*, 'friendship,' from Skt. *maitra*.

c. 1590.—"A **met'h** fetches fodder and assists in caparisoning the elephant. **Met'hs** of all classes get on the march 4 *dáms* daily, and at other times 3½."—*Āīn*, ed. *Blochmann*, i. 125.

1810.—"In some families **mates** or assistants are allowed, who do the drudgery."—*Williamson, V. M.* i. 241.

1837.—"One **matee**."—See *Letters from Madras*, 106.

1872.—"At last the morning of our departure came. A crowd of porters stood without the veranda, chattering and squabbling, and the **mate** distributed the boxes and bundles among them."—*A True Reformer*, ch. vi.

1873.—"To procure this latter supply (of green food) is the daily duty of one of the attendants, who in Indian phraseology is termed a **mate**, the title of Mahout being reserved for the head keeper" (of an elephant).—*Sat. Rev.* Sept. 6, 302.

MATRANEE, s. Properly Hind. from Pers. *mihtarānī*; a female sweeper (see **MEHTAR**). [In the following extract the writer seems to mean *Bhaṭhiyāran* or *Bhaṭhiyārin*, the wife of a *Bhaṭhiyāra* or inn-keeper.

[1785.—"... a handsome serai ... where a number of people, chiefly women, called **metrahnees**, take up their abode to attend strangers on their arrival in the city."—*Diary*, in *Forbes, Or. Mem.* 2nd ed. ii. 404.]

MATROSS, s. An inferior class of soldier in the Artillery. The word is quite obsolete, and is introduced here because it seems to have survived a good deal longer in India than in England, and occurs frequently in old Indian narratives. It is Germ. *matrose*, Dutch *matroos*, 'a sailor,' identical no doubt with Fr. *matelot*. The origin is so obscure that it seems hardly worth while to quote the conjectures regarding it. In the establishment of a company of Royal Artillery in 1771, as given in Duncan's Hist. of that corps, we have besides sergeants and corporals, "4 Bombardiers, 8 Gunners, 34 *Matrosses*, and 2 Drummers." A definition of the Matross is given in our 3rd quotation. We have not ascertained when the term was disused in the R.A. It appears in the Establishment as given by Grose in 1801 (*Military Antiq.* i. 315). As far as Major Duncan's book informs us, it appears first in 1639, and has disappeared by 1793, when we find the men of an artillery force divided (excluding sergeants, corporals, and bombardiers) into First Gunners, *Second Gunners*, and Military Drivers.

1673.—"There being in pay for the Honourable East India Company of English and Portuguese, 700, reckoning the **Montrosses** and Gunners."—*Fryer*, 38.

1745.—"... We were told with regard to the Fortifications, that no Expense should be grudged that was necessary for the Defence of the Settlement, and in 1741, a Person was sent out in the character of an Engineer for our Place; but ... he lived not to come among us; and therefore, we could only judge of his Merit and Qualifications by the Value of his Stipend, Six Pagodas a Month, or about Eighteen Pence a Day, scarce the Pay of a common **Matross.** ..."—Letter from *Mr. Barnett* to the *Secret Committee*, in *Letter to a Proprietor of the E.I. Co.*, p. 45.

1757.—"I have with me one Gunner, one **Matross**, and two Lascars."—Letter in *Dalrymple, Or. Repert.* i. 203.

1779.—"**Matrosses** are properly apprentices to the gunner, being soldiers in the royal regiment of artillery, and next to them; they assist in loading, firing, and spunging the great guns. They carry firelocks, and march along with the guns and store-waggons, both as a guard, and to give their assistance in every emergency."—*Capt. G. Smith's Universal Military Dictionary.*

1792.—"Wednesday evening, the 25th inst., a **Matross** of Artillery deserted from the Mount, and took away with him his firelock, and nine rounds of powder and ball."—*Madras Courier*, Feb. 2.

[1800.—"A serjeant and two **matrosses** employed under a general committee on the captured military stores in Seringapatam."—*Wellington Suppl. Desp.* ii. 32 (*Stanf. Dict.*).]

MAUMLET, s. Domestic Hind. *māmlat*, for 'omelet'; [*Māmlēt* is 'marmalade'].

MAUND, s. The authorised Anglo-Indian form of the name of a weight (Hind. *man*, Mahr. *maṇ*), which, with varying values, has been current over Western Asia from time immemorial. Professor Sayce traces it (*mana*) back to the Accadian language.[1] But in any case it was the Babylonian name for 1/60 of a talent, whence it passed, with the Babylonian weights and measures, almost all over the ancient world. Compare the *men* or *mna* of Egyptian hieroglyphic inscriptions, preserved in the *emna* or *amna* of the Copts, the Hebrew *māneh*, the Greek *μνᾶ*, and the Roman *mina*. The introduction of the word into India may have occurred during the extensive commerce of the Arabs with that country during the 8th and 9th centuries; possibly at an earlier date. Through the Arabs also we find an old Spanish word *almena*, and in old French *almène*, for a weight of about 20 lbs. (*Marcel Devic*).

The quotations will show how the Portuguese converted *man* into *mão*, of which the English made *maune*, and so (probably by the influence of the old English word *maund*)[2] our present form, which occurs as early as 1611. Some of the older travellers, like Linschoten, misled by the Portuguese *mão*, identified it with the word for 'hand' in that language, and so rendered it.

The values of the *man* as weight, even in modern times, have varied immensely, *i.e.* from little more than 2 *lbs.* to upwards of 160. The 'Indian Maund,' which is the standard of weight in British India, is of 40 *sers*, each *ser* being divided into 16 *chhiṭāks*; and this is the general scale of subdivision in the local weights of Bengal, and Upper and Central India, though the value of the *ser* varies. That of the standard *ser* is 80 tolas or rupee-weights, and thus the *maund* = 82 2/7 *lbs.* avoirdupois. The Bombay maund (or *man*) of 48 *sers* = 28 *lbs.*; the Madras one of 40 *sers* = 25 *lbs.* The Palloda *man* of Ahmadnagar contained 64 *sers*, and was = 163¼ *lbs.* This is the largest *man* we find in the '*Useful Tables*.' The smallest Indian *man* again is that of Colachy in Travancore, and that = 18 *lbs.* 12 *oz.* 13 *dr.* The Persian *Tabrīzī man* is, however, a little less than 7 *lbs.*; the *man shāhī* twice that; the smallest of all on the list named is the Jeddah *man* = 2 *lbs.* 3 *oz.* 9¾ *dr.*

B.C. 692.—In the "Eponymy of Zazai," a house in Nineveh, with its shrubbery and gates, is sold for one **maneh** of silver according to the royal standard. Quoted by *Sayce*, u.s.

B.C. 667.—We find Nergal-sarra-nacir lending "four **manehs** of silver, according to the **maneh** of Carchemish."—*Ibid.*

c. B.C. 524.—"Cambyses received the Libyan presents very graciously, but not so the gifts of the Cyrenaeans. They had sent no more than 500 **minae** of silver, which Cambyses, I imagine, thought too little. He therefore snatched the money from them, and with his own hand scattered it among the soldiers."—*Herodot.* iii. ch. 13 (E.T. by *Rawlinson*).

c. A.D. 70.—"Et quoniam in mensuris quoque ac ponderibus crebro Graecis nominibus utendum est, interpretationem eorum semel in hoc loco ponemus: ... **mna**, quam nostri **minam** vocant pendet drachmas Atticas c."—*Pliny*, xxi., at end.

c. 1020.—"The gold and silver ingots amounted to 700,400 **mans** in weight."—*Al'Utbi*, in *Elliot*, ii. 35.

1040.—"The Amír said:—'Let us keep fair measure, and fill the cups evenly.' ... Each

1 See *Sayce, Principles of Comparative Philology*, 2nd ed. 208–211.

2 "*Maund*, a kind of great Basket or Hamper, containing eight Bales, or two Fats. It is commonly a quantity of 8 bales of unbound Books, each Bale having 1000 lbs. weight."—*Giles Jacob, New Law Dict.*, 7th ed., 1756, s.v

goblet contained half a **man**."—*Baihaki, ibid.* ii. 144.

c. 1343.—

"The **Mena** of Sarai makes in Genoa weight . . . . . lb. 6 oz. 2
The **Mena** of Organci (*Urghanj*) in Genoa . . . . . . lb. 3 oz. 9
The **Mena** of Oltrarre (*Otrār*) in Genoa . . . . lb. 3 oz. 9
The **Mena** of Armalecho (*Almaligh*) in Genoa . . . . lb. 2 oz. 8
The **Mena** of Camexu (*Kancheu* in N. W. China) . . . . lb. 2"

Pegolotti, 4.

1563.—"The value of stones is only because people desire to have them, and because they are scarce, but as for virtues, those of the loadstone, which staunches blood, are very much greater and better attested than those of the emerald. And yet the former sells by **maos**, which are in Cambay ... equal to 26 *arratels* each, and the latter by *ratis*, which weigh 3 grains of wheat."—*Garcia*, f. 159*v*.

1598.—"They have another weight called **Mao**, which is a Hand, and is 12 pounds."—*Linschoten*, 69; [Hak. Soc. i. 245].

1610.—"He was found ... to have sixtie **maunes** in Gold, and euery **maune** is five and fiftie pound weight."—*Hawkins*, in *Purchas*, i. 218.

1611.—"Each **maund** being three and thirtie pound English weight."—*Middleton, ibid.* i. 270.

[1645.—"As for the weights, the ordinary **mand** is 69 *livres*, and the *livre* is of 16 *onces*; but the **mand**, which is used to weigh indigo, is only 53 *livres*. At Surat you speak of a *seer*, which is 1¾ *livres*, and the *livre* is 16 *onces*."—*Tavernier*, ed. *Ball*, i. 38.]

c. 1665.—"Le **man** pese quarante livres par toutes les Indes, mais ces livres ou *serres* sont differentes selon les Pais."—*Thevenot*, v. 54.

1673.—"A *Lumbrico* (Sconce) of pure Gold, weighing about one **Maund** and a quarter, which is Forty-two pounds."—*Fryer*, 78.

"The Surat **Maund** ... is 40 *Sear*, of 20 *Pice* the *Sear*, which is 37*l.*
The Pucka **Maund** at *Agra* is double as much, where is also the
Ecbarry **Maund** which is 40 *Sear*, of 30 *Pice* to the *Sear* ..."

Ibid. 205.

1683.—"Agreed with Chittur Mullsaw and Muttradas, Merchants of this place (Hugly), for 1,500 Bales of ye best Tissinda Sugar, each bale to weigh 2 **Maunds**, 6½ *Seers*, Factory weight."—*Hedges, Diary*, April 5; [Hak. Soc. i. 75].

1711.—"Sugar, Coffee, Tutanague, all sorts of Drugs, &c., are sold by the **Maund** Tabrees; which in the Factory and Custom house is nearest 6¾*l. Avoirdupoiz.* ... Eatables, and all sorts of Fruit ... &c. are sold by the **Maund** *Copara* of 7¾*l.* ... The **Maund** Shaw is two **Maunds** *Tabrees*, used at Ispahan."—*Lockyer*, 230.

c. 1760.—Grose says, "the **maund** they weigh their indicos with is only 53 *lb.*" He states the *maund* of Upper India as 69*lb.*; at Bombay, 28 *lb.*; at Goa, 14 *lb.*; at Surat, 37½ *lb.*; at Coromandel, 25 *lb.*; in Bengal, 75 *lb.*

1854.—"... You only consent to make play when you have packed a good **maund** of traps on your back."—*Life of Lord Lawrence*, i. 433.

MAYLA, s. Hind. *melā*, 'a fair,' almost always connected with some religious celebration, as were so many of the medieval fairs in Europe. The word is Skt. *mela*, *melaka*, 'meeting, concourse, assembly.'

[1832.—"A party of foreigners ... wished to see what was going on at this far-famed **mayllah**. ..."—*Mrs. Meer Hassan Ali, Observations*, ii. 321–2.]

1869.—"Le **Mela** n'est pas précisément une foire telle que nous l'entendent; c'est le nom qu'on donne aux réunions de pèlerins et des marchands qui ... se rendent dans les lieux considérés comme sacrés, aux fêtes de certaine dieux indiens et des personnages reputés saints parmi les musulmans."—*Garcin de Tassy, Rel. Mus.* p. 26.

MEHTAR, s. A sweeper or scavenger. This name is usual in the Bengal Presidency, especially for the domestic servant of this class. The word is Pers. comp. *mihtar* (Lat. *major*), 'a great personage,' 'a prince,' and has been applied to the class in question in irony, or rather in consolation, as the domestic tailor is called **caleefa**. But the name has so completely adhered in this application, that all sense of either irony or consolation has perished; *mehtar* is a sweeper and nought else. His wife is the **Matranee**. It is not unusual to hear two *mehtars* hailing each other as *Mahārāj!* In Persia the menial application of the word seems to be different (see below). The same class of servant is usually called in W. India *bhangī* (see BUNGY), a name which in Upper India is applied to the caste generally and specially to those not in the service of Europeans. [Examples of the word used in the honorific sense will be found below.]

c. 1800.—"**Maitre.**" See under BUNOW.

1810.—"The **mater**, or sweeper, is considered

the lowest menial in every family."—*Williamson, V. M.* i. 276–7.

1828.—"... besides many **mehtars** or stable-boys."—*Hajji Baba in England*, i. 60.

[In the honorific sense:

[1824.—"In each of the towns of Central India, there is ... a **mehtur**, or head of every other class of the inhabitants down to the lowest."—*Malcolm, Central India*, 2nd ed. i. 555.

[1880.—"On the right bank is the fort in which the **Mihter** or **Bādshāh**, for he is known by both titles, resides."—*Biddulph, Tribes of the Hindoo Kush*, 61.]

MEM-SAHIB, s. This singular example of a hybrid term is the usual respectful designation of a European married lady in the Bengal Presidency; the first portion representing *ma'am. Madam Sahib* is used at Bombay; *Doresani* (see DORAY) in Madras. (See also BURRA BEEBEE.)

MENDY, s. Hind. *mehndī*, [*meṅhdī*, Skt. *mendhikā*;] the plant *Lawsonia alba*, Lam., of the N. O. *Lythraceae*, strongly resembling the English privet in appearance, and common in gardens. It is the plant whose leaves afford the *henna*, used so much in Mahommedan countries for dyeing the hands, &c., and also in the process of dyeing the hair. *Mehndī* is, according to Royle, the *Cyprus* of the ancients (see *Pliny*, xii. 24). It is also the *camphire* of Canticles i. 14, where the margin of A. V. has erroneously *cypress* for *cyprus*.

[1813.—"After the girls are betrothed, the ends of the fingers and nails are dyed red, with a preparation from the **Mendey**, or hinna shrub."—*Forbes, Or. Mem.* 2nd ed. i. 55; also see i. 22.]

c. 1817.—"... his house and garden might be known from a thousand others by their extraordinary neatness. His garden was full of trees, and was well fenced round with a ditch and **mindey** hedge."—*Mrs. Sherwood's Stories*, ed. 1873, p. 71.

MINCOPIE, n.p. This term is attributed in books to the Andaman islanders as their distinctive name for their own race. It originated with a vocabulary given by Lieut. Colebrooke in vol. iv. of the *Asiatic Researches*, and was certainly founded on some misconception. Nor has the possible origin of the mistake been ascertained. [Mr. Man (*Proc. Anthrop. Institute*, xii. 71) suggests that it may have been a corruption of the words *min kaich!* 'Come here!']

MOFUSSIL, s., also used adjectively, "The provinces,"—the country stations and districts, as contra-distinguished from 'the Presidency'; or, relatively, the rural localities of a district as contra-distinguished from the **sudder** or chief station, which is the residence of the district authorities. Thus if, in Calcutta, one talks of the Mofussil, he means anywhere in Bengal out of Calcutta; if one at Benares talks of going into the *Mofussil*, he means going anywhere in the Benares division or district (as the case might be) out of the city and station of Benares. And so over India. The word (Hind. from Ar.) *mufaṣṣal* means properly 'separate, detailed, particular,' and hence 'provincial,' as *mufaṣṣal 'adālat*, a 'provincial court of justice.' This indicates the way in which the word came to have the meaning attached to it.

About 1845 a clever, free-and-easy newspaper, under the name of *The* **Mofussilite**, was started at Meerut, by Mr. John Lang, author of *Too Clever by Half*, &c., and endured for many years.

1781.—"... a gentleman lately arrived from the **Moussel**" (plainly a misprint).—*Hicky's Bengal Gazette*, March 31.

"A gentleman in the **Mofussil**, Mr. P., fell out of his chaise and broke his leg. ..."—*Ibid.*, June 30.

1810.—"Either in the Presidency or in the **Mofussil**. ..."—*Williamson, V. M.* ii. 499.

1836.—"... the **Mofussil** newspapers which I have seen, though generally disposed to cavil at all the acts of the Government, have often spoken favourably of the measure."—*T. B. Macaulay*, in *Life*, &c. i. 399.

MOGUL, n.p. This name should properly mean a person of the great nomad race of Mongols, called in Persia, &c., *Mughals*; but in India it has come, in connection with the nominally Mongol, though essentially rather *Turk*, family of Baber, to be applied to all foreign Mahommedans from the countries on the W. and N.W. of India, except the Pathāns. In fact these people themselves make a sharp distinction between the *Mughal Irānī*, of Pers. origin (who is a Shīah), and the *M. Tūrānī* of Turk origin (who is a Sunni). *Beg* is the characteristic affix of the Mughal's name, as *Khān* is of the Pathān's. Among the Mahommedans of S. India the *Moguls* or *Mughals* constitute a strongly marked caste. [They are also clearly distinguished in the Punjab and N.W.P.] In the quotation from Baber below, the name still retains its original application. The passage illustrates the tone in which Baber always speaks of his kindred of the Steppe, much as Lord Clyde used sometimes to speak of "confounded Scotchmen."

In Port. writers *Mogol* or *Mogor* is often used for "Hindostān," or the territory of the **Great Mogul**.

1247.—"Terra quaedam est in partibus orientis ... quae **Mongal** nominatur. Haec terra quondam populos quatuor habuit: unus Yeka **Mongal**, id est magni Mongali. ..."—*Joannis de Plano Carpini, Hist. Mongalorum*, 645.

1253.—"Dicit nobis supradictus Coiac. ... 'Nolite dicere quod dominus noster sit christianus. Non est christianus, sed **Moal**'; quia enim nomen christianitatis videtur eis nomen cujusdem gentis ... volentes nomen suum, hoc est **Moal**, exaltare super omne nomen, nec volunt vocari *Tartari*."—*Itin. Willielmi de Rubruk*, 259.

1298.—"... **Mungul**, a name sometimes applied to the Tartars."—*Marco Polo*, i. 276 (2nd ed.).

c. 1300.—"Ipsi verò dicunt se descendisse de Gog et Magog. Vnde ipsi dicuntur **Mogoli**, quasi corrupto vocabulo *Magogoli*."—*Ricoldus de Monte Crucis*, in *Per. Quatuor*, p. 118.

c. 1308.—"*Ὁ δὲ Νογᾶς ... ὃς ἅμα πλίσταις δυνάμεσιν ἐξ ὁμογενῶν Τοχάρων, οὓς αὐτοι Μουγουλίους λέγουσι, ἔξαποσταλεις ἐκ τῶν κατὰ τὰς Κασπίας ἀρχόντων τοῦ γένους οὓς Κάνιδας στομάζουσιν.*"—*Georg. Pachymeres, de Mich. Palaeol.*, lib. v.

c. 1340.—"In the first place from Tana to Gintarchan may be 25 days with an ox-waggon, and from 10 to 12 days with a horse-waggon. On the road you will find plenty of **Moccols**, that is to say of armed troopers."—*Pegolotti*, on the Land Route to Cathay, in *Cathay*, &c., ii. 287.

1404.—"And the territory of this empire of Samarkand is called the territory of **Mogalia**, and the language thereof is called **Mugalia**, and they don't understand this language on this side of the River (the Oxus) ... for the character which is used by those of Samarkand beyond the river is not understood or read by those on this side the river; and they call *that* character **Mongali**, and the Emperor keeps by him certain scribes who can read and write this **Mogali** character."—*Clavijo*, § ciii. (Comp. *Markham*, 119–120.)

c. 1500.—"The **Moghul** troops, which had come to my assistance, did not attempt to fight, but instead of fighting, betook themselves to dismounting and plundering my own people. Nor is this a solitary instance; such is the uniform practice of these wretches the **Moghuls**; if they defeat the enemy they instantly seize the booty; if they are defeated, they plunder and dismount their own allies, and betide what may, carry off the spoil."—*Baber*, 93.

1534.—"And whilst Badur was there in the hills engaged with his pleasures and luxury, there came to him a messenger from the King of the **Mogores** of the kingdom of Dely, called Bobor Mirza."—*Correa*, iii. 571.

1536.—"Dicti **Mogores** vel à populis Persarum **Mogoribus**, vel quod nunc Turkae à Persis **Mogores** appellantur."—Letter from *K. John III.* to *Pope Paul III.*

1555.—"Tartaria, otherwyse called **Mongal**, As Vincentius wryteth, is in that parte of the earthe, where the Easte and the northe joine together."—*W. Watreman, Fardle of Faciouns.*

1563.—"This Kingdom of Dely is very far inland, for the northern part of it marches with the territory of Coraçone (Khorasan). ... The **Mogores**, whom we call Tartars, conquered it more than 30 years ago. ..."—*Garcia*, f. 34.

[c. 1590.—"In his time (Naṣirn'ddīn Maḥmūd) the **Mughals** entered the Panjab ..."—*Āīn*, ed. *Jarrett*, ii. 304.

[c. 1610.—"The greatest ships come from the coast of Persia, Arabia, **Mogor**."—*Pyrard de Laval*, Hak. Soc. i. 258.

[1636.—India "containeth many Provinces and Realmes, as Cambaiar, Delli, Decan, Bishagar, Malabar, Narsingar, Orixa, Bengala, Sanga, **Mogores**, Tipura, Gourous, Ava, Pegua, Aurea Chersonesus, Sina, Camboia, and Campaa."—*T. Blundevil, Description and use of Plancius his Mappe, in Eight Treatises*, ed. 1626, p. 547.]

c. 1650.—"Now shall I tell how the royal house arose in the land of the **Monghol**. ... And the Ruler (Chingiz Khan) said, ... 'I will that this people Bèdè, resembling a precious crystal, which even to the completion of my enterprise hath shown the greatest fidelity in every peril, shall take the name of *Köke* (Blue) **Monghol**. ..."—*Sanang Setzen*, by *Schmidt*, pp. 57 and 71.

1741.—"Ao mesmo tempo que a paz se ajusterou entre os referidos generaes **Mogor** e Marata."—*Bosquejo das Possessôes Portug. na Oriente—Documentos Comprovaticos*, iii. 21 (Lisbon 1853).

1764.—"Whatever **Moguls**, whether Oranies or Tooranies, come to offer their services should be received on the aforesaid terms."—*Paper of Articles* sent to Major Munro by the *Nawab*, in *Long*, 360.

c. 1773.—"... the news-writers of Rai Droog frequently wrote to the Nawaub ... that the besieged Naik ... had attacked the batteries of the besiegers, and had killed a great number of the **Moghuls**."—*H. of Hydur*, 317.

1781.—"Wanted an European or **Mogul** Coachman that can drive four Horses in hand."—*India Gazette*, June 30.

1800.—"I pushed forward the whole of the Mahratta and **Mogul** cavalry in one body. ..."—*Sir A. Wellesley* to *Munro, Munro's Life*, i. 268.

1803.—"The **Mogul** horse do not appear very active; otherwise they ought certainly to keep the **pindarries** at a greater distance."—*Wellington*, ii. 281.

In these last two quotations the term is applied distinctively to Hyderabad troops.

1855.—"The **Moguls** and others, who at the present day settle in the country, intermarrying with these people (Burmese Mahommedans) speedily sink into the same practical heterodoxies."—*Yule, Mission to Aca*, 151.

MOGUL, THE GREAT, n.p. Sometimes '*The Mogul*' simply. The name by which the Kings of Delhi of the House of Timur were popularly styled, first by the Portuguese (*o grão Mogor*) and after them by Europeans generally. It was analogous to **the Sophy** (q.v.), as applied to the Kings of Persia, or to the 'Great Turk' applied to the Sultan of Turkey. Indeed the latter phrase was probably the model of the present one. As noticed under the preceding article, **MOGOL, MOGOR**, and also *Mogolistan* are applied among old writers to the *dominions* of the Great Mogul. We have found no native idiom precisely suggesting the latter title; but *Mughal* is thus used in the *Araish-i-Mahfil* below, and *Mogolistan* must have been in some native use, for it is a form that Europeans would not have invented.

c. 1563.—"Ma già dodici anni il **gran Magol** Re Moro d'Agra et del Deli ... si è impatronito di tutto il Regno de Cambaia."—*V. di Messer Cesare Federici*, in *Ramusio*, iii.

1572.—

"A este o Rei Cambayco soberbissimo
Fortaleza darà na rica Dio;
Porque contra o **Mogor** poderosissimo
Lhe ajude a defender o senhorio..."
Camões, x. 64.

By Burton:

"To him Cambaya's King, that haughtiest Moor,
shall yield in wealthy Diu the famous fort
that he may gain against the **Grand Mogor**
'spite his stupendous power, your firm support ..."

[1609.—"When you shall repair to the **Greate Magull**."—*Birdwood, First Letter Book*, 325.

[1612.—"Hecchabar (Akbar) the last deceased Emperor of Hindustan, the father of the present **Great Mogul**."—*Danvers, Letters*, i. 163.]

1615.—"Nam praeter **Magnum Mogor** cui hodie potissima illius pars subjecta est; qui tum quidem Mahometicae religioni deditus erat, quamuis eam modo cane et angue peius detestetur, vix scio an illius alius rex Mahometana sacra coleret."—*Jarric*, i. 58.

"... prosecuting my travaile by land, I entered the confines of the **great Mogor**. ..."—*De Monfart*, 15.

1616.—"It (Chitor) is in the country of one Rama, a Prince newly subdued by the **Mogul**."—*Sir T. Roe*. [In Hak. Soc. (i. 102) for "the **Mogul**" the reading is "this King."]

"The Seuerall Kingdomes and Prouinces subject to the **Great Mogoll** Sha Selin Gehangier."—*Idem*. in *Purchas*, i. 578.

"... the base cowardice of which people hath made The **Great Mogul** sometimes use this proverb, that one Portuguese would beat three of his people ... and he would further add that one Englishman would beat three Portuguese. The truth is that those Portuguese, especially those born in those Indian colonies, ... are a very low poor-spirited people. ..."—*Terry*, ed. 1777, 153.

["... a copy of the articles granted by the **Great Mogoll** may partly serve for precedent."—*Foster, Letters*, iv. 222.]

1623.—"The people are partly Gentile and partly Mahometan, but they live mingled together, and in harmony, because the **Great Mogul**, to whom Guzerat is now subject ... although he is a Mahometan (yet not altogether that, as they say) makes no difference in his states between one kind of people and the other."—*P. della Valle*, ii. 510; [Hak. Soc. i. 30, where Mr. Grey reads "Gran Moghel"].

1644.—"The King of the inland country, on the confines of this island and fortress of Dlu, is the **Mogor**, the greatest Prince in all the East."—*Bocarro*, MS.

1653.—"**Mogol** est vn terme des Indes qui signifie blanc, et quand nous disons le **grand Mogol**, que les Indiens appellent Schah Geanne Roy du monde, c'est qu'il est effectiuement blanc ... nous l'appellons grand Blanc ou **grand Mogol**, comme nous appellons le Roy des Ottomans grand Turq."—*De la Boullaye-le-Gouz*, ed. 1657, pp. 549–550.

"This Prince, having taken them all, made fourscore and two of them abjure their faith, who served him in his wars against the **Great Mogor**, and were every one of them miserably slain in that expedition."—*Cogan's Pinto*, p. 25.

The expression is not in Pinto's original, where it is *Rey dos Mogores* (cap. xx.).

c. 1663.—"Since it is the custom of *Asia* never to approach Great Persons with Empty Hands, when I had the Honour to kiss the Vest of the **Great Mogol** *Aureng Zebe*, I presented him with Eight *Roupees* ..."—*Bernier*, E.T. p. 62; [ed. *Constable*, 200].

1665.—

"... Samarchand by Oxus, Temir's throne,
To Paquin of Sinaean Kings; and thence
To Agra and Lahor of **Great Mogul**...'
Paradise Lost, xi. 389–91.

c. 1665.—"L'Empire du **Grand-Mogol**, qu'on nomme particulierement le **Mogolistan**, est le plus étendu et le plus puissant des Roiaumes des Indes. ... Le **Grand-Mogol** vient en ligne directe de Tamerlan, dont les descendants qui se sont établis aux Indes, se sont fait appeller **Mogols**. ..."—*Thevenot*, v. 9.

1672.—"In these beasts the **Great Mogul** takes his pleasure, and on a stately Elephant he rides in person to the arena where they fight."—*Baldaeus* (Germ. ed.), 21.

1673.—"It is the Flower of their Emperor's Titles to be called the **Great Mogul**, *Burrore* (read *Burrow*, see Fryer's Index) **Mogul** *Podeshar*, who ... is at present *Auren Zeeb*."—*Fryer*, 195.

1716.—**Gram Mogol**. Is as much as to say 'Head and king of the Circumcised,' for **Mogol** in the language of that country signifies circumcised"(!)—*Bluteau*, s.v.

1727.—"Having made what observations I could, of the Empire of *Persia*, I'll travel along the Seacoast towards *Industan*, or the **Great Mogul's** Empire."—*A. Hamilton*, i. 115, [ed. 1744].

1780.—"There are now six or seven fellows in the tent, gravely disputing whether Hyder is, or is not, the person commonly called in Europe the **Great Mogul**."—Letter of *T. Munro*, in *Life*, i. 27.

1783.—"The first potentate sold by the Company for money, was the **Great Mogul**—the descendant of Tamerlane."—*Burke*, *Speech on Fox's E.I. Bill*, iii. 458.

1786.—"That Shah Allum, the prince commonly called the **Great Mogul**, or, by eminence, the King, is or lately was in possession of the ancient capital of Hindostan. ..."—*Art. of Charge against Hastings*, in *Burke*, vii. 189.

1807.—"L'Hindoustan est depuis quelque temps dominé par une multitude de petits souverains, qui s'arrachent l'un l'autre leurs possessions. Aucun d'eux ne reconnait comme il faut l'autorité légitime du **Mogol**, si ce n'est cependant Messieurs les Anglais, lesquels n'ont pas cessé d'être soumis à son obéissance; en sort qu'actuellement, c'est à dire en 1222 (1807) ils reconnaissent l'autorité suprême d'Akbar Schah, fils de Schah Alam."—*Afsos*, *Araish-i-Mahjil*, quoted by *Garcin de Tassy*, *Rel. Mus.* 90.

MOGUL BREECHES, s. Apparently an early name for what we call **long-drawers** or **pyjamas** (qq.v.).

1625.—"... let him have his shirt on and his **Mogul breeches**; here are women in the house."—*Beaumont & Fletcher*, *The Fair Maid of the Inn*, iv. 2.

In a picture by Vandyke of William 1st Earl of Denbigh, belonging to the Duke of Hamilton, and exhibited at Edinburgh in July 1883, the subject is represented as out shooting, in a red striped shirt and *pyjamas*, no doubt the "Mogul breeches" of the period.

MOHUR, GOLD, s. The official name of the chief gold coin of British India, Hind. from Pers. *muhr*, a (metallic) seal, and thence a gold coin. It seems possible that the word is taken from *mihr*, 'the sun,' as one of the secondary meanings of that word is 'a golden circlet on the top of an umbrella, or the like' (*Vullers*). [Platts, on the contrary, identifies it with Skt. *mudrā*, 'a seal.']

The term *muhr*, as applied to a coin, appears to have been popular only and quasi-generic, not precise. But that to which it has been most usually applied, at least in recent centuries, is a coin which has always been in use since the foundation of the Mahommedan Empire in Hindustan by the Ghūrī Kings of Ghazni and their freedmen, circa A.D. 1200, tending to a standard weight of 100 *ratis* of pure gold, or about 175 grains, thus equalling in weight, and probably intended then to equal ten times in value, the silver coin which has for more than three centuries been called **Rupee**.

There is good ground for regarding this as the theory of the system.[1] But the gold coins, especially, have deviated from the theory considerably; a deviation which seems to have commenced with the violent innovations of Sultan Mahommed Tughlak (1325–1351), who raised the gold coin to 200 grains, and diminished the silver coin to 140 grains, a change which may have been connected with the enormous influx of gold into Upper India, from the plunder of

1 See *Cathay*, &c., pp. ccxlvii.-ccl.; and Mr. E. Thomas, *Pathán Kings of Delhi*, *passim*.

the immemorial accumulations of the Peninsula in the first quarter of the 14th century. After this the coin again settled down in approximation to the old weight, insomuch that, on taking the weight of 46 different *mohurs* from the lists given in Prinsep's *Tables*, the average of pure gold is 167·22 grains.[1]

The first gold mohur struck by the Company's Government was issued in 1766, and declared to be a legal tender for 14 sicca rupees. The full weight of this coin was 179·66 grs., containing 149·72 grs. of gold. But it was impossible to render it current at the rate fixed; it was called in, and in 1769 a new mohur was issued to pass as legal tender for 16 sicca rupees. The weight of this was 190·773 grs. (according to Regn. of 1793, 190·894), and it contained 190·086 grs. of gold. Regulation xxxv. of 1793 declared these **gold mohurs** to be a legal tender in all public and private transactions. Regn. xiv. of 1818 declared, among other things, that "it has been thought advisable to make a slight deduction in the intrinsic value of the **gold mohur** to be coined at this Presidency (Fort William), in order to raise the value of fine gold to fine silver, from the present rates of 1 to 14·861 to that of 1 to 15. The **gold mohur** will still continue to pass current at the rate of 16 rupees." The new gold mohur was to weigh 204·710 grs., containing fine gold 187·651 grs. Once more Act xvii. of 1835 declared that the only gold coin to be coined at Indian mints should be (with proportionate subdivisions) a **gold mohur** or "15 rupee piece" of the weight of 180 grs. troy, containing 165 grs. of pure gold; and declared also that no gold coin should thenceforward be a legal tender of payment in any of the territories of the E.I. Company. There has been since then no substantive change.

A friend (W. Simpson, the accomplished artist) was told in India that **gold mohur** was a corruption of *gol*, ('round') *mohr*, indicating a distinction from the square mohurs of some of the Delhi Kings. But this we take to be purely fanciful.

1690.—"The **Gold Moor**, or Gold Roupie, is valued generally at 14 of Silver; and the Silver Roupie at Two Shillings Three Pence."—*Ovington*, 219.

1726.—"There is here only also a State mint where **gold Moors**, silver *Ropyes*, *Peysen* and other money are struck."—*Valentijn*, v. 166.

1758.—"80,000 rupees, and 4000 **gold mohurs**, equivalent to 60,000 rupees, were the military chest for immediate expenses."—*Orme*, ed. 1803, ii. 364.

[1776.—"Thank you a thousand times for your present of a parcel of **morahs**."—*Mrs. P. Francis*, to her husband, in *Francis Letters*, i. 286.]

1779.—"I then took hold of his hand: then he (Francis) took out **gold mohurs**: and offered to give them to me: I refused them; he said 'Take that (offering both his hands to me), 'twill make you great men, and I will give you 100 **gold mohurs** more.'"—*Evidence of* Rambux Jemadar, *on Trial of* Grand *v.* Francis, quoted in *Echoes of Old Calcutta*, 228.

1785.—"Malver, hairdresser from Europe, proposes himself to the ladies of the settlement to dress Hair daily, at two **gold mohurs** per month, in the latest fashion with gauze flowers, &c. He will also instruct the slaves at a moderate price."[2]—In *Seton-Karr*, i. 119.

1797.—"Notwithstanding he (the Nabob) was repeatedly told that I would accept nothing, he had prepared 5 lacs of rupees and 8000 **gold Mohurs** for me, of which I was to have 4 lacs, my attendants one, and your Ladyship the gold."—Letter in *Mem. of Lord Teignmouth*, i. 410.

1809.—"I instantly presented to her a nazur (see NUZZER) of nineteen **gold mohurs** in a white handkerchief."—*Lord Valentia*, i. 100.

1811.—"Some of his fellow passengers ... offered to bet with him sixty **gold mohurs**."—*Morton's Life of Leyden*, 83.

1829.—"I heard that a private of the Company's Foot Artillery passed the very noses of the prize-agents, with 500 **gold mohurs** (sterling 1000*l.*) in his hat or cap."—*John Shipp*, ii. 226.

[c. 1847.—"The widow is vexed out of patience, because her daughter Maria has got a place beside Cambric, the penniless curate, and not by Colonel **Goldmore**, the rich widower

1 The average was taken as follows:—(1). We took the whole of the weight of gold in the list at p. 43 ("Table of the Gold Coins of India") with the omission of four pieces which are exceptionally debased; and (2), the first twenty-four pieces in the list at p. 50 ("Supplementary Table"), omitting two exceptional cases, and divided by the whole number of coins so taken. See the tables at end of Thomas's ed. of *Prinsep's Essays*.

2 Was this ignorance, or slang? Though slave-boys are occasionally mentioned, there is no indication that slaves were at all the usual substitute for domestic servants at this time in European families.

from India."—*Thackeray, Book of Snobs*, ed. 1879, p. 71.]

MOHURRUM, s. Ar. *Muḥarram* (*'sacer'*), properly the name of the 1st month of the Mahommedan lunar year. But in India the term is applied to the period of fasting and public mourning observed during that month in commemoration of the death of Hassan and of his brother Husain (A.D. 669 and 680) and which terminates in the ceremonies of the *'Ashūrā-a*, commonly however known in India as "*the Mohurrum*." For a full account of these ceremonies see *Herklots, Qanoon-e-Islam*, 2nd ed. 98–148. [*Perry, Miracle Play of Hasan and Husain.*] And see in this book **HOBSON-JOBSON**.

1869.—"*Fête du Martyre de Huçain.* ... On la nomme généralement **Muharram** du nom du mois ... et plus spécialement *Dahâ*, mot persan dérivé de *dah* 'dix,' ... les dénominations viennent de ce que la fête de Hucain dure dix jours."—*Garcin de Tassy, Rel. Mus.* p. 31.

MOLLY, or (better) **MALLEE**, s. Hind. *mālī*, Skt. *mālika*, 'a garland-maker,' or a member of the caste which furnishes gardeners. We sometimes have heard a lady from the Bengal Presidency speak of the daily homage of "the **Molly** with his **dolly**," viz. of the *mālī* with his *dālī*.

1759.—In a Calcutta wages tariff of this year we find—

"House **Molly** ... ... 4 Rs."

In *Long*, 182.

MOLUCCAS, n.p. The 'Spice Islands,' strictly speaking the five Clove Islands, lying to the west of Gilolo, and by name Ternate (*Tarnāti*), Tidore (*Tidori*), Mortir, Makian, and Bachian. [See Mr. Gray's note on *Pyrard de Laval*, Hak. Soc. ii. 166.] But the application of the name has been extended to all the islands under Dutch rule, between Celebes and N. Guinea. There is a Dutch governor residing at Amboyna, and the islands are divided into 4 residencies, viz. Amboyna, Banda, Ternate and Manado. The origin of the name Molucca, or *Maluco* as the Portuguese called it, is not recorded; but it must have been that by which the islands were known to the native traders at the time of the Portuguese discoveries. The early accounts often dwell on the fact that each island (at least three of them) had a king of its own. Possibly they got the (Ar.) name of *Jazīrat-al-Mulūk*, 'The Isles of the Kings.'

Valentijn probably entertained the same view of the derivation. He begins his account of the islands by saying:

"There are many who have written of the **Moluccos** and *of their Kings*, but we have hitherto met with no writer who has given an exact view of the subject" (*Deel*, i. *Mol.* 3).

And on the next page he says:

"For what reason they have been called Moluccos we shall not here say; for we shall do this circumstantially when we shall speak of the **Molukse** *Kings* and their customs."

But we have been unable to find the fulfilment of this intention, though probably it exists in that continent of a work somewhere. We have also seen a paper by a writer who draws much from the quarry of Valentijn. This is an article by Dr. Van Muschenbroek in the *Proceedings* of the International Congress of Geog. at Venice in 1881 (ii. pp. 596, *seqq.*), in which he traces the name to the same origin. He appears to imply that the chiefs were known among themselves as **Molokos**, and that this term was substituted for the indigenous *Kolano*, or King. "Ce nom, ce titre restèrent, et furent même peu à peu employés, non seulement pour les chefs, mais aussi pour l'état même. A la longue les îles et les états *des* **Molokos** devinrent les îles et les états **Molokos**." There is a good deal that is questionable, however, in this writer's deductions and etymologies. [Mr. Skeat remarks: "The islands appear to be mentioned in the Chinese history of the Tang dynasty (618–696) as **Mi-li-ku**, and if this be so the name is perhaps too old to be Arab."]

c. 1430.—"Has (Javas) ultra xv dierum cursu duae reperiuntur insulae, orientem versus. Altera Sandai appellatur, in qua nuces muscatae et maces; altera Bandam nomine, in qua sola gariofali producuntur."—*N. Conti*, in *Poggius*.

1501.—The earliest mention of these islands by this name, that we know, is in a letter of Amerigo Vespucci, who in 1501, among the places heard of by Cabral's fleet, mentions the **Maluche Islands**.

1510.—"We disembarked in the island of **Monoch**, which is much smaller than Bandan; but the people are worse. ... Here the cloves grow, and in many other neighbouring islands, but they are small and uninhabited."—*Varthema*, 246.

1514.—"Further on is Timor, whence comes sandalwood, both the white and the red; and further on still are the **Maluc**, whence come the cloves. The bark of these trees I am sending you; an excellent thing it is; and so are the flowers."—*Letter of Giovanni da Empoli*, in *Archivio Stor. Ital.*, p. 81.

1515.—"From Malacca ships and junks are come with a great quantity of spice, cloves, mace, nut(meg), sandalwood, and other rich things. They have discovered the **five Islands of Cloves**; two Portuguese are lords of them, and rule the land with the rod. 'Tis a land of much meat, oranges, lemons, and clove-trees, which grow there of their own accord, just as trees in the woods with us ... God be praised for such favour, and such grand things!"—*Another letter of do., ibid.* pp. 85–86.

1516.—"Beyond these islands, 25 leagues towards the north-east, there are five islands, one before the other, which are called the islands of **Maluco**, in which all the cloves grow. ... *Their Kings are Moors*, and the first of them is called *Bachan*, the second *Maquian*, the third is called *Motil*, the fourth *Tidory*, and the fifth *Ternaty* ... every year the people of Malaca and Java come to these islands to ship cloves. ..."—*Barbosa*, 201–202.

1518.—"And it was the monsoon for **Maluco**, dom Aleixo despatched dom Tristram de Meneses thither, to establish the trade in clove, carrying letters from the King of Portugal, and presents for the Kings of the isles of Ternate and Tidore where the clove grows."—*Correa*, ii. 552.

1521.—"Wednesday the 6th of November ... we discovered four other rather high islands at a distance of 14 leagues towards the east. The pilot who had remained with us told us these were the **Maluco** islands, for which we gave thanks to God, and to comfort ourselves we discharged all our artillery ... since we had passed 27 months all but two days always in search of **Maluco**."—*Pigafetta, Voyage of Magellan*, Hak. Soc. 124.

1553.—"We know by our voyages that this part is occupied by sea and by land cut up into many thousand islands, these together, sea and islands, embracing a great part of the circuit of the Earth ... and in the midst of this great multitude of islands are those called **Maluco**. ... (These) five islands called **Maluco** ... stand all within sight of one another embracing a distance of 25 leagues ... we do not call them **Maluco** because they have no other names; and we call them *five* because in that number the clove grows naturally. ... Moreover we call them in combination **Maluco**, as here among us we speak of the Canaries, the Terceiras, the Cabo-Verde islands, including under these names many islands each of which has a name of its own."—*Barros*, III. v. 5.

"... li molti viaggi dalla città di Lisbona, e dal mar rosso a Calicut, et insino alle **Molucche**, done nascono le spezierie."—*G. B. Ramusio, Pref. sopra il Libro del Magn.* M. Marco Polo.

1665.—

"As when far off at sea a fleet descried
Hangs in the clouds, by equinoctial winds
Close sailing from Bengala, or the Isles
Of *Ternate* and *Tidore*, whence merchants
bring
Their spicy drugs..."

Paradise Lost, ii. 636–640.

MONKEY-BREAD TREE, s. The Baobab, *Adansonia digitata*, L. "a fantastic-looking tree with immense elephantine stem and small twisted branches, laden in the rains with large white flowers; found all along the coast of Western India, but whether introduced by the Mahommedans from Africa, or by ocean-currents wafting its large light fruit, full of seed, across from shore to shore, is a nice speculation. A sailor once picked up a large seedy fruit in the Indian Ocean off Bombay, and brought it to me. It was very rotten, but I planted the seeds. It turned out to be *Kigelia pinnata* of E. Africa, and propagated so rapidly that in a few years I introduced it all over the Bombay Presidency. The Baobab however is generally found most abundant about the old ports frequented by the early Mahommedan traders" (*Sir G. Birdwood, MS.*) We may add that it occurs sparsely about Allahabad, where it was introduced apparently in the Mogul time; and in the Gangetic valley as far E. as Calcutta, but always *planted*. There are, or were, noble specimens in the Botanic Gardens at Calcutta, and in Mr. Arthur Grote's garden at Alipūr. [See *Watt, Econ. Dict.* i. 105.]

MONSOON, s. The name given to the periodical winds of the Indian seas, and of the seasons which they affect and characterize. The original word is the Ar. *mausim*, 'season,' which the Portuguese corrupted into *monção*, and our people into *monsoon*. Dictionaries (except Dr. Badger's) do not apparently give the Arabic word *mausim* the technical sense of *monsoon*. But there can be no doubt that it had that sense among the Arab pilots from whom the Portuguese adopted the word. This is shown by the quotations from the Turkish Admiral Sidi 'Ali. "The rationale of the term is well put in the *Beirūt Moḥīt*, which says: '*Mausim* is used of anything that comes round but once a year, like the festivals. In Lebanon the *mausim* is the season of working with the silk,'—which is the important season there, as the season of navigation is in Yemen." (*W. R. S.*)

The Spaniards in America would seem to have a word for *season* in analogous use for a recurring wind, as may be gathered from *Tom Cringle*.[1] The Venetian, Leonardo Ca' Masser (below) calls the monsoons *li tempi*. And the quotation from *Garcia De Orta* shows that in his time the Portuguese sometimes used the word for *season* without any apparent reference to the wind. Though **monção** is general with the Portuguese writers of the 16th century, the historian Diogo de Couto always writes **moução**, and it is possible that the *n* came in, as in some other cases, by a habitual misreading of the written *u* for *n*. Linschoten in Dutch (1596) has **monssoyn** and **monssoen** (p. 8; [Hak. Soc. i. 33]). It thus appears probable that we get our *monsoon* from the Dutch. The latter in modern times seem to have commonly adopted the French form **mousson**. [Prof. Skeat traces our *monsoon* from Ital. *monsone*.] We see below (*Ces. Feder.*) that **Monsoon** was used as synonymous with "the half year," and so it is still in S. India.

1505.—"De qui passano el colfo de Colocut che sono leghe 800 de pacizo (? passeggio): aspettano *li tempi* che sono nel principio dell' Autuno, e con le cole fatte (?) passano."—*Leonardo di Ca' Masser*, 26.

[1512.—"... because the **mauçam** for both the voyages is at one and the same time."—*Albuquerque, Cartas*, p. 30.]

1553.—"... and the more, because the voyage from that region of Malaca had to be made by the prevailing wind, which they call **monção**, which was now near its end. If they should lose eight days they would have to wait at least three months for the return of the time to make the voyage."—*Barros*, Dec. II. liv. ii. cap. iv.

1554.—"The principal winds are four, according to the Arabs, ... but the pilots call them by names taken from the rising and setting of certain stars, and assign them certain limits within which they begin or attain their greatest strength, and cease. These winds, limited by space and time, are called **Mausim**."—*The Mohit*, by *Sidi 'Ali Kapudān*, in *J. As. Soc. Beng.* iii. 548.

"Be it known that the ancient masters of navigation have fixed the time of the **monsoon** (in orig. doubtless *mausim*), that is to say, the time of voyages at sea, according to the year of Yazdajird, and that the pilots of recent times follow their steps. ..." (*Much detail on the* **monsoons** *follows*.)—*Ibid.*

1563.—"The season (**monção**) for these (*i.e.* mangoes) in the earlier localities we have in April, but in the other later ones in May and June; and sometimes they come as a *rodolho* (as we call it in our own country) in October and November."—*Garcia*, f. 134*c*.

1568.—"Come s'arriua in vna città la prima cosa si piglia vna casa a fitto, ò per mesi ò per anno, seconda che si disegnà di starui, e nel Pegù è costume di pigliarla per **Moson**, cioè per sei mesi."—*Ces. Federici*, in *Ramusio*, iii. 394.

1585-6.—"But the other goods which come by sea have their fixed season, which here they call **Monzão**."—*Sassetti*, in *De Gubernatis*, p. 204.

1599.—"Ora nell anno 1599, essendo venuta la **Mansone** a proposito, si messero alla vela due navi Portoghesi, le quali eran venute dalla città di Goa in Amacao (see MACAO)."—*Carletti*, ii. 206.

c. 1610.—"Ces **Monssons** ou **Muessons** sont vents qui changent pour l'Esté ou pour l'Hyver de six mois en six mois."—*Pyrard de Laval*, i. 199; see also ii. 110; [Hak. Soc. i. 280; in i. 257 **Monsons**; in ii. 175, 235, **Muesons**].

[1615.—"I departed for Bantam having the time of the year and the opportunity of the **Monethsone**."—*Foster, Letters*, iii. 268.

["The **Monthsone** will else be spent."—*Sir T. Roe*, Hak. Soc. i. 36.]

1616.—"... quos Lusitani patriâ voce **Moncam** indigetant."—*Jarric*, i. 46.

Sir T. Roe writes **Monson.**

1627.—"Of *Corea* hee was also told that there are many bogges, for which cause they have Waggons with broad wheeles, to keepe them from sinking, and obseruing the **Monson** or season of the wind ... they have sayles fitted to these waggons, and so make their Voyages on land."—*Purchas, Pilgrimage*, 602.

1634.—

"Partio, vendo que o tempo em vao gastava,
E que a **monção** di navegar passava."

Malaca, Conquistada, iv. 75.

1644.—"The winds that blow at Diu from the commencement of the change of season in September are sea-breezes, blowing from time to time from the S., S.W., or N.W., with no certain **Monsam** wind, and at that time one can row across to Dio with great facility."—*Bocarro*, MS.

1 "Don Ricardo began to fret and fidget most awfully—'Beginning of the *seasons*'—why, we may not get away for a week, and all the ships will be kept back in their loading."—Ed. 1863, p. 309.

c. 1665.—"... and it would be true to say, that the sun advancing towards *one* Pole, causeth on that side two great regular currents, viz., that of the Sea, and that of the Air which maketh the **Mounson**-*wind*, as he causeth two opposite ones, when he returns towards the other Pole."—*Bernier*, E.T. 139–40; [ed. *Constable*, 436; see also 109].

1673.—"The northern **Monsoons** (if I may so say, being the name imposed by the first Observers, *i.e.* **Motiones**) lasting hither."—*Fryer*, 10.

"A constellation by the Portugals called *Rabodel Elephanto* (see ELEPHANTA, **b.**) known by the breaking up of the **Munsoons**, which is the last Flory this Season makes."—*Ibid.* 48. He has also **Mossoons** or **Monsoons**, 46.

1690.—"Two **Mussouns** are the Age of a Man."—Bombay Proverb in *Ovington's Voyage*, 142.

[**"Mussoans.**" See under ELEPHANTA, **b.**]

1696.—"We thought it most advisable to remain here, till the next **Mossoon**."—*Bowyear*, in *Dalrymple*, i. 87.

1783.—"From the Malay word **moossin**, which signifies season."—*Forrest, V. to Mergui*, 95.

"Their prey is lodged in England; and the cries of India are given to seas and winds, to be blown about, in every breaking up of the **monsoon**, over a remote and unhearing ocean."—*Burke's Speech on Fox's E.I. Bill*, in *Works*, iii. 468.

MOOLLAH, s. Hind. *mullā*, corr. from Ar. *maulā*, a der. from *wilā*, 'propinquity.' This is the legal bond which still connects a former owner with his manumitted slave; and in virtue of this bond the patron and client are both called *maulā*. The idea of patronage is in the other senses; and the word comes to mean eventually 'a learned man, a teacher, a doctor of the Law.' In India it is used in these senses, and for a man who reads the Ḳorān in a house for 40 days after a death. When oaths were administered on the Ḳorān, the servitor who held the book was called *Mullā Ḳorānī*. *Mullā* is also in India the usual Mussulman term for 'a schoolmaster.'

1616.—"Their **Moolaas** employ much of their time like Scrieueners to doe businesse for others."—*Terry*, in *Purchas*, ii. 1476.

[1617.—"He had shewed it to his **Mulaies**."—*Sir T. Roe*, Hak. Soc. ii. 417.]

1638.—"While the Body is let down into the grave, the kindred mutter certain Prayers between their Teeth, and that done all the company returns to the house of the deceased, where the **Mollas** continue their Prayers for his Soul, for the space of two or three days. ..."—*Mandelslo*, E.T. 63.

1673.—"At funerals, the **Mullahs** or Priests make Orations or Sermons, after a Lesson read out of the *Alchoran*."—*Fryer*, 94.

1680.—"The old **Mulla** having been discharged for misconduct, another by name Cozzee (see CAZEE) Mahmud entertained on a salary of 5 Pagodas per mensem, his duties consisting of the business of writing letters, &c., in Persian, besides teaching the Persian language to such of the Company's servants as shall desire to learn it."—*Ft. St. Geo. Consn.* March 11. *Notes and Exts.* No. iii. p. 12; [also see *Pringle, Diary, Ft. St. Geo.*, 1st ser. ii. 2, with note].

1763.—"The **Mulla** in Indostan superintends the practice, and punishes the breach of religious duties."—*Orme*, reprint, i. 26.

1809.—"The British Government have, with their usual liberality, continued the allowance for the **Moolahs** to read the Koran."—*Ld. Valentia*, i. 423.

[1842.—See the classical account of the **Moollahs** of Kabul in *Elphinstone's Caubul*, ed. 1842, i. 281 *seqq.*]

1879.—"... struck down by a fanatical crowd impelled by a fierce **Moola**."—*Sat. Rev.* No. 1251, p. 484.

MOOLVEE, s. Popular Hind. *mulvī*, Ar. *maulavī*, from same root as *mullā* (see MOOLLAH). A Judge, Doctor of the Law, &c. It is a usual prefix to the names of learned men and professors of law and literature. (See LAW-OFFICER.)

1784.—

"A Pundit in Bengal or **Molavee**
 May daily see a carcase burn;
But you can't furnish for the soul of ye
 A dirge sans ashes and an urn."

N. B. Halhed, see *Calc. Review*, xxvi. 79.

MOONG, MOONGO, s. Or. 'green-gram'; Hind. *mūng*, [Skt. *mudga*]. A kind of vetch (*Phaseolus Mungo*, L.) in very common use over India; according to Garcia the *mesce* (*māsh?*) of Avicenna. Garcia also says that it was popularly recommended as a diet for fever in the Deccan; [and is still recommended for this purpose by native physicians (*Watt, Econ. Dict.* vi. pt. i. 191)].

c. 1336.—"The **munj** again is a kind of *māsh*, but its grains are oblong and the colour is light green. **Munj** is cooked along with rice, and eaten with butter. This is what they call *Kichrī* (see KEDGEREE), and it is the diet on which one breakfasts daily."—*Ibn Batuta*, iii. 131.

1557.—"The people were obliged to bring hay, and corn, and **mungo**, which is a certain species of seed that they feed horses with."—*Albuquerque*, Hak. Soc. ii. 132.

1563.—

"*Servant-maid.*—That girl that you brought from the Deccan asks me for **mungo**, and says that in her country they give it them to eat, husked and boiled. Shall I give it her?

"*Orta.*—Give it her since she wishes it; but bread and a boiled chicken would be better. For she comes from a country where they eat bread, and not rice."—*Garcia*, f. 145.

[1611.—"... for 25 maunds **Moong**, 28m. 09 p."—*Danvers*, *Letters*, i. 141.]

MOONSHEE, s. Ar. *munshi*, but written in Hind. *munshī*. The verb *insha*, of which the Ar. word is the participle, means 'to educate' a youth, as well as 'to compose' a written document. Hence 'a secretary, a reader, an interpreter, a writer.' It is commonly applied by Europeans specifically to a native teacher of languages, especially of Arabic, Persian, and Urdū, though the application to a native amanuensis in those tongues, and to any respectable, well-educated native gentleman is also common. The word probably became tolerably familiar in Europe through a book of instruction in Persian bearing the name (viz. "*The Persian Moonshee, by F. Gladwyn*," 1st ed. s.a., but published in Calcutta about 1790–1800).

1777.—"**Moonshi**. A writer or secretary."—*Halhed*, *Code*, 17.

1782.—"The young gentlemen exercise themselves in translating ... they reason and dispute with their **munchees** (tutors) in Persian and Moors. ..."—*Price's Tracts*, i. 89.

1785.—"Your letter, requiring our authority for engaging in your service a **Mûnshy**, for the purpose of making out passports, and writing letters, has been received."—*Tippoo's Letters*, 67.

"A lasting friendship was formed between the pupil and his **Moonshee**. ... The **Moonshee**, who had become wealthy, afforded him yet more substantial evidence of his recollection, by earnestly requesting him, when on the point of leaving India, to accept a sum amounting to £1600, on the plea that the latter (*i.e.* Shore) had saved little."—*Mem. of Lord Teignmouth*, i. 32–33.

1814.—"They presented me with an address they had just composed in the Hindoo language, translated into Persian by the Durbar **munsee**."—*Forbes*, *Or. Mem.* iii. 365; [2nd ed. ii. 344].

1817.—"Its authenticity was fully proved by ... and a Persian **Moonshee** who translated."—*Mill*, *Hist.* v. 127.

1828.—"... the great **Moonshi** of State himself had applied the whole of his genius to selecting such flowers of language as would not fail to diffuse joy, when exhibited in those dark and dank regions of the north."—*Hajji Baba in England*, i. 39.

1867.—"When the Mirza grew up, he fell among English, and ended by carrying his rupees as a **Moonshee**, or a language-master, to that infidel people."—*Select Writings of Viscount Strangford*, i. 265.

MOOR, **MOORMAN**, s. (and adj. **MOORISH**). A Mahommedan; and so from the habitual use of the term (*Mouro*), by the Portuguese in India, particularly a Mahommedan inhabitant of India.

In the Middle Ages, to Europe generally, the Mahommedans were known as the *Saracens*. This is the word always used by Joinville, and by Marco Polo. Ibn Batuta also mentions the fact in a curious passage (ii. 425–6). At a later day, when the fear of the Ottoman had made itself felt in Europe, the word *Turk* was that which identified itself with the Moslem, and thus we have in the Collect for Good Friday,—"Jews, *Turks*, Infidels, and Heretics." But to the Spaniards and Portuguese, whose contact was with the Musulmans of Mauritania who had passed over and conquered the Peninsula, all Mahommedans were **Moors**. So the Mahommedans whom the Portuguese met with on their voyages to India, on what coast soever, were alike styled *Mouros;* and from the Portuguese the use of this term, as synonymous with Mahommedan, passed to Hollanders and Englishmen.

The word then, as used by the Portuguese discoverers, referred to religion, and implied no nationality. It is plain indeed from many passages that the *Moors* of Calicut and Cochin were in the beginning of the 16th century people of mixt race, just as the **Moplahs** are now. The Arab, or Arabo-African occupants of Mozambique and Melinda, the Sumālis of Magadoxo, the Arabs and Persians of Kalhāt and Ormuz, the Boras of Guzerat, are all **Mouros** to the Portuguese writers, though the more intelligent among these are quite conscious of the impropriety of the term. The *Moors* of the Malabar coast were middlemen, who had adopted a profession of Islam for their own convenience, and in order to minister for their own profit to the constant traffic of merchants from Ormuz and the Arabian ports. Similar influences still affect the boatmen of the same coast, among whom it has become a sort of custom in certain families, that different members should profess respectively Mahommedanism, Hinduism, and Christianity.

The use of the word *Moor* for Mahommedan died out pretty well among educated Europeans in the Bengal Presidency in the beginning of the last century, or even earlier, but probably held its ground a good deal longer among the British soldiery, whilst the adjective *Moorish* will be found in our quotations nearly as late as 1840. In Ceylon, the Straits, and the Dutch Colonies, the term *Moorman* for a Musalman is still in common use. Indeed the word is still employed by the servants of Madras officers in speaking of Mahommedans, or of a certain class of these. **Moro** is still applied at Manilla to the **Musulman** Malays.

1498.—"... the **Moors** never came to the house when this trading went on, and we became aware that they wished us ill, insomuch that when any of us went ashore, in order to annoy us they would spit on the ground, and say 'Portugal, Portugal.'"—*Roteiro de V. da Gama*, p. 75.

"For you must know, gentlemen, that from the moment you put into port here (Calecut) you caused disturbance of mind to the **Moors** of this city, who are numerous and very powerful in the country."—*Correa*, Hak. Soc. 166.

1499.—"We reached a very large island called Sumatra, where pepper grows in considerable quantities. ... The Chief is a **Moor**, but speaking a different language."—*Santo Stefano*, in *India in the XVth Cent.* [7].

1505.—"Adì 28 zugno vene in Venetia insieme co Sier Alvixe de Boni un sclav **moro** el qual portorono i spagnoli da la insula spagniola."—*MS.* in *Museo Civico* at Venice. Here the term **Moor** is applied to a native of Hispaniola!

1513.—"Hanc (Malaccam) rex **Maurus** gubernabat."—*Emanuelis Regis Epistola*, f. 1.

1553.—"And for the hatred in which they hold them, and for their abhorrence of the name of *Frangue*, they call in reproach the Christians of our parts of the world *Frangues* (see FIRINGHEE), just as we improperly call *them* again **Moors**."—*Barros*, IV. iv. 16.

c. 1560.—"When we lay at Fuquien, we did see certain **Moores**, who knew so little of their secte that they could say nothing else but that Mahomet was a **Moore**, my father was a **Moore**, and I am a **Moore**."—*Reports of the Province of China*, done into English by *R. Willes*, in *Hakl.* ii. 557.

1563.—"And as to what you say of Ludovico Vartomano, I have spoken both here and in Portugal, with people who knew him here in India, and they told me that he went about here in the garb of a **Moor**, and that he came back among us doing penance for his sins; and that the man never went further than Calecut and Cochin, nor indeed did we at that time navigate those seas that we now navigate."—*Garcia*, f. 30.

1569.—"... always whereas I have spoken of Gentiles is to be understood Idolaters, and whereas I speak of **Moores**, I mean Mahomets secte."—*Caesar Frederike*, in *Hakl.* ii. 359.

1610.—"The King was fled for feare of the King of Makasar, who ... would force the King to turne **Moore**, for he is a Gentile."—*Midleton*, in *Purchas*, i. 239.

1611.—"Les **Mores** du pay faisoiēt courir le bruict, que les notres avoient esté battus."—*Wytfliet, H. des Indes*, iii. 9.

1648.—"King Jangier (Jehāngīr) used to make use of a reproach: That one *Portugees* was better than three **Moors**, and one Hollander or Englishman better than two Portugees."—*Van Twist*, 59.

c. 1665.—"Il y en a de **Mores** et de Gentils *Raspoutes* (see RAJPOOT) parce que je savois qu'ils servent mieux que les **Mores** qui sont superbes, and ne veulent pas qu'on se plaigne d'eux, quelque sotise ou quelque tromperie qu'ils fassent."—*Thevenot*, v. 217.

1673.—"Their Crew were all **Moors** (by which Word hereafter must be meant those of the Mahometan faith) apparell'd all in white."—*Fryer*, p. 24.

"They are a Shame to our Sailors, who can hardly ever work without horrid Oaths and hideous Cursing and Imprecations; and these **Moormen**, on the contrary, never set their Hands to any Labour, but that they sing a Psalm or Prayer, and conclude at every joint Application of it, 'Allah, Allah,' invoking the Name of God."—*Ibid.* pp. 55–56.

1685.—"We putt out a peece of a Red Ancient to appear like a **Moor's** Vessel: not judging it safe to be known to be English; Our nation having lately gott an ill name by abusing ye Inhabitants of these Islands: but no boat would come neer us ..." (in the Maldives).—*Hedges*, *Diary*, March 9; [Hak. Soc. i. 190].

1688.—"**Lascars**, who are **Moors** of India."—*Dampier*, ii. 57.

1689.—"The place where they went ashore was a Town of the **Moors**: Which name our Seamen give to all the Subjects of the great Mogul, but especially his *Mahometan* Subjects;

calling the Idolators, Gentous or *Rashboots* (see RAJPOOT)."—*Dampier*, i. 507.

1747.—"We had the Misfortune to be reduced to almost inevitable Danger, for as our Success chiefly depended on the assistance of the **Moors**, We were soon brought to the utmost Extremity by being abandoned by them."—*Letter from Ft. St. Geo. to the Court*, May 2 (India Office MS. Records).

1752.—"His successor Mr. Godehue ... even permitted him (Dupleix) to continue the exhibition of those marks of **Moorish** dignity, which both Murzafa-jing and Salla-bad-jing had permitted him to display."—*Orme*, i. 367.

1757.—In Ives, writing in this year, we constantly find the terms **Moormen** and **Moorish**, applied to the forces against which Clive and Watson were acting on the Hoogly.

1763.—"From these origins, time has formed in India a mighty nation of near ten millions of Mahomedans, whom Europeans call **Moors**."—*Orme*, ed. 1803, i. 24.

1770.—"Before the Europeans doubled the Cape of Good Hope, the **Moors**, who were the only maritime people of India, sailed from Surat and Bengal to Malacca."—*Raynal* (tr. 1777), i. 210.

1781.—"Mr. Hicky thinks it a Duty incumbent on him to inform his friends in particular, and the Public in General, that an attempt was made to Assassinate him last Thursday Morning between the Hours of One and two o'Clock, by two armed Europeans aided and assisted by a **Moorman**. ..."—*Hicky's Bengal Gazette*, April 7.

1784.—"Lieutenants Speediman and Rutledge ... were bound, circumcised, and clothed in **Moorish** garments."—In *Seton-Karr*, i. 15.

1797.—"Under the head of castes entitled to a favourable term, I believe you comprehend Brahmans, **Moormen**, merchants, and almost every man who does not belong to the Sudra or cultivating caste. ..."—*Minute of Sir T. Munro*, in *Arbuthnot*, i. 17.

1807.—"The rest of the inhabitants, who are **Moors**, and the richer Gentoos, are dressed in various degrees and fashions."—*Ld. Minto in India*, p. 17.

1829.—"I told my **Moorman**, as they call the Mussulmans here, just now to ask the drum-major when the mail for the *Pradwan* (?) was to be made up."—*Mem. of Col. Mountain*, 2nd ed. p. 80.

1839.—"As I came out of the gate I met some young **Moorish** dandies on horseback; one of them was evidently a 'crack-rider,' and began to show off."—*Letters from Madras*, p. 290.

MOORS, THE, s. The Hindustani language was in the 18th century commonly thus styled. The idiom is a curious old English one for the denomination of a language, of which 'broad Scots' is perhaps a type, and which we find exemplified in 'Malabars' (see MALABAR) for Tamil, whilst we have also met with *Bengals* for Bengālī, with *Indostans* for Urdū, and with *Turks* for Turkish. The term *Moors* is probably now entirely obsolete, but down to 1830, at least, some old officers of the Royal army and some old Madras civilians would occasionally use the term as synonymous with what the former would also call 'the black language.' [**Moors** for Urdū was certainly in use among the old European pensioners at Chunār as late as 1892.]

The following is a transcript of the title-page of Hadley's Grammar, the earliest English Grammar of Hindustani:[1]

"Grammatical Remarks | on the | Practical and Vulgar Dialect | Of the | Indostan Language | commonly called **Moors** | with a Vocabulary | English and **Moors**. The Spelling according to | The Persian Orthography | Wherein are | References between Words resembling each other in | Sound and different in Significations | with Literal Translations and Explanations of the Com- | pounded Words and Circumlocutory Expressions | For the more easy attaining the Idiom of the Language | The whole calculated for

The Common Practice in Bengal.
"—Si quid novisti rectius istis,
Candidus imperti; si non his utere mecum."
By Capt. GEORGE HADLEY.
London:
Printed for T. Cadell in the Strand.
MDCCLXXII."

Captain Hadley's orthography is on a detestable system. He writes *chookerau*, *chookeree*, for *chhokrā*, *chhokrī* ('boy, girl'); *dolchinney* for *dāl-chīnī* ('cinnamon'), &c. His etymological ideas also are loose. Thus he gives 'shrimps = *chînghra mutchee*, 'fish with legs and claws,' as if the word was from *chang* (Pers.), 'a hook or claw.' *Bāgḍor*, 'a halter,' or as he writes, *baug-doore*, he derives from *dūr*, 'distance,' instead of *ḍor*, 'a rope.' He has no knowledge of the instrumental case with terminal *ne*, and he does not seem to be aware that *ham* and *tum* (*hum* and *toom*, as he writes) are in reality plurals ('we'

1 Hadley, however, mentions in his preface that a small pamphlet had been received by Mr. George Bogle in 1770, which he found to be the mutilated embryo of his own grammatical scheme. This was circulating in Bengal "at his expence."

and 'you'). The grammar is altogether of a very primitive and tentative character, and far behind that of the R. C. Missionaries, which is referred to s.v. **Hindostanee**. We have not seen that of Schulz (1745) mentioned under the same.

1752.—"The Centinel was sitting at the top of the gate, singing a **Moorish** song."—*Orme*, ed. 1803, i. 272.

1767.—"In order to transact Business of any kind in this Countrey, you must at least have a smattering of the Language for few of the Inhabitants (except in great Towns) speak English. The original Language, of this Countrey (or at least the earliest we know of) is the Bengala or Gentoo. ... But the politest Language is the **Moors** or Mussulmans and Persian. ... The only Language that I know anything of is the Bengala, and that I do not speak perfectly, for you may remember that I had a very poor knack at learning Languages."—*MS. Letter of James Rennell*, March 10.

1779.—

"*C.* What language did Mr. Francis speak?

W. (*Meerum Kitmutgar*). The same as I do, in broken **Moors**."—*Trial of* Grand *v.* Philip Francis, quoted in *Echoes of Old Calcutta*, 226.

1783.—"**Moors**, by not being written, bars all close application."—Letter in *Life of Colebrooke*, 13.

"The language called '**Moors**' has a written character differing both from the Sanskrit and Bengalee character, it is called *Nagree*, which means 'writing.'"—Letter in *Mem: of Ld. Teignmouth*, i. 104.

1784.—

"Wild perroquets first silence broke,
Eager of dangers near to prate;
But they in English never spoke,
And she began her **Moors** of late."

Plassey Plain, a Ballad by *Sir W. Jones*, in *Works*, ii. 504.

1788.—"*Wants Employment*. A young man who has been some years in Bengal, used to common accounts, understands *Bengallies*, **Moors**, Portuguese. ..."—In *Seton-Karr*, i. 286.

1789.—"... sometimes slept half an hour, sometimes not, and then wrote or talked Persian or **Moors** till sunset, when I went to parade."—Letter of *Sir T. Munro*, i. 76.

1802.—"All business is transacted in a barbarous mixture of **Moors**, Mahratta, and Gentoo."—*Sir T. Munro*, in *Life*, i. 333.

1803.—"Conceive what society there will be when people speak what they don't think, in **Moors**."—*M. Elphinstone*, in *Life*, i. 108.

1804.—"She had a **Moorish** woman interpreter, and as I heard her give orders to her interpreter in the **Moorish** language ... I must consider the conversation of the first authority."—*Wellington*, iii. 290.

"*The Stranger's Guide to the* Hindoostanic, *or Grand Popular Language of India, improperly called* **Moorish**; *by* J. Borthwick Gilchrist: *Calcutta.*"

MORT-DE-CHIEN, s. A name for cholera, in use, more or less, up to the end of the 18th century, and the former prevalence of which has tended probably to the extraordinary and baseless notion that epidemic cholera never existed in India till the governorship of the Marquis of Hastings. The word in this form is really a corruption of the Portuguese **mordexim**, shaped by a fanciful French etymology. The Portuguese word again represents the Konkani and Mahratti *moḍachī*, *moḍshī*, or *moḍwashī*, 'cholera,' from a Mahr. verb *moḍnen*, 'to break up, to sink' (as under infirmities, in fact 'to collapse'). The Guzaratī appears to be *moṛchi* or *moṛachi*.

[1504.—Writing of this year Correa mentions the prevalence of the disease in the Samorin's army, but he gives it no name. "Besides other illness there was one almost sudden, which caused such a pain in the belly that a man hardly survived 8 hours of it."—*Correa*, i. 489.]

1543.—Correa's description is so striking that we give it almost at length: "This **winter** they had in Goa a mortal distemper which the natives call **morxy**, and attacking persons of every quality, from the smallest infant at the breast to the old man of fourscore, and also domestic animals and fowls, so that it affected every living thing, male and female. And this malady attacked people without any cause that could be assigned, falling upon sick and sound alike, on the fat and the lean; and nothing in the world was a safeguard against it. And this malady attacked the stomach, caused as some experts affirmed by chill; though later it was maintained that no cause whatever could be discovered. The malady was so powerful and so evil that it immediately produced the symptoms of strong poison; *e.g.*, vomiting, constant desire for water, with drying of the stomach; and cramps that contracted the hams and the soles of the feet, with such pains that the patient seemed dead, with the eyes broken and the nails of the fingers and toes black and crumpled. And for this malady our physicians never found any cure; and the patient was carried off in one day, or at the most in a day and night; insomuch that not ten in a hundred recovered, and those who did recover were such as were healed in haste with medicines of little importance known to the natives. So great was the mortality this season that the bells were tolling all day ...

insomuch that the governor forbade the tolling of the church bells, not to frighten the people ... and when a man died in the hospital of this malady of **morexy** the Governor ordered all the experts to come together and open the body. But they found nothing wrong except that the paunch was shrunk up like a hen's gizzard, and wrinkled like a piece of scorched leather. ..."—*Correa*, iv. 288–289.

1563.—

"*Page.*—Don Jeronymo sends to beg that you will go and visit his brother immediately, for though this is not the time of day for visits, delay would be dangerous, and he will be very thankful that you come at once.

"*Orta.*—What is the matter with the patient, and how long has he been ill?

"*Page.*—He has got **morxi**; and he has been ill two hours.

"*Orta.*—I will follow you.

"*Ruano.*—Is this the disease that kills so quickly, and that few recover from? Tell me how it is called by our people, and by the natives, and the symptoms of it, and the treatment you use in it.

"*Orta.*—Our name for the disease is *Collerica passio*; and the Indians call it *morxi*; whence again by corruption we call it **mordexi**. ... It is sharper here than in our own part of the world, for usually it kills in four and twenty hours. And I have seen some cases where the patient did not live more than ten hours. The most that it lasts is four days; but as there is no rule without an exception, I once saw a man with great constancy of virtue who lived twenty days continually throwing up ("*curgínosa*"?) ... bile, and died at last. Let us go and see this sick man; and as for the symptoms you will yourself see what a thing it is."—*Garcia*, ff. 74*v*, 75.

1578.—"There is another thing which is useless called by them *canarin*, which the Canarin Brahman physicians usually employ for the *collerica passio* sickness, which they call **morxi**; which sickness is so sharp that it kills in fourteen hours or less."—*Acosta, Tractado*, 27.

1598.—"There reigneth a sicknesse called **Mordexijn** which stealeth uppon men, and handleth them in such sorte, that it weakeneth a man, and maketh him cast out all that he hath in his bodie, and many times his life withall."—*Linschoten*, 67; [Hak. Soc. i. 235; **Morxi** in ii. 22].

1599.—"The disease which in India is called **Mordicin**. This is a species of Colic, which comes on in those countries with such force and vehemence that it kills in a few hours; and there is no remedy discovered. It causes evacuations by stool or vomit, and makes one burst with pain. But there is a herb proper for the cure, which bears the same name of **mordescin**."—*Carletti*, 227.

1602.—"In those islets (off Aracan) they found bad and brackish water, and certain beans like ours both green and dry, of which they ate some, and in the same moment this gave them a kind of dysentery, which in India they corruptly call **mordexim**, which ought to be *morxis*, and which the Arabs call *sachaiza* (Ar. *hayẓat*), which is what Rasis calls *sahida*, a disease which kills in 24 hours. Its action is immediately to produce a sunken and slender pulse, with cold sweat, great inward fire, and excessive thirst, the eyes sunken, great vomitings, and in fact it leaves the natural power so collapsed (*derriboula*) that the patient seems like a dead man."—*Couio*, Dec. IV. liv. iv. cap. 10.

c. 1610.—"Il regne entre eux vne autre maladie qui vient a l'improviste, ils la nomment **Mordesin**, et vient auec grande douleur des testes, et vomissement, et crient fort, et le plus souvent en meurent."—*Pyrard de Laval*, ii. 19; [Hak. Soc. ii. 13].

1631.—"Pulvis ejus (Calumbac) ad scrup. unius pondus sumptus cholerae prodest, quam **Mordexi** incolae vocant."—*Jac. Bontii*, lib. iv. p. 43.

1638.—"... celles qui y regnent le plus, sont celles qu'ils appellent **Mordexin**, qui tue subitement."—*Mandelslo*, 265.

1648.—See also the (questionable) *Voyages Fameux du Sieur Victor le Blanc*, 76.

c. 1665.—"Les Portugais appellent **Mordechin** les quatre sortes de Coliques qu'on souffre dans les Indes ou elles sont frequentes ... ceux qui ont la quatrième soufrent les trois maux ensemble, à savoir le vomissement, le flux de ventre, les extremes douleurs, et je crois que cette derniere est le Colera-Morbus."—*Thevenot*, v. 324.

1673.—"They apply Cauteries most unmercifully in a **Mordisheen**, called so by the Portugals, being a Vomiting with Looseness."—*Fryer*, 114.

[1674.—"The disease called **Mordechi** generally commences with a violent fever, accompanied by tremblings, horrors and vomitings; these symptoms are generally followed by delirium and death." He prescribes a hot iron applied to the soles of the feet. He attributes the disease to indigestion, and remarks bitterly that at least the prisoners of the Inquisition were safe from this disease.—*Dellon, Relation de l'Inquisition de Goa*, ii. ch. 71.]

1690.—"The **Mordechine** is another Disease ... which is a violent Vomiting and Looseness."—*Ovington*, 350.

c. 1690.—*Rumphius*, speaking of the **Jack**-fruit (q.v.): "Non nisi vacuo stomacho edendus est, alias enim ... plerumque oritur *Passio Cholerica*, Portugallis **Mordexi** dicta."—*Herb. Amb.*, i. 106.

1702.—"Cette grande indigestion qu'on appelle aux Indes **Mordechin**, et que quelques uns de nos Français ont appellée **Mort-de-Chien**."—*Lettres Edif.*, xi. 156.

Bluteau (s.v.) says **Mordexim** is properly a failure of digestion which is very perilous in those parts, unless the native remedy be used. This is to apply a thin rod, like a spit, and heated, under the heel, till the patient screams with pain, and then to slap the same part with the sole of a shoe, &c.

1705.—"Ce mal s'appelle **mort-de-chien**."—*Luillier*, 113.

The following is an example of literal translation, as far as we know, unique:

1716.—"The extraordinary distempers of this country (I. of Bourbon) are the *Cholick*, and what they call the *Dog's Disease*, which is cured by burning the heel of the patient with a hot iron."—*Acct. of the I. of Bourbon*, in *La Roque's Voyage to Arabia the Happy*, &c., E.T. London, 1726, p. 155.

1727.—"... the **Mordexin** (which seizes one suddenly with such oppression and palpitation that he thinks he is going to die on the spot)."—*Valentijn*, v. (Malabar) 5.

c. 1760.—"There is likewise known, on the Malabar coast chiefly, a most violent disorder they call the **Mordechin**; which seizes the patient with such fury of purging, vomiting, and tormina of the intestines, that it will often carry him off in 30 hours."—*Grose*, i. 250.

1768.—"This (cholera morbus) in the East Indies, where it is very frequent and fatal, is called **Mort-de-chien**."—*Lind, Essay on Diseases incidental to Hot Climates*, 248.

1778.—In the Vocabulary of the Portuguese *Grammatica Indostana*, we find **Mordechim**, as a Portuguese word, rendered in Hind. by the word *badazmi*, *i.e. bad-hazmī*, 'dyspepsia' (p. 99). The most common modern Hind. term for cholera is Arab. *haiẓah*. The latter word is given by Garcia de Orta in the form *hachaiza*, and in the quotation from Couto as *sachaiza* (?). Jahāngīr speaks of one of his nobles as dying in the Deccan, of *haiẓah*, in A.D. 1615 (see note to *Elliot*, vi. 346). It is, however, perhaps not to be assumed that *haiẓah* always means cholera. Thus Macpherson mentions that a violent epidemic, which raged in the Camp of Aurangzīb at Bījapur in 1689, is called so. But in the history of Khāfi Khān (*Elliot*, vii. 337) the general phrases *ta'ūn* and *wabā* are used in reference to this disease, whilst the description is that of bubonic plague.

1781.—"Early in the morning of the 21st June (1781) we had two men seized with the **mort-de-chien**."—*Curtis, Diseases of India*, 3rd ed., Edinb., 1807.

1782.—"Les indigestions appellées dans l'Inde **Mort-de-chien**, sont fréquentes. Les Castes qui mangent de la viande, nourriture trop pesante pour un climat si chaud, en sont souvent attaquées. ..."—*Sonnerat*, i. 205. This author writes just after having described two epidemics of cholera under the name of *Flux aigu*. He did not apprehend that this was in fact the real **Mort-de-chien**.

1783.—"A disease generally called '**Mort-de-chien**' at this time (during the defence of Onore) raged with great violence among the native inhabitants."—*Forbes, Or. Mem.* iv. 122.

1796.—"Far more dreadful are the consequences of the above-mentioned intestinal colic, called by the Indians *shani*, **mordexim** and also *Nircomben*. It is occasioned, as I have said, by the winds blowing from the mountains ... the consequence is that malignant and bilious slimy matter adheres to the bowels, and occasions violent pains, vomiting, fevers, and stupefaction; so that persons attacked with the disease die very often in a few hours. It sometimes happens that 30 or 40 persons die in this manner, in one place, in the course of the day. ... In the year 1782 this disease raged with so much fury that a great many persons died of it."—*Fra Paolino*, E.T. 409–410 (orig. see p. 353). As to the names used by Fra Paolino, for his *Shani* or *Ciani*, we find nothing nearer than Tamil and Mal. *sanni*, 'convulsion, paralysis.' (Winslow in his *Tamil Dict.* specifies 13 kinds of *sanni*. *Komben* is explained as 'a kind of cholera or smallpox' (!); and *nir-komben* ('water-k.') as a kind of cholera or bilious diarrhœa.) Paolino adds: "La *droga amara* costa assai, e non si poteva amministrare a tanti miserabili che perivano. Adunque in mancanza di questa droga amara noi distillasimo in *Tàgara*, o acqua vite di coco, molto sterco di cavalli (!), e l'amministrammo agl' infermi. Tutti quelli che prendevano questa guarivano."

1808.—"**Môrchee** or **Mortshee** (Guz.) and *Môdee* (Mah.). A morbid affection in which the symptoms are convulsive action, followed by evacuations of the first passage up and down, with intolerable tenesmus, or twisting-like sensation in the intestines, corresponding remarkably with the cholera-morbus of European synopsists, called by the country people in England (?) **morti-sheen**, and by others **mord-du-chien** and **Maua des chienes**, as if it had come from France."—*R. Drummond, Illustrations*, &c. A curious notice; and the author was, we presume, from his title of "Dr.," a medical man. We suppose for *England* above should be read *India*.

The next quotation is the latest instance of the *familiar* use of the word that we have met with:

1812.—"General M—— was taken very ill three or four days ago; a kind of fit—**mort de chien**—the doctor said, brought on by eating too many radishes."—*Original Familiar Correspondence between Residents in India*, &c., Edinburgh, 1846, p. 287.

1813.—"**Mort de chien** is nothing more than the highest degree of Cholera **Morbus**."—*Johnson, Infl. of Tropical Climate*, 405.

The second of the following quotations evidently refers to the outbreak of cholera mentioned, after Macpherson, in the next paragraph.

1780.—"I am once or twice a year (!) subject to violent attacks of **cholera morbus**, here called **mort-de-chien**. ..."—*Impey to Dunning*, quoted by *Sir James Stephen*, ii. 339.

1781.—"The Plague is now broke out in Bengal, and rages with great violence; it has swept away already above 4000 persons. 200 or upwards have been buried in the different Portuguese churches within a few days."—*Hicky's Bengal Gazette*, April 21.

These quotations show that cholera, whether as an epidemic or as sporadic disease, is no new thing in India. Almost in the beginning of the Portuguese expeditions to the East we find apparent examples of the visitations of this terrible scourge, though no precise name is given in the narratives. Thus we read in the Life of Giovanni da Emboli, an adventurous young Florentine who served with the Portuguese, that, arriving in China in 1517, the ships' crews were attacked by a *pessima malatia di frusso* (virulent flux) of such kind that there died thereof about 70 men, and among these Giovanni himself, and two other Florentines (*Vita*, in *Archiv. Stor. Ital.* 33). Correa says that, in 1503, 20,000 men died of a like disease in the army of the Zamorin. We have given above Correa's description of the terrible Goa pest of 1543, which was most evidently cholera. Madras accounts, according to Macpherson, first mention the disease at Arcot in 1756, and there are frequent notices of it in that neighbourhood between 1763 and 1787. The Hon. R. Lindsay speaks of it as raging at Sylhet in 1781, after carrying off a number of the inhabitants of Calcutta (*Macpherson*, see the quotation of 1781 above). It also raged that year at Ganjam, and out of a division of 5000 Bengal troops under Col. Pearse, who were on the march through that district, 1143 were in a few days sent into hospital, whilst "death raged in the camp with a horror not to be described." The earliest account from the pen of an English physician is by Dr. Paisley, and is dated Madras, Feby. 1774. In 1783 it broke out at Hardwār Fair, and is said, in less than 8 days, to have carried off 20,000 pilgrims. The paucity of cases of cholera among European troops in the returns up to 1817, is ascribed by Dr. Macnamara to the way in which facts were disguised by the current nomenclature of disease. It need not perhaps be denied that the outbreak of 1817 marked a great recrudescence of the disease. But it is a fact that some of the more terrible features of the epidemic, which are then spoken of as quite new, had been prominently described at Goa nearly three centuries before.

See on this subject an article by Dr. J. Macpherson in *Quarterly Review*, for Jany. 1867, and a *Treatise on Asiatic Cholera*, by C. Macnamara, 1876. To these, and especially to the former, we owe several facts and references; though we had recorded quotations relating to **mordexin** and its identity with cholera some years before even the earlier of these publications.

MOSQUE, s. There is no room for doubt as to the original of this word being the Ar. *masjid*, 'a place of worship,' literally the place of *sujūd*, *i.e.* 'prostration.' And the probable course is this. *Masjid* becomes (1) in Span. *mezquita*, Port. *mesquita*;[1] (2) Ital. *meschita*, *moschea*; French (old) *mosquete*, *mosquée*; (3) Eng. *mosque*. Some of the quotations might suggest a different course of modification, but they would probably mislead.

Apropos of *masjid* rather than of mosque we have noted a ludicrous misapplication of the word in the advertisement to a newspaper story. "*Musjeed* the Hindoo: Adventures with the Star of India in the Sepoy Mutiny of 1857." The *Weekly Detroit Free Press, London*, July 1, 1882.

1336.—"Corpusque ipsius perditissimi

1 According to Pyrard *mesquite* is the word used in the Maldive Islands. It is difficult to suppose the people would adopt such a word from the Portuguese. And probably the form both in east and west is to be accounted for by a hard pronunciation of the Arabic *j*, as in Egypt now; the older and probably the most widely diffused. [See Mr. Gray's note in Hak. Soc. ii. 417.]

Pseudo-prophetae ... in civitate quae Mecha dicitur ... pro maximo sanctuario conservatur in pulchrâ ipsorum Ecclesiâ quam **Mulscket** vulgariter dicunt."—*Gul. de Boldensele*, in *Canisii Thesaur. ed. Basnage*, iv.

1384.—"Sonvi le **mosquette**, cioe chiese de' Saraceni ... dentro tutte bianche ed intonicate ed ingessate."—*Frescobaldi*, 29.

1543.—"And with the stipulation that the 5000 *larin tangas* which in old times were granted, and are deposited for the expenses of the **mizquitas** of Baçaim, are to be paid from the said duties as they always have been paid, and in regard to the said **mizquitas** and the prayers that are made in them there shall be no innovation whatever."—Treaty at Baçaim of the Portuguese with King Bador of Çanbaya (Bahādur Shāh of Guzerat) in *S. Botelho, Tombo*, 137.

1553.—"... but destined yet to unfurl that divine and royal banner of the Soldiery of Christ ... in the Eastern regions of Asia, amidst the infernal **mesquitas** of Arabia and Persia, and all the **pagodes** of the heathenism of India, on this side and beyond the Ganges."—*Barros*, I. i. 1.

[c. 1610.—"The principal temple, which they call *Oucourou* **misquitte**" (*Hukuru miskitu*, 'Friday mosque').—*Pyrard de Laval*, Hak. Soc. i. 72.]

1616.—"They are very jealous to let their women or **Moschees** be seen."—*Sir T. Roe*, in *Purchas*, i. 537; [Hak. Soc. ii. 21].

[1623.—"We went to see upon the same Lake a **meschita**, or temple of the Mahometans."—*P. della Valle*, Hak. Soc. i. 69.]

1634.—

"Que a de abominação **mesquita** immũda
Casa, a Deos dedicada hoje se veja."
Malaca Conquistada, l. xii. 43.

1638.—Mandelslo unreasonably applies the term to all sorts of pagan temples, *e.g.*—

"Nor is it only in great Cities that the *Benjans* have their many **Mosqueys**. ..."—E.T. 2nd ed. 1669, p. 52.

"The King of *Siam* is a *Pagan*, nor do his Subjects know any other Religion. They have divers **Mosquees**, Monasteries, and Chappels."—*Ibid.* p. 104.

c. 1662.—"... he did it only for love to their Mammon; and would have sold afterwards for as much more St. Peter's ... to the Turks for a **Mosquito**."—*Cowley*, Discourse concerning the Govt. of O. Cromwell.

1680.—Consn. Ft. St. Geo. March 28: "Records the death of Cassa Verona ... and a dispute arising as to whether his body should be burned by the *Gentues* or buried by the *Moors*, the latter having stopped the procession on the ground that the deceased was a Mussleman and built a **Musseet** in the Towne to be buried in, the Governor with the advice of his Council sent an order that the body should be burned as a *Gentue*, and not buried by the *Moors*, it being apprehended to be of dangerous consequence to admit the Moors such pretences in the Towne."—*Notes and Exts.* No. iii. p. 14.

1719.—"On condition they had a **Cowle** granted, exempting them from paying the Pagoda or **Musqueet** duty."—In *Wheeler*, ii. 301.

1727.—"There are no fine Buildings in the City, but many large Houses, and some Caravanserays and **Muscheits**."—*A. Hamilton*, i. 161; [ed. 1774, i. 163].

c. 1760.—"The Roman Catholic Churches, the Moorish **Moschs**, the Gentoo Pagodas, the worship of the Parsees, are all equally unmolested and tolerated."—*Grose*, i. 44.

[1862.—"... I slept at a **Musheed**, or village house of prayer."—*Brinckman, Rifle in Cashmere*, 78.]

MOSQUITO, s. A gnat is so called in the tropics. The word is Spanish and Port. (dim. of *mosca*, 'a fly'), and probably came into familiar English use from the East Indies, though the earlier quotations show that it was *first* brought from S. America. A friend annotates here: "Arctic mosquitoes are worst of all; and the Norfolk ones (in the Broads) beat Calcutta!"

It is related of a young Scotch lady of a former generation who on her voyage to India had heard formidable, but vague accounts of this terror of the night, that on seeing an elephant for the first time, she asked: "Will yon be what's called a **musqueetae**?"

1539.—"To this misery was there adjoyned the great affliction, which the Flies and Gnats (*por parte dos atabôes e* **mosquitos**), that coming out of the neighbouring Woods, bit and stung us in such sort, as not one of us but was gore blood."—*Pinto* (orig. cap. xxiii.), in *Cogan*, p. 29.

1582.—"We were oftentimes greatly annoyed with a kind of flie, which in the Indian tongue is called *Tiquari*, and the Spanish call them **Muskitos**."—*Miles Phillips*, in *Hakl.* iii. 564.

1584.—"The 29 Day we set Saile from Saint Iohns, being many of vs stung before upon Shoare with the **Muskitos**; but the same night we tooke a Spanish Frigat."—*Sir Richard Greenevile's Voyage*, in *Hakl.* iii. 308.

1616 and 1673.—See both *Terry* and *Fryer* under **Chints**.

1662.—"At night there is a kind of insect that plagues one mightily; they are called

Muscieten,—it is a kind that by their noise and sting cause much irritation."—*Saar*, 68–69.

1673.—"The greatest Pest is the **Mosquito**, which not only wheals, but domineers by its continual Hums."—*Fryer*, 189.

1690.—(The Governor) "carries along with him a *Peon* or Servant to Fan him, and drive away the busie Flies, and troublesome **Musketoes**. This is done with the Hair of a Horse's Tail."—*Ovington*, 227–8.

1740.—"... all the day we were pestered with great numbers of **muscatos**, which are not much unlike the gnats in *England*, but more venomous. ..."—*Anson's Voyage*, 9th ed., 1756, p. 46.

1764.—

"**Mosquitos**, sandflies, seek the sheltered roof,
And with full rage the stranger guest assail,
Nor spare the sportive child."

—*Grainger*, bk. i.

1883.—"Among rank weeds in deserted Bombay gardens, too, there is a large, speckled, unmusical **mosquito**, raging and importunate and thirsty, which will give a new idea in pain to any one that visits its haunts."—*Tribes on My Frontier*, 27.

MUDDÁR, s. Hind. *madār*, Skt. *mandāra; Calotropis procera*, R. Brown, N.O. *Asclepiadaceae*. One of the most common and widely diffused plants in uncultivated plains throughout India. In Sind the bark fibre is used for halters, &c., and experiment has shown it to be an excellent material worth £40 a ton in England, if it could be supplied at that rate; but the cost of collection has stood in the way of its utilisation. The seeds are imbedded in a silky floss, used to stuff pillows. This also has been the subject of experiment for textile use, but as yet without practical success. The plant abounds with an acrid milky juice which the Rājputs are said to employ for infanticide. (*Punjab Plants.*) The plant is called **Ak** in Sind and throughout N. India.

MUDDLE, s. (?) This word is only known to us from the clever—perhaps too clever—little book quoted below. The word does not seem to be known, and was probably a misapprehension of **budlee**. [Even Mr. Brandt and Mrs. Wyatt are unable to explain this word. The former does not remember hearing it. Both doubt its connection with **budlee**. Mrs. Wyatt suggests with hesitation Tamil *muder*, "boiled rice," *mudei-palli*, "the cook-house."]

1836-7.—"Besides all these acknowledged and ostensible attendants, each servant has a kind of **muddle** or double of his own, who does all the work that can be put off upon him without being found out by his master or mistress."—*Letters from Madras*, 38.

"They always come accompanied by their Vakeels, a kind of Secretaries, or interpreters, or flappers,—their **muddles** in short; everybody here has a **muddle**, high or low."—*Letters from Madras*, 86.

MUFTY, s.

a. Ar. *Muftī*, an expounder of the Mahommedan Law, the utterer of the *fatwā* (see FUTWAH). Properly the *Muftī* is above the *Kāẓī* who carries out the judgment. In the 18th century, and including Regulation IX. of 1793, which gave the Company's Courts in Bengal the reorganization which substantially endured till 1862, we have frequent mention of both *Cauzies* and *Mufties* as authorized expounders of the Mahommedan Law; but, though Kāẓīs were nominally maintained in the Provincial Courts down to their abolition (1829–31), practically the duty of those known as Kāẓīs became limited to quite different objects and the designation of the Law-officer who gave the *futwā* in our District Courts was *Maulavī*. The title *Muftī* has been long obsolete within the limits of British administration, and one might safely say that it is practically unknown to any surviving member of the Indian Civil Service, and never was heard in India as a living title by any Englishman now surviving. (See CAZEE, LAW-OFFICER, MOOLVEE).

b. A slang phrase in the army, for 'plain clothes.' No doubt it is taken in some way from **a**, but the transition is a little obscure. [It was perhaps originally applied to the attire of dressing-gown, smoking-cap, and slippers, which was like the Oriental dress of the *Muftī* who was familiar in Europe from his appearance in Moliere's *Bourgeois Gentilhomme*. Compare the French *en Pekin*.]

a.—

1653.—"Pendant la tempeste vne femme **Industani** mourut sur notre bord; vn **Moufti** Persan de la Secte des Schaï (see SHEEAH) assista à cette derniere extrémité, luy donnant esperance d'vne meilleure vie que celle-cy, et d'vn Paradis, où l'on auroit tout ce que l'on peut desirer ... et la fit changer de Secte. ..."—*De la Boullaye-le-Gouz*, ed. 1657, p. 281.

1674.—"Resolve to make a present to the Governors of Changulaput and Pallaveram, old friends of the Company, and now about to go to Golcondah, for the marriage of the former with the daughter of the King's **Mufti** or Churchman."—*Fort St. Geo. Consn.*, March 26. In *Notes and Exts.*, No. i. 80.

1767.—"3d. You will not let the **Cauzy** or **Mufty** receive anything from the tenants unlawfully."—*Collectors' Instructions*, in *Long*, 511.

1777.—"The **Cazi** and **Muftis** now deliver in the following report, on the right of inheritance claimed by the widow and nephew of Shabaz Beg Khan. ..."—*Report on the Patna Cause*, quoted in *Stephen's Nuncomar and Impey*, ii. 167.

1793.—"§ XXXVI. The **Cauzies** and **Muftis** of the provincial Courts of Appeal, shall also be **cauzies** and **mufties** of the courts of circuit in the several divisions, and shall not be removable, except on proof to the satisfaction of the Governor-General in Council that they are incapable, or have been guilty of misconduct. ..."—*Reg. IX. of* 1793.

[c. 1855.—
"Think'st thou I fear the dark vizier,
Or the **mufti's** vengeful arm?"
Bon Gaultier, The Cadi's Daughter.]

MUGGUR, s. Hind. and Mahr. *magar* and *makar*, from Skt. *makara* 'a sea-monster' (see MACAREO). The destructive broad-snouted crocodile of the Ganges and other Indian rivers, formerly called *Crocodilus biporcatus*, now apparently subdivided into several sorts or varieties.

1611.—"Alagaters or Crocodiles there called **Murgur** *match*. ..."—*Hawkins*, in *Purchas*, i. 436. The word is here intended for *magar-mats* or *machh*, 'crocodile-fish.'

[1876.—See under NUZZER.]

1878.—"The **muggur** is a gross pleb, and his features stamp him as low-born. His manners are coarse."—*Ph. Robinson, In My Indian Garden*, 82–3.

1879.—"En route I killed two crocodiles; they are usually called alligators, but that is a misnomer. It is the **mugger** ... these **muggers** kill a good many people, and have a playful way of getting under a boat, and knocking off the steersman with their tails, and then swallowing him afterwards."—*Pollok, Sport*, &c., i. 168.

1881.—"Alligator leather attains by use a beautiful gloss, and is very durable ... and it is possible that our rivers contain a sufficient number of the two varieties of crocodile, the **muggar** and the *garial* for the tanners and leather-dressers of Cawnpore to experiment upon."—*Pioneer Mail*, April 26.

***MULL**, s. A contraction of **Mulligatawny**, and applied as a distinctive sobriquet to members of the Service belonging to the Madras Presidency, as Bengal people are called **Qui-his**, and Bombay people **Ducks** or **Benighted**.

[1837.—"The **Mulls** have been excited also by another occurrence ... affecting rather the trading than fashionable world."—*Asiatic Journal*, December, p. 251.]

[1852.—"... residents of Bengal, Bombay, and Madras are, in Eastern parlance. designated 'Qui Hies,' 'Ducks,' and '**Mulls**.'"—*Notes and Queries*, 1st ser. v. 165.]

1860.—"It ys ane darke Londe, and ther dwellen ye *Cimmerians* whereof speketh *Homerus Poeta* in his *Odysseia*, and to thys Daye thei clepen *Tenebrosi* or 'ye Benyghted ffolke.' Bot thei clepen hemselvys **Mullys** from *Mulligataunee* wh[ch] ys ane of theyr goddys from w[ch] thei ben ysprong."—Ext. from a lately discovered MS. of *Sir John Maundeville*.

MULLIGATAWNY, s. The name of this well-known soup is simply a corruption of the Tamil *milagu-tannīr*, 'pepper-water'; showing the correctness of the popular belief which ascribes the origin of this excellent article to Madras, whence—and not merely from the complexion acquired there—the sobriquet of the preceding article.

1784.—
"In vain our hard fate we repine;
In vain on our fortune we rail;
On **Mullaghee-tawny** we dine,
Or **Congee**, in Bangalore Jail."
Song by a Gentleman of the Navy (one of Hyder's Prisoners), in *Seton-Karr*, i. 18.

[1823.— ... in a brasen pot was **mulugu tanni**, a hot vegetable soup, made chiefly from pepper and capsicums."—*Hoole, Missions in Madras*, 2nd ed. 249.]

MUNCHEEL, MANJEEL, s. This word is proper to the S.W. coast; Malayal. *manjīl*, *mañehal*, from Skt. *mancha*. It is the name of a kind of hammock-litter used on that coast as a substitute for palankin or dooly. It is substantially the same as the **dandy** of the Himālaya, but more elaborate. Correa describes but does not name it.

1561.—"... He came to the factory in a litter which men carried on their shoulders. These are made with thick canes, bent upwards and arched, and from them are suspended some clothes half a fathom in width, and a fathom and a half in length; and at the extremities pieces of wood to sustain the cloth hanging from the pole; and upon this cloth a mattress of the same size as the cloth ... the whole very splendid, and as rich as the gentlemen ... may desire."—*Correa, Three Voyages*, &c., p. 199.

1811.—"The Inquisition is about a quarter of a mile distant from the convent, and we proceeded thither in **manjeels**."—*Buchanan, Christian Researches*, 2nd ed., 171.

1819.—"**Muncheel**, a kind of litter resembling a sea-cot or hammock, hung to a long pole, with a moveable cover over the whole, to keep off the sun or rain. Six men will run with one from one end of the Malabar coast to the other, while twelve are necessary for the lightest palanquin."—*Welsh*, ii. 142.

1844.—"**Muncheels**, with poles complete. ... Poles, **Muncheel**-, Spare."—*Jameson's Bombay Code, Ordnance Nomenclature.*

1862.—"We ... started ... in **Munsheels** or hammocks, slung to bamboos, with a shade over them, and carried by six men, who kept up unearthly yells the whole time."—*Markham, Peru and India*, 353.

c. 1886.—"When I landed at Diu, an officer met me with a **Muncheel** for my use, viz. a hammock slung to a pole, and protected by an awning."—*M.-Gen. R. H. Keatinge.*

A form of this word is used at Réunion, where a kind of palankin is called "le **manchy**." It gives a title to one of Leconte de Lisle's Poems:

c. 1858.—

"Sous un nuage frais de claire mousseline
Tous les dimanches au matin,
Tu venais à la ville en **manchy** de rotin,
Par les rampes de la colline."

Le **Manchy**.

The word has also been introduced by the Portuguese into Africa in the forms *maxilla*, and *machilla.*

1810.—"... tangas, que elles chamão **maxilas**."—*Annaes Maritimas*, iii. 434.

1880.—"The Portuguese (in Quilliman) seldom even think of walking the length of their own street, and ... go from house to house in a sort of palanquin, called here a **machilla** (pronounced *masheela*). This usually consists of a pole placed upon the shoulders of the natives, from which is suspended a long plank of wood, and upon that is fixed an old-fashioned-looking chair, or sometimes two. Then there is an awning over the top, hung all round with curtains. Each **machilla** requires about 6 to 8 bearers, who are all dressed alike in a kind of livery." —*A Journey in E. Africa*, by *M. A. Pringle*, p. 89.

MUNGOOSE, s. This is the popular Anglo-Indian name of the Indian ichneumons, represented in the South by *Mangusta Mungos* (Elliot), or *Herpestes griseus* (Geoffroy) of naturalists, and in Bengal by *Herpestes malaccensis*. [Blanford (*Mammalia*, 119 *seqq.*) recognises eight species, the "Common Indian Mungoose" being described as *Herpestes mungo.*] The word is Telugu, *mangīsu*, or *mungīsa*. In Upper India the animal is called *newal*, *neolā*, or *nyaul*. Jerdon gives *mangūs* however as a Deccani and Mahr. word; [Platts gives it as dialectic, and very doubtfully derives it from Skt. *makshu*, 'moving quickly.' In Ar. it is *bint-'arūs*, 'daughter of the bridegroom,' in Egypt *kitt* or *katt Farāūn*, 'Pharaoh's cat' (*Burton, Ar. Nights*, ii. 369].

1673.—"... a **Mongoose** is akin to a Ferret. ..."—*Fryer*, 116.

1681.—"The knowledge of these antidotal herbs they have learned from the **Mounggutia**, a kind of Ferret."—*Knox*, 115.

1685.—"They have what they call a **Mangus**, creatures something different from ferrets; these hold snakes in great antipathy, and if they once discover them never give up till they have killed them."—*Ribeyró*, f. 56*v*.

Bluteau gives the following as a quotation from a *History of Ceylon*, tr. from Portuguese into French, published at Paris in 1701, p. 153. It is in fact the gist of an anecdote in Ribeyro.

"There are persons who cherish this animal and have it to sleep with them, although it is ill-tempered, for they prefer to be bitten by a **mangus** to being killed by a snake."

1774.—"He (the Dharma Raja of Bhootan) has got a little lap-dog and a **Mungoos**, which he is very fond of."—*Bogle's Diary*, in *Markham's Tibet*, 27.

1790.—"His (Mr. Glan's) experiments have also established a very curious fact, that the ichneumon, or **mungoose**, which is very common in this country, and kills snakes without danger to itself, does not use antidotes ... but that the poison of snakes is, to this animal, innocent."—Letter in *Colebrooke's Life*, p. 40.

1329.—"Il **Mongùse** animale simile ad una donnola."—*Papi*, in *de Gubernatis, St. dei Viagg. Ital.*, p. 279.

MUNTRA, s. Skt. *mantra*, 'a text of the Vedas; a magical formula.'

1612.—"... Trata da causa primeira, segundo os livros que tem, chamados Terum **Mandra** moie" (*mantra-mūla*, *mūla* 'text').—*Couto*, Dec. V. liv. vi. cap. 3.

1776.—"**Mantur**—a text of the Shaster."—*Halhed, Code*, p. 17.

1817.—"... he is said to have found the great **mantra**, spell or talisman."—*Mill, Hist.* ii. 149.

MUSIC. There is no matter in which the sentiments of the people of India differ more from those of Englishmen than on that of music, and curiously enough the one kind of Western music which they appreciate, and seem to enjoy, is that of the bagpipe. This is testified by Captain Munro in the passage quoted below; but it was also shown during Lord Canning's visit to Lahore in 1860, in a manner which dwells in the memory of one of the present writers. The escort consisted of part of a Highland regiment. A venerable Sikh chief who heard the pipes exclaimed: 'That is indeed music! it is like that which we hear of in ancient story, which was so exquisite that the hearers became insensible (*behosh*).'

1780.—"The bagpipe appears also to be a favourite instrument among the natives. They have no taste indeed for any other kind of music, and they would much rather listen to this instrument a whole day than to an organ for ten minutes."—*Munro's Narrative*, 33.

MUSK, s. We get this word from the Lat. *muschus*, Greek μόσχος, and the latter must have been got, probably through Persian, from the Skt. *mushka*, the literal meaning of which is rendered in the old English phrase 'a cod of musk.' The oldest known European mention of the article is that which we give from St. Jerome; the oldest medical prescription is in a work of Aetius, of Amida (c. 540). In the quotation from Cosmas the word used is μόσχος, and *kastūri* is a Skt. name, still, according to Royle, applied to the musk-deer in the Himālaya. The transfer of the name to (or from) the article called by the Greeks καστόριον, which is an analogous product of the beaver, is curious. The Musk-deer (*Moschus moschiferus*, L.) is found throughout the Himālaya at elevations rarely (in summer) below 8000 feet, and extends east to the borders of Szechuen, and north to Siberia.

c. 390.—"Odoris autem suavitas, et diversa thymiamata, et amomum, et cyphi, oenanthe, **muscus**, et peregrini muris pellicula, quod dissolutis et amatoribus conveniat, nemo nisi dissolutus negat."—*St. Jerome*, in Lib. Secund. *adv. Jovinianum*, ed. *Vallarsii*, ii. col. 337.

c. 545.—"This little animal is the **Musk** (μόσχος). The natives call it in their own tongue καστοῦρι. They hunt it and shoot it, and binding tight the blood collected about the navel they cut this off, and this is the sweet smelling part of it, and what we call **musk**."—*Cosmas Indicopleustes*, Bk. xi.

["**Muske** commeth from Tartaria. ... There is a certaine beast in Tartaria, which is wilde and big as a wolfe, which beast they take aliue, and beat him to death with small stanes yᵗ his blood may be spread through his whole body, then they cut it in pieces, and take out all the bones, and beat the flesh with the blood in a mortar very smal, and dry it, and make purses to put it in of the skin, and these be the Cods of **Muske**."—*Caesar Frederick*, in *Hakl.* ii. 372.]

1673.—"**Musk**. It is best to buy it in the Cod ... that which openeth with a bright *Mosk* colour is best."—*Fryer*, 212.

MUSK-RAT, s. The popular name of the *Sorex caerulescens*, Jerdon, [*Crocidura caerulea*, Blanford], an animal having much the figure of the common shrew, but nearly as large as a small brown rat. It diffuses a strong musky odour, so penetrative that it is commonly asserted to affect bottled beer by running over the bottles in a cellar. As Jerdon judiciously observes, it is much more probable that the corks have been affected before being used in bottling; [and Blanford (*Mammalia*, 237) writes that "the absurd story ... is less credited in India than it formerly was, owing to the discovery that liquors bottled in Europe and exported to India are not liable to be tainted."] When the female is in heat she is often seen to be followed by a string of males giving out the odour strongly. Can this be the *mus peregrinus* mentioned by St. Jerome (see MUSK), as P. Vincenzo supposes?

c. 1590.—"Here (in Tooman Bekhrad, n. of Kabul R.) are also **mice** that have a fine **musky scent**."—*Ayeen*, by *Gladwin* (1800) ii. 166; [ed. *Jarrett*, ii. 406].

[1598.—"They are called sweet smelling **Rattes**, for they have a smell as if they were full of **Muske**."—*Linschoten*, Hak. Soc. i. 303.]

1653.—"Les rats d'Inde sont de deux sortes. ... La deuxiesme espece que les Portugais appellent *cheroso* ou odoriferant est de la figure d'vn furet" (a ferret), "mais extremement petit, sa morseure est veneneuse. Lorsqu'il entre en vne chambre l'on le sent incontinent, et l'on l'entend crier *krik, krik, krik*."—*De la Boullaye-le-Gouz*, ed. 1657, p. 256. I may note on this that Jerdon says of the *Sorex murinus*,—the large musk-rat of China, Burma, and the Malay countries, extending into Lower Bengal and Southern India, especially the Malabar coast, where it is said to be the common species (therefore probably that known to our author),—that the bite is considered venomous by the natives (*Mammals*, p. 54), [a belief for which, according to Blanford (*l.c.* p. 236), there is no foundation].

1672.—P. Vincenzo Maria, speaking of his first acquaintance with this animal (*il ratto del musco*), which occurred in the Capuchin Convent at Surat, says with simplicity (or malignity?): "I was astonished to perceive an odour so fragrant[1] in the vicinity of those most religious Fathers, with whom I was at the moment in conversation."—*Viaggio*, p. 385.

1681.—"This country has its vermin also. They have a sort of Rats they call **Musk-rats**, because they smell strong of musk. These the inhabitants do not eat of, but of all other sorts of Rats they do."—*Knox*, p. 31.

1789.—H. Munro in his *Narrative* (p. 34) absurdly enough identifies this animal with the **Bandicoot**, q.v.

1813.—See *Forbes, Or. Mem.* i. 42; [2nd. ed. i. 26].

MUSLIN, s. There seems to be no doubt that this word is derived from Mosul (Mauṣal or Mauṣil) on the Tigris,[2] and it has been from an old date the name of a texture, but apparently not always that of the thin semi-transparent tissue to which we now apply it. Dozy (p. 323) says that the Arabs employ *mausili* in the same sense as our word, quoting the *Arabian Nights* (Macnaghten's ed., i. 176, and ii. 159), in both of which the word indicates the material of a *fine* turban. [Burton (i. 211) translates 'Mosul stuff,' and says it may mean either of 'Mosul fashion,' or muslin.] The quotation from Ives, as well as that from Marco Polo, seems to apply to a different texture from what we call muslin.

1298.—"All the cloths of gold and silk that are called **Mosolins** are made in this country (Mausul)."—*Marco Polo*, Bk. i. chap. 5.

c. 1544.—"*Almussoli* est regio in Mesopotamia, in qua texuntur telae ex bombyce valde pulchrae, quae apud Syros et Aegyptios et apud mercatores Venetos appellantur **mussoli**, ex hoc regionis nomine. Et principes Aegyptii et Syri, tempore sestatis sedentes in loco honorauiliori induunt vestes ex hujusmodi **mussoli**."—*Andreae Bellunensis*, Arabicorum nominum quae in libris. *Avicennae* sparsim legebantur *Interpretatio*.

1573.—"... you have all sorts of Cotton-works, Handkerchiefs, long Fillets, Girdles ... and other sorts, by the *Arabians* called **Mossellini** (after the Country *Mussoli*, from whence they are brought, which is situated in Mesopotamia), by us **Muslin**."—*Rauwolff*, p. 84.

c. 1580.—"For the rest the said Agiani (misprint for Bagnani, **Banyans**) wear clothes of white **mussolo** or *sessa* (?); having their garments very long and crossed over the breast."—*Gasparo Balbi*, f. 33*b*.

1673.—"Le drap qu'on estend sur les matelas est d'une toille aussy fine que de la **mousceline**."—App. to *Journal d'Ant. Galland*, ii. 198.

1685.—"I have been told by several, that **muscelin** (so much in use here for cravats) and *Calligo* (!), and the most of the Indian linens, are made of nettles, and I see not the least improbability but that they may be made of the fibres of them."—*Dr. Hans Sloane to Mr. Ray*, in *Ray Correspondence*, 1848, p: 163.

c. 1760.—"This city (Mosul)'s manufacture is **Mussolin** [read **Mussolen**] (a cotton cloth) which they make very strong and pretty fine, and sell for the European and other markets."—*Ives, Voyage*, p. 324.

MUSNUD, s. H.—Ar. *masnad*, from root *sanad*, 'he leaned or rested upon it.' The large cushion, &c., used by native Princes in India, in place of a throne.

1752.—"Salabat-jing ... went through the ceremony of sitting on the **musnud** or throne."—*Orme*, ad. 1803, i. 250.

1757.—"On the 29th the Colonel went to the Soubah's Palace, and in the presence of all the Rajahs and great men of the court, led him to the **Musland**. ..."—*Reflexions by Luke Scrafton, Esq.*, ed. 1770, p. 93.

1803.—"The Peshwah arrived yesterday, and is to be seated on the **musnud**."—*A. Wellesley*, in *Munro's Life*, i. 343.

1809.—"In it was a **musnud**, with a carpet, and a little on one side were chairs on a white cloth."—*Ld. Valentia*, i. 346.

1824.—"They spread fresh carpets, and prepared the royal **musnud**, covering it with a magnificent shawl."—*Hajji Baba*, ed. 1835, p. 142.

1827.—"The Prince Tippoo had scarcely dismounted from his elephant, and occupied the **musnud**, or throne of cushions."—*Sir W. Scott, Surgeon's Daughter*, ch. xiv.

MUSSALLA, s. P.—H. (with change of sense from Ar. *maṣāliḥ*, pl. of *maslaḥa*)

1 "*Stupiva* d'vdire tanta fragranza." The Scotchman is laughed at for "feeling" a smell, but here the Italian *hears* one!

2 We have seen, however, somewhere an ingenious suggestion that the word really came from *Maisolia* (the country about Masulipatam, according to Ptolemy), which even in ancient times was famous for fine cotton textures.

'materials, ingredients,' lit. 'things for the good of, or things or affairs conducive to good.' Though sometimes used for the ingredients of any mixture, *e.g.* to form a cement, the most usual application is to spices, curry-stuffs and the like. There is a tradition of a very gallant Governor-General that he had found it very tolerable, on a sharp but brief campaign, to "rough it on **chuprassies** and **mussaulchees**" (qq.v.), meaning *chupatties* and *mussalla.*

1780.—"A dose of **marsall**, or purgative spices."—*Munro, Narrative,* 85.

1809.—"At the next hut the woman was grinding **missala** or curry-stuff on a flat smooth stone with another shaped like a rolling pin."—*Maria Graham,* 20.

MUSSUCK, s. The leathern water-bag, consisting of the entire skin of a large goat, stript of the hair and dressed, which is carried by a *bhishti* (see BHEESTY). Hind. *mashak,* Skt. *maśaka.*

[1610.—"**Mussocke.**" See under RUPEE.

[1751.—"7 hands of **Musuk**" (probably meaning *Bhistis*).—In *Yule, Hedges' Diary,* Hak. Soc. II. xi.]

1842.—"Might it not be worth while to try the experiment of having '**mussucks**' made of waterproof cloth in England!"—*Sir G. Arthur,* in *Ind. Adm. of Lord Ellenborough,* 220.

MUSSULMAN, adj. and s. Mahommedan. *Muslim,* 'resigning' or 'submitting' (*sc.* oneself to God), is the name given by Mahommed to the Faithful. The Persian plural of this is *Muslimân,* which appears to have been adopted as a singular, and the word *Muslimān* or *Musalmān* thus formed. [Others explain it as either from Ar. pl. *Muslimīn,* or from *Muslim-mān,* 'like a Muslim,' the former of which is adopted by Platts as most probable.]

1246.—"Intravimus terram **Biserminorum**. Isti homines linguam Comanicam loquebantur, et adhuc loquuntur; sed legem Sarracenorum tenent."—*Plano Carpini,* in *Rec. de Vogages,* &c. iv. 750.

c. 1540.—"... disse por tres vezes, *Lah, hilah, hilah, lah Muhamed roçol halah, o* **Massoleymoens** *e homes justos da santa ley de Mafamede.*"—*Pinto,* ch. lix.

1559.—"Although each horde (of Tartars) has its proper name, *e.g.* particularly the horde of the Savolhensians ... and many others, which are in truth Mahometans; yet do they hold it for a grievous insult and reproach to be called and styled *Turks*; they wish to be styled **Besermani**, and by this name the Turks also desire to be styled."—*Herberstein,* in *Ramusio,* ii. f. 171.

[1568.—"I have noted here before that if any Christian will become a **Busorman**, ... and be a Mahumetan of their religion, they give him any gifts ..."—*A. Edward,* in *Hakl.* i. 442.]

c. 1580.—"Tutti sopradetti Tartari seguitano la fede de' Turchi et alla Turchesca credono, ma si tēgono a gran vergogna, e molto si corrociano l'esser detti Turchi, secondo che all' incontro godono d'esser **Besurmani**, cioè gēte eletta, chiamati."—*Descrittione della Sarmatia Evropea* del magn. caval. *Aless. Gvagnino,* in *Ramusio,* ii. Pt. ii. f. 72.

1619.—"... i **Musulmani**, cioè i salvati: che cosa pazzamente si chiamano fra di loro i maomettani."—*P. della Valle,* i. 794.

"The precepts of the **Moslemans** are first, circumcision ..."—*Gabriel Sionita,* in *Purchas,* ii. 1504.

1653.—"... son infanterie d'Indistannis **Mansulmans**, ou Indiens de la secte des Sonnis."—*De la Boullaye-le-Gouz,* ed. 1657, 233.

1673.—"Yet here are a sort of bold, lusty, and most an end, drunken Beggars of the **Musslemen** Cast, that if they see a Christian in good clothes, mounted on a stately horse ... are presently upon their Punctilio's with God Almighty, and interrogate him, Why he suffers him to go a Foot, and in Rags, and this *Coffery* (see CAFFER) (Unbeliever) to vaunt it thus?"—*Fryer,* 91.

1788.—"We escape an ambiguous termination by adopting *Moslem* instead of *Musulman* in the plural number."—*Gibbon,* pref. to vol. iv.

MUSTEES, MESTIZ, &c., s. A **half-caste**. A corruption of the Port. *mestiço,* having the same meaning; "a mixling; applied to human beings and animals born of a father and mother of different species, like a mule" (*Bluteau*); French, *métis* and *métif.*

1546.—"The Governor in honour of this great action (the victory at Diu) ordered that all the **mestiços** who were in Dio should be inscribed in the Book, and that pay and subsistence should be assigned to them,—subject to the King's confirmation. For a regulation had been sent to India that no **mestiço** of India should be given pay or subsistence; for, as it was laid down, it was their duty to serve for nothing, seeing that they had their houses and heritages in the country, and being on their native soil were bound to defend it."—*Correa,* iv. 580.

1552.—"... the sight of whom as soon as they came, caused immediately to gather about them a number of the natives, Moors in belief, and Negroes with curly hair in appearance, and some of them only swarthy, as being **mistiços**."—*Barros*, I. ii. 1.

1586.—"... che se sono nati qua di donne indiane, gli domandano **mestizi**."—*Sassetti*, in *De Gubernatis*, 188.

1588.—"... an Interpretour ... which was a **Mestizo**, that is halfe an Indian, and halfe a Portugall."—*Candish*, in *Hakl.* iv. 337.

c. 1610.—"Le Capitaine et les Marchands estoient **Mestifs**, les autres Indiens Christianisez."—*Pyrard de Laval*, i. 165; [Hak. Soc. i. 78; also see i. 240]. This author has also **Métifs** (ii. 10; [Hak. Soc. i. 373]), and again: "... qu'ils appellent **Metices**, c'est à dire **Metifs**, meslez" (ii. 23; [Hak. Soc. ii. 38]).

"Ie vy vne moustre generalle de tous les Habitans portans armes, tant Portugais que **Metices** et Indiens, and se trouuerent environ 4000."—*Moquet*, 352.

[1615.—"**A Mestiso** came to demand passage in our junck."—*Cocks's Diary*, Hak. Soc. i. 216.]

1653.—(At Goa) "Les **Mestissos** sont da plusieurs sortes, mais fort mesprisez des **Reinols** et Castissos (see CASTEES, parce qu'il y a eu vn peu de sang noir dans la generation de leurs ancestres ... la tache d'auoir eu pour ancestre une Indienne leur demeure iusques à la centiesme generation: ils peuuent toutesfois estre soldats et Capitaines de forteresses ou de vaisseaux, sils font profession de suiure les armes, et s'ils se iettent du costé de l'Eglise ils peuuent estre Lecteurs, mais non Prouinciaux."—*De la Boullaye-le-Gouz*, ed. 1657, p. 226.

c. 1665.—"And, in a word, *Bengale* is a country abounding in all things; and 'tis for this very reason that so many Portuguese, **Mesticks**, and other Christians are fled thither."—*Bernier*, E.T. 140; [ed. *Constable*, 438].

[1673.—"Beyond the Outworks live a few Portugals **Musteroes** or **Misteradoes**."—*Fryer*, 57.]

1678.—"Noe Roman Catholick or Papist, whether English or of any other nation shall bear office in this Garrison, and shall have no more pay than 80 **fanams** per mensem, as private centinalls, and the pay of those of the Portuguez nation, as Europeans, **Musteeses**, and **Topasees**, is from 70 to 40 **fanams** per mensem."—*Articles and Orders ... of Ft. St. Geo.*, Madraspatam. In *Notes and Exts.*, i. 88.

1699.—"Wives of Freemen, **Mustees**."—Census of Company's Servants on the Coast, in *Wheeler*, i. 356.

1727.—"A poor Seaman had got a pretty **Mustice** Wife."—*A. Hamilton*, ii. 10; [ed. 1744, ii. 8].

1781.—"Eloped from the service of his Mistress a Slave Boy aged 20 years, or thereabouts, pretty white or colour of **Musty**, tall and slinder."—*Hicky's Bengal Gazette*, Feb. 24.

1799.—"August 13th. ... Visited by appointment ... Mrs. Carey, the last survivor of those unfortunate persons who were imprisoned in the Black Hole of Calcutta. ... This lady, now fifty-eight years of ago, as she herself told me, is ... of a fair **Mesticia** colour. ... She confirmed all which Mr. Holwell has said. ..."—*Note by* Thomas Boileau (an attorney in Calcutta, the father of Major-Generals John Theophilus and A. H. E. Boileau, R.E. (Bengal)), quoted in *Echoes of Old Calcutta*, 34.

1834.—"You don't know these Baboos. ... Most of them now-a-days have their **Misteesa** *Beebees*, and their Moosulmaunees, and not a few their *Gora* Beebees likewise."—*The Baboo*, &c., 167–168.

1868.—"These **Mestizas**, as they are termed, are the native Indians of the Philippines, whose blood has to a great extent perhaps been mingled with that of their Spanish rulers. They are a very exclusive people ... and have their own places of amusement ... and **Mestiza** balls, to which no one is admitted who does not don the costume of the country."—*Collingwood, Rambles of a Naturalist*, p. 296.

MUTTONGOSHT, s. (*i.e.* 'Muttonflesh.') Anglo-Indian domestic Hind. for 'Mutton.'

MYDAN, MEIDAUN, s. Hind. from Pers. *maidān*. An open space, an esplanade, parade-ground or green, in or adjoining a town; a *piazza* (in the Italian sense); any open plain with grass on it; a *chaugān* (see CHICANE ground; a battle-field. In Ar., usually, a hippodrome or race-course.

c. 1330.—"But the brethren were meanwhile brought out to the **Medan**, *i.e.*, the piazza of the City, where an exceeding great fire had been kindled. And Friar Thomas went forward to cast himself into the fire, but as he did so a certain Saracen caught him by the hood ..."—*Friar Odoric*, in *Cathay*, 63.

1618.—"When it is the hour of complines, or a little later to speak exactly, it is the time for the promenade, and every one goes on horseback to the **meidan**, which is always kept clean, watered by a number of men whose business this is, who water it carrying the water in skins slung over the shoulder, and usually well shaded and very cool."—*P. della Valle*, i. 707.

c. 1665.—"Celui (Quervansera) des Étrangers est bien plus spacieux que l'autre et est quarré, et tous deux font face au **Meidan**."—*Thevenot*, v. 214.

1670.—"Before this house is a great square

meidan or promenade, planted on all sides with great trees, standing in rows."—*Andriesz*, 35.

1673.—"The **Midan**, or open Space before the Caun's Palace, is an Oblong and Stately Piatzo, with real not belied Cloisters."—*Fryer*, 249.

1828.—"All this was done with as much coolness and precision, as if he had been at exercise upon the **maidaun**."—*The Kuzzilbash*, i. 223.

[1859. "A 24-pound howitzer, hoisted on to the maintop of the Shannon, looked menacingly over the **Maidan** (at Calcutta) ..."—*Oliphant, Narrative of Ld. Elgin's Mission*, i. 60.

MYNA, MINA, &c. s. Hind. *mainā*. A name applied to several birds of the family of starlings. The common *myna* is the *Acridotheres tristis* of Linn.; the southern Hill-Myna is the *Gracula*, also *Eulabes religiosa* of Linn.; the Northern Hill-Myna, *Eulabes intermedia* of Hay (see *Jerdon's Birds*, ii. Pt. i. 325, 337, 339). Of both the first and last it may be said that they are among the most teachable of imitative birds, articulating words with great distinctness, and without Polly's nasal tone. We have heard a wild one (probably the first), on a tree in a field, spontaneously echoing the very peculiar call of the black partridge from an adjoining jungle, with unmistakable truth. There is a curious description in Aelian (*De Nat. An.* xvi. 2) of an Indian talking bird which we thought at one time to be the *Myna*; but it seems to be nearer the **Shāmā**, and under that head the quotation will be found. [Mr. M'Crindle (*Invasion of India*, 186) is in favour of the *Myna*.]

[1590.—"The **Mynah** is twice the size of the *Shárak*, with glossy black plumage, but with the bill, wattles and tail coverts yellow. It imitates the human voice and speaks with great distinctness."—*Āīn*, ed. *Jarrett*, iii. 121.]

1631.—Jac. Bontius describes a kind of **Myna** in Java, which he calls *Pica, seu potius Sturnus Indicus*. "The owner, an old Mussulman woman, only lent it to the author to be drawn, after great persuasion, and on a stipulation that the beloved bird should get no swine's flesh to eat. And when he had promised accordingly, the *avis pessima* immediately began to chaunt: *Orang Nasarani catjor macan babi!* i.e. 'Dog of a Christian, eater of swine!'"—Lib. v. cap. 14, p. 67.

[1664.—"In the Duke's chamber there is a bird, given him by Mr. Pierce, the surgeon, comes from the East Indys, black the greatest part, with the finest collar of white about the neck; but talks many things and neyes like the horse, and other things, the best almost that ever I heard bird in my life."—*Pepys, Diary*, April 25. Prof. Newton in Mr. Wheatley's ed. (iv. 118) is inclined to identify this with the Myna, and notes that one of the earliest figures of the bird is by Eleazar Albin (*Nat. Hist. of Birds*, ii. pl. 38) in 1738.

[1703.—"Among singing birds that which in Bengall is called the **Minaw** is the only one that comes within my knowledge."—In *Yule, Hedges' Diary*, Hak. Soc. ii. cccxxxiv.]

1803.—"During the whole of our stay two **minahs** were talking almost incessantly, to the great delight of the old lady, who often laughed at what they said, and praised their talents. Her hookah filled up the interval."—*Ld. Valentia*, i. 227–8.

1813.—"The **myneh** is a very entertaining bird, hopping about the house, and articulating several words in the manner of the starling."—*Forbes, Or. Mem.* i. 47; [2nd ed. i. 32.]

1817.—"Of all birds the *chiong* (**miner**) is the most highly prized."—*Raffles, Java*, i. 260.

1875.—"A talking **mina** in a cage, and a rat-trap, completed the adornments of the veranda."—*The Dilemma*, ch. xii.

1878.—"The **myna** has no wit. ... His only way of catching a worm is to lay hold of its tail and pull it out of its hole,—generally breaking it in the middle and losing the bigger half."—*Ph. Robinson, In My Indian Garden*, 28.

1879.—"So the dog went to a **mainá**, and said: 'What shall I do to hurt this cat!'"—*Miss Stokes, Indian Fairy Tales*, 18.

"... beneath
Striped squirrels raced, the **mynas** perked
and picked.
The **nine brown sisters** chattered in the
thorn ..."

E. Arnold, The Light of Asia, Book. i.

N

***NABÓB**, s. Port. *Nabâbo*, and Fr. *Nabab*, from Hind. *Nawāb*, which is the Ar. pl. of sing. *Nāyab*, 'a deputy,' and was applied in a singular sense[1] to a delegate of the supreme chief, viz. to a Viceroy or chief Governor under the Great Mogul, *e.g.* the *Nawāb* of Surat, the *Nawāb* of Oudh, the *Nawāb* of Arcot, the *Nawāb Nāzim* of Bengal. From this use it became a title of rank without

1 Dozy says (2nd ed. 323) that the plural form has been adopted by mistake. Wilson says 'honorifically.' Possibly in this and other like cases it came from popular misunderstanding of the Arabic plurals. So we have omra, *i.e. umarā*, pl. of *amīr* used singularly and forming a plural *umrāyān*.

necessarily having any office attached. It is now a title occasionally conferred, like a peerage, on Mahommedan gentlemen of distinction and good service, as *Rāī* and *Rājā* are upon Hindus.

Nabob is used in two ways: (a) simply as a corruption and representative of *Nawāb*. We get it direct from the Port. *nabâbo*, see quotation from Bluteau below. (b) It began to be applied in the 18th century, when the transactions of Clive made the epithet familiar in England, to Anglo-Indians who returned with fortunes from the East; and Foote's play of 'The **Nabob**' (*Nábob*) (1768) aided in giving general currency to the word in this sense.

a.—

1604.—"... delante del **Nauabo** que es justicia mayor."—*Guerrero, Relacion*, 70.

1615.—"There was as **Nababo** in Surat a certain Persian Mahommedan (*Mouro Parsio*) called Mocarre Bethião, who had come to Goa in the time of the Viceroy Ruy Lourenço de Tavora, and who being treated with much familiarity and kindness by the Portuguese ... came to confess that it could not but be that truth was with their Law. ..."—*Bocarro*, p. 354.

1616.—"Catechumeni ergo parentes viros aliquot inducunt honestos et assessores **Nauabi**, id est, judicis supremi, cui consiliarii erant, uti et Proregi, ut libellum famosum adversus Pinnerum spargerent."—*Jarric, Thesaurus*, iii. 378.

1652.—"The **Nahab**[1] was sitting, according to the custom of the Country, bare-foot, like one of our Taylors, with a great number of Papers sticking between his Toes, and others between the Fingers of his left hand, which Papers he drew sometimes from between his Toes, sometimes from between his Fingers, and order'd what answers should be given to every one."—*Tavernier*, E.T. ii. 99; [ed. *Ball*, i. 291].

1653.—"... il prend la qualité de **Nabab** qui vault autant à dire que monseigneur."—*De la Boullaye-le-Gouz* (ed. 1657), 142.

1666.—"The ill-dealing of the **Nahab** proceeded from a scurvy trick that was play'd me by three Canary-birds at the Great Mogul's Court. The story whereof was thus in short ..."—*Tavernier*, E.T. ii. 57; [ed. *Ball*, i. 134].

1673.—"Gaining by these steps a nearer intimacy with the **Nabob**, he cut the new Business out every day."—*Fryer*, 183.

1675.—"But when we were purposing next day to depart, there came letters out of the Moorish Camp from the **Nabab**, the field-marshal of the Great Mogul. ..."—*Heiden Vervaarlijke Schip-Breuk*, 52.

1682.—"... Ray Nundelall ye **Nábabs** *Duan*, who gave me a most courteous reception, rising up and taking of me by ye hands, and ye like at my departure, which I am informed is a greater favour than he has ever shown to any *Franke*. ..."—*Hedges, Diary*, Oct. 27; [Hak. Soc. i. 42]. Hedges writes *Nabob, Nabab, Navab, Navob*.

1716.—"**Nabâbo**. Termo do Mogol. He o Titolo do Ministro que he Cabeca."—*Bluteau*, s.v.

1727.—"A few years ago, the **Nabob** or Vice-Roy of *Chormondel*, who resides at *Chickakal*, and who superintends that Country for the Mogul, for some Disgust he had received from the Inhabitants of Diu Islands, would have made a Present of them to the Colony of Fort St. George."—*A. Hamilton*, i. 374; [ed. 1744].

1742.—"We have had a great man called the **Nabob** (who is the next person in dignity to the Great Mogul) to visit the Governor. ... His lady, with all her women attendance, came the night before him. All the guns fired round the fort upon her arrival, as well as upon his; *he* and *she* are **Moors**, whose women are never seen by any man upon earth except their husbands."—Letter from Madras in *Mrs. Delany's Life*, ii. 169.

1743.—"Every governor of a fort, and every commander of a district had assumed the title of **Nabob** ... one day after having received the homage of several of these little lords, Nizam ul muluck said that he had that day seen no less than eighteen **Nabobs** in the Carnatic."—*Orme*, Reprint, Bk. i. 51.

1752.—"Agreed ... that a present should be made the **Nobab** that might prove satisfactory."—In *Long*, 33.

1773.—

"And though my years have passed in this
hard duty,
No Benefit acquired—no **Nabob's** booty."

Epilogue at Fort Marlborough, by *W. Marsden*, in *Mem*. 9.

1787.—

"Of armaments by flood and field;
Of **Nabobs** you have made to yield."

Ritson, in *Life and Letters*, i. 124.

1807.—"Some say that he is a Tailor who brought out a long bill against some of Lord Wellesley's staff, and was in consequence provided for; others say he was an adventurer, and sold knicknacks to the **Nabob** of Oude."—*Sir T. Munro*, in *Life*, i. 371.

1809.—"I was surprised that I had heard nothing from the **Nawaub** of the Carnatic."—*Ld. Valentia*, i. 381.

1 The word is so misprinted throughout this part of the English version.

c. 1858.—
"Le vieux **Nabab** et la Begum d'Arkate."
Leconte de Lisle, ed. 1872, p. 156.

b.—

[1764.—"Mogul Pitt and **Nabob** Bute."—*Horace Walpole, Letters*, ed. 1857, iv. 222 (*Stanf. Dict.*).]

1773.—"I regretted the decay of respect for men of family, and that a **Nabob** would not carry an election from them.

"Johnson: Why, sir, the **Nabob** will carry it by means of his wealth, in a country where money is highly valued, as it must he where nothing can be had without money; but if it comes to personal preference, the man of family will always carry it."—*Boswell, Journal of a Tour to the Hebrides*, under Aug. 25.

1777.—"In such a revolution ... it was impossible but that a number of individuals should have acquired large property. They did acquire it; and with it they seem to have obtained the detestation of their countrymen, and the appellation of **nabobs** as a term of reproach.—*Price's Tracts*, i. 13.

1780.—"The Intrigues of a **Nabob**, or Bengal the Fittest Soil for the Growth of Lust, Injustice, and Dishonesty. Dedicated to the Hon. the Court of Directors of the East India Company. By Henry Fred. Thompson. Printed for the Author." (A base book).

1783.—"The office given to a young man going to India is of trifling consequence. But he that goes out an insignificant boy, in a few years returns a great **Nabob**. Mr. Hastings says he has two hundred and fifty of that kind of raw material, who expect to be speedily manufactured into the merchantlike quality I mention."—*Burke, Speech on Fox's E.I. Bill*, in *Works and Corr.*, ed. 1852, iii. 506.

1787.—"The speakers for him (Hastings) were Burgess, who has completely done for himself in one day; Nichols, a lawyer; Mr. Vansittart, a **nabob**; Alderman Le Mosurier, a smuggler from Jersey; ... and Dempster, who is one of the good-natured candid men who connect themselves with every bad man 'they can find."—*Ld. Minto*, in *Life*, &c., i. 126.

1848.—"'Isn't he very rich?' said Rebecca.

"'They say all Indian **Nabobs** are enormously rich.'"—*Vanity Fair*, ed. 1867, i. 17.

1872.—"Ce train de vie facile ... suffit à me faire décerner ... le surnom de **Nabob** par les bourgeois et les visiteurs de la petite ville."—*Rev. des Deux Mondes*, xcviii. 938.

1874.—"At that time (c. 1830) the Royal Society was very differently composed from what it is now. Any wealthy or well-known person, any M.P. ... or East Indian **Nabob**, who wished to have F.R.S. added to his name, was sure to obtain admittance."—*Geikie, Life of Murchison*, i. 197.

1878.—"... A Tunis?—interrompit le duc. ... Alors pourquoi ce nom de **Nabab**?—Bah! les Parisiens n'y regardent pas de si près. Pour eux tout riche étranger est un **Nabab**, n'importe d'où il vienne."—*Le* **Nabab**, par *Alph. Daudet*, ch. i.

It is purism quite erroneously applied when we find **Nabob** in this sense miswritten *Nawab*; thus:

1878.—"These were days when India, little known still in the land that rules it, was less known than it had been in the previous generation, which had seen Warren Hastings impeached, and burghs[1] bought and sold by Anglo-Indian **Nawabs**."—*Smith's Life of Dr John Wilson*, 30.

But there is no question of purism in the following delicious passage:

1878.—"If ... the spirited proprietor of the Daily Telegraph had been informed that our aid of their friends the Turks would have taken the form of a tax upon paper, and a concession of the Levis to act as Commanders of Regiments of Bashi-Bozouks, with a request to the Generalissimo to place them in as forward a position as **Nabob** was given in the host of King David, the harp in Peterborough Court would not have twanged long to the tune of a crusade in behalf of the Sultan of Turkey."—*Truth*, April 11, p. 470. In this passage in which the wit is equalled only by the scriptural knowledge, observe that *Nabob* = Naboth, and *Naboth* = Uriah.

NANKEEN, s. A cotton stuff of a brownish yellow tinge, which was originally imported from China, and derived its name from the city of Nanking. It was not dyed, but made from a cotton of that colour, the *Gossypium religiosum* of Roxb., a variety of *G. herbaceum*. It was, however, imitated with dyed cotton in England, and before long exports of this imitation were made to China. Nankeen appears to be known in the Central Asia markets under the modified name of **Nanka** (see below).

1793-4.—"The land in this neighbourhood produces the cloth usually called **Nankeens** in Europe ... in that growing in the province of Kiangnan, of which the city of Nan-kin is the capital, the down is of the same yellow tinge

1 Qu. *boroughs?* The writer does injustice to his country when he speaks of *burghs* being bought and sold. The representation of Scotch *burghs* before 1832 was bad, but it never was purchassable. There are no *burghs* in England.

which it possesses when spun and woven into cloth."—*Staunton's Narr. of Ld. Macartney's Embassy*, ii. 425.

1794-5.—"The colour of **Nam-King** is thus natural, and not subject to fade. ... The opinion (that it was dyed) that I combat was the cause of an order being sent from Europe a few years ago to dye the pieces of **Nam-King** of a deeper colour, because of late they had grown paler."—*Van Braam's Embassy*, E.T. ii. 141.

1797.—"*China Investment per Upton Castle* ... Company's broad and narrow **Nankeen**, brown **Nankeen**."—In *Seton-Karr*, ii. 605.

c. 1809.—"Cotton in this district (*Puraniya* or *Purneea*) is but a trifling article. There are several kinds mentioned. ... The *Kukti* is the most remarkable, its wool having the colour of **nankeen** cloth, and it seems in fact to be the same material which the Chinese use in that manufacture."—*F. Buchanan*, in *Eastern India*, iii. 244. [See *Watt, Econ. Dict.* iv. 16, 29.]

1838.—"**Nanka** is imported in the greatest quantity (to Kabul) from Russia, and is used for making the outer garments for the people, who have a great liking to it. It is similar to **nankeen** cloth that comes to India from China, and is of a strong durable texture."—*Report by Baines*, in *Punjab Trade Report*, App. p. ix. See also p. clxvii.

1848.—"'Don't be trying to deprecate the value of the lot, Mr. Moss,' Mr. Hammerdown said; 'let the company examine it as a work of art—the attitude of the gallant animal quite according to natur'; the gentleman in a **nankeen**-jacket, his gun in hand, is going to the chase; in the distance a *banyhann* tree (see BANYAN-TREE) and a **pagody**."—*Vanity Fair*, i. 178.

NASSICK, n.p. *Nāsik*; Νασίκα of *Ptolemy* (vii. i. 63); an ancient city of Hindu sanctity on the upper course of the Godavery R., and the headquarter of a district of the same name in the Bombay Presidency. A curious discussion took place at the R. Geog. Society in 1867, arising out of a paper by Mr. (afterwards Sir) George Campbell, in which the selection of a capital for British India was determined on logical principles in favour of Nassick. But logic does not decide the site of capitals, though government by logic is quite likely to lose India. Certain highly elaborated magic squares and magic cubes, investigated by the Rev. A. H. Frost (*Cambridge Math. Jour.*, 1857) have been called by him *Nasik* squares, and Nasik cubes, from his residence in that ancient place (see *Encyc. Britan.* 9th ed. xv. 215).

***NAUTCH**, s. A kind of ballet-dance performed by women; also any kind of stage entertainment; an European ball. Hind. and Mahr. *nāch*, from Skt. *nṛitya*, dancing and stage-playing, through Prakrit *nachcha*. The word is in European use all over India. [A *poggly nautch* (see POGGLE) is a fancy-dress ball. Also see POOTLY NAUTCH.] Browning seems fond of using this word, and persists in using it wrongly. In the first of the quotations below he calls Fifine the 'European *nautch*,' which is like calling some Hindu dancing-girl 'the Indian ballet.' He repeats the mistake in the second quotation.

[1809.—"You Europeans are apt to picture to yourselves a **Nach** as a most attractive spectacle, but once witnessed it generally dissolves the illusion."—*Broughton, Letters from a Mahratta Camp*, ed. 1892, p. 142.]

1823.—"I joined Lady Macnaghten and a large party this evening to go to a **nâch** given by a rich native, Rouplall Mullich, on the opening of his new house."—*Mrs. Heber*, in *Heber*, ed. 1844, i. 37.

[1829.—"... a dance by black people which they calls a **Notch**. ..."—*Oriental Sport. Mag.* ed. 1873, i. 129.]

c. 1831.—"Elle (Begum Sumrou) fit enterrer vivante une jeune esclave, dont elle était jalouse, et donna à son mari un **nautch** (bal) sur cette horrible tombe."—*Jacquemont, Correspondance*, ii. 221.

1872.—
"... let be there was no worst
Of degradation spared Fifine; ordained
from first
To last, in body and soul, for one life-long
debauch,
The Pariah of the North, the European
Nautch!" *Fifine at the Fair*, 31.

1876.—
"... I locked in the swarth little lady—I swear,
From the head to the foot of her,—well quite
as bare!
'No **Nautch** shall cheat me,' said I, taking
my stand
At this bolt which I draw... ."
Natural Magic, in *Pacchiarotto*, &c.

NAUTCH-GIRL, s. (See BAYADÈRE, DANCING-GIRL.) The last quotation is a glorious jumble, after the manner of the compiler.

[1809.—"**Nach Girls** are exempted from all taxes, though they pay a kind of voluntary one monthly to a Fuqeer. ..."—*Broughton, Letters from a Mahratta Camp*, ed. 1892, p. 113-4.]

1825.—"The **Nâch women** were, as usual,

ugly, huddled up in huge bundles of red petticoats; and their exhibition as dull and insipid to an European taste, as could well be conceived."—*Heber*, ii. 102.

1836.—"In India and the East dancing-girls are trained called *Almeh*, and they give a fascinating entertainment called a **natch**, for which they are well paid."—In *R. Phillips, A Million of Facts*, 322.

NEELÁM, LEELÁM, s. Hind. *nīlām*, from Port. *leilão*. An auction or public **outcry**, as it used to be called in India (corresponding to Scotch *roup*; comp. Germ. *rufen*, and *outroop* of Linschoten's translator below). The word is, however, Oriental in origin, for Mr. C. P. Brown (MS. notes) points out that the Portuguese word is from Ar. *i'lām* (*al-i'lām*), 'proclamation, advertisement.' It is omitted by Dozy and Engelmann. How old the custom in India of prompt disposal by auction of the effects of a deceased European is, may be seen in the quotation from Linschoten.

1515.—"Pero d'Alpoym came full of sorrow to Cochin with all the apparel and servants of Afonso d'Alboquerque, all of which Dom Gracia took charge of; but the Governor (Lopo Soares) gave orders that there should be a **leilão** (auction) of all the wardrobe, which indeed made a very poor show. Dom Gracia said to D. Aleixo in the church, where they met: The Governor your uncle orders a **leilão** of all the old wardrobe of Afonso d'Alboquerque. I can't praise his intention, but what he has done only adds to my uncle's honour; for all the people will see that he gathered no rich Indian stuffs, and that he despised everything but to be foremost in honour."—*Correa*, ii. 469.

[1527.—"And should any man die, they at once make a **Leylam** of his property."—India Office MSS., *Corpo Chronologico*, vol. i. Letter of *Fernando Nunes* to the King, Sept. 7.

[1554.—"All the spoil of Mombasa that came into the general stock was sold by **leilão**."—*Castanheda*, Bk. ii. ch. 13.]

1598.—"In Goa there is holden a daylie assemblie ... which is like the meeting upõ the burse in Andwarpe ... and there are all kindes of Indian commodities to sell, so that in a manner it is like a Faire ... it beginneth in ye morning at 7 of the clocke, and continueth till 9 ... in the principal streete of the citie ... and is called the **Leylon**, which is as much as to say, as an *outroop* ... and when any man dieth, all his goods are brought thether and sold to the last pennieworth, in the same outroop, whosoever they be, yea although they were the Viceroyes goodes. ..."—*Linschoten*, ch. xxix.; [Hak. Soc. i. 184; and compare *Pyrard de Laval*, Hak. Soc. ii. 52, who spells the word **Laylon**].

c. 1610.—"... le mary vient frapper à la porte, dont la femme faisant fort l'estonnée, prie le Portugais de se cacher dans vne petite cuue à pourcelaine, et l'ayant fait entrer là dedans, et ferme tres bien à clef, ouurit la porte a son mary, qui ... le laissa tremper là iusqu'au lendemain matin, qu'il fit porter ceste cuue au marché, ou **lailan** ainsi qu'ils appellént. ..."—*Mocquet*, 344.

Linschoten gives an engraving of the *Rua Direita* in Goa, with many of these auctions going on, and the superscription: "*O* **Leilao** *que se faz cada dia pola menhã na Rua direita de Goa.*" The Portuguese word has taken root at Canton Chinese in the form *yélang;* but more distinctly betrays its origin in the Amoy form *lé-lang* and Swatow *loylang* (see *Giles;* also *Dennys's Notes and Queries*, vol. i.).

NEEM, s. The tree (N.O. *Meliaceae*) *Azadirachta indica*, Jussieu; Hind. *nīm* (and *nīb*, according to Playfair, *Taleef Shereef*, 170), Mahr. *nimb*, from Skt. *nimba*. It grows in almost all parts of India, and has a repute for various remedial uses. Thus poultices of the leaves are applied to boils, and their fresh juice given in various diseases; the bitter bark is given in fevers; the fruit is described as purgative and emollient, and as useful in worms, &c., whilst a medicinal oil is extracted from the seeds; and the gum also is reckoned medicinal. It is akin to the *bakain*, on which it grafts readily.

1563.—"*R.* I beg you to recall the tree by help of which you cured that valuable horse of yours, of which you told me, for I wish to remember it.

"*O.* You are quite right, for in sooth it is a tree that has a great repute as valuable and medicinal among nations that I am acquainted with, and the name among them all is **nimbo**. I came to know its virtues in the Balaghat, because with it I there succeeded in curing sore backs of horses that were most difficult to clean and heal; and these sores were cleaned very quickly, and the horses very quickly cured. And this was done entirely with the leaves of this tree pounded and put over the sores, mixt with lemon-juice. ..."—*Garcia*, f. 153.

1578.—"There is another tree highly medicinal ... which is called **nimbo**; and the Malabars call it *Bepole* [Malayāl. *vēppu*]."—*Acosta*, 284.

[1813.—"... the principal square ... regularly planted with beautiful **nym** or **lym**-trees."—*Forbes, Or. Mem.* 2nd ed. ii. 445.

[1856.—"Once on a time Guj Singh ... said to those around him, 'Is there any one who would leap down from that **limb** tree into the court?'"—*Forbes, Rās Mālā*, ed. 1878, p. 465.]

1877.—"The elders of the Clans sat every day on their platform, under the great **neem** tree in the town, and attended to all complaints."—*Meadows Taylor, Story*, &c., ii. 85.

NIGGER, s. It is an old brutality of the Englishman in India to apply this title to the natives, as we may see from Ives quoted below. The use originated, however, doubtless in following the old Portuguese use of *negros* for "the **blacks**" (q.v.), with no malice prepense, without any intended confusion between Africans and Asiatics.

1548.—"Moreover three blacks (**negros**) in this territory occupy lands worth 3000 or 4000 pardaos of rent; [they are related to one another, and are placed as guards in the outlying parts."—*S. Botelho, Cartas*, 111.

1582.—"A **nigroe** of John *Cambrayes*, Pilot to *Paulo de la Gama*, was that day run away to the Moores."—*Castañeda*, by N. L., f. 19.

[1608.—"The King and people **niggers**."—*Danvers, Letters*, i. 10.]

1622.—Ed. Grant, purser of the Diamond, reports capture of vessels, including a junk "with some stoor of **negers**, which was devided bytwick the Duch and the English."—*Sainsbury*, iii. p. 78.

c. 1755.—"You cannot affront them (the natives) more than to call them by the name of **negroe**, as they conceive it implies an idea of slavery."—*Ives, Voyage*, p. 23.

c. 1757.—"Gli Gesuiti sono missionarii e parocchi de' **negri** detti Malabar."—*Della Tomba*, 3.

1760.—"The Dress of this Country is entirely linnen, save Hats and Shoes; the latter are made of tanned Hides as in England ... only that they are no thicker than coarse paper. These shoes are neatly made by **Negroes**, and sold for about 10*d*. a Pr. each of which will last two months with care."—*MS. Letter of James Rennell*, Sept. 30.

1866.—"Now the political creed of the frequenters of dawk bungalows is too uniform ... it consists in the following tenets ... that Sir Mordaunt Wells is the greatest judge that ever sat on the English bench; and that when you hit a **nigger** he dies on purpose to spite you."—*The Dawk Bungalow*, p. 225.

***NIPA**, s. Malay *nīpah*.

a. The name of a stemless palm (*Nipa fruticans*, Thunb.), which abounds in estuaries from the Ganges delta eastwards, through Tenasserim and the Malay countries, to N. Australia, and the leaves of which afford the chief material used for thatch in the Archipelago. "In the Philippines," says Crawfurd, "but not that I am aware of anywhere else, the sap of the *Nipa* ... is used as a beverage, and for the manufacture of vinegar, and the distillation of spirits. On this account it yields a considerable part of the revenue of the Spanish Government" (*Desc. Dict.* p. 301). But this fact is almost enough to show that the word is the same which is used in sense **b**; and the identity is placed beyond question by the quotations from Teixeira and Mason.

b. Arrack made from the sap of a palm tree, a manufacture by no means confined to the Philippines. The Portuguese, appropriating the word *Nipa* to this spirit, called the tree itself *nipeira*.

a.—

1611.—"Other wine is of another kind of palm which is called **Nipa** (growing in watery places), and this is also extracted by distillation. It is very mild and sweet, and clear as pure water; and they say it is very wholesome. It is made in great quantities, with which ships are laden in Pegu and Tanasarim, Malaca, and the Philippines or Manila; but that of Tanasarim exceeds all in goodness."—*Teixeira, Relaciones*, i. 17.

1613.—"And then on from the marsh to the **Nypeiras** or wild-palms of the rivulet of Paret China."—*Godinho de Eredia*, 6.

"And the wild palms called **Nypeiras** ... from those flowers is drawn the liquor which is distilled into wine by an alembic, which is the best wine of India."—*Ibid.* 16*v*.

[1817.—"In the maritime districts, *atapi* or thatch, is made almost exclusively from the leaves of the **nípa** or *búyu*."—*Raffles, H. of Java*, 2nd ed. i. 185.]

1848.—"Steaming amongst the low swampy islands of the Sunderbunds ... the paddles of the steamer tossed up the large fruits of the **Nipa** *fruticans*, a low stemless palm that grows in the tidal waters of the Indian ocean, and bears a large head of nuts. It is a plant of no interest to the common observer, but of much to the geologist, from the nuts of a similar plant abounding in the tertiary formations at the mouth of the Thames, having floated about there in as great profusion as here, till buried deep in the silt and mud that now form the island of Sheppey."—*Hooker, Himalayan Journals*, i. 1–2.

1860.—"The **Nipa** is very extensively cultivated in the Province of Tavoy. From incisions in the stem of the fruit, toddy is extracted, which has very much the flavour of mead, and this extract, when boiled down, becomes sugar."—*Mason's Burmah*, p. 506.

1874.—"It (sugar) is also got from **Nipa** *fruticans*, Thunb., a tree of the low coast-regions, extensively cultivated in Tavoy."—*Hanbury and Flückiger*, 655.

These last quotations confirm the old travellers who represent Tenasserim as the great source of the **Nipa** spirit.

b.—

c. 1567.—"Euery yeere is there lade (at Tenasserim) some ships with Verzino, **Nipa**, and Benjamin."—*Ces. Federici* (E.T. in *Hakl.*), ii. 359.

1568.—"**Nipa**, qual' è vn Vino eccellentissimo che nasce nel fior d'vn arbore chiamato **Niper**, il cui liquor si distilla, e se ne fa vna beuanda eccellentissima."—*Ces. Federici*, in *Ramusio*, iii. 392*v*.

1583.—"I Portoghesi e noi altri di queste bande di quà non mangiamo nel Regno di Pegù pane di grano ... ne si beve vino; ma una certa acqua lambiccata da vn albero detto **Annippa**, ch' è alla bocca assai gustevole; ma al corpo giova e nuoce, secondo le complessioni de gli huomini."—*G. Balbi*, f. 127.

1591.—"Those of Tanaseri are chiefly freighted with Rice and **Nipar** wine, which is very strong."—*Barker's Account of Lancaster's Voyage*, in *Hakl.* ii. 592.

In the next two quotations *nipe* is confounded with coco-nut spirit.

1598.—"Likewise there is much wine brought thether, which is made of Cocus or Indian Nuttes, and is called **Nype** *de Tanassaria*, that is *Aqua-Composita of Tanassaria*."—*Linschoten*, 30; [Hak. Soc. i. 103].

"The Sura, being distilled, is called *Fula* (see FOOL'S RACK) or **Nipe**, and is an excellent *Aqua Vitae* as any is made in Dort."—*Ibid.* 101; [Hak. Soc. ii. 49].

[1616.—"One jar of **Neepe**."—*Foster, Letters*, iv. 162].

1623.—"In the daytime they did nothing but talk a little with one another, and some of them get drunk upon a certain wine they have of raisins, or on a kind of aqua vitæ with other things mixt in it, in India called **nippa**, which had been given them."—*P. della Valle*, ii. 669; [Hak. Soc. ii. 272].

We think there can be little doubt that the slang word **nip**, for a small dram of spirits, is adopted from **nipa**. [But compare Dutch *nippen*, 'to take a dram.' The old word *nippitatum* was used for 'strong drink'; see *Stanf. Dict.*]

NIRVÁNA, s. Skt. *nirvāṇa*. The literal meaning of this word is simply 'blown out,' like a candle. It is the technical term in the philosophy of the Buddhists for the condition to which they aspire as the crown and goal of virtue, viz. the cessation of sentient existence. On the exact meaning of the term see Childer's *Pali Dictionary*, s.v. *nibbāna*, an article from which we quote a few sentences below, but which covers ten double-column pages. The word has become common in Europe along with the growing interest in Buddhism, and partly from its use by Schopenhauer. But it is often employed very inaccurately, of which an instance occurs in the quotation below from Dr. Draper. The oldest European occurrence of which we are aware is in *Purchas*, who had met with it in the Pali form common in Burma, &c., *nibban*.

1626.—"After death they (the Talapoys) beleeve three Places, one of Pleasure *Scuum* (perhaps *sukham*) like the Mahumitane Paradise; another of Torment *Naxac* (read *Narac*); the third of Annihilation which they call **Niba**."—*Purchas, Pilgrimage*, 506.

c. 1815.—"... the state of **Niban**, which is the most perfect of all states. This consists in an almost perpetual extacy, in which those who attain it are not only free from troubles and miseries of life, from death, illness and old age, but are abstracted from all sensation; they have no longer either a thought or a desire."—*Sangermano, Burmese Empire*, p. 6.

1858.—"... Transience, Pain, and Unreality ... these are the characters of all existence, and the only true good is exemption from these in the attainment of **nirwāna**, whether that be, as in the view of the Brahmin or the theistic Buddhist, absorption into the supreme essence; or whether it be, as many have thought, absolute nothingness; or whether it be, as Mr. Hodgson quaintly phrases it, the *ubi* or the *modus* in which the infinitely attenuated elements of all things exist, in this last and highest state of abstraction from all particular modifications such as our senses and understandings are cognisant of."—*Yule, Mission to Ava*, 236.

"When from between the sál trees at Kusinára he passed into **nirwána**, he (Buddha) ceased, as the extinguished fire ceases."—*Ibid.* 239.

1869.—"What Bishop Bigandet and others represent as the popular view of the **Nirvâna**, in contradistinction to that of the Buddhist divines, was, in my opinion, the conception of Buddha and his disciples. It represented the entrance of the soul into rest, a subduing of all wishes and desires, indifference to joy and pain, to good and evil, an absorption of the soul into itself, and a freedom from the circle of existences from birth to death, and from death to a new birth. This is still the meaning which educated people attach to it, whilst **Nirvâna** suggests rather a kind of Mohammedan Paradise or of blissful Elysian fields to the minds of the larger masses."—*Prof. Max Müller, Lecture on Buddhistic Nihilism*, in *Trübner's Or. Record*, Oct. 16.

1875.—"**Nibbānam.** Extinction; destruction; annihilation; annihilation of being, **Nirvāṇa**; annihilation of human passion, Arhatship or final sanctification. ... In Trübner's Record for July, 1870, I first propounded a theory which meets all the difficulties of the question, namely, that the word **Nirvāṇa** is used to designate two different things, the state of blissful sanctification called Arhatship, and the annihilation of existence in which Arhatship ends."—*Childers, Pali Dictionary*, pp. 265–266.

"But at length reunion with the universal intellect takes place; **Nirwana** is reached, oblivion is attained ... the state in which we were before we were born."—*Draper, Conflict*, &c., 122.

1879.—
"And how—in fulness of the times—it fell
That Buddha died ...
And how a thousand thousand crores since then
Have trod the Path which leads whither he went
Unto **Nirvâna** where the Silence lives."
Sir E. Arnold, Light of Asia, 237.

***NOKAR**, s. A servant, either domestic, military, or civil, also pl. *Nokar-logue*, 'the servants.' Hind. *naukar*, from Pers. and *naukar-lōg*. Also *naukar-chākar*, 'the servants,' one of those jingling double-barrelled phrases in which Orientals delight even more than Englishmen (see LOOTY). As regards Englishmen, compare hugger-mugger, hurdy-gurdy, tip-top, highty-tighty, higgledy-piggledy, hocus-pocus, tit for tat, topsy-turvy, harum-scarum, roly-poly, fiddle-faddle, rump and stump, slip-slop. In this case *chākar* (see CHACKUR) is also Persian. *Naukar* would seem to be a Mongol word introduced into Persia by the hosts of Chinghiz. According to I. J. Schmidt, *Forschungen im Gebiete der Volker Mittel Asiens*, p. 96, **nükur** is in Mongol, 'a comrade, dependent, or friend.'

c. 1407.—"L'Emir Khodaidad fit partir avec ce député son serviteur (**naukar**) et celui de Mirza Djihanghir. Ces trois personnages joignent la cour auguste. ..."—*Abdurrazzāk*, in *Notices et Extraits*, XIV. i. 146.

c. 1660.—"Mahmúd Sultán ... understood accounts, and could reckon very well by memory the sums which he had to receive from his subjects, and those which he had to pay to his '**naukars**' (apparently armed followers)."—*Abulghāzi*, by *Desmaisons*, 271.

[1810.—"**Noker.**" See under CHACKUR.

[1834.—"Its (Balkh) present population does not amount to 2000 souls; who are chiefly ... the remnant of the Kara **Noukur**, a description of the militia established here by the Afgans."—*Burnes, Travels into Bokhara*, i. 238.]

1840.—"**Noker**, 'the servant'; this title was borne by Tuli the fourth son of Chenghiz Khan, because he was charged with the details of the army and the administration."—*Hammer, Golden Horde*, 460.

***NON-REGULATION**, adj. The style of certain Provinces of British India (administered for the most part under the more direct authority of the Central Government in its Foreign Department), in which the ordinary Laws (or **Regulations**, as they were formerly called) are not in force, or are in force only so far as they are specially declared by the Government of India to be applicable. The original theory of administration in such Provinces was the union of authority in all departments under one district chief, and a kind of paternal despotism in the hands of that chief But by the gradual restriction of personal rule, and the multiplication of positive laws and rules of administration, and the division of duties, much the same might now be said of the difference between *Regulation* and *Non-regulation* Provinces that a witty Frenchman said of Intervention and Non-intervention:—"La *Non-intervention* est une phrase politique et technique qui veut dire enfin à-peu-près la même chose que *l'Intervention*."

Our friend Gen. F. C. Cotton, R.E., tells us that on Lord Dalhousie's visit to the Neilgherry Hills, near the close of his government, he was riding with the Governor-General to visit some new building. Lord Dalhousie said to him: "It is not a thing that one must say in public, but I would give a great deal that the whole of India should be *Non-regulation*."

The Punjab was for many years the greatest example of a Non-regulation Province. The chief survival of that state of things is that there, as in Burma and a few other provinces, military men are still eligible to hold office in the civil administration.

1860.—"... Nowe what ye ffolke of Bengala worschyppen Sir Jhone discourseth lityl. This moche wee gadere. Some worschyppin ane Idole yclept Regulacioun and some worschyppen Non-regulacion (*veluti* Gog et Magog). ..."—Ext. from a MS. of *The Travels of Sir John Mandevill in the E. Indies*, lately discovered.

1867.—"... We believe we should indicate the sort of government that Sicily wants, tolerably well to Englishmen who know anything of India, by saying that it should be treated in great measure as a '**non-regulation**' province."—*Quarterly Review*, Jan. 1867, p. 135.

1883.—"The Delhi district, happily for all, was a **non-regulation** province."—*Life of Ld. Lawrence*, i. 44.

NULLAH, s. Hind. *nālā*. A watercourse; not necessarily a dry watercourse, though this is perhaps more frequently indicated in the Anglo-Indian use.

1776.—"When the water falls in all the **nullahs**. ..."—*Halhed's Code*, 52.

c. 1785.—"Major Adams had sent on the 11th Captain Hebbert ... to throw a bridge over Shinga **nullah**."—*Carraccioli, Life of Clive*, i. 93.

1789.—"The ground which the enemy had occupied was entirely composed of sandhills and deep **nullahs**. ..."—*Munro, Narrative*, 224.

1799.—"I think I can show you a situation where two embrasures might be opened in the bank of the **nullah** with advantage."—*Wellington, Despatches*, i. 26.

1817.—"On the same evening, as soon as dark, the party which was destined to open the trenches marched to the chosen spot, and before daylight formed a **nullah** ... into a large parallel."—*Mill's Hist.* v. 377.

1843.—"Our march tardy because of the **nullahs**. Watercourses is the right name, but we get here a slip-slop way of writing quite contemptible."—*Life of Sir C. Napier*, ii. 310.

1860.—"The real obstacle to movement is the depth of the **nullahs** hollowed out by the numerous rivulets, when swollen by the rains."—*Tennent's Ceylon*, ii. 574.

***NUMERICAL AFFIXES, COEFFICIENTS, or DETERMINATIVES.**[1] What is meant by these expressions can perhaps be best elucidated by an extract from the *Malay Grammar* of the late venerable John Crawfurd:

"In the enumeration of certain objects, the Malay has a peculiar idiom which, as far as I know, does not exist in any other language of the Archipelago. It is of the same nature as the word 'head,' as we use it in the tale of cattle, or 'sail' in the enumeration of ships; but in Malay it extends to many familiar objects. *Alai*, of which the original meaning has not been ascertained, is applied to such tenuous objects as leaves, grasses, &c.; *Batang*, meaning 'stem,' or 'trunk,' to trees, logs, spears, and javelins; *Bantak*, of which the meaning has not been ascertained, to such objects as rings; *Bidang*, which means 'spreading' or 'spacious,' to mats, carpets, thatch, sails, skins, and hides; *Biji*, 'seeds,' to corn, seeds, stones, pebbles, gems, eggs, the eyes of animals, lamps, and candlesticks," and so on. Crawfurd names 8 or 9 other terms, one or other of which is always used in company with the numeral, in ennumerating different classes of objects, as if, in English, idiom should compel us to say 'two *stems* of spears,' 'four *spreads* of carpets,' 'six *corns* of diamonds.' As a matter of fact we do speak of 20 *head* of cattle, 10 *file* of soldiers, 100 *sail* of ships, 20 *pieces* of cannon, a dozen *stand* of rifles. But still the practice is in none of these cases obligatory, it is technical and exceptional; insomuch that I remember, when a boy, in old Reform-Bill days, and when disturbances were expected in a provincial town, hearing it stated by a well-informed lady that a great proprietress in the neighbourhood was so alarmed that she had ordered from town *a whole stand of muskets!*

To some small extent the idiom occurs also in other European languages, including French and German. Of French I don't remember any example now except *tête* (de betail), nor of German except *Stück*, which is, however, almost as universal as the Chinese *piecey*. A quaint example dwells in my memory of a German courier, who, when asked whether he had any employer at the moment, replied: '*Ja freilich! dreizehn* Stück *Amerikaner!*'

The same peculiar idiom that has been described in the extract from Crawfurd as existing in Malay, is found also in Burmese. The Burmese affixes seem to be more numerous, and their classification to be somewhat more arbitrary and sophisticated. Thus *oos*, a root implying 'chief' or 'first,' is applied to kings, divinities, priests, &c.; *Yauk*, 'a male,' to rational beings not divine; *Gaung*, 'a brute beast,' to irrational beings;

1 Other terms applied have been *Numeralia*, Quantitative Auxiliaries, Numeral Auxiliaries, Segregatives, &c.

Pya implying superficial extent, to dollars, countries, dishes, blankets, &c.; *Lun*, implying rotundity, to eggs, loaves, bottles, cups, toes, fingers, candles, bamboos, hands, feet, &c.; *Tseng* and *Gyaung*, 'extension in a straight line,' to rods, lines, spears, roads, &c.

The same idiom exists in Siamese, and traces of it appear in some of the vocabularies that have been collected of tribes on the frontier of China and Tibet, indicated by the fact that the numerals in such vocabularies in various instances show identity of origin in the essential part of the numeral, whilst a different aspect is given to the whole word by a variation in what appears to be the numeral-affix[1] (or what Mr. Brian Hodgson calls the 'servile affix'). The idiom exists in the principal vernaculars of China itself, and it is a transfer of this idiom from Chinese dialects to Pigeon-English which has produced the *piecey*, which in that quaint jargon seems to be used as the universal numerical affix ("Two *piecey* cooly," "three *piecey* dollar," &c.).

This one **pigeon** phrase represents scores that are used in the vernaculars. For in some languages the system has taken what seems an extravagant development, which must form a great difficulty in the acquisition of colloquial use by foreigners. Some approximate statistics on this subject will be given below.

The idiom is found in Japanese and Corean, but it is in these cases possibly not indigenous, but an adoption from the Chinese.

It is found in several languages of C. America, *i.e.* the Quiché of Guatemala, the Nahault of Mexico Proper; and in at least two other languages (Tep and Pirinda) of the same region. The following are given as the coefficients or determinatives chiefly used in the (Nahualt or) Mexican. Compare them with the examples of Malay and Burmese usage already given:

Tetl (a stone) used for roundish or cylindrical objects; *e.g.* eggs, beans, cacao beans, cherries, prickly-pears, Spanish loaves, &c., also for books, and fowls:

Pantli (?) for long rows of persons and things; also for walls and furrows:

Tlamantli (from *mana*, to spread on the ground), for shoes, dishes, basins, paper, &c., also for speeches and sermons:

Olotl (maize-grains) for ears of maize, cacao-pods, bananas: also for flint arrow-heads (see *W. v. Humboldt*, *Kawi-Sprache*, ii. 265).

I have, by the kind aid of my friend Professor Terrien de la Couperie, compiled a list of nearly fifty languages in which this curious idiom exists. But it takes up too much space to be inserted here. I may, however, give his statistics of the number of such determinatives, as assigned in the grammars of some of these languages In Chinese vernaculars, from 33 in the Shanghai vernacular to 110 in that of Fuchan. In Corean, 12; in Japanese, 16; in Annamite, 106; in Siamese, 24; in Shan, 42; in Burmese, 40; in Malay and Javanese, 19.

If I am not mistaken, the propensity to give certain technical and appropriated titles to couples of certain beasts and birds, which had such an extensive development in old English sporting phraseology, and still partly survives, had its root in the same state of mind, viz. difficulty in grasping the idea of abstract numbers, and a dislike to their use. Some light to me was, many years ago, thrown upon this feeling, and on the origin of the idiom of which we have been speaking, by a passage in a modern book, which is the more noteworthy as the author does not make any reference to the existence of this idiom in any language, and possibly was not aware of it:

"On entering into conversation with the (Red) Indian, it becomes speedily apparent that he is unable to comprehend the idea of abstract numbers. They exist in his mind only as associated ideas. He has a distinct conception of five dogs or five deer, but he is so unaccustomed to the idea of number as a thing apart from specific objects, that I have tried in vain to get an Indian to admit that the idea of the number five, as associated in his mind with five dogs, is identical, as far as number is concerned, with that of five fingers."—(*Wilson's Pre-historic Man*, 1st ed. ii. 470.) [Also see *Tylor*, *Primitive Culture*, 2nd ed. i. 252 *seqq.*].

Thus it seems probable that the use of the *numeral* co-efficient, whether in the Malay idiom or in our old sporting phraseology, is a kind of *survival* of the effort to bridge the difficulty felt, in identifying abstract numbers as applied to different objects, by the introduction of a common concrete term.

Traces of a like tendency, though probably

1 See Sir H. Yule's *Introductory Essay* to Capt. Gill's *River of Golden Sand*, ed. 1883, pp. [127], [128].

grown into a mere fashion and artificially developed, are common in Hindustani and Persian, especially in the official written style of *munshīs*, who delight in what seemed to me, before my attention was called to the Indo-Chinese idiom, the wilful surplusage (*e.g.*) of two 'sheets' (*fard*) of letters, also used with quilts, carpets, &c.; three 'persons' (*nafar*) of barḳandāzes; five 'rope' (*rās*) of buffaloes; ten 'chains' (*zanjīr*) of elephants; twenty 'grips' (*ḳabẓa*) of swords, &c. But I was not aware of the extent of the idiom in the *munshī's* repertory till I found it displayed in Mr. Carnegy's *Kachahri Technicalities*, under the head of *Muḥāwara* (Idioms or Phrases). Besides those just quoted, we there find *'adad* ('number') used with coins, utensils, and sleeveless garments; *dāna* ('grain') with pearls and coral beads; *dast* ('hand') with falcons, &c., shields, and robes of honour; *jild* (volume, lit. 'skin') with books; *muhār* ('nose-bit') with camels; *ḳiṭa* ('portion,' *piecey!*) with precious stones, gardens, tanks, fields, letters; *manzil* ('a stage on a journey, an alighting place') with tents, boats, houses, carriages, beds, howdas, &c.; *sāz* ('an instrument') with guitars, &c.; *silk* ('thread') with necklaces of all sorts, &c. Several of these, with others purely Turkish, are used also in Osmanli Turkish.[1]

NUZZER, s. Hind. from Ar. *nazr* or *nazar* (prop. *nadhr*), primarily 'a vow or votive offering'; but, in ordinary use, a ceremonial, properly an offering from an inferior to a superior, the converse of *in'ām*. The root is the same as that of *Nazarite* (Numbers, vi. 2).

[1765.—"The congratulatory **nazirs**, &c., shall be set opposite my ordinary expenses; and if ought remains, it shall go to Poplar, or some other hospital."—Letter of *Ld. Clive*, Sept. 30, in *Verelst, View of Bengal*, 127.

[c. 1775.—"The Governor lays before the board two bags ... which were presented to him in **nizzers**. ..."—Progs. of Council, quoted by Fox in speech against W. Hastings, in *Bond*, iv. 201.]

1782.—"Col. Monson was a man of high and hospitable household expenses; and so determined against receiving of presents, that he would not only not touch a **nazier** (a few silver rupees, or perhaps a gold mohor) always presented by **country** gentlemen, according to their rank. ..."—*Price's Tracts*, ii. 61.

1785.—"Presents of ceremony, called **nuzzers**, were to many a great portion of their subsistence. ..."—Letter in *Life of Colebrooke*, 16.

1786.—Tippoo, even in writing to the French Governor of Pondichery, whom it was his interest to conciliate, and in acknowledging a present of 500 muskets, cannot restrain his insolence, but calls them "sent by way of **nuzr**."—*Select Letters of Tippoo*, 377.

1809.—"The Aumil himself offered the **nazur** of fruit."—*Ld. Valentia*, i. 453.

[1832.—"I ... looked to the Meer for explanation; he told me to accept Muckabeg's '**nuzza**.'"—*Mrs. Meer Hassan Ali, Obsèrvns.* i. 193.]

1876.—"The Standard has the following curious piece of news in its Court Circular of a few days ago:—

'Sir Salar Jung was presented to the Queen by the Marquis of Salisbury, and offered his **Muggur** as a token of allegiance, which her Majesty touched and returned.'"—*Punch*, July 15.

For the true sense of the word so deliciously introduced instead of **Nuzzer**, see MUGGUR.

O

OMLAH, s. This is properly the Ar. pl. *'amalat*, *'amalā*, of *'āmil* It is applied on the Bengal side of India to the native officers, clerks, and other staff of a civil court or **cutcherry** (q.v.) collectively.

c. 1778.—"I was at this place met by the **Omlah** or officers belonging to the establishment, who hailed my arrival in a variety of boats dressed out for the occasion."—*Hon. R. Lindsay*, in *Lives of the Lindsays*, iii. 167.

1866.—"At the worst we will hint to the **Omlahs** to discover a fast which it is necessary they shall keep with great solemnity."—*Trevelyan*, *The Dawk Bungalow*, in *Fraser*, lxxiii. 390.

The use of an English plural, *omlahs*, here is incorrect and unusual; though *omrahs* is used (see next word).

1878.—"... the subordinate managers, young, inexperienced, and altogether in the hands of the **Omlah**."—*Life in the Mofussil*, ii. 6.

OMRAH, s. This is properly, like the last word, an Ar. pl. (*Umarā*, pl. of *Amīr*—see

1 Some details on the subject of these determinatives, in reference to languages on the eastern border of India, will be found in Prof. Max Müller's letter to Bunsen in the latter's *Outlines of the Phil. of Universal History*, 1. 896 *seqq.*; as well as in W. von Humboldt, quoted above. Prof. Max Müller refers to Humboldt's *Complete Works*, vi. 402; but this I have not been able to find, nor, in either writer, any suggested *rationale* of the idiom.

AMEER), and should be applied collectively to the higher officials at a Mahommedan Court, especially that of the Great Mogul. But in old European narratives it is used as a singular for a lord or grandee of that Court; and indeed in Hindustani the word was similarly used, for we have a Hind. plural *umarāyān*, 'omrahs.' From the remarks and quotations of Blochmann, it would seem that *Manṣabdārs* from the commandant of 1000 upwards, were styled *umarā-i-kabār*, or *umara-i-'izām*, 'Great Amīrs'; and these would be the *Omrahs* properly. Certain very high officials were styled *Amīr-ul-Umarā* (*Āīn*, i. 239–240), a title used first at the Court of the Caliphs.

1616.—"Two **Omrahs** who are great Commanders."—*Sir T. Roe.*

["The King lately sent out two **Vmbras** with horse to fetch him in."—*Ibid.* Hak. Soc. ii. 417; in the same page he writes *Vmreis*, and in ii. 445, *Vmraes.*]

c. 1630.—"Howbeit, out of this prodigious rent, goes yearely many great payments: to his Leiftenants of Provinces, and **Vmbrayes** of Townes and Forts."—*Sir T. Herbert*, p. 55.

1638.—"Et sous le commandement de plusieurs autres seigneurs de ceux qu'ils appellent **Ommeraudes**."—*Mandelslo*, Paris, 1659, p. 174.

1653.—"Il y a quantité d'elephans dans les Indes ... les **Omaras** s'en seruent par grandeur."—*De la Boullaye-le-Gouz*, ed. 1657, p. 250.

c. 1664.—"It is not to be thought that the **Omrahs**, or Lords of the Mogul's Court, are sons of great Families, as in *France* ... these **Omrahs** then are commonly but Adventurers and Strangers of all sorts of Nations, some of them slaves; most of them without instruction, which the Mogul thus raiseth to Dignities as he thinks good, and degrades them again, as he pleaseth."—*Bernier*, E.T. 66; [ed. *Constable*, 211].

c. 1666.—"Les **Omras** sont les grand seigneurs du Roiaume, qui sont pour la plupart Persans ou fils de Persans."—*Thevenot*, v. 307.

1673.—"The President ... has a Noise of Trumpets ... an Horse of State led before him, a *Mirchal* (a Fan of Ostrich Feathers) to keep off the Sun, as the **Ombrahs** or Great Men have."—*Fryer*, 86.

1676.—

"Their standard, planted on the battlement,
Despair and death among the soldiers sent;
You the bold **Omrah** tumbled from the wall,
And shouts of victory pursued the fall."

Dryden, Aurengzebe, ii. 1.

1710.—"Donna Juliana ... let the Heer Ambassador know ... that the Emperor had ordered the **Ammaraws** Enay Ullah Chan (&c.) to take care of our interests."—*Valentijn*, iv. *Suratte*, 284.

1727.—"You made several complaints against former Governors, all of which I have here from several of my **Umbras**."—*Firmān of Aurangzīb*, in *A. Hamilton*, ii. 227; [ed. 1744, i. 231].

1791.—"... les **Omrahs** ou grands seigneurs Indiens. ..."—*B. de St. Pierre, La Chaumière Indienne*, 32.

OOJYNE, n.p. *Ujjayanī*, or, in the modern vernacular, *Ujjain*, one of the most ancient of Indian cities, and one of their seven sacred cities. It was the capital of King Vikramaditya, and was the first meridian of Hindu astronomers, from which they calculated their longitudes.

The name of Ujjain long led to a curious imbroglio in the interpretation of the Arabian geographers. Its meridian, as we have just mentioned, was the zero of longitude among the Hindus. The Arab writers borrowing from the Hindus wrote the name apparently *Azīn*, but this by the mere omission of a diacritical point became *Arīn*, and from the Arabs passed to medieval Christian geographers as the name of an imaginary point on the equator, the intersection of the central meridian with that circle. Further, this point, or transposed city, had probably been represented on maps, as we often see cities on medieval maps, by a cupola or the like. And hence the "Cupola of *Arin* or *Arym*," or the "Cupola of the Earth" (*Al-ḳubba al-arḍh*) became an established commonplace for centuries in geographical tables or statements. The idea was that just 180° of the earth's circumference was habitable, or at any rate cognizable as such, and this meridian of *Arin* bisected this habitable hemisphere. But as the western limit extended to the Fortunate Isles, it became manifest to the Arabs that the central meridian could not be so far east as the Hindu meridian of *Arin* (or of *Lanka*, *i.e.* Ceylon). (See quotation from the *Aryabhatta*, under JAVA.) They therefore shifted it westward, but shifted the mystic *Arin* along the equator westward also. We find also among medieval European students (as with Roger Bacon, below), a confusion between Arin and Syene. This Reinaud supposes to have arisen from the Ἐσσινὰ ἐμπόριον of Ptolemy, a place which he locates on the Zanzibar coast, and approximating to the shifted position of

Arin. But it is perhaps more likely that the confusion arose from some survival of the real name *Azīn*. Many conjectures were vainly made as to the origin of *Arym*, and M. Sedillot was very positive that nothing more could be learned of it than he had been able to learn. But the late M. Reinaud completely solved the mystery by pointing out that *Arin* was simply a corruption of *Ujjain*. Even in Arabic the mistake had been thoroughly ingrained, insomuch that the word *Arīn* had been adopted as a generic name for a place of medium temperature or qualities (see *Jorjānī*, quoted below).

c. A.D. 150.—"Ὀζηνὴ βασίλειον Τιαστανοῦ."—*Ptol.* VII. i. 63.

c. 930.—"The Equator passes between east and west through an island situated between Hind and Habash (Abyssinia), and a little south of these two countries. This point, half way between north and south is cut by the point (meridian?) half way between the Eternal Islands and the extremity of China; it is what is called *The Cupola of the Earth*."—*Maṣ'ūdī*, i. 180–181.

c. 1020.—"Les Astronomes ... ont fait correspondre la ville d'**Odjein** avec le lieu qui dans le tableau des villes inséré dans les tables astronomiques a reçu le nom d'**Arin**, et qui est supposé situé sur les bords de la mer. Mais entre **Odjein** et la mer, il y a près de cent *yodjanas*."—*Al-Birūnī*, quoted by *Reinaud, Intro. to Abulfeda*, p. ccxlv.

c. 1267.—"Meridianum vero latus Indiae descendit a tropico Capricorni, et secat aequinoctialem circulum apud Montem Maleum et regiones ei conterminos et transit per *Syenem*, quae nunc **Arym** vocatur. Nam in libro cursuum planetarum dicitur quod duplex est *Syene;* una sub solstitio ... alia sub aequinoctiali circulo, de quâ nunc est sermo, distans per xc gradus ab occidente, sed magis ab oriente elongatur propter hoc, quod longitudo habitabilis major est quam medietas coeli vel terrae, et hoc versus orientem."—*Roger Bacon, Opus Majus*, ed. London, 1633, p. 195.

c. 1300.—"Sous la ligne équinoxiale, au milieu du monde, là où il n'y a pas de latitude, se trouve le point de la corrélation servant de centre aux parties que se coupent entre elles. ... Dans cet endroit et sur ce point se trouve le lieu nommé *Coupole de* **Azin** ou *Coupole de* **Arin**. Là est un château grand, élevé et d'un accès difficile. Suivant Ibn-Alaraby, c'est le séjour des démons et la trône d'Eblis. ... Les Indiens parlent également de ce lieu, et débitent des fables à son sujet."—*Arabic Cosmography*, quoted by *Reinaud*, p. ccxliii.

c. 1400.—"**Arin** (*al-arīn*). Le lieu d'une proportion moyenne dans les choses ... un point sur la terre à une hauteur égale des deux poles, en sorte que la nuit n'y empiète point sur la durée du jour, ni le jour sur la durée de la nuit. Ce mot a passé dans l'usage ordinaire, pour signifier d'une manière générale un lieu d'une temperature moyenne."—Livre de *Definitions* du *Seïd Scherif Zeineddin* ... fils de *Mohammed Djordjani*, trad. de *Silv. de Sacy, Not. et Extr.* x. 39.

1498.—"Ptolemy and the other philosophers, who have written upon the globe, thought that it was spherical, believing that this hemisphere was round as well as that in which they themselves dwelt, the centre of which was in the island of **Arin**, which is under the equinoctial line, between the Arabian Gulf and the Gulf of Persia."—*Letter of Columbus*, on his Third Voyage, to the King and Queen. *Major's Transl.*, Hak. Soc. 2nd ed. 135.

[c. 1583.—"From thence we went to **Vgini** and Serringe. ..."—*R. Fitch* in *Hakl.* ii. 385.

[1616.—"**Vgen**, the Cheefe Citty of Malwa."—*Sir T. Roe*, Hak. Soc. ii. 379.]

c. 1659.—"Dara having understood what had passed at **Eugenes**, fell into that choler against *Kasem Kan*, that it was thought he would have cut off his head."—*Bernier*, E.T. p. 13; [ed. *Constable*, 41].

1785.—"The *City* of **Ugen** is very ancient, and said to have been the *Residence* of the Prince Bicker Majit, whose Æra is now Current among the Hindus."—*Sir C. Malet*, in *Dalrymple, Or. Rep.* i. 268.

[**OORD, OORUD**, s. Hind. *uṛad*. A variety of *dāl* (see DHALL) or pulse, the produce of Phaseolus radiatus. "*Urd* is the most highly prized of all the pulses of the genus *Phaseolus*, and is largely cultivated in all parts of India" (*Watt, Econ. Dict.* vi. pt. i. 102, *seqq.*).

[1792.—"The stalks of the **oord** are hispid in a lesser degree than those of **moong**."—*Asiat. Res.* vi. 47.

[1814.—"**Oord.**" See under POPPER.

[1857.—"The **Oordh** Dal is in more common use than any other throughout the country."—*Chevers, Man. of Medical Jurisprudence*, 309.]

OORDOO, s. The Hindustani language. The (Turki) word *urdū* means properly the camp of a Tartar Khān, and is, in another direction, the original of our word *horde* (Russian *orda*), [which, according to Schuyler (*Turkistan*, i. 30, note), "is now commonly used by the Russian soldiers and Cossacks in a very amusing manner as a contemptuous term for an Asiatic"]. The 'Golden Horde' upon the Volga was not properly (*pace* Littré) the name of a tribe of Tartars, as is often supposed, but was the style of the Royal Camp, eventually Palace, of the Khāns of the House of Batu at Sarai. *Horde* is said by Pihan, quoted by Dozy (*Oosterl.* 43) to have been introduced into French by Voltaire in his *Orphelin de la Chine.* But Littré quotes it as used in the 16th century. *Urda* is now used in Turkistan, *e.g.* at Tashkend, Khokhand, &c., for a 'citadel' (*Schuyler, loc. cit.* i. 30). The word *urdū*, in the sense of a royal camp, came into India probably with Baber, and the royal residence at Delhi was styled *urdū-i-mu'allā*, 'the Sublime Camp.' The mixt language which grew up in the court and camp was called *zabān-i-urdū*, 'the Camp Language,' and hence we have elliptically *Urdū*. On the Peshawar frontier the word *urdū* is still in frequent use as applied to the camp of a field-force.

1247.—"Post haec venimus ad primam **ordam** Imperatoris, in quâ erat una de uxoribus suis; et quia nondum videramus Imperatorem, noluerint nos vocare nec intromittere ad **ordam** ipsius."—*Plano Carpini*, p. 752.

1254.—"Et sicut populus Israel sciebat, unusquisque ad quam regionem tabernaculi deberet figere tentoria, ita ipsi sciunt ad quod latus curie debeant se collocare. ... Unde dicitur curia **Orda** lingua eorum, quod sonat medium, quia semper est in medio hominum suorum. ..."—*William of Rubruk*, p. 267.

1404.—"And the Lord (Timour) was very wroth with his Mirassaes (Mirzas), because he did not see the Ambassador at this feast, and because the *Truximan* (Interpreter) had not been with them ... and he sent for the *Truximan* and said to him: 'How is it that you have enraged and vexed the Lord? Now since you were not with the Frank ambassadors, and to punish you, and ensure your always being ready, we order your nostrils to be bored, and a cord put through them, and that you be led through the whole **Ordo** as a punishment.'"—*Clavijo*, § cxi.

c. 1440.—"What shall I saie of the great and innumerable moltitude of beastes that are in this **Lordo**? ... if you were disposed in one daie to bie a thousande or ij.[ml] horses you shulde finde them to sell in this **Lordo**, for they go in heardes like sheepe. ..."—*Josafa Barbaro*, old E.T. Hak. Soc. 20.

c. 1540.—"Sono diuisi i Tartari in **Horde**, e **Horda** nella lor lingua significa ragunāza di popolo vnito e concorde a similitudine d'vna città."—*P. Jovio, delle Cose della Moscovia*, in *Ramusio*, ii. f. 133.

1545.—"The Tartars are divided into certain groups or congregations, which they call **hordes.** Among which the Savola **horde** or group is the first in rank."—*Herberstein*, in *Ramusio*, ii. 171.

[1560.—"They call this place (or camp) **Ordu** bazaar."—*Tenreiro*, ed. 1829, ch. xvii. p. 45.]

1673.—"**L'Ourdy** sortit d'Andrinople pour aller au camp. Le mot *ourdy* signifie camp, et sous ce nom sont compris les mestiers que sont necessaires pour la commodité du voyage."—*Journal d'Ant. Galland*, i. 117.

[1753.—"That part of the camp called in Turkish the **Ordubazar** or camp-market, begins at the end of the square fronting the guard-rooms. ..."—*Hanway, Hist. Account*, i. 247.]

***OPIUM**, s. This word is in origin Greek, not Oriental. [The etymology accepted by Platts, Skt. *ahiphena*, 'snake venom' is not probable.] But from the Greek *ὄπιον* the Arabs took *afyūn* which has sometimes reacted on old spellings of the word. The collection of the *ὀπὸς*, or juice of the poppy-capsules, is mentioned by Dioscorides (c. A.D. 77), and Pliny gives a pretty full account of the drug as *opion* (see *Hanbury and Flückiger*, 40). The Opium-poppy was introduced into China, from Arabia, at the beginning of the 9th century, and its earliest Chinese name is **A-fu-yung**, a representation of the Arabic name. The Arab. *afyūn* is sometimes corruptly called *afīn*, of which *afīn*, 'imbecile,' is a popular etymology. Similarly the Bengalees derive it from *afiheno*, 'serpent-home.' [A number of early references to opium smoking have been collected by Burnell, *Linschoten*, Hak. Soc. ii. 113.]

c. A.D. 70.—"... which juice thus drawne, and thus prepared, hath power not onely to provoke sleepe, but if it be taken in any great quantitie, to make men die in their sleepe: and this our Physicians call **opion**. Certes I have knowne many come to their death by this meanes; and namely, the father of Licinius Cecinna late deceased, a man by calling a Pretour, who not being able to endure the intollerable pains and torments of a certaine disease, and being wearie of his life, at Bilbil in Spaine, shortened his owne daies by taking **opium**."—*Pliny*, in *Holland's* transl. ii. 68.

(*Medieval*).—

"Quod venit a Thebis, **opio** laudem
perhibebis;

Naribus horrendum, rufum laus dictat emendum."

Otho Cremonensis.

1511.—"Next day the General (Alboquerque) sent to call me to go ashore to speak to the King; and that I should say on his part ... that he had got 8 Guzzarate ships that he had taken on the way because they were enemies of the King of Portugal; and that these had many rich stuffs and much merchandize, and **arfiun** (for so they call *opio tebaico*) which they eat to cool themselves; all which he would sell to the King for 300,000 ducats worth of goods, cheaper than they could buy it from the Moors, and more such matter."—Letter of *Giovanni da Empoli*, in *Archivio Storico Italiano*, 55.

[1513.—"Opium (**oafyam**) is nothing else than the milk of poppies."—*Alboquerque, Cartas*, p. 174.]

1516.—"For the return voyage (to China) they ship there (at Malacca) Sumatra and Malabar pepper, of which they use a great deal in China, and drugs of Cambay, much *anfiam*, which we call **opium**. ..."—*Barbosa*, 206.

1563.—"*R.* I desire to know for certain about **amfiao**, what it is, which is used by the people of this country; if it is what we call **opium**, and whence comes such a quantity as is expended, and how much may be eaten every day?

* * * * *

"*O.* ... that which I call of Cambaia come for the most part from one territory which is called Malvi (*Mālwā*). ... I knew a secretary of Nizamoxa, a native of Coraçon, who every day eat three *tóllas*, or a weight of 10½ cruzados ... though he was a well educated man, and a great scribe and notary, he was always dozing or sleeping; yet if you put him to business he would speak like a man of letters and discretion; from this you may see what habit will do."—*Garcia*, 153*v* to 155*v*.

1568.—"I went then to Cambaya ... and there I bought 60 parcels of **Opium**, which cost me two thousand and a hundreth duckets, every ducket at foure shillings two pence."—*Master C. Frederike*, in *Hakl.* ii. 371. The original runs thus, showing the looseness of the translation: "... comprai sessanta *man* **d'Anfion**, che mi costò 2100 ducati serafini, che a nostro conto possono valere 5 lire I'vno."—In *Ramusio*, iii. 396*v*.

1598.—"**Amfion**, so called by the Portingales, is by Arabians, Mores, and Indians called **Affion**, in latine **Opio** or **Opium**. ... The Indians use much to eat *Amfion*. ... Hee that useth to eate it, must eate it daylie, otherwise he dieth and consumeth himselfe ... likewise hee that hath never eaten it, and will venture at the first to eate as much as those that dayly use it, it will surely kill him. ..."—*Linschoten*, 124; [Hak. Soc. ii. 112].

[c. 1610.—"Opium, or as they (in the Maldives) call it, **Aphion**."—*Pyrard de Laval*, Hak. Soc. i. 195.

[1614.—"The waster washer who to get **Affanan** hires them (the cloths) out a month."—*Foster, Letters*, ii. 127.

[1615.—"... Coarse chintz, and **ophyan**."—*Ibid.* iv. 107].

1638.—"Turcae **opium** experiuntur, etiam in bona quantitate, innoxium et confortativum; adeo ut etiam ante praelia ad fortitudinem illud sumant; nobis vero, nisi in parvâ quantitate, et cum bonis correctivis lethale est."—*Bacon, H. Vitae et Mortis* (ed. Montague) x. 188.

1644.—"The principal cause that this monarch, or rather say, this tyrant, is so powerful, is that he holds in his territories, and especially in the kingdom of Cambaya, those three plants of which are made the **Anfiam**, and the anil (see ANILE), and that which gives the *Algodam*" (Cotton).—*Bocarro*, MS.

1694.—"This people, that with *amphioen* or **opium**, mixed with tobacco, drink themselves not merely drunk but mad, are wont to fall furiously upon any one whom they meet, with a naked *kris* or dagger in the hand, and to stab him, though it be but a child, in their mad passion, with the cry of *Amock* (see A MUCK), that is 'strike dead,' or 'fall on him.' ..."—*Valentijn*, iv. (*China*, &c.) 124.

1726.—"It will hardly be believed ... that Java alone consumes monthly 350 packs of **opium**, each being of 136 *catis*, though the E. I. Company make 145 catis out of it. ..."—*Valentijn*, iv. 61.

1727.—"The Chiefs of Calecut, for many years had vended between 500 and 1000 chests of *Bengal* **Ophium** yearly up in the inland Countries, where it is very much used."—*A. Hamilton*, i. 315; [ed. 1744, i. 317 *seq.*.].

1770.—"Patna ... is the most celebrated place in the world for the cultivation of **opium**. Besides what is carried into the inland parts, there are annually 3 or 4000 chests exported, each weighing 300 lbs. ... An excessive fondness for opium prevails in all the countries to the east of India. The Chinese emperors have suppressed it in their dominions, by condemning to the flames every vessel that imports this species of poison."—*Raynal* (tr. 1777), i. 424.

ORANGE, s. A good example of plausible but entirely incorrect etymology is that of orange from Lat. *aurantium*. The latter word is in fact an ingenious medieval fabrication. The word doubtless came from the Arab. *nāranj*, which is again a form of Pers.

nārang, or *nārangī*, the latter being still a common term for the orange in Hindustan. The Persian indeed may be traced to Skt. *nāgarañga*, and *nārañga*, but of these words no satisfactory etymological explanation has been given, and they have perhaps been Sanscritized from some southern term. Sir W. Jones, in his article on the Spikenard of the Ancients, quotes from Dr. Anderson of Madras, "a very curious philological remark, that in the Tamul dictionary, most words beginning with *nar* have some relation to fragrance; as *narukeradu*, to yield an odour; *nártum pillei*, lemon-grass; *nártei*, citron; *nárta manum* (read *mārum*), the wild orange-tree; *nárum panei*, the Indian jasmine; *nárum alleri*, a strong smelling flower; and *nártu*, which is put for *nard* in the Tamul version of our scriptures." (See *As. Res.* vol. ii. 414). We have not been able to verify many of these Tamil terms. But it is true that in both Tamil and Malayalam *naṛu* is 'fragrant.' See, also, on the subject of this article, *A. E. Pott*, in Lassen's *Zeitschrift f. d. Kunde des Morgenlandes*, vii. 114 *seqq.*

The native country of the orange is believed to be somewhere on the northern border of India. A wild orange, the supposed parent of the cultivated species, both sweet and bitter, occurs in Garhwāl and Sikkim, as well as in the Kāṣia country, the valleys of which last are still abundantly productive of excellent oranges. [See *Watt, Econ. Dict.* ii. 336 *seqq.*] It is believed that the orange first known and cultivated in Europe was the bitter or Seville orange (see *Hanbury and Flückiger*, 111–112).

From the Arabic, Byzantine Greek got νεράντζιον, the Spaniards *naranja*, old Italian *narancia*, the Portuguese *laranja*, from which last, or some similar form, by the easy detachment of the *l* (taken probably, as in many other instances, for an article), we have the Ital. *arancio*, L. Latin *aurantium*, French *orange*, the modification of these two being shaped by *aurum* and *or*. Indeed, the quotation from Jacques de Vitry possibly indicates that some form like *al-arangi* may have been current in Syria. Perhaps, however, his phrase *ab indigenis nuncupantur* may refer only to the Frank or quasi-Frank settlers, in which case we should have among them the birthplace of our word in its present form. The reference to this passage we derived in the first place from Hehn, who gives a most interesting history of the introduction of the various species of *citrus* into Europe. But we can hardly think he is right in supposing that the Portuguese first brought the sweet orange (*Citrus aurantium dulce*) into Europe from China, c. 1548. No doubt there may have been a reintroduction of some fine varieties at that time.[1] But as early as the beginning of the 14th century we find Abulfeda extolling the fruit of Cintra. His words, as rendered by M. Reinaud, run: "Au nombre des dependances de Lisbonne est la ville de Schintara; à Schintara on recueille des pommes admirables pour la grosseur et le gout" (244[2]). That these *pommes* were the famous Cintra oranges can hardly be doubted. For Baber (*Autobiog.* 328) describes an orange under the name of *Sangtarah*, which is, indeed, a recognised Persian and Hind. word for a species of the fruit. And this early propagation of the sweet orange in Portugal would account not only for such wide diffusion of the name of *Cintra*, but for the persistence with which the alternative name of *Portugals* has adhered to the fruit in question. The familiar name of the large sweet orange in Sicily and Italy is *portogallo*, and nothing else; in Greece πορτογαλέα, in Albanian *protokale*, among the Kurds *portoghāl*; whilst even colloquial Arabic has *burtuḳān*. The testimony of Maṣ'ūdī as to the introduction of the orange into Syria before his time (c. A.D. 930), even if that were (as it would seem) the Seville orange, renders it quite possible that better qualities should have reached Lisbon or been developed there during the Saracenic occupation. It was indeed suggested in our hearing by the late Sir Henry M. Elliot that *sangtarah* might be interpreted as *sang-tar*, 'green stones' (or in fact 'moist pips'); but we hardly think he would have started this had the passage in Abulfeda been brought to his notice. [In the *Āīn* (ed. *Gladwin*, 1800, ii. 20) we read: "Sircar Silhet. ... Here grows a delicious fruit

1 There seems to have been great oscillation of traffic in this matter. About 1873, one of the present writers, then resident at Palermo, sent, in compliance with a request from Lahore, a collection of plants of many (about forty) varieties of *citrus* cultivated in Sicily, for introduction into the Punjab. This despatch was much aided by the kindness of Prof. Todaro, in charge of the Royal Botanic Garden at Palermo.

2 In Reiske's version "poma stupendae moliset excellentissima."—*Büsching's Magasin*, iv. 230.

called *Soontara*, in colour like an orange, but of an oblong form." This passage reads in Col. Jarrett's translation (ii. 124): "There is a fruit called *Suntarah* in colour like an orange but large and very sweet." Col. Jarrett disputes the derivation of *Sangtarah* from *Cintra*, and he is followed by Mr. H. Beveridge, who remarks that Humayun calls the fruit *Sanatra*. Mr. Beveridge is inclined to think that *Santra* is the *Indian* hill name of the fruit, of which *Sangtarah* is a corruption, and refers to a village at the foot of the Bhutan Hills called *Santrabārī*, because it had orange groves.]

A.D. c. 930.—"The same may be said of the orange-tree (*Shajr-ul-* **nāranj**) and of the round citron, which were brought from India after the year (A.H.) 300, and first sown in 'Oman. Thence they were transplanted to Basra, to 'Irāk, and to Syria ... but they lost the sweet and penetrating odour and beauty that they had in India, having no longer the benefits of the climate, soil, and water peculiár to that country."—*Maṣ'ūdī*, ii. 438–9.

c. 1220.—"In parvis autem arboribus quaedam crescunt alia poma citrina, minoris quantitatis frigida et acidi seu pontici (*bitter*) saporis, quae poma **orenges** ab indigenis nuncupantur."—*Jacobus Vitriacus*, in *Bongars*. These were apparently our Seville oranges.

c. 1290.—"In the 18th of Edward the first a large Spanish Ship came to Portsmouth; out of the cargo of which the Queen bought one frail of Seville figs, one frail of raisins or grapes, one bale of dates, two hundred and thirty pomegranates, fifteen citrons, and seven oranges (*Poma de* **orenge**)."—*Manners and Household Expenses of England in the 13th and 15th Centuries*, Roxb. Club, 1841, p. xlviii. The Editor deigns only to say that 'the MS. is in the Tower.' [Prof. Skeat writes (9 ser. *Notes and Queries*, v. 321): "The only known allusion to oranges, previously to 1400, in any piece of English literature (I omit household documents) is in the '*Alliterative Poems*,' edited by Dr. Morris, ii. 1044. The next reference, soon after 1400, is in Lydgate's '*Minor Poems*,' ed. Halliwell, p. 15. In 1440 we find **oronge** in the '*Promptorium Parvulorum*,' and in 1470 we find **orenges** in the '*Paston Letters*,' ed. Gairdner, ii. 394."]

1481.—"Item to the galeman (galley man) brought the lampreis and **oranges** ... iiij*d*."—*Household Book* of John D. of Norfolk, Roxb. Club, 1844, p. 38.

c. 1526.—"They have besides (in India) the **nâranj** [or Seville orange, Tr.] and the various fruits of the orange species. ... It always struck me that the word **nâranj** was accented in the Arab fashion; and I found that it really was so; the men of Bajour and Siwâd call *nâranj nârank*" (or perhaps rather **nârang**).—*Baber*, 328. In this passage Baber means apparently to say that the right name was *nārang*, which had been changed by the usual influence of Arabic pronunciation into *nāranj*.

1883.—"Sometimes the foreign products thus cast up (on Shetland) at their doors were a new revelation to the islanders, as when a cargo of **oranges** was washed ashore on the coast of Delting, the natives boiled them as a new kind of potatoes."—*Saty. Review*, July 14, p. 57.

ORANG-OTANG, ORANG-OUTAN, &c. s. The great man-like ape of Sumatra and Borneo; *Simia Satyrus*, L. This name was first used by Bontius (see below). It is Malay, *ōrăng-ūtăn*, 'homo sylvaticus.' The proper name of the animal in Borneo is *mias*. Crawfurd says that it is never called *orang-utan* by 'the natives.' But that excellent writer is often too positive—especially in his negatives! Even if it be not (as is probable) anywhere a recognised specific name, it is hardly possible that the name should not be sometimes applied popularly. We remember a tame hooluck belonging to a gentleman in E. Bengal, which was habitually known to the natives as *janglī ādmī*, literally = *orang-utan*. [There seems reason to believe that Crawfurd was right after all. Mr. Scott (*Malayan Words in English*, p. 87) writes: "But this particular application of *ōrang ūtan* to the ape does not appear to be, or ever to have been, familiar to the Malays generally; Crawfurd (1852) and Swettenham (1889) omit it, Pijnappel says it is 'Low Malay,' and Klinkert (1893) denies the use entirely. This uncertainty is explained by the limited area in which the animal exists within even native observation. Mr. Wallace could find no natives in Sumatra who 'had ever heard of such an animal,' and no 'Dutch officials who knew anything about it.' Then the name came to European knowledge more than 260 years ago; in which time probably more than one Malay name has faded out of general use or wholly disappeared, and many other things have happened." Mr. Skeat writes: "I believe Crawfurd is absolutely right in saying that it is never called *ōrang-ūtan* by the natives. It is much more likely to have been a sailor's mistake or joke than an error on the part of the Malays who know better. Throughout the Peninsula *ōrang-ūtan* is the name applied to the wild tribes, and though the *mawas* or *mias* is known to the Malays only by tradition, yet in tradition the two are never confused; and in those islands where the *mawas* does exist he is never called *ōrang-ūtan*, the word *ōrang* being reserved exclusively to describe the human species."]

1631.—"Loqui vero eos easque posse Iavani aiunt, sed non velle, ne ad labores cogantur; ridicule mehercules. Nomen ei induunt **Ourang Outang**, quod 'hominem silvae' significat, eosque nasci affirmant e libidine mulierum Indarum, quae se Simiis et Cercopithecis detestanda libidine uniunt."—*Bontii, Hist. Nat.* v. cap. 32, p. 85.

1668.—"Erat autem hic satyrus quadrupes: sed ab humanâ specie quam prae se fert, vocatur Indis **Ourang-outang**: sive homo silvestris."—*Licetus de Monstris*, 338.

[1701.—"**Orang-outang** sive Homo Sylvestris: or the Anatomy of a Pygmie compared with that of a Monkey, an Ape, and a Man. ..."—Title of work by *E. Tyson* (*Scott*).]

1727.—"As there are many species of wild Animals in the Woods (of Java) there is one in particular called the **Ouran-Outang**."—*A. Hamilton*, ii. 131; [ed. 1744, ii. 136].

1783.—"Were we to be driven out of India this day, nothing would remain to tell that it had been possessed, during the inglorious period of our dominion, by any thing better than the **ourang-outang** or the tiger."—*Burke, Sp. on Fox's E. India Bill, Works*, ed. 1852, iii. 468.

1802.—"Man, therefore, in a state of nature, was, if not the **ourang-outang** of the forests and mountains of Asia and Africa at the present day, at least an animal of the same family, and very nearly resembling it."—*Ritson, Essay on Abstinence from Animal Food*, pp. 13–14.

1811.—"I have one slave more, who was given me in a present by the Sultan of Pontiana. ... This gentleman is Lord Monboddo's genuine **Orang-outang**, which in the Malay language signifies literally *wild man*. ... Some people think seriously that the **oran-outang** was the original patriarch and progenitor of the whole Malay race."—*Lord Minto, Diary in India*, 268–9.

1868.—"One of my chief objects ... was to see the **Orang-utan** ... in his native haunts."—*Wallace, Malay Archip.* 39.

In the following passage the term is applied to a tribe of men:

1884.—"The Jacoons belong to one of the wild aboriginal tribes ... they are often styled **Orang Utan**, or men of the forest."—*Cavenagh, Rem. of an Indian Official*, 293.

ORMUS, ORMUZ, n.p. Properly *Hurmuz* or *Hurmūz*, a famous maritime city and minor kingdom near the mouth of the Persian Gulf. The original place of the city was on the northern shore of the Gulf, some 30 miles east of the site of Bandar Abbās or **Gombron**; but about A.D. 1300, apparently to escape from Tartar raids, it was transferred to the small island of Gerūn or Jerūn, which may be identified with the *Organa* of Nearchus, about 12 m. westward, and five miles from the shore, and this was the seat of the kingdom when first visited and attacked by the Portuguese under Alboquerque in 1506. It was taken by them about 1515, and occupied permanently (though the nominal reign of the native kings was maintained), until wrested from them by Shāh 'Abbās, with the assistance of an English squadron from Surat, in 1622. The place was destroyed by the Persians, and the island has since remained desolate, and all but uninhabited, though the Portuguese citadel and water-tanks remain. The islands of Hormuz, Kishm, &c., as well as Bandar 'Abbās and other ports on the coast of Kerman, had been held by the Sultans of Omān as fiefs of Persia, for upwards of a century, when in 1854 the latter State asserted its dominion, and occupied those places in force (see *Badger's Imams of Omān*, &c., p. xciv.).

B.C. c. 325.—"They weighed next day at dawn, and after a course of 100 stadia anchored at the mouth of the river Anamis, in a country called **Harmozeia**."—*Arrian, Voyage of Nearchus*, ch. xxxiii., tr. by *M'Crindle*, p. 202.

c. A.D. 150.—(on the coast of Carmania)
"Ἅρμουζα πόλις.
Ἁρμοζον ἄκρον." *Ptol.* VI. viii. 5.

c. 540.—At this time one Gabriel is mentioned as (Nestorian) Bishop of **Hormuz** (see *Assemani*, iii. 147–8).

c. 655.—"Nobis ... visum est nihilominus velut ad sepulchra mortuorum, quales vos esse video, geminos hosce Dei Sacerdotes ad vos allegare; Theodorum videlicet Episcopum **Hormuzdadschir** et Georgium Episcopum Susatrae."—Syriac Letter of the *Patriarch Jesujabus, ibid.* 133.

1298.—"When you have ridden these two days you come to the Ocean Sea, and on the shore you find a City with a harbour, which is called **Hormos**."—*Marco Polo*, Bk. i. ch. xix.

c. 1330.—"... I came to the Ocean Sea. And the first city on it that I reached is called **Ormes**, a city strongly fenced and abounding in costly wares. The city is on an island some five miles distant from the main; and on it there grows no tree, and there is no fresh water."—*Friar Odoric*, in *Cathay*, &c., 56.

c. 1331.—"I departed from 'Omān for the country of **Hormuz**. The city of Hormuz stands on the shore of the sea. The name is also called Moghistān. The new city of **Hormuz** rises in face of the first in the middle of the sea, separated from it only by a channel 3 parasangs in width. We arrived at New **Hormuz**, which forms an island of which the capital is called Jaraun. ... It is a mart for Hind and Sind."—*Ibn Batuta*, ii. 230.

1442.—"**Ormus** (qu. *Hurmūz?*), which is now called Djerun, is a port situated in the middle of the sea, and which has not its equal on the face of the globe."—*Abdurrazzāk*, in *India in XV. Cent.* p. 5.

c. 1470.—"**Hormuz** is 4 miles across the water, and stands on an Island."—*Athan. Nikitin, ibid.* p. 8.

1503.—"Habitant autem ex eorum (Francorum) gente homines fere viginti in urbe Cananoro: ad quos profecti, postquam ex **Hormizda** urbe ad eam Indorum civitatem Cananorum venimus, significavimus illis nos esse Christianos, nostramque conditionem et gradum indicavimus; et ab illis magno cum gaudio suscepti sumus. ... Eorundem autem Francorum regio Portugallus vocatur, una ex Francorum regionibus; eorumque Rex Emanuel appellatur; Emmanuelem oramus ut illum custodiat."—Letter from *Nestorian Bishops* on Mission to India, in *Assemani*, iii. 591.

1505.—"In la bocha di questo mare (di Persia) è vn altra insula chiamata **Agramuzo** doue sono perle infinite: (e) caualli che per tutte quelle parti sono in gran precio."—Letter of *K. Emanuel*, p. 14.

1572.—

"Mas vê a illa Gerum, como discobre
O que fazem do tempo os intervallos;
Que da cidade **Armuza**, que alli esteve
Ella o nome despois, e gloria teve."
Camões, x. 103.

By Burton:

"But see you Gerum's isle the tale unfold
of mighty things which Time can make or mar;
for of **Armuza**-town yon shore upon
the name and glory this her rival won."

1575.—"Touchant le mot **Ormuz**, il est moderne, et luy a esté imposé par les Portugais, le nom venant de l'accident de ce qu'ils cherchoient que c'estoit que l'Or; tellement qu'estant arrivez là, et voyans le trafic de tous biens, auquel le pais abonde, ils dirent *Vssi esta Or mucho*, c'est à dire, Il y a force d'Or; et pource ils donnerēt le nom d'**Ormucho** à la dite isle."—*A. Thevet; Cosmographie Univ.*, liv. x. i. 329.

1623.—"Non volli lasciar di andare con gl' Inglesi in **Hormuz** a veder la forteza, la città, e ciò che vi era in fine di notabile in quell' isola,"—*P. della Valle*, ii. 463. Also see ii. 61.

1667.—

"High on a throne of royal state, which far
Outshone the wealth of **Ormus** and of Ind,
Or where the gorgeous East with richest hand
Showers on her kings barbaric pearl and gold."
Paradise Lost, ii. 1-4.

OTTO, OTTER, s. Or usually 'Otto of Roses,' or by imperfect purists '*Attar* of Roses,' an essential oil obtained in India from the petals of the flower, a manufacture of which the chief seat is at Ghāzipur on the Ganges. The word is the Arab. *'iṭr*, 'perfume.' From this word are derived *'aṭṭār*, a 'perfumer or druggist,' *'aṭṭārī*, adj., 'pertaining to a perfumer.' And a relic of Saracen rule in Palermo is the *Via Latterini*, 'the street of the perfumers' shops.' We find the same in an old Spanish account of Fez:

1573.—"Issuing thence to the Cayzerie by a gate which faces the north there is a handsome street which is called *of the* **Atarin**, which is the Spicery."—*Marmol, Affrica*, ii. f. 88.

[*'Itr* of roses is said to have been discovered by the Empress Nūr-jahān on her marriage with Jahāngīr. A canal in the palace garden was filled with rose-water in honour of the event, and the princess, observing a scum on the surface, caused it to be collected, and found it to be of admirable fragrance, whence it was called *'iṭr-i-Jahāngīrī*.]

1712.—Kaempfer enumerating the departments of the Royal Household in Persia names: "*Pharmacopoeia* ... **Atthaar** *choneh*, in quâ medicamenta, et praesertim variae virtutis opiata, pro Majestate et aulicis praeparantur. ..."—*Am. Exot.* 124.

1759.—"To presents given, &c.

* * * * *

"1 **otter** box set with diamonds
"*Sicca Rs.* 3000 ... ... 3222 3 6."
Accts. of Entertainment to Jugget Set, in *Long*, 89.

c. 1790.—"Elles ont encore une prédilection particulière pour les huiles oderiferantes, surtout pour celle de rose, appelée **otta**."—*Haafner*, ii. 122.

1824.—"The **attar** is obtained after the rose-water is made, by setting it out during the night and till sunrise in the morning in large open vessels exposed to the air, and then skimming off the essential oil which floats at the top."—*Heber*, ed. 1844, i. 154.

***OUTCRY**, s. Auction. This term seems to have survived a good deal longer in India than in England. (See NEELAM). The old Italian expression for auction seems to be identical in sense, viz. *gridaggio*, and the auctioneer *gridatore*, thus:

c. 1343.—"For jewels and plate; and (other) merchandize that is sold by **outcry** (*gridaggio*), *i.e.* by auction (*oncanto*) in Cyprus, the buyer pays the crier (*gridatore*) one quarter *carat* per bezant on the price bid for the thing bought through the crier, and the seller pays nothing except," &c.—*Pegolotti*, 74.

1627.—"Out-crie *of goods to be sold.* G(allicè) Encánt. Incánt. (I(talicè).—Incánto. ... H(ispanicè). Almoneda, *ab* Al.*articulus, et Arab.* nedeye, *clamare, vocare.* ... B(atavicè). At-roep."—*Minsheu*, s.v.

[1700.—"The last week Mr. Proby made a **outcry** of lace."—In *Yule, Hedges' Diary*, Hak. Soc. ii. cclix.]

1782.—"On Monday next will be sold by Public **Outcry** ... large and small China silk Kittisals (KITTYSOL). ..."—*India Gazette*, March 31.

1787.—"Having put up the Madrass Galley at **Outcry** and nobody offering more for her than 2300 Rupees, we think it more for the Company's Int. to make a Sloop of Her than let Her go at so low a price."—*Ft. William MS. Reports*, March.

[1841.—"When a man dies in India, we make short work with him; ... an '**outcry**' is held, his goods and chattels are brought to the hammer. ..."—*Society in India*, ii. 227.]

***OVERLAND**. Specifically applied to the Mediterranean route to India, which in former days involved usually the land journey from Antioch or thereabouts to the Persian Gulf; and still in vogue, though any land journey may now be entirely dispensed with, thanks to M. Lesseps.

1612.—"His Catholic Majesty the King Philip III. of Spain and II. of Portugal, our King and Lord, having appointed Dom Hieronymo de Azevedo to succeed Ruy Lourenço de Tavira ... in January 1612 ordered that a courier should be despatched **overland** (*por terra*) to this Government to carry these orders and he, arriving at Ormuz at the end of May following. ..."—*Bocarro, Decada*, p. 7.

1629.—"The news of his Exploits and Death being brought together to King *Philip* the Fourth, he writ with his own hand as follows. *Considering the two Pinks that were fitting for* India *may be gone without an account of my Concern for the Death of* Nunno Alvarez Botello, *an Express shall immediately be sent* **by Land** with advice."—*Faria y Sousa* (Stevens), iii. 373.

1673.—"French and Dutch Jewellers coming **overland** ... have made good Purchase by buying Jewels here, and carrying them to Europe to Cut and Set, and returning thence sell them here to the Ombrahs (see OMRAH), among whom were Monsieur Tavernier. ..."—*Fryer*, 89.

1675.—"Our last to you was dated the 17th August past, **overland**, transcripts of which we herewith send you."—*Letter from Court to Ft. St. Geo.* In *Notes and Exts.* No. i. p. 5.

1676.—"Docket Copy of the Company's General **Overland**.

"'Our Agent and Councel Fort St. George.

* * * * *

"'The foregoing is copy of our letter of 28th June **overland**, which we sent by three several conveyances for Aleppo.'"—*Ibid.* p. 12.

1684.—"That all endeavors would be used to prevent my going home the way I intended, by Persia, and so **overland**."—*Hedges, Diary*, Aug. 19; [Hak. Soc. i. 155].

c. 1686.—"Those Gentlemen's Friends in the Committee of the Company in *England*, acquainted them by Letters **over Land**, of the Danger they were in, and gave them Warning to be on their guard."—*A. Hamilton*, i. 196; [ed. 1744, i. 195].

1737.—"Though so far apart that we can only receive letters from Europe once a year, while it takes 18 months to get an answer, we Europeans get news almost every year **over land** by Constantinople, through Arabia or Persia. ... A few days ago we received the news of the Peace in Europe; of the death of Prince Eugene; of the marriage of the P. of Wales with the Princess of Saxe-Gotha. ..."—Letter of the *Germ. Missionary Sartorius*, from Madras, Feb. 16. In *Notices of Madras, and Cuddalore*, &c. 1858, p. 159.

1763.—"We have received **Overland** the news of the taking of Havannah and the Spanish Fleet, as well as the defeat of the Spaniards in Portugall. We must surely make an advantageous Peace, however I'm no Politician."—*MS. Letter of James Rennell*, June 1, fr. Madras.

1774.—"Les Marchands à Bengale envoyèrent un Vaisseau à *Suès* en 1772, mais il fut endommagé dans le Golfe de Bengale, et obligé de retourner; en 1773 le Sr. *Holford* entreprit encore ce voyage, réussit cette fois, et fut ainsi le premier Anglois qui eut conduit un vaisseau à *Suès*. ... On s'est déjà servi plusieurs fois de cette route comme d'un chemin de poste; car le Gouvernement des Indes envoye actuellement dans des cas d'importance ses Couriers par *Suès* en Angleterre, et peut presqu'avoir plutôt reponse de *Londres* que leurs lettres ne peuvent venir en Europe par le Chemin ordinaire du tour du Cap de bonne esperance."—*Niebuhr, Voyage*, ii. 10.

1776.—"We had advices long ago from England, as late as the end of May, by way of Suez. This is a new Route opened by Govr. Hastings, and the Letters which left Marseilles the 3rd June arrived here the 20th August. This, you'll allow, is a ready communication with Europe, and may be kept open at all times, if we chuse to take a little pains."—*MS. Letter from James Rennell*, Oct. 16, "from Islamabad, capital of Chittigong."

1781.—"On Monday last was Married Mr. George Greenley to Mrs. Anne Barrington, relict of the late Capt. William B——, who unfortunately perished on the Desart, in the attack that was made on the Carravan of Bengal Goods under his and the other Gentlemen's care between Suez and Grand Cairo."—*India Gazette*, March 7.

1782.—"When you left England with an intention to pass **overland** and by the route of the Red Sea into India, did you not know that no subject of these kingdoms can lawfully reside in India ... without the permission of the United Company of Merchants? ..."—*Price, Tracts*, i. 130.

1783.—"... Mr. Paul Benfield, a gentleman whose means of intelligence were known to be both extensive and expeditious, publicly declared, from motives the most benevolent, that he had just received **overland** from England certain information that Great Britain had finally concluded a peace with all the belligerent powers in Europe."—*Munro's Narrative*, 317.

1786.—"The packet that was coming to us **overland**, and that left England in July, was cut off by the wild Arabs between Aleppo and Bussora."—*Lord Cornwallis*, Dec. 28, in *Correspondence*, &c., i. 247.

1793.—"Ext. of a letter from Poonamallee, dated 7th June.

'The dispatch by way of Suez has put us all in a commotion.'"—*Bombay Courier*, June 29.

1803.—"From the Governor General to the Secret Committee, dated 24th Decr. 1802. Recd. **Overland**, 9th May 1803."—*Mahratta War Papers* (Parliamentary).

P

PADDY, s. Rice in the husk; but the word is also, at least in composition, applied to growing rice. The word appears to have in some measure, a double origin.

There is a word *batty* used by some writers on the west coast of India, which has probably helped to propagate our uses of *paddy*. This seems to be the Canarese *batta* or *bhatta*, 'rice in the husk,' which is also found in Mahr. as *bhāt* with the same sense, a word again which in Hind. is applied to 'cooked rice.' The last meaning is that of Skt. *bhaktā*, which is perhaps the original of all these forms.

But in Malay *pādī* [according to Mr. Skeat, usually pronounced *pădi*] Javan. *pārī*, is 'rice in the straw.' And the direct parentage of the word in India is thus apparently due to the Archipelago; arising probably out of the old importance of the export trade of rice from Java (see *Raffles, Java*, i. 239–240, and *Crawfurd's Hist.* iii. 345, and *Descript. Dict.*, 368). Crawfurd, (*Journ. Ind. Arch.*, iv. 187) seems to think that the Malayo-Javanese word may have come from India with the Portuguese. But this is impossible, for as he himself has shown (*Desc. Dict.*, u.s.), the word *pārī*, more or less modified, exists in all the chief tongues of the Archipelago, and even in Madagascar, the connection of which last with the Malay regions certainly was long prior to the arrival of the Portuguese.

1580.—"Certaine Wordes of the naturall language of Jaua ... **Paree**, ryce in the huske."—*Sir F. Drake's Voyage*, in *Hakl.* iv. 246.

1598.—"There are also divers other kinds of Rice, of a lesse price, and slighter than the other Ryce, and is called **Batte** ..."—*Linschoten*, 70; [Hak. Soc. i. 246].

1600.—"In the fields is such a quantity of rice, which they call bate, that it gives its name to the kingdom of Calou, which is called on that account *Batecalou*."—*Lucena, Vida do Padre F. Xavier*, 121.

1615.—"... oryzae quoque agri feraces quam **Batum** incolae dicunt."—*Jarric, Thesaurus*, i. 461.

1673.—"The Ground between this and the great Breach is well ploughed, and bears good **Batty**."—*Fryer*, 67, see also 125. But in the Index he has **Paddy**.

1798.—"The **paddie** which is the name given to the rice, whilst in the husk, does not grow ... in compact ears, but like oats, in loose spikes."—*Stavorinus*, tr. i. 231.

1837.—"Parrots brought 900,000 loads of hill-**paddy** daily, from the marshes of Chandata,—mice husking the hill-**paddy**, without breaking it, converted it into rice."—*Turnour's Mahawanso*, 22.

1871.—"In Ireland Paddy makes riots, in Bengal raiyats make **paddy**; and in this lies the difference between the **paddy** of green Bengal, and the Paddy of the Emerald Isle."—*Govinda Samanta*, ii. 25.

1878.—"Il est établi un droit sur les riz et les **paddys** exportés de la Colonie, excepté pour le Cambodge par la voie du fleuve."—*Courrier de Saigon*, Sept. 20.

PADDY-FIELD, s. A rice-field, generally in its flooded state.

1759.—"They marched onward in the plain towards Preston's force, who, seeing them coming, halted on the other side of a long morass formed by **paddy-fields**."—*Orme*, ed. 1803, iii. 430.

1800.—"There is not a single **paddy-field** in the whole county, but plenty of cotton ground swamps, which in this wet weather are delightful."—*Wellington* to *Munro*, in *Despatches*, July 3.

1809.—"The whole country was in high cultivation, consequently the **paddy-fields** were nearly impassable."—*Ld. Valentia*, i. 350.

PADRE, s. A priest, clergyman, or minister, of the Christian Religion; when applied by natives to their own priests, as it sometimes is when they speak to Europeans, this is only by way of accommodation, as 'church' is also sometimes so used by them.

The word has been taken up from the Portuguese, and was of course applied originally to Roman Catholic priests only. But even in that respect there was a peculiarity in its Indian use among the Portuguese. For P. della Valle (see below) notices it as a singularity of their practice at Goa that they gave the title of *Padre* to secular priests, whereas in Italy this was reserved to the *religiosi* or regulars. In Portugal itself, as Bluteau's explanation shows, the use is, or was formerly, the same as in Italy; but, as the first ecclesiastics who went to India were monks, the name apparently became general among the Portuguese there for all priests.

It is a curious example of the vitality of words that this one which had thus already in the 16th century in India a kind of abnormally wide application, has now in that country a still wider, embracing all Christian ministers. It is applied to the Protestant clergy at Madras early in the 18th century. A bishop is known as **Lord** (see LAT) **padre**. See LAT *Sahib*.

According to Leland the word is used in China in the form *pa-ti-li*.

1541.—"Chegando à Porta da Igreja, o sahirão a receber oito **Padres**."—*Pinto*, ch. lxix. (see *Cogan*, p. 85).

1584.—"It was the will of God that we found there two **Padres**, the one an Englishman, and the other a Flemming."—*Fitch*, in *Hakl.* ii. 381.

"... had it not pleased God to put it into the minds of the archbishop and other two **Padres** of Jesuits of S. Paul's Colledge to stand our friends, we might have rotted in prison."—*Newberrie, ibid.* ii. 380.

c. 1590.—"Learned monks also come from Europe, who go by the name of **Pádre**. They have an infallible head called *Pápá*. He can change any religious ordinances as he may think advisable, and kings have to submit to his authority."—*Badāonī*, in *Blochmann's Āīn*, i. 182.

c. 1606.—"Et ut adesse **Patres** comperiunt, minor exclamat **Padrigi, Padrigi**, id est Domine Pater, Christianus sum."—*Jarric*, iii. 155.

1614.—"The **Padres** make a church of one of their Chambers, where they say Masse twice a day."—*W. Whittington*, in *Purchas*, i. 486.

1616.—"So seeing Master Terry whom I brought with me, he (the King) called to him, **Padre** you are very welcome, and this house is yours."—*Sir T. Roe*, in *Purchas*, i. 564; [Hak. Soc. ii. 385].

1623.—"I Portoghesi chiamano anche i preti secolari **padri**, come noi i religiosi ..."—*P. della Valle*, ii. 586; [Hak. Soc. i. 142].

1665.—"They (Hindu Jogis) are impertinent enough to compare themselves with our Religious Men they meet with in the *Indies*. I have often taken pleasure to catch them, using much ceremony with them, and giving them great respect; but I soon heard them say to one another, This *Franguis* knows who we are, he hath been a great while in the *Indies*, he knows that we are the **Padrys** of the *Indians*. A fine comparison, said I, within myself, made by an impertinent and idolatrous rabble of Men!"—*Bernier*, E.T. 104; [ed. *Constable*, 323].

1675.—"The **Padre** (or Minister) complains to me that he hath not that respect and place of preference at Table and elsewhere that is due unto him. ... At his request I promised to move it at ye next meeting of ye Councell. What this little Sparke may enkindle, especially should it break out in ye Pulpit, I cannot foresee further than the inflaming of ye dyning Roome w[ch] sometimes is made almost intollerable hot upon other Acc[ts]."—*Mr. Puckle's Diary at Metchlapatam*, MS. in India Office.

1676.—"And whiles the French have no settlement near hand, the keeping French **Padrys** here instead of Portugueses, destroys the encroaching growth of the Portugall interest, who used to entail Portugalism as well as

Christianity on all their converts."—*Madras Consns.*, Feb. 29, in *Notes and Exts.* i. p. 46.

1680.—"... where as at the Dedication of a New Church by the French **Padrys** and Portugez in 1675 guns had been fired from the Fort in honour thereof, neither **Padry** nor Portugez appeared at the Dedication of our Church, nor as much as gave the Governor a visit afterwards to give him joy of it."—*Ibid.* Oct. 28. No. III. p. 37.

c. 1692.—"But their greatest act of tyranny (at Goa) is this. If a subject of these misbelievers dies, leaving young children, and no grown-up son, the children are considered wards of the State. They take them to their places of worship, their churches ... and the **padris**, that is to say the priests, instruct the children in the Christian religion, and bring them up in their own faith, whether the child be a Mussulman *saiyid* or a Hindú *bráhman*."—*Kháfi Khán*, in *Elliot*, vii. 345.

1711.—"The Danish **Padre** Bartholomew Ziegenbalgh, requests leave to go to Europe in the first ship, and in consideration that he is head of a Protestant Mission, espoused by the Right Reverend the Lord Archbishop of Canterbury ... we have presumed to grant him his passage."—In *Wheeler*, ii. 177.

1726.—"May 14. Mr. Leeke went with me to St. Thomas's Mount. ... We conversed with an old **Padre** from Silesia, who had been 27 years in India. ..."—*Diary of the Missionary Schultze* (in *Notices of Madras*, &c., 1858), p. 14.

"May 17. The minister of the King of Pegu called on me. From him I learned, through an interpreter, that Christians of all nations and professions have perfect freedom at Pegu; that even in the Capital two French, two Armenian, and two Portuguese **Patres**, have their churches. ..."—*Ibid.* p. 15.

1803.—"Lord Lake was not a little pleased at the Begum's loyalty, and being a little elevated by the wine ... he gallantly advanced, and to the utter dismay of her attendants, took her in his arms, and kissed her. ... Receiving courteously the proffered attention, she turned calmly round to her astonished attendants—'It is,' said she, 'the salute of a **padre** (or priest) to his daughter.'"—*Skinner's Mil. Mem.* i. 293.

1809.—"The **Padre**, who is a half cast Portuguese, informed me that he had three districts under him."—*Ld. Valentia*, i. 329.

1830.—"Two fat naked Brahmins, bedaubed with paint, had been importuning me for money ... upon the ground that they were **padres**."—*Mem. of Col. Mountain*, iii.

1876.—"There is **Padre** Blunt for example,—we always call them **Padres** in India, you know,—makes a point of never going beyond ten minutes, at any rate during the hot weather."—*The Dilemma*, ch. xliii.

PAGODA, s. This obscure and remarkable word is used in three different senses.

a. An idol temple; and also specifically, in China, a particular form of religious edifice, of which the famous "Porcelain tower" of Nanking, now destroyed, may be recalled as typical. In the 17th century we find the word sometimes misapplied to places of Mahommedan worship, as by Faria-y-Sousa, who speaks of the "**Pagoda** of Mecca."

b. An idol.

c. A coin long current in S. India. The coins so called were both gold and silver, but generally gold. The gold *pagoda* was the *varāha* or *hūn* of the natives; the former name (fr. Skt. for 'boar') being taken from the Boar avatār of Vishnu, which was figured on a variety of ancient coins of the South; and the latter signifying 'gold,' no doubt identical with *sonā*, and an instance of the exchange of *h* and *s*.

Accounts at Madras down to 1818 were kept in *pagodas*, *fanams*, and *kās* (see CASH); 8 *kās* = 1 *fanam*, 42 *fanams* = 1 *pagoda*. In the year named the rupee was made the standard coin.[1] The pagoda was then reckoned as equivalent to 3½ rupees.

In the suggestions of etymologies for this word, the first and most prominent meaning alone has almost always been regarded, and doubtless justly; for the other uses are deduceable from it. Such suggestions have been many.

Thus Chinese origins have been propounded in more than one form; *e.g. Pao-t'ah*, 'precious pile,' and *Poh-kuh-t'ah* ('white-bones-pile').[2] Anything can be made out of Chinese monosyllables in the way of etymology; though no doubt it is curious that the first at least of these phrases is actually applied by the Chinese to the polygonal towers which in China foreigners specially call *pagodas*. Whether it be possible that this phrase may have been in any measure formed in imitation of *pagoda*, so constantly in the mouth of foreigners, we cannot say (though it would not be a solitary example of such borrowing—see NEELAM); but we can say with confidence that it is impossible *pagoda* should have been taken from the

1 Prinsep's *Useful Tables*, by E. Thomas, p. 19.
2 Giles, *Glossary of References*, s.v.

Chinese. The quotations from Corsali and Barbosa set that suggestion at rest.

Another derivation is given (and adopted by so learned an etymologist as H. Wedgwood) from the Portuguese *pagão*, 'a pagan.' It is possible that this word may have helped to facilitate the Portuguese adoption of *pagoda;* it is not possible that it should have given rise to the word. A third theory makes *pagoda* a transposition of dagoba. The latter is a genuine word, used in Ceylon, but known in Continental India, since the extinction of Buddhism, only in the most rare and exceptional way.

A fourth suggestion connects it with the Skt. *bhagavat*, 'holy, divine,' or *Bhagavatī*, applied to Durgā and other goddesses; and a fifth makes it a corruption of the Pers. *but-kadah*, 'idol-temple'; a derivation given below by Ovington. There can be little doubt that the origin really lies between these two.

The two contributors to this book are somewhat divided on this subject:—

(1) Against the derivation from *bhagavat*, 'holy,' or the Mahr. form *bhagavant*, is the objection that the word *pagode* from the earliest date has the final *e*, which was necessarily pronounced. Nor is *bhagavant* a name for a temple in any language of India. On the other hand *but-kadah* is a phrase which the Portuguese would constantly hear from the Mahommedans with whom they chiefly had to deal on their first arrival in India. This is the view confidently asserted by Reinaud (*Mémoires sur l'Inde*, 90), and is the etymology given by Littré.

As regards the coins, it has been supposed, naturally enough, that they were called *pagoda*, because of the figure of a temple which some of them bear; and which indeed was borne by the *pagodas* of the Madras Mint, as may be seen in Thomas's *Prinsep*, pl. xlv. But in fact coins with this impress were first struck at Ikkeri at a date *after* the word *pagode* was already in use among the Portuguese. However, nearly all bore on one side a rude representation of a Hindu deity (see *e.g.* Kṛishṇarāja's pagoda, c. 1520), and sometimes two such images. Some of these figures are specified by Prinsep (*Useful Tables*, p. 41), and Varthema speaks of them: "These *pardai* ... have two devils stamped upon one side of them, and certain letters on the other" (115–116). Here the name may have been appropriately taken from *bhagavat* (A. B.).

On the other hand, it may be urged that the resemblance between *butkadah* and *pagode* is hardly close enough, and that the derivation from *but-kadah* does not easily account for all the uses of the word. Indeed, it seems admitted in the preceding paragraph that *bhagavat* may have had to do with the origin of the word in one of its meanings.

Now it is not possible that the word in all its applications may have had its origin from *bhagavat*, or some current modification of that word? We see from Marco Polo that such a term was currently known to foreign visitors of S. India in his day—a term almost identical in sound with *pagoda*, and bearing in his statement a religious application, though not to a temple.[1] We thus have four separate applications of the word *pacauta*, or *pagoda*, picked up by foreigners on the shores of India from the 13th century downwards, viz. to a Hindu ejaculatory formula, to a place of Hindu worship, to a Hindu idol, to a Hindu coin with idols represented on it. Is it not possible that *all* are to be traced to *bhagavat*, 'sacred,' or to *Bhagavat* and *Bhagavatī*, used as names of divinities—of Buddha in Buddhist times or places, of Kṛishṇa and Durgā in Brahminical times and places? (uses which are *fact*). How common was the use of *Bhagavatī* as the name of an object of worship in Malabar, may be seen from an example. Turning to Wilson's work on the Mackenzie MSS., we find in the list of local MS. tracts belonging to Malabar, the repeated occurrence of *Bhagavati* in this way. Thus in this section of the book we have at p. xcvi. (vol. ii.) note of an account "of a temple of *Bhagavati*"; at p. ciii. "Temple of Mannadi *Bhagavati* goddess ..."; at p. civ. "Temple of Mangombu *Bhagavati* ..."; "Temple of Paddeparkave *Bhagavati* ..."; "Temple of the goddess

1 "The prayer that they say daily consists of these words: '*Pacauta! Pacauta! Pacauta!*' And this they repeat 104 times."—(Bk. iii. ch. 17.) The word is printed in Ramusio *pacauca;* but no one familiar with the constant confusion of *c* and *t* in medieval manuscript will reject this correction of M. Pauthier. Bishop Caldwell observes that the word was probably *Bagavā*, or *Pagavā*, the Tamil form of *Bhagavata*, "Lord"; a word reiterated in their sacred formulæ by Hindus of all sorts, especially Vaishnava devotees. The words given by Marco Polo, if written "*Pagoda! Pagoda! Pagoda!*" would be almost undistinguishable in sound from *Pacauta*.

Pannáyennar Kave *Bhagavati* ..."; "Temple of the goddess Patáli *Bhagavati* ..."; "Temple of *Bhagavati* ..."; p. cvii., "Account of the goddess *Bhagavati* at, &c. ..."; p. cviii., "Acc. of the goddess Yalanga *Bhagavati*," "Acc. of the goddess Vallur *Bhagavati*." The term *Bhagavati* seems thus to have been very commonly attached to objects of worship in Malabar temples (see also *Fra Paolino*, p. 79 and p. 57, quoted under c. below). And it is very interesting to observe that, in a paper on "Coorg Superstitions," Mr. Kittel notices parenthetically that Bhadrā Kālī (*i.e.* Durgā) is "also called **Pogŏdi**, *Pavodi*, a *tadbhava* of **Bagavati**" (*Ind. Antiq.* ii. 170)—an incidental remark that seems to bring us very near the possible origin of *pagode*. It is most probable that some form like *pagodi* or *pagode* was current in the mouths of foreign visitors before the arrival of the Portuguese; but if the word was of Portuguese origin there may easily have been some confusion in their ears between *Bagavati* and *but-kadah* which shaped the new word. It is no sufficient objection to say that *bhagavati* is not a term applied by the natives to a temple; the question is rather what misunderstanding and mispronunciation by foreigners of a native term may probably have given rise to the term?—(H. Y.)

Since the above was written, Sir Walter Elliot has kindly furnished a note, of which the following is an extract:—

"I took some pains to get at the origin of the word when at Madras, and the conclusion I came to was that it arose from the term used generally for the object of their worship, viz., *Bhagavat*, 'god'; *bhagavati*, 'goddess.'

"Thus, the Hindu temple with its lofty *gopuram* or propylon at once attracts attention, and a stranger enquiring what it was, would be told, 'the house or place of *Bhagavat*.' The village divinity throughout the south is always a form of *Durga*, or, as she is commonly called, simply '*Devi*' (or *Bhagavati*, 'the goddess'). ... In like manner a figure of *Durga* is found on most of the gold *Huns* (*i.e. pagoda* coins) current in the Dakhan, and a foreigner inquiring what such a coin was, or rather what was the form stamped upon it, would be told it was 'the goddess,' *i.e.*, it was '*Bhagavati*.'"

As my friend, Dr. Burnell, can no longer represent his own view, it seems right here to print the latest remarks of his on the subject that I can find. They are in a letter from Tanjore, dated March 10, 1880:—

"I think I overlooked a remark of yours regarding my observation that the *e* in *Pagode* was pronounced, and that this was a difficulty in deriving it from *Bhagavat*. In modern Portuguese *e* is *not* sounded, but verses show that it was in the 16th century. Now, if there is a final vowel in *Pagoda*, it must come from *Bhagavati;* but though the goddess is and was worshipped to a certain extent in S. India, it is by other names (*Amma*, &c.). Gundert and Kittel give '*Pogodi*' as a name of a Durga temple, but assuredly this is no corruption of *Bhagavati*, but *Pagoda!* Malayālam and Tamil are full of such adopted words. *Bhagavati* is little used, and the goddess is too insignificant to give rise to *pagoda* as a general name for a temple.

"*Bhagavat* can only appear in the S. Indian languages in its (Skt.) nominative form *bhagavān* (Tamil *paγuvān*). As such, in Tamil and Malayālam it equals Vishnu or Siva, which would suit. But *pagoda* can't be got out of *bhagavān;* and if we look to the N. Indian forms, *bhagavant*, &c., there is the difficulty about the *e*, to say nothing about the *nt*."

The use of the word by Barbosa at so early a date as 1516, and its application to a particular class of temples must not be overlooked.

a.—

1516.—"There is another sect of people among the Indians of Malabar, which is called *Cujaven* [*Kushavan, Logan, Malabar*, i. 115]. ... Their business is to work at baked clay, and tiles for covering houses, with which the temples and Royal buildings are roofed. ... Their idolatry and their idols are different from those of the others; and in their houses of prayer they perform a thousand acts of witchcraft and necromancy; they call their temples **pagodes**, and they are separate from the others."—*Barbosa*, 135. This is from Lord Stanley of Alderley's translation from a Spanish MS. The Italian of Ramusio reads: "nelle loro orationi fanno molte strigherie e necromãtie, le quali chiamano **Pagodes**, differenti assai dall' altre" (*Ramusio*, i. f. 308*v.*). In the Portuguese MS. published by the Lisbon Academy in 1812, the words are altogether absent; and in interpolating them from Ramusio the editor has given the same sense as in Lord Stanley's English.

1516.—"In this city of Goa, and all over India, there are an infinity of ancient buildings of the Gentiles, and in a small island near this, called Dinari, the Portuguese, in order to build the city, have destroyed an ancient temple called **Pagode**, which was built with marvellous art, and with ancient figures wrought to the greatest perfection in a certain black stone, some of which remain standing, ruined and shattered, because these Portuguese care nothing about them. If I can come by one of these shattered images I will send it to your Lordship, that you may perceive how much in old times sculpture was esteemed in every part of the world."—Letter of *Andrea Corsali* to *Giuliano de'Medici*, in *Ramusio*, i. f. 177.

1543.—"And with this fleet he anchored at Coulão and landed there with all his people. And the Governor (Martim Afonso de Sousa) went thither because of information he had of a **pagode** which was quite near in the interior, and which, they said, contained much treasure. ... And the people of the country seeing that the Governor was going to the **pagode**, they sent to offer him 50,000 pardaos not to go."—*Correa*, iv. 325–326.

1554.—"And for the monastery of Santa Fee 845,000 *reis* yearly, besides the revenue of the **Paguodes** which His Highness bestowed upon the said House, which gives 600,000 reis a year. ..."—*Botelho, Tombo*, in *Subsidios*, 70.

1563.—"They have (at Bacaim) in one part a certain island called Salsete, where there are two **pagodes** or houses of idolatry."—*Garcia*, f. 211*v*.

1582.—"... **Pagode**, which is the house of praiers to their Idolls."—*Castañeda* (by N. L.), f. 34.

1594.—"And as to what you have written to me, viz., that although you understand how necessary it was for the increase of the Christianity of those parts to destroy all the **pagodas** and mosques (*pagodes e mesquitas*), which the Gentiles and the Moors possess in the fortified places of this State. ..." (The King goes on to enjoin the Viceroy to treat this matter carefully with some theologians and canonists of those parts, but not to act till he shall have reported to the King).—Letter from the *K. of Portugal* to the *Viceroy*, in *Arch. Port. Orient.*, Fasc. 3, p. 417.

1598.—"... houses of Diuels [Divels] which they call **Pagodes**."—*Linschoten*, 22; [Hak. Soc. i. 70].

1606.—Gouvea uses **pagode** both for a temple and for an idol, *e.g.*, see f. 46*v*, f. 47.

1630.—"That he should erect **pagods** for God's worship, and adore images under green trees."—*Lord, Display*, &c.

1638.—"There did meet us at a great **Pogodo** or **Pagod**, which is a famous and sumptuous Temple (or Church)."—*W. Bruton*, in *Hakl.* v. 49.

1674.—"Thus they were carried, many flocking about them, to a **Pagod** or Temple" (*pagode* in the orig.).—*Stevens' Faria y Sousa*, i. 45.

1674.—"**Pagod** (quasi Pagan-God), an Idol or false god among the Indians; also a kind of gold coin among them equivalent to our Angel."—*Glossographia*, &c., by T. S.

1689.—"A **Pagoda** ... borrows its Name from the *Persian* word *Pout*, which signifies Idol; thence *Pout-Gheda*, a Temple of False Gods, and from thence **Pagode**."—*Ovington*, 159.

1696.—"... qui eussent élévé des **pagodes** au milieu des villes."—*La Bruyère, Caractères*, ed. *Jouast*, 1881, ii. 306.

[1710.—"In India we use this word pagoda (**pagodes**) indiscriminately for idols or temples of the Gentiles."—*Oriente Conquistado*, vol. i. Conq. i. Div. i. 53.]

1717.—"... the **Pagods**, or Churches."—*Phillip's Account*, 12.

1727.—"There are many ancient **Pagods** or Temples in this country, but there is one very particular which stands upon a little Mountain near *Vizagapatam*, where they worship living Monkies."—*A. Hamilton, i.* 380 [ed. 1744].

1736.—"**Págod** [incert. etym.], an idol's temple in China."—*Bailey's Dict.* 2nd ed.

1763.—"These divinities are worshipped in temples called **Pagodas** in every part of Indostan."—*Orme, Hist.* i. 2.

1781.—"During this conflict (at Chillumbrum), all the Indian females belonging to the garrison were collected at the summit of the highest **pagoda**, singing in a loud and melodious chorus hallelujahs, or songs of exhortation, to their people below, which inspired the enemy with a kind of frantic enthusiasm. This, even in the heat of the attack, had a romantic and pleasing effect, the musical sounds being distinctly heard at a considerable distance by the assailants."—*Munro's Narrative*, 222.

1809.—

"In front, with far stretch'd walls, and many
 a tower,
Turret, and dome, and pinnacle elate,
The huge **Pagoda** seemed to load the land."
 Kehama, viii. 4.

[1830.—"... **pagodas**, which are so termed from *paug*, an idol, and *ghoda*, a temple (!) ..."—*Mrs. Elwood, Narrative of a Journey Overland from England*, ii. 27.]

1855.—"... Among a dense cluster of palm-trees and small **pagodas**, rises a colossal Gaudama, towering above both, and, Memnon-like, glowering before him with a placid and eternal smile."—*Letters from the Banks of the Irawadee, Blackwood's Mag.*, May, 1856.

b.—

1498.—"And the King gave the letter with

his own hand, again repeating the words of the oath he had made, and swearing besides by his **pagodes**, which are their idols, that they adore for gods. ..."—*Correa, Lendas*, i. 119.

1582.—"The Divell is oftentimes in them, but they say it is one of their Gods or **Pagodes**."—*Castañeda* (tr. by N. L.), f. 37.

[In the following passage from the same author, as Mr. Whiteway points out, the word is used in both senses, a temple and an idol:

"In Goa I have seen this festival in a **pagoda**, that stands in the island of Divar, which is called Çapatu, where people collect from a long distance; they bathe in the arm of the sea between the two islands, and they believe ... that on that day the idol (**pagode**) comes to that water, and they cast in for him much betel and many plantains and sugar-canes; and they believe that the idol (**pagode**) eats those things."—*Castanheda*, ii. ch. 34. In the orig., **pagode** when meaning a temple has a small, and when the idol, a capital, *P.*]

1584.—"La religione di queste genti non si intende per esser differenti sette fra loro; hanno certi lor **pagodi** che son gli idoli. ..."—Letter of *Sassetti*, in *De Gubernatis*, 155.

1587.—"The house in which his **pagode** or idol standeth is covered with tiles of silver."—*R. Fitch*, in *Hakl.* ii. 391.

1598.—"... The **Pagodes**, their false and divelish idols."—*Linschoten*, 26; [Hak. Soc. i. 86].

1630.—"... so that the Bramanes under each green tree erect temples to **pagods**. ..."—*Lord, Display*, &c.

c. 1630.—"Many deformed **Pagothas** are here worshipped; having this ordinary evasion that they adore not Idols, but the *Deumos* which they represent."—*Sir T. Herbert*, ed. 1665, p. 375.

1664.—

"Their classic model proved a maggot,
Their Directory an Indian **Pagod**."
Hudibras, Pt. II. Canto i.

1693.—"... For, say they, what is the **Pagoda**? it is an image or stone. ..."—In *Wheeler*, i. 269.

1727.—"... the Girl with the Pot of Fire on her Head, walking all the Way before. When they came to the End of their journey ... where was placed another black stone **Pagod**, the Girl set her Fire before it, and run stark mad for a Minute or so."—*A. Hamilton*, i. 274 [ed. 1744].

c. 1737.—

"See thronging millions to the **Pagod** run,
And offer country, Parent, wife or son."
Pope, Epilogue to Sat. I.

1814.—"Out of town six days. On my return, find my poor little **pagod**, Napoleon, pushed off his pedestal;—the thieves are in Paris."—Letter of *Byron's*, April 8, in *Moore's Life*, ed. 1832, iii. 21.

c.—

c. 1566.—"Nell' vscir poi li caualli Arabi di Goa, si paga di datio quaranta due **pagodi** per cauallo, et ogni **pagodo** val otto lire alla nostra moneta; e sono monete d'oro; de modo che li caualli Arabi sono in gran prezzo in que' paesi, come sarebbe trecento quattro cento, cinque cento, a fina mille ducati l'vno."—*C. Federici*, in *Ramusio*, iii. 388.

1597.—"I think well to order and decree that the **pagodes** which come from without shall not be current unless they be of forty and three points (assay?) conformable to the first issue, which is called of *Agra*, and which is of the same value as that of the *San Tomes*, which were issued in its likeness."—*Edict of the King*, in *Archiv. Port. Orient.* iii. 782.

1598.—"There are yet other sorts of money called **Pagodes**. ... They are Indian and Heathenish money with the picture of a Diuell vpon them, and therefore are called **Pagodes**. ..."—*Linschoten*, 54 and 69; [Hak. Soc. i. 187, 242].

1602.—"And he caused to be sent out for the Kings of the Decan and Canara two thousand horses from those that were in Goa, and this brought the King 80,000 **pagodes**, for every one had to pay forty as duty. These were imported by the Moors and other merchants from the ports of Arabia and Persia; in entering Goa they are free and uncharged, but on leaving that place they have to pay these duties."—*Couto*, IV. vi. 6.

["... with a sum of gold **pagodes**, a coin of the upper country (Balagate), each of which is worth 500 *reis* (say 11s. 3d.; the usual value was 360 *reis*)."—*Ibid.* VII. i. 11.]

1623.—"... An Indian Gentile Lord called Rama Rau, who has no more in all than 2000 **pagod** [**paygods**] of annual revenue, of which again he pays about 800 to Venktapà Naieka, whose tributary he is. ..."—*P. della Valle*, ii. 692; [Hak. Soc. ii. 306].

1673.—"About this time the Rajah ... was weighed in Gold, and poised about 16,000 **Pagods**."—*Fryer*, 80.

1676.—"For in regard these **Pagods** are very thick, and cannot be clipt, those that are Masters of the trade, take a Piercer, and pierce the **Pagod** through the side, halfway or more, taking out of one piece as much Gold as comes to two or three Sous."—*Tavernier*, E.T. 1684, ii. 4; [*Ball*, ii. 92].

1780.—"Sir Thomas Rumbold, Bart., resigned the Government of Fort St. George on the Mg. of the 9th inst., and immediately went on board the General Barker. It is confidently reported that he has not been able to accumulate a very large Fortune, considering the long time he has been at Madrass; indeed people say it amounts to only 17 Lacks and a half of **Pagodas**, or a little more than £600,000 sterling."—*Hicky's Bengal Gazette*, April 15.

1785.—"Your servants have no Trade in this country, neither do you pay them high wages, yet in a few years they return to England with many lacs of **pagodas**."—*Nabob of Arcot*, in *Burke's Speech on the Nabob's Debts, Works*, ed. 1852, iv. 18.

1796.—"La Bhagavadi, moneta d'oro, che ha l'immagine della dea Bhagavadi, nome corrotto in **Pagodi o Pagode** dagli Europei, è moneta rotonda, convessa in una parte ..."—*Fra Paolino*, 57.

1803.—"It frequently happens that in the bazaar, the star **pagoda** exchanges for 4 rupees, and at other times for not more than 3."—*Wellington, Desp.*, ed. 1837, ii. 375.

PAGODA-TREE. A slang phrase once current, rather in England than in India, to express the openings to rapid fortune which at one time existed in India. [For the original meaning, see the quotation from Ryklof Van Goens under BO TREE. Mr. Skeat writes: "It seems possible that the idea of a coin tree may have arisen from the practice, among some Oriental nations at least, of making **cash** in moulds, the design of which is based on the plan of a tree. On the E. coast of the Malay Peninsula the name *cashtree* (*poko' pitis*) is applied to cash cast in this form. Gold and silver tributary trees are sent to Siam by the tributary States: in these the leaves are in the shape of ordinary tree leaves."]

1877.—"India has been transferred from the regions of romance to the realms of fact ... the mines of Golconda no longer pay the cost of working, and the **pagoda-tree** has been stripped of all its golden fruit."—*Blackwood's Magazine*, 575.

1881.—"It might be mistaken ... for the work of some modern architect, built for the Nabob of a couple of generations back, who had enriched himself when the **pagoda-tree** was worth the shaking."—*Sat. Review*, Sept. 3, p. 307.

PÁLAGILÁSS, s. This is domestic Hind. for 'Asparagus' (*Panjab N. & Q.* ii. 189).

***PALANKEEN, PALANQUIN**, s. A box-litter for travelling in, with a pole projecting before and behind, which is borne on the shoulders of 4 or 6 men—4 always in Bengal, 6 sometimes in the Telugu country.

The origin of the word is not doubtful, though it is by no means clear how the Portuguese got the exact form which they have handed over to us. The nasal termination may be dismissed as a usual Portuguese addition, such as occurs in *mandarin*, *Baçaim* (*Wasai*), and many other words and names as used by them. The basis of all the forms is Skt. *paryañka*, or *palyañka*, 'a bed,' from which we have Hind. and Mahr. *palang*, 'a bed,' Hind. *pālkī*, 'a palankin,' [Telugu *pallakī*, which is perhaps the origin of the Port. word], Pali *pallanko*, 'a couch, bed, litter, or palankin' (*Childers*), and in Javanese and Malay *palañgki*, 'a litter or sedan' (*Crawfurd*).[1]

It is curious that there is a Spanish word *palanca* (L. Lat. *phalanga*) for a pole used to carry loads on the shoulders of two bearers (called in Sp. *palanquinos*); a method of transport more common in the south than in England, though even in old English the thing has a name, viz. 'a cowlestaff' (see *N.E.D.*). It is just possible that this word (though we do not find it in the Portuguese dictionaries) may have influenced the form in which the early Portuguese visitors to India took up the word.

The *thing* appears already in the *Rāmāyana*. It is spoken of by Ibn Batuta and John Marignolli (both c. 1350), but neither uses this Indian name; and we have not found evidence of *pālkī* older than Akbar (see *Elliot*, iv. 515, and *Āīn*, i. 254).

As drawn by Linschoten (1597), and as described by Grose at Bombay (c. 1760), the palankin was hung from a bamboo which bent in an arch over the vehicle; a form perhaps not yet entirely obsolete in native use. Williamson (*V. M.*, i. 316 *seqq.*) gives an account of the different changes in the fashion of palankins, from which it would appear that the present form must have come into use about the end of the 18th century. Up to 1840–50 most people in Calcutta kept a

1 In *Canticles*, iii. 9, the "ferculum quod *fecit sibi rex Salomon de lignis Libani*" is in the Hebrew *appiryōn*, which has by some been supposed to be Greek φορεῖον; highly improbable, as the litter came to Greece from the East. Is it possible that the word can be in some way taken from *paryañka?* The R. V. has *palanquin*. [See the discussion in *Encyclopaedia Biblica*, iii. 2804 *seq.*].

palankin and a set of bearers (usually natives of Orissa), but the practice and the vehicle are now almost, if not entirely, obsolete among the better class of Europeans. Till the same period the palankin, carried by relays of bearers, laid out by the post-office, or by private **chowdries** (q.v.), formed the chief means of accomplishing extensive journeys in India, and the elder of the present writers has undergone hardly less than 8000 or 9000 miles of travelling in going considerable distances (excluding minor journeys) after this fashion. But in the decade named, the palankin began, on certain great roads, to be superseded by the *dawk*-**garry** (a **Palkee-garry** or palankin-carriage, horsed by ponies posted along the road, under the post-office), and in the next decade to a large extent by railway, supplemented by other wheel-carriage, so that the palankin is now used rarely, and only in out-of-the-way localities.

c. 1340.—"Some time afterwards the pages of the Mistress of the Universe came to me with a *dūla*. ... It is like a bed of state ... with a pole of wood above ... this is curved, and made of the Indian cane, solid and compact. Eight men, divided into two relays, are employed in turn to carry one of these; four carry the palankin whilst four rest. These vehicles serve in India the same purpose as donkeys in Egypt; most people use them habitually in going and coming. If a man has his own slaves, he is carried by them; if not he hires men to carry him. There are also a few found for hire in the city, which stand in the bazars, at the Sultan's gate, and also at the gates of private citizens."—*Ibn Batuta*, iii. 386.

c. 1350.—"Et eciam homines et mulieres portant super scapulas in lecticis de quibus in Canticis: *ferculum fecit sibi Salomon de lignis Libani*, id est lectulum portatilem sicut portabar ego in Zayton et in India."—*Marignolli* (see *Cathay*, &c., p. 331).

1515.—"And so assembling all the people made great lamentation, and so did throughout all the streets the women, married and single, in a marvellous way. The captains lifted him (the dead Alboquerque), seated as he was in a chair, and placed him on a **palanquim**, so that he was seen by all the people; and João Mendes Botelho, a knight of Afonso d'Alboquerque's making (who was) his Ancient, bore the banner before the body."—*Correa, Lendas*, II. i. 460.

1563.—"... and the branches are for the most part straight except some ... which they twist and bend to form the canes for **palenquins** and portable chairs, such as are used in India."—*Garcia*, f. 194.

1567.—"... with eight Falchines (*fachini*), which are hired to carry the **palanchines**, eight for a **Palanchine** (*palanchino*), foure at a time."—*C. Frederike*, in *Hakl.* ii. 348.

1598.—"... after them followeth the bryde between two *Commeres*, each in their **Pallamkin**, which is most costly made."—*Linschoten*, 56; [Hak. Soc. i. 196].

1606.—"The **palanquins** covered with curtains, in the way that is usual in this Province, are occasion of very great offences against God our Lord" ... (the Synod therefore urges the Viceroy to prohibit them altogether, and) ... "enjoins on all ecclesiastical persons, on penalty of sentence of excommunication, and of forfeiting 100 *pardaos* to the church court[1] not to use the said **palanquins**, made in the fashion above described."—4th Act of 5th Council of Goa, in *Archiv. Port. Orient.*, fasc. 4. (See also under BOY.)

The following is the remonstrance of the city of Goa against the ecclesiastical action in this matter, addressed to the King:

1606.—"Last year this City gave your Majesty an account of how the Archbishop Primate proposed the issue of orders that the women should go with their **palanquins** uncovered, or at least half uncovered, and how on this matter were made to him all the needful representations and remonstrances on the part of the whole community, giving the reasons against such a proceeding, which were also sent to Your Majesty. Nevertheless in a Council that was held this last summer, they dealt with this subject, and they agreed to petition Your Majesty to order that the said **palanquins** should travel in such a fashion that it could be seen who was in them.

"The matter is of so odious a nature, and of such a description that Your Majesty should grant their desire in no shape whatever, nor give any order of the kind, seeing this place is a frontier fortress. The reasons for this have been written to Your Majesty; let us beg Your Majesty graciously to make no new rule; and this is the petition of the whole community to Your Majesty."—*Carta, que a Cidade de Goa escrevea a Sua Magestade, o anno de* 1606. In *Archiv. Port. Orient.*, fasc. iº. 2ª. Edição, 2ª, Parte, 186.

1608–9.—"If comming forth of his Pallace, hee (Jahāngīr) get vp on a Horse, it is a signe that he goeth for the Warres; but if he be vp vpon an Elephant or **Palankine**, it will bee but an hunting Voyage."—*Hawkins*, in *Purchas*, i. 219.

---

1 "*Pagos do aljube.*" We are not sure of the meaning.

1616.—"... *Abdala Chan*, the great governour of *Amadauas*, being sent for to Court in disgrace, comming in Pilgrim's Clothes with fortie servants on foote, about sixtie miles in counterfeit humiliation, finished the rest in his **Pallankee**."—*Sir T. Roe*, in *Purchas*, i. 552; [Hak. Soc. ii. 278, which reads **Palanckee**, with other minor variances].

In Terry's account, in *Purchas*, ii. 1475, we have a **Pallankee**, and (p. 1481) **Palanka**; in a letter of Tom Coryate's (1615) **Palankeen**.

1623.—"In the territories of the Portuguese in India it is forbidden to men to travel in **palankin** (*Palanchino*) as in good sooth too effeminate a proceeding; nevertheless as the Portuguese pay very little attention to their laws, as soon as the rains begin to fall they commence getting permission to use the **palankin**, either by favour or by bribery; and so, gradually, the thing is relaxed, until at last nearly everybody travels in that way, and at all seasons."—*P. della Valle*, i. 611; [comp. Hak. Soc. i. 31].

1659.—"The designing rascal (Sivají) ... conciliated Afzal Khán, who fell into the snare. ... Without arms he mounted the **pálkí**, and proceeded to the place appointed under the fortress. He left all his attendants at the distance of a long arrow-shot. ... Sivají had a weapon, called in the language of the Dakhin *bichúá* (*i.e.* 'scorpion') on the fingers of his hand, hidden under his sleeve. ..."—*Kháfi Khán*, in *Elliot*, vii. 259. See also p. 509.

c. 1660.—"... From *Golconda* to *Maslipatan* there is no travelling by waggons. ... But instead of Coaches they have the convenience of **Pallekies**, wherein you are carried with more speed and more ease than in any part of India."—*Tavernier*, E.T. ii. 70; [ed. *Ball*, i. 175]. This was quite true up to our own time. In 1840 the present writer was carried on that road, a stage of 25 miles in little more than 5 hours, by 12 bearers, relieving each other by sixes.

1672. The word occurs several times in Baldaeus as **Pallinkijn**. Tavernier writes **Palleki** and sometimes **Pallanquin** [*Ball*, i. 45, 175, 390, 392]; Bernier has **Paleky** [ed. *Constable*, 214, 283, 372].

1673.—"... ambling after these a great pace, the **Palankeen**-Boys support them four of them, two at each end of a *Bambo*, which is a long hollow Cane ... arched in the middle ... where hangs the **Palenkeen**, as big as an ordinary Couch, broad enough to tumble in. ..."—*Fryer*, 34.

1678.—"The permission you are pleased to give us to buy a **Pallakee** on the Company's Acct. Shall make use off as Soone as can possible meet wth one y[t] may be fitt for y[e] purpose. ..."—MS. Letter from *Factory* at *Ballasore* to the *Council* (of Fort. St. George), March 9, in India Office.

1682.—Joan Nieuhof has **Palakijn**. *Zee en Lant-Reize*, ii. 78.

["The Agent and Council ... allowed him (Mr. Clarke) 2 pag[os] p. mensem more towards the defraying his **pallanquin** charges, he being very crazy and much weaken'd by his sicknesse."—*Pringle, Diary Ft. St. Geo.* 1st ser. i. 34.]

1720.—"I desire that all the free Merchants of my acquaintance do attend me in their **palenkeens** to the place of burial."—Will of *Charles Davers*, Merchant, in *Wheeler*, ii. 340.

1726.—"... **Palangkyn** dragers" (palankin-bearers).—*Valentijn, Ceylon*, 45.

1736.—"**Palanquin**, a kind of chaise or chair, borne by men on their shoulders, much used by the Chinese and other Eastern peoples for travelling from place to place."—*Bailey's Dict.* 2nd ed.

1750-52.—"The greater nobility are carried in a **palekee**, which looks very like a hammock fastened to a pole."—*Toreen's Voyage to Suratte, China*, &c., ii. 201.

1754-58.—In the former year the Court of Directors ordered that Writers in their Service should "lay aside the expense of either horse, chair, or **Palankeen**, during their Writership." The Writers of Fort William (4th Nov. 1756) remonstrated, begging "to be indulged in keeping a **Palankeen** for such months of the year as the excessive heats and violent rains make it impossible to go on foot without the utmost hazard of their health." The Court, however, replied (11 Feb. 1756): "We very well know that the indulging Writers with **Palankeens** has not a little contributed to the neglect of business we complain of, by affording them opportunities of rambling"; and again, with an obduracy and fervour too great for grammar (March 3, 1758): "We do most positively order and direct (and will admit of no representation for postponing the execution of) that no Writer whatsoever be permitted to keep either **palankeen**, horse, or chaise, during his Writership, on pain of being immediately dismissed from our service."—In *Long*, pp. 54, 71, 130.

1780.—"The Nawaub, on seeing his condition, was struck with grief and compassion; but ... did not even bend his eyebrow at the sight, but lifting up the curtain of the **Palkee** with his own hand, he saw that the eagle of his (Ali Ruza's) soul, at one flight had winged its way to the gardens of Paradise."—*H. of Hydur*, p. 429.

1784.—

"The Sun in gaudy **palanqueen**
  Curtain'd with purple, fring'd with gold,
Firing no more heav'n's vault serene,

Retir'd to sup with Ganges old."

Plassy Plain, a ballad by *Sir W. Jones; in Life and Works*, ed. 1807, ii. 503.

1804.—"Give orders that a **palanquin** may be made for me; let it be very light, with the pannels made of canvas instead of wood, and the poles fixed as for a dooley. Your Bengally **palanquins** are so heavy that they cannot be used out of Calcutta."—*Wellington* (to Major Shaw), June 20.

The following measures a change in ideas. A palankin is now hardly ever used by a European, even of humble position, much less by the opulent:

1808.—"**Palkee**. A litter well known in India, called by the English **Palankeen**. A Guzerat punster (aware of no other) hazards the Etymology *Pa-lakhee* [*pāo-lākhī*] a thing requiring an annual income of a quarter Lack to support it and corresponding luxuries."—*R. Drummond, Illustrations*, &c.

"The conveyances of the island (Madeira) are of three kinds, viz.: horses, mules, and a litter, ycleped a **palanquin**, being a chair in the shape of a bathing-tub, with a pole across, carried by two men, as doolees are in the east."—*Welsh, Reminiscences*, i. 282.

1809.—

"Woe! Woe! around their **palankeen**, As on
a bridal day
With symphony and dance and song,
Their kindred and their friends come on,
The dance of sacrifice! The funeral song!"

Kehama, i. 6.

c. 1830.—"Un curieux indiscret reçut un galet dans la tête; on l'emporta baigné de sang, couché dans un **palanquin**."—*V. Jacquemont, Corr.* i. 67.

1880.—"It will amaze readers in these days to learn that the Governor-General sometimes condescended to be carried in a **Palanquin**—a mode of conveyance which, except for long journeys away from railroads, has long been abandoned to portly Baboos, and Eurasian clerks."—*Sat. Rev.*, Feb. 14.

1881.—"In the great procession on Corpus Christi Day, when the Pope is carried in a **palanquin** round the Piazza of St. Peter, it is generally believed that the cushions and furniture of the **palanquin** are so arranged as to enable him to bear the fatigue of the ceremony by sitting whilst to the spectator he appears to be kneeling."—*Dean Stanley, Christian Institutions*, 231.

PALE ALE. The name formerly given to the beer brewed for Indian use. (See BEER.)

1784.—"London Porter and **Pale Ale**, light and excellent, Sicca Rupees 150 per hhd."—Advt. in *Seton-Karr*, i. 39.

1793.—"For sale ... **Pale Ale** (per hhd.) ... Rs. 80."—*Bombay Courier*, Jan. 19.

[1801.—"1. **Pale Ale**; 2. strong ale; 3. small beer; 4. brilliant beer; 5. strong porter; 6. light porter; 7. brown stout."—Advt. in *Carey, Good Old Days*, i. 147.]

1848.—"Constant dinners, tiffins, **pale ale**, and claret, the prodigious labour of cutchery, and the refreshment of brandy pawnee, which he was forced to take there, had this effect upon Waterloo Sedley."—*Vanity Fair*, ed. 1867, ii. 258.

1853.—"Parmi les cafés, les cabarets, les gargotes, l'on rencontre çà et là une taverne anglaise placardée de sa pancarte de porter simple et double, d'old Scotch ale, d'*East India* **Pale beer**."—*Th. Gautier, Constantinople*, 22.

1867.—

"Pain bis, galette ou panaton,
Fromage à la pie ou Stilton,
Cidre ou **pale-ale** de Burton,
Vin de brie, ou branne-mouton."

Th. Gautier à Ch. Garnier.

PALEMPORE, s. A kind of chintz bed-cover, sometimes made of beautiful patterns, formerly made at various places in India, especially at Sadras and Masulipatam, the importation of which into Europe has become quite obsolete, but under the greater appreciation of Indian manufactures has recently shown some tendency to revive. The etymology is not quite certain,—we know no place of the name likely to have been the eponymic,—and possibly it is a corruption of a hybrid (Hind. and Pers.) *palang-posh*, 'a bed-cover,' which occurs below, and which may have been perverted through the existence of Salempore as a kind of stuff. The probability that the word originated in a perversion of *palang-posh*, is strengthened by the following entry in Bluteau's *Dict.* (*Suppt.* 1727.)

"CHAUDUS or CHAUDEUS são huns panos grandes, que servem para cobrir camas e outras cousas. São pintados de cores muy vistosas, e alguns mais finos, a que chamão **palangapuzes**. Fabricão-se de algodão em Bengala e Choromandel,"—*i.e.* *"Chaudus* ou *Chaudeus"* (this I cannot identify, perhaps the same as *Choutar* among **Piece-goods**) "are a kind of large cloths serving to cover beds and other things. They are painted with gay colours, and there are some of a finer description which are called **palangposhes**," &c.

[For the mode of manufacture at Masulipatam, see *Journ. Ind. Art.* iii. 14. Mr.

Pringle (*Madras Selections*, 4th ser. p. 71, and *Diary Ft. St. Geo.* 1st ser. iii. 173) has questioned this derivation. The word may have been taken from the State and town of *Pālanpur* in Guzerat, which seems to have been an emporium for the manufactures of N. India, which was long noted for chintz of this kind.]

1648.—"Int Governe van *Raga mandraga* ... werden veel ... **Salamporij** ... gemaeckt."—*Van den Broecke*, 87.

1673.—"Staple commodities (at Masulipatam) are calicuts white and painted, **Palempores**, Carpets."—*Fryer*, 34.

1813.—

"A stain on every bush that bore
A fragment of his **palampore**,
His breast with wounds unnumber'd riven,
His back to earth, his face to heaven ..."

Byron, The Giaour.

1814.—"A variety of tortures were inflicted to extort a confession; one was a sofa, with a platform of tight cordage in network, covered with a **palampore**, which concealed a bed of thorns placed under it: the collector, a corpulent Banian, was then stripped of his *jama* (see JAMMA), or muslin robe, and ordered to lie down."—*Forbes, Or. Mem.* ii. 429; [2nd ed. ii. 54].

1817.—"... these cloths ... serve as coverlids, and are employed as a substitute for the Indian **palempore**."—*Raffles, Java*, 171; [2nd ed. i. 191].

[1855.—

"The jewelled amaun of thy zemzem is bare,
And the folds of thy **palampore** wave in
the air."

Bon Gaultier, Eastern Serenade.]

1862.—"Bala posh, or **Palang posh**, quilt or coverlet, 300 to 1000 rupees."—*Punjab Trade Report*, App. p. xxxviii.

1880.—"... and third, the celebrated **palampores**, or 'bed-covers,' of Masulipatam, Fatehgarh, Shikarpur, Hazara, and other places, which in point of art decoration are simply incomparable."—*Birdwood, The Industrial Arts of India*, 260.

PALKEE-GARRY, s. A 'palankin-coach,' as it is termed in India; *i.e.* a carriage shaped somewhat like a palankin on wheels; Hind. *pālkī-gāṛī*. The word is however one formed under European influences. ["The system of conveying passengers by palkee carriages and trucks was first established between Cawnpore and Allahabad in May 1843, and extended to Allyghur in November of the same year; Delhi was included in June 1845, Agra and Meerut about the same time; the now-going line not being, however, ready till January 1846" (*Carey, Good Old Days*, ii. 91).]

1878.—"The Governor-General's carriage ... may be jostled by the hired '**palki-gharry**,' with its two wretched ponies, rope harness, nearly naked driver, and wheels whose sinuous motions impress one with the idea that they must come off at the next revolution."—*Life in the Mofussil*, i. 38.

This description applies rather to the **cranchee** (q.v.) than to the palkee-garry, which is (or used to be) seldom so sordidly equipt. [Mr. Kipling's account of the Calcutta *palki gari* (*Beast and Man*, 192) is equally uncomplimentary.]

PANDY, s. The most current colloquial name for the Sepoy mutineer during 1857–58. The surname *Pāṇḍē* [Skt. *Paṇḍita*] was a very common one among the high-caste Sepoys of the Bengal army, being the title of a *Jōt* [*got, gotra*] or subdivisional branch of the Brahmins of the Upper Provinces, which furnished many men to the ranks. "The first two men hung" (for mutiny) "at Barrackpore were **Pandies** by caste, hence all sepoys were **Pandies**, and ever will be so called" (*Bourchier*, as below). "In the Bengal army before the Mutiny, there was a person employed in the quarter-guard to strike the gong, who was known as the *gunta* **Pandy**" (*M.-G. Keatinge*). *Ghanṭā*, 'a gong or bell.'

1857.—"As long as I feel the entire confidence I do, that we shall triumph over this iniquitous combination, I cannot feel gloom. I leave this feeling to the **Pandies**, who have sacrificed honour and existence to the ghost of a delusion."—*H. Greathed, Letters during the Siege of Delhi*, 99.

"We had not long to wait before the line of guns, howitzers, and mortar carts, chiefly drawn by elephants, soon hove in sight. ... Poor **Pandy**, what a pounding was in store for you! ..."—*Bourchier, Eight Months' Campaign against the Bengal Sepoy Army*, 47.

PAPAYA, PAPAW, s. This word seems to be from America like the insipid, not to say nasty, fruit which it denotes (*Carica papaya*, L.). A quotation below indicates that it came by way of the Philippines and Malacca. [The Malay name, according to Mr. Skeat, is *betik*, which comes from the same Ar. form as **pateca**, though *papaya* and *kapaya* have been introduced by Europeans.] Though of little esteem, and though the tree's peculiar quality of rendering fresh meat tender which is familiar in the W. Indies, is little known or taken advantage of, the tree is found in gardens and compounds all over India, as far north as Delhi. In the N.W. Provinces it is called by the native gardeners *aranḍ-kharbūza*, 'castor-oil-tree-melon,' no doubt from the superficial resemblance of its foliage to that of the *Palma Christi*. According to Moodeen Sheriff it has a Perso-Arabic name *'anbah-i-Hindī*; in Canarese it is called *P'arangi-haṇṇu* or *-mara* ('Frank or Portuguese fruit, tree'). The name *papaya* according to Oviedo as quoted by Littré ("*Oviedo*, t. 1. p. 333, Madrid, 1851,"—we cannot find it in *Ramusio*) was that used in Cuba, whilst the Carib name was *ababai*.[1] [Mr. J. Platt, referring to his article in 9th Ser. *Notes & Queries*, iv. 515, writes: "Malay *papaya*, like the Accra term *kpakpa*, is a European loan word. The evidence for Carib origin is, firstly, Oviedo's *Historia*, 1535 (in the ed. of 1851, vol. i. 323): 'Del arbol que en esta isla Española llaman *papaya*, y en la tierra firme los llaman los Españoles los higos del mastuerço, y en la provincia de Nicaragua llaman a tal arbol *olocoton*.' Secondly, Breton, *Dictionnaire Caraibe*, has: '*Ababai*, papayer.' Gilij, *Saggio*, 1782, iii. 146 (quoted in *N. & Q.*, *u.s.*), says the Otamic word is *pappai*."] Strange liberties are taken with the spelling. Mr. Robinson (below) calls it *popeya*; Sir L. Pelly (*J.R.G.S.* xxxv. 232), *poppoi* (*ὦ πόποι!*). **Papaya** is applied in the Philippines to Europeans who, by long residence, have fallen into native ways and ideas.

c. 1550.—"There is also a sort of fruit resembling figs, called by the natives **Papaie** ... peculiar to this kingdom" (Peru).—*Girol. Benzoni*, 242.

1598.—"There is also a fruite that came out of the Spanish Indies, brought from beyond ye *Philipinas* or *Lusons* to *Malacca*, and frõ thence to *India*, it is called **Papaios**, and is very like a *Mellon* ... and will not grow, but alwaies two together, that is male and female ... and when they are diuided and set apart one from the other, then they yield no fruite at all. ... This fruite at the first for the strangeness thereof was much esteemed, but now they account not of it."—*Linschoten*, 97; [Hak. Soc. ii. 35].

c. 1630.—"... **Pappaes**, Cocoes, and Plantains, all sweet and delicious. ..."—*Sir T. Herbert*, ed. 1665, p. 350.

c. 1635.—

"The Palma Christi and the fair **Papaw**
Now but a seed (preventing Nature's Law)
In half the circle of the hasty year,
Project a shade, and lovely fruits do wear."
Waller, Battle of the Summer Islands.

1658.—"Utraque Pinoguaçu (mas. et fœmina), Mamoeira Lusitanis dicta, vulgò **Papay**, cujus fructum *Mamam* vocant a figura, quia mammae instar pendet in arbore ... carne lutea instar melonum, sed sapore ignobiliori. ..."—*Gul. Pisonis ... de Indiae utriusque Re Naturali et Medicâ*, Libri xiv. 159–160.

1673.—"Here the flourishing **Papaw** (in Taste like our Melons, and as big, but growing on a Tree leaf'd like our Fig-tree. ..."—*Fryer*, 19.

1705.—"Il y a aussi des ananas, des **Papées**. ..."—*Luillier*, 33.

1764.—

"Thy temples shaded by the tremulous palm,
Or quick **papaw**, whose top is necklaced
round
With numerous rows of particoloured fruit."
Grainger, Sugar Cane, iv.

[1773.—"**Paw Paw**. This tree rises to, 20 feet, sometimes single, at other times it is divided into several bodies."—*Ives*, 480.]

1878.—"... the rank **popeyas** clustering beneath their coronal of stately leaves."—*Ph. Robinson, In My Indian Garden*, 50.

***PARIAH, PARRIAR**, &c., s.

a. The name of a low caste of Hindus in Southern India, constituting one of the most numerous castes, if not *the* most numerous, in the Tamil country. The word in its present shape means properly 'a drummer.' Tamil *paṛai* is the large drum, beaten at certain festivals, and the hereditary beaters of it are called (sing.) *paṛaiyan*, (pl.) *paṛaiyar*. [Dr. Oppert's theory (*Orig. Inhabitants*, 32 *seq.*) that the word is a form of *Pahaṛiyā*, 'a mountaineer' is not probable.] In the city of Madras this caste forms one fifth of the whole population, and from it come (unfortunately) most of the domestics in European service in that part of India. As with other castes low in caste-rank they are also low in habits, frequently eating carrion and other objectionable food, and addicted to drink. From their coming into contact with and under observation of Europeans, more habitually than any similar caste, the name *Pariah* has come to be regarded as applicable to the whole body of the lowest castes,

1 See also *De Candolle, Plantes Cultivées*, p. 234.

or even to denote outcastes or people without any caste. But this is hardly a correct use. There are several castes in the Tamil country considered to be lower than the *Pariahs*, *e.g.* the caste of shoemakers, and the lowest caste of washermen. And the *Pariah* deals out the same disparaging treatment to these that he himself receives from higher castes. The Pariahs "constitute a well-defined, distinct, ancient caste, which has 'subdivisions' of its own, its own peculiar usages, its own traditions, and its own jealousy of the encroachments of the castes which are above it and below it. They constitute, perhaps, the most numerous caste in the Tamil country. In the city of Madras they number 21 per cent. of the Hindu people."—*Bp. Caldwell, u. i.*, p. 545. Sir Walter Elliot, however, in the paper referred to further on includes under the term *Paraiya* all the servile class not recognised by Hindus of caste as belonging to their community.

A very interesting, though not conclusive, discussion of the ethnological position of this class will be found in Bp. Caldwell's *Dravidian Grammar* (pp. 540–554). That scholar's deduction is, on the whole, that they are probably Dravidians, but he states, and recognises force in, arguments for believing that they may have descended from a race older in the country than the proper Dravidian, and reduced to slavery by the first Dravidians. This last is the view of Sir Walter Elliot, who adduces a variety of interesting facts in its favour, in his paper on the *Characteristics of the Population of South India.*[1]

Thus, in the celebration of the Festival of the Village Goddess, prevalent all over Southern India, and of which a remarkable account is given in that paper, there occurs a sort of Saturnalia in which the Pariahs are the officiating priests, and there are several other customs which are most easily intelligible on the supposition that the Pariahs are the representatives of the earliest inhabitants and original masters of the soil. In a recent communication from this venerable man he writes: 'My brother (Col. C. Elliot, C.B.) found them at Raipur, to be an important and respectable class of cultivators. The Pariahs have a sacerdotal order amongst themselves.' [The view taken in the *Madras Gloss.* is that "they are distinctly Dravidian without fusion, as the Hinduized castes are Dravidian with fusion."]

The mistaken use of *pariah*, as synonymous with out-caste, has spread in English parlance over all India. Thus the lamented Prof. Blochmann, in his *School Geography of India*: "Outcasts are called **pariahs**." The name first became generally known in Europe through Sonnerat's *Travels* (pub. in 1782, and soon after translated into English). In this work the **Parias** figure as the lowest of castes. The common use of the term is however probably due, in both France and England, to the appearance in the Abbé Raynal's famous *Hist. Philosophique des Établissements dans les Indes*, formerly read very widely in both countries, and yet more perhaps to its use in Bernardin de St. Pierre's preposterous though once popular tale, *La Chaumière Indienne*, whence too the misplaced halo of sentiment which reached its acme in the drama of Casimir Delavigne, and which still in some degree adheres to the name. It should be added that Mr. C. P. Brown says expressly: "The word *Paria* is unknown" (in *our* sense?) "to all natives, unless as learned from us."

b. See PARIAH-DOG.

1516.—"There is another low sort of Gentiles, who live in desert places, called **Pareas**. These likewise have no dealings with anybody, and are reckoned worse than the devil, and avoided by everybody; a man becomes contaminated by only looking at them, and is excommunicated. ... They live on the *imane* (*iname, i.e.* yams), which are like the root of *iucca* or *batate* found in the West Indies, and on other roots and wild fruits."—*Barbosa*, in *Ramusio*, i. f. 310. The word in the Spanish version transl. by Lord Stanley of Alderley is *Pareni*, in the Portuguese of the Lisbon Academy, *Parcens*. So we are not

1 Sir W. Elliot refers to the Asoka inscription (Edict II.) as bearing *Palaya* or *Paraya*, named with Choḍa (or Chola), Kerala, &c., as a country or people "in the very centre of the Dravidian group ... a reading which, if it holds good, supplies a satisfactory explanation of the origin of the Paria name and nation" (in *J. Ethnol. Soc.* N.S., 1869, p. 103). But apparently the reading has not held good, for M. Senart reads the name *Pāṁdya* (see *Ind. Ant.* ix. 287). [Mr. V. A. Smith writes: "The Girnar text is very defective in this important passage, which is not in the Dhauli text; that text gives only 11 out of the 14 edicts. The capital of the *Pāṁdiyan* Kingdom was Madura. The history of the kingdom is very imperfectly known. For a discussion of it see *Sewell, Lists of Antiquities, Madras,* vol. ii. Of course it has nothing to do with Parias."]

quite sure that *Pareas* is the proper reading, though this is probable.

1626.—"... The **Pareas** are of worse esteeme."—(*W. Methold*, in) *Purchas, Pilgrimage*, 553.

"... the worst whereof are the abhorred **Piriawes** ... they are in publike Justice the hateful executioners, and are the basest, most stinking, ill-favored people that I have seene."—*Ibid.* 998–9.

1648.—"... the servants of the factory even will not touch it (beef) when they put it on the table, nevertheless there is a caste called **Pareyaes** (they are the most contemned of all, so that if another Gentoo touches them, he is compelled to be dipt in the water) who eat it freely."—*Van de Broecke*, 82.

1672.—"The **Parreas** are the basest and vilest race (accustomed to remove dung and all uncleanness, and to eat mice and rats), in a word a contemned and stinking vile people."—*Baldaeus* (Germ. ed.), 410.

1711.—"The Company allow two or three Peons to attend the Gate, and a **Parrear** Fellow to keep all clean."—*Lockyer*, 20.

"And there ... is such a resort of basket-makers, Scavengers, people that look after the buffaloes, and other **Parriars**, to drink Toddy, that all the Punch-houses in Madras have not half the noise in them."—*Wheeler*, ii. 125.

1716.—"A young lad of the Left-hand Caste having done hurt to a **Pariah** woman of the Right-Hand Caste (big with child), the whole caste got together, and came in a tumultuous manner to demand justice."—*Ibid.* 230.

1717.—"... **Barrier**, or a sort of poor people that eat all sort of Flesh and other things, which others deem unclean."—*Phillips, Account*, &c., 127.

1726.—"As for the separate generations and sorts of people who embrace this religion, there are, according to what some folks say, only 4; but in our opinion they are 5 in number, viz.:

α. The Bramins.

β. The Settreas.

γ. The Weynyas or Veynsyas.

δ. The Sudras.

ε. The **Perrias**, whom the High-Dutch and Danes call **Barriars**."—*Valentijn, Chorom.* 73.

1745.—"Les **Parreas** ... sont regardés comme gens de la plus vile condition, exclus de tous les honneurs et prérogatives. Jusques-là qu'on ne sçauroit les souffrir, ni dans les Pagodes des Gentils, ni dans les Eglises des Jesuites."—*Norbert*, i. 71.

1750.—"*K.* Es ist der Mist von einer Kuh, denselben nehmen die **Parreyer**-Weiber, machen runde Kuchen daraus, und wenn sie in der Sonne genug getrocken sind, so verkauffen sie dieselbigen *Fr.* O Wunder! Ist das das Feuerwerk, das ihr hier halt?"—*Madras*, &c., *Halle*, p. 14.

1770.—"The fate of these unhappy wretches who are known on the coast of Coromandel by the name of **Parias**, is the same even in those countries where a foreign dominion has contributed to produce some little change in the ideas of the people."—*Raynal, Hist. &c.*, see ed. 1783, i. 63.

"The idol is placed in the centre of the building, so that the **Parias** who are not admitted into the temple may have a sight of it through the gates."—*Raynal* (tr. 1777), i. p. 57.

1780.—"If you should ask a common *cooly*, or porter, what cast he is of, he will answer, 'the same as master, **pariar**-*cast*.'"—*Munro's Narrative*, 28–9.

1787.—"... I cannot persuade myself that it is judicious to admit **Parias** into battalions with men of respectable casts. ..."—*Col. Fullarton's View of English Interests in India*, 222.

1791.—"Le *masalchi* y courut pour allumer un flambeau; mais il revient un peu après, pris d'haleine, criant: 'N'approchez pas d'ici; il y a un **Paria!**' Aussitôt la troupe effrayée cria: 'Un **Paria!** Un **Paria!** Le docteur, croyant que c'était quelque animal féroce, mit la main sur ses pistolets. 'Qu'est ce que qu'un **Paria**?' demanda-t-il à son porte-flambeau."—*B. de St. Pierre, La Chaumière Indienne*, 48.

1800.—"The **Parriar**, and other impure tribes, comprising what are called the *Punchum Bundum*, would be beaten, were they to attempt joining in a Procession of any of the gods of the Brahmins, or entering any of their temples."—*Buchanan's Mysore*, i. 20.

c. 1805–6.—"The Dubashes, then all powerful at Madras, threatened loss of cast and absolute destruction to any Brahmin who should dare to unveil the mysteries of their language to a **Pariar** *Frengi*. This reproach of *Pariar* is what we have tamely and strangely submitted to for a long time, when we might with a great facility have assumed the respectable character of *Chatriya*."—*Letter of Leyden*, in *Morton's Memoir*, ed. 1819, p. lxvi.

1809.—"Another great obstacle to the reception of Christianity by the Hindoos, is the admission of the **Parias** in our Churches. ..."—*Ld. Valentia*, i. 246.

1821.—

"Il est sur ce rivage une race flêtrie,
Une race étrangère au sein de sa patrie.
Sans abri protecteur, sans temple hospitalier,
Abominable, impie, horrible au peuple entier.
Les **Parias**; le jour à regret les éclaire,
La terre sur son sein les porte avec colère.

* * * * *

Eh bien! mais je frémis; tu vas me fuir
peut-être;
Je suis un **Paria**. . . ."
Casimir Delavigne, Le Paria, Acte 1. Sc. 1.

1843.—"The Christian **Pariah**, whom both sects curse, Does all the good he can and loves his brother."—*Forster's Life of Dickens*, ii. 31.

1873.—"The Tamilas hire a **Pariya** (*i.e.* drummer) to perform the decapitation at their Badra Kâli sacrifices."—*Kittel*, in *Ind. Ant.* ii. 170.

1878.—"L'hypothèse la plus vraisemblable, en tout cas la plus heureuse, est celle qui suppose que le nom propre et spécial de cette race [*i.e.* of the original race inhabiting the Deccan before contact with northern invaders] était le mot '**paria**'; ce mot dont l'orthographe correcte est **pareiya**, derivé de *par'ei*, 'bruit, tambour,' et à très-bien, pu avoir le sens de 'parleur, doué de la parole'"(?)—*Hovelacque et Vinson, Etudes de Linguistique*, &c., Paris, 67.

1872.—
"Fifine, ordained from first to last,
In body and in soul
For one life-long debauch,
The **Pariah** of the north,
The European *nautch*."
Browning, Fifine at the Fair.

Very good rhyme, but no reason. See under NAUTCH.

The word seems also to have been adopted in Java, *e.g.*:

1860.—"We Europeans ... often ... stand far behind compared with the poor **pariahs**."—*Max Havelaar*, ch. vii.

PARIAH-ARRACK, s. In the 17th and 18th centuries this was a name commonly given to the poisonous native spirit commonly sold to European soldiers and sailors. [See FOOL'S RACK.]

1671-72.—"The unwholesome liquor called **Parrier-arrack**. ..."—*Sir W. Langhorne*, in *Wheeler*, iii. 422.

1711.—"The Tobacco, Beetle, and **Pariar Arack**, on which such great profit arises, are all expended by the Inhabitants."—*Lockyer*, 13.

1754.—"I should be very glad to have your order to bring the ship up to Calcutta ... as ... the people cannot here have the opportunity of intoxicating and killing themselves with **Pariar Arrack**."—In *Long*, 51.

PARIAH-DOG, s. The common ownerless yellow dog, that frequents all inhabited places in the East, is universally so called by Europeans, no doubt from being a low-bred casteless animal; often elliptically '**pariah**' only.

1789.—"... A species of the common cur, called a **pariar-dog**."—*Munro, Narr.* p. 36.

1810.—"The nuisance may be kept circling for days, until forcibly removed, or until the **pariah dogs** swim in, and draw the carcase to the shore."—*Williamson, V. M.* ii. 261.

1824.—"The other beggar was a **Pariah dog**, who sneaked down in much bodily fear to our bivouac."—*Heber*, ed. 1844, i. 79.

1875.—"Le Musulman qui va prier à la mosquée, maudit les **parias** honnis."—*Rev. des Deux Mondes*, April, 539.

[1883.—"**Paraya Dogs** are found in every street."—*T. V. Row, Man. of Tanjore Dist.* 104.]

PARIAH-KITE, s. The commonest Indian kite, *Milvus Govinda*, Sykes, notable for its great numbers, and its impudence. "They are excessively bold and fearless, often snatching morsels off a dish *en route* from kitchen to hall, and even, according to Adams, seizing a fragment from a man's very mouth" (*Jerdon*). Compare quotation under BRAHMINY KITE.

[1880.—"I had often supposed that the scavenger or **Pariah Kites** (*Milvus govinda*), which though generally to be seen about the tents, are not common in the jungles, must follow the camp for long distances, and today I had evidence that such was the case. ..."—*Ball, Jung le Life*, 655.]

PARSEE, n.p. This name, which distinguishes the descendants of those emigrants of the old Persian stock, who left their native country, and, retaining their Zoroastrian religion, settled in India to avoid Mahommedan persecution, is only the old form of the word for a Persian, viz., *Pārsī*, which Arabic influences have in more modern times converted into *Fārsī*. The Portuguese have used both *Parseo* and *Perseo*. From the latter some of our old travellers have taken the form *Persee*; from the former doubtless we got *Parsee*. It is a curious example of the way in which different accidental mouldings of the same word come to denote entirely different ideas, that Persian, in this form, in Western India, means a Zoroastrian fire-worshipper, whilst *Pathi*, a Burmese corruption of the same word, in Burma means a Mahommedan.

c. 1328.—"There be also other pagan-folk in this India who worship fire; they bury not their dead, neither do they burn them, but cast them into the midst of a certain roofless tower, and there expose them totally uncovered to the fowls of heaven. These believe in two First Principles, to wit, of Evil and of Good, of Darkness and of Light."—*Friar Jordanus*, 21.

1552.—"In any case he dismissed them with favour and hospitality, showing himself glad of the coming of such personages, and granting them protection for their ships as being (**Parseos**) Persians of the Kingdom of Ormuz."—*Barros*, I. viii. 9.

"... especially after these were induced by the Persian and Guzerati Moors (*Mouros*, **Parseos** *e Guzarates*) to be converted from heathen (*Gentios*) to the sect of Mahamed."—*Ibid.* II. vi. i.

[1563.—"There are other herb-sellers (*mercadores de boticas*) called Coaris, and in the Kingdom of Cambay they call them **Esparcis**, and we Portuguese call them Jews, but they are not, only Hindus who came from Persia and have their own writing."—*Garcia*, p. 213.]

1616.—"There is one sect among the Gentiles, which neither burne nor interre their dead (they are called **Parcees**) who incircle pieces of ground with high stone walls, remote from houses or Road-wayes, and therein lay their Carcasses, wrapped in Sheetes, thus having no other Tombes but the gorges of rauenous Fowles."—*Terry*, in *Purchas*, ii. 1479.

1630.—"Whilst my observation was bestowed on such inquiry, I observed in the town of Surrat, the place where I resided, another Sect called the **Persees**. ..."—*Lord, Two Forraigne Sects.*

1638.—"Outre les Benjans il y a encore vne autre sorte de Payens dans le royaume de *Gusuratte*, qu'ils appellent **Parsis**. Ce sont des Perses de Fars, et de Chorasan."—*Mandelslo* (Paris, 1659), 213.

1648.—"They (the **Persians** of India, *i.e. Parsees*) are in general a fast-gripping and avaricious nation (not unlike the Benyans and the Chinese), and very fraudulent in buying and selling."—*Van Twist*, 48.

1653.—"Les Ottomans appellent *gueuure* vne secte de Payens, que nous connaissons sous le nom d'adorateurs du feu, les Persans sous celuy d'*Atechperés*, et les Indous sous celuy de **Parsi**, terme dont ils se nomment eux-mesmes."—*De la Boullaye-le-Gouz*, ed. 1657, p. 200.

1672.—"Non tutti ancora de' Gentili sono d' vna medesima fede. Alcuni descendono dalli **Persiani**, li quali si conoscono dal colore, ed adorano il fuoco. ... In Suratte ne trouai molti. ..."—*P. F. Vincenzo Maria, Viaggio*, 234.

1673.—"On this side of the Water are people of another Offspring than those we have yet mentioned, these be called **Parseys** ... these are somewhat white, and I think nastier than the Gentues. ..."—*Fryer*, 117.

"The **Parsies**, as they are called, are of the old Stock of the Persians, worship the Sun and Adore the Elements; are known only about Surat."—*Ibid.* p. 197.

1689.—"... the **Persies** are a Sect very considerable in India. ..."—*Ovington*, 370.

1726.—"... to say a word of a certain other sort of Heathen who have spread in the City of Suratte and in its whole territory, and who also maintain themselves in Agra, and in various places of Persis, especially in the Province of Kerman, at Yezd, and in Ispahan. They are commonly called by the Indians **Persees** or **Parsis**, but by the Persians *Gaurs* or *Gebbers*, and also *Atech Peres* or adorers of Fire."—*Valentijn*, iv. (*Suratte*) 153.

1727.—"The **Parsees** are numerous about Surat and the adjacent Countries. They are a remnant of the ancient Persians."—*A. Hamilton*, ch. xiv; [ed. 1744, i. 159].

1877.—"... en se levant, le **Parsi**, après s'être lavé les mains et la figure avec l'urine du taureau, met sa ceinture en disant: Souverain soit Ormuzd, abattu soit Ahrimān."—*Darmesteter*, *Ormuzd et Ahriman*, p. 2.

PATCHOULI, PATCH-LEAF, also **PUTCH** and **PUTCHA-LEAF,** s. In Beng. *pachapāt*; Deccani Hind. *pacholī*. The latter are trade names of the dried leaves of a labiate plant allied to mint (*Pogostemon patchouly*, Pelletier). It is supposed to be a cultivated variety of *Pogostemon Heyneanus*, Bentham, a native of the Deccan. It is grown in native gardens throughout India, Ceylon, and the Malay Islands, and the dried flowering spikes and leaves of the plant, which are used, are sold in every bazar in Hindustan. The *pacha-pāt* is used as an ingredient in tobacco for smoking, as hair-scent by women, and especially for stuffing mattresses and laying among clothes as we use lavender. In a fluid form *patchouli* was introduced into England in 1844, and soon became very fashionable as a perfume.

The origin of the word is a difficulty. The name is alleged in Drury, and in Forbes Watson's *Nomenclature* to be Bengāli. Littré says the word *patchouli* is *patchey-elley*, 'feuille de patchey'; in what language we know not; perhaps it is from Tamil *pachcha*, 'green,' and *êlâ*, *êlam*, an aromatic perfume for the hair. [The *Madras Gloss.* gives Tamil *paççilai*, *paççai*, 'green,' *ilai*, 'leaf.']

1673.—"*Note*, that if the following Goods from *Acheen* hold out the following *Rates*, the Factor employed is no further responsible.

* * * * *

Patch Leaf, 1 *Bahar Maunds* 7 20 *sear*."—*Fryer*, 209.

PAWN, s. The **betel**-leaf (q.v.) Hind. *pān*, from Skt. *parṇa*, 'a leaf.' It is a North Indian term, and is generally used for the combination of betel, areca-nut, lime, &c., which is politely offered (along with otto of roses) to visitors, and which intimates the termination of the visit. This is more fully termed **pawn-sooparie** (*supārī*, [Skt. *supriya*, 'pleasant,'] is Hind. for areca). "These leaves are not vsed to bee eaten alone, but because of their bitternesse they are eaten with a certaine kind of fruit, which the *Malabars* and *Portugalls* call *Arecca*, the *Gusurates* and *Decanijns Suparijs*. ..." (In *Purchas*, ii. 1781).

1616.—"The King giving mee many good words, and two pieces of his **Pawne** out of his Dish, to eate of the same he was eating. ..."—*Sir T. Roe*, in *Purchas*, i. 576; [Hak. Soc. ii. 453].

[1623.—"... a plant, whose leaves resemble a Heart, call'd here **pan**, but in other parts of India, Betle."—*P. della Valle*, Hak. Soc. i. 36.]

1673.—"... it is the only Indian entertainment, commonly called **Pawn**."—*Fryer*, p. 140.

1809.—"On our departure **pawn** and roses were presented, but we were spared the *attar*, which is every way detestable."—*Ld. Valentia*, i. 101.

***PAWNEE**, s. Hind. *pānī*, 'water.' The word is used extensively in Anglo-Indian compound names, such as **bilayutee pawnee**, 'soda-water,' brandy-**pawnee**, *Khush-bo* **pawnee** (for European scents), &c., &c. An old friend, Gen. J. T. Boileau, R.E. (Bengal), contributes from memory the following Hindi ode to Water, on the Pindaric theme *ἄριστον μὲν ὕδωρ*, or the Thaletic one *ἀρχὴ δὲ τῶν πάντων ὕδωρ*!

"**Pānī** kūā, pānī tāl;
Pānī āṭā, pānī dāl;
Pānī bāgh, pānī ramnā;
Pānī Gangā, pānī Jumnā;
Pānī haṅstā, pānī rotā;
Pānī jagtā, pānī sotā;
Pānī bāp, pānī mā;
Barā nām **Pānī** kā!"

Thus rudely done into English:

"Thou, Water, stor'st our Wells and Tanks,
Thou fillest Gunga's, Jumna's banks;
Thou Water, sendest daily food,
And fruit and flowers and needful wood;
Thou, Water, laugh'st, thou, Water, weepest;
Thou, Water, wak'st, thou, Water, sleepest;
—Father, Mother, in thee blent,—
Hail, O glorious element!"

PAWNEE, KALLA, s. Hind. *kālā pāṇī*, *i.e.* 'Black Water'; the name of dread by which natives of the interior of India designate the Sea, with especial reference to a voyage across it, and to transportation to penal settlements beyond it. "Hindu servants and sepoys used to object to cross the Indus, and called *that* the **kālā pānī**. I think they used to assert that they lost caste by crossing it, which might have induced them to call it by the same name as the ocean,—or possibly they believed it to be part of the river that flows round the world, or the country beyond it to be outside the limits of Aryavartta" (*Note by Lt.-Col. J. M. Trotter*).

1823.—"An agent of mine, who was for some days with Cheetoo" (a famous Pindārī leader), "told me he raved continually about **Kala Panee**, and that one of his followers assured him when the Pindarry chief slept, he used in his dreams to repeat these dreaded words aloud."—*Sir J. Malcolm*, *Central India* (2nd ed.), i. 446.

1833.—"**Kala Pany**, dark water, in allusion to the Ocean, is the term used by the Natives to express transportation. Those in the interior picture the place to be an island of a very dreadful description, and full of malevolent beings, and covered with snakes and other vile and dangerous nondescript animals."—*Mackintosh*, *Acc. of the Tribe of Ramoosies*, 44.

***PEEPUL**, s. Hind. *pīpal*, Skt. *pippala*, *Ficus religiosa*, L.; one of the great fig-trees of India, which often occupies a prominent place in a village, or near a temple. The *Pīpal* has a strong resemblance, in wood and foliage, to some common species of poplar, especially the aspen, and its leaves with their long footstalks quaver like those of that tree. This trembling is popularly attributed to spirits agitating each leaf. And hence probably the name of 'Devil's tree' given to it, according to Rheede ('*Hort. Mal.* i. 48), by Christians in Malabar. It is possible therefore that the name is identical with that of the poplar. Nothing would be more natural than that the Aryan immigrants, on first seeing this Indian tree, should give it the name of the poplar which they had known in more northern latitudes (*popul-us*, *pappel*, &c.). Indeed, in Kumāon, a true sp. of poplar (*Populus ciliata*) is called by the people *gar-pipal* (qu. *ghar*, or 'house'-peepul? [or rather perhaps as another name for it is *pahāṛī*, from *gir*, *giri*, 'a mountain']). Dr. Stewart also says of this *Populus*: "This tree grows to a large size, occasionally reaching. 10 feet in girth, and from its leaves resembling those of the pipal ... is frequently called by that name by plainsmen" (*Punjab Plants*, p. 204). A young *peepul* was shown to one of the present writers in a garden at Palermo as *populo delle Indie*. And the recognised name of the peepul in French books appears to be *peuplier d'Inde*. Col. Tod notices the resemblance (*Rajasthan*, i. 80), and it appears that Vahl called it *Ficus populifolia*. (See also *Geograph. Magazine*, ii. 50). In Balfour's *Indian Cyclopaedia* it is called by the same name in translation, 'the poplar-leaved Fig-tree.' We adduce these facts the more copiously perhaps because the suggestion of the identity of the names *pippala* and *populus* was somewhat scornfully rejected by a very learned scholar. The tree is peculiarly destructive to buildings, as birds drop the seeds in the joints of the masonry, which becomes thus penetrated by the spreading roots of the tree. This is alluded to in a quotation below. "I remember noticing among many Hindus, and especially among Hinduized Sikhs, that they often say *Pīpal ko jātā hūṅ* ('I am going to the Peepul Tree'), to express 'I am going to say my prayers.'" (*Lt.-Col. John Trotter*. (See BO-TREE.)

c. 1550.—"His soul quivered like a **pipal** leaf."—*Rāmāyana of Tulsi Dás*, by *Growse* (1878), ii. 25.

[c. 1590.—"In this place an arrow struck Sri Kishn and buried itself in a **pipal** tree on the banks of the *Sarsuti*."—*Āīn*, ed. *Jarrett*, ii. 246.]

1806.—"Au sortir du village un **pipal** élève sa tête majestueuse. ... Sa nombreuse posterité l'entoure au loin sur la plaine, telle qu'une armée de géans qui entrelacent fraternellement leurs bras informes."—*Haafner*, i. 149. This writer seems to mean a **banyan**. The *peepul* does not drop roots in that fashion.

1817.—"In the second ordeal, an excavation in the ground ... is filled with a fire of **pippal** wood, into which the party must walk barefoot, proving his guilt if he is burned; his innocence, if he escapes unhurt."—*Mill* (quoting from Halhed), ed. 1830, i. 280.

1826.—"A little while after this he arose, and went to a **Peepul**-tree, a short way off, where he appeared busy about something, I could not well make out what."—*Pandurang Hari*, 26; [ed. 1873, i. 36, reading **Peepal**].

1836.—"It is not proper to allow the English, after they have made made war, and peace has been settled, to remain in the city. They are accustomed to act like the **Peepul** tree. Let not Younger Brother therefore allow the English to remain in his country."—Letter from *Court of China* to *Court of Ava*. See *Yule, Mission to Ava*, p. 265.

1854.—"Je ne puis passer sons silence deux beaux arbres ... ce sont le **peuplier** *d'Inde* à larges feuilles, arbre reputé sacré. ..."—*Pallegoix, Siam*, i. 140.

1861.—

"... Yonder crown of umbrage hoar
Shall shield her well; the **Peepul** whisper
  a dirge
And Caryota drop her tearlike store
Of beads; whilst over all slim Casuarine
Points upwards, with her branchlets ever
  green,
To that remaining Rest where Night and
  Tears are o'er."

Barrackpore Park, 18*th Nov.* 1861.

PEKING, n.p. This name means 'North-Court,' and in its present application dates from the early reigns of the Ming Dynasty in China. When they dethroned the Mongol descendants of Chinghiz and Kublai (1368) they removed the capital from Taitu or Khānbāligh (*Cambaluc* of Polo) to the great city on the Yangtsze which has since been known as *Nan-King* or 'South-Court.' But before many years the Mongol capital was rehabilitated as the imperial residence, and became *Pe-King* accordingly. Its preparation for reoccupation began in 1409. The first English mention that we have met with is that quoted by Sainsbury, in which we have the subjects of more than one allusion in Milton.

1520.—"Thomé Pires, quitting this pass, arrived at the Province of Nanquij, at its chief city called by the same name, where the King dwelt, and spent in coming thither always travelling north, four months; by which you may take note how vast a matter is the empire of this gentile prince. He sent word to Thomé Pires that he was to wait for him at **Pequij**, where he would despatch his affair. This city is in another province so called, much further north, in which the King used to dwell for the most part, because it was on the frontier of the Tartars. ..."—*Barros*, III. vi. 1.

1541.—"This City of **Pequin** ... is so prodigious, and the things therein so remarkable, as I do almost repent me for undertaking to discourse of it. ... For one must not imagine it to be, either as the City of *Rome*, or *Constantinople*, or *Venice*, or *Paris*, or *London*, or *Sevill*, or *Lisbon*.

... Nay I will say further, that one must not think it to be like to Grand *Cairo* in *Egypt*, *Tauris* in *Persia*, *Amadaba* (Amadabad, **Avadavat**) in *Cambaya*, *Bisnaga(r)* in *Narsingaa*, *Goura* (Gouro) in *Bengala*, *Ava* in *Chalen*, *Timplan* in *Calaminham*, *Martaban* (Martavão) and *Bagou* in *Pegu*, *Guimpel* and *Tinlau* in *Siammon*, *Odia* in the Kingdom of *Sornau*, *Passavan* and *Dema* in the Island of *Java*, *Pangor* in the Country of the *Lequiens* (no Lequio) *Usangea* (Uzãgnè) in the *Grand Cauchin*, *Lancama* (Laçame) in *Tartary*, and *Meaco* (Mioco) in *Jappun* ... for I dare well affirm that all those same are not to be compared to the least part of the wonderful City of **Pequin**. ..."—*Pínto* (in *Cogan*), p. 136 (orig. cap. cvii.).

[c. 1586.—"The King maketh alwayes his abode in the great city **Pachin**, as much as to say in our language ... the towne of the kingdome."—*Reports of China*, in *Hakl.* ii. 546.]

1614.—"Richard Cocks writing from Ferando understands there are great cities in the country of Corea, and between that and the sea mighty bogs, so that no man can travel there; but great waggons have been invented to go upon broad flat wheels, under sail as ships do, in which they transport their goods ... the deceased Emperor of Japan did pretend to have conveyed a great army in these sailing waggons, to assail the Emperor of China in his City of **Paquin**."—In *Sainsbury*, i. 343.

166*.—

"from the destined walls
Of Cambalu, seat of Cathaian Can,
And Samarchand by Oxus, Temer's throne,
To **Paquin** of Sinaean Kings..."
Paradise Lost, xi. 387–390.

PELICAN, s. This word, in its proper application to the *Pelicanus onocrotalus*, L., is in no respect peculiar to Anglo-India, though we may here observe that the bird is called in Hindi by the poetical name *gagan-bheṛ*, *i.e.* 'Sheep of the Sky,' which we have heard natives with their strong propensity to metathesis convert into the equally appropriate *Gangā-bheṛī* or 'Sheep of the Ganges.' The name may be illustrated by the old term 'Cape-sheep' applied to the albatross.[1] But *Pelican* is habitually misapplied by the British soldier in India to the bird usually called **Adjutant** (q.v.). We may remember how Prof. Max Müller, in his Lectures on Language, tells us that the Tahitians show respect to their sovereign by ceasing to employ in common language those words which form part or the whole of his name, and invent new terms to supply their place. "The object was clearly to guard against the name of the sovereign being ever used, even by accident, in ordinary conversation," 2nd ser. 1864, p. 35, [*Frazer, Golden Bough*, 2nd ed. i. 421 *seqq.*]). Now, by an analogous process, it is possible that some martinet, holding the office of adjutant, at an early date in the Anglo-Indian history, may have resented the ludicrously appropriate employment of the usual name of the bird, and so may have introduced the entirely inappropriate name of *pelican* in its place. It is in the recollection of one of the present writers that a worthy northern matron, who with her husband had risen from the ranks in the —th Light Dragoons, on being challenged for speaking of "the *pelicans* in the barrack-yard," maintained her correctness, conceding only that "some ca'd them **paylicans**, some ca'd them **audjutants**."

1829.—"This officer ... on going round the yard (of the military prison) ... discovered a large beef-bone recently dropped. The sergeant was called to account for this ominous appearance. This sergeant was a shrewd fellow, and he immediately said,—'Oh Sir, the **pelicans** have dropped it.' This was very plausible, for these birds will carry enormous bones; and frequently when fighting for them they drop them, so that this might very probably have been the case. The moment the dinner-trumpet sounds, whole flocks of these birds are in attendance at the barrack-doors, waiting for bones, or anything that the soldiers may be pleased to throw to them."—*Mem. of John Shipp*, ii. 25.

***PENANG LAWYER**, s. The popular name of a handsome and hard (but sometimes brittle) walking-stick, exported from Penang and Singapore. It is the stem of a miniature palm (*Licuala acutifida*, Griffith). The sticks are prepared by scraping the young stem with glass, so as to remove the epidermis and no more. The sticks are then straightened by fire and polished (*Balfour*). The name is popularly thought to have originated in a jocular supposition that law-suits in Penang were decided by the *lex baculina*. But there can be little doubt that it is a corruption of some native term, and

1 "... great diversion is found ... in firing balls at birds, particularly the *albitross*, a large species of the swan, commonly seen within two or three hundred miles round the Cape of Good Hope, and which the French call *Montons* (Moutons) du *Cap*."—*Munro's Narrative*, 13. The confusion of genera here equals that mentioned in our article above.

pinang liyar, 'wild areca' [or *pinang lāyor*, "fire-dried areca," which is suggested in *N.E.D.*], may almost be assumed to be the real name. [Dennys (*Descr. Dict.* s.v.) says from "*Layor*, a species of cane furnishing the sticks so named." But this is almost certainly wrong.]

1883.—(But the book—an excellent one—is without date—more shame to the *Religious Tract Society* which publishes it). "Next morning, taking my '**Penang lawyer**' to defend myself from dogs. ..." The following note is added: "A **Penang lawyer** is a heavy walking-stick, supposed to be so called from its usefulness in settling disputes in Penang."—*Gilmour, Among the Mongols*, 14.

PEON, s. This is a Portuguese word *peão* (Span. *peon*); from *pé*, 'foot,' and meaning a 'footman' (also a *pawn* at chess), and is not therefore a corruption, as has been alleged, of Hind. *piyāda*, meaning the same; though the words are, of course ultimately akin in root. It was originally used in the sense of 'a foot-soldier'; thence as 'orderly' or messenger. The word *Sepoy* was used within our recollection, and perhaps is still, in the same sense in the city of Bombay. The transition of meaning comes out plainly in the quotation from Ives. In the sense of 'orderly,' *peon* is the word usual in S. India, whilst **chuprassy** (q.v.) is more common in N. India, though *peon* is also used there. The word is likewise very generally employed for men on police service. [Mr. Skeat notes that *Piyun* is used in the Malay States, and *Tambi* or *Tanby* at Singapore]. The word had probably become unusual in Portugal by 1600; for Manoel Correa, an early commentator on the Lusiads (d. 1613), thinks it necessary to explain **piões** by 'gente de pé.'

1503.—"The Çamorym ordered the soldier (**pião**) to take the letter away, and strictly forbade him to say anything about his having seen it."—*Correa, Lendas*, I. i. 421.

1510.—"So the Sabayo, putting much trust in this (Rumi), made him captain within the city (Goa) and outside of it put under him a captain of his with two thousand soldiers (**piães**) from the Balagate. ..."—*Ibid.* II. i. 51.

1563.—"The pawn (**pião**) they call *Piada*, which is as much as to say a man who travels on foot."—*Garcia*, f. 37.

1575.—

"O Rey de Badajos era alto Mouro
Con quatro mil cavallos furiosos,
Innumeros **piões**, darmas e de ouro,
Guarnecidos, guerreiros, e lustrosos."
Camões, iii. 66.

By Burton:

"The King of Badajos was a Moslem bold,
with horse four thousand, fierce and furious knights,
and countless **Peons**, armed and dight with gold,
whose polisht surface glanceth lustrous light."

1609.—"The first of February the Capitaine departed with fiftie **Peons**. ..."—*W. Finch*, in *Purchas*, i. 421.

c. 1610.—"Les **Pions** marchent après le prisonnier, lié avec des cordes qu'ils tiennent."—*Pyrard de Laval*, ii. 11; [Hak. Soc. ii. 17; also i. 428, 440; ii. 16].

[1616.—"This Shawbunder (see SHABUNDER) imperiously by a couple of **Pyons** commanded him from me."—*Foster, Letters*, iv. 351.]

c. 1630.—"The first of *December*, with some **Pe-unes** (or black Foot-boyes, who can pratle some English) we rode (from Swally) to Surat."—*Sir T. Herbert*, ed. 1638, p. 35. [For "black" the ed. of 1677 reads "olive-coloured," p. 42.]

1666.—"... siete cientos y treinta y tres mil **peones**."—*Faria y Sousa*, i. 195.

1673.—"The Town is walled with Mud, and Bulwarks for Watch-Places for the English **peons**."—*Fryer*, 29.

"... **Peons** or servants to wait on us."—*Ibid.* 26.

1687.—"Ordered that ten **peons** be sent along the coast to Pulicat ... and enquire all the way for goods driven ashore."—In *Wheeler*, i. 179.

1689.—"At this Moors Town, they got a **Peun** to be their guide to the Mogul's nearest Camp. ... These **Peuns** are some of the Gentous or *Rashbouts* (see RAJPOOT), who in all places along the Coast, especially in Seaport Towns, make it their business to hire themselves to wait upon Strangers."—*Dampier*, i. 508.

"**A Peon** of mine, named *Gemal*, walking abroad in the Grass after the Rains, was unfortunately bit on a sudden by one of them" (a snake).—*Ovington*, 260.

1705.—"..., **pions** qui sont ce que nous appellons ici des Gardes ..."—*Luillier*, 218.

1745.—"Dès le lendemain je fis assembler dans la Forteresse où je demeurois en qualité d'Aumonier, le Chef des **Pions**, chez qui s'étaient fait les deux mariages."—*Norbert, Mém.* iii. 129.

1746.—"As the Nabob's behaviour when Madras was attacked by De la Bourdonnais, had caused the English to suspect his assurances of assistance, they had 2,000 **Peons** in the defence of Cuddalore. ..."—*Orme*, i. 81.

c. 1760.—"**Peon**. One who waits about the

house to run on messages; and he commonly carries under his arm a sword, or in his sash a *krese*, and in his hand a ratan, to keep the rest of the servants in subjection. He also walks before your palanquin, carries **chits** (q.v.) or notes, and is your bodyguard."—*Ives*, 50.

1763.—"Europeans distinguish these undisciplined troops by the general name of **Peons**."—*Orme*, ed. 1803, i. 80.

1772.—Hadley, writing in Bengal, spells the word **pune**; but this is evidently phonetic.

c. 1785.—"... **Peons**, a name for the infantry of the Deckan."—*Carraccioli's Life of Clive*, iv. 563.

1780–90.—"I sent off annually from Sylhet from 150 to 200 (elephants) divided into 4 distinct flocks. ... They were put under charge of the common **peon**. These people were often absent 18 months. On one occasion my servant Manoo ... after a twelve-months' absence returned ... in appearance most miserable; he unfolded his girdle, and produced a scrap of paper of small dimensions, which proved to be a banker's bill amounting to 3 or 4,000 pounds,—his own pay was 30 shillings a month. ... When I left India Manoo was still absent on one of these excursions, but he delivered to my agents as faithful an account of the produce as he would have done to myself. ..."—*Hon. R. Lindsay*, in *Lives of the Lindsays*, iii. 77.

1842.—"... he was put under arrest for striking, and throwing into the Indus, an inoffensive **Peon**, who gave him no provocation, but who was obeying the orders he received from Captain ——. The Major General has heard it said that the supremacy of the British over the native must be maintained in India, and he entirely concurs in that opinion, but it must be maintained by justice."—*Gen. Orders*, &c., *of Sir Ch. Napier*, p. 72.

1873.—"Pandurang is by turns a servant to a shopkeeper, a **peon**, or orderly, a groom to an English officer ... and eventually a pleader before an English Judge in a populous city."—*Saturday Review*, May 31, p. 728.

PEPPER, s. The original of this word, Skt. *pippali*, means not the ordinary pepper of commerce ('black pepper') but *long pepper*, and the Sanskrit name is still so applied in Bengal, where one of the long-pepper plants, which have been classed sometimes in a different genus (*Chavica*) from the black pepper, was at one time much cultivated. There is still indeed a considerable export of long pepper from Calcutta; and a kindred species grows in the Archipelago. Long pepper is mentioned by Pliny, as well as white and black pepper; the three varieties still known in trade, though with the kind of error that has persisted on such subjects till quite recently, he misapprehends their relation. The proportion of their ancient prices will be found in a quotation below.

The name must have been transferred by foreign traders to black pepper, the staple of export, at an early date, as will be seen from the quotations. *Pippalimūla*, the root of long pepper, still a stimulant medicine in the native pharmacopoeia, is probably the πεπέρεως ῥίζα of the ancients (*Royle*, p. 86).

We may say here that *Black pepper* is the fruit of a perennial climbing shrub, *Piper nigrum*, L., indigenous in the forests of Malabar and Travancore, and thence introduced into the Malay countries, particularly Sumatra.

White pepper is prepared from the black by removing the dark outer layer of pericarp, thereby depriving it of a part of its pungency. It comes chiefly *viâ* Singapore from the Dutch settlement of Rhio, but a small quantity of fine quality comes from Tellicherry in Malabar.

Long pepper is derived from two shrubby plants, *Piper officinarum*, C.D.C., a native of the Archipelago, and *Piper longum*, L., indigenous in Malabar, Ceylon, E. Bengal, Timor, and the Philippines. Long pepper is the fruit-spike gathered and dried when not quite ripe (*Hanbury and Flückiger*, *Pharmacographia*). All these kinds of pepper were, as has been said, known to the ancients.

c. 70 A.D.—"The cornes or graines ... lie in certaine little huskes or cods. ... If that be plucked from the tree before they gape and open of themselves, they make that spice which is called **Long pepper**; but if as they do ripen, they cleave and chawne by little and little, they shew within the **white pepper**: which afterwards beeing parched in the Sunne, chaungeth colour and waxeth blacke, and therewith riveled also ... **Long pepper** is soone sophisticated, with the senvie or mustard seed of Alexandria: and a pound of it is worth fifteen Roman deniers. The **white** costeth seven deniers a pound, and the **black** is sold after foure deniers by the pound."—*Pliny*, tr. by *Phil. Holland*, Bk. xii. ch. 7.

c. 80–90.—"And there come to these marts great ships, on account of the bulk and quantity of **pepper** and malabathrum. ... The **pepper** is brought (to market) here, being produced largely only in one district near these marts, that which is called *Kottonarikē*."—*Periplus*, § 56.

c. A.D. 100.—"The **Pepper**-tree (πέπερι δένδρον) is related to grow in India; it is short, and the fruit as it first puts it forth is long, resembling pods; and this long **pepper** has within it (grains) like small millet, which are what grow to be the perfect (black) **pepper**. At the proper season it opens and puts forth a cluster bearing the berries such as we know them. But those that are like unripe grapes, which constitute the **white pepper**, serve the best for eye-remedies, and for antidotes, and for theriacal potencies."—*Dioscorides, Mat. Med.* ii. 188.

c. 545.—"This is the **pepper-tree**" (there is a drawing). "Every plant of it is twined round some lofty forest tree, for it is weak and slim like the slender stems of the vine. And every bunch of fruit has a double leaf as a shield; and it is very green, like the green of rue."—*Cosmas*, Book xi.

c. 870.—"The mariners say every bunch of **pepper** has over it a leaf that shelters it from the rain. When the rain ceases the leaf turns aside; if rain recommences the leaf again covers the fruit."—*Ibn Khurdādba*, in *Journ. As.* 6th ser. tom. v. 284.

1166.—"The trees which bear this fruit are planted in the fields which surround the towns, and every one knows his plantation. The trees are small, and the *pepper* is originally white, but when they collect it they put it into basons and pour hot water upon it; it is then exposed to the heat of the sun, and dried ... in the course of which process it becomes of a black colour."—*Rabbi Benjamin*, in *Wright*, p. 114.

c. 1330.—"L'albore che fa il **pepe** è fatto come l'elera che nasce su per gli muri. Questo pepe sale su per gli arbori che l'uomini piantano a modo de l'elera, e sale sopra tutti li arbori più alti. Questo pepe fa rami a modo dell' uve; ... e maturo si lo vendemiano a modo de l'uve e poi pongono il pepe al sole a seccare come uve passe, e nulla altra cosa si fa del **pepe**."—*Odoric*, in *Cathay*, App. xlvii.

PERGUNNAH, s. Hind. *pargana* [Skt. *pragaṇ*, 'to reckon up'], a subdivision of a 'District'.

c. 1500.—"The divisions into *súbas* (see SOUBA) and **parganas**, which are maintained to the present day in the province of Tatta, were made by these people" (the Samma Dynasty).—*Tárikh-i-Táhirí*, in *Elliot*, i. 273.

1535.—"Item, from the three **praguanas**, viz., Anzor, Cairena, Panchenaa 133, 260 *fedeas*."—*S. Botelho, Tombo*, 139.

[1614.—"I wrote him to stay in the **Pregonas** near Agra."—*Foster, Letters*, ii. 106.]

[1617.—"For that Muckshud had also newly answered he had mist his **prigany**."—*Sir T. Roe*, Hak. Soc. ii. 415.]

1753.—"Masulipatnam ... est capitale de ce qu'on appelle dans l'Inde un Sercar (see SIRCAR), qui comprend plusieurs **Perganés**, ou districts particuliers."—*D'Anville*, 132.

1812.—"A certain number of villages with a society thus organised, formed a **pergunnah**."—*Fifth Report*, 16.

PERGUNNAHS, THE TWENTY-FOUR, n.p. The official name of the District immediately adjoining and inclosing, though not administratively including, Calcutta. The name is one of a character very ancient in India and the East. It was the original 'Zemindary of Calcutta' granted to the English Company by a 'Subadar's Perwana' in 1757–58. This grant was subsequently confirmed by the Great Mogul as an unconditional and rent-free **jagheer** (q.v.). The quotation from Sir Richard Phillips' *Million of Facts*, illustrates the development of 'facts' out of the moral consciousness. The book contains many of equal value. An approximate parallel to this statement would be that London is divided into Seven Dials.

1765.—"The lands of the **twenty-four Purgannahs**, ceded to the Company by the treaty of 1757, which subsequently became Colonel *Clive's* jagghier, were rated on the King's books at 2 lac and 22,000 rupees."—*Holwell, Hist. Events*, 2nd ed., p. 217.

1812.—"The number of convicts confined at the six stations of this division (independent of *Zillah* **Twenty-four pergunnahs**, is about 4,000. Of them probably nine-tenths are dacoits."—*Fifth Report*, 559.

c. 1831.—"Bengal is divided in **24 Pergunnahs**, each with its judge and magistrate, registrar, &c."—*Sir R. Phillips, Million of Facts*, stereot. ed. 1843, 927.

***PERI**, s. This Persian word for a class of imaginary sprites, rendered familiar in the verses of Moore and Southey, has no blood-relationship with the English *Fairy*, notwithstanding the exact compliance with Grimm's Law in the change of initial consonant. The Persian word is *parī*, from '*par*, 'a feather, or wing'; therefore 'the winged one'; [so F. Johnson, *Pers. Dict.*; but the derivation is very doubtful;] whilst the genealogy of *fairy* is apparently Ital. *fata*, French *fée*, whence *féerie* ('fay-dom') and thence *fairy*.

[c. 1500?—"I am the only daughter of a Jinn

chief of noblest strain and my name is **Peri-Banu.**"—*Arab. Nights, Burton*, x. 264.]

1800.—

"From cluster'd henna, and from orange
groves,
That with such perfumes fill the breeze
As **Peris** to their Sister bear,
When from the summit of some lofty tree
She hangs encaged, the captive of the Dives."
Thalaba, xi. 24.

1817.—

"But nought can charm the luckless **Peri**;
Her soul is sad—her wings are weary."
Moore, Paradise and the **Peri**.

PESHAWUR, n.p. *Peshāwar*. This name of what is now the frontier city and garrison of India towards Kābul, is sometimes alleged to have been given by Akbar. But in substance the name is of great antiquity, and all that can be alleged as to Akbar is that he is said to have modified the old name, and that since his time the present form has been in use. A notice of the change is quoted below from Gen. Cunningham; we cannot give the authority on which the statement rests. Peshāwar could hardly be called a frontier town in the time of Akbar, standing as it did according to the administrative division of the *Āīn*, about the middle of the Sūba of Kābul, which included Kashmīr and all west of it. We do not find that the modern form occurs in the text of the *Āīn* as published by Prof. Blochmann. In the translation of the *Tabakāt-i-Akbarī* of Nizāmu-d-din Ahmad (died 1594–95), in Elliot, we find the name transliterated variously as *Peshāwar* (v. 448), *Parsháwar* (293), *Parshor* (423), *Pershor* (424). We cannot doubt that the Chinese form *Folausha* in Fah-hian already expresses the name *Parashāwar*, or *Parshāwar*.

c. 400.—"From Gandhâra, going south 4 days' journey, we arrive at the country of **Fo-lau-sha**. In old times Buddha, in company with all his disciples, travelled through this country."—*Fah-hian*, by *Beal*, p. 34.

c. 630.—"The Kingdom of Kien-to-lo (Gândhâra) extends about 1000 *li* from E. to W. and 800 *li* from S. to N. On the East it adjoins the river *Sin* (Indus). The capital of this country is called **Pu-lu-sha-pu-lo** (Purashapura). ... The towns and villages are almost deserted. ... There are about a thousand convents, ruined and abandoned; full of wild plants, and presenting only a melancholy solitude. ..."—*Hwen T'sang, Pèl. Boud.* ii. 104–105.

c. 1001.—"On his (Mahmúd's) reaching **Purshaur**, he pitched his tent outside the city. There he received intelligence of the bold resolve of Jaipál, the enemy of God, and the King of Hind, to offer opposition."—*Al-Utbi*, in *Elliot*, ii. 25.

c. 1020.—"The aggregate of these waters forms a large river opposite the city of **Parsháwar.**"—*Al-Bīrūnī*, in *Elliot*, i. 47. See also 63.

1059.—"The Amír ordered a letter to be despatched to the minister, telling him 'I have determined to go to Hindustán, and pass the winter in Waihind, and Marminára, and **Barshúr**. ..."—*Baihaki*, in *Elliot*, ii. 150.

c. 1220.—"**Farshābūr**. The vulgar pronunciation is **Barshāwūr**. A large tract between Ghazna and Lahor, famous in the history of the Musulman conquest."—*Yāḳūt*, in *Barbier de Maynard, Dict. de la Perse*, 418.

1519.—"We held a consultation, in which it was resolved to plunder the country of the Aferîdî Afghâns, as had been proposed by Sultan Bayezîd, to fit up the fort of **Pershâwer** for the reception of their effects and corn, and to leave a garrison in it."—*Baber*, 276.

c. 1555.—"We came to the city of **Purshawar**, and having thus fortunately passed the *Kotal* we reached the town of Joshāya. On the Kotal we saw rhinoceroses, the size of a small elephant."—*Sidi 'Ali*, in *J. As.* Ser. i. tom. ix. 201.

c. 1590.—"Tumān Bagrām, which they call **Parshāwar**; the spring here is a source of delight. There is in this place a great place of worship which they call Gorkhatri, to which people, especially Jogis, resort from great distances."—*Āīn* (orig.), i. 592; [ed. *Jarrett*, ii. 404. In iii. 69, **Parasháwar**].

1754.—"On the news that **Peishor** was taken, and that Nadir Shah was preparing to pass the Indus, the Moghol's court, already in great disorder, was struck with terror."—*H. of Nadir Shah*, in *Hanway*, ii. 363.

1783.—"The heat of Peshour seemed to me more intense, than that of any country I have visited in the upper parts of India. Other places may be warm; hot winds blowing over tracts of sand may drive us under the shelter of a wetted skreen; but at **Peshour**, the atmosphere, in the summer solstice, becomes almost inflammable."—*G. Forster*, ed. 1808, ii. 57.

1863.—"Its present name we owe to Akbar, whose fondness for innovation led him to change the ancient **Parashâwara**, of which he did not know the meaning, to **Peshâwar**, or the 'frontier town.' Abul Fazl gives both names."—*Cunningham, Arch. Reports*, ii. 87. Gladwin does in his translation give both names; but see above.

PESHCUSH, s. Pers: *pesh-kash*. Wilson

interprets this as literally 'first-fruits.' It is used as an offering or tribute, but with many specific and technical senses which will be found in Wilson, *e.g.* a fine on appointment, renewal, or investiture; a quit-rent, a payment exacted on lands formerly rent-free, or in substitution for service no longer exacted; sometimes a present to a great man, or (loosely) for the ordinary Government demand on land. **Peshcush**, in the old English records, is most generally used in the sense of a present to a great man.

1653,—"**Pesket** est vn presant en Turq."—*De la Boullaye-le-Gouz*, ed. 1657, p. 553.

1657.—"As to the **Piscash** for the King of Golcundah, if it be not already done, we do hope with it you may obteyn our liberty to coyne silver Rupees and copper Pice at the Fort, which would be a great accommodation to our Trade. But in this and all other **Piscashes** be as sparing as you can."—*Letter of Court to Ft. St. Geo.*, in *Notes and Exts.*, No. i. p. 7.

1673.—"Sometimes sending **Pishcashes** of considerable value."—*Fryer*, 166.

1675.—"Being informed that Mr. Mohun had sent a **Piscash** of Persian Wine, Cases of Stronge Water, &c. to ye Great Governour of this Countrey, that is 2*d*. or 3*d*. pson in ye kingdome, I went to his house to speake abt. it, when he kept me to dine with him."—*Puckle's Diary*, MS. in India Office.

[1683.—"**Piscash.**" (See under FIRMAUN.)]

1689.—"But the **Pishcushes** or Presents expected by the *Nabobs* and *Omrahs* retarded our Inlargement for some time notwithstanding."—*Ovington*, 415.

1754.—"After I have refreshed my army at DELHIE, and received the subsidy (*Note.*—'This is called a **Peischcush**, or present from an inferior to a superior. The sum agreed for was 20 crores') which must be paid, I will leave you in possession of his dominion."—*Hist. of Nadir Shah*, in *Hanway*, ii. 371.

1761.—"I have obtained a promise from his Majesty of his royal confirmation of all your possessions and priviledges, provided you pay him a proper **pishcush**. ..."—*Major Carnac* to the Governor and Council, in *Van Sittart*, i. 119.

1811.—"By the *fixed or regulated sum* ... the Sultan ... means the **Paishcush**, or tribute, which he was bound by former treaties to pay to the Government of Poonah; but which he does not think proper to ... designate by any term denotive of inferiority, which the word *Paishcush* certainly is."—*Kirkpatrick*, Note on *Tippoo's Letters*, p. 9.

***PESHWA**, s. from Pers. 'a leader, a guide.' The chief minister of the Mahratta power, who afterwards, supplanting his master, the descendant of Sivaji, became practically the prince of an independent State and chief of the Mahrattas. The Peshwa's power expired with the surrender to Sir John Malcolm of the last Peshwa, Bājī Rāo, in 1817. He lived in wealthy exile, and with a *jāgīr* under his own jurisdiction, at Bhitūr, near Cawnpoor, till January 1851. His adopted son, and the claimant of his honours and allowances, was the infamous Nānā Sāhib.

Mr C. P. Brown gives a feminine *peshwīn*: "The princess Gangā Bāī was *Peshwīn* of Purandhar." (MS. notes).

1673.—"He answered, it is well, and referred our Business to *Moro Pundit* his **Peshua**, or Chancellour, to examine our Articles, and give an account of what they were."—*Fryer*, 79.

1803.—"But how is it with the **Peshwah**? He has no minister; no person has influence over him, and he is only guided by his own caprices."—*Wellington Desp.*, ed. 1837, ii. 177.

In the following passage (*quando-quidem dormitans*) the Great Duke had forgotten that things were changed since he left India, whilst the editor perhaps did not know:

1841.—"If you should draw more troops from the Establishment of Fort St. George, you will have to place under arms the subsidiary force of the Nizam, the **Peishwah**, and the force in Mysore, and the districts ceded by the Nizam in 1800–1801."—Letter from the *D. of Wellington*, in *Ind. Adm. of Lord Ellenborough*, 1874. (Dec. 29). The Duke was oblivious when he spoke of the Peshwa's Subsidiary Force in 1841.

PETERSILLY, s. This is the name by which 'parsley' is generally called in N. India. We have heard it quoted there as an instance of the absurd corruption of English words in the mouths of natives. But this case at least might more justly be quoted as an example of accurate transfer. The word is simply the Dutch term for 'parsley,' viz. **petersilie**, from the Lat. *petroselinum*, of which *parsley* is itself a double corruption through the French *persil*. In the Arabic of Avicenna the name is given as *fatrasiliūn*.

[**PHOOLKAREE**, s. Hind. *phūlkārī*, 'flowered embroidery.' The term applied in N. India to the cotton sheets embroidered in silk by village women, particularly Jats. Each girl is supposed to embroider one of these for her marriage. In recent years a considerable demand has arisen for specimens of this kind of needlework among English ladies, who use them for screens and other decorative purposes. Hence a considerable manufacture has sprung up of which an account will be found in a note by Mrs. F. A. Steel, appended to Mr. H. C. Cookson's *Monograph on the Silk Industry of the Punjab* (1886–7), and in the *Journal of Indian Art*, ii. 71 *seqq*.

[1887.—"They (native school girls) were collected in a small inner court, which was hung with the pretty **phulcarries** they make here (Rawal Pindi), and which ... looked very Oriental and gay."—*Lady Dufferin, Viceregal Life*, 336.]

PICE, s. Hind. *paisā*, a small copper coin, which under the Anglo-Indian system of currency is ¼ of an anna, ⅟₆₄ of a rupee, and somewhat less than ⅗ of a farthing. *Pice* is used slangishly for money in general. By Act XXIII. of 1870 (cl. 8) the following copper coins are current:—1. Double *Pice* or Half-anna, 2. *Pice* or ¼ anna. 3. *Half-pice* or ⅛ anna. 4. *Pie* or ⅟₁₂. anna. No. 2 is the only one in very common use. As with most other coins, weights, and measures, there used to be **pucka** pice, and **cutcha** pice. The distinction was sometimes between the regularly minted copper of the Government and certain amorphous pieces of copper which did duty for small change (*e.g.* in the N.W. Provinces within memory), or between single and double pice, *i.e.* ¼ anna-pieces and ½ anna-pieces.

c. 1590.—"The *dám* ... is the fortieth part of the rupee. At first this coin was called **Paisah**."—*Āīn*, ed. *Blochmann*, i. 31.

[1614.—"Another coin there is of copper, called a **Pize**, whereof you have commonly 34 in the mamudo."—*Foster, Letters*, iii. 11.]

1615.—"**Pice**, which is a Copper Coyne; twelve Drammes make one **Pice**. The English Shilling, if weight, will yeeld thirtie three *Pice* and a halfe."—*W. Peyton*, in *Purchas*, i. 530.

1616.—"Brasse money, which they call **Pices**, whereof three or thereabouts countervail a Peny."—*Terry*, in *Purchas*, ii. 1471.

1648.—"... de **Peysen** zijn kooper gelt. ..."—*Van Twist*, 62.

1653.—"**Peça** est vne monnoye du Mogol de la valeur de 6 deniers."—*De la Boullaye-le-Gouz*, ed. 1657, p. 553.

1673.—"**Pice**, a sort of Copper Money current among the Poorer sort of People ... the Company's Accounts are kept in Book-rate **Pice**, viz. 32 to the Mam. [i.e. and 80 **Pice** to the Rupee."—*Fryer*, 205.

1676.—"The Indians have also a sort of small Copper-money; which is called **Pecha**. ... In my last Travels, a *Roupy* went at Surat for nine and forty **Pecha's**."—*Tavernier*, E.T. ii. 22; [ed. *Ball*, i. 27].

1689.—"Lower than these (pice), bitter-Almonds here (at Surat) pass for Money, about Sixty of which make a **Pice**."—*Ovington*, 219.

1726.—"1 *Ana* makes 1½ stuyvers or 2 **peys**."—*Valentijn*, v. 179. [Also see under MOHUR GOLD.]

1768.—"Shall I risk my cavalry, which cost 1000 rupees each horse, against your cannon balls that cost two **pice**?—No.—I will march your troops until their legs become the size of their bodies."—*Hyder Ali*, Letter to *Col. Wood*, in *Forbes, Or. Mem.* iii. 287; [2nd ed. ii. 300].

c. 1816.—"'Here,' said he, 'is four **pucker-pice** for Mary to spend in the bazar; but I will thank you, Mrs. Browne, not to let her have any fruit. ..."—*Mrs. Sherwood's Stories*, 16, ed. 1863.

PICOTTAH, s. This is the term applied in S. India to that ancient machine for raising water, which consists of a long lever or yard, pivotted on an upright post, weighted on the short arm and bearing a line and bucket on the long arm. It is the *ḍhenklī* of Upper India, the *shādūf* of the Nile, and the old English *sweep*, *swape*, or *sway-pole*. The machine is we believe still used in the Terra Incognita of market-gardens S.E. of London. The name is Portuguese, *picota*, a marine term now applied to the handle of a ship's pump and post in which it works—a 'pump-brake.' The *picota* at sea was also used as a pillory, whence the employment of the word as quoted from Correa. The word is given in the Glossary attached to the "Fifth Report" (1812), but with no indication of its source. Fryer (1673, pub. 1698) describes the thing without giving it a name. In the following the word is used in the marine sense:

1524.—"He (V. da Gama) ordered notice to be given that no seaman should wear a cloak, except on Sunday ... and if he did, that it should be taken from him by the constables (*lhe serra tomada polos meirinhos*), and the man put in the **picota** in disgrace, for one day. He found great fault with men of military service wearing cloaks, for in that guise they did not look like soldiers."—*Correa, Lendas*, II. ii. 822.

1782.—"Pour cet effet (arroser les terres) on emploie une machine appellée **Picôte**. C'est une bascule dressée sur le bord d'un puits ou d'un réservoir d'eaux pluviales, pour en tirer l'eau, et la conduire ensuite où l'on veut."—*Sonnerat, Voyage*, i. 188.

c. 1790.—"Partout les **pakotiés**, ou puits à bascule, étoient en mouvement pour fournir l'eau nécessaire aux plantes, et partout on entendoit les jardiniers égayer leurs travaux par des chansons."—*Haafner*, ii. 217.

1807.—"In one place I saw people employed in watering a rice-field with the *Yatam*, or **Pacota**, as it is called by the English."—*Buchanan, Journey through Mysore*, &c., i. 15. [Here *Yatam*, is Can. *yāta* Tel. *ētamu*, Mal. *ēttam*.]

1871.—
"Aye, e'en **picotta**-work would gain
By using such bamboos."
Gover, Folk Songs of S. India, 184.]

***PIECE-GOODS**. This, which is now the technical term for Manchester cottons imported into India, was originally applied in trade to the Indian cottons exported to England, a trade which appears to have been deliberately killed by the heavy duties which Lancashire procured to be imposed in its own interest, as in its own interest it has recently procured the abolition of the small import duty on English piece-goods in India.[1] [In 1898 a duty at the rate of 3 per cent. on cotton goods was reimposed.]

***PIGEON ENGLISH**. The vile jargon which forms the means of communication at the Chinese ports between Englishmen who do not speak Chinese, and those Chinese with whom they are in the habit of communicating. The word "*business*" appears in this kind of talk to be corrupted into "*pigeon*," and hence the name of the jargon is supposed to be taken. [For examples see *Chamberlain, Things Japanese*, 3rd ed. pp. 321 *seqq.*; *Ball, Things Chinese*, 3rd ed. 430 *seqq.* (See BUTLER ENGLISH.)]

1880.—"... the English traders of the early days. ... instead of inducing the Chinese to make use of correct words rather than the misshapen syllables they had adopted, encouraged them by approbation and example, to establish **Pigeon English**—a grotesque gibberish which would be laughable if it were not almost melancholy."—*Capt. W. Gill, River of Golden Sand*, i. 156.

1883.—"The '**Pidjun English**' is revolting, and the most dignified persons demean themselves by speaking it. ... How the whole English-speaking community, without distinction of rank, has come to communicate with the Chinese in this baby talk is extraordinary."—*Miss Bird, Golden Chersonese*, 37.

***PIG-STICKING**. This is Anglo-Indian hog-hunting, or what would be called among

---

1 It is an easy assumption that this export trade from India was killed by the development of machinery in England. We can hardly doubt that this cause would have killed it in time. But it was not left to any such lingering and natural death. Much time would be required to trace the whole of this episode of "ancient history." But it is certain that this Indian trade was not killed by natural causes: *it was killed by prohibitory duties*. These duties were so high in 1783 that they were declared to operate as a premium on smuggling, and they were *reduced* to 18 per cent. *ad valorem*. In the year 1796–97 the value of piece-goods from India imported into England was £2,776,682, or one-third of the whole value of the imports from India, which was £8,252,309. And in the sixteen years between 1793–4 and 1809–10 (inclusive) the imports of Indian piece-goods amounted in value to £26,171,125.

In 1799 the duties were raised. I need not give details, but will come down to 1814, just before the close of the war, when they were, I believe, at a maximum. The duties then, on "plain white calicoes," were:—

	£	s.	d.	
Warehouse duty	4	0	0	per cent.
War enhancement	1	0	0	"
Customs duty	50	0	0	"
War enhancement	12	10	0	"
Total	67	10	0	{per cent. on value.

There was an Excise duty upon British manufactured and printed goods of 3½*d.* per square yard, and of twice that amount on foreign (Indian) calico and muslin printed in Great Britain, and the whole of both duty and excise upon such goods was recoverable as draw back upon re-exportation. But on the exportation of Indian white goods there was no drawback recoverable; and stuffs printed in India were at this time, so far as we can discern, *not admitted through the English Custom-house at all* until 1826, when they were admitted on a duty of 3½*d.* per square yard.

(See in the *Statutes*, 43 Geo. III. *capp.* 68, 69, 70; 54 Geo. III. *cap.* 36; 6 Geo. IV. *cap.* 3; also *Macpherson's Annals of Commerce*, iv. 426).

In Sir A. Arbuthnot's publication of *Sir T. Munro's Minutes* (*Memoir*, p. cxxix.) he quotes a letter of Munro's to a friend in Scotland, written about 1825, which shows him surprisingly before his age in the matter of Free Trade, speaking with reference to certain measures of Mr. Huskisson's. The passage ends thus: "India is the country that has been worst used in the new arrangements. All her products ought undoubtedly to be imported freely into England, upon paying the same duties, and no more, which English duties [?manufactures] pay in India. When I see what is done in Parliament against India, I think that I am reading about Edward III. and the Flemings."

a people delighting more in lofty expression, 'the chase of the Wild Boar.' When, very many years since, one of the present writers, destined for the Bengal Presidency, first made acquaintance with an Indian mess-table, it was that of a Bombay regiment at Aden—in fact of that gallant corps which is now known as the 103rd Foot, or Royal Bombay Fusiliers. Hospitable as they were, the opportunity of enlightening an aspirant Bengalee on the short-comings of his Presidency could not be foregone. The chief counts of indictment were three: 1st. The inferiority of the Bengal Horse Artillery system; 2nd. That the Bengalees were guilty of the base effeminacy of drinking beer out of champagne glasses; 3rd. That in pig-sticking they *threw* the spear at the boar. The two last charges were evidently ancient traditions, maintaining their ground as facts down to 1840 therefore; and showed how little communication practically existed between the Presidencies as late as that year. Both the allegations had long ceased to be true, but probably the second had been true in the 18th century, as the third certainly had been. This may be seen from the quotation from R. Lindsay, and by the text and illustrations of Williamson's *Oriental Field Sports* (1807), [and much later (see below)]. There is, or perhaps we should say more diffidently there was, still a difference between the Bengal practice in pig-sticking, and that of Bombay. The Bengal spear is about 6½ feet long, loaded with lead at the butt so that it can be grasped almost quite at the end and carried with the point down, inclining only slightly to the front; the boar's charge is received on the right flank, when the point, raised to 45° or 50° of inclination, if rightly guided, pierces him in the shoulder. The Bombay spear is a longer weapon, and is carried under the armpit like a dragoon's lance. Judging from Elphinstone's statement below we should suppose that the Bombay as well as the Bengal practice originally was to throw the spear, but that both independently discarded this, the **Qui-his** adopting the short overhand spear, the **Ducks** the long lance.

1679.—"In the morning we went a hunting of wild Hoggs with Kisna Reddy, the chief man of the Islands" (at mouth of the Kistna) "and about 100 other men of the island (Dio) with lances and Three score doggs, with whom we killed eight Hoggs great and small, one being a Bore very large and fatt, of greate weight."—*Consn. of Agent and Council of Fort St. Geo.* on Tour. In *Notes and Exts.* No. II.

The party consisted of Streynsham Master "Agent of the Coast and Bay," with "Mr. Timothy Willes and Mr. Richard Mohun of the Councell, the Minister, the Chyrurgeon, the Schoolmaster, the Secretary, and two Writers, an Ensign, 6 mounted soldiers and a Trumpeter," in all 17 Persons in the Company's Service, and "Four Freemen, who went with the Agent's Company for their own pleasure, and at their own charges." It was a Tour of Visitation of the Factories.

1773.—The Hon. R. Lindsay *does* speak of the "Wild-boar chase"; but he wrote after 35 years in England, and rather eschews Anglo-Indianisms:

"Our weapon consisted only of a short heavy spear, three feet in length, and well poised; the boar being found and unkennelled by the spaniels, runs with great speed across the plain, is pursued on horseback, and the first rider who approaches him throws the javelin. ..."—*Lives of the Lindsays*, iii. 161.

1807.—"When (the hog) begins to slacken, the attack should be commenced by the horseman who may be nearest pushing on to his left side; into which the spear should be thrown, so as to lodge behind the shoulder blade, and about six inches from the backbone."—*Williamson*,

---

Sir A. Arbuthnot adds very appropriately a passage from a note by the late Prof. H. H. Wilson in his continuation of James Mill's *History of India* (1845, vol. i. pp. 538–539), a passage which we also gladly insert here:

"It was stated in evidence (in 1813) that the cotton and silk goods of India, up to this period, could be sold for a profit in the British market at a price from 50 to 60 per cent. lower than those fabricated in England. It consequently became necessary to protect the latter by duties of 70 or 80 per cent. on their value, or by positive prohibition. Had this not been the case, had not such prohibitory duties and decrees existed, the mills of Paisley and of Manchester would have been stopped in their outset, and could hardly have been again set in motion, even by the powers of steam. They were created by the sacrifice of the Indian manufactures. Had India been independent, she would have retaliated; would have imposed preventive duties upon British goods, and would thus have preserved her own productive industry from annihilation. This act of self-defence was not permitted her; she was at the mercy of the stranger. British goods were forced upon her without paying any duty; and the foreign manufacturer employed the arm of political injustice to keep down and ultimately strangle a competitor with whom he could not contend on equal terms."

Oriental Field Sports, p. 9. (*Left* must mean hog's *right*.) This author says that the bamboo shafts were 8 or 9 feet long, but that *very short* ones had formerly been in use; thus confirming Lindsay.

1816.—"We hog-hunt till two, then tiff, and hawk or course till dusk ... we do not throw our spears in the old way, but poke with spears longer than the common ones, and never part with them."—*Elphinstone's Life*, i. 311.

[1828.—"... the boar who had made good the next cane with only a slight scratch from a spear thrown as he was charging the hedge."—*Orient. Sport. Mag.* reprint 1873, i. 116.]

1848.—"Swankey of the Body-Guard himself, that dangerous youth, and the greatest buck of all the Indian army now on leave, was one day discovered by Major Dobbin, *tête-á-tête* with Amelia, and describing the sport of **pigsticking** to her with great humour and eloquence."—*Vanity Fair*, ii. 288.

1866.—"I may be a young **pig-sticker**, but I am too old a sportsman to make such a mistake as that."—*Trevelyan, The Dawk Bungalow*, in *Fraser*, lxxiii. 387.

1873.—"**Pigsticking** may be very good fun. ..."—*A True Reformer*, ch. i.

1876.—"You would perhaps like tiger-hunting or **pig-sticking**; I saw some of that for a season or two in the East. Everything here is poor stuff after that."—*Daniel Deronda*, ii. ch. xi.

1878.—"In the meantime there was a '**pig-sticking**' meet in the neighbouring district."—*Life in the Mofussil*, i. 140.

PIG-TAIL, s. This term is often applied to the Chinaman's long plait of hair, by transfer from the *queue* of our grandfathers, to which the name was much more appropriate. Though now universal among the Chinese, this fashion was only introduced by their Manchu conquerors in the 17th century, and was "long resisted by the natives of the Amoy and Swatow districts, who, when finally compelled to adopt the distasteful fashion, concealed the badge of slavery beneath cotton turbans, the use of which has survived to the present day" (*Giles, Glossary of Reference*, 32). Previously the Chinese wore their unshaven back hair gathered in a net, or knotted in a chignon. De Rhodes (Rome, 1615, p. 5) says of the people of Tongking, that "*like the Chinese* they have the custom of gathering the hair in fine nets under the hat."

1879.—"One sees a single Sikh driving four or five Chinamen in front of him, having knotted their **pigtails** together for reins."—*Miss Bird, Golden Chersonese*, 283.

PILAU, PILOW, PILÁF, &c., s. Pers. *pulāo*, or *pilāv*, Skt. *pulāka*, 'a ball of boiled rice.' A dish, in origin purely Mahommedan, consisting of meat, or fowl, boiled along with rice and spices. Recipes are given by Herklots, ed. 1863, App. xxix.; and in the *Āīn-i-Akbarī* (ed. *Blochmann*, i. 60), we have one for *kīma pulāo* (*kīma* = 'hash') with several others to which the name is not given. The *name* is almost as familiar in England as **curry**, but not the *thing*. It was an odd circumstance, some 45 years ago, that the two surgeons of a dragoon regiment in India were called *Currie* and *Pilleau*.

1616.—"Sometimes they boil pieces of flesh or hens, or other fowl, cut in pieces in their rice, which dish they call **pillaw**. As they order it they make it a very excellent and a very well tasted food."—*Terry*, in *Purchas*, ii. 1471.

c. 1630.—"The feast begins: it was compounded of a hundred sorts of **pelo** and candied dried meats."—*Sir T. Herbert*, ed. 1638, p. 133, [and for varieties, p. 310].

[c. 1660.—"... my elegant hosts were fully employed in cramming their mouths with as much **Pelau** as they could contain. ..."—*Bernier*, ed. *Constable*, 121.]

1673.—"The most admired Dainty wherewith they stuff themselves is **Pullow**, whereof they will fill themselves to the Throat and receive no hurt, it being so well prepared for the Stomach."—*Fryer*, 399. See also p. 93. At p. 404 he gives a recipe.

1682.—"They eate their **pilaw** and other spoone-meate withoute spoones, taking up their pottage in the hollow of their fingers."—*Evelyn, Diary*; June 19.

1687.—"They took up their Mess with their Fingers, as the Moors do their **Pilaw**, using no Spoons."—*Dampier*, i. 430.

1689.—"**Palau**, that is Rice boil'd ... with Spices intermixt, and a boil'd Fowl in the middle, is the most common *Indian* Dish."—*Ovington*, 397.

1711.—"They cannot go to the Price of a **Pilloe**, or boil'd Fowl and Rice; but the better sort make that their principal Dish."—*Lockyer*, 231.

1793.—"On a certain day ... all the Musulman officers belonging to your department shall be entertained at the charge of the *Sircar*, with a public repast, to consist of **Pullao** of the first sort."—*Select Letters of Tippoo S.*, App. xlii.

c. 1820.—

"And nearer as they came, a genial savour
Of certain stews, and roast-meats, and **pilaus**,

Things which in hungry mortals' eyes find favour."—*Don Juan*, v. 47.

1848.—"'There's a **pillau**, Joseph, just as you like it, and Papa has brought home the best turbot in Billingsgate.'"—*Vanity Fair*, i. 20.

PISHPASH, s. Apparently a factitious Anglo-Indian word, applied to a slop of rice-soup with small pieces of meat in it, much used in the Anglo-Indian nursery. [It is apparently P. *pash-pash*, 'shivered or broken in pieces'; from Pers. *pashīdan*.]

1834.—"They found the Secretary disengaged, that is to say, if surrounded with huge volumes of Financial Reports on one side, and a small silver tray holding a mess of **pishpash** on the other, can be called disengaged."—*The Baboo*, &c. i. 85.

PLANTAIN, s. This is the name by which the *Musa sapientum* is universally known to Anglo-India. Books distinguish between the *Musa sapientum* or plantain, and the *Musa paradisaica* or banana; but it is hard to understand where the line is supposed to be drawn. Variation is gradual and infinite.

The botanical name *Musa* represents the Ar. *mauz*, and that again is from the Skt. *mocha*. The specific name *sapientum* arises out of a misunderstanding of a passage in Pliny, which we have explained under the head **Jack**. The specific *paradisaica* is derived from the old belief of Oriental Christians (entertained also, if not originated by the Mahommedans) that this was the tree from whose leaves Adam and Eve made themselves aprons. A further mystical interest attached also to the fruit, which some believed to be the forbidden apple of Eden. For in the pattern formed by the core or seeds, when the fruit was cut across, our forefathers discerned an image of the Cross, or even of the Crucifix. Medieval travellers generally call the fruit either *Musa* or 'Fig of Paradise,' or sometimes 'Fig of India,' and to this day in the W. Indies the common small plantains are called 'figs.' The Portuguese also habitually called it 'Indian Fig.' And this perhaps originated some confusion in Milton's mind, leading him to make the **Banyan** (*Ficus Indica* of Pliny, as of modern botanists) the Tree of the aprons, and greatly to exaggerate the size of the leaves of that *ficus*.

The name **banana** is never employed by the English in India, though it is the name universal in the London fruit-shops, where this fruit is now to be had at almost all seasons, and often of excellent quality, imported chiefly, we believe, from Madeira, [and more recently from Jamaica. Mr. Skeat adds that in the Strait Settlements the name **plantain** seems to be reserved for those varieties which are only eatable when cooked, but the word **banana** is used indifferently with **plantain**, the latter being on the whole perhaps the rarer word].

The name *plantain* is no more originally Indian than is *banana*. It, or rather *platano*, appears to have been the name under which the fruit was first carried to the W. Indies, according to Oviedo, in 1516; the first edition of his book was published in 1526. That author is careful to explain that the plant was *improperly* so called, as it was quite another thing from the *platanus* described by Pliny. Bluteau says the word is Spanish. We do not know how it came to be applied to the *Musa*. [Mr. Guppy (8 ser. *Notes & Queries*, viii. 87) suggests that "the Spaniards have obtained *platano* from the Carib and Galibi words for *banana*, viz., *balatanna* and *palatana*, by the process followed by the Australian colonists when they converted a native name for the casuarina trees into 'she-oak'; and that we can thus explain how *platano* came in Spanish to signify both the plane-tree and the banana" Prof. Skeat (*Concise Dict.* s.v.) derives plantain from Lat. *planta*, 'a plant'; properly 'a spreading sucker or shoot'; and says that the plantain took its name from its spreading leaf.] The rapid spread of the plantain or banana in the West, whence both names were carried back to India, is a counterpart to the rapid diffusion of the **ananas** in the Old World of Asia. It would seem from the translation of Mendoça that in his time (1585) the Spaniards had come to use the form *plantano*, which our Englishmen took up as *plantan* and *plantain*. But even in the 1736 edition of Bailey's Dict. The only explanation of plantain given is as the equivalent of the Latin *plantago*, the field-weed known by the former name. *Platano* and *Plantano* are used in the Philippine Islands by the Spanish population.

1336.—"Sunt in Syriâ et Aegypto poma oblonga quae Paradisi nuncupantur optimi saporis, mollia, in ore cito dissolubilia: per transversum quotiescumque ipsa incideris invenies *Crucifixum* ... diu non durant, unde per mare ad nostras partes duci non possunt incorrupta."—*Gul. de Boldensele.*

c. 1350.—"Sunt enim in orto illo Adae de Seyllano primo *musae*, quas incolae ficus vocant ... et istud vidimus oculis nostris quod ubicunque inciditur per transversum, in utrâque parte incisurae videtur ymago hominis *crucifixi* ... et de istis foliis ficûs Adam et Eva fecerunt sibi perizomata. ..."—*John de' Marignolli*, in *Cathay*, &c. p. 352.

1384.—"And there is again a fruit which many people assert to be that regarding which our first father Adam sinned, and this fruit they call *Muse* ... in this fruit you see a very great miracle, for when you divide it anyway, whether lengthways or across, or cut it as you will, you shall see inside, as it were, the image of the *Crucifix*; and of this we comrades many times made proof."—*Viaggio di Simone Sigoli* (Firenze, 1862, p. 160).

1526 (tr. 1577).—"There are also certayne plantes whiche the Christians call **Platani**. In the myddest of the plant, in the highest part thereof, there groweth a cluster with fourtie or fiftie **platans** about it. ... This cluster ought to be taken from the plant, when any one of the **platans** begins to appeare yelowe, at which time they take it, and hang it in their houses, where all the cluster waxeth rype, with all his **platans**."—*Ociedo*, transl. in *Eden's Hist. of Travayle*, f. 208.

1552 (tr. 1582).—"Moreover the Ilande (of Mombas) is verye pleasaunt, having many orchards, wherein are planted and are groweing. ... Figges of the Indias. ..."—*Castañeda*, by N. L., f. 22.

1579.—"... a fruit which they call *Figo* (Magellane calls it a figge of a span long, but it is no other than that which the Spaniards and Portingalls have named **Plantanes**)."—*Drake's Voyage*, Hak. Soc. p. 142.

1585 (tr. 1588).—"There are mountaines very thicke of orange trees, siders [*i.e. cedras*, 'citrons'], limes, **plantanos**, and palmas."—*Mendoça*, by *R. Parke*, Hak. Soc. ii. 330.'

1588.—"Our Generall made their wiues to fetch vs **Plantans**, Lymmons, and Oranges, Pine-apples, and other fruits."—*Voyage of Master Thomas Candish*, in *Purchas*, i. 64.

1588 (tr. 1604).—"... the first that shall be needefulle to treate of is the **Plantain** (*Platano*), or **Plantano**, as the vulgar call it. ... The reason why the Spaniards call it **platano** (for the Indians had no such name), was, as in other trees for that they have found some resemblance of the one with the other, even as they called some fruites prunes, pines, and cucumbers, being far different from those which are called by those names in Castille. The thing wherein was most resemblance, in my opinion, between the **platanos** at the Indies and those which the ancients did celebrate, is the greatnes of the leaves. ... But, in truth, there is no more comparison nor resemblance of the one with the other than there is, as the Proverb saith, betwixt an egge and a chesnut."—*Joseph de Acosta*, transl. by E. G., Hak. Soc. i. 241.

1593.—"The **plantane** is a tree found in most parts of Afrique and America, of which two leaves are sufficient to cover a man from top to toe."—*Hawkins, Voyage into the South Sea*, Hak. Soc. 49.

1610.—"... and every day failed not to send each man, being one and fiftie in number, two cakes of white bread, and a quantitie of Dates and **Plantans**. ..."—*Sir H. Middleton*, in *Purchas*, i. 254.

c. 1610.—"Ces Gentils ayant pitié de moy, il y eut vne femme qui me mit ... vne seruiete de feuilles de **plantane** accommodées ensemble auec des espines, puis me ietta dessus du rys cuit auec vne certaine sauce qu'ils appellent *caril* (see CURRY). ..."—*Mocquet, Voyages*, 292.

["They (elephants) require ... besides leaves of trees, chiefly of the Indian fig, which we call Bananes and the Turks **plantenes**."—*Pyrard de Laval*, Hak. Soc. ii. 345.]

1616.—"They have to these another fruit we English there call a **Planten**, of which many of them grow in clusters together ... very yellow when they are Ripe, and then they taste like unto a *Norwich* Pear, but much better."—*Terry*, ed. 1665, p. 360.

c. 1635.—

"... with candy **Plantains** and the juicy Pine,
On choicest Melons and sweet Grapes they dine,
And with Potatoes fat their wanton Swine."
Waller, Battle of the Summer Islands.

c. 1635.—

"Oh how I long my careless Limbs to lay
Under the **Plantain's** Shade; and all the Day
With amorous Airs my Fancy entertain."
Waller, Battle of the Summer Islands.

c. 1660.—

"The Plant (at Brasil *Bacone* call'd) the Name
Of the Eastern **Plane-tree** takes, but not the same:
Bears leaves so large, one single Leaf can shade
The Swain that is beneath her Covert laid;
Under whose verdant Leaves fair Apples grow,
Sometimes two Hundred on a single Bough... ."
Cowley, of Plants, Bk. v.

1664—

"Wake, Wake Quevera! Our soft rest must cease,

And fly together with our country's peace.
No more must we sleep under **plantain** shade,
Which neither heat could pierce nor cold invade;
Where bounteous Nature never feels decay,
And opening buds drive falling fruits away."

Dryden, Prologue to the Indian Queen.

1673.—"Lower than these, but with a Leaf far broader, stands the curious **Plantan**, loading its tender Body with a Fruit, whose clusters emulate the Grapes of *Canaan*, which burthened two men's shoulders."—*Fryer*, 19.

1686.—"The **Plantain** I take to be King of all Fruit, not except the Coco itself."—*Dampier*, i. 311.

1689.—"... and now in the Governour's Garden (at St. Helena) and some others of the Island are quantities of **Plantins**, **Bonanoes**, and other delightful Fruits brought from the East. ..."—*Ovington*, 100.

1764.—

"But round the upland huts, bananas plant;
A wholesome nutriment bananas yield,
And sunburnt labour loves its breezy shade,
Their graceful screen let kindred **plantanes** join,
And with their broad vans shiver in the breeze."

Grainger, Bk. iv.

1805.—"The **plantain**, in some of its kinds, supplies the place of bread."—*Orme, Fragments*, 479.

***PLASSEY**, n.p. The village *Palāsī*, which gives its name to Lord Clive's famous battle (June 23, 1757). It is said to take its name from the *pālas* (or **dhawk**) tree.

1748.—"... that they have great reason to complain of Ensign English's conduct in not waiting at **Placy** ... and that if he had staid another day at **Placy**, as Tullerooy Caun was marching with a large force towards Cutway, they presume the Mahrattas would have retreated inland on their approach and left him an open passage. ..."—*Letter from Council at Cossimbazar*, in *Long*, p. 2.

[1757.—Clive's original report of the battle is dated on the "plain of **Placis**."—*Birdwood, Report on Old Records*, 57.]

1768–71.—"General Clive, who should have been the leader of the English troops in this battle (**Plassy**), left the command to Colonel Coote, and remained hid in his palankeen during the combat, out of the reach of the shot, and did not make his appearance before the enemy were put to flight."—*Stavorinus*, E.T. i. 486. This stupid and inaccurate writer says that several English officers who were present at the battle related this "anecdote" to him. This, it may be hoped, is as untrue as the rest of the story. Even to such a writer one would have supposed that Clive's mettle would be familiar.

***POGGLE, PUGGLY**, &c., s. Properly Hind. *pāgal*; 'a madman, an idiot'; often used colloquially by Anglo-Indians. A friend belonging to that body used to adduce a macaronic adage which we fear the non-Indian will fail to appreciate: "**Pagal** *et pecunia jaldè separantur!*" [See NAUTCH.]

1829.—"It's true the people call me, I know not why, the **pugley**."—*Mem. John Shipp*, ii. 255.

1866.—"I was foolish enough to pay these **budmashes** beforehand, and they have thrown me over. I must have been a **paugul** to do it."—*Trevelyan, The Dawk Bungalow*, 385.

[1885.—"He told me that the native name for a regular picnic is a '**Poggle**-*khana*,' that is, a fool's dinner."—*Lady Dufferin, Viceregal Life*, 88.]

POLO, s. The game of hockey on horseback, introduced of late years into England, under this name, which comes from Baltī; *polo* being properly in the language of that region the ball used in the game. The game thus lately revived was once known and practised (though in various forms) from Provence to the borders of China (see CHICANE). It had continued to exist down to our own day, it would seem, only near the extreme East and the extreme West of the Himālaya, viz. at Manipur in the East (between Cachar and Burma), and on the West in the high valley of the Indus (in Ladāk, Balti, Astōr and Gilgit, and extending into Chitrāl). From the former it was first adopted by our countrymen at Calcutta, and a little later (about 1864) it was introduced into the Punjab, almost simultaneously from the Lower Provinces and from Kashmīr, where the summer visitors had taken it up. It was first played in England, it would seem at Aldershot, in July 1871, and in August of the same year at Dublin in the Phœnix Park. The next year it was played in many places.[1] But the first mention we can find in the *Times* is a notice of a match at Lillie-Bridge, July 11, 1874, in the next day's paper. There is mention of the game in the *Illustrated London News* of July 20, 1872, where it is treated as a new invention by British officers in India. [According

1 See details in the *Field* of Nov. 15, 1884, p. 667, courteously given in reply to a query from the present writer.

to the author of the *Badminton Library* treatise on the game, it was adopted by Lieut. Sherer in 1854, and a club was formed in 1859. The same writer fixes its introduction into the Punjab and N.W.P. in 1861–62. See also an article in *Baily's Magazine* on "The Early History of Polo." (June 1890). The Central Asian form is described, under the name of *Baiga* or *Kok-büra*, 'grey wolf,' by Schuyler (*Turkistan*, i. 268 *seqq.*) and that in Dardistan by Biddulph (*Tribes of the Hindoo Koosh*, 84 *seqq.*).] In Ladāk it is not indigenous, but an introduction from Baltistan. See a careful and interesting account of the game of those parts in Mr. F. Drew's excellent book, *The Jummoo and Kashmir Territories*, 1875, pp. 380–392.

We learn from Professor Tylor that the game exists still in Japan, and a very curious circumstance is that the polo *racket*, just as that described by Jo. Cinnamus in the extract under **CHICANE** has survived there. [See *Chamberlain, Things Japanese*, 3rd ed. 333 *seqq.*]

1835.—"The ponies of Muneepoor hold a very conspicuous rank in the estimation of the inhabitants. ... The national game of Hockey, which is played by every male of the country capable of sitting a horse, renders them all expert equestrians; and it was by men and horses so trained, that the princes of Muneepoor were able for many years not only to repel the aggressions of the Burmahs, but to save the whole country ... and plant their banners on the banks of the Irrawattee."—*Pemberton's Report on the E. Frontier of Br. India*, 31–32.

1838.—"At Shighur I first saw the game of the Chaughán, which was played the day after our arrival on the **Mydan** or plain laid out expressly for the purpose. ... It is in fact hocky on horseback. The ball, which is larger than a cricket ball, is only a globe made of a kind of willow-wood, and is called in Tibeti '**Pulu**.' ... I can conceive that the Chaughán requires only to be seen to be played. It is the fit sport of an equestrian nation. ... The game is played at almost every valley in Little Tibet and the adjoining countries ... Ladakh, Yessen, Chitral, &c.; and I should recommend it to be tried on the Hippodrome at Bayswater. ..."—*Vigne, Travels in Kashmir, Ladakh, Iskardo*, &c. (1842), ii. 289–392.

1848.—"An assembly of all the principal inhabitants took place at Iskardo, on some occasion of ceremony or festivity. ... I was thus fortunate enough to be a witness of the chaugan, which is derived from Persia, and has been described by Mr. Vigne as hocky on horseback. ... Large quadrangular enclosed meadows for this game may be seen in all the larger villages of Balti, often surrounded by rows of beautiful willow and poplar trees."—*Dr. T. Thomson, Himalaya and Tibet*, 260–261.

1875.—

"**Polo**, Tent-pegging, Hurlingham, the Rink,
I leave all these delights."

Browning, Inn Album, 23.

POOJA, s. Properly applied to the Hindu ceremonies in idol-worship; Skt. *pūjā*; and colloquially to any kind of rite. Thus *jhaṇḍā kī pūjā*, or 'Pooja of the flag,' is the sepoy term for what in St. James's Park is called 'Trooping of the colours.' [Used in the plural, as in the quotation of 1900, it means the holidays of the Durgā Pūjā or **Dussera**.]

[1776.—"... the occupation of the *Bramin* should be ... to cause the performance of the **poojen**, *i.e.* the worship to *Dewtàh*. ..."—*Halhed, Code*, ed. 1781, Pref. xcix.

[1813.—"... the Pundits in attendance commenced the **pooja**, or sacrifice, by pouring milk and curds upon the branches, and smearing over the leaves with wetted rice."—*Broughton, Letters*, ed. 1892, p. 214.]

1826.—"The person whose steps I had been watching now approached the sacred tree, and having performed **puja** to a stone deity at its foot, proceeded to unmuffle himself from his shawls. ..."—*Pandurang Hari*, 26; [ed. 1873, i. 34].

1866.—"Yes, Sahib, I Christian boy. Plenty **poojah** do. Sunday time never no work do."—*Trevelyan, The Dawk Bungalow*, in *Fraser*, lxxiii. 226.

1874.—"The mass of the ryots who form the population of the village are too poor to have a family deity. They are forced to be content with ... the annual **pujahs** performed ... on behalf of the village community."—*Cal. Rev.* No. cxvii. 195.

1879.—"Among the curiosities of these lower galleries are little models of costumes and country scenes, among them a grand **pooja** under a tree."—*Sat. Rev.* No. 1251, p. 477.

[1900.—"Calcutta has been in the throes of the **Pujahs** since yesterday."—*Pioneer Mail*, 5 Oct.].

POORÁNA, s. Skt. *purāṇa*, 'old,' hence 'legendary,' and thus applied as a common name to 18 books which contain the legendary mythology of the Brahmans.

1612.—"... These books are divided into bodies, members, and joints (*cortos, membros, e articulos*) ... six which they call *Xastra* (see

SHASTER), which are the bodies; eighteen which they call **Puraná**, which are the members; twenty-eight called *Agamon*, which are the joints."—*Couto*, Dec. V. liv. vi. cap. 3.

1651.—"As their **Poranas**, *i.e.* old histories, relate."—*Rogerius*, 153.

[1667.—"When they have acquired a knowledge of Sanscrit ... they generally study the **Purana**, which is an abridgment and interpretation of the Beths" (see VEDAS).—*Bernier*, ed. *Constable*, p. 335.]

c. 1760.—"Le **puran** comprend dix-huit livres qui renferment l'histoire sacrée, qui contient les dogmes de la religion des Bramines."—*Encyclopédie*, xxvii. 807.

1806.—"Ceux-ci, calculoient tout haut de mémoire tandis que d'autres, plus avancés, lisoient, d'un ton chantant, leurs **Pourans**."—*Haafner*, i. 130.

POOTLY NAUTCH, s. Properly Hind. *kāṭh-putlī-nāch*, 'wooden-puppet-dance.' A puppet show.

c. 1817.—"The day after tomorrow will be my lad James Dawson's birthday, and we are to have a **puttully-nautch** in the evening."—*Mrs. Sherwood's Stories*, 291.

POPPER-CAKE, in Bombay, and in Madras **popadam**, ss. These are apparently the same word and thing, though to the former is attributed a Hind. and Mahr. origin *pāpaṛ*, Skt. *parpaṭa*, and to the latter a Tamil one, *pappaḍam*, as an abbreviation of *paruppu-aḍam*, 'lentil cake.' [The *Madras Gloss*. gives Tel. *appadam*, Tam. *appalam*, and Mal. *pappatam*, from *parippu*, '**dhall**,' *ata*, 'cake.'] It is a kind of thin scone or wafer, made of any kind of pulse or lentil flour, seasoned with assafoetida, &c., friend in oil, and in W. India baked crisp, and often eaten at European tables as an accompaniment to curry. It is not bad, even to a novice.

1814.—"They are very fond of a thin cake, or wafer, called **popper**, made from the flour of *oord* or *mash* ... highly seasoned with assafoetida; a salt called **popper**-*khor*; and a very hot massaula (see MUSSALLA), compounded of turmeric, black pepper, ginger, garlic, several kinds of warm seeds, and a quantity of the hottest Chili pepper."—*Forbes, Or. Mem.* ii. 50; [2nd ed. i. 347].

1820.—"**Papaḍoms** (fine cakes made of gram-flour and a fine species of alkali, which gives them an agreeable salt taste, and serves the purpose of yeast, making them rise, and become very crisp when fried. ..."—*As. Researches*, xiii. 315.

"**Paper**, the flour of *ooreed* (see OORD), salt, assa-foetida, and various spices, made into a paste, rolled as thin as a wafer, and dried in the sun, and when wanted for the table baked crisp. ..."—*T. Coates*, in *Tr. Lit. Soc. Bo.* iii. 194.

PORCELAIN, s. The history of this word for China-ware appears to be as follows. The family of univalve mollusks called *Cypraeidae*, or **Cowries**, (q.v.) were in medieval Italy called *porcellana* and *porcelletta*, almost certainly from their strong resemblance to the body and back of a pig, and not from a grosser analogy suggested by Mahn (see in Littré *sub voce*). That this is so is strongly corroborated by the circumstance noted by Dr. J. E. Gray (see *Eng. Cyc. Nat. Hist.* s.v. *Cypraeidae*) that *Pig* is the common name of shells of this family on the English coast; whilst *Sow* also seems to be a name of one or more kinds. The enamel of this shell seems to have been used in the Middle Ages to form a coating for ornamental pottery, &c., whence the early application of the term *porcellana* to the fine ware brought from the far East. Both applications of the term, viz. to cowries and to China-ware, occur in *Marco Polo* (see below). The quasi-analogous application of *pig* in Scotland to earthen-ware, noticed in an imaginary quotation below, is probably quite an accident, for there appears to be a Gaelic *pige*, 'an earthen jar,' &c. (see *Skeat*, s.v. *piggin*). We should not fail to recall Dr. Johnson's etymology of *porcelaine* from *"pour cent années,"* because it was believed by Europeans that the materials were matured under ground 100 years! (see quotations below from Barbosa, and from Sir Thomas Brown).

c. 1250.—Capmany has the following passage in the work cited. Though the same writer published the Laws of the Consulado del Mar in 1791, he has deranged the whole of the chapters, and this, which he has quoted, is omitted altogether!

"In the XLIVth chap. of the maritime laws of Barcelona, which are undoubtedly not later than the middle of the 13th century, there are regulations for the return cargoes of the ships trading with Alexandria. ... In this are enumerated among articles brought from Egypt ... cotton in bales and spun wool *de capells* (for hats?), **porcelanas**, alum, elephants' teeth. ..."—*Memorias, Hist. de Barcelona*, I. Pt. ii. p. 44.

1298.—"Il out monoie en tel mainere con je voz dirai, car il espendent **porcelaine** blance, celle qe se trovent en la mer et qe se metent au cuel des chienz, et vailent les quatre-vingt **porcelaines** un saic d'arjent qe sunt deus venesians gros. ..."—*Marco Polo*, oldest French text, p. 132.

"Et encore voz di qe en ceste provence, en une cité qe est apellé Tinugui, se font escuelle de **porcellaine** grant et pitet les plus belles qe l'en peust deviser."—*Ibid.* 180.

c. 1328.—"Audivi quòd ducentas civitates habet sub se imperator ille (Magnus Tartarus) majores quàm Tholosa; et ego certè credo quòd plures habeant homines. ... Alia non sunt quae ego sciam in isto imperio digna relatione, nisi vasa pulcherrima, et nobilissima, atque virtuosa **porseleta**."—*Jordani Mirabilia*, p. 59.

In the next passage it seems probable that the shells, and not China dishes, are intended.

c. 1343.—"... ghomerabica, vernice, armoniaco, zaffiere, coloquinti, **porcellánc**, mirra, mirabolani ... si vendono a Vinegia a cento di peso sottile" (*i.e.* by the **cutcha** hundredweight).—*Pegolotti, Practica della Mercatura*, p. 134.

c. 1440.—"... this Cim and Macinn that I haue before named arr ii verie great provinces, thinhabitants whereof arr idolaters, and there make they vessells and disshes of **Porcellana**."—*Giosafa Barbaro*, Hak. Soc. 75.

In the next the shells are clearly intended:

1442.—"*Gabelle di Firenze* ... **Porcielette** marine, la libra ... soldi ... denari 4."—*Uzzano, Prat. della Mercatura*, p. 23.

1461.—"**Porcellane** pezzi 20, cioè 7 piattine, 5 scodelle, 4 grandi e una piccida, piattine 5 grandi, 3 scodelle, una biava, e due bianche."—*List of Presents sent by the* Soldan of Egypt *to the Doge* Pasquale Malepiero. In *Muratori, Rerum Italicarum Scriptores*, xxi. col. 1170.

1475.—"The seaports of Cheen and Machin are also large. **Porcelain** is made there, and sold by the weight and at a low price."—*Nikitin*, in *India in the XVth Cent.*, 21.

1487.—"... le mando lo inventario del presente del Soldano dato a Lorenzo ... vasi grandi di **Porcellana** mai più veduti simili ne meglio lavorati. ..."—*Letter of P. da Bibbieno to Clar. de' Medici*, in *Roscoe's Lorenzo*, ed. 1825, ii. 371.

1502.—"In questo tempo abrusiorno xxi nave sopra il porto di Calechut; et de epse hebbe tãte drogarie e speciarie che caricho le dicte sei nave. Praeterea me ha mandato sei vasi di **porzellana** excellitissimi et grãdi: quatro bochali de argento grandi cõ certi altri vasi al modo loro per credentia."—*Letter of K. Emanuel*, 13.

1516.—"They make in this country a great quantity of **porcelains** of different sorts, very fine and good, which form for them a great article of trade for all parts, and they make them in this way. They take the shells of sea-snails (? *caracoli*), and eggshells, and pound them, and with other ingredients make a paste, which they put underground to refine for the space of 80 or 100 years, and this mass of paste they leave as a fortune to their children. ..."—*Barbosa*, in *Ramusio*, i. 320*v*.

1553.—(In China) "The service of their meals is the most elegant that can be, everything being of very fine **procelana** (although they also make use of silver and gold plate), and they eat everything with a fork made after their fashion, never putting a hand into their food, much or little."—*Barros*, III. ii. 7.

1554.—(After a suggestion of the identity of the *vasa murrhina* of the ancients): "Ce nom de **Porcelaine** est donné à plusieurs coquilles de mer. Et pource qu'vn beau Vaisseau d'vne coquille de mer ne se pourroit rendre mieux à propos suyuãt le nom antique, que de l'appeller de **Porcelaine** i'ay pensé que les coquilles polies et luysantes, resemblants à Nacre de perles, ont quelque affinité auec la matière des vases de **Porcelaine** antiques: ioinct aussi que le peuple Frãçois nomme les patesnostres faictes de gros vignols, patenostres de **Porcelaine**. Les susdicts vases de **Porcelaine** sont transparents, et coustent bien cher au Caire, et disent mesmement qu'ilz les apportent des Indes. Mais cela ne me sembla vraysemblable: car on n'en voirroit pas ai grande quantité, ne de si grãdes pieces, s'il failloit apporter de si loing. Vne esguiere, vn pot, ou vn autre vaisseau pour petite qu'elle soit, couste vn ducat: si c'est quelque grãd vase, il coustera d'auantage."—*P. Belon, Observations*, f. 134.

c. 1560.—"And because there are many opinions among the Portugals which have not beene in *China*, about where this **Porcelane** is made, and touching the substance whereof it is made, some saying, that it is of oysters shels, others of dung rotten of a long time, because they were not enformed of the truth, I thought it conuenient to tell here the substance. ..."—*Gaspar da Cruz*, in *Purchas*, iii. 177.

[1605-6.—"... China dishes or **Puselen**."—*Birdwood, First Letter Book*, 77.

[1612.—"Balanced one part with sandal wood, **Porcelain** and pepper."—*Danvers, Letters*, i. 197.]

1615.—"If we had in England beds of **porcelain** such as they have in China,—which **porcelain** is a kind of plaster buried in the earth, and by length of time congealed and glazed into that substance; this were an artificial mine, and part of that substance. ..."—*Bacon, Argument on Impeachment of Waste*; *Works*, by *Spedding*, &c., 1859, vii. 528.

c. 1630.—"The *Bannyans* all along the sea-shore pitch their Booths ... for there they sell Callicoes, China-satten, **Purcellain**-ware, scrutores or Cabbinets. ..."—*Sir T. Herbert*, ed. 1665, p. 45.

1650.—"We are not thoroughly resolved concerning **Porcellane** or China dishes, that according to common belief they are made of earth, which lieth in preparation about an hundred years underground; for the relations thereof are not only divers but contrary; and Authors agree not herein. ..."—*Sir Thomas Browne, Vulgar Errors*, ii. 5.

[1652.—"Invited by Lady Gerrard I went to London, where we had a greate supper; all the vessels, which were innumerable, were of **Porcelan**, she having the most ample and richest collection of that curiositie in England."—*Evelyn, Diary*, March 19.]

1726.—In a list of the treasures left by Akbar, which is given by Valentijn, we find:

"In **Porcelyn**, &c., Ropias 2507747."—iv. (*Suratte*), 217.

1880.—"'Vasella quidem delicatiora et caerulea et venusta, quibus inhaeret nescimus quid elegantiae, **porcellana** vocantur, quasi (sed nescimus quare) a *porcellis*. In partibus autem Britanniae quae septentrionem spectant, vocabulo forsan analogo, vasa grossiora et fusca *pigs* appellant barbari, quasi (sed quare iterum nescimus) a *porcis*.' *Narrischchen und Weitgeholt, Etymol. Universale*, s.v. 'Blue China.'"—Motto to *An Ode in Brown Pig, St. James's Gazette*, July 17.

PRACRIT, s. A term applied to the older vernacular dialects of India, such as were derived from, or kindred to, Sanskrit. Dialects of this nature are used by ladies, and by inferior characters, in the Sanskrit dramas. These dialects, and the modern vernaculars springing from them, bear the same relation to Sanskrit that the "Romance" languages of Europe bear to Latin, an analogy which is found in many particulars to hold with most surprising exactness. The most completely preserved of old Prakrits is that which was used in Magadha, and which has come down in the Buddhist books of Ceylon under the name of Pali. The first European analysis of this language bears the title "*Institutiones Linguac* **Pracriticae**. *Scripsit Christianus Lassen*, Bonnae ad Rhenum, 1837." The term itself is Skt. *prākṛita*, 'natural, unrefined, vulgar,' &c.

1801.—"*Sanscrita* is the speech of the Celestials, framed in grammatical institutes, **Pracrita** is similar to it, but manifold as a provincial dialect, and otherwise."—*Sanskrit Treatise*, quoted by *Colebrooke*, in *As. Res.* vii. 199.

PRESIDENCY (and **PRESIDENT**), s. The title 'President,' as applied to the Chief of a principal Factory, was in early popular use, though in the charters of the E.I.C. its first occurrence is in 1661 (see *Letters Patent*, below). In Sainsbury's *Calendar* we find letters headed "to Capt. Jourdain, president of the English at Bantam" in 1614 (i. 297–8); but it is to be doubted whether this wording is in the original. A little later we find a "proposal by Mr. Middleton concerning the appointment of two especial factors, at Surat and Bantam, to have authority over all other factors; Jourdain named." And later again he is styled "John Jourdain, Captain of the house" (at Bantam; see pp. 303, 325), and "Chief Merchant at Bantam" (p. 343).

1623.—"Speaking of the Dutch Commander, as well as of the English **President**, who often in this fashion came to take me for an airing, I should not omit to say that both of them in Surat live in great style, and like the grandees of the land. They go about with a great train, sometimes with people of their own mounted, but particularly with a great crowd of Indian servants on foot and armed, according to custom, with sword, target, bow and arrows."—*P. della Valle*, ii. 517.

"Our boat going ashore, the **President** of the English Merchants, who usually resides in Surat, and is chief of all their business in the E. Indies, Persia, and other places dependent thereon, and who is called Sign. Thomas Rastel[1] ... came aboard in our said boat, with a minister of theirs (so they term those who do the priest's office among them)."—*Ibid.* ii. 501–2; [Hak. Soc. i. 19].

1638.—"As soon as the Commanders heard that the (English) **President** was come to Suhaly, they went ashore. ... The two dayes following were spent in feasting, at which the Commanders of the two Ships treated the **President**, who afterwards returned to *Suratta*. ... During my abode at *Suratta*, I wanted for no divertisement; for I ... found company at the *Dutch* **President's**, who had his Farms there ... inasmuch as I could converse with them in their own Language."—*Mandelslo*, E.T., ed. 1669, p. 19.

1638.—"Les Anglois ont bien encore vn bureau à Bantam, dans l'Isle de Jaua, mais il a son **President** particulier, qui ne depend point

1 Thomas Rastall or Rastell went out apparently in 1615, in 1616 is mentioned as a "chief merchant of the fleet at Swally Road," and often later as chief at Surat (see *Sainsbury*, i. 476, and ii. *passim*).

de celuy de *Suratta*."—*Mandelslo*, French ed. 1659, p. 124.

"A mon retour à *Suratta* ie trouvay dans la loge des Anglois plus de cinquante marchands, que le **President** auoit fait venir de tous les autres Bureaux, pour rendre compte de leur administration, et pour estre presens à ce changement de Gouuernement."—*Ibid.* 188.

1661.—"And in case any Person or Persons, being convicted and sentenced by the **President** and Council of the said Governor and Company, in the said East Indies, their Factors or Agents there, for any Offence by them done, shall appeal from the same, that then, and in every such case, it shall and may be lawful to and for the said **President** and Council, Factor or Agent, to seize upon him or them, and to carry him or them home Prisoners to England."—*Letters Patent to the Governor and Company of Merchants of London, trading with the E. Indies*, 3d April.

1670.—The Court, in a letter to Fort St. George, fix the amount of tonnage to be allowed to their officers (for their private investments) on their return to Europe:

"**Presidents** and Agents, at Surat, Fort St. George, and Bantam . 5 *tonns*.
Chiefes, at Persia, the Bay, Mesulapatam, and Macassar: Deputy at Bombay, and Seconds at Surat, Fort St. George, and Bantam. . . . . 3 *tonns*."

In *Notes and Exts.*, No. i. p. 3.

1702.—"Tuesday 7th Aprill. ... In the morning a Councill ... afterwards having some Discourse arising among us whether the charge of hiring Calashes, &c., upon Invitations given us from the Shabander or any others to go to their Countrey Houses or upon any other Occasion of diverting our Selves abroad for health, should be charged to our Honble Masters account or not, the **President** and Mr. Loyd were of opinion to charge the same. ... But Mr. Rouse, Mr. Ridges, and Mr. Master were of opinion that Batavia being a place of extraordinary charge and Expense in all things, the said Calash hire, &c., ought not to be charged to the Honourable Company's Account."—*MS. Records in India Office.*

The book containing this is a collocation of fragmentary MS. diaries. But this passage pertains apparently to the proceedings of President Allen Catchpole and his council, belonging to the Factory of Chusan, from which they were expelled by the Chinese in 1701–2; they stayed some time at Batavia on their way home. Mr. Catchpole (or Ketchpole) was soon afterwards chief of an English settlement made upon Pulo Condore, off the Cambojan coast. In 1704–5, we read that he reported favourably on the prospects of the settlement, requesting a supply of young **writers**, to learn the Chinese language, anticipating that the island would soon become an important station for Chinese trade. But Catchpole was himself, about the end of 1705, murdered by certain people of Macassar, who thought he had broken faith with them, and with him all the English but two (see *Bruce's Annals*, 483–4, 580, 606, and *A. Hamilton*, ii. 205 [ed. 1744]). The Pulo Condore enterprise thus came to an end.

1727.—"About the year 1674, **President** Aungier, a gentleman well qualified for governing, came to the Chair, and leaving Surat to the Management of Deputies, came to *Bombay*, and rectified many things."—*A. Hamilton*, i. 188.

***PUCKA**, adj. Hind. *pakkā*, 'ripe, mature, cooked'; and hence substantial, permanent, with many specific applications, of which examples have been given under the habitually contrasted term **cutcha** (q.v.). One of the most common uses in which the word has become specific is that of a building of brick and mortar, in contradistinction to one of inferior material, as of mud, matting, or timber. Thus:

[1756.—"... adjacent houses; all of them of the strongest **Pecca** work, and all most proof against our Mettal on ye Bastions." *Capt. Grant, Report on Siege of Calcutta*, ed. by Col. Temple, *Ind. Ant.*, 1890, p. 7.]

1784.—"The House, Cook-room, bottle-connah, godown, &c., are all **pucka**-built."—In *Seton-Karr*, i. 41.

1824.—"A little above this beautiful stream, some miserable **pucka** sheds pointed out the Company's warehouses."—*Heber*, ed. 1844, i. 259–60.

1842.—"I observe that there are in the town (Dehli) many buildings **pucka**-built, as it is called in India."—*Wellington* to Ld. Ellenborough, in *Indian Adm.* of *Ld. E.*, p. 306.

1857.—"Your Lahore men have done nobly. I should like to embrace them; Donald, Roberts, Mac, and Dick are, all of them, **pucca** trumps."—*Lord Lawrence*, in *Life*, ii. 11.

1869.—"... there is no surer test by which to measure the prosperity of the people than the number of **pucka** houses that are being built."—*Report of a Sub-Committee* on Proposed Indian Census.

This application has given rise to a substantive

pucka, for work of brick and mortar, or for the composition used as cement and plaster.

1727.—"Fort William was built on an irregular Tetragon of Brick and Mortar, called **Puckah**, which is a Composition of Brick-dust, Lime, Molasses, and cut Hemp, and when it comes to be dry, it is as hard and tougher than firm Stone or Brick."—*A. Hamilton*, ii. 19; [ed. 1744, ii. 7].

The word was also sometimes used substantively for "*pucka pice*" (see CUTCHA).

c. 1817.—"I am sure I strive, and strive, and yet last month I could only lay by eight rupees and four **puckers**."—*Mrs. Sherwood's Stories*, 66.

In (Stockdale's) *Indian Vocabulary* of 1788 we find another substantive use, but it was perhaps even then inaccurate.

1788.—"**Pucka**—A putrid fever, generally fatal in 24 hours."

Another habitual application of **pucka** and **cutcha** distinguishes between two classes of weights and measures. The existence of twofold weight, the **pucka** ser and the **cutcha**, used to be very general in India. It was equally common in Medieval Europe. Almost every city in Italy had its libra *grossa* and libra *sottile* (*e.g.* see *Pegolotti*, 4, 34, 153, 228, &c.), and we ourselves still have them, under the names of *pound avoirdupois* and *pound troy*.

1673.—"The **Maund Pucka** at *Agra* is double as much (as the Surat *Maund*)."—*Fryer*, 205.

1760.—"Les **pacca** cosses ... repondent à une lieue de l'Isle de France."—*Lett. Edif.* xv. 189.

1803.—"If the rice should be sent to Coraygaum, it should be in sufficient quantities to give 72 **pucca** seers for each load."—*Wellington, Desp.* (ed. 1837), ii. 43.

In the next quotation the terms apply to the temporary or permanent character of the appointments held.

1866.—"*Susan*. Well, Miss, I don't wonder you're so fond of him. He is such a sweet young man, though he is **cutcha**. Thank goodness, my young man is **pucka**, though he is only a subordinate Government Salt Chowkee."—*Trevelyan, The Dawk Bungalow*, 222.

The remaining quotations are examples of miscellaneous use:

1853.—"'Well, Jenkyns, any news?' 'Nothing **pucka** that I know of.'"—*Oakfield*, ii. 57.

1866.—"I cannot endure a swell, even though his whiskers are **pucka**."—*Trevelyan, The Dawk Bungalow*, in *Fraser*, lxxiii. 220.

The word has spread to China:

"Dis **pukka** sing-song makee show
How smart man make mistake, galow."
Leland, Pidgin English Sing-Song, 54.

***PUCKEROW**, v. This is properly the imperative of the Hind. verb *pakṛānā*, 'to cause to be seized,' *pakṛāo*, 'cause him to be seized'; or perhaps more correctly of a compound verb *pakaṛāo*, 'seize and come,' or in our idiom, 'Go and seize.' But *puckerow* belongs essentially to the dialect of the European soldier, and in that becomes of itself a verb 'to *puckerow*,' *i.e.* to lay hold of (generally of a recalcitrant native). The conversion of the Hind. imperative into an Anglo-Indian verb infinitive, is not uncommon; compare **bunow**, **dumbcow**, **gubbrow**, **lugow**, &c.

1866.—"Fanny, I am **cutcha** no longer. Surely you will allow a lover who is **pucka** to **puckero**!"—*Trevelyan, The Dawk Bungalow*, 390.

PUGGRY, PUGGERIE, s. Hind. *pagṛī*, 'a turban.' The term being often used in colloquial for a scarf of cotton or silk wound round the hat in turban-form, to protect the head from the sun, both the thing and name have of late years made their way to England, and may be seen in London shop-windows.

c. 1200.—"Prithirâja ... wore a **pagari** ornamented with jewels, with a splendid *toro*. In his ears he wore pearls; on his neck a pearl necklace."—*Chand Bardai* E.T. by *Beames, Ind. Ant.* i. 282.

[1627.—"... I find it is the common mode of the Eastern People to shave the head all save a long lock which superstitiously they leave at the very top, such especially as wear **Turbans**, Mandils, Dustars, and **Puggarees**."—*Sir T. Herbert*, ed. 1677. p. 140.]

1673.—"They are distinguished, some according to the consanguinity they claim with Mahomet, as a Siad is akin to that Imposture, and therefore only assumes to himself a Green Vest and **Puckery** (or Turbat). ..."—*Fryer*, 93; [comp. 113].

1689.—"... with a **Puggaree** or Turbant upon their Heads."—*Ovington*, 314.

1871.—"They (the Negro Police in Demarara) used frequently to be turned out to parade in George Town streets, dressed in a neat uniform, with white **puggries** framing in their ebony faces."—*Jenkins, The Coolie*.

***PUNCH**, s. This beverage, according to the received etymology, was named from the Pers. *panj*, or Hind. and Mahr. *pānch*, both meaning 'five'; because composed of five ingredients, viz. arrack, sugar, lime-juice, spice, and water. Fryer may be considered to give something like historical evidence of its origin; but there is also something of Indian idiom in the suggestion. Thus a famous horse-medicine in Upper India is known as *battīsī*, because it is supposed to contain 32 ('*battīs*') ingredients. Schiller, in his *Punschlied*, sacrificing truth to trope, omits the spice and makes the ingredients only 4: "*Vier* Elemente Innig gesellt, Bilden das Leben, Bauen die Welt."

The Greeks also had a "Punch," πενταπλόα, as is shown in the quotation from Athenaeus. Their mixture does not sound inviting. Littré gives the etymology correctly from the Pers. *panj*, but the 5 elements *à la française*, as tea, sugar, spirit, cinnamon, and lemon-peel,—no water therefore!

Some such compound appears to have been in use of the beginning of the 17th century under the name of **Larkin**. Both Dutch and French travellers in the East during that century celebrate the beverage under a variety of names which amalgamate the drink curiously with the vessel in which it was brewed. And this combination in the form of **Bole-ponjis** was adopted as the title of a Miscellany published in 1851, by H. Meredith Parker, a Bengal civilian, of local repute for his literary and dramatic tastes. He had lost sight of the original authorities for the term, and his quotation is far astray. We give them correctly below.

c. 210.—"On the feast of the Scirrha at Athens he (Aristodemus on Pindar) says a race was run by the young men. They ran this race carrying each a vine-branch laden with grapes, such as is called *ōschus*; and they ran from the temple of Dionysus to that of Athena Sciras. And the winner receives a cup such as is called '**Five-fold**,' and of this he partakes joyously with the band of his comrades. But the cup is called πενταπλόα because it contains wine and honey and cheese and flour, and a little oil."—*Athenaeus*, XI. xcii.

1638.—"This voyage (Gombroon to Surat) ... we accomplished in 19 days. ... We drank English beer, Spanish sack, French wine, Indian spirit, and good English water, and made good **Palepunzen**."—*Mandelslo*, (Dutch ed. 1658), p. 24. The word **Palepunzen** seems to have puzzled the English translator (John Davis, 2nd ed. 1669), who has "excellent good sack, *English* beer, *French* wines, *Arak, and other refreshments.*" (p. 10).

1653.—"**Bolleponge** est vn mot Anglois, qui signifie vne boisson dont les Anglois vsent aux Indes faite de sucre, suc de limon, eau de vie, fleur de muscade, et biscuit roty."—*De la Boullaye-le-Gouz*, ed. 1657, p. 534.

[1658.—"Arriued this place where found the Bezar almost Burnt and many of the People almost starued for want of Foode which caused much Sadnes in Mr. Charnock and my Selfe, but not soe much as the absence of your Company, which wee haue often remembered in a bowle of the cleerest **Punch**, hauing noe better Liquor."—*Hedges, Diary*, Hak. Soc. iii. cxiv.]

1659.—"Fürs Dritte, **Pale bunze** getituliret, von halb Wasser, halb Brantwein, dreyssig, vierzig Limonien, deren Körnlein ausgespeyet werden, und ein wenig Zucker eingeworfen; wie dem Geschmack so angenehm nicht, also auch der Gesundheit nicht."—*Saar*, ed. 1672, 60.

[1662.—"Amongst other spirituous drinks, as **Punch**, &c., they gave us Canarie that had been carried to and fro from the Indies, which was indeed incomparably good."—*Evelyn, Diary*, Jan. 16.]

c. 1666.—"Neánmoins depuis qu'ils (les Anglois) ont donné ordre, aussi bien que les Hollandois, que leurs equipages ne boivent point tant de **Bouleponges** ... il n'y a pas tant de maladies, et il ne leur meurt plus tant de monde. **Bouleponge** est un certain breuvage composé d'arac ... avec du suc de limons, de l'eau, et un peu de muscade rapée dessus: il est assez agréable au gout, mais c'est la peste du corps et de la santé."—*Bernier*, ed. 1723, ii. 335 (Eng. Tr. p. 141); [ed. *Constable*, 441].

1670.—"Doch als men zekere andere drank, die zij **Paleponts** noemen, daartusschen drinkt, zo word het quaat enigsins geweert."—*Andriesz*, 9. Also at p. 27, "**Palepunts**."

We find this blunder of the compound word transported again to England, and explained as a 'hard word.'

1672.—Padre Vincenzo Maria describes the thing, but without a name:

"There are many fruites to which the Hollanders and the English add a certain beverage that they compound of lemon-juice, aqua-vitae, sugar, and nutmegs, to quench their thirst, and this, in my belief, augments not a little the evil influence."—*Viaggio*, p. 103.

1673.—"At Nerule is the best *Arach* or *Nepa* (see NIPA) *de Goa*, with which the *English* on this Coast make that enervating Liquor called **Paunch** (which is *Indostan* for Five), from Five Ingredients; as the Physicians name their Composition *Diapente*; or from four things, *Diatessaron*."—*Fryer*, 157.

1674.—"**Palapuntz**, a kind of Indian drink, consisting of *Aqua-vitae*, Rose-water, juyce of Citrons and Sugar."—*Glossographia*, &c., by T. E.

[1675.—"Drank part of their boules of **Punch** (a liquor very strange to me)."—*H. Teonge, Diary*, June 1.]

1682.—"Some (of the Chinese in Batavia) also sell Sugar-beer, as well as cooked dishes and Sury, arak or Indian brandy; wherefrom they make *Mussak* and **Follepons**, as the Englishmen call it."—*Nieuhoff, Zee en Lant-Reize*, ii. 217.

1683.—"... Our owne people and mariners who are now very numerous, and insolent among us, and (by reason of **Punch**) every day give disturbance."—*Hedges, Diary*, Oct. 8; [Hak. Soc. i. 123].

1688.—"... the soldiers as merry as **Punch** could make them."—In *Wheeler*, i. 187.

1689.—"Bengal (Arak) is much stronger spirit than that of Goa, tho' both are made use of by the Europeans in making **Punch**."—*Ovington*, 237–8.

1694.—"If any man comes into a victualling house to drink **punch**, he may demand one quart good Goa *arak*, half a pound of sugar, and half a pint of good lime water, and make his own **punch**. ..."—*Order Book of Bombay Govt.*, quoted by *Anderson*, p. 281.

1705.—"Un bon repas chez les Anglais ne se fait point sans *bonne* **ponse** qu'on sert dans un grand vase."—*Sieur Luillier, Voy. aux Grandes Indes*, 29.

1771.—"Hence every one (at Madras) has it in his Power to eat well, tho' he can afford no other Liquor at Meals than **Punch**, which is the common Drink among Europeans, and here made in the greatest Perfection."—*Lockyer*, 22.

1724.—"Next to *Drams*, no Liquor deserves more to be stigmatised and banished from the Repasts of the *Tender, Valetudinary*, and *Studious*, than **Punch**."—*G. Cheyne, An Essay on Health and Longevity*, p. 58.

1791.—"Dès que l'Anglais eut cessé de manger, le Paria ... fit un signe à sa femme, qui apporta ... une grande calebasse pleine de **punch**, qu'elle avoit preparé, pendant le souper, avec de l'eau, et du jus de citron, et du jus de canne de sucre. ..."—*B. de St. Pierre, Chaumière Indienne*, 56.

PUNCH-HOUSE, s. An Inn or Tavern; now the term is chiefly used by natives (sometimes in the hybrid form **Punch-ghar**, [which in Upper India is now transferred to the meeting-place of a Municipal Board]) at the Presidency towns, and applied to houses frequented by seamen. Formerly the word was in general Anglo-Indian use. [In the Straits the Malay *Panchaus* is, according to Mr. Skeat, still in use, though obolescent.].

1661.—"... the Commandore visiting us, wee delivering him another examination of a Persee (**Parsee**), who kept a **Punch-house**, where the murder was committed. ..."—*Forrest, Bombay Letters, Home Series*, i. 189.]

1671–2.—"It is likewise enordered and declared hereby that no Victuallar, **Punch-house**, or other house of Entertainment shall be permitted to make stoppage at the pay day of their wages. ..."—*Rules*, in *Wheeler*, iii. 423.

1676.—Major Puckle's "Proposals to the Agent about the young men at Metchlepatam.

"That some pecuniary mulct or fine be imposed ... for misdemeanours.

* * * * *

"6. Going to **Punch** or **Rack-houses** without leave or warrantable occasion.

"Drubbing any of the Company's **Peons** or servants."

* * * * *

—In *Notes and Exts.*, No. I. p. 40.

1688.—"... at his return to Achen he constantly frequented an English **Punch-house**, spending his Gold very freely."—*Dampier*, ii. 134.

"Mrs. Francis, wife to the late Lieutenant Francis killed at Hoogly by the Moors, made it her petition that she might keep a **Punch-house** for her maintenance."—In *Wheeler*, i. 184.

1697.—"Monday, 1st April ... Mr. Cheesely having in a **Punch-house**, upon a quarrel of words, drawn his Sword ... and being taxed therewith, he both doth own and justify the drawing of the sword ... it thereupon ordered not to wear a sword while here."—In *Wheeler*, i. 320.

1727.—"... Of late no small Pains and Charge have been bestowed on its Buildings (of the Fort at Tellichery); but for what Reason I know not ... unless it be for small Vessels ... or to protect the Company's Ware-house, and a small **Punch-house** that stands on the Sea-shore. ..."—*A. Hamilton*, i. 299 [ed. 1744].

1789.—"Many ... are obliged to take up their residence in dirty **punch-houses**."—*Munro's Narrative*, 22.

1810.—"The best house of that description which admits boarders, and which are commonly called **Punch-houses**."—*Williamson, V.M.* i. 135.

PUNCHAYET, s. Hind. *panchāyat*, from *pānch*, 'five.' A council (properly of 5 persons) assembled as a Court of Arbiters or Jury; or as a committee of the people of a village, of the members of a Caste, or what-not, to decide on questions interesting the body generally.

1778.—"*The Honourable* William Hornby, Esq., *President and Governor of His Majesty's Castle and Island of Bombay*, &c.

"The humble Petition of the Managers of the **Panchayet** of Parsis at Bombay. ..."—*Dosambhai Framji, H. of the Parsis*, 1884, ii. 219.

1810.—"The Parsees ... are governed by their own **panchaït** or village Council. The word **panchait** literally means a Council of five, but that of the Guebres in Bombay consists of thirteen of the principal merchants of the sect."—*Maria Graham*, 41.

1813.—"The carpet of justice was spread in the large open hall of the durbar, where the arbitrators assembled: there I always attended, and agreeably to ancient custom, referred the decision to a **panchaeït** or jury of five persons."—*Forbes, Or. Mem.*, ii. 359; [in 2nd ed. (ii. 2) **Panchaut**].

1819.—"The **punchayet** itself, although in all but village causes it has the defects before ascribed to it, possesses many advantages. The intimate acquaintance of the members with the subject in dispute, and in many cases with the characters of the parties, must have made their decisions frequently correct, and ... the judges being drawn from the body of the people, could act on no principles that were not generally understood."—*Elphinstone*, in *Life*, ii. 89.

1821.—"I kept up **punchayets** because I found them ... I still think that the **punchayet** should on no account be dropped, that it is an excellent institution for dispensing justice, and in keeping up the principles of justice, which are less likely to be observed among a people to whom the administration of it is not at all intrusted."—*Ibid.* 124.

1826.—"... when he returns assemble a **punchayet**, and give this cause patient attention, seeing that Hybatty has justice."—*Pandurang Hari*, 31; [ed. 1873, i. 42].

1832.—Bengal Regn. VI. of this year allows the judge of the Sessions Court to call in the alternative aid of a **punchayet**, in lieu of assessors, and so to dispense with the **futwa**. See LAW-OFFICER.

1853.—"From the death of Runjeet Singh to the battle of Sobraon, the Sikh Army was governed by **'Punchayets'** or **'Punches'**—committees of the soldiery. These bodies sold the Government to the Sikh chief who paid the highest, letting him command until murdered by some one who paid higher."—*Sir C. Napier*, *Defects of Indian Government*, 69.

1873.—"The Council of an Indian Village Community most commonly consists of five persons ... the **panchayet** familiar to all who have the smallest knowledge of India."—*Maine*, *Early Hist. of Institutions*, 221.

***PUNDIT**, s. Skt. *paṇḍita*, 'a learned man.' Properly a man learned in Sanskrit lore. The Pundit of the Supreme Court was a Hindu **Law-Officer**, whose duty it was to advise the English Judges when needful on questions of Hindu Law. The office became extinct on the constitution of the 'High Court,' superseding the Supreme Court and Sudder Court, under the Queen's Letters Patent of May 14, 1862.

In the Mahratta and Telegu countries, the word *Paṇḍit* is usually pronounced *Pant* (in English colloquial *Punt*); but in this form it has, as with many other Indian words in like case, lost its original significance, and become a mere personal title, familiar in Mahratta history, *e.g.* the Nānā Dhundo*pant* of evil fame.

Within the last 30 or 35 years the term has acquired in India a peculiar application to the natives trained in the use of instruments, who have been employed beyond the British Indian frontier in surveying regions inaccessible to Europeans. This application originated in the fact that two of the earliest men to be so employed, the explorations by one of whom acquired great celebrity, were masters of village schools in our Himālayan provinces. And the title *Pundit* is popularly employed there much as *Dominie* used to be in Scotland. The *Pundit* who brought so much fame on the title was the late Nain Singh, C.S.I. [See Markham, *Memoir of Indian Surveys*, 2nd ed. 148 *seqq.*]

1574.—"I hereby give notice that ... I hold it good, and it is my pleasure, and therefore I enjoin on all the **pandits** (*panditos*) and Gentoo physicians (*phisicos gentios*) that they ride not through this City (of Goa) or the suburbs thereof on horseback, nor in **andors** and palanquins, on pain of paying, on the first offence 10 *cruzados*, and on the second 20, *pera o sapal*,[1] with the forfeiture of such horses, **andors**, or palanquins, and on the third they shall become the galley-slaves of the King my Lord. ..."—*Procl.* of the Governor *Antonio Moriz Barreto*, in *Archiv. Port. Orient.* Fascic. 5, p. 899.

1 *Pera o sapal*, *i.e.* 'for the marsh. We cannot be certain of the meaning of this; but we may note that in 1543 the King, as a favour to the city of Goa, and for the commodity of its shipping and the landing of goods, &c., makes a grant "of the marsh inundated with sea-water (*do* sapal *alagado dagoa salgada*) which extends along the river-side from the houses of Antonio Correa to the houses of Afonso Piquo, which grant is to be perpetual ... to serve for a landing-place and quay for the merchants to moor and repair their ships, and to erect their **bankshalls** (*bangaçaes*), and never to be turned away to any other purpose." Possibly the fines went into a fund for the drainage of this *sapal* and formation of landing-places. See *Archiv. Port. Orient.*, Fasc. 2, pp. 130–131.

1604.—"... llamando tãbien en su compania los **Põditos**, le presentaron al Nauabo."—*Guerrero, Relaçion*, 70.

1616.—"... Brachmanae una cum **Panditis** comparentes, simile quid iam inde ab orbis exordio in Indostane visum negant."—*Jarric, Thesaurus*, iii. 81–82.

1663.—"A **Pendet** Brachman or *Heathen* Doctor whom I had put to serve my Agah ... would needs make his Panegyrick ... and at last concluded seriously with this: *When you put your Foot into the Stirrup, My Lord, and when you march on Horseback in the front of the Cavalry, the Earth trembleth under your Feet, the eight Elephants that hold it up upon their Heads not being able to support it.*"—*Bernier*, E.T., 85; [ed. *Constable*, 264].

1688.—"Je feignis donc d'être malade, et d'avoir la fièvre on fit venir aussitôt un **Pandite** ou médicin Gentil."—*Dellon, Rel. de l'Inq. de Goa*, 214.

1785.—"I can no longer bear to be at the mercy of our **pundits**, who deal out Hindu law as they please; and make it at reasonable rates, when they cannot find it ready made."—Letter of *Sir W. Jones*, in Mem. by *Ld. Teignmouth*, 1807, ii. 67.

1791.—"Il était au moment de s'embarquer pour l'Angleterre, plein de perplexité et d'ennui, lorsque les brames de Bénarés lui apprirent que le brame supérieur de la fameuse pagode de Jagrenat ... était seul capable de resoudre toutes les questions de la Société royale de Londres. C'était en effect le plus fameux **pandect**, ou docteur, dont on eût jamais oui parler."—*B. de St. Pierre, La Chaumière Indienne.* The preceding exquisite passage shows that the blunder which drew forth Macaulay's flaming wrath, in the quotation lower down, was not a new one.

1798.—"... the most learned of the **Pundits** or Bramin lawyers, were called up from different parts of Bengal."—*Raynal, Hist.* i. 42.

1856.—"Besides ... being a **Pundit** of learning, he (Sir David Brewster) is a bundle of talents of various kinds."—*Life and Letters of Sydney Dobell*, ii. 14.

1860.—"Mr. Vizetelly next makes me say that the principle of limitation is found 'amongst the **Pandects** of the Benares. ...' The Benares he probably supposes to be some Oriental nation. What he supposes their Pandects to be I shall not presume to guess. ... If Mr. Vizetelly had consulted the Unitarian Report, he would have seen that I spoke of the **Pundits** of Benares, and he might without any very long and costly research have learned where Benares is and what a Pundit is."—*Macaulay*, Preface to his *Speeches*.

1877.—"Colonel Y——. Since Nain Singh's absence from this country precludes my having the pleasure of handing to him in person, this, the Victoria or Patron's Medal, which has been awarded to him, ... I beg to place it in your charge for transmission to the **Pundit**."—*Address* by *Sir R. Alcock*, Prest. R. Geog. Soc., May 28.

"Colonel Y—— in reply, said: ... Though I do not know Nain Singh personally, I know his work. ... He is not a topographical automaton, or merely one of a great multitude of native employés with an average qualification. His observations have added a larger amount of important knowledge to the map of Asia than those of any other living man, and his journals form an exceedingly interesting book of travels. It will afford me great pleasure to take steps for the transmission of the Medal through an official channel to the **Pundit**."—*Reply to the President*, same date.

***PUNJAUB**, n.p. The name of the country between the Indus and the Sutlej. The modern Anglo-Indian province so-called, now extends on one side up beyond the Indus, including Peshāwar, the Derajāt, &c., and on the other side up to the Jumna, including Delhi. [In 1901 the Frontier Districts were placed under separate administration.] The name is Pers. *Panj-āb*, 'Five Rivers.' These rivers, as reckoned, sometimes include the Indus, in which case the five are (1) Indus, (2) Jelam or Behat, the ancient *Vitasta* which the Greeks made Ὑδάσπης (*Strabo*) and Βιδάσπης (*Ptol.*), (3) Chenāb, ancient *Chandrabāgha* and *Asiknī*. Ptolemy preserves a corruption of the former Sanskrit name in Σανδαβάλ, but it was rejected by the older Greeks because it was of ill omen, *i.e.* probably because Grecized it would be Ξανδροφάγος, 'the devourer of Alexander.' The alternative *Āsiknī* they rendered Ἀκεσίνης. (4) Rāvī, the ancient *Airāvatī*, Ὑάρωτης (*Strabo*), Ὑδραώτης (*Arrian*), Ἄδρις or Ῥούαδις (*Ptol.*). (5) Biās, ancient *Vipāsā*, Ὕφασις (Arrian), Βιβάσιος (*Ptol.*). This excluded the Sutlej, *Satadru*, *Hesydrus* of Pliny, Ζαράδρος or Ζαδάδρης (*Ptol.*), as Timur excludes it below. We may take in the Sutlej and exclude the Indus, but we can hardly exclude the Chenāb as Wassāf does below.

No corresponding term is used by the Greek geographers. "Putandum est nomen **Panchanadae** Graecos aut omnino latuisse, aut casu quodam non ad nostra usque tempora pervenisse, quod in tanta monumentorum ruina facile accidere potuit" (*Lassen, Pentapotamia*, 3). Lassen however has termed the country *Pentepotamia* in a learned Latin dissertation on its ancient geography. Though the actual word *Panjāb* is Persian, and dates from Mahommedan times, the corresponding Skt. *Panchanada* is ancient and genuine, occurring in the *Mahābhārata* and *Rāmāyaṇa*. The name *Panj-āb* in older Mahommedan writers is applied to the Indus river, after receiving the rivers of the country which we call *Punjaub*. In that sense *Panj-nad*, of equivalent meaning, is still occasionally used. [In S. India the term is sometimes applied to the country watered by the Tumbhadra, Wardha, Malprabha, Gatprabha and Kistna (*Wilks, Hist. Sketches*, Madras reprint, i. 405).]

We remember in the newspapers, after the second Sikh war, the report of a speech by a clergyman in England, who spoke of the deposition of "the bloody **Punjaub** of Lahore."

B.C. *x*.—"Having explored the land of the Pahlavi and the country adjoining, there had then to be searched **Panchanada** in every part; the monkeys then explore the region of Kashmīr with its woods of acacias."—*Rāmāyaṇa*, Bk. iv. ch. 43.

c. 940.—Maṣ'ūdī details (with no correctness) the five rivers that form the Mihrān or Indus. He proceeds: "When the **Five Rivers** which we have named have past the House of Gold which is Mūltān, they unite at a place three days distant from that city, between it and Mansūra at a place called Doshāb."—i. 377–8.

c. 1020.—"They all (Sind, Jhailam, Irāwa, Biah) combine with the Satlader (Sutlej) below Múltán, at a place called **Panjnad**, or 'the junction of the five rivers.' They form a very wide stream."—*Al-Birūnī*, in *Elliot*, i. 48.

c. 1300.—"After crossing the **Panj-āb**, or five rivers, namely Sind, Jelam, the river of Loháwar (*i.e.* of *Lahore*, viz. the Rāvī), Satlút, and Bīyah. ..."—*Wassāf*, in *Elliot*, iii. 36.

c. 1333.—"By the grace of God our caravan arrived safe and sound at **Banj-āb**, *i.e.* at the River of the Sind. *Banj* (*panj*) signifies 'five,' and *āb*, 'water;' so that the name signifies 'the Five Waters.' They flow into this great river, and water the country."—*Ibn Batuta*, iii. 91.

c. 1400.—"All these (united) rivers (Jelam, Chenáb, Rávi, Bíyáh, Sind) are called the Sind or **Panj-áb**, and this river falls into the Persian Gulf near Thatta."—*The Emp. Timur*, in *Elliot*, iii. 476.

[c. 1630.—"He also takes a Survey of **Pang-ob** ..."—*Sir T. Herbert*, ed. 1677, p. 63. He gives a list of the rivers in p. 70.]

1648.—"... **Pang-ab**, the chief city of which is Lahor, is an excellent and fruitful province, for it is watered by the five rivers of which we have formerly spoken."—*Van Twist*, 3.

"The River of the ancient Indus, is by the Persians and Magols called **Pang-ab**, *i.e.* the Five Waters."—*Ibid.* i.

1710.—"He found this ancient and famous city (Lahore) in the Province **Panschaap**, by the side of the broad and fish-abounding river Rari (for *Ravi*)."—*Valentijn*, iv. (*Suratte*), 282.

1790.—"Investigations of the religious ceremonies and customs of the Hindoos, written in the Carnatic, and in the **Punjab**, would in many cases widely differ."—*Forster*, Preface to *Journey*.

1793.—"The Province, of which Lahore is the capital, is oftener named **Panjab** than Lahore."—*Rennell's Memoir*, 3rd ed. 82.

1804.—"I rather think ... that he (Holkar) will go off to the **Punjaub**. And what gives me stronger reason to think so is, that on the seal of his letter to me he calls himself '*the Slave of Shah Mahmoud, the King of Kings*.' Shah Mahmoud is the brother of Zemaun Shah. He seized the musnud and government of Caubul, after having defeated Zemaun Shah two or three years ago, and put out his eyes."—*Wellington, Desp.* under March 17.

1815.—"He (Subagtageen) ... overran the fine province of the **Punjaub**, in his first expedition."—*Malcolm, Hist. of Persia*, i. 316.

PUNKAH, s. Hind. *pankhā*.

a. In its original sense a portable fan, generally made from the leaf of the **palmyra** (*Borassus flabelliformis*, or 'fan-shaped'), the natural type and origin of the fan. Such *pankhās* in India are not however formed, as Chinese fans are, like those of our ladies; they are generally, whether large or small, of a bean-shape, with a part of the dried leaf-stalk adhering, which forms the handle.

b. But the specific application in Anglo-Indian colloquial is to the large fixed and swinging fan, formed of cloth stretched on a rectangular frame, and suspended from the ceiling, which is used to agitate the air in hot weather. The date of the introduction of this machine into India is not known to us. The quotation from Linschoten shows that some such apparatus was known in the 16th century, though this comes out clearly in the French version alone; the original Dutch, and the old English translation are here unintelligible, and indicate that Linschoten (who apparently never was at Ormuz) was describing, from hearsay, something that he did not understand. More remarkable passages are those which we take from Dozy, and from El-Fakhrī, which show that the true Anglo-Indian *punka* was known to the Arabs as early as the 8th century.

a.—

1710.—"Aloft in a Gallery the King sits in his chaire of State, accompanied with his Children and chiefe Vizier ... no other without calling daring to goe vp to him, saue onely two **Punkaws** to gather wind."—*W. Finch*, in *Purchas*, i. 439. The word seems here to be used improperly for the men who plied the fans. We find also in the same writer a verb to **punkaw**:

"... behind one **punkawing**, another holding his sword."—*Ibid.* 433.

Terry does not use the word:

1616.—"... the people of better quality, lying or sitting on their Carpets or Pallats, have servants standing about them, who continually beat the air upon them with *Flabella's*, or Fans, of stiffned leather, which keepe off the flyes from annoying them, and cool them as they lye."—Ed. 1665, p. 405.

1663.—"On such occasions they desire nothing but ... to lie down in some cool and shady place all along, having a servant or two to fan one by turns, with their great **Pankas**, or Fans."—*Bernier*, E.T., p. 76; [ed. *Constable*, 241].

1787.—"Over her head was held a **punker**."—*Sir C. Malet*, in Parl. Papers, 1821, '*Hindoo Widows*.'

1809.—"He ... presented me ... two **punkahs**."—*Lord Valentia*, i. 428.

1881.—"The chair of state, the *sella gestatoria*, in which the Pope is borne aloft, is the ancient palanquin of the Roman nobles, and, of course, of the Roman Princes ... the fans which go behind are the **punkahs** of the Eastern Emperors, borrowed from the Court of **Persia**."—*Dean Stanley, Christian Institutions*, 207.

b.—

c. 1150-60.—"Sous le nom de *Khaich* on entend des étoffes de mauvais toile de lin qui servent à différents usages. Dans ce passage de Rhazès (c. A.D. 900) ce sont des ventilateurs faits de cet étoffe. Ceci se pratique de cette manière: on en prend un morceau de la grandeur d'un tapis, un peu plus grand ou un peu plus petit selon les dimensions de la chambre, et on le rembourre avec des objets qui ont de la consistance et qui ne plient pas facilement, par exemple avec du sparte. L'ayant ensuite suspendu au milieu de la chambre, on le fait tirer et lacher doucement et continuellement par un homme placé dans le haut de l'appartement. De cette manière il fait beaucoup de vent et rafraichit l'air. Quelquefois on le trempe dans de l'eau de rose, et alors il parfume l'air en même temps qu'il le rafraichit."—*Glossaire sur le Mançouri*, quoted in *Dozy et Engelmann*, p. 342. See also *Dozy, Suppt. aux Dictt. Arabes*, s.v. *Khaich*.

1166.—"He (Ibn Hamdun the Kātib) once recited to me the following piece of his composition, containing an enigmatical description of a linen fan: (1)

"'Fast and loose, it cannot touch what it tries to reach; though tied up it moves swiftly, and though a prisoner it is free. Fixed in its place it drives before it the gentle breeze; though its path lie closed up it moves on in its nocturnal journey.'"—Quoted by *Ibn Khallikan*, E.T. iii. 91.

"(1) The *linen fan* (*Mirwaha-t al Khaish*) is a large piece of linen, stretched on a frame, and suspended from the ceiling of the room. They make use of it in Irâk. See de Sacy's *Hariri*, p. 474."—Note by *MacGuckin de Slane*, *ibid.* p. 92.

c. 1300.—"One of the innovations of the Caliph Manṣūr (A.D. 753–774) was the *Khaish* of linen in summer, a thing which was not known before his time. But the Sāsānian Kings used in summer to have an apartment freshly plastered (with clay) every day, which they inhabited, and on the morrow another apartment was plastered for them."—*El-Fakhrī*, ed. *Ahlwardt*, p. 188.

1596.—"And (they use) instruments like swings with fans, to rock the people in, and to make wind for cooling, which they call *cattaventos*."—Literal Transln. from *Linschoten*, ch. 6.

1598.—"And they vse certaine instruments like Waggins, with bellowes, to beare all the people in, and to gather winde to coole themselves withall, which they call *Cattaventos*."—*Old English Translation*, by W. P., p. 16; [Hak. Soc. i. 52].

The French version is really a brief description of the punka:

1610.—"Ils ont aussi du Cattaventos qui sont certains instruments pendus en l'air es quels se faisant donner le bransle ils font du vent qui les rafraichit."—Ed. 1638, p. 17.

The next also perhaps refers to a suspended punka:

1662.—"... furnished also with good Cellars with great *Flaps* to stir the Air, for reposing in the fresh Air from 12 till 4 or 5 of the Clock, when the Air of these Cellars begins to be hot and stuffing."—*Bernier*, p. 79; [ed. *Constable*, 247].

1807.—"As one small concern succeeds another, the **punkah** vibrates gently over my eyes."—*Lord Minto in India*, 27.

1810.—"Were it not for the **punka** (a large frame of wood covered with cloth) which is suspended over every table, and kept swinging, in order to freshen the air, it would be scarcely possible to sit out the melancholy ceremony of an Indian dinner."—*Maria Graham*, 30.

Williamson mentions that **punkahs** "were suspended in most dining halls,"—*Vade Mecum*, i. 281.

1823.—"**Punkas**, large frames of light wood covered with white cotton, and looking not unlike enormous fire-boards, hung from the ceilings of the principal apartments."—*Heber*, ed. 1844, i. 28.

1852.—

"Holy stones with scrubs and slaps
(Our Christmas waits!) prelude the day;
For holly and festoons of bay
Swing feeble **punkas**,—or perhaps
A windsail dangles in collapse."

Christmas on board a P. and O., near the Equator.

1875.—"The **punkah** flapped to and fro lazily overhead."—*Chesney, The Dilemma*, ch. xxxviii.

Mr. Busteed observes: "It is curious that in none of the lists of servants and their duties which are scattered through the old records in the last century (18th), is there any mention of the **punka**, nor in any narratives referring to domestic life in India then, that have come under our notice, do we remember any allusion to its use. ... The swinging **punka**, as we see it to-day, was, as every one knows, an innovation of a later period. ... This dates from an early year in the present century."—*Echoes of Old Calcutta*, p. 115. He does not seem, however, to have found any positive evidence of the date of its introduction. ["Hanging punkahs are said by one authority to have originated in Calcutta by accident towards the close of the last (18th) century. It is reported that a clerk in a Government office suspended the leaf of a table, which was accidentally waved to and fro by a visitor. A breath of cool air followed the movement, and suggested the idea which was worked out and resulted in the present machine" (*Carey, Good Old Days of John Company*, i. 81). Mr. Douglas says that punkahs were little used by Europeans in Bombay till 1810. They were not in use at Nuncomar's trial in Calcutta (1775), *Bombay and W. India*, ii. 253.]

PURDAH, s. Hind. from Pers. *parda*, 'a curtain'; a *portière*; and especially a curtain screening women from the sight of men; whence a woman of position who observes such rules of seclusion is termed *pardanishīn*, 'one who sits behind a curtain.'

1809.—"On the fourth (side) a **purdah** was stretched across."—*Ld. Valentia*, i. 100.

1810.—"If the disorder be obstinate, the doctor is permitted to approach the **purdah** (*i.e.* curtain, or screen) and to put *the hand* through a small aperture ... in order to feel the patient's pulse."—*Williamson, V. M.* i. 130.

[1813.—"My travelling palankeen formed my bed, its **purdoe** or chintz covering my curtains."—*Forbes, Or. Mem.* 2nd ed. ii. 109.]

1878.—"Native ladies look upon the confinement behind the **purdah** as a badge of rank, and also as a sign of chastity, and are exceedingly proud of it."—*Life in the Mofussil*, i. 113.

[1900.—"Charitable aid is needed for the **purdah** women."—*Pioneer Mail*, Jan. 21.]

PURWANNA, PERWAUNA, s. Hind. from Pers. *parwāna*, 'an order; a grant or letter under royal seal; a letter of authority from an official to his subordinate; a license or pass.'

1682.—"... we being obliged at the end of two months to pay Custom for the said goods, if in that time we did not procure a **Pherwanna** for the *Duan* of Decca to excuse us from it."—*Hedges, Diary*, Oct. 10; [Hak. Soc. i. 34].

1693.—"... Egmore and Pursewaukum were lately granted us by the Nabob's **purwannas**."—*Wheeler*, i. 281.

1759.—"**Perwanna**, under the Coochuck (or the small seal) of the Nabob Vizier Ulma Maleck, Nizam ul Muluck Bahadour, to Mr. John Spenser."—In *Cambridge's Acct. of the War*, 230.

1774.—"As the peace has been so lately concluded, it would be a satisfaction to the Rajah to receive your **parwanna** to this purpose before the departure of the caravan."—*Bogle's Diary*, in *Markham's Tibet*, p. 50. But Mr. Markham changes the spelling of his originals.

PUTTÁN, PATHÁN, n.p. Hind. *Paṭhān*. A name commonly applied to Afghans, and especially to people in India of Afghan descent. The derivation is obscure. Elphinstone derives it from *Pushtūn* and *Pukhtūn*, pl. *Pukhtāna*, the name the Afghans give to their own race, with which Dr. Trumpp [and Dr. Bellew (*Races of Afghanistan*, 25) agree. This again has been connected with the *Pactyica* of Herodotus (iii. 102, iv. 44).] The Afghans have for the name one of the usual fantastic etymologies which is quoted below (see quotation,

c. 1611). The Mahommedans in India are sometimes divided into four classes, viz. *Paṭhāns; Mughals* (see **MOGUL**), *i.e.* those of Turki origin; *Shaikhs*, claiming Arab descent; and *Saiyyids*, claiming also to be descendants of Mahommed.

1553.—"This State belonged to a people called **Patane**, who were lords of that hill-country. And as those who dwell on the skirts of the Pyrenees, on this side and on that, are masters of the passes by which we cross from Spain to France, or vice versâ, so these **Patan** people are the masters of the two entrances to India, by which those who go thither from the landward must pass. ..."—*Barros*, IV. vi. 1.

1563.—"... This first King was a **Patane** of certain mountains that march with Bengala."—*Garcia, Coll.* f. 34.

1572.—

"Mas agora de nomes, et de usança,
Novos, et varios são os habitantes,
Os Delijs, os **Patãnes** que em possança
De terra, e gente são mais abundantes."
Camões, vii. 20.

[By Aubertin:

"But now inhabitants of other name
And customs new and various there are found,
The Delhis and **Patans**, who in the fame
Of land and people do the most abound."]

1610.—"A **Pattan**, a man of good stature."—*Hawkins*, in *Purchas*, i. 220.

c. 1611.—"... the mightiest of the Afghan people was Kais. ... The Prophet gave Kais the name of Abd Ulrasheed ... and ... predicted that God would make his issue so numerous that they, with respect to the establishment of the Faith, would outvie all other people; the angel Gabriel having revealed to him that their attachment to the Faith would, in strength, be like the wood upon which they lay the keel when constructing a ship, which wood the seamen call *Pathan*: on this account he conferred upon Abd Ulrasheed the title of **Pathan**[1] also."—*Hist. of the Afghans*, E.T., by *Dorn*, i. 38.

[1638.—"... Ozmanchan a **Puttanian** ..."—*Sir T. Herbert*, ed. 1677, p. 76.]

1648.—"In general the Moors are a haughty and arrogant and proud people, and among them the **Pattans** stand out superior to the others in dress and manners."—*Van Twist*, 58.

1666.—"Martin Affonso and the other Portuguese delivered them from the war that the **Patanes** were making on them."—*Faria y Sousa, Asia Portuguesa*, i. 343.

1673.—"They are distinguished, some according to the Consanguinity they claim with *Mahomet;* as a *Siad* is a kin to that Imposture. ... A *Shiek* is a Cousin too, at a distance, into which Relation they admit all new made Proselytes. *Meer* is somewhat allied also. ... The rest are adopted under the Name of the Province ... as *Mogul*, the Race of the *Tartars* ... **Patan**, *Duccan*."—*Fryer*, 93.

1681.—"En estas regiones ay vna cuyas gentes se dizen los **Patanes**."—*Martinez de la Puente, Compendio*, 21.

1726.—"... The *Patans* (**Patanders**) are very different in garb, and surpass in valour and stout-heartedness in war."—*Valentijn, Choro.* 109.

1757.—"The Colonel (Clive) complained bitterly of so many insults put upon him, and reminded the Soubahdar how different his own conduct was, when called upon to assist him against the **Pytans**."—*Ives*, 149.

1763.—"The northern nations of India, although idolaters ... were easily induced to embrace Mahomedanism, and are at this day the Affghans or **Pitans**."—*Orme*, i. 24, ed. 1803.

1789.—"Moormen are, for the most part, soldiers by profession, particularly in the cavalry, as are also ... **Pitans**."—*Munro, Narr.* 49.

1798.—"... Afghans, or as they are called in India, **Patans**."—*G. Forster, Travels*, ii. 47.

[**PUTTEE, PUTTY**, s. Hind. *paṭṭī*.

a. A piece or strip of cloth, bandage; especially used in the sense of a ligature round the lower part of the leg used in lieu of a gaiter, originally introduced from the Himālaya, and now commonly used by sportsmen and soldiers. A special kind of cloth appears in the old trade-lists under the name of **puteahs**.

1875.—"Any one who may be bound for a long march will put on leggings of a peculiar sort, a bandage about 6 inches wide and four yards long, wound round from the ankle up to just below the knee, and then fastened by an equally long string, attached to the upper end, which is lightly wound many times round the calf of the leg. This, which is called **patawa**, is a much cherished piece of dress."—*Drew, Jummoo*, 175.

1900.—"The **Puttee** leggings are excellent for peace and war, on foot or on horseback."—*Times*, Dec. 24.

b. In the N.W.P. "an original share in a joint or coparcenary village or estate comprising

1 We do not know what word is intended, unless it be a special use of Ar. *batan*, 'the interior or middle of a thing.' Dorn refers to a note, which does not exist in his book. Bellew gives the title conferred by the Prophet as "*Pīhtān* or *Pāthān*, a term which in the Syrian language signifies a rudder." Somebody else interprets it as 'a mast.'

many villages; it is sometimes defined as the smaller subdivision of a mahal or estate" (*Wilson*). Hence **Putteedaree**, *paṭṭi-dārī* used for a tenure of this kind.

1852.—"Their names were forthwith scratched off the collector's books, and those of their eldest sons were entered, who became forthwith, in village and cutcherry parlance, **lumberdars** of the shares of their fathers, or in other words, of **puttee** Shere Singh and **puttee** Baz Singh."—*Raikes, Notes on the N.W.P.* 94.

c. In S. India, soldiers' pay.

1810.—"... hence in ordinary acceptation, the pay itself was called **puttee**, a Canarese word which properly signifies a written statement of any kind."—*Wilks, Hist. Sketches*, Madras reprint, i. 415.]

PUTTYWALLA, s. Hind. *paṭṭāwālā*, *paṭṭī-wālā* (see PUTTEE), 'one with a belt.' This is the usual Bombay term for a messenger or orderly attached to an office, and bearing a belt and brass badge, called in Bengal **chuprassy** or **peon** (qq.v.), in Madras usually by the latter name.

1878.—"Here and there a belted Government servant, called a **Puttiwālā**, or **Paṭṭawālā**, because distinguished by a belt. ..."—*Monier Williams, Modern India*, 34.

PYE, s. A familiar designation among British soldiers and young officers for a **Pariah-dog** (q.v.); a contraction, no doubt, of the former word.

[1892.—"We English call him a **pariah**, but this word, belonging to a low, yet by no means degraded class of people in Madras, is never heard on native lips as applied to a dog, any more than our other word '**pie**.'"—*L. Kipling, Beast and Man*, 266.]

***PYJAMMAS**, s. Hind. *pāē-jāma* (see JAMMA), lit. 'leg-clothing.' A pair of loose drawers or trowsers, tied round the waist. Such a garment is used by various persons in India, *e.g.* by women of various classes, by Sikh men, and by most Mahommedans of both sexes. It was adopted from the Mahommedans by Europeans as an article of *dishabille* and of night attire, and is synonymous with **Long Drawers**, **Shulwáurs**, and **Mogul-breeches**. [For some distinctions between these various articles of dress see Forbes-Watson, (*Textile Manufactures*, 57).] It is probable that we English took the habit like a good many others from the Portuguese. Thus Pyrard (c. 1610) says, in speaking of Goa Hospital: "Ils ont force *calsons* sans quoy ne couchent iamais les Portugais des Indes" (ii. p. 11; [Hak. Soc. ii. 9]). The word is now used in London shops. A friend furnishes the following reminiscence: "The late Mr. B——, tailor in Jermyn Street, some 40 years ago, in reply to a question why **pyjammas** had feet sewn on to them (as was sometimes the case with those furnished by London outfitters) answered: 'I believe, Sir, it is because of the **White Ants**!'"

[1828.—

"His chief joy smoking a cigar
In loose **Paee-jams** and native slippers."

Orient. Sport. Mag., reprint 1873, i. 64.]

1881.—"The rest of our attire consisted of that particularly light and airy white flannel garment, known throughout India as a **pajama** suit."—*Haekel, Ceylon*, 329.

Q

QUI-HI, s. The popular distinctive nickname of the Bengal Anglo-Indian, from the usual manner of calling servants in that Presidency, viz. '*Koī hai?*' 'Is any one there?' The Anglo-Indian of Madras was known as a **Mull**, and he of Bombay as a **Duck** (qq.v.).

1816.—"The Grand Master, or Adventures of **Qui Hi** in Hindostan, a Hudibrastic Poem; with illustrations by Rowlandson."

1825.—"Most of the household servants are Parsees, the greater part of whom speak English. ... Instead of '**Koee hue**,' Who's there? the way of calling a servant is 'boy,' a corruption, I believe, of '*bhae*,' brother."—*Heber*, ed. 1844, ii. 98. [But see under BOY.]

c. 1830.—"J'ai vu dans vos gazettes de Calcutta les clameurs des **quoihaés** (sobriquet des Européens Bengalis de ce côté) sur la chaleur."—*Jacquemont, Corresp.* ii. 308.

R

RAINS, THE, s. The common Anglo-Indian colloquial for the Indian rainy season. The same idiom, *as chuvas*, had been already in use by the Portuguese. (See WINTER).

c. 1666.—"Lastly, I have imagined that if in *Delhi*, for example, the **Rains** come from the East, it may yet be that the Seas which are Southerly to it are the origin of them, but that they are forced by reason of some Mountains ... to turn aside and discharge themselves another way. ..."—*Bernier*, E.T., 138; [ed. *Constable*, 433].

1707.—"We are heartily sorry that the **Rains** have been so very unhealthy with you."—Letter in *Orme's Fragments*.

1750.—"The **Rains** ... setting in with great violence, overflowed the whole country."—*Orme, Hist.*, ed. 1803, i. 153.

1868.—"The place is pretty, and although it is '**the Rains**,' there is scarcely any day when we cannot get out."—*Bp. Milman*, in *Memoir*, p. 67.

RAJA, RAJAH, s. Skt. *rājā*, 'king.' The word is still used in this sense, but titles have a tendency to degenerate, and this one is applied to many humbler dignitaries, petty chiefs, or large Zemindars. It is also now a title of nobility conferred by the British Government, as it was by their Mahommedan predecessors, on Hindus, as Nawāb is upon Moslem. *Rāī, Rāo, Rānā, Rāwal, Rāya* (in S. India), are other forms which the word has taken in vernacular dialects or particular applications. The word spread with Hindu civilisation to the eastward, and survives in the titles of Indo-Chinese sovereigns, and in those of Malay and Javanese chiefs and princes.

It is curious that the term *Rājā* cannot be traced, so far as we know, in any of the Greek or Latin references to India, unless the very questionable instance of Pliny's *Rachias* be an exception. In early Mahommedan writers the now less usual, but still Indian, forms *Rāō* and *Rāī*, are those which we find. (Ibn Batuta, it will be seen, regards the words for king in India and in Spain as identical, in which he is fundamentally right.) Among the English vulgarisms of the 18th century again we sometimes find the word barbarised into *Roger*.

c. 1338.—"... Bahā-uddīn fled to one of the heathen Kings called the Rāī Kanbīlah. The word **Rāī** among those people, just as among the people of Rūm, signifies 'King.'"—*Ibn Batuta*, iii. 318. The traveller here refers, as appears by another passage, to the Spanish *Rey*.

1612.—"In all this part of the East there are 4 castes. ... The first caste is that of the **Rayas**, and this is a most noble race from which spring all the Kings of Canara. ..."—*Couto*, V. vi. 4.

[1615.—"According to your direction I have sent per Orincay Beege **Roger's** junk six peculles of lead."—*Foster, Letters*, iv. 107.

[1623.—"A **Ragia**, that is an Indian Prince."—*P. della Valle*, Hak. Soc. i. 84.]

1683.—"I went a hunting with ye **Ragea**, who was attended with 2 or 300 men, armed with bows and arrows, swords and targets."—*Hedges, Diary*, March 1; [Hak. Soc. i. 66].

1786.—Tippoo with gross impropriety addresses Louis XVI. as "the **Rajah** of the French."—*Select Letters*, 369.

***RAJPOOT**, s. Hind. *Rājpūt*, from Skt. *Rājaputra*, 'King's Son.' The name of a great race in India, the hereditary profession of which is that of arms. The name was probably only a honorific assumption; but no race in India has furnished so large a number of princely families. According to Chand, the great medieval bard of the Rājpūts, there were 36 clans of the race, issued from four *Kshatriyas* (Parihār, Pramār, Solankhī, and Chauhān) who sprang into existence from the sacred *Agnikuṇḍa* or Firepit on the summit of Mount Abū. Later bards give five eponyms from the firepit, and 99 clans. The Rājpūts thus claim to be true *Kshatriyas*, or representatives of the second of the four fundamental castes, the Warriors; but the Brahmans do not acknowledge the claim, and deny that the true Kshatriya is extant. Possibly the story of the fireborn ancestry hides a consciousness that the claim is factitious. "The Rajpoots," says Forbes, "use animal food and spirituous liquors, both unclean in the last degree to their puritanic neighbours, and are scrupulous in the observance of only two rules,—those which prohibit the slaughter of cows, and the remarriage of widows. The clans are not forbidden to eat together, or to intermarry, and cannot be said in these respects to form separate castes" (*Rās-mālā*, reprint 1878, p. 537).

An odd illustration of the fact that to partake of animal food, and especially of the heroic repast of the flesh of the wild boar killed in the chase (see Terry's representation of this below), is a Rājpūt characteristic, occurs to the memory of one of the present writers. In Lord Canning's time the young Rājpūt Rāja of Alwar had betaken himself to degrading courses, insomuch that the Viceroy felt constrained, in open **durbar** at Agra, to admonish him. A veteran political officer, who was present, inquired of the agent at the Alwar Court what had been the nature of the conduct thus rebuked. The reply was that the young prince had become the habitual associate of low and profligate Mahommedans, who had so influenced his conduct that among other indications, he *would not eat wild pig*. The old Political, hearing this, shook his head very gravely, saying, 'Would not eat *Wild Pig!* Dear! Dear! Dear!' It seemed the *ne plus ultra* of Rājpūt degradation! The older travellers give the name in the quaint form *Rashboot*, but this is not confined to Europeans, as the quotation from Sidi 'Ali shows; though the aspect in which the old English travellers regarded the tribe, as mainly a pack of banditti, might have made us think the name to be shaped by a certain sense of aptness. The Portuguese again frequently call them *Reys Butos*, a form in which the true etymology, at least partially, emerges.

1516.—"There are three qualities of these Gentiles, that is to say, some are called **Razbutes**, and they, in the time that their King was a Gentile, were Knights, the defenders of the Kingdom, and governors of the Country."—*Barbosa*, 50.

1533.—"Insomuch that whilst the battle went on, Saladim placed all his women in a large house, with all that he possessed, whilst below the house were combustibles for use in the fight; and Saladim ordered them to be set fire to, whilst he was in it. Thus the house suddenly blew up with great explosion and loud cries from the unhappy women; whereupon all the people from within and without rushed to the spot, but the **Resbutos** fought in such a way that they drove the Guzarat troops out of the gates, and others in their hasty flight cast themselves from the walls and perished."—*Correa*, iii. 527.

"And with the stipulation that the 200 *pardaos*, which are paid as allowance to the *lascarins* of the two small forts which stand between the lands of Baçaim and the **Reys buutos**, shall be paid out of the revenues of Baçaim as they have been paid hitherto."—*Treaty of Nuno da Cunha* with the *K. of Cambaya*, in *Subsidios*, 137.

c. 1554.—"But if the caravan is attacked, and the *Bāts* kill themselves, the **Rashbūts**, according to the law of the *Bāts*, are adjudged to have committed a crime worthy of death."—*Sidi 'Ali Kapudān*, in *J. As.*, Ser. I., tom. ix. 95.

[1602.—"**Rachebidas**."—*Couto*, Dec. viii. ch. 15.]

c. 1614.—"The next day they embarked, leaving in the city, what of those killed in fight and those killed by fire, more than 800 persons, the most of them being **Regibutos**, *Moors* of great valour; and of ours fell eighteen. ..."—*Bocarro, Decada*, 210.

[1614.—"... in great danger of thieves called **Rashbouts**. ..."—*Foster, Letters*, ii. 260.]

1616.—"... it were fitter he were in the Company of his brother ... and his safetie more regarded, then in the hands of a **Rashboote** Gentile. ..."—*Sir T. Roe*, i. 553–4; [Hak. Soc. ii. 282].

"The **Rashbootes** eate Swines-flesh most hateful to the Mahometans."—*Terry*, in *Purchas*, ii. 1479.

1638.—"These **Rasboutes** are a sort of Highway men, or Tories."—*Mandelslo*, Eng. by *Davies*, 1669, p. 19.

1648.—"These **Resbouts** (Resbouten) are held for the best soldiers of Gusuratta."—*Van Twist*, 39.

[c. 1660.—"The word **Ragipous** signifies *Sons of Rajas*."—*Bernier*, ed. *Constable*, 39.]

1673.—"Next in esteem were the *Rashwaws*, **Rashpoots**, or Souldiers."—*Fryer*, 27.

1689.—"The place where they went ashore was at a Town of the *Moors*, which name our Seamen give to all the Subjects of the Great Mogul, but especially his Mahometan Subjects; calling the Idolaters *Gentous* or **Rashbouts**."—*Dampier*, i. 507.

1791.—"... Quatre cipayes ou **reispoutes** montés sur des chevaux persans, pour l'escorter."—*B. de St. Pierre*; *Chaumière Indienne*.

RAMASAMMY, s. This corruption of *Rāmaswāmi* ('Lord Rāma'), a common Hindū proper name in the South, is there used colloquially in two ways:

(**a**). As a generic name for Hindūs, like 'Tommy Atkins' for a British soldier. Especially applied to Indian coolies in Ceylon, &c.

(**b**). For a twisted roving of cotton in a tube (often of wrought silver) used to furnish light for a cigar (see FULEETA). Madras use:

a.—

[1843.—"I have seen him almost swallow it, by Jove, like **Ramo Samee**, the Indian juggler."—*Thackeray*, *Book of Snobs*, ch. i.]

1880.—"... if you want a clerk to do your work or a servant to attend on you, ... you would take on a saponaceous Bengali Baboo, or a servile abject Madrasi **Ramasammy**. ... A Madrasi, even if wrongly abused, would simply call you his father, and his mother, and his aunt, defender of the poor, and epitome of wisdom, and would take his change out of you in the bazaar accounts."—*Cornhill Mag.*, Nov., pp. 582–3.

RAMDAM, s. Hind. from Ar. *ramaẓān* (*ramaḍhān*). The ninth Mahommedan lunar month, viz. the month of the Fast.

1615.—"... at this time, being the preparation

to the **Ramdam** or Lent."—*Sir T. Roe,* in *Purchas,* i. 537; [Hak. Soc. i. 21; also 58, 72, ii. 274].

1623.—"The 29th June: I think that (to-day?) the Moors have commenced their **ramadhan**, according to the rule by which I calculate."—*P. della Valle,* ii. 607; [Hak. Soc. i. 179].

1686.—"They are not ... very curious or strict in observing any Days or Times of particular Devotions, except it be **Ramdam** time as we call it. ... In this time they fast all Day. ..."—*Dampier,* i. 343.

***RAMOOSY,** n.p. The name of a very distinct caste in W. India, Mahr. *Rāmosī,* [said to be from Mahr. *ranavāsī,* 'jungle-dweller']; originally one of the thieving castes. Hence they came to be employed as hereditary watchmen in villages, paid by cash or by rent-free lands, and by various petty dues. They were supposed to be responsible for thefts till the criminals were caught; and were often themselves concerned. They appear to be still commonly employed as hired **chokidars** by Anglo-Indian households in the west. They come chiefly from the country between Poona and Kolhapūr. The surviving traces of a Ramoosy dialect contain Telegu words, and have been used in more recent days as a secret slang. [See an early account of the tribe in: "An Account of the Origin and Present condition of the tribe of **Ramoosies**, including the Life of the Chief Oomíah Naik, by *Capt. Alexander Mackintosh* of the Twenty-seventh Regiment, Madras Army," Bombay 1833.]

[1817.—"His Highness must long have been aware of **Ramoosees** near the Mahadeo pagoda."—*Elphinstone's Letter* to *Peshwa,* in *Papers relating to E.I. Affairs,* 23.]

1833.—"There are instances of the **Ramoosy** Naiks, who are of a bold and daring spirit, having a great ascendancy over the village **Patells** and *Koolkurnies,* but which the latter do not like to acknowledge openly ... and it sometimes happens that the village officers participate in the profits which the **Ramoosies** derive from committing such irregularities."—*Macintosh, Acc. of the Tribe of Ramoossies,* p. 19.

1883.—"Till a late hour in the morning he (the chameleon) sleeps sounder than a **ramoosey** or a chowkeydar; nothing will wake him."—*Tribes on My Frontier.*

RAM-RAM! The commonest salutation between two Hindus meeting on the road; an invocation of the divinity.

[1652.—"... then they approach the idol waving them (their hands) and repeating many times (the words) **Ram, Ram,** *i.e.* God, God."—*Tavernier,* ed. *Ball,* i. 263.]

1673.—"Those whose Zeal transports them no further than to die at home, are immediately Washed by the next of Kin, and bound up in a Sheet; and as many as go with him carry them by turns on a Colt-staff; and the rest run almost naked and shaved, crying after him **Ram, Ram.**"—*Fryer,* 101.

1726.—"The wives of Bramines (when about to burn) first give away their jewels and ornaments, or perhaps a pinang, which is under such circumstances a great present, to this or that one of their male or female friends who stand by, and after taking leave of them, go and lie over the corpse, calling out only **Ram, Ram.**"—*Valentijn,* v. 51.

[1828.—See under SUTTEE.]

c. 1885.—Sir G. Birdwood writes: "In 1869–70 I saw a green parrot in the Crystal Palace aviary very doleful, dull, and miserable to behold. I called it 'pretty poll,' and coaxed it in every way, but no notice of me would it take. Then I bethought me of its being a Mahratta *poput,* and hailed it **Ram Ram**! and spoke in Mahratti to it; when at once it roused up out of its lethargy, and hopped and swung about, and answered me back, and cuddled up close to me against the bars, and laid its head against my knuckles. And every day thereafter, when I visited it, it was always in an eager flurry to salute me as I drew near to it."

RANEE, s. A Hindu queen; *rānī,* fem. of *rājā,* from Skt. *rājnī* (= *regina*).

1673.—"*Bedmure* (Bednūr) ... is the Capital City, the Residence of the **Ranna,** the Relict of *Sham Shunker Naig.*"—*Fryer,* 162.

1809.—"The young **Rannie** may marry whomsoever she pleases."—*Lord Valentia,* i. 364.

1879.—"There were once a Raja and a **Ráné** who had an only daughter."—*Miss Stokes, Indian Fairy Tales,* 1.

RANGOON, n.p. Burm. *Ran-gun,* said to mean 'War-end'; the chief town and port of Pegu. The great Pagoda in its immediate neighbourhood had long been famous under the name of Dagon, but there was no town in modern times till Rangoon was founded by Alompra during his conquest of Pegu, in 1755. The name probably had some kind of intentional assonance to *Da-gun,* whilst it "proclaimed his forecast of the immediate destruction of his enemies." Occupied by the British forces in May 1824, and again, taken by storm, in 1852, Rangoon has since the latter date been the capital, first of the British province of Pegu, and latterly of British Burma. It is now a flourishing port with a population of 134,176 (1881); [in 1891, 180,324].

RASEED, s. Hind. *rasīd*. A native corruption of the English 'receipt,' shaped, probably, by the Pers. *rasīda*, 'arrived'; viz. an acknowledgment that a thing has 'come to hand.'

1877.—"There is no Sindi, however wild, that cannot now understand '**Rasíd**' (receipt), and '*Apíl*' (appeal)."—*Burton, Sind Revisited*, i. 282.

RATTAN, s. The long stem of various species of Asiatic climbing palms, belonging to the genus *Calamus* and its allies, of which canes are made (not 'bamboo-canes,' improperly so called), and which, when split, are used to form the seats of cane-bottomed chairs and the like. From Malay *rotan*, [which Crawfurd derives from *rawat*, 'to pare or trim'], applied to various species of *Calamus* and *Daemonorops* (see *Filet*, No. 696 *et seq.*). Some of these attain a length of several hundred feet, and are used in the Himālaya and the Kāsia Hills for making suspension bridges, &c., rivalling rope in strength.

1511.—"The Governor set out from Malaca in the beginning of December, of this year, and sailed along the coast of Pedir. ... He met with such a contrary gale that he was obliged to anchor, which he did with a great anchor, and a cable of **rótas**, which are slender but tough canes, which they twist and make into strong cables."—*Correa, Lendas*, ii. 269.

1563.—"They took thick ropes of **rotas** (which are made of certain twigs which are very flexible) and cast them round the feet, and others round the tusks."—*Garcia*, f. 90.

1598.—"There is another sorte of the same reedes which they call **Rota**: these are thinne like twigges of Willow for baskets. ..."—*Linschoten*, 28; [Hak. Soc. i. 97].

c. 1610.—"Il y a vne autre sorte de canne qui ne vient iamais plus grosse que le petit doigt ... et il ploye comme osier. Ils l'appellent **Rotan**. Ils en font des cables de nauire, et quantité de sortes de paniers gentiment entre lassez."—*Pyrard de Laval*, i. 237; [Hak. Soc. i. 331, and see i. 207].

1673.—"... The Materials Wood and Plaister, beautified without with folding windows, made of Wood and latticed with **Rattans**. ..."—*Fryer*, 27.

1844.—"In the deep vallies of the south the vegetation is most abundant and various. Amongst the most conspicuous species are ... the **rattan** winding from trunk to trunk and shooting his pointed head above all his neighbours."—*Notes on the Kasia Hills and People*, in *J.A.S.B.* vol. xiii. pt. ii. 615.

REGULATION, s. A law passed by the Governor-General in Council, or by a Governor (of Madras or Bombay) in Council. This term became obsolete in 1833, when legislative authority was conferred by the Charter Act (3 & 4 Will. IV. cap. 85) on those authorities; and thenceforward the term used is *Act*. By 13 Geo. III. cap. 63, § xxxv., it is enacted that it shall be lawful for the G.-G. and Council of Fort William in Bengal to issue Rules or Decrees and Regulations for the good order and civil government of the Company's settlements, &c. This was the same Charter Act that established the Supreme Court. But the authorised compilation of "*Regulations of the Govt. of Fort William in force at the end of* 1853," begins only with the Regulations of 1793, and makes no allusion to the earlier Regulations. No more does Regulation XLI. of 1793, which prescribes the form, numbering, and codifying of the Regulations to be issued. The fact seems to be that prior to 1793, when the enactment of Regulations was systematized, and the Regulations began to be regularly numbered, those that were issued partook rather of the character of resolutions of Government and circular orders than of Laws.

1868.—"The new Commissioner ... could discover nothing prejudicial to me, except, perhaps, that the **Regulations** were not sufficiently observed. The sacred **Regulations!** How was it possible to fit them on such very irregular subjects as I had to deal with?"—*Lt.-Col. Lewin, A Fly on the Wheel*, p. 376.

1880.—"The laws promulgated under this system were called **Regulations**, owing to a lawyer's doubts as to the competence of the Indian authorities to infringe on the legislative powers of the English Parliament, or to modify the 'laws and customs' by which it had been decreed that the various nationalities of India were to be governed."—*Saty. Review*, March 13, p. 335.

RESIDENT, s. This term has been used in

two ways which require distinction. Thus (**a**) up to the organization of the Civil Service in Warren Hastings's time, the chiefs of the Company's commercial establishments in the provinces, and for a short time the European chiefs of districts, were termed *Residents*. But later the word was applied (**b**) also to the representative of the Governor-General at an important native Court, *e.g.* at Lucknow, Delhi, Hyderabad, and Baroda. And this is the only meaning that the term now has in British India. In Dutch India the term is applied to the chief European officer of a province (corresponding to an Indian **Zillah**) as well as to the Dutch representative at a native Court, as at Solo and Djokjocarta.

a.—

1748.—"We received a letter from Mr. Henry Kelsall, **Resident** at Ballasore."—*Ft. William. Consn.*, in *Long*, 3.

1760.—"*Agreed,* Mr. Howitt the present **Resident** in Rajah Tillack Chund's country (*i.e.* Burdwan) for the collection of the tuncahs, be wrote to. ..."—*Ibid.* March 29, *Ibid.* 244.

c. 1778.—"My pay as **Resident** (at Sylhet) did not exceed 500*l.* per annum, so that fortune could only be acquired by my own industry."—*Hon. R. Lindsay*, in *Lives of the L.'s*, iii. 174.

b.—

1798.—"Having received overtures of a very friendly nature from the Rajah of Berar, who has requested the presence of a British **Resident** at his Court, I have despatched an ambassador to Nagpore with full powers to ascertain the precise nature of the Rajah's views."—*Marquis Wellesley, Despatches*, i. 99.

RESSALDAR, Ar.—P.—H. *Risāladār* (Ressala). Originally in Upper India the commander of a corps of Hindustani horse, though the second quotation shows it, in the south, applied to officers of infantry. Now applied to the native officer who commands a ressala in one of our regiments of "Irregular Horse." This title is applied honorifically to overseers of post-horses or stables. (See *Panjab Notes & Queries*, ii. 84.)

[c. 1590.—"Besides, there are several copyists who write a good hand and a lucid style. They receive the *yáddásht* (memorandum) when completed, keep it with themselves, and make a proper abridgement of it. After signing it, they return this instead of the *yaddásht*, when the abridgement is signed and sealed by the Wāqi'ahnawīs, and the **Risalahdar** (in orig. *risālah*). ..."—*Āīn*, i. 259.]

1773.—"The Nawaub now gave orders to the **Risaladárs** of the regular and irregular infantry, to encircle the fort, and then commence the attack with their artillery and musketry."—*H. of Hydur Naik*, 327.

1803.—"The **rissaldars** finding so much money in their hands, began to quarrel about the division of it, while Perron crossed in the evening with the bodyguard."—*Mil. Mem. of James Skinner*, i. 274.

c. 1831.—"Le lieutenant de ma troupe a bonne chance d'être fait Capitaine (**ressel-dar**)."—*Jacquemont, Corresp.* ii. 8.

RHINOCEROS, s. We introduce this word for the sake of the quotations, showing that even in the 16th century this animal was familiar not only in the Western Himālaya, but in the forests near Peshāwar. It is probable that the nearest rhinoceros to be found at the present time would be not less than 800 miles, as the crow flies, from Peshāwar.

c. 1387.—"In the month of Zi-l Ka'da of the same year he (Prince Muhammed Khan) went to the mountains of Sirmor (W. of the Jumna) and spent two months in hunting the **rhinoceros** and the elk."—*Táríkh-i-Mubárak-Sháhí*, in *Elliot*, iv. 16.

1398.—(On the frontier of Kashmīr). "Comme il y avoit dans ces Pays un lieu qui par sa vaste étendue, et la grande quantité de gibiers, sembloit inviter les passans à chasser. ... Timur s'en donna le divertissement ... ils prisent une infinité de gibiers, et l'on tua plusiers **rhinoceros** à coups de sabre et de lances, quoique cet animal ... a la peau si ferme, qu'on ne peut la percer que par des efforts extraordinaires."—*Petis de la Croix, H. de Timur-Bec*, iii. 159.

1519.—"After sending on the army towards the river (Indus), I myself set off for Sawâti, which they likewise call Karak-Khaneh (*kark-khāna*, 'the rhinoceros-haunt'), to hunt the **rhinoceros**. We started many **rhinoceroses**, but as the country abounds in brushwood, we could not get at them. A she rhinoceros, that had whelps, came out, and fled along the plain; many arrows were shot at her, but ... she gained cover. We set fire to the brushwood, but the rhinoceros was not to be found. We got sight of another, that, having been scorched in the fire, was lamed and unable to run. We killed it, and every one cut off a bit as a trophy of the chase."—*Baber*, 253.

1554.—"Nous vinmes à la ville de *Pourschewer* (**Peshawur**), et ayant heureusement passe le *Koutel* (**Kotul**), nous gagnâmes la ville de Djouschayeh. Sur le *Koutel* nous apercûmes des **rhinoceros**, dont la grosseur approchait celle d'un elephant. ..."—*Sidi 'Ali*, in *J. As.*, 1st ser. tom. ix. 201–202.

RICE, s. The well-known cereal, *Oryza sativa*, L. There is a strong temptation to derive the Greek *ὀρύζα*, which is the source of our word through It. *riso*, Fr. *riz*, etc., from the Tamil *ariśi*, 'rice deprived of husk,' ascribed to a root *ari*, 'to separate.' It is quite possible that Southern India was the original seat of rice cultivation. Roxburgh (*Flora Indica*, ii. 200) says that a wild rice, known as *Newaree* [Skt. *nīvāra*, Tel. *nivvāri*] by the Telinga people, grows abundantly about the lakes in the Northern Circars, and he considers this to be the original plant.

It is possible that the Arabic *al-ruzz* (*arruzz*) from which the Spaniards directly take their word *arroz*, may have been taken also directly from the Dravidian term. But it is hardly possible that *ὀρύζα* can have had that origin. The knowledge of rice apparently came to Greece from the expedition of Alexander, and the mention of *ὀρύζα* by Theophrastus, which appears to be the oldest, probably dates almost from the lifetime of Alexander (d. B.C. 323). Aristobulus, whose accurate account is quoted by Strabo (see below), was a companion of Alexander's expedition, but seems to have written later than Theophrastus. The term was probably acquired on the Oxus, or in the Punjab. And though no Skt. word for rice is nearer *ὀρύζα* than *vrīhi*, the very common exchange of aspirant and sibilant might easily give a form like *vrīsi* or *brīsi* (comp. *hindū*, *sindū*, &c.) in the dialects west of India. Though no such exact form seems to have been produced from old Persian, we have further indications of it in the Pushtu, which Raverty writes, sing. 'a grain of rice' *w'rijza'h*, pl. 'rice' *w'rijzey*, the former close to *oryza*. The same writer gives in *Barakai* (one of the uncultivated languages of the Kabul country, spoken by a 'Tajik' tribe settled in Logar, south of Kabul, and also at Kanigoram in the Waziri country) the word for rice as *w'rizza*, a very close approximation again to *oryza*. The same word is indeed given by Leech, in an earlier vocabulary, largely coincident with the former, as *rizza*. The modern Persian word for husked rice is *birinj*, and the Armenian *brinz*. A nasal form, deviating further from the hypothetical *brīsi* or *vrīsi*, but still probably the same in origin, is found among other languages of the Hindū Kūsh tribes, *e.g.* Burishki (Khajuna of Leitner) *bron*; Shina (of Gilgit), *briūn*; Khowar of the Chitral Valley (Arniyah of Leitner), *grinj* (*Biddulph, Tribes of Hindoo Koosh*, App., pp. xxxiv., lix., cxxxix.).

1298.—"Il hi a forment et **ris** asez, mès il ne menuient pain de forment por ce que il est en cele provence enferme, mès menuient **ris** et font poison (*i.e.* drink) de **ris** con especes qe molt e(s)t biaus et cler et fait le home evre ausi con fait le vin."—*Marc Pol.* Geo. Text, 132.

B.C. c. 320–300.—"*Μᾶλλον δὲ σπείρουσι τὸ καλούμενον ὄρυζον, ἐξ οὗ το ἕψημα· τοῦτο δὲ ὅμοιον τῇ ζειᾷ, καὶ περιπτισθὲν οἷον χόνδρος, ευπεπτον δὲ τὴν ὄψιν πεφυκὸς ὅμοιον ταῖς αἴραις, καὶ τὸν πολύν χρόνον ἐν ὕδατι. Ἀποχεῖται δὲ οὒκ εἰς στάχυν, ἀλλ' οἷον φόβην ὥσπερ ὁ κέγχρος καὶ ὁ ἔλυμος.*"—*Theophrast. de Hist. Plantt.*, iv. c. 4.

B.C. c. 20.—"The rice (*ὄρυζα*), according to Aristobulus, stands in water, in an enclosure. It is sowed in beds. The plant is 4 cubits in height, with many ears, and yields a large produce. The harvest is about the time of the setting of the Pleiades, and the grain is beaten out like barley.

"It grows in Bactriana, Babylonia, Susis, and in the Lower Syria."—*Strabo*, xv. i. § 18, in Bohn's E.T. iii. 83.

B.C. 300.—"Megasthenes writes in the second Book of his *Indica*. The Indians, says he, at their banquets have a table placed before each person. This table is made like a buffet, and they set upon it a golden bowl, into which they first help boiled rice (*ὄρυζαν*), as it might be boiled groats, and then a variety of cates dressed in Indian fashions."—*Athenaeus*, iv. § 39.

A.D. c 70.—"Hordeum Indis sativum et silvestre, ex quo panis apud eos praecipuus et alica. Maxime quidem **oryza** gaudent, ex qua tisanam conficiunt quam reliqui mortales ex hordeo. ..."—*Pliny*, xviii. 13. Ph. Holland has here got so wrong a reading that we abandon him.

A.D. c. 80–90.—"Very productive is this country (*Syrastrēnē* or Penins. Guzerat) in wheat and rice (*ὀρύζης*) and sessamin oil and butter[1] (see GHEE) and cotton, and the abounding Indian piece-goods made from it."—*Periplus*, § 41.

ROC, s. The *Rukh* or fabulous colossal bird of Arabian legend. This has been treated of at length by one of the present writers in *Marco Polo* (Bk. iii. ch. 33, notes); and here we shall only mention one or two supplementary facts.

M. Marre states that *rūḳ-rūḳ* is applied by

1 Müller and (very positively) Fabricius discard *Βουτύρου* for *Βοσμόρου*, which "no fellow understands." A. Hamilton (i. 136) mentions "Wheat, Pulse, and *Butter*" as exports from *Mangaroul* on this coast. He does *not* mention *Bosmoron!*

the Malays to a bird of prey of the vulture family, a circumstance which *possibly* may indicate the source of the Arabic name, as we know it to be of some at least of the legends. [See Skeat, *Malay Magic*, 124.]

In one of the notes just referred to it is suggested that the roc's quills, spoken of by Marco Polo in the passage quoted below (a passage which evidently refers to some real object brought to China), might possibly have been some vegetable production such as the great frond of the *Ravenala* of Madagascar (*Urania speciosa*), cooked to pass as a bird's quill. Mr. Sibree, in his excellent book on Madagascar (*The Great African Island*, 1880), noticed this, but pointed out that the object was more probably the immensely long midrib of the *rofia* palm (*Sagus Raphia*). Sir John Kirk, when in England in 1882, expressed entire confidence in this identification, and on his return to Zanzibar in 1883 sent four of these midribs to England. These must have been originally from 36 to 40 feet in length. The leaflets were all stript, but when entire the object must have strongly resembled a Brobdingnagian feather. These roc's quills were shown at the Forestry Exhibition in Edinburgh, 1884. Sir John Kirk wrote:

"I send to-day per S.S. Arcot ... four fronds of the Raphia palm, called here *Moale*. They are just as sold and shipped up and down the coast. No doubt they were sent in Marco Polo's time in exactly the same state—*i.e.* stripped of their leaflets and with the tip broken off. They are used for making stages and ladders, and last long if kept dry. They are also made into doors, by being cut into lengths, and pinned through."

Some other object has recently been shown at Zanzibar as part of the wings of a great bird. Sir John Kirk writes that this (which he does not describe particularly) was in the possession of the R. C. priests at Bagamoyo, to whom it had been given by natives of the interior, and these declared that they had brought it from Tanganyika, and that it was part of the wing of a gigantic bird. On another occasion they repeated this statement, alleging that this bird was known in the Udoe (?) country, near the coast. The priests were able to communicate directly with their informants, and certainly believed the story. Dr. Hildebrand also, a competent German naturalist, believed in it. But Sir John Kirk himself says that 'what the priests had to show was most undoubtedly the whalebone of a comparatively small whale' (see letter of the present writer in *Athenaeum*, March 22nd, 1884).

(c. 1000?).—"El Haçan fils d'Amr et d'autres, d'après ce qu'ils tenaient de maint-personnages de l'Inde, m'ont rapporté des choses bien extraordinaires, au sujet des oiseaux du pays de Zabedj, de Khmêr (*Kumār*) du Senf et autres regions des parages de l'Inde. Ce que j'ai vu de plus grand, en fait de plumes d'oiseaux, c'est un tuyau que me montra Abou' l-Abbas de Siraf. Il était long de deux aunes environs capable, semblait-il, de contenir une outre d'eau.

"'J'ai vu dans l'Inde, me dit le capitaine Ismaïlawéih, chez un des principaux marschands, un tuyau de plume qui était près de sa maison, et dans lequel on versait de l'eau comme dans une grande tonne. ... Ne sois pas étonné, me dit-il, car un capitaine du pays des Zindjs m'a conté qu'il avait vu chez le roi de Sira un tuyan de plume qui contenait vingt-cinq outres d'eau.'"—*Livre des Mervailles d'Inde.* (*Par Van der Lith* et *Marcel Devic*, pp. 62–63.)

***ROGUE** (Elephant), s. An elephant (generally, if not always a male) living in apparent isolation from any herd, usually a bold marauder, and a danger to travellers. Such an elephant is called in Bengal, according to Williamson, *saun*, *i.e. sān* [Hind. *sānd*, Skt. *shaṇḍa*]; sometimes it would seem *gunḍā* [Hind. *gunḍā*, 'a rascal']; and by the Sinhalese *hora*. The term *rogue* is used by Europeans in Ceylon, and its origin is somewhat obscure. Sir Emerson Tennent finds such an elephant called, in a curious book of the 18th century, *ronkedor* or *runkedor*, of which he supposes that *rogue* may perhaps have been a modification. That word looks like Port. *roncador*, 'a snorer, a noisy fellow, a bully,' which gives a plausible sense. But Littré gives *rogue* as a colloquial French word conveying the idea of arrogance and rudeness. In the following passage which we have copied, unfortunately without recording the source, the word comes still nearer the sense in which it is applied to the elephant: "On commence à s'apperceuoir dés Bayonne, que l'humeur de ces peuples tient vn peu de celle de ses voisins, et qu'ils sont *rogues* et peu communicatifs avec l'Estranger." After all however it is most likely that the word is derived from an English use of the word. For Skeat shows that *rogue*, from the French sense of 'malapert, saucy, rude, surly,' came to be applied as a cant term to beggars, and is used, in some old English passages which he quotes, exactly in the sense of our modern 'tramp.' The transfer to a vagabond elephant would be easy. Mr. Skeat refers to Shakespeare:—

"And wast thou fain, poor father,
To hovel thee with swine, and **rogues**
forlorn?"
K. Lear, iv. 7.

1878.—"Much misconception exists on the subject of **rogue** or solitary elephants. The usually accepted belief that these elephants are turned out of the herds by their companions or rivals is not correct. Most of the so-called solitary elephants are the lords of some herds near. They leave their companions at times to roam by themselves, usually to visit cultivation or open country ... sometimes again they make the expedition merely for the sake of solitude. They, however, keep more or less to the jungle where their herd is, and follow its movements."—*Sanderson*, p. 52.

ROHILLA, n.p. A name by which Afghāns, or more particularly Afghāns settled in Hindustan, are sometimes known, and which gave a title to the province *Rohilkaṇd*, and now, through that, to a Division of the N.W. Provinces embracing a large part of the old province. The word appears to be Pushtu, *rōhēlah* or *rōhēlai*, adj., formed from *rōhu*, 'mountain,' thus signifying 'mountaineer of Afghānistān.' But a large part of E. Afghānistān specifically bore the name of *Roh*. Keene (*Fall of the Moghul Monarchy*, 41) puts the rise of the Rohillas of India in 1744, when 'Ali Mahommed revolted, and made the territory since called Rohilkhand independent. A very comprehensive application is given to the term *Roh* in the quotation from Firishta. A friend (Major J. M. Trotter) notes here: "The word **Rohilla** is little, if at all, used now in Pushtu, but I remember a line of an ode in that language, '*Sádik* **Rohilai** *yam pa Hindubár gad*,' meaning, 'I am a simple mountaineer, compelled to live in Hindustan'; *i.e.* 'an honest man among knaves.'"

c. 1452.—"The King ... issued *farmáns* to the chiefs of the various Afghán Tribes. On receipt of the *farmáns*, the Afgháns of **Roh** came as is their wont, like ants and locusts, to enter the King's service. ... The King (Bahlol Lodi) commanded his nobles, saying,—'Every Afghán who comes to Hind from the country of **Roh** to enter my service, bring him to me. I will give him a *jágír* more than proportional to his deserts.'"—*Táríkh-i-Shír-Sháhí*, in *Elliot*, iv. 307.

c. 1542.—"Actuated by the pride of power, he took no account of clanship, which is much considered among the Afghans, and especially among the **Rohilla** men."—*Ibid.* 428.

c. 1612.—"**Roh** is the name of a particular mountain [-country], which extends in length from Swád and Bajaur to the town of Siwí belonging to Bhakar. In breadth it stretches from Hasan Abdál to Kábul. Kandahár is situated in this territory."—*Firishta's Introduction*, in *Elliot*, vi. 568.

1726.—"... 1000 other horsemen called **Ruhelahs**."—*Valentijn*, iv. (*Suratte*), 277.

1745.—"This year the Emperor, at the request of Suffder Jung, marched to reduce Ali Mahummud Khan, a **Rohilla** adventurer, who had, from the negligence of the Government, possessed himself of the district of Kutteer (*Kathehar*), and assumed independence of the royal authority."—In Vol. II. of *Scott's* E.T. of *Hist. of the Dekkan*, &c., p. 218.

1763.—"After all the **Rohilas** are but the best of a race of men, in whose blood it would be difficult to find one or two single individuals endowed with good nature and with sentiments of equity; in a word they are **Afghans**."—*Seir Mutaqherin*, iii. 240.

1786.—"That the said Warren Hastings ... did in September, 1773, enter into a private engagement with the said Nabob of Oude ... to furnish them, for a stipulated sum of money to be paid to the E. I. Company, with a body of troops for the declared purpose of 'thoroughly extirpating the nation of the **Rohillas**'; a nation from whom the Company had never received, or pretended to receive, or apprehend, any injury whatever."—*Art. of Charge against Hastings*, in *Burke*, vi. 568.

ROOK, s. In chess the *rook* comes to us from Span. *roque*, and that from Ar. and Pers. *rukh*, which is properly the name of the famous gryphon, the **roc** of Marco Polo and the *Arabian Nights*. According to Marcel Devic it meant 'warrior.' It is however generally believed that this form was a mistake in transferring the Indian *rath* (see RUT) or 'chariot,' the name of the piece in India.

ROOMAUL, s. Hind. from Pers. *rūmāl* (lit. 'face-rubber,') a towel, a handkerchief. ["In modern native use it may be carried in the hand by a high-born *parda* lady attached to her *batwa* or tiny silk handbag, and ornamented with all sorts of gold and silver trinkets; then it is a handkerchief in the true sense of the word. It may be carried by men, hanging on the left shoulder, and used to wipe the hands or face; then, too, it is a handkerchief. It may be as big as a towel, and thrown over both shoulders by men, the ends either hanging loose or tied in a knot in front; it then serves the purpose of a *gulúband* or muffler. In the case of children it is tied round the neck as a neckkerchief, or round the waist for mere show. It may be used by women much as the 18th century tucker was used in England in Addison's time" (*Yusuf Ali, Mon. on Silk*, 79; for its use to mark a kind of shawl, see Forbes Watson, *Textile Manufactures*, 123).] In ordinary Anglo-Indian Hind. it is the word for a 'pocket handkerchief.' In modern trade it is applied to thin silk piece-goods with handkerchief-patterns. We are not certain of its meaning in the old trade of piece-goods, *e.g.*:

[1615.—"2 handkerchiefs **Rumall** cottony."—*Cocks's Diary*, Hak. Soc. i. 179.

[1665.—"Towel, **Rumale**."—*Persian Glossary*, in *Sir T. Herbert*, ed. 1677, p. 100.

[1684.—"**Romalls** Courge ... 16."—*Pringle, Diary Ft. St. Geo.*, 1st ser. iii. 119.]

1704.—"Price Currant (Malacca) ... **Romalls**, Bengall ordinary, per Corge, 26 Rix Dlls."—*Lockyer*, 71.

1726.—"**Roemaals**, 80 pieces in a pack, 45 ells long, 1½ broad."—*Valentijn*, v. 178.

Rūmāl was also the name technically used by the **Thugs** for the handkerchief with which they strangled their victims.

[c. 1833.—"There is no doubt but that all the Thugs are expert in the use of the handkerchief, which is called **Roomal** or *Paloo.* ..."—*Wolff, Travels*, ii. 180.]

***ROY**, s. A common mode of writing the title *rāī* (see RAJA); which sometimes occurs also as a family name, as in that of the famous Hindu Theist Rammohun **Roy**.

RUM-JOHNNY, s. Two distinct meanings are ascribed to this vulgar word, both, we believe, obsolete.

a. It was applied, according to Williamson, (*V.M.*, i. 167) to a low class of native servants who plied on the wharves of Calcutta in order to obtain employment from new-comers. That author explains it as a corruption of *Ramaẓānī*, which he alleges to be one of the commonest of Mahommedan names. [The *Meery-jhony Gully* of Calcutta (*Carey, Good Old Days*, i. 139) perhaps in the same way derived its name from one *Mīr Jān*.]

1810.—"Generally speaking, the present *banians*, who attach themselves to the captains of European ships, may without the least hazard of controversion, be considered as nothing more or less than **Rum-johnnies** 'of a larger growth.'"—*Williamson, V.M.*, i. 191.

b. Among soldiers and sailors, 'a prostitute'; from Hind. *rāmjanī*, Skt. *rāmā-janī*, 'a pleasing woman,' 'a dancing-girl.'

[1799.—"... and the **Rámjenís** (Hindu dancing women) have been all day dancing and singing before the idol."—*Colebrooke*, in *Life*, 153.]

1814.—"I lived near four years within a few miles of the solemn groves where those voluptuous devotees pass their lives with the **ramjannies** or dancing-girls attached to the temples, in a short of luxurious superstition and sanctified indolence unknown in colder climates."—*Forbes, Or. Mem.* iii. 6; [2nd ed. ii. 127].

[1816.—"But we must except that class of females called **ravjannees**, or dancing-girls, who are attached to the temples."—*Asiatic Journal*, ii. 375, quoting *Wathen, Tour to Madras and China*.]

RUPEE, s. Hind. *rūpiya*, from Skt. *rūpya*, 'wrought silver.' The standard coin of the Anglo-Indian monetary system, as it was of the Mahommedan Empire that preceded ours. It is commonly stated (as by Wilson, in his article on this word, which contains much valuable and condensed information) that the rupee was introduced by Sher Shāh (in 1542). And this is, no doubt, formally true; but it is certain that a coin substantially identical with the rupee, *i.e.* approximating to a standard of 100 *ratis* (or 175 grains troy) of silver, an ancient Hindu standard, had been struck by the Mahommedan sovereigns of Delhi in the 13th and 14th centuries, and had formed an important part of their currency. In fact, the capital coins of Delhi, from the time of Iyaltimish (A.D. 1211–1236) to the accession of Mahommed Tughlak (1325) were gold and silver pieces, respectively of the weight just mentioned. We gather from the statements of Ibn Batuta and his contemporaries that the gold coin, which the former generally calls **tanga** and sometimes *gold* **dīnār**, was worth 10 of the silver coin, which he calls **dīnār**, thus indicating that the relation of gold to silver value was, or had recently been, as 10 : 1. Mahommed Tughlak remodelled the currency, issuing gold pieces of 200 grs. and silver pieces of 140 grs.—an indication probably of a great "depreciation of gold" (to use our modern language) consequent on the enormous amount of gold bullion obtained from the plunder of Western and Southern India. Some years later (1330) Mahommed developed his notable scheme of a forced currency, consisting entirely of copper tokens. This threw everything into confusion, and it was not till six years later that any sustained issues of ordinary coin were recommenced. From about this time the old standard of 175 grs. was readopted for gold, and was maintained till the time of Sher Shāh. But it does not appear that the old standard was then resumed for silver. In the reign of Mahommed's successor Feroz Shāh, Mr. E. Thomas's examples show the gold coin of 175 grs. standard running parallel with continued issues of a silver (or professedly silver) coin of 140 grs.; and this, speaking briefly, continued to be the case to the end of the Lodi dynasty (*i.e.* 1526). The coinage seems to have sunk into a state of great irregularity, not remedied by Baber (who struck *ashrafis* and *dirhams*, such as were used in Turkestan) or Humāyūn, but the reform of which was undertaken by Sher Shāh, as above mentioned.

His silver coin of 175–178 grs. was that which popularly obtained the name of *rūpiya*, which has continued to our day. The weight, indeed, of the coins so styled, never very accurate in native times, varied in different States, and the purity varied still more. The former never went very far on either side of 170 grs., but the quantity of pure silver contained in it sunk in some cases as low as 140 grs., and even, in exceptional cases, to 100 grs. Variation however was not confined to native States. Rupees were struck in Bombay at a very early date of the British occupation. Of these there are four specimens in the Br. Mus. The first bears *obv.* 'The Rvpee of Bombaim. 1677. By AUTHORITY of Charles the Second; *rev.* King of Great Britaine. France. and Ireland.' Wt. 167·8 gr. The fourth bears *obv.* 'Hon. Soc. Ang. Ind. ori.' with a shield; *rev.* 'A. Deo. Pax. et. Incrementum:—Mon. Bombay. Anglic. Regim^s. A^o 7°.' Weight 177·8 gr. Different *Rupees* minted by the British Government were current in the three Presidencies, and in the Bengal Presidency several were current; viz. the *Sikka* (see sicca) Rupee, which latterly weighed 192 grs., and contained 176 grs. of pure silver; the *Farrukhābād*, which latterly weighed 180 grs.,[1] containing 165·215 of pure silver; the *Benares* Rupee (up to 1819), which weighed 174·76 grs., and contained 168·885 of pure silver. Besides these there was the *Chalānī* or 'current' rupee of account, in which the Company's accounts were kept, of which 116 were equal to 100 *sikkas*. ["The *bharī* or Company's Arcot rupee was coined at Calcutta, and was in value 3½ per cent. less than the Sikka rupee" (*Beveridge, Bakarganj*, 99).] The Bombay Rupee was adopted from that of Surat, and from 1800 its weight was 178·32 grs.; its pure silver 164·94. The Rupee at Madras (where however the standard currency was of an entirely different character, see pagoda) was originally that of the Nawāb of the Carnatic (or 'Nabob of Arcot') and was usually known as the *Arcot* Rupee. We find its issues varying from 171 to 177 grs. in weight, and from 160 to 170 of pure silver; whilst in 1811 there took place an abnormal coinage, from Spanish dollars, of rupees with a weight of 188 grs. and 169·20 of pure silver.

Also from some reason or other, perhaps from commerce between those places and the 'Coast,' the Chittagong and Dacca currency (*i.e.* in the extreme east of Bengal) "formerly consisted of Arcot rupees; and they were for some time coined expressly for those districts at the Calcutta and Dacca Mints. (!) (*Prinsep, Useful Tables*, ed. by *E. Thomas*, 24.)

These examples will give some idea of the confusion that prevailed (without any reference to the vast variety besides of native coinages), but the subject is far too complex to be dealt with minutely in the space we can

---

1 The term *Sonaut* rupees, which was of frequent occurrence down to the reformation and unification of the Indian coinage in 1833, is one very difficult to elucidate. The word is properly *sanwāt*, pl. of Ar. *sana(t)*, a year. According to the old practice in Bengal, coins deteriorated in value, in comparison with the rupee of account, when they passed the third year of their currency, and these rupees were termed *Sanwāt* or *Sonaut*. But in 1773, to put a stop to this inconvenience, Government determined that all rupees coined in future should bear the impression of the 19th *san* or year of Shāh 'Alam (the Mogul then reigning). And in all later uses of the term *Sonaut* it appears to be equivalent in value to the Farrukhābād rupee, or the modern "Company's Rupee" (which was of the same standard).

afford to it in such a work as this. The first step to reform and assimilation took place under Regulation VII. of 1833, but this still maintained the exceptional **Sicca** in Bengal, though assimilating the rupees over the rest of India. The *Sicca* was abolished as a coin by Act XIII. of 1836; and the universal rupee of British territory has since been the "Company's Rupee," as it was long called, of 180 grs. weight and 165 pure silver, representing therefore in fact the *Farrukhābād* Rupee.

1610.—"This armie consisted of 100,000 horse at the least, with infinite number of Camels and Elephants: so that with the whole baggage there could not bee lesse than fiue or sixe hundred thousand persons, insomuch that the waters were not sufficient for them; a **Mussocke** (see MUSSUCK) of water being sold for a **Rupia**, and yet not enough to be had."—*Hawkins*, in *Purchas*, i. 427.

[1615.—"**Roupies** Jangers (*Jahāngīrī*) of 100 *pisas*, which goeth four for five ordinary roupies of 80 *pisas* called *Cassanes*, and we value them at 2*s*. 4*d*. per piece: *Cecaus* (see SICCA) of Amadavrs which goeth for 86 *pisas; Challennes* of Agra, which goeth for 83 *pisas*."—*Foster*, *Letters*, iii. 87.]

1616.—"**Rupias** monetae genus est, quarum singulae xxvi assibus gallicis aut circiter aequivalent."—*Jarric*, iii. 83.

"... As for his Government of Patan onely, he gave the King eleven Leckes of **Rupias** (the **Rupia** is two shillings, two-pence sterling) ... wherein he had Regall Authoritie to take what he list, which was esteemed at five thousand horse, the pay of every one at two hundred Rupias by the yeare."—*Sir T. Roe*, in *Purchas*, i. 548; [Hak. Soc. i. 239, with some differences of reading].

"They call the peeces of money **roopees**, of which there are some of divers values, the meanest worth two shillings and threepence, and the best two shillings and ninepence sterling."—*Terry*, in *Purchas*, ii. 1471.

["This money, consisting of the two-shilling pieces of this country called **Roopeas**."—*Foster*, *Letters*, iv. 229.]

1648.—"Reducing the **Ropie** to four and twenty Holland Stuyvers."—*Van Twist*, 26.

1653.—"**Roupie** est vne mõnoye des Indes de la valeur de 30*s*." (*i.e. sous*).—*De la Boullaye-le-Gouz*, ed. 1657, p. 355.

c. 1666.—"And for a **Roupy** (in Bengal) which is about half a Crown, you may have 20 good Pullets and more; Geese and Ducks, in proportion."—*Bernier*, E.T. p. 140; [ed. *Constable*, 438].

1673.—"The other was a Goldsmith, who had coined copper **Rupees**."—*Fryer*, 97.

1677.—"We do, by these Presents ... give and grant unto the said Governor and Company ... full and free Liberty, Power, and Authority ... to stamp and coin ... Monies, to be called and known by the Name or Names of **Rupees**, **Pices**, and **Budgrooks**, or by such other Name or Names ..."—*Letters Patent of Charles II.* In *Charters of the E.I. Co.*, p. 111.

1771.—"We fear the worst however; that is, that the Government are about to interfere with the Company in the management of Affairs in India. Whenever that happens it will be high Time for us to decamp. I know the Temper of the King's Officers pretty well, and however they may decry our manner of acting they are ready enough to grasp at the **Rupees** whenever they fall within their Reach."—*MS. Letter of James Rennell*, March 31.

RUT, s. Hind. *rath*, 'a chariot.' Now applied to a native carriage drawn by a pony, or oxen, and used by women on a journey. Also applied to the car in which idols are carried forth on festival days. [See ROOK.]

[1810–17.—"Tippoo's **Aumil** ... wanted iron, and determined to supply himself from the **rut**, (a temple of carved wood fixed on wheels, drawn in procession on public occasions, and requiring many thousand persons to effect its movement)."—*Wilks*, *Sketches*, Madras reprint, ii. 281.

[1813.—"In this camp **hackeries** and **ruths**, as they are called when they have four wheels, are always drawn by bullocks, and are used, almost exclusively, by the *Baees*, the Nach girls, and the bankers."—*Broughton*, *Letters*, ed. 1892, p. 117.]

1829.—"This being the case I took the liberty of taking the **rut** and horse to camp as prize property."—*Mem. of John Shipp*, ii. 183.

RYOT, s. Ar. *ra'īyat*, from *ra'ā*, 'to pasture,' meaning originally, according to its etymology, 'a herd at pasture'; but then 'subjects' (collectively). It is by natives used for 'a subject' in India, but its specific Anglo-Indian application is to 'a tenant of the soil'; an individual occupying land as a farmer or cultivator. In Turkey the word, in the form *raiya*, is applied to the Christian subjects of the Porte, who are not liable to the conscription, but pay a poll-tax in lieu, the *Kharāj*, or *Jizya*.

[1609.—"**Riats** or clownes." (See under DOAI.)]

1776.—"For some period after the creation

of the world there was neither Magistrate nor Punishment ... and the **Ryots** were nourished with piety and morality."—*Halhed, Gentoo Code*, 41.

1789.—
"To him in a body the **Ryots** complain'd
That their houses were burnt, and their
cattle distrain'd."
The Letters of Simpkin the Second, &c. 11.

1790.—"A **raiyot** is rather a farmer than a husbandman."—*Colebrooke*, in *Life*, 42.

1809.—"The **ryots** were all at work in their fields."—*Lord Valentia*, ii. 127.

1813.—
"And oft around the cavern fire
On visionary schemes debate,
To snatch the **Rayahs** from their fate."
Byron, Bride of Abydos.

1820.—"An acquaintance with the customs of the inhabitants, but particularly of the **rayets**, the various tenures ... the agreements usual among them regarding cultivation, and between them and soucars respecting loans and advances ... is essential to a judge."—*Sir T. Munro*, in *Life*, ii. 17.

1870.—"**Ryot** is a word which is much ... misused. It is Arabic, but no doubt comes through the Persian. It means 'protected one,' 'subject,' 'a commoner,' as distinguished from '*Raees*' or 'noble.' In a native mouth, to the present day, it is used in this sense, and not in that of tenant."—*Systems of Land Tenure* (Cobden Club), 166.

The title of a newspaper, in English but of native editing, published for some years back in Calcutta, corresponds to what is here said; it is *Raees and* **Raiyat**.

1877.—"The great financial distinction between the followers of Islam ... and the **rayahs** or infidel subjects of the Sultan, was the payment of *haratch* or capitation tax."—*Finlay, H. of Greece*, v. 22 (ed. 1877).

1884.—"Using the rights of conquest after the fashion of the Normans in England, the Turks had everywhere, except in the Cyclades, ... seized on the greater part of the most fertile lands. Hence they formed the landlord class of Greece; whilst the **Rayahs**, as the Turks style their non-Mussulman subjects, usually farmed the territories of their masters on the *metayer* system."—*Murray's Handbook for Greece* (by A. F. Yule), p. 54.

RYOTWARRY, adj. A technicality of modern coinage. Hind. from Pers. *ra'iyatwār*, formed from the preceding. The *ryotwarry* system is that under which the settlement for land revenue is made directly by the Government agency with each individual cultivator holding land, not with the village community, nor with any middleman or landlord, payment being also received directly from every such individual. It is the system which chiefly prevails in the Madras Presidency; and was elaborated there in its present form mainly by Sir T. Munro.

1824.—"It has been objected to the **ryotwari** system that it produces unequal assessment and destroys ancient rights and privileges: but these opinions seem to originate in some misapprehension of its nature."—*Minutes*, &c., of *Sir T. Munro*, i. 265. We may observe that the spelling here is not Munro's. The Editor, Sir A. Arbuthnot, has followed a system (see Preface, p. x.); and we see in *Gleig's Life* (iii. 355) that Munro wrote '**Rayetwar**.'

S

SAFFLOWER, s. The flowers of the annual *Carthamus tinctorius*, L. (N.O. *Compositae*), a considerable article of export from India for use of a red dye, and sometimes, from the resemblance of the dried flowers to saffron, termed 'bastard saffron.' The colouring matter of safflower is the basis of *rouge*. The name is a curious modification of words by the 'striving after meaning.' For it points, in the first half of the name, to the analogy with saffron, and in the second half, to the object of trade being a flower. But neither one nor the other of these meanings forms any real element in the word. *Safflower* appears to be an eventual corruption of the Arabic name of the thing, *'usfūr*. This word we find in medieval trade-lists (*e.g.* in Pegolotti) to take various forms such as *asfiore, asfrole, astifore, zaffrole, saffiore*; from the last of which the transition to *safflower* is natural. In the old Latin translation of Avicenna it seems to be called *Crocus hortulanus*, for the corresponding Arabic is given *hasfor*. Another Arabic name for this article is *ḳurṭum*, which we presume to be the origin of the botanist's *carthamus*. In Hind. It is called *kusumbha* or *kusum*. Bretschneider remarks that though the two plants, saffron and safflower, have not the slightest resemblance, and belong to two different families and classes of the nat. system, there has been a certain confusion between them among almost all nations, including the Chinese.

c. 1200.—"**'Usfur** ... *Abu Hanifa*. This plant yields a colouring matter, used in dyeing. There are two kinds, cultivated and wild, both of which grow in Arabia, and the seeds of which are called *al-ḳurṭum*."—*Ibn Baithar*, ii. 196.

c. 1343.—"**Affiore** vuol esser fresco, e asciutto, e colorito rosso in colore di buon zafferano, e non giallo, e chiaro a modo di famminella di zafferano, e che non sia trasandato, che quando è vecchio e trasandato si spolverizza, e fae vermini."—*Pegolotti*, 372.

1612.—"The two Indian ships aforesaid did discharge these goods following ... **oosfar**, which is a red die, great quantitie."—*Capt. Saris*, in *Purchas*, i. 347.

[1667-8.—"... madder, **safflower**, argoll, castoreum. ..."—*List of Goods imported*, in *Birdwood, Report on Old Records*, 76.]

1810.—"Le safran bâtard ou carthame, nommé dans le commerce *safranon*, est appelé par les Arabes ... **osfour** ou ... *Kortom*. Suivant M. Sonnini, le premier nom désigne la plante; et le second, ses graines."—*Silv. de Sacy*, Note on *Abdallatif*, p. 123.

1813.—"**Safflower** (*Cussom*, Hind., *Asfour* Arab.) is the flower of an annual plant, the *Carthamus tinctorius*, growing in Bengal and other parts of India, which when well-cured is not easily distinguishable from saffron by the eye, though it has nothing of its smell or taste."—*Milburn*, ii. 238.

SAFFRON, s. Arab. *za'farān*. The true saffron (*Crocus salivus*, L.) in India is cultivated in Kashmīr only. In South India this name is given to *turmeric*, which the Portuguese called *açafrão da terra* ('country saffron.') The Hind. name is *haldī*, or in the Deccan *halad*, [Skt. *haridra, hari*, 'green, yellow']. Garcia de Orta calls it *croco Indiaco*, 'Indian saffron.' Indeed, Dozy shows that the Arab. *kurkum* for turmeric (whence the bot: Lat. *curcuma*) is probably taken from the Greek κρόκος or obl. κρόκον. Moodeen Sherif says that *kurkum* is applied to saffron in many Persian and other writers.

c. 1200.—"The Persians call this root *al-Hard*, and the inhabitants of Basra call it *al-Kurkum*, and *al-Kurkum* is **Saffron**. They call these plants **Saffron** because they dye yellow in the same way as Saffron does."—*Ibn Baithar*, ii. 370.

1563.—"*R*. Since there is nothing else to be said on this subject, let us speak of what we call 'country **saffron**.'

"*O*. This is a medicine that should be spoken of, since it is in use by the Indian physicians; it is a medicine and article of trade much exported to Arabia and Persia. In this city (Goa) there is little of it, but much in Malabar, *i.e.* in Cananor and Calecut. The Canarins call the root *alad;* and the Malabars sometimes give it the same name, but more properly call it *mangale*, and the Malays *cunhet*; the Persians, *darzard*, which is as much as to say 'yellow-wood.' The Arabs call it *habet;* and all of them, each in turn, say that this saffron does not exist in Persia, nor in Arabia, nor in Turkey, except what comes from India."—*Garcia*, f. 78*v*. Further on he identifies it with *curcuma*.

1726.—"Curcuma, or Indian **Saffron**."—*Valentijn, Chor.* 42.

SAGO, s. From Malay *sāgū*. The farinaceous pith taken out of the stem of several species of a particular genus of palm, especially *Metroxylon laeve*, Mart., and *M. Rumphii*, Willd., found in every part of the Indian Archipelago, including the Philippines, wherever there is proper soil. They are most abundant in the eastern part of the region indicated, including the Moluccas and N. Guinea, which probably formed the original habitat; and in these they supply the sole bread of the natives. In the remaining parts of the Archipelago, *sago* is the food only of certain wild tribes, or consumed (as in Mindanao) by the poor only, or prepared (as at Singapore, &c.) for export. There are supposed to be five species producing the article.

1298.—"They have a kind of trees that produce flour, and excellent flour it is for food. These trees are very tall and thick, but have a very thin bark, and inside the bark they are crammed with flour."—*Marco Polo*, Bk. iii. ch. xi.

1330.—"But as for the trees which produce flour, tis after this fashion. ... And the result is the best *pasta* in the world, from which they make whatever they choose, cates of sorts, and excellent bread, of which I, Friar Odoric, have eaten."—*Fr. Odoric*, in *Cathay*, &c., 32.

1522.—"Their bread (in Tidore) they make of the wood of a certain tree like a palm-tree, and they make it in this way. They take a piece of this wood, and extract from it certain long black thorns which are situated there; then they pound it, and make bread of it which they call **sagu**. They make provision of this bread for their sea voyages."—*Pigafetta*, Hak. Soc. p. 136. This is a bad description, and seems to refer to the **Sagwire**, not the true sago-tree.

1552.—"There are also other trees which are called **çagus**, from the pith of which bread is made."—*Castanheda*, vi. 24.

1553.—"Generally, although they have some millet and rice, all the people of the Isles of Maluco eat a certain food which they call **Sagum**, which is the pith of a tree like a palm-tree, except that the leaf is softer and smoother, and the green of it is rather dark."—*Barros*, III. v. 5.

1579.—"... and a Kind of meale which they call **Sago**, made of the toppes of certaine trees, tasting in the Mouth like some curds, but melts away like sugar."—*Drake's Voyage*, Hak. Soc. p. 142.

Also in a list of "Certaine Wordes of the Naturall Language of Iaua"; "**Sagu**, bread of the Countrey."—*Hakl.* iv. 246.

c. 1690.—"Primo **Sagus** genuina, Malaice **Sagu**, sive *Lapia tuni*, h.e. vera *Sagu*."—*Rumphius*, i. 75. (We cannot make out the language of *lapia tuni*.)

1727.—"And the inland people subsist mostly on **Sagow**, the Pith of a small Twig split and dried in the Sun."—*A. Hamilton*, ii. 93; [ed. 1744].

SAHIB, s. The title by which, all over India, European gentlemen, and it may be said Europeans generally, are addressed, and spoken of, when no disrespect is intended, by natives. It is also the general title (at least where Hindustani or Persian is used) which is affixed to the name or office of a European, corresponding thus rather to *Monsieur* than to Mr. For *Colonel Ṣāḥib, Collector Ṣāḥib, Lord Ṣāḥib*, and even *Sergeant Ṣāḥib* are thus used, as well as the general vocative *Ṣāḥib!* 'Sir!' In other Hind. use the word is equivalent to 'Master'; and it is occasionally used as a specific title both among Hindus and Musulmans, *e.g. Appa Ṣāḥib, Tīpū Ṣāḥib;* and generically is affixed to the titles of men of rank when indicated by those titles, as *Khān Ṣāḥib, Nawāb Ṣāḥib, Rājā Ṣāḥib*. The word is Arabic, and originally means 'a companion'; (sometimes a companion of Mahommed). [In the *Arabian Nights* it is the title of a Wazīr (*Burton*, i. 218).]

1673.—"... To which the subtle Heathen replied, **Sahab** (i.e. Sir), why will you do more than the Creator meant?"—*Fryer*, 417.

1689.—"Thus the distracted Husband in his *Indian* English confest, *English fashion*, **Sab**, best fashion, have one Wife best for one Husband."—*Ovington*, 326.

1853.—"He was told that a '**Sahīb**' wanted to speak with him."—*Oakfield*, ii. 252.

1878.—"... forty Elephants and five **Sahibs** with guns and innumerable followers."—*Life in the Mofussil*, i. 194.

SAIVA, s. A worshipper of *Śiva*; Skt. *Śaiva*, adj., 'belonging to Siva.'

1651.—"The second sect of the Bramins, '**Seiviá**' ... by name, say that a certain *Eswara* is the supreme among the gods, and that all the others are subject to him."—*Rogerius*, 17.

1867.—"This temple is reckoned, I believe, the holiest shrine in India, at least among the **Shaivites**."—*Bp. Milman*, in *Memoirs*, p. 48.

***SALA**, s. Hind. *sālā*, 'brother-in-law,' *i.e.* wife's brother; but used elliptically as a low term of abuse.

[1856.—"Another reason (for infanticide) is the blind pride which makes them hate that any man should call them **sala**, or Sussoor—brother-in-law, or father-in-law."—*Forbes, Rās Mālā*, ed. 1878, 616.]

1881.—"Another of these popular Paris sayings is '*et ta soeur*?' which is as insulting a remark to a Parisian as the apparently harmless remark **sālā**, 'brother-in-law,' is to a Hindoo."—*Sat. Rev.*, Sept. 10, 326.

SALAAM, s. A salutation; properly oral salutation of Mahommedans to each other. Arab. *salām*, 'peace.' Used for any act of salutation; or for 'compliments.'

[c. 60 B.C.—

"*Ἀλλ' εἰ μὲν Σύρος ἐσσὶ "Σαλὰμ," εἰ δ' οὖν σύ γε φοῖνιξ*

"*Ναίδιος," εἰ δ' Ἕλλην "Χαῖρε"· τὸ δ' αὐτὸ φράσον.*"

—*Meleagros*, in *Anthologia Palatina*, vii. 149.

The point is that he has been a bird of passage, and says good-bye now to his various resting-places in their own tongue.]

1513.—"The ambassador (of Bisnagar) entering the door of the chamber, the Governor rose from the chair on which he was seated, and stood up while the ambassador made him great **çalema**."—*Correa, Lendas*, II. i. 377. See also p. 431.

1552.—"The present having been seen he took the letter of the Governor, and read it to him, and having read it told him how the Governor sent him his **çalema**, and was at his command with all his fleet, and with all the Portuguese. ..."—*Castanheda*, iii. 445.

1611.—"**Çalema**. The salutation of an inferior."—*Cobarruvias, Sp. Dict.* s.v.

1626.—"Hee (Selim *i.e.* Jahāngīr) turneth ouer his Beades, and saith so many words, to wit three thousand and two hundred, and then presenteth himself to the people to receive their **salames** or good morrow. ..."—*Purchas, Pilgrimage*, 523.

1638.—"En entrant ils se saluent de leur **Salom** qu'ils accompagnent d'vne profonde inclination."—*Mandelslo*, Paris, 1659, 223.

1648.—"... this salutation they call **salam**;

and it is made with bending of the body, and laying of the right hand upon the head."—*Van Twist*, 55.

1689.—"The **Salem** of the Religious Bramins, is to join their Hands together, and spreading them first, make a motion towards their Head, and then stretch them out."—*Ovington*, 183.

1694.—"The Town Conicopolies, and chief inhabitants of Egmore, came to make their **Salaam** to the President."—*Wheeler*, i. 231.

1717.—"I wish the Priests in Tranquebar a Thousand fold **Schalam**."—*Philipp's Acct.* 62.

1809.—"The old priest was at the door, and with his head uncovered, to make his **salaams**."—*Ld. Valentia*, i. 273.

1813.—

"'Ho! who art thou?'—'This low **salam**
Replies, of Moslem faith I am.'"

Byron, The Giaour.

1832.—"Il me rendit tous les **salams** que je fis autrefois au "Grand Mogol."—*Jacquemont, Corresp.* ii. 137.

1844.—"All chiefs who have made their **salam** are entitled to carry arms personally."—*G. O. of Sir C. Napier*, 2.

***SALIGRAM**, s. Skt. *Śālagrāma* (this word seems to be properly the name of a place, 'Village of the Sāltree'—a real or imaginary *tīrtha* or place of sacred pilgrimage, mentioned in the *Mahābhārata*). [Other and less probable explanations are given by Oppert, *Anc. Inhabitants*, 337.] A pebble having mystic virtues, found in certain rivers, *e.g.* Gandak, Son, &c. Such stones are usually marked by containing a fossil ammonite. The *śālagrāma* is often adopted as the representative of some god, and the worship of any god may be performed before it.[1] It is daily worshipped by the Brahmans; but it is especially connected with Vaishnava doctrine. In May 1883 a *śālagrāma* was the ostensible cause of great popular excitement among the Hindus of Calcutta. During the proceedings in a family suit before the High Court, a question arose regarding the identity of a *śālagrāma*, regarded as a household god. Counsel on both sides suggested that the thing should be brought into court. Mr. Justice Norris hesitated to give this order till he had taken advice. The attorneys on both sides, Hindus, said there could be no objection; the Court interpreter, a high-caste Brahman, said it could not be brought into Court, *because of the coir-matting*, but it might with perfect propriety be brought into the corridor for inspection; which was done. This took place during the excitement about the "Ilbert Bill," giving natives magisterial authority in the provinces over Europeans; and there followed most violent and offensive articles in several native newspapers reviling Mr. Justice Norris, who was believed to be hostile to the Bill. The editor of the *Bengallee* newspaper, an educated man, and formerly a member of the covenanted Civil Service, the author of one of the most unscrupulous and violent articles, was summoned for contempt of court. He made an apology and complete retractation, but was sentenced to two months' imprisonment.

c. 1590.—"**Salgram** is a black stone which the Hindoos hold sacred. ... They are found in the river Sown, at the distance of 40 cose from the mouth."—*Ayeen, Gladwin's* E.T. 1800, ii. 25; [ed. *Jarrett*, ii. 150].

1782.—"Avant de finir l'histoire de Vichenou, je ne puis me dispenser de parler de la pierre de **Salagraman**. Elle n'est autre chose qu'une coquille petrifiée du genre des *cornes d'Ammon*: les Indiens prétendent qu'elle represente Vichenon, parcequ'ils en ont découvert de neuf nuances différentes, ce qu'ils rapportent aux neuf incarnations de ce Dieu. ... Cette pierre est aux sectateurs de Vichenou ce que le Lingam est à ceux de Chiven."—*Sonnerat*, i. 307.

[1822.—"In the Nerbuddah are found those types of Shiva, called **Solgrammas**, which are sacred pebbles held in great estimation all over India."—*Wallace, Fifteen Years in India*, 296.]

1824.—"The **shalgramŭ** is black, hollow, and nearly round; it is found in the Gunduk River, and is considered a representation of Vishnoo. ... The **Shalgramŭ** is the only stone that is naturally divine; all the other stones are rendered sacred by incantations."—*Wanderings of a Pilgrim*, i. 43.

1885.—"My father had one (a **Salagram**). It was a round, rather flat, jet black, small, shining stone. He paid it the greatest reverence possible, and allowed no one to touch it, but worshipped it with his own hands. When he became ill, and as he would not allow a woman to touch it, he made it over to a Brahman ascetic with a money present."—*Sundrábái*, in *Punjab*

1 Like the Βαιτύλιον which the Greeks got through the Semitic nations. In Photius there are extracts from Damascius (*Life of Isidorus the Philosopher*), which speak of the stones called *Baitulos* and *Baitulion*, which were objects of worship, gave oracles, and were apparently used in healing. These appear, from what is stated, to have been meteoric stones. There were many in Lebanon (see *Phot. Biblioth.*, ed. 1653, pp. 1047, 1062–3).

Notes and Queries, ii. 109. The **śālagrāma** is in fact a Hindu fetish.

SAMPAN, s. A kind of small boat or skiff. The word appears to be Javanese and Malay. It must have been adopted on the Indian shores, for it was picked up there at an early date by the Portuguese; and it is now current all through the further East. [The French have adopted the Annamite form *tamban*.] The word is often said to be originally Chinese, '*sanpan*,' = 'three boards,' and this is possible. It is certainly one of the most ordinary words for a boat in China. Moreover, we learn, on the authority of Mr. E. C. Baber, that there is another kind of boat on the Yangtse which is called *wu-pan*, 'five boards.' Giles however says: "From the Malay *sampan* = three boards"; but in this there is some confusion. The word has no such meaning in Malay.

1510.—"My companion said, 'What means then might there be for going to this island?" They answered: 'That it was necessary to purchase a **chiampana**,' that is a small vessel, of which many are found there."—*Varthema*, 242.

1516.—"They (the Moors of Quilacare) perform their voyages in small vessels which they call **champana**."—*Barbosa*, 172.

c. 1540.—"In the other, whereof the captain was slain, there was not one escaped, for *Quiay Panian* pursued them in a **Champana**, which was the Boat of his Junk."—*Pinto* (*Cogan*, p. 79), orig. ch. lix.

1552.—"... **Champanas**, which are a kind of small vessels."—*Castanheda*, ii. 76; [rather, Bk. ii. ch. xxii. p. 76].

1613.—"And on the beach called the Bazar of the *Jaos* ... they sell every sort of provision in rice and grain for the Jaos merchants of Java Major, who daily from the dawn are landing provisions from their junks and ships in their boats or **Champenas** (which are little skiffs). ..."—*Godinho de Eredia*, 6.

[1622.—"Yt was thought fytt ... to trym up a China **Sampan** to goe with the fleete. ..."—*Cock's Diary*, Hak. Soc. ii. 122.]

1648.—In *Van Spilbergen's Voyage* we have **Champane**, and the still more odd **Champaigne**. [See under TOPAZ.]

1702.—"**Sampans** being not to be got we were forced to send for the Sarah and Eaton's Long-boats."—*MS. Correspondence in 1. Office from China Factory* (at Chusan), Jan. 8.

c. 1788.—"Some made their escape in prows, and some in **sampans**."—*Mem. of a Malay Family*, 3.

1868.—"The harbour is crowded with men-of-war and trading vessels ... from vessels of several hundred tons burthen down to little fishing-boats and passenger **sampans**."—*Wallace, Malay Archip.* 21.

SANDAL, SANDLE, SANDERS, SANDAL-WOOD, s. From Low Latin santalum, in Greek *σάνταλον*, and in later Greek *σάνδανον*; coming from the Arab. *ṣandal*, and that from Skt. *chandana*. The name properly belongs to the fragrant wood of the *Santalum album*, L. Three woods bearing the name *santalum*, white, yellow, and red, were in official use in the Middle Ages. But the name Red Sandalwood, or Red Sanders, has been long applied, both in English and in the Indian vernaculars, to the wood of *Pterocarpus santalina*, L., a tree of S. India, the wood of which is inodorous, but which is valued for various purposes in India (pillars, turning, &c.), and is exported as a dye-wood. According to Hanbury and Flückiger this last was the *sanders* so much used in the cookery of the Middle Ages for colouring sauces, &c. In the opinion of those authorities it is doubtful whether the red sandal of the medieval pharmacologists was a kind of the real odorous sandal-wood, or was the wood of *Pteroc. santal.* It is possible that sometimes the one and sometimes the other was meant. For on the one hand, even in modern times, we find Milburn (see below) speaking of the three colours of the real sandal-wood; and on the other hand we find Matthioli in the 16th century speaking of the red sandal as inodorous.

It has been a question how the *Pterocarpus santalina* came to be called sandal-wood at all. We may suggest, as a possible origin of this, the fact that its powder "mixed with oil is used for bathing and purifying the skin" (*Drury*, s.v.), much as the true sandal-wood powder also is used in the East.

c. 545.—"And from the remoter regions, I speak of Tzinista and other places of export, the imports to Taprobane are silk, aloeswood, cloves, **Sandalwood** (*τζάνδανη*), and so forth. ..."—*Cosmas*, in *Cathay*, &c., clxxvii.

1298.—"Encore sachiez que en ceste ysle a arbres de **sandal** vermoille ausi grant come sunt les arbres des nostre contrée ... et il en ont bois come nos avuns d'autres arbres sauvajes."—*Marco Polo*, Geog. Text, ch. exci.

c. 1390.—"Take powdered rice and boil it in almond milk ... and colour it with **Saunders**."—Recipe quoted by *Wright, Domestic Manners*, &c., 350.

1554.—"Le **Santal** donc croist es Indes Orientales et Occidentales: en grandes Forestz, et fort espesses. Il s'en treuue trois especes: mais le plus pasle est le meilleur: le blanc apres: le rouge est mis au dernier ranc, pource qu'il n'a aucune odeur: mais les deux premiers sentent fort bon."—*Matthioli* (old Fr. version), liv. i. ch. xix.

1563.—"The **Sandal** grows about Timor, which produces the largest quantity, and it is called **chundana**; and by this name it is known in all the regions about Malaca; and the Arabs, being those who carried on the trade of those parts, corrupted the word and called it **sandal**. Every Moor, whatever his nation, calls it thus ..."—*Garcia*, f. 185*v*. He proceeds to speak of the **sandalo** *vermelho* as quite a different product, growing in Tenasserim and on the Coromandel Coast.

1584.—"...**Sandales** wilde from Cochin. **Sandales** domestick from Malacca. ..."—*Wm. Barrett*, in *Hakl.* ii. 412.

1613.—"... certain renegade Christians of the said island, along with the Moors, called in the Hollanders, who thinking it was a fine opportunity, went one time with five vessels, and another time with seven, against the said fort, at a time when most of the people ... were gone to Solor for the **Sandal** trade, by which they had their living."—*Bocarro, Decada*, 723.

1615.—"Committee to procure the commodities recommended by Capt. Saris for Japan, viz. ... pictures of wars, steel, skins, **sanders-wood**."—*Sainsbury*, i. 380.

1813.—"When the trees are felled, the bark is taken off; they are then cut into billets, and buried in a dry place for two months, during which period the white ants will eat the outer wood without touching the **sandal**; it is then taken up and ... sorted into three kinds. The deeper the colour, the higher is the perfume; and hence the merchants sometimes divide **sandal** into red, yellow, and white; but these are all different shades of the same colour."—*Milburn*, i. 291.

1825.—"REDWOOD, properly RED **Saunders**, is produced chiefly on the Coromandel Coast, whence it has of late years been imported in considerable quantity to England, where it is employed in dyeing. It ... comes in round billets of a thickish red colour on the outside, a deep brighter red within, with a wavy grain; no smell or taste."—*Ibid.* ed. 1825, p. 249.

SANSKRIT, s. The name of the classical language of the Brahmans, *Saṃskṛita*, meaning in that language 'purified' or 'perfected.' This was obviously at first only an epithet, and it is not of very ancient use in this specific application. To the Brahmans Sanskrit was the *bhāsha*, or language, and had no particular name. The word Sanskrit is used by the protogrammarian Pānini (some centuries before Christ), but not as a denomination of the language. In the latter sense, however, both 'Sanskrit' and 'Prakrit' (**Pracrit**) are used in the *Bṛihat Samhitā* of Varāhamihira, c. A.D. 504, in a chapter on omens (lxxxvi. 3), to which Prof. Kern's translation does not extend. It occurs also in the *Mrichch'hakatikā*, translated by Prof. H. H. Wilson in his *Hindu Theatre*, under the name of the 'Toy-cart'; in the works of Kumārila Bhatta, a writer of the 7th century; and in the *Pāṇinīyā Śīkshā*, a metrical treatise ascribed by the Hindus to Pāṇini, but really of comparatively modern origin.

There is a curiously early mention of Sanskrit by the Mahommedan poet Amīr Khusrū of Delhi, which is quoted below. The first mention (to our knowledge) of the word in any European writing is in an Italian letter of Sassetti's, addressed from Malabar to Bernardo Davanzati in Florence, and dating from 1586. The few words on the subject, of this writer, show much acumen.

In the 17th and 18th centuries such references to this language as occur are found chiefly in the works of travellers to Southern India, and by these it is often called *Grandonic*, or the like, from *grantha*, 'a book' *i.e.* a book of the classical Indian literature. The term *Sanskrit* came into familiar use after the investigations into this language by the English in Bengal (viz. by Wilkins, Jones, &c.) in the last quarter of the 18th century. [See Macdonell, *Hist. of Sanskrit Lit.* ch. i.]

A.D. *x?*—"*Maitreya.* Now, to me, there are two things at which I cannot choose but laugh, a woman reading **Sanskrit**, and a man singing a song: the woman snuffles like a young cow when the rope is first passed through her nostrils; and the man wheezes like an old Pandit repeating his bead-roll."—*The Toy-Cart*, E.T. in *Wilson's Works*, xi. 60.

A.D. *y?*—"Three-and-sixty or four-and-sixty sounds are there originally in Prakrit (PRACRIT) even as in **Sanskrit**, as taught by the Svayambhū."—*Pāṇinīyā Śīkshā*, quoted in *Weber's Ind. Studien* (1858), iv. 348. But see also *Weber's Akadem. Vorlesungen* (1876), p. 194.

1318.—"But there is another language, more select than the other, which all the Brahmans use. Its name from of old is **Sahaskrit**, and the common people know nothing of it."—*Amīr Khusrū*, in *Elliot*, iii. 563.

1586.—"Sono scritte le loro scienze tutte in una lingua che dimandano **Samscruta**, che vuol dire 'bene articolata': della quale non si ha memoria quando fusse parlata, con avere (com' io dico) memorie antichissime. Imparanla come noi la greca e la latina, e vi pongono molto maggior tempo, si che in 6 anni o 7 sene fanno padroni: et ha la lingua d'oggi molte cose comuni con quella, nella quale sono molti de' nostri nomi, e particularmente de numeri il 6, 7, 8, e 9, *Dio, serpe*, et altri assai."—*Sassetti*, extracted in *De Gubernatis*, *Storia*, &c., Livorno, 1875, p. 221.

c. 1590.—"Although this country (Kashmīr) has a peculiar tongue, the books of knowledge are **Sanskrit** (or Sahanskrit). They also have a written character of their own, with which they write their books. The substance which they chiefly write upon is *Tūs*, which is the bark of a tree,[1] which with a little pains they make into leaves, and it lasts for years. In this way ancient books have been written thereon, and the ink is such that it cannot be washed out."—*Āīn* (orig.), i. p. 563; [ed. *Jarrett*, ii. 351].

1623.—"The Jesuites conceive that the Bramenes are of the dispersion of the Israelites, and their Bookes (called **Samescretan**) doe somewhat agree with the Scriptures, but that they understand them not."—*Purchas*, *Pilgrimage*, 559.

1651.—"... *Souri* signifies the Sun in **Samscortam**, which is a language in which all the mysteries of Heathendom are written, and which is held in esteem by the Bramines just as Latin is among the Learned in Europe."—*Rogerius*, 4.

In some of the following quotations we have a form which it is difficult to account for:

c. 1666.—"Their first study is in the **Hanscrit**, which is a language entirely different from the common *Indian*, and which is only known by the *Pendets*. And this is that Tongue, of which Father *Kircher* hath published the Alphabet received from Father *Roa*. It is called *Hanscrit*, that is, a pure Language; and because they believe this to be the Tongue in which God, by means of *Brahma*, gave them the four *Beths* (see VEDA), which they esteem *Sacred Books*, they call it a Holy and Divine Language."—*Bernier*, E.T. 107; [ed. *Constable*, 335].

1673.—"... who founded these, their Annals nor their **Sanscript** deliver not."—*Fryer*. 161.

1689.—"... the learned Language among them is called the **Sanscreet**."—*Ovington*, 248.

1694.—"Indicus ludus *Tchûpur*, sic nominatus veterum Brachmanorum linguâ Indicè dictâ **Sanscroot**, seu, ut vulgo, exiliori sono elegantiae causâ **Sanscreet**, non autem **Hanscreet** ut minus recte eam nuncupat Kircherus."—*Hyde*, *De Ludis Orientt.*, in *Syntagma Diss.* ii. 264.

1726.—"Above all it would be a matter of general utility to the Coast that some more chaplains should be maintained there for the sole purpose of studying the *Sanskrit* tongue (*de* **Sanskritze** *taal*) the head-and-mother tongue of most of the Eastern languages, and once for all to make an exact translation of the *Vedam* or Law book of the Heathen. ..."—*Valentijn*, *Choro.* p. 72.

1760.—"They have a learned language peculiar to themselves, called the **Hanscrit.** ..."—*Grose*, i. 202.

1774.—"This code they have written in their own language, the **Shanscrit**. A translation of it is begun under the inspection of one of the body, into the Persian language, and from that into English."—*W. Hastings*, to *Lord Mansfield*, in *Gleig*, i. 402.

1778.—"The language as well as the written character of Bengal are familiar to the Natives ... and both seem to be base derivatives from the **Shanscrit**."—*Orme*, ed. 1803, ii. 5.

1782.—"La langue **Samscroutam**, *Samskret*, **Hanscrit** ou *Grandon*, est la plus étendue: ses caractères multipliés donnent beaucoup de facilité pour exprimer ses pensées, ce qui l'a fait nommer langue divine par le P. Pons."—*Sonnerat*, i. 224.

1794.—
"With Jones, a linguist, **Sanskrit**, Greek, or
Manks."
Pursuits of Literature, 6th ed. 286.

1796.—"La madre di tutte le lingue Indiane è la **Samskrda**, cioè, *lingua perfetta*, piena, *ben digerita*. *Krda* opera perfetta o compita, *Sam*, simul, *insieme*, e vuol dire lingua tutta insieme *ben digerita*, legata, *perfetta*."—*Fra Paolino*, p. 258.

SAREE, s. Hind. *sāṛī*, *sāṛhī*. The cloth which constitutes the main part of a woman's dress in N. India, wrapt round the body and then thrown over the head.

1598.—"... likewise they make whole pieces or webbes of this hearbe, sometimes mixed and woven with silke. ... Those webs are named **sarijn** ..."—*Linschoten*, 28; [Hak. Soc. i. 96].

1785.—"... Her clothes were taken off, and a red silk covering (a **saurry**) put upon her."—*Acct. of a Suttee*, in *Seton-Karr*, i. 90.

SARONG, s. **Malay**. *sārung;* the body-cloth, or long kilt, tucked or girt at the waist,

1 Of the birch-tree, Sansk. *bhurja*, *Betula Bhojpattra*, Wall., the exfoliating outer bark of which is called *tōz*.

and generally of coloured silk or cotton, which forms the chief article of dress of the Malays and Javanese. The same article of dress, and the name (*saran*) are used in Ceylon. It is an old Indian form of dress, but is now used only by some of the people of the south; *e.g.* on the coast of Malabar, where it is worn by the Hindus (white), by the Mappilas of that coast, and the Labbais of Coromandel (coloured), and by the *Bants* of Canara, who wear it of a dark blue. With the Labbais the coloured *sarong* is a modern adoption from the Malays. Crawfurd seems to explain *sarung* as Javanese, meaning first 'a case or sheath,' and then a wrapper or garment. But, both in the Malay islands and in Ceylon, the word is no doubt taken from Skt. *sāranga*, meaning 'variegated' and also 'a garment.'

[1830.—"... the cloth or **sarong**, which has been described by Mr. Marsden to be 'not unlike a Scots highlander's plaid in appearance, being a piece of party-coloured cloth, about 6 or 8 feet long, and 3 or 4 feet wide, sewed together at the ends, forming, as some writers have described it, a wide sack without a bottom.' With the *Maláyus*, the **sarong** is either worn slung over the shoulders as a sash, or tucked round the waist and descending to the ankles, so as to enclose the legs like a petticoat."—*Raffles, Java*, i. 96.]

1868.—"He wore a **sarong** or Malay petticoat, and a green jacket."—*Wallace, Mal. Arch.* 171.

SATIN, s. This is of course English, not Anglo-Indian. The common derivation [accepted by Prof. Skeat (*Concise Dict.* 2nd ed. s.v.] is with Low Lat. *seta*, 'silk,' Lat. *seta*, *saeta*, 'a bristle, a hair,' through the Port. *setim*. Dr. Wells Williams (*Mid. King.*, ii. 123) says it is probably derived eventually from the Chinese *sz'-tün*, though intermediately through other languages. It is true that *sz'tün* or *sz'twan* is a common (and ancient) term for this sort of silk texture. But we may remark that trade-words adopted directly from the Chinese are comparatively rare (though no doubt the intermediate transit indicated would meet this objection, more or less). And we can hardly doubt that the true derivation is that given in *Cathay and the Way Thither*, p. 486; viz. from *Zaitun* or *Zayton*, the name by which Chwan-chau, the great medieval port of western trade in Fokien, was known to western traders. We find that certain rich stuffs of damask and satin were called from this place, by the Arabs, *Zaitūnia;* the Span. *aceytuni* (for 'satin'), the medieval French *zatony*, and the medieval Ital. *zetani*, afford intermediate steps.

c. 1350.—"The first city that I reached after crossing the sea was *Zaitūn*. ... It is a great city, superb indeed; and in it they make damasks of velvet as well as those of satin (*kimkhā*—see KINCOB), which are called from the name of the city **zaitūnia**."—*Ibn Batuta*, iv. 269.

1352.—In an inventory of this year in *Douet d'Arcq* we have: "**Zatony** at 4 *écus* the ell" (p. 342).

1405.—"And besides, this city (Samarkand) is very rich in many wares which come to it from other parts. From Russia and Tartary come hides and linens, and from Cathay silk-stuffs, the best that are made in all that region, especially the **setunis**, which are said to be the best in the world, and the best of all are those that are without pattern."—*Clavijo* (translated anew—the passage corresponding to Markham's at p. 171). The word **setuni** occurs repeatedly in Clavijo's original.

1440.—In the *Libro de Gabelli*, &c., of Giov. da Uzzano, we have mention among silk stuffs, several times, of "**zetani** *vellutati*, and other kinds of **zetani**."—*Della Decima*, iv. 58, 107, &c.

1441.—"Before the throne (at Bijanagar) was placed a cushion of **zaitūnī** satin, round which three rows of the most exquisite pearls were sewn."—*Abdurrazzāk*, in *Elliot*, iv. 120. (The original is "*darpesh-i-takht bālishī az* **atlas-i-zaitūnī**"; see *Not. et Exts.* xiv. 376. Quatremère (*ibid.* 462) translated '*un carreau de satin* olive,' taking *zaitūn* in its usual Arabic sense of 'an olive tree.') Also see *Elliot*, iv. 113.

***SATSUMA**, n.p. Name of a city and formerly of a principality (daimioship) in Japan, the name of which is familiar not only from the deplorable necessity of bombarding its capital Kagosima in 1863 (in consequence of the murder of Mr. Richardson, and other outrages, with the refusal of reparation), but from the peculiar cream-coloured pottery made there and now well known in London shops.

1615.—"I said I had receued suffition at his highnes hands in havinge the good hap to see the face of soe mightie a King as the King of **Shashma**; whereat he smiled."—*Cocks's Diary*, i. 4–5.

1617.—"Speeches are given out that the *cuboques* or Japon players (or whores) going from hence for Tushma to meete the Corean ambassadors, were set on by the way by a boate of **Xaxma** theeves, and kild all both men and women, for the money they had gotten at Firando."—*Ibid.* 256.

SEBUNDY, s. Hind. from Pers. *sihbandī* (*sih*, 'three'). The *rationale* of the word is obscure to us. [Platts says it means 'three-monthly or quarterly payment.' The *Madras Gloss.* less probably suggests Pers. *sipāhbandī* (see SEPOY), 'recruitment.'] It is applied to irregular native soldiery, a sort of militia, or imperfectly disciplined troops for revenue or police duties, &c. Certain local infantry regiments were formerly officially termed *Sebundy*. The last official appearance of the title that we can find is in application to "The *Sebundy* Corps of Sappers and Miners" employed at Darjeeling. This is in the E.I. Register down to July, 1869, after which the title does not appear in any official list. Of this corps, if we are not mistaken, the late Field-Marshal Lord Napier of Magdala was in charge, as Lieut. Robert Napier, about 1840. An application to Lord Napier, for corroboration of this reminiscence of many years back, drew from him the following interesting note:—

"Captain Gilmore of the (Bengal) Engineers was appointed to open the settlement of Darjeeling, and to raise two companies of **Sebundy** Sappers, in order to provide the necessary labour.

"He commenced the work, obtained some (Native) officers and N.C. officers from the old Bengal Sappers, and enlisted about half of each company.

"The first season found the little colony quite unprepared for the early commencement of the **Rains**. All the **Coolies**, who did not die, fled, and some of the Sappers deserted. Gilmore got sick; and in 1838 I was suddenly ordered from the extreme border of Bengal—Nyacollee—to relieve him for one month. I arrived somehow, with a pair of pitarahs as my sole possession.

"Just then, our relations with Nepaul became strained, and it was thought desirable to complete the **Sebundy** Sappers with men from the Border Hills unconnected with Nepaul—Garrows and similar tribes. Through the Political Officer the necessary number of men were enlisted and sent to me.

"When they arrived I found, instead of the 'fair recruits' announced, a number of most unfit men; some of them more or less crippled, or with defective sight. It seemed probable that, by the process known to us in India as *uddlee buddlee* (see BUDLEE), the original recruits had managed to insert substitutes during the journey! I was much embarrassed as to what I should do with them; but night was coming on, so I encamped them on the newly opened road, the only clear space amid the dense jungle on either side. To complete my difficulty it began to rain, and I pitied my poor recruits! During the night there was a storm—and in the morning, to my intense relief, they had all disappeared!

"In the expressive language of my sergeant, there was not a '*visage*' of the men left.

"The **Sebundies** were a local corps, designed to furnish a body of labourers fit for mountain-work. They were armed, and expected to fight if necessary. Their pay was 6rs. a month, instead of a Sepoy's 7½. The pensions of the Native officers were smaller than in the regular army, which was a ground of complaint with the Bengal Sappers, who never expected in accepting the new service that they would have lower pensions than those they enlisted for.

"I eventually completed the corps with Nepaulese, and, I think, left them in a satisfactory condition.

"I was for a long time their only sergeant-major. I supplied the Native officers and N.C. officers from India with a good pea-jacket each, out of my private means, and with a little gold-lace made them smart and happy.

"When I visited Darjeeling again in 1872, I found the remnant of my good Sapper officers living as pensioners, and waiting to give me an affectionate welcome.

* * * * *

"My month's acting appointment was turned into four years. I walked 30 miles to get to the place, lived much in hovels and temporary huts thrown up by my Hill-men, and derived more benefit from the climate than from my previous visit to England. I think I owe much practical teaching to the Hill-men, the Hills and the Climate. I learnt the worst the elements could do to me—very nearly—excepting earthquakes! And I think I was thus prepared for any hard work."

c. 1778.—"At Dacca I made acquaintance with my venerable friend John Cowe. He had served in the Navy so far back as the memorable siege of Havannah, was reduced when a lieutenant, at the end of the American War, went out in the Company's military service, and here I found him in command of a regiment of **Sebundees**, or native militia."—*Hon. R. Lindsay*, in *L. of the Lindsays*, iii. 161.

1785.—"The Board were pleased to direct that in order to supply the place of the **Sebundy** corps, four regiments of Sepoys be employed in securing the collection of the revenues."—In *Seton-Karr*, i. 92.

"One considerable charge upon the Nabob's country was for extraordinary **sibbendies**, sepoys and horsemen, who appear to us to be a very unnecessary incumbrance upon the revenue."—Append, to *Speech on Nab. of Arcot's Debts*, in *Burke's Works*, iv. 18, ed. 1852.

1796.—"The Collector at Midnapoor having reported the **Sebundy** Corps attached to that Collectorship, Sufficiently Trained in their Exercise; the Regular Sepoys who have been Employed on that Duty are to be withdrawn."—G. O. Feb. 23, in *Suppt.* to *Code of Military Regs.*, 1799, p. 145.

1803.—"The employment of these people therefore ... as **sebundy** is advantageous ... it lessens the number of idle and discontented at the time of general invasion and confusion."—*Wellington, Desp.* (ed. 1837), ii. 170.

1812.—"**Sebundy**, or provincial corps of native troops."—*Fifth Report*, 38.

1861.—"Sliding down Mount Tendong, the summit of which, with snow lying there, we crossed, the **Sebundy** Sappers were employed cutting a passage for the mules; this delayed our march exceedingly."—*Report of Capt. Impey, R.E.*, in *Gawler's Sikhim*, p. 95.

SEEDY, s. Hind. *sīdī*; Arab. *saiyid*, 'lord' (whence the *Cid* of Spanish romantic history), *saiyidī*, 'my lord'; and Mahr. *siddhī*. Properly an honorific name given in Western India to African Mahommedans, of whom many held high positions in the service of the kings of the Deccan. Of these at least one family has survived in princely position to our own day, viz. the Nawāb of Jangīra, near Bombay. The young heir to this principality, Siddhī Ahmad, after a minority of some years, was installed in the Government in Oct., 1883. But the proper application of the word in the ports and on the shipping of Western India is to negroes in general. [It "is a title still applied to holy men in Marocco and the Maghrib; on the East African coast it is assumed by negro and negroid Moslems, *e.g.* Sidi Mubarak Bombay; and 'Seedy boy' is the Anglo-Indian term for a Zanzibarman" (*Burton, Ar. Nights*, iv. 231).]

c. 1563.—"And among these was an Abyssinian (*Abexim*) called **Cide** Meriam, a man reckoned a great cavalier, and who entertained 500 horse at his own charges, and who greatly coveted the city of Daman to quarter himself in, or at the least the whole of its pergunnas (*parganas*—see PERGUNNAH) to devour."—*Couto*, VII. x. 8.

[c. 1610.—"The greatest insult that can be passed upon a man is to call him **Cisdy**—that is to say 'cook.'"—*Pyrard de Laval*, Hak. Soc. i. 173.]

1673.—"An *Hobsy* or African Coffery (they being preferred here to chief employments, which they enter on by the name of **Siddies**)."—*Fryer*, 147.

"He being from a *Hobsy Caphir* made a free Denizen ... (who only in this Nation arrive to great Preferment, being the Frizled Woolly-pated Blacks) under the known style of **Syddies**. ..."—*Ibid.* 168.

1679.—"The protection which the **Siddees** had given to Gingerah against the repeated attacks of Sevagi, as well as their frequent annoyance of their country, had been so much facilitated by their resort to Bombay, that Sevagi at length determined to compel the English Government to a stricter neutrality, by reprisals on their own port."—*Orme, Fragments*, 78.

1690.—"As he whose Title is *most Christian*, encouraged him who is its principal Adversary to invade the Rights of Christendom, so did Senor Padre *de Pandara*, the Principal Jesuite and in an adjacent Island to *Bombay*, invite the **Síddy** to exterminate all the Protestants there."—*Ovington*, 157.

1750-60.—"These (islands) were formerly in the hands of Angria and the **Siddies** or Moors."—*Grose*, i. 58.

1759.—"The Indian seas having been infested to an intolerable degree by pirates, the Mogul appointed the **Siddee**, who was chief of a colony of Coffrees (**Caffer**), to be his Admiral. It was a colony which, having been settled at Dundee-Rajapore, carried on a considerable trade there, and had likewise many vessels of force."—*Cambridge's Account of the War*, &c., p. 216.

1800.—"I asked him what he meant by a **Siddee**. He said a *hubshee*. This is the name by which the Abyssinians are distinguished in India."—*T. Munro*, in *Life*, i. 287.

1814.—"Among the attendants of the Cambay Nabob ... are several Abyssinian and Caffree slaves, called by way of courtesy **Seddees** or Master."—*Forbes, Or. Mem.* iii. 167; [2nd ed. ii. 225].

1832.—"I spoke of a **Sindhee**" (*Siddhee*) "or *Habshee*, which is the name for an Abyssinian in this country lingo."—*Mem. of Col. Mountain*, 121.

1885.—"The inhabitants of this singular tract (Soopah plateau in N. Canara) were in some parts Mahrattas, and in others of Canarese race, but there was a third and less numerous section, of pure African descent called **Sidhis** ... descendants of fugitive slaves from Portuguese settlements ... the same ebony coloured, large-limbed men as are still to be found on the African coast, with broad, good-humoured, grinning faces."—*Gordon S. Forbes, Wild Life in Canara*, &c., 32-33.

[1896.—
"We've shouted on seven-ounce nuggets,
We've starved on a **Seedee** boy's pay."
R. Kipling, The Seven Seas.]

SEERPAW, s. Pers. through Hind. *sar-ā-pā*—'cap-a-pie.' A complete suit, presented as a *Khilat* (**Killut**) or dress of honour, by the sovereign or his representative.

c. 1666.—"He ... commanded, there should be given to each of them an embroider'd Vest, a Turbant, and a Girdle of Silk Embroidery, which is that which they call **Ser-apah**, that is, an Habit from head to foot."—*Bernier*, E.T. 37; [ed. *Constable*, 147].

1673—"Sir George Oxendine ... had a *Collat* (**Killut**) or **Serpaw**, a Robe of Honour from Head to Foot, offered him from the Great Mogul."—*Fryer*, 87.

1680.—"Answer is returned that it hath not been accustomary for the Governours to go out to receive a bare *Phyrmaund* (**Firmaun**), except there come therewith a **Serpow** or a Tasheriffe (**Tashreef**)."—*Ft. St. Geo. Consn.* Dec. 2, in *N. & E.* No. iii. 40.

1715.—"We were met by Padre Stephanus, bringing two **Seerpaws**."—In *Wheeler*, ii. 245.

1727.—"As soon as he came, the King embraced him, and ordered a **serpaw** or a royal Suit to be put upon him."—*A. Hamilton*, i. 171 [ed. 1744].

1735.—"The last Nabob (Sadatulla) would very seldom suffer any but himself to send a **Seerpaw**; whereas in February last Sunta Sahib, Subder Ali Sahib, Jehare Khan and Imaum Sahib, had all of them taken upon them to send distinct **Seerpaws** to the President."—In *Wheeler*, iii. 140.

1759.—"Another deputation carried six costly **Seerpaws**; these are garments which are presented sometimes by superiors in token of protection, and sometimes by inferiors in token of homage."—*Orme*, i. 159.

SEETULPUTTY, s. A fine kind of mat made especially in Eastern Bengal, and used to sleep on in the cold weather. [They are made from the split stems of the *mukta pata, Phrynium dichotomum*, Roxb. (see *Watt, Econ. Dict.* vi. pt. i. 216 *seq.*).] Hind. *sītalpaṭṭī*, 'cold-slip.' Williamson's spelling and derivation (from an Arab. word impossibly used,) are quite erroneous.

1810.—"A very beautiful species of mat is made ... especially in the south-eastern districts ... from a kind of reedy grass. ... These are peculiarly slippery, whence they are designated '**seekul-putty**' (*i.e.* polished sheets). ... The principal uses of the '**seekul-putty**' are to be laid under the lower sheet of a bed, thereby to keep the body cool."—*Williamson, V. M.* ii. 41.

[1818.—"Another kind (of mat) the **shēētŭlŭpatēēs**, laid on beds and couches on account of their coolness, are sold from one roopee to five each."—*Ward, Hindoos*, i. 106.]

1879.—In *Fallon's Dicty.* we find the following Hindi riddle:—

*"Chīnī kā piyālā ṭūṭā, kóī joṛtā nahīn;
Mālī jī kā bāg lagā, koī toṛtā nahīn;
Sītal-pāṭī bichhī, koī sotā náhīn;
Rāj-bansī mūā, koī rotā nahīn."*

Which might be rendered:

"A china bowl that, broken, none can join;
A flowery field, whose blossoms none purloin;
A royal scion slain, and none shall weep;
A **sītalpaṭṭī** spread where none shall sleep."

The answer is an Egg; the Starry Sky; a Snake (*Rāj-bansī*, 'royal scion,' is a placatory name for a snake); and the Sea.

SEPOY, SEAPOY, s. In Anglo-Indian use a native soldier, disciplined and dressed in the European style. The word is Pers. *sipāhī*, from *sipāh*, 'soldiery, an army'; which J. Oppert traces to old Pers. *spāda*, 'a soldier' (*Le peuple et la Langue des Mèdes*, 1879, p. 24). But *Sbah* is a horseman in Armenian; and sound etymologists connect *sipāh* with *asp*, 'a horse'; [others with Skt. *padāti*, 'a foot-soldier']. The original word *sipāhī* occurs frequently in the poems of Amīr Khusrū (c. A.D. 1300), bearing always probably the sense of a 'horse-soldier,' for all the important part of an army then consisted of horsemen. See *spāhī* below.

The word *sepoy* occurs in Southern India before we had troops in Bengal; and it was probably adopted from Portuguese. We have found no English example in print older than 1750, but probably an older one exists. The India Office record of 1747 from Fort St. David's is the oldest notice we have found in extant MS. [But see below.]

c. 1300.—"Pride had inflated his brain with wind, which extinguished the light of his intellect, and a few **sipāhīs** from Hindustan, without any religion, had supported the credit of his authority."—*Amīr Khusrū*, in *Elliot*, iii. 536.

[1665.—"Souldier—**Suppya** and Haddee."—*Persian Gloss.* in *Sir T. Herbert*, ed. 1677, p. 99.]

1682.—"As soon as these letters were sent away, I went immediately to Ray Nundelall's to have y^e **Seapy**, or Nabob's horseman, consigned to me, with order to see y^e *Perwanna* put in execution; but having thought better of it, ye Ray desired me to have patience till tomorrow morning. He would then present me to the Nabob, whose commands to y^e **Seapy** and Bulchunds *Vekeel* would be more powerful and advantageous to me than his own."—*Hedges, Diary*, Hak. Soc. i. 55, *seq.* Here we see the word still retaining the sense of 'horseman' in India.

[1717.—"A Company of **Sepoys** with the colours."—*Yule*, in *ditto*, II. ccclix. On this Sir H. Yule notes: "This is an occurrence of the word **sepoy**, in its modern signification, 30 years earlier than any I had been able to find when publishing the A.-I. Gloss. I have one a year earlier, and expect now to find it earlier still."

[1733.—"You are next ... to make a complete survey ... of the number of fighting **Sepoys**. ..."—*Forrest, Bombay Letters*, ii. 55.]

1737.—"Elle com tota a força desponivel, que eram 1156 soldados pagos em que entraram 281 chegados na não Mercês, e 780 **sypaes** ou *lascarins* (**lascar**), recuperon o territorio."—*Bosquejo das Possessões Portuguezas no Oriente*, &c., *por Joaquim Pedro Celestino Soares*, Lisboa, 1851, p. 58.

1746.—"The Enemy, by the best Intelligence that could be got, and best Judgment that could be formed, had or would have on Shore next Morning, upwards of 3000 *Europeans*, with at least 500 *Coffrys*, and a number of **Cephoys** and Peons."—*Ext. of Diary*, &c., in App. to *A Letter to a Propr. of the E.I. Co.*, London, 1750, p. 94.

[1746.—Their strength on shore I compute 2000 Europeans **Seapiahs** and 300 Coffrees."—*Letter from Madras*, Oct. 9, in *Bengal Consultations. Ibid.* p. 600, we have **Seapies**.]

1747.—"At a Council of War held at Fort St. David the 25th December, 1747.

Present:—

Charles Floyer, Esq., Governor.

George Gibson	John Holland
John Crompton	John Rodolph de Gingens
William Brown	John Usgate

Robert Sanderson.

* * *

"It is further ordered that Captn. Crompton keep the Detachment under his Command at Cuddalore, in a readiness to march to the Choultry over against the Fort as soon as the Signal shall be made from the Place, and then upon his firing two Muskets, Boats shall be sent to bring them here, and to leave a serjeant at Cuddalore Who shall conduct his **Seapoys** to the Garden Guard, and the Serjeant shall have a Word by which He shall be received at the Garden."—*Original MS. Proceedings* (in the India Office).

The Council of Fort St. David write to Bombay, March 16th, "if they could not supply us with more than 300 Europeans, We should be glad of Five or Six Hundred of the best Northern People their way, as they are reported to be much better than ours, and not so liable to Desertion."

In Consn. May 30th they record the arrival of the ships Leven, Warwick, and Ilchester, Princess Augusta, "on the 28th inst., from Bombay, (bringing) us a General from that Presidency,[1] as entered No. 38, advising of having sent us by them sundry stores and a Reinforcement of Men, consisting of 70 European Soldiers, 200 *Topasses* (**Topaz**), and 100 well-trained **Seapoys**, all of which under the command of Capt. Thomas Andrews, a Good Officer... ."

And under July 13th. "... The Reinforcement of **Sepoys** having arrived from Tellicherry, which, with those that were sent from Bombay, making a formidable Body, besides what are still expected; and as there is far greater Dependance to be placed on those People than on our own **Peons** ... many of whom have a very weakly Appearance, Agreed, that a General Review be now had of them, that all such may be discharged, and only the Choicest of them continued in the Service."—*MS. Records in India Office.*

1752.—"... they quitted their entrenchments on the first day of March, 1752, and advanced in order of battle, taking possession of a rising ground on the right, on which they placed 50 Europeans; the front consisted of 1500 **Sipoys**, and one hundred and twenty or thirty French."—*Complete Hist. of the War in India*, 1761, pp. 9–10.

1758.—A Tabular Statement (*Mappa*) of the Indian troops, 20th Jan. of this year, shows "Corpo de **Sipaes**" with 1162 "**Sipaes** promptos."—*Bosquejo*, as above.

"A stout body of near 1000 **Sepoys** has been raised within these few days."—In *Long*, 134.

[1759.—"Boat rice extraordinary for the Gentoo **Seapois**. ..."—*Ibid.* 174.]

1763.—"The Indian natives and Moors, who are trained in the European manner, are called **Sepoys**."—*Orme*, i. 80.

1763.—"Major Carnac ... observes that your establishment is loaded with the expense of more Captains than need be, owing to the unnecessarily making it a point that they should be Captains who command the **Sepoy** Battalions, whereas such is the nature of **Sepoys** that it requires a peculiar genius and talent to be qualified for that service, and the Battalion should be given only to such who are so without

1 Not a general officer, but a letter from the body of the Council.

regard to rank."—*Court's Letter*. of March 9. In *Long*, 290.

1770.—"England has at present in India an establishment to the amount of 9800 European troops, and 54,000 **sipahis** well armed and disciplined."—*Raynal* (tr. 1777), i. 459.

1774.—"**Sipai** sono li soldati Indiani."—*Della Tomba*, 297.

1778.—"La porta del Ponente della città si custodiva dalli **sipais** soldati Indiani radunati da tutte le tribù, e religioni."—*Fra Paolino, Viaggio*, 4.

1780.—"Next morning the **sepoy** came to see me. ... I told him that I owed him my life. ... He then told me that he was not very rich himself, as his pay was only a pagoda and a half a month—and at the same time drew out his purse and offered me a rupee. This generous behaviour, so different to what I had hitherto experienced, drew tears from my eyes, and I thanked him for his generosity, but I would not take his money."—*Hon. J. Lindsay's Imprisonment, Lives of Lindsays*, iii. 274.

1782.—"As to Europeans who run from their natural colours, and enter into the service of the country powers, I have heard one of the best officers the Company ever had ... say that he considered them no otherwise than as so many **Seapoys**; for acting under blacks they became mere blacks in spirit."—*Price, Some Observations*, 95–96.

1789.—

"There was not a captain, nor scarce a
 seapoy,
But a Prince would depose, or a Bramin
 destroy."

Letter of Simpkin the Second, &c., 8.

1803.—"Our troops behaved admirably; the **sepoys** astonished me."—*Wellington* ii. 384.

1827.—"He was betrothed to the daughter of a **Sipahee**, who served in the mud-fort which they saw at a distance rising above the jungle."—*Sir W. Scott, The Surgeon's Daughter*, ch. xiii.

1836.—"The native army of the E. I. Company. ... Their formation took place in 1757. They are usually called **sepoys**, and are light and short."—In *R. Phillips, A Million of Facts*, 718.

1881.—"As early as A.D. 1592 the chief of Sind had 200 natives dressed and armed like Europeans: these were the first '**sepoys**.'"—*Burton's Camoens, A Commentary*, ii. 445.

The French write *cipaye* or *cipai:*

1759.—"De quinze mille **Cipayes** dont l'armée est censée composée, j'en compte à peu près huit cens sur la route de Pondichery, chargé de sucre et de poivre et autres marchandises, quant aux Coulis, ils sont tous employés pour le même objet."—*Letter of Lally to the Governor of Pondicherry*, in *Cambridge's Account*, p. 150.

c. 1835–38.—

"Il ne criant ni Kriss ni zagaies,
Il regarde l'homme sans fuir,
Et rit des balles des **cipayes**
Qui rebondissent sur son cuir."

Th. Gautier, L'Hippopotame.

Since the conquest of Algeria the same word is common in France under another form, viz., *spāhī*. But the *Spāhī* is totally different from the *sepoy*, and is in fact an irregular horseman. With the Turks, from whom the word is taken, the *spāhī* was always a horseman.

1554.—"Aderant magnis muneribus praepositi multi, aderant praetoriani equites omnes **Sphai**, Garipigi, Ulufagi, Gianizarorum magnus numerus, sed nullus in tanto conventu nobilis nisi ex suis virtutibus et fortibus factis."—*Busbeq, Epistolae*, i. 99.

[1562.—"The **Spachi**, and other orders of horsemen."—*J. Shute, Two Comm.* (Tr.) fol. 53 ro. *Stanf. Dict.* where many early instances of the word will be found.]

1672.—"Mille ou quinze cents **Spahiz**, tous bien équippés et bien montés ... terminoient toute ceste longue, magnifique, et pompeuse cavalcade."—*Journal d'Ant. Galland*, i. 142.

1675.—"The other officers are the *sardar* (**Sirdar**), who commands the Janizaries ... the **Spahi** *Aga*, who commands the **Spahies** or *Turkish* Horse."—*Wheeler's Journal*, 348.

[1686.—"I being providentially got over the river before the **Spie** employed by them could give them intelligence."—*Hedges, Diary*, Hak. Soc. i. 229.]

1738.—"The Arab and other inhabitants are obliged, either by long custom ... or from fear and compulsion, to give the **Spahees** and their company the *mounah* ... which is such a sufficient quantity of provision for ourselves, together with straw and barley for our mules and horses."—*Shaw's Travels in Barbary*, ed. 1757, p. xii.

1786.—"Bajazet had two years to collect his forces ... we may discriminate the janizaries ... a national cavalry, the **Spahis** of modern times."—*Gibbon*, ch. lxv.

1877.—"The regular cavalry was also originally composed of tribute children. ... The **sipahis** acquired the same preeminence among the cavalry which the janissaries held among the infantry, and their seditious conduct rendered them much sooner troublesome to the Government."—*Finlay, H. of Greece*, ed. 1877, v. 37.

SERAI, **SERYE**, s. This word is used to represent two Oriental words entirely different.

a. Hind. from Pers. *sarā, sarāī*. This means originally an edifice, a palace. It was especially used by the Tartars when they began to build palaces. Hence *Sarāī*, the name of more than one royal residence of the Mongol Khāns upon the Volga, the *Sarra* of Chaucer. The Russians retained the word from their Tartar oppressors, but in their language *sarai* has been degraded to mean 'a shed.' The word, as applied to the Palace of the Grand Turk, became, in the language of the Levantine Franks, *serail* and *serraglio*. In this form, as P. della Valle lucidly explains below, the "striving after meaning" connected the word with Ital. *serrato*, 'shut up'; and with a word *serraglio* perhaps previously existing in Italian in that connection. [*Seraglio*, according to Prof. Skeat (*Concise Dict.* s.v.) is "formed with suffix *-aglio* (L. *-aculum*) from Late Lat. *serare*, 'to bar, shut in'—Lat. *sera*, a 'bar, bolt'; Lat. *serere*, 'to join together.'] It is this association that has attached the meaning of 'women's apartments' to the word. *Sarai* has no such specific sense.

But the usual modern meaning in Persia, and the only one in India, is that of a building for the accommodation of travellers with their pack-animals; consisting of an enclosed yard with chambers round it.

Recurring to the Italian use, we have seen in Italy the advertisement of a travelling menagerie as *Serraglio di Belve*. A friend tells us of an old Scotchman whose ideas must have run in this groove, for he used to talk of 'a *Serragle* of blackguards.' In the Diary in England of Annibale Litolfi of Mantua the writer says: "On entering the tower there is a *Serraglio* in which, from grandeur, they keep lions and tigers and cat-lions." (See *Rawdon Brown's Calendar of Papers in Archives of Venice*, vol. vi. pt. iii. 1557–8. App.) [The *Stanf. Dict.* quotes Evelyn as using the word of a place where persons are confined: 1644. "I passed by the Piazza Judea, where their *seraglio* begins" (*Diary*, ed. 1872, i. 142).]

c. 1584.—"At **Saraium** Turcis palatium principis est, vel aliud amplum aedificium, non a *Czar*[1] voce Tatarica, quae regem significat, dictum; vnde Reineccius **Saragliam** Turcis vocari putet, ut *regiam*. Nam aliae quoque domus, extra Sultani regiam, nomen hoc ferunt ... vt ampla Turcorum hospitia, sive diversoria publica, quae vulgo *Caravasarias* (**Caravanseray**) nostri vocant."—*Leunclavius*, ed. 1650, p. 403.

1609.—"... by it the great **Suray**, besides which are diuers others, both in the city and suburbs, wherein diuers neate lodgings are to be let, with doores, lockes, and keys to each."—*W. Finch*, in *Purchas*, i. 434.

1614.—"This term **serraglio**, so much used among us in speaking of the Grand Turk's dwelling ... has been corrupted into that form from the word **serai**, which in their language signifies properly 'a palace.' ... But since this word *serai* resembles *serraio*, as a Venetian would call it, or *seraglio* as we say, and seeing that the palace of the Turk is (*serrato* or) shut up all round by a strong wall, and also because the women and a great part of the courtiers dwell in it barred up and shut in, so it may perchance have seemed to some to have deserved such a name. And thus the real term **serai** has been converted into **serraglio**."—*P. della Valle*, i. 36.

1615.—"Onely from one dayes Journey to another the *Sophie* hath caused to bee erected certaine kind of great harbours, or huge lodgings (like hamlets) called *caravan-***sara**, or **surroyes**, for the benefite of *Caravanes*. ..."—*De Montfart*, 8.

1616.—"In this kingdome there are no Innes to entertaine strangers, only in great Townes and Cities are faire Houses built for their receit, which they call **Sarray**, not inhabited, where any Passenger may haue roome freely, but must bring with him his Bedding, his Cooke, and other necessaries."—*Terry*, in *Purchas*, ii. 1475.

1638.—"Which being done we departed from our **Serray** (or Inne)."—*W. Bruton*, in *Hakl.* v. 49.

1648.—"A great **sary** or place for housing travelling folk."—*Van Twist*, 17.

[1754.—"... one of the Sciddees (**seedy**) officers with a party of men were lodged in the **Sorroy**. ..."—*Forrest, Bombay Letters*, i. 307.]

1782.—"The stationary tenants of the **Serauee**, many of them women, and some of them very pretty, approach the traveller on his entrance, and in alluring language describe to him the varied excellencies of their several lodgings."—*Forster, Journey*, ed. 1808, i. 86.

1825.—"The whole number of lodgers in and about the **serai**, probably did not fall short of 500 persons. What an admirable scene for an Eastern romance would such an inn as this afford!"—*Heber*, ed. 1844, ii. 122.

1850.—"He will find that, if we omit only three names in the long line of the Delhi Emperors, the comfort and happiness of the people were never contemplated by them;

1 On another B.M. copy of an earlier edition than that quoted, and which belonged to Jos. Scaliger, there is here a note in his autograph: "Id est *Caesar*, non est vox Tatarica, sed Viudica seu Illyrica, ex Latino detorta."

and with the exception of a few **saráís** and bridges,—and these only on roads traversed by the imperial camps—he will see nothing in which purely selfish considerations did not prevail."—*Sir H. M. Elliot,* Original Preface to *Historians of India, Elliot,* I. xxiii.

b. A long-necked earthenware (or metal) flagon for water; a goglet. This is Ar.—P. *ṣurāḥī*. [This is the *ḳorak* or *kulleh* of Egypt, of which Lane (*Mod. Egypt.* ed. 1871, i. 186 *seq.*) gives an account with illustrations.]

c. 1666.—"... my *Navab* having vouchsafed me a very particular favour, which is, that he hath appointed to give me every day a new loaf of his house, and a **Souray** of the water of *Ganges* ... **Souray** is that Tin-flagon full of water, which the Servant that marcheth on foot before the Gentleman on horseback, carrieth in his hand, wrapt up in a sleeve of red cloath."—*Bernier,* E.T. 114; [ed. *Constable,* 356].

1808.—"We had some bread and butter, two **surahees** of water, and a bottle of brandy."—*Elphinstone,* in *Life,* i. 183.

[1880.—"The best known is the gilt silver work of Cashmere, which is almost confined to the production of the water-vessels or **sarais**, copied from the clay goblets in use throughout the northern parts of the Panjab."—*Birdwood, Indust. Arts of India,* 149.]

SERANG, s. A native boatswain, or chief of a **lascar** crew; the skipper of a small native vessel. The word is Pers. *sarhang,* 'a commander or overseer.' In modern Persia it seems to be used for a colonel (see *Wills,* 80).

1599.—"... there set sail two Portuguese vessels which were come to Amacao (**Macao**) from the City of Goa, as occurs every year. They are commanded by Captains, with Pilots, quartermasters, clerks, and other officers, who are Portuguese; but manned by sailors who are Arabs, Turks, Indians, and Bengalis, who serve for so much a month, and provide themselves under the direction and command of a chief of their own whom they call the **Saranghi**, who also belongs to one of these nations, whom they understand, and recognise and obey, carrying out the orders that the Portuguese Captain, Master, or Pilot may give to the said **Saranghi**."—*Carletti, Viaggi,* ii. 206.

1690.—"Indus quem de hoc Ludo consului fuit scriba satis peritus ab officio in nave suâ dictus *le* **saràng**, Anglicè **Boatswain** seú **Boson**."—*Hyde, De Ludis Orientt.* in *Syntagma,* ii. 264.

[1822.—"... the ghaut **syrangs** (a class of men equal to the kidnappers of Holland and the crimps of England). ..."—*Wallace, Fifteen Years in India,* 256.]

SETT, s. Properly Hind. *seth,* which according to Wilson is the same word with the Chetti or *Sheṭṭi* of the Malabar Coast, the different forms being all from Skt. *śreshṭha,* 'best, or chief,' *śresṭhi,* 'the chief of a corporation, a merchant or banker.' C. P. Brown entirely denies the identity of the S. Indian *sheṭṭi* with the Skt. word.

1740.—"The **Sets** being all present at the Board inform us that last year they dissented to the employment of Fillick Chund (&c.), they being of a different caste; and consequently they could not do business with them."—In *Long,* p. 9.

1757.—"To the **Seats** Mootabray and Roopchund the Government of Chandunagore was indebted a million and a half Rupees."—*Orme,* ii. 138 of reprint (Bk. viii.).

1770.—"As soon as an European arrived the Gentoos, who know mankind better than is commonly supposed, study his character ... and lend or procure him money upon bottomry, or at interest. This interest, which is usually 9 per cent. at this is higher when he is under a necessity of borrowing of the **Cheyks.**

"These **Cheyks** are a powerful family of Indians, who have, time immemorial, inhabited the banks of the Ganges. Their riches have long ago procured them the management of the bank belonging to the Court. ..."—*Raynal,* tr. 1777, i. 427. Note that by *Cheyks* the Abbé means **Setts.**

[1883.—"... from the Himalayas to Cape Comorin a security endorsed by the Mathura **Seth** is as readily convertible into cash as a Bank of England Note in London or Paris."—*F. S. Growse, Mathura,* 14.]

***SETTLEMENT**, s. In the Land Revenue system of India, an estate or district is said to be *settled,* when instead of taking a quota of the year's produce the Government has agreed with the cultivators, individually or in community, for a fixed sum to be paid at several periods of the year, and not liable to enhancement during the term of years for which the agreement or *settlement* is made. The operation of arranging the terms of such an agreement, often involving tedious and complicated considerations and enquiries, is known as the process of *settlement.* A *Permanent Settlement* is that in which the annual payment is fixed in perpetuity. This was introduced in Bengal by Lord Cornwallis in 1793, and does not exist except within that great Province, [and a few districts in the Benares division of the N.W.P., and in Madras.]

SHAHBASH! interj. 'Well done!' 'Bravo!' Pers. *Shāh-bāsh*. 'Rex fias!'[1] [Rather *Shād-bāsh*, 'Be joyful.']

c. 1610.—"Le Roy fit rencontre de moy ... me disant vn mot qui est commun en toute l'Inde, à savoir **Sabatz**, qui veut dire grand mercy, et sert aussi à louer vn homme pour quelque chose qu'il a bien fait."—*Pyrard de Laval*, i. 224.

[1843.—"I was awakened at night from a sound sleep by the repeated **savāshes**! *wāh! wāhs!* from the residence of the thanndar."—*Davidson, Travels in Upper India*, i. 209.]

SHABUNDER, s. Pers. *Shāhbandar*, lit. 'King of the Haven,' Harbour-Master. This was the title of an officer at native ports all over the Indian seas, who was the chief authority with whom foreign traders and ship-masters had to transact. He was often also head of the Customs. Hence the name is of prominent and frequent occurrence in the old narratives. Portuguese authors generally write the word *Xabander*; ours *Shabunder* or *Sabundar*. The title is not obsolete, though it does not now exist in India; the quotation from Lane shows its recent existence in Cairo, [and the Persians still call their Consuls *Shāh-bandar* (*Burton, Ar. Nights*, iii. 158)]. In the marine Malay States the *Shābandar* was, and probably is, an important officer of State. The passages from Lane and from Tavernier show that the title was not confined to seaports. At Aleppo Thevenot (1663) calls the corresponding official, perhaps by a mistake, '*Scheik* **Bandar**' (*Voyages*, iii. 121). [This is the office which King Mihrjān conferred upon Sindbad the Seaman, when he made him "his agent for the port and registrar of all ships that entered the harbour" (*Burton*, iv. 351)].

c. 1350.—"The chief of all the Musulmans in this city is Mahommed **Shāhbandar**."—*Ibn Batuta*, iv. 100.

c. 1539.—"This King (of the Batas) understanding that I had brought him a Letter and a Present from the Captain of *Malaca*, caused me to be entertained by the **Xabandar**, who is he that with absolute Power governs all the affairs of the Army."—*Pinto* (orig. cap. xv.), in *Cogan's Transl.* p. 18.

1552.—"And he who most insisted on this was a Moor, **Xabandar** of the Guzarates" (at Malacca).—*Caslanheda*, ii. 359.

1553.—"A Moorish lord called Sabayo (**Sabaio**) ... as soon as he knew that our ships belonged to the people of these parts of Christendom, desiring to have confirmation on the matter, sent for a certain Polish Jew who was in his service as **Shabandar** (*Xabandar*), and asked him if he knew of what nation were the people who came in these ships. ..."—*Barros*, I. iv. 11.

1561.—"... a boatman, who, however, called himself **Xabandar**."—*Correa, Lendas*, ii. 80.

1599.—"The **Sabandar** tooke off my Hat, and put a Roll of white linnen about my head. ..."—*J. Davis*, in *Purchas*, i. 12.

1606.—"Then came the **Sabendor** with light, and brought the Generall to his house."—*Middleton's Voyage*, E. (4).

1610.—"The **Sabander** and the Governor of *Mancock* (a place scituated by the River). ..."—*Peter Williamson Floris*, in *Purchas*, i. 322.

[1615.—"The opinion of the **Sabindour** shall be taken."—*Foster, Letters*, iv. 79.]

c. 1650.—"Coming to Golconda, I found that the person whom I had left in trust with my chamber was dead: but that which I observ'd most remarkable, was that I found the door seal'd with two Seals, one being the Cadi's or chief Justice's, the other the **Sha-Bander's** or Provost of the Merchants."—*Tavernier*, E.T. Pt. ii. 136; [ed. *Ball*, ii. 70].

1673.—"The **Shawbunder** has his Grandeur too, as well as receipt of Custom, for which he pays the King yearly 22,000 *Thomands*."—*Fryer*, 222.

1688.—"When we arrived at Achin, I was carried before the **Shabander**, the chief Magistrate of the City. ..."—*Dampier*, i. 502.

1711.—"The Duties the Honourable Company require to be paid here on Goods are not above one fifth Part of what is paid to the **Shabander** or Custom-Master."—*Lockyer*, 223.

1726.—Valentyn, v. 313, gives a list of the **Sjahbandars** of Malakka from 1641 to 1725. They are names of Dutchmen.

1759.—"I have received a long letter from the Shahzada, in which he complains that you have begun to carry on a large trade in salt, and betel nut, and refuse to pay the duties on those articles ... which practice, if continued, will oblige him to throw up his post of **Shahbunder** Droga (**Daroga**)."—*W. Hastings* to the Chief at Dacca, in *Van Sittart*, i. 5.

1768.—"... two or three days after my arrival (at Batavia), the landlord of the hotel where I lodged told me he had been ordered by the **shebandar** to let me know that my carriage, as well as others, must stop, if I should meet the Governor, or any of the council; but I desired him to acquaint the **shebandar** that I could not

1 "At pueri ludentes, *Rex eris*, aiunt,
Si recte facies."—*Hor. Ep.* I. i.

consent to perform any such ceremony."—*Capt. Carteret*, quoted by transl. of *Stavorinus*, i. 281.

1795.—"The descendant of a Portuguese family, named Jaunsee, whose origin was very low ... was invested with the important office of **Shawbunder**, or intendant of the port, and receiver of the port customs."—*Symes*, p. 160.

1837.—"The Seyd Mohammad El Mahroockee, the **Shahbendar** (chief of the Merchants of Cairo) hearing of this event, suborned a common fellah. ..."—*Lane's Mod. Egyptians*, ed. 1837, i. 157.

SHADE (TABLE-SHADE, WALL-SHADE), s. A glass guard to protect a candle or simple oil-lamp from the wind. The oldest form, in use at the beginning of the last century, was a tall glass cylinder which stood on the table, the candlestick and candle being placed bodily within in. In later days the universal form has been that of an inverted dome fitting into the candlestick, which has an annular socket to receive it. The *wall-shade* is a bracket attached to the wall, bearing a candle or cocoa-nut oil lamp, protected by such a shade. In the wine-drinking days of the earlier part of last century it was sometimes the subject of a challenge, or forfeit, for a man to empty a wall-shade filled with claret. The second quotation below gives a notable description of a captain's outfit when taking the field in the 18th century.

1780.—"Borrowed last Month by a Person or Persons unknown, out of a private Gentleman's House near the Esplanade, a very elegant Pair of Candle **Shades**. Whoever will return the same will receive a reward of 40 *Sicca Rupees*.—N.B. The Shades have private marks."—*Hicky's Bengal Gazette*, April 8.

1789.—"His tent is furnished with a good large bed, mattress, pillow, &c., a few camp-stools or chairs, a folding table, a pair of **shades** for his candles, six or seven trunks with table equipage, his stock of linen (at least 24 shirts); some dozens of wine, brandy, and gin; tea, sugar, and biscuit; and a hamper of live poultry and his milchgoat."—*Munro's Narrative*, 186.

1817.—"I am now finishing this letter by candle-light, with the help of a handkerchief tied over the **shade**."—*T. Munro*, in *Life*, i. 511.

[1838.—"We brought carpets, and chandeliers, and **wall shades** (the great staple commodity of Indian furniture), from Calcutta. ..."—*Miss Eden, Up the Country*, 2nd ed. i. 182.]

SHAITAN, Ar. 'The Evil One; Saṭan.' *Shaitān kā bhāī*, 'Brother of the Arch-Enemy,' was a title given to Sir C. Napier by the Amīrs of Sind and their followers. He was not the first great English soldier to whom this title had been applied in the East. In the romance of *Cœur de Lion*, when Richard entertains a deputation of Saracens by serving at table the head of one of their brethren, we are told:

"Every man sat stylle and pokyd othir;
They saide: 'This is the *Develys brothir*,
That sles our men, and thus hem eetes ..."

[c. 1630.—"But a Mountebank or Impostor is nick-named **Shitan**. Tabib, *i.e.* the Devil's Chirurgion."—*Sir T. Herbert*, ed. 1677, p. 304.

1753.—"God preserve me from the **Scheithan** Alragim."—*Hanway*, iii. 90.]

1863.—"Not many years ago, an eccentric gentleman wrote from Sikkim to the Secretary of the Asiatic Society in Calcutta, stating that, on the snows of the mountains there were found certain mysterious foot-steps, *more than* 30 *or* 40 *paces asunder*, which the natives alleged to be **Shaitan's**. The writer at the same time offered, if Government would give him leave of absence for a certain period, etc., to go and trace the author of these mysterious vestiges, and thus this strange creature would be discovered *without any expense to Government*. The notion of catching **Shaitan** *without any expense to Government* was a sublime piece of Anglo-Indian tact, but the offer was not accepted."—*Sir H. Yule, Notes to Friar Jordanus*, 37.

***SHAMAN, SHAMANISM**, s. These terms are applied in modern times to superstitions of the kind that connects itself with exorcism and "devil-dancing" as their most prominent characteristic, and which are found to prevail with wonderful identity of circumstance among non-Caucasian races over parts of the earth most remote from one another; not only among the vast variety of Indo-Chinese tribes, but among the Dravidian tribes of India, the Veddahs of Ceylon, the races of Siberia, and the red nations of N. and S. America. "Hinduism has assimilated these 'prior superstitions of the sons of Tur,' as Mr. Hodgson calls them, in the form of Tantrika mysteries, whilst, in the wild performance of the Dancing Dervishes at Constantinople, we see, perhaps, again, the infection of Turanian blood breaking out from the very heart of Mussulman orthodoxy" (see *Notes to Marco Polo*, Bk. II. ch. 50). The characteristics of Shamanism is the existence of certain sooth-sayers or medicine-men, who profess a special art of dealing with the mischievous spirits who are supposed to produce illness and other calamities, and who invoke these spirits and ascertain the means of appeasing them, in trance produced by fantastic ceremonies and convulsive dancings.

The immediate origin of the term is the title of the spirit-conjuror in the Tunguz language, which is *shaman*, in that of the Manchus becoming *saman*, pl. *samasa*. But then in Chinese *Sha-măn* or *Shi-măn* is used for a Buddhist ascetic, and this would seem to be taken from the Skt. *śramana*, Pali *samana*. Whether the Tanguz word is in any way connected with this or adopted from it, is a doubtful question. W. Schott, who has treated the matter elaborately (*Über den Doppelsinn des Wortes* Schamane *und über den tungusichen* Schamanen-*Cultus am Hofe der Mandju Kaisern*, Berlin Akad. 1842), finds it difficult to suppose any connection. We, however, give a few quotations relating to the two words in one series. In the first two the reference is undoubtedly to Buddhist ascetics.

c. B.C. 320.—"*Τοὺς δὲ Σαρμάνας, τοὺς μὲν ἐντιμοτάτους Ὑλοβίους φησὶν ὀνομάζεσθαι, ζῶντας ἐν ταῖς ὕλαις ἀπὸ φύλλων καὶ καρπῶν ἀγρίων, ἐσθῆτας δ' ἔχειν ἀπὸ φλοιῶν δενδρείων, ἀφροδισίων χωρὶς καὶ οἴνου.*"—From *Megasthenes*, in *Strabo*, xv.

c. 712.—"All the **Samanís** assembled and sent a message to Bajhrá, saying, "We are *násik* devotees. Our religion is one of peace and quiet, and fighting and slaying is prohibited, as well as all kinds of shedding of blood."—*Chach Náma*, in *Elliot*, i. 158.

1829.—"*Kami* is the Mongol name of the spirit-conjuror or sorcerer, who before the introduction of Buddhism exercised among the Mongols the office of Sacrificer and Priest, as he still does among the Tunguzes, Manjus, and other Asiatic tribes. ... In Europe they are known by the Tunguz name **schaman**; among the Manjus as **saman**, and among the Tibetans as *Hlaba*. The Mongols now call them with contempt and abhorrence *Böh* or *Böghe*, *i.e.* 'Sorcerer,' 'Wizard,' and the women who give themselves to the like fooleries *Udugun*."—*I. J. Schmidt, Notes to Sanang Setzen*, p. 416.

1871.—"Among Siberian tribes, the **shamans** select children liable to convulsions as suitable to be brought up to the profession, which is apt to become hereditary with the epileptic tendencies it belongs to."—*Tylor, Primitive Culture*, ii. 121.

SHAMPOO, v. To knead and press the muscles with the view of relieving fatigue, &c. The word has now long been familiarly used in England. The Hind. verb is *chāmpnā*, from the imperative of which, *chāmpō*, this is most probably a corruption, as in the case of **Bunow**, **Puckerow**, &c. The process is described, though not named, by Terry, in 1616: "Taking thus their ease, they often call their Barbers, who tenderly gripe and smite their Armes and other parts of their bodies instead of exercise, to stirre the bloud. It is pleasing wantonnesse, and much valued in these hot climes." (In *Purchas*, ii. 1475). The process was familiar to the Romans under the Empire, whose slaves employed in this way were styled *tractator* and *tractatrix*. [Perhaps the earliest reference to the practice is in Strabo (*McCrindle, Ancient India*, 72).] But with the ancients it seems to have been allied to vice, for which there is no ground that we know in the Indian custom.

1748.—"**Shampooing** is an operation not known in Europe, and is peculiar to the Chinese, which I had once the curiosity to go through, and for which I paid but a trifle. However, had I not seen several China merchants **shampooed** before me, I should have been apprehensive of danger, even at the sight of all the different instruments. ..." (The account is good, but too long for extract.)—*A Voyage to the E. Indies in* 1747 *and* 1748. London, 1762, p. 226.

1750–60.—"The practice of **champing**, which by the best intelligence I could gather is derived from the Chinese, may not be unworthy particularizing, as it is little known to the modern Europeans. ..."—*Grose*, i. 113. This writer quotes *Martial*, iii. Ep. 82, and *Seneca*, Epist. 66, to show that the practice was known in ancient Rome.

1800.—"The Sultan generally rose at break of day: after being **champoed**, and rubbed, he washed himself, and read the Koran for an hour."—*Beatson, War with Tippoo*, p. 159.

[1810.—"**Shampoeing** may be compared to a gentle kneading of the whole person, and is the same operation described by the voyagers to the Southern and Pacific ocean."—*Wilks, Hist. Sketches*, Madras reprint, i. 276.]

'Then whilst they fanned the children, or **champooed** them if they were restless, they used to tell stories, some of which dealt of marvels as great as those recorded in the 1001 Nights."—*Mrs. Sherwood, Autobiog.* 410.

"That considerable relief is obtained from **shampoing**, cannot be doubted; I have repeatedly been restored surprisingly from severe fatigue. ..."—*Williamson, V. M.* ii. 198.

1813.—"There is sometimes a voluptuousness in the climate of India, a stillness in nature, an indescribable softness, which soothes the mind, and gives it up to the most delightful sensations: independent of the effects of opium, **champoing**, and other luxuries indulged in by oriental sensualists.'—*Forbes, Or. Mem.* i. 35; [2nd ed. i. 25.]

SHASTER, s. The Law books or Sacred Writings of the Hindus. From Skt. *śāstra*, 'a rule,' a religious code, a scientific treatise.

1612.—"... They have many books in their Latin. ... Six of these they call **Xastra**, which are the bodies; eighteen which they call *Purána* (**Poorana**), which are the limbs."—*Couto*, V. vi. 3.

1630.—"... The Banians deliver that this book, by them called the **Shaster**, or the Book of their written word, consisted of these three tracts."—*Lord's Display*, ch. viii.

1651.—In *Rogerius*, the word is everywhere misprinted **Iastra**.

1717.—"The six **Sastrangól** contain all the Points and different Ceremonies in Worship. ..."—*Phillips's Account*, 40.

1765.—"... at the capture of *Calcutta*, A.D. 1756, I lost many curious *Gentoo* manuscripts, and among them two very correct and valuable copies of the *Gentoo* **Shastah**."—*J. Z. Holwell, Interesting Hist. Events*, &c., 2d ed., 1766, i. 3.

1770.—"The **Shastah** is looked upon by some as a commentary on the *vedam*, and by others as an original work."—*Raynal* (tr 1777), i. 50.

1776.—"The occupation of the Bramin should be to read the *Beids*, and other **Shasters**."—*Halhed, Gentoo Code*, 39.

[**SHASTREE**, s. Hind. *śāstrī* (see SHASTER). A man of learning, one who teaches any branch of Hindu learning, such as law.

[1824.—"Gungadhur **Shastree**, the minister of the Baroda state, ... was murdered by Trimbuckjee under circumstances which left no doubt that the deed was perpetrated with the knowledge of Bajerow."—*Malcolm, Central India*, 2nd ed. i. 307.]

***SHAWL**, s. Pers. and Hind. *shāl*, also *doshāla*, 'a pair of shawls.' The Persian word is perhaps of Indian origin, from Skt. *śavala*, 'variegated.' Sir George Birdwood tells us that he has found among the old India records "Carmania **shells**" and "Carmania **shawools**," meaning apparently *Kermān shawls*. He gives no dates unfortunately. [In a book of 1685 he finds "**Shawles** Carmania" and "Carmania Wooll"; in one of 1704, "**Chawools**" (*Report on Old Records*, 27, 40). Carmania goats are mentioned in a letter in *Forrest, Bombay Letters*, i. 140.] In Meninski (published in 1680) *shāl* is defined in a way that shows the humble sense of the word originally:

"Panni viliores qui partim albi, partim cineritii, partim nigri esse solent ex lana et pillis caprinis; hujusmodi pannum seu telam injiciunt humeris Dervisii ... instar stolae aut pallii." To this he adds, "Datur etiam sericea ejusmodi tela, fere instar nostri multitii, sive simplicis sive duplicati." For this the 2nd edition a century later substitutes: "*Shāl-i-Hindī*" (Indian shawl). "Tela *sericea* subtilissima ex India adferri solita."

c. 1590.—"In former times **shawls** were often brought from Kashmír. People folded them in four folds, and wore them for a very long time. ... His Majesty encourages in every possible way the (*shāl-bāfī*) manufacture of **shawls** in Kashmír. In Lahór also there are more than 1000 workshops."—*Āīn* i. 92. [Also see ed. *Jarrett*, ii. 349, 355.]

c. 1665.—"Ils mettent sur eux a toute saison, lorsqu'ils sortent, une **Chal**, qui est une maniere de toilette d'une laine très-fine qui se fait a Cachmir. Ces **Chals** ont environ deux aunes (the old French *aune*, nearly 47 inches English) de long sur une de large. On les achete vingt-cinq ou trente écus si elles sont fines. Il y en a même qui coûtent cinquante écus, mais ce sont les trés-fines."—*Thevenot*, v. 110.

c. 1666.—"Ces **chales** sont certaines pièces d'étoffe d'une aulne et demie de long, et d'une de large ou environ, qui sont brodées aux deux bouts d'une espèce de broderie, faite au métier, d'un pied ou environ de large. ... J'en ai vu de ceux que les *Omrahs* font faire exprès, qui coutoient jusqu'à cent cinquante Roupies; des autres qui sont de cette laine du pays, je n'en al pas vu qui passaient 50 Roupies."—*Bernier*, ii. 280–281; [ed. *Constable*, 402].

1717.—"... Con tutto ciò preziosissime nobilissime e senza comparazione magnifiche sono le tele che si chiamano **Scial**, si nella lingua Hindustana, come ancora nella lingua Persiana. Tali **Scial** altro non sono, che alcuni manti, che si posano sulla testa, e facendo da man destra, e da man sinistra scendere le due metà, con queste si cinge. ..."—*MS. Narrative of Padre Ip. Desideri.*

[1662.—"Another rich Skarf, which they call **schal**, made of a very fine stuff."—*J. Davies, Ambassador's Trav.*, Bk. vi. 235, *Stanf. Dict.*]

1727.—"When they go abroad they wear a **Shawl** folded up, or a piece of White Cotton Cloth lying loose on the Top of their Heads."—*A. Hamilton*, ii. 50; [**Shaul** in ed. 1744, ii. 49].

c. 1760.—"Some **Shawls** are manufactured

there. ... Those coming from the province of Cachemire on the borders of Tartary, being made of a peculiar kind of silky hair, that produces from the loom a cloth beautifully bordered at both ends, with a narrow flowered selvage, about two yards and a half long, and a yard and a half wide ... and according to the price, which is from ten pounds and upwards to fifteen shillings, join, to exquisite fineness, a substance that renders them extremely warm, and so pliant that the fine ones are easily drawn through a common ring on the finger."—*Grose*, i. 118.

1781.—Sonnerat writes **challes**. He says: "Ces étoffes (faites avec la laine des moutons de Tibet) surpassent nos plus belles soieries en finesse."—*Voyage*, i. 52.

It seems from these extracts that the large and costly shawl, woven in figures over its whole surface, is a modern article. The old shawl, we see, was from 6 to 8 feet long, by about half that breadth; and it was most commonly white, with only a *border* of figured weaving at each end. In fact what is now called a Rampoor Chudder when made with figured ends is probably the best representation of the old shawl.

SHEEAH, SHIA, s. Arab. *shīʻa*, *i.e.* 'sect.' A follower (more properly the followers collectively) of the Mahommedan 'sect,' or sects rather, which specially venerate 'Ali, and regard the Imāms (see IMAUM), his descendants, as the true successors to the Caliphate. The Persians (since the accession of the 'Sophy' dynasty, (q.v.)) are *Shīʻas*, and a good many of the Moslems in India. The sects which have followed more or less secret doctrines, and the veneration of hereditary quasi-divine heads, such as the Karmathites and Ismaelites of Musulman history, and the modern Bohras and "Mulāḥis," may generally be regarded as *Shīʻa*. [See the elaborate article on the sect in *Hughes, Dict. of Islām*, 572 *seqq.*]

c. 1309.—"... dont encore il est ainsi, que tuit cil qui croient en la loy Haali dient que cil qui croient en la loy Mahommet sont mescréant; et aussi tuit cil qui croient en la loy Mahommet dient que tuit cil qui croient en la loy Haali sont mescréant."—*Joinville*, 252.

1553.—"Among the Moors have always been controversies ... which of the four first Caliphs was the most legitimate successor to the Caliphate. The Arabians favoured Bubac, Homar, and Otthoman, the Persians (*Parseos*) favoured Alle, and held the others for usurpers, and as holding it against the testament of Mahamed ... to the last this schism has endured between the Arabians and the Persians. The latter took the appellation **Xiá**, as much as to say 'Union of one Body,' and the Arabs called them in reproach *Raffady* [*Rāfiḍī*, a heretic (lit. 'deserter')], as much as to say 'People astray from the Path,' whilst they call themselves **Çuny** (see SUNNEE), which is the contrary."—*Barros*, II. x. 6.

1620.—"The Sonnite adherents of tradition, like the Arabs, the Turks, and an infinite number of others, accept the primacy of those who actually possess it. The Persians and their adherents who are called *Shias* (**Sciai**), *i.e.* 'Sectaries,' and are not ashamed of the name, believe in the primacy of those who have only claimed it (without possessing it), and obstinately contend that it belongs to the family of Alì only."—*P. della Valle*, ii. 75; [conf. Hak. Soc. i. 152].

1626.—"He is by Religion a Mahumetan, descended from Persian Ancestors, and retaineth their opinions, which differing in many points from the Turkes, are distinguished in their Sectes by tearmes of **Seaw** and *Sunnee*."—*Purchas, Pilgrimage*, 995.

1653.—"Les Persans et *Keselbaches* se disent **Schaì** ... si les Ottomans estoient **Schaìs**, ou de la Secte de Haly, les Persans se feroient *Sonnis* qui est la Secte des Ottomans."—*De la Boullaye-le-Gouz*, ed. 1657, 106.

1673.—"His Substitute here is a **Chias** Moor."—*Fryer*, 29.

1798.—"In contradistinction to the *Soonis*, who in their prayers cross their **hands** on the lower part of the breast, the **Schiahs** drop their arms in straight lines."—*G. Forster, Travels*, ii. 129.

1805.—"The word **Sh'eeah**, or **Sheeut**, properly signifies a troop or sect ... but has become the distinctive appellation of the followers of Aly, or all those who maintain that he was the first legitimate *Khuleefah*, or successor to Moohummad.—"*Baillie, Digest of Mah. Law*, II. xii.

1869.—"La tolerance indienne est venue diminuer dans l'Inde le fanatisme Musulman. Là *Sunnites* et **Schiites** n'ont point entre eux cette animosité qui divise les Turcs et les Persans ... ces deux sectes divisent les musulmans de l'Inde; mais comme je viens de dire, elles n'excitent généralement entre eux aucune animosité."—*Garcin de Tassy, Rel. Mus.*, p. 12.

SHERBET, s. Though this word is used in India by natives in its native (Arab. and Pers.) form *sharbat*,[1] 'draught,' it is not a

1 In both written alike, but the final *t* in Arabic is generally silent, giving *sharba*, in Persian

word now specially in Anglo-Indian use. The Arabic seems to have entered Europe by several different doors. Thus in Italian and French we have *sorbetto* and *sorbet*, which probably came direct from the Levantine or Turkish form *shurbat* or *shorbat*; in Sp. and Port. we have *xarabe*, *axarabe* (*ash-sharāb*, the standard Ar. *sharāb*, 'wine or any beverage'), and *xarope*, and from these forms probably Ital. *sciroppo*, *siroppo*, with old French *ysserop* and mod. French *sirop*; also English *syrup*, and more directly from the Spanish, *shrub*. Mod. Span. again gets, by reflection from French or Italian, *sorbete* and *sîrop* (see *Dozy*, 17, and *Marcel Devic*, s.v. *sirop*). Our *sherbet* looks as if it had been imported direct from the Levant. The form *shrāb* is applied in India to all wines and spirits and prepared drinks, *e.g.* Port-*shraub*, Sherry-*shraub*, **Lall-shraub**, Brandy-*shraub*, Beer-*shraub*. Beer-*shraub*.

c. 1334.—"... They bring cups of gold, silver, and glass, filled with sugar-candy-water; *i.e.* syrup diluted with water. They call this beverage **sherbet**" (*ash-shurbat*).—*Ibn Batuta*, iii. 124.

1554.—"... potio est gratissima praesertim ubi multa nive, quae Constantinopoli nullo tempore deficit, fuerit refirgerata, *Arab* **Sorbet** vocant, hoc est, potionem Arabicam."—*Busbeq.* Ep. i. p. 92.

1578.—"The physicians of the same country use this **xarave** (of tamarinds) in bilious and ardent fevers."—*Acosta*, 67.

c. 1580.—"Et saccharo potum jucundissimum parant quem **Sarbet** vocant."—*Prosper Alpinus*, Pt. i. p. 70.

1611.—"In Persia there is much good wine of grapes which is called **Xaràb** in the language of the country."—*Teixeira*, i. 16.

c. 1630.—"Their liquor may perhaps better delight you; 'tis faire water, sugar, rose-water, and juyce of Lemons mixt, call'd **Sherbets** or **Zerbets**, wholsome and potable."—*Sir T. Herbert*, ed. 1638, p. 241.

1682.—"The Moores ... dranke a little milk and water, but not a drop of wine; they also dranke a little **sorbet**, and *jacolatt*."—*Evelyn's Diary*, Jan 24.

1827.—"On one occasion, before Barak-el-Hadgi left Madras, he visited the Doctor, and partook of his **sherbet**, which he preferred to his own, perhaps because a few glasses of rum or brandy were usually added to enrich the compound."—*Sir W. Scott, The Surgeon's Daughter*, ch. x.

1837.—"The Egyptians have various kinds of **sherbets**. ... The most common kind (called simply **shurbát** or **shurbát** *sook'har* ...) is merely sugar and water ... lemonade (*ley'moónáteh*, or **sharáb** *elleymoón*) is another."—*Lane, Mod. Egypt.*, ed. 1837, i. 206.

1863.—"The Estate overseer usually gave a dance to the people, when the most dissolute of both sexes were sure to be present, and to indulge too freely in the **shrub** made for the occasion."—*Waddell, 29 Years in the W. Indies*, 17.

---

sharbat, So we get *minaret* from Pers. and Turk. *munārat*, in Ar. (and in India) *munāra* (*manār*, *manāra*].

SHIKAR, s. Hind. from Pers. *shikār*, 'la chasse'; sport (in the sense of shooting and hunting); game.

c. 1590.—"*Āīn*, 27. *Of Hunting* (orig. *Āīn-i-***Shikār**). Superficial worldly observers see in killing an animal a sort of pleasure, and in their ignorance stride about, as if senseless, on the field of their passions. But deep enquirers see in hunting a means of acquisition of knowledge. ... This is the case with His Majesty."—*Āīn*, i. 282.

1609–10.—"**Sykary**, which signifieth, seeking, or hunting."—*W. Finch*, in *Purchas*, i. 428.

1800.—"250 or 300 horsemen ... divided into two or three small parties, supported by our infantry, would give a proper **shekar**; and I strongly advise not to let the Mahratta boundary stop you in the pursuit of your game."—*Sir A. Wellesley* to *T. Munro*, in *Life of Munro*, iii. 117.

1847.—"Yet there is a charm in this place for the lovers of **Shikar**."—*Dry Leaves from Young Egypt*, 3.

[1859.—"Although the jungles literally swarm with tigers, a **shickar**, in the Indian sense of the term, is unknown."—*Oliphant, Narr. of Mission*, i. 25.]

1866.—"May I ask what has brought you out to India, Mr. Cholmondeley? Did you come out for **shikar**, eh?"—*Trevelyan, The Dawk Bungalow*, in *Fraser*, lxxiii. 222.

In the following the word is wrongly used in the sense of **Shikaree**.

[1900.—"That so experienced a **shikar** should have met his death emphasises the necessity of caution."—*Field*, Sept. 1.]

SHIKAREE, SHEKARRY, s. Hind. *shikārī*, a sportsman. The word is used in three ways:

a. As applied to a native expert, who either brings in game on his own account, or accompanies European sportsmen as guide and aid.

[1822.—"**Shecarries** are generally Hindoos

of low cast, who gain their livelihood entirely by catching birds, hares, and all sorts of animals."—*Johnson, Sketches of Field Sports*, 25.]

1879.—"Although the province (Pegu) abounds in large game, it is very difficult to discover, because there are no regular **shikarees** in the Indian acceptation of the word. Every village has its local **shikaree**, who lives by trapping and killing game. Taking life as he does, contrary to the principles of his religion, he is looked upon as damned by his neighbours, but that does not prevent their buying from him the spoils of the chase."—*Pollok, Sport in Br. Burmah*, &c., i. 13.

b. As applied to the European sportsman himself: *e.g.* "Jones is well known as a great *Shikaree*." There are several books of sporting adventure written *circa* 1860–75 by Mr. H. A. Leveson under the name of 'The Old **Shekarry**.'

[**c.** A shooting-boat used in the Cashmere lakes.

[1875.—"A **shikārī** is a sort of boat, that is in daily use with the English visitors; a light boat manned, as it commonly is, by six men, it goes at a fast pace, and, if well fitted with cushions, makes a comfortable conveyance. A *bandūqī shikāri* is the smallest boat of all; a shooting punt, used in going after wild fowl on the lakes."—*Drew, Jummoo*, &c., 181.]

***SHIKHÓ**, n. and v. Burmese word. The posture of a Burmese in presence of a superior, *i.e.* kneeling with joined hands and bowed head in an attitude of worship. Some correspondence took place in 1883, in consequence of the use of this word by the then Chief Commissioner of British Burma, in an official report, to describe the attitude used by British envoys at the Court of Ava. The statement (which was grossly incorrect) led to remonstrance by Sir Arthur Phayre. The fact was that the envoy and his party sat on a carpet, but the attitude had no analogy whatever to that of *shikho*, though the endeavour of the Burmese officials was persistent to involve them in some such degrading attitude. (See KOWTOW.)

1855.—"Our conductors took off their shoes at the gate, and the Woondouk made an ineffectual attempt to induce the Envoy to do likewise. They also at four different places, as we advanced to the inner gate, dropt on their knees and **shikhoed** towards the palace."—*Yule, Mission to Ava*, 82.

1882.—"Another ceremony is that of **shekhoing** to the spire, the external emblem of the throne. All Burmans must do this at each of the gates, at the foot of the steps, and at intervals in between. ..."—*The Burman, His Life and Notions*, ii. 206.

SHISHMUHULL, s. Pers. *shīshamaḥal*, lit. 'glass apartment' or palace. This is or was a common appendage of native palaces, viz. a hall or suite of rooms lined with mirror and other glittering surfaces, usually of a gimcrack aspect. There is a place of exactly the same description, now gone to hideous decay, in the absurd Villa Palagonia at Bagheria near Palermo.

1835.—"The **Shīsha-mahal**, or house of glass, is both curious and elegant, although the material is principally pounded talc and looking-glass. It consists of two rooms, of which the walls in the interior are divided into a thousand different panels, each of which is filled up with raised flowers in silver, gold, and colours, on a ground-work of tiny convex mirrors."—*Wanderings of a Pilgrim*, i. 365.

SHRAUB, SHROBB, s. Ar. *sharāb*; Hind. *sharāb, shrāb*, 'wine.' See under SHERBET.

SHROFF, s. A money-changer, a banker. Ar. *ṣarrāf, ṣairafi, ṣairaf.* The word is used by Europeans in China as well as in India, and is there applied to the experts who are employed by banks and mercantile firms to check the quality of the dollars that pass into the houses (see *Giles* under next word). Also **shroffage**, for money-dealer's commission. From the same root comes the Heb. *sōrēf*, 'a goldsmith.' Compare the figure in *Malachi*, iii. 3: "He shall sit as a refiner and purifier of silver; and he shall purify the sons of Levi." Only in Hebrew the goldsmith tests metal, while the *ṣairaf* tests *coins*. The Arab poet says of his mare: "Her forefeet scatter the gravel every midday, as the dirhams are scattered at their testing by the *sairaf*" (W. R. S.)

1554.—"*Salaries of the officers of the Custom Houses, and other charges for these which the Treasurers have to pay* ... Also to the **Xarrafo**, whose charge it is to see to the money, two *pardaos* a month, which make for a year seven thousand and two hundred *reis*."—*Botelho, Tombo*, in *Subsidios*, 238.

1560.—"There are in the city many and very wealthy **carafos** who change money."—*Tenreiro*, ch. i.

1584.—"5 **tangas** make a *seraphin* of gold; but if one would change them into *basaruchies* he may have 5 tangas and 16 *basaruchies*, which ouerplus they call **cerafagio**. ..."—*Barret*, in *Hakl.* ii. 410.

1585.—"This present year, because only two ships came to Goa, (the *reals*) have sold at 12 per cent. of **Xarafaggio** (shroffage), as this commission is called, from the word **Xaraffo**, which is the title of the banker."—*Sassetti*, in *De Gubernatis, Storia*, p. 203.

1598.—"There is in every place of the street exchangers of money, by them called **Xaraffos**, which are all christian Jewes."—*Linschoten*, 66; [Hak. Soc. i. 231, and see 244.]

c. 1610.—"Dans ce Marché ... aussi sont les changeurs qu'ils nomment **Cherafes**, dont il y en a en plusieurs autres endroits; leurs boutiques sont aux bouts des ruës et carrefours, toutes couuertes de monnoye, dont ils payent tribut au Roy."—*Pyrard de Laval*, ii. 39; [Hak. Soc. ii. 67].

[1614.—"... having been borne in hand by our **Sarafes** to pay money there."—*Foster*, *Letters*, iii. 282. The "**Sheriff** of Bantam" (*ibid.* iv. 7) may perhaps be a **shroff**, but compare **Shereef**.]

1673.—"It could not be improved till the Governor had released the **Shroffs** or Bankers."—*Fryer*, 413.

1697-8.—"In addition to the cash and property which they had got by plunder, the enemy fixed two *lacs* of rupees as the price of the ransom of the prisoners. ... To make up the balance, the **Sarráfs** and merchants of Nandurbár were importuned to raise a sum, small or great, by way of loan. But they would not consent."—*Kháfi Khán*, in *Elliot*, vii. 362.

1750.—"... the Irruption of the *Morattoes* into *Carnatica*, was another event that brought several eminent **Shroffs** and wealthy Merchants into our Town; insomuch, that I may say, there was hardly a **Shroff** of any Note, in the *Mogul* empire but had a House in it; in a word, *Madrass* was become the Admiration of all the Country People, and the Envy of all our *European* Neighbours."—*Letter to a Proprietor of the E. I. Co.* 53-54.

1809.—"I had the satisfaction of hearing the Court order them (*i.e.* Gen. Martin's executors) to pay two lacs and a half to the plaintiff, a **shroff** of Lucknow."—*Ld. Valentia*, i. 243.

[1891.—"The banker in Persia is looked on simply as a small tradesman—in fact the business of the **Serof** is despised."—*Wills, in the Land of the Lion and the Sun*, 192].

SHROFF, TO, v. This verb is applied properly to the sorting of different rupees or other coins, so as to discard refuse, and to fix the various amounts of discount or *agio* upon the rest, establishing the value in standard coin. Hence figuratively 'to sift,' choosing the good (men, horses, facts, or what not) and rejecting the inferior.

[1554.—(See under BATTA, b.)]

1878.—"**Shroffing** schools are common in Canton, where teachers of the art keep bad dollars for the purpose of exercising their pupils; and several works on the subject have been published there, with numerous illustrations of dollars and other foreign coins, the methods of scooping out silver and filling up with copper or lead, comparisons between genuine and counterfeit dollars, the difference between native and foreign milling, etc., etc."—*Giles, Glossary of Reference*, 129.

1882.—(The **Compradore**) "derived a profit from the process of **shroffing** which (the money received) underwent before being deposited in the Treasury."—*The Fankwae at Canton*, 55.

***SHULWAURS**, s. Trousers, or drawers rather, of the Oriental kind, the same as **pyjammas**, **long-drawers**, or **mogul-breeches** (qq.v). The Persian is *shalwār*, which according to Prof. Max Müller is more correctly *shulvār*, from *shul*, 'the thigh,' related to Latin *crus, cruris*, and to Skt. *kshura* or *khura*, 'hoof' (see *Pusey* on *Daniel*, 570). Be this as it may, the Ar. form is *sirwāl* (vulg. *sharwāl*), pl. *sarāwīl*, [which Burton (*Arab. Nights*, i. 205) translates 'bag-trousers' and 'petticoat-trousers,'"the latter being the divided skirt of the future."] This appears in the ordinary editions of the Book of Daniel in Greek, as σαράβαρα, and also in the Vulgate, as follows: "Et capillus capitis eorum non esset adustus, et **sarabala** eorum non fuissent immutata, et odor ignis non transisset per eos" (iii. 27). The original word is *sarbālīn*, pl. of *sarbāla*. Luther, however, renders this *Mantel*; as the A.V. also does by *coats;* [the R. V. *hosen*]. On this Prof. Robertson-Smith writes:

"It is not certain but that Luther and the A.V. are right. The word *sarbālīn* means 'cloak' in the Gemara; and in Arabic *sirbāl* is 'a garment, a coat of mail.' Perhaps quite an equal weight of scholarship would now lean (though with hesitation) towards the cloak or coat, and against the breeches theory.

"The Arabic word occurs in the Traditions of the Prophet (*Bokhāri*, vii. 36).

"Of course it is certain that σαράβαρα comes from the Persian, but not through Arabic. The Bedouins did not wear trowsers in the time of Ammianus, and don't do so now.

"The ordinary so-called LXX. editions of Daniel contain what is really the post-Christian version of Theodotion. The true LXX. text has ὑποδήματα.

"It may be added that Jerome says that both

Aquila and Symmachus wrote *saraballa*." [The *Encycl. Biblica* also prefers the rendering of the A.V. (i. 607), and see iii. 2934.]

The word is widely spread as well as old; it is found among the Tartars of W. Asia as *jālbār*, among the Siberians and Bashkirds as *sālbār*, among the Kalmaks as *shālbūr*, whilst it reached Russia as *sharawari*, Spain as *zaraguelles*, and Portugal as *zarelos*. A great many Low Latin variations of the word will be found in Ducange, *serabula*, *serabulla*, *sarabella*, *sarabola*, *sarabura*, and more! [And Crawfurd (*Desc. Dict.* 124) writes of Malay dress: "Trowsers are occasionally used under the *sarung* by the richer classes, and this portion of dress, like the imitation of the turban, seems to have been borrowed from the Arabs, as is implied by its Arabic name, *sarual*, corrupted *saluwar*."]

In the second quotation from Isidore of Seville below it will be seen that the word had in some cases been interpreted as 'turbans.'

A.D. (?).—"*Καὶ ἐθεώρουν τοῦς ἄνδρας ὅτι οὐκ ἐκυρίευσε το πῦρ τοῦ σώματος αὐτῶν καὶ ἡ θρὶξ τῆς κεφαλῆς αὐτῶν οὐκ ἐφλογίσθη καὶ τα σαράβαρα αὐτῶν οὐκ ἠλλοιώθη, καὶ ὀσμὴ πυρὸς οὐκ ἦν ἐν αὐτοῖς.*"—Gr. Tr. of *Dan.* iii. 27.

c. A.D. 200.—"*Ἐν δὲ τοῖς Σκύθαις Ἀντιφάνης ἔφη Σαράβαρα καὶ χιτῶνας πάντας ἐνδεδυκότας.*"—*Julius Pollux*, *Onomast.* vii. 13, sec. 59.

c. A.D. 500.—"*Σαράβαρα, τὰ περὶ τάς κνημῖδας* (sic) *ἐνδύματα.*"—*Hesychius*, s.v.

c. 636.—"**Sarabara** sunt fluxa ac sinuosa vestimenta de quibus legitur in Daniele. ... Et Publius: Vt quid ergo in ventre tuo Parthi **Sarabara** suspenderunt? Apud quosdam autem **Sarabarae** quaedã capitum tegmina nuncupantur qualia videmus in capite Magorum picta."—*Isidorus Hispalensis*, *Orig. et Etym.*, lib. xix., ed. 1601, pp. 263–4.

c. 1000?—"*Σαράβαρα,—ἐσθὴς Περσική ἔνιοι δὲ λέγουσι βρακία.*"—*Suidas*, s.v.

which may be roughly rendered:

"A garb outlandish to the Greeks,
Which some call **Shalwārs**, some call
Breeks!"

c. 900.—"The deceased was unchanged, except in colour. They dressed him then with **sarāwīl**, overhose, boots, a *ḳurṭak* and *khaftān* of gold cloth, with golden buttons, and put on him a golden cap garnished with sable."—*Ibn Foszlān*, in *Fraehn*, 15.

c. 1300.—"Disconsecratur altare eorum, et oportet reconciliari per episcopum ... si intraret ad ipsum aliquis qui non esset Nestorius; si intraret eciam ad ipsum quicumque sine **sorrabulis** vel capite cooperto."—*Ricoldo of Monte Croce*, in *Peregrinatores Quatuor*, 122.

1330.—"Haec autem mulieres vadunt discalceatae portantes **sarabulas** usque ad terram."—*Friar Odoric*, in *Cathay*, &c., App. iv.

c. 1495.—"The first who wore **sarāwīl** was Solomon. But in another tradition it is alleged that Abraham was the first."—The '*Beginnings*,' by *Soyuti*, quoted by *Fraehn*, 113.

1567.—"Portauano braghesse quasi alla turchesca, et anche **saluarī**."—*C. Federici*, in *Ramusio*, iii. f. 389.

1824.—"... tell me how much he will be contented with? Can I offer him five *Temauns*, and a pair of crimson **Shulwaurs**?"—*Hajji Baba*, ed. 1835, p. 179.

1881.—"I used to wear a red shirt and velveteen **sharovary**, and lie on the sofa like a gentleman, and drink like a Swede."—*Ten Years of Penal Servitude in Siberia*, by *Fedor Dostoyeffski*, E.T. by Maria v. Thilo, 191.

SIAM, n.p. This name of the Indo-Chinese Kingdom appears to come to us through the Malays, who call it *Siyăm*. From them we presume the Portuguese took their Reyno de *Sião* as Barros and Couto write it, though we have in Correa *Siam* precisely as we write it. Camões also writes *Syão* for the kingdom; and the statement of De la Loubère quoted below that the Portuguese used Siam as a national, not a geographical, expression cannot be accepted in its generality, accurate as that French writer usually is. It is true that both Barros and F. M. Pinto use *os Siames* for the nation, and the latter also uses the adjective form *o reyno Siame*. But he also constantly says *rey de Sião*. The origin of the name would seem to be a term **Sien**, or *Siam*, identical with **Shan**. "The kingdom of Siam is known to the Chinese by the name *Sien-lo*. ... The supplement to Matwanlin's *Encyclopædia* describes *Sien-lo* as on the seaboard, to the extreme south of Chen-ching (or Cochin China). 'It originally consisted of two kingdoms, **Sien** and *Lo-hoh*. The Sien people are the remains of a tribe which in the year (A.D. 1341) began to come down upon the Lo-hoh and united with the latter into one nation.'" See *Marco Polo*, 2nd ed., Bk. iii. ch. 7, note 3. The considerations there adduced indicate that the *Lo* who occupied the coast of the Gulf before the descent of the *Sien*, belonged to the Laotian Shans, *Thainyai*, or Great T'ai, whilst the *Sien* or Siamese Proper were the *Tai Noi*, or Little T'ai. ["The name *Siam* ...

whether it is 'a barbarous Anglicism derived from the Portuguese or Italian word *Sciam*,' or is derived from the Malay *Sayam*, which means 'brown.'"—*J. G. Scott, Upper Burma Gazetteer*, i. pt. i. 205.]

1516.—"Proceeding further, quitting the kingdom of Peeguu, along the coast over against Malaca there is a very great kingdom of pagans which they call Danseam (of **Anseam**); the king of which is a pagan also, and a very great lord."—*Barbosa* (Lisbon, Acad.), 369. It is difficult to interpret this *An***seam**, which we find also in C. Federici below in the form **Asion**. But the *An* is probably a Malay prefix of some kind.

c. 1522.—"The king (of Zzuba) answered him that he was welcome, but that the custom was that all ships which arrived at his country or port paid tribute, and it was only 4 days since that a ship called the Junk of **Ciama**, laden with gold and slaves, had paid him his tribute, and to verify what he said, he showed them a merchant of the said **Ciama**, who had remained there to trade with the gold and slaves."—*Pigafetta*, Hak. Soc. 85.

"All these cities are construsted like ours, and are subject to the king of **Siam**, who is named Siri Zacebedera, and who inhabits Iudia."—*Ibid*. 156.

1525.—"In this same Port of Pam (Pahang), which is in the kingdom of **Syam**, there was another junk of Malaqua, the captain whereof was Alvaro da Costaa, and it had aboard 15 Portuguese, at the same time that in Joatane (Patane) they seized the ship of Andre de Bryto, and the junk of Gaspar Soarez, and as soon as this news was known they laid hands on the junk and the crew and the cargo; it is presumed that the people were killed, but it is not known for certain."—*Lembrança das Cousas da India*, 6.

1572.—

"Vês Pam, Patâne, reinos e a longura
De **Syão**, que estes e outros mais sujeita;
Olho o rio Menão que se derrama
Do grande lago, que Chiamay se chiama."

Camões, x. 25.

By Burton:

"See Pam, Patane and in length obscure,
Siam that ruleth all with lordly sway;
behold Menam, who rolls his lordly tide
from source Chiámái called, lake long and wide."

c. 1567.—"Va etiandio ogn' anno per l'istesso Capitano (di Malacca) vn nauilio in **Asion**, a caricare di *Verzino*" (Brazilwood).—*Ces. Federici*, in *Ramusio*, iii. 396.

"Fu già **Sion** vna grandissima Città e sedia d'Imperio, ma l'anno MDLXVII fu pressa dal Re del Pegu, qual caminando per terra quattro mesi di viaggio, con vn esercito d'vn million, e quattro cento mila uomini da guerra, la venne ad assediare ... e lo so io percioche mi ritrouai in Pegù sei mesi dopo la sua partita."—*Ibid*.

1598.—"... The King of **Sian** at this time is become tributarie to the king of Pegu. The cause of this most bloodie battaile was, that the king of **Sian** had a white Elephant."—*Linschoten*, p. 30; [Hak. Soc. i. 102. In ii. 1 **Sion**].

[1611.—"We have news that the Hollanders were in **Shian**."—*Danvers, Letters*, i. 149.]

1688.—"The Name of **Siam** is unknown to the *Siamese*. 'Tis one of those words which the *Portugues* of the *Indies* do use, and of which it is very difficult to discover the Original. They use it as the Name of the Nation and not of the Kingdom: And the Names of *Pegu, Lao, Mogul*, and most of the Names which we give to the Indian Kingdoms, are likewise National Names."—*De la Loubère*, E.T. p. 6.

SICCA, s. As will be seen by reference to the article RUPEE, up to 1835 a variety of rupees had been coined in the Company's territories. The term *sicca* (*sikkā*, from Ar. *sikka*, 'a coining die,'—and 'coined money,'—whence Pers. *sikka zadan*, 'to coin') had been applied to newly coined rupees, which were at a **batta** or premium over those worn, or assumed to be worn, by use. In 1793 the Government of Bengal, with a view to terminating, as far as that Presidency was concerned, the confusion and abuses engendered by this system, ordered that all rupees coined for the future should bear the impress of the 19th year of Shāh 'Alam (the "Great Mogul" then reigning), and this rupee, "19 *San* **Sikkah**," 'struck in the 19th year,' was to be the legal tender in Bengal, Bahar, and Orissa. This rupee, which is the Sicca of more recent monetary history, weighed 192 grs. troy, and then contained 176·13 grs. of pure silver. The "Company's Rupee," which introduced uniformity of coinage over British India in 1835, contained only 165 grs. silver. Hence the *Sicca* bore to the Company's Rupee (which was based on the old Farrukhābād rupee) the proportion of 16: 15 nearly. The *Sicca* was allowed by Act VII. of 1833 to survive as an exceptional coin in Bengal, but was abolished as such in 1836. It continued, however, a ghostly existence for many years longer in the form of certain Government Book-debts in that currency. (See also CHICK.)

1537.—"... Sua senhoria avia d'aver por bem que as **siquas** das moedas corressem em seu nome per todo o Reino do Guzerate, asy em Dio como nos otros luguares que forem del Rey de Portuguall."—*Treaty of Nuno da Cunha with Nizamamede Zamom (Mahommed Zamam) concerning Cambaya*, in *Botelho, Tombo*, 225.

1537.—"... e quoanto á moeda ser chapada de sua *sita* (read **sica**) pois já lhe concedia."—*Ibid.* 226.

[1615.—"... **cecaus** of Amadavrs which goeth for eight-six *pisas* (see PICE) ..."—*Foster, Letters*, iii. 87.]

1683.—"Having received 25,000 Rupees **Siccas** for Rajamaul."—*Hedges, Diary*, April 4; [Hak. Soc. i. 75].

1705.—"Les roupies **Sicca** valent à Bengale 39 sols."—*Luillier*, 255.

1779.—"In the 2nd Term, 1779, on Saturday, March 6th: Judgment was pronounced for the plaintiff. Damages fifty thousand **sicca rupees**.

"... 50,000 **Sicca Rupees** are equal to five thousand one hundred and nine pounds, two shillings and elevenpence sterling, reckoning according to the weight and fineness of the silver."—*Notes of Mr. Justice Hyde* on the case *Grand v. Francis*, in *Echoes of Old Calcutta*, 243. [To this Mr. Busteed adds: "Nor does there seem to be any foundation for the other time-honoured story (also repeated by Kaye) in connection with this judgment, viz., the alleged interruption of the Chief Justice, while he was delivering judgment, by Mr. Justice Hyde, with the eager suggestion or reminder of '**Siccas, Siccas**, Brother Impey,' with the view of making the damages as high at the awarded figure as possible. Mr. Merivale says that he could find no confirmation of the old joke. ... The story seems to have been first promulgated in a book of 'Personal Recollections' by John Nicholls, M.P., published in 1822."—*Ibid.* 3rd ed. 229].

* * *

1833.—

"III.—The weight and standard of the Calcutta **sicca** rupee and its sub-divisions, and of the Furruckabad rupee, shall be as follows:—

	Weight.	*Fine.*	*Alloy.*
	Grains.	Grains.	Grains.
Calcutta **sicca** rupee	192	176	16

* * * * * *

"IV.—The use of the **sicca** weight of 179·666 grains, hitherto employed for the receipt of bullion at the Mint, being in fact the weight of the Moorshedabad rupee of the old standard ... shall be discontinued, and in its place the following unit to be called the Tola shall be introduced."—*India Regulation VII.* of 1833.

[**SICKMAN**, s. adj. The English *sick man* has been adopted into Hind. sepoy patois as meaning 'one who has to go to hospital,' and generally *sikmān ho jānā* means 'to be disabled.'

[1665.—"That **sickman** Chaseman."—In *Yule, Hedges' Diary*, Hak. Soc. II. cclxxx.

[1843.—"... my hired cart was broken—(or, in the more poetical garb of the sepahee, '**seek mān** *hogya*,' *i.e.* become a sick man)."—*Davidson, Travels*, i. 251.]

SIKH, SEIKH, n.p. Panjābi-Hind. *Sikh*, 'a disciple,' from Skt. *Śishya*; the distinctive name of the disciples of Nānak Shāh who in the 16th century established that sect, which eventually rose to warlike predominance in the Punjab, and from which sprang Ranjīt Singh, the founder of the brief Kingdom of Lahore.

c. 1650–60.—"The Nanac-Panthians, who are known as composing the nation of the **Sikhs**, have neither idols, nor temples of idols. ..." (Much follows.)—*Dabistān*, ii. 246.

1708–9.—"There is a sect of infidels called *Gurú* (see GOOROO), more commonly known as **Sikhs**. Their chief, who dresses as a fakír, has a fixed residence at Láhore. ... This sect consists principally of *Játs* and *Khatrís* of the Panjáb and of other tribes of infidels. When Aurangzeb got knowledge of these matters, he ordered these deputy *Gurús* to be removed and the temples to be pulled down."—*Khāfi Khān*, in *Elliot*, vii. 413.

1756.—"April of 1716, when the Emperor took the field and marched towards Lahore, against the **Sykes**, a nation of Indians lately reared to power, and bearing mortal enmity to the Mahomedans."—*Orme*, ii. 22. He also writes **Sikes**.

1781.—"Before I left *Calcutta*, a gentleman with whom I chanced to be discoursing of that sect who are distinguished from the worshippers of *Brăhm*, and the followers of MAHOMMED by the appellation **Seek**, informed me that there was a considerable number of them settled in the city of *Patna*, where they had a College for teaching the tenets of their philosophy."—*Wilkins*, in *As. Res.* i. 288.

1781–2.—"In the year 1128 of the Hedjra" (1716) "a bloody action happened in the plains of the Pendjab, between the **Sycs** and the Imperialists, in which the latter, commanded by Abdol-semed-Khan, a famous Viceroy of that province, gave these inhuman freebooters a great defeat, in which their General, Benda, fell into the victors' hands. ... He was a **Syc** by profession, that is one of those men attached to the tenets of Guru-Govind, and who from their birth or from the moment of their admission never cut or shave either their beard or whiskers or any hair whatever of their body. They form a particular Society as well as a sect, which distinguishes itself by wearing almost always blue cloaths, and going armed at all times. ..." &c.—*Seir Mutaqherin*, i. 87.

1782.—"News was received that the **Seiks** had crossed the Jumna."—*India Gazette*, May 11.

1783.—"Unhurt by the **Sicques**, tigers, and thieves, I am safely lodged at Nourpour."—*Forster, Journey*, ed. 1808, i. 247.

1784.—"The **Seekhs** are encamped at the distance of 12 cose from the Pass of Dirderry, and have plundered all that quarter."—In *Seton-Karr*, i. 13.

1790.—"Particulars relating to the seizure of Colonel Robert Stewart by the **Sicques**."—*Calc. Monthly Register*, &c., i. 152.

1810.—Williamson (*V.M.*) writes **Seeks**.

The following extract indicates the prevalence of a very notable error:—

1840.—"Runjeet possesses great personal courage, a quality in which the **Sihks** (*sic*) are supposed to be generally deficient."—*Osborne, Court and Camp of Runjeet Singh*, 83.

We occasionally about 1845-6 saw the word written by people in Calcutta, who ought to have known better, **Sheiks**.

SILBOOT, SILPET, SLIPPET, s. Domestic Hind. corruptions of 'slipper.' The first is an instance of "striving after meaning" by connecting it in some way with 'boot.' [The Railway 'sleeper' is in the same way corrupted into *silīpat*.]

SILLADAR, adj. and s. Hind. from Pers. *silaḥ-dār*, 'bearing or having arms,' from Ar. *silaḥ*, 'arms.' [In the *Arabian Nights* (*Burton*, ii. 114) it has the primary sense of an 'armour-bearer.'] Its Anglo-Indian application is to a soldier, in a regiment of irregular cavalry, who provides his own arms and horse; and sometimes to regiments composed of such men—"a corps of **Silladar** Horse." [See Irvine, *The Army of the Indian Moghuls*, (*J. R. As. Soc.*, July 1896, p. 549).]

1766.—"When this intelligence reached the Nawaub, he leaving the whole of his troops and baggage in the same place, with only 6000 stable horse, 9000 **Sillahdārs**, 4000 regular infantry, and 6 guns ... fell bravely on the Mahrattas. ..."—*Mir Hussein Ali, H. of Hydur Naik*, 173.

1804.—"It is my opinion, that the arrangement with the Soubah of the Deccan should be, that the whole of the force ... should be **silladar** horse."—*Wellington*, iii. 671.

1813.—"Bhàou ... in the prosecution of his plan, selected Malhar Row Holcar, a **Silledar** or soldier of fortune."—*Forbes, Or. Mem.* iii. 349.

SIMKIN, s. Domestic Hind. for champagne, of which it is a corruption; sometimes **samkīn**.

1853—"'The dinner was good, and the iced **simkin**, Sir, delicious.'"—*Oakfield*, ii. 127.

SINGALESE, CINGHALESE, n.p. Native of Ceylon; pertaining to Ceylon. The word is formed from *Siṉhala*, 'Dwelling of Lions,' the word used by the natives for the Island, and which is the origin of most of the names given to it (see CEYLON). The explanation given by De Barros and Couto is altogether fanciful, though it leads them to notice the curious and obscure fact of the introduction of Chinese influence in Ceylon during the 15th century.

1552.—"That the Chinese (*Chijs*) were masters of the Choromandel Coast, of part of Malabar, and of this Island of Ceylon, we have not only the assertion of the Natives of the latter, but also evidence in the buildings, names, and language that they left in it ... and because they were in the vicinity of this Cape Galle, the other people who lived from the middle of the Island upwards called those dwelling about there **Chingálla**, and their language the same, as much as to say the language, or the people of the **Chins of Galle**."—*Barros*, III. ii. 1.

1583.—(The Cauchin Chineans) "are of the race of the **Chingalays**, which they say are the best kinde of all the Malabars."—*Fitch*, in *Hakl.* ii. 397.

1598.—"... inhabited with people called **Cingalas**. ..."—*Linschoten*, 24; [Hak. Soc. i. 77; in i. 81, **Chingalas**].

c. 1610.—"Ils tiennent donc que ... les premiers qui y allerent, et qui les peuplerent (les Maldives) furent ... les **Cingalles** de l'Isle de Ceylan."—*Pyrard de Laval*, i. 185; [Hak. Soc. i. 105, and see i. 266].

1612.—Couto, after giving the same explanation of the word as Barros, says: "And as they spring from the Chins, who are the falsest heathen of the East ... so are they of this island the weakest, falsest, and most tricky people in all India, insomuch that, to this day, you never find faith or truth in a **Chingalla**."—V. i. 5.

1681.—"The **Chinguleys** are naturally a people given to sloth and laziness: if they can but anyways live, they abhor to work." ...—*Knox*, 32.

SINGAPORE, SINCAPORE, n.p. This name was adopted by Sir Stamford Raffles in favour of the city which he founded, February 23, 1819, on the island which had always retained the name since the Middle Ages. This it derived from *Siṇhapura*, Skt. 'Lion-city,' the name of a town founded by Malay or Javanese settlers from Sumatra, probably in the 14th century, and to which Barros ascribes great commercial importance. The Indian origin of the name, as of many other names and phrases which survive from the old Indian civilisation of the Archipelago, had been forgotten, and the origin which Barros was taught to ascribe to it is on a par with his etymology of **Singalese** quoted in the preceding article. The words on which his etymology is founded are no doubt Malay: *singah*, 'to tarry, halt, or lodge,' and *pora-pora*, 'to pretend'; and these were probably supposed to refer to the temporary occupation of Sinhapura, before the chiefs who founded it passed on to Malacca. [It may be noted that Dennys (*Desc. Dict.* s.v.) derives the word from *singha*, 'a place of call,' and *pura*, 'a city.' In Dalboquerque's *Comm.* Hak. Soc. iii. 73, we are told: "Singapura, whence the city takes its name, is a channel through which all the shipping of those parts passes, and signifies in his Malay language, '*treacherous delay*'" See quotation from Barros below.]

The settlement of Hinduized people on the site, if not the name, is probably as old as the 4th century, A.D., for inscriptions have been found there in a very old character. One of these, on a rock at the mouth of the little river on which the town stands, was destroyed some 40 or 50 years ago for the accommodation of some wretched bungalow.

The modern Singapore and its prosperity form a monument to the patriotism, sagacity, and fervid spirit of the founder. According to an article in the *Geogr. Magazine* (i. 107) derived from Mr. Archibald Ritchie, who was present with the expedition which founded the colony, Raffles, after consultation with Lord Hastings, was about to establish a settlement for the protection and encouragement of our Eastern trade, in the Nicobar Islands, when his attention was drawn to the superior advantages of Singapore by Captains Ross and Crawford of the Bombay Marine, who had been engaged in the survey of those seas. Its great adaptation for a mercantile settlement had been discerned by the shrewd, if somewhat vulgar, Scot, Alexander Hamilton, 120 years earlier. It seems hardly possible, we must however observe, to reconcile the *details* in the article cited, with the letters and facts contained in the *Life of Raffles*; though probably the latter had, at some time or other, received information from the officers named by Mr. Ritchie.

1512.—"And as the enterprise was one to make good booty, everybody was delighted to go on it, so that they were more than 1200 men, the soundest and best armed of the garrison, and so they were ready incontinently, and started for the Strait of **Cincapura**, where they were to wait for the junks."—*Correa*, ii. 284–5.

1551.—"Sed hactenus Deus nobis adsit omnibus. Amen. Anno post Christum natum, MDLI. *Ex Freto* **Syncapurano**."—*Scti. Franc. Xaverii* Epistt. Pragae, 1667, Lib. III. viii.

1553.—"Anciently the most celebrated settlement in this region of Malaca was one called **Cingapura**, a name which in their tongue means 'pretended halt' (*falsa dimora*); and this stood upon a point of that country which is the most southerly of all Asia, and lies, according to our graduation, in half a degree of North Latitude ... before the foundation of Malaca, at this same **Cingapura** ... flocked together all the navigators of the Seas of India from West and East. ..."—*Barros*, II. vi. 1. [The same derivation is given in the *Comm. of Dalboquerque*, Hak. Soc. iii. 73.]

1572.—

"Mas na ponta da terra **Cingapura**
Verás, onde o caminho as naos se estreita;
Daqui, tornando a costa á Cynosura,
Se incurva, e para a Aurora se endireita."
Camões, x. 125.

By Burton:

"But on her Lands-end throned see **Cingapúr**,
where the wide sea-road shrinks to narrow way:
Thence curves the coast to face the Cynosure,
and lastly trends Aurora-wards its lay."

1598.—"... by water the coast stretcheth to the Cape of **Singapura**, and from thence it runneth upwards [inwards] againe. ...—"*Linschoten*, 30; [Hak. Soc. i. 101].

1599.—"In this voyage nothing occurred worth relating, except that, after passing the Strait of **Sincapura**, situated in one degree and a half, between the main land and a variety of islands ... with so narrow a channel that from the ship you could jump ashore, or touch the branches of the trees on either side, our vessel struck on a shoal."—*Viaggi di Carletti*, ii. 208–9.

1606.—"The 5th May came there 2 Prows from the King of Johore, with the Shahbander (**Shabunder**) of **Singapoera**, called Siri Raja Nagara. ..."—*Valentijn*, v. 331.

1616.—"Found a Dutch man-of-war, one of a fleet appointed for the siege of Malaca, with the aid of the King of Acheen, at the entrance of the Straits of **Singapore**."—*Sainsbury*, i. 458.

1727.—"In anno 1703 I called at *Johore* on my Way to China, and he treated me very kindly, and made me a Present of the Island of **Sincapure**, but I told him it could be of no use to a private Person, tho' a proper Place for a Company to settle a Colony in, lying in the Center of Trade, and being accommodated with good Rivers and safe Harbours, so conveniently situated that all Winds served Shipping, both to go out and come in."—*A. Hamilton*, ii. 98; [ed. 1744, ii. 97].

1818.—"We are now on our way to the eastward, in the hope of doing something, but I much fear the Dutch have hardly left us an inch of ground. ... My attention is principally turned to Johore, and you must not be surprised if my next letter to you is dated from the site of the ancient city of **Singapura**."—*Raffles*, Letter to Marsden, dated *Sandheads*, Dec. 12.

SIRCAR, s. Hind. from Pers. *sarkār*, 'head (of) affairs.' This word has very divers applications; but its senses may fall under three heads.

a. The State, the Government, the Supreme authority; also 'the Master' or head of the domestic government. Thus a servant, if asked 'Whose are those horses?' in replying 'They are the *sarkār's*,' may mean according to circumstances, that they are Government horses, or that they belong to his own master.

b. In Bengal the word is applied to a domestic servant who is a kind of house-steward, and keeps the accounts of household expenditure, and makes miscellaneous purchases for the family; also, in merchants' offices, to any native accountant or native employed in making purchases, &c.

c. Under the Mahommedan Governments, as in the time of the Mogul Empire, and more recently in the Deccan, the word was applied to certain extensive administrative divisions of territory. In its application in the Deccan it has been in English generally spelt **Circar**.

a.—

[1759.—"... there is no separation between your Honour ... and this **Sircar**. ..."—*Forrest, Bombay Letters*, ii. 129.]

1800.—"Would it not be possible and proper to make people pay the **circar** according to the exchange fixed at Seringapatam?"—*Wellington*, i. 60.

[1866.—"... the **Sirkar** Buhadoor gives me four rupees a month. ..."—*Confessions of an Orderly*, 43.]

b.—

1777.—"There is not in any country in the world, of which I have any knowledge, a more pernicious race of vermin in human shape than are the numerous cast of people known in Bengal by the appellation of **Sircars**; they are educated and trained to deceive."—*Price's Tracts*, i. 24.

1810.—"The **Sircar** is a genius whose whole study is to handle money, whether receivable or payable, and who contrives either to confuse accounts, when they are adverse to his view, or to render them most expressively intelligible, when such should suit his purpose."—*Williamson, V.M.* i. 200.

1822.—"One morning our **Sircar**, in answer to my having observed that the articles purchased were highly priced, said, 'You are my father and my mother, and I am your poor little child. I have only taken 2 annas in the rupee dustoorie'" (**dustoor**).—*Wanderings of a Pilgrim*, i. 21–22.

1834.—"'And how the deuce,' asked his companion, 'do you manage to pay for them?' 'Nothing so easy,—I say to my **Sirkar**: 'Baboo, go pay for that horse 2000 rupees, and it is done, Sir, as quickly as you could dock him.'"—*The Baboo and Other Tales*, i. 13.

c.—

c. 1590.—"In the fortieth year of his majesty's reign, his dominions consisted of 105 **Sircars**, subdivided into 2737 kusbahs" "the revenue of which he settled for ten years at 3 Arribs, 62 **Crore**, 97 **Lacks**, 55,246 **Dams**" (q.v. 3,62,97,55,246 *dāms* = about 9 millions sterling).—*Ayeen*, E.T. by Gladwin, 1800, ii. 1; [ed. *Jarrett*, ii. 115.]

SIRDAR, s. Hind. from Pers. *sardār*, and less correctly *sirdār*, 'leader, a commander, an officer'; a chief, or lord; the head of a set of palankin-bearers, and hence the '*sirdār-bearer*,' or elliptically 'the *Sirdār*,' is in Bengal the style of the valet or body-servant, even when he may have no others under him (see BEARER). [**Sirdār** is now the official title of the Commander-in-Chief of the Egyptian army; **Sirdār** *Bahādur* is an Indian military distinction.]

[c. 1610.—"... a captain of a company, or, as they call it, a **Sardare**."—*Pyrard de Laval*, Hak. Soc. i. 254.

[1675.—"**Sardar**." See under SEPOY.]

1808.—"I, with great difficulty, knocked up some of the villagers, who were nearly as much afraid as Christie's Will, at the visit of a **Sirdār**" (here an *officer*).—*Life of Leyden.*

[c. 1817.—"... the bearers, with their **Sirdaur**, have a large room with a verandah before it."—*Mrs. Sherwood, Last Days of Boosy*, 63.]

1826.—"Gopee's father had been a **Sirdar** of some consequence."—*Pandurang Hari*, 174; [ed. 1873, i. 252].

SIRDRÁRS, s. This is the name which native valets (**bearer**) give to common drawers (underclothing). A friend (Gen. R. Maclagan, R.E.) has suggested the origin, which is doubtless "short drawers" in contradistinction to **Long-drawers**, or **Pyjamas** (qq.v.). A common bearer's pronunciation is *sirdrāj*; as a chest of drawers is also called '**Drāj** *kā almairā*' (see **ALMYRA**).

SIRRIS, s. Hind. *siris*, Skt. *shirisha*, *shri*, 'to break,' from the brittleness of its branches; the tree *Acacia Lebbek*, Benth., indigenous in S. India, the Sātpura range, Bengal, and the sub-Himālayan tract; cultivated in Egypt and elsewhere. A closely kindred sp., *A. Julibrissin*, Boivin, affords a specimen of scientific 'Hobson-Jobson'; the specific name is a corruption of *Gulāb-reshm*, 'silk-flower.'

1808.—"Quelques anneés après le mort de Dariyaî, des charpentiers ayant abattu un arbre de **Seris**, qui croissoit auprès de son tombeau, le coupèrent en plusieurs pièces pour l'employer à des constructions. Tout-à-coup une voix terrible se fit entendre, la terre se mit à trembler et le tronc de cet arbre se releva de lui-même. Les ouvriers épouvantés s'enfuirent, et l'arbre ne tarda pas à reverdir."—*Afsōs, Arāyish-i-Mahfil*, quoted by *Garcin de Tassy, Rel. Mus.* 88.

[c. 1890.—
"An' it fell when **sirris**-shaws were sere,
And the nichts were long and mirk."
R. Kipling, Departmental Ditties, The Fall of Jock Gillespie.]

SITTING-UP. A curious custom, in vogue at the Presidency towns more than a century ago, and the nature of which is indicated by the quotations. Was it of Dutch origin?

1777.—"Lady Impey **sits up** with Mrs. Hastings; *vulgo* toad-eating."—*Ph. Francis's Diary*, quoted in *Busteed, Echoes of Old Calcutta*, 124; [3rd ed. 125].

1780.—"When a young lady arrives at Madras, she must, in a few days afterwards **sit up** to receive company, attended by some beau or master of the ceremonies, which perhaps continues for a week, or until she has seen all the fair sex, and gentlemen of the settlement."—*Munro's Narr.*, 56.

1795.—"You see how many good reasons there are against your scheme of my taking horse instantly, and hastening to throw myself at the lady's feet; as to the other, of proxy, I can only agree to it under certain conditions. ... I am not to be forced to **sit up**, and receive male or female visitors. ... I am not to be obliged to deliver my opinion on patterns for caps or petticoats for any lady. ..."—*T. Munro to his Sister*, in *Life*, i. 169.

1810.—"Among the several justly exploded ceremonies we may reckon that ... of '**Sitting up**.' ... This '**Sitting up**,' as it was termed, generally took place at the house of some lady of rank or fortune, who, for three successive nights, threw open her mansion for the purpose of receiving all ... who chose to pay their respects to such ladies as might have recently arrived in the country."—*Williamson, V.M.* i. 113.

SLAVE. We cannot now attempt a history of the former tenure of slaves in British India, which would be a considerable work in itself. We only gather a few quotations illustrating that history.

1676.—"Of three Theeves, two were executed and one made a **Slave**. We do not approve of putting any to death for theft, nor that any of our own nation should be made a **Slave**, a word that becomes not an Englishman's mouth."—*The Court to Ft. St. Geo.*, March 7. In *Notes and Exts.* No. i. p. 18.

1682.—"... making also proclamation by beat of drum that if any **Slave** would run away from us he should be free, and liberty to go where they pleased."—*Hedges, Diary*, Oct. 14; [Hak. Soc. i. 38].

["There being a great number of **Slaves** yearly exported from this place, to ye great grievance of many persons whose Children are very commonly stollen away from them, by those who are constant traders in this way, the Agent, &c., considering the Scandall that might accrue to ye Government, &c., the great losse that many parents may undergoe by such actions, have order'd that noe more **Slaves** be sent off the shoare again."—*Pringle, Diary, Ft. St. Geo.*, 1st ser. i. 70.]

1752.—"Sale of **Slaves** ... Rs. 10: 1: 3."—Among Items of Revenue. In *Long*, 34.

1637.—"We have taken into consideration the most effectual and speedy method for supplying our settlements upon the West Coast with **slaves**, and we have therefore fixed upon two ships for that purpose ... to proceed from hence to Madagascar to purchase as many as can be procured, and the said ships conveniently carry, who are to be delivered by the captains of those ships to our agents at Fort Marlborough at the rate of £15 a head."—*Court's Letter* of Dec. 8. In *Long*, 293.

1764.—"That as an inducement to the Commanders and Chief Mates to exert themselves in procuring as large a number of **Slaves** as the Ships can conveniently carry, and to encourage the Surgeons to take proper care of them in the passage, there is to be allowed 20 shillings for every **slave** shipped at Madagascar, to be divided, viz., 13s. 4d. a head to the Commander, and 6s. 8d. to the Chief Mate, also for every one delivered at Fort Marlborough the Commander is to be allowed the further sum of 6s. 8d. and the Chief Mate 3s. 4d. The Surgeon is likewise to be allowed 10s. for each **slave** landed at Fort Marlborough."—*Court's Letter*, Feb. 22. In *Long*, 366.

1778.—Mr. Busteed has given some curious extracts from the charge-sheet of the Calcutta Magistrate in this year, showing **slaves** and **slave-girls**, of Europeans, Portuguese, and Armenians, sent to the magistrate to be punished with the rattan for running away and such offences.—*Echoes of Old Calcutta*, 117 *seqq.* [Also see extracts from newspapers, &c., in *Carey, Good Old Days*, ii. 71 *seqq.*].

1782.—"On Monday the 29th inst. will be sold by auction ... a bay Buggy Horse, a Buggy and Harness ... some cut Diamonds, a quantity of China Sugarcandy ... a quantity of the best Danish Claret ... deliverable at Serampore; two **Slave Girls** about 6 years old; and a great variety of other articles."—*India Gazette*, July 27.

1785.—"Malver. Hair-dresser from Europe, proposes himself to the ladies of the settlement to dress hair daily, at two gold mohurs per month, in the latest fashion, with gauze flowers, &c. He will also instruct the **slaves** at a moderate price."—In *Seton-Karr*, i. 119. This was surely a piece of slang. Though we hear occasionally, in the advertisements of the time, of slave boys and girls, the domestic servants were not usually of that description.

1794.—"50 Rupees Reward for Discovery.

"Run off about four Weeks ago from a Gentleman in Bombay, A Malay **Slave** called Cambing or Rambing. He stole a Silk Purse, with 45 Venetians, and some Silver Buttons. ..."—*Bombay Courier*, Feb. 22.

SNAKE-STONE, s. This is a term applied to a substance, the application of which to the part where a snake-bite has taken effect, is supposed to draw out the poison and render it innocuous. Such applications are made in various parts of the Old and New Worlds. The substances which have this reputation are usually of a porous kind, and when they have been chemically examined have proved to be made of charred bone, or the like. There is an article in the 13th vol. of the *Asiatic Researches* by Dr. J. Davy, entitled *An Analysis of the Snake-Stone*, in which the results of the examination of three different kinds, all obtained from Sir Alex. Johnstone, Chief Justice of Ceylon, is given. (1) The first kind was of round or oval form, black or brown in the middle, white towards the circumference, polished and somewhat lustrous, and pretty enough to be sometimes worn as a neck ornament; easily cut with a knife, but not scratched by the nail. When breathed on it emitted an earthy smell, and when applied to the tongue, or other moist surface, it adhered firmly. This kind proved to be of bone partially calcined. (2) We give below a quotation regarding the second kind. (3) The third was apparently a bezoar, rather than a snake-stone. There is another article in the *As. Res.* xvi. 382 *seqq.* by Captain J. D. Herbert, on *Zehr Mohereh, or* **Snake-Stone**. Two kinds are described which were sold under the name given (*Zahr muhra*, where *zahr* is 'poison,' *muhra*, 'a kind of polished shell,' 'a bead,' applied to a species of bezoar). Both of these were mineral, and not of the class we are treating of.

c. 1666.—"C'est dans cette Ville de Diu que se font les **Pierres de Cobra** si renommées: elles sont composées de racines qu'on brûle, et dont on amasse les cendres pour les mettre avec une sorte de terre qu'ils ont, et les brûler encore une fois avec cette terre; et après cela on en fait la pâte dont ces Pierres sont formées. ... Il faut faire sortir avec une éguille, un peu de sang de la plaie, y appliquer la Pierre, et l'y laisser jusqu'à ce qu'elle tombe d'elle même."—*Thevenot*, v. 97.

1673.—"Here are also those Elephant Legged St. *Thomeans*, which the unbiassed Enquirers will tell you chances to them two ways: By the Venom of a certain Snake, by which the *Jaugies* (see JOGEE) or Pilgrims furnish them with a Factitious Stone (which we call a **snake-stone**), and is a Counter-poyson of all deadly Bites; if it stick, it attracts the Poyson; and put into Milk it recovers itself again, leaving its virulency therein, discovered by its Greenness."—*Fryer*, 53.

c. 1676.—"There is the **Serpent's stone** not to be forgot, about the bigness of a *double* (doubloon?); and some are almost oval, thick in the middle and thin about the sides. The Indians report that it is bred in the head of certain Serpents. But I rather take it to be a story of the Idoloter's Priests, and that the Stone is rather a composition of certain Drugs. ... If the Person bit be not much wounded, the place must be incis'd; and the Stone being appli'd thereto, will not fall off till it has drawn all the poison to it: To cleanse it you must steep it in Womans-milk, or for want of that, in Cows-milk. ... There are two ways to try whether the **Serpent-stone** be true or false. The first is, by putting the Stone in your mouth, for there it will give a leap, and fix to the Palate. The other is by putting it in a glass full of water; for if the Stone be true, the water will fall a boyling, and rise in little bubbles. ..."—*Tavernier*, E.T., Pt. ii. 155; [ed. *Ball*, ii. 152]. Tavernier also speaks of another **snake-stone** alleged to be found behind the hood of the Cobra: "This Stone being rubb'd against another Stone, yields a slime, which being drank in water," &c. &c.—*Ibid.*

1690.—"The thing which he carried ... is a Specific against the Poison of Snakes ... and therefore obtained the name of **Snake-stone**. It is a small artificial Stone. ... The Composition of it is Ashes of burnt Roots, mixt with a kind of Earth, which is found at Diu. ..."—*Ovington*, 260–261.

1712.—"**Pedra de Cobra**: ita dictus lapis, vocabulo a Lusitanis imposito, adversus viperarum morsus praestat auxilium, externè applicatus. In serpente, quod vulgò credunt, non invenitur, sed arte secretâ fabricatur à Brahmanis. Pro dextro et felici usu, oportet adesse geminos, ut cum primus veneno saturatus vulnusculo decidit, alter surrogari illico in locum possit. ... Quo ipso feror, ut istis lapidibus nibil efficaciæ inesse credam, nisi quam actuali frigiditate suâ, vel absorbendo praestant."—*Kaempfer, Amoen. Exot.* 395–7.

1772.—"Being returned to Roode-Zand, the much celebrated **Snake-stone** (*Slangesteen*) was shown to me, which few of the farmers here could afford to purchase, it being sold at a high price, and held in great esteem. It is imported from the *Indies*, especially from Malabar, and cost several, frequently 10 or 12, rix dollars. It is round, and convex on one side, of a black colour, with a pale ash-grey speck in the middle, and tubulated with very minute pores. ... When it is applied to any part that has been bitten by a serpent, it sticks fast to the wound, and extracts the poison; as soon as it is saturated, it falls off of itself. ..."—*Thunberg*, *Travels*, E.T. i. 155 (*A Journey into Caffraria*).

1796.—"Of the remedies to which cures of venomous bites are often ascribed in India, some are certainly not less frivolous than those employed in Europe for the bite of the viper; yet to infer from thence that the effects of the poison cannot be very dangerous, would not be more rational than to ascribe the recovery of a person bitten by a Cobra de Capello, to the application of a **snake-stone**, or to the words muttered over the patient by a Bramin."—*Patrick Russell, Account of Indian Serpents*, 77.

1820.—"Another kind of **snake-stone** ... was a small oval body, smooth and shining, externally black, internally grey; it had no earthy smell when breathed on, and had no absorbent or adhesive power. By the person who presented it to Sir Alexander Johnstone it was much valued, and for adequate reason if true, 'it had saved the lives of four men.'"—*Dr. Davy*, in *As. Res.* xiii. 318.

1860.—"The use of the *Pamboo-Kaloo*, or **snake-stone**, as a remedy in cases of wounds by venomous serpents, has probably been communicated to the Singhalese by the itinerant snake-charmers who resort to the island from the Coast of Coromandel; and more than one well-authenticated instance of its successful application has been told to me by persons who had been eye-witnesses." ... (These follow.) "... As to the **snake-stone** itself, I submitted one, the application of which I have been describing, to Mr. Faraday, and he has communicated to me, as the result of his analysis, his belief that it is 'a piece of charred bone which has been filled with blood, perhaps several times, and then charred again.' ... The probability is, that the animal charcoal, when instantaneously applied, may be sufficiently porous and absorbent to extract the venom from the recent wound, together with a portion of the blood, before it has had time to be carried into the system. ..."—*Tennent*, *Ceylon*, i. 197–200.

1861.—"'Have you been bitten?' 'Yes, Sahib,' he replied, calmly; 'the last snake was a vicious one, and it has bitten me. But there is no danger,' he added, extracting from the recesses of his mysterious bag a small piece of white stone. This he wetted, and applied to the wound, to which it seemed to adhere ... he apparently suffered no ... material hurt. I was thus effectually convinced that snake-charming is a real art, and not merely clever conjuring, as I had previously imagined. These so-called **snake stones** are well known throughout India."—*Lt.-Col. T. Lewin, A Fly on the Wheel*, 91–92.

1872.—"With reference to the **snake-stones**, which, when applied to the bites, are said to absorb and suck out the poison, ... I have only to say that I believe they are perfectly powerless to produce any such effect ... when we reflect on the quantity of poison, and the force and depth with and to which it is injected ... and the extreme rapidity with which it is hurried along in the vascular system to the nerve centres, I think it is obvious that the application of one of these stones can be of little use in a real bite of a deadly snake, and that a belief in their efficacy is a dangerous delusion."—*Fayrer, Thanatophidia of India*, pp. 38, 40.

[1880.—"It is stated that in the pouch-like throat appendages of the older birds (**adjutants**), the fang of a snake is sometimes to be found. This, if rubbed above the place where a poisonous snake has bitten a man, is supposed to prevent the venom spreading to the vital parts of the body. Again, it is believed that a so-called '**snake-stone**' is contained within the head of the adjutant. This, if applied to a snake-bite, attaches itself to the punctures, and extracts all the venom. ..."—*Ball, Jungle Life*, 82.]

SOLA, vulg. **SOLAR**, s. This is properly Hind. *sholā*, corrupted by the Bengālī inability to utter the shibboleth, to *solā*, and often again into *solar* by English people, led astray by the usual "striving after meaning." *Sholā* is the name of the plant *Aeschynomene aspera*, L. (N.O. *Leguminosae*), and is particularly applied to the light pith of that plant, from which the light thick Sola **topees**, or pith hats, are made. The material is also used to pad the roofs of palankins, as a protection against the sun's power, and for various minor purposes, *e.g.* for slips of tinder, for making models, &c. The word, until its wide diffusion within the last 45 years, was peculiar to the Bengal Presidency. In the Deccan the thing is called *bhenḍ*, Mahr. *bhenḍa*, and in Tamil. *neṭṭi*, ['breaking with a crackle.'] **Solar** hats are now often advertised in London. [Hats made of elder pith were used in S. Europe in the early 16th century. In Albert Dürer's *Diary in the Netherlands* (1520–21) we find: "Also Tomasin has given me a plaited hat of elder-pith" (*Mrs. Heaton, Life of Albrecht Dürer*, 269). Miss Eden, in 1839, speaks of Europeans wearing "broad white feather hats to keep off the sun" (*Up the Country*, ii. 56). Illustrations of the various shapes of Sola hats used in Bengal about 1854 will be found in *Grant, Rural Life in Bengal*, 105 *seq.*]

1836.—"I stopped at a fisherman's, to look at the curiously-shaped floats he used for his very large and heavy fishing-nets; each float was formed of eight pieces of **sholā**, tied together by the ends. ... When this light and spongy pith is wetted, it can be cut into thin layers, which pasted together are formed into hats; Chinese paper appears to be made of the same material."—*Wanderings of a Pilgrim*, ii. 100.

1872.—"In a moment the flint gave out a spark of fire, which fell into the **solá**; the sulphur match was applied; and an earthen lamp. ..."—*Govinda Samanta*, i. 10.

1878.—"My **solar** topee (pith hat) was whisked away during the struggle."—*Life in the Mofussil*, i. 164.

1885.—"I have slipped a pair of galoshes over my ordinary walking-boots; and, with my **solar topee** (or sun helmet) on, have ridden through a mile of deserted streets and through bazaars, in a grilling sunshine."—*A Professional Visit in Persia, St. James's Gazette*, March 9.

SOMBRERO, s. Port. *sumbreiro*. In England we now understand by this word a broad-brimmed hat; but in older writers it is used for an *umbrella*. **Summerhead** is a name in the Bombay Arsenal (as M.-Gen. Keatinge tells me) for a great umbrella. I make no doubt that it is a corruption (by 'striving after meaning') of **Sombreiro**, and it is a capital example of **Hobson-Jobson**.

1503.—"And the next day the Captain-Major before daylight embarked armed with all his people in the boats, and the King (of Cochin) in his boats which they call *tones* ... and in the *tone* of the King went his **Sombreiros**, which are made of straw, of a diameter of 4 palms, mounted on very long canes, some 3 or 4 fathoms in height. These are used for state ceremonial, showing that the King is there in person, as it were his pennon or royal banner, for no other lord in his realm may carry the like."—*Correa*, i. 378.

1516.—"And besides the page I speak of who carries the sword, they take another page who carries a **sombreiro** with a stand to shade his master, and keep the rain off him; and some of these are of silk stuff finely wrought, with many fringes of gold, and set with stones and seed pearl. ..."—*Barbosa*, Lisbon ed. 298.

1553.—"At this time Dom Jorge discerned a great body of men coming towards where he was standing, and amid them a **sombreiro** on a lofty staff, covering the head of a man on horseback, by which token he knew it to be some noble person. This **sombreiro** is a fashion in India coming from China, and among the Chinese no one may use it but a gentleman, for it is a token of nobility, which we may describe as a one-handed *pallium* (having regard to those which we use to see carried by four, at the reception of some great King or Prince on his entrance into a city). ..."—*Barros*, III. x. 9. Then follows a minute description of the **sombreiro** or **umbrella**.

[1599.—"... a great broad **sombrero** or shadow in their hands to defend them in the Summer from the Sunne, and in the Winter from the Raine."—*Hakl.* II. i. 261 (*Stanf. Dict.*).

[1602.—In his character of D. Pedro Mascarenhas, the Viceroy, Couto says he was anxious to change certain habits of the Portuguese in India: "One of these was to forbid the tall **sombreiros** for warding off the rain and sun, to relieve men of the expence of paying those who carried them; he himself did not have one, but used a woollen umbrella with small cords (?), which they called for many years *Mascarenhas*. Afterwards finding the sun intolerable and the rain immoderate, he permitted the use of tall umbrellas, on the condition that private slaves should bear them, to save the wages of the Hindus who carry them, and are called **boys de sombreiro** (see BOY)."—*Couto*, Dec. VII. Bk. i. ch. 12.]

c. 1630.—"Betwixt towns men usually travel in Chariots drawn by Oxen, but in Towns upon **Palamkeens**, and with **Sombreros** *de Sol* over them."—*Sir T. Herbert*, ed. 1665, p. 46.

1657.—"A costé du cheval il y a un homme qui esvente *Wistnou*, afin qu'il ne reçoive point d'incommodité soit par les mouches, ou par la chaleur; et à chaque costé on porte deux **Zombreiros**, afin que le Soleil ne luise pas sur luy. ..."—*Abr. Roger*, Fr. Tr. ed. 1670, p. 223.

1673.—"None but the Emperor have a **Sumbrero** among the *Moguls*."—*Fryer*, 36.

1727.—"The *Portuguese* ladies ... sent to beg the Favour that he would pick them out some lusty *Dutch* men to carry their *Palenqueens* and **Somereras** or Umbrellas."—*A. Hamilton*, i. 338; [ed. 1744, i. 340].

1768-71.—"Close behind it, followed the heir-apparent, on foot, under a **sambreel**, or sunshade, of state."—*Stavorinus*, E.T. i. 87.

[1845.—"No open umbrellas or **summer-heads** allowed to pass through the gates."—*Public Notice on Gates of Bombay Town*, in *Douglas, Glimpses of Old Bombay*, 86.]

SONTHALS, n.p. Properly *Santāls*, [the name being said to come from a place called *Saont*, now Silda in Mednipur, where the tribe remained, for a long time (*Dalton, Descr. Eth.* 210-11)]. The name of a non-Aryan people belonging to the Kolarian class, extensively settled in the hilly country to the west of the Hoogly R. and to the south of Bhāgalpur, from which they extended tò Balasore at interval, sometimes in considerable masses, but more generally much scattered. The territory in which they are chiefly settled is now formed into a separate district called Santāl Parganas, and sometimes *Santalia*. Their settlement in this tract is, however, quite modern; they have emigrated thither from the S.W. In Dr. F. Buchanan's statistical account of Bhāgalpur and its Hill people the Santāls are not mentioned. The earliest mention of this tribe that we have found is in Mr. Sutherland's Report on the Hill People, which is printed in the Appendix to Long. No date is given there, but we learn from Mr. Man's book, quoted below, that the date is 1817. [The word is, however, much older than this. Forbes (*Or. Mem.* ii. 374 *seq.*) gives an account taken from Lord Teignmouth of witch tests among the **Soontaar**.

[1798.—"... amongst a wild and unlettered tribe, denominated **Soontaar**, who have reduced the detection and trial of persons suspected of witchcraft to a system."—*As. Res.* iv. 359.]

1817.—"For several years many of the industrious tribes called **Sonthurs** have established themselves in these forests, and have been clearing and bringing into cultivation large tracts of lands. ..."—*Sutherland's Report*, quoted in *Long*, 569.

1867.—"This system, indicated and proposed by Mr. Eden,[1] was carried out in its integrity under Mr. George Yule, C.B., by whose able management, with Messrs. Robinson and Wood as his deputies, the **Sonthals** were raised from misery, dull despair, and deadly hatred of the government, to a pitch of prosperity which, to my knowledge, has never been equalled in any other part of India under the British rule. The Regulation Courts, with their horde of leeches in the shape of badly paid, and corrupt Amlah (**Omlah**) and pettifogging **Mooktears**, were abolished, and in their place a Number of active English gentlemen, termed Assistant Commissioners, and nominated by Mr. Yule, were set down among the **Sonthals**, with a Code of Regulations drawn up by that gentleman, the pith of which may be summed up as follows:—

"'To have no medium between the **Sonthal** and the **Hakim**, *i.e.* Assistant Commissioner.

"'To patiently hear any complaint made by the **Sonthal** from his own mouth, without any written petition or charge whatever, and without any **Amlah** or Court at the time.

"'To carry out all criminal work by the aid of the villagers themselves, who were to bring in the accused, with the witnesses, to the Hakim, who should immediately attend to their statements, and punish them, if found guilty, according to the tenor of the law.'

"These were some of the most important of the golden rules carried out by men who

1 This is apparently a mistake. The proposals were certainly original with Mr. Yule.

recognised the responsibility of their situation; and with an adored chief, in the shape of Yule, for their ruler, whose firm, judicious, and gentlemanly conduct made them work with willing hearts, their endeavours were crowned with a success which far exceeded the expectations of the most sanguine. ..."—*Sonthalia and the Sonthals*, by *E. G. Man*, Barrister-at-Law, &c. Calcutta, 1867, pp. 125–127.

SOODRA, SOODER, s. Skt. *śudra*, [usually derived from root. *śuć*, 'to be afflicted,' but probably of non-Aryan origin]. The (theoretical) Fourth Caste of the Hindus. In South India, there being no claimants of the 2nd or 3rd classes, the highest castes among the (so-called) *Śudras* come next after the Brahmans in social rank, and *śudra* is a note of respect, not of the contrary as in Northern India.

1630.—"The third Tribe or Cast, called the **Shudderies**."—*Lord, Display*, &c., ch. xii.

1651.—"La quatrième lignée est celle des **Soudraes**; elle est composée du commun peuple: cette lignée a sous soy beaucoup et diverses familles, dont une chacune prétend surpasser l'autre. ..."—*Abr. Roger*, Fr. ed. 1670, p. 8.

[c. 1665.—"The fourth caste is called **Charados** or **Soudra**."—*Tavernier*, ed. *Ball*, ii. 184.

[1667.—"... and fourthly, the tribe of **Seydra**, or artisans and labourers."—*Bernier*, ed. *Constable*, 325.]

1674.—"The ... **Chudrer** (these are the Nayres)."—*Faria y Sousa*, ii. 710.

1717.—"The Brahmens and the **Tschuddirers** are the proper persons to satisfy your Enquiries."—*Phillips, An Account of the Religion*, &c., 14.

1858.—"Such of the Aborigines as yet remained were formed into a fourth class, the **Çudra**, a class which has no rights, but only duties."—*Whitney, Or. and Ling. Studies*, ii. 6.

1867.—"A Brahman does not stand aloof from a **Soudra** with a keener pride than a Greek Christian shows towards a Copt."—*Dixon, New America*, 7th ed. i. 276.

SOPHY, n.p. The name by which the King of Persia was long known in Europe—"The *Sophy*," as the Sultan of Turkey was "The Turk" or "Grand Turk," and the King of Delhi the "Great Mogul." This title represented *Sūfī*, *Safavī*, or *Safī*, the name of the dynasty which reigned over Persia for more than two centuries (1449–1722, nominally to 1736). The first king of the family was Isma'il, claiming descent from 'Ali and the Imāms, through a long line of persons of saintly reputation at Ardebil. The surname of Sūfī or Safī assumed by Isma'il is generally supposed to have been taken from Shaikh Safī-ud-dīn, the first of his more recent ancestors to become famous, and who belonged to the class of Sūfīs or philosophic devotees. After Isma'il the most famous of the dynasty was Shāh Abbās (1585–1629).

c. 1524.—"Susiana, quae est Shushan Palatium illud regni **Sophii**."—*Abraham Peritsol*, in *Hyde, Syntagma Dissertt.* i. 76.

1560.—"De que o **Sufi** foy contente, e mandou gente em su ajuda."—*Terceiro*, ch. i.

"Quae regiones nomine Persiae ei regnantur quem Turcae *Chislibas*, nos **Sophi** vocamus."—*Busbeq. Epist.* iii. (171).

1561.—"The Queenes Maiesties *Letters to the great* **Sophy** *of Persia, sent by* M. Anthonie Ienkinson.

"Elizabetha Dei gratia Angliae Franciae et Hiberinae Regina, &c. Potentissimo et inuictissimo Principi, Magno **Sophi** Persarum, Medorum, Hircanorum, Carmanorum, Margianorum, populorum cis et vltra Tygrim fluuium, et omnium intra Mare Caspium et Persicum Sinum nationum atque Gentium Imperatori salutem et rerum prosperarum foelicissimum incrementum."—In *Hakl.* i. 381.

[1568.—"The King of Persia (whom here we call the great **Sophy**) is not there so called, but is called the Shaugh. It were dangerous to call him by the name of **Sophy**, because that **Sophy** in the Persian tongue is a beggar, and it were as much as to call him The great beggar."—*Geffrey Ducket, ibid.* i. 447.]

1598.—"And all the Kings continued so with the name of Xa, which in Persia is a King, and Ishmael is a proper name, whereby Xa Ismael, and Xa Thamas are as much as to say King Ismael, and King Thamas, and of the Turkes and Rumes are called **Suffy** or **Soffy**, which signifieth a great Captaine."—*Linschoten*, ch. xxvii.; [Hak. Soc. i. 173].

1601.—

"*Sir Toby*. Why, man, he's a very devil: I have not seen such a firago ...

"They say, he has been fencer to the **Sophy**."—*Twelfth Night*, III. iv.

[c. 1610.—"This King or **Sophy**, who is called the Great Chaa."—*Pyrard de Laval*, Hak. Soc. ii. 253.]

1619.—"Alla porta di Sciah **Sofi**, si sonarono nacchere tutto il giorno: ed insomma tutta la città e tutto il popolo andò in allegrezza, concorrendo infinita gente alla meschita di Schia **Sofi**, a far *Gratiarum actionem*."—*P. della Valle*, i. 808.

1626.—
"Were it to bring the Great Turk bound in chains
Through France in triumph, or to couple up
The **Sophy** and great Prester-John together;
I would attempt it."
Beaum. & Fletch., The Noble Gentleman, v. 1.

c. 1630.—"Ismael at his Coronation proclaim'd himself King of *Persia* by the name of *Pot-shaw-Ismael*-**Sophy**. Whence that word **Sophy** was borrowed is much controverted. Whether it be from the Armenian idiom, signifying Wooll, of which the Shashes are made that ennobled his new order. Whether the name was from **Sophy** his grandsire, or from the Greek word *Sophos* imposed upon *Aydar* at his conquest of *Trebizond* by the Greeks there, I know not. Since then, many have called the Kings of Persia **Sophy's**: but I see no reason for it; since *Ismael's* son, grand and great grandsons Kings of *Persia* never continued that name, till this that now reigns, whose name indeed is *Soffee*, but casuall."—*Sir T. Herbert*, ed. 1638, 286.

1643.—"Y avoit vn Ambassadeur Persien qui auoit esté enuoyé en Europe de la part du Grand **Sophy** Roy de Perse."—*Mocquet, Voyages*, 269.

1665.—
"As when the Tartar from his Russian foe,
By Astracan, over the snowy plains
Retires; or Bactrian **Sophy**, from the horns
Of Turkish crescent, leaves all waste beyond
The realm of Aladule, in his retreat
To Tauris or Casbeen... ."
Paradise Lost, x. 431 *seqq.*

1673.—"But the **Suffee's** Vicar-General is by his Place the Second Person in the Empire, and always the first Minister of State."—*Fryer* 338.

1681.—"La quarta parte comprehende el Reyno de Persia, cuyo Señor se llama en estos tiempos, el Gran **Sophi**."—*Martinez, Compendio*, 6.

1711.—"In Consideration of the Company's good Services ... they had half of the Customs of *Gombroon* given them, and their successors, by a Firman from the **Sophi** or Emperor."—*Lockyer*, 220.

1727.—"The whole Reign of the last **Sophi** or King, was managed by such Vermin, that the *Ballowches* and *Mackrans* ... threw off the Yoke of Obedience first, and in full Bodies fell upon their Neighbours in *Caramania*."—*A. Hamilton*, i. 108; [ed. 1744, i. 105].

1815.—"The **Suffavean** monarchs were revered and deemed holy on account of their descent from a saint."—*Malcolm, H. of Pers.* ii. 427.

1828.—"It is thy happy destiny to follow in the train of that brilliant star whose light shall shed a lustre on Persia, unknown since the days of the earlier **Soofees**."—*J. B. Fraser, The Kuzzilbash*, i. 192.

SOUBA, SOOBAH, s. Hind. from Pers. *ṣūba*. A large Division or Province of the Mogul Empire (*e.g.* the *Ṣūbah* of the Deccan, the *Ṣūbah* of Bengal). The word is also frequently used as short for *Sūbadār* (see SOUBADAR), 'the Viceroy' (over a *ṣūba*). It is also "among the Marațhas sometimes applied to a smaller division comprising from 5 to 8 *țarafs*" (*Wilson*).

c. 1594.—"In the fortieth year of his majesty's reign, his dominions consisted of 105 **Sircars**. ... The empire was then parcelled into 12 grand divisions, and each was committed to the government of a **Soobadar** ... upon which occasion the Sovereign of the world distributed 12 Lacks of beetle. The names of the **Soobahs** were Allahabad, Agra, Owdh, Ajmeer, Ahmedabad, Bahar, Bengal, Dehly, Cabul, Lahoor, Multan, and Malwa: when his majesty conquered Berar, Khandeess, and Ahmednagur, they were formed into three **Soobahs**, increasing the number to 15."—*Ayeen*, ed. *Gladwin*, ii. 1–5; [ed. *Jarrett*, ii. 115].

1753.—"Princes of this rank are called **Subahs**. *Nizam al muluck* was **Subah** of the *Decan* (or Southern) provinces. ... The Nabobe of *Condanore, Cudapah, Carnatica, Yalore*, &c., the Kings of *Tritchinopoly, Mysore, Tanjore*, are subject to this **Subah**-ship. Here is a subject ruling a larger empire than any in Europe, excepting that of the Muscovite."—*Orme, Fragments*, 398–399.

1760.—"Those Emirs or Nabobs, who govern great Provinces, are stiled **Subahs**, which imports the same as Lord-Lieutenants or Vice-Roys."—*Memoirs of the Revolution in Bengal*, p. 6.

1763.—"From the word **Soubah**, signifying a province, the Viceroy of this vast territory (the Deccan) is called **Soubahdar**, and by the Europeans improperly **Soubah**."—*Orme*, i. 35.

1765.—"Let us have done with this ringing of changes upon **Soubahs**; there's no end to it. Let us boldly dare to be **Soubah** ourselves. ..."—*Holwell, Hist. Events*, &c., i. 183.

1783.—"They broke their treaty with him, in which they stipulated to pay 400,000*l.* a year to the **Subah** of Bengal."—*Burke's Speech on Fox's India Bill, Works*, iii. 468.

1804.—"It is impossible for persons to have behaved in a more shuffling manner than the **Soubah's** servants have. ..."—*Wellington*, ed. 1837, iii. 11.

1809.—"These (pillars) had been removed from a sacred building by Monsieur Dupleix, when he assumed the rank of **Soubah**."—*Lord Valentia*, i. 373.

1823.—"The Delhi Sovereigns whose vast empire was divided into **Soubahs**, or Governments, each of which was ruled by a **Soubahdar** or Viceroy."—*Malcolm, Cent. India*, i. 2.

SOUBADAR, SUBADAR, s. Hind. from Pers. *ṣūbadār*, 'one holding a *ṣūba*' (see SOUBA).

a. The Viceroy, or Governor of a *ṣūba*.

b. A local commandant or chief officer.

c. The chief native officer of a company of Sepoys; under the original constitution of such companies, its actual captain.

a. See **SOUBA**.

b.—

1673.—"The **Subidar** of the Town being a Person of Quality ... he (the Ambassador) thought good to give him a Visit."—*Fryer*, 77.

1805.—"The first thing that the **Subidar** of Vire Rajendra Pettah did, to my utter astonishment, was to come up and give me such a shake by the hand, as would have done credit to a Scotsman."—Letter in *Leyden's Life*, 49.

c.—

1747.—"14th September ... Read the former from Tellicherry adviseing that ... in a day or two they shall despatch another **Subidar** with 129 more Sepoys to our assistance."—MS. *Consultations at Fort St. David*, in *India Office*.

1760.—"One was the **Subahdar**, equivalent to the Captain of a Company."—*Orme*, iii. 610.

c. 1785.—"... the **Subahdars** or commanding officers of the black troops."—*Carraccioli, L. of Clive*, iii. 174.

1787.—"A Troop of Native Cavalry on the present Establishment consists of 1 European Subaltern, 1 European Serjeant, 1 **Subidar**, 3 **Jemadars**, 4 **Havildars**, 4 Naiques, 1 Trumpeter, 1 Farrier, and 68 Privates."—*Regns. for the Hon. Comp.'s Black Troops on the Coast of Coromandel*, &c., p. 6.

SOWAR, SUWAR, s. Pers. *sawār*, 'a horseman.' A native cavalry soldier; a mounted orderly. In the Greek provinces in Turkey, the word is familiar in the form *σουβάρις*, pl. *σουβαρίδες*, for a mounted gendarme. [The regulations for *suwārs* in the Mogul armies are given by *Blochmann, Āīn*, i. 244 *seq.*]

1824-5.—"... The **sowars** who accompanied him."—*Heber*, Orig. i. 404.

1827.—"Hartley had therefore no resource save to keep his eye steadily fixed on the lighted match of the **sowar** ... who rode before him."—*Sir W. Scott, The Surgeon's Daughter*, ch. xiii.

[1830.—"... Meerza, an **Asswar** well known on the Collector's establishment."—*Or. Sport. Mag.* reprint 1873, i. 390.]

SOWAR, SHOOTER, s. Hind. from Pers. *shutur-sawār*, the rider of a dromedary or swift camel. Such riders are attached to the establishment of the Viceroy on the march, and of other high officials in Upper India. The word *sowar* is quite misused by the Great Duke in the passage below, for a camel-*driver*, a sense it never has. The word written, or intended, may however have been **surwaun**

[1815.—"As we approached the camp his oont-**surwars** (camel-riders) went ahead of us."—*Journal, Marquess of Hastings*, i. 337.]

1834.—"I ... found a fresh horse at Sufter Jung's tomb, and at the Kutub a couple of riding camels and an attendant **Shutur Suwar**."—*Mem. of Col. Mountain*, 129.

[1837.—"There are twenty **Shooter Suwars** (I have not an idea how I ought to spell those words), but they are native soldiers mounted on swift camels, very much *trapped*, and two of them always ride before our carriage."—*Miss Eden, Up the Country*, i. 31.]

1840.—"Sent a **Shuta Sarwar** (camel driver) off with an express to Simla."—*Osborne, Court and Camp of Runj. Singh*, 179.

1842.—"At Peshawur, it appears by the papers I read last night, that they have camels, but no **sowars**, or drivers."—Letter of *D. of Wellington*, in *Indian Administration of Ld. Ellenborough*, 228.

1857.—"I have given general notice of the **Shutur Sowar** going into Meerut to all the Meerut men."—*H. Greathed's Letters during Siege of Delhi*, 42.

SOWARRY, SUWARREE, s. Hind. from Pers. *sawārī*. A cavalcade, a cortège of mounted attendants.

1803.—"They must have tents, elephants, and other **sewary**; and must have with them a sufficient body of troops to guard their persons."—*A. Wellesley*, in *Life of Munro*, i. 346.

1809.—"He had no **sawarry**."—*Ld. Valentia*, i. 388.

1814.—"I was often reprimanded by the Zemindars and native officers, for leaving the **suwarree**, or state attendants, at the outer gate of the city, when I took my evening excursion."—*Forbes, Or. Mem.* iii. 420; [2nd ed. ii. 372].

[1826.—"The '**aswary**,' or suite of Trimbuckje, arrived at the palace."—*Pandurang Hari*, ed. 1873, i. 119.]

1827.—"Orders were given that on the next

day all should be in readiness for the **Sowarree**, a grand procession, when the Prince was to receive the Begum as an honoured guest."—*Sir Walter Scott, The Surgeon's Daughter*, ch. xiv.

c. 1831.—"Je tâcherai d'éviter toute la poussière de ces immenses **sowarris**."—*Jacquemont, Corresp.* ii. 121.

[1837.—"The Raja of Benares came with a very magnificent **surwarree** of elephants and camels."—*Miss Eden, Up the Country*, i. 35.]

SOY, s. A kind of condiment once popular. The word is Japanese *si-yau* (a young Japanese fellow-passenger gave the pronunciation clearly as *sho-yu*.—A. B.), Chin. *shi-yu*. [Mr. Platts (9 ser. *N. & Q.* iv. 475) points out that in Japanese as written with the native character *soy* would not be *siyau*, but *siyau-yu*; in the Romanised Japanese this is simplified to *shoyu* (colloquially this is still further reduced, by dropping the final vowel, to *shoy* or *soy*). Of this monosyllable only the *so* represents the classical *siyau*; the final consonant (*y*) is a relic of the termination *yu*. The Japanese word is itself derived from the Chinese, which at Shanghai is *sze-yu*, at Amoy; *si-iu*, at Canton, *shi-yau*, of which the first element means 'salted beans,' or other fruits, dried and used as condiments; the second element merely means 'oil.'] It is made from the beans of a plant common in the Himālaya and E. Asia, and much cultivated, viz. *Glycine Soja*, Sieb. and Zucc. (*Soya hispida*, Moench.), boiled down and fermented. [In India the bean is eaten in places where it is cultivated, as in Chutia Nāgpur (*Watt, Ecom. Dict.* iii. 510 *seq.*)]

1679.—"... Mango and **Saio**, two sorts of sauces brought from the East Indies."—*Journal of John Locke*, in *Ld. King's Life of L.*, i. 249.

1688.—"I have been told that **soy** is made with a fishy composition, and it seems most likely by the Taste; tho' a Gentleman of my Acquaintance who was very intimate with one that sailed often from Tonquin to Japan, from whence the true *Soy* comes, told me that it was made only with Wheat and a sort of Beans mixt with Water and Salt."—*Dampier*, ii. 28.

1690.—"... **Souy**, the choicest of all Sawces."—*Ovington*, 397.

1712.—"Hoc legumen in coquinâ Japonicâ utramque replet paginam; ex eo namque conficitur: tum puls *Miso* dicta, quae ferculis pro consistentiâ, et butyri loco additur, butyrum enim hôc coelô res ignota est; tum **Sooju** dictum embamma, quod nisi ferculis, certè frictis et ássatis omnibus affunditur."—*Kaempfer, Amoen. Exot.* p. 839.

1776.—An elaborate account of the preparation of Soy is given by *Thunberg, Travels*. E.T. iv. 121–122; and more briefly by Kaempfer on the page quoted above.

[1900.—"Mushrooms shred into small pieces, flavoured with *shoyu*" (**soy**).—*Mrs. Frazer, A Diplomatist's Wife in Japan*, i. 238.]

SPIN, s. An unmarried lady; popular abbreviation of 'Spinster.' [The Port. equivalent *soltera* (*soltiera*) was used in a derogatory sense (*Gray*, note on *Pyrard de Laval*, Hak. Soc. ii. 128).]

SQUEEZE, s. This is used in Anglo-Chinese talk for an illegal exaction. It is, we suppose, the translation of a Chinese expression. It corresponds to the *malatolta* of the Middle Ages, and to many other slang phrases in many tongues.

1882.—"If the licence (of the Hong merchants) ... was costly, it secured to them uninterrupted and extraordinary pecuniary advantages; but on the other hand it subjected them to 'calls' or '**squeezes**' for contributions to public works, ... for the relief of districts suffering from scarcity ... as well as for the often imaginary ... damage caused by the overflowing of the 'Yangtse Keang' or the 'Yellow River.'"—*The Fankwae at Canton*, p. 36.

STATION, s. A word of constant recurrence in Anglo-Indian colloquial. It is the usual designation of the place where the English officials of a district, or the officers of a garrison (not in a fortress) reside. Also the aggregate society of such a place.

[1832.—"The nobles and gentlemen are frequently invited to witness a '**Station** ball.' ..."—*Mrs. Meer Hassan Ali, Observations*, i. 196.]

1866.—

"And if I told how much I ate at one Mofussil **station**,
I'm sure 'twould cause at home a most extraordinary sensation."
Travelyan, The Dawk Bungalow, in *Fraser*, lxxiii. p. 391.

"Who asked the **Station** to dinner, and allowed only one glass of Simkin to each guest."—*Ibid.* 231.

SUDDEN DEATH. Anglo-Indian slang for a fowl served as a spatchcock, the standing dish at a dawk-bungalow in former days. The bird was caught in the yard, as the traveller entered, and was on the table by the time he had bathed and dressed.

[c. 1848.—"'**Sudden death**' means a young chicken about a month old, caught, killed, and grilled at the shortest notice."—*Berncastle, Voyage to China*, i. 193.]

SUDDER, adj., but used as s. Literally 'chief,' being Ar. *sadr*. This term had a technical application under Mahommedan rule to a chief Judge, as in the example quoted below. The use of the word seems to be almost confined to the Bengal Presidency. Its principal applications are the following:

a. Sudder Board. This is the 'Board of Revenue,' of which there is one at Calcutta, and one in the N.W. Provinces at Allahabad. There is a Board of Revenue at Madras, but not called '**Sudder** Board' there.

b. Sudder Court, *i.e.* 'Sudder **Adawlut** (*sadr 'adālat*). This was till 1862, in Calcutta and in the N.W.P., the chief court of appeal from the **Mofussil** or District Courts, the Judges being members of the Bengal Civil Service. In the year named the Calcutta Sudder Court was amalgamated with the Supreme Court (in which English Law had been administered by English Barrister-Judges), the amalgamated Court being entitled the *High Court of Judiciary*. A similar Court also superseded the Sudder Adawlut in the N.W.P.

c. Sudder Ameen, *i.e.* chief **Ameen** (q.v.). This was the designation of the second class of native Judge in the classification which was superseded in Bengal by Act XVI. of 1868, in Bombay by Act XIV. of 1869, and in Madras by Act III. of 1873. Under that system the highest rank of native Judge was **Principal Sudder Ameen**; the 2nd rank, **Sudder Ameen**; the 3rd, Moonsiff. In the new classification there are in Bengal Subordinate Judges of the 1st, 2nd and 3rd grade, and Munsiffs of 4 grades; in Bombay, Subordinate Judges of the 1st class in 3 grades, and 2nd class in 4 grades; and in Madras Subordinate Judges in 3 grades, and Munsiffs in 4 grades.

d. Sudder Station. The chief station of a district, viz. that where the Collector, Judge, and other chief civil officials reside, and where their Courts are.

c. 1340.—"The **Sadr**-*Jihān* ('Chief of the Word') *i.e.* the **Kadī**-*al-Kuḍāt* ('Judge of Judges') (CAZEE) ... possesses ten townships, producing a revenue of about 60,000 tankas. He is also called **Ṣadr**-*al-Islām*."—*Shihābuddīn Dimishkī*, in *Notes et Exts.* xiii. 185.

SUFEENA, s. Hind. *sạfina*. This is the native corr. of *subpoena*. It is shaped, but not much distorted, by the existence in Hind. of the Ar. word *safina* for 'a blank-book, a note-book.'

SUGAR, s. This familiar word is of Skt. origin. *Sarkara* originally signifies 'grit or gravel,' thence crystallised sugar, and through a Prakrit form *sakkara* gave the Pers. *shakkar*, the Greek σάκχαρ and σάκχαρον, and the late Latin *saccharum*. The Ar. is *sukkar*, or with the article *as-sukkar*, and it is probable that our modern forms, It. *zucchero* and *succhero*, Fr. *sucre*, Germ. *Zucker*, Eng. *sugar*, came as well as the Sp. *azucar*, and Port. *assucar*, from the Arabic direct, and not through Latin or Greek. The Russian is *sakhar*; Polish *zukier*; Hung. *zukur*. In fact the ancient knowledge of the product was slight and vague, and it was by the Arabs that the cultivation of the sugar-cane was introduced into Egypt, Sicily, and Andalusia. It is possible indeed, and not improbable, that palm-sugar (see JAGGERY) is a much older product than that of the cane. [This is disputed by Watt (*Econ. Dict.* vi. pt. i. p. 31), who is inclined to fix the home of the cane in E. India.] The original habitat of the cane is not known; there is only a slight and doubtful statement of Loureiro, who, in speaking of Cochin-China, uses the words "habitat et colitur," which may imply its existence in a wild state, as well as under cultivation, in that country. De Candolle assigns its earliest production to the country extending from Cochin-China to Bengal.

Though, as we have said, the knowledge which the ancients had of sugar was very dim, we are disposed greatly to question the thesis, which has been so confidently maintained by Salmasius and later writers, that the original *saccharon* of Greek and Roman writers was not sugar but the siliceous concretion sometimes deposited in bamboos, and used in medieval medicine under the name **tabasheer**. It is just possible that Pliny in the passage quoted below may have jumbled up two different things, but we see no sufficient evidence even of this. In White's Latin Dict. we read that by the word *saccharon* is meant (not sugar but) "a sweet juice distilling from the joints of the bamboo."

This is nonsense. There is no such sweet juice distilled from the joints of the bamboo; nor is the substance *tabashīr* at all sweet. On the contrary it is slightly bitter and physicky in taste, with no approach to sweetness. It is a hydrate of silica. It could never have been called "honey" (see Dioscorides and Pliny below); and the name of *bamboo-sugar* appears to have been given it by the Arabs merely because of some resemblance of its concretions to lumps of sugar. [The same view is taken in the *Encycl. Brit.* 9th ed. xxii. 625, quoting *Not. et Extr.*, xxv. 267.] All the erroneous notices of *σάκχαρον* seem to be easily accounted for by lack of knowledge; and they are exactly paralleled by the loose and inaccurate stories about the origin of camphor, of lac, and what-not, that may be found within the boards of this book.

In the absence or scarcity of sugar, honey was the type of sweetness, and hence the name of *honey* applied to sugar in several of these early extracts. This phraseology continued down to the Middle Ages, at least in its application to uncrystallised products of the sugar-cane, and analogous substances. In the quotation from Pegolotti we apprehend that his three kinds of honey indicate honey, treacle, and a syrup or treacle made from the sweet pods of the carob-tree.

Sugar does not seem to have been in early Chinese use. The old Chinese books often mention *shi-mi* or 'stone-honey' as a product of India and Persia. In the reign of Taitsung (627–650) a man was sent to Gangetic India to learn the art of sugar-making; and Marco Polo below mentions the introduction from Egypt of the further art of refining it. In India now, *Chīnī* (Chinese) is applied to the whiter kinds of common sugar; *Miṣrī* or Egyptian, to sugar-candy; loaf-sugar is called *kand*.

c. A.D. 60.—

"Quâque ferens rapidum diviso gurgite fontem
Vastis Indus aquis mixtum non sentit Hydaspen:
Quique bibunt tenerâ dulcis ab arundine succos. ..."
Lucan, iii. 235.

"Aiunt inveniri apud Indos mel in arundinum foliis, quod aut nos illius cœli, aut ipsius arundinis humor dulcis et pinguis gignat."—*Seneca, Epist.* lxxxiv.

c. A.D. 65.—"It is called *σάκχαρον*, and is a kind of honey which solidifies in India, and in Arabia Felix; and is found upon canes, in its substance resembling salt, and crunched by the teeth as salt is. Mixed with water and drunk, it is good for the belly and stomach, and for affections of the bladder and kidneys."—*Dioscorides, Mat. Med.* ii. c. 104.

c. A.D. 70.—"**Saccharon** et Arabia fert, sed laudatius India. Est autem mel in harundinibus collectum, commium modo candidum, dentibus fragile, amplissimum nucis abellanae magnitudine, ad medicinae tantum usum."—*Plin. Hist. Nat.* xii. 8.

c. 170.—"But all these articles are hotter than is desirable, and so they aggravate fevers, much as wine would. But *oxymeli* alone does not aggravate fever, whilst it is an active purgative. ... Not undeservedly, I think, that **saccharum** may also be counted among things of this quality. ..."—*Galen, Methodus Medendi*, viii.

c. 636.—"In Indicis stagnis nasci arundines calamique dicuntur, ex quorum radicibus expressum suavissimum succum bibunt. Vnde et Varro ait:

Indica non magno in arbore crescit arundo;
Illius et lentis premitur radicibus humor,
Dulcia qui nequeant succo concedere mella."
Isidori Hispalensis Originum, Lib. xvii. cap. vii.

c. 1220.—"Sunt insuper in Terra (Sancta) *canamellae* de quibus **zucchara** ex compressione eliquatur."—*Jacobi Vitriaci, Hist. Jherosolym*, cap. lxxxv.

1298.—"Bangala est une provence vers midi. ... Il font grant merchandie, car il ont espi e galanga e gingiber e succare et de maintes autres chieres espices."—*Marco Polo*, Geog. Text, ch. cxxvi.

1298.—"Je voz di que en ceste provences." (Quinsai or Chekiang) "naist et se fait plus **sucar** que ne fait en tout le autre monde, et ce est encore grandissime vente."—*Ibid.* ch. cliii.

1298.—"And before this city" (a place near Fu-chau) "came under the Great Can these people knew not how to make fine **sugar** (*zucchero*); they only used to boil and skim the juice, which, when cold, left a black paste. But after they came under the Great Can some men of Babylonia" (*i.e.* of Cairo) "who happened to be at the Court proceeded to this city and taught the people to refine **sugar** with the ashes of certain trees."—*Idem.* in *Ramusio*, ii. 49.

c. 1343.—"In Cyprus the following articles are sold by the hundred-weight (*cantara di peso*) and at a price in besants: Round pepper, sugar in powder (*polvere di* **zucchero**) ... sugars in loaves (**zuccheri** *in pani*), bees' honey, sugar-cane honey, and carob-honey (*mele d'ape, mele di cannameli, mele di carrube*). ..."—*Pegolotti*, 64.

"Loaf sugars are of several sorts, viz. **zucchero** *muchhera*, *caffettino*, and *bambillonia*; and *musciatto*, and *dommaschino*; and the *mucchera* is the best sugar there is; for it is more thoroughly boiled, and its paste is whiter, and more solid, than any other sugar; it is in the form of the *bambillonia* sugar like this Δ; and of this *mucchara* kind but little comes to the west, because nearly the whole is kept for the mouth and for the use of the Soldan himself.

"**Zucchero** *caffettino* is the next best after the *muccara* ...

"**Zucchero** *Bambillonia* is the best next after the best *caffettino*.

"**Zucchero** *musciatto* is the best after that of *Bambillonia*.

* * * * *

"**Zucchero** *chandi*, the bigger the pieces are, and the whiter, and the brighter, so much is it the better and finer, and there should not be too much small stuff.

"Powdered sugars are of many kinds, as of Cyprus, of Rhodes, of the Cranco of Monreale, and of Alexandria; and they are all made originally in entire loaves; but as they are not so thoroughly done, as the other sugars that keep their loaf shape ... the loaves tumble to pieces, and return to powder, and so it is called powdered sugar ..." (and a great deal more).—*Ibid.* 362–365. We cannot interpret most of the names in the preceding extract. *Bambillonia* is 'Sugar of Babylon,' *i.e.* of Cairo, and *Dommaschino* of Damascus. *Mucchera* (see CANDY (SUGAR), the second quotation), *Caffettino*, and *Musciatto*, no doubt all represent Arabic terms used in the trade at Alexandria, but we cannot identify them.

c. 1345.—"J'ai vu vendre dans le Bengale ... un *rithl* de sucre (**al-sukkar**), poids de Dihly, pour quatre drachmes."—*Ibn Batuta*, iv. 211.

1516.—"Moreover they make in this city (Bengala, *i.e.* probably Chittagong) much and good white cane **sugar** (acuquere *branco de canas*), but they do not know how to consolidate it and make loaves of it, so they wrap up the powder in certain wrappers of raw hide, very well stitched up; and make great loads of it, which are despatched for sale to many parts, for it is a great traffic."—*Barbosa*, Lisbon ed. 362.

[1630.—"Let us have a word or two of the prices of **suger** and **suger candy**."—*Forrest*, *Bombay Letters*, i. 5.]

1807.—"Chacun sait que par effet des regards de Farid, des monceaux de terre se changeaient en sucre. Tel est le motif du surnom de **Schakar** *ganj*, 'tresor de sucre' qui lui a été donné."—*Arāish-i-Maḥfil*, quoted by *Garcin de Tassy*, *Rel. Mus.* 95. (This is the saint, Farīd-uddīn Shakarganj (d. A.D. 1268) whose shrine is at *Pāk Pattan* in the Punjab.) [See *Crooke*, *Popular Religion*, &c. i. 214 *seqq.*]

1810.—"Although the sugar cane is supposed by many to be indigenous in India, yet it has only been within the last 50 years that it has been cultivated to any great extent. ... Strange to say, the only sugar-candy used until that time" (20 years before the date of the book) "was received from China; latterly, however, many gentlemen have speculated deeply in the manufacture. We now see sugar-candy of the first quality manufactured in various places of Bengal, and I believe that it is at least admitted that the raw sugars from that quarter are eminently good."—*Williamson, V. M.* ii. 133.

SULTAN, s. Ar. *sulṭān*, 'a Prince, a Monarch.' But this concrete sense is, in Arabic, post-classical only. The classical sense is abstract 'dominion.' The corresponding words in Hebrew and Aramaic have, as usual, *sh* or *s*. Thus *sholṭān* in Daniel (*e.g.* vi. 26—"in the whole dominion of my kingdom") is exactly the same word. The concrete word, corresponding to *sultān* in its post-classical sense, is *shallīt*, which is applied to Joseph in Gen. xlii. 6—"governor." So Saladin (Yūsuf Salāh-ad-dīn) was not the first Joseph who was *sultan* of Egypt. ["In Arabia it is a not uncommon proper name; and as a title it is taken by a host of petty kinglets. The Abbaside Caliphs (as Al-Wásik ...) formerly created these Sultans as their regents. Al Tá'i bi'llah (A.D. 974) invested the famous Sabuktagin with the office ... Sabuktagin's son, the famous Mahmúd of the Ghaznavite dynasty in 1002, was the first to adopt 'Sultán' as an independent title some 200 years after the death of Harún-al-Rashíd" (*Burton, Arab. Nights*, i. 188.)]

c. 950.—"*Ἐπὶ δὲ τῆς Βασιλείας Μιχαὴλ τοῦ υἱοῦ Θεοφίλου ἀνῆλθεν ἀπὸ Ἀφρικῆς στόλος λς´ κομπαρίων, ἔχων κεφαλὴν τὸν τε Σολδανὸν καὶ τὸν Σάμαν καὶ τὸν Καλφοῦς, καὶ ἐχειρώσαντο διαφόρους πόλεις τῆς Δαλματίας.*"—*Constant. Porphyrog.*, *De Thematibus*, ii. Thēma xi.

c. 1075 (written c. 1130).—"... *οἱ καὶ καθελόντες Πέρσας τε καὶ Σαρακηνοὺς αὐτοὶ κύριοι τῆς Περσίδος γεγόνασι σουλτάνον τὸν Στραγγολίπιδα*[1] *ὀνομάσαντες, ὅπερ σημαίνει παρ᾽ αὐτοῖς Βασιλεὺς καὶ παντοκράτωρ.*"—*Nicephorus Bryennius*, *Comment*, i. 9.

c. 1124.—"De divitiis **Soldani** mira referunt, et de incognitis speciebus quas in oriente viderunt. **Soldanus** dicitur quasi *solus dominus*, quia cunctis praeest Orientis prinicipibus."—*Ordericus Vitalis*, *Hist. Eccles.* Lib. xi. In Paris ed. of *Le Prevost*, 1852, iv. 256–7.

1165.—"Both parties faithfully adhered to this

---

1 Togrul Beg, founder of the Seljuk dynasty, called by various Western writers *Tangrolipiz*, and (as here) *Stràngolipes.*

arrangement, until it was interrupted by the interference of Sanjar-Shah ben Shah, who governs all Persia, and holds supreme power over 45 of its Kings. This prince is called in Arabic **Sultan** ul-Fars-al-Khabir (supreme commander of Persia)."—*R. Benjamin*, in *Wright*, 105–106.

c. 1200.—"Endementres que ces choses coroient einsi en Antioche, li message qui par Aussiens estoient alé au **soudan** de Perse por demander aide s'en retournoient."—*Guillaume de Tyr*, Old Fr. Tr. i. 174.

1298.—"Et quaint il furent là venus, adonc Bondocdaire qe **soldan** estoit de Babelonie vent en Armenie con grande host, et fait grand domajes por la contrée."—*Marco Polo*, Geog. Text, ch. xiii.

1307.—"Post quam vero Turchi occupaverunt terrã illã et habitaverũt ibidem, elegerũt dominũ super eos, et illum vocaverunt **Soldã** quod idem est quod rex in idiomate Latinorũ."—*Haitoni Armeni de Tartaris Liber*, cap. xiii. in *Novus Orbis*.

1309.—"En icelle grant paour de mort où nous estiens, vindrent à nous jusques à treize ou quatorze dou consoil dou **soudan**, trop richement appareillé de dras d'or et de soie, et nous firent demander (par un frere de l'Ospital qui savoit sarrazinois), de par le **soudan**, se nous vorriens estre delivre, et nous deimes que oil, et ce pooient il bien savoir."—*Jainville, Credo*. Joinville often has **soudanc**, and sometimes **saudanc**.

1498.—"Em este lugar e ilha a que chamão Moncobiquy estavá hum senhor a que elles chamavam **Colyytam** que era como visorrey."—*Roteiro de V. da Gama*, 26.

c. 1586.
"Now Tamburlaine the mighty **Soldan** comes,
And leads with him the great Arabian King."
Marlowe, Tamb. the Great, iv. 3.

[1596.— "... this scimitar
That slew the Sophy and a Persian prince
That won three fields of **Sultan** Solyman."
Merchant of Venice, II. i. 26.]

[**SUMJAO**, v. This is properly the imp. of the H. verb *samjhānā*, 'to cause to know, warn, correct,' usually with the implication of physical coercion. Other examples of a similar formation will be found under PUCKEROW.

[1826.—"... in this case they apply themselves to **sumjao**, the defendant."—*Pandurang Hari*, ed. 1873, ii. 170.]

SUNDERBUNDS, n.p. The well-known name of the tract of intersecting creeks and channels, swampy islands, and jungles, which constitutes that part of the Ganges Delta nearest the sea. The limits of the region so-called are the mouth of the Hoogly on the west, and that of the Megna (*i.e.* of the combined great Ganges and Brahmaputra) on the east, a width of about 220 miles. The name appears not to have been traced in old native documents of any kind, and hence its real form and etymology remain uncertain. *Sundara-vana*, 'beautiful forest'; *Sundarī-vana*, or *-ban*, 'forest of the *Sundarī* tree'; *Chandra-ban*, and *Chandra-band*, 'moon-forest' or 'moon-embankment'; *Chanda-bhanda*, the name of an old tribe of salt-makers;[1] *Chandra dīp-ban* from a large zemindary called Chandra-dīp in the Bakerganj district at the eastern extremity of the Sunderbunds; these are all suggestions that have been made. Whatever be the true etymology, we doubt if it is to be sought in *sundara* or *sundarī*. [As to the derivation from the *Sundarī* tree which is perhaps most usually accepted, Mr. Beveridge (*Man. of Bakarganj*, 24, 167, 32) remarks that this tree is by no means common in many parts of the Bakarganj Sunderbunds; he suggests that the word means 'beautiful wood' and was possibly given by the Brahmans.] The name has never (except in one quotation below) been in English mouths, or in English popular orthography, *Soonderbunds*, but *Sunderbunds*, which implies (in correct transliteration) an original *sandra* or *chandra*, not *sundara*. And going back to what we conjecture may be an early occurrence of the name in two Dutch writers, we find this confirmed. These two writers, it will be seen, both speak of a famous **Sandery**, or *Santry*, Forest in Lower Bengal, and we should be more positive in our identification were it not that in Van der Broucke's map (1660) which was published in Valentijn's *East Indies* (1726) this Sandery Forest is shown on the *west* side of the Hoogly R., in fact about due west of the site of Calcutta, and a little above a place marked as *Basanderi*, located near the exit into the Hoogly of what represents the old Saraswati R., which enters the former at Sānkrāl, not far below the Botanical Gardens, and 5 or 6 miles below Fort William. This has led Mr. Blochmann to identify the *Sanderi Bosch* with the old

1 These are mentioned in a copper tablet inscription of A.D. 1136; see *Blochmann*, as quoted further on, p. 226.

Mahall *Basandhari* which appears in the *Āīn* as belonging to the Sirkār of Sulīmānābād (*Gladwin's Ayeen*, ii. 207, *orig.* i. 407; *Jarrett*, ii. 140; *Blochm.* in *J.A.S.B.* xlii. pt. i. p. 232), and which formed one of the original "xxiv. Pergunnas."[1] Undoubtedly this is the *Basanderi* of V. den Broucke's map; but it seems possible that some confusion between *Basanderi* and Bosch Sandery (which would be *Sandarban* in the vernacular) may have led the map-maker to misplace the latter. We should gather from Schulz[2] that he passed the Forest of Sandry about a Dutch mile below Sankral, which he mentions. But his statement is so nearly identical with that in Valentijn that we apprehend they have no *separate* value. Valentijn, in an earlier page, like Bernier, describes the Sunderbunds as the resort of the Arakan pirates, but does not give a name (p. 169).

1661.—"We got under sail again" (just after meeting the Arakan pirates) "in the morning early, and went past the **Forest of Santry**, so styled because (as has been credibly related) Alexander the Great with his mighty army was hindered by the strong rush of the ebb and flood at this place, from advancing further, and therefore had to turn back to Macedonia."—*Walter Schulz*, 155.

c. 1666.—"And thence it is" (from piratical raids of the Mugs, &c.) "that at present there are seen in the mouth of the *Ganges*, so many fine Isles quite deserted, which were formerly well peopled, and where no other Inhabitants are found but wild Beasts, and especially Tygers."—*Bernier*, E.T. 54; [ed. *Constable*, 442].

1726.—"This (Bengal) is the land wherein they will have it that Alexander the Great, called by the Moors, whether Hindostanders or Persians, *Sulthaan Iskender*, and in their historians *Iskender Doulcarnain*, was ... they can show you the exact place where King Porus held his court. The natives will prate much of this matter; for example, that in front of the SANDERIE-WOOD (*Sanderie Bosch*, which we show in the map, and which they call properly after him *Iskenderie*) he was stopped by the great and rushing streams."—*Valentijn*, v. 179.

1728.—"But your petitioners did not arrive off **Sunderbund Wood** till four in the evening, where they rowed backward and forward for six days; with which labour and want of provisions three of the people died."—*Petition of Sheik Mahmud Ameen and others*, to Govr. of Ft. St. Geo., in *Wheeler*, iii. 41.

1764.—"On the 11th Bhaudan, whilst the Boats were at Kerma in **Soonderbund**, a little before daybreak, Captain Ross arose and ordered the Manjee to put off with the **Budgerow**. ..."—*Native Letter regarding Murder of Captain John Ross by a Native Crew.* In *Long*, 383. This instance is an exception to the general remark made above that the English popular orthography has always been *Sunder*, and not *Soonder-bunds*.

1786.—"If the Jelinghy be navigable we shall soon be in Calcutta; if not, we must pass a second time through the **Sundarbans**."—Letter of *Sir W. Jones*, in *Life*, ii. 83.

"A portion of the **Sunderbunds** ... for the most part overflowed by the tide, as indicated by the original Hindoo name of **Chunderbund**, signifying mounds, or offspring of the moon."—*James Grant*, in App. to *Fifth Report*, p. 260. In a note Mr. Grant notices the derivation from "Soondery wood," and "Soonder-ban," 'beautiful wood,' and proceeds: "But we adhere to our own etymology rather ... above all, because the richest and greatest part of the **Sunderbunds** is still comprized in the ancient Zemindarry pergunnah of *Chunder deep*, or lunar territory."

1792.—"Many of these lands, what is called the **Sundra bunds**, and others at the mouth of the Ganges, if we may believe the history of Bengal, was formerly well inhabited."—*Forrest, V. to Mergui*, Pref. p. 5.

1793.—"That part of the delta bordering on the sea, is composed of a labyrinth of rivers and creeks, ... this tract known by the name of the Woods, or **Sunderbunds**, is in extent equal to the principality of Wales."—*Rennell, Mem. of Map of Hind.*, 3rd ed., p. 359.

1853.—"The scenery, too, exceeded his expectations; the terrible forest solitude of the **Sunderbunds** was full of interest to an European imagination."—*Oakfield*, i. 38.

[**SUNNEE**, **SOONNEE**, s. Ar. *sunnī*, which is really a Pers. form and stands for that which is expressed by the Ar. *Ahlu's-Sunnah*, 'the people of the Path,' a 'Traditionist.' The term applied to the large Mahommedan sect who acknowledge the first four Khalīfahs to have been the rightful descendants of the Prophet, and are thus

1 Basandhari is also mentioned by Mr. James Grant (1786) in his *View of the Revenues of Bengal*, as the Pergunna of *Belia-bussendry*; and by A. Hamilton as a place on the Damūdar, producing much good sugar (*Fifth Report*, p. 405; *A. Ham.* ii. 4). It would seem to have been the present Pergunna of Balia, some 13 or 14 miles west of the northern part of Calcutta. See *Hunter's Bengal Gas.* i. 365.

2 So called in the German version which we use; but in the Dutch original he is *Schouter*.

opposed to the **Sheeahs**. The latter are much less numerous than the former, the proportion being, according to Mr. Wilfrid Blunt's estimate, 15 millions Shiahs to 145 millions of Sunnis.

[c. 1590.—"The Mahommedans (of Kashmīr) are partly **Sunnies**, and others of the sects of Aly and Noorbukhshy; and they are frequently engaged in wars with each other."—*Ayeen*, by *Gladwin*, ii. 125; ed. *Jarrett*, ii. 352.

[1623.—"The other two ... are **Sonni**, as the Turks and Moghol."—*P. della Valle*, Hak. Soc. i. 152.

[1812.—"A fellow told me with the gravest face, that a lion of their own country would never hurt a **Sheyah** ... but would always devour a **Sunni**."—*Morier, Journey through Persia*, 62.]

SUNNUD, s. Hind. from Ar. *sanad.* A diploma, patent, or deed of grant by the government of office, privilege, or right. The corresponding Skt.—H. is *śāsana.*

[c. 1590.—"A paper authenticated by proper signatures is called a **sunnud**. ..."—*Ayeen*, by *Gladwin*, i. 214; ed. *Blockmann*, i. 259.]

1758.—"They likewise brought **sunnuds**, or the commission for the nabobship."—*Orme*, *Hist.*, ed. 1803, ii. 284.

1759.—"That your Petitioners, being the Bramins, &c. ... were permitted by **Sunnud** from the President and Council to collect daily alms from each shop or doocan of this place, at 5 cowries per diem."—In *Long*, 184.

1776.—"If the path to and from a House ... be in the Territories of another Person, that Person, who always hath passed to and fro, shall continue to do so, the other Person aforesaid, though he hath a Right of Property in the Ground, and hath an attested **Sunnud** thereof, shall not have Authority to cause him any Let or Molestation."—*Halhed, Code*, 100–101.

1799.—"I enclose you **sunnuds** for pension for the **Killadar** of Chittledroog."—*Wellington*, i. 45.

1800.—"I wished to have traced the nature of landed property in Soondah ... by a chain of **Sunnuds** up to the 8th century."—*Sir T. Munro*, in *Life*, i. 249.

1809.—"This **sunnud** is the foundation of all the rights and privileges annexed to a Jageer (**Jagheer**)."—*Harrington's Analysis*, ii. 410.

SUNYÁSEE, s. Skt. *sannyāsī*, lit. 'one who resigns, or abandons,' *scil.* 'worldly affairs'; a Hindu religious mendicant. The name of Sunnyásee was applied familiarly in Bengal, c. 1760–75, to a body of banditti claiming to belong to a religious fraternity, who, in the interval between the decay of the imperial authority and the regular establishment of our own, had their head-quarters in the forest-tracts at the foot of the Himālaya. From these they used to issue periodically in large bodies, plundering and levying exactions far and wide, and returning to their asylum in the jungle when threatened with pursuit. In the days of Nawāb Mīr Kāsim 'Ali (1760–64) they were bold enough to plunder the city of Dacca; and in 1766 the great geographer James Rennell, in an encounter with a large body of them in the territory of Koch Bihār, was nearly cut to pieces. Rennell himself, five years later, was employed to carry out a project which he had formed for the suppression of these bands, and did so apparently with what was considered at the time to be success, though we find the depredators still spoken of by W. Hastings as active, two or three years later.

[c. 200 A.D.—"Having thus performed religious acts in a forest during the third portion of his life, let him become a **Sannyasi** for the fourth portion of it, abandoning all sensual affection."—*Manu*, vi. 33.

[c. 1590.—"The fourth period is **Sannyása**, which is an extraordinary state of austerity that nothing can surpass. ... Such a person His Majesty calls **Sannyásí**."—*Āīn*, ed. *Jarrett*, iii. 278.]

1616.—"Sunt autem **Sanasses** apud illos Brachmanes quidam, sanctimoniae opinione habentes, ab hominum scilicet consortio semoti in solitudine degentes et nonnūnquã totũ nudi corpus in publicũ prodeuntes."—*Jarric, Thes.* i. 663.

1626.—"Some (an vnlearned kind) are called **Sannases**."—*Purchas, Pilgrimage*, 549.

1651.—"The **Sanyasys** are people who set the world and worldly joys, as they say, on one side. These are indeed more precise and strict in their lives than the foregoing."—*Rogerius*, 21.

1674.—"**Saniade**, or **Saniasi**, is a dignity greater than that of Kings."—*Faria y Sousa, Asia Port.* ii. 711.

1726.—"The **San-yasés** are men who, forsaking the world and all its fruits, betake themselves to a very strict and retired manner of life."—*Valentijn, Choro.* 75.

1766.—"The **Sanashy** Faquirs (part of the same Tribe which plundered Dacca in Cossim Ally's Time[1]) were in arms to the number of 7 or 800 at the Time I was surveying Báár (a small

1 This affair is alluded to in one of the extracts in *Long* (p. 342): "Agreed ... that the Fakiers who were made prisoners at the retaking of Dacca may be employed as Coolies in the repair of

Province near Boutan), and had taken and plundered the Capital of that name within a few Coss of my route. ... I came up with Morrison immediately after he had defeated the **Sanashys** in a pitched Battle. ... Our Escorte, which were a few Horse, rode off, and the Enemy with drawn Sabres immediately surrounded us. Morrison escaped unhurt, Richards, my Brother officer, received only a slight Wound, and fought his Way off; my Armenian Assistant was killed, and the Sepoy Adjutant much wounded. ... I was put in a **Palankeen**, and Morrison made an attack on the Enemy and cut most of them to Pieces. I was now in a most shocking Condition indeed, being deprived of the Use of both my Arms, ... a cut of a Sable (*sic*) had cut through my right Shoulder Bone, and laid me open for nearly a Foot down the Back, cutting thro' and wounding some of my Ribs. I had besides a Cut on the left Elbow wh[ch] took off the Muscular part of the breadth of a Hand, a Stab in the Arm, and a large Cut on the head. ..."—MS. Letter from *James Rennell*, dd. August 30, in possession of his grandson *Major Rodd.*

1767.—"A body of 5000 **Sinnasses** have lately entered the Sircar Sarong country; the Phousdar sent two companies of Sepoys after them, under the command of a serjeant ... the **Sinnasses** stood their ground, and after the Sepoys had fired away their ammunition, fell on them, killed and wounded near 80, and put the rest to flight. ..."—Letter to *President at Ft. William*, from *Thomas Rumbold, Chief at Patna*, dd. April 20, in *Long*, p. 526.

1773.—"You will hear of great disturbances committed by the **Sinassies**, or wandering Fackeers, who annually infest the provinces about this time of the year, in pilgrimage to Juggernaut, going in bodies of 1000 and sometimes even 10,000 men."—Letter of *Warren Hastings*, dd. February 2, in *Gleig*, i. 282.

"At this time we have five battalions of Sepoys in pursuit of them."—Do. do., March 31, in *Gleig*, i. 294.

1774.—"The history of these people is curious. ... They ... rove continually from place to place, recruiting their numbers with the healthiest children they can steal. ... Thus they are the stoutest and most active men in India. ... Such are the **Senassies**, the gypsies of Hindostan."—Do. do., dd. August 25, in *Gleig*, 303–4. See the same vol., also pp. 284, 296–7–8, 395.

1826.—"Being looked upon with an evil eye by many persons in society, I pretended to bewail my brother's loss, and gave out my intention of becoming a **Sunyasse**, and retiring from the world."—*Pandurang Hari*, 394; [ed. 1873, ii. 267; also i. 189].

the Factory."—*Procgs. of Council at Ft. William*, Dec. 5, 1769.

SUPREME COURT. The designation of the English Court established at Fort William by the Regulation Act of 1773 (13 Geo. III. c. 63), and afterwards at the other two Presidencies. Its extent of jurisdiction was the subject of acrimonious controversies in the early years of its existence; controversies which were closed by 21 Geo. III. c. 70, which explained and defined the jurisdiction of the Court. The use of the name came to an end in 1862 with the establishment of the 'High Court,' the bench of which is occupied by barrister judges, judges from the Civil Service, and judges promoted from the native bar.

The Charter of Charles II., of 1661, gave the Company certain powers to administer the laws of England, and that of 1683 to establish Courts of Judicature. That of Geo. I. (1726) gave power to establish at each Presidency Mayor's Courts for civil suits, with appeal to the Governor and Council, and from these, in cases involving more than 1000 **pagodas**, to the King in Council. The same charter constituted the Governor and Council of each Presidency a Court for trial of all offences except high treason. Courts of Requests were established by charter of Geo. II., 1753. The Mayor's Court at Madras and Bombay survived till 1797, when (by 37 Geo. III. ch. 142) a Recorder's Court was instituted at each. This was superseded at Madras by a Supreme Court in 1801, and at Bombay in 1823.

SURKUNDA, s. Hind. *sarkandā*, [Skt. *śara*, 'reed-grass,' *kāṇḍa*, 'joint, section']. The name of a very tall reed-grass, *Saccharum Sara*, Roxb., perhaps also applied to *Saccharum procerum*, Roxb. These grasses are often tall enough in the riverine plains of Eastern Bengal greatly to overtop a tall man standing in a howda on the back of a tall elephant. It is from the upper part of the flower-bearing stalk of *surkunda* that **sirky** is derived. A most intelligent visitor to India was led into a curious mistake about the name of this grass by some official, who ought to have known better. We quote the passage. ——'s story about the main branch of a river channel probably rests on no better foundation.

1875.—"As I drove yesterday with ——, I asked him if he knew the scientific name of the tall grass which I heard called tiger-grass at Ahmedabad, and which is very abundant here (about Lahore). I think it is a *saccharum*, but am not quite sure. 'No,' he said, 'but the people in the neighbourhood call it **Sikunder's Grass**, as they still call the main branch of a river 'Sikander's channel.' Strange, is it not?—how that great individuality looms through history."—*Grant Duff, Notes of an Indian Journey*, 105.

***SUTTEE**, s. The rite of widow-burning; *i.e.* the burning of the living widow along with the corpse of her husband, as practised by people of certain castes among the Hindus, and eminently by the Rājpūts.

The word is properly Skt. *satī*, 'a good woman,' 'a true wife,' and thence specially applied, in modern vernaculars of Sanskrit parentage, to the wife who was considered to accomplish the supreme act of fidelity by sacrificing herself on the funeral pile of her husband. The application of this substantive to the suicidal act, instead of the person, is European. The proper Skt. term for the act is *sahagamana*, or 'keeping company,' [*sahamaraṇa*, 'dying together'].[1] A very long series of quotations in illustration of the practice, from classical times downwards, might be given. We shall present a selection.

We should remark that the word (*satī* or *suttee*) does not occur, so far as we know, in any European work older than the 17th century. And then it only occurs in a disguised form (see quotation from P. Della Valle). The term *masti* which he uses is probably *mahā-satī*, which occurs in Skt. Dictionaries ('a wife of great virtue'). Della Valle is usually eminent in the correctness of his transcriptions of Oriental words. This conjecture of the interpretation of *masti* is confirmed, and the traveller himself justified, by an entry in Mr. Whitworth's Dictionary of a word *Masti-kalla* used in Canara for a monument commemorating a *sati*. *Kalla* is stone and *masti* = *mahā-satī*. We have not found the term exactly in any European document older than Sir C. Malet's letter of 1787, and Sir W. Jones's of the same year (see below).

Suttee is a Brahmanical rite, and there is a Sanskrit ritual in existence (see *Classified Index to the Tanjore MSS.*, p. 135*a*). It was introduced into Southern India with the Brahman civilisation, and was prevalent there chiefly in the Brahmanical Kingdom of Vijayanagar, and among the Mahrattas. In Malabar, the most primitive part of S. India, the rite is forbidden (*Anāchāranirṇaya*, v. 26). The cases mentioned by Teixeira below, and in the *Lettres Édifiantes*, occurred at Tanjore and Madura. A (Mahratta) Brahman at Tanjore told one of the present writers that he had to perform commemorative funeral rites for his grandfather and grandmother on the same day, and this indicated that his grandmother had been a *satī*.

The practice has prevailed in various regions besides India. Thus it seems to have been an early custom among the heathen Russians, or at least among nations on the Volga called Russians by Maṣ'ūdī and Ibn Foẓlān. Herodotus (Bk. v. ch. 5) describes it among certain tribes of Thracians. It was in vogue in Tonga and the Fiji Islands. It has prevailed in the island of Bali within our own time, though there accompanying Hindu rites, and perhaps of Hindu origin,—certainly modified by Hindu influence. A full account of Suttee as practised in those Malay Islands will be found in Zollinger's account of the Religion of Sassak in *J. Ind. Arch.* ii. 166; also see Friedrich's *Bali* as in note preceding. [A large number of references to *Suttee* are collected in Frazer, *Pausanias*, iii. 198 *seqq.*]

In Diodorus we have a long account of the rivalry as to which of the two wives of Kēteus, a leader of the Indian contingent in the army of Eumenes, should perform **suttee**. One is rejected as with child. The history of the other terminates thus:

B.C. 317.—"Finally, having taken leave of those of the household, she was set upon the pyre by her own brother, and was regarded with wonder by the crowd that had run together to the spectacle, and heroically ended her life; the whole force with their arms thrice marching round the pyre before it was kindled. But she, laying herself beside her husband, and even at the violence of the flame giving utterance to no unbecoming cry, stirred pity indeed in others of the spectators, and in some excess of eulogy; not but what there were some of the Greeks present who reprobated such rites as

---

1 But it is worthy of note that in the Island of Bali one manner of accomplishing the rite is called **Satia** (Skt. *satyā*, 'truth,' from *sat*, whence also *satī*). See *Crawfurd, H. of Ind. Archip.* ii. 243, and *Friedrich*, in *Verhandelingen van het Batav. Genootschap*. xxiii. 10.

barbarous and cruel. ..."—*Diod. Sic. Biblioth.* xix. 33–34.

c. B.C. 30.

"Felix Eois lex funeris una maritis
Quos Aurora suis rubra colorat equis;
Namque ubi mortifero jacta est fax ultima lecto
Uxorum fusis stat pia turba comis;
Et certamen habet leti, quae viva sequatur
Conjugium; pudor est non licaisse mori.
Ardent victrices; et flammae pectora praebent,
Imponuntque suis ora perusta viris."

Propertius,[1] Lib. iii. xiii. 15–22.

c. B.C. 20.—"He (Aristobulus) says that he had heard from some persons of wives burning themselves voluntarily with their deceased husbands, and that those women who refused to submit to this custom were disgraced."—*Strabo*, xv. 62 (E.T. by *Hamilton and Falconer*, iii. 112).

A.D. c. 390.—"Indi, ut omnes fere barbari uxores plurimas habent. Apud eos lex est, ut uxor carissima cum defuncto marito cremetur. Hae igitur contendunt inter se de amore viri, et ambitio summa certantium est, ac testimonium castitatis, dignam morte decerni. Itaque victrix in habitu ornatuque pristino juxta cadaver accubat, amplexans illud et deosculans et suppositos ignes prudentiae laude contemnens."—*St. Jerome, Advers. Jovinianum*, in ed. *Vallars*, ii. 311.

c. 851.—"All the Indians burn their dead. Serendib is the furthest out of the islands dependent upon India. Sometimes when they burn the body of a King, his wives cast themselves on the pile, and burn with him; but it is at their choice to abstain."—*Reinaud, Relation*, &c. i. 50.

c. 1200.—"Hearing the Raja was dead, the Parmâri became a **satí**:—dying she said—The son of the Jadavanî will rule the country, may my blessing be on him!"—*Chand Bardai*, in *Ind. Ant.* i. 227. We cannot be sure that *satí* is in the original, as this is a *condensed* version by Mr. Beames.

1298.—"Many of the women also, when their husbands die and are placed on the pile to be burnt, do burn themselves along with the bodies."—*Marco Polo*, Bk. iii. ch. 17.

c. 1322.—"The idolaters of this realm have one detestable custom (that I must mention). For when any man dies they burn him; and if he leave a wife they burn her alive with him, saying that she ought to go and keep her husband company in the other world. But if the woman have sons by her husband she may abide with them, an she will."—*Odoric*, in *Cathay*, &c., i. 79.

Also in Zampa or **Champa**: "When a married man dies in this country his body is burned, and his living wife along with it. For they say that she should go to keep company with her husband in the other world also."—*Ibid.* 97.

c. 1328.—"In this India, on the death of a noble, or of any people of substance, their bodies are burned; and eke their wives follow them alive to the fire, and for the sake of worldly glory, and for the love of their husbands, and for eternal life, burn along with them, with as much joy as if they were going to be wedded. And those who do this have the higher repute for virtue and perfection among the rest."—*Fr. Jordanus*, 20.

c. 1343.—"The burning of the wife after the death of her husband is an act among the Indians recommended, but not obligatory. If a widow burns herself, the members of the family get the glory thereof, and the fame of fidelity in fulfilling their duties. She who does not give herself up to the flames puts on coarse raiment and abides with her kindred, wretched and despised for having failed in duty. But she is not compelled to burn herself." (There follows an interesting account of instances witnessed by the traveller.)—*Ibn Batuta*, ii. 138.

c. 1430.—"In Mediâ vero Indiâ mortui comburuntur, cumque his, ut plurimum vivae uxores ... una pluresve, prout fuit matrimonii conventio. Prior ex lege uritur, etiam quae unica est. Sumuntur autem et aliae uxores quaedam eo pacto, ut morte funus suâ exornent, isque haud parvus apud eos honos ducitur ... submisso igne uxor ornatiori cultu inter tubas tibicinasque et cantus, et ipsa psallentis more alacris rogum magno comitatu circuit. Adstat interea et sacerdos ... hortando suadens. Cum circumierit illa saepius ignem prope suggestum consistit, vestesque exuens, loto de more prius corpore, tum sindonem albam induta, ad exhortationem dicentis in ignem prosilit."—*N. Conti*, in *Poggius de Var. Fort.* iv.

c. 1520.—"There are in this Kingdom (the Deccan) many heathen, natives of the country, whose custom it is that when they die they are burnt, and their wives along with them; and if these will not do it they remain in disgrace with all their kindred. And as it happens oft times that they are unwilling to do it, their Bramin kinsfolk persuade them thereto, and this in order that such a fine custom should not be broken and fall into oblivion."—*Sommario de' Genti*, in *Ramusio*, i. f. 329.

"In this country of **Camboja** ... when the King dies, the lords voluntarily burn themselves, and so do the King's wives at the same time, and

1 The same poet speaks of Evadne, who threw herself at Thebes on the burning pile of her husband Capaneus (I. xv. 21), a story which Paley thinks must have come from some early Indian legend.

so also do other women on the death of their husbands."—*Ibid.* f. 336.

1522.—"They told us that in Java Major it was the custom, when one of the chief men died, to burn his body; and then his principal wife, adorned with garlands of flowers, has herself carried in a chair by four men ... comforting her relations, who are afflicted because she is going to burn herself with the corpse of her husband ... saying to them, 'I am going this evening to sup with my dear husband and to sleep with him this night.' ... After again consoling them (she) casts herself into the fire and is burned. If she did not do this she would not be looked upon as an honourable woman, nor as a faithful wife."—*Pigafetta*, E.T. by *Lord Stanley of A.*, 154.

c. 1566.—Cesare Federici notices the rite as peculiar to the Kingdom of "*Bezeneger*": "vidi cose stranie e bestiali di quella gentilitâ; vsano primamente abbrusciare i corpi morti cosi d'huomini come di donne nobili; e si l'huomo è maritato, la moglie è obligata ad abbrusciarsi viva col corpo del marito."—*Orig.* ed. p. 36. This traveller gives a good account of a Suttee.

1583.—"In the interior of Hindústán it is the custom when a husband dies, for his widow willingly and cheerfully to cast herself into the flames (of the funeral pile), although she may not have lived happily with him. Occasionally love of life holds her back, and then her husband's relations assemble, light the pile, and place her upon it, thinking that they thereby preserve the honour and character of the family. But since the country had come under the rule of his gracious Majesty [Akbar], inspectors had been appointed in every city and district, who were to watch carefully over these two cases, to discriminate between them, and to prevent any woman being forcibly burnt."—*Abu'l Fazl, Akbar Námah*, in *Elliot*, vi. 69.

1583.—"Among other sights I saw one I may note as wonderful. When I landed (at Nogapatam) from the vessel, I saw a pit full of kindled charcoal; and at that moment a young and beautiful woman was brought by her people on a litter, with a great company of other women, friends of hers, with great festivity, she holding a mirror in her left hand, and a lemon in her right hand. ..."—and so forth.—*G. Balbi*, f. 82*v*. 83.

1586.—"The custom of the countrey (Java) is, that whensoever the King doeth die, they take the body so dead and burne it, and preserve the ashes of him, and within five dayes next after, the wines of the said King so dead, according to the custome and vse of their countrey, every one of them goe together to a place appointed, and the chiefe of the women which was nearest to him in accompt, hath a ball in her hand, and throweth it from her, and the place where the ball resteth, thither they goe all, and turne their faces to the Eastward, and every one with a dagger in their hand (which dagger they call a crise (see **CREASE**), and is as sharpe as a rasor), stab themselues in their owne blood, and fall a-groueling on their faces, and so ende their dayes."—*T. Candish*, in *Hakl.* iv. 338. This passage refers to Blambangan at the east end of Java, which till a late date was subject to Bali, in which such practices have continued to our day. It seems probable that the Hindu rite here came in contact with the old Polynesian practices of a like kind, which prevailed *e.g.* in Fiji, quite recently. The narrative referred to below under 1633, where the victims were the slaves of a deceased queen, points to the latter origin. W. Humboldt thus alludes to similar passages in old Javanese literature: "Thus we may reckon as one of the finest episodes in the *Brata Yuda*, the story how **Satya Wati**, when she had sought out her slain husband among the wide-spread heap of corpses on the battlefield, stabs herself by his side with a dagger."—*Kawi-Sprache*, i. 89 (and see the whole section, pp. 87–95).

[c. 1590.—"When he (the Rajah of Asham) dies, his principal attendants of both sexes voluntarily bury themselves alive in his grave."—*Āīn*, ed. *Jarrett*, ii. 118.]

1598.—The usual account is given by *Linschoten*, ch. xxxvi., with a plate; [Hak. Soc. i. 249].

[c. 1610.—See an account in *Pyrard de Laval*, Hak. Soc. i. 394.]

1611.—"When I was in India, on the death of the Naique of Maduré, a country situated between that of Malauar and that of Choromandel, 400 wives of his burned themselves along with him."—*Teixeira*, i. 9.

c. 1620.—"The author ... when in the territory of the Karnátik ... arrived in company with his father at the city of Southern Mathura (Madura), where, after a few days, the ruler died and went to hell. The chief had 700 wives, and they all threw themselves at the same time into the fire."—*Muhammad Sharíf Hanafi*, in *Elliot*, vii. 139.

1623.—"When I asked further if force was ever used in these cases, they told me that usually it was not so, but only at times among persons of quality, when some one had left a young and handsome widow, and there was a risk either of her desiring to marry again (which they consider a great scandal) or of a worse mishap,—in such a case the relations of her husband, if they were very strict, would compel her, even against her will, to burn ... a barbarous and cruel law indeed! But in short, as regarded Giaccamà, no one exercised either compulsion or persuasion; and she did the thing of her own free choice; both her kindred and herself exulting in it, as in an act magnanimous (which in sooth it was) and held in high honour among them. And when I asked about the ornaments and flowers that she wore, they told me this was customary as a sign of the joyousness of the **Mastì** (*Mastì* is what they call a woman who gives herself up to be burnt upon the death of her husband)."—*P. della Valle*, ii. 671; [Hak. Soc. ii. 275, and see ii. 266 *seq.*].

1633.—"The same day, about noon, the queen's body was burnt without the city, with two and twenty of her female slaves; and we consider ourselves bound to render an exact account of the barbarous ceremonies practised in this place on such occasions as we were witness to. ..."—*Narrative of a Dutch Mission to Bali*, quoted by *Crawfurd, H. of Ind. Arch.*, ii. 244–253, from *Prevost*. It is very interesting, but too long for extract.

c. 1650.—"They say that when a woman becomes a **Sattee**, that is burns herself with the deceased, the Almighty pardons all the sins committed by the wife and husband and that they remain a long time in paradise; nay if the husband were in the infernal regions, the wife by this means draws him from thence and takes him to paradise. ... Moreover the **Sattee**, in a future birth, returns not to the female sex ... but she who becomes not a **Sattee**, and passes her life in widowhood, is never emancipated from the female state. ... It is however criminal to force a woman into the fire, and equally to prevent her who voluntarily devotes herself."—*Dabistān*, ii. 75–76.

c. 1650–60.—Tavernier gives a full account of the different manners of *Suttee*, which he had witnessed often, and in various parts of India, but does not use the word. We extract the following:

c. 1648.—"... there fell of a sudden so violent a Shower, that the Priests, willing to get out of the Rain, thrust the Woman all along into the Fire. But the Shower was so vehement, and endured so long, that the Fire was quench'd, and the Woman was not burn'd. About midnight she arose, and went and knock'd at one of her Kinsmen's Houses, where Father *Zenom* and many *Hollanders* saw her, looking so gastly and grimly, that it was enough to have scar'd them; however the pain she endur'd did not so far terrifie her, but that three days after, accompany'd by her Kindred, she went and was burn'd according to her first intention."—*Tavernier*, E.T. ii. 84; [ed. *Ball*, i. 219].

Again:

"In most places upon the Coast of Coromandel, the Women are not burnt with their deceas'd Husbands, but they are buried alive with them in holes, which the Bramins make a foot deeper than the tallness of the man and woman. Usually they chuse a Sandy place; so that when the man and woman are both let down together, all the Company with Baskets of Sand fill up the hole above half a foot higher than the surface of the ground, after which they jump and dance upon it, till they believe the woman to be stifl'd."—*Ibid.* 171; [ed. *Ball*, ii. 216].

c. 1667.—Bernier also has several highly interesting pages on this subject, in his "Letter written to M. Chapelan, sent from Chiras in Persia." We extract a few sentences: "Concerning the Women that have actually burn'd themselves, I have so often been present at such dreadful spectacles, that at length I could endure no more to see it, and I retain still some horrour when I think on't. ... The Pile of Wood was presently all on fire, because store of Oyl and Butter had been thrown upon it, and I saw at the time through the Flames that the Fire took hold of the Cloaths of the Woman. ... All this I saw, but observ'd not that the Woman was at all disturb'd; yea it was said, that she had been heard to pronounce with great force these two words, *Five, Two*, to signifie, according to the Opinion of those who hold the Souls Transmigration, that this was the 5th time she had burnt herself with the same Husband, and that there remain'd but *two* times for perfection; as if she had at that time this Remembrance, or some Prophetical Spirit."—E.T. p. 99; [ed. *Constable*, 306 *seqq.*].

1677.—Suttee, described by A. Bassing, in *Valentijn* v. (*Ceylon*) 300.

1713.—"Ce fut cette année de 1710, que mourut le Prince de Marava, âgé de plus de quatre-vingt-ans; ses femmes, en nombre de quarante sept, se brûlèrent avec le corps du Prince. ..." (details follow).—*Père Martin* (of the Madura Mission), in *Lett. Edif.* ed. 1781, tom. xii., pp. 123 *seqq.*

1727.—"I have seen several burned several Ways. ... I heard a Story of a Lady that had received Addresses from a Gentleman who afterwards deserted her, and her Relations died shortly after the Marriage ... and as the Fire was well kindled ... she espied her former Admirer, and beckned him to come to her. When he came she took him in her Arms, as if she had a Mind to embrace him; but being stronger than he, she carried him into the Flames in her Arms, where they were both consumed, with the Corpse of her Husband."—*A. Hamilton*, i. 278; [ed. 1744, i. 280].

"The Country about (Calcutta) being overspread with *Paganisms*, the Custom of Wives burning themselves with their deceased Husbands, is also practised here. Before the *Mogul's* War, Mr. *Channock* went one time with his Ordinary Guard of Soldiers, to see a young

Widow act that tragical Catastrophe, but he was so smitten with the Widow's Beauty, that he sent his Guards to take her by Force from her Executioners, and conducted her to his own Lodgings. They lived lovingly many Years, and had several Children; at length she died, after he had settled in *Calcutta*, but instead of converting her to *Christianity*, she made him a Proselyte to *Paganism*, and the only part of *Christianity* that was remarkable in him, was burying her decently, and he built a Tomb over her, where all his Life after her Death, he kept the anniversary Day of her Death. by sacrificing a Cock on her Tomb, after the *Pagan* Manner."—*Ibid.* [ed. 1744], ii. 6–7. [With this compare the curious lines described as an Epitaph on "Joseph Townsend, Pilot of the Ganges" (5 ser. *Notes & Queries*, i. 466 *seq.*).]

1774.—"Here (in Bali) not only women often kill themselves, or burn with their deceased husbands, but men also burn in honour of their deceased masters."—*Forrest, V. to N. Guinea*, 170.

1787.—"Soon after I and my conductor had quitted the house, we were informed the **suttee** (for that is the name given to the person who so devotes herself) had passed. ..."—*Sir C. Malet*, in *Parly. Papers of* 1821, p. 1 ("Hindoo Widows").

"My Father, said he (Pundit Rhadacaunt), died at the age of one hundred years, and my mother, who was eighty years old, became a **sati**, and burned herself to expiate sins."—Letter of *Sir W. Jones*, in *Life*, ii. 120.

1792.—"In the course of my endeavours I found the poor **suttee** had no relations at Poonah."—Letter from *Sir C. Malet*, in *Forbes, Or. Mem.* ii. 394; [2nd ed. ii. 28, and see i 178, in which the previous passage is quoted].

1808.—"These proceedings (Hindu marriage ceremonies in Guzerat) take place in the presence of a Brahmin. ...' And farther, now the young woman vows that her affections shall be fixed upon her Lord alone, not only in all this life, but will follow in death, or to the next, that she will die, that she may burn with him, through as many transmigrations as shall secure their joint immortal bliss. Seven successions of **suttees** (a woman seven times born and burning, thus, as often) secure to the loving couple a seat among the gods."—*R. Drummond.*

1809.—

"O sight of misery!
You cannot hear her cries ... their sound
In that wild dissonance is drowned; ...
But in her face you see
The supplication and the agony ...
See in her swelling throat the desperate strength
That with vain effort struggles yet for life;
Her arms contracted now in fruitless strife,
Now wildly at full length,
Towards the crowd in vain for pity spread, ...
They force her on, they bind her to the dead."
Kehama, i. 12.

In all the poem and its copious notes, the word **suttee** does not occur.

[1815.—"In reference to this mark of strong attachment (of Sati for Siva), a Hindoo widow burning with her husband on the funeral pile is called **sutee**."—*Ward, Hindoos*, 2nd ed. ii. 25.]

1828.—"After having bathed in the river, the widow lighted a brand, walked round the pile, set it on fire, and then mounted cheerfully: the flame caught and blazed up instantly; she sat down, placing the head of the corpse on her lap, and repeated several times the usual form, 'Ram, Ram, **Suttee**; Ram, Ram, **Suttee**.'"—*Wanderings of a Pilgrim*, i. 91–92.

1829.—"*Regulation XVII.*

"A Regulation for declaring the practice of **Suttee**; or of burning or burying alive the widows of Hindoos, illegal, and punishable by the Criminal Courts."—Passed by the *G.-G. in C.*, Dec. 4.

1839.—"Have you yet heard in England of the horrors that took place at the funeral of that wretched old Runjeet Singh? *Four* wives, and *seven* slave-girls were burnt with him; not a word of remonstrance from the British Government."—*Letters from Madras*, 278.

1843.—"It is lamentable to think how long after our power was firmly established in Bengal, we, grossly neglecting the first and plainest duty of the civil magistrate, suffered the practices of infanticide and **suttee** to continue unchecked."—*Macaulay's Speech on Gates of Somnauth.*

1856.—"The pile of the **sutee** is unusually large; heavy cart-wheels are placed upon it, to which her limbs are bound, or sometimes a canopy of massive logs is raised above it, to crush her by its fall. ... It is a fatal omen to hear the **sutee's** groan; therefore as the fire springs up from the pile, there rises simultaneously with it a deafening shout of 'Victory to Umbâ! Victory to Ranchor!' and the horn and the hard rattling drum sound their loudest, until the sacrifice is consumed."—*Râs Mâlâ*, ii. 435; [ed. 1878, p. 691].

[1870.—A case in this year is recorded by Chevers, *Ind. Med. Jurispr.* 665.]

1871.—"Our bridal finery of dress and feast too often proves to be no better than the Hindu woman's 'bravery,' when she comes to perform **suttee**."—*Cornhill Mag.* vol. xxiv. 675.

1872.—"La coutume du suicide de la **Sati** n'en est pas moins fort ancienne, puisque déjà les Grecs d'Alexandre la trouvèrent en usage chez un peuple au moins du Penjâb. Le premier témoignage brahmanique qu'on en trouve est celui de la *Brihaddevatâ* qui, peut-être, remonte tout aussi haut. A l'origine elle parait avoir été propre à l'aristocratie militaire."—*Barth, Les Religions de l'Inde*, 39.

SWAMY, SAMMY, s. This word is a corruption of Skt. *suāmin*, 'Lord.' It is especially used in S. India, in two senses: (**a**) a Hindu idol, especially applied to those of Śiva or Subramanyam; especially, as **Sammy**, in the dialect of the British soldier. This comes from the usual Tamil pronunciation *sāmi*. (**b**) The Skt. word is used by Hindus as a term of respectful address, especially to Brahmans.

a.—

1755.—"Towards the upper end there is a dark repository, where they keep their **Swamme**, that is their chief god."—*Ives*, 70.

1794.—"The gold might for us as well have been worshipped in the shape of a **Sawmy** at Juggernaut."—*The Indian Observer*, p. 167.

1838.—"The Government lately presented a shawl to a Hindu idol, and the Government officer ... was ordered to superintend the delivery of it ... so he went with the shawl in his tonjon, and told the Bramins that they might come and take it, for that he would not touch it with his fingers to present it to a **Swamy**."—*Letters from Madras*, 183.

b.—

1516.—"These people are commonly called **Jogues** (see JOGEE), and in their own speech they are called **Zoame**, which means Servant of God."—*Barbosa*, 99.

1615.—"Tune ad suos conversus: Eia Brachmanes, inquit, quid vobis videtur? Illi mirabundi nihil praeter **Suami**, **Suami**, id est Domine, Domine, retulerunt."—*Jarric, Thes.*, i. 664.

***SWAMY-HOUSE, SAMMY-HOUSE**, s. An idol-temple, or pagoda. The *Sammy-house* of the Delhi ridge in 1857 will not soon be forgotten.

1760.—"The French cavalry were advancing before their infantry; and it was the intention of Colliaud that his own should wait until they came in a line with the flank-fire of the field-pieces of the **Swamy-house**."—*Orme*, iii. 443.

1829.—"Here too was a little detached **Swamee-house** (or chapel) with a lamp burning before a little idol."—*Mem. of Col. Mountain*, 99.

1857.—"We met Wilby at the advanced post, the '**Sammy House**,' within 600 yards of the Bastion. It was a curious place for three brothers to meet in. The view was charming. Delhi is as green as an emerald just now, and the Jumma Musjid and Palace are beautiful objects, though held by infidels."—*Letters written during the Siege of Delhi*, by *Hervey Greathed*, p. 112.

SYCE, s. Hind. from Ar. *sāïs*. A groom. It is the word in universal use in the Bengal Presidency. In the South horse-keeper is more common, and in Bombay a vernacular form of the latter, viz. *ghoṛāwālā*. The Ar. verb, of which *sāïs* is the participle, seems to be a loan-word from Syriac, *sausī*, 'to coax.'

[1759.—In list of servants' wages: "**Syce**, Rs. 2."—In *Long*, 182.]

1779.—"The **bearer** and **scise**, when they returned, came to the place where I was, and laid hold of Mr. Ducarell. I took hold of Mr. Shee and carried him up. The bearer and **scise** took Mr. Ducarell out. Mr. Keeble was standing on his own house looking, and asked, 'What is the matter?' The bearer and **scise** said to Mr. Keeble, 'These gentlemen came into the house when my master was out.'"—*Evidence on Trial of* Grand *v.* Francis, in *Echoes of Old Calcutta*, 230.

1810.—"The **Syce**, or groom, attends but one horse."—*Williamson, V.M.* i. 254.

c. 1858?—

"Tandis que les **çais** veillent
les chiens rodeurs." *Leconte de Lisle.*

T

TAJ, s. Pers. *tāj*, 'a crown.' The most famous and beautiful mausoleum in Asia; the *Tāj Mahal* at Agra, erected by Shāh Jahān over the burial-place of his favourite wife Mumtāz-i-Mahal ('Ornament of the Palace') Banū Begam.

1663.—"I shall not stay to discourse of the Monument of *Ekbar*, because whatever beauty is there, is found in a far higher degree in that of **Taj Mehale**, which I am now going to describe to you ... judge whether I had reason to say that the *Mausoleum*, or Tomb of **Taj-Mehale**, is something worthy to be admired. For my part I do not yet well know, whether I am somewhat infected still with Indianisme; but I must needs say, that I believe it ought to be reckoned amongst the Wonders of the World. ..."—*Bernier*, E.T. 94–96; [ed. *Constable*, 293].

1665.—"Of all the Monuments that are to be seen at *Agra*, that of the Wife of *Cha-Jehan* is the most magnificent; she caus'd it to be set up on purpose near the *Tasimacan*, to which all strangers must come, that they should admire it. The *Tasimacan* [? Tāj-i-mukām, 'Place of the Tāj'] is a great *Bazar*, or Market-place, comprised of six great courts, all encompass'd with Portico's; under which there are Warehouses for Merchants. ... The monument of this *Begum* or *Sultaness*, stands on the East side of the City. ... I saw the beginning and compleating of this great work, that cost two and twenty years labour, and 20,000 men always at work."—*Tavernier*, E.T. ii. 50; [ed. *Ball*, i. 109].

1856.—

"But far beyond compare, the glorious **Taj**,
Seen from old Agra's towering battlements,
And mirrored clear in Jumna's silent stream;
Sun-lighted, like a pearly diadem
Set royal on the melancholy brow
Of withered Hindostan; but, when the moon
Dims the white marble with a softer light,
Like some queened maiden, veiled in dainty lace,
And waiting for her bridegroom, stately, pale,
But yet transcendent in her loveliness."

The Banyan Tree.

***TALEE**, s. Tam. *tāli*. A small trinket of gold which is fastened by a string round the neck of a married woman in S. India. It may be a curious question whether the word may not be an adaptation from the Ar. *tahlīl*, "qui signifie proprement: prononcer la formule *lâ ilâha illâ 'llâh*. ... Cette formule, écrite sur un morceau de papier, servait d'amulette ... le tout était renfermé dans un étui auquel on donnait le nom de *tahlīl*" (*Dozy & Engelmann*, 346). These Mahommedan *tahlīls* were worn by a band, and were the origin of the Span. word *tali*, 'a baldrick.' [But the *talee* is a Hindu, not a Mahommedan ornament, and there seems no doubt that it takes its name from Skt. *tāla*, 'the palmyra,' it being the original practice for women to wear this leaf dipped in saffron-water (*Mad. Gloss*, s.v. *Logan, Malabar*, i. 134).] The Indian word appears to occur first in Abraham Rogerius, but the custom is alluded to by early writers, *e.g.* Gouvea, *Synodo*, f. 43*v*.

1651.—"So the Bridegroom takes this **Tali**, and ties it round the neck of his bride."—*Rogerius*, 45.

1672.—"Among some of the Christians there is also an evil custom, that they for the greater tightening and fast-making of the marriage bond, allow the Bridegroom to tie a **Tali** or little band round the Bride's neck; although in my time this was as much as possible denounced, seeing that it is a custom derived from Heathenism."—*Baldaeus, Zeylon* (German), 408.

1674.—"The bridegroom attaches to the neck of the bride a line from which hang three little pieces of gold in honour of the three gods: and this they call **Tale**; and it is the sign of being a married woman."—*Faria y Sousa, Asia Port.*, ii. 707.

1704.—"Praeterea, quum moris hujus Regionis sit, ut infantes sex vel septem annorum, interdum etiam in teneriori aetate, ex genitorum consensu, matrimonium indissolubile de praesenti contrahant, per impositionem **Talii**, seu aureae tesserae nuptialis, uxoris collo pensilis: missionariis mandamus ne hujusmodi irrita matrimonia inter Christianos fieri permittant."—*Decree of Card. Tournon*, in *Norbert, Mem. Hist.* i. 155.

1726.—"And on the betrothal day the **Tali**, or bride's betrothal band, is tied round her neck by the Bramin ... and this she must not untie in her husband's life."—*Valentijn, Choro.* 51.

[1813.—"... the **tali**, which is a ribbon with a gold head hanging to it, is held ready; and, being shown to the company, some prayers and blessings are pronounced; after which the bridegroom takes it, and hangs it about the bride's neck."—*Forbes, Or. Mem.* 2nd ed. ii. 312.]

TAMARIND, s. The pod of the tree which takes its name from that product, *Tamarindus indica*, L., N.O. *Leguminosae*. It is a tree cultivated throughout India and Burma for the sake of the acid pulp of the pod, which is laxative and cooling, forming a most refreshing drink in fever. The tree is not believed by Dr. Brandis to be indigenous in India, but is supposed to be so in tropical Africa. The origin of the name is curious. It is Ar. *tamar-u'l-Hind*, 'date of India,' or perhaps rather in Persian form, *tamar-i-Hindī*. It is possible that the original name may have been *thamar*, 'fruit' of India, rather than *tamar*, 'date.'

1298.—"When they have taken a merchant vessel, they force the merchants to swallow a stuff called **Tamarindi**, mixed in sea-water, which produces a violent purging."—*Marco Polo*, 2nd ed., ii. 383.

c. 1335.—"L'arbre appelé *ḥammar*, c'est à dire **al-tamar-al-Hindi**, est un arbre sauvage qui couvre les montagnes."—*Masālik-al-abṣar*, in *Not. et Ext.* xiii. 175.

1563.—"It is called in Malavar *puli*, and in Guzerat *ambili*, and this is the name they have among all the other people of this India; and the Arab calls it **tamarindi**, because *tamar*, as you well know, is our *tamara*, or, as the Castilians say, *datil* [*i.e.* date], so that **tamarindi** are 'dates of India'; and this was because the Arabs could not think of a name more appropriate on account of its having stones inside, and not because either the tree or the fruit had any resemblance."—*Garcia*, f. 200. [*Puli* is the Malayāl. name; *ambilii* is probably Hind. *imlī*, Skt. *amlikā*, 'the tamarind.']

c. 1580.—"In febribus verò pestilentibus, atque omnibus aliis ex putridis, exurentibus, aquam, in qua multa copia **Tamarindorum** infusa fuerit cum saccharo ebibunt."—*Prosper Alpinus* (*De Plantis Aegypt.*) ed. Lugd. Bat. 1735, ii. 20.

1582.—"They have a great store of **Tamarindos**. ..."—*Castañeda*, by N. L. f. 94.

[1598.—"**Tamarinde** is by the Aegyptians called *Derelside* (qu. *dār-al-sayyida*, 'Our Lady's tree'?)."—*Linschoten*, Hak. Soc. ii. 121.]

1611.—"That wood which we cut for firewood did all hang trased with cods of greene fruit (as big as a Bean-cod in England) called **Tamerim**; it hath a very soure tast, and by the Apothecaries is held good against the Scurvie."—*N. Dounton*, in *Purchas*, i. 277.

[1623.—"**Tamarinds**, which the Indians call *Hambele*" (*imlī*, as in quotation from Garcia above).—*P. della Valle*, Hak. Soc. i. 92.]

1829.—"A singularly beautiful **Tamarind** tree (ever the most graceful, and amongst the most magnificent of trees). ..."—*Mem. of Col. Mountain*, 98.

1877.—"The natives have a saying that sleeping beneath the '**Date of Hind**' gives you fever, which you cure by sleeping under a *nim* tree (*Melia azedirachta*), the lilac of Persia."—*Burton, Sind Revisited*, i. 92. The *nim* (see NEEM) (*pace* Capt. Burton) is not the 'lilac of Persia'. The prejudice against encamping or sleeping under a tamarind tree is general in India. But, curiously, Bp. Pallegoix speaks of it as the practice of the Siamese "to rest and play under the beneficent shade of the **Tamarind**."—(*Desc. du Royaume Thai ou Siam*, i. 136).

TANA, THANA, s. A Police station. Hind. *thāna, thānā*, [Skt. *sthāna*, 'a place of standing, a post']. From the quotation following it would seem that the term originally meant a fortified post, with its garrison, for the military occupation of the country; a meaning however closely allied to the present use.

c. 1640-50.—"**Thánah** means a corps of cavalry, matchlockmen, and archers, stationed within an enclosure. Their duty is to guard the roads, to hold the places surrounding the **Thánah**, and to despatch provisions to the next **Thánah**."—*Pádisháh námah*, quoted by *Blochmann*, in *Āīn*, i. 345.

TANADAR, THANADAR, s. The chief of a police station (see TANA), Hind. *thānadār*. This word was adopted in a more military sense at an early date by the Portuguese, and is still in habitual use with us in the civil sense.

1516.—In a letter of 4th Feb. 1515 (*i.e.* 1516), the King Don Manoel constitutes João Machado to be **Tanadar** and captain of land forces in Goa.—*Archiv. Port. Orient.* fasc. 5, 1-3.

1519.—"Senhor Duarte Pereira; this is the manner in which you will exercise your office of **Tannadar** of this Isle of Tycoari (*i.e.* Goa), which the Senhor Capitão will now encharge you with."—*Ibid.* p. 35.

c. 1548.—"In Aguaci is a great mosque (*mizquita*), which is occupied by the **tenadars**, but which belongs to His Highness; and certain *petayas*, (yards?) in which *bate* (**paddy**) is collected, which also belong to His Highness."—*Tombo* in *Subsidios*, 216.

1602.—"So all the force went aboard of the light boats, and the Governor in his bastard-galley entered the river with a grand clangour of music, and when he was in mid-channel there came to his galley a boat, in which was the **Tanadar** of the City (Dabul), and going aboard the galley presented himself to the Governor with much humility, and begged pardon of his offences. ..."—*Couto*, IV. i. 9.

[1813.—"The third in succession was a **Tandar**, or petty officer of a district. ..."—*Forbes*, *Or. Mem.* 2nd ed. ii. 5.]

TANK, s. A reservoir, an artificial pond or lake, made either by excavation or by damming. This is one of those perplexing words which seem to have a double origin, in this case one Indian, the other European.

As regards what appears to be the Indian word, Shakespear gives: "*Tānk'h* (in Guzerat), an underground reservoir for water." [And so Platts.] Wilson gives: "*Tánkeṇ* or *ṭákeṇ*, Mahr. ... *Tánkh* (said to be Guzeráthí). A reservoir of water, an artificial pond, commonly known to Europeans in India as a **Tank**. *Ṭánki*, Guz. A reservoir of water; a small well." R. Drummond, in his *Illustrations of Guzerattee*, &c., gives: "*Tanka* (Mah.) and *Tankoo* (Guz.) Reservoirs, constructed of stone or brick or lime, of larger and lesser size, generally inside houses. ... They are almost entirely covered at top, having but a small aperture to let a pot or bucket down." ... "In the towns of Bikaner," says Tod, "most families have large cisterns or reservoirs called *Tankas*, filled by the rains" (*Rajputana*, ii. 202). Again, speaking of towns in the desert of Márwár, he says; "they collect the rain water in reservoirs called *Tanka*, which they are obliged to use sparingly, as it is said to produce night blindness" (ii. 300). Again, Dr. Spilsbury (*J.A.S.B.* ix. pt. 2, 891), describing a journey in the Nerbudda Basin, cites the word, and notes: "I first heard this word used by a native in the Betool district; on asking him if at the top of Bowergurh there was any spring, he said No, but there was a *Tanka* or place made of *pukka* (stone and cement) for holding water." Once more, in an Appendix to the Report of the Survey of India for 1881–1882, Mr. G. A. MacGill, speaking of the rain cisterns in the driest part of Rajputana, says: "These cisterns or wells are called by the people *tánkás*" (*App.* p. 12). See also quotation below from a Report by Major Strahan. It is not easy to doubt the genuineness of the word, which may possibly be from Skt. *taḍaga, taṭāga, taṭāka*, 'a pond, pool, or tank.'

Fr. Paolino, on the other hand, says the word *tanque* used by the Portuguese in India was *Portoghesa corrotta*, which is vague. But in fact *tanque* is a word which appears in all Portuguese dictionaries, and which is used by authors so early after the opening of communication with India (we do not know if there is an instance actually earlier) that we can hardly conceive it to have been borrowed from an Indian language, nor indeed could it have been borrowed from Guzerat and Rajpūtāna, to which the quotations above ascribe the vernacular word. This Portuguese word best suits, and accounts for that application of *tank* to large sheets of water which is habitual in India. The indigenous Guzerati and Mahratti word seems to belong rather to what we now call a *tank* in England; *i.e.* a small reservoir for a house or ship. Indeed the Port. *tanque* is no doubt a form of the Lat. *stagnum*, which gives It. *stagno*, Fr. old *estang* and *estan*, mod. *étang*, Sp. *estanque*, a word which we have also in old English and in Lowland Scotch, thus:

1589.—"They had in them **stanges** or pondes of water full of fish of sundrie sortes."—*Parkes's Mendoza*, Hak. Soc. ii. 46.

c. 1785.—
"I never drank the Muses' **stank**,
  Castalia's burn and a' that;
But there it streams, and richly reams,
  My Helicon I ca' that."—*Burns*.

It will be seen that Pyrard de Laval uses *estang*, as if specifically, for the *tank* of India.

1498.—"And many other saints were there painted on the walls of the church, and these wore diadems, and their portraiture was in a divers kind, for their teeth were so great that they stood an inch beyond the mouth, and every saint had 4 or 5 arms, and below the church stood a great **tanque** wrought in cut stone like many others that we had seen by the way."—*Roteiro de Vasco da Gama*, 57.

"So the Captain Major ordered Nicolas Coelho to go in an armed boat, and see where the water was, and he found in the said island (Anchediva) a building, a church of great ashlar work which had been destroyed by the Moors, as the country people said, only the chapel had been covered with straw, and they used to make their prayers to three black stones which stood in the midst of the body of the chapel. Moreover they found just beyond the church a **tanque** of wrought ashlar in which we took as much water as we wanted; and at the top of the whole island stood a great **tanque** of the depth of 4 fathoms, and moreover we found in front of the church a beach where we careened the ship Berrio."—*Ibid.* 95.

1510.—"Early in the morning these Pagans go to wash at a **tank**, which **tank** is a pond of still water (—*ad uno* **Tancho** *il qual* **Tancho** *è una fossa d'acqua morta*)."—*Varthema*, 149.

"Near to Calicut there is a temple in the midst of a **tank**, that is, in the middle of a pond of water."—*Ibid.* 175.

1553.—"In this place where the King (Bahádur Sháh) established his line of battle, on one side there was a great river, and on the other a **tank** (*tanque*) of water, such as they are used to make in those parts. For as there are few streams to collect the winter's waters, they make these **tanks** (which might be more properly called lakes), all lined with stone. They are so big that many are more than a league in compass."—*Barros*, IV. vi. 5.

c. 1610.—"Son logis estoit éloigné près d'vne lieuë du palais Royal, situé sur vn **estang**, et basty de pierres, ayant bien demy lieuë de tour, comme rous les autres **estangs**."—*Pyrard de Laval*, ed. 1679, i. 262; [Hak. Soc. i. 367].

[1615.—"I rode early ... to the **tancke** to take the ayre."—*Sir T. Roe*, Hak. Soc. i. 78.]

1616.—"Besides their Rivers ... they have many Ponds, which they call **Tankes**."—*Terry*, in *Purchas*, ii. 1470.

1638.—"A very faire **Tanke**, which is a square pit paved with gray marble."—*W. Bruton*, in *Hakl.* v. 50.

1648.—"... a standing water or **Tanck**. ..." —*Van Twist, Gen. Beschr.* 11.

1672.—"Outside and round about Suratte, there are elegant and delightful houses for recreation, and stately cemeteries in the usual fashion of the Moors, and also divers **Tanks** and reservoirs built of hard and solid stone."—*Baldaeus*, p. 12.

1673.—"Within a square Court, to which a stately Gate-house makes a Passage, in the middle whereof a **Tank** vaulted. ..."—*Fryer*, 27.

1754.—"The post in which the party intended to halt had formerly been one of those reservoirs of water called **tanks**, which occur so frequently in the arid plains of this country."—*Orme*, i. 354.

1799.—"One crop under a **tank** in Mysore or the Carnatic yields more than three here."—*T. Munro*, in *Life*, i. 241.

1809.—
"Water so cool and clear,
The peasants drink not from the humble well.
* * * * *
Nor **tanks** of costliest masonry dispense
To those in towns who dwell,
The work of kings in their beneficence."
Kehama, xiii. 6.

1883.—"... all through sheets[1] 124, 125, 126, and 131, the only drinking water is from '**tankas**,' or from '*tobs*.' The former are circular pits puddled with clay, and covered in with wattle and daub domes, in the top of which are small trap doors, which are kept locked; in these the villages store rain-water; the latter are small and somewhat deep ponds dug in the valleys where the soil is clayey, and are filled by the rain; these latter of course do not last long, and then the inhabitants are entirely dependent on their **tankas**, whilst their cattle migrate to places where the well-water is fit for use."—*Report* on Cent. Ind. and Rajputana Topogr. Survey (Bickaneer and Jeysulmeer). By *Major C. Strachan*, R.E., in *Report of the Survey in India*, 1882–83; App. p. 4. [The writer in the *Rajputana Gazetteer* (Bikanir) (i. 182) calls these covered pits *kund*, and the simple excavations *sār*.]

TASHREEF, s. This is the Ar. *tashrīf*, 'honouring'; and thus "conferring honour upon anyone, as by paying him a visit, presenting a dress of honour, or any complimentary donation" (*Wilson*). In Northern India the general use of the word is as one of ceremonious politeness in speaking of a visit from a superior or from one who is treated in politeness as a superior; when such an one is invited to 'bring his *tashrīf*,' *i.e.* 'to carry the honour of his presence,' 'to condescend to visit'——. The word always implies superiority on the part of him to whom *tashrīf* is attributed. It is constantly used by polite natives in addressing Europeans. But when the European in return says (as we have heard said, through ignorance of the real meaning of the phrase), 'I will bring my *tashrīf*,' the effect is ludicrous in the extreme, though no native will betray his amusement. In S. India the word seems to be used for the dress of honour conferred, and in the old Madras records, rightly or wrongly, for any complimentary present, in fact a *honorarium*. Thus in Wheeler we find the following:

1674.—"He (Lingapa, naik of Poonamalee) had, he said, carried a **tasheriff** to the English, and they had refused to take it. ..."—*Op. cit.* i. 84.

1680.—"It being necessary to appoint one as the Company's Chief Merchant (Verona being deceased), resolved Bera Pedda Vincatadry, do succeed and the **Tasheriffs** be given to him and the rest of the principal Merchants, viz., 3 yards Scarlett to Pedda Vincatadry, and 2½ yards each to four others... .

"The Governor being informed that Verona's young daughter was melancholly and would not eat because her husband had received no **Tasheriff**, he also is **Tasherifd** with 2½ yards Scarlet cloth."—*Fort St. Geo. Consns.*, April 6. In *Notes and Exts.*, Madras, 1873, p. 15.

1685.—"Gopall Pundit having been at great charge in coming hither with such a numerous retinue ... that we may engage him ... to continue his friendship, to attain some more and better privileges there (at Cuddalore) than we have as yet—It is ordered that he with his attendants be **Tasherift** as followeth" (a list of presents follows).—In *Wheeler*, i. 148. [And see the same phrase in *Pringle, Diary*, &c., i. 1].

TATTY, s. Hind. *ṭaṭṭī* and *ṭaṭi*, [which Platts connects with Skt. *tantra*, 'a thread, the warp in a loom']. A screen or mat made of the roots of fragrant grass with which door or window openings are filled up in the season of hot winds. The screens being kept wet, their fragrant evaporation as the dry winds blow upon them cools and refreshes the house greatly, but they are only efficient when such winds are blowing. See also THERMANTIDOTE. The principle of the *tatty* is involved in the quotation from Dr. Fryer, though he does not mention the grass-mats.

c. 1665.—"... or having in lieu of Cellarage certain *Kas-Kanays*, that is, little Houses of

1 These are sheets of the *Atlas of India*, within Bhawalpur and Jeysalmīr, on the borders of Bikaner.

Straw, or rather of odoriferous Roots, that are very neatly made, and commonly placed in the midst of a Parterre ... that so the Servants may easily with their Pompion-bottles, water them from without."—*Bernier*, E.T. 79; [ed. *Constable*, 247].

1673.—"They keep close all day for 3 or 4 Months together ... repelling the Heat by a coarse wet Cloath, continually hanging before the chamber-windows."—*Fryer*, 47.

[1789.—The introduction of **tatties** into Calcutta is mentioned in a letter from Dr. Campbell, dated May 10, 1789:—"We have had very hot winds and delightful cool houses. Everybody uses **tatties** now. ... Tatties are however dangerous when you are obliged to leave them and go abroad, the heat acts so powerfully on the body that you are commonly affected with a severe catarrh."—In *Carey, Good Old Days*, i. 80.]

1808.—"... now, when the hot winds have set in, and we are obliged to make use of **tattees**, a kind of screens made of the roots of a coarse grass called Kus."—*Broughton's Letters*, 110; [ed. 1892, p. 83].

1809.—"Our style of architecture is by no means adapted to the climate, and the large windows would be insufferable, were it not for the **tattyes** which are easily applied to a house one story high."—*Ld. Valentia*, i. 104.

1810.—"During the hot winds **tats** (a kind of mat), made of the root of the koosa grass, which has an agreeable smell, are placed against the doors and windows."—*Maria Graham*, 125.

1814.—"Under the roof, throughout all the apartments, are iron rings, from which the **tattees** or screens of sweet scented grass, were suspended."—*Forbes, Or. Mem.* iv. 6; [2nd ed. ii. 392].

1828.—"An early breakfast was over; the well watered **tatties** were applied to the windows, and diffused through the apartment a cool and refreshing atmosphere which was most comfortably contrasted with the white heat and roar of the fierce wind without."—*The Kuzzilbash*, I. ii.

***TAZEEA**, n. A.—P.—H. *ta'ziya*, 'mourning for the dead.' In India the word is applied to the **taboot**, or representations, in flimsy material, of the tombs of Hussein and Hassan which are carried about in the Muharram (see **MOHURRUM**) processions. In Persia it seems to be applied to the whole of the mystery-play which is presented at that season. At the close of the procession the *ta'ziyas* must be thrown into water; if there be no sufficient mass of water they should be buried. [See Sir L. Pelly, *The Miracle Play of Hasan and Husain.*] The word has been carried to the W. Indies by the coolies, whose great festival (whether they be Mahommedans or Hindus) the Muharram has become. And the attempt to carry the *Tazeeas* through one of the towns of Trinidad, in spite of orders to the contrary, led in the end of 1884 to a sad catastrophe. [Mahommedan Lascars have an annual celebration at the London Docks.]

1809.—"There were more than a hundred **Taziyus**, each followed by a long train of Fuqueers, dressed in the most extravagant manner, beating their breasts ... such of the Mahratta Surdars as are not Brahmuns frequently construct **Taziyus** at their own tents, and expend large sums of money upon them."—*Broughton, Letters*, 72; [ed. 1892, 53].

1869.—"En lisant la description ... de ces fêtes on croira souvent qu'il s'agit de fêtes hindous. Telle est par exemple la solennité du **ta'zia** ou *deuil*, établie en commemoration du martyre de Huçaïn, laquelle est semblable en bien de points à celle du *Durga-pujâ*. ... Le **ta'ziya** dure dix jours comme le *Durga-pujâ*. Le dixième jour, les Hindous précipitent dans la rivière la statue de la déesse au milieu d'une foule immense, avec un grand appareil et au son de mille instruments de musique; la même chose a lieu pour les représentations du tombeau de Huçaïn."—*Garcin de Tassy, Rel. Musulm.* p. 11.

***TEA**, s. Crawfurd alleges that we got this word in its various European forms from the Malay *Te*, the Chinese name being *Chhâ*. The latter is indeed the pronunciation attached, when reading in the 'mandarin dialect,' to the character representing the tea-plant, and is the form which has accompanied the knowledge of tea to India, Persia, Portugal, Greece (τσάι) and Russia. But though it may be probable that *Te*, like several other names of articles of trade, may have come to us through the Malay, the word is, not the less, originally Chinese, *Tê* (or *Tay* as Medhurst writes it) being the utterance attached to the character in the Fuhkíen dialect. The original pronunciation, whether direct from Fuh-kien or through the Malay, accompanied the introduction of tea to England as well as other countries of Western Europe. This is shown by several couplets in Pope, *e.g.*

1711.—

"... There stands a structure of majestic frame
Which from the neighbouring Hampton
takes its name.

* * * * *

"Here thou, great ANNA, whom three Realms obey,
Dost sometimes counsel take, and sometimes **tea**." *Rape of the Lock*, iii.

Here *tay* was evidently the pronunciation, as in Fuh-kien. The *Rape of the Lock* was published in 1711. In Gray's *Trivia*, published in 1720, we find *tea* rhyme to *pay*, in a passage needless to quote (ii. 296). Fifty years later there seems no room for doubt that the pronunciation had changed to that now in use, as is shown by Johnson's extemporised verses (c. 1770):

"I therefore pray thee, Renny, dear,
That thou wilt give to me
With cream and sugar soften'd well,
Another dish of **tea**"—and so on.
Johnsoniana, ed. *Boswell*, 1835, ix. 194.

The change must have taken place between 1720 and 1750, for about the latter date we find in the verses of Edward Moore:

"One day in July last at **tea**,
And in the house of Mrs. P."
The Trial of Sarah, &c.

[But the two forms of pronunciation seem to have been in use earlier, as appears from the following advertisement in *The Gazette* of Sept. 9, 1658 (quoted in 8 ser. *N. & Q.* vi. 266): "That excellent, and by all Physitians approved, China Drink, called by the Chineans Toha, by other nations Tay, alias Tee, is sold at the Sultaness Head, a coffee house in Sweetings Rents by the Royal Exchange, London."] And in *Zedler's Lexicon* (1745) it is stated that the English write the word either *Tee* or *Tea*, but pronounce it *Tiy*, which seems to represent our modern pronunciation. ["Strange to say, the Italians, however, have two names for tea, *cia* and *te*, the latter, of course, is from the Chinese word *te*, noticed above, while the former is derived from the word *ch'a*. It is curious to note in this connectión that an early mention, if not the first notice, of the word in English is under the form *cha* (in an English Glossary of A.D. 1671); we are also told that it was once spelt *tcha*—both evidently derived from the Cantonese form of the word: but 13 years later we have the word derived from the Fokienese *te*, but borrowed through the French and spelt as in the latter language *the*; the next change in the word is early in the following century when it drops the French spelling and adopts the present from of *tea*, though the Fokienese pronunciation, which the French still retain, is not dropped for the modern pronunciation of the now wholly Anglicised word *tea* till comparatively lately. It will thus be seen that we, like the Italians, might have had two forms of the word, had we not discarded the first, which seemed to have made but little lodgement with us, for the second" (*Ball, Things Chinese*, 3rd ed. 583 *seq.*).]

Dr. Bretschneider states that the Tea-shrub is mentioned in the ancient Dictionary *Rh-ya*, which is believed to date long before our era, under the names *Kia* and *K'u-tu* (*K'u* = 'bitter'), and a commentator on this work who wrote in the 4th century A.D. describes it, adding "From the leaves can be made by boiling a hot beverage" (*On Chinese Botanical Works*, &c., p. 13). But the first distinct mention of tea-cultivation in Chinese history is said to be a record in the annals of the T'ang Dynasty under A.D. 793, which mentions the imposition in that year of a duty upon tea. And the first western mention of it occurs in the next century, in the notes of the Arab traders, which speak not only of tea, but of this fact of its being subject to a royal impost. Tea does not appear to be mentioned by the medieval Arab writers upon Materia Medica, nor (strange to say) do any of the European travellers to Cathay in the 13th and 14th centuries make mention of it. Nor is there any mention of it in the curious and interesting narrative of the Embassy sent by Shāh Rukh, the son of the great Timur, to China (1419–21).[1] The first European work, so far as we are aware, in which *tea* is named, is Ramusio's (posthumous) Introduction to Marco Polo, in the second volume of his great collection of *Navigationi e Viaggi*. In this he repeats the account of Cathay which he had heard from Hajji Mahommed, a Persian merchant who visited Venice. Among other matters the Hajji detailed the excellent properties of *Chiai-Catai* (*i.e.* Pers. *Chā-i-Khitāī*, 'Tea of China'), concluding with an assurance that

1 Mr. Major, in his Introduction to Parke's *Mendoza* for the Hak. Soc. says of this embassy, that at their halt in the desert 12 marches from Su-chau, they were regaled "with a variety of strong liquors, *together with a pot of Chinese tea*." It is not stated by Mr. Major whence he took the account; but there is nothing about tea in the translation of M. Quatremère (*Not. et Ext.* xiv. pt. 1), nor in the Persian text given by him, nor in the translation by Mr. Rehatsek in the *Ind. Ant.* ii. 75 *seqq.*

if these were known in Persia and in Europe, traders would cease to purchase rhubarb, and would purchase this herb instead, a prophecy which has been very substantially verified. We find no mention of tea in the elaborate work of Mendoça on China. The earliest notices of which we are aware will be found below. Milburn gives some curious extracts from the E.I. Co.'s records as to the early importation of tea into England. Thus, 1666, June 30, among certain "raretys," chiefly the production of China, provided by the Secretary of the Company for His Majesty, appear:

"22¾ *lbs.* of **thea** at 50*s.* per *lb.*=£56 17 6
For the two cheefe persons
that attended his Majesty,
thea . . . . . . 6 15 6"

In 1667 the E.I. Co.'s first order for the importation of tea was issued to their agent at Bantam: "to send home by these ships 100lb. weight of the best **tey** that you can get." The first importation actually made for the Co. was in 1669, when two canisters were received from Bantam, weighing 143½ lbs. (*Milburn*, ii. 531.) [The earliest mention of tea in the Old Records of the India Office is in a letter from Mr. R. Wickham, the Company's Agent at Firando, in Japan, who, writing, June 27, 1615, to Mr. Eaton at Miaco, asks for "a pt. of the best sort of **chaw**" (see *Birdwood, Report on Old Records*, 26, where the early references are collected).]

A.D. 851.—"The King (of China) reserves to himself ... a duty on salt, and also on a certain herb which is drunk infused in hot water. This herb is sold in all the towns at high prices; it is called **sākh**. It has more leaves than the *ratb'ah* (Medicago sativa recens) and something more of aroma, but its taste is bitter. Water is boiled and poured upon this herb. The drink so made is serviceable under all circumstances."—*Relation*, &c., trad. par *Reinaud*, i. 40.

c. 1545.—"Moreover, seeing the great delight that I above the rest of the party took in this discourse of his, he (Chaggi Memet, *i.e.* Hajji Mahommed) told me that all over the country of Cathay they make use of another plant, that is of its leaves, which is called by those people **Chiai** *Catai*; it is produced in that district of Cathay which is called Cachanfu. It is a thing generally used and highly esteemed in all those regions. They take this plant whether dry or fresh, and boil it well in water, and of this decoction they take one or two cups on an empty stomach; it removes fever, headache, stomach-ache, pain in the side or joints; taking care to drink it as hot as you can bear; it is good also for many other ailments which I can't now remember, but I know gout was one of them. And if any one chance to feel his stomach oppressed by overmuch food, if he will take a little of this decoction he will in a short time have digested it. And thus it is so precious and highly esteemed that every one going on a journey takes it with him, and judging from what he said these people would at any time gladly swap a sack of rhubarb for an ounce of *Chiai Catai*. These people of Cathay say (he told us) that if in our country, and in Persia, and the land of the Franks, it was known, merchants would no longer invest their money in *Rauend Chini* as they call rhubarb."—*Ramusio, Dichiaratione*, in ii. f. 15.

c. 1560.—"Whatsoever person or persones come to any mans house of qualitee, hee hath a custome to offer him in a fine basket one Porcelane ... with a kinde of drinke which they call **cha**, which is somewhat bitter, red, and medicinali, which they are wont to make with a certayne concoction of herbes."—*Da Cruz*, in *Purchas*, iii. 180.

1565.—"Ritus est Japoniorum ... benevolentiae causâ praebere spectanda, quae apud se pretiosissima sunt, id est, omne instrumentum necessarium ad potionem herbae cujusdam in pulverem redactae, suavem gustu, nomine **Chia**. Est autem modus potionis ejusmodi: pulveris ejus, quantum uno juglandis putamine continetur, conjiciunt in fictile vas ex eorum genere, quae procellana (**Porcelain**) vulgus appellat. Inde calenti admodum aquâ dilutum ebibunt. Habent autem in eos usus ollam antiquissimi operis ferream, figlinum poculum, cochlearia, infundibulum eluendo figlino, tripodem, foculum denique potioni caleficiendae."—Letter from Japan, of *L. Almeida*, in *Maffei*, *Litt. Select. ex India*, Lib. iv.

1588.—"Caeterum (apud Chinenses) ex herba quadam expressus liquor admodum salutaris, nomine **Chia**, calidus hauritur, ut apud Iaponios."—*Maffei, Hist. Ind.* vi.

"Usum vitis ignorant (Japonii): oryzâ exprimunt vinum: Sed ipsi quoque ante omnia delectantur haustibus aquae poene ferventis, insperso quem supra diximus pulvere **Chia**. Circa eam potionem diligentissimi sunt, ac principes interdum viri suis ipsi manibus eidem temperandae ac miscendae, amicorum honoris causae, dant operam."—*Ibid.* Lib. xii.

1598.—"... the aforesaid warme water is made with the powder of a certaine hearbe called **chaa**."—*Linschoten*, 46; [Hak. Soc. i. 157].

1611.—"Of the same fashion is the **cha** of China, and taken in the same manner; except that the *Cha* is the small leaf of a herb, from a certain plant brought from Tartary, which was shown me when I was at Malaca."—*Teixeira*, i. 19.

1616.—"I bought 3 **chaw** cups covered with silver plates. ..."—*Cocks, Diary*, Hak. Soc. i. 202, [and see ii. 11].

1626.—"They vse much the powder of a certaine Herbe called **Chia**, of which they put as much as a Walnut-shell may containe, into a dish of Porcelane, and drinke it with hot water."—*Purchas, Pilgrimage*, 587.

1631.—"*Dur.* You have mentioned the drink of the Chinese called **Thee**; what is your opinion thereof? ... *Bont.* ... The Chinese regard this beverage almost as something sacred ... and they are not thought to have fulfilled the rites of hospitality to you until they have served you with it, just like the Mahometans with their Caveah (see. COFFEE). It is of a drying quality, and banishes sleep ... it is beneficial to asthmatic and wheezing patients."—*Jac. Bontius, Hist. Nat. et Med. Ind. Or.* Lib. i. Dial. vi. p. 11.

1638.—"Dans les assemblées ordinaires (à Sourat) que nous faisions tous les iours, nous ne prenions que du **Thè**, dont l'vsage est fort cummun par toutes les Indes."—*Mandelslo*, ed. Paris, 1659, p. 113.

1658.—"Non mirum est, multos. etiam nunc in illo errore versari, quasi diversae speciei plantae essent **The** et **Tsia**, cum è contra eadem sit, cujus decoctum Chinensibus **The**, Iaponensibus **Tsia** nomen audiat; licet horum **Tsia**, ob magnam contributionem et coctionem, nigrum **The** appellatur."—*Bontii Hist. Nat.* Pisonis Annot. p. 87.

1660.—(September) "28th. ... I did send for a cup of **tea** (a China drink) of which I never had drank before."—*Pepys's Diary.* [Both Ld. Braybrooke (4th ed. i. 110) and Wheatley (i. 249) read **tee**, and give the date as Sept. 25.]

1667.—(June) "28th. ... Home and there find my wife making of **tea**; a drink which Mr. Pelling, the Potticary, tells her is good for her cold and defluxions."—*Ibid.* [*Wheatley*, vi. 398].

1672.—"There is among our people, and particularly among the womankind a great abuse of **Thee**, not only that too much is drunk ... but this is also an evil custom to drink it with a full stomach; it is better and more wholesome to make use of it when the process of digestion is pretty well finished. ... It is also a great folly to use sugar candy with **Thee**."—*Baldaeus*, Germ. ed. 179. (This author devotes five columns to tea, and its use and abuse in India).

1677.—"Planta dicitur **Chà**, vel ... Cià, ... cujus usus in *Chinae* claustris nescius in Europae quoque paulatim sese insinuare attentat. ... Et quamvis Turcarum *Cave* (see COFFEE) et Mexicanorum *Ciocolata* eundem praesteut effectum, **Cià** tamen, quam nonulli quoque **Te** vocant, ea multum superat," etc.—*Kircher, China Illust.* 180.

"Maer de **Cià** (of **Thee**) sonder achting op eenije tijt te hebben, is novit schadelijk."—*Vermeulen*, 30.

1683.—"Lord Russell ... went into his chamber six or seven times in the morning, and prayed by himself, and then came out to Tillotson and me; he drunk a little **tea** and some sherry."—*Burnet, Hist. of Own Time*, Oxford ed. 1823, ii. 375.

1683.—

"Venus her Myrtle, Phœbus has his Bays;
Tea both excels which She[1] vouchsafes to praise,
The best of Queens, and best of Herbs we owe
To that bold Nation which the Way did show
To the fair Region where the Sun does rise,
Whose rich Productions we so justly prize."—*Waller.*

1690.—"... Of all the followers of *Mahomet* ... none are so rigidly Abstemious as the *Arabians* of *Muscatt*. ... For **Tea** and **Coffee**, which are judg'd the privileg'd Liquors of all the *Mahometans*, as well as *Turks*, as those of *Persia*, *India*, and other parts of *Arabia*, are condemned by them as unlawful. ..."—*Ovington*, 427.

1726.—"I remember well how in 1681 I for the first time in my life drank **thee** at the house of an Indian Chaplain, and how I could not understand how sensible men could think it a treat to drink what tasted no better than hay-water."—*Valentijn*, v. 190.

1789.—

"And now her vase a modest Naiad fills
With liquid crystal from her pebbly rills;
Piles the dry cedar round her silver urn,
(Bright climbs the blaze, the crackling faggots burn).
Culls the green herb of China's envy'd bowers,
In gaudy cups the steaming treasure pours;
And sweetly smiling, on her bended knee,
Presents the fragrant quintessence of **Tea**."

Darwin, Botanic Garden, Loves of the Plants, Canto ii.

1844.—"The Polish word for tea, *Herbata*, signifies more properly 'herb,' and in fact there is little more of the genuine Chinese beverage in the article itself than in its name, so that we often thought with longing of the delightful Russian **Tshaī**, genuine in word and fact."—*J. I. Kohl, Austria*, p. 444.

The following are some of the names given in the market to different kinds of tea, with their etymologies.

1. **(TEA), BOHEA**. This name is from the *Wu-i* (dialectically *Bú-î*)-shan Mountains in the N.W. of Fuh-kien, one of the districts

1 Queen Catharine.

most famous for its black tea. In Pope's verse, as Crawfurd points out, *Bohea* stands for a tea in use among fashionable people. Thus:

"To part her time 'twixt reading and **bohea**,
To muse, and spill her solitary tea."
Epistle to Mrs Teresa Blount.

[The earliest examples in the *N.E.D.* carry back the use of the word to the first years of the 18th century.]

1711.—"There is a parcel of extraordinary fine **Bohee Tea** to be sold at 26*s*. per Pound, at the sign of the Barber's Pole, next door to the Brazier's Shop in Southampton Street in the Strand."—Advt. in the *Spectator* of April 2, 1711.

1711.—
"Oh had I rather unadmired remained
On some lone isle or distant northern land;
Where the gilt chariot never marks the way,
Where none learn ombre, none e'er taste **bohea.**"
Belinda, in *Rape of the Lock*, iv. 153.

The last quotation, and indeed the first also, shows that the word was then pronounced *Bohay*. At a later date *Bohea* sank to be the market name of one of the lowest qualities of tea, and we believe it has ceased altogether to be name quoted in the tea-market. The following quotations seem to show that it was the general name for "black-tea."

1711.—"**Bohea** is of little Worth among the *Moors* and *Gentoos* of India, *Arrabs* and *Persians* ... that of 45 Tale would not fetch the Price of green Tea of 10 Tale a **Pecull**."—*Lockyer*, 116.

1721.—
"Where Indus and the double Ganges flow,
On odorif'rous plains the leaves do grow,
Chief of the treat, a plant the boast of fame,
Sometimes called green, **Bohea's** the greater name."
Allan Ramsay's Poems, ed. 1800, i. 213–14.

1726.—"Anno 1670 and 1680 there was knowledge only of **Boey** Tea and Green Tea, but later they speak of a variety of other sorts ... **Congo** ... **Pego** ... *Tongge*, *Rosmaryn Tea*, rare and very dear."—*Valentijn*, iv. 14.

1727.—"In September they strip the Bush of all its Leaves, and, for Want of warm dry Winds to cure it, are forced to lay it on warm Plates of Iron or Copper, and keep it stirring gently, till it is dry, and that Sort is called **Bohea**."—*A. Hamilton*, ii. 289; [ed. 1744, ii. 288].

But Zedler's *Lexicon* (1745) in a long article on **Thee** gives **Thee Bohea** as "the worst sort of all." The other European trade-names, according to Zedler, were **Thee-Peco**, **Congo** which the Dutch called the best, but **Thee Cancho** was better still and dearer, and **Chaucon** best of all.

2. (**TEA**) **CAMPOY**, a black tea also. *Kam-pui*, the Canton pron. of the characters *Kien-pei*, "select-dry (over a fire)."

3. (**TEA**) **CONGOU** (a black tea). This is *Kang-hu* (**tê**) the Amoy pronunciation of the characters *Kung-fu*, 'work or labour.' [Mr. Pratt (9 ser. *N. & Q.* iv. 26) writes: "The *N.E.D.* under *Congou* derives it from the standard Chinese *Kung-fu* (which happens also to be the Cantonese spelling); 'the omission of the *f*,' we are told, 'is the foreigner's corruption.' It is nothing of the kind. The Amoy name for this tea is *Konghu*, so that the omission of the *f* is due to the local Chinese dialect."]

4. **HYSON** (a green tea). This is *He-* (*hei* and *ai* in the south) *-ch'un*, 'bright spring,' [which Mr. Ball (*Things Chinese*, 586) writes *yu-ts'in*, 'before the rain'], characters which some say formed the **hong** name of a tea-merchant named Le, who was in the trade in the dist. of Hiu-ning (S.W. of Hang-chau) about 1700; others say that *He-chun* was Le's daughter, who was the first to separate the leaves, so as to make what is called **Hyson**. [Mr. Ball says that it is so called, "the young hyson being half-opened leaves plucked in April before the spring rains."]

c. 1772.—
"And Venus, goddess of the eternal smile,
Knowing that stormy brows but ill become
Fair patterns of her beauty, hath ordained
Celestial **Tea**;—a fountain that can cure
The ills of passion, and can free from frowns.
* * * * *
To her, ye fair! in adoration bow!
Whether at blushing morn, or dewy eve,
Her smoking cordials greet your fragrant board
With **Hyson**, or **Bohea**, or **Congo** crown'd."
R. Fergusson, Poems.

5. **OOLONG** (bl. tea). *Wu-lung*, 'black dragon'; respecting which there is a legend to account for the name. ["A black snake (and snakes are sometimes looked upon as dragons in China) was coiled round a plant of this tea, and hence the name" (*Ball, op. cit.* 586).]

6. **PEKOE** (do.). *Pak-ho*, Canton pron. of characters *pŏh-hao*, 'white-down.'

7. **POUCHONG** (do.). *Pao-chung*, 'fold-sort.' So called from its being packed in small paper packets, each of which is supposed to be the produce of one choice tea-plant. Also

called **Padre**-*souchong*, because the priests in the Wu-i hills and other places prepare and pack it.

8. **SOUCHONG** (do.). *Siu-chung*, Canton for *Siao-chung*, 'little-sort.'

1781.—"Les Nations Européennes retirent de la Chine des thés connus sous les noms de thé **bouy**, thé vert, et **thé saothon**."—*Sonnerat*, ii. 249.

9. **TWANKAY** (green tea). From *T'un-k'i*, the name of a mart about 15 m. S.W. of Hwei-chau-fu in Nganhwei. Bp. Moule says (perhaps after W. Williams?) from *T'un-k'i*, name of a stream near Yen-shau-fu in Chi-kiang. [Mr. Pratt (*loc. cit.*) writes; "The Amoy *Tun-ke* is nearer, and the Cantonese *Tun-kei* nearer still, its second syllable being absolutely the same in sound as the English. The Twankay is a stream in the E. of the province of Nganhwui, where Twankay tea grows."] *Twankay* is used by Theodore Hook as a sort of slang for 'tea.'

10. **YOUNG HYSON**. This is called by the Chinese *Yü-t'sien*, 'rain-before,' or '*Yu-before*,' because picked before *Kuh-yu*, a term falling about 20th April (see HYSON above). According to Giles it was formerly called, in trade, *Uchain*, which seems to represent the Chinese name. In an "*Account of the Prices at which Teas have been put up to Sale, that arrived in England in* 1784, 1785" (MS. India Office Records) the Teas are (from cheaper to dearer):—

"**Bohea Tea.**	Singlo (?),
Congou,	**Hyson.**"
Souchong,	

TEA-CADDY, s. This name, in common English use for a box to contain tea for the daily expenditure of the household, is probably corrupted, as Crawfurd suggests, from **catty**, a weight of 1⅓ *lb.* (q.v.). A '*catty-box*,' meaning a box holding a *catty*, might easily serve this purpose and lead to the name. This view is corroborated by a quotation which we have given under **caddy** (q.v.) A friend adds the remark that in his youth 'Tea-caddy' was a Londoner's name for Harley Street, due to the number of E.I. Directors and proprietors supposed to inhabit that district.

TEAPOY, s. A small tripod table. This word is often in England imagined to have some connection with *tea*, and hence, in London shops for japanned ware and the like, a *teapoy* means a tea-chest fixed on legs. But this is quite erroneous. *Tipāī* is a Hindustāni, or perhaps rather an Anglo-Hindustāni word for a tripod, from Hind. *tīn*, 3, and Pers. *pāē*, 'foot'. The legitimate word from the Persian is *sipāī* (properly *sihpāya*), and the legitimate Hindi word *tirpad* or *tripad*, but *tipāī* or *tepoy* was probably originated by some European in analogy with the familiar **charpoy** (q.v.) or 'four-legs,' possibly from inaccuracy, possibly from the desire to avoid confusion with another very familiar word **sepoy, seapoy**. [Platts, however, gives *tipāī* as a regular Hind. word, Skt. *tri-pād-ikā*.] The word is applied in India not only to a three-legged table (or any very small table, whatever number of legs it has), but to any tripod, as to the tripod-stands of surveying instruments, or to trestles in carpentry. *Sihpāya* occurs in 'Ali of Yezd's history of Timur, as applied to the trestles used by Timur in bridging over the Indus (*Elliot*, iii. 482). A teapoy is called in Chinese by a name having reference to tea:—viz. *Ch'a-chi'rh*. It has 4 legs.

[c. 1809.—"(Dinajpoor) **Sepaya**, a wooden stand for a lamp or candle with three feet."—*Buchanan, Eastern India*, ii. 945.]

1844.—"'Well, to be sure, it does seem odd—very odd;'—and the old gentleman chuckled,—'most odd to find a person who don't know what a **tepoy** is. ... Well, then, a **tepoy** or *tinpoy* is a thing with three feet, used in India to denote a little table, such as that just at your right.'

"'Why, that table has four legs,' cried Peregrine.

"'It's a **tepoy** all the same,' said Mr. Havethelacks."—*Peregrine Pulleney*, i. 112.

TEAK, s. The tree, and timber of the tree, known to botanists as *Tectona grandis*, L., N.O. *Verbenaceae*. The word is Malayāl. *tekka*, Tam. *tekku*. No doubt this name was adopted owing to the fact that Europeans first became acquainted with the wood in Malabar, which is still one of the two great sources of supply; Pegu being the other. The Skt. name of the tree is *śāka*, whence the modern Hind. name *sāgwān* or *sāgūn* and the Mahr. *śāg*. From this last probably was taken *sāj*, the name of teak in Arabic and Persian. And we have doubtless the same word in the σαγαλίνα of the Periplus, one of the exports from Western India, a form which may be illustrated by the Mahr. adj. *sāgalī*, 'made of the teak, belonging to teak.' The last fact shows, in some degree, how old the export of teak is from India. Teak beams, still undecayed, exist in the walls of the great palace of the Sassanid Kings at Seleucia or Ctesiphon, dating from the middle of the 6th century. [See *Birdwood, First Letter Book*, Intro. XXIX.] Teak has continued to recent times to be imported into Egypt. See *Forskal*, quoted by Royle (*Hindu Medicine*, 128). The *gopher-wood* of Genesis is translated *sāj* in the Arabic version of the Pentateuch (Royle). [It was probably cedar (see *Encycl. Bibl.* s.v.)]

Teak seems to have been hardly known in Gangetic India in former days. We can find no mention of it in Baber (which however is indexless), and the only mention we can find in the *Āīn*, is in a list of the weights of a cubic yard of 72 kinds of wood, where the name "*Ságaun*" has not been recognised as teak by the learned translator (see *Blochmann's* E.T. i. p. 228).

c. A.D. 80.—"In the innermost part of this Gulf (the Persian) is the Port of Apologos, lying near Pasine Charax and the river Euphrates.

"Sailing past the mouth of the Gulf, after a course of 6 days you reach another port of Persia called Omana. Thither they are wont to despatch from Barygaza, to both these ports of Persia, great vessels with brass, and timbers and beams of **teak** (ξύλων σαγαλίνων καὶ δοκῶν), and horns and spars of shisham (σασαμίνων), and of ebony. ..."—*Peripl. Maris Erythr.* § 35-36.

c. 800.—(under Hārūn al Rashīd) "Faẓl continued his story '... I heard loud wailing from the house of Abdallah ... they told me he had been struck with the *judām*, that his body was swollen and all black. ... I went to Rashīd to tell him, but I had not finished when they came to say Abdallah was dead. Going out at once I ordered them to hasten the obsequies. ... I myself said the funeral prayer. As they let down the bier a slip took place, and the bier and earth fell in together; an intolerable stench arose ... a second slip took place. I then called for planks of *teak* (**sāj**). ..."—Quotation in *Maṣ'ūdī, Prairies d'Or*, vi. 298-299.

c. 880.—"From Kol to Sindān, where they collect **teak**-*wood* (**sāj**) and cane, 18 farsakhs."—*Ibn Khurdādba*, in *J. As. S.* VI. tom. v. 284.

c. 940.—"... The *teak-tree* (**sāj**). This tree, which is taller than the date-palm, and more bulky than the walnut, can shelter under its branches a great number of men and cattle, and you may judge of its dimensions by the logs that arrive, of their natural length, at the depôts of Basra, of 'Irāk, and of Egypt. ..."—*Maṣ'ādī*, iii. 12.

Before 1200.—Abu'l-ḍhali' the Sindian, describing the regions of Hind, has these verses:

* * * * *

"By my life! it is a land where, when the rain falls,
Jacinths and pearls spring up for him who wants ornaments.
There too are produced **musk** and **camphor** and *ambergris* and *agila*,

* * * * *

And ivory there, and *teak* (**al-sāj**) and aloeswood and sandal... ."

Quoted by *Kazwini*, in *Gildemeister*, 217-218.

The following order, in a King's Letter to the Goa Government, no doubt refers to Pegu teak, though not naming the particular timber:

1597.—"We enjoin you to be very vigilant not to allow the Turks to export any timber from the Kingdom of Pegu, nor from that of Achem and you must arrange how to treat this matter, particularly with the King of Achem."—In *Archiv. Port. Orient.* fasc. ii. 669.

1602.—"... It was necessary in order to appease them, to give a promise in writing that the body should not be removed from the town, but should have public burial in our church in sight of everybody; and with this assurance it was taken in solemn procession and deposited in a box of *teak* (**teca**), which is a wood not subject to decay. ..."—*Sousa, Oriente Conquist.* (1710). ii. 265.

["Of many of the roughest thickets of bamboos and of the largest and best wood in the world, that is **teca**."—*Couto*, Dec. VII. Bk. vi. ch. 6. He goes on to explain that all the ships and boats made either by Moors or Gentiles since the Portuguese came to India, were of this wood which came from the inexhaustible forests at the back of Damaun.]

1631.—Bontius gives a tolerable cut of the foliage, &c., of the Teak-tree, but writing in the Archipelago does not use that name, describing it under the title "*Quercus Indica*, Kiati Malaiis dicta."—Lib. vi. cap. 16. On this Rheede, whose plate of the tree is, as usual, excellent (*Hortus Malabaricus*, iv. tab. 27), observes justly that the teak has no resemblance to an oak-tree, and also that the Malay name is not *Kiati* but *Jati*. *Kiati* seems to be a mistake of some kind growing out of *Kayu-jati*, 'Teak-wood.

1644.—"Hã nestas terras de Damam muyta e boa madeyra de **Teca**, a milhor de toda a India, a tambem de muyta parto do mundo, porque com ser muy fasil de laurar he perduravel, e particullarmente nam lhe tocando agoa."—*Bocarro, MS.*

1675.—"At Cock-crow we parted hence and observed that the Sheds here were round thatched and lined with broad Leaves of **Teke** (the Timber Ships are built with) in Fashion of a Bee-hive."—*Fryer*, 142.

"... **Teke** by the Portuguese, **Sogwan** by the Moors, is the firmest Wood they have for Building ... in Height the lofty Pine exceeds it not, nor the sturdy Oak in Bulk and Substance. ... This Prince of the Indian Forest was not so attractive, though mightily glorious, but that ..."—*Ibid.* 178.

1727.—"*Gundavee* is next, where good Quantities of **Teak** Timber are cut, and exported, being of excellent Use in building of Houses or Ships."—*A. Hamilton*, i. 178; [ed. 1744].

1744.—"**Tecka** is the name of costly wood which is found in the Kingdom of Martaban in the East Indies, and which never decays."—*Zeidler, Univ. Lexicon*, s.v.

1759.—"They had endeavoured to burn the **Teak** *Timbers* also, but they lying in a *swampy place*, could not take fire."—*Capt. Alwes, Report on Loss of Negrais*, in *Dalrymple*, i. 349.

c. 1760.—"As to the wood it is a sort called **Teak**, to the full as durable as oak."—*Grose*, i. 108.

1777.—"Experience hath long since shewn, that ships built with oak, and joined together with wooden trunnels, are by no means so well calculated to resist the extremes of heat and damp, in the tropical latitudes of Asia, as the ships which are built in India of **tekewood**, and bound with iron spikes and bolts."—*Price's Tracts*, i. 191.

1793.—"The **teek** forests, from whence the marine yard at Bombay is furnished with that excellent species of ship-timber, lie along the western side of the Gaut mountains ... on the north and north-east of Basseen. ... I cannot close this subject without remarking the unpardonable negligence we are guilty of in delaying to build **teak** ships of war for the service of the Indian seas."—*Rennell, Memoir*, 3rd ed. 260.

[1800.—"**Tayca**, *Tectona Robusta*."—*Buchanan, Mysore*, i. 26.]

***THAKOOR**, s. Hind. *ṭhākur*, from Skt. *ṭhakkura*, 'an idol, a deity.' Used as a term of respect, Lord, Master, &c., but with a variety of specific applications, of which the most familiar is as the style of Rājpūt nobles. It is also in some parts the honorific designation of a barber, after the odd fashion which styles a tailor *khalīfa* (see CALEEFA); a *bihishtī*, *jama'-dār* (see JEMADAR); a sweeper, **mehtar**. And in Bengal it is the name of a Brahman family, which its members have Anglicised as *Tagore*, of whom several have been men of character and note, the best known being Dwārkanāth Tagore, "a man of liberal opinions and enterprising character" (*Wilson*), who died in London in 1840.

[c. 1610.—"The nobles in blood (in the Maldives) add to their name **Tacourou**."—*Pyrard de Laval*, Hak. Soc. i. 217.

[1798.—"The **Thacur** (so Rajput chieftains are called) was naked from the waist upwards, except the sacrificial thread or scarf on his shoulders and a turban on his head."—*L. of Colebrooke*, 462.

[1881.—"After the sons have gone to their respective offices, the mother changing her clothes retires into the **thakur***ghar* (the place of worship), and goes through her morning service. ..."—*S. C. Bose, The Hindoos as they are*, 13.]

THERMANTIDOTE, s. This learned word ("heat-antidote") was applied originally, we believe, about 1830–32 to the invention of the instrument which it designates, or rather to the application of the instrument, which is in fact a winnowing machine fitted to a window aperture, and incased in wet **tatties** (q.v.), so as to drive a current of cooled air into a house during hot, dry weather. We have a dim remembrance that the invention was ascribed to Dr. Spilsbury.

1831.—"To the 21st of June, this oppressive weather held its sway; our only consolation grapes, iced-water, and the **thermantidote**, which answers admirably, almost too well, as on the 22d. I was laid up with rheumatic fever and lumbago, occasioned ... by standing or sleeping before it."—*Wanderings of a Pilgrim*, i. 208.

[Mrs Parkes saw for the first time a **thermantidote** at Cawnpore in 1830.—*Ibid.* i. 134.]

1840.—"... The thermometer at 112° all day in our tents, notwithstanding tatties, **phermanticiotes**,[1] and every possible invention that was likely to lessen the stifling heat."—*Osborne, Court and Camp of Runjeet Singh*, 132.

1853.—"... then came punkahs by day, and next punkahs by night, and then tatties, and then **therm-antidotes**, till at last May came round again, and found the unhappy Anglo-Indian world once more surrounded with all the necessary but uncomfortable sweltering panoply of the hot weather."—*Oakfield*, i. 263–4.

1878.—"They now began (c. 1840) to have the benefit of **thermantidotes**, which however were first introduced in 1831; the name of the

1 This book was printed in England, whilst the author was in India; doubtless he was innocent of this quaint error.

inventor is not recorded."—*Calcutta Rev.* cxxiv. 718.

1880.—"... low and heavy punkahs swing overhead; a sweet breathing of wet *khaskhas* grass comes out of the **therm-antidote**."—*Sir Ali Baba*, 112.

***THUG**, s. Hind. *ṭhag*, Mahr. *ṭhak*, Skt. *sṭhaga*, 'a cheat, a swindler.' And this is the only meaning given and illustrated in R. Drummond's *Illustrations of Guzerattee*, &c. (1808). But it has acquired a specific meaning, which cannot be exhibited more precisely or tersely than by Wilson: "Latterly applied to a robber and assassin of a peculiar class, who sallying forth in a gang ... and in the character of wayfarers, either on business or pilgrimage, fall in with other travellers on the road, and having gained their confidence, take a favourable opportunity of strangling them by throwing their handkerchiefs round their necks, and then plundering them and burying their bodies." The proper specific designation of these criminals was *phānsīgar* or *phānsigar*, from *phansī*, 'a noose.'

According to Mackenzie (in *As. Res.* xiii.) the existence of gangs of these murderers was unknown to Europeans till shortly after the capture of Seringapatam in 1799, when about 100 were apprehended in Bangalore. But Fryer had, a century earlier, described a similar gang caught and executed near Surat. The *Phānsigars* (under that name) figured prominently in an Anglo-Indian novel called, we think, "The English in India," which one of the present writers read in early boyhood, but cannot now trace. It must have been published between 1826 and 1830.

But the name of *Thug* first became thoroughly familiar not merely to that part of the British public taking an interest in Indian affairs, but even to the mass of Anglo-Indian society, through the publication of the late Sir William Sleeman's book "*Ramaseeana*; or a Vocabulary of the peculiar language used by the **Thugs**, with an Introduction and Appendix, descriptive of that Fraternity, and of the Measures which have been adopted by the Supreme Government of India for its Suppression," Calcutta, 1836; and by an article on it which appeared in the *Edinburgh Review*, for Jan. 1837, (lxiv. 357). One of Col. Meadows Taylor's Indian romances also, *Memoirs of a Thug* (1839), has served to make the name and system familiar. The suppression of the system, for there is every reason to believe that it was brought to an end, was organised in a masterly way by Sir W. (then Capt.) Sleeman, a wise and admirable man, under the government and support of Lord William Bentinck. [The question of the Thugs and their modern successors has been again discussed in the *Quarterly Review*, Oct. 1901.]

c. 1665.—"Les Voleurs de ce pais-là sont les plus adroits du monde; ils ont l'usage d'un certain lasset à noeud coulant, qu'ils savent jetter si subtilement au col d'un homme, quand ils sont à sa portée, qu'ils ne le manquent jamais; en sorte qu'en un moment ils l'étranglent ..." &c.—*Thevenot*, v. 123.

1673.—"They were Fifteen, all of a Gang, who used to lurk under Hedges in narrow Lanes, and as they found Opportunity, by a Device of a Weight tied to a Cotton Bow-string made of Guts, ... they used to throw it upon Passengers, so that winding it about their Necks, they pulled them from their Beasts and dragging them upon the Ground strangled them, and possessed themselves of what they had ... they were sentenced to *Lex Talionis*, to be hang'd; wherefore being delivered to the *Catwal* or Sheriff's Men, they led them two Miles with Ropes round their Necks to some Wild Date-trees: In their way thither they were chearful, and went singing, and smoaking Tobacco ... as jolly as if going to a Wedding; and the Young Lad now ready to be tied up, boasted, That though he were not 14 Years of Age, he had killed his Fifteen Men. ..."—*Fryer*, 97.

1785.—"Several men were taken up for a most cruel method of robbery and murder, practised on travellers, by a tribe called **phanseegurs**, or stranglers ... under the pretence of travelling the same way, they enter into conversation with the strangers, share their sweetmeats, and pay them other little attentions, until an opportunity offers of suddenly throwing a rope round their necks with a slip-knot, by which they dexterously contrive to strangle them on the spot."—*Forbes, Or. Mem.* iv. 13; [2nd ed. ii. 397].

1808.—"**Phanseeo.** A term of abuse in Guzerat, applied also, truly, to thieves or robbers who strangle children in secret or travellers on the road."—*R. Drummond, Illustrations*, s.v.

1820.—"In the more northern parts of India these murderers are called **Thegs**, signifying deceivers."—*As. Res.* xiii. 250.

1823.—"The **Thugs** are composed of all castes, Mahommedans even were admitted: but the great majority are Hindus; and among these the Brahmins, chiefly of the Bundelcund tribes, are in the greatest numbers, and generally direct the operations of the different bands."—*Malcolm, Central India*, ii. 187.

1831.—"The inhabitants of Jubbulpore were this morning assembled to witness the execution of 25 **Thugs**. ... The number of **Thugs** in the neighbouring countries is enormous; 115, I believe, belonged to the party of which 25 were executed, and the remainder are to be transported; and report says there are as many in Sauger Jail."—*Wanderings of a Pilgrim*, i. 201–202.

1843.—"It is by the command, and under the special protection of the most powerful goddesses that the **Thugs** join themselves to the unsuspecting traveller, make friends with him, slip the noose round his neck, plunge their knives in his eyes, hide him in the earth, and divide his money and baggage."—*Macaulay, Speech on Gates of Somnauth.*

1874.—"If a **Thug** makes strangling of travellers a part of his religion, we do not allow him the free exercise of it."—*W. Newman*, in *Fortnightly Rev.*, N.S. xv. 181.

[Tavernier writes: "The remainder of the people, who do not belong to either of these four castes, are called *Pauzecour*." This word Mr. Ball (ii. 185) suggests to be equivalent to either **pariah** or **phansigar**. Here he is in error. *Pauzecour* is really Skt. *Pancha-Gauḍa*, the five classes of northern Brahmans, for which see *Wilson*, (*Indian Caste*, ii. 124 *seqq.*).]

TIBET, n.p. The general name of the vast and lofty table-land of which the Himālaya forms the southern marginal range, and which may be said roughly to extend from the Indus elbow, N.W. of Kashmīr, to the vicinity of Sining-fu in Kansuh and to Tatsienlu on the borders of Szechuen, the last a distance of 1800 miles. The origin of the name is obscure, but it came to Europe from the Mahommedans of Western Asia; its earliest appearance being in some of the Arab Geographies of the 9th century.

Names suggestive of *Tibet* are indeed used by the Chinese. The original form of these (according to our friend Prof. Terrien de la Couperie) was *Tu-pot*; a name which is traced to a prince so called, whose family reigned at Liang-chau, north of the Yellow R. (in modern Kansuh), but who in the 5th century was driven far to the southwest, and established in eastern Tibet a State to which he gave the name of *Tu-pot*, afterwards corrupted into *Tu-poh* and *Tu-fan*. We are always on ticklish ground in dealing with derivations from or through the Chinese. But it is doubtless possible, perhaps even probable, that these names passed into the western form *Tibet*, through the communication of the Arabs in Turkestan with the tribes on their eastern border. This may have some corroboration from the prevalence of the name *Tibet*, or some proximate form, among the Mongols, as we may gather both from Carpini and Rubruck in the 13th century (quoted below), and from Sanang Setzen, and the Mongol version of the *Bodhimor* several hundred years later. These latter write the name (as represented by I. J. Schmidt), *Tūbet* and *Tōbōt*.

[c. 590.—"**Tobbat**." See under INDIA.]

851.—"On this side of China are the countries of the Taghazghaz and the Khākān of **Tibbat**; and that is the termination of China on the side of the Turks."—*Relation*, &c., tr. par *Reinaud*, pt. i. p. 60.

c. 880.—"Quand un étranger arrive au *Tibet* (*al*-**Tibbat**), il éprouve, sans pouvoir s'en rendre compte, un sentiment de gaieté et de bien être qui persiste jusqu'au départ."—*Ibn Khurdādba*, in *J. As.* Ser. vi. tom. v. 522.

c. 910.—"The country in which lives the goat which produces the musk of China, and that which produces the musk of **Tibbat** are one and the same; only the Chinese get into their hands the goats which are nearest their side, and the people of **Tibbat** do likewise. The superiority of the musk of **Tibbat** over that of China is due to two causes; first, that the musk-goat on the **Tibbat** side of the frontier finds aromatic plants, whilst the tracts on the Chinese side only produce plants of a common kind."—*Relation*, &c., pt. 2, pp. 114–115.

c. 930.—"This country has been named **Tibbat** because of the establishment there of the Himyarites, the word *thabat* signifying to fix or establish oneself. That etymology is the most likely of all that have been proposed. And it is thus that Di'bal, son of Alī-al-Khuzā'ī, vaunts this fact in a poem, in which when disputing with Al-Kumair he exalts the descendants of Ḳaṭlān above those of Nizāar, saying:

"'Tis they who have been famous by their
writings at the gate of Merv,
And who were writers at the gate of Chin,
'Tis they who have bestowed on Samarkand
the name of Shamr,
And who have transported thither the
Tibetans" (*Al*-**Tubbatīna**).[1]

Mas'ūdī, i. 352.

1 This refers to an Arab legend that Samarkand was founded in very remote times by Tobba'-al-Akbar, Himyarite King of Yemen, (see *e.g.*

c. 976.—"From the sea to **Tibet** is 4 months' journey, and from the sea of Fārs to the country of Kanauj is 3 months' journey."—*Ibn Haukal*, in *Elliot*, i. 33.

c. 1020.—"Bhútesar is the first city on the borders of **Tibet**. There the language, costume, and appearance of the people are different. Thence to the top of the highest mountain, of which we spoke ... is a distance of 20 parasangs. From the top of it **Tibet** looks red and Hind black."—*Al-Birūnī*, in *Elliot*, i. 57.

1075.—"*Τοῦ μόσχου, διάφορα εἴδη εἰσίν · ὧν ὁ κρείττων γίνεται ἐν πόλει τινὶ πολὺ τοῦ Χοράσῃ ἀνατολικοτέρα, λεγομένη Τουπάτα · ἔστι δὲ τὴν χροιὰν ὑπόξανθον · τοῦτου δὲ ἧπτον ὁ ἀπὸ τῆς Ἰνδιάς μετακομιζόμενος · ῥέπει δὲ ἐπὶ τὸ μελάντερον · καὶ τούτου πάλιν ὑποδεέστερος ὁ ἀπὸ τῶν Σίνων ἀγόμενος · πάντες δε ἐν ὀμφαλῷ ἀπογεννῶνται ζώου τινὸς μονοκέρωτος μέγιστου ὁμοιόυ δορκάδος*."—*Symeon Seth*, quoted by *Bochart, Hieroz*. III. xxvi.

1165.—"This prince is called in Arabic Sultan-al-Fars-al-Kábar ... and his empire extends from the banks of the Shat-al-Arab to the City of Samarkand ... and reaches as far as **Thibet**, in the forests of which country that quadruped is found which yields the musk."—*Rabbi Benjamin*, in *Wright's Early Travels*, 106.

c. 1200.—
"He went from Hindustan to the
Tibat-land... .
From **Tibat** he entered the boundaries of
Chīn."
Sikandar Nāmah, E.T. by *Capt. H. W. Clarke*, R.E., p. 585.

1247.—"Et dum reverteretur exercitus ille, videlicet Mongalorum, venit ad terram Buri-**Thabet**, quos bello vicerunt: qui sunt pagani. Qui consuetudinem mirabilem imo potius miserabilem habent: quia cum alicujus pater humanae naturae debitum solvit, omnem congregant parentelam ut comedant eum, sicut nobis dicebatur pro certo."—*Joan. de Plano Carpini*, in *Rec. de Voyages*, iv. 658.

1253.—"Post istos sunt **Tebet**, homines solentes comedere parentes suos defunctos, ut causa pietatis non facerent aliud sepulchrum eis nisi viscera sua."—*Rubruq*. in *Recueil de Voyages*, &c. iv. 289.

1298.—"**Tebet** est une grandisime provence qve lengajes ont por elles, et sunt ydres. ... Il sunt maint grant laironz ... il sunt mau custumés; il ont grandismes chenz mastin qe sunt grant come asnes et sunt mout buen a prendre bestes sauvajes."—*Marco Polo*, Geog. Text. ch. cxvi.

1330.—"Passando questa provincia grande perveni a un altro gran regno che si chiama **Tibet**, ch'ene ne confini d'India ed e tutta al gran Cane ... la gente di questa contrada dimora in tende che sono fatte di feltri neri. La principale cittade è fatta tutta di pietre bianche e nere, e tutte le vie lastricate. In questa cittade dimora il Atassi (Abassi?) che viene a dire in nostro modo il Papa."—*Fr. Odorico*, Palatine MS., in *Cathay*, &c. App. p. lxi.

c. 1340.—"The said mountain (*Karāchīl*, the Himālaya) extends in length a space of 3 months' journey, and at the base is the country of **Thabbat**, which has the antelopes which give musk."—*Ibn. Batuta*, iii. 438–439.

Edrisi, by *Jaubert*, ii. 198), and the following: "The author of the *Treatise on the Figure of the Earth* says on this subject: "This is what was told me by Abu-Bakr-Dimashkī—"I have seen over the great gate of Samarkand an iron tablet bearing an inscription, which, according to the people of the place, was engraved in Himyarite characters, and as an old tradition related, had been the work of "Tobba." ' "—*Shihābuddīn Dimashkī*, in *Not, et Ext*. xiii. 254.

TICCA, and vulg. **TICKER**, adj. This is applied to any person or thing engaged by the job, or on contract. Thus a *ticca garry* is a hired carriage, a *ticca doctor* is a surgeon not in the regular service but temporarily engaged by Government. From Hind. *ṭhīka*, *ṭhīkah*, 'hire, fare, fixed price.'

[1813.—"**Teecka**, hire, fare, contract, job."—*Gloss. to Fifth Report*, s.v.]

1827.—"A Rule, Ordinance and Regulation for the good Order and Civil Government of the Settlement of Fort William in Bengal, and for regulating the number and fare of **Teeka Palankeens**, and **Teeka Bearers** in the Town of Calcutta ... registered in the Supreme Court of Judicature, on the 27th June, 1827."—*Bengal Regulations* of 1827.

1878.—"Leaving our servants to jabber over our heavier baggage, we got into a '**ticca gharry**,' 'hired trap,' a bit of civilization I had hardly expected to find so far in the Mofussil."—*Life in the Mofussil*, ii. 94.

[**TICKA**, s. Hind. *ṭikā*, Skt. *tilaka*, a mark on the forehead made with coloured earth or unguents, as an ornament, to mark sectarial distinction, accession to the throne, at betrothal, &c; also a sort of spangle worn on the forehead by women. The word has now been given the additional meaning of the mark made in vaccination, and the *ṭīkāwālā Ṣāḥib* is the vaccination officer.

[c. 1796.—"... another was sent to Kutch to bring thence the **tika**. ..."—*Mir Hussein Ali, Life of Tipu*, 251

[1832.—"In the centre of their foreheads is

a **teeka** (or spot) of lamp-black."—*Herklots, Qanoon-e-Islam*, 2nd ed. 139.

[c. 1878.—"When a sudden stampede of the children, accompanied by violent yells and sudden falls, has taken place as I entered a village, I have been informed, by way of apology, that it was not I whom the children feared, but that they supposed that I was the **Tikawala** *Sahib*."—*Panjab Gazetteer, Rohtak*, p. 9.]

TICKY-TOCK. This is an unmeaning refrain used in some French songs, and by foreign singing masters in their scales. It would appear from the following quotations to be of Indian origin.

c. 1755.—"These gentry (the band with nautch-girls) are called **Tickytaw** boys, from the two words **Ticky** and **Taw**, which they continually repeat, and which they chaunt with great vehemence."—*Ives*, 75.

[c. 1883.—"Each pair of boys then, having privately arranged to represent two separate articles ... comes up to the captains, and one of the pair says **dik dik, daun daun**, which apparently has about as much meaning as the analogous English nursery saying, 'Dickory, dickory dock.' "—*Panjab Gazetteer, Hoshiārpur*, p. 35.]

***TIFFIN**, s. Luncheon, Anglo-Indian and Hindustani, at least in English households. Also **to Tiff**, v. to take luncheon. Some have derived this word from Ar. *tafannun*, 'diversion, amusement,' but without history, or evidence of such an application of the Arabic word. Others have derived it from Chinese *ch'ih-fan*, 'eat-rice,' which is only an additional example that anything whatever may be plausibly resolved into Chinese monosyllables. We believe the word to be a local survival of an English colloquial or slang **term**. Thus we find in the *Lexicon Balatronicum*, compiled originally by Capt. Grose (1785): "*Tiffing*, eating or drinking out of meal-times," besides other meanings. Wright (*Dict. of Obsolete and Provincial English*) has: "*Tiff*, s. (1) a draught of liquor, (2) small beer;" and Mr. Davies (*Supplemental English Glossary*) gives some good quotations both of this substantive and of a verb "*to tiff*," in the sense of 'take off a draught.' We should conjecture that Grose's sense was a modification of this one, that his "*tiffing*" was a participial noun from the verb *to tiff*, and that the Indian **tiffin** is identical with the participial noun. This has perhaps some corroboration both from the form "*tiffing*" used in some earlier Indian examples, and from the Indian use of the verb "**to Tiff**." [This view is accepted by Prof. Skeat, who derives *tiff* from Norweg. *tev*, 'a drawing in of the breath, sniff,' *teva*, 'to sniff' (*Concise Dict.* s.v.; and see 9 ser. *N. & Q.* iv. 425, 460, 506; v. 13).] Rumphius has a curious passage which we have tried in vain to connect with the present word; nor can we find the words he mentions in either Portuguese or Dutch Dictionaries. Speaking of **Toddy** and the like he says:

"Homines autem qui eas (potiones) colligunt ac praeparant, dicuntur Portugallico nomine *Tiffadores*, atque opus ipsum *Tiffar*; nostratibus Belgis *tyfferen*" (*Herb. Amboinense*, i. 5).

We may observe that the comparatively late appearance of the word **tiffin** in our documents is perhaps due to the fact that when dinner was early no lunch was customary. But the word, to have been used by an English novelist in 1811, could not then have been new in India.

We now give examples of the various uses:

TIFF, s. In the old English senses (in which it occurs also in the form *tip*, and is probably allied to *tipple* and *tipsy*); [see Prof. Skeat, quoted above].

(1) For a draught:

1758.—"*Monday* ... *Seven*. Returned to my room. Made a **tiff** of warm punch, and to bed before nine."—*Journal of a Senior Fellow*, in the *Idler*, No. 33.

(2) For small beer:

1604.—

"... make waste more prodigal
Than when our beer was good, that John may float
To Styx in beer, and lift up Charon's boat
With wholsome waves: and as the conduits ran
With claret at the Coronation,
So let your channels flow with single **tiff**,
For John I hope is crown'd... ."
On John Dawson, Butler of Christ Church, in *Bishop Corbet's Poems*, ed. 1807, pp. 207–8.

TO TIFF, v. in the sense of taking off a draught.

1812.—

"He **tiff'd** his punch and went to rest."
Combe, Dr. Syntax, I. Canto v.

(This is quoted by Mr. Davies.)

TIFFIN (the Indian substantive).

1784.—

"Each temperate day

With health glides away,
No **Triffings**[1] our forenoons profane,"
—*Memoirs of the Late War in Asia*, by *An officer of Colonel Baillie's Detachment*, ii. *Appendix*, p. 293.

1807.—"Many persons are in the habit of sitting down to a repast at one o'clock, which is called **tiffen**, and is in fact an early dinner."—*Cordiner's Ceylon*, i. 83.

1810.—"The (Mahommedan) ladies, like ours, indulge in **tiffings** (slight repasts), it being delicate to eat but little before company."—*Williamson, V.M.* i. 352.

(published 1812) "The dinner is scarcely touched, as every person eats a hearty meal called **tiffin**, at 2 o'clock, at home."—*Maria Graham*, 29.

1811.—"Gertrude was a little unfortunate in her situation, which was next below Mrs. Fashionist, and who ... detailed the delights of India, and the *routine* of its day; the changing linen, the *curry-combing* ... the idleness, the dissipation, the sleeping and the necessity of sleep, the gay **tiffings**, were all delightful to her in reciting. ..."—*The Countess and Gertrude, or Modes of Discipline*, by *Laetitia Maria Hawkins*, ii. 12.

1824.—"The entreaty of my friends compelled me to remain to breakfast and an early **tiffin**. ..."—*Seely, Wonders of Ellora*, ch. iii.

c. 1832.—"Reader! I, as well as Pliny, had an uncle, an East Indian Uncle ... everybody has an Indian Uncle. ... He is not always so orientally rich as he is reputed; but he is always orientally munificent. Call upon him at any hour from two till five, he insists on your taking **tiffin**; and such a **tiffin!** The English corresponding term is luncheon: but how meagre a shadow is the European meal to its glowing Asiatic cousin."—*De Quincey, Casuistry of Roman Meals*, in *Works*, iii. 259.

1847.—"'Come home and have some **tiffin**, Dobbin,' a voice cried behind him, as a pudgy hand was laid on his shoulder. ... But the Captain had no heart to go a-feasting with Joe Sedley."—*Vanity Fair*, ed. 1867, i. 235.

1850.—"A vulgar man who enjoys a champagne **tiffin** and swindles his servants ... may be a pleasant companion to those who do not hold him in contempt as a vulgar knave, but he is not a gentleman."—*Sir C. Napier, Farewell Address.*

1853.—"This was the case for the prosecution. The court now adjourned for **tiffin**."—*Oakfield*, i. 319.

1882.—"The last and most vulgar form of 'nobbling' the press is well known as the luncheon or **tiffin** trick. It used to be confined to advertising tradesmen and hotel-keepers, and was practised on newspaper reporters. Now it has been practised on a loftier scale. ..."—*Saty. Rev.*, March 25, 357.

1 [In note "Luncheon."]

TO TIFF, in the Indian sense.

1803.—"He hesitated, and we were interrupted by a summons to **tiff** at Floyer's. After **tiffin** Close said he should be glad to go."—*Elphinstone*, in *Life*, i. 116.

1814.—"We found a pool of excellent water, which is scarce on the hills, and laid down to **tiff** on a full soft bed, made by the grass of last year and this. After **tiffing**, I was cold and unwell."—*Ibid.* p. 283. *Tiffing* here is a participle, but its use shows how the noun **tiffin** would be originally formed.

1816.—
"The huntsman now informed them all
They were to **tiff** at Bobb'ry Hall.
Mounted again, the party starts,
Upsets the **hackeries** and carts,
Hammals and **palanquins** and **doolies.**
Dobies (see DHOBY) and burrawas (?) and
coolies."
The Grand Master, or Adventures of Qui Hi, by *Quiz* (Canto viii.).

[Burrawa is probably H. *bharuā*, 'a pander.']

1829.—"I was **tiffing** with him one day, when the subject turned on the sagacity of elephants. ..."—*John Shipp*, ii. 267.

1859.—"Go home, Jack. I will **tiff** with you to-day at half-past two."—*J. Lang, Wanderings in India*, p. 16.

The following, which has just met our eye, is bad grammar, according to Anglo-Indian use:

1885.—"'Look here, RANDOLPH, don't you know,' said Sir PEEL, ... 'Here you've been gallivanting through India, riding on elephants, and **tiffining** with Rajahs. ...' "—*Punch, Essence of Parliament*, April 25, p. 204.

***TIGER**, s. The royal tiger was apparently first known to the Greeks by the expedition of Alexander, and a little later by a live one which Seleucus sent to Athens. The animal became, under the Emperors, well known to the Romans, but fell out of the knowledge of Europe in later days, till it again became familiar in India. The Greek and Latin τίγρις, *tigris*, is said to be from the old Persian word for an arrow, *tigra*, which gives the modern Pers. (and Hind.) *tīr*.[2] Pliny

2 Sir H. Rawlinson gives *tigra* as old Persian for an arrow (see *Herod.* vol. iii. p. 552). Vüllers seems to consider it rather an induction than a known word for an arrow. He says: "Besides the name of that river (Tigris) *Arvand*, which often occurs

says of the *River* Tigris: "*a celeritate* **Tigris** *incipit vocari. Ita appellant Medi sagittam*" (vi. 27). In speaking of the animal and its "*velocitatis tremendae,*" Pliny evidently glances at this etymology, real or imaginary. So does Pausanias probably, in his remarks on its colour. [This view of the origin of the name is accepted by Schrader (*Prehist. Ant. of the Aryan Peoples*, E.T. 250), who writes: "Nothing like so far back in the history of the Indo-Europeans does the lion's dreadful rival for supremacy over the beasts, the tiger, go. In India the songs of the Rigveda have nothing to say about him; his name (*vyághrá*) first occurs in the Atharvaveda, *i.e.* at a time when the Indian immigration must have extended much farther towards the Ganges; for it is in the reeds and grasses of Bengal that we have to look for the tiger's proper home. Nor is he mentioned among the beasts of prey in the Avesta. The district of Hyrcania, whose numerous tigers the later writers of antiquity speak of with especial frequency, was then called *Vehrkana*, 'wolf-land.' It is, therefore, not improbable ... that the tiger has spread in relatively late times from India over portions of W. and N. Asia."]

c. B.C. 325.—"The Indians think the **Tiger** (*τὸν τίγριν*) a great deal stronger than the elephant. Nearchus says he saw the skin of a tiger, but did not see the beast itself, and that the Indians assert the **tiger** to be as big as the biggest horse; whilst in swiftness and strength there is no creature to be compared to him. And when he engages the elephant he springs on its head, and easily throttles it. Moreover, the creatures which we have seen and call *tigers* are only jackals which are dappled, and of a kind bigger than ordinary jackals."—*Arrian, Indica*, xv. We apprehend that this big dappled jackal (*θῶς*) is meant for a *hyaena*.

---

in the *Shāhnāma*, and which properly signifies 'running' or 'swift'; another Medo-persic name *Tigra* is found in the cuneiform inscriptions, and is cognate with the Zend word *tedjao*, *tedjerem*, and Pehlvi *tedjera*, *i.e.* 'a running river,' which is entered in Anquetil's vocabulary. And these, along with the Persian *tej* 'an arrow,' *tegh* 'a sword,' *tekh* and *teg* 'sharp,' are to be referred to the Zend root *tikhsh*, Skt. *tij*, 'to sharpen.' The Persian word *tīr*, 'an arrow,' may be of the same origin, since its primitive form appears to be *tīgra*, from which it seems to come by elision of the g, as the Skt. *tīr*, 'arrow,' comes from *tīvra* for *tīgra*, where *v* seems to have taken the place of g. From the word *tīgra* ... seem also to be derived the usual names of the river Tigris, Pers. *Dishla*, Ar. *Dijah*" (Vüllers, s.v. *tīr*).

c. B.C. 322.—"In the island of Tylos ... there is also another wonderful thing they say ... for there is a certain tree, from which they cut sticks, and these are very handsome articles, having a certain variegated colour, like the skin of a **tiger**. The wood is very heavy; but if it is struck against any solid substance it shivers like a piece of pottery."—*Theophrastus, H. of Plants*, Bk. v. c. 4.

c. B.C. 321.—"And Ulpianus ... said: 'Do we anywhere find the word used a masculine, *τὸν τίγριν*? for I know that Philemon says thus in his Neaera:

'*A*. We've seen the **tigress** (*τὴν τίγριν*) that
Seleucus sent us;
Are we not bound to send Seleucus back
Some beast in fair exchange?' "

In *Athenaeus*, xiii. 57.

c. B.C. 320.—"According to Megasthenes, the largest **tigers** are found among the Prasii, almost twice the size of lions, and of such strength that a tame one led by four persons seized a mule by its hinder leg, overpowered it, and dragged it to him."—*Strabo*, xv. ch. 1, § 37 (*Hamilton* and *Falconer's* E.T. iii. 97).

c. B.C. 19.—"And Augustus came to Samos, and again passed the winter there ... and all sorts of embassies came to him; and the Indians who had previously sent messages proclaiming friendship, now sent to make a solemn treaty, with presents, and among other things including **tigers**, which were then seen for the first time by the Romans; and if I am not mistaken by the Greeks also."—*Dio Cassius*, liv. 9. [See *Merivale, Hist. Romans*, ed. 1865, iv. 176.]

c. B.C. 19.—
... duris genuit te cautibus horrens
Caucasus, Hyrcanaeque admôrunt ubera
tigres." *Aen.* iv. 366–7.

c. A.D. 70.—"The Emperor Augustus ... in the yeere that Q. Tubero and Fabius Maximus were Consuls together ... was the first of all others that shewed a tame **tygre** within a cage: but the Emperour Claudius foure at once. ... **Tygres** are bred in Hircania and India: this beast is most dreadful for incomparable swiftness."—*Pliny*, by *Ph. Holland*, i. 204.

c. 80–90.—"Wherefore the land is called **Dachanabadēs**, (see DECCAN) for the South is called *Dachanos* in their tongue. And the land that lies in the interior above this towards the East embraces many tracts, some of them of deserts or of great mountains, with all kinds of wild beasts, panthers and **tigers** (*τίγρεις*) and elephants, and immense serpents (*δράκοντας*) and hyenas (*κροκόττας*) and *cynocephala* of many species, and many and populous nations till you come to the Ganges."—*Periplus*, § 50.

c. A.D. 180.—"That beast again, in the talk of Ctesias about the Indians, which is alleged to be called by them *Martióra* (*Martichóra*), and by the Greeks *Androphagus* (Maneater), I am convinced is really the **tiger** (*τὸν τίγριν*). The story that he has a triple range of teeth in each jaw, and sharp prickles at the tip of his tail which he shoots at those who are at a distance, like the arrows of an archer,—I don't believe it to be true, but only to have been generated by the excessive fear which the beast inspires. They have been wrong also about his colour;—no doubt when they see him in the bright sun-light he takes that colour and looks red; or perhaps it may be because of his going so fast, and because even when not running he is constantly darting from side to side; and then (to be sure) it is always from a long way off that they see him."—*Pausanias*, IX. xxi. 4. [See Frazer's tr. i. 470; v. 86. *Martichoras* is here Pers. *mardumkhwūr*, 'eater of men.']

1298.—"Enchore sachiés qe le Grant Sire a bien leopars asez qe tuit sunt bon da chacer et da prendre bestes. ... Il ha plosors lyons grandismes, greignors asez qe cele de Babilonie. Il sunt de mout biaus poil et de mout biaus coleor, car il sunt tout vergés por lonc, noir et vermoil et blance. Il sunt afaités a prandre sengler sauvajes et les bueff sauvajes, et orses et asnes sauvajes et cerf et cavriolz et autres bestes."—*Marco Polo*, *Geog. Text*, ch. xcii. Thus Marco Polo can only speak of this huge animal, striped black and red and white, as of a *Lion*. And a medieval Bestiary has a chapter on the **Tigre** which begins: "Une Beste est qui est apelée **Tigre**, c'est une maniere de serpent."—(In *Cahier et Martin, Mélanges d' Archéol.* ii. 140).

1474.—"This meane while there came in certain men sent from a Prince of India, wth certain strange beastes, the first whereof was a *leonza* ledde in a chayne by one that had skyll, which they call in their languaige *Babureth*. She is like vnto a lyonesse; but she is redde coloured, streaked all over wth black strykes; her face is redde wth certain white and blacke spottes, the bealy white, and tayled like the lyon: seemyng to be a marvailouse fiers beast."—*Josafa Barbaro*, Hak. Soc. pp. 53–54. Here again is an excellent description of a tiger, but that name seems unknown to the traveller. *Babureth* is in the Ital. original *Baburth*, Pers. *babr*, a **tiger**.

1553.—"... Beginning from the point of Çingapura and all the way to Pulloçambilam, *i.e.* the whole length of the Kingdom of Malaca ... there is no other town with a name except this City of Malaca, only some havens of fishermen, and in the interior a very few villages. And indeed the most of these wretched people sleep at the top of the highest trees they can find, for up to a height of 20 palms the **tigers** can seize them at a leap; and if anything saves the poor people from these beasts it is the bonfires they keep burning at night, which the tigers are much afraid of. In fact these are so numerous that many come into the city itself at night in search of prey. And it has happened, since we took the place, that a tiger leapt into a garden surrounded by a good high timber fence, and lifted a beam of wood with three slaves who were laid by the heels, and with these made a clean leap over the fence."—*Barros*, II. vi. 1. Lest I am doing the great historian wrong as to this Munchausen-like story, I give the original: "E jà aconteoeo ... saltar hum tigre em hum quintal cercado de madeira bem alto, e levou hum tronco de madeira com trez (tres?) escravos que estavam prezos nelle, com os quaes saltou de claro em claro per cima da cerca."

1583.—"We also escaped the peril of the multitude of **tigers** which infest those tracts" (the Pegu delta) "and prey on whatever they can get at. And although we were on that account anchored in midstream, nevertheless it was asserted that the ferocity of these animals was such that they would press even into the water to seize their prey."—*Gasparo Balbi*, f. 94*v*.

1586.—"We went through the wildernesse because the right way was full of thieves, when we passed the country of *Gouren*, where we found but few Villages, but almost all Wildernesse, and saw many Buffes, Swine, and Deere, Grasse longer than a man, and very many **Tigres**."—*R. Fitch*, in *Purchas*, ii. 1736.

1675.—"Going in quest whereof, one of our Soldiers, a Youth, killed a **Tigre-Royal**; it was brought home by 30 or 40 *Combies*, the Body tied to a long Bamboo, the Tail extended ... it was a **Tigre** of the Biggest and Noblest Kind, Five Feet in Length beside the Tail, Three and a Half in Height, it was of a light Yellow, streaked with Black, like a Tabby Cat ... the Visage Fierce and Majestick, the Teeth gnashing. ..."—*Fryer*, 176.

1683.—"In y[e] afternoon they found a great **Tiger**, one of y[e] black men shot a barbed arrow into his Buttock. Mr. French-feild and Capt. Raynes alighted off their horses and advanced towards the thicket where y[e] Tiger lay. The people making a great noise, y[e] Tiger flew out upon Mr. Frenchfeild, and he shot him with a brace of Bullets into y[e] breast: at which he made a great noise, and returned again to his den. The Black Men seeing of him wounded fell upon him, but the Tiger had so much strength as to kill 2 men, and wound a third, before he died. At Night y[e] Ragea sent me the Tiger."—*Hedges, Diary*, Hak. Soc. i. 66–67.

1754.—"There was a *Charter* granted to the *East India Company*. Many Disputes arose about it, which came before Parliament; all Arts were used to corrupt or delude the Members; among others a **Tyger** *was baited* with Solemnity, on the Day the great Question was to come on. This was such a Novelty, that several of the Members were drawn off from their Attendance, and absent on the Division. ..."—*A Collection of Letters relating to the E.I. Company*, &c. (Tract), 1754, p. 13.

1869.—"Les **tigres** et les léopards sont considérés, autant par les Hindous que par les musalmans, comme étant la propriété des *pirs*: aussi les naturels du pays ne sympathisent pas avec les Européens pour la chasse du **tigre**."—*Garcin de Tassy, Rel. Mus.* p. 24.

1872.—"One of the Frontier Battalion soldiers approached me, running for his life. ... This was his story:—

'Sahib, I was going along with the letters ... which I had received from your highness ... a great **tiger** came out and stood in the path. Then I feared for my life; and the **tiger** stood, and I stood, and we looked at each other. I had no weapon but my kukri ... and the Government letters. So I said, 'My lord **Tiger**, here are the Government letters, the letters of the Honourable Kumpany Bahadur ... and it is necessary for me to go on with them.' The tiger never ceased looking at me, and when I had done speaking he growled, but he never offered to get out of the way. On this I was much more afraid, so I kneeled down and made obeisance to him; but he did not take any more notice of that either, so at last I told him I should report the matter to the Sahib, and I threw down the letters in front of him, and came here as fast as I was able. Sahib, I now ask for your justice against that **tiger**.' "—*Lt. Col. T. Lewin, A Fly on the Wheel*, p. 444.

TOBACCO, s. On this subject we are not prepared to furnish any elaborate article, but merely to bring together a few quotations touching on the introduction of tobacco into India and the East, or otherwise of interest.

[? c. 1550.—"... Abū Kīr would carry the cloth to the market-street and sell it, and with its price buy meat and vegetables and **tobacco**. ..."—*Burton, Arab. Nights*, vii. 210. The only mention in the *Nights* and the insertion of some scribe.]

"It has happened to me several times, that going through the provinces of Guatemala and Nicaragua I have entered the house of an Indian who had taken this herb, which in the Mexican language is called **tabacco**, and immediately perceived the sharp fetid smell of this truly diabolical and stinking smoke, I was obliged to go away in haste, and seek some other place."—*Girolamo Benzoni*, Hak. Soc. p. 81. [The word *tabaco* is from the language of Hayti, and meant, first, the pipe, secondly, the plant, thirdly, the sleep which followed its use (*Mr. J. Platt*, 9 ser. *N. & Q.* viii. 322).]

1585.—"Et hi" (viz. Ralph Lane and the first settlers in Virginia) "reduces Indicam illam plantam quam **Tabaccam** vocant et *Nicotiam*, qua contra cruditates ab Indis edocti, usi erant, in Angliam primi, quod suam, intulerunt. Ex illo sane tempore usu coepit esse creberrimo, et magno pretio, dum quam plurimi graveolentem illius fumum, alii lascivientes, alii valetudini consulentes, per tubulum testaceum inexplebili aviditate passim hauriunt, et mox e naribus efflant; adeo ut tabernae **Tabaccanae** non minus quam cervisiariae et vinariae passim per oppida habeantur. Ut Anglorum corpora (quod salse ille dixit) qui hac plantâ tantopere delectantur in Barbarorum naturam degenerasse videantur; quum iisdem quibus Barbari delectentur et sanari se posse credant."—*Gul. Camdeni, Annal. Rerum Anglicanum* ... regn. *Elizabetha*, ed. 1717, ii. 449.

1592.—

"Into the woods thence forth in haste shee went
To seeke for hearbes that mote him remedy;
For shee of herbes had great intendiment,
Taught of the Nymphe which from her infancy
Her nourced had in true Nobility:
This whether yt divine **Tobacco** were,
Or Panachaea, or Polygony,
Shee fownd, and brought it to her patient deare
Who al this while lay bleding out his hart-blood neare."

The Faerie Queen, III. v. 32.

1597.—"His Lordship" (E. of Essex at Villafranca) "made no answer, but called for **tobacco**, seeming to give but small credit to this alarm; and so on horseback, with these noblemen and gentlemen on foot beside him, took **tobacco**, whilst I was telling his Lordship of the men I had sent forth, and the order I had given them. Within some quarter of an hour, we might hear a good round volley of shot betwixt the 30 men I had sent to the chapel, and the enemy, which made his Lordship cast his pipe from him, and listen to the shooting."—*Commentaries of Sir Francis Vere*, p. 62.

1598.—"*Cob.* Ods me I marle what pleasure or felicity they have in taking this roguish **tobacco**. It is good for nothing but to choke a man, and fill him full of smoke and embers: there were four died out of one house last week with taking of it, and two more the bell went for yesternight; one of them they say will never scape it; he voided a bushel of soot yesterday upward and downward ... its little better than rats-bane or rosaker."—*Every Man in his Humour*, iii. 2.

1604.—"Oct. 19. Demise to Tho. Lane and

Ph. Bold of the new Impost of 6*s.* 8*d.*, and the old Custom of 2*d.* per pound on **tobacco.**"—*Calendar of State Papers, Domestic*, James I., p. 159.

1604 or 1605.—"In Bijápúr I had found some **tobacco.** Never having seen the like in India, I brought some with me, and prepared a handsome pipe of jewel work. ... His Majesty (Akbar) was enjoying himself after receiving my presents, and asking me how I had collected so many strange things in so short a time, when his eye fell upon the tray with the pipe and its appurtenances: he expressed great surprise and examined the **tobacco**, which was made up in pipefuls; he inquired what it was, and where I had got it. The Nawab Khán-i-'Azam replied: 'This is **tobacco**, which is well known in Mecca and Medina, and this doctor has brought it as a medicine for your Majesty.' His Majesty looked at it, and ordered me to prepare and take him a pipeful. He began to smoke it, when his physician approached and forbade his doing so" ... (omitting much that is curious). "As I had brought a large supply of tobacco and pipes, I sent some to several of the nobles, while others sent to ask for some; indeed all, without exception, wanted some, and the practice was introduced. After that the merchants began to sell it, so the custom of smoking spread rapidly."—*Asad Beg*, in *Elliot*, vi. 165–167.

1610.—"The *Turkes* are also incredible takers of Opium ... carrying it about with them both in peace and in warre; which they say expelleth all feare, and makes them couragious; but I rather think giddy headed. ... And perhaps for the self same cause they also delight in **Tobacco**; they take it through reeds that have ioyned vnto them great heads of wood to containe it: I doubt not but lately taught them, as brought them by the English: and were it not sometimes lookt into (for *Morat Bassa* not long since commanded a pipe to be thrust through the nose of a *Turke*, and so to be led in derision through the Citie,) no question but it would prove a principall commodity. Neverthelesse they will take it in corners, and are so ignorant therein, that that which in England is not saleable, doth passe here amongst them for most excellent."—*Sandys, Journey*, 66.

1615.—"Il **tabacco** ancora usano qui" (at Constantinople) "di pigliar in conversazione per gusto: ma io non ho voluto mai provarne, e ne avera cognizione in Italia che molti ne pigliano, ed in particolare il signore cardinale Crescenzio qualche volta per medicamento insegnatogli dal Signor don Virginio Orsino, che primo di tutti, se io non fallo, gli anni addietro lo portò in Roma d'Inghilterra."—*P. della Valle*, i. 76.

1616.—"Such is the miraculous omnipotence of our strong tasted **Tobacco**, as it cures al sorts of diseases (which neuer any drugge could do before) in all persons and at all times. ... It cures the gout in the feet and (which is miraculous) in that very instant when the smoke thereof, as light, flies vp into the head, the virtue thereof, as heauy, runs down to the litle toe. It helps all sorts of argues. It refreshes a weary man, and yet makes a man hungry. Being taken when they goe to bed, it makes one sleepe soundly, and yet being taken when a man is sleepie and drousie, it will, as they say, awake his braine, and quicken his vnderstanding. ... O omnipotent power of **Tobacco**! And if it could by the smoake thereof chase out deuils, as the smoake of *Tobias* fish did (which I am sure could smell no stronglier) it would serve for a precious Relicke, both for the Superstitious Priests, and the insolent Puritanes, to cast out deuils withall."—*K. James I., Counter-blaste to Tobacco*, in *Works*, pp. 219–220.

1617.—"As the smoking of tobacco (**tambákú**) had taken very bad effect upon the health and mind of many persons, I ordered that no one should practise the habit. My brother Sháh 'Abbás, also being aware of its evil effects, had issued a command against the use of it in Irán. But Khán-i-'Alam was so much addicted to smoking, that he could not abstain from it, and often smoked."—*Memoirs of Jahángír*, in *Elliot*, v. 851. See the same passage rendered by *Blochmann*, in *Ind. Antiq.* i. 164.

1623.—"Incipit nostro seculo in immensum crescere usus **tobacco**, atque afficit homines occulta quidem delectatione, ut qui illi semel assueti sint, difficile postea abetinent."—*Bacon, H. Vitae et Mortis*, in *B. Montague's* ed. x. 189.

We are unable to give the date or Persian author of the following extract (though clearly of the 17th century), which with an introductory sentence we have found in a fragmentary note in the handwriting of the late Major William Yule, written in India about the beginning of last century:[1]

"Although **Tobacco** be the produce of an European Plant, it has nevertheless been in use by our Physicians medicinally for some time past. Nay, some creditable People even have been friendly to the use of it, though from its having been brought sparingly in the first instance from Europe, its rarity prevented it from coming into general use. The Culture of this Plant, however, became speedily almost universal, within a short period after its introduction into Hindostaun; and the produce of

1 Some notice of Major Yule, whose valuable Oriental MSS. were presented to the British Museum after his death, will be found in Dr. Rieu's Preface to the *Catalogue of Persian MSS.* (vol. iii. p. xviii.).

it rewarded the Cultivator far beyond every other article of Husbandry. This became more especially the case in the reign of Shah Jehaun (commenced A.H. 1037) when the Practice of Smoking pervaded all Ranks and Classes within the Empire. Nobles and Beggars, Pious and Wicked, Devotees and Free-thinkers, poets, historians, rhetoricians, doctors and patients, high and low, rich and poor, all! all seemed intoxicated with a decided preference over every other luxury, nay even often over the necessaries of life. To a stranger no offering was so acceptable as a Whiff, and to a friend one could produce nothing half so grateful as a **Chillum.** So rooted was the habit that the confirmed Smoker would abstain from Food and Drink rather than relinquish the gratification he derived from inhaling the Fumes of this deleterious Plant! Nature recoils at the very idea of touching the Saliva of another Person, yet in the present instance our Tobacco smokers pass the moistened Tube from one mouth to another without hesitation on the one hand, and it is received with complacency on the other! The more acrid the Fumes so much the more grateful to the Palate of the Connoisseur. The Smoke is a Collyrium to the Eyes, whilst the Fire, they will tell you, supplies to the Body the waste of radical Heat. Without doubt the **Hookah** is a most pleasing Companion, whether to the Wayworn Traveller or to the solitary Hermit. It is a Friend in whose Bosom we may repose our most confidential Secrets; and a Counsellor upon whose advice we may rely in our most important Concerns. It is an elegant Ornament in our private Appartments: it gives joy to the Beholder in our public Halls. The Music of its sound puts the warbling of the Nightingale to Shame, and the Fragrance of its Perfume brings a Blush on the Cheek of the Rose. Life in short is prolonged by the Fumes inhaled at each inspiration, whilst every expiration of them is accompanied with extatic delight. ..."—(*cœtera desunt*).

c. 1760.—"**Tambákú.** It is known from the *Maásir-i-Rakímí* that the **tobacco** came from Europe to the Dakhin, and from the Dakhin to Upper India, during the reign of Akbar Sháh (1556–1605), since which time it has been in general use."—*Bahár-i'-Ajam*, quoted by *Blochmann*, in *Ind. Antiq.* i. 164.

1878.—It appears from Miss Bird's *Japan* that tobacco was not cultivated in that country till 1605. In 1612 and 1615 the Shogun prohibited both culture and use of **tabako.**—See the work, i. 276–77. [According to Mr. Chamberlain (*Things Japanese*, 3rd ed. p. 402) by 1651 the law was so far relaxed that smoking was permitted, but only out-of-doors.]

TODDY, s. A corruption of Hind. *tāṛī*, *i.e.* the fermented sap of the *tāṛ* or palmyra, Skt. *tāla*, and also of other palms, such as the date, the coco-palm, and the *Caryota urens*; palm-wine. *Toddy* is generally the substance used in India as yeast, to leaven bread. The word, as is well known, has received a new application in Scotland, the immediate history of which we have not traced. The *tāla*-tree seems to be indicated, though confusedly, in this passage of Megasthenes from Arrian:

c. B.C. 320.—"Megasthenes tells us ... the Indians were in old times nomadic ... were so barbarous that they wore the skins of such wild animals as they could kill, and subsisted (?) on the bark of trees; that these trees were called in the Indian speech **tala**, and that there grew on them as there grows at the tops of the (date) palm trees, a fruit resembling balls of wool."—*Arrian, Indica*, vii., tr. by McCrindle.

c. 1330.—"... There is another tree of a different species, which ... gives all the year round a white liquor, pleasant to drink, which tree is called **tari**."—*Fr. Jordanus*, 16.

[1554.—"There is in Gujaret a tree of the palm-tribe, called **tari** agadji (millet tree). From its branches cups are suspended, and when the cut end of a branch is placed into one of these vessels, a sweet liquid, something of the nature of **arrack**, flows out in a continuous stream ... and presently changes into a most wonderful wine."—*Travels of Sidi Ali Reïs, trans. A. Vambéry*, p. 29.]

1611.—"Palmiti Wine, which they call **Taddy**."—*N. Dounton*, in *Purchas*, i. 298.

[1614.—"A sort of wine that distilleth out of the Palmetto trees, called **Tadie**."—*Foster*, *Letters*, iii. 4.]

1615.—
"... And then more to glad yee
Weele have a health to al our friends in
Tadee."
Verses to T. Coryat, in *Crudities*, iii. 47.

1623.—"... on board of which we stayed till nightfall, entertaining with conversation and drinking **tari**, a liquor which is drawn from the coco-nut trees, of a whitish colour, a little turbid, and of a somewhat rough taste, though with a blending in sweetness, and not unpalatable, something like one of our *vini piccanti*. It will also intoxicate, like wine, if drunk over freely."—*P. della Valle*, ii. 530; [Hak. Soc. i. 62].

[1634.—"The **Toddy**-tree is like the Date of Palm; the Wine called **Toddy** is got by wounding and piercing the Tree, and putting a Jar or Pitcher under it, so as the Liquor may drop into it."—*Sir T. Herbert*, in *Harris*, i. 408.]

1648.—"The country ... is planted with palmito-trees, from which a sap is drawn called

Terry, that they very commonly drink."—*Van Twist*, 12.

1653.—"... le **tari** qui est le vin ordinaire des Indes."—*De la Boullaye-le-Gouz*, 246.

1673.—"The Natives singing and roaring all Night long; being drunk with **Toddy**, the Wine of the Cocoe."—*Fryer*, 53.

"As for the rest, they are very respectful, unless the Seamen and Soldiers get drunk, either with **Toddy** or Bang."—*Ibid.* 91.

1686.—"Besides the Liquor or Water in the Fruit, there is also a sort of Wine drawn from the Tree called **Toddy**, which looks like Whey."—*Dampier*, i. 293.

1705.—"... cette liqueur s'appelle **tarif**."—*Luillier*, 43.

1710.—This word was in common use at Madras.—*Wheeler*, ii. 125.

1750.—"*J.* Was vor Leute trincken **Taddy**? *C.* Die Soldaten, die Land Portugiesen, die Parreier (see PARIAH) und Schiffleute trincken diesen **Taddy**."—*Madras, oder Fort St. George*, &c., Halle, 1750.

1857.—"It is the unfermented juice of the Palmyra which is used as food: when allowed to ferment, which it will do before midday, if left to itself, it is changed into a sweet, intoxicating drink called 'kal' or '**toddy**.' "—*Bp. Caldwell, Lectures on Tinnevelly Mission*, p. 33.

¶ "The Rat, returning home full of **Toddy**, said, If I meet the Cat, I will tear him in pieces."—Ceylon Proverb, in *Ind. Antiq.* i. 59.

Of the Scotch application of the word we can find but one example in Burns, and, strange to say, no mention in Jameson's Dictionary:

1785.—

"The lads an' lasses, blythely bent
To mind baith saul an' body,
Sit round the table, weel content
An' steer about the **toddy**...."
Burns, The Holy Fair.

1798.—"Action of the case, for giving her a dose in some **toddy**, to intoxicate and inflame her passions."—*Roots's Reports*, i. 80.

1804.—

"... I've nae fear for't;
For siller, faith, ye ne'er did care for't,
Unless to help a needful body,
An' get an antrin glass o' **toddy**."
Tannakill, Epistle to James Barr.

TOM-TOM, s. *Ṭamṭam*, a native drum. The word comes from India, and is chiefly used there. Forbes (*Rās-Mālā*, ii. 401) [ed. 1878, p. 665] says the thing is so called because used by criers who beat it *tām-tām*, 'place by place,' *i.e.* first at one place, then at another. But it is rather an *onomatopoeia*, not belonging to any language in particular. In Ceylon it takes the form *tamaṭṭama*, in Tel. *tappeta*, in Tam. *tambattam*; in Malay it is *tontoṅ*, all with the same meaning. [When badminton was introduced at Satāra natives called it *Ṭamṭam phūl khel*, *ṭam-ṭam* meaning 'battledore,' and the shuttlecock looked like a flower (*phūl*). Tommy Atkins promptly turned this into "*Tom Fool*" (*Calcutta Rev.* xcvi. 346).] In French the word *tamtam* is used, not for a drum of any kind, but for a Chinese **gong** (q.v.). M. Littré, however, in the Supplement to his Dict., remarks that this use is erroneous.

1693.—"It is ordered that to-morrow morning the **Choultry** Justices do cause the **Tom Tom** to be beat through all the Streets of the Black Town. ..."—In *Wheeler*, i. 268.

1711.—"Their small Pipes, and **Tom Toms**, instead of Harmony made the Discord the greater."—*Lockyer*, 235.

1755.—In the Calcutta Mayor's expenses we find:

"**Tom Tom**, R. 1 1 0."—In *Long*, 56.

1764.—"You will give strict orders to the Zemindars to furnish Oil and Musshauls, and **Tom Toms** and Pikemen, &c., according to custom."—*Ibid.* 391.

1770.—"... An instrument of brass which the Europeans lately borrowed from the Turks to add to their military music, and which is called a **tam**" (!).—*Abbé Raynal*, tr. 1777, i. 30.

1789.—"An harsh kind of music from a **tom-tom** or drum, accompanied by a loud rustic pipe, sounds from different parties throughout the throng. ..."—*Munro, Narrative*, 73.

1804.—"I request that they may be hanged; and let the cause of their punishment be published in the bazar by beat of **tom-tom**."—*Wellington*, iii. 186.

1824.—"The Mahrattas in my vicinity kept up such a confounded noise with the **tamtams**, cymbals, and pipes, that to sleep was impossible."—*Seely, Wonders of Ellora*, ch. iv.

1836.—For the use of the word by Dickens, see under GUM-GUM.

1862.—"The first musical instruments were without doubt percussive sticks, calabashes, **tomtoms**."—*Herbert Spencer, First Principles*, 356.

1881.—"The **tom-tom** is ubiquitous. It knows no rest. It is content with depriving man of his. It selects by preference the hours of the night as the time for its malign influence to assert its most potent sway. It reverberates its dull unmeaning monotones through the fitful dreams which sheer exhaustion brings. It inspires delusive hopes by a brief lull only to break forth with refreshed vigour into wilder ecstacies of maniacal fury—accompanied with nasal incantations and protracted howls. ..."—*Overland Times of India*, April 14.

TONGA, s. A kind of light and small two-wheeled vehicle, Hind. *tāngā*, [Skt. *tamanga*, 'a platform']. The word has become familiar of late years, owing to the use of the *tonga* in a modified form on the roads leading up to Simla, Darjeeling, and other hill-stations. [Tavernier speaks of a carriage of this kind, but does not use the word:

[c. 1665.—"They have also, for travelling, small, very light, carriages which contain two persons; but usually one travels alone ... to which they harness a pair of oxen only. These carriages, which are provided, like ours, with curtains and cushions, are not slung. ..."—*Tavernier*, ed. *Ball*, i. 44.]

1874.—"The villages in this part of the country are usually superior to those in Poona or Sholápur, and the people appear to be in good circumstances. ... The custom too, which is common, of driving light **Tongas** drawn by ponies or oxen points to the same conclusion."—*Settlement Report of Násik*.

1879.—"A **tongha** dâk has at last been started between Rajpore and Dehra. The first tongha took only 5½ hours from Rajpore to Saharunpore."—*Pioneer Mail*.

1880.—"In the (*Times*) of the 19th of April we are told that 'Syud Mahomed Padshah has repulsed the attack on his fort instigated by certain *moolahs* of **tonga** *dâk*.' ... Is the relentless **tonga** a region of country or a religious organization? ... The original telegram appears to have contemplated a full stop after 'certain *moollahs*.' Then came an independent sentence about the **tonga** *dâk* working admirably between Peshawur and Jellalabad, but the sub-editor of the *Times*, interpreting the message referred to, made sense of it in the way we have seen, associating the ominous mystery with the *moollahs*, and helping out the other sentence with some explanatory ideas of his own."—*Pioneer Mail*, June 10.

1881.—"Bearing in mind Mr. Framji's extraordinary services, notably those rendered during the mutiny, and ... that he is crippled for life ... by wounds received while gallantly defending the mail **tonga** cart in which he was travelling, when attacked by dacoits. ..."—Letter from *Bombay Govt. to Govt. of India*, June 17, 1881.

TOOLSY, s. The holy Basil of the Hindus (*Ocimum sanctum*, L.), Skt. *tulsī* or *tulasī*, frequently planted in a vase upon a pedestal of masonry in the vicinity of Hindu temples or dwellings. Sometimes the ashes of deceased relatives are preserved in these domestic shrines. The practice is alluded to by Fr. Odoric as in use at Tana, near Bombay (see *Cathay*, i. 59, c. 1322); and it is accurately described by the later ecclesiastic quoted below. See also *Ward's Hindoos*, ii 203. The plant has also a kind of sanctity in the Greek Church, and a character for sanitary value at least on the shores of the Mediterranean generally.

[c. 1650.—"They who bear the **tulasī** round the neck ... they are Vaishnavas, and sanctify the world."—*Bhaktā Mālā*, in *H. H. Wilson's Works*, i. 41.]

1672.—"Almost all the Hindus ... adore a plant like our *Basilico gentile*, but of more pungent odour. ... Every one before his house has a little altar, girt with a wall half an ell high, in the middle of which they erect certain pedestals like little towers, and in these the shrub is grown. They recite their prayers daily before it, with repeated prostrations, sprinklings of water, &c. There are also many of these maintained at the bathing-places, and in the courts of the pagodas."—*P. Vincenzo Maria*, 300.

1673.—"They plaster Cow-dung before their Doors; and so keep themselves clean, having a little place or two built up a Foot Square of Mud, where they plant *Calaminth*, or (by them called) **Tulce**, which they worship every Morning, and tend with Diligence."—*Fryer*, 199.

1842.—"Veneram a planta chamada **Tulosse**, por dizerem é do pateo dos Deoses, e por isso é commun no pateo de suas casas, e todas as manhãs lhe vão tributar veneração."—*Annaes Maritimos*, iii. 453.

1872.—"At the head of the ghát, on either side, is a sacred **tulasi** plant ... placed on a high pedestal of masonry."—*Govinda Samanta*, i. 18.

The following illustrates the esteem attached to Toolsy in S. Europe:

1885.—"I have frequently realised how much prized the basil is in Greece for its mystic properties. The herb, which they say grew on Christ's grave, is almost worshipped in the Eastern Church. On St. Basil's day women take sprigs of this plant to be blessed in church. On returning home they cast some on the floor of the house, to secure luck for the ensuing year. They eat a little with their household, and no sickness, they maintain, will attack them for a year. Another bit they put in their cupboard, and firmly believe that their embroideries and silken raiment will be free from the visitation of rats, mice, and moths, for the same period."—*J. T. Bent, The Cyclades*, p. 328.

TOPAZ, TOPASS, &c., s. A name used in the 17th and 18th centuries for dark-skinned or half-caste claimants of Portuguese descent, and Christian profession. Its application is generally, though not universally, to soldiers of this class, and it is possible that it was originally a corruption of Pers. (from Turkish) *top-chī*, 'a gunner.' It may be a slight support to this derivation that Italians were employed to cast guns for the Zamorin at Calicut from a very early date in the 16th century, and are frequently mentioned in the annals of Correa between 1503 and 1510. Various other etymologies have however been given. That given by Orme below (and put forward doubtfully by Wilson) from *topī*, 'a hat,' has a good deal of plausibility, and even if the former etymology be the true *origin*, it is probable that this one was often in the minds of those using the term, as its true connotation. It may have some corroboration not only in the fact that Europeans are to this day often spoken of by natives (with a shade of disparagement) as **Topeewalas** (q.v.) or 'Hat-men,' but also in the pride commonly taken by all persons claiming European blood in wearing a hat; indeed Fra Paolino tells us that this class call themselves *gente de chapeo* (see also the quotation below from Ovington). Possibly however this was merely a misrendering of *topaz* from the assumed etymology. The same Fra Paolino, with his usual fertility in error, propounds in another passage that *topaz* is a corruption of *do-bhāshiya*, 'two-tongued' (in fact is another form of **Dubash**, q.v.), viz. using Portuguese and a debased vernacular (pp. 50 and 144). [The *Madras Gloss.* assumes Mal. *tópáshi* to be a corruption of **dubash**.] The *Topaz* on board ship is the sweeper, who is at sea frequently of this class.

1602.—"The 12th ditto we saw to seaward another *Champaigne* (**Sampan**) wherein were 20 men, Mestiços (see MUSTEES) and **Toupas**."—*Van Spilbergen's Voyage*, p. 34, pub. 1648.

[1672.—"**Toepasses**." See under MADRAS.]

1673.—"To the Fort then belonged 300 *English*, and 400 **Topazes**, or Portugal Firemen."—*Fryer*, 66. In his glossarial Index he gives "**Topazes**, Musketeers."

1680.—"It is resolved and ordered to entertain about 100 **Topasses**, or Black Portuguese, into pay."—In *Wheeler*, i. 121.

1686.—"It is resolved, as soon as English soldiers can be provided sufficient for the garrison, that all **Topasses** be disbanded, and no more entertained, since there is little dependence on them."—In *ditto*, 159.

1690.—"A Report spread abroad, that a Rich Moor Ship belonging to one *Abdal Ghaford*, was taken by *Hat-men*, that is, in their (the Moors) Dialect, Europeans."—*Ovington*, 411.

1705.—"... **Topases**, qui sont des gens du pais qu'on élève et qu'on habille à la Françoise, lesquels ont esté instruits dans la Religion Catholique par quelques uns de nos Missionnaires."—*Luillier*, 45–46.

1711.—"The Garrison consists of about 250 Soldiers, at 91 Fanhams, or 1*l.* 2*s.* 9*d.* per Month, and 200 **Topasses**, or black Mungrel Portuguese, at 50, or 52 Fanhams per Month."—*Lockyer*, 14.

1727.—"Some Portuguese are called **Topasses** ... will be served by none but Portuguese Priests, because they indulge them more and their Villany."—*A. Hamilton*, [ed. 1744, i. 326].

1745.—"Les Portugais et les autres Catholiques qu'on nomme Mestices (see MUSTEES) et **Topases**, également comme les naturels du Pays y viennent sans distinction pour assister aux Divins mystères."—*Norbert*, ii. 31.

1747.—"The officers upon coming in report their People in general behaved very well, and could not do more than they did with such a handful of men against the Force the Enemy had, being as they believe at least to be one thousand Europeans, besides **Topasses**, Coffrees (see CAFFER), and Seapoys (see SEPOY), altogether about Two Thousand (2000)."—*MS. Consns. at Ft. St. David*, March 1. (In India Office).

1749.—"600 effective *Europeans* would not have cost more than that Crowd of useless **Topasses** and *Peons* of which the Major Part of our Military has of late been composed."—In *A Letter to a Proprietor of the E.I. Co.* p. 57.

"The **Topasses** of which the major Part of the Garrison consisted, every one that knows *Madrass* knows it to be a black, degenerate, wretched Race of the antient *Portuguese*, as proud and bigotted as their Ancestors, lazy, idle, and vitious withal, and for the most Part as weak and feeble in Body as base in Mind, not one in ten possessed of any of the necessary Requisites of a Soldier."—*Ibid.* App. p. 103.

1756.—"... in this plight, from half an hour after eleven till near two in the morning, I sustained the weight of a heavy man, with his knees on my back, and the pressure of his whole body on my head; a Dutch sergeant, who had taken his seat upon my left shoulder, and a **Topaz** bearing on my right."—*Holwell's Narr. of the Black Hole*, [ed. 1758, p. 19].

1758.—"There is a distinction said to be made by you ... which, in our opinion, does no way square with rules of justice and equity, and that is the exclusion of Portuguese **topasses**, and other Christian natives, from any share of the money granted by the Nawab."—*Court's Letter*, in *Long*, 133.

c. 1785.—"**Topasses**, black foot soldiers, descended from Portuguese marrying natives, called **topasses** because they wear hats."—*Carraccioli's Clive*, iv. 564. The same explanation in *Orme*, i. 80.

1787.—"... Assuredly the mixture of Moormen, Rajahpoots, Gentoos, and Malabars in the same corps is extremely beneficial. ... I have also recommended the corps of **Topasses** or descendants of Europeans, who retain the characteristic qualities of their progenitors."—*Col. Fullarton's View of English Interests in India*, 222.

1789.—"**Topasses** are the sons of Europeans and black women, or low Portuguese, who are trained to arms."—*Munro, Narr.* 321.

1817.—"**Topasses**, or persons whom we may denominate Indo-Portuguese, either the mixed produce of Portuguese and Indian parents, or converts to the Portuguese, from the Indian, faith."—*J. Mill, Hist.* iii. 19.

TOPEE, s. A hat, Hind. *ṭopī*. This is sometimes referred to Port. *topo*, 'the top' (also *tope*, 'a top-knot,' and *topete*, a 'toupee'), which is probably identical with English and Dutch *top*, L. German *topp*, Fr. *topet*, &c. But there is also a simpler Hind. word *ṭop*, for a helmet or hat, and the quotation from the Roteiro Vocabulary seems to show that the word existed in India when the Portuguese first arrived. With the usual tendency to specialize foreign words, we find this word becomes specialized in application to the **sola** hat.

1498.—In the vocabulary ("*Este he a linguajem de Calicut*") we have: "barrete (*i.e.* a cap): **tupy**."—*Roteiro*, 118.

The following expression again, in the same work, seems to be Portuguese, and to refer to some mode in which the women's hair was dressed: "Trazem em a moleera huuns **topetes** por signall que sam Christãos."—*Ibid.* 52.

1849.—"Our good friend Sol came down in right earnest on the waste, and there is need of many a fold of twisted muslin round the white **topi**, to keep off his importunacy."—*Dry Leaves from Young Egypt*, 2.

1883.—"**Topee**, a solar helmet."—*Wills, Modern Persia*, 263.

TOPEEWALA, s. Hind. *ṭopīwālā*, 'one who wears a hat,' generally a European, or one claiming to be so. Formerly by Englishmen it was habitually applied to the dark descendants of the Portuguese. R. Drummond says that in his time (before 1808) *Topeewala* and **Puggry**_wala_ were used in Guzerat and the Mahratta country for 'Europeans' and 'natives.' [The S. Indian form is *Toppikār*.] The author of the Persian *Life of Hydur Naik* (Or. Tr. Fund, by Miles) calls Europeans *Kalāh-posh*, *i.e.* 'hat-wearers' (p. 85).

1803.—"The descendants of the Portuguese ... unfortunately the ideas of Christianity are so imperfect that the only mode they hit upon of displaying their faith is by wearing hats and breeches."—*Sydney Smith, Works*, 3d. ed. iii. 5.

[1826.—"It was now evident we should have to encounter the **Topee wallas**."—*Pandurang Hari*, ed. 1873, i. 71.]

1874.—"... you will see that he will not be able to protect us. All **topiwálás** ... are brothers to each other. The magistrates and the judge will always decide in favour of their white brethren."—*Govinda Samanta*, ii. 211.

TOUCAN, s. This name is very generally misapplied by Europeans to the various species of Horn-bill, formerly all styled *Buceros*, but now subdivided into various genera. Jerdon says: "They (the hornbills) are, indeed, popularly called Toucans throughout India; and this appears to be their name in some of the Malayan isles; the word signifying 'a worker,' from the noise they make." This would imply that the term did originally belong to a species of hornbill, and not to the S. American *Rhamphastes* or *Zygodactyle*. *Tukang* is really in Malay a 'craftsman or artificer'; but the dictionaries show no application to the bird. We have here, in fact, a remarkable instance of the coincidences which often justly perplex etymologists, or would perplex them if it were not so much their habit to seize on one solution and despise the others. Not only is *tukang* in Malay 'an artificer,' but, as Willoughby tells us, the Spaniards called the real S. American toucan '*carpintero*' from the noise he makes. And yet there seems no doubt that *Toucan* is a Brazilian name for a Brazilian bird. See the quotations, and especially Thevet's, with its date.

The Toucan is described by Oviedo (c.

1535), but he mentions only the name by which "the Christians" called it,—in Ramusio's Italian *Picuto* (? *Beccuto*; *Sommario*, in *Ramusio*, iii. f. 60). [Prof. Skeat (*Concise Dict.* s.v.) gives only the Brazilian derivation. The question is still further discussed, without any very definite result, save that it is probably an imitation of the cry of the bird, in *N. & Q.* 9 ser. vii. 486; viii. 22, 67, 85, 171, 250.]

1556.—"Sur la coste de la marine, la plus frequẽte marchandise est le plumage d'vn oyseau, qu'ils appellent en leur langue **Toucan**, lequel descrivons sommairement puis qu'il vient à propos. Cest oyseau est de la grandeur d'vn pigeon. ... Au reste cest oyseau est merveilleusement difforme et monstrueux, ayant le bec plus gros et plus long quasi que le reste du corps."—*Les Singularitez de la France Antarticque, autrement nommée Amerique. ... Par T. André Theuet, Natif d'Angoulesme*, Paris, 1558, f. 91.

1648.—"**Tucana** sive **Toucan** Brasiliensibus: avis picae aut palumbi magnitudine. ... Rostrum habet ingens et nonnumquam palmum longum, exterius flavam. ... Mirum est autem videri possit quomodo tantilla avis tam grande rostrum ferat; sed levissimum est."—*GeorgI MarcgravI de Liebstad, Hist. Rerum Natur. Brasiliae*. Lib. V. cap. xv., in *Hist. Natur. Brasil.* Lugd. Bat. 1648, p. 217.

See also (1599) *Aldrovandus, Ornitholog.* lib. xii. cap. 19, where the word is given **toucham**.

Here is an example of misapplication to the Hornbill, though the latter name is also given:

1885.—"Soopah (in N. Canara) is the only region in which I have met with the **toucan** or great hornbill. ... I saw the comical looking head with its huge aquiline beak, regarding me through a fork in the branch; and I account it one of the best shots I ever made, when I sent a ball ... through the head just at its junction with the handsome orange-coloured helmet which surmounts it. Down came the **toucan** with outspread wings, dead apparently; but when my peon Manoel raised him by the thick muscular neck, he fastened his great claws on his hand, and made the wood resound with a succession of roars more like a bull than a bird."—*Gordon Forbes, Wild Life in Canara*, &c. pp. 37–38.

***TRAGA**, s. [Molesworth gives "S. *trāgā*, Guz. *trāgu*"; *trāga* does not appear in Monier-Williams's Skt. Dict., and Wilson queries the word as doubtful. Dr. Grierson writes: "I cannot trace its origin back to Skt. One is tempted to connect it with the Skt. root *trai*, or *trā*, 'to protect,' but the termination *gā* presents difficulties which I cannot get over. One would expect it to be derived from some Skt. word like *trāka*, but no such word exists."] The extreme form of **dhurna** (q.v.) among the Rājputs and connected tribes, in which the complainant puts himself, or some member of his family, to torture or death, as a mode for bringing vengeance on the oppressor. The tone adopted by some persons and papers at the time of the death of the great Charles Gordon, tended to imply their view that his death was a kind of *traga* intended to bring vengeance on those who had sacrificed him. [For a case in Greece, see *Pausanias*, X. i. 6. Another name for this self-sacrifice is *Chandi*, which is perhaps Skt. *ćaṇḍa*, 'passionate' (see *Malcolm, Cent. India*, 2nd ed. ii. 137). Also compare the *jūhar* of the Rājputs (*Tod, Annals*, Calcutta reprint, i. 74). And for *Kūr*, see *As. Res.* iv. 357 *seqq.*]

1803.—A case of **traga** is recorded in Sir Jasper Nicoll's Journal, at the capture of Gawilgarh, by Sir A. Wellesley. See note to *Wellington*, ed. 1837, ii. 387.

1813.—"Every attempt to levy an assessment is succeeded by the **Tarakaw**, a most horrid mode of murdering themselves and each other."—*Forbes, Or. Mem.* ii. 91; [2nd ed. i. 378; and see i. 244].

1819.—For an affecting story of **Traga**, see *Macmurdo*, in *Bo. Lit. Soc. Trans.* i. 281.

TUMASHA, s. An entertainment, a *spectacle* (in the French sense), a popular excitement. It is Ar. *tamāshi*, 'going about to look at anything entertaining.' The word is in use in Turkestan (see *Schuyler*, below).

1610.—"Heere are also the ruines of *Ranichand* (*qu.* Ramchand's?) Castle and Houses which the Indians acknowledge for the great God, saying that he took flesh vpon him to see the **Tamasha** of the World."—*Finch*, in *Purchas*, i. 436.

1631.—"Hic quoque meridiem prospicit, ut spectet **Thamasham** id est pugnas Elephantum Leonum Buffalorum et aliarum ferarum. ..."—*De Laet, De Imperio Magni Mogolis*, 127. (For this quotation I am indebted to a communication from Mr. Archibald Constable of the Oudh and Rohilkund Railway.—*Y.*)

1673.—"... We were discovered by some that told our Banyan ... that two Englishmen were come to the **Tomasia**, or Sight. ..."—*Fryer*, 159.

1705.—"**Tamachars**. Ce sont des réjouissances que les Gentils font en l'honneur de quelqu'unes de leurs divinitez."—*Luillier, Tab. des Matières.*

1840.—"Runjeet replied, 'Don't go yet; I am going myself in a few days, and then we will have *burra* **tomacha**.' "—*Osborne, Court and Camp of Runjeet Singh*, 120–121.

1876.—"If you told them that you did not want to buy anything, but had merely come for **tomasha**, or amusement, they were always ready to explain and show you everything you wished to see."—*Schuyler's Turkistan*, i. 176.

TUMLET, s. Domestic Hind. *tāmlet*, being a corruption of *tumbler*.

TUMTUM, s. A dog-cart. We do not know the origin. [It is almost certainly a corr. of English *tandem*, the slang use of which in the sense of a conveyance (according to the *Stanf. Dict.*) dates from 1807. Even now English-speaking natives often speak of a dog-cart with a single horse as a *tandem*.]

1866.—"We had only 3 coss to go, and we should have met a pair of **tumtums** which would have taken us on."—*Trevelyan, The Dawk Bungalow*, 384.

[1889.—"A G.B.T. cart once married a bathing-machine, and they called the child **Tum-tum**."—*R. Kipling, The City of Dreadful Night*, 74.]

TURBAN, s. Some have supposed this well-known English word to be a corruption of the P.—H. *sirband*, 'head-wrap,' as in the following:

1727.—"I bought a few **seerbunds** and *sannoes* there (at Cuttack) to know the difference of the prices."—*A. Hamilton*, i. 394.

This, however, is quite inconsistent with the history of the word. Wedgewood's suggestion that the word may be derived from Fr. *turbin*, 'a whelk,' is equally to be rejected. It is really a corruption of one which, though it seems to be out of use in modern Turkish, was evidently used by the Turks when Europe first became familiar with the Ottomans and their ways. This is set forth in the quotation below from Zedler's *Lexicon*, which is corroborated by those from Rycaut and from Galland, &c. The proper word was apparently *dulband*. Some modern Persian dictionaries give the only meaning of this as 'a sash.' But Meninski explains it as 'a cloth of fine white muslin; a wrapper for the head'; and Vüllers also gives it this meaning, as well as that of a 'sash or belt.'[1] In doing so he quotes Shakespear's Dict., and marks the use as 'Hindustani-Persian.' But a merely Hindustani use of a Persian word could hardly have become habitual in Turkey in the 15th and 16th centuries. The use of *dulband* for a turban was probably genuine Persian, adopted by the Turks. Its etymology is apparently from Arab. *dul*, *'volvere,'* admitting of application to either a girdle or a head-wrap. From the Turks it passed in the forms *Tulipant*, *Tolliban*, *Turbant*, &c., into European languages. And we believe that the flower *tulip* also has its name from its resemblance to the old Ottoman turban, [a view accepted by Prof. Skeat (*Concise Dict.* s.v. *tulip, turban*)].[2]

1487.—"... tele bambagine assai che loro chiamano **turbanti**; tele assai colla salda, che lor chiamano *sexe* (sash). ..."—Letter on presents from the Sultan to L. de' Medici, in *Roscoe's Lorenzo*, ed. 1825, ii. 371–72.

c. 1490.—"Estradiots sont gens comme Genetaires: vestuz, à pied et à cheval, comme les Turcs, sauf la teste, où ils ne portent ceste toille qu'ils appellent **tolliban**, et sont durs gens, et couchent dehors tout l'an et leurs chevaulx."—*Ph. de Commynes*, Liv. VIII. ch. viii. ed. *Dupont* (1843), ii. 456. Thus given in Danett's translation (1595): "These Estradiots are soldiers like to the Turkes Ianizaries, and attired both on foote and on horsebacke like to the Turks, save that they weare not vpon their head such a great roule of linnen as the Turkes do called (*sic*) **Tolliban**."—p. 325.

1586-8.—"... the King's Secretarie, who had upon his head a peece of died linen cloth folded vp like vnto a Turkes **Tuliban**."—*Voyage of Master Thomas Candish*, in *Hakl.* iv. 33.

1588.—"In this canoa was the King's Secretarie, who had on his head a piece of died linen cloth folded vp like vnto a Turkes **Tuliban**."—*Cavendish, ibid.* iv. 337.

c. 1610.—"... un gros **turban** blanc à la Turque."—*Pyrard de Laval*, i. 98; [Hak. Soc. i. 132 and 165].

1611.—Cotgrave's French Dict. has: "**Toliban**: m. A **Turbant** or Turkish hat.

"**Tolopan**, as **Turbant**.

"**Turban**: m. A **Turbant**; a Turkish hat, of white and fine linnen wreathed into a rundle;

1 The Pers. *partala* is always used for a 'waist-belt' in India, but in Persia also for a turban.

2 Busbecq (1554) says: "... ingens ubique florum copia offerebatur, Narcissorum, Hyacinthorum, et eorum quos Turcae **Tulipan** vocant."—*Epist.* i. Elzevir ed. p. 47.

broad at the bottom to enclose the head, and lessening, for ornament, towards the top."

1615.—"... se un Cristiano fosse trovato con **turbante** bianco in capo, sarebbe perciò costretto o a rinegare o a morire. Questo **turbante** poi lo portano Turchi, di varie forme."—*P. della Valle*, i. 96.

1615.—"The Sultan of Socotora ... his clothes are *Surat* Stuffes, after the Arabs manner ... a very good **Turbant**, but bare footed."—*Sir T. Roe*, [Hak. Soc. i. 32].

"Their Attire is after the Turkish fashion, **Turbants** only excepted, insteed whereof they have a kind of Capp, rowled about with a black **Turbant**."—*De Monfart*, 5.

1619.—"Nel giorno della qual festa tutti Persiani più spensierati, e fin gli uomini grandi, e il medesimo rè, si vestono in abito succinto all uso di Mazanderan; e con certi berrettini, non troppo buoni, in testa, perchè i **turbanti** si guasterebbono e sarebbero di troppo impaccio. ..."—*P. della Valle*, ii. 31; [Hak. Soc. comp. i. 43].

1630.—"Some indeed have sashes of silke and gold, **tulipanted** about their heads. ..."—*Sir T. Herbert*, p. 128.

"His way was made by 30 gallant young gentlemen vested in crimson saten; their **Tulipants** were of silk and silver wreath'd about with cheynes of gold."—*Ibid.* p. 139.

1672.—"On the head they wear great **Tulbands** (*Tulbande*) which they touch with the hand when they say *salam* to any one."—*Baldaeus* (Germ. version), 33.

"Trois **Tulbangis** venoient de front après luy, et ils portoient chascun un beau **tulban** orné et enrichy d'aigrettes."—*Journ. d'Ant. Galland*, i. 139.

1673.—"The mixture of Castes or Tribes of all *India* are distinguished by the different Modes of binding their **Turbats**."—*Fryer*, 115.

1674.—"El **Tanadar** de un golpo cortò las repetidas bueltas del **turbante** a un Turco, y la cabeça asta la mitad, de que cayò muerte."—*Faria y Sousa, Asia Port.* ii. 179–180.

"**Turbant**, a Turkish hat," &c.—*Glossographia, or a Dictionary interpreting the Hard Words of whatsoever language, now used in our refined English Tongue*, &c., the 4th ed., by *T.E.*, of the Inner Temple, Esq. In the Savoy, 1674.

1676.—"*Mahamed Alibeg* returning into *Persia* out of *India* ... presented *Cha-Sefi* the second with a Coco-nut about the bigness of an Austrich-egg ... there was taken out of it a **Turbant** that had 60 cubits of calicut in length to make it, the cloath being so fine that you could hardly feel it."—*Tavernier*, E.T. p. 127; [ed. *Ball*, ii. 7].

1687.—In a detail of the high officers of the Sultan's Court we find:

"5. The **Tulbentar** Aga, he that makes up his **Turbant**."

A little below another personage (apparently) is called **Tulban**-*oghlani* ('The Turban Page')—*Ricaut, Present State of the Ottoman Empire*, p. 14.

1711.—"Their common Dress is a piece of blew Callico, wrap'd in a Role round their Heads for a **Turbat**."—*Lockyer*, 57.

1745.—"The Turks hold the Sultan's **Turban** in honour to such a degree that they hardly dare touch it ... but he himself has, among the servants of his privy chamber, one whose special duty it is to adjust his **Turban**, or head-tire, and who is thence called **Tulbentar** or **Dulbentar** *Aga*, or. **Dulbendar** *Aga*, also called by some **Dulbend** *Oghani* (*Oghlani*), or Page of the Turban."—*Zedler, Universal Lexicon*, s.v.

c. 1760.—"They (the Sepoys) are chiefly armed in the country manner, with sword and target, and wear the Indian dress, the **turbant**, the cabay or vest, and **long drawers**."—*Grose*, i. 39.

1843.—"The mutiny of Vellore was caused by a slight shown to the Mahomedan **turban**; the mutiny of Bangalore by disrespect said to have been shown to a Mahomedan place of worship."—*Macaulay, Speech on Gates of Somnauth.*

TYCONNA, TYEKANA, s. A room in the basement or cellarage, or dug in the ground, in which it has in some parts of India been the practice to pass the hottest part of the day during the hottest season of the year. Pers. *tah-khāna*, 'nether-house,' *i.e.* 'subterraneous apartment.' ["In the centre of the court is an elevated platform, the roof of a subterraneous chamber called a *zeera zemeon*, whither travellers retire during the great heats of the summer" (*Morier, Journey through Persia*, &c., 81). Another name for such a place is *sardābeh* (*Burton, Ar. Nights*, i. 314).]

1663.—"... in these hot Countries, to entitle an House to the name of Good and Fair it is required it should be ... furnish'd also with good **Cellars** with great Flaps to stir the Air, for reposing in the fresh Air from 12 till 4 or 5 of the Clock, when the Air of these Cellars begins to be hot and stuffing. ..."—*Bernier*, E.T. 79; [ed. *Constable*, 247].

c. 1763.—"The throng that accompanied that minister proved so very great that the floor of the house, which happened to have a **Tah-Qhana**, and possibly was at that moment under a secret influence, gave way, and the body, the Vizir, and all his company fell into the apartment underneath."—*Seir Mutaqherin*, iii. 19.

1842.—"The heat at Jellalabad from the end of April was tremendous, 105° to 110° in the shade. Everybody who could do so lived in underground chambers called **tykhánás.** Broadfoot dates a letter 'from my den six feet under ground.' "—*Mrs. Mackenzie, Storms and Sunshine of a Soldier's Life*, i. 298. [The same author in her *Life in the Mission* (i. 330) writes **taikhana.**]

TYPHOON, s. A tornado or cyclone-wind; a sudden storm, a '**norwester**' (q.v.). Sir John Barrow (see *Autobiog.* 57) ridicules "learned antiquarians" for fancying that the Chinese took *typhoon* from the Egyptian *Typhon*, the word being, according to him, simply the Chinese syllables, *ta-fung*, 'Great Wind.' His ridicule is misplaced. With a monosyllabic language like the Chinese (as we have remarked elsewhere) you may construct a plausible etymology, to meet the requirements of the sound alone, from anything and for anything. And as there is no evidence that the word is in Chinese use at all, it would perhaps be as fair a suggestion to derive it from the English "*tough 'un.*" Mr. Giles, who seems to think that the balance of evidence is in favour of this (Barrow's) etymology, admits a serious objection to be that the Chinese have special names for the *typhoon*, and rarely, if ever, speak of it vaguely as a 'great wind.' The fact is that very few words of the class used by seafaring and trading people, even when they refer to Chinese objects, are directly taken from the Chinese language. *E.g. Mandarin, pagoda, chop, cooly, tutenague*;—none of these are Chinese. And the probability is that Vasco and his followers got the *tufão*, which our sailors made into *touffon* and then into *typhoon*, as they got the *monção* which our sailors made into *monsoon*, direct from the Arab pilots.

The Arabic word is *ṭūfān*, which is used habitually in India for a sudden and violent storm. Lane defines it as meaning 'an overpowering rain, ... Noah's flood,' etc. And there can be little doubt of its identity with the Greek τυφῶν or τυφών. [But Burton (*Ar. Nights*, iii. 257) alleges that it is pure Arabic, and comes from the root *ṭauf*, 'going round.'] This word τυφών (the etymologists say, from τυφώ, 'I raise smoke') was applied to a demon-giant or Titan, and either directly from the etym. meaning or from the name of the Titan (as in India a whirlwind is called 'a **Devil** or Pisachee') to a 'waterspout,' and thence to analogous stormy phenomena. 'Waterspout' seems evidently the meaning of τυφών in the *Meteorologica* of Aristotle (γίγνεται μὲν οὖν τυφὼν ... κ.τ.λ.) iii. 1; the passage is exceedingly difficult to render clearly); and also in the quotation which we give from Aulus Gellius. The word *may* have come to the Arabs either in maritime intercourse, or through the translations of Aristotle. It occurs (*al-ṭūfān*) several times in the Koran; thus in *sura*, vii. 134, for a flood or storm, one of the plagues of Egypt, and in s. xxix. 14 for the Deluge.

Dr. F. Hirth, again (*Journ. R. Geog. Soc.* i. 260), advocates the quasi-Chinese origin of the word. Dr. Hirth has found the word *T'ai* (and also with the addition of *fung*, 'wind') to be really applied to a certain class of cyclonic winds, in a Chinese work on Formosa, which is a re-issue of a book originally published in 1694. Dr. Hirth thinks *t'ai* as here used (which is not the Chinese word *ta* or *tai*, 'great,' and is expressed by a different character) to be a local Formosan term; and is of opinion that the combination *t'ai-fung* is "a sound so near that of *typhoon* as almost to exclude all other conjectures, if we consider that the writers using the term in European languages were travellers distinctly applying it to storms encountered in that part of the China Sea." Dr. Hirth also refers to F. Mendes Pinto and the passages (quoted below) in which he says *tufão* is the Chinese name for such storms. Dr. Hirth's paper is certainly worthy of much more attention than the scornful assertion of Sir John Barrow, but it does not induce us to change our view as to the origin of *typhoon*.

Observe that the Port. *tufão* distinctly represents *ṭūfān* and not *t'ai-fung*, and the oldest English form '*tuffon*' does the same, whilst it is not by any means unquestionable that these Portuguese and English forms were first applied in the China Sea, and not in the Indian Ocean. Observe also Lord Bacon's use of the word *typhones* in his Latin below; also that *ṭūfān* is an Arabic word, at least as old as the Koran, and closely allied in sound and meaning to τυφών, whilst it is habitually used for a storm in Hindustani. This is shown by the quotations below (1810–1836); and Platts defines *ṭūfān* as "a violent storm of wind and rain, a tempest, a **typhoon**; a flood, deluge, inundation, the universal deluge" etc.; also *ṭūfānī*, "stormy, tempestuous ... boisterous, quarrelsome, violent, noisy, riotous."

Little importance is to be attached to Pinto's linguistic remarks such as that quoted, or even to the like dropt by Couto. We apprehend that Pinto made exactly the same mistake that Sir John Barrow did; and we need not wonder at it, when so many of our countrymen in India have supposed **hackery** to be a Hindustani word, and when we find even the learned H. H. Wilson assuming tope (in the sense of 'grove') to be in native Hindustani use. Many instances of such mistakes might be quoted. It is just possible, though not we think very probable, that some contact with the Formosan term may have influenced the modification of the old English form *tuffon* into *typhoon*. It is much more likely to have been influenced by the analogies of *monsoon*, *simoom*; and it is quite possible that the Formosan mariners took up their (unexplained) *t'ai-fung* from the Dutch or Portuguese.

On the origin of the Ar. word the late Prof. Robertson-Smith forwarded the following note:

"The question of the origin of *Ṭūfān* appears to be somewhat tangled.

"*Τυφῶν*, 'whirlwind, waterspout,' connected with *τῦφος* seems pure Greek; the combination in Baal-*Zephon*, Exod. xiv. 2, and *Sephóni*, the northern one, in Joel, ii. 20, suggested by Hitzig, appears to break down, for there is no proof of any Egyptian name for Set corresponding to Typhon.

"On the other hand *Ṭūfān*, the deluge, is plainly borrowed from the Aramaic. *Ṭūfān*, for Noah's flood, is both Jewish, Aramaic and Syriac, and this form is not borrowed from the Greek, but comes from a true Semitic root *ṭūf* 'to overflow.'

"But again, the sense of *whirlwind* is not recognised in classical Arabic. Even Dozy in his dictionary of later Arabic only cites a modern French-Arabic dictionary (Bocthor's) for the sense, *Tourbillon, trombe*. Bistání in the *Moḥít el Moḥít* does not give this sense, though he is pretty full in giving modern as well as old words and senses. In Arabic the root *ṭūf* means 'to go round,' and a combination of this idea with the sense of sudden disaster might conceivably have given the new meaning to the word. On the other hand it seems simpler to regard this sense as a late loan from some modern form of *τυφών*, *typho*, or *tifone*. But in order finally to settle the matter one wants examples of this sense of *ṭūfān*."

[Prof. Skeat (*Concise Dict.* s.v.) gives: "Sometimes claimed as a Chinese word meaning 'a great wind' ... but this seems to be a late mystification. In old authors the forms are *tuffon, tuffoon, tiphon*, &c.—Arab. *ṭūfān*, a hurricane, storm. Gk. *τυφών*, better *τυφώς*, a whirlwind. The close accidental coincidence of these words in sense and form is very remarkable, as Whitney notes."]

c. A.D. 160.—"... dies quidem tandem illuxit: sed nichil de periculo, de saevitiâve remissum, quia turbines etiam crebriores, et coelum atrum et fumigantes globi, et figurae quaedam nubium metuendae, quas *τυφῶνας* vocabant, impendere, imminere, et depressurae navem videbantur."—*Aul. Gellius*, xix. 2.

1540.—"Now having ... continued our Navigation within this Bay of *Cauchin-china* ... upon the day of the nativity of our Lady, being the eight of *September*, for the fear that we were in of the new Moon, during the which there oftentimes happens in this Climate such a terrible storm of wind and rain, as it is not possible for ships to withstand it, which by the Chineses is named **Tufan**" (*o qual tormento os Chins chamão* **tufão**).—*Pinto* (orig. cap. I.) in *Cogan*, p. 60.

"... in the height of forty and one degrees, there arose so terrible a Southwind, called by the Chineses **Tufaon** (*un tempo do Sul, a q̃ Chins chamão* **tufão**)."—*Ibid.* (cap. lxxix.), in *Cogan*, p. 97.

1554.—"Não se ouve por pequena maravilha cessarem os **tufões** na paragem da ilha de Sãchião."—Letter in *Sousa, Oriente Conquist.* i. 680.

[c. 1554.—"... suddenly from the west arose a great storm known as fil **Tofani** [literally 'Elephant's flood, comp. ELEPHANTA, b.]."—*Travels of Sidi Ali, Reïs*, ed. *Vambéry*, p. 17.]

1567.—"I went aboorde a shippe of Bengala, at which time it was the yeere of **Touffon**, concerning which **Touffon** ye are to vnderstand that in the East Indies often times, there are not stormes as in other countreys; but every 10 or 12 yeeres there are such tempests and stormes that it is a thing incredible ... neither do they know certainly what yeere they will come."—*Master Caesar Frederike*, in *Hakl.* ii. 370 [369].

1575.—"But when we approach'd unto it (Cyprus), a Hurricane arose suddenly, and blew so fiercely upon us, that it would our great Sail round about our main Mast. ... These Winds arise from a Wind that is called by the Greeks **Typhon**; and *Pliny* calleth it *Vertex* and *Vortex*; but as dangerous as they are, as they arise suddenly, so quickly are they laid again also."—*Rauwolff's Travels*, in *Ray's Collection*, ed. 1705, p. 320. Here the traveller seems to intimate (though we are not certain) that *Typhon* was then applied in the Levant to such winds; in any case it was exactly the *ṭūfān* of India.

1602.—"This Junk seeking to make the port of Chincheo met with a tremendous storm such as the natives call **Tufão**, a thing so overpowering and terrible, and bringing such violence, such earthquake as it were, that it appears as if all the spirits of the infernal world had got into the waves and seas, driving them in a whirl till their fury seems to raise a scud of flame, whilst in the space of one turning of the sand-glass the wind shall veer round to every point of the compass, seeming to blow more furiously from each in succession.

"Such is this phenomenon that the very birds of heaven, by some natural instinct, know of its coming 8 days beforehand, and are seen to take their nests down from the tree-tops and hide them in crevices of rock. Eight days before, the clouds also are seen to float so low as almost to graze men's heads, whilst in these days the seas seem beaten down as it were, and of a deep blue colour. And before the storm breaks forth, the sky exhibits a token well-known to all, a great object which seamen call the Ox-Eye (*Olho de Boi*) all of different colours, but so gloomy and appalling that it strikes fear in all who see it. And as the Bow of Heaven, when it appears, is the token of fair weather, and calm, so this seems to portend the Wrath of God, as we may well call such a storm. ..." &c.—*Couto*, V. viii. 12.

1610.—"But at the breaking vp, commeth alway a cruell Storme, which they call the **Tuffon**, fearfull even to men on land; which is not alike extreame euery yeare."—*Finch*, in *Purchas*, i. 423.

1613.—"E porque a terra he salitrosa e ventosa, he muy sogeita a tempestades, ora menor aquella chamada Ecnephia (*Εκνεφιας*), ora maior chamada **Tiphon** (*Τυφων*), aquelle de ordinario chamamos **Tuphão** ou Tormenta desfeita ... e corre com tanta furia e impeto que desfas os tectos das casas e aranca arvores, e as vezes do mar lança as embarcações em terra nos campos do sertão."—*Godinho de Eredia*, f. 36*v*.

1615.—"And about midnight Capt. Adams went out in a bark abord the *Hozeander* with many other barks to tow her in, we fearing a **tuffon**."—*Cocks's Diary*, i. 50.

1624.—"3. **Typhones** majores, qui per latitudinem aliquam corripiunt, et correpta sorbent in sursum, raro fiunt; at vortices, sive turbines exigui et quasi ludicri, frequenter.

"4. Omnes procellae et **typhones**, et turbines majores, habent manifestum motum praecipitii, aut vibrationis deorsum magis quam alii venti."—*Bacon, Hist. Ventorum*, in *B. Montagu's* ed. of Works, x. 49. In the translation by R. G. (1671) the words are rendered "the greater **typhones**."—*Ibid.* xiv. 268.

1626.—"*Francis Fernandez* writeth, that in the way from Malacca to Iapan they are encountred with great stormes which they call **Tuffons**, that blow foure and twentie houres, beginning from the North to the East, and so about the Compasse."—*Purchas, Pilgrimage*, 600.

1688.—"**Tuffoons** are a particular kind of violent Storms blowing on the Coast of Tonquin ... it comes on fierce and blows very violent, at N.E. twelve hours more or less. ... When the Wind begins to abate it dies away suddenly, and falling flat calm it continues so an Hour, more or less; then the Wind comes round about to the S.W. and it blows and rains as fierce from thence, as it did before at N.E. and as long."—*Dampier*, ii. 36.

1712.—"Non v'è spavento paragonabile a quello de' naviganti, quali in mezzo all' oceano assaltati d'ogni intorno da turbini e da **tifoni**."—*P. Paolo Segnero, Mann. dell' Anima*, Ottobre 14. (Borrowed from Della Crusca Voc.).

1721.—"I told them they were all strangers to the nature of the **Moussoons** and **Tuffoons** on the coast of India and China."—*Shelvocke's Voyage*, 383.

1727.—"... by the Beginning of *September*, they reacht the Coast of China, where meeting with a **Tuffoon**, or a North East Storm, that often blows violently about that Season, they were forced to bear away for Johore."—*A. Hamilton*, ii. 89; [ed. 1744, ii. 88].

1727.—

"In the dread Ocean, undulating wide,
Beneath the radiant line that girts the globe,
The circling **Typhon**, whirl'd from point to point,
Exhausting all the rage of all the Sky..."

Thomson, Summer.

1780.—Appended to Dunn's New Directory, 5th ed. is:—

"PROGNOSTIC of a **Tuffoon** *on the Coast of China*. By ANTONIO PASCAL DE ROSA, *a Portuguese Pilot of* MACAO."

c. 1810.—(Mr. Martyn) "was with us during a most tremendous **touffan**, and no one who has not been in a tropical region can, I think, imagine what these storms are."—*Mrs. Sherwood's Autobiog.* 382.

1826.—"A most terrific **toofaun** ... came on that seemed likely to tear the very trees up by the roots."—*John Shipp*, ii. 285.

"I thanked him, and enquired how this **toofan** or storm had arisen."—*Pandurang Hari*, [ed. 1873, i. 50].

1836.—"A hurricane has blown ever since

gunfire; clouds of dust are borne along upon the rushing wind; not a drop of rain; nothing is to be seen but the whirling clouds of the **tūfān**. The old peepul-tree moans, and the wind roars in it as if the storm would tear it up by the roots."—*Wanderings of a Pilgrim*, ii. 53.

1840.—"Slavers throwing overboard the Dead and Dying. **Typhoon** coming on.

"'Aloft all hands, strike the topmasts and
belay;
Yon angry setting sun, and fierce-edge
clouds
Declare the **Typhoon's** coming' &c.
(*Fallacies of Hope*)."

J. M. W. Turner, in the R.A. Catalogue.

Mr. Ruskin appears to have had no doubt as to the etymology of **Typhoon**, for the rain-cloud from this picture is engraved in *Modern Painters*, vol. iv. as "The Locks of **Typhon**." See Mr. Hamerton's *Life of Turner*, pp. 288, 291, 345.

Punch parodied Turner in the following imaginary entry from the R.A. Catalogue:

"34.—A **Typhoon** bursting in a Simoon over the Whirlpool of Maelstrom, Norway, with a ship on fire, an eclipse and the effect of a lunar rainbow."

1853.—"... pointing as he spoke to a dark dirty line which was becoming more and more visible in the horizon:

"'By Jove, yes!' cried Stanton, 'that's a **typhaon** coming up, sure enough.' "—*Oakfield*, i. 122.

1859.—"The weather was sultry and unsettled, and my Jemadar, Ramdeen Tewarry ... opined that we ought to make ready for the coming **tuphan** or tempest. ... A darkness that might be felt, and that no lamp could illumine, shrouded our camp. The wind roared and yelled. It was a hurricane."—*Lt.-Col. Lewin, A Fly on the Wheel*, p. 62.

Compare the next quotation, from the same writer, with that given above from Couto respecting the *Olho de Boi*:

1885.—"The district was subject to cyclonic storms of incredible violence, fortunately lasting for a very short time, but which often caused much destruction. These storms were heralded by the appearance above the horizon of clouds known to the natives by the name of 'lady's eyebrows,' so called from their being curved in a narrow black-arched wisp, and these most surely foretold the approach of the tornado."—*Ibid.* 176.

U

UMBRELLA, s. This word is of course not Indian or Anglo-Indian, but the *thing* is very prominent in India, and some interest attaches to the history of the word and thing in Europe. We shall collect here a few quotations bearing upon this. The knowledge and use of this serviceable instrument seems to have gone through extraordinary eclipses. It is frequent as an accompaniment of royalty in the Nineveh sculptures; it was in general Indian use in the time of Alexander; it occurs in old Indian inscriptions, on Greek vases, and in Greek and Latin literature; it was in use at the court of Byzantium, and at that of the Great Khan in Mongolia, in medieval Venice, and more recently in the semi-savage courts of Madagascar and Ashantee. Yet it was evidently a strange object, needing particular description, to John Marignolli (c. 1350), Ruy Clavijo (c. 1404), Barbosa (1516), John de Barros (1553), and Minsheu (1617). See also **SOMBRERO**.

c. B.C. 325.—"*Τοὺς δὲ πωγώνας λέγει Νέαρχος ὅτι βάπτονται Ἰνδοὶ ... και σκιάδια ὅτι προβάλλονται, τοῦ θέρεος, ὅσοι οὐκ ἠμελημένοι Ἰνδῶν.*"—*Arrian, Indica*, xvi.

c. B.C. 2.

"Ipse tene distenta suis **umbracula** virgis;
Ipse face in turba, qua venit illa, locum."

Orid, Art. Amat. ii. 209–210.

c. A.D. 5.

"Aurea pellebant rapidos **umbracula** soles
Quae tamen Herculeae sustinuere manus."

Ibid. Fasti, ii. 311–312.

c. A.D. 100.

"En, cui tu viridem **umbellam**, cui succina
mittas
Grandia natalis quoties redit..."

Juvenal, ix. 50–51.

c. 200.—"... *ἔπεμψε δὲ καὶ κλίνην αὔτῳ ἀργυρόποδα, καὶ στρωμνὴν, καὶ σκηνὴν οὐρανόροφον ἀνθίνην, καὶ θρόνον ἀργυροῦν, καὶ ἐπίχρυσον σκιάδιον* ..."—*Athenaeus*, Lib. ii. Epit. § 31.

c. 380.—"Ubi si inter aurata flabella laciniis sericis insiderint muscae, vel per foramen **umbraculi** pensilis radiolus irruperit solis, queruntur quod non sunt apud Cimmerios nati."—*Ammianus Marcellinus*, XXVIII. iv.

1248.—"Ibi etiam quoddam **Solinum** (*v.* **Soliolum**), sive tentoriolum, quod portatur super caput Imperatoris, fuit praesentatum eidem, quod totum erat praeparatum cum gemmis."—*Joan. de Plano Carpini*, in *Rec. de V.*, iv. 759–760.

c. 1292.—"Et a haute festes porte Monsignor

le Dus une corone d'or ... et la ou il vait a hautes festes si vait apres lui un damoiseau qui porte une **unbrele** de dras à or sur son chief..."

and again:

"Et apres s'en vet Monsignor li Dus desos **l'onbrele** que li dona Monsignor l'Apostoille; et cele **onbrele** est d'un dras (a) or, que la porte un damosiaus entre ses mains, que s'en vet totes voies apres Monsignor li Dus."—Venetian Chronicle of *Martino da Canale, Archiv. Stor. Ital.*, I. Ser. viii. 214, 560.

1298.—"Et tout ceus ... ont par commandement que toutes fois que il chevauchent doivent avoir sus le chief un palieque que on dit **ombrel**, que on porte sur une lance en senefiance de grant seigneurie."—*Marco Polo*, Text of *Pauthier*, i. 256–7.

c. 1332.—(At Constantinople) "the inhabitants, military men or others, great and small, winter and summer, carry over their heads huge **umbrellas** (*ma hallāt*)."—*Ibn Batuta*, ii. 440.

c. 1335.—"Whenever the Sultan (of Delhi) mounts his horse, they carry an **umbrella** over his head. But when he starts on a march to war, or on a long journey, you see carried over his head seven umbrellas, two of which are covered with jewels of inestimable value."—*Shihābuddīn Dimishkī*, in *Not. et Exts.* xiii. 190.

1404.—"And over her head they bore a **shade** (**sombra**) carried by a man, on a shaft like that of a lance; and it was of white silk, made like the roof of a round tent, and stretched by a hoop of wood, and this shade they carry over the head to protect them from the sun."—*Clavijo*, § cxxii.

1541.—"Then next to them marches twelve men on horseback, called Peretandas, each of them carrying an **Umbrello** of carnation Sattin, and other twelve that follow with banners of white damask."—*Pinto*, in *Cogan's* E.T., p. 135.

In the original this runs:

"Vão doze homẽs a cavallo, que se chamão peretandas, cõ **sombreyros** de citim cramesim nas mãos *a modo de esparacels postos em cesteas muyto compridas* (like tents upon very long staves) et outros doze cõ bãndeyras de damasco branco."

[c. 1590.—"*The Ensigns of Royalty* ... 2. The *Chatr*, or **umbrella**, is adorned with the most precious jewels, of which there are never less than seven. 3. The *Sáibán* is of an oval form, a yard in length, and its handle, like that of the umbrella, is covered with brocade, and ornamented with precious stones. One of the attendants holds it, to keep off the rays of the sun. It is also called *Áftábgír*."—*Āīn*, i. 50.]

1617.—"An 𝔘𝔪𝔟𝔯𝔢𝔩𝔩, a *fashion of* round and broade fanne, wherewith the Indians, *and from them our great ones preserve themselves from the heate of the scorching sunne.* G. Ombraire, m. Ombrelle, f. I. Ombrélla. L. Vmbella, *ab vmbra*, the shadow, *est enim* instrumentum quo solem à facie arcent ¶ Iuven. Gr. σκιάδιον, diminut. a σκία, i. vmbra. T. 𝔖𝔠𝔥𝔞𝔟𝔥𝔲𝔱, q. 𝔰𝔠𝔥𝔞𝔱𝔥𝔲𝔱, *à* 𝔰𝔠𝔥𝔞𝔱𝔱𝔢𝔫, i. *vmbra*, et 𝔥𝔲𝔱, i. *pileus, á quo*, et B. 𝔖𝔠𝔥𝔦𝔫𝔥𝔬𝔢𝔡𝔱. Br. *Teggidel, à teg.* i. pulchrum forma, et *gidd*, pro *riddio*, i. protegere; *haec enim vmbellae finis.*"—*Minsheu* (1st ed. s.v.).

1644.—"Here (at Marseilles) we bought **umbrellas** against the heats."—*Evelyn's Diary*, 7th Oct.

1677.—(In this passage the word is applied to an awning before a shop. "The Streets are generally narrow ... the better to receive the advantages of **Umbrello's** extended from side to side to keep the sun's violence from their customers."—*Fryer*, 222.

1681.—"After these comes an Elephant with two Priests on his back; one whereof is the Priest before spoken of, carrying the painted Stick on his shoulder. ... The other sits behind him, holding a round thing like an **Vmbrello** over his head, to keep off Sun or Rain."—*Knox's Ceylon*, 79.

1709.—"... The Young Gentleman belonging to the Custom-house that for fear of rain borrowed the **Umbrella** at Will's Coffee-house in Cornhill of the Mistress, is hereby advertised that to be dry from head to foot in the like occasion he shall be welcome to the Maid's pattens."—*The Female Tatler*, Dec. 12, quoted in *Malcolm's Anecdotes*, 1808, p. 429.

1712.

"The tuck'd up semstress walks with hasty strides
While streams run down her oil'd **umbrella's** sides."

Swift, A City Shower.

1715.

"Good housewives all the winter's rage despise,
Defended by the riding hood's disguise;
Or underneath the **Umbrella's** oily shade
Safe through the wet on clinking pattens tread.
"Let Persian dames the **Umbrella's** ribs display
To guard their beauties from the sunny ray;
Or sweating slaves support the shady load
When Eastern monarchs show their state abroad;
Britain in winter only knows its aid
To guard from chilly showers the walking maid."

Gay, Trivia, i.

1850.—*Advertisement posted at the door of one of the Sections of the* British Association *meeting at* Edinburgh.

"The gentleman, who carried away a brown silk **umbrella** from the —— Section yesterday, may have the cover belonging to it, which is of no further use to the Owner, by applying to the Porter at the Royal Hotel."—(*From Personal Recollection.*)—It is a curious parallel to the advertisement above from the *Female Tatler.*

UPAS, s. This word is now, like **Juggernaut**, chiefly used in English as a customary metaphor, and to indicate some institution that the speaker wishes to condemn in a compendious manner. The word *upas* is Javanese for poison; [Mr. Scott writes: "The Malay word *ūpas*, means simply 'poison.' It is Javanese *hupas*, Sundanese *upas*, Balinese *hupas*, 'poison.' It commonly refers to vegetable poison, because such are more common. In the Lampong language *upas* means 'sickness.'"] It became familiar in Europe in connection with exaggerated and fabulous stories regarding the extraordinary and deadly character of a tree in Java, alleged to be so called. There are several trees in the Malay Islands producing deadly poisons, but the particular tree to which such stories were attached is one which has in the last century been described under the name of *Antiaris toxicaria*, from the name given to the poison by the Javanese proper, viz. *Antjar*, or *Anchar* (the name of the tree all over Java), whilst it is known to the Malays and people of Western Java as *Upas*, and in Celebes and the Philippine Islands as *Ipo* or *Hipo*. [According to Mr. Scott "the Malay name for the 'poison-tree,' or any poison-tree, is *pōhun ūpas, pūhun ūpas*, represented in English by **bohonupas**. The names of two poison-trees, the Javanese *anchar* (Malay also *anchar*) and *chetik*, appear occasionally in English books ... The Sundanese name for the poison tree is *bulo ongko*."] It was the poison commonly used by the natives of Celebes and other islands for poisoning the small bamboo darts which they used (and in some islands still use) to shoot from the blow-tube.

The story of some deadly poison in these islands is very old, and we find it in the *Travels* of Friar Odoric, accompanied by the mention of the disgusting antidote which was believed to be efficacious, a genuine Malay belief, and told by a variety of later and independent writers, such as Nieuhof, Saar, Tavernier, Cleyer, and Kaempfer.

The subject of this poison came especially to the notice of the Dutch in connection with its use to poison the arrows just alluded to, and some interesting particulars are given on the subject by Bontius, from whom a quotation is given below, with others. There is a notice of the poison in De Bry, in Sir T. Herbert (whencesoever he borrowed it), and in somewhat later authors about the middle of the 17th century. In March 1666 the subject came before the young Royal Society, and among a long list of subjects for inquiry in the East occur two questions pertaining to this matter.

The illustrious Rumphius in his *Herbarium Amboinense* goes into a good deal of detail on the subject, but the tree does not grow in Amboyna where he wrote, and his account thus contains some ill-founded statements, which afterwards lent themselves to the fabulous history of which we shall have to speak presently. Rumphius however procured from Macassar specimens of the plant, and it was he who first gave the native name (*Ipo*, the Macassar form) and assigned a scientific name, *Arbor toxicaria*.[1] Passing over with simple mention the notices in the appendix to John Ray's *Hist. Plantarum*, and in Valentijn (from both of which extracts will be found below), we come to the curious compound of the loose statements of former writers magnified, of the popular stories current among Europeans in the Dutch colonies, and of pure romantic invention, which first appeared in 1783, in the *London Magazine*. The professed author of this account was one Foersch, who had served as a junior surgeon in the Dutch East Indies.[2] This person describes the tree, called **bohon-upas**, as situated "about 27 leagues[3] from Batavia, 14 from Soura Karta, the seat of the Emperor, and between 18 and 20 leagues from Tinkjoe" (probably for *Tjukjoe, i.e.* Djokjo-Karta), "the present residence of the Sultan of Java." Within a radius of 15 to 18 miles round the tree no human creature, no living thing could exist. Condemned malefactors were employed to fetch the poison; they were protected by

1 It must be kept in mind that though Rumphius (George Everard Rumpf) died in 1693, his great work was not printed till nearly fifty years afterwards (1741).

2 Foersch was a surgeon of the third class at Samarang in the year 1773.—*Horsfield*, in *Bat. Trans.* as quoted below.

3 This distance is probably a clerical error. It is quite inconsistent with the other two assigned.

special arrangements, yet not more than 1 in 10 of them survived the adventure. Foersch also describes executions by means of the Upas poison, which he says he witnessed at Sura Karta in February 1776.

The whole paper is a very clever piece of sensational romance, and has impressed itself indelibly, it would seem, on the English language; for to it is undoubtedly due the adoption of that standing metaphor to which we have alluded at the beginning of this article. This effect may, however, have been due not so much directly to the article in the *London Magazine* as to the adoption of the fable by the famous ancestor of a man still more famous, Erasmus Darwin, in his poem of the *Loves of the Plants*. In that work not only is the essence of Foersch's story embodied in the verse, but the story itself is quoted at length in the notes. It is said that Darwin was warned of the worthlessness of the narrative, but was unwilling to rob his poem of so sensational an episode.

Nothing appears to be known of Foersch except that there was really a person of that name in the medical service in Java at the time indicated. In our article **ANACONDA** we have adduced some curious particulars of analogy between the Anaconda-myth and the Upas-myth, and intimated a suspicion that the same hand may have had to do with the spinning of both yarns.

The extraordinary *éclat* produced by the Foerschian fables led to the appointment of a committee of the Batavian Society to investigate the true facts, whose report was published in 1789. This we have not yet been able to see, for the report is not contained in the regular series of the *Transactions* of that Society; nor have we found a refutation of the fables by M. Charles Coquebert referred to by Leschenault in the paper which we are about to mention. The poison tree was observed in Java by Deschamps, naturalist with the expedition of D'Entrecasteaux, and is the subject of a notice by him in the *Annales de Voyages*, vol. i., which goes into little detail, but appears to be correct as far as it goes, except in the statement that the Anchar was confined to Eastern Java. But the first thorough identification of the plant, and scientific account of the facts was that of M. Leschenault de la Tour. This French savant, when about to join a voyage of discovery to the South Seas, was recommended by Jussieu to take up the investigation of the Upas. On first enquiring at Batavia and Samarang, M. Leschenault heard only fables akin to Foersch's romance, and it was at Sura Karta that he first got genuine information, which eventually enabled him to describe the tree from actual examination.

The tree from which he took his specimens was more than 100 ft. in height, with a girth of 18 ft. at the base. A Javanese who climbed it to procure the flowers had to make cuts in the stem in order to mount. After ascending some 25 feet the man felt so ill that he had to come down, and for some days he continued to suffer from nausea, vomiting, and vertigo. But another man climbed to the top of the tree without suffering at all. On another occasion Leschenault, having had a tree of 4 feet girth cut down, walked among its broken branches, and had face and hands besprinkled with the gum-resin, yet neither did he suffer; he adds, however, that he had washed immediately after. Lizards and insects were numerous on the trunk, and birds perched upon the branches. M. Leschenault gives details of the preparation of the poison as practised by the natives, and also particulars of its action, on which experiment was made in Paris with the material which he brought to Europe. He gave it the scientific name by which it continues to be known, viz. *Antiaris toxicaria* (N.O. *Artocarpeae*).[1]

M. Leschenault also drew the attention of Dr. Horsfield, who had been engaged in the botanical exploration of Java some years before the British occupation, and continued it during that period, to the subject of the Upas, and he published a paper on it in the *Batavian Transactions* for 1813 (vol. vii.). His account seems entirely in accordance with that of Leschenault, but is more detailed and complete, with the result of numerous observations and experiments of his own. He saw the *Antiaris* first in the Province of Poegar, on his way to Banyuwangi. In Blambangan

1 Leschenault also gives the description of another and still more powerful poison, used in a similar way to that of the *Antiaris*, viz. the *tieute*, called sometimes *Upas Raja*, the plant producing which is a *Strychnos*, and a creeper. Though, as we have said, the name *Upas* is generic, and is applied to this, it is not *the* Upas of English metaphor, and we are not concerned with it here. Both kinds are produced and prepared in Java. The *Ipo* (a form of *Upas*) of Macassar is the *Antiaris*; the *ipo* of the Borneo Dayaks in the *Tieute*.

(eastern extremity of Java) he visited four or five trees; he afterwards found a very tall specimen growing at Passaruwang, on the borders of Malang, and again several young trees in the forests of Japāra, and one near Onārang. In all these cases, scattered over the length of Java, the people knew the tree as *anchar*.

Full articles on the subject are to be found (by Mr. J. J. Bennet) in Horsfield's *Plantae Javanicae Rariores*, 1838–52, pp. 52 *seqq*., together with a figure of a flowering branch pl. xiii.; and in Blume's *Rumphia* (Brussels, 1836), pp. 46 *seqq*., and pls. xxii., xxiii.; to both of which works we have been much indebted for guidance. Blume gives a drawing, for the truth of which he vouches, of a tall specimen of the trees. These he describes as "*vastas, arduas, et a ceteris segregatas*,"—solitary and eminent, on account of their great longevity, (possibly on account of their being spared by the axe?), but not for any such reason as the fables allege. There is no lack of adjoining vegetation; the spreading branches are clothed abundantly with parasitical plants, and numerous birds and squirrels frequent them. The stem throws out 'wings' or buttresses (see Horsfield in the *Bat. Trans*., and Blume's Pl.) like many of the forest trees of Further India. Blume refers, in connection with the origin of the prevalent fables, to the real existence of exhalations of carbonic acid gas in the volcanic tracts of Java, dangerous to animal life and producing sterility around, alluding particularly to a paper by M. Loudoun (a Dutch official of Scotch descent), in the *Edinburgh New Phil. Journal* for 1832, p. 102, containing a formidable description of the Guwo Upas or Poison Valley on the frontier of the Pekalongan and Banyumas provinces. We may observe, however, that, if we remember rightly, the exaggerations of Mr. Loudoun have been exposed and ridiculed by Dr. Junghuhn, the author of "*Java*." And if the Foersch legend be compared with some of the particulars alleged by several of the older writers, *e.g.* Camell (in Ray), Valentijn, Spielman, Kaempfer, and Rumphius, it will be seen that the *basis* for a great part of that *putida commentatio*, as Blume calls it, is to be found in them.

George Colman the Younger founded on the Foerschian Upas-myth, a kind of melodrama, called the *Law of Java*, first acted at Covent Garden May 11, 1822. We give some quotations below.[1]

Lindley, in his *Vegetable Kingdom*, in a short notice of *Antiaris toxicaria*, says that, though the accounts are greatly exaggerated, yet the facts are notable enough. He says cloth made from the tough fibre is so acrid as to verify the Shirt of Nessus. My friend Gen. Maclagan, noticing Lindley's remark to me, adds: "Do you remember in our High School days (at Edinburgh) a grand Diorama called **The Upas Tree**? It showed a large wild valley, with a single tree in the middle, and illustrated the safety of approach on the windward side, and the desolation it dealt on the other."

[For some details as to the use of the Upas poison, and an analysis of the Arrow-poisons of Borneo by Dr. L. Lewin (from *Virchow's Archiv. fur Pathol. Anat.* 1894, pp. 317–25) see *Ling Roth, Natives of Sarawak*, ii. 188 *seqq*. and for superstitions connected with these poisons, *Skeat, Malay Magic*, 426.]

c. 1330.—"En queste isole sono molte cose maravigliose e strane. Onde alcuni arbori li sono ... che fanno veleno pessimo ... Quelli uomini sono quasi tutti corsali, e quando vanno a battaglia portano ciascuno uno canna in mano, di lunghezza d'un braccio e pongono in capo de la canna uno ago di ferro atossiato in quel veleno, e sofiano nella canna e l'ago vola e percuotelo dove vogliono, e'ncontinente quelli ch'è percosso muore. Ma egli hanno la tina piene di sterco d'uomo e una iscodella di sterco guarisce l'uomo da queste cotali ponture."—*Storia di Frate Odorigo*, from Palatina MS., in *Cathay, &c.*, App., p. xlix.

c. 1630.—"And (in Makasser) which is no lesse infernall, the men use long canes or trunks (cald Sempitans), out of which they can (and use it) blow a little pricking quill, which if it draw the lest drop of blood from any part of the body, it makes him (though the strongest man living) die immediately; some venoms operate in an houre, others in a moment, the veynes and body (by the virulence of the poyson) corrupting and rotting presently, to any man's terrour and amazement, and feare to live where such abominations predominate."—*Sir T. Herbert*, ed. 1638, p. 329.

c. 1631.—"I will now conclude; but I first must say something of the poison used by the

1 I remember when a boy reading the whole of Foersch's story in a fascinating book, called *Wood's Zoography*, which I have not seen for half a century, and which, I should suppose from my recollection, was more sensational than scientific.—*Y.*

King of Macassar in the Island of Celebes to envenom those little arrows which they shoot through blowing-tubes, a poison so deadly that it causes death more rapidly than a dagger. For one wounded ever so lightly, be it but a scratch bringing blood, or a prick in the heel, immediately begins to nod like a drunken man, and falls dead to the ground. And within half an hour of death this putrescent poison so corrupts the flesh that it can be plucked from the bones like so much *mucus*. And what seems still more marvellous, if a man (*e.g.*) be scratched in the thigh, or higher in the body, by another point which is *not* poisoned, and the still warm blood as it flows down to the feet be merely touched by one of these poisoned little arrows, swift as wind the pestilent influence ascends to the wound, and with the same swiftness and other effects snatches the man from among the living.

"These are no idle tales, but the experience of eye-witnesses, not only among our countrymen, but among Danes and Englishmen."—*Jac. Bontii*, lib. v. cap. xxxiii.

1646.—"Es wachst ein Baum auf *Maccasser*, einer Cüst auf der Insul *Celebes*, der ist treflich vergiftet, dass wann einer nur an einem Glied damit verletzet wird, und man solches nit alsbald wegschlägt, der Gift geschwind zum Hertzen eilet, und den Garaus machet" (then the antidote as before is mentioned). ... "Mit solchem Gift schmieren die *Bandanesen* Ihre lange Pfeil, die Sie von grossen Bögen, einer Mannsläng hoch, hurtig schiessen; in *Banda* aber tähten Ihre Weiber grossen Schaden damit. Denn Sie sich auf die Bäume setzten, und kleine Fischgeräht damit schmierten, und durch ein gehöhlert Röhrlein, von einem Baum, auf unser Volck schossen, mit grossen machtigen Schaden."—*Saar, Ost-Indianische Funfzehen-Jahrige Kriegs-Dienste* ... 1672, pp. 46–47.

1667.—"*Enquiries for* Suratt, *and other parts of the East Indies*.

* * * * *

"19. Whether it be true, that the only Antidote hitherto known, against the famous and fatal *macassar-poison*, is *human ordure*, taken inwardly? And what substance that poison is made of?"—*Phil. Trans.* vol. ii. Anno 1667 (Proceedings for March 11, 1666, *i.e.* N.S. 1667), d. 417.

1682.—"The especial weapons of the Makassar soldiers, which they use against their enemies, are certain pointed arrowlets about a foot in length. At the foremost end these are fitted with a sharp and pointed fish-tooth, and at the butt with a knob of spongy wood.

"The points of these arrows, long before they are to be used, are dipt in poison and then dried.

"This poison is a sap that drips from the bark of the branches of a certain tree, like resin, from pine-trees.

"The tree grows on the Island Makasser, in the interior, and on three or four islands of the Bugisses round about Makassar. It is about the height of the clove-tree, and has leaves very similar.

"The fresh sap of this tree is a very deadly poison; indeed its virulence is incurable.

"The arrowlets prepared with this poison are not, by the Makasser soldiers, shot with a bow, but blown from certain blow-pipes (*uit zekere spatten gespat*); just as here, in the country, people shoot birds by blowing round pellets of clay.

"They can with these in still weather hit their mark at a distance of 4 rods.

"They say the Makassers themselves know no remedy against this poison ... for the poison presses swiftly into the blood and vital spirits, and causes a violent inflammation. They hold (however) that the surest remedy for this poison is ..." (and so on, repeating the antidote already mentioned).—*Joan Nieuhof's Zee en Land Reize*, &c., pp. 217–218.

c. 1681.—"*Arbor Toxicaria*, **Ipo**.

"I have never yet met with any poison more horrible and hateful, produced by any vegetable growth, than that which is derived from this lactescent tree.

* * * * *

Moreover beneath this tree, and in its whole circumference to the distance of a stone-cast, no plant, no shrub, or herbage will grow; the soil beneath it is barren, blackened, and burnt as it were ... and the atmosphere about it is so polluted and poisoned that the birds which alight upon its branches become giddy and fall dead * * * all things perish which are touched by its emanations, insomuch that every animal shuns it and keeps away from it, and even the birds eschew flying by it.

"No man dares to approach the tree without having his arms, feet, and head wrapped round with linen ... for Death seems to have planted his foot and his throne beside this tree. ..." (He then tells of a venomous basilisk with two feet in front and fiery eyes, a crest, and a horn, that dwelt under this tree).* * *

"The Malays call it *Cayu* **Upas**, but in Macassar and the rest of Celebes it is called **Ipo**.

* * * * *

"It grows in desert places, and amid bare hills, and is easily discerned from afar, there being no other tree near it."

* * * * *

—*Rumphii*; *Herbarium Amboinense*, ii. 263–268.

1685.—"I cannot omit to set forth here an account of the poisoned missiles of the

Kingdom of *Macassar*, which the natives of that kingdom have used against our soldiers, bringing them to sudden death. It is extracted from the Journal of the illustrious and gallant admiral, H. Cornelius Spielman. ... The natives of the kingdom in question possess a singular art of shooting arrows by blowing through canes, and wounding with these, insomuch that if the skin be but slightly scratched the wounded die in a twinkling."

(Then the old story of the only antidote)...

The account follows extracted from the Journal.

* * * * *

"There are but few among the Macassars and Bugis who possess the real knowledge needful for selecting the poison, so as to distinguish between what is worthless and what is highest quality. ... From the princes (or Rajas) I have understood that the soil in which the trees affording the poison grow, for a great space round about produces no grass nor any other vegetable growth, and that the poison is properly a water or liquid, flowing from a bruise or cut made in the bark of those trees, oozing out as sap does from plants that afford milky juices. ... When the liquid is being drawn from the wounded tree, no one should carelessly approach it so as to let the liquid touch his hands, for by such contact all the joints become stiffened and contracted. For this reason the collectors make use of long bamboos, armed with sharp iron points. With these they stab the tree with great force, and so get the sap to flow into the canes, in which it speedily hardens."—Dn. Corn. Spielman ... *de Telis deleterio Veneno infectis in* Macassar, *et aliis Regnis Insulae* Celebes; *ex ejus Diario extracta. Huic praemittitur brevis narratio de hac materia Dn.* Andreae Cleyeri. In *Miscellanea Curiosa, sive Ephemeridum. ... Academiae Naturae Curiosorum,* Dec. II. Annus Tertius. Anni MDCLXXXIV., Norimbergae (1685), pp. 127 *seqq.*

1704.—"**Ipo** seu **Hypo** arbor est mediocris, folio parvo, et obscure virenti, quae tam malignae et nocivae qualitatis, ut omne vivens umbrâ suâ interimat, unde narrant in circuitu, et umbrae distinctu, plurima ossium mortuorum hominum animaliumque videri. Circumvicinas etiam plantas enecat, et aves insidentes interficere ferunt, si Nucis Vomicae *Igasur*, plantam non invenerint, qua reperta vita quidem donantur et servantur, sed defluvium patiuntur plumarum. ... **Hypo** lac Indi *Camucones* et *Sambales,* Hispanis infensissimi, longis, excipiunt arundineis perticis, sagittis intoxicandis deservitùrum irremediabile venenum, omnibus aliis alexipharmacis superius, praeterquam stercore humano propinato. An Argensolae *arbor comosa,* quam *Insulae Celebes* ferunt, cujus umbra occidentalis mortifera, orientalis antidotum? ..."—*De Quibusdam Arboribus Venenatis,* in *Herbarum aliarumque Stirpium in Insula Luzone ...* a Revdo Patre Georgio Camello, S.J. *Syllabus ad* Joannem Raium *transmissus.* In Appendix, p. 87, of *Joan. Raii Hist. Plantarum.* Vol. III. (London 1704).

1712.—"Maxima autem celebritas radiculae enata est, ab eximia illa virtute, quam adversus toxicum Macassariense praestat, exitiale illud, et vix alio remedio vincibile. Est venenum hoc succus lacteus et pinguis, qui collegitur ex recens sauciata arbore quadam, indigenes **Ipu**, Malajis Javanisque **Upà** dictâ, in abditis locis sylvarum Insulae Celebes ... crescente ... cujus genuinum et in solâ Macassariâ germinantis succum, qui colligere suscipiunt, praesentissimis vitae periculis se exponant necesse est. Nam ad quaerendam arborem loca dumis beluisque infesta penetranda sunt, inventa vero, nisi eminus vulneretur, et ab eâ parte, a qua ventus adspirat, vel aura incumbit, aggressores erumpento halitu subito suffocabit. Quam sortem etiam experiri dicuntur volucres, arborem recens vulneratam transvolantes. Collectio exitiosi liquoris, morti ob patrata maleficia damnatis committitur, eo pacto, ut poena remittatur, si liquorem reportaverint ... Sylvam ingrediuntur longâ instructi arundine ... quam altera extremitate ... ex asse acuunt, ut ad pertundendam arboris corticem valeat. ... Quam longe possunt, ab arbore constituti, arundinis aciem arbori valide intrudunt, et liquoris, ex vulnere effluentis, tantum excipiunt, quantum arundinis cavo ad proximum usque internodium capi potest. ... Reduces, supplicio et omni discrimine defuncti, hoc vitae suae λυτρον Regi offerunt. Ita narrarunt mihi populares Celebani, hodie Macassari dicti. Quis autem veri quicquam ex Asiaticorum ore referat, quod figmentis non implicatur ...?"—*Kaempfer, Amoen. Exot.*, 575–576.

1726.—"But among all sorts of trees, that occur here, or hereabouts, I know of none more pernicious than the sap of the Macassar Poison tree * * * They say that there are only a few trees of this kind, occuring in the district of *Turatte* on Celebes, and that none are employed except, at a certain time of the year when it is procurable, those who are condemned to death, to approach the trees and bring away the poison. ... The poison must be taken with the greatest care in Bamboos, into which it drips slowly from the bark of the trees, and the persons collected for this purpose must first have their hands, heads, and all exposed parts, well wound round with cloths. ..."—*Valentijn,* iii. 218.

1783.—"The following description of the BOHON **Upas**, or POISON TREE, which grows in the Island of Java, and renders it unwholesome by its noxious vapours, has been procured for the *London Magazine*, from Mr. Heydinger, who was employed to translate it from the original Dutch, by the author, Mr. Foersch, who, we are informed, is at present abroad, in the capacity of surgeon on board an English vessel...

* * * * *

"'In the year 1774, I was stationed at Batavia, as a surgeon, in the service of the Dutch East India Company. During my residence there I received several different accounts of the *Bohon*-**Upas**, and the violent effects of its poison. They all then seemed incredible to me, but raised my curiosity in so high a degree, that I resolved to investigate this subject thoroughly. ... I had procured a recommendation from an old Malayan priest to another priest, who lives on the nearest habitable spot to the tree, which is about fifteen or sixteen miles distant. The letter proved of great service to me on my undertaking, as that priest is employed by the Emperor to reside there, in order to prepare for eternity the souls of those who, for different crimes, are sentenced to approach the tree, and to procure the poison. ... Malefactors, who, for their crimes, are sentenced to die, are the only persons to fetch the poison; and this is the only chance they have of saving their lives. ... They are then provided with a silver or tortoise-shell box, in which they are to put the poisonous gum, and are properly instructed how to proceed, while they are upon their dangerous expedition. Among other particulars, they are always told to attend to the direction of the winds; as they are to go towards the tree before the wind, so that the effluvia from the tree are always blown from them. ... They are afterwards sent to the house of the old priest, to which place they are commonly attended by their friends and relations. Here they generally remain some days, in expectation of a favourable breeze. During that time the ecclesiastic prepares them for their future fate by prayers and admonitions. When the hour of their departure arrives the priest puts them on a long leather cap with two glasses before their eyes, which comes down as far as their breast, and also provides them with a pair of leather gloves...

"The worthy old ecclesiastic has assured me, that during his residence there, for upwards of thirty years, he had dismissed above seven hundred criminals in the manner which I have described; and that scarcely two out of twenty returned," ... &c. &c.—*London Magazine*, Dec. 1783, pp. 512–517.

The paper concludes:

"[We shall be happy to communicate any authentic papers of Mr. Foersch to the public through the London Magazine.]"

1789.—
"No spicy nutmeg scents the vernal gales,
Nor towering plantain shades the midday
  vales,

* * * * *

No step retreating, on the sand impress'd,
Invites the visit of a second guest;

* * * * *

Fierce in dread silence on the blasted heath
Fell **Upas** sits, the Hydra Tree of death;
Lo! from one root, the envenom'd soil below,
A thousand vegetative serpents grow ..." etc.

Darwin, *Loves of the Plants*; in *The Botanic Garden*, Pt. II.

1808.—"*Notice sur le* Pohon **Upas** *ou Arbre à* Poison; *Extrait d'un Voyage inédit dans l'Intérieur de l'Ile de Java, par* L. A. Deschamps, D.M.P., *l'un des compagnons du Voyage du Général d'Entrecasteaux.*

"C'est au fond des sombre forêts de l'ile de Java que la nature a caché le *pohun* **upas**, l'arbre le plus dangereux du règne végétal, pour le poison mortel qu'il renferme, et plus celèbre encore par les fables dont on l'a rendu le sujet. ..."—*Annales des Voyages*, i. 69.

1810.—"Le poison fameux dont se servent les Indiens de l'Archipel des *Moluques*, et des iles de la *Sonde*, connu sous le nom **d'ipo** et **upas**, a interessé plus que tous les autres la curiosité des Européens, parce que les relations qu'on en a donné ont été exagérées et accompagnées de ce merveilleux dont les peuples de l'Inde aiment à orner leurs narrations. ..."—*Leschenault de la Tour*, in Mémoire sur le Strychnos Tieute *et l'*Antiaris toxicaria, *plantes venimeuses de l'Ile de* Java. ... In *Annales du Museum d'Histoire Naturelle*, Tom. XVIième, p. 459.

1813.—"The literary and scientific world has in few instances been more grossly imposed upon than in the account of the *Pohon* **Upas**, published in Holland about the year 1780. The history and origin of this forgery still remains a mystery. Foersch, who put his name to the publication, certainly was ... a surgeon in the Dutch East India Company's service about the time. ... I have been led to suppose that his literary abilities were as mean as his contempt for truth was consummate. Having hastily picked up some vague information regarding the **Oopas**, he carried it to Europe, where his notes were arranged, doubtless by a different hand, in such a form as by their plausibility and appearance of truth, to be generally credited. ... But though the account just mentioned ... has been demonstrated to be an extravagant forgery, the existence of a tree in Java, from whose sap a poison is prepared, equal in fatality, when thrown into the circulation, to the strongest animal poisons hitherto known, is a fact."—*Horsfield*, in *Batavian Trans*. vol. vii. art. x. pp. 2–4.

1822.—"The Law of Java," a Play ... *Scene.* Kérta-Sûra, and a desolate Tract in the Island of Java.

* * * * * *

"Act I. Sc. 2.

Emperor. The haram's laws, which cannot be repealed,
Had not enforced me to pronounce your death,

* * * * * *

One chance, indeed, a slender one, for life,
All criminals may claim.

Parbaya. Aye, I have heard
Of this your cruel mercy;—'tis to seek
That tree of Java, which, for many a mile,
Sheds pestilence;—for where the **Upas** grows
It blasts all vegetation with its own;
And, from its desert confines, e'en those brutes
That haunt the desert most shrink off, and tremble.
Thence if, by miracle, a man condemned
Bring you the poison that the tree exudes,
In which you dip your arrows for the war,
He gains a pardon,—and the palsied wretch
Who scaped the **Upas**, has escaped the tyrant."

* * * * * *

"Act II. Sc. 4.

Pengoose. Finely dismal and romantic, they say, for many miles round the **Upas**; nothing but poisoned air, mountains, and melancholy. A charming country for making *Mems* and *Nota benes!*"

* * * * * *

"Act III. Sc. 1.

Pengoose. ... That's the Divine, I suppose, who starts the poor prisoners, for the last stage to the **Upas tree**; an Indian Ordinary of Newgate.

Servant, your brown Reverence! There's no people in the parish, but, I believe, you are the rector?

(*Writing*). "The reverend Mister Orzinga U.C.J.—The **Upas** Clergyman of Java."

George Colman the Younger.

[1844.—"We landed in the Rajah's boat at the watering place, near the **Upas** tree. ...—Here follows an interesting account by Mr Adams, in which he describes how "the mate, a powerful person and of strong constitution, felt so much stupified as to be compelled to withdraw from his position on the tree."—*Capt. Sir E. Belcher, Narr. of the Voyage of H.M.S. Samarang*, i. 180 *seqq.*]

1868.—"The Church of Ireland offers to us, indeed, a great question, but even that question is but one of a group of questions. There is the Church of Ireland, there is the land of Ireland, there is the education of Ireland ... they are all so many branches from one trunk, and that trunk is the Tree of what is called Protestant ascendancy. ... We therefore aim at the destruction of that system of ascendancy, which, though it has been crippled and curtailed by former measures, yet still must be allowed to exist; it is still there like a tall tree of noxious growth, lifting its head to heaven, and darkening and poisoning the land as far as its shadow can extend; it is still there, gentlemen, and now at length the day has come when, as we hope, the axe has been laid to the root of that tree, and it nods and quivers from its top to its base. ..."—Mr. Gladstone's *Speech at Wigan*, Oct. 23. In this quotation the orator indicates the **Upas tree** without naming it. The name was supplied by some commentators referring to this indication at a later date:

1873.—"It was perfectly certain that a man who possessed a great deal of imagination might, if he stayed out sufficiently long at night, staring at a small star, persuade himself next morning that he had seen a great comet; and it was equally certain that such a man, if he stared long enough at a bush, might persuade himself that he had seen a branch of the **Upas Tree**."—Speech of Lord Edmond Fitzmaurice on the 2nd reading of the University Education (Ireland) Bill, March 3.

"It was to regain office, to satisfy the Irish irreconcilables, to secure the Pope's brass band, and not to pursue 'the glorious traditions of English Liberalism,' that Mr. Gladstone struck his two blows at the **Upas tree**."—Mr. Joseph Chamberlain, in *Fort. Rev.* Sept. pp. 289–90.

1876.—"... the **Upas-tree** superstition."—*Contemp. Rev.* May.

1880.—"Lord Crichton, M.P. ... last night said ... there was one topic which was holding all their minds at present ... what was this conspiracy which, like the **Upas-tree** of fable, was spreading over the land, and poisoning it? ..."—In *St. James's Gazette*, Nov. 11, p. 7.

1885.—"The dread **Upas** dropped its fruits.

"Beneath the shady canopy of this tall fig no native will, if he knows it, dare to rest, nor will he pass between its stem and the wind, so strong is his belief in its evil influence.

"In the centre of a tea estate, not far off from my encampment, stood, because no one could be found daring enough to cut it down, an immense specimen, which had long been a nuisance to the proprietor on account of the lightning every now and then striking off, to the damage of the shrubs below, large branches, which none of his servants could be induced to remove. One day, having been pitchforked together and burned, they were considered disposed of: but next morning the whole of his labourers awoke, to their intense alarm, afflicted with a painful eruption. ... It was then remembered that the smoke of the burning branches had been blown by the wind through the village. ..." (Two Chinamen were engaged to cut down and remove the tree, and did not suffer; it was ascertained that they had smeared their bodies with coco-nut oil.)—*H. O. Forbes, A Naturalist's Wanderings*, 112–113.

[Mr. Bent (*Southern Arabia*, 72, 89) tells a similar story about the collection of frankincense, and suggests that it was based on the custom of employing slaves in this work, and on an interpretation of the name Hadrimaut, said to mean 'valley of death.']

UPPER ROGER, s. This happy example of the Hobson-Jobson dialect occurs in a letter dated 1755, from Capt. Jackson at Syrian in Burma, which is given in Dalrymple's *Oriental Repertory*, i. 192. It is a corruption of the Skt. *yuva-rāja*, 'young King,' the Caesar or Heir-Apparent, a title borrowed from ancient India by most of the Indo-Chinese monarchies, and which we generally render in Siam as the 'Second King.'

URZ, **URZEE**, and vulgarly **URJEE**, s. P.—H. *'arẓ* and *'arẓī*, from Ar. *'arz*, the latter a word having an extraordinary variety of uses even for Arabic. A petition or humble representation either oral or in writing; the technical term for a request from an inferior to a superior; 'a sifflication' as one of Sir Walter Scott's characters calls it. A more elaborate form is *'arẓ-dāsht*, 'memorializing.' This is used in a very barbarous form of Hobson-Jobson below.

1606.—"Every day I went to the Court, and in every eighteen or twentie dayes I put up **Ars** or Petitions, and still he put mee off with good words. ..."—*John Mildenhall*, in *Purchas*, i. (Bk. iii.) 115.

[1614.—"Until Mocrob Chan's **erzedach** or letter came to that purpose it would not be granted."—*Foster, Letters*, ii. 178. In p. 179 "By whom I **erzed** unto the King again."

[1687.—"The **arzdest** with the Estimauze (*Iltimās*, 'humble representation') concerning your twelve articles. ..."—In *Yule, Hedges' Diary*, Hak. Soc. II. lxx.

[1688.—"Capt. Haddock desiered the Agent would write his **arzdost** in answer to the Nabob's Perwanna (**Purwanna**)."—*Ibid.* II. lxxxiii.]

1690.—"We think you should **Urzdaast** the Nabob to writt purposely for yᵉ releasmᵗ of Charles King, it may Induce him to put a great Value on him."—Letter from Factory at Chuttanutte to *Mr. Charles Eyre* at Ballasore, d. November 5 (MS. in India Office).

1782.—"Monsr. de Chemant refuses to write to Hyder by *arzoasht* (read **arzdasht**), and wants to correspond with him in the same manner as Mons. Duplex did with Chanda Sahib; but the Nabob refuses to receive any letter that is not in the stile of an **arzee** or petition."—*India Gazette*, June 22.

c. 1785.—"... they (the troops) constantly applied to our colonel, who for presenting an **arzee** to the King, and getting him to sign it for the passing of an account of 50 lacks, is said to have received six lacks as a reward. ..."—*Carraccioli, Life of Clive*, iii. 155.

1809.—"In the morning ... I was met by a minister of the Rajah of Benares, bearing an **arjee** from his master to me. ..."—*Ld. Valentia*, i. 104.

1817.—"The Governor said the Nabob's Vakeel in the **Arzee** already quoted, directed me to forward to the presence that it was his wish, that your Highness would write a letter to him."—*Mill's Hist.* iv. 436.

V

***VACCINATION**. Vaccine was first imported into Bombay viâ Bussora in 1802. "Since then," says R. Drummond, "the British Governments in Asia have taken great pains to preserve and diffuse this mild instrument of salvation." [Also see *Forbes, Or. Mem.* 2nd ed. ii. 374.]

VAKEEL, s. An attorney; an authorised representative. Arab. *wakīl*.

[c. 1630.—"A Scribe, **Vikeel**."—*Persian Gloss*, in *Sir T. Herbert*, ed. 1677, p. 316.]

1682.—"If Mr. Charnock had taken the paines to present these 2 Perwannas (**Purwanna**) himself, 'tis probable, with a small present, he might have prevailed with Bulchund to have our goods freed. However, at this rate any pitifull **Vekeel** is as good to act yᵉ Company's Service as himself."—*Hedges, Diary*, Dec. 7; [Hak. Soc. i. 54].

[1683.—"... a copy whereof your **Vackel** James Price brought you from Dacca."—In *Yule, ibid.* II. xxiii.]

1691.—"*November* the 1st, arriv'd a **Pattamar** or *Courrier*, from our **Fakeel**, or Sollicitor at Court. ..."—*Ovington*, 415.

1811.—"The Raja has sent two **Vakeels** or ambassadors to meet me here. ..."—*Ld. Minto in India*, 268.

c. 1847.—"If we go into Court I suppose I must employ a **Vehicle**."—Letter from an European subordinate to one of the present writers.

VEDAS. The Sacred Books of the Brahmans, *Veda* being 'knowledge.' Of these books there are nominally four, viz. the *Rig*, *Yajur*, *Sāma* and *Atharva* Vedas.

The earliest direct intimation of knowledge of the existence of the Vedas appears to be in the book called *De Tribus Impostoribus*, said to have been printed in 1598, in which they are mentioned.[1] Possibly this knowledge came through the Arabs. Though thus we do not trace back any direct allusion to the Vedas in European books, beyond the year 1600 or thereabouts, there seems good reason to believe that the Jesuit missionaries had information on the subject at a much earlier date. St. Francis Xavier had frequent discussions with Brahmans, and one went so far as to communicate to him the *mantra "Om śrīnārāyaṇanāmah."* In 1559 a learned Brahman at Goa was converted by Father Belchior Carneyro, and baptized by the name of Manuel. He afterwards (with the Viceroy's sanction!) went by night and robbed a Brahman on the mainland who had collected many MSS., and presented the spoil to the Fathers, with great satisfaction to himself and them (*Sousa*, *Orient. Conquist.* i. 151–2).

It is probable that the information concerning the Hindu religion and sacred books which was attained even in Europe by the end of the 16th century was greater than is commonly supposed, and greater than what we find in print would warrant us to assume. A quotation from San Roman below illustrates this in a general way. And in a constitution of Gregory XV. dated January 31, 1623, there is mention of rites called *Haiteres* and *Tandié*, which doubtless represent the Vedic names *Aitareya* and *Tāṇḍya* (see *Norbert*, i. 39). Lucena's allusion below to the "four parts" of Hindu doctrine must have reference to the Vedas, and his information must have come from reports and letters, as he never was in India. In course of time, however, what had been known seems to have been forgotten, and even Halhed (1776) could write about 'Beids of the Shaster!' (see *Code*, p. xiii.). This shows that though he speaks also of the 'Four Beids' (p. xxxi.) he had no precise knowledge.

In several of the earlier quotations of the word it will be seen that the form used is *Vedam* or *Veidam*. This is the Tamil form. And it became prevalent during the 18th century in France from Voltaire's having constituted himself the advocate of a Sanskrit Poem, called by him *l'Ezour Vedam*, and which had its origin in S. India. This was in reality an imitation of an Indian *Purāna*, composed by some missionary in the 17th century (probably by R. de' Nobili), to introduce Christian doctrines; but Voltaire supposed it to be really an ancient Indian book. Its real character was first explained by Sonnerat (see the Essay by F. W. Ellis, in *As. Res.* xi.). The first information regarding the real Vedas was given by Colebrooke in 1805 (*As. Res.* viii.). Orme and some authors of the 18th and early part of the 19th century write *Bede*, which represents the N. Indian vernacular form *Bed*. Both forms, *Bed* and *Vedam*, are known to Fleury, as we see below.

On the subject of the Vedas, see *Weber's Hist. of Indian Lit.*, *Max Müller's Ancient Sanskrit Lit.*, *Whitney's Oriental and Linguistic Studies*, vol. i. [and *Macdonell's Hist. of Sanskrit Lit.*, pp. 29 *seqq.*].

c. 1590.—"*The Brahmins.* These have properly six duties. 1. The study of the **Bedes.**"—*Ayeen*, by *Gladwin*, ii. 393; [ed. *Jarrett*, iii. 115].

"Philologists are constantly engaged in translating Hindi, Greek, Arabic, and Persian books ... Háj Ibrahím of Sarhind translated into Persian the *At'harban* (*i.e. Atharva* **Veda**) which, according to the Hindus is one of the four divine books."—*Ibid.* by *Blochmann*, i. 104–105.

1600.—"... Consta esta doutrina de quatro partes. ..."—*Lucena V. de P. Franc. Xavier*, 95.

1602.—"These books are divided into bodies,

1 So wrote A. B. I cannot find the book in the B. Museum Library.—*Y.* [A bibliographical account of this book will be found in "*La Traité des Trois Imposteurs, et précédé d'une notice philologique et bibliographique par Philomneste Junior* (*i.e.* Brunet), Paris and Brussels, 1867. Also see 7 Ser. *N. & Q.* viii. 449 *seqq.*; 9 Ser. ix. 55. The passage about the Vedas seems to be the following: "Et Sectarii istorum, ut et *Vedae* et Brachmanorum ante MCCC retro secula obstant collectanea, ut de Sinensibus nil dicam. Tu, qui in angulo Europae hic delitescis, ista neglegis, negas; quam bene videas ipse. Eadem facilitate enim isti tua negant. Et quid non miraculorum superesset ad convincendos orbis incolas, si mundum ex Scorpionis ovo conditum et progenitum terramque Tauri capiti impositam, et rerum prima fundamentis ex prioribus III. Vedae libris constarent, nisi invidus aliquis Deorum filius haec III. prima volumina furatus esset!"]

limbs, and joints; and their foundations are certain books which they call **Vedáos**, which are divided into four parts."—*Couto*, V. vi. 3.

1603.—"Tienen muchos libros, de mucha costa y escriptura, todos llenos de agueros y supersticiones, y de mil fabulas ridiculas que son sus evangelios. ... Todo esto es tan sin fundamento, que algunos libros han llegado a Portugal, que se han traydo de la India, y han venido algunos Iogues que se convertieron à la Fè."—*San Roman, Hist. de la India Oriental*, 47.

1651.—"The **Vedam**, or the Heathen's book of the Law, hath brought great Esteem unto this Tribe (the Bramines)."—*Rogerius*, 3.

c. 1667.—"They say then that God, whom they call *Achar*, that is to say, Immoveable or Immutable, hath sent them four Books which they call **Beths**, a word signifying *Science*, because they pretend that in these Books all Sciences are comprehended. The first of these Books is called *Athenba-(Atherba-)* **bed**, the second *Zagur*-**bed**, the third *Rek*-**bed**, the fourth *Sama*-**bed**."—*Bernier*, E.T. 104; [ed. *Constable*, 325].

1672.—"Commanda primieramente il **Veda** (che è tutto il fondamento della loro fede) l'adoratione degli Idoli."—*P. Vincenzo*, 313.

"Diese vier Theile ihres **Vedam** oder" Gesetzbuchs werden genant *Roggo* **Vedam**, *Jadura* **Vedam**, *Sama* **Vedam**, und *Tarawana* **Vedam**. ..."—*Baldaeus*, 556.

1689.—"Il reste maintenant à examiner sur quelles preuves les Siamois ajoutent foi à leur Bali, les Indiens à leur **Beth** ou **Vedam**, les Musulmans à leur Alcoran."—*Fleury*, in *Lett. Edif.* xxv. 65.

1726.—"Above all it would be a matter of general utility to the Coast that some more chaplains should be maintained there for the sole purpose of studying the Sanskrits tongue (*de Sanskritse taal*), the head and mother tongue of most eastern languages, and once for all to make a translation of the **Vedam**, or Lawbook of the Heathen (which is followed not only by the Heathen on this Coast, but also, in whole or in part, in Ceylon, Malabar, Bengal, Surat, and other neighbouring Kingdoms), and thereby to give such preachers further facilities for the more powerful conviction of the Heathen here and elsewhere, on their own ground, and for the disclosure of many mysteries and other matters, with which we are now unacquainted. ... This Lawbook of the Heathen, called the **Vedam**, had in the very old times 4 parts, though one of these is now lost. ... These parts were named *Roggo* **Vedam**, *Sadura* or *Issoure* **Vedam**, *Sama* **Vedam**, and *Tarawana* or *Adderawana* **Vedam**."—*Valentijn, Keurlijke Beschryving van Choromandel*, in his *East Indies*, v. pp. 72–73.

1745.—"Je commençais à douter si nous n'avions point été trompés par ceux qui nous avoient donné l'explication de ces cérémonies qu'ils nous avoient assurés être très-conformes à leur **Vedam**, c'est à dire au Livre de leur loi."—*Norbert*, iii. 132.

c. 1760.—"**Vedam**—s.m. *Hist. Superst.* C'est un livre pour qui les Brames ou Nations idolâtres de l'Indostan ont la plus grande vénération ... en effet, on assure que le **Vedam** est écrit dans une langue beaucoup plus ancienne que le *Sanskrit*, qui est la langue savante, connue des bramines. Le mot **Vedam** signifie science."—*Encylopédie*, xxx. 32. This information was taken from a letter by Père Calmette, S.J. (see *Lett. Edif.*), who anticipated Max Müller's chronological system of Vedic literature, in his statement that some parts of the *Veda* are at least 500 years later than others.

1765.—"If we compare the great purity and chaste manners of the Shastah (**Shaster**), with the great absurdities and impurities of the **Viedam**, we need not hesitate to pronounce the latter a corruption of the former."—*J. Z. Holwell, Interesting Hist. Events*, &c., 2nd ed. i. 12. This gentleman also talks of the **Bhades** and the **Viedam** in the same line without a notion that the word was the same (see *ibid.* Pt. ii. 15, 1767).

c. 1770.—"The Bramin, bursting into tears, promised to pardon him on condition that he should swear never to translate the **Bedas** or sacred volumes. ... From the Ganges to the Indus the **Vedam** is universally received as the book that contains the principles of religion."—*Raynal*, tr. 1777, i. 41–42.

c. 1774.—"Si crede poi como infallibile che dai quattro suddette **Bed**, che in Malabar chiamano **Vedam**, Bramah medesimo ne retirasse sei *Sastrah*, cioè scienze."—*Della Tomba*, 102.

1777.—"The word **Vēd**, or **Vēdă**, signifies Knowledge or Science. The sacred writings of the Hindoos are so distinguished, of which there are four books."—*C. Wilkins*, in his *Hĕĕtopădēs*, 298.

1778.—"The natives of Bengal derive their religion from a Code called the **Shaster**, which they assert to be the genuine scripture of Bramah, in preference to the **Vedam**."—*Orme*, ed. 1803, ii. 5.

1778.—

"Ein indischer Brahman, geboren auf der Flur,
Der nichts gelesen als den **Weda** der Natur."
Rückert, Weisheit der Bramanen, i. 1.

1782.—"... pour les rendre (les *Pouranons*) plus authentiques, ils ajoutèrent qu'ils étoient tirés du **Védam**; ce que n'étoit pas facile à vérifier, puisque depuis très long-tems les Védams ne sont plus connus."—*Sonnerat*, ii. 21.

1789.—

"Then Edmund begg'd his Rev'rend Master

T'instruct him in the *Holy* **Shaster**.
No sooner does the Scholar ask,
Than *Goonisham* begins the task,
Without a book he glibly reads
Four of his own invented **Bedes**."
Simpkin the Second, 145.

1791.—"Toute verité ... est renfermée dans les quatre **beths**."—*St. Pierre, Chaumière Indienne.*

1794–97.—"... or Hindoo **Vedas** taught."
Pursuits of Literature, 6th ed. 359.

VERANDA, s. An open pillared gallery round a house. This is one of the very perplexing words for which at least two origins may be maintained, on grounds equally plausible. Besides these two, which we shall immediately mention, a third has sometimes been alleged, which is thus put forward by a well-known French scholar:

"Ce mot (**véranda**) n'est lui-méme qu'une transcription inexacte du Persan *beramada*, perche, terrasse, balcon."—*C. Defrémery*, in *Revue Critique*, 1869, 1st Sem. p. 64.

Plausible as this is, it may be rejected. Is it not, however, possible that *barāmada*, the literal meaning of which is 'coming forward, projecting,' may be a Persian 'striving after meaning,' in explanation of the foreign word which they may have borrowed?

Williams, again, in his Skt. Dict. (1872) gives '*varaṇḍa* ... a veranda, a portico. ...' Moreover Beames in his *Comparative Grammar of Modern Aryan Languages*, gives Sansk. *baraṇḍa*, 'portico,' Bengali *bārāṇḍā*, Hind. *varaṇḍā*, adding: "Most of our wiseacre *literateurs* (qu. *littérateurs*?) in Hindustan now-a-days consider this word to be derived from Pers. *barāmadah*, and write it accordingly. It is, however, good Sanskrit" (i. 153). Fortunately we have in Bishop Caldwell a proof that comparative grammar does not preclude good manners. Mr. Beames was evidently in entire ignorance of the facts which render the origin of the Anglo-Indian word so curiously ambiguous; but we shall *not* call him the "wise-acre grammarian." *Varaṇḍa*, with the meaning in question, does not, it may be observed, belong to the older Sanskrit, but is only found in comparatively modern works.[1]

Littré also gives as follows (1874): "Etym. *Verandah*, mot rapporté de l'Inde par les Anglais, est la simple dégénérescence, dans les langues modernes de l'Inde, du Sansc. *veranda*, colonnade, de *var*, couvrir."

1 This last remark is due to A. B.

That the word as used in England and in France was brought by the English from India need not be doubted. But either in the same sense, or in one closely analogous, it appears to have existed, quite independently, in Portuguese and Spanish; and the manner in which it occurs without explanation in the very earliest narrative of the adventure of the Portuguese in India, as quoted below, seems almost to preclude the possibility of their having learned it in that country for the first time; whilst its occurrence in P. de Alcala can leave no doubt on the subject. [Prof. Skeat says: "If of native Span. origin, it may be Span. *vara* a rod, rail. Cf. L. *uarus*, crooked" (*Concise Dict.* s.v.).]

1498.—"E vêo ter comnosco onde estavamos lançados, em huma **varanda** onde estava hum grande castiçall d'arame que nos alumeava."—*Roteiro da Viagem de Vasco da Gama*, 2nd ed., 1861, p. 62, *i.e.* "... and came to join us where we had been put in a **varanda**, where there was a great candlestick of brass that gave us light. ..." And Correa, speaking of the same historical passage, though writing at a later date, says: "When the Captain-Major arrived, he was conducted through many courts and **verandas** (*muitos pateos e* **varandas**) to a dwelling opposite that in which the king was. ..."—*Correa*, by *Stanley*, 193, compared with original *Lendas*, I. i. 98.

1505.—In Pedro de Alcala's Spanish-Arabic Vocabulary we have:

"**Varandas**—*Târbuç*.
Varandas assi *çârgaba, çârgab*."

Interpreting these Arabic words, with the assistance of Prof. Robertson Smith, we find that *târbuç* is, according to Dozy (*Suppt.* I. 430), *darbūz*, itself taken from *darābazīn* (τραπέζιον), 'a stair-railing, fireguard, balcony, &c.'; whilst *çârgab* stands for *sarjab*, a variant (*Abul W.*, p. 735, i.) of the commoner *sharjab*, 'a lattice, or anything latticed,' such as a window,—'a balcony, a balustrade.'

1540.—"This said, we entred with her into an outward court, all about invironed with Galleries (*cercado a roda de duas ordens de* **varandas**) as if it had been a Cloister of Religious persons. ..."—*Pinto* (orig. cap. lxxxiii.), in *Cogan*, 102.

1553 (but relating events of 1511).

"... assentou Affonso d'Alboquerque com elles, que primeiro que sahissem em terra, item ao seguinte dia, quando agua estivesse estofa, dez bateis a queimar alguns baileus, que são como **varandas** sobre o mar."—*Barros*, II. vi. 3.

1563.—"*R.* ... nevertheless tell me what the tree is like. *O.* From this **varanda** you can see the trees in my garden: those little ones have been planted two years, and in four they give excellent fruit. ..."—*Garcia*, f. 112.

1602.—"De maneira, que quando ja El Rey (de Pegu) chegava, tinha huns formosos Pacos de muitas camaras, **varandas**, retretes, cozinhas, em que se recolhia com suas mulheres. ..."—*Couto*, Dec. vi. Liv. vii., cap. viii.

1611.—"**Varanda.** Lo entreado de los corridores, por ser como varas, per otro nombre vareastes quasi varafustes."—*Cobarruvias.*

1631.—In Haex, Malay-Latin Vocabulary, we have as a *Malay* word, "**Baranda,** Contignatio vel Solarium."

1644.—"The fort (at Cochin) has not now the form of a fortress, consisting all of houses; that in which the captain lives has a **Varanda** fronting the river, 15 paces long and 7 wide. ..."—*Bocarro*, MS. f. 313.

1710.—"There are not wanting in Cambaya great buildings with their courts, **varandas**, and chambers."—*De Sousa, Oriente Conquist.* ii. 152.

1711.—"The Building is very ancient . . and has a paved Court, two large **Verandas** or Piazzas."—*Lockyer*, 20.

c. 1714.—"**Varanda.** Obra sacada do corpo do edificio, cuberta o descuberta, na qual se costuma passear, tomar o sol, o fresco, &c. *Pergula.*"—*Bluteau*, s.v.

1729.—"**Baranda.** Especie de corredor o balaustrada que ordinariamente se colocà debante de los altares o escaléras, compuesta de balaustres de hierro, bronce, madera, o otra materia, de la altura de un medio cuerpo, y su uso es para adorno y reparo. Algunos escriven esta voce con *b.* Lat. Peribolus, Lorica clathrata."—*Golis, Hist. de Nueva España*, lib. 3, cap. 15. "Alajá-base la pieza por la mitad con un **baranda** o biombo que sin impedir la vista señalava termino al concorso."—*Dicc. de la Ling. Cast. por la R. Acad.*

1754.—Ives, in describing the Cave of Elephanta, speaks twice of "the **voranda** or open gallery."—p. 45.

1756.—"... as soon as it was dark, we were all, without distinction, directed by the guard set over us to collect ourselves into one body, and sit down quietly under the arched **Veranda**, or Piazza, to the west of the Black-hole prison. ..."—*Holwell's Narr. of the Black Hole* [p. 3]; [in *Wheeler, Early Records*, 229].

c. 1760.—"... Small ranges of pillars that support a pent-house or shed, forming what is called, in the Portuguese linguafranca, **Verandas.**"—*Grose*, i. 53.

1781.—"On met sur le devant une petite galerie appellée **varangue**, et formée par le toit."—*Sonnerat*, i. 54. There is a French nautical term, *varangue*, 'the ribs or floor-timbers of a ship,' which seems to have led this writer astray here.

1783.—"You are conducted by a pretty steep ascent up the side of a rock, to the door of the cave, which enters from the North. By it you are led first of all into a **feerandah**(!) or piazza which extends from East to West 60 feet."—*Acct. of some Artificial Caves in the Neighbourhood of Bombay* (Elephanta), by *Mr. W. Hunter*, Surgeon in the E. Indies. In *Archaeologia*, vii. 287.

"The other gate leads to what in this country is called a **veranda** or **feranda** (printed *seranda*), which is a kind of piazza or landing-place before you enter the hall."—*Letter* (on Caves of Elephanta, &c.), from *Hector Macneil*, Esq., *ibid.* viii. 254.

1796.—"... Before the lowest (storey) there is generally a small hall supported by pillars of teka (**Teak**) wood, which is of a yellow colour and exceedingly hard. This hall is called **varanda**, and supplies the place of a parlour."—*Fra Paolino*, E.T.

1809.—"In the same **verandah** are figures of natives of every cast and profession."—*Ld. Valentia*, i. 424.

1810.—"The **viranda** keeps off the too great glare of the sun, and affords a dry walk during the rainy season."—*Maria Graham*, 21.

c. 1816.—"... and when Sergeant Browne bethought himself of Mary, and looked to see where she was, she was conversing up and down the **verandah**, though it was Sunday, with most of the rude boys and girls of the barracks."—*Mrs. Sherwood's Stories*, p. 47, ed. 1873.

VIZIER, WUZEER, s. Ar.—H. *wazīr*, 'a minister,' and usually the principal minister, under a (Mahommedan) prince. [In the Koran (cap. xx. 30) Moses says: "Give a **wazir** of my family, Harūn (Aaron) my brother." In the *Āin* we have a distinction drawn between the *Vakīl*, or prime minister, and the *Vazīr*, or minister of finance (ed. *Blochmann*, i. 527).] In India the Nawāb of Oudh was long known as the Nawāb Wazīr, the founder of the quasi-independent dynasty having been Sa'ādat'Alī Khān, who became Sūbadār of Oudh c. 1732, and was also Wazīr of the Empire, a title which became hereditary in his family. The title of Nawāb Wazīr merged in that of *pādshāh*, or King, assumed by Ghāzī-ud-dīn Haidar in 1820, and up to his death still borne or claimed by the ex-King Wājíd 'Alī Shāh, under surveillance in Calcutta. As most titles degenerate, *Wazīr* has in Spain become *alguazil*, 'a constable,' in Port. *alvasil*, 'an alderman.'

[1612.—"Jeffer Basha **Vizier** and Viceroy of the Province."—*Danvers, Letters*, i. 173.]

1614.—"Il primo **visir**, sopra ogni altro, che era allora Nasuh bascià, genero del Gran Signore, venne ultimo di tutti, con grandissima e ben adorna cavalcata, enfin della quale andava egli solo con molta gravita."—*P. della Valle* (from Constantinople), i. 43.

W

WHISTLING TEAL, s. This in Jerdon is given as *Dendrocygna Awsuree* of Sykes. Latin names given to birds and beasts might at least fulfil one object of Latin names, in being intelligible and pronounceable by foreign nations. We have seldom met with a more barbarous combination of impossible words than this. A numerous flock of these whistlers is sometimes seen in Bengal sitting in a tree, a curious habit for ducks.

WHITE JACKET, s. The old custom in the hot weather, in the family or at bachelor parties, was to wear this at dinner; and one or more dozens of white jackets were a regular item in an Indian outfit. They are now, we believe, altogether, and for many years obsolete. [They certainly came again into common use some 20 years ago.] But though one reads under every generation of British India that they had gone out of use, they did actually survive to the middle of the last century, for I can remember a white-jacket dinner in Fort William in 1849. [The late Mr. Bridgman of Gorakhpur, whose recollection of India dated from the earlier part of the last century told me that in his younger days the rule at Calcutta was that the guest always arrived at his host's house in the full evening-dress of the time, on which his host meeting him at the door expressed his regret that he had not chosen a cooler dress; on which the guest's Bearer always, as if by accident, appeared from round the corner with a nankeen jacket, which was then and there put on. But it would have been opposed to etiquette for the guest to appear in such a dress without express invitation.]

1803.—"It was formerly the fashion for gentlemen to dress in **white jackets** on all occasions, which were well suited to the country, but being thought too much an undress for public occasions, they are now laid aside for English cloth."—*Ld. Valentia*, i. 240.

[c. 1848.—"... **a white jacket** being evening dress for a dinner-party. ..."—*Berncastle, Voyage to China, including a Visit to the Bombay Pres.* i. 93.]

WINTER, s. This term is constantly applied by the old writers to the *rainy season*, a usage now quite unknown to Anglo-Indians. It may have originated in the fact that winter is in many parts of the Mediterranean coast so frequently a season of rain, whilst rain is rare in summer. Compare the fact that *shitā* in Arabic is indifferently 'winter,' or 'rain'; the winter season being the rainy season. *Shitā* is the same word that appears in *Canticles* ii. 11: "The winter (*sethāv*) is past, the rain is over and gone."

1513.—"And so they set out, and they arrived at Surat (*Çurrate*) in May, when the **winter** had already begun, so they went into **winter**-quarters (*polo que envernarão*), and in September, when the **winter** was over, they went to Goa in two foists and other vessels, and in one of these was the ganda (rhinoceros), the sight of which made a great commotion when landed at Goa. ..."—*Correa*, ii. 373.

1563.—"*R.* ... In what time of the year does this disease (*morxi*, **Mort-de-chien**) mostly occur?

"*O.* ... It occurs mostly in June and July (which is the **winter**-time in this country). ..."—*Garcia*, f. 76*y*.

c. 1567.—"Da Bezeneger a Goa sono d'estate otto giornate di viaggio: ma noi lo facessimo di mezo **l'inverno**, il mese de Luglio."—*Cesare Federici*, in *Ramusio*, iii. 389.

1583.—"Il **uerno** in questo paese è il Maggio, Giugno, Luglio e Agosto, e il resto dell' anno è state. Ma bene è da notare che qui la stagione nõ si può chiamar **uerno** rispetto al freddo, che nõ vi regna mai, mà solo per cagione de' venti, e delle gran pioggie. ..."—*Gasparo Balbi*, f. 67*v*.

1584.—"Note that the Citie of Goa is the principall place of all the Oriental India, and the **winter** thus beginneth the 15 of May, with very great raine."—*Barret*, in *Hakl.* ii. 413.

1610.—"The **Winter** heere beginneth about the first of Iune and dureth till the twentieth of September, but not with continuall raines as at Goa, but for some sixe or seuen dayes every change and full, with much wind, thunder and raine."—*Finch*, in *Purchas*, i. 423.

c. 1610.—"**L'hyver** commence au mois d'Avril, et dure six mois."—*Pyrard de Lacal*, i. 78: [Hak. Soc. i. 104, and see i. 64, ii. 34].

1643.—"... des Galiottes (qui sortent tous les ans pour faire la guerre aux Malabares ... et cela est enuiron la May-Septembre, lors que leur **hyuer** est passé. ..."—*Mocquet*, 347.

1653.—"Dans les Indes il y a deux Estez et deux **Hyuers**, ou pour mieux dire vn Printemps perpetuel, parce que les arbres y sont tousiours verds: Le premier Esté commance au mois de Mars, et finit au mois de May, que est la commancement de l'**hyuer** de pluye, qui continue iusques en Septembre pleuuant incessament ces quatre mois, en sorte que les Karauanes, ny les Patmars ne vont ne viennent: i'ay esté quarante iours sans pouuoir sortir de la maison. ... Le second Esté est depuis Octobre iusques en Decembre, au quel mois il commance à faire froid ... ce froid est le second **Hyuer** qui finit au mois de Mars."—*De la Boullaye-le-Gouz*, ed. 1657, p. 244–245.

1665.—"**L'Hyver** se sait sentir. El commença en Juin per quantité de pluies et de tonneres."—*Thevenot*, v. 311.

1678.—"... In **Winter** (when they rarely stir) they have a *Mumjama*, or Wax Cloth to throw over it. ..."—*Fryer*, 410.

1691.—"In orâ Occidentali, quae *Malabarorum* est, **hyems** â mense Aprili in Septembrem usque dominatur: in littore verò Orientali, quod Hollandi de Kust van Choromandel, *Oram Coromandellae* vocant trans illos montes, in iisdem latitudinis gradibus, contrariô planè modô â Septembri usque ad Aprilem **hyemem** habent."—*Iobi Lusdofi*, ad suam Historiam *Commentarius*, 101.

1770.—"The mere breadth of these mountains divides summer from winter, that is to say, the season of fine weather from the rainy ... all that is meant by **winter** in India is the time of the year when the clouds ... are driven violently by the winds against the mountains," &c.—*Raynal*, tr. 1777, i. 34.

WRITER, s.

(**a**). The rank and style of the junior grade of covenanted civil servants of the E.I. Company. Technically it has been obsolete since the abolition of the old grades in 1833. The term no doubt originally described the duty of these young men; they were the clerks of the factories.

(**b**). A copying clerk in an office, native or European.

a.—

1673.—"The whole Mass of the Company's Servants may be comprehended in those Classes, viz., Merchants, Factors, and **Writers**."—*Fryer*, 84.

[1675-6.—See under FACTOR.]

1676.—"There are some of the **Writers** who by their lives are not a little scandalous."—*Letter from a Chaplain*, in *Wheeler*, i. 64.

1683.—"Mr. Richard More, one that came out a **Writer** on y[e] *Herbert*, left this World for a better. Y[e] Lord prepare us all to follow him!"—*Hedges*, *Diary*, Aug.22; [Hak. Soc. i. 105].

1747.—"82. Mr. ROBERT CLIVE, Writer in the Service, being of a Martial Disposition, and having acted as a Volunteer in our late Engagements, We have granted him an Ensign's Commission, upon his Application for the same."—Letter from the *Council at Ft. St. David* to the *Honble. Court of Directors*, dd. 2d. May, 1747 (MS. in India Office).

1758.—"As we are sensible that our junior servants of the rank of **Writers** at Bengal are not upon the whole on so good a footing as elsewhere, we do hereby direct that the future appointments to a **Writer** for salary, diet money, and all allowances whatever, be 400 Rupees per annum, which mark of our favour and attention, properly attended to, must prevent their reflections on what we shall further order in regard to them as having any other object or foundation than their particular interest and happiness."—*Court's Letter*, March 3, in *Long*, 129. (The 'further order' is the prohibition of *palankins*, &c.—see PALANKEEN.)

c. 1760.—"It was in the station of a covenant servant and **writer**, to the East India Company, that in the month of March, 1750, I embarked."—*Grose*, i. 1.

1762.—"We are well assured that one great reason of the **Writers** neglecting the Company's business is engaging too soon in trade. ... We therefore positively order that none of the **Writers** on your establishment have the benefit or liberty of Dusticks (see DUSTUCK) until the times of their respective writerships are expired, and they commence **Factors**, with this exception. ..."—*Court's Letter*, Dec. 17, in *Long*, 287.

1765.—"Having obtained the appointment of a **Writer** in the East India Company's service at Bombay, I embarked with 14 other passengers ... before I had attained my sixteenth year."—*Forbes*, *Or. Mem.* i. 5; [2nd ed. i. 1].

1769.—"The **Writers** of Madras are exceedingly proud, and have the knack of forgetting their old acquaintances."—*Ld. Teignmouth*, *Mem.* i. 20.

1788.—"In the first place all the persons who go abroad in the Company's civil service, enter as clerks in the counting-house, and are called by a name to correspond with it, **Writers**. In that condition they are obliged to serve five years."—*Burke*, *Speech on Hastings' Impeachment*, Feb. 1788. In *Works*, vii. 292.

b.—

1764.—"*Resolutions and orders.*—That no **Moonshee**, **Linguist**, Banian (see BANYAN), or **Writer** be allowed to any officer except the

Commander-in-Chief and the commanders of detachments. ..."—*Ft. William Consns.* In *Long*, 382.

[1860.—"Following him are the krānees (see **CRANNY**), or **writers**, on salaries varying, according to their duties and abilities, from five to thirty roopees."—*Grant, Rural L. in Bengal*, 138–9.]

Y

YAK, s. The Tibetan ox (*Bos grunniens*, L., *Poëphagus* of Gray), belonging to the Bisontine group of *Bovinae*. It is spoken of in Bogle's Journal under the odd name of the "cow-tailed cow," which is a literal sort of translation of the Hind. name *chāorī gāo*, *chāorīs* (see **CHOWRY**), having been usually called "cow-tails" in the 18th century. [The usual native name for the beast in N. India is *suragā'o*, which comes from Skt. *surabhi*, 'pleasing.'] The name **yak** does not appear in Buffon, who calls it the 'Tartarian cow,' nor is it found in the 3rd ed. of Pennant's *H. of Quadrupeds* (1793), though there is a fair account of the animal as *Bos grunniens* of Lin, and a poor engraving. Although the word occurs in Della Penna's account of Tibet, written in 1730, as quoted below, its first appearance in print was, as far as we can ascertain, in Turner's *Mission to Tibet*. It is the Tib. *gYak*, Jäsche's Dict. *gyag*. The animal is mentioned twice, though in a confused and inaccurate manner, by Aelian; and somewhat more correctly by Cosmas. Both have got the same fable about it. It is in medieval times described by Rubruk. The domestic yak is in Tibet the ordinary beast of burden, and is much ridden. Its hair is woven into tents, and spun into ropes; its milk a staple of diet, and its dung of fuel. The wild yak is a magnificent animal, standing sometimes 18 hands high, and weighing 1600 to 1800 lbs., and multiplies to an astonishing extent on the high plateaux of Tibet. The use of the tame yak extends from the highlands of Khokand to Kuku-khotan or Kwei-hwaching, near the great northern bend of the Yellow River.

c. A.D. 250.—"The Indians (at times) carry as presents to their King tame tigers, trained panthers, four-horned oryxes, and cattle of two different races, one kind of great swiftness, and another kind that are terribly wild, that kind of cattle from (the tails of) which they make fly-flaps. ..."—*Aelian, de Animalibus*, xv. cap. 14.

Again:

"There is in India a grass-eating[1] animal, which is double the size of the horse, and which has a very bushy tail very black in colour.[2] The hairs of the tail are finer than human hair, and the Indian women set great store by its possession. ... When it perceives that it is on the point of being caught, it hides its tail in some thicket ... and thinks that since its tail is not seen, it will not be regarded as of any value, for it knows that the tail is the great object of fancy."—*Ibid.* xvi. 11.

c. 545.—"This Wild Ox is a great beast of India, and from it is got the thing called *Tupha*, with which officers in the field adorn their horses and pennons. They tell of this beast that if its tail catches in a tree he will not budge but stands stock-still, being horribly vexed at losing a single hair of its tail; so the natives come and cut his tail off, and then when he has lost it altogether, he makes his escape."—*Cosmas Indicopleustes*, Bk. xi. Transl. in *Cathay*, &c., p. clxxiv.

[c. 1590.—In a list of things imported from the "northern mountains" into Oudh, we have "tails of the *Kutās* cow."—*Āīn*, ed. *Jarrett*, ii. 172; and see 280.]

1730.—"Dopo di che per circa 40 giorni di camino non si trova più abitazioni di case, ma solo alcune tende con quantità di mandre di **Iak**, ossiano bovi pelosi, pecore, cavalli. ..."—*Fra Orazio della Penna di Billi, Breve Notizia del Thibet* (published by Klaproth in *Journ. As.* 2d. ser.) p. 17.

1783.—"... on the opposite side saw several of the black chowry-tailed cattle. ... This very singular and curious animal deserves a particular description. ... The **Yak** of Tartary, called *Soora Goy* in Hindostan. ..."—*Turner's Embassy* (pubd. 1800), 185–6. [Sir H. Yule identifies *Soora Goy* with *Ch'āorī Gāī*; but, as will be seen above, the H. name is *surāgāo*.]

In the publication at the latter date appears the excellent plate after Stubbs, called "the **Yak** *of Tartary*," still the standard representation of the animal. [Also see Turner's paper (1794) in the *As. Res.*, London reprint of 1798, iv. 365 *seqq.*]

Though the two following quotations from Abbé Hue do not contain the word *yak*, they are pictures by that clever artist which we can hardly omit to reproduce:

1851.—"Les bœufs à long poils étaient de véritables caricatures; impossible de figurer rien de plus drôle; ils marchaient les jambes

1 Ποηφάγος, whence no doubt Gray took his name for the genus.

2 The tails usually brought for sale are those of the tame Yak, and are *white*. The tail of the wild Yak is black, and of much greater size.

écartées, et portaient péniblement un énorme système de stalactites, quí leur pendaient sous le ventre jusqu'à terre. Ces pauvres bêtes étaient si informes et tellement recouvertes de glaçons qu'il semblait qu'on les eût mis confire dans du sucre candi."—*Huc et Gabet, Souvenirs d'un Voyage*, &c. ii. 201; [E.T. ii. 108].

"Au moment où nous passâmes le Mouroui Oussou sur la glace, un spectacle assez bizarre s'offrit à nos yeux. Déjà nous avions remarqué de loin ... des objets informes et noirâtres rangés en file en travers de ce grand fleuve. ... Ce fut seulement quand nous fûmes tout près, que nous pûmes reconnaître plus de 50 bœufs sauvages incrustés dans la glace. Ils avaient voulu, sans doute, traverser le fleuve à la nage, au moment de la concrétion des eaux, et ils s'étaient trouvés pris par les glaçons sans avoir la force de s'en débarrasser et de continuer leur route. Leur belle tête, surmontée de grandes cornes, était encore à découvert; mais la reste du corps était pris dans la glace, qui était si transparente qu'on pouvait distinguer facilement la position de ces imprudentes bêtes; on eût dit qu'elles étaient encore à nager. Les aigles et les corbeaux leur avaient arraché les yeux."—*Ibid.* ii. 219; [E.T. ii. 119 *seq.* and for a further account of the animal see ii. 81].

Z

ZEMINDAR, s. Pers. *zamīn-dār*, 'landholder.' One holding land on which he pays revenue to the Government direct, and not to any intermediate superior. In Bengal Proper the zemindars hold generally considerable tracts, on a permanent settlement of the amount to be paid to Government. In the N.W. Provinces there are often a great many zemindars in a village, holding by a common settlement, periodically renewable. In the N.W. Provinces the rustic pronunciation of the word *zamīndār* is hardly distinguishable from the ordinary Anglo-Indian pronunciation of *jama'-dār* (see JEMADAR), and the form given to *zamīndār* in early English records shows that this pronunciation prevailed in Bengal more than two centuries ago.

1683.—"We lay at Bogatchera, a very pleasant and delightfull Country, ye **Gemidar** invited us ashore, and showed us Store of Deer, Peacocks, &c., but it was not our good fortune to get any of them."—*Hedges, Diary*, April 11; [Hak. Soc. i. 77, also i. 89].

[1686.—"He has ordered downe 300 horse under the conduct of three **Jemidars**."—In ditto, II. lvi.]

1697.—"Having tried all means with the **Jemidar** of the Country adjacent to us to let us have the town of *De Calcutta* at the usual Hire or Rent, rather than fail, having promised him ¼ Part more than the Place at present brings him in, and all to no Purpose, he making frivolous and idle Objections, that he will not let us have any Part of the Country in the Right Honourable Company's name, but that we might have it to our use in any of the Natives Names; the Reason he gives for it is, that the Place will be wholly lost to him—that we are a Powerful People—and that he cannot be possessed of his Country again when he sees Occasion—whereas he can take it from any of the Natives that rent any Part of his Country at his Pleasure.

* * * * *

October 31st, 1698. "The Prince having given us the three towns adjacent to our Settlement, viz. *De Calcutta, Chutanutte*, and *Gobinpore*, or more properly may be said the **Jemmidarship** of the said towns, paying the said Rent to the King as the **Jemidars** have successively done, and at the same time ordering the **Jemmidar** of the said towns to make over their Right and Title to the English upon their paying to the **Jemidar(s)** One thousand Rupees for the same, it was agreed that the Money should be paid, being the best Money that ever was spent for so great a Privilege; but the **Jemmidar(s)** making a great Noise, being unwilling to part with their Countrey ... and finding them to continue in their averseness, notwithstanding the Prince had an officer upon them to bring them to a Compliance, it is agreed that 1,500 Rupees be paid them, provided they will relinquish their title to the said towns, and give it under their Hands in Writing, that they have made over the same to the Right Honourable Company."—*Ext of Consns. at Chuttanutte*, the 29th December (Printed for Parliament in 1788).

In the preceding extracts the *De* prefixed to Calcutta is Pers. *deh.* 'village,' or 'township,' a common term in the language of Indian Revenue administration. An 'Explanation of Terms' furnished by W. Hastings to the Fort William Council in 1759 thus explains the word: "**Deeh**—the ancient limits of any village or parish. Thus, '**Deeh** Calcutta' means only that part which was originally inhabited."—(In *Long*, p. 176.)

1707-8.—In a "List of Men's Names, &c., immediately in the Service of the Hon[ble] Vnited Comp[y]. in their Factory of Fort William, Bengal * * * *

New Co. 1707/8

* * * *

Mr. William Bugden ... **Jemidar** or
* * rent gatherer.

1713. * *
Mr. Edward Page ... **Jemendar.**"
MS. Records in India Office.

1762.—"One of the articles of the Treaty with Meer Jaffier says the Company shall enjoy the **Zemidary** of the Lands from Calcutta down to Culpee, they paying what is paid in the King's Books."—*Holograph* (unpublished) *Letter of Ld. Clive*, in India Office Records, *dated* Berkeley Square, Jan. 21.

1776.—"The Countrey **Jemitdars** remote from Calcutta, treat us frequently with great Insolence; and I was obliged to retreat with only an officer and 17 Sepoys near 6 Miles in the face of 3 or 400 Burgundasses, who lined the Woods and Kept a straggling Fire all y[e] Way."—*MS. Letter of Major James Rennell*, dd. August 5.

1778.—"This avaricious disposition the English plied with presents, which in 1698 obtained his permission to purchase from the **Zemindar**, or Indian proprietor, the town of Sootanutty, Calcutta and Govindpore."—*Orme*, ii. 17.

1809.—"It is impossible for a province to be in a more flourishing state: and I must, in a great degree, attribute this to the total absence of **zemindars**."—*Ld. Valentia*, i. 456. He means *zemindars* of the Bengal description.

1812.—"... the **Zemindars**, or hereditary Superintendents of Land."—*Fifth Report*, 13.

[1818.—"The Bengal farmers, according to some, are the tenants of the Honourable Company; according to others, of the **Jumidarus**, or land-holders."—*Ward, Hindoos*, i. 74.]

1822.—"Lord Cornwallis's system was commended in Lord Wellesley's time for some of its parts, which we now acknowledge to be the most defective. Surely you will not say it has no defects. The one I chiefly alluded to was its leaving the ryots at the mercy of the **zemindars**."—*Elphinstone*, in *Life*, ii. 182.

1843.—"Our plain clothing commands far more reverence than all the jewels which the most tawdry **Zemindar** wears."—*Macaulay, Speech on Gates of Somnauth.*

1871.—"The **Zemindars** of Lower Bengal, the landed proprietary established by Lord Cornwallis, have the worst reputation as landlords, and appear to have frequently deserved it."—*Maine, Village Communities*, 163.

***ZENANA**, s. Pers. *zanāna*, from *zan*, 'woman'; the apartments of a house in which the women of the family are secluded. This Mahommedan custom has been largely adopted by the Hindus of Bengal and the Mahrattas. **Zanāna** is also used for the women of the family themselves. The growth of the admirable Zenana Missions has of late years made this word more familiar in England. But we have heard of more than one instance in which the objects of this Christian enterprise have been taken to be an amiable aboriginal tribe—"the **Zenanas**."

[1760.—"I am informed the Dutch chief at Bimlipatam has ... embarked his **jenninora** on board a sloop bound to Chinsurah. ..."—In *Long*, 236.]

1761.—"... I asked him where the Nabob was? Who replied, he was asleep in his **Zunana**."—*Col. Coote*, in *Van Sittart*, i. 111.

1780.—"It was an object with the Omrahs or great Lords of the Court, to hold captive in their **Zenanahs**, even hundreds of females."—*Hodges, Travels*, 22.

1782.—"Notice is hereby given that one *Zoraveer*, **consumah** to Hadjee Mustapha of Moorshedabad these 13 years, has absconded, after stealing. ... He has also carried away with him two Women, heretofore of Sujah Dowlah's **Zenana**; purchased by Hadjee Mustapha when last at Lucknow, one for 300 and the other for 1200 Rupees."—*India Gazette*, March 9.

1786.—
"Within the **Zenana**, no longer would they
In a starving condition impatiently stay,
But break out of prison, and all run away."
Simpkin the Second, 42.

"Their behaviour last night was so furious, that there seemed the greatest probability of their proceeding to the uttermost extremities, and that they would either throw themselves from the walls, or force open the doors of the **zenanahs**."—*Capt. Jaques*, quoted in *Articles of Charge against Hastings*, in *Burke*, vii. 27.

1789.—"I have not a doubt but it is much easier for a gentleman to support a whole **zenana** of Indians than the extravagance of one English lady."—*Munro's Narr.* 50.

1790.—"In a Mussleman Town many complaints arise of the *Passys* or Toddy Collectors climbing the Trees and overlooking the **Jenanas** or Women's apartments of principal Natives."—*Minute* in a letter from *Bd. of Revenue* to Govt. of Bengal, July 12.—MS. in India Office.

1809.—"Musulmauns ... even carried their depravity so far as to make secret enquiries respecting the females in their districts, and if they heard of any remarkable for beauty, to have them forcibly removed to their **zenanas**."—*Lord Valentia*, i. 415.

1817.—"It was represented by the Rajah that they (the bailiffs) entered the house, and endeavoured to pass into the **zenana**, or women's apartments."—*J. Mill, Hist.* iv. 294.

1826.—"The women in the **zananah**, in their impotent rage, flew at Captain Brown, who came off minus a considerable quantity of skin from his face."—*John Shipp*, iii. 49.

1828.—"'Thou sayest Tippoo's treasures are in the fort?' 'His treasures and his **Zenana**; I may even be able to secure his person.'"—*Sir W. Scott, The Surgeon's Daughter*, ch. xii.

ZEND, ZENDAVESTA, s. Zend is the name which has been commonly applied, for more than a hundred years to that dialect of the ancient Iranian (or Persian) language in which the Avesta or Sacred Books of Zorastrianism or the old Persian religion are written. The application of the name in this way was quite erroneous, as the word *Zand* when used alone in the Parsi books indicates a 'commentary or explanation,' and is in fact applied only to some **Pahlavi** translation, commentary, or gloss. If the name Zend were now to be used as the designation of any language it would more justly apply to the Pahlavi itself. At the same time Haug thinks it probable that the term Zand was originally applied to a commentary written in the same language as the Avesta itself, for in the Pahlavi translations of the Yasna, a part of the Avesta, where the scriptures are mentioned, Avesta and Zend are coupled together, as of equal authority, which could hardly have been the case if by Zend the translator meant his own work. No name for the language of the ancient scriptures has been found in the Parsi books; and *Avesta* itself has been adopted by scholars in speaking of the language. The fragments of these scriptures are written in two dialects of the Eastern Iranian, one, the more ancient, in which the *Gāthas* or hymns are written; and a later one which was for many centuries the spoken and written language of Bactria.

The word *Zand*, in Haug's view, may be referred to the root *zan*, 'to know'; Skt. *jnā*, Gr. *γνο*, Lat. *gno* (as in *agnosco, cognosco*), so that its meaning is 'knowledge.' Prof. J. Oppert, on the other hand, identifies it with old Pers. *zannda*, 'prayer.'

Zendavesta is the name which has been by Europeans popularly applied to the books just spoken of as the Avesta. The term is undoubtedly an inversion, as, according to Haug, "the Pahlavi books always style them *Avistâk va Zand* (Avesta and Zend)" *i.e.* the Law with its traditional and authoritative explanation. *Abastâ*, in the sense of law, occurs in the funeral inscription of Darius at Behistūn; and this seems now the most generally accepted origin of the term in its application to the Parsi sacred books. (This is not, however, the explanation given by Haug.) Thus, '*Avesta* and Zend' signify together 'The Law and the Commentary.'

The Avesta was originally much more extensive than the texts which now exist, which are only fragments. The Parsi tradition is that there were twenty-one books called *Nasks*, the greater part of which were burnt by Alexander in his conquest of Persia; possibly true, as we know that Alexander did burn the palace at Persepolis. The collection of fragments which remains, and is known as the Zend-avesta, is divided, in its usual form, into two parts. I. The Avesta properly so called, containing (*a*) the *Vendîdâd*, a compilation of religious laws and of mythical tales; (*b*) the *Vispêrad*, a collection of litanies for the sacrifice; and (*c*) the *Yasna*, composed of similar litanies and of 5 hymns or *Gâthas* in an old dialect. II. The *Khorda*, or small, *Avesta*, composed of short prayers for recitation by the faithful at certain moments of the day, month, or year, and in presence of the different elements, with which certain other hymns and fragments are usually included.

The term Zendavesta, though used, as we see below, by Lord in 1630, first became familiar in Europe through the labours of Anquetil du Perron, and his publication of 1771. [The Zend-Avesta has now been translated in *Sacred Books of the East*, by J. Darmesteter, L. H. Mills; *Pahlavi Texts*, by E. W. West.]

c. 930.—"Zarādasht, the son of Asbimām, ... had brought to the Persians the book **al-Bastāh** in the old Fārsī tongue. He gave a commentary on this, which is the **Zand**, and to this commentary yet another explanation which was called **Bazand**. ..."—*Maṣ'ūdī*, ii. 167. [See *Haug, Essays*, p. 11.]

c. 1030.—"The chronology of this same past, but in a different shape, I have also found in the book of Hamza ben Alhusain Alisfahâni, which he calls '*Chronology of great nations of the past and present*.' He says that he has endeavoured to correct his account by means of the **Abastâ**, which is the religious code (of the Zoroastrians). Therefore I have transferred it into this place of my book."—*Al-Birûnî, Chronology of Ancient Nations*, by *Sachau*, p. 112.

"Afterwards the wife gave birth to six other children, the names of whom are known in the **Avastâ**."—*Ibid.* p. 108.

1630.—"Desirous to add anything to the

ingenious that the opportunities of my Travayle might conferre vpon mee, I ioyned myselfe with one of their Church men called their *Daroo*, and by the interpretation of a *Parsee*, whose long imployment in the Companies Service, had brought him to mediocrity in the *English* tongue, and whose familiarity with me, inclined him to further my inquiries: I gained the knowledge of what hereafter I shall deliver as it was compiled in a booke writ in the Persian Characters containing their Scriptures, and in their own language called their ZVNDAVASTAVV."—*Lord, The Religion of the Persees, The Proeme.*

[c. 1630.—"Being past the Element of Fire and the highest Orbs (as saith their **Zundavastaio**) ..."—*Sir T. Herbert*, 2nd ed. 1677, p. 54.]

1653.—"Les ottomans appellent *gueuures* vne secte de Payens que nous connoissons sous le nom d'adorateurs du feu, les Persans sous celuy d'*Atechperes*, et les Indou sous celuy de Parsi, terme dont ils se nommẽt eux-mesmes. ... Ils ont leur Saincte Escriture ou **Zundeuastavv**, en deux volumes composée par vn nommé Zertost, conduit par vn Ange nommé Abraham ou plus-tost Bahaman Vinshauspan. ..."—*De la Boullaye-le-Gouz*, ed. 1657, pp. 200–201.

1700.—"Suo itaque Libro (Zerdusht) ... alium affixit specialem Titulum **Zend**, seu alias **Zendavestâ**; vulgus sonat *Zund* et *Zundavastaw*. Ita ut quamvis illud ejus Opus variis Tomis, sub distinctis etiam nominibus, constet, tamen quidvis ex dictorum Tomorum quovis, satis propriè et legitimè citari possit, sub dicto generali nomine, utpote quod, hac ratione, in operum ejus complexu seu Syntagmate contineri intelligatur. ... Est autem **Zend** nomen Arabicum: et **Zendavestâ** conflatum est ex superaddito nomine *Hebraeo-Chaldaico, Eshta*, *i.e.* ignis, unde *Εστία* ... supra dicto nomine *Zend* apud Arabes, significatur *Igniarium* seu *Focile*. ... Cum itaque nomine **Zend** significetur *Igniarium*, et **Zendavestâ** *Igniarium et Ignis*," &c.—*T. Hyde, Hist. Rel. Vet. Persarum eorunique Magorum*, cap. xxv., ed. Oxon. 1760, pp. 335–336.

1771.—"Persuadé que les usages modernes de l'Asie doivent leur origine aux Peuples et aux Religions qui l'ont subjuguée, je me suis proposé d'étudier dans les sources l'ancienne Théologie des Nations habituées dans les Contrées immenses qui sont à l'Est de l'Euphrate, et de consulter sur leur Histoire, les livres originaux. Ce plan m'a engagé à remonter aux Monumens les plus anciens. Je les ai trouvé de deux espèces: les prémiers écrits en Samskretan; ce sont les Vedes, Livres sacrés des Pays, qui de l'Indus s'étendent aux frontières de la Chine: les seconds écrits en **Zend**, ancienne Langue du Nord de la Perse; c'est le **Zend Avesta**, qui passe pour avoir été la Loi des Contrées bornées par l'Euphrate, le Caucase, l'Oxus, et la mer des Indes."—*Anquetil du Perron, Zend-Avesta, Ouvrage de Zoroastre—Documens Préliminaires*, p. iii.

"Dans deux cens ans, quand les Langues **Zend** et Pehlvie seront devenues en Europe familières aux Sçavans, on pourra, en rectifiant les endroits où je me serai trompé, donner une Traduction plus exacte du **Zend-Avesta**, et ci ce que je dis ici excitant l'émulation, avance le terme que je viens de fixer, mes fautes m'auront conduit au but que je me suis proposé."—*Ibid.* Preface, xvii.

1884.—"The supposition that some of the books were destroyed by Alexander the Great is contained in the introductory chapter of the Pehlevi *Viraf-Nama*, a book written in the Sassanian times, about the 6th or 7th century, and in which the event is thus chronicled:—'The wicked, accursed Guna Mino (the evil spirit), in order to make the people sceptical about their religion, instigated the accursed Alexiedar (Alexander) the Ruman, the inhabitant of Egypt, to carry war and hardships to the country of Iran (Persia). He killed the monarch of Iran, and destroyed and made desolate the royal court. And this religion, that is, all the books of **Avesta** and **Zend**, written with gold ink upon prepared cow-skins, was deposited in the archives of Stakhar (Istakhar or Persepolis) of Papak. The accursed, wretched, wicked *Ashmogh* (destroyer of the pious), Alexiedar the evildoer, took them (the books) out and burnt them.'"—*Dosabhai Framji, H. of the Parsis*, ii. 158–159.

ZINGARI, n.p. This is of course not Anglo-Indian, but the name applied in various countries of Europe, and in various modifications, *zincari*, *zingani*, *zincali*, *chingari*, *zigeuner*, &c., to the gypsies.

Various suggestions as to its derivation have been made on the supposition that it is of Indian origin. Borrow has explained the word as 'a person of mixt blood,' deriving it from the Skt. *sankara*, 'made up.' It is true that *varṅa sankara* is used for an admixture of castes and races (*e.g.* in *Bhāgavad Gītā*, i. 41, &c.), but it is not the name of any caste, nor would people to whom such an opprobrious epithet had been applied be likely to carry it with them to distant lands. A writer in the *Saturday Review* once suggested the Pers. *zīngar*, 'a saddler.' Not at all probable. In Sleeman's *Ramaseeana* or Vocabulary of the peculiar Language used by the Thugs (Calcutta, 1836), p. 85, we find:

"**Chingaree**, a class of Multani Thugs, sometimes called *Naiks*, of the Mussulman faith. They proceed on their expeditions in the character of Brinjaras, with cows and bullocks laden with merchandize, which they expose for sale at their encampments, and thereby attract their victims. They use the rope of their bullocks instead of the *roomal* in strangling. They are an ancient tribe of Thugs, and take their wives and children on their expeditions."

[These are the Chāngars of whom Mr. Ibbetson (*Panjab Ethnog.* 308) gives an account. A full description of them has been given by Dr. G. W. Leitner (*A Sketch of the Changars and of their Dialect*, Lahore, 1880), in which he shows reason to doubt any connection between them and the Zingari.]

De Goeje (*Contributions to the Hist. of the Gypsies*) regards that people as the Indian *Zoṭṭ* (*i.e. Jatt* of Sind). He suggests as possible origins of the name first *shikārī* (see SHIKAREE), and then Pers. *changī*, 'harper,' from which a plural *changān* actually occurs in Lane's *Arabian Nights*, iii. 730, note 22. [These are the Al-Jink, male dancers (see *Burton, Ar. Nights*, viii. 18).]

If the name is to be derived from India, the term in Sleeman's *Vocabulary* seems a more probable origin than the others mentioned here. But is it not more likely that *zingari*, like Gipsy and Bohemian, would be a name given *ab extra* on their appearing in the West, and not carried with them from Asia?

NOTES ON THE ENTRIES

EPIGRAPHS

2 The first epigraph, as with all entries in square brackets, is a 1903 addition by Crooke. Of the remaining six quotations, three were contributed by Burnell, three by Yule. The epigraphs were routinely omitted from later reprints of *Hobson-Jobson*, perhaps because of their excessive number and diversity. But they seem entirely characteristic of the length and complexity of the collaborative work as a whole. Some of the epigraphs contradict one other: the quotation from Verstegan, for instance, resists the use of words of foreign origin, whereas that from Purchas celebrates the intoxicating 'draught of English-Indian liquor'; the reworked quotation from Ovid implies that essential meaning survives translation, whereas the extract from Iamblichus suggests that some idioms are untranslatable.

Verstegan: Richard Verstegan's *A Restitution of Decayed Intelligence* (1605) attacks the introduction of words from other languages into English. Given Verstegan's linguistic xenophobia, the book might appear a surprising choice for an epigraph for *Hobson-Jobson*, but a vein of cultural superiority runs through the glossary.

Ovid: the epigraph reworks Ovid's Latin original, substituting 'vocem' (voice) for 'animam' (soul) in a passage describing Pythagoras' concept of metempsychosis, or the transmigration of souls:

As pliant wax
Is moulded to new forms and does not stay
As it has been nor yet keep the self-same form
Yet is the self-same wax, be well assured
The soul is always the same spirit, though
It passes into different forms.

Ovid, *Metamorphoses*, trans. B. More
(Boston: Cornhill, 1922)

Plinii: from the preface of Pliny the Elder's massive *Natural History* (AD 77). 'Nor do we doubt that there are many things that have escaped us also; for we are but human and beset with duties, and we pursue this sort of interest in our spare moments.' Pliny, *Natural History*, trans. H. Rackham (Cambridge, Mass.: Loeb, 1938).

Martialis: from the Latin *Epigrams* of Martial (*c.* AD 40–104). The poet is asking Caesar for recognition:

This boon, if I have failed to please you, will be some consolation to me;
If I have succeeded in pleasing you, will be some reward.

Martial, *Epigrams*, trans. H. G. Bohn (London: G. Bell, 1897)

DEDICATION

4 George Udny Yule (1813–86), Henry Yule's older brother. He had a successful career in India, serving as chief commissioner of Oudh, resident of Hyderabad, and member of the Governor General's Council.

To an excellent and dearly beloved brother,
A most delightful friend
This, nearly fifteen years
A pastime and a solace,
And a work of no small labour
Finally completed,
An old man to an old man
He dedicates.

PREFACE

5 *Ars longa, vita brevis*: Latin translation of Hippocrates' Greek aphorism, 'Art is long, life is short'.

horae subsicivae: Latin for 'leisure hours'.

INTRODUCTORY REMARKS

11 *impeachment of Hastings*: the impeachment of Warren Hastings, former Governor General of Bengal, on charges of misgovernment in India, was one of the great political trials of eighteenth-century Britain, running from 1787 until Hastings's acquittal in 1795.

12 *great Dictionary*: *The New English Dictionary*.

18 *Burghers and Antiburghers*: sects in the Scottish Presbyterian Church.

veluti Gog et Magog!: 'like Gog and Magog'. Gog and Magog feature in the Bible (Ezekiel 38–9 and Revelation 20) as enemies of Israel and Christ.

Sir Charles Napier: commander of the British Army and governor of Sind. For Napier's orders, see illustrative quotation dated 1844, under entry for HINDOSTANEE.

as we have indicated: the tendency to convert the Hindustani imperative into the infinitive reveals the British linguistic habit of command. The imperative is in the 'familiar' form, which does not indicate respect. Many of the verbs cited suggest either distrust (*bunow* to sham, *fozilow* to flatter) or coercion (*puckerow* to lay hold of, *dumbcow* to browbeat, *sumjow* to correct).

19 *Chinghiz*: Genghis Khan.

21 *nomen gentile*: Latin, 'clan name'.

23 *etwas schwankende yulische Orthographie*: German, 'Yule's somewhat inconsistent spelling'.

GLOSSARY

ACHÁR *Crosse and Blackwell*: the Company of Crosse & Blackwell was founded in 1829 and pioneered the import and export of spices, pickles, and sauces to and from India.

AFGHÁN: Henry Yule wrote the entry on Afghanistan for the 9th edition of *Encyclopaedia Britannica* (1875).

AKALEE *Wahābis of Sikhism*: the Wahabis are a reform movement within Sunni Islam.

the annexation of the Panjab: the Punjab was annexed by the British in 1849, following the Second Anglo-Sikh War.

ALLIGATOR *lacertine*: lizard-like.

ALLIGATOR-PEAR: now known as the avocado.

A MUCK: the spectre of drugged men running amok is one of the stereotypical British images of the Malays, as the length of the entry indicates.

ANACONDA *Mr H. W. Bates entirely disbelieved it*: Henry Walter Bates (1825–92) was a naturalist who specialized in the flora and fauna of Amazonia. He was at the heart of scientific and geographical circles, serving as secretary to the Royal Geographical Society for twenty-seven years.

ANDAMAN: Henry Yule wrote the entry on the Andaman Islands for the 9th edition of the *Encyclopaedia Britannica* (1875) Arthur Conan Doyle seems to have drawn on this article in his representation of the savage Andaman Islander, Tonga, in *The Sign of Four* (1890).

ANGENGO *"Sterne's Eliza"*: Eliza Draper, born at the East India Company factory at Anjengo, in 1744. She met Laurence Sterne, author of *Tristram Shandy* (1760–7) on a visit to England in 1767. Sterne fell in love with her, but she returned to her husband in India.

ANILE *a native satirical drama Nīl-Darpan*: the oppressive conduct of British indigo planters led to the 1859 rebellion of Bengali peasants known as the 'blue mutiny'. In 1860 James Long, a British missionary in Bengal, translated Dinabandhu Mitra's play *Nil Darpan* (*The Indigo Mirror*) into English, at the request of a commission investigating the condition of the indigo cultivators. The play dramatized the brutal and oppressive methods of British planters. Outraged at this depiction, indigo planters brought a legal case against Long, charging him with slander. Long was convicted, fined, and imprisoned for a month.

since the days of Impey: Sir Elijah Impey (1732–1809), Chief Justice in Calcutta during Warren Hastings's tenure as Governor General, was involved in a number of scandals. The most notorious was the case of Maharaja Nandakumar, who had accused Hastings of bribery. In 1775 Nandakumar was charged with forgery and sentenced to death by Impey.

ANNA *applied colloquially to persons of mixt parentage*: such phrases speak of the nineteenth-century British fear of miscegenation (see also the entry for CHEECHEE).

APOLLO BUNDER *A friend here queries: 'By Mr. Shapira?'*: in 1883, Moses Wilhelm Shapira, a Jerusalem antiquarian book dealer, offered a scroll for sale to the British Museum, claiming it was an early version of the Book of Deuteronomy. Biblical scholars deemed it a fake, and Shapira was publicly humiliated. The tentative attribution to Shapira should alert the reader's suspicions: the 'MS. of Sir John Mandeville, lately discovered' was written by Henry Yule himself, a mock medieval account of India, published in the anonymous *Fragments of Unprofessional Papers* (Calcutta, 1862). It is cited a number of times in the glossary (with variant spellings of Mandeville's name).

ART, EUROPEAN *artists . . . for European patrons, and after European patterns*: this alludes to the 1880s debate over the quality of Indian arts and crafts. Critics, such as George Birdwood (who was a contributor to *Hobson-Jobson*), lamented the declining quality of Indian arts and crafts, emphasizing the detrimental effect of European influence, education, and mechanization on traditional techniques and designs.

ARYAN: the idea that language was linked to race was current in the nineteenth century. The theory was expounded in particular by the Comte de Gobineau in his 1853 *Essai sur l'inégalité des races humaines* (cited in the entry's illustrative quotations). Gobineau argued that language and intelligence were determined by physical features, and that some races were essentially inferior. The use of the term 'Aryan' to denote the people who spoke Indo-European languages was popularized by the influential Sanskrit scholar and philologist Friedrich Max Müller (cited twice in the illustrative quotations for this entry). Early in his career, Max Müller assumed the identity of the Aryan languages and peoples, but with the rise of race science, he revised his views, and denied the link. After the Indian Rebellion of 1857–8, many British commentators reacted against the idea that the British and Indians were in any way related, and refuted the idea of an Aryan race.

BABOO: the British notion of the effeminate Bengali was a long-standing stereotype. The language of the English-educated Babu was caricatured as pompous yet flawed; as in, for instance, the supposedly humorous compilation: *'Baboo English': On our Mother Tongue as our Aryan Brethren Understand It* (1890). The most famous literary baboo is Hurree Chunder Mookerjee in Kipling's *Kim* (1901).

BAMBOO: the many uses of the versatile bamboo were often noted by British travel writers. The 1886 Colonial and Indian Exhibition in South Kensington had a 'Bamboo Trophy' or arch displaying the different species of bamboo and a wide variety of bamboo artefacts.

BANCHOOT, BETEECHOOT: the terms are deemed too obscene to translate other than through rather imprecise biblical allusion. They mean 'sister-fucker' and 'daughter-fucker' respectively. In 1 Samuel 20: 30, King Saul is angry with his son, Jonathan, and so insults him by cursing his mother as a whore. The King James Version reads: 'Then Saul's anger was kindled against Jonathan, and he said unto him, Thou son of the perverse rebellious *woman*, do not I know that thou hast chosen the son of Jesse to thine own confusion, and unto the confusion of thy mother's nakedness?'

BANDANNA: the East India Company purchased bandannas along with many Indian textiles for sale in West Africa, the West Indies and America as part of the slave trade. See also the notes to GUINEA-CLOTHS and MADRAS.

BANYAN *called these Hindus of Guzerat Bagnani*: the seventeenth-century Carmelite Vincenzo Maria links the term 'banyan' to the Italian *bagno* (bath): 'they are called *Bagnani* by the Portuguese, because of the frequency and superstition with which they wash themselves many times a day'.

BANYAN-TREE: the banyan tree was considered one of the botanical wonders of India, represented by many travel writers and artists. With its apparently endless capacity for rooting and expansion, it appealed to writers and poets, as the quotations from Jonson, Milton, and Southey here testify.

Epistle from a Lady in England to a Lady in Avignon: the title of Tickell's poem should read *Epistle from a Lady in England to a Gentleman in Avignon*.

BATTA *the reduction of full batta to half batta*: the army's outrage at this economizing measure was so intense that there were threats of a mutiny in 1828.

BAYADÈRE *the idol of Somnāth*: in 1842 Lord Ellenborough marked British victory in Afghanistan with a symbolic gesture and proclamation, much criticized at the time. He claimed to have recovered the ancient gates of the Hindu temple of Somnath in Gujarat, carried off to Afghanistan by Mahmud of Ghazni in 1024. Ellenborough proclaimed that he had revenged Somnath, thus aligning himself with the Hindu population and alienating Indian Muslims. The gates later proved to be replicas.

BEEBEE: the definition omits to mention that in the eighteenth century the title Beebee denoted Indian women who lived with British men in long-term relationships.

BENIGHTED, THE *Fragments of Sir J. Maundevile*: by Henry Yule (see note to APOLLO BUNDER).

BERYL *Professor Max Müller*: Friedrich Max Müller (1823–1900) held the chair of comparative philology at Oxford and was a pioneer scholar of Sanskrit, mythology, religion, and philosophy. He was an intellectual hero and friend to both Burnell and Yule.

BHEESTY *Ganga Din*: Crooke added this reference to Kipling's poem 'Gunga Din' to the 1903 edition. Kipling's portrayal of the much-abused, yet devoted Gunga Din echoes *Hobson-Jobson*'s characterization of the *bihishtī* as courageous and faithful. The model may have been Juma, the *bihishtī* to the Corps of Guides at the Siege of Delhi, celebrated for service to the

British during the 1857 Rebellion. The lexicon and poem coincide to construct the *bihishtī* as a type of the heroic, loyal Indian servant.

BILDAR *Ye Dreme of an Executive Engineere*: the poem is by Henry Yule, published in the anonymous *Fragments of Unprofessional Papers* (Calcutta, 1862).

BLACK ACT *Recent agitation caused by the "Ilbert Bill"*: proposed in 1883, the Ilbert Bill generated great controversy in both Britain and India. Under the Bill, Indian magistrates would adjudicate in cases involving Europeans. The fierce opposition to the Bill by British indigo and tea planters contributed to the growth of Indian nationalist sentiment. The Indian National Congress was founded two years later, in 1885.

BUGGY *the Hunterian spelling-controversy*: when compiling the *Imperial Gazetteer of India* in the 1870s, William Wilson Hunter (1840–1900) proposed a system of transliteration for Indian place names. Initially his proposal met with opposition, but his method was subsequently adopted by the government, and remains the basis for the official system of romanization in India today.

CABUL, CAUBOOL *now so familiar*: the name of Kabul would have been familiar to the nineteenth-century British public, following the city's occupation by the British in two Anglo-Afghan Wars of 1839–42 and 1878–80.

CANDAHAR *the object of so much political interest*: following the close of the Second Anglo-Afghan War in 1880, there was considerable public debate concerning the extent of British presence in Afghanistan. As a member of the Council of India, Yule advocated the British retention of Kandahar, a town of commercial and strategic importance, situated on the roads leading to Herat and Kabul. But financial and military considerations led to the withdrawal of British troops from Kandahar in 1881.

CASTE: from the mid-nineteenth century on, the British administration in India was preoccupied with the issue of caste. Census-taking practices and ethnographic studies tended to reinforce and extend caste distinctions. This process of systemization resulted in caste becoming the defining element of Indian identity.

CHOLERA, AND CHOLERA MORBUS *The Disease*: cholera epidemics were greatly feared by the British in India; mortality rates were especially high among the rural poor and lower ranks of the army. The glossary has two entries on cholera (see the long article on MORT-DE-CHIEN), a measure of the terror inspired by the disease.

COMPOUND *Campon . . . appellantur*: 'Campon: a joining-together or association; hence a name given also to villages and small localities.'

Maison . . . entoure: 'House surrounded by a plot of land.'

Village . . . l'entoure: 'Fortified village, or, in a town a separate and generally enclosed quarter, inhabited by people of the same nationality, Malays,

Siamese, Chinese, Bugis, etc. This word properly signifies an enclosure, a pen, and by extension an enclosed quarter, district, or fortified village. The word *Kampong* sometimes also denotes a house of some importance with an enclosed area that is dependent on and surrounds it.'

CONGEE *Mr. Draper, the husband of Sterne's Eliza*: see note to ANGENGO.

Hunc medicus . . . pereamve rapinis?: 'But his physician, a man of very quick wit and a loyal friend, revives him by this device . . . "Come now, take this drop of rice-gruel." "What's the cost?" "Oh, a trifle." "How much, I say?" "Eight pence." "Alack! What matters it, whether I die by sickness, or by theft and robbery?"' Horace, *Satires,* II. iii. 147–57, trans. H. Rushton Fairclough (London: Heinemann, 1942).

COOLY *nomen gentile*: Latin, 'clan name'.

COTWAL, CUTWAUL *"Ketaul . . . d'Ozbegs"*: '*Ketaul*, fortress guard, chief of a garrison; name of a tribe of Ozbegs'.

COUNTRY *the great Ritter*: Carl Ritter (1779–1859), German geographer.

dormitans Homerus: 'a nodding Homer'.

Seide: German for silk.

COWLE *The Emperor Sigismund gave Cowle to John Huss—and broke it*: Sigismund (1369–1437, King of Hungary, Germany, Bohemia; 1433–7, Holy Roman Emperor) guaranteed safe conduct to the Bohemian religious reformer Jan Huss (1369–1415), but had him arrested, condemned as a heretic, and burnt at the stake.

DACOIT, DACOO *The term, being current in Bengal, got into the Penal Code*: in colonial India, certain groups were identified as criminal tribes or dacoits. It was an offence to be a member of a gang of dacoits. According to the Indian Penal Code of 1860, a robbery committed by five or more was classified as dacoity and carried a more severe penalty than robbery.

DARJEELING, DĀRJĪLING *an outrage committed by the Sikkim Minister*: in 1848, the British superintendent of Darjeeling, Archibald Campbell, accompanied the botanist Joseph Hooker on an expedition to Sikkim, and crossed the border into Tibet. They were turned back by Tibetan troops and imprisoned for some months in Sikkim. Reports of their ill treatment were used to justify the British annexation of the Sikkim Terai and portions of the Sikkim Hills. Hooker, later director of Kew Gardens, was himself a contributor to *Hobson-Jobson*.

DATURA *One of the present writers has judicially convicted many*: Burnell served as a district judge in the Madras Civil Service.

DEWAUN *et hoc genus omne*: Latin, 'and everything of the kind'.

DEWAUNY *"Diwaen begì, id est . . . disponendi facultatem habet"*: 'The Diwaen *begi*, that is, the Highest Authority in criminal Justice . . . in cases of robbery and piracy and homicide has jurisdiction not only in this royal capital but also throughout the whole kingdom.'

DOAI! DWYE! *the old Norman Haro! Haro! viens à mon aide, mon Prince!*: the 'Clameur de Haro' is a customary cry for justice, 'Come to my aid, my Prince!', still extant in the Channel Islands (see Burnell's footnote to entry).

DRAVIDIAN: As with 'aryan' (see note to entry), the term 'Dravidian' was applied both to a language group and race.

DUCKS *Extract from a MS. of the Travels of Sir John Maudevill*: by Henry Yule (see note to APOLLO BUNDER).

EKTENG: Yule cites his own writing as evidence of sound association across languages.

ELEPHANT *mutatis mutandis*: Latin phrase, 'the necessary changes having been made'.

FACTOR *vis inertiae*: Latin phrase from Newtonian physics, 'the force of inertia'.

FACTORY: the entry has been abridged to exclude the list of East India Company Factories.

FAILSOOF *φιλόσοφος*: Greek, 'philosopher'.

FAKEER: the figure of the *fakir* is one of the well-established Indian types noted by European writers. It was this image that Churchill drew on in his notorious 1931 speech that characterized Gandhi as 'a seditious Middle Temple lawyer of the type well-known in the East, now posing as a fakir, striding half naked up the steps of the Viceregal palace'.

FIREFLY *alleged rhythmical or synchronous flashing of fireflies when visible in great numbers*: current research indicates that large groups of tropical firefly species do indeed flash in synchrony.

GALLEVAT *quod minime reris!*: 'little though you may think this!'; a quotation from the prophecy of the Sibyl to Aeneas in Virgil's *Aeneid*, vi. 97. The Sibyl predicts that the Trojans will find help where they least expect it, from a Greek city (their former enemy). The allusion to the *Aeneid* suggests a parallel (frequently drawn by nineteenth-century writers) between the British and Roman empires.

GINGHAM *"Guingamp, ville de Bretagne, où il y a des fabriques de tissus"*: 'Guingamp, a Breton town where cloth is manufactured.'

GOOJUR *formerly notorious for thieving propensities*: following Gujar involvement in the 1857–8 Rebellion, the British regarded Gujars with suspicion. Under the 1871 Criminal Tribes Act, Gujars were categorized as a criminal tribe, subject to surveillance and possible resettlement.

GOORKA, GOORKALLY *the best soldiers of modern India*: the martial reputation of Gurkhas continues to this day; the British Army maintains a Brigade of Gurkhas, recruited exclusively from Nepal.

GORA: Rabindranath Tagore's 1910 novel *Gora*, written in part as a response to

Kipling's *Kim*, has as its central protagonist an Irish orphan Gora, brought up in ignorance of his origins by a Bengali couple.

GRIFFIN, GRIFF: the figure of the griffin is memorably satirized by the artist Charles d'Oyly in his 1828 illustrated poem, *Tom Raw the Griffin*.

GRUNTH *The Granth has been translated by Dr Trumpp*: the preface to the Adi Granth (1877) written by the German missionary Ernest Trumpp, condemned the Sikh scripture as 'incoherent and shallow in the extreme'.

GUINEA-CLOTHS, GUINEA-STUFFS *West African trade*: the East India Company supplied textiles for use in the transatlantic slave trade. See notes to BANDANNA and MADRAS.

GUTTA PERCHA: the naturally occurring rubber revolutionized nineteenth-century communications when used as insulation for submarine telegraph cables. It also transformed the lives of the middle classes, when used to produce dental fillings and rain-resistant golf balls.

GYM-KHANA: the term was associated with horse-riding events only in the 1930s.

HARAMZADA: the glossary tends to euphemize terms of abuse (see notes on BANCHOOT and SALA); 'haramzada' means 'bastard'.

HIMALÝA *"Whose snowy ridge the roving Tartar bounds"*: John Milton, *Paradise Lost*, iii. 432.

"a montibus . . . significante": 'the Hemodi Mountains, a projection of which is called the Imaus, which in the vernacular means "snowy"'. Pliny, *Natural History*, vol. ii, trans H. Rackham (Cambridge, Mass.: Loeb, 1961).

HING *Teufels dreck . . . stercus!*: devil's dung, i.e. not food but excrement of the devil!

HOME: in an attempt to preserve a sense of national and cultural identity, the British in India typically returned to Britain for education, periods of leave, and retirement.

INDIA, INDIES *the Court of the E.I.C.*: the EIC is the East India Company (see also INTERLOPER and PRESIDENCY).

INDIGO: indigo was one of India's major exports in the first half of the nineteenth century. By the 1870s chemists discovered methods of synthesizing artificial indigo, and commercial production began in Germany at the end of the century.

JADOOGUR: Freemasonry had been established in India since the eighteenth century, gaining ground through its association with the army in the nineteenth century. By the final quarter of the nineteenth century, anglicized Indians began to be admitted to Masonic lodges. Rudyard Kipling joined the Masons in 1886 and recalled meeting Muslim, Hindu, Sikh, Arya

Samaj, and Jewish Masons. The most famous literary *Jadoo-Gher* features in Kipling's *Kim*.

JAGHEER, JAGHIRE: in eighteenth-century Britain, the term 'jagheer' was associated with charges of British corruption in India. In 1772–3, Robert Clive faced questions from a parliamentary inquiry into the jagheer worth £27,000 per year, granted to him by Mir Jafar, the Nawab of Bengal.

JAWAUB *"Grove nods at grove . . . reflects the other"*: Alexander Pope, 'Epistle IV', *Moral Essays*.

JOGEE: the figure of the ascetic yogi, sometimes combined or confused with the Muslim fakir, is one of the Indian types much noted by European travel writers.

the stuff which has of late been propagated . . . the doctrine of the Jogis: founded in New York in 1875 by Madame Helena Blavatsky, Colonel Henry Olcott, and William Judge, the Theosophical Society established its headquarters in Adyar, Madras, in 1882. It was a spiritualist movement that drew on various religious traditions and claimed knowledge of the secret teachings of the Buddha, 'esoteric Buddhism'. The Theosophical Society attracted both followers in America and India and ridicule from scholars, as the tone of the glossary's entry suggests. The society still operates from its Adyar Headquarters today, with members across the world.

JUGGURNAUT: the gloss plays down accounts of religious suicide at the Jagannath festival. Lurid tales of devotees crushed to death under the temple car were standard in European travel literature, and often cited by evangelical and missionary writers as evidence of heathen barbarity. Used figuratively, juggernaut came to mean an inexorable force, or an idea or institution that commanded self-sacrificial devotion. Juggernaut acquired its current British meaning of a large lorry only in the 1960s, when newspapers started to campaign against heavy goods vehicles in towns and villages.

JUNKAMEER: in transcribing Burnell's final letter, Yule pays tribute to his deceased co-author and friend. The note gives a sense of the collaborative process, the easy exchange of ideas, and delight in problem solving.

JUTE *so important an export . . . material for manufacture in Great Britain as well as in India*: the centres of jute manufacture in Britain and India were Dundee and Calcutta. At the time of the glossary's publication, Calcutta was poised to overtake Dundee as the world's leading jute producer. The market for jute was immense since it was used for packing foodstuffs and raw materials across the globe.

KHUTPUT *Sir James Outram's struggles with the rascality*: James Outram was removed from his post as Resident of Baroda in 1852 for exposing the system of corruption (*khatpat*) prevalent in the government. He set out his case in *Baroda Intrigues and Bombay Khutput* (1853).

KOTOW, KOWTOW *Lord Amherst's refusal to perform it at Pekin in 1816*: British diplomats considered the kowtow a ritual that compromised national prestige and dignity. When he was received by the Qing emperor in 1793, Lord Macartney went down on bended knee rather than prostrate himself. In 1816, Lord Amherst refused to perform the kowtow and was denied an imperial audience altogether. Similar concerns surrounded the Burmese court ritual of the shikhó (see entry and note).

KUBBERDAUB *chokidārs*: watchmen.

KYFE *dolce far niente*: Italian, 'sweet idleness'.

LACK: the term 'lakh' was associated with the legendary wealth acquired by unscrupulous East India Company servants in the eighteenth century. It was said that the interjection 'Alas and alack-a-day!' was converted to an after-dinner toast: 'A lass and a lakh a day!'

LATTEEAL: the British indigo planters of Bengal kept strong men to coerce peasants and settle land disputes. Their oppressive measures led to a rebellion of indigo cultivators in 1859 (see note to ANILE).

LINGAM *The great idol of Somnāth*: see note to BAYADÈRE.

MADRAS *large bright-coloured handkerchiefs*: for the association between the East India Company's trade in textiles and the transatlantic slave trade, see notes on BANDANNA and GUINEA-CLOTHS.

MAHOUT *Μαμάτραι . . . Ινδοῖς*: 'Mamatrae: that is what the generals are called by the Indians.' Hesychius of Alexandria, *Alphabetical Collection of All Words*.

MULL *Ext. from a lately discovered MS. of Sir John Maundeville*: see note to APOLLO BUNDER.

NABÓB [*footnote*] *The representation of Scotch burghs before 1832 . . . was never purchasable*: the 1832 Reform Act extended the franchise to middle-class urban men by redistributing parliamentary seats. *Burgh* is the Scottish spelling of *borough*.

NAUTCH: until the mid-nineteenth century, the British were frequently both guests and patrons at nautches. But the increased segregation of the British community and missionary disapproval meant that this Indo-British social practice fell into disuse.

NIPA *We think . . . that the slang word* nip *. . . is adopted from* nipa: the gloss seems to be mistaken. The *Oxford English Dictionary* derives 'nip' from 'nipperkin', the amount of alcohol contained in a small vessel or nipperkin, a term possibly derived from the Dutch *nippen*, to sip.

NOKAR *one of those jingling double-doubled phrases in which Orientals delight even more than Englishmen*: but the examples of rhyming reduplication that follow suggest the authors' considerable relish for wordplay, manifested too in the glossary's title: *Hobson-Jobson*.

NON-REGULATION *"La Non-Intervention . . . la même chose que l'Intervention"*: 'Non-Intervention is a political and technical phrase that comes to mean more or less the same thing as Intervention.'

Ext. from a MS. of The Travels of Sir John Mandevill: see note to APOLLO BUNDER.

NUMERICAL AFFIXES: the entry is anomalous in that it does not relate to a particular word or phrase. The article is rather a contribution to contemporary philological discussion, using linguistic evidence to formulate general rules about human development, after the manner of Friedrich Max Müller (cited in a footnote at the end of the entry).

'Ja freilich! dreizehn Stück Amerikaner!': 'Yes, of course! Thirteen Americans!' (*Stück*: 'piece(s)' or 'item(s)' is untranslatable, since English does not have a comparable idiom.)

OPIUM: the entry is conspicuously silent on the significance of opium in Anglo-Chinese relations and to the British economy. From the late eighteenth century, the East India Company held the monopoly on opium production in Bengal. The company sold the opium to independent British traders who smuggled it into China, making a 2,000% profit for the company on each chest of opium sold. So great were the returns that the British government was prepared to back the illegal trade with force. The two Opium Wars of 1839–42 and 1856–60 compelled the Chinese authorities to open China to British trade and ultimately legalize the import of opium into China. By the mid-nineteenth century, opium made up nearly a third of all of India's exports. The trade reached its peak in 1880 with the export of more than 6,500 tons of Indian-grown opium to China.

OUTCRY: the high mortality rates of Europeans in India meant that outcries or auctions were held regularly to dispose of a deceased person's goods. See also NEELÁM.

OVERLAND *M. Lesseps*: Ferdinand de Lesseps (1805–94) was responsible for the construction of the Suez Canal. Opened in 1869, the Suez Canal allowed goods, passengers, and troops to be transported between Britain and India with much greater speed and economy than the previous route around the Cape. The Suez Canal reduced the distance between London and Calcutta by over 2,000 miles and the travel time by around two weeks.

PALANKEEN, PALANQUIN [*footnote*] *"ferculum* quod *fecit sibi rex Salomon de lignis Libani"*: 'King Solomon made himself a chariot of the wood of Lebanon'. Canticles (Song of Solomon) 3: 9 (King James Version).

PARIAH, PARRIAR *As with other castes low in caste-rank they are also low in habits*: the entry seems to replicate upper-caste Hindu notions of lower-caste impurity. European distaste for *paraiyar*s was common; compare, for instance, the comments of the French Catholic missionary Jean Antoine Dubois in his *Description of the Character, Manners and Customs of the People of India* (London, 1817): 'if the caste of the Pariahs be held in low and vile repute, it must be admitted that it deserves to be so, by the conduct of the individuals and the sort of life which they lead' (p. 458).

PAWNEE *ἄριστον μὲν ὕδωρ*: 'water is best'. Pindar, Olympian 1.1.

ἀρχὴ δὲ τῶν πάντων ὕδωρ: according to later writers, Thales taught that 'water is the source of everything'.

PEEPUL *a very learned scholar*: this is a reprise of an earlier scholarly spat between the philologist Isaac Taylor and Henry Yule. In *Etruscan Researches* (1874), Taylor asserted that there was no credible Aryan etymology for *populus*, the poplar tree. Yule contested this in 'Some Unscientific Notes on the History of Plants', *Geographical Magazine* (Feb. 1875), 49, arguing for the identity of *populus* with the Sanskrit *pippala*, the peepal tree.

PENANG LAWYER *lex baculina*: law of the stick.

The most famous literary 'penang lawyer' is the walking stick scrutinized by Dr Watson and Sherlock Holmes at the start of Conan Doyle's *The Hound of the Baskervilles* (1902).

PERI *Grimm's Law*: the German philologist Jacob Grimm identified the relationship between certain initial consonants in Indo-European and Germanic languages. It is singularly appropriate for this entry on sprites that Grimm is better known as one of the editors of *Grimms' Fairy Tales* (1812).

PESHWA *Nānā Sāhib*: the popular name for Dandhu Panth (*c.*1834–60) who headed the uprising at Kanpur during the Indian Rebellion of 1857–8.

PIECE-GOODS: as the tone of the entry and footnote suggests, Yule was vehement in his belief that Indian cloth production had been irretrievably damaged by custom duties. As a member of the Council of India, he opposed the abolition of duty on British manufactured cotton goods exported to India. The entry has been abridged to exclude a list of the various kinds of Indian piece-goods.

PIGEON ENGLISH *vile jargon*: the contempt for pidgin English was a common nineteenth-century British response. The accompanying quotations suggest that the disdain for pidgin arises from the idea that English traders were responsible for establishing the language in the first place, and that it is not just the lower classes who used it. See also BUTLER-ENGLISH.

PIG-STICKING *enlightening an aspirant Bengalee on the short-comings of his Presidency*: rivalry between the British residents of Calcutta, Bombay, and Madras is apparent in a number of entries. See BENIGHTED, THE, and CHILLUMCHEE.

PLASSEY *Lord Clive's famous battle*: British rule in India was conventionally dated from 1757, the defeat of the Nawab of Bengal, Siraj-ud-Daulah, at the Battle of Plassey. The outcome of the battle was decided before the armies took to the field. Mir Jafar, Siraj-ud-Daulah's rival, sided with the British, and induced many of the Nawab's troops to defect.

POGGLE, PUGGLY *macaronic*: a combination of Latin words and vernacular words with Latinate endings.

Pagal et pecunia jaldè separantur!: a Latin and Hindi version of the English proverb 'A fool and his money are soon parted'.

PUCKA: the word 'pukka' is now best known in Britain as a London slang term for genuine or excellent.

PUCKEROW: the adoption of the Hindustani imperative as an infinitive is one of the characteristics of the British language of command. In addition, the imperative is in the 'familiar' form, which implies lack of respect. The definition supplied expresses both the violence of colonial rule and Indian resistance: 'to lay hold of (generally of a recalcitrant native)'.

PUNCH *"Vier . . . Welt"*: 'Four elements, join'd in | Harmonious Strife, | Shadow the world forth, | And typify Life'. The first stanza of Friedrich Schiller's 'Punch Song', in *The Poems of Schiller*, trans. Edgar A. Bowring (London: John W. Parker & Son, 1851), 117. The poem was set to music by Franz Schubert.

PUNDIT *the Nānā Dhundopant of evil fame*: the Indian rebel leader, also known as Nana Sahib. See note to PESHWA.

Colonel Y——: Yule actively promoted Nain Singh's cause at the Royal Geographical Society. Here he quotes from a speech he himself made when he accepted the Royal Geographical Society's patron's medal on Nain Singh's behalf.

PUNJAUB *"Putandum est nomen* Panchanadae . . . *accidere potuit"*: 'It is thought that the name "Panchanada" either was wholly unknown to the Greeks or for some reason has simply not survived into our time—as could easily happen amidst the widespread loss of ancient records.'

PYJAMMAS *"Ils ont force calsons sans quoy ne couchent iamais les Portugais des Indes"*: 'They have a large stock of drawers, without which no Portuguese in India ever sleeps'. *The Voyage of François Pyrard of Laval*, trans. Albert Gray, ii (London: Hakluyt Society, 1888), 9.

RAJPOOT *The name of a great race in India, the hereditary profession . . . of arms*: the British identified the Rajputs as one of India's 'martial races', considered particularly suited to military service.

RAMOOSY *one of the thieving castes*: under the Criminal Tribes Act of 1871, the Ramosi of Bombay Presidency were kept under official surveillance and the possible penalty of relocation.

ROGUE *the following passage which we have copied, unfortunately without recording the source*: the missing source is François d'Aerssen van Sommerdyck, *Le Voyage d'Espagne* (Cologne, 1666), 4.

"On commence à s'apperceuoir dés Bayonne . . . avec l'Estranger": 'It is notice-

able from Bayonne onwards that the inhabitants' temper rather takes after that of their neighbours, and that they are cold and incommunicative with outsiders.'

ROY *Rammohun* Roy: the social, political, and religious reformer Ram Mohan Roy (1772–1833) was one of the founders of the theistic Brahmo Samaj reform movement.

SALA *used elliptically as a low term of abuse*: the gloss is itself elliptical in the definition of obscenity. Used offensively, *sala* implies a sexual relationship with someone's sister.

SALIGRAM *In May 1883 a śālagrāma . . . Hindus of Calcutta*: the protests originated in an editorial, published in *The Bengalee* by the Indian nationalist leader Surendranath Banerjee, who condemned Justice Norris's treatment of the *saligram* as sacrilegious. Banerjee apologized, but was found guilty of contempt of court and sentenced to two months' imprisonment. His sentence provoked protest in Bengal and other Indian cities, helping to unify the nascent nationalist movement. Two years later, the Indian National Congress held its first meeting, with Banerjee as one of the founder members.

"Ilbert Bill": see note to BLACK ACT.

SATSUMA *the deplorable necessity of bombarding its capital Kagosima*: a striking instance of British gunboat diplomacy; the destruction of the city of Kagoshima in 1863 entailed the loss of perhaps 18,000 civilian lives. The bombardment was the British response to the Japanese authorities' anti-foreign policy and specifically the refusal to pay an indemnity and to hand over those responsible for a British merchant's death. The gloss diminishes the gravity of the Anglo-Satsuma War by pairing it with a description of pottery. But there is an implicit link between the two: Satsuma ware only became fashionable in Europe after the forcible opening of Japan to Western trade.

SETTLEMENT *Permanent Settlement*: the social and political repercussions of the Permanent Settlement of Bengal were multiple. The sums that landowners had to pay to the British government, and that peasants had to pay to landowners, did not allow for fluctuations in the harvest. In bad years, peasants could be turned off the land for non-payment, and landholders have their estates confiscated and resold by the government. Traditional obligations between landowner and peasant were eroded. Peasants migrated to city slums, and large estates were carved up into smaller holdings. A new landed middle-class emerged, whose interests were closely tied to the British.

SHAMAN, SHAMANISM *sons of Tur . . . Turanian*: the term 'Turanian' is a loosely defined linguistic and racial category used by nineteenth-century philologists and anthropologists to designate non-Aryan peoples (see note to ARYAN).

SHAWL: from the late eighteenth to the late nineteenth century, the Kashmir shawl was one of the most desirable of British fashion items. Men in lucrative Indian posts might send a shawl home as a gift to female relatives, as we see in novels such as Thackeray's *Vanity Fair* (1848) and Gaskell's *Cranford* (1853). But the expense of the genuine article encouraged the development of a domestic shawl industry in Norwich and Paisley that copied Indian designs at a fraction of the price.

SHIKHÓ: from the outraged tone of the gloss, it is evident that Yule was of the opinion that British dignity would be compromised by prostration. As the secretary to Arthur Phayre's mission to Ava in 1855, Yule objected even to the removal of shoes when visiting temples and court buildings. Rather than be humiliated by stockinged feet, the British party declined to visit the sites. They only took off their shoes before entering the royal reception chamber itself.

SHULWAURS *'Et capillus . . . et* sarabala . . . *per eos'*: 'nor was an hair of their head singed, neither were their coats changed, nor the smell of fire had passed on them'. Daniel 3: 27, King James Version. The quotation comes from the story of Shadrach, Meshach, and Abednego who survive Nebuchadnezzar's fiery furnace unscathed.

SUTTEE: as the length of this entry indicates, the claim to have witnessed a sati became a standard topos in European travel accounts published up to the early nineteenth century. The sati was variously represented as an extraordinarily devoted widow, as the deluded victim of wily Brahmins, or, occasionally, as a lucky escapee. The gloss does not mention the controversy surrounding sati in the early decades of the nineteenth century. Missionaries condemned the rite as barbaric, particularly after 1813, when the British authorities legalized voluntary sati. The practice was outlawed in 1829 under William Bentinck. The entry, notably, does not celebrate Bentinck's act as evidence of the benevolent and progressive nature of British rule, only alluding to it through citation of the 1829 Regulation in the illustrative quotations.

SWAMY-HOUSE, SAMMY-HOUSE *The Sammy-house of the Delhi ridge in 1857 will not soon be forgotten*: during the 1857 Siege of Delhi, the 'Sammy House' was the site of a British battery which came under sustained attack from Indian rebel troops.

TALEE *"qui signifie proprement . . . donnait le nom de tahlīl"*: 'which strictly means: to recite the phrase *lâ ilâha illâ 'llâh* . . . This formula, inscribed on a piece of paper, served as an amulet . . . the whole contained in a case known as *tahlīl*'.

TAZEEA *a sad catastrophe*: the festival of Muharram was transported with Indian indentured labourers to the Caribbean. In Trinidad, it was known as Hosay (the name, derived, like *Hobson-Jobson*, from the ritual lament 'Ya Hassan! Ya Hosain!'). In 1884 the British authorities, nervous after two years of strikes on the Trinidad sugar plantations, banned the Hosay procession. When the festival went ahead in defiance, British forces opened fire on the procession, killing twenty-two of the participants, and injuring a hundred more.

TEA: Chinese tea was by far the most significant commodity traded by the East India Company. From the mid-eighteenth century, the demand for tea in Britain grew exponentially. By 1800, the tax levied on tea accounted for one-tenth of all British import duties. The British broke the Chinese monopoly on the production of tea with the successful cultivation of the tea plant in Assam from the 1830s. By the late 1860s, the quantity of tea imported by Britain from India overtook that from China.

THAKOOR *Dwārkanāth Tagore*: a prominent industrial entrepreneur and philanthropist, Dwarkanath Tagore (1794–1846) advocated educational reform and the abolition of sati. He was the grandfather of the renowned poet, novelist, and composer Rabindranath Tagore.

THUG: colonial anxiety over Indian criminality erupted in the 1830s with the campaign against thuggee, headed by W. E. Sleeman. As constructed by the British, Thugs ritually strangled and robbed unsuspecting travellers, out of devotion to the goddess Kali. They were supposed to belong to an extensive cult with its own secret language, documented by Sleeman in the *Ramaseeana* (1836). Between 1831 and 1837, more than three thousand individuals were arrested as thugs, with over four hundred executions. Sleeman himself was credited with the suppression of the system of thuggee. Public awareness of thuggee was largely based on Sleeman's own writing and Philip Meadow Taylor's popular novel, *Confessions of a Thug* (1839).

TIFFIN *"Homines autem . . . nostratibus Belgis tyfferen"*: 'Now those who collect and prepare these refreshments are known by the Portuguese name "Tiffadores", and the occupation itself is called "Tiffar"; our Belgians call it "tyfferen".'

TIGER: the British considered the Bengal tiger a beast of malign ferocity. The tiger was particularly associated with Tipu Sultan (1750–99), the great adversary of the British in Mysore. Adopted as the sultan's emblem, the tiger featured prominently on court artefacts, many of which were looted after the fall of Mysore. Most famous of all was 'Tippoo's Tiger', the clockwork model of a tiger mauling a prostrate European soldier, placed on public display, first at the East India Company's Museum and then the South Kensington Museum. To combat the perceived threat of tigers, the British hunted them enthusiastically. From 1800, a bounty of 10 rupees was awarded for every tiger killed. George Udny Yule, Henry Yule's elder brother and the dedicatee of *Hobson-Jobson*, was a renowned tiger hunter. 'By 1856 the roll of his slain tigers exceeded four hundred, some of them of special fame,' wrote Amy Yule; 'after that he continued slaying his tigers, but ceased to count them' (Henry Yule, *The Book of Ser Marco Polo*, 3rd edn. (London, 1903), p. lxxiii).

TRAGA *the death of the great Charles Gordon*: General Charles Gordon (1833–85) was already a popular military hero, but his death elevated him to the status of imperial martyr. In 1884, Gladstone sent Gordon to Khartoum to evacuate Egyptian forces under attack from Sudanese rebels, led by Muhammad Ahmed al-Mahdi. Defying orders, Gordon did not attempt an evacuation, and rebel forces besieged the city. The British press and public called for a relief force to be sent to Khartoum, but Gladstone did not respond immediately. After a ten-month siege, Khartoum was taken by the rebels and Gordon killed. The British relief force arrived two days later. The news of Gordon's death triggered an unprecedented display of public grief in Britain; the devout Gordon was mourned as a Christian martyr and Gladstone blamed for his sacrifice.

VACCINATION: smallpox was one of the major causes of mortality in India. The British introduced vaccination to counter the widespread folk practice of variolation (inoculation with live smallpox material). Vaccination was intended to prove the superiority of Western medicine and the benign nature of British rule, but many Indians regarded the procedure as invasive and offensive on religious grounds. Legislation was introduced in the 1870s and 1880s for compulsory vaccination in particular urban and military environments.

ZENANA *Zenana Missions*: in the second half of the nineteenth century, the Zenana Missions focused their evangelizing efforts on elite Indian women within their own homes. Along with Christianity, the Zenana Missions aimed to promote European forms of domesticity among Indian women. Female missionaries entered the zenana or women's quarters to teach reading and embroidery to girls and women. Later in the century, the Zenana Missions extended their activity to include medical work, recruiting female doctors as missionaries.

The Oxford World's Classics Website

www.worldsclassics.co.uk

- Browse the full range of Oxford World's Classics online
- Sign up for our monthly e-alert to receive information on new titles
- Read extracts from the Introductions
- Listen to our editors and translators talk about the world's greatest literature with our Oxford World's Classics audio guides
- Join the conversation, follow us on Twitter at OWC_Oxford
- Teachers and lecturers can order inspection copies quickly and simply via our website

www.worldsclassics.co.uk

MORE ABOUT OXFORD WORLD'S CLASSICS

American Literature

British and Irish Literature

Children's Literature

Classics and Ancient Literature

Colonial Literature

Eastern Literature

European Literature

Gothic Literature

History

Medieval Literature

Oxford English Drama

Philosophy

Poetry

Politics

Religion

The Oxford Shakespeare

A SELECTION OF **OXFORD WORLD'S CLASSICS**

	Late Victorian Gothic Tales
	Literature and Science in the Nineteenth Century
JANE AUSTEN	**Emma**
	Mansfield Park
	Persuasion
	Pride and Prejudice
	Selected Letters
	Sense and Sensibility
MRS BEETON	**Book of Household Management**
MARY ELIZABETH BRADDON	**Lady Audley's Secret**
ANNE BRONTË	**The Tenant of Wildfell Hall**
CHARLOTTE BRONTË	**Jane Eyre**
	Shirley
	Villette
EMILY BRONTË	**Wuthering Heights**
ROBERT BROWNING	**The Major Works**
JOHN CLARE	**The Major Works**
SAMUEL TAYLOR COLERIDGE	**The Major Works**
WILKIE COLLINS	**The Moonstone**
	No Name
	The Woman in White
CHARLES DARWIN	**The Origin of Species**
THOMAS DE QUINCEY	**The Confessions of an English Opium-Eater**
	On Murder
CHARLES DICKENS	**The Adventures of Oliver Twist**
	Barnaby Rudge
	Bleak House
	David Copperfield
	Great Expectations
	Nicholas Nickleby

A SELECTION OF OXFORD WORLD'S CLASSICS

CHARLES DICKENS	The Old Curiosity Shop Our Mutual Friend The Pickwick Papers
GEORGE DU MAURIER	Trilby
MARIA EDGEWORTH	Castle Rackrent
GEORGE ELIOT	Daniel Deronda The Lifted Veil and Brother Jacob Middlemarch The Mill on the Floss Silas Marner
EDWARD FITZGERALD	The Rubáiyát of Omar Khayyám
ELIZABETH GASKELL	Cranford The Life of Charlotte Brontë Mary Barton North and South Wives and Daughters
GEORGE GISSING	New Grub Street The Nether World The Odd Women
EDMUND GOSSE	Father and Son
THOMAS HARDY	Far from the Madding Crowd Jude the Obscure The Mayor of Casterbridge The Return of the Native Tess of the d'Urbervilles The Woodlanders
JAMES HOGG	The Private Memoirs and Confessions of a Justified Sinner
JOHN KEATS	The Major Works Selected Letters
CHARLES MATURIN	Melmoth the Wanderer
HENRY MAYHEW	London Labour and the London Poor

A SELECTION OF **OXFORD WORLD'S CLASSICS**

William Morris	**News from Nowhere**
John Ruskin	**Praeterita**
	Selected Writings
Walter Scott	**Ivanhoe**
	Rob Roy
	Waverley
Mary Shelley	**Frankenstein**
	The Last Man
Robert Louis Stevenson	**Strange Case of Dr Jekyll and Mr Hyde and Other Tales**
	Treasure Island
Bram Stoker	**Dracula**
W. M. Thackeray	**Vanity Fair**
Frances Trollope	**Domestic Manners of the Americans**
Oscar Wilde	**The Importance of Being Earnest and Other Plays**
	The Major Works
	The Picture of Dorian Gray
Ellen Wood	**East Lynne**
Dorothy Wordsworth	**The Grasmere and Alfoxden Journals**
William Wordsworth	**The Major Works**
Wordsworth and Coleridge	**Lyrical Ballads**

TROLLOPE IN OXFORD WORLD'S CLASSICS

ANTHONY TROLLOPE	The American Senator
	An Autobiography
	Barchester Towers
	Can You Forgive Her?
	Cousin Henry
	Doctor Thorne
	The Duke's Children
	The Eustace Diamonds
	Framley Parsonage
	He Knew He Was Right
	Lady Anna
	The Last Chronicle of Barset
	Orley Farm
	Phineas Finn
	Phineas Redux
	The Prime Minister
	Rachel Ray
	The Small House at Allington
	The Warden
	The Way We Live Now

A SELECTION OF **OXFORD WORLD'S CLASSICS**

Hans Christian Andersen	**Fairy Tales**
J. M. Barrie	**Peter Pan in Kensington Gardens and Peter and Wendy**
L. Frank Baum	**The Wonderful Wizard of Oz**
Frances Hodgson Burnett	**The Secret Garden**
Lewis Carroll	**Alice's Adventures in Wonderland and Through the Looking-Glass**
Carlo Collodi	**The Adventures of Pinocchio**
Kenneth Grahame	**The Wind in the Willows**
Anthony Hope	**The Prisoner of Zenda**
Thomas Hughes	**Tom Brown's Schooldays**
Charles Perrault	**The Complete Fairy Tales**
Anna Sewell	**Black Beauty**
Robert Louis Stevenson	**Kidnapped** **Treasure Island**

A SELECTION OF **OXFORD WORLD'S CLASSICS**

	Bhagavad Gita
	The Bible Authorized King James Version *With Apocrypha*
	The Book of Common Prayer
	Dhammapada
	The Gospels
	The Koran
	The Pañcatantra
	The Sauptikaparvan (from the Mahabharata)
	The Tale of Sinuhe and Other Ancient Egyptian Poems
	The Qur'an
	Upanisads
ANSELM OF CANTERBURY	**The Major Works**
THOMAS AQUINAS	**Selected Philosophical Writings**
AUGUSTINE	**The Confessions** **On Christian Teaching**
BEDE	**The Ecclesiastical History**
KĀLIDĀSA	**The Recognition of Śakuntalā**
LAOZI	**Daodejing**
RUMI	**The Masnavi**
ŚĀNTIDEVA	**The Bodhicaryāvatāra**